Film Exhibition and Distribution in Ireland, 1909–2010

D1345829

For Matthew and Stephen

FILM EXHIBITION AND DISTRIBUTION IN IRELAND, 1909–2010

KEVIN ROCKETT
WITH EMER ROCKETT

FOUR COURTS PRESS

Set in 9 on 12.5 point Sabon for
FOUR COURTS PRESS LTD
7 Malpas Street, Dublin 8, Ireland
www.fourcourtspress.ie
and in North America
FOUR COURTS PRESS
c/o ISBS, 920 N.E. 58th Avenue, Suite 300, Portland, OR 97213.

A catalogue record for this title

ISBN 978–1–84682–316–9

Printed in England
by Antony Rowe Ltd, Chippenham, Wilts.

Contents

LIST OF ILLUSTRATIONS   7

LIST OF ABBREVIATIONS   10

ACKNOWLEDGMENTS   11

PREFACE   12

PROLOGUE   13

PART I: COMMERCIAL CINEMA EXHIBITION AND DISTRIBUTION

1   Film Distribution and Exhibition, 1909–29   15
    Ireland's first full-time cinema: James Joyce and the Volta   15
    The first cinema building boom, and early exhibition practices throughout
    Ireland   22
    Distribution: from sale to hire and from first-run to second-run cinemas 38
    Going to the pictures during the silent period   41
    The struggle over Sunday opening in Dublin and Belfast   47
    From crisis to stability   60

2   Economic Protectionism and Foreign Oligopoly, 1929–46   72
    The second Irish cinema building boom, 1929–39   72
    Economic nationalism and British exhibition: 'alien penetration' in the 1930s   84
    Northern Ireland's exhibition wars in the 1930s and 1940s   96
    Other effects of war on Irish exhibition, north and south   106
    The nature of competition: exhibition   108
    The nature of competition: distribution   111

3   Dividing the Spoils: British and American Film Interests in Ireland after
    the Second World War   115
    J. Arthur Rank's cinema empire   115
    Cinema taxation   125
    The post-war audience   140
    Innovation, retrenchment and reorganization   149

4   The Emergence of Ward Anderson and the Challenge from
    New Distribution Technologies   159
    The Ward Anderson companies   159
    Investigating monopoly practices   166
    Further decline in the 1980s   175
    The challenge from new distribution technologies   179

5   **Multiplexes and the Renewal of Irish Exhibition**   193
    Defining the multiplex   193
    The multiplex in Ireland   201
    Ward Anderson and the multiplex   210
    The megaplex   214
    Other developments in Irish exhibition from the late 1990s   217

PART 2: ALTERNATIVE FILM PRACTICES

6   **Alternative Exhibition**   229
    Irish Film Society/Cumann na Scannán   229
    Federation of Irish Film Societies/Access>CINEMA   242
    Cultural cinema in Northern Ireland   246
    Commercial art cinema in the Irish Republic   249
    Project Cinema Club   252
    Irish Film Theatre   253
    Irish Film Institute cinemas (including the Light House Cinema,
    Abbey Street)   260
    Dedicated full-time art cinemas outside the capital   265
    Film festivals in Cork, Dublin, Galway, Derry, Belfast and elsewhere   270

7   **Irish Catholic Film Policies in the 1920s and 1930s**   293
    The Catholic hierarchy and the immorality of imported popular culture 293
    Father Richard Devane's crusade for an Irish film institute   299
    The state responds   307
    The Catholic hierarchy and film policy   314

8   **Establishing a Catholic-Sanctioned Film Culture in Ireland**   319
    Establishing an Irish (Catholic) film institute   319
    The National Irish Film Institute of Ireland, 1945–82   336
    The perennial controversy: children and the cinema   341
    Archbishop McQuaid and the screening of religious themed films   353

PART 3: CINEMA BUILDINGS IN IRELAND

9   **Irish Cinemas**   366
    The cinema building   366
    A note on sources and scope of cinemas' list   367
    List of cinemas and public venues screening films in Ireland
    (arranged by county)   369

    Appendix
    Irish Cinema and Other Statistics   455

    Coda   480

NOTES   482
SELECT BIBLIOGRAPHY   608
INDEX OF CINEMA LOCATIONS   612
GENERAL INDEX   616

Illustrations

Plates between pages 128 and 129.

1. Irish film exhibitors at Gresham Hotel, Dublin, 1939.
2. Frank Chambers, Dublin-based exhibitor.
3. John Yeats Moore, exhibitor, 1913.
4. Norman Whitten, proprietor, General Film Supply, Dublin.
5. Michael J. Tighe, Cork-based exhibitor, c.1920.
6. Izidore Isaac Bradlaw, Princess Cinema, Rathmines, Dublin.
7. J.J. King, Phibsboro' Picture House, Dublin.
8. Frederick A. Sparling, Bohemian Cinema, Phibsborough, Dublin.
9. Cathal McGarvey, manager, Phoenix Picture Palace, Ellis Quay, Dublin.
10. Alex McEwan who had cinemas in Cork, Limerick and Waterford.
11. J.E. MacDermott, proprietor, The Picture House, Quinsboro' Road, Bray, Co. Wicklow
12. James T. Jameson, proprietor, Irish Animated Picture Company, Dublin.
13. Michael Curran, Belfast-based exhibitor.
14. A.D. Coon, travelling exhibitor based in Co. Donegal.
15. Youghal, Co. Cork, exhibitor James Horgan with son Joseph.
16. Horgan's Orchestra, Youghal, Co. Cork.
17. Staff outside the Dorset Picture Hall, Dublin, 1910s.
18. Cinema queue outside the Corinthian, Dublin, 1928.
19. Cinema queue outside the Metropole, Dublin, 1937.
20. Dr John Charles McQuaid, archbishop of Dublin, 1941–72.
21. Fr Richard S. Devane, SJ.
22. Council of the National Film Insitute of Ireland, 1954.
23. Members of the Irish Film Society, 1937.
24. Cork Film Festival director Michael Hannigan, film archivist Liam O'Leary and Irish Film Institute director David Kavanagh, 1990.
25. Kevin Rockett and Thekla Beere, 1990.
26. Dermot Breen, director, Cork Film Festival, 1956–78.
27. Michael Dwyer, journalist and founder of Dublin Film Festival and Dublin International Film Festival.
28. Crowd outside Savoy Cinema during first Cork Film Festival, 1956.
29. Colin Farrell at the Dublin International Film Festival, 2010.
30. Galway Film Fleadh at Town Hall Theatre.
31. Exhibitor Leo Ward and Irish Film Board chairman James Morris, 2008.
32. Louis Elliman and Cecil B. De Mille.
33. Exhibitor Kevin Anderson outside the Savoy Cinema, Dublin, 2004.

34. Exhibitor Albert Kelly outside the Classic Cinema, Harold's Cross, Dublin.
35. Exhibitor Paul Ward.
36. Exhibitor Paul Anderson.
37. Exhibitors Ossie Spurling and Andrew O'Gorman.
38. Exhibitor Michael McAdam.
39. Tie-in items for sale relating to *The Singing Fool* at the Capitol, Dublin, 1929.
40. Irish Film Institute entrance and shop.

Plates between pages 288 and 289.

41. Volta Cinema, Dublin, 1909–47.
42. Kelvin Picture Palace, Belfast, 1910–72.
43. The Picture House, Dublin.
44. Electric Theatre, Larne.
45. Pillar Picture House, Dublin.
46. Grafton Picture House, Dublin.
47. Horgan's Picture Theatre (exterior), Youghal, Co. Cork.
48. Horgan's Picture Theatre (interior), Youghal, Co. Cork.
49. Interior of the Savoy Cinema, Patrick Street, Cork.
50. Metropole, Dublin.
51. Regal Cinema (exterior), Portadown, Co. Armagh, May 1933.
52. Regal Cinema (interior), Portadown, Co. Armagh, May 1933.
53. Ritz Cinema (exterior), Belfast, November 1936.
54. Ritz Cinema (interior), Belfast, November 1936.
55. Green Cinema (interior), Dublin, December 1935.
56. Stadium Cinema (interior), Belfast, October 1937.
57. Pavilion Cinema (interior), Cork, cafe.
58. Cameo Cinema (interior), Cork.
59. Aftermath of the Drumcollogher cinema fire, 1926.
60. Aftermath of fire at Park Street Cinema, Dundalk, 1961.
61. Demolition of Capitol, Dublin, 1972.
62. Demolition of the Ritz Cinema, Athlone, Co. Westmeath, 1999.
63. Meeting House Square, Temple Bar, Dublin.
64. Movie Junction drive-in cinema, Cork, 2010.
65. Cinema One of Irish Film Institute, Eustace Street, Dublin.
66. Eye Cinema, Galway.
67. Vue, Liffey Valley, Dublin.
68. Movies@Dundrum, Dublin.
69. Cineworld, Parnell Street, Dublin.
70. Movie House, City Side, Belfast.
71. Coon's travelling cinema van.
72. Cinemobile.

Plates between pages 448 and 449.

73. Grace Gifford cartoon of Horace Plunkett, c.1910–15.
74. Dublin Cinematograph Theatre opening programme, 1910.
75. *Beatrice Cenci* advertisement, 1909.
76. Kelvin Picture House opening advertisement, 1910.
77. Dorset Picture Hall programme, c.1913.
78. Coliseum Cinema, Cork, with synchronous sound-image films, 1915.

79. Princess Picture Palace, Belfast, programme, *c.*1919.
80. Gaiety Theatre poster for D.W. Griffith's *The Birth of a Nation* (1915).
81. Programme cover, La Scala Theatre and Opera House, opened in 1920.
82. Programme cover, Metropole, Dublin, opened in 1922.
83. Shannon Cinema, Athlone, programme, 1925.
84. Capitol Theatre and Cinema, Dublin, programme, 1927.
85. Corinthian Theatre/Cinema, Dublin, programme, 1927.
86. Galway cinema bills, 1936.
87. Erne Cinema, Ballyshannon, Co. Donegal, programme, 1963.
88. Stella Cinema, Rathmines, programme, 1949.
89. Galway Film Fleadh opening programme, 1989.
90. Foyle Film Festival opening programme, 1987.
91. Cinemagic, Belfast, advertisement, 2010.
92. Cork Film Festival advertisement, 2006.
93. Dublin Film Festival advertisement, 1993.
94. 3D Digital advertisement, 2009.
95. XD-Theatre advertisement, 2010.
96. Darklight Festival programme, 2006.

Drop-ins

Elliman advert, 1947, p. 158.
Archbishop McQuaid's invitation to premiere of *The Quiet Man* (1952), p. 365.
Cinema tickets, p. 610.

ACKNOWLEDGMENTS

1, 2, 3, 4, 5, 16, 17, 18, 19, 32, 39, 41, 43, 44, 45, 46, 49, 50, 55, 57, 59, 71, 77, 78, 79, 80, National Library of Ireland; 6, 7, 8, 9, 10, 11, *Irish Limelight*, NLI; 12, *Bioscope*, November 1911, NLI; 14, 15, 22, 24, 25, 40, 47, 48, 60, 65, 72, 88, Irish Film Institute; 20, Blackrock College; 21, Irish Jesuit Archive; 23, 42, 74, 81, 82, 83, 84, 85, 87, 89, 90, 95, 96, authors' collection; 26, 28, 58, courtesy of *Irish Examiner*; 27, 29, 31, courtesy of Dublin International Film Festival and Pat Redmond; 30, Galway Film Fleadh; 33, 34, 61, 62, 69, courtesy of *Irish Times*; 35, 36, courtesy of *Sunday Business Post*; 37, 68, Movies@Dundrum; 38, 70, Movie House, Belfast; 51, 52, 53, 54, 56, courtesy of National Museums Northern Ireland, Collection Ulster Museum; 60, Paul Kavanagh; 63, courtesy of Temple Bar Cultural Trust; 64, courtesy of Diane Cusack; 66, Eye Cinema, Galway; 67, Vue Entertainment; 73, courtesy of National Gallery of Ireland; 75, *Cinefono e RFC* no. 77, 18 September 1909 (advert.); 76, Kelvin's opening advert., December 1910; 91, 2010 advert.; 92, festival advert., 2005; 93, Dublin Film Festival programme advert. 1993; 94, 2009 advertisement.

For their assistance in sourcing the illustrations, thanks especially to Honora Faul and Brian McKenna, NLI; Rebecca Grant, IFI; Michelle Ashmore, Ulster Museum; Anne Hodge and Louise Morgan, NGI; Sarah Smyth and Gráinne Humphreys, Dublin International Film Festival; Miriam Allen, Galway Film Fleadh; Michael Hannigan, Cork Film Festival; Donald Taylor Black; Irene Stevenson, *Irish Times*; Anne Kearney, *Irish Examiner*; Bryan Walshe, *Sunday Business Post*; and the film exhibition companies which supplied photographs.

Abbreviations

BFI	British Film Institute
CRO	Companies Registration Office
DCA	Dublin City Archives
DDA	Dublin Diocesan Archive
DIA	*Dictionary of Irish Architects, 1720–1940* (www.dia.ie)
FJ	*Freeman's Journal*
IFI	Irish Film Institute
IFS	Irish Film Society
IT	*Irish Times*
KRS	Kinematograph Renters Society
KW	*Kinematograph Weekly/Kine Weekly*
KYB	*Kinematograph Year Book*
NAI	National Archives of Ireland
NFI	National Film Institute of Ireland
NLI	National Library of Ireland
RIA	Royal Irish Academy
RPC	Restrictive Practices Commission
TC	*To-day's Cinema*
TCD	Trinity College Dublin

Acknowledgments

Firstly, thanks are due to the Irish Research Council for the Humanities and Social Sciences for the awarding in 2005–6 of a Research Fellowship to Kevin Rockett, while Trinity College's Arts & Sciences' Benefactions fund provided a grant for the purchase of illustrations. Thanks also are due to the following libraries and archives: National Archives of Ireland; Dublin Diocesan Archive; Irish Film Institute library; National Library of Ireland; Irish Jesuit Archive; Dublin City Archive; and Irish Film Board.

Colleagues who have provided access to their own private archives include John Hill, who made available his material on Northern Ireland and the cinema, and Roddy Flynn. The cinemas list (chapter 9) has been enhanced by work undertaken particularly by Eugene Finn, but also Brendan McCall, Harvey O'Brien, John Lynch (Listowel), Declan McLaughlin (Limerick) and Martin McLoone (Derry). We are grateful to Four Courts Press, especially Martin Fanning, for encouraging and embracing the project.

Preface

In the introduction to *Cinema and Ireland* (1987), which offered a history of film production in Ireland as well as a consideration of representations of Ireland and the Irish in British and America cinemas, it was noted that there remained to be written a complementary history of Irish film exhibition and distribution. Though part of that story was told in *Irish film censorship* (2004), it has taken until now to complete what is, in effect, the third part of the history of cinema in Ireland. While this book has its origins in my D.Phil thesis (University of Ulster, 1989), where preliminary work on exhibition and distribution in Ireland was outlined, it was only during 2005–6 when I was awarded an Irish Research Council for the Humanities and Social Sciences Research Fellowship that sustained work on the project began in earnest.

As the project grew, I enlisted the help of my wife Emer, who had already undertaken additional research for and extensively refined my last major study, *Irish film censorship*, and who, subsequently, and concurrent with this project, worked with me on a self-contained but complementary volume to the history of cinema exhibition entitled *Magic lantern, panorama and moving picture shows in Ireland, 1786–1909*.

To Emer my sincerest thanks for helping me shape and complete this history, and to our boys to whom the book is dedicated my gratitude for their forbearance.

Kevin Rockett,
Trinity College Dublin,
April 2011

Prologue

'By Jove!' he exclaimed; 'it's a living picture!'[1] The lights dim, and so begins the history of cinema; of a technology that owes to the competing discourses and traditions of science and art, while all the time being bound to and by economics; of a form of mass diversion or entertainment; of a communication medium formed by and distributed according to ideological – social, political and religious – as much as practical determinations. It is no less an admission ticket to the velvet seats, the smell of popcorn,[2] the sticky carpet and to our love affair with the silvered screen and motion pictures, or (new) living pictures, or the flicks; with a reality framed, reformed, enhanced, extended beyond the frame, made assaultive and visceral; with a communal grammar that denies the cultural individualism and atomization of its audience (which it, in part, has cultivated)[3] and, at times, even its own content; and with, what is, in effect, a filter through which we can understand a society, a culture, a history and the intra- and interrelationships of these. The opening credits can now begin; the advertisers and the concession stand satisfied. But no, the Irish Catholic writer May Nevin[4] whose words we borrowed insists we do not read selectively, that we acknowledge the *full* story.

Returning to her story, a story of embracing the light, of turning to the Virgin Mary – the advice Archbishop John Charles McQuaid gave to the nascent National Film Institute of Ireland when he told them 'only the limitless power of Our Blessed Lady can avail to defeat the particular evils that the Institute attempts to combat'[5] – it becomes clear that the 'living picture' in question is just a traditional painting, albeit a masterpiece, and not a film. However, it assumes importance not for its formal or aesthetic qualities, but because, as one of the story's characters Protestant Major Hargrave sees it, 'the artist has actually put life into his pictures.' This masterpiece subsequently proves central to Hargrave's conversion to Catholicism and his reuniting with his son. Of course, a similar though literal achievement of a painter capturing life had been imagined already by the more famous Irish writer Oscar Wilde in his novel *The picture of Dorian Gray* (1891), which has come to be regarded as an apt analogy for cinema.

While Nevin's sentimental story has significance in the context of this book as it serves to illustrate the importance of visual representations within a society, it is also of note given that in addition to exploring the nature of private reflective viewing it implicitly addresses the nature of exhibition and picture-going as an activity independent perhaps of its thematic concerns. Indeed, in the short story when the priest sees Hargrave at his church, surprised, he welcomes him by saying, 'You have come

to see our new set of stations? ... They are a fine set.' Though it is this latter activity
– group or mass picture-going, rather than private viewing – that is at the heart of this
study, more specifically the book's focus is on the commercial distribution and exhibition of moving-pictures.

Given that cinema as 'New Living Pictures' and the related and at times competing pre-cinema originating picture-based entertainments are treated in the complementary volume *Magic lantern, panorama and moving picture shows in Ireland, 1786–
1909*, this allows this book to concentrate on the development of cinema in Ireland
from the opening of Ireland's first full-time permanent commercial cinema in 1909,
though certainly in the pre-multiplex era the cinema continued to be referred to popularly by many as 'the pitchers' or the picture house.[6] At all times, the interest remains
not so much on the cinema buildings themselves (and their architecture) or the films,
but on the economic, cultural and political environments in which they operated. In
this way, issues around nationhood and the struggle for Irish self-determination,
Ireland's relative marginal status, government policy, and internal and international
economics, including taxation and funding, are explored.

While part 1 of the book concentrates on commercial cinema, part 2 examines
alternative exhibition practices including film clubs and societies, festivals, and more
broadly, the area of cultural cinema. Central to this is the exploration of Catholic film
policy vis-à-vis both the secular world, and its own internal struggles between the competing ideologies of rigid and exclusive authoritarianism and a more inclusive vocationalism and inter-denominationalism. The final section of the book offers a listing
of all the cinemas or places of public film exhibition on the entire island of Ireland,
from the beginnings of cinema in the 1890s to the present, at which time there are
roughly 600 screens with over 70,000 seats, achieving attendances of just under
450,000 per week. For contemporary readers, what is perhaps most striking about the
list is the extent of cinema's penetration even in the early years of cinema throughout
the island, in every county, town and even village.

To conclude, *Film exhibition and distribution in Ireland, 1909–2010* is an attempt
to present a social, cultural and economic history of film exhibition and distribution
in Ireland. As such, it is unique in the Irish context in that it offers a broad-based
account of an entire sector, one that highlights the challenges facing peripheral countries such as Ireland and their necessarily marginal economic status. One disturbing
feature that emerges in considering this history is how successive Irish governments
have failed to engage with and support an Irish cinema on its own terms rather than
within some use-value system. As a result, the book is principally concerned with
imported rather than indigenously produced cinema, though it should be stated that
this largely imported form of culture has been and continues to be enjoyed by Irish
people, chiefly, in Irish-owned buildings and cinemas around the island of Ireland.

CHAPTER I

Film Distribution and Exhibition, 1909–29

'Not less slow than in other countries, our people have come to regard the motion pictures as a mighty force which no other agency has yet surpassed.'

Irish Limelight, 1917[1]

IRELAND'S FIRST FULL-TIME CINEMA: JAMES JOYCE AND THE VOLTA

Notwithstanding that Dublin's Volta has come to be regarded as Ireland's first full-time cinema, it is important to note that prior to its opening on 20 December 1909 at least six venues, including the Rotunda, Dublin, had been or were regularly screening films. Furthermore, while one of these, Belfast's Royal Hippodrome, which opened on 2 November 1907, claimed to be the first Irish theatre to incorporate cinema projection apparatus into its design (though it remained a variety house until 1931), another, the Queen's Theatre in Dublin, enjoyed a brief period as a *de facto* picture palace. Famous for its presentation of Irish melodramas,[2] from 2 March 1908 to January 1909, the Queen's became home to the Colonial Picture Combine,[3] and accordingly was promoted as 'The People's Popular Picture Palace',[4] where audiences could, like those at the Rotunda, take pleasure in the 'full band' and 'good singers' that accompanied the film programme. Diarist Joseph Holloway (architect of the Abbey Theatre, and later, in the 1920s and 1930s, deputy to official film censor James Montgomery),[5] provides not just an account of its opening night, but, displaying his customary distaste for the moving picture audience, an insight into what is commonly understood as the different pleasures afforded by cinema and theatre: cinema's expressive, visceral, and communal engagement, in contrast to theatre's cerebral and contained experience.

According to Holloway, small boys thronged the theatre 'eager to gain admittance' and to see the show's highlight, the pioneering Australian film about the Irish-Australian outlaw Ned Kelly, *The Story of the Kelly Gang* (Charles Tait, 1906). This, incidentally, he deemed to be 'full of the horrors of the "penny dreadfuls".' After a series of shorts – a comedy about a man's first row on a river; a dramatic story featuring the 'sorrows of a clown'; and a crime film *His Rival's Necklace* (1907, GB), in which an actress, suspected of stealing a rival's necklace, escapes to a cottage where she encounters the

real thief[6] – the programme's main event, perhaps the longest narrative film[7] to have
been made worldwide by 1906, was announced 'amid "sensation"' in a 'house [that]
was agog with excitement'. Unable to stay for the complete duration of the film due
to another engagement, he noted that as he left the theatre, the film was *'dramatically
and excitingly* unfolding itself amid noisy applause' [emphasis added], while the street
outside 'was a hive of childhood' with long queues already forming for the 9p.m. show,
an hour later. His conclusion was that the night had provided proof 'that crude melodrama even in "living pictures" is what appeals to the youthful mind ever eager for
thrilling events.'[8] Although the drama and excitement clearly registered with the children, perhaps it appealed no less to him. As the *Evening Telegraph* put it, the 'whole
picture-drama … was followed with breathless interest.'[9]

In this regard, it is of note that the third Dublin film venue pre-1909, the Grafton
Station or Savoy Station, offered an explicitly visceral film-based entertainment, one
that owed much more explicitly to the (topographical or travel based) moving-
panorama than regular cinema did.[10] On the former premises of the Savoy Theatre of
Varieties near the junction of Grafton Street and South Anne Street,[11] it was opened
on 3 June 1907 as a Hale's Tours' venue by Will C. Pepper and featured the 'New
Dublin Railway'. The entrance was designed in the shape of a platform with dummy
telegraph wires overhead, and coupling chains were attached to the carriages to generate a realistic response.[12] As elsewhere, this short-lived phenomenon,[13] ending in early
1909 when its English parent went bankrupt,[14] offered a very particular experience
whereby for 6d. a spectator-'tourist' could sit in a railway carriage for a ten minute
'ride' and watch screened scenes from the front of the train – a phantom ride.
Appropriate 'lurching' of the carriage, suggesting movement, and sound effects, such
as felling trees in *Lumber Camp* and *A Trip through the Canadian Rockies* (two of the
films screened on the opening programme), completed the illusion. The running commentary was by Mike Nono, a well-known Irish step-dancer. While it was Pepper, the
venue's manager, who had brought Hale's Tours to Ireland, the person who operated
the apparatus was Arthur Bursey, a native of the Isle of Wight, who had come to Dublin
in 1901. He recalled in 1955 how the 'throbbing engine … beat out the familiar rhythm
of a train at full speed, and with a floor designed on the "Rocking Horse" principle
the sensation of the swish of the railway carriages was well conveyed as the scenes on
the screen swept around the corners of the tracks.'[15]

Meanwhile in Belfast, the first 'cinemas' included St George's Hall, 39 High Street,
opened by Entertainment Halls Ltd on 17 August 1908 with a capacity of 1,500 persons;[16] and the Star Picture Palace, Church Street, a variety house, which operated for
less than two years from 14 September 1908. (The premature closure of the Star was
likely due to its inability to meet the new safety requirements of the 1909
Cinematograph Act.)[17] However, despite the importance of these venues and the fact
that circuits throughout Ireland were well established by the end of the first decade of
the 1900s, ultimately, none of these venues can rival the Volta in terms of the consistency and longevity of film exhibition. (The Volta, after all, operated, albeit under different personnel, for almost forty years.)

The conventional and generally accepted view of the Volta's origins lie in Eva Joyce's observation to older brother James that Dublin offered an excellent business opportunity for film entrepreneurs, given that smaller cities such as Trieste, where James was living, could support commercially-successful cinemas. Fuelled by her idea, but lacking the capital, Joyce convinced four Triestine businessmen who had among their business enterprises film exhibition interests in Trieste and Bucharest known as the International Cinematograph Society Volta, to fund the project. On 20 December 1909, with their financial backing, and having spent two months overseeing the renovations of a disused hardware store at 45 Mary Street, a short distance from O'Connell Street, Joyce opened the 320-seat Volta.[18]

Given that no alternative version of these events has been uncovered, and that Joyce's own account, as published in the *Letters,* provides no clue to the project's inception, or reveals his *precise* motivation behind it, it is easy to understand how Eva's narrative has been uncritically accepted even though such an origin-narrative necessarily fails to recognize the successful film exhibition practices established in Dublin, particularly at the Rotunda during the 1900s, something with which Joyce had to be familiar. The fact that he stayed at 44 Fontenoy Street, the family home, during his visit to Dublin from 29 July to 9 September 1909 would have meant that not only would he have frequently passed the nearby Rotunda where films were being screened at this time, and, as such, would have been aware of film's popularity among the middle classes, but also it is likely that he attended the Rotunda screenings (even if he makes no such reference in his published letters to having done so at this time or earlier). Conceivably, this (in)direct experience, rather than Eva's suggestion, may have contributed to the idea that the Dublin cinema audience could be more regularized and, perhaps with thoughts of the financial shortcomings of students and young people (rather than the largely uneducated working-class audience for whom he showed some distaste), broadened.

Arguably, a more urgent and personal artistic motivation for setting up a cinema in Dublin presented itself to him shortly after his return to Italy. This was the release in Rome on 1 October 1909 of *Beatrice Cenci* (Mario Caserini, 1909, Italy),[19] a rape-revenge narrative based on fact, and, importantly in this context, popularized in play form by one of Joyce's literary heroes, Percy Bysshe Shelley. Within just over a fortnight (16 October), Joyce had signed a contract with the Volta's backers and when the cinema opened three months later, this film, much to the surprise of the *Freeman's Journal*, was included as part of the programme. Though praising Joyce for his role in establishing the Volta, it stated, in perhaps what was the first rebuke in relation to any film shown in Ireland, that *The Tragic Story of Beatrice Cenci* (perhaps Joyce's title) was 'hardly as exhilarating a subject as one would desire on the eve of the festive season.' Nevertheless, the reviewer continued, 'it was very much appreciated and applauded.'[20] While there is no written evidence to associate Joyce with *any* film screened at the Volta, particularly after 2 January 1910 when Joyce left Dublin to return to Trieste, something usually not acknowledged,[21] it is fair to assume that Joyce was involved in the decision to screen *Beatrice Cenci* as the cinema's opening film. Such an assumption can be made on the basis of Joyce's initial involvement with the cinema and the first three programmes; his interest in both film and Shelley;[22] and that he may have seen *Beatrice Cenci*, or, at least, have been aware of its existence, prior to his return to Dublin. Indeed, on 15 June 1910, the day following the sale of the Volta, Ettore Schmitz (pseud. Italo Svevo) wrote to Joyce, and, having noted how 'excited' Joyce had been over the 'cynematograph-affair' (sic), undoubtedly made a reference to the film when he remarked somewhat cryptically, 'I remembered your face so startled by such wickedness.'[23]

A week after its Italian release, *Beatrice Cenci* was reviewed very favourably in the British film trade publication the *Bioscope*, which 'strongly advised' British exhibitors to book it.[24] Though the film, as a result of cinematic conventions, censorship restraints and its length at approximately ten minutes,[25] must have been markedly different from Shelley's play, it nevertheless tells the same basic tale of frustrated desire, familial abuse, intrigue and murder. Beatrice wishes to marry a young nobleman, but her father, Count Cenci, opposes the relationship. In order to thwart the marriage, he decides to have his daughter forcibly brought to one of his other castles and engages a man (who has entered his service in order to avenge the death of his lover killed by order of the count), to take Beatrice and her mother 'to durance vile'. The count treats Beatrice 'very brutally' and though an attempt is made to stab the count, his suit of mail saves him. A plot is then concocted between Beatrice's lover and the avenging lover to murder the count. His wine is drugged, and suffering its effects, the count retires to his room, where, with the 'connivance' of the count's wife, 'whom he has so badly treated', he is murdered. Beatrice then marries the nobleman, but at the wedding feast she is arrested and accused of her father's murder, whereupon she is imprisoned and tortured. At her trial she denies her guilt, but, threatened with further torture, confesses that she was party to the crime and is sentenced to death. She is publicly beheaded at the Bridge of St Angelo, Rome.[26]

Filmed at the Cenci castle (with the permission of the government),[27] where the main events took place in 1599, and the Bridge of St Angelo, according to *Bioscope*, the film's 'artistic production' was set to 'rivet the attention' of all who would see it, and sustain the production company Cines' 'high reputation'. Though the journal also noted the 'historically correct' nature of the costumes, it is impossible to assess from contemporary accounts of the film, of which unfortunately no copy seems to have survived, whether the themes of rape and incest overarching the story were included. If they were, it is most likely to have been at the level of *mise-en-scène*, rather than as explicit narrative elements.

The relatively short period between the Dublin and Rome screenings of *Beatrice Cenci* belies the difficulties Joyce experienced in realizing the Dublin cinema project. Though he might well have surrendered himself to the cinema's particular onscreen 'wickedness', he, nonetheless, found his time in Dublin irksome. Indeed even prior to the delay in the issuing of the cinema's music licence and his suffering an 'attack of rheumatic inflammation of the iris of the eye' which caused him on 2 January 1910 to leave Ireland 'at once', a day earlier than he had been contracted to stay in the country,[28] 'with black bandages over both [his] eyes',[29] an ironic end to his involvement with the visual medium, he was already frustrated. On 25 October, for example, only four days after arriving in the capital, he wrote to Nora expressing his resentment at wasting his day 'among the common Dublin people whom I hate and despise', while adding, presumably in the context of work on the cinema premises, that he was 'dreadfully busy from morning to night'.[30] Two days later, he wrote again, this time telling her of 'a disgusting audience' he encountered at his visit to the theatre and that he felt '(as I always feel) a stranger in my own country ... I loathe Ireland and the Irish.'[31]

With the transformation of the premises at 45 Mary Street largely completed by early December 1909, Joyce became increasingly impatient at the delay in the cinema's opening; 'I ... am of course dead sick of Dublin', he complained to his brother Stanislaus in Trieste on 2 December.[32] In addition to some problems with the electricity that continued until the middle of the month, and the late arrival of the film projector, another impediment to the cinema's opening was that the recorder, Lopdell O'Shaughnessy, the court official responsible for the issuing of music licences – an essential requirement for any entertainment venue intending to include music, even if only as accompaniment – was away. Although Joyce had to wait until 29 December for an appointment with the recorder in order to secure the music licence, as the cinema actually opened nine days earlier, the Volta must have, in the initial period, perhaps with some dispensation, operated without a music licence. Nevertheless, it certainly had the other licence required to operate as a cinema: a standard one-year cinema licence, which would take effect from 1 January 1910, the date from which the 1909 Cinematograph Act stipulated that cinema licences were required. This had been issued in December by Dublin corporation's Walter Butler, inspector of theatres and other places of public resort, whom Joyce had met on 23 October, two days after having arrived in Dublin.[33]

If, unlike other venues in Ireland, there was no uncertainty as to the Volta's identity as a full-time cinema, the audience policy pursued was at best contradictory, a confusion perhaps also expressed aesthetically in the cinema's colour scheme of crimson and light blue, colours associated with sensual and cerebral amusement respectively. This may have been the result of a deliberate attempt by Joyce to move away from the type of 'disgusting audience' he had experienced in Dublin. Perhaps the thought was that if the focus was put on the entertainment rather than the internal audience dynamic then the issue of class might be elided or problematized and the cultural meaning of the film would assume most importance.

In any case, it seems that Joyce (or his business partners, who arrived in Dublin on 17–19 November, and after a short stay at Finn's Hotel moved to the premises above the Volta, where they resided until they left Dublin on 25 December), sought to attract the middle-class clientele frequenting the Rotunda. For example, not only did the cinema's façade with its classical garlands signal a traditional theme,[34] but a five-person orchestra played at the inaugural event, and an indication was given that future screenings would feature the novelty of opera films or 'operatic pictures, describing the stories of famous operas'.[35] As explained in *Bioscope*, the opera would be played on 'a specially prepared disc, while the orchestra accompanies the unravelling of the plot by rapid but artistic, playing of a selection from the composer's music for the opera.'[36] Indeed, it was the intention 'to introduce to Dublin the quick continental system at low prices, presenting only the newest films, with a constant change of subject', a process facilitated by the renting rather than the purchase of films.[37] Additionally, the cinema included 200 Windsor (or tea-room) chairs. Yet, despite this, on the other hand, plain forms, or benches, were provided for children and the poor, even though such a small auditorium would not have easily permitted any real social class segregation as was possible in a larger theatre, thus making the venue unattractive for the (self-consciously) middle classes, many of whom would have been uncomfortable already with the cinema's location on the edge of a tenement district.

While the middle and skilled working class would have had sufficient surplus to spend on entertainment, this was not always the case with the unskilled and labouring classes. A prolonged economic crisis in Dublin during 1904 to 1912 led to high unemployment and depressed wages for most workers. Among the estimated 90,000 adult males in Dublin in 1911 there was as much as 20 per cent unemployment, while 25,000 of the workforce were unskilled workers, a factor that further depressed wages.[38] Thus, Joyce introduced 'popular prices' to cater for these groups. With admission prices set at 2*d.*, 4*d.* and 6*d.* and continuous performances from 5p.m. to 10p.m., it was much cheaper to attend than the Rotunda, but there, programmes included live performances and lasted on average three to five times longer than the Volta's which were typically only thirty to forty minutes. Of course, such pricing would have also facilitated students and other middle-class youths.

Though 'terrible weather' gave it 'poor houses' initially, by 23 December, Joyce, 'awfully tired after all the worry', reported to Stanislaus that it was doing 'fairly well'.[39] Nevertheless, such cinemas were operating as marginal businesses. The typical running costs for a London cinema in 1910 amounted to £43 17s. per week,[40] while a surviving February 1910 expenses sheet for the Volta suggests somewhat similar, though slightly lesser, costs. The weekly expenses at the Volta included advertising (in *Sinn Féin*, *Dublin Evening Mail* and on trams), which came to £3 15s. 2*d.*; orchestra: £4; wages totalling £3 18s. for projectionist Guido Lenardon (£2 2s.) and two other staff members (£1, and 16s. each); electricity: £3 18s. 1.5*d.*; and miscellaneous payments, including 15s. to boys, probably for distributing handbills on the street; and one can only speculate as to what 2s. 8*d.* worth of sawdust was used for.[41] While the listed expenditure only amounts to roughly £20, a number of other considerable outgoings, including film hire (which would have been presumably in excess of £10), the cost of carriage of films, premises' rental or mortgage, rates, and the salary for the manager (Lorenzo Novak, who had arrived in Dublin on 2 December and was the brother-in-law of the most important of the venture's promoters, Antonio Machnich) were not recorded, and so, if factored in would then serve to push costs to a level just below that for London. (Unfortunately, no figures seem to have survived for box office income at the cinema, though weekly profits for similar ventures in London were estimated to be in the £10–£20 range.)[42] The multiplicity of factors affecting the Volta (such as for example, the fact that neither Novak or Lenardon spoke fluent English, and film supply lines from Trieste may have been erratic) led to its failure to generate sufficient profits to sustain the venture.[43] As a result, the owners decided in April 1910 to dispose of the cinema, and, thus, on 14 June 1910, the Volta was sold to the British film exhibition company Provincial Cinematograph Theatres Ltd[44] for £1,000, a loss of £600 for the Triestine businessmen. It seems that Provincial, which had already opened the prestigious 270-seat Picture House at 51 Lower O'Connell Street on 9 April 1910, and would open on 17 April 1911 another fashionable venue, the Grafton Street Picture House, 72 Grafton Street, only bought the cinema as a defensive strategy.

As Luke McKernan shows,[45] two-thirds of the films that were screened at the Volta during December 1909–April 1910 were fiction titles. Thirty-two were French, thirty-one Italian, and about five were American or British. Nine of the Italian films, including *Beatrice Cenci,* were from the major Italian production company Cines, which specialized in historical and costume films and had a London office. All evidence suggests that the material screened was general cinema fare and included 'travelogues', such as another Cines' title *A Little Jules Verne* (1907), and historical subjects such as one on Nero, shown while Joyce was in Dublin, and similar to ones already screened at the Rotunda. Some of the films seem to have been released in Italy *after* Joyce's departure for Dublin, and thus were selected and collected by the partners who had experience of the film business – something, of course, Joyce did not have.

Commentators from Ellmann on have accepted that the preponderance of European films often without English intertitles was responsible for the Volta's demise. However, such intertitles did not become generalized in the cinema until about 1912, but even before then French and Italian films with intertitles were being distributed in Britain and the USA, for whose markets they would have been translated. Nevertheless, it seems that sheets with English text were given out to the Volta's audience. As outlined above in the discussion of pre-Volta Dublin film exhibition, Irish audiences had been seeing and enjoying such films for some time. As is manifest in the already cited reviews of *Beatrice Cenci,* the hostility to such European films which many commentators assumed to have existed in Britain and Ireland is clearly absent, while the popularity of later Italian epics including *Quo Vadis?* (Enrico Guazzoni, 1913, Italy) and *Cabiria* (Giovanni Pastrone, 1914, Italy) confirms that European films were not just for a middle class or restricted audience. Nevertheless, what had changed by 1909, and hence affected the Volta, was the rise of an alternative American, and to a lesser extent, British cinema.

With the desire to attract a broader range of patrons, theatres and cine-variety houses were including popular genre films, such as crime and melodrama, which were being produced in abundance in America in particular. As a result, the Rotunda, and later the Volta, were caught in a dilemma: whether to continue to cater primarily for a higher paying middle-class clientele, or respond with popular productions aimed at a 'proletarian' market. The issue, as will be seen in the next chapter, was resolved when the exhibition market became clearly demarcated between first-run and second-run venues. While films such as *Beatrice Cenci* and other historical subjects including *Nero*

(Luigi Maggi, Arturo Ambrosio, 1909, Italy), contained elements that appealed to both classes – an historical epic, tragic and melodramatic in its narrative, together with real locations, and European art aspects – it may be that these films did not fully address the needs of any one type of audience. The failure, then, of the Volta under Joyce's and Novak's management was not simply down to the screening of European films, but the attempt to look both ways at once.

THE FIRST CINEMA BUILDING BOOM, AND EARLY EXHIBITION PRACTICES THROUGHOUT IRELAND

Mirroring the expansion of film exhibition and the development of cinemas in Britain from 1910 onwards, Ireland saw the number of premises where films were being shown regularly increase dramatically during the years 1910 to 1914, while in the north of Ireland this growth was maintained throughout the war with Belfast seeing the opening of a number of cinemas in the period 1915 to 1917. As Nicholas Hiley has outlined with regard to Britain, the cultural and economic base of the cinema boom in this period had much in common with the roller-skating phenomenon of 1909–10, at which time individual rinks were attracting as many as 3,000 patrons on weekdays and 5,000 on Saturdays. Not only did the short-lived craze (which by the end of 1909 had resulted in over 300 rink companies with nominal capital of over £2 million), clearly show to private investors the possible profits to be made from such entertainments, but when skating faded in early 1910 with hundreds of rink companies facing bankruptcy, the cinema industry stepped into the entertainment breech. Indeed, notwithstanding that the British cinema industry was 'built on very shaky foundations'[46] with the earliest purpose-built cinemas erected by independent small-scale showmen, even by 1909 the cinema industry was hoping to emulate the overwhelming success of the skating sector with many small cinemas able to generate profits of as much as £100 per week.[47] Comprising of seventy-eight cinema companies with a combined nominal capital of £708,000,[48] the industry in Britain had already undergone a transformation in terms of funding with investment now coming from private limited companies, many of which were or had been involved in the skating rage, a phenomenon also enjoyed to some extent in Ireland.[49] Furthermore, and as was pointed out by an *Irish Times'* article,[50] although the number of cinemas multiplied both in Ireland and in Britain in a way similar to the roller skating industry, it was, nevertheless, unlikely to share the fate of skating given that cinema had 'still room for indefinite development' not least with regard to colour photography which was still in its infancy, and sound, but also, as was highlighted in the article, in terms of content, which was largely limited at that stage to amusement rather than education or stimulating dramatic art with 'really good acting'.[51]

Just as 'the provincial middle classes [in Britain] proved themselves eager to invest in this new form of entertainment',[52] Ireland was no different, and excepting the anomalies of the single investment by the Italians and the Irish interests of the British-based

Provincial Cinematograph Theatres, most of those who entered film exhibition in Ireland were small-scale local entrepreneurs with other business interests and with limited amounts of capital. Exemplary is John J. Farrell, who, on 19 May 1911, opened the 379-seat Electric Theatre, 45 Talbot Street, near Amiens Street railway station, Dublin, in the converted premises of his tobacconist/stationery shop and boot and shoe warehouse.[53] In contrast to Britain, which had between 600 and 1,000 cinemas at the end of 1909, film exhibition in Ireland developed later. As a result, when it did occur, mostly from 1910 onwards, it was underpinned by the Cinematograph Act 1909, which sought to foreground issues of public safety. Therefore, badly constructed or poorly adapted buildings, such as the unattractive 'penny gaff' shop-front cinemas, which were a feature of the early phase of British cinemas, were largely absent in Ireland.

That said, many Irish venues were nothing more than cheaply built rectangular halls, which were sparsely decorated, had little architectural merit and had limited seating. Indeed, Ireland's first cinema, the Volta, was, despite its façade, 'a plain, comfortless hall' with wooden benches and 'a few rows in the front which had hard kitchen chairs for the *elite* who could afford the top price' of 6*d*.[54] Furthermore, the majority of cinemas that opened in Dublin prior to the First World War, including the Volta, were not specifically built as cinemas, as was the case in London where more than 80 per cent of 1914 cinema licences were held by purpose-built venues, but were converted buildings. While most had been adapted from shops or warehouses, some had more unusual origins. The most curious conversion was that of the Bethesda chapel,[55] 22–23 Upper Dorset Street, at the corner with Granby Row. Developed by M. William Shanly, 'the great chair contractor',[56] and with alterations by architects Bachelor and Hicks, who made 'no attempt to disguise the fact' that it had been a chapel,[57] the cinema opened with 520 seats on the ground floor and 250 in the gallery, though *Irish Builder* said the hall could seat 1,000.[58] It continued as a cinema until 1981[59] under various names, including, informally, as Shanly's Picture Hall from 1910 to 1911; the Dorset Picture Hall, from 13 May 1911, the date on which it officially opened; the Plaza Picture Hall, from 26 September 1927; the Picture Palace Theatre when owned by J.J. Farrell; Plaza Cinema; and the Plaza Cinerama from 1967 to 1976. By the time of the cinema's official opening, Shanly, perhaps as a result of his business interests in seating, already owned five cinemas in England.[60]

In terms of building cost, it seems that British and Irish cinemas were not radically different, though the few known Irish figures are somewhat less, particularly in the context that most Irish cinemas were renovations of existing buildings. While Rachael Low has estimated that the cost of building Britain's first cinema, Lancashire's Central Hall, Colne, which opened in February 1907, or any 'small and modest' cinema in 1907 was approximately £2,000, and that in 1914 a cinema such as Edinburgh's Palace Cinema, the 'last word in sumptuousness', cost £19,000, Ireland's first cinema, the Volta, cost its backers, including the losses incurred in running the cinema, £1,600. The Sandford Cinema, Ranelagh, which opened in 1914 at the end of the initial phase of cinema adaptation, cost less than £4,000, excluding the value of the premises.[61] Although this amount is comparable to Alfred H. Poulter's outlay of £3,000 for his

354-seat Picture House, 55 Lower Camden Street, Dublin, which opened on 25 October 1912,[62] it is less than the £5,000 investment by Provincial in their 'very pretty' 450-seat Grafton Street Picture House which had opened three years earlier on 17 April 1911.[63] Situated on Ireland's most fashionable thoroughfare, this prestigious cinema boasted a small Wedgwood lounge as well as a smoke room.[64] In 1913, in a clear indication of its popularity, the cinema closed for renovation and expansion and reopened eight months later in February 1914 with 800 seats.

Presumably, though running costs in Ireland were similar to those in Britain, where, according to Low, 'if a suitable hall could be hired it was still possible in 1914 to run a modest show on relatively small capital', no doubt, Irish costs were somewhat less, due to the depressed economy, and lower still in secondary locations. In Britain, projection equipment seems to have cost between £20 and £100; electrical installation, £20 upwards; while the average weekly wages covering an operator, pianist, cashier, doorman-cleaner and young attendant, was roughly £12. As such the wage bill was comparable to the cost of film hire with £10 sufficient in 1909 for the hire of 5,000ft of 'the very best' first-run films for a week, though 'the average programme' would have cost only £7 to £8. However, by 1912, with the advent of the long feature film (with multiple reels of film of approximately ten minutes each), the cost of first-run product had risen to between £20 and £24 per week, with a second-run programme costing £16. Consequently, it was only the large, luxurious first-run houses that were able to afford such top prices, so the distinction between first and second-run was already well established before the First World War.[65]

Belying the general trend during this period of small-scale cinema development by individual middle-class entrepreneurs in Ireland, one of Britain's largest exhibition companies, Provincial Cinematograph Theatres Ltd, opened on 9 April 1910 the Picture House on Dublin's O'Connell Street, continuing the trend established in the eighteenth century of viewing the street as the country's most important commercial entertainment location. With continuous performances from Monday 11 April from 2p.m. until 10.30p.m., the cinema, Provincial's first Irish venue, offered through its aluminum screen greater visual comfort to the viewer ('the picture being remarkably clear and quite free from flickering').[66] Regarded rightly as 'the first of its kind'[67] in Ireland, it effectively consolidated the class differentiation between the more modest cinemas such as the Volta, which largely catered for the working classes, and those that were developed in central Dublin shortly after the opening of the Picture House and which similarly sought a middle class patronage and, as such, followed the pricing pattern of the Picture House with seat prices of 6d. and 1s.

Within two months of the opening of the O'Connell Street venue, Provincial extended its portfolio to include a second Dublin cinema by acquiring the Volta, but it was not integrated into Provincial's corporate structure in the way that might have been expected, or in the manner that Dan Lowrey's music hall had been incorporated into Moss and Stoll's circuit with its London headquarters largely determining the programme of the Dame Street venue. Instead, the acquisition of the Volta seems to have been a defensive move designed to shut down a competitor, albeit one in a secondary

location, at a moment of financial vulnerability. As the chairman of Provincial, financier (and sportsman) Sir William Bass, said in 1912, it was one of the 'small theatres
of a secondary type, which was comparatively unimportant' to them.[68] In 1912, the
company leased the Volta to 'a syndicate of Dublin gentlemen',[69] perhaps including
J.T. Jameson, before disposing of it for £875 (£125 less than they paid for it) to J.J.
Farrell, Robert ('Bob') O'Russ and others in September 1915.[70] By then, Provincial
already had another Dublin cinema, the fashionable Grafton Street Picture House,
which had opened on 17 April 1911; a 680-seat picture house in Belfast on Royal
Avenue, which opened on 19 June 1911;[71] and seven other cinemas in Britain.

An insight into the operation of Provincial is provided by records of its annual general meeting of 29 February 1912. According to these, the admission figure in the year
to 31 January 1912 was four million; while, notwithstanding its rapid expansion, its
trading profit was £47,104, allowing it to reward its shareholders with a 10 per cent
dividend. Although trading details for the individual cinemas were not given, unusually, the receipts from the three cinema cafes operated by Provincial, two of which were
in Irish cinemas (at the Grafton and in Belfast) and the sales of chocolates, cigarettes
and programmes, were reported by chairman Bass as £1,650. This represented an
increase of 125 per cent on the previous year's takings. As will be discussed later, such
revenues sometimes amounted to a quarter of a cinema's gross income, a revelation
perhaps unsurprising to contemporary cinemagoers who pay grossly inflated prices for
soft drinks, sweets, popcorn and other food at cinemas. Also outlined was Provincial's
de facto centralized corporate policy. The company, which was structured into departments (including catering, plant maintenance, advertising and accountancy), not only
had all accounts from the theatres and cafes checked and paid for by head office, but
also the booking of films was done centrally to ensure 'a clean, interesting and well
varied programme'. 'Nothing is ever shown at our theatres', the chairman told the
annual general meeting, 'which has not been seen and approved by our film department.' Programmes usually comprised of two or three films of general interest, dealing with scenery, travel, natural history, popular science, industry, or similar subjects,
interspersed with dramatic and humorous films and current events.[72]

Perhaps it was because of this lack of regional autonomy that Provincial's Dublin
manager, W.H. Huish, resigned in April 1912, though there may have been tensions
between Huish and his staff given that a Mr Marshall 'travelled specially' from
Provincial's London headquarters in February 1912 to see whether any Dublin
employee of the company had 'a legitimate grievance, and if so to redress it.'
Nevertheless, *Bioscope* reported that nothing substantial was stated at this general
meeting of the staff of the O'Connell Street, Grafton Street and Volta cinemas.[73] In an
interview with *Bioscope* following his resignation two months later, Huish predicted
that within a year there would be 400 Irish cinemas, a number of which he hoped
would be his.[74] While this figure was not achieved before the First World War, at which
time in county Dublin there were approximately forty-five cinemas, forty of which
were full-time,[75] and in Dublin city there were twenty-five[76] or twenty-six[77] venues with
a total of 15,000 seats,[78] at least twenty-one of which were exclusively or primarily

devoted to film screenings, what is of note with regard to Huish is that the form of relationship he had with Provincial was one endured by all subsequent Irish branch managers of foreign distributors and exhibitors, and, marked by a lack of decision-making power at a local level, remained a source of dissension throughout the rest of the century. Indeed, echoing the relationship between second-run and first-run cinemas, and notwithstanding 'the craze for building cinematograph theatres in Dublin'[79] and Belfast, Ireland, north and south, had a marginalized film-economic relationship with other countries, a theme which will recur throughout this book.

In July 1913 Provincial became the first such company to have its shares quoted on the stock exchange, while by 1914, the year in which Associated Provincial Picture Houses Ltd was established with the aim of further increasing Provincial's exhibition interests, the company had twenty-six cinemas, eighteen of which were first-run venues. By then, in Britain, there were between 4,000 and 4,500 cinemas, with only between 15 and 20 per cent of these constituting the 109 cinema circuits with a circuit defined as a chain of two or more cinemas. While thirteen 'circuits' had an average of fifteen cinemas each, these comprised as little as almost one-third of the circuit market, or 4 to 6 per cent of total cinemas. Therefore, it is clear that the majority of picture houses were owned, as was the case in Ireland, by small-scale entrepreneurs and that Britain, which at this time had a film exhibition market about twenty times larger than Ireland's, was not yet dominated by corporations.[80]

Despite Provincial's success in Ireland, in 1917, perhaps because of reasons associated with the difficulties that faced Irish exhibition during the First World War, which are discussed below, it sold the Picture House, Sackville Street, to Robert Morrison who renamed it the Sackville Picture House. The company also disposed of the Belfast Picture House to Northern Theatres. Nevertheless, it opened on 24 December 1923 the 1,810-seat Classic, 13–25 Castle Lane, whose status is reflected in the comment that 'no other [Belfast] cinema could match the Classic.'[81] During the expansion and consolidation of British exhibition from the late 1920s to the Second World War, Provincial Cinematograph Theatres was taken over in February 1929 by Gaumont, which emerged as one of the three dominant exhibition circuits in Britain (the two others were Associated British Pictures and Odeon Cinemas). While Dublin's Grafton, opened by Provincial in 1911, was sold to the Ellis family in the 1930s, Gaumont retained the Classic with even its name changed in 1950 to the Gaumont.

Aside from Provincial's investment in Ireland, and outside Dublin city centre, the Rathmines Picture Palace, or Princess Cinema, 145 Lower Rathmines Road, which opened on 24 March 1913, appears to have been the first custom-built cinema in Dublin and certainly one of the few large-scale projects undertaken in this period. The only cinemas to be designed specifically as such and built on cleared sites were the Manor Street Picture House, 60–61 Manor Street, Stoneybatter, renamed in the mid-1930s as the Broadway; the Bohemian Picture House, 154–55 Phibsboro Road; and the Coliseum, 24 Henry Street, also known as the Picture Palace Theatre; all three of which opened during 1914–15. Later, a number of O'Connell Street cinemas – the Grand Central, the Metropole, La Scala, and the Savoy – were built on sites which had been made derelict during the 1916 Rising, in the case of the former two, rebuilt on sites of former cinemas.[82]

Designed by George L. O'Connor, the Rathmines Picture Palace was developed by the Rathmines Amusement Company. Incorporated on 30 October 1912, the company's directors, most, if not all, of whom were Jewish, included Izidore Isaac Bradlaw, a Briton of Russian origin who was a dentist based at 51 Grafton Street; British-born brothers Joseph Michael Karmel, a merchant tailor, and Nathan Karmel, a tailor's cutter, the company's secretary; and Harry E. Taylor, a 'gentleman', who was also associated with the clothing business.[83] Offering a continuous programme from 3p.m. to 10.30p.m. and charging admission prices of 3*d.*, 6*d.* and 1*s.*, it was managed by James J. Worth, previously of Abercorn Hall,[84] or Picturedrome, 3 Harcourt Road. (Built in the 1880s for religious meetings, the Abercorn had been used, like other such venues, for cinema screenings. It was a 'primitive' marginal cinema with a 'bare board floor, … long stools without backrests for seating',[85] and a cheap admission policy of 2*d.*, which catered 'especially for the working classes and the poorer children of the district'.)[86] Just ten weeks after its opening, the new Rathmines Picture Palace, for some undetermined reason, closed on 27 May 1913, but reopened six months later on 13 December as the Princess Cinema, with Bradlaw still in charge.[87] On 18 July 1914, the cinema, which continued the practice of screening local events such as the procession of civic bodies through the streets of Dublin on 15 July and the festival of folk dancing in Phoenix Park, was visited by the lord lieutenant and Lady Aberdeen who attended a sponsored film.[88]

While most film exhibitors in Dublin (as elsewhere in Ireland) were like Bradlaw and did not confine their involvement with cinema to a single venture,[89] or were, moreover, small businessmen with other interests, two families, led by Maurice Elliman and John J. Farrell, respectively, both of whom came from relatively humble small-shopkeeper beginnings, came to dominate within the sector. Although James T. Jameson, who, from at least 1904, had been showing films in Rathmines town hall, and, as discussed in the companion volume, the central figure in Irish Animated Picture Co., was also prominent within Irish film exhibition until 1916, or later. In 1910, from 23 April to 11 June, for example, Jameson had an extended run of the *Funeral of Edward VII*[90] at Rathmines town hall, a building that he subsequently leased from 1912 as a full-time exhibition venue.[91] The same year he advertised the first season of colour films at the Rotunda;[92] but in the increasingly competitive environment, he was forced to reduce the entrance fee. Thus, 'Jameson's Movies', as they were advertised during the First World War, set admission rates at the Rotunda of 3*d.* to 1*s.* 3*d.* By then, Jameson seems to have begun to minimize his involvement in, or to leave completely, the exhibition business, such that William Kay, who had been proprietor of the Grand Cinema, O'Connell Street, destroyed in the 1916 Rising, took over the Rotunda in October 1916[93] and continued in charge following its reopening after refurbishment on 3 May 1920.

Born on 8 March 1872, in the small village of Kovno, near Riga, Latvia, where his mother had a wine shop, Maurice Elliman left home in 1892 in the wake of the anti-Jewish pogroms that were sweeping czarist Russia and its neighbours. He walked to

Hamburg, Germany, from where he took a ship to Liverpool and went on to Dublin, arriving in Ireland when he was 20 years old. Eight years later, around 1900, he opened a small greengrocer's shop in Aungier Street, close to where he opened his first cinema, and where he lived above the shop.[94] His first association with show business seems to have been 'shortly before 1910' when he had a travelling show which included a boxing booth and a cinematograph.[95] Nevertheless, his role in this and in the Coliseum Theatre of Living Pictures, 16–17 Redmond's Hill, which Richard ('Dickie') H. Graham seems also to have been associated with,[96] and was operational from at least March 1910 (when it received a Dublin corporation licence) until 28 August 1911 (when it was completely destroyed following a fire in the exterior projection box),[97] is somewhat unclear.[98] We know, however, that Elliman was to the forefront of Irish Amusement Company which, on 1 December 1911 on the site of a former billiard saloon, opened the 300-seat Brunswick Cinema Theatre, 30 Great Brunswick Street (now Pearse Street), near the fire station. Elliman's co-directors in Irish Amusement Company were A. Sim; O.S. Baker; and I.I. Bradlaw, who later, as mentioned above, was the primary instigator of the Princess Cinema. The venture did not last and was one of many casualties of the cinema boom of the 1910s, as increasingly cinemagoers demanded more comfortable cinemas with better facilities, though, of course, other cinemas failed simply due to under capitalization. (By 1919 the premises was being used by the Brunswick Motor Exchange.) A week after the Brunswick opened, another Elliman cinema, the 400-seat Theatre de Luxe, 84–86 Lower Camden Street, was opened on 16 December 1912 by his Dublin Kinematograph Theatres Ltd. Designed by architect Frederick Hayes with an oriel window on the first floor its admission prices were set at 3*d.* and 6*d.* Backing for the venture had come from Elliman's Camden Street business neighbours, Rourkes' Bakery and Corrigans' undertakers.[99] Just over fourteen months later, on 28 February 1914, he opened the Blackrock Cinema Theatre, 13 Main Street, Blackrock, with 700 seats.

In what was the beginning of a major expansion of his exhibition interests, in 1920 Elliman demolished the narrow and compact Theatre de Luxe, and, having acquired the adjoining building (no. 85), built, at a cost of £30,000, an enlarged cinema with 1,200 seats. In 1934, the cinema underwent further remodelling and, with an art deco façade from a design by Alfred E. Jones of Jones & Kelly, was renamed the New Super Theatre de Luxe before it closed on 29 June 1974.[1] In February 1922, another Elliman company, Metropole and Allied Cinemas Company Ltd, opened the 883-seat[2] Metropole Cinema, 35–39 Lower O'Connell Street, on the derelict site of the former Metropole Hotel, which had been destroyed during the 1916 Rising. His eldest son, Abe, who began his film career in the Theatre de Luxe, was installed as the Metropole's general manager,[3] thus ensuring a family dynasty that would last until the 1970s and was described as the 'most influential family in Irish entertainment management'.[4] However, as we will see, it was not Abe, but his brother Louis who became, by the 1930s, the dominant player in the business.

John J. Farrell, the *pater familias* of the Farrells, a family, which, for over thirty years was to the fore of Irish film exhibition, was, until 1918, in the unusual and at times potentially conflicting position of not just owning and running cinemas, but also of having power and influence over how cinemas and film might be regulated. This double role came about as a consequence of his membership of Dublin corporation from 1899 to 1918 and his position as an alderman. Like other such local councils in Britain and Ireland, it was the responsibility of Dublin corporation to issue cinema licences under the 1909 Cinematograph Act to venues within its jurisdiction, in this case to Dublin city venues. Notwithstanding incidents where Dublin cinemas were fined or refused licences, such as the Abercorn Hall being fined in 1911 for using cinematograph machines without a licence, or 'Dickie' Graham's Irish Cinema Theatre, 113 Capel Street,[5] which in the years 1912 to 1914 found itself repeatedly unable to comply with licensing requirements;[6] rarely did Dublin cinemas encounter difficulties with the licensing authority with regard to safety issues, the primary focus of the act and for which it had been designed following a series of disastrous fires in Europe and elsewhere. This owes in part to Dublin corporation having an experienced inspector of entertainment venues in Walter Butler, but also to the fact that Irish cinema building and, more usually, the adaptation of existing structures, largely occurred after the introduction of the 1909 act, and, as such, were designed according to the corporation's bye-laws which were strictly enforced.

As might be expected then, very few fires broke out in Dublin cinemas in this period; those that did included at the Coliseum Picture House, Redmond's Hill in August 1911, as noted above, and the Kingstown's Pavilion Cinema, Marine Road, in November 1915 (though this was outside the jurisdiction of Dublin corporation). Both cinemas were destroyed with only the Pavilion rebuilt. More contained fires broke out in the operation rooms of Clontarf Town Hall in October 1917[7] from which the operator and his young assistant narrowly escaped (Clontarf had been incorporated with Dublin corporation's boundaries in 1900);[8] Rathmines Town Hall in September 1918;[9] and the Rotunda Picture House in July 1920.[10] Given that legislation required that projection booths had to be situated outside the cinema hall, there was no great threat to the audience, and in all cases, no panic ensued. In addition, the Bohemian Picture Theatre, 154–55 Phibsborough Road, had at least three fires, including in 1925[11] and a more extensive one in 1927, when its organ (installed in 1914 and valued at £3,000) was destroyed, as were the stage, the orchestral stalls, and the greater portion of the roof.[12] While the cause of the 1927 fire was unknown (it did not start in the projection box), one of the earlier fires was believed to have been started by a cigarette-end. Despite the relatively few fire incidents, in 1929 the issue of fire safety was raised in the Dáil following a fire at the Grand Central, O'Connell Street, on 16 September 1929, but it was stated by the minister for justice, James Fitzgerald-Kenney, that there was 'no evidence that there is any necessity for further legislation' and that the fire was not of a serious nature, something disputed by Dublin North Fianna Fáil TD Eamon Cooney who argued that it was 'of a very serious nature and that certain influences were used to prevent a prosecution, and the consequent publicity'.[13] Nevertheless, it was nationally accepted that cinemas in Irish cities, most especially in Dublin, were above reproach. As an *Irish Times* article stated, they were of the best possible description, equipped with the most up-to-date safety appliances, and with as much fire-proof material as was possible in their construction. It could be said of some of these cinemas, particularly in Dublin, that if they went on fire to-morrow the only things that would burn in them would be the seats and the stage, and in a few days these could be replaced and the walls repainted.[14]

Furthermore, Dublin, as well as nearby Rathmines and Pembroke, and Cork, had 'really efficient fire brigades', while other local authorities in centres including Limerick, Waterford, and Galway also had fire engines, which though perhaps not sufficient to fight a big fire would be 'useful in extinguishing small fires before they had time to get a hold on a building.'[15]

Outside Dublin where expertise the calibre of Butler's was lacking, it was usually left to the police to ensure compliance with the new regulations. However, according to Justice Fahy speaking in 1930 at Wexford court on the occasion of fining Augustus McCormack, proprietor of a travelling cinema show, for not having the fire appliances required under the Cinematograph Act 1909, there was 'a great laxity in supervision of cases of this kind.'[16] While often it was when film shows were presented as part of travelling circuses or other such entertainments that they became subject to official scrutiny (such as, for example, in July 1910 when the chief secretary's office was forwarded a report following police investigation of a covered van being used by a Miss Basco for film shows as part of her travelling circus in Newcastle West, Co. Limerick, which, in the end, was deemed to pose only an 'infinitesimal' risk),[17] provincial cinemas more generally were slack in their observation of the regulations laid down under the 1909 act. The potential danger that such venues posed was largely due to the fact that a significant number of them were poor conversions of barns, garages, stores and other spaces, some of which were timber-built, and at times, were not exclusively dedicated to film screenings with part of the property being used to store wood and other flammable items. Furthermore, unlike the tents used by fairground film exhibitors, which, as Mr Bowen explained on the occasion of travelling cinema owner Mr McCormack's successful application for a licence, were not dangerous as 'people can run out on all sides',[18] many of these 'cinemas' were either without adequate exits or had obstructed passageways, while a majority had poor, if any, anti-fire fittings. As one insurance man stated in a letter to the *Irish Times* in 1926, 'so-called fire-proof chambers … are inadequate to prevent fire from spreading',[19] with one such fire-proof projection box described elsewhere as being made of wood with a thin lining of metal like tin.[20]

Consequently, it is hardly surprising that numerous cinemas outside Dublin were destroyed by fires with examples in the silent period including Kildare's Star Cinema, Dublin Road, destroyed in 1917[21] and again in December 1925;[22] Newtownards' Picture House, Regent Street, destroyed in December 1919;[23] Limerick's Tivoli Cinema, Assembly Mall, and Cork's Lee Cinema, Winthrop Street, both seriously damaged by fire in 1920 (July and December, respectively); Lurgan's Cinema and Hippodrome, Church Place, Main Street, destroyed in August 1922;[24] Powell's Cinema Hall, Main

Street, Roscrea, destroyed on 28 November 1924;[25] Galway's Victoria Cinema Theatre, Victoria Place, burned down on 20 July 1926;[26] an occasional venue in Church Street in the small village of Drumcollogher, Co. Limerick, burned in September 1926, to which we will return; the Letterkenny Recreation and Cinema Hall destroyed by fire on 7 May 1928;[27] and the Francis Street cinema in Fermoy, Co. Cork, where fire broke out in the early hours of the morning and gutted the building in October 1929.[28]

Unfortunately, such a pattern also marks the 1930s with many incidents in 1930 such as the fires in Tipperary at Cashel's Cinema, Main Street (January),[29] in Cork at the Pavilion Cinema and Cafe, Patrick Street (February), and in Limerick at Abbey Cinema, George's Quay (April);[30] and thereafter at the Rock Cinema, Ballyshannon in 1932;[31] at Youghal in August 1935 where fire in the neighbouring cinemas of Horgan's Picture Theatre (damaged) and Hurst's Picture Palace (completely destroyed) left the town without a cinema for some time;[32] at Coleraine where the Palladium, Society Street, which burnt in September 1936;[33] and the 1938 fires in Carlow's Cinema Palace, Burrin Street, in Carrickmacross' Gem Cinema,[34] and in Cork's Washington Cinema, Washington Street.[35] Such a list, of course, does not include all the minor fires, which, akin to those at the Clontarf or Rathmines Town Halls cited above, were extinguished quickly and caused little damage or interruption to regular screenings.[36]

While at least some companies refused 'to insure cinemas in county districts where the buildings [had] been converted, instead of being specially built' given that they were potentially 'death-traps',[37] what is remarkable about the list above is that only one fire, that of Drumcollogher, Co. Limerick, in September 1926, resulted in serious injuries or fatalities. Perhaps, more remarkable is the fact that after Drumcollogher, which was the worst cinema fire in Britain and Ireland, with forty-eight people,[38] or almost one-third of the audience killed, safety regulations continued to be ignored, and, despite a number of prosecutions, such as in Limerick in 1927 when reference was made by the presiding Justice Flood to Drumcollogher, who noted that the corporation, the civic guards and the legal system represented in this case by himself 'had a duty to perform to the public',[39] a strict enforcement policy was not adopted with the result that fires remained a feature of cinema exhibition in provincial parts of Ireland. Nevertheless, the history of cinema exhibition in most parts of the world in this period is punctuated with such tragedies.[40]

From the 1940s to the end of the century, however, serious cinema fires throughout Ireland became less common, with an average of three per decade. By then, the converted non-purpose built cinema, the type at the centre of the Drumcollogher disaster, had become a thing of the past, while the use of inflammable nitrate film ceased by the early 1950s. Indeed, the Drumcollogher cinema was nothing more than a room measuring 60ft by 20ft on the upper floor of a two-storey wooden shed on Church Street, the ground floor of which was used as a store for timber and glass. Accessed by a wooden ladder with a handrail, the upstairs, which had two small, but barred windows at one end, and a small partitioned room, sometimes used as a dressing room by amateur theatre groups, had been used, on at least five occasions prior to the night of the fire, Sunday, 5 September 1926, by the Hurleys of Charleville to show films.

Ironically, the reason that the Drumcollogher building was used at all on that fateful Sunday was because of another cinema's observation of the Cinematograph Act. Given that the Assembly Rooms Picturedrome, Cork, just forty miles away from Drumcollogher, complied with the terms of their six-day licence (the only type issued by Cork corporation at the time) it meant that the popular western melodrama, Clifford Smith's 1925 *The White Outlaw*, which had begun its run the previous Friday, was potentially available for screening elsewhere on the Sunday.[41] Having become aware of the planned 5 September screening in Drumcollegher, Sergeant Long of the local garda station, formerly a fireman, contacted proprietor Patrick Brennan, film renter and local hackney-car owner William Forde, and projectionist Patrick Downing, who worked at the Assembly Rooms Picturedrome, and drew their attention to the provisions of the Cinematograph Act as it affected public safety. Nevertheless, it seems that Long's strictures regarding the provision of blankets, sand and water, as well as clear exits, were ignored.

With no internal electrics – a lorry parked outside provided power for the projector – Forde, who was collecting money at a table beside the narrow door at the top of the access ladder, had to rely on two candles for light. However, when Downing, having chosen to leave the protective metal cases of the films at the Assembly Rooms because of their considerable weight, placed the uncovered combustible nitrate film on the table with the candles, they caught fire. The fire spread rapidly, and only those behind the projector managed to escape through the narrow doorway, the rest being trapped by the flames as they found that the window exits were seemingly barred. Parish clerk John Gleeson and at least six others managed to escape through the bars. As a former member of the IRA, which used to meet there, Gleeson had partly cut the bars in the event that should the Black and Tans raid their meeting place, they could escape. After a small number had escaped through the window, a large woman got stuck in it, thus blocking this escape route.

The victims of the Drumcollogher fire were buried in a communal grave marked by a large Celtic cross in the grounds of the local Catholic church, St Bartholomew's, while an international relief fund was launched to help the fifty-three children left dependent. A fund-raising show was held at La Scala, Dublin, on 10 September at which the popular American entertainer Will Rogers played. In all, £16,000 was raised for the relatives of the victims and for the memorial cross. The inquest found Downing guilty of negligence and Forde of carelessness with regard to the candles. When the inquest concluded, Forde, Downing, and Brennan were charged with manslaughter, but at their trial, which concluded on 15 December 1926, Brennan was found not guilty, while the jury could not agree a verdict in the cases against Forde and Downing, both of whom were later acquitted.[42] Forde emigrated to Australia and died there in 1929, apparently as a result of his adding arsenic instead of baking powder while making bread, causing three deaths, including his own.[43] Later in 1929, in a sad reflection of the poor enforcement of the act, an almost identical venue to the Drumcollogher one, a two-story building with cinema room above a garage and stores, was gutted in nearby Fermoy.[44]

Despite the initial motivation and intention behind the Cinematograph Act, its wording was interpreted by British and Irish courts as allowing local authorities to take on powers of film censorship, an altogether more subjective and more culturally and socially powerful activity than decisions limited to structure and safety. Consequently, J.J. Farrell found himself engaged in the struggle over censorship as he tried to find a balance between protecting his own and his industry's economic interests and resisting during the 1910s a restrictive film censorship policy while at the same time maintaining good relations with powerful lay and religious constituents and opinion-makers.[45]

Following the establishment of his first cinema, the Electric, Talbot Street, albeit in a secondary location, Farrell opened on 19 December 1912 his second cinema, the 920-seat Mary Street Picture House, 12–13 Mary Street, a short distance from the Volta. Also known as the Irish Kinematograph, and later popularly referred to as the 'Maro' (or 'Mero'/'Mayro'), it was built on the site of Beakey's cabinet factory to a design by George L. O'Connor, who was later described by *Bioscope* as a 'specialist in cinema design'.[46] Featuring a moulded arched entrance, panelled recessed walls, decorative arches and a curved ceiling,[47] it was one of the best equipped and largest cinemas at the time.

Two years later, Farrell opened the small, 372-seat[48] Pillar Picture House, 62 Upper O'Connell Street, opposite Nelson's Pillar, on 2 December 1914[49] from a design by Aubrey V. O'Rourke, another architect who would become closely associated with Irish cinema design. As a result of 'crowded houses' enjoyed from its opening, this 'newest, and perhaps prettiest and most select' of Dublin's cinemas was 'unaffected by slackness of business owing to the war.'[50] *Irish Builder and Engineer*[51] reported that the approach to the cinema was covered with a semi-circular veranda, which followed the sweep of a broad arch, and the opening under was filled in with Sicilian marble and leaded glass. It added that the vestibule was 'very effectively' treated with walnut and satinwood panelling with a fibrous plaster frieze of figured plaques and swag work. The ceiling was elaborately ornamented and had a semi-circular dome of leaded glass. The staircase to the balcony was also panelled in walnut, and the enclosing walls artistically decorated in fibrous work. The interior was 'modern classic' in design. Though situated close to the General Post Office, it survived the 1916 Rising and continued as a cinema until March 1945.[52]

Another early cinema that Farrell was involved with was the Phibsborough (or Phibsboro) Picture House, 36 Madras Place (now 376 North Circular Road). Initiated by William King, a farmer of Belcamp House, Raheny, planning for the cinema began when in 1913 he joined with Farrell, Henry Hibbert and Thomas Wood to form the Phibsboro Picture House Company, which subsequently built the cinema from a design by Aubrey V. O'Rourke. Though it opened in May 1914 with 387 seats, following reconstruction in 1915, it had 600 seats. The cinema, managed by Robert O'Russ, continued under King's ownership until 1938 when it was bought by Maurice Elliman's Metropole and Allied Cinemas Company.[53]

Just like Elliman, who had built the Metropole on a derelict 1916 site, Farrell acquired the site of the former Dublin Bread Company, 6–7 Lower O'Connell Street, which had been similarly ruined during the rising, on which to build an 800-seat cinema. Opened on 10 October 1921, Farrell's new cinema was called Grand Central Cinema, a reference to William Kay's small luxurious Grand Cinema that had occupied the adjoining site, no. 8, until it was destroyed during the rising. According to *Bioscope*, Kay's Grand, which had opened in 1913 as part of the Kay family owned Grand Hotel and restaurant, was 'one of the coziest and most popular cinemas in Dublin [whose] loss [would] be severely felt.'[54] The new cinema, an impressive building, was adorned with distinctive neo-classical fronting and imposing glass canopy from designs by three teams of architects: O'Callaghan and Webb; Higginbottom and Stafford; and Vincent Kelly. It also boasted a large balcony that could accommodate over half the audience[55] and, to maximize the spectators' field of vision, it was steeply raked, a feature that led some patrons to complain of vertigo.[56] The building was destroyed by fire on 13 September 1946 and was sold three years later to Hibernian Bank. It continues to operate as a bank.

Paralleling the expansion of cinemas in Dublin (both in the primary sites of O'Connell and Grafton streets and the secondary locations elsewhere in the city and county), Belfast's engagement with the sector was no less dramatic. While the first regular venues for film screenings in Belfast were St George's Hall, 39 High Street, with a capacity of 1,500 persons (operating from 17 August 1908 to 1916); Star Picture Palace, Church Street (operating from 14 September 1908 to 1910);[57] and the Royal Hippodrome (operating from 2 November 1907 to 1931), the first full-time cinema to open was the Electric Picture Palace. Situated at 19–21 York Street, the small 250-seat cinema was opened by Fred Stewart on 1 August 1910,[58] nearly eight months after the establishment of Dublin's Volta, or over three years after Britain's first cinema in Colne, Lancashire, which opened in February 1907, the same year that London's first cinema was located in the New Egyptian Hall, Piccadilly.

Stewart's second cinema was the 335-seat Panopticon, 44–46 High Street, which opened on 22 February 1912 (and after refurbishment was known as the Lyric from 13 October 1924). Possibly it was when Stewart planned to open the larger New York Cinema that the Electric was closed down (on 6 March 1915). The 800-seat New York opened on 31 July 1916, though it, too, closed six years later, at the end of December 1922, perhaps because of the Troubles. Nevertheless, Stewart remained active within Belfast exhibition, later owning the Crumlin Picture House, Crumlin Road.

Though the two cinemas at Newtownards Road, Belfast, were both named the Princess, they were not affiliated to each other. On 16 September 1910, at 308 Newtownards Road, W.T. Anderson opened the 1,200-seat Princess Picture Palace which seems to have catered for the lower end of the market. Two years later, on 29 July 1912, a rival, Ferris ('Paddy') Pounds who went on to become a key figure in the Irish Theatres cinema circuit (the main competitor to the Curran circuit, discussed in the next chapter), opened his cinema across the road at number 307, cheekily calling his 1,000-seat picture house the New Princess Palace. Contrasting the 'uninspiring' entrance of the first Princess, Pounds' featured coloured lights and a distinctive windmill-like tower.

Before the end of 1910 a number of other neighbourhood cinemas opened. These included the 500-seat Shankill Picturedrome, 148 Shankill Road, by Shankill Picturedrome (Belfast) Ltd; the 632-seat Kelvin Picture Palace, Fisherwick Place, College Square East; and the 200-seat Shaftesbury Pictoria, Shaftesbury Square, which, although the first cinema in Belfast to run continuous programmes from 3p.m. to 11p.m., closed in 1917, probably as a result of competition from larger and more profitable cinemas. The following year, the 900-seat Picturedrome, 112 Mountpottinger Road, opened on 25 February 1911.[59] Managed during its first year by 'Paddy' Pounds, the Picturedrome, which was originally owned, though only briefly, by Belfast Picturedrome Ltd before being bought by Mount Pottinger Cinemas Ltd and later integrated into the Irish Theatres circuit, was the first major Belfast cinema to be built on one level, or in stadium-style. Thus, by the time Provincial Cinematograph Theatres opened the 680-seat Belfast Picture House, Royal Avenue, on 19 June 1911, unlike in Dublin where the Volta was the only full-time cinema that preceded Provincial's entrance to the cinema market, in Belfast there were already at least seven full-time cinema venues, though most of these were akin to the down-market Volta. Like its Dublin venues, when Provincial opened in Belfast it consciously sought out a middle class patronage with its swish café, printed programme and resident orchestra.

Validating the pattern evident elsewhere in Ireland and Britain of established businessmen unconnected with the cinema entering the sector, coal merchant John Donnelly opened on 18 December 1912 the 600-seat West Belfast Picture Theatre, 80 Albert Street, situated in an alleyway behind Albert Street. Its first manager, Joseph Cavanagh, who seems to have bought the cinema from Donnelly in 1914, went on to run a number of other cinemas. On 9 October 1913, ten months after the establishment of the West Belfast Picture Theatre, Shankill Road grocer Joe McKibben, who would become another major figure in Belfast exhibition by the time of his death in 1921, opened his first cinema – the 1,150-seat West End Picture House, 108 Shankill Road – which remained in his family until 1960 when it shut down.

With little capital behind it, the 'quite spartan' Central Picture Theatre, 18–20 Smithfield, converted from a jeweller's shop, was opened by Central Belfast Picture Theatre Ltd on 22 December 1913. The same day, Clonard Hall Company opened the 1,200-seat Clonard Picture House, 140 Falls Road, which, also known as the Slieve Donard, was one of the 'finest suburban cinemas' built in Belfast before the First World War.[60] The following year, on 23 March 1914, the 850-seat Crumlin Road Picture House, built by Crumlin Picture House Ltd, the owners of the Panopticon Cinema (later the Lyric), opened. Like other establishments, it created different sections within the cinema by contrasting plush seats and Wilton carpet for the more expensive parts of the house, with hard benches and cork flooring for the cheap front stalls.

Although it was the case that the majority of these cinemas did not embellish the exteriors or interiors with attractive or unusual features, the 550-seat Kinema House, Great Victoria Street, opened by Great Northern Kinema Company on 7 April 1914, was a rare exception. Designed in an old English timbered style, it had a spacious foyer with a miniature fountain and waterfall, while the rear wall of the auditorium featured an Irish landscape painting with a castle, the projection holes corresponding to the castle windows.[61] Though the Kinema House, through its ambience and location, was an attractive middle-class venue, the 1,000-seat Imperial Picture House, Cornmarket, which was opened on 7 December 1914 by Mr (later Sir) Crawford McCullagh, JP, who would remain closely associated with Belfast cinemas into the 1940s, 'was the most important cinema' in Belfast until the Classic was built in 1923.[62] Indeed, the day after the Imperial's opening, the *Belfast Newsletter*[63] noted that as well as occupying a central site in the city, it 'leaves nothing to be desired' with its Tudor or early Jacobean period style; a ceiling of 'a refined Greek character'; and an 'Empire' tea-room.

Unlike in Dublin, where a depressed war-time economy, which affected all businesses, resulted in the ending of the first cinema building boom, Belfast saw a continuing expansion of cinema exhibition with a further eight venues opened during 1915 to 1917. Belfast Coliseum Ltd, for example, whose managing director was Andy T. Wright, opened the 900-seat Coliseum Cinema, Grosvenor Road, on 8 February 1915. Built in 1909 as the Alexandra Theatre and later renamed the Palladium, the conversion cost the company £11,000.[64] During this period, Wright was, perhaps, Ireland's most important exhibitor/distributor. An investor in Dublin's Phoenix Cinema, 7–9 Ellis Quay, which was officially opened on 3 December 1912 by Dublin's lord mayor, Lorcan G. Sherlock,[65] and in the 600-seat Cinema Palace, Harper's Lane, Wexford town; in 1914, Wright already controlled twenty-nine cinemas and was head of distributors Films Ltd.[66]

Catering for the cheaper end of the market, the Queen's, 250–56 York Road, commenced its business around 8 December 1915, while its investors, Belfast Gaiety Picture Theatre Co., established the equally downmarket 968-seat cine-variety house, the Gaiety, 157–63 North Street, on 14 November 1916. Seeking to satisfy the opposing religious and political constituencies of the Shankill and Falls roads, Michael Open[67] reports that the cinema divided its week with three days allocated to each group. One surprising early entrant into film exhibition was the Willowfield Unionist Club of the Unionist Party in south-east Belfast which on 20 December 1915 provided the 800-seat hall that was the Willowfield Picture House. Less than three months later, on 6 March 1916, Joe McKibben opened what was his last cinema, the 1,200-seat Midland Picture House, 7–9 Canning Street, a prominent site close to York Street station, while Duncairn Picture Theatre, 12 Duncairn Gardens, also with 1,200 seats, opened on 3 July 1916. Built by Will White's Duncairn Picture Theatre Co., it was regarded as a building of 'exceptional quality' possessing 'originality of ... design' and being 'extremely attractive and very large'. The building's design incorporated a tea lounge at the top of the staircase from where it was possible to view the films, and retail outlets on the ground floor.[68]

The 850-seat Lyceum, Antrim Road/New Lodge Road, opened on 11 December 1916. Within a week, on 16 December, the 1,200-seat Royal Cinema, Arthur Square (Cornmarket), began screenings. Owned by Fred Warden, the expensively-equipped venue was built as a reconstruction of the Theatre Royal. On 30 October 1917, W.J. Hogan, owner of the Clonard, Falls Road, through his Popular Picture Palace Ltd, opened the 1,100-seat Popular Picture Theatre, 49–55 Newtownards Road, while publican P.J. Kelly launched the Tivoli, 2 Christian Place (off Irwin Street, Smithfield), on 1 July 1918, but it closed in the 1920s.

As in Dublin, during the 1910s religious and other halls were used for regular or sporadic film screenings. These venues included in 1916 the 1,900-seat Albert Hall, Shankill Road, where the licensee was Revd H. Montgomery; the 2,000-seat Assembly Hall, Fisherwick Place and Howard Street, where the licensee was Henry Scott; the 600-seat East Belfast YMCA, 183 Albertbridge Road, leased by Andrew MacMillan; the 850-seat Macquiston Institute, Cregagh Road, leased by J.W.A. Hamilton; the 1,200-seat People's Hall, York Street, where the licensee was Revd W. McGuire; the 1,500-seat St Mary's Hall, Bank Street; the 1,500-seat Wellington Hall, Wellington Place, leased by D.A. Black; and the 630-seat Woodvale Hall, Cambral Street. In summary, by the end of 1914, there were sixteen venues in Belfast where films were being shown full-time, while a further ten opened before the end of the war. By 1920, even though some early venues had closed, there were twenty-six cinemas in Belfast, a number not too dissimilar to Dublin.

Outside of Dublin and Belfast, and a number of major provincial cities including Cork, Waterford, Limerick, Galway and Derry, all of which had no more than a few full-time cinemas (something which remained true even during the expansionary period of cinema building in the 1930s), the experience of cinema in Ireland during the 1910s was periodic, and was largely confined to two or three visits per year from a travelling cinematograph show. One such travelling show was James T. Jameson's Irish Animated, which began its tours in the early 1900s. In addition to visiting the major urban areas, Irish Animated took in smaller provincial centres, particularly in the south and south-west, which was also served by the Ormonde family from Kilkenny, who had been touring there (and the rest of Ireland) for many years with their circus, variety and film screening combination. Unlike other touring exhibitors, Irish Animated often offered a highly sophisticated film screening experience. For example, during their three-day visit to Skibbereen's Town Hall in June 1910 both the Rotunda's orchestra, under the baton of Harry Peters, and the Irish baritone W.R. Goggin, also performed.[69] Reflecting, no doubt, its popularity, Irish Animated returned five months later.[70] While other nearby venues, including at Bandon,[71] were visited by the company, a more permanent presence in the south-west was established when Jameson, from December 1912 until at least 1914, rented the recently-built 800-seat Tralee Theatre Royal for use as a cinema for £50 per month.[72] However, the use of the theatre as a cinema met with some resistance, particularly from publicans, who felt it was leading to a loss of business. The chairman of the local council in supporting Jameson asked those opposing the cinema not to 'deprive the people of the town and the working classes of Tralee of the entertainment and [not to] lose the money to the town.' Jameson, reporting that he was paying £22 per week to permanent staff, and thus creating local employment, later pointed out he was not just taking money out of the town, but contributing to the local economy.[73] The cinema thrived and as one sympathetic patron told the *Echo*, the 'vast audience' for the hugely-popular Italian epic *Quo Vadis?* (1913) was a 'remarkable spectacle' because it was 'representative of every section of the people, [who were] keenly appreciating what one might well have thought no one but the most highly cultured would be able to appreciate.' There was a 'church-like decorum' at the Theatre Royal with 'groups of urchins excitedly discussing classic drama!'[74]

The travelling shows outside provincial towns, especially in small villages, were far more basic. Maurice Butler (born 1907) who remembers seeing films in the 1910s at a 'Fancy Fair' in Rush, Co. Dublin, or a cine-variety show run by the Purcell family, describes the shows as having taken place on a fit-up stage where the construction was a half-tent, half-wooden structure measuring about 40ft by 25ft. For safety reasons, the projector was mounted in a caravan adjoining the tent, with a projection hole cut in the wall opposite the screen. The young boy, overawed by the films, was disappointed to discover that 'all the action seemed to be taking place in a perpetual shower of rain', which he later found out 'was the result of the film being run too often through a faulty projector'![75] In this and later periods, including in the 1950s, travelling shows such as those run by the Daniels' family in Donegal, Monaghan and other parts of the north-west included films.[76] Recalling his experience with travelling exhibitors in the village of Granagh, Co. Limerick, in the early 1950s, David O'Riordan recollects a range of such seasonal visitors, including Brian Lyons' Super Talkies; Ben Bono from Dublin; the Hayes Brothers, whose tent and equipment were destroyed during a fire while visiting the village; McCormacks; Gazettes; and the Courtneys, who would 'have special shows on Sunday nights'.[77] Indeed, while similar 16mm screenings, usually under the control of the parish priest, were a feature of Sunday nights in a great many village halls, including that of Slieverue, Co. Kilkenny, where the principal author saw his first films in the 1950s, given the improvements in public and private transport and Slieverue's proximity to Waterford city which, only three miles away, boasted three full-time cinemas, such travelling shows were already being made obsolete.[78]

Although travelling film shows were a feature of rural life for many decades, and were given an impetus with the post-Second World War availability of 16mm film projectors such that fixed site exhibitors sought to have them curtailed,[79] by the First World War most provincial towns had cinemas, though as already noted, often not custom-built ones, nevertheless, these fixed sites came to dominate rural exhibition. Furthermore, a number of these cinema halls formed mini-circuits or clusters of two (or more). In Co. Louth, for example, the Dundealgan [Dundalk] Electric Theatres Ltd rented from 1912 the 450-seat Town Hall Buildings, Crowe Street, Dundalk, and from 1914, the nearby Whitworth Hall, near St Lawrence Gate, Drogheda, with the same person, Mr O'Mahoney, managing both venues.[80] Such a practice of a local entrepreneur renting an existing premises prior to the construction of custom-built cinemas (often as late as the 1930s) was repeated throughout the island.

DISTRIBUTION: FROM SALE TO HIRE AND FROM FIRST-RUN TO
SECOND-RUN CINEMAS

Britain and Ireland, by comparison with other western countries, were late in transforming the film distribution business from sale to hire. By 1906 hiring had almost completely replaced free sale in the USA, whereas in 'primitive' Britain, so described as it was deemed backward due to its reliance on sales of films as there were only four hiring companies, while in Ireland there is no evidence that there was any such specialist company, with the result that during cinema's first decade, exhibitors, both in Britain and Ireland, either directly, or indirectly through middlemen whose activity was 'extremely lively throughout the period', had to purchase films on the open market.[81] In this way, any number of copies of a film regardless of subject could be sold at the uniform price of 6*d*. per foot, though in 1906, Pathé, in a move subsequently accepted by the other producer-distributors/distributors, reduced the price to 4*d*. per foot. Given such expense, many exhibitors, including perhaps Irish Animated, recouped at least part of the cost by selling the discarded films on the second-hand market, with the price determined by the age and quality of the print. With the shift towards renting, the cost to a renter-distributor to acquire a full programme was in the region of £100, with the rent price set at between £2 2*s*. and £6 (1909). As a result, to ensure decent returns on the capital employed, renter-distributors literally exhausted prints such that the number of prints in circulation was often huge. For example, there were 400 copies of Cecil Hepworth's famous *Rescued by Rover* (1905) in circulation for four or five years.[82]

A vigorous campaign in Britain during 1910, in which Irish exhibitors were far from disinterested, was designed to stave off the attempts by the powerful Kinematograph Manufacturers' Association and the newly formed Incorporated Association of Film Renters, formed in 1910, to control the market. Under a secret agreement between the two, the aim was to fix prices and limit the time in which films were in circulation. Furthermore, it sought to eliminate completely the sale of films. This 'strangulation' of the open market and the introduction of the 'American system of trusts' led to 'a state of war in the trade' over the fear of monopoly practices being imposed on small exhibitors and the marginalization of small distributors. These threats led to the formation in 1912 of the defensive Cinematograph Exhibitors' Association (CEA) of Great Britain. By 1914, this representative body of cinema owners had 965 members with 1,465 theatres. Irish exhibitors, like their Scottish counterparts, at least initially seem to have remained aloof from the new body, and in time separate exhibitors' organizations were set up in Ireland, though association was maintained with the London-based CEA, and in the case of Northern Ireland a formal relationship was established in 1942. When Pathé, the largest manufacturers of film in Europe, broke ranks and announced in early 1913 that it would bypass renters and deal directly with exhibitors, the trade was put into further disarray with the cartel and monopolistic tendencies of the manufacturers and large renters undermined. After a period of intense negotiations, the three trade associations agreed on a new scheme whereby a three-year licensing system for films was introduced, but with the condition that films would be returned to a clearing house for checking at the end of years one and two. This not only ensured that prints would be of reasonable quality, but imposing a year's circulation effectively ended the outright sale of film. Those who failed to cooperate with the scheme would be boycotted.[83]

The rise of the longer (three reel or more) film and the feature film after 1910 effectively settled the issue with price differentiation distinguishing between cheaply-produced movies and prestigious or 'exclusive' drama films. By then, the latter were being auctioned to the highest bidder and rented to an exhibitor for an exclusive run in a particular district, a process which later became known as the 'barring' system. Whereas a popular title could have been acquired for as little as £12 in the early to mid-1900s, the auction prices for Enrico Guazzoni's Cines-produced monumental spectacular epics *Quo Vadis?* the most expensive and successful film of its age, and *Anthony and Cleopatra* (*Marcantonio e Cleopatra*, 1913, Italy), were £6,700 and £8,100, respectively, while the prestigious British productions *The Battle of Waterloo* (Charles Weston, 1913) and *East Lynne* (Bert Haldane, 1913) were auctioned for the 'quite exceptional' prices of £5,000 and £4,000.[84] The result was a sharp demarcation between 'exclusive' or first-run cinemas, which could command high prices, and second-run venues. In Ireland, however, because of its geographical marginalization, the films came later to first-run venues. Nevertheless, when films such as those mentioned were finally shown in Dublin, they were screened initially in prestigious locations, often middle-class theatre venues with premium prices.

Since indigenous Irish fiction film production did not properly begin until 1915, all films screened in Ireland had to be imported, and, therefore, came from London, or, later, were mediated through the Dublin regional offices of foreign companies. Consequently, a major impediment to screening first-run product at an early stage was the travel time taken for a film to reach Ireland, which, typically, added up to two days to a rental. Thus, for an Irish exhibitor to offer a three-day run of a title, the (British) renter was effectively without the print for up to five days, suffering two days loss of income. As *Bioscope*'s 'Paddy' reported in 1912,

> It was difficult to secure special feature or exclusive films for Ireland ... A film, hired from Monday till Wednesday, could not be dispatched to England until the Thursday; therefore, by the time it arrived the company hiring it would have lost about two days. He found, in consequence, that a second or third release was generally the most suitable.[85]

The economics of this inevitably led to a less attractive programme, albeit at a cheaper rental cost, not just for (delayed) first-run venues but for those in secondary locations. That said, the number of films available for hire in Britain and Ireland greatly increased from 4,144 in 1910 to 7,554 by 1913, a rise which no doubt was important in the cinema building expansionary period of 1910 to 1914. In 1910, the country of origin of these titles, all of which, theoretically, at least, were available to Irish exhibitors, were France, 36 per cent, over half of which, 22 per cent, came from Pathé; USA, 28 per cent; Italy, 17 per cent; Britain, 15 per cent; and others, including Denmark and Germany, 4 per cent; while 60 per cent of the releases came from just six companies: Pathé, Gaumont, Vitagraph, Lux, Edison and the single British representative, Hepworth, which accounted for nearly half the British output, but was only one-quarter Pathé's size. In all, in 1910 six foreign companies (Cines, Edison, Essanay, Nordisk, Pathé and Vitagraph), had their own offices in England, while another thirty-four released through English agents.[86] Of course, with the outbreak of the First World War such variety was eliminated, such that by 1918 Irish screens were dominated by Anglo-American product.

Notwithstanding such geographical/economic disadvantage, Ireland continued to develop as a film territory. At one level, this is reflected in the film trade journal *Bioscope*'s introduction in February 1912 of a regular 'Pictures in Ireland' column with an Irish contributor, 'Paddy'; and *Kinematograph and Lantern Weekly*'s inclusion of 'Irish Notes' as a regular feature shortly afterwards. (Dublin's *Evening Telegraph*, however, only introduced a weekly 'Kinematograph Notes and News' in early 1917.) At another level, Ireland's profitability as a film territory is indicated in British Gaumont's opening in April 1913 of a Dublin premises on Lord Edward Street. Custom-built, it included a preview theatre for showing films prior to hire or purchase, and, as a producer of newsreels, facilities for processing and printing films.[87]

A number of other companies and individuals were also active in Irish film distribution at this time, including Hibernian Films Ltd, also based at 13 Lord Edward Street; Film Services Ltd, similarly located and which supplied, among other items, Uyama carbons for projectors; James T. Jameson; the Ideal Film Renting Co., 40 Dawson Street; Green Isle Film Agency, 34 Windsor Road, Dublin, which was run in 1915 by Godfrey Kilroy; Weisker Brothers, 205 Great Brunswick Street; and Norman Whitten's General Film Supply, 17 Brunswick Street, which later became an important supplier of newsreels with its *Irish Events* series, 1917–20. According to *Kine Weekly* in 1915, General Film Supply made 'a speciality of cheap programs for the smaller country towns in Ireland'.[88] While a Gaumont advertisement in 1916 sought offers for Charlie Chaplin films in Ireland and for the Irish exhibition rights for twenty-eight Keystone 'exclusives',[89] a British-based company, Harma & Co. of Wardour Street, London, in 1917 offered to sell ('no Renting proposition will be entertained') territorial rights for Ireland of about twenty films, together or separately, including three Cecil M. Hepworth films (*Comin' through the Rye*, 1916; *The Marriage of William Ashe*, 1916; and *The Cobweb*, 1917); *The House of Fortescue* (Frank Wilson, 1916); *The Happy Warrior* (F. Martin Thornton, 1917); and *A Master of Men* (Wilfred Noy, 1917).[90] With trade shows having become common in Dublin and Belfast by 1914, by 1917, 'several of the leading [distribution] firms' had representatives in Ireland.[91]

GOING TO THE PICTURES DURING THE SILENT PERIOD

The expansion in the number of buildings adapted as cinemas in Dublin during 1910–14 owes perhaps less to the rise in the wealth of the working and middle classes than to other interconnecting factors. These included the comparative cheapness and greater availability of the film product; the increasing attraction and sophistication of film in terms of narrative and spectacle, which by this stage had largely replaced the early craze and interest in film technology; and the appeal of a shared communal space, which was characterized in the first instance as pleasure-giving rather than as being part of, or governed by, the instrumental rational order of capitalism, the state, or the church. However, the most crucial dynamic in the mix was the double realization by businessmen, particularly small- to middle-size investors, no doubt aware of trends in Britain and elsewhere, that film entertainment, having already considerably 'matured' and 'developed', but not to the point of exhaustion, was most likely here to stay, an idea widely accepted in cultural comment,[92] and that film exhibition could, given the basic level of infrastructure required to open a cinema, produce an acceptable or modest return on relatively small investment.

Nevertheless, in 1914, given that British cinema-owners were achieving on average as little as 12.5 per cent of capacity over about fifteen weekly screenings, or recording attendances of 1,400 per week where the average cinema seated about 850 people,[93] it is likely that, as Hiley argues, 'there were few profits to be made from local cinema companies, despite the investment of an estimated £13.9 million of public and private capital.'[94] More fundamentally, on the eve of the First World War, as many as 1,000 British cinemas, or one in five, were 'on the verge of bankruptcy'.[95] But then, as is suggested by the admission differential in Britain of four million admissions per week in 1911 when there were approximately 2,000 purpose-built cinemas, and only seven million admissions per week in 1914, when the number of cinemas had expanded to 5,000, it was not audience demand (which in Britain peaked as late as 1915), or even film production (which peaked in 1912), but cinema building by private investors (which peaked in 1910) that led to the explosion in exhibition venues. As such, it was only a matter of time before the optimism within the film exhibition sector would be given a serious reality check. As always, local events could also erode business activity and profits.

During the latter part of 1913, film exhibitors in Dublin, and especially the Elliman family, were given a sharp reminder of the social divisions in the capital. As an attempt to smash the Irish Transport and General Workers' Union (ITGWU), Dublin's most powerful businessman, William Martin Murphy, who also headed the Employers' Federation, demanded that his workers sign a declaration disowning the union. Those who refused to sign the declaration were locked out, beginning with Murphy's own *Independent* newspapers on 15 August 1913. By the following month, 404 other Dublin employers had come to support him. The union called a general strike on 26 August, which was followed by the 'Bloody Sunday' clashes between strikers and police on 31 August in which 400 were injured. A bitter and violent seven-month struggle ensued during the course of which poverty and destitution became widespread among the estimated 100,000 men, women and children, directly or indirectly, affected.

In this volatile cauldron an incendiary strike poster, 'Appeal to the People of Dublin', was circulated in which the 'locked out' workers at Elliman's Theatre de Luxe called on the public 'not to support the dishonourable tactics adopted by the sweating employers' of the cinema which was being 'worked by BLACKLEGS'. It seems that 'a man of exemplary character', Thomas Dalton, was dismissed on 6 September 1913 because of his activities as a workers' spokesman as part of a deputation to a cinema managers' meeting, even though the chairman, alderman Dr McWalter BL, had promised that no one would be 'victimised'. However, the 'dishonourable' manager of the Theatre de Luxe broke this promise. The cinema was subsequently picketed and hand-billed for a month, but 'when the proprietors found that the public would not support these SCABS and BLACKLEGS', they sought arbitration, which took place on 12 October 1913. According to the poster, even though both sides had agreed to abide by the decision of Dr McWalter's court of arbitration,[96] the 'unanimous award' in favour of Dalton (which included his reinstatement), was not observed by the proprietors of the Theatre de Luxe, who were accused of having no honour. In a reference to the 1691 treaty that had ended the Williamite wars in Ireland, but whose provisions of religious and political equality for Catholics were not implemented, the poster stated that the judgment was 'broken like the "the treaty of Limerick ere the ink was dry"'. The arbitration agreement also provided for the formal dismissal of the 'present staff' and their reinstatement on their rejoining the National Association of Theatrical Employees (NATE), a stipulation that seems to indicate that the industrial dispute may have been over trade union recognition; and that any police court proceedings were to be withdrawn, a clause that clearly referred to the charges against Dalton, Richard Menehan and John Forsythe, with regard to their (alleged) 'us[e of] abusive and insulting words' outside the cinema on 29 and 30 September. On those dates they had been distributing hand-bills, apparently issued by NATE, and carrying illuminated placards with the words 'The Home of Scabs'. It was reported that the 'scabs' had been members of NATE, but had been expelled when they did not support colleagues – presumably Dalton and the others –who were being 'victimised'. As such though it appears that there was not an official strike, in the hothouse atmosphere of the Dublin Lock-Out it was often a case that workers were either regarded as trade union members or if not, as 'scabs'.[97]

While the tone and content of the picketing of the cinema and of the poster reflect the nature of employer/employee relations in Dublin at this time,[98] the poster also takes a decidedly nativist bias towards the end in its call for public support against the 'alien employers'. Presented as 'men of no principle who have refused to obey' the decision of the arbitration committee, they were identified as William Petrie, Sackville Street and Usher's Quay; Maurice Elliman, a fruit shop owner of a premises beside the Princess Cinema, Rathmines, who 'should have been called Judas only Judas had the manhood to hang himself'; Jacob Elliman, framemaker, Exchequer Street; and George J. Nesbitt, a director of Theatre de Luxe, who was regarded as 'a gentleman [who had] been misled'. The large-sized poster ends with the rallying cries: 'Workers Stand Together. Down with Scabs, Blacklegs and Sweaters and don't support the Theatre de Luxe, Camden St. Now or Never. Workers Support Your Own.'[99]

Returning to the broader economic context within Ireland during the cinema-building boom, a fuller understanding of film exhibition's expansion and cinema-going emerges. According to Mary Daly, while many skilled workers' income in the pre-First World War period was identical to that during the late 1870s, 'virtually all' unskilled workers' wages had risen, thus enabling a greater number of the working class to enjoy paid entertainments. Nevertheless, it remained the case that many unskilled workers, commonly earning in this period £1 per week, still lived in conditions of poverty. Given that a 1905 survey of working-class household budgets had found that there was 'no margin' on £1 per week for a family of five for spending on 'unnecessary items',[1] and that the cost of food increased in the period 1910 to 1914, it would seem there was little or no surplus available for cinema attendance either by adults, or by children who could avail of the cheapest seats. Yet, it must be remembered that cinema-going, particularly in the context of the 1*d*. admission or 'Penny Rush', was a *very* cheap entertainment. This is starkly evident in a comparison of the costs of cinema admission and the most popular sweets, which ranged from 0.5*d*. to 1*d*.; and the fact that the popular soft drink of the period, Vimto, sold for 2*d*., twice the 1*d*. cinema ticket.[2] Luke McKernan has argued in the very similar context of lower social economic groups in London that many working-class people, most especially children who constituted up to half of the London cinema audience, '*did* find the money, and it was on their support that the cinema in London flourished in the first place.'[3]

While for this period there is little material on the actual means children employed in order to gain admission to the cinema, in Belfast during the depression of the late 1920s/1930s we know that children obtained money in a number of innovative ways including collecting wooden boxes and making bundles of sticks which sold at three bundles for 1*d*. – the cost of matinee admission at some cinemas; collecting 'kitchen refuse' or 'skins' as pig feed for which 2*d*. was paid per bucket of swill; and the collecting of horse manure, which was sold to allotment owners.[4] In Dublin in the 1920s and 1930s, working-class children often used tradable empty jam jars, worth a halfpenny (0.5*d*.) each, as payment and indeed received as change, at the cinema box office of several cinemas.[5] This practice continued even during the 1940s with different glassware empties having specific values, and, according to Des McGuinness, fixed rates of exchange operated:

hair oil bottles:	0.125*d*.
sauce bottles:	0.25*d*.
1 lb. jam jars:	0.5*d*.
2 lb. jam jars:	1*d*.
wine bottles:	2*d*.
large stone jars:	5*d*.[6]

Similarly, in 1930s Belfast, stone jam jars could be exchanged in cinema lobbies for 2*d*. before going to the box office.[7]

While the First World War led to a surge in cinema-going in Britain, with an increase to 38 per cent of its potential, such was not the case in Ireland, though Irish admission figures are, with one exception, unavailable for the 1910s. That exception is provided by the 1917 report of the cinema commission which offers the relatively reliable figure of approximately 20 million Irish admissions out of a total of just over 1 billion (1,075,875,000) UK admissions to the 4,500 cinemas in Britain and Ireland.[8] This figure of 20 million admissions for the whole island of Ireland compares to the daily 20 million admissions in the USA for the same year when about one in five of the total population visited daily one of the 15,000 cinemas.[9] Based on an average estimated admission price in Ireland during the 1910s of 6*d.* (a reasonable suggestion given that a large number of second-run venues catering for children charged only 1*d.* or 2*d.* admission, that many cinemas had 6*d.* as their top price, and ticket prices at first-run venues usually did not exceed 1*s.* or 12*d.*), the value of gross box office income was probably no more than £500,000 per annum for the whole island of Ireland and £300,000 per annum for the area which would become the Irish Free State in 1922. However, bearing in mind that the majority of people did not live in urban areas and thus did not have ready access to the cinema, a fact verified in the 1926 Irish Free State census of population, which revealed that at least two-thirds of the population lived outside towns and villages, it is possible that the 1917 cinema report figure was too generously rounded and hence the estimated gross box office, if anything, is too high. Nevertheless, it seems to be reasonably in line with the results of the first reliable survey of Irish Free State exhibition, which took place in 1934–35, when gross box office income was calculated at £895,000 from 18.25 million admissions.[10] In any case, during this period, while travelling exhibitors provided a social and cultural service, if not necessarily making a lucrative living for themselves, by visiting on a weekly basis villages and towns where, exempting the public house and home music sessions, popular indoor entertainment was largely absent, it was the Dublin market in the south and the Belfast market in the north that were central to the profitability or otherwise of film companies. In 1911, for example, Dublin with a population of 386,386 represented 12 per cent of what became the Irish Free State, while in 1926, with a population of 408,148, this had risen to 13.7 per cent.[11] Yet, Thekla Beere estimated that in the mid-1930s, Dublin accounted for about 60 per cent of Irish box office.[12]

As was the case elsewhere, in Dublin, notwithstanding the existence of such cinemas as the top-class Provincial and the Grafton, the initial experience of filmed entertainment by many middle class people was often in prestigious theatres. Thus, *Cabiria* (Giovanni Pastrone, 1914), 'one of the most interesting films ever exhibited in Dublin',[13] was first shown at the Theatre Royal in November 1915 for almost three weeks, while D.W. Griffith's epic *The Birth of a Nation* (1915), screened at Belfast's prestigious Grand Opera House in August 1916,[14] was shown from September 1916 in Dublin's Gaiety where its two-week run was extended for a third week due to demand.[15] Though such venues were necessarily pervaded by middle-class respectability, more generally, the film entertainment audience, especially as constituted in the cinemas located at secondary sites, the majority of cinemas, provides a contrast to the theatre's audience in terms of age profile, social class, and gender composition. The *Freeman's Journal* in 1913 during the course of its review of the premiere Dublin screening of the earliest major life of Christ, *From the Manger to the Cross* (Sidney Olcott, 1912), at the Phoenix Picture Palace, Ellis Quay, describes the make-up of the adult audience:

> The audience as a whole was the class commonly seen in picture palaces, young
> lads of the clerk and shop assistant type and men of the artisan and labouring
> classes. The proportion of women was smaller than usual.[16]

Paddy Crosbie in his memoir of his childhood, *Your dinner's poured out!*, one of the
most interesting of such 'authentic' if often impressionistic working-class histories of
Dublin, similarly highlighted the gender imbalance but with regard to the Phoenix's
children's audience later in the decade and in the 1920s, where 'girls were always a
minority group'.[17]

According to Crosbie, going to the cinema, in his case the local Phoenix, known
colloquially as the 'Feeno' or the Ellis, for the Penny Rush, which in later decades
became the Two-, Three-, and Four-Penny Rush, was 'the big event of the week' in the
late 1910s and 1920s. Outside the cinema, an attendant with a cane kept order over
the crowd of what Crosbie (exaggeratedly?) estimated as 3,000 children all eager to
secure their entrance into the cinema, which had seats for less than half this number.
While initially the venue opened in December 1912 with either 750 or 950 seats,[18]
within a few months of opening it was renovated and recommenced business on 3
March 1913, with 1,200 seats, though some reports suggest it may have had 1,500
seats.[19] Consequently, the aisles were packed and there was intense competition for
seats. As there was no 'class distinction' at the 'Feeno' at least with regard to such
shows, children were free to choose the 'woodeners', 'cushioners' or 'upstairs', depending on their position in the queue. However, given the conditions that pertained, including some boys urinating in the auditorium, it is unlikely that any middle-class children,
particularly girls, were either let or wanted to attend the Phoenix. In what may be
unrepresentative of the majority behaviour, Crosbie recalls that being positioned directly
below the front line of the balcony was the worst place to be since nobody would go
the toilet during the programme for fear of losing their seat. As a result,

> most boys relieved themselves where they were ... [and] the boys in the front
> row of the balcony performed this feat down on the boys beneath. Downstairs,
> the floor was built at a slant and the accumulated urine trickled down to where
> the old lady played the piano.[20]

Such a description is far from the idealized romantic memories usually associated with
cinema-going during the silent period or later even when the cinema is remembered as
a primitive space with little more than a series of wooden benches. Nevertheless,
Crosbie remembers with affection the comradeship, the longing from week to week,
and the enjoyment and celebration afforded by the total event from home to cinema
and back again which was the feature of their week.

Despite the fact that class was not foregrounded in the experience of attending the
Feeno, class, or social standing and money, did feature as an important issue and determined which cinema a child might attend. Indeed, Crosbie gives a telling description
of class discrimination within the community, which pervaded even attendance at his
local church and was subsequently replayed in the practice of cinema-going:

There was a positive class distinction in most of the Catholic churches during my boyhood. In Arran Quay itself, there was a barrier rail separating the Body of the church from the Sanctuary. The offering at the Sanctuary door was 2*d.*; the offering at the doors to the Body and the Gallery was 1*d.* Holy Communion was administered first to those in the Sanctuary; then the priest proceeded down to the dividing rails to the so-called lower class. In the Sanctuary were publicans, shopkeepers, businessmen and their families, plus those who thought they were a cut above the rest … After joining the altar society, I noticed something else. Even amongst the altar-boys there was an indefinable division between sons of shopkeepers and publicans and sons of ordinary working people. The former kept together in a group; they went to the large picture-houses down town [that is, O'Connell Street and environs] and had never been at the Penny Rush in the Feeno.[21]

THE STRUGGLE OVER SUNDAY OPENING IN DUBLIN AND BELFAST

While Saturday was the main cinema-going day for children, due to the five-and-a-half or six-day working week for most working-class employees, Sunday was the most important day for adults and, as such, was the most lucrative day of the week for cinema owners. Therefore, any attempt by local councils, whose remit included the issuing of cinema licences, acting under pressure from religious and other organizations, to close cinemas on Sundays was fiercely resisted by exhibitors. Indeed, even before the cinema there had been continuous struggles over alcohol consumption and public entertainments on the Sabbath.

More broadly, in the nineteenth century, campaigns by Irish reform movements to reduce alcohol consumption merged with the issue of religious observance, especially among Ulster Presbyterians, who sought to make the Sabbath an exclusive day of worship. Consequently, as part of this interconnected push towards teetotalism, or even prohibition, and the foregrounding of religious practice on the Sabbath, considerable energy was expended on trying to have public houses and retail shops that sold alcohol closed on Sundays, though Catholics and nationalists remained suspicious of the Sabbatarian agenda, finding in it an inherent racism and social class bias.[22] However, given that half the population in Dublin and a quarter in Belfast, according to an 1876 police survey, attended public houses on Sundays, 'Sunday drinking in the main urban areas was simply too popular for the government to dare abolish it totally.' To do so, the police feared, would create, particularly in Dublin where 660 of the 765 pubs within the six square miles between the canals opened on Sundays, 'widespread discontent, resulting in illicit drinking on a massive scale and public disorder'.[23] As a result, Dublin was one of only four locations to be exempted from the Sunday closing regulations.

While not all Protestants or Catholics sought to eradiate Sunday drinking, all groups did seek to provide alternative attractive recreations as a means of weaning people off alcohol and away from the public house or 'whisky shop' where perhaps more than alcohol might be offered. Thus, according to Elizabeth Malcolm, Catholic priest Father Theobold Mathew's temperance meetings were 'primarily a form of recreation [which] substituted for the old entertainments associated with drink.'[24] Held from 1838 to his death in 1856 these large public meetings regularly ended up as (apparently alcohol-free) all-night signing, dancing and music sessions such that a German visitor to one such event in Kilrush in 1843 was struck by 'the "extravagance" and the "intemperance" of this so-called temperance movement'.[25] The events organized by Protestant groups (including, the anti-drink lantern slide shows and the screenings of early films which were *not* produced in Ireland) were not imbued with the same sense of physical or emotional pleasure as Fr Mathew's 'carnival' ones. Instead, they tended to be motivated by puritan denial, or, at least, were supervised educational uplift events.

In response to the recognition of the dominance of drink within the culture, evident not least in the paucity of cafes, restaurants or other places where food and drink could be consumed in a non-exclusively alcohol only environment, from the 1830s alternative venues to the public house began to be established. While these included the coffee stalls run by the Dublin Total Abstinence Society around the city which catered for travellers, porters and cab drivers who might otherwise go to the pub, one of the most successful of these alternative venues was their Temperance Hall and Coffee Palace at 6 Townsend Street, Dublin. Close to the Theatre Royal, the hall had opened in 1875 as a public meeting house and entertainment venue, but by 1882 incorporated coffee rooms, misleadingly referred to as 'bar-rooms' which, despite its serving only non-alcoholic drinks, attempted to reproduce the atmosphere and layout of a public house.[26] In late 1908, the society introduced film screenings as part of their 'reforming' recreation, and, following a change in management and brief closure, reopened on 30 March 1909 as 'The Palace' or Palace Theatre, with the American Moving Picture Company, as a cine-variety venue.[27] Despite its popularity, the cinema, also known as the Cinema Palace, closed in December 1913, but under G. Butler and Sons, musical instrument makers, Monument House, O'Connell Bridge, reopened as the Cinema Royal on 23 December with 500 seats. Granted a belated cinema licence in 1914, the cinema ceased business when the Dublin Total Abstinence Society went into liquidation in 1915.[28]

George's Hall, 63 South Great George's Street, owned by the Dublin Central Mission, was another Protestant 'missionary' organization granted a licence in 1914 to screen films on Saturdays in a hall for seventy people.[29] By then, film production had decisively shifted away from the proselytizing, educational, or topical aspects of early cinema towards popular genres, which, even if featuring 'moral' endings (retribution for doing bad), had transgressive elements and often included risqué scenes. Therefore, while some reformers and anti-drink campaigners viewed the cinema as preferable to the public house and did not call for cinemas to close or to close completely on Sundays – Catholic leaders, for example, happy with the compromise of Sunday evening closure (usually from between 7p.m. and 8p.m., or 6.30p.m. to 8.30p.m.) to coincide with religious ceremonies[30] – others, more particularly Protestants informed by the nineteenth-century struggle against drink and reflecting Protestantism's strict observance of the Sabbath, took a less flexible approach. In Britain, at least initially, it was neither religion nor morality that were to the fore in the opposition to Sunday opening, but labour, largely driven by the National Organization of Cinematograph Operators, who sought to have Sundays work-free.

Though the Sabbath was regarded by the main churches in Ireland as a day of religious worship on which work, most especially paid employment, should not be undertaken unless in exceptional circumstances, in general, the Protestant faith — or its more puritanical elements — has also treated it as a day to be *devoid* of personal pleasure. Even as late as the 1960s and beyond in Northern Ireland, where local authorities were under the political control of extreme Sabbatarians, such as those of Ian Paisley's Democratic Unionist Party, some public entertainment complexes, including swimming pools, were closed on Sundays. (Indeed, the Sunday closing of public houses in Northern Ireland was not changed until the 1990s.) Catholics, by contrast, have more loosely interpreted the day as one where rest and relaxation, including attendance at public entertainments, such as sporting events and the cinema, are generally permitted once such activities do not interfere with the performance of personal religious duties. Perhaps, unsurprisingly then, alcohol consumption was allowed in public houses on Sundays for four decades after independence in southern Ireland providing the drinker was a *bona fide* traveller, that is, a person who lived three miles or more from the pub, a law extensively broken in rural areas, but by the early 1960s the wider availability of motor cars made such a law obsolete. The precedent in British law relating to the Sabbath lay in the Sunday Observance Acts of 1625 to 1780, which forbade premises being used on Sundays 'for public entertainment or amusement' where patrons were charged admittance.

While the 1780 act applied to a wide spectrum of entertainments, the 1843 Theatres' Act applied only to venues registered or licensed as places of entertainment. As a result of this, prior to the introduction of the Cinematograph Act 1909, no legislation covered the screening of films in *unlicensed* shops, halls or fairgrounds.[31] Thereafter, of course, *all* venues where films were shown were required to hold a cinema licence issued by the relevant local authority. Notwithstanding that the act, operational from 1 January 1910, had been ostensibly designed to ensure public safety in cinemas, it, nonetheless, served to (re)ignite the controversy over Sunday opening with the influential London county council only granting to cinemas within its jurisdiction six-day licences though with a possibility of Sunday opening for 'charity' screenings. The majority of councils that allowed Sunday opening stipulated that 20 per cent (or more) of gross box office takings on that day had to be donated to charity. While exhibitors challenged this, the courts not only upheld the councils' regulations, but also confirmed that the act gave powers to local authorities beyond matters of health and safety, such as over a film's content or the imposing of general and specific conditions to screenings. In turn, this led to the establishment of the British Board of Film Censors in 1913 as a 'voluntary' industry response to the extension of local authority power over the content of films screened. Although exhibitors, in a bid to stave off further regulation of Sunday opening, abided by the charity 'clause', a (cynical) goodwill gesture that was particularly important in the context of the First World War, many tried to claim that by using non-inflammable (or safety film), of which little was in circulation given that it became dry and brittle and thus had a far shorter life than regular or inflammable film,[32] that they by-passed or were outside the terms of reference of the 1909 Cinematograph Act which specially referred to 'inflammable' film. However, in 1914 Middlesex county council successfully prosecuted such an exhibitor who had defied the licence restrictions on Sunday by invoking the 'inflammable' film clause. Unsurprisingly, other cases followed in its wake, with the majority resulting in similar outcomes.[33]

Mirroring London county council's broad interpretation of the act, other local authorities in Britain and Ireland felt justified in inserting into their annual cinema licence restrictions on when cinemas could open and on the content of films.[34] The former, which was largely determined by the dominant religion of the district, could have a considerable impact on the viability and profitability of a cinema, particularly if it was decided that the cinema had to close completely on Sunday. In 1916, when the autonomous Rathmines urban district council (a predominantly middle-class area with a significant Protestant presence unlike in Dublin city), voted to close cinemas in its district on Sundays, the Sandford reported that there was 'such a marked difference' between Sunday box office, worth £750 per annum, and the rest of the week, that the cinema would be forced to close unless the decision was rescinded.[35]

Towards the end of 1911, Dublin corporation's law agent, Ignatius J. Rice, following a query about prohibiting tenants from occupying the upper floors of cinemas,[36] validated the council's action when he offered the opinion that the corporation had been empowered under the Cinematograph Act to 'use their discretion' to impose conditions within cinema licences. During this same meeting, a more significant opinion was offered concerning the division of authority between the law courts' officer, the recorder, whose responsibilities included the issuing of music licences, which, given the practice of accompanying films with music, cinemas also needed, and Dublin corporation's public health committee (PHC), the body that was directly responsible for administering the 1909 act. Following the practice with regard to theatres and music halls, the recorder issued six-day only music licences to cinemas. When the Volta and the Dublin Electric cinemas breached the six-day music licence by presenting a Sunday programme[37] the secretary to the chief commissioner of police, perhaps alerted by Thomas Lopdell O'Shaughnessy KC,[38] the last recorder in Dublin, serving from 1905 to 1924, at which time the post was abolished, wrote to the PHC requesting that the committee take action against the exhibitors. Stating that the police would assist in the prosecution, the secretary added that clergy from two churches adjoining the premises were 'strongly opposed' to cinemas being open on Sundays.

The PHC subsequently sought advice from the law agent who reported that as the cinema licence had not included any restriction on Sunday screenings, though it was within their power should they choose to impose such on future licences, the matter did not concern them. Though he acknowledged that it was the job of the police to bring proceedings against exhibitors for breaches of the music licence under part 4 of the Public Health Act 1890, he cautioned, in an echo of anti-drink reformers such as Father Mathew, that

> it would be well for the Committee to consider whether it ought to deprecate any action by the Police which would tend to deprive the poorer classes of the City of an innocent and healthy form of recreation which could do them no harm, and might do a great deal of good by offering a counter attraction to other less desirable forms of amusement.[39]

With such an unenthusiastic response from Dublin corporation's law agent, the recorder[40] directly approached the PHC in 1913 and quickly influenced the committee, over which he had no authority, to establish restrictions on Sunday opening. While these usually ensured that cinemas remained closed before 2p.m. and during evening religious services (mostly within the time period of 6.30 to 8.30p.m.), some cinemas in Dublin were only granted six-day licences.

The location of the cinema impacted in a fundamental way on the difficulties that might arise in the would-be exhibitor's acquisition of a licence. Unsurprisingly, perhaps, local churches, regardless of persuasion, were, on numerous occasions, to the fore in objecting to cinemas. Controversy surrounded the granting of a cinema licence in 1912 to the Irish National Foresters' Hall, 41 Rutland (Parnell) Square West due to its proximity to St Kevin's House, a residence for Catholic girls supervised by Revd J.P. Dowling OP, manager at no. 42, and Revd J.O. George Dougherty, rector, St Mary's parish, at no. 39. There was also a Catholic nurses' home at no. 34. Despite the objections, the licence was granted initially for a 432-seat cinema.

Similarly, in 1912, the Quaker community, whose Meeting Room, or 'church', was on Eustace Street, objected to the nearby Dame Street Picture House, 17 Dame Street, a 360-seat venue. The cinema opened on 24 December 1912, but only with a six-day licence which was standard for middle-class cinemas, particularly those located in the fashionable shopping districts of Sackville and Grafton streets, where the 'better class' of patron had sufficient leisure time, Monday through to Saturday, to shop and view films. Nevertheless, given that Dame Street was a business and administrative thoroughfare with the imposing Bank of Ireland and Trinity College at one end, and City Hall and Dublin Castle at the other, with the Stock Exchange running off it, and as such, hardly an 'unfashionable' street, the cinema's owners somewhat disingenuously argued that the street was 'frequented largely by the working class' and that the object of their application had been to facilitate working-class people attending Sunday screenings. The recorder responded by saying that while he 'had great sympathy with the working people' and 'did not see why Sunday should be a day of gloom' – 'he had no Puritanical views' on the matter – he regarded the Dame Street Picture House in a similar light to those 'superior' cinemas of the class which were not allowed to open on Sundays by the London county council.[41] He also objected to its proximity to Dublin Castle, 'the residence of the representative of the Sovereign.' Replying, the cinema's manager said that Sunday business was 'the mainstay of the theatre, as they took more money on that day than they did for half of the week.' It was to no avail as the recorder ruled on 2 April 1913 that the cinema could not have a seven-day licence.[42] In response, John Carley of the Dame Street Picture House sent a 'memorial' on 22 July 1913 to the lord lieutenant of Ireland seeking amelioration of the recorder's decision. Citing twelve cinemas where Sunday opening was allowed – Phoenix Picture Palace; Irish Cinema, Capel Street; Dorset Street Picture House; Picture House and Theatre de Luxe, Camden Street; Picturedrome, Harcourt Road; Great Brunswick Street Picture House; Princess, Rathmines; Mary Street Picture House; Volta; World's Fair Picturedrome; and the Electric, Talbot Street – Carley stated that having invested £3,500 in order to provide 'a decent, innocent, and instructive form of entertainment suitable to the needs of the inhabitants ... which would be a material advantage to the populace', he now sought a temporary seven-day licence until the annual licence season came around again in October.[43] Seeking further information and opinion, the lord lieutenant had Inspector Cornelius Kiernan of the Dublin Metropolitan Police (DMP) prepare a report for the chief secretary's office. Sent on 26 July, Kiernan's report, which supported the recorder's ruling, argued that those attending nearby Christ Church cathedral, St Andrew's church, George's Hall, and the Quakers' Friends' meeting house on Eustace Street, 'might be obstructed' if Sunday opening was permitted as they were on 'the route' to the cinema.[44] Ironically, the Quakers' Meeting Room is now Cinema 1 of the Irish Film Institute complex, while the Dame Street Picture House, which closed down in 1920, perhaps financially weakened by the Sabbatarian restrictions, became in 1924 the premises of the official film censor, a status it retained into the 1930s.

Given such social class differentiation in the issuing of six- or seven-day licences in the city, it is not surprising that when Maurice Elliman's son Jacob applied to the recorder on behalf of the Blackrock Picture House in 1915 for a seven-day licence, he was refused on the basis that 'it was more a residential than a working-class place' and was offered a six-day licence which he finally accepted.[45] The Picture House, 30 Great Brunswick Street, run by his brother Abe which was adjoining a working class district, was, however, granted a seven-day licence. Nevertheless, on Sundays it was not permitted to open before 1p.m. or between 7p.m. and 8p.m., 'when the humbler type of the Protestant population used their churches', while no music could be played between 8p.m. and 9p.m. The recorder was keen to point out that 'the religious views of every class in the community should be respected in these matters.'[46]

While in the initial period the main Grafton and Sackville street cinemas prospered without Sunday opening – a condition accepted by the English-owned Provincial Cinematograph Company whose ethos was most likely to favour a Sabbatarian restriction – later heavy investment made little commercial sense and caused many exhibitors to seek to have their licence extended to seven days. Such a move can be clearly seen with regard to La Scala Theatre and Opera House, 4–8 Princes Street North, just off O'Connell Street. Opened in 1920 on the first day of the Dublin Horse Show (10 August) on the quarter acre site of the former premises of the *Freeman's Journal* and Alex Thom, which had been destroyed during the 1916 Rising, the site cost £12,500. Though a government grant of £21,286 was awarded 'to make good the ravages of the bombardment', the building contract for the theatre was said in 1918 to be £26,275, making the total cost for what then was planned as a 1,500 seat venue (1,100 on ground floor; 400 in balcony), about £40,000.[47] However, when La Scala Theatre and Opera House was completed, it was reported to have 3,200 seats (stalls and two double catilevered balconies) plus thirty-two boxes and was built at (the perhaps exaggerated) cost of £120,000.[48] The sumptuous building included tearooms, a lounge and a bar on each floor; a ballroom; smoke and dressing rooms; and a ground floor restaurant. The picture screen was 50 feet from the front row of the parterre, while the stage was able to accommodate the largest shows.[49] Prior to realizing the project, on 2 September 1918 the promoter of the theatre sought a letter's patent, or permit, which would confer on the venue unrestricted theatrical rights, including the right to open on Sundays. Though the owners of the Gaiety, Queen's and Empire theatres opposed the submission, the applicant pointed out to the privy council chamber, Dublin Castle, in the presence of the attorney general and the solicitor-general, that such a letter was provided for in a law dating back to George V. Notwithstanding that this law was an anomaly, with Dublin the only location where such a patent was required, the application prevailed.[50] Armed with the letter's patent, on 10 October 1920 La Scala began Sunday film shows. Notwithstanding the Empire Theatre's opposition to La Scala's patent application, and the fact that it was located near to the Quaker Meeting House and other religious venues, such as Christ Church cathedral, the Empire also showed films on Sundays, from 8p.m.

With city centre competition increasing following the opening of La Scala, other exhibitors sought to have the Sabbath ruling modified. For example, shortly before the issuing of the annual licence, solicitor John Burke on behalf of J.J. Farrell, who owned the Pillar Picture House situated no more than 100 meters from La Scala, which Farrell had acquired in 1926 and renamed the Capitol Theatre the following year, wrote to the Dublin Metropolitan Police superintendent at Store Street station saying he intended to apply for a change in the Pillar's six-day music licence so as to allow the cinema to open on Sundays from 2p.m. to 6.30p.m. and from 8p.m. to 10.30p.m., the same as the existing provision within seven-day cinema licences.[51] Two weeks later, a briefing document, 'Cinema performances on Sunday',[52] prepared by the DMP, was sent to the chief crown solicitor's office as part of its review of the La Scala patent process.[53] Confusion and a degree of paralysis seem to have gripped the office of the under-secretary for Ireland, C.M. Martin-Jones, who handled the issue. However, a change in policy was effected when, in early January 1921, the chief commissioner of the DMP met a delegation from the Dublin and South of Ireland Cinematograph Exhibitors' Association (DSICEA) concerned at the twin impediments to their business, the military curfew due to the War of Independence and the six-day licence for certain cinemas. Reporting that Sunday was 'formerly in many cases their most profitable time', they wanted a relaxation of the measure. Though they complained that La Scala's patent had given it an unfair business advantage by allowing it to open on Sundays, when it was 'thronged' with patrons, it was not their intention to have La Scala's rights denied or restricted, but, in a view supported by the chief commissioner, extended to other venues.

Following the meeting, the chief commissioner made representations on behalf of the DSICEA to Martin-Jones,[54] who responded by enquiring about the attitude of the recorder to such a change. In early February 1921, the chief commissioner replied[55] to the under-secretary stating that the recorder had granted temporary permission for nine cinemas – The Bohemian; Dame Street Picture House; Dorset Picture Hall; Dublin Electric Theatre; Mary Street Picture House; Phibsborough Picture House; Theatre de Luxe; Palace Cinema; and Phoenix Picture Palace – which held a six-day only licence to open on Sundays though not between the hours of 6.30p.m. to 8.30p.m. While it is not known exactly what happened behind the scenes that led to this modification of the recorder's policy, it can be speculated that it was 'encouraged' by the combined force of the chief commissioner and under-secretary. Although some flexibility was evident in the situation as it pertained in Dublin city, this was not the case in adjoining districts where the Sabbath was regarded as sacrosanct. Notwithstanding that the recorder modified the strict Sabbatarian music licence with regard to better-off areas, he was the initiator of the campaign for Sunday closing in the autonomous Rathmines and Rathgar urban district.

Difficulties for the Rathmines and Rathgar exhibitors began to surface in May 1915 when the *Freeman's Journal* published a call by Alfred Poulter of the Camden Street Picture House, about a mile from Rathmines Town Hall and the Princess Cinema, to end the closure of Dublin cinemas on a Sunday during 6.30p.m. to 8.30p.m. and so bring parity with the Rathmines and Rathgar cinemas, which were permitted to stay open all day. In response, Recorder Lopdell-O'Shaugnessy stated that it was a 'disgrace and discredit to the Rathmines council that they allowed such an outrage to proceed.'[56] Prior to this it seems that the cinema practice within Rathmines and Rathgar urban district was without controversy. In February 1915, for example, the district's energetic and conscientious buildings' inspector, Sam W. Dixon, reported to the urban district council clerk, Seacome Mason, that as a result of his frequent visits to the district's two cinemas, the Princess and Town Hall on Rathmines Road, 'no complaint, of any kind has been received from the public attending these picture houses',[57] while H. Coleman, managing director of Sandford Cinema Co. Ltd, 5 Lower Sandford Road, Ranelagh, gave assurance to UDC's chairman, F.P. Fawcett, in advance of the cinema's opening on 9 November 1914 that not only would the 'greatest care' be exercised in selecting films but that the directors could 'guarantee that nothing objectionable will be permitted'.[58]

In June 1915, one month after his intervention, the recorder repeated his attacks on Rathmines council's licensing policy, describing the situation pertaining in the district as 'a very discreditable state of affairs'.[59] A week later, perhaps in response to councillors' queries, which had been clearly prompted by Lopdell-O'Shaugnessy's involvment, Seacome Mason wrote to the council's solicitor, William Shannon, enquiring as to what amendments could be made to the licences.[60] However, Shannon informed him that no action could be taken until the issued licences expired in March 1916.[61] Mason then sought voluntary action by the exhibitors requesting that they open on Sunday only between 3p.m and 6p.m. and between 8p.m. and 10.30p.m., somewhat along the lines of Dublin city.[62] Nathan Karmel of the Princess, pointing out that Sunday was not just 'by far the best day' for box office but that sufficient money was not taken before 7p.m. or 7.30p.m. on ordinary weekdays even to pay for the electric light, replied that the company's directors were seeking a meeting with the councillors, 'the matter being of an exceptionally serious nature.'[63] The Sandford responded by arguing that since films were booked well in advance, the restricted Sunday hours would upset the working of the cinema 'to a considerable extent'.[64]

Given that the Town Hall cinema, owned by the council, was the only venue in the district to have been issued with a six-day licence, it was, at this stage, unaffected by the debate. Later, however, in January 1916 the licensee of the Town Hall, James T. Jameson, sought the right to open on Sundays.[65] Perhaps as a result of the council's refusal, he forfeited the lease for which he had been paying £16 10s. per week rent in 1915.[66] Despite the six-day operational status of the venue its rent later considerably increased. Frederick A. Sparling of the Bohemian Cinema, Phibsborough, who rented the hall from 17 August 1917 paid £23 per week, while from 1 March 1919, the new lessee, William Kay, who, as noted, had taken over the Rotunda in 1916 and later in partnership with local publican Anthony O'Grady was one of the promoters of the Stella Cinema, Rathmines, perhaps the most important cinema outside Dublin city centre,[67] paid £25 10s. per week rent.[68] It is clear from the 242 per cent rental increase within four years that the market for cinema was extremely buoyant and profitable, at least in this predominantly middle class area. Nevertheless, it was only so in a context of non-investment or capitalization. Just as La Scala's promoters needed to secure Sunday business in order to make their investment viable, the Rathmines and Rathgar UDC's subsequent imposition of Sunday closure of cinemas within their district largely contributed to the liquidation in 1917 of the Sandford whose opening in late 1914 marked the end of the cinema-building boom. From its opening in 1914, the Sandford had been supported and driven by the profits generated on Sundays.

The campaign for Sunday closure continued and in late October 1915, Revd Ernest Henry Lewis-Crosby, the Church of Ireland rector in Rathmines, 1914–24, and later dean of Christ Church cathedral, 1938–61, asked the council to meet with a deputation of clergy 'of the various communions in the Township'.[69] The delegation, which included himself, Archdeacon Fricker, and Revd D. Sandys, met the council on 3 November. Displaying an antipathy to cinema in general and pointing out that 'the present was not a time when people should be encouraged to dissipate time or money', the delegation pronounced that such 'abominable places … did not provide the moral uplift to be expected' on a Sunday. Sunday cinema opening was, they declared, 'a disgrace' and 'most monstrous', a position with which the chairman of the council expressed his 'very sympathetic feeling'.[70]

At its December meeting presided over by Revd Lewis-Crosby, Rathmines parish church passed a resolution proposed by Professor W.E.E. Thrift, a fellow of Trinity College Dublin, calling for the closure of cinemas on Sundays. On 2 January 1916, Rathgar Presbyterian church passed a similar resolution. In an effort to stem the tide against Sunday opening the Sandford and Princess cinemas elicited the support of the

Rathmines' Ratepayers' Protection Association, a representative body of the business community. In a submission to Mason, Hugh Higginson, the association's secretary, stated that 90 per cent of the local residents were in favour of Sunday opening. It was, he said, the only day for many working-class people to go to the cinema, where, he strategically added, they could see friends and relations fighting in the war. In the absence of cinema, they would go to the pub or, as he euphemistically described brothels, 'so-called clubs' and other places of very 'doubtful' reputation. He also mobilized bourgeois arguments of the social control of the working classes when he stated that 'by bringing them to a "centre" they can be supervised and kept in some sort of order and respectability.' Indeed, the police 'had noticed a considerable improvement in respect of the working classes in particular.' The cinema was the lesser of two evils, he said, and preferable to the pub. It was 'the only source available to [working-class people] of healthy and harmless enjoyment which they look forward to, from week to week.'[71]

It was all in vain as two days later, on 5 January, the campaign for Sunday closure was won. After a tied vote of councillors, the chairman cast his vote in favour of a motion closing cinemas *completely* on Sundays. As a means of reinforcing the decision, many churches, including a 'ladies' meeting' of the Methodist congregation, Brighton Road, Rathgar, passed resolutions congratulating the council on 'the wisdom shown in this matter of Public morals'.[72] Concerned that the exhibitors might succeed in reversing the decision, the Presbyterian church asked the council to meet a deputation before its next meeting on 2 February.[73]

Unsurprisingly, immediately following the council's 5 January decision the local exhibitors began agitating against the resolution. While John Carley, secretary of the Irish branch of the Cinematograph Exhibitors' Association of Great Britain and Ireland, unsuccessfully, it seems, requested that the council convene, prior to their next official meeting, with a group of interested representatives, including Dublin corporation alderman and exhibitor J.J. Farrell and either David Frame or Izidore Bradlaw representing the CEA (Ireland). Realizing that they had little chance in reversing the decision completely, the exhibitors concentrated on seeking to establish Sunday opening on a par with Dublin city. Bradlaw wrote to the council chairman to that effect within a month of the resolution having been passed.[74] Nathan Karmel wrote to Mason, the UDC's clerk, on 14 February and, reinforcing the message, stated bluntly that if Sunday cinema was not allowed, the Princess would close down losing the district income of £500 in municipal light and rates. He also included a list of seventeen Dublin and Wicklow cinemas, including the Theatre de Luxe and the Picture House on nearby Camden Street, which were open on Sunday.[75]

Oblivious to any business implications, the Zion church, Rathgar, declared that Sunday films 'ought to be rigidly prohibited'.[76] Similarly, the Methodist churches of Dublin and adjoining townships passed a resolution on 3 February supporting the council decision of 5 January,[77] while, shortly afterwards, the Presbyterian church in Ireland approved a resolution 'strongly' urging the members of the council 'to resist the efforts' being made to reverse the decision.[78] The Rathmines' Young Women's Christian Association also declared that 'anything that interferes with the sanctities of the Sabbath is opposed to the best interests of the young womanhood' of the area.[79] (It will be noted that the Catholic church seems to have stayed aloof, at least publicly, on the issue.) Nevertheless, a 'reasonable compromise' was sought by Councillor T. Kennedy, who submitted a motion to the council that would alter the 5 January resolution by allowing cinemas to open on Sundays from 2.30 p.m to 6.30p.m. and from 8p.m. to 10.30p.m. in line with what pertained in Dublin city.[80]

Seacome Mason asked William Shannon, the council's solicitor (with whom he was already busy amending the cinema licences to take account of the January resolution), for legal advice regarding Kennedy's proposal.[81] The matter was of particular urgency as new licences were issued each March. Kennedy's motion was defeated and, much to the annoyance of the Ratepayers' Association,[82] the January resolution was confirmed on 1 March. The council also took the opportunity to approve a further condition of the licence in the form of a resolution, which stated that the council 'reserves to themselves the right to veto any film in this Township on report', powers already accrued to local authorities via the Cinematograph Act 1909.[83] Since Dublin corporation's public health committee did not have a role in Rathmines censorship, this resolution in effect allowed the UDC to restrict further whatever censorship decisions were taken on particular films in Dublin city. It was a view other local authorities also took when they felt that Dublin city's decisions were inadequate to their local needs. Before the end of March, Mason wrote to Superintendent Kiernan of Rathmines police station informing him of the Sunday closing resolution and asking that it be enforced against the Sandford and Princess cinemas.[84]

It was not censorship, however, but economic survival that most concerned the proprietors of the Princess and Sandford cinemas. An anxious Karmel of the Princess was first to write to Mason seeking, once again, reconsideration of Sunday closure, and seeking parity with Dublin city. Pointing to the reduction in staff numbers at the Princess, the £100 loss in electric light to the municipality, and to the fact that several of the company's directors and shareholders 'had been ruined by the recent [Easter] rebellion', he stated that Sunday opening was imperative to 'enable us to carry on our business.'[85] The UDC, however, took no action at its next meeting on 8 June.

The following month, A.J. Harris Whitney of the Sandford, who emphasized that his cinema endeavoured to put on the 'purest' programme of films, also wrote to the UDC clerk hoping to influence a change in the council's policy. In a three-page letter Whitney outlined the financial structure of the Sandford, including debts of £1,550 (£1,100 of which was payable to the builder who still retained the building's title deeds and who was being paid £50 per quarter), arguing that, despite expenses and staff being cut to a minimum, it was 'impossible to pay the rent and other outgoings' from week-days alone, given that Sundays were worth £750 in box office income. Put in other terms, he explained that the company's shareholders, 'men of probity and standing', almost all of whom were Rathmines residents, having invested over £2,000 in the company,[86] only expected what the city cinemas were allowed. He also highlighted the fact that the shareholders would not be the sole financial losers. In addition to the loss of employment, light, and rates, Whitney estimated that the government would lose

£250 per annum of the recently introduced entertainments' tax, while traders were owed £300.[87]

Whitney's plea was deferred at the July sitting, while on 2 August it was decided to postpone consideration of any change until the next licence period, March 1917.[88] In a desperate attempt to gain both income and prestige for the Princess, Karmel wrote to Mason requesting approval for classical music concerts on Sundays, but Mason reported that the local authority had no power to grant such permission.[89] Shortly before the 1917 renewal of the licence both Karmel and Whitney repeated their entreaties. Whitney, reporting that 'the position of the company [was] very serious', once again stated that it was 'only equitable to extend to us the privilege of exhibiting harmless and entertaining films' on Sundays which would allow the cinema's liabilities to be met.[90] Nevertheless, there was no change in the licence conditions in 1917, and later in the year Whitney's fears were realized when the Sandford was put into liquidation. The interest in the cinema was bought from the liquidator by John Healy, 11 Woodstock Gardens, Ranelagh, who, following some renovations, reopened the cinema on 26 December 1917.[91]

Despite continuing efforts by Karmel and Healy, who wrote to Mason ingeniously contextualizing the struggle for Sunday cinema opening with regard to the provision in recent decades of a Sunday train service and Sunday excursions, and concert and museum-going on the Sabbath,[92] no change was made in the licence in 1918, 1919, or 1920.[93] However, the tide of opinion, demonstrated by the outcome of an application by a Kingstown cinema in early 1919 and, ironically, led by Dublin's recorder, was beginning to flow in the exhibitors' favour.

Mr O'Connor, manager of the Picture House, 9–10 Upper George's Street, Kingstown, whose proprietor, Robert Morrison, also owned the Sackville Street Picture House, applied to the recorder to have the Sunday opening privileges in operation at the Kingstown Pavilion extended to the Picture House. Reflecting how the two main churches differed on the matter, Canon Murphy, Kingstown's Catholic parish priest, supported the application, provided the evening show did not commence before 8.30p.m., while according to Canon H. Kennedy of the Mariners' church, representing Protestant churches, Sunday cinema was

> objectionable, especially with regard to young people, amongst whom it tended to induce a spirit of dissipation and frivolity incompatible with the sacredness of the day.[94]

In his judgment the recorder favoured the Dublin status quo, observing that he had granted licences

> in certain districts where it had been represented to him that there was a large population who earned their bread by labour through the week, and that it was better for them to have rational amusement on Sundays than to devote their attention to drink. As Canon Murphy had said, they must look at things as they were.

He granted a licence for Sunday opening from 2p.m. to 6.30p.m. and from 8.30p.m. to 10p.m. with no one under-16 allowed at the evening show.

The ending of the restrictions regarding Sunday screenings came so quickly to Rathmines that the churches had little time to build a campaign against the change. Nathan Karmel of the Princess Cinema wrote to Mason in September 1920 stating that his company planned to open a new cinema in Rathmines, but before incurring any expenditure they needed a guarantee that they would be allowed the same privileges as operated in the urban districts of Dublin, Blackrock, Kingstown, Dalkey, Bray and Greystones.[95] Recognizing that the Rathmines and Rathgar urban district council were now completely out of touch with what pertained in the Greater Dublin area, Rathmines and Rathgar UDC voted on 3 November to permit Sunday film shows from 2p.m to 5p.m and from 8.30p.m. to 10.30p.m., though the Town Hall was not accorded this privilege. Despite objections by the churches following the decision, the Sunday partial opening remained in force until the district was incorporated into Dublin corporation in 1930. Perhaps as a consequence of the 1920 policy change, another cinema project was allowed to develop with the incorporation in November 1921 of the Stella Picture Co. Ltd, which seems to have originated with the partnership on 24 April 1921, six months after Sunday restrictions were modified, of Anthony O'Grady, licensed vintner and grocer of nearby Leinster Road, and William Kay of Sutton, Co. Dublin, whose involvement with film exhibition included his Grand Cinema, O'Connell Street, and as lessee of the Rotunda and Rathmines Town Hall. From a design by Higginbotham and Stafford, the Stella Cinema, Rathmines, opened on 29 January 1923. The well-appointed building, complete with luxurious décor and a small dance hall, had 1,000 seats and was regarded as one of the largest in Ireland at the time, and the second largest in Dublin after La Scala.[96]

After the passage of the Censorship of Films Act 1923, which removed the power of local authorities provided for under the 1909 Cinematograph Act to censor the content of films, Dublin corporation took the opportunity to refine its annual licence. While it confirmed its by then Sunday opening from 2.30p.m. to 6.30p.m. and from 8.30p.m. to 10.30p.m., it changed the hours when children could attend the cinema. As a result, children of school-going age were precluded from attending between 9a.m. and 3p.m. unless accompanied by a parent or guardian, while under-14s had to leave by 9.30p.m. unless similarly accompanied. The latter provision amended an earlier clause in which under-12s had to leave cinemas by 7p.m. Elsewhere in the Irish Free State cinema licensing was not so flexible. In Limerick, for example, complete Sunday closing was introduced in 1927,[97] while in Dundalk where only charity screenings were permitted, suspicions seem to have been aroused about the *bona fides* of the promoters of some of these screenings.[98] Ironically, in light of the battles which would emerge there in later decades, Belfast was one of only seventeen Irish council areas where Sunday opening was permitted in 1914, a result, perhaps, of the proceeds often being donated to war charities, a policy also observed in Britain.[99]

FROM CRISIS TO STABILITY

(a) Dublin, Belfast, and the effects of war

Within the decade 1914 to 1924, no less than four major conflicts impacted on Ireland: the First World War (1914–18); the 1916 Rising; the (Irish) War of Independence (1919–21); and the Irish Civil War (1922–24). Apart from the more immediate practical, political and social implications of these wars, in which literally thousands of Irish fought, died or were seriously injured, when understood in terms of film distribution, the Partition Act of 1920 and the Anglo-Irish treaty of 1921 which brought about the division of Ireland into two regions had most impact. These new entities were the largely Catholic-nationalist twenty-six-county Irish Free State in the south, which comprised three-quarters of the Irish population, and the predominantly Protestant-unionist dominated six counties in the north-east of the country, which retained alignment with Britain. Nevertheless, even though the two regions developed, usually independently of each other, their own laws and business practices, and that the smaller of the two, which was largely dependent on the British imperial government and tended to be 'impotent' when it came to control over the statelet's revenue manifest in 'repeated begging expeditions' to England during the inter-war period,[1] there remained in the post-partition decades a friendly interaction between cross-border film exhibition interests.

While the First World War necessarily impacted on the complete island of Ireland, the negative consequences of the war were most pronounced in areas outside of the industrialized north-east, which, including Derry and more importantly Belfast with its shipbuilding and other heavy industrial plants, was essential to the British war effort, and hence did not suffer to the same extent the poverty experienced elsewhere in Ireland. The grim reality in wartime Dublin is most starkly expressed in a 1917 pamphlet entitled *Starvation in Dublin*, which argued that 'the primary poverty prevailing in the city before the war had been converted into actual starvation by wartime conditions and worried that serious disorder could break out if nothing was done to relieve it.'[2] Although proportionately in relation to Britain consumption of meat per head in Dublin remained the same at half the British figure, wages in Dublin grew much more slowly than in munitions-producing Britain, while with brewing and distilling cutbacks, unemployment in Dublin rose in mid-1917 to a peak.[3] The depressed conditions throughout most of Ireland in turn translated into poorer cinema attendance as working-class families, who heretofore had constituted a significant proportion of the audience, had even less discretionary surplus than they had in the past.

An additional strain on the fledgling exhibition business and, indeed, on the working classes' ability to access filmed entertainment was the introduction of an entertainment tax in the 1916 Finance (New Duties) Act which was weighted against lower-priced admission tickets. Thus, tickets costing up to 2*d.*, had 0.5*d.* tax added, and those 2.5*d.* to 6*d.*, had 1*d.* tax; 6.5*d.* to 2s. 6*d.*, 2*d.* tax; and 2s. 6*d.* to 5s., 3*d.* tax, while the even more expensive tickets for such middle-class venues as theatres and concert halls, had 6*d.* added for tickets costing 5s. to 7s. 6*d.* and 1s. tax added to seats of 7s. 6*d.* to

12s. 6d., and an extra 1s. for every 10s. or part of 10s.[4] As the cheapest priced cinemas in working-class areas were most affected, the failure of such cinemas began to be ascribed to the tax, as a result of which the film trade in Ireland and Britain began to campaign for revised rates of tax. However, the government was more than satisfied with the new revenue stream, reporting that 80 per cent of the tax collected came from tickets costing 6d. or less,[5] and chose not only to ignore the industry's pleas, but actually increased some of the tax rates in 1917. While the 0–2d. rate remained at 0.5d., with effect from 1 October 1917 the 2d. tax rate now applied from 4.5d. to 6d.; the 3d. tax to tickets from 6.5d. to 1s.; 4d. tax from 1s. to 2s.; and 6d. tax from 2s. 1d. to 3s.[6] Following further campaigning by the film trade, changes introduced in the 1918 Finance Act were postponed and later modified by the government before being introduced from 1 October 1918. The most important change was the making of tickets up to 2d. tax free, while those from 2d. to 2.5d. had 0.5d. tax added; and those 6.5d. to 7d., had the tax reduced to 2d. from 3d.[7] In 1919 a further slight modification was introduced with seats from 4.5d. to 5d. now paying 1.5d. tax, instead of 2d.[8] Despite these changes, the greatest proportion of the tax, which was 'bitterly resented' by exhibitors, and which had increased from £3 million in 1917 to £11.7 million by 1921,[9] was still being paid by the lower-end or secondary cinemas where prices were usually less than one shilling, though cinema seats generally rarely exceeded 2s. 6d. In Ireland, however, some exhibitors chose to absorb the tax for fear of further audience decline; one Dublin cinema manager even reduced the 4d. ticket price to 1d.[10]

A further cause of concern for Irish cinema-owners during the war was the Daylight Saving Time Act. While the act put clocks forward by one hour during the summer period, because of Ireland's geographical position further west of mainland Britain it had, in effect, already an average of an additional thirty minutes of daylight all year round. From the government's viewpoint such bright late evenings had the purpose of saving precious fuel and artificial light consumption, but from the film exhibitor's perspective, it was a 'burden' as it indirectly encouraged people to stay outdoors and away from indoor activities such as the cinema. As *Irish Limelight* observed, 'only those inside the industry realize how crushing this burden has proved itself to be.'[11]

Such was the state of the industry that in October 1916 a delegation of Irish exhibitors visited London to impress 'upon the responsible authorities' that the sector 'was reaching ... breaking point.' Unable to continue under such conditions, *Irish Limelight* reported in January 1918 that 'a number of once prosperous cinemas have closed their doors' and correctly predicted that 'many more will fail to successfully negotiate the difficulties' of the next 'Summer Time' period.[12] With the 'margin of profit reaching vanishing point due to increased costs', the existence of entertainments tax, and cinema admissions remaining at pre-war levels,[13] it was clear that the positive conditions that had prevailed during 1910 to 1914, and which had allowed for the sector's expansion, had considerably altered such that the number of cinema licences issued by Dublin corporation began to fluctuate in the latter half of the decade. While, as noted, Dublin corporation issued at least twenty-five licences in 1914, only eighteen were granted in 1917, twenty in 1918, and nineteen in 1919. Nevertheless, in 1922, following the end of the War of Independence, the number of cinema licences issued increased to twenty-eight.

Local events and conditions, however, were also detrimental to the sector as evidenced during Easter week 1916 when the indiscriminate shelling of the O'Connell Street area by the British military, as they sought to suppress the rising and make a public statement of its power through reducing the street to rubble, resulted in a number of cinemas being destroyed or damaged. Located in close proximity to the General Post Office (the headquarters of the rising), the Grand Cinema at 8 Lower Sackville Street, the Coliseum at 24 Henry Street, and the nearby World's Fair at 30 Henry Street, were all destroyed, while other cinemas, including the Carlton at 52 Upper Sackville Street, which had been opened at the end of December 1915 by cinema proprietor Frank W. Chambers[14] and manufacturer George P. Fleming, and the Masterpiece at 100 Talbot Street, were seriously damaged. The subsequent War of Independence with its persistent street skirmishes and the introduction of a 10p.m. curfew, which meant that cinemas had to close by 9p.m. even though few opened in the afternoon, cast a further cloud over film exhibition in Dublin.

Consequently, by December 1920, the Dublin and South of Ireland Exhibitors' Association (DSIEA), seeing the curfew as a further 'severe blow to the industry' and deeming themselves to be in a 'precarious position', gave a week's notice to their employees, saying it was provisional from week to week. Furthermore, a DSIEA delegation headed by chairman David Frame[15] met the Irish advisory committee of the British-based Kinematograph Renters Society for the first time in a formal session. The exhibitors claimed that many of their members were considering closing down completely, but had postponed such action pending renegotiation of film rental terms in a way that 'would prove ameliorative to exhibitors during the present abnormal and disastrous circumstances.' Following an invitation by the KRS committee's chairman, S. Ormsby Scott, who expressed sympathy for their position, the exhibitors, while noting that films commanding a large rental were the greatest burden, proposed a percentage reduction on all rentals materializing during the current crisis, with such price decreases made on a sliding scale. Subsequent to a lengthy discussion of the proposal, the delegation withdrew to allow the renters' body to deliberate, but, despite earlier expressions of sympathy, no dispensation was recommended to the London headquarters, or was granted. This, as Ormsby Scott explained, was largely because it was an 'indisputable fact' that any such concession would lead to concessions for other towns where curfews were in place, something which 'would spell disaster for the renting side of the business.' Belfast, for example, was affected by a 10.30 p.m. curfew order, which, according to *Bioscope*, was 'very detrimental' to cinemas there.[16] Frame concluded that the only course of action open to him was to advise his members to close 'until the clouds rolled by'.[17]

Of course, cinemas continued to be established throughout the country during the insurrectionary period, and on 23 December 1917, Horgan's Picture Theatre, Friar Street, Youghal, Co. Cork, was opened by James Horgan with his brothers Thomas and Philip, next door to Hurst's Picture Palace which had been operating since 1914.

Why this cinema is of particular interest is that it is the only Irish venue for which income and expenditure data from the 1910s and later decades is known to exist. While an extant receipt book from the cinema records that it took £9 10s. at the box office on its opening night, other such books cover most of the period to July 1919. (More complete business records from the cinema in the 1930s are discussed in chapter 2.) Gross box office takings' records for 1918 (see accompanying table), for which all but five weeks (24 April to 31 May) survive show that for the other weeks during which the cinema was open (forty-three only as it was closed in November due to a flu pandemic)[18] the income was almost £545, or approximately £12 7s. per week. Unsurprisingly, there is a significant difference between the summer and Christmas holiday periods, and ordinary time, though October is actually higher than June, July or August.[19] How this income was distributed is unknown as expenditure data has not survived.

Horgan's Picture Theatre gross box office takings, 1918	
January	£39 11s. 11.5d.
February	£33 18s. 5.5d.
March	£44 17s. 6d.
April (to 24th)	£32 9s. 4.5d.
May	No data available
June	£61 8s. 9.5d.
July	£61 3s.
August	£55 14s. 5.5d.
September	£37 6s. 1d.
October	£70 8s. 6.5d.
November	Closed due to flu pandemic
December	£106 13s. 4d.
TOTAL (43 weeks)	£544 18s. 4.5d.

Though the *Irish Times* in its review of 1921 reported that the 'outstanding feature' of the year had been the 'abnormal slump which set in early' due to the 'stringent' curfew order and 'by persistent street skirmishing', it could also note that, following the declaration of the Anglo-Irish truce in July 1921 and the passing of an exceptionally fine summer, 'a recovery almost equally abnormal' took place. The resurgence, the paper suggested, owed in part to the release of Charlie Chaplin's *The Kid* (1921) and *A Yankee in King Arthur's Court* (aka *The Connecticut Yankee at King Arthur's Court*, Emmett J. Flynn, 1920), which brought audiences back in 'overwhelming numbers'.[20] Indeed, some months earlier, in October 1921, the same paper had confidently asserted that Dublin was 'gradually shedding some of its old traditions' and 'arising' as a 'new city', 'new customs [were] coming into vogue', with the amusements of the previous generation giving way 'to suit the tastes of the modern.

Nowhere is this more pronounced than in the realms where motion pictures hold sway.'[21] At this time, it was reported that the city and its immediate suburbs had twenty-seven venues exclusively devoted to showing films while two 'elaborate' cinemas were due to open shortly.

Anticipating, at least for the monied classes, a 'new city' with 'new customs', and seeing within that a more prosperous future for the cinema, as early as during the War of Independence, large-scale cinema building projects were being developed. In May 1920, Dr Isaac Epell, who later was writer and producer of *Irish Destiny* (George Dewhurst, 1926) – the first fiction film to deal with the War of Independence and a rare triumph in early indigenous cinema – rebranded the Antient Concert Rooms, 42 Brunswick Street, as the 600-seat Palace Cinema. Three months later, despite the continuing unrest with shootings taking place all over the capital, La Scala Theatre, Prince's Street, opened in the shadow of the burnt-out GPO. A year later, the Corinthian, Eden Quay, designed by Thomas F. McNamara with 700 seats, opened on 6 August 1921. Within six months, two further cinemas, both built on sites made derelict by the rising, began business. These, as already discussed, were J.J. Farrell's 1,000-seat Grand Central Cinema on the old DBC O'Connell street site which, costing £60,000,[22] had 'one of the best front elevations in Ireland from an artistic point of view',[23] and Maurice Elliman's Metropole Cinema, complete with restaurant, on the former premises of the Metropole Hotel. The nearby cinema at 51 Lower O'Connell Street, originally the Provincial Picture House, having survived the rising, was renamed in 1917 following its sale by Provincial Cinematograph Theatres to Robert Morrison. Outside of the city centre, Robert Graves ('Daddy') Kirkham opened the Inchicore Cinema, 29–35 Tyrconnell Road, one of the earliest suburban cinemas.

The opening of these new cinemas, and their obvious need to attract affluent clientele, led the *Irish Times* at the end of 1921 to favourably compare the cinema with the Christmas pantomime:

> The film has become a serious competitor with the pantomime for Christmas favour. While it may not possess the glamour of pantomime, the cinema has other compensating qualities which make it an attractive medium for supplementing the season's festivities. The secret of its growing popularity is its value as a family resort, a place where in an interval of shopping, a business interlude, or after the day's work friends can foregather at their ease in congenial surroundings.[24]

Perhaps the paper's real motivation behind recommending the cinema was its affinity with 'high art' culture through the increasing use of live orchestral music. The article continued:

> The strains of an orchestra also add to the charm of a good film, and happily most picture houses are now recognising the merit of appropriate music. With the slow, but gradual improvement in the standard of pictures and the increasing importance of the musical programme, the number of cinema patrons is

appreciably on the rise. A more intellectual atmosphere without becoming in any sense 'high brow' is gradually creeping into the picture theatres, and the more general it becomes the better.

Regardless of this possible civilizing influence, with the exception of the O'Connell Street area, it remained the case that most of those who attended the cinema were from the working and lower middle classes.

Notwithstanding the development of the film exhibition sector, with four new cinemas opening or reopening in the O'Connell Street area during 1920–2, Dublin was by no means exceptional in the number of cinemas per head of population with regard to the rest of the island. In 1923, there was an estimated thirty-one cinemas in the greater Dublin area. Given that, according to the 1926 census, Dublin city and its four adjoining urban districts had a population of 418,981, representing 14.1 per cent of the total country's population, roughly speaking this averages out as one cinema per 13,500 persons. This may be compared to the rest of the Free State where there were approximately 120 other cinemas and halls where films were screened, which loosely represents one 'cinema' per 21,000 persons. In other words, the ratio of cinemas per head of population, Dublin to the rest of the Free State was something in the region of 1:1.5. Nevertheless, with the exception of the large conurbations of Waterford, Cork, Limerick and Galway, the cinemas outside Dublin and particularly those outside the city centre tended to be smaller and included irregular or part-time venues. As such, it is likely that the ratio of cinema seats per head was 1:2 as Dublin had twice the per capita amount of the rest of the state. Indeed, the Beere survey in the mid-1930s, which estimated that 60 per cent of the Irish Free State cinema seats were in the Dublin region, confirms this figure.

While, as noted, several Dublin cinemas were destroyed by British artillery fire during the 1916 Rising and suffered further attacks during the War of Independence, throughout the civil war, and particularly during Mary MacSwiney's hunger strike in 1922, many were subject to intimidation and closure threats.[25] Additionally, a small number of cinemas were bombed during this period. These include the accidental explosion, in March 1923, of the rear doors of the Pillar Picture House, 62 Upper O'Connell Street, during an effort to disable a power line supplying La Scala;[26] the attempt, on 13 April 1923, to blow up the Corinthian Cinema, 4–6 Eden Quay;[27] on 27 April 1923 an explosion of a landmine placed on the entrance steps of the Grand Central Cinema, 6–7 Lower O'Connell Street, damaging the lobby and causing the cinema to close briefly;[28] and on 20 November 1925 a bomb attack on the Masterpiece Picture Theatre, 99 Talbot Street, because it was showing films to which republicans objected.[29]

As might be expected then, Belfast also suffered during the 'Troubles' of the early 1920s when at least three cinemas were bombed: the West Belfast Picture Theatre, the Clonard, and the Diamond,[30] while a cinema attendant was killed in 1922 when three shots were fired into the Crumlin Road Picture House, though the motivation for the attack was not revealed.[31] (Of course, this pales in comparison to the devastation visited on Northern Ireland's cinemas by the IRA in the post-1969 Troubles, as is detailed

in part three of the book.) Nevertheless, despite such hostile social and political circumstances, Belfast, like Dublin, saw new cinemas being built in this period, two of
which were very much local or neighbourhood cinemas that did not look beyond their
immediate surroundings for patrons. The first of these, located in a Protestant area,
was the down-market 700-seat Sandro, 71–73 Sandy Row, which was owned by Sandro
Theatres Ltd, opened in 1919. As it had no proper cinema screen, the films were projected on the whitewashed front wall of the cinema. However, the walls of its auditorium surprisingly included ornate plaster mouldings decorated with sixteenth-century
scenes.[32] The second, the 600-seat Diamond Picture House, 35 Falls Road, was similarly 'bottom-of-the-market', but had, at least, a small screen. Owned by Joe McKibben
who already had two other cinemas, it was located in a Catholic community and its
'ultra-local' status led it to advertise its film shows only outside the cinema.[33] By contrast, Classic Cinemas opened the Classic, 13–25 Castle Lane, on 24 December 1923.
Not only had it 1,807 seats, making it one of the city's largest cinemas, but also it
offered a luxurious and sumptuous interior in the 'atmospheric' American style popular in the 1920s. Like Dublin's Savoy six years later, which would also boast the
'atmospheric' aesthetic, it became the benchmark against which the city's cinemas were
measured. Yet, it is the small, barn-like, more down-market, everyday 'cinemas' with
plain forms and wooden chairs as much as, and perhaps more than, the swanky palaces
epitomized by the Classic, Savoy, or those located in the primary O'Connell Street and
Grafton Street areas, that remain central to the memory of cinema-going in 1920s
Ireland.

(b) Partition and trade relations
The imminence of independence led to a fracturing of film trade relationships across
the border as Irish Free State members withdrew from the Cinematograph Exhibitors
Association of Great Britain and Ireland. In 1917, following a campaign by *Irish
Limelight* for an Irish exhibitors' 'defensive alliance' to combat the 'moral' campaign
against cinema and to deal with trade disputes, the first specifically Irish film trade
body was established. Initially known as the Dublin and South and West of Ireland
Picture House Exhibitors' Association, it was also referred to as the Dublin and South
of Ireland Cinematograph Exhibitors' Association, before it was renamed in 1920 as
the Theatre and Cinema Association of Ireland, sometimes shortened to the Irish
Cinema Association.[34] Among its first actions was the presenting, by a small delegation led by David Frame, of an ambulance to Dublin corporation. Introduced to the
lord mayor by alderman and exhibitor John J. Farrell, Frame, as chairman of Farrell's
own Dublin Electric Theatre since 1911, the Dame Street cinema and the Phoenix, and
with interests in Cork's Coliseum Cinema and the Curragh Picture House, was one of
the country's foremost exhibitors. Within three years, the organization, which by this
time had thirty-eight members, had been joined by a smaller body which operated in
the south and south-west of the country, and another based in Belfast.[35] However, such
fragmentation of the market across three independent organizations did not work to
maximize Irish exhibitors' bargaining power with regard to the London-based dis-

tributors' body, the Kinematograph Renters' Society (KRS). Acting as the European headquarters for distribution of Hollywood product, the KRS's establishment in 1915 served to formalize the two-tier nature of British and Irish distribution and exhibition. By the end of 1918, the KRS had twenty-five renter-members, while a year later, the organization included thirty full members and twenty-eight provincial ones mainly based in Manchester, Leeds, Newcastle, Birmingham, Cardiff and Dublin.[36]

Though lamenting the 'negligible quantity' of Irish films produced, in 1921 the *Irish Times*, noting that most of the leading distribution firms in London had branch offices in Dublin and Belfast, declared that renting or distribution in Ireland was 'fairly well developed'.[37] Having identified the international companies as Gaumont, Weisker Brothers, Pathé-Frères, Famous-Lasky, Ideal Films, Film Booking Offices Ltd, and Western Import Co. Ltd, the paper went on to list the several Irish firms which, purchasing films or acting as agents for the leading renting houses, were distributing to the 200 theatres throughout the island of Ireland. These distributors included J.T. Jameson (Vitagraph); General Film Supply (Astra and Phillips); National Films Ltd (Stoll); Express Film Agency (Moss Empires and Grangers); Levi & Sons (Butchers); and Phoenix Film Ltd. The only Belfast distributor named was J.Y. Moore Ltd, whose eponymous principal later became chairman of Irish Theatres Ltd. The article also detailed the new distribution pattern within the Irish market whereby 'first-run' films were rented on an exclusive basis to a particular cinema, in a system known as reserving, or 'barring', while 'second-run' films were rented without any such restrictions. Such a system largely remained in place until the 1980s with certain distributors eventually becoming associated with particular cinemas.

Another company from this period was the independent Irish Film Service whose managing director was Mr R.G. Aitken. With trade shows presented by Mr C.A. Robb, the company, established in 1920, had a Dublin office at Dame Street, and two in Belfast: at 6 Skipper Street and 2 Sandy Row.[38] Similarly, Bradbury Films Ltd also had Dublin and Belfast offices.[39] Like most distributors at this time, it, too, held regular trade shows in both Dublin and Belfast.[40] However, given that by the late 1920s many distributors chose to operate from their Liverpool offices with regard to Northern Ireland, which resulted in extra carriage charges and landing formalities for films at Belfast, trade shows were being held with less regularity in Belfast.[41] Notwithstanding that the European Motion Picture Company's unprecedented departure from Northern Ireland in July 1928[42] fuelled concerns of distribution going fully off-shore to Liverpool (which, even as late as 1945, was generating 'alarm' among exhibitors),[43] the Northern Ireland market retained a certain buoyancy with Radio Pictures' Irish boss, Walter McNally, using the Picture House, Royal Avenue, for trade screenings in 1930, shortly after the John McCormack vehicle and Irish location film, *Song O' My Heart* (Frank Borzage, 1930), had set a new box office record there.[44]

Despite the many non-American European renting companies in both Britain and Ireland in the 1920s, which provided an outlet for the distribution of British films, given that much of this material was, as Rachael Low comments, so 'poor', subsidiaries of American companies increasingly became more dominant in the sector, thus 'con-

firming the vicious circle of small [British] output and poor distribution facilities.'[45] By
the early 1920s, 38 per cent of films in British and Irish distribution came through just
six large firms, all of which handled American films. These were Film Booking Offices
Ltd, Famous-Lasky, Fox, Goldwyn, Vitagraph and Western Import Co. Ltd. While as
early as 1917, both Fox and Vitagraph had representatives in Dublin, by 1921, in keeping with the establishment by large renters of regional offices in cities such as
Birmingham, Leeds, Liverpool, Manchester and Newcastle,[46] Famous-Lasky, Film
Booking Offices and Western Import all had opened Dublin branch offices.

The concept of 'block booking' – introduced in America by Famous Players-Lasky
Corporation[47] to ensure that all of their 104 films made annually were bought (at times
unseen) by exhibitors as a package (the notorious '104 policy' or 'P104') – came to
Britain in 1916 when Essanay Manufacturing Film Company demanded that in order
to secure exhibition rights for their Charlie Chaplin films,[48] an exhibitor was forced
to takes three reels of other film. Furthermore, Essanay stopped selling its films to
renters on the open market, but rented directly to cinemas on an exclusive-contract
basis. This considerably altered the market such that during the following five years
Britain (and, of course, Ireland in tow) went from being 'one of the most flexible, open
markets in the world to one of the most rigid, closed ones'.[49] With open play dates
eliminated and films booked one to two years in advance, local productions as well as
those from less popular companies or countries found that there were no slots available for their films. While other countries such as Germany, France and the USSR in
particular 'sought distinctive alternatives' to Hollywood films that could be made more
cheaply, 'British producers opted for the most part to imitate Hollywood' and lacking
sufficient capital, 'the results were a series of pale copies [of American films] which
simply could not compete on the international market.'[50] As a result, it is unsurprising that British films were always at a disadvantage in Ireland as elsewhere, with
America accounting for 75 per cent or more of the films released in Ireland, and Britain
only reaching 20 per cent when sound cinema more or less completely eliminated foreign-language films from Irish screens.[51]

Following the collapse of European production during the First World War,
Paramount (part of the Famous Players-Lasky Corporation)[52] increased its output to
220 titles per year and distributed these to 5,000 cinemas in the USA. In an effort to
contain Paramount's grip on exhibition, in 1917 twenty-seven major American first-
run cinemas formed First National Exhibitors' Circuit (FNEC), which by 1921 had
established a production unit and was connected to 3,500 cinemas in the USA. Seeking,
in turn, to protect his interests, Famous Players-Lasky's Adolph Zukor began buying
cinemas, and by 1926 controlled more than one thousand venues. By the end of 1926
in Britain, Famous-Lasky, or Paramount as it was called from 1927, had cinemas in
Manchester and Birmingham,[53] a pre-release theatre in London, the Plaza, and from
1928, a second such venue, the Carlton. Meanwhile, it also gained a foothold in Ireland,
when through Famous Lasky Film Services Ltd and later through Paramount Film
Services Ltd, it became the lessee of Dublin's prestigious first-run La Scala. As such it
was the first (and, in this period, only) American company to invest in Irish exhibi-

tion. Taken over the previous year by J.J. Farrell and other investors, including George P. Fleming, one of La Scala's original backers,[54] it was renamed the Capitol Cinema, and on 1 August reopened with Paramount's own *The Kid Brother* (Ted Wilde, 1927). Less than twenty-one months later on 21 April 1929, its high status was confirmed when it screened the first commercially released talking picture, *The Singing Fool* (Lloyd Bacon, 1928), using Western Union equipment.[55] Nevertheless, its attempt to enter the Belfast market was less successful. In 1931, for example, it was reported that its promised super cinema was postponed due to the economic depression, and, though Paramount seems to have become involved with the Picture House, Royal Avenue, with a view to erecting a super cinema on it and an adjoining site, progress on this, too, was postponed,[56] while the Picture House itself reopened in November 1934 after refurbishment.[57] Other American companies also pursued vertical integration of the three arms of the industry – production, distribution and exhibition – with five such groups formed by the mid-1920s. Joining Paramount (the first and most aggressive of the American companies in its expansion overseas), and the already cited First National, were Universal (especially from 1915), Fox Film Corporation (1915), and Metro-Goldwyn-Mayer (MGM; 1924).

While pre-release was developing as an additional and important element in the profits of the Hollywood majors, this inevitably provoked protests from exhibitors who regarded a pre-release in a prestigious venue at often high prices as eating into their income. Indeed, preempting the protectionist Irish attitudes of the 1930s, a suggestion was made in 1925 that London county council should only license cinemas that were entirely British-owned. Unsurprisingly, when Zukor's company leased the two Birmingham cinemas in 1926, British 'exhibitors talked wildly about boycotts', but Paramount announced that it was not interested in developing a circuit, stating that it only planned to use one of the cinemas as a showcase venue. As Rachael Low notes,

> there was no real danger of an American invasion of exhibition. Most big American firms had pre-release cinemas in London by the end of the twenties … and there was little reason for American producers or renters to seek further participation in ordinary British exhibition, which was already completely dominated by [American] films.[58]

Indeed by the 1940s Paramount had sold all but its two West End outlets, though it had consolidated an arrangement whereby its films were released on the Odeon circuit.[59] Meanwhile, in Ireland, the company did not renew its lease on the Capitol after 1934, though as the cinema's 1930s' tag line had it, the Dublin cinema remained 'The Home of Paramount Pictures', with Paramount productions such as *Frenchman's Creek* (Mitchell Leisen, 1944) continuing to premiere there[60] throughout the 1940s.[61]

By the mid-1920s, the number of films available to British exhibitors had fallen from 891 in 1920 to 709. While all of these, theoretically, should have been also available to Irish exhibitors, the introduction of national film censorship from January 1924 interfered with the supply of films in the Irish Free State and created further problems

for exhibitors and distributors, not the least of which was the requirement for distributors to pay for the censoring of films in order to ensure that the censorship system
would be self-financing. In the ten-year period of 1926 to 1935, distributors paid an
average of just under £2,500 per annum to the Irish censor for certifying films.[62] With
a ban or cut issued with regard to 20 per cent of the films viewed, renters decided to
boycott the Irish market from February to July 1924. A joint exhibitors/distributors'
committee was established which distributed hundreds of thousands of leaflets in cinemas, while slides flashed similar propaganda messages on cinema screens.[63] The boycott, however, was faced down by the authorities who told a distributors' delegation
visiting Dublin that Ireland would rather have no films than the ones rejected.[64]
Annually, from 1924 to the end of the decade, just over five million feet of drama film
was submitted, typically roughly 10 per cent was banned and a further 15 per cent
cut.[65] In contrast, while the British Board of Film Censors banned just six films in 1926,
one of which was the Irish feature film *Irish Destiny*, the Irish censor rejected 115 titles.
Such a level of restriction on product inevitably had an adverse effect on profits and
continued to depress the market.

Meanwhile, the share of British-made releases had declined in the home market
from a respectable 25 per cent in 1914 to only 10 per cent in 1924 and dropped to just
2 per cent the following year.[66] Seeking some level of parity with the enormity of the
American market, focus was placed on the idea of the British empire as a single unit.
Thus, the Moyne committee's reliable 1934 estimate was that while there were 14,500
cinemas with 10 million seats in the USA, the British empire had 7,900 cinemas with
5.593 million seats, of which 4,300 cinemas with 3.872 million seats were in Britain.[67]
(Nonetheless, American companies were already firmly entrenched in these territories.)
At a more practical level, the British responded with the introduction, through the
Cinematograph Films Act 1927, of a screen quota system. Such a system was already
well-established in other European countries by this date, with Germany, for example,
linking imports with home film production such that by the mid-1920s renters had to
distribute one German film for every foreign import.[68] Given that there had been only
one significant indigenous feature film – *Irish Destiny* – and a few short comedies produced in Ireland in the 1920s, none of which got much distribution outside the country, it was unlikely that such a system could be emulated there.

With effect from January 1928, the British quota act hoped to restrict blind and
advance booking and ensure the distribution of a proportion of British films. Rental
agreements were to be eventually restricted to six months, while a renter's quota of
British product was set at 7.5 per cent in 1929, rising to 20 per cent in 1936–38. The
crucial reference, however, to production companies was that they were to be 'British
companies' which could be owned and run by non-British nationals rather than 'British-
controlled companies'. Consequently, the large American production and distribution
companies filled the requirements under the act with cheap 'British' productions popularly referred to as 'quota quickies', with the result that there was a 'disastrous decline
in [the] quality' of British films, which, it should be remembered, was already poor by
comparison with USA films.[69] Furthermore, as part of the process of evading the restric-

tions on blind booking, a practice known as 'penciling-in' came into play, such that the old system remained largely intact.[70] The American distribution companies asserted their dominance in Britain (and Ireland) in the 1920s and 1930s and easily brushed aside the challenge from native film interests. When Irish exhibitors with the support of the media and state sought to do something similar in the 1930s and 1940s, not just with regard to American renters, but British exhibitors, they were no more successful than their British counterparts.

Speaking during the censorship of films bill debate in the Dáil in 1923 the minister for home affairs, Kevin O'Higgins, identified the cinema's annual audience as about 10 million or only 3.5 admissions per person per year and primarily as consisting of those aged 8 to 17 years old.[71] Even proceeding on the basis that he mistakenly gave the Dublin figure as the national one,[72] and that as such the national annual audience was in the region of 16 to 17 million or up to 6 admissions per person per year, the number attending the cinema (many paying only children's prices) was relatively modest. As a result, film exhibition in Ireland cannot have been a very profitable business, except, perhaps, for the small number of high quality central Dublin cinemas that were able to attract the middle classes. These cinemas were also the first to compete for the new sound technology. While Michael Curran's Belfast Lyceum Cinema was the first in the city to show fully synchronous sound films on 20 November 1926,[73] the first screening in Ireland of a modern talkie was on 21 April 1929 when Dublin's Capitol Cinema presented *The Singing Fool* staring Al Jolson. A major national event, during its first two weeks alone, approximately 100,000 people attended, 40 per cent of whom were from outside the capital,[74] while the number of patrons during the film's third week exceeded that of either the first two weeks.[75] On 29 April 1929 Belfast Picture House reopened with the film.[76] Synchronous sound filming in Ireland began when two months later Gordon Lewis filmed in sound the mass during the Catholic Emancipation centenary celebrations at the Phoenix Park for *Fox Movietone News* and *Pathé Gazette*.[77] By October, eight Dublin cinemas had installed sound. The Savoy, which opened the following month as a state-of-the-art cinema and which remains Dublin's premier venue, joined these. Located at 19 Upper O'Connell Street on the site of the former Crown and Granville hotels destroyed during the civil war, it cost between £200,000 and £250,000 with the projection equipment alone costing approximately £10,000. That such a venue opened is an indication that, notwithstanding issues around product, distribution, and modest enough audience numbers, as the 1930s dawned the future was relatively bright for the Irish distribution and exhibition business, which was valued at almost one million pounds annually.[78]

CHAPTER 2

Economic Protectionism and Foreign Oligopoly, 1929–46

'Considering the extent to which we have to rely on an Anglo-American monopoly for our film supplies, it is evident that we cannot alter fundametally the manner of film distribution.'

Report of the inter-departmental committee on the film industry, 1942.[1]

THE SECOND IRISH CINEMA BUILDING BOOM, 1929–39

(a) Irish Free State

During the first three decades of cinema in Ireland, very few films were made in the country and as a result almost all films shown were from Europe (particularly France, Italy and Britain) and the USA, with the American product rising from 26 per cent of all films distributed in Britain (and, thus, Ireland) in early 1911, to 52 per cent at the outbreak of the First World War, and to 82 per cent by the end of 1917.[2] The distribution of these films, both American and European, largely remained outside Irish control since companies operated the Irish market either directly from their London offices, or indirectly, as those few companies that had an Irish branch office, located in Dublin or Belfast, tended to refer decisions of importance to their London headquarters. This practice of referral is reflected in particular through the Dublin-based Irish *advisory* committee of the renters' organization, the Kinematograph Renters' Society.[3]

The only integrated Irish production and distribution company as cinema matured in the 1910s was General Film Supply (GFS). This was established in 1913 by Norman Whitten, an English-born cameraman, who had worked with Cecil Hepworth, the most prominent British filmmaker before the First World War.[4] Besides producing Irish newsreel material, the company made two recruiting films – *Britannia's Message* (1914) and *Sons of John Bull* (1914) – as well as producing Ireland's first animated film, *Ten Days Leave* (1917). The latter film, drawn by newspaper cartoonist Jack Leah[5] and photographed by J. Gordon Lewis, may have been directed by Englishman Jack Warren,[6] editor of *Irish Limelight*, which, following GFS's establishment in 1917 of the *Irish Events* newsreel, lauded the company's activities.

[General Film Supply] have launched a new industry in Ireland ... and should ... provide a good deal of employment directly and indirectly... Even at the present time the company is a gratifying contrast ... to many film businesses which are making big money in Ireland – for directors in England and America – and spending as little of it as they possibly can [in Ireland].[7]

Though many of the titles that GFS carried were made in the USA or by American companies working in Ireland, such as those filmed by Kalem during 1910–12,[8] their advertisements, as summed up in their tag-line, 'Irish films for Irish picture-goers', emphasized the Irishness of their product which was epitomized best by their innovative indigenous documentaries, including *Irish Pilgrimage to Lourdes* (1917) and *Court Laundry* (1917).[9] Despite the company's success, suggested in the fact that by December 1917 it claimed to have three million feet of film for hire,[10] their pioneering newsreel series, *Irish Events*, ended in 1920. Nevertheless, 1920 also saw the company extend its activities into feature film production with Whitten's well-received *In the Days of St Patrick*,[11] which was photographed by *Irish Events'* cameraman Lewis, who, with Whitten, had supplied Irish newsreel material to Pathé throughout the 1910s. Demonstrating the difficulty of Irish filmmakers maintaining their independence in the small Irish market, Lewis continued to work as Pathé's Irish newsreel cameraman, and in 1934 was appointed manager of Pathé's new Dublin office.[12]

At least one area of the film business, however, that is exhibition, was largely under Irish control (notwithstanding that one of Ireland's leading exhibitors, Maurice Elliman,[13] was born in Latvia and only arrived in Ireland as a teenager). During the silent period, apart from the brief interlude by the Italians with regard to the Volta, the only non-Irish companies operating in the market were the British-owned Provincial Cinematograph Company, which was taken over by Gaumont in February 1929, and the American-owned Paramount. Though Provincial had first-run cinemas located in Dublin on Lower O'Connell Street (from 1910 to 1917, the Picture House), and Grafton Street (from 1911), and in Belfast on Royal Avenue (from 1911 to the 1920s, the Belfast Picture House) and Castle Lane where their prestigious Classic opened in 1923,[14] by the time Gaumont took over Provincial, only the Grafton and Classic remained. Gaumont, which in turn was taken over by Rank in 1941, subsequently sold its single Dublin cinema to the Ellis family in the 1930s, and did not reenter the southern Irish exhibition market.[15] Paramount, on the other hand, only ever had the one venue; this was the Capitol which had been renamed as such in 1927 when the company had acquired the lease of Dublin's premier cine-variety venue La Scala.

In the sound period, a new (foreign) player entered the Irish exhibition market: the highly aggressive and expansionist Associated British Pictures (ABP). An emerging force in the British film industry, it had interests in production (through Elstree Studios and British International Pictures [BIP], one of whose directors was Alfred Hitchcock); distribution (through Wardour Films Ltd and as agent for First National Pathé); and exhibition (through Associated British Cinemas [ABC]). Established in 1928 as a subsidiary of the production-centred BIP, ABC had grown from three distinct British exhibition circuits, one of which, comprising of about sixteen cinemas under the Savoy Cinemas banner, and with sites for large cinemas planned for Brighton and Dublin, had been developed from a Scottish base by John Maxwell, the majority owner of ABP's affiliated companies. In all, there were forty-three or forty-four cinemas in the new group and though Maxwell unsuccessfully bid for Provincial's ninety-two cinemas, forcing Gaumont to pay a premium price for the company, he quickly added a further eleven cinemas to the ABC chain. Additionally, in 1929, many smaller chains were added to the circuit while ABC also saw the opening of other cinemas, including Dublin's unequalled Savoy.

By May 1931, ABC, with more than 230,000 cinema seats, was registering an impressive 1.75 million admissions *weekly*, or about 91 million admissions annually.[16] The full impact of these figures is best understood through a comparison with Irish figures. According to the first authoritative study of film exhibition and distribution in the Irish Free State, carried out during 1934–5 by statistician Thekla Beere,[17] it was estimated that there were 190 cinemas with a total of 111,438 seats, recording 18.25 million admissions annually (or 0.35 million admissions *weekly*). Put differently, the entire Irish film market had less than half the amount of seats controlled by the single company ABC, while the total annual number of admissions to Irish cinemas was only a fifth of the total admissions to ABC cinemas. Yet, ABC never achieved dominance within the Irish market and during the 1930s had an unsettled relationship with Ireland.

Dublin's Savoy, Upper O'Connell Street, which cost 'almost' £200,000,[18] was the largest and most impressive cinema in the Free State. Designed by London-based architect F.C. Mitchell,[19] about 1,000 Irish people had been employed in its construction and, where possible, Irish companies had participated both in the building and fitting out of the new complex.[20] Behind a rather bland façade, the building offered a 3,000-seat[21] magnificent Venetian 'atmospheric' auditorium complete with blue ceiling with twinkling stars designed and executed by Mr W.E. Greenwood and a 300-seat restaurant. These were staffed by 150 people, who were, like those who built the cinema, 'as far as possible', Irish.[22]

The significance of ABC's investment and the Savoy's importance was evident in the fact that the opening ceremony on 29 November 1929 was performed by no less than the president of the executive council of the Irish Free State, William Cosgrave, and also in the fact that reclusive John Maxwell attended. In describing the opening night, which included a screening of *On With the Show* (Alan Crosland, 1929, USA), one of the first sound-era musicals in colour,[23] the *Saturday Herald* breathlessly sketched the experience of walking through the cinema:

> An air of expectancy prevailed, and the vast audience were like children longing to see what this marvellous building was like, nor were they disappointed. Having mounted the wide stairway and noted the beauty of design and the harmony of decoration, one stood in a different world ... Coming back to earth, a vast amphitheatre stretched to the sides and back, while in front on a stage bright with gold the No. 1 Army Band, under the direction of Col. Fritz Brase, was playing Wagner's wonderful 'Meistersinger' Prelude ... The President, in a

happy speech, declared the house open, and congratulated the proprietors and all concerned in the construction, decoration, and organisation of the building. He also spoke appreciably of the trade and industrial prosperity which follows on a large undertaking of this nature.[24]

To develop the Irish business, in July 1930, ABC established an Irish subsidiary, Associated Irish Cinemas Ltd (AIC), under ABC managing director J.E. (John Edward) Pearce who was an Irish Free State citizen.[25] Though incorporated in Ireland, and registered at Dublin's Savoy, it was run by Pearce from ABC's London headquarters, 32 Shaftesbury Avenue, but, as a subsidiary of ABC, which was registered in Britain, it probably could take advantage of reciprocal British-Irish taxation arrangements which would have facilitated AIC's avoidance of Irish tax.[26] A month after opening, it took on a debenture loan of £92,000, presumably to develop other Irish cinemas.[27] Indeed, in May 1932, AIC opened Cork's premier cinema, the even more spectacular, if smaller, 2,249-seat Savoy Cinema and Restaurant, Patrick Street. By this time Maxwell had taken over from Pearce as managing director of ABC, though Pearce continued to run the Irish subsidiary from London. In February 1933, AIC took on a further debenture loan of £40,000,[28] and, just over a year later in April 1934, through the takeover of the Dublin Theatre Co. by Pearce and other AIC shareholders,[29] it acquired Dublin's prestigious Theatre Royal, Hawkins Street, for which it announced an ambitious £250,000 ten-month reconstruction project.[30] The same year, however, a new public company Irish Cinemas Ltd was formed to take over the entire business and assets of AIC Ltd for an undisclosed sum.[31] The company's directors, three of whom were Irish citizens (J.E. Pearce [chairman]; John McCann, a director of the Royal Bank of Ireland; and John Xavier Murphy, a director of the Bank of Ireland, though he died in 1937) and two were from Yorkshire (Horace and Fred Moore),[32] proposed that the company would operate additional cinemas and restaurants throughout the Free State, with Limerick, where a site had been acquired already, mentioned as the first such venture.

Despite their impressive portfolio boosted by their 'association' with the Dublin Theatre Co., which had recently opened the largest theatre in the country – the 3,850-seat Theatre Royal[33] – Irish Cinemas Ltd posted a dividend of only 2.5 per cent in the financial year to 31 August 1937, compared with 5 per cent the previous year.[34] Considering the quality of their assets, not least of which were the Savoys, this can only be regarded as a poor performance. However, in January 1939, following 'secret negotiations conducted over a considerable period',[35] the biggest cinema merger in the history of the Irish film trade occurred when the Elliman group acquired a 'controlling interest' in the company. While by this time Irish Cinemas Ltd owned all the ordinary shares in Dublin Theatre Company,[36] the Elliman group, which controlled the private company Metropole and Allied Cinemas headed by Maurice Elliman who was also managing director of Dublin Kinematograph Theatres Ltd, owned the Queen's;[37] two first-run Dublin cinemas, the Metropole and the Corinthian;[38] and two others, the Theatre de Luxe[39] and Phibsboro Picture House,[40] which in 1934 and 1938, respectively, had been enlarged and brought to 'Super' status.

Following the merger, the combined group, operating under the Irish Cinemas' banner, controlled ten venues. As well as the cine-variety focused Queen's and Theatre Royal with its small 750-seat Regal Cinema, which prior to the cinema's opening in April 1938 had been the Royal's Regal restaurant, it owned eight full-time cinemas with a total of about 15,110 seats,[41] four restaurants and the Metropole ballroom. The new board formed to run the group comprised of three members of the Irish Cinemas' board and four representatives of Metropole and Allied Cinemas. Horace Moore, who had already replaced Pearce as chairman of the company, became chairman of Irish Cinemas, while Maurice Elliman became general manager. No financial details of the merger were revealed as Elliman stated that the merger was a private transaction.

Though the deal was reported prominently as a 'booking merger' designed to enhance future bargaining capacity with distributors,[42] a secondary objective was, in effect, the 'squeez[ing] out' of ABC's new first-run cinema, the Adelphi, Middle Abbey Street, Dublin. Initiated by an Irish company, Adelphi Ltd, the principals of which were William H. Freeman and William M. Middleton,[43] and designed by ABC house architect, William Riddell Glen, working with Irish architect Robert Donnelly, the Adelphi opened on 12 January 1939[44] with 2,304 seats and standing room for 500.[45] Given that ABC was the parent company of AIC, the company subsumed by the independent Irish Cinemas Ltd, before it 'merged' with Metropole and Allied Cinemas, made this motivation somewhat ironic. It was even more ironic as prior to this merger 'a proposition' had been made by Irish Cinemas to John Maxwell.[46]

In any case, no Irish circuit[47] or combine could hope to match the number of cinemas or cinema seats controlled by ABC and hence equal the bargaining power that flowed from this. Indeed, following ABC's take over in October 1937 of the 139-cinema British Union Cinemas chain, through which it gained over 9,000 Northern Ireland cinema seats across seven venues,[48] one of which, the Ritz, Belfast, was later described as 'the show place of Northern Ireland … slick, ultra-modern, [and] completely beautiful',[49] ABC controlled 460 cinemas, 115 more than arch-rival Gaumont.[50] Prior to this, ABC's interests in Northern Ireland had been limited to the Belfast variety house, the Hippodrome (from 1935, Royal Hippodrome), Great Victoria Street, which it bought in 1931 and reopened as a full-time first-run sound (Western Electric) cinema on 20 July with George Dobler continuing as manager[51] before selling it in December 1938 to an independent.

Nevertheless, despite Irish Cinemas' small size, relative, that is, to the leading British companies, within five years, the Elliman-led company had been transformed with chairman John McCann able to report a company tax payment of £14,630 and an impressive profit of £40,800 in the year ended 31 August 1945. This was due to a 'considerable increase in cinema attendance.' The profit yielded during the previous two years was also healthy with £31,000 taken in 1943, and £37,268 in 1944.[52]

Meanwhile, Maurice Elliman's son Louis, a pharmaceutical chemist, followed his brothers into the film business. Though he served as Dublin branch manager for First National (later Warner Bros) until 1932, at which time he established himself as an independent distributor before becoming managing director of the Gaiety Theatre in

1936 (a position he retained until his death in 1965, aged 62),[53] more significantly, in the context of this study, Louis, through Western Cinemas Ltd, of which he was also managing director, was the force behind the building of two of Ireland's most important modern cinemas. These were the Ritzes in Athlone (987 seats: about 750 stalls and 250 balcony), and in Clonmel (980 seats), which opened on 14 February 1940 and 1 March 1940, respectively, and which aimed to show first class films recently screened in Dublin in luxurious conditions, but for low admission prices of 4*d*., 1*s*., 1*s*. 4*d*., and 1*s*. 8*d*.[54] Designed by Bill O'Dwyer of the country's premier modernist architectural firm, Michael Scott & Associates,[55] they incorporated many features of modern Dutch architecture, and, consequently, offered a stark contrast to the rest of the surrounding architecture and provided relief from the dreary repetitiveness of Victorian buildings common in provincial towns. As Sean Rothery comments, 'with its white walls, large areas of glass, flat roofs and porthole windows the [Athlone] Ritz must have seemed an exotic, exciting and even bizarre newcomer to this old market town.'[56] Another Ritz, the 1,054-seat cinema which had opened almost two years earlier in Carlow in June 1938,[57] and in which Louis Elliman was also involved through Carlow Cinema Ltd, was similarly described by the *Irish Times*, as 'represent[ing] the last word in cinema glamour.'[58] The paper also remarked that 'perhaps no other type of enterprise so faithfully indicates the prosperity of a town as the erection of a luxury premises can do.'

One of the most interesting modernist cinemas built in Dublin in the 1930s was the Stephen's Green Cinema, 127 St Stephen's Green West, close to the College of Surgeons. Constructed on the site of Dublin's only Turkish baths, the cinema was developed by Stephen's Green Cinema Ltd, whose principals included chairman Sir Thomas W. Robinson, also chair of Kingstown Ltd, operators of the Pavilion Gardens Cinema, Dún Laoghaire;[59] F.J. McDonnell BL, PC, who became the cinema's managing director; and Michael J. Deasy, who, previously had been the manager of the Cinema Palace, Burrin Street, Carlow, became the cinema's manager. Designed by architects Jones & Kelly, the cinema, which had a rather plain frontage – 'a vertical cube, four storeys high, with horizontal steel windows'[60] – but a splendid art deco interior, opened on 18 December 1935 with 1,000 seats on the ground floor and 500 in the balcony. In its opening souvenir programme, the proprietors were keen to emphasize that in contrast to an atmosphere 'suggest[ive of] a Monastery or Viennese Palace' which prevails in other cinemas, including, though unnamed, Dublin's Savoy and the recently opened Theatre Royal, and which was moreover out of kilter with the tone and aesthetic of the entertainments provided, the 'decorative treatment' of the Stephen's Green Cinema

> does not follow any particular style. And is almost devoid of any of the usual more or less-intricately woven and highly-coloured establishments. Instead, a simple but nevertheless bold treatment has been provided, … the atmosphere produced by the perfect combination of shape and surface with light, can be altered from time to time to gain accord with the venue of screen action.[61]

Throughout the 1930s the Farrells, led by John J., and mostly through Capitol and Allied Theatres, continued, until the 1960s, to be a dominant force within Irish film exhibition,[62] even if many of their cinemas were in secondary locations or were relatively small. While by the late 1930s, day-to-day running of the cinemas had passed to his sons Patrick (Paddy) and Peter, John J. remained chairman until his death at the age of 83 of the various holding companies which included Capitol & Allied Theatres, Ltd; Capitol and Provincial Cinemas, Ltd; Capitol (Cork), Ltd; and Irish Kinematograph Co. Though the period 1939 to 1946 saw three of their cinemas close – the Mary Street cinema in 1939; the Pillar Picture House on O'Connell Street in 1945; and the Grand Central, also on O'Connell Street, in 1946 when it was destroyed by fire[63] – the similar period of 1937 to 1945 brought four new cinemas to the family. These were the Picture House, 51 Lower O'Connell Street, formerly owned by Provincial Cinematograph Company, which was reopened by the Farrells on 27 March 1937 as the Astor; the 1,550-seat New Electric on Talbot Street, which opened in April 1938 to replace John J. Farrell's first cinema, the 379-seat Electric, which had been destroyed by fire earlier in the year;[64] and the 1945 acquisitions of the Volta and Phoenix following the death of previous owner Rudolph Ahearne. However, perhaps reflecting a confused policy, in October 1947 the Volta ceased business.[65] Incidentally, and, considering the rivalry between James T. Jameson and John J. Farrell in Dublin exhibition in the early part of the century, ironically, the Rotunda also came under Capitol and Allied's control. On 23 September 1954, it was reopened by Patrick Farrell, the company's managing director, as the 1,222-seat Ambassador Cinema, and remained part of Capitol & Allied until the effective demise of the company in 1977.

The 1930s also saw the emergence of a number of new exhibition entrepreneurs. The Ellis family, who, as already mentioned, were involved in Irish Cinemas Ltd, bought, through Jack Ellis, the Grafton Street Picture House from Gaumont. They also rebuilt and extended the Carlton Picture House, Upper O'Connell Street, one of Dublin's 'supers', situated directly opposite the Savoy; while in 1938 on 16 April, Jack Ellis and others opened the 2,000-seat[66] new Carlton Cinema. Incorporating two adjoining premises, numbers 53 and 54,[67] and with a design by architects Robinson and O'Keefe,[68] the cinema's interior and foyer featured Celtic as well as musical instrument motifs, while its classical façade was complemented by two art-deco light beacons that shone into the sky. (Following complaints from air traffic controllers at Dublin Airport, the beacons were turned off.)

Another exhibitor active at this time was Leonard Ging, who concentrated on suburban Dublin sites. On 18 November 1929, Ging (with partners Patrick J. Whelan, his brother-in-law, and Joseph Lyons) opened what was to be the first of five suburban cinemas that he would build, the 1,469-seat Grand Cinema, Fairview. Four years later, he added a balcony to the cinema, while further work in the 1940s increased its seating to 1,750. Meanwhile, on 19 October 1934, he opened the 1,038-seat Drumcondra Grand Cinema, 20–24 Upper Drumcondra Road, which was designed by Harry J. Lyons and decorated in silver and green with amber lighting.[69] The 729-seat Sutton Grand, Sutton Cross, followed in January 1937,[70] and two years later, on 16 April

1938, the 500-seat Strand Cinema, North Strand Road, another Harry Lyons design, opened. This latter cinema was subsequently extended on to adjoining land and reopened on 16 March 1945 with 1,426 seats.[71]

Yet another person to emerge as an exhibitor in the 1930s was Walter McNally, an opera singer who continued his singing career even while heavily engaged in film distribution as RKO's Irish agent, and as an exhibitor. By 1931, he was managing director of four cinemas in Dublin, including the Grand Central, O'Connell Street, as well as owner of cinemas in Athlone, Westport, and the Empire Theatre in Galway.[72] In 1934, following difficulties with the Empire's licensing on the grounds of safety, McNally built and opened the 1,254-seat Savoy, Galway, with an investment of £18,000 through Galway Cinemas Ltd.[73] Following his death in August 1945,[74] McNally's son Hubert (known as Bertie), who had entered the business as manager of Capitol and Allied Theatres' Astor, O'Connell Street, which closed in 1946, took over from his father as Irish manager for RKO in September 1945,[75] and subsequently joined forces with Louis Elliman, who became chairman of Amalgamated Cinemas (Ireland) Ltd, which controlled eighteen provincial theatres. In 1949, Bertie, with his brother Dr Patrick McNally, invested in the last cinema to be built by Leonard Ging, the 1,634-seat Cabra Grand. However, shortly after its completion the cinema, which had one of Ireland's largest proscenium arches at thirteen metres wide, was sold in April 1949 to Rank's Irish Cinemas Ltd. Four years later, Bertie opened the Astor, Eden Quay, Dublin, as a specialist foreign-language cinema with manager Tommy Gogan in charge until his death in 1961, and ran it until his own death in 1976.

Finally, a further exhibitor to emerge in this period was Manchester-born businessman Maurice Baum, who moved to Ireland in the 1930s.[76] Having opened on 5 November 1936 the 1,500-seat[77] Rialto Cinema, 27–31 South Circular Road, Dublin, Baum went on to acquire the 600-seat Picture House, Quinsboro' Road, Bray, first opened in 1920; another Bray cinema, the 600-seat Roxy; and the 750-seat Rialto, Fitzwilliam Square, in Wicklow town. This small circuit was typical of Irish circuits in this period, with most groupings limited to between two and four cinemas, which were usually located in the same or adjoining counties. In addition to the Leinster circuit, Baum also had, for a time at least, one other cinema, the 400-seat Roxy, Ballaghadereen, Co. Roscommon, which he sold in 1944 to the local clergy.[78] While clerical involvement in film exhibition, facilitated by the widespread availability of 16mm films after the Second World War, was largely limited to screenings in village parish halls, occasionally, the religious ran full-time cinemas, including the 750-seat Magnet Cinema, Dundalk. Opened by Fr J. Stokes Horn on Easter Sunday 1936, all profits were devoted to parish churches and schools.[79] However, in Clones, Co. Monaghan, in 1943, morality and commerce were unhappy bedfellows with the committee, under clerical guidance, which ran the local cinema at St Joseph's Temperance hall, decreeing that only married couples were allowed to sit together, thus banning courting couples, or brothers and sisters, from being beside each other in the cinema's darkness.[80] The ban was lifted eighteen months later, perhaps in anticipation of the imminent opening of a new cinema in the town.[81]

While the Elliman, Farrell, and Ellis families together with Leonard Ging, Walter McNally and Maurice Baum were to the forefront of the development of Irish cinemas, a significant number of independently-run cinemas opened throughout the 1930s. In December 1934, P.J. Whelan's Associated Picture Houses Ltd opened the 1,700-plus-seat Tivoli Cinema, 135–8 Francis Street,[82] while in February 1935, James O'Neill opened the Astoria, Serpentine Avenue, Ballsbridge. (The Astoria was often referred to as the shed or shack. This was due to the fact that previous to the cinema's opening, an unlicensed shed on the premises had been used occasionally to show films from at least 1919. In 1940, the Astoria was renamed the Ritz in order to allow O'Neill carry the Astoria name to his new cinema on Glasthule Road.)[83] In 1936, the Leinster, Dolphin's Barn, was opened by Dublin's Lord Mayor Alfie Byrne in one of many such ceremonies by him in the 1930s.[84] In 1938, Associated Picture Houses, which had five cinemas at the time of managing director Patrick Whelan's death in 1944, opened the James V. McCrane designed Regent[85] on the site of the Blackrock Picture Theatre, which had closed in 1929; while Sundrive Cinema Ltd opened the Classic, Terenure. The following year, 1939, Portlaoise exhibitors Joseph Egan and J.L. Kelly in association with Peter Ging, converted the former premises of the Irish Omnibus Company into the 350-seat Tower Cinema, Monastery Road, Clondalkin, Co. Dublin;[86] and in April of that year Associated Picture Houses paid £14,500 for the Fountain Cinema, 36–7 James's Street, which had opened in 1923, and renamed it the Lyric.[87]

In order to achieve greater bargaining power, mergers between small provincial circuits were being considered. In the south-east, for example, Martin Breen (managing director of the Regal and Theatre Royal, Waterford, and owner of Waterford's Bridge hotel; the Savoy, New Ross; Ritz, also New Ross, and the Rex, Tramore), and James J. Kavanagh (managing director of the Paramount and Ormonde cinemas circuit based in Arklow, Co. Wicklow), publicized a merger in 1944.[88] Though they announced plans to open jointly new cinemas,[89] the amalgamation does not seem to have occurred given that by 1947 Kavanagh had nine cinemas in the adjoining counties of Wicklow, Wexford, Waterford and Cork, while Breen, partly overlapping these locations, had seven cinemas in Waterford, Wexford, Kilkenny and Tipperary.[90] The opportunity to cut costs by consolidating these two groups was lost, as was the possibility of creating one of the country's largest circuits, which would have had a virtual monopoly in five of the twenty-six counties. Nevertheless, by 1952, Kavanagh's circuit included twelve cinemas, ten of which, at Arklow, Gorey, Dungarvan, Greystones, Midleton, Kanturk, Rathdrum, Carnew, Cobh and Fermoy, were Ormondes. He added the Ormonde, Stillorgan, Co. Dublin, in 1954, and he also owned the Paramount Cinema, Arklow (where he also had two ballrooms: the Marquee and Mayfair); the Desmond Cinema, Cappoquin; and the Castle Cinema, Ferns.[91]

(b) Northern Ireland

The pattern of a few large and numerous small circuits, which pertained in the south of Ireland, was replicated in Northern Ireland. However, as noted, British exhibitors, notably ABC and Gaumont, had a much more prominent presence in Northern Ireland,

especially in Belfast and Derry, than in the south, in part facilitated by the closer sym-
metry in the taxation and legal systems of mainland Britain and Northern Ireland.
Similar to Dublin, Northern Ireland, particularly Belfast and Derry, also witnessed a
significant cinema-building boom during the 1930s. Such was the growth in cinema-
building that existing exhibitors (in both jurisdictions), as discussed below, sought to
have it curtailed. While twenty-seven cinema licences were issued in Belfast in 1934,[92]
in the four years between October 1933 (when the Apollo, Ormeau Road/Agincourt
Avenue opened) and October 1937 (when the Stadium, 351–3 Shankill Road, opened)
a total of seventeen new cinemas with about 21,000 seats entered the Belfast (city and
suburbs) cinema market. Indeed, British-based Union cinemas, before its take-over by
ABC in October 1937, engaged in a breakneck expansion during the mid-1930s by
adding no less than three Belfast venues (Majestic, Ritz and Strand) between December
1935 and November 1936.[93]

The emergence of province-wide circuits was also a significant feature of the decade.
By the mid-1940s, apart from the large British circuits already cited, there were three
significant local circuits active in the provinces. These were Irish Theatres Ltd, Michael
Curran & Sons, and Supreme Cinemas Ltd, which combined, had about forty cinemas. Additionally, there were fourteen other circuits, each with two to four venues and
which accounted for thirty-four cinemas.

Though Irish Theatres, which vied with Curran's as the largest local circuit, was not
registered as a company until 1935 (when its share capital was £2,000 [shares £1] and
its signatories were Messrs J. Yeats Moore and E. King, both of Belfast),[94] it was actually
formed in the 1920s by Englishman Ferris ('Paddy') Pounds as a federation of
independent exhibitors seeking to increase their bargaining power with distributors.
According to Sir Dawson Bates, the company's registering solicitor, speaking in 1942,
at which time he was Northern Ireland minister for home affairs, Irish Theatres had been
set-up to book films, and had never 'erected a picture house in its existence'.[95] By the
late 1930s, it incorporated cinemas both within and beyond Belfast. Outside the city, it
controlled the Picture Houses at Larne, Lisburn, Coleraine[96] and Banbridge, the latter
venue opened in the mid-1910s by James U. Finney, who was a director of Irish Theatres
Ltd;[97] the Savoy in Newry, also Finney's; and the Regal in Enniskillen, which opened in
1936, incidentally, the name of the cinema opened in Larne by Pounds (who remained
a principal figure in Irish Theatres), and J.Y. Moore of Irish Electric Palaces Ltd in 1937
which replaced the Picture House, also known as the Electric Palace. The circuit's Belfast
cinemas included the Picturedrome, 112 Mountpottinger Road (from 1924), of which
Pounds had been manager from its opening in February 1911 until late 1912, when he
left to manage his own cinema, the 1,000-seat New Princess Palace, Newtownards Road,
which opened the previous July and which also became part of the circuit;[98] the mixed
venue Alhambra, North Street, one of Belfast's oldest and most famous theatres; the
Coliseum, Grosvenor Road/Durham Street which started up in 1915 (having previously
been the Alexandra theatre); the 1,200-seat Windsor, Donegall Road, which started in
1935; the 1,250-seat Forum, Crumlin Road, which opened in 1937; and the 1,400-seat
Stadium, Shankill Road, also opened in 1937. The latter cinema had been envisaged as

a 'typical working class' cinema of the future by Pounds whose halls more generally were regarded by *Kine Weekly* as catering for 'industrial patronage', which, given the dominance of Protestants within industry, not least Harland and Wolff shipbuilding with its 10,000 strong workforce, might be better characterized as Protestant working-class patronage. As its name suggests, it was built on the stadium principle, albeit modified somewhat to suit the proscenium arch. With 'a gently sloping, raised balcony, just like in a circus or a boxing ring', it was a 'business-like building devoid of all garish decoration' with 'just the necessary amount of appeal', neither 'dull [n]or depressing'.[99]

The second indigenous circuit, Michael Curran & Sons, Ltd, also known as Curran Theatres Ltd, was established by Michael Curran (*c.*1872–1940) in 1934. By the time of Curran's death in 1940, the circuit had ten cinemas.[1] These were the 2,000-plus seat Tonic, Bangor, which, opened in 1936 by Bangor Cinemas Ltd (one of the Curran subsidiaries), had a Compton organ and was one of the island's largest cinemas; the Frontier in Newry from at least 1935; the 1,650-seat Strand, Derry's largest cinema, which Curran bought from Billy James, who had built it the previous year in 1934;[2] Derry's Midland Cinema, Waterside, also acquired from James by 1937 (though his Majestic in Portrush did not pass to the Currans until the 1940s); and six venues in Belfast, five of which had been opened in the period 1933 to 1936. These were the 1,100-seat Apollo, Ormeau Road/Agincourt Avenue (opened by J.H. McVea in 1933);[3] the opulent and expensive to run 1,275-seat Astoria, Upper Newtownards Road (opened in 1934 as the first cinema to be built by the Curran group);[4] the 1,300-seat[5] Regal Cinema, 386 Lisburn Road,[6] which, similar in design to the Astoria, was opened by Fred Curran in October 1935;[7] the smaller, but no less comfortable, 1,000-seat Capitol, 407 Antrim Road, which opened a month later; and the 1,380-seat Broadway, 278 Falls Road, which opened in December 1936 and included a 'particularly spectacular' lighting system around the screen curtains.[8] All of these suburban cinemas, as James Doherty notes, 'boasted facilities which were on par with the downtown ones.'[9] The final Belfast cinema owned by the group at this time was the Lyceum, Antrim Road/New Lodge Road. Opened in 1916 by Irish Electric Palaces Ltd, the company formed in 1911 by Michael Curran, I. Moore and Andy T. Wright,[10] which was also behind Larne's (and indeed Curran's) first cinema, the Electric Palace (later integrated into the Pounds-led Irish Theatres' circuit), the Lyceum (incidentally fitted out by Michael Curran in his capacity as Belfast's preferred electrical contractor of cinemas)[11] was acquired by Curran as his share of the splitting of the original Irish Theatres circuit, after which he severed his connections with Irish Electric Palaces. On 20 November 1926, the Lyceum became the first Belfast cinema to show fully synchronous sound films and in March 1930 'went "all talkie" with *Noah's Ark*' (Michael Curtiz, 1929).[12]

After Michael Curran's death, his six sons took control of the business, each taking responsibility for managing individual cinemas as well as jointly maintaining the electrical business.[13] Thereafter, it seems the group gained only one additional Belfast cinema. This was the Picture House, Royal Avenue, in 1947, which was subsequently renamed the Regent.[14] In contrast to the Irish Theatres' circuit, Currans, with their quality, luxurious cinemas, mostly looked to a (lower) middle-class audience. According to *Kine Weekly* reporter Melchior A.A. Sinkins, writing in 1944, the typical patrons comprised of 'the black-coated worker', or 'the family man', municipal or civil servant, and the bank and insurance clerk. Given that these were 'by all pre-war and war standards grossly underpaid', Currans' top admission price was only 1s. 9d.[15] Indeed, the pre-war admission price for many of the basic local or suburban working-class cinemas seems to have been as low as 3d. to 6d.[16] Elsewhere in his overview of Irish exhibitors, Sinkins characterized James Curran's running of the circuit as having a 'cold, clockwork-like efficiency'.[17] Sinkins, who described Curran, one of Michael Curran's sons, as a 'family man, shrewd booker, acute, and a man of firm convictions about politics, both Trade and national, and a little bit distant', regarded the interview as 'the most miserable twenty minutes of [his] life' not least because it showed him 'there can be dangers, quite unconnected with trade problems, in controlling a large number of kinema theatres'.[18]

The smaller Supreme Cinemas Ltd circuit, formed by Maurice Logan, T.J. Furey and V. ('Bertie') Walsh in 1936, began with the opening of the Picture House, Maghera-felt.[19] On 12 December that year, it opened the 1,200-seat Park Cinema, Old Park Road, Belfast. While by the mid-1940s it had acquired only one further cinema, the Sandro, in the crowded Belfast market, it had nine cinemas elsewhere in Northern Ireland. These were in Co. Antrim in Ballyclare, Ballymena (where it had two), Randalstown and Whitehead; in Co. Derry in Maghera and Magherafelt; in Co. Down in Bangor; and in Co. Tyrone in Dungannon. In September 1956, T.J. Furey opened the Supreme group's thirteenth cinema, the 1,000-seat Metro, Dundonald, near Belfast, while a few weeks later, Maurice Logan, another one of the group's three directors, opened its fourteenth cinema, the New Reo at Ballyclare, with a similar seating capacity.[20]

Given the extent of cinema building, fears were raised periodically about 'the menace of over-building', 'overseating' and 'redundancy'. When the Strand, as noted, Derry's largest cinema, was being built in 1934 by Billy James, who already owned the city's Midland Cinema, Derry's other five exhibitors recommended that the local authority not issue the new cinema with a licence on the grounds of redundancy, as, they argued, there were already sufficient cinemas for the 40,000 inhabitants.[21] The following year, the White Cinema Club, the local exhibitors' body, announced it would 'take action',[22] but there was little it could do.[23] As *Kine Weekly* commented, existing regulations made it 'impossible' for a cinema to be rejected on grounds of redundancy, though it cautioned that newcomers to the trade maybe did not realize the difficulties and problems that they would have to face.[24] Small towns which could perhaps only support one cinema, now sometimes had three, while the many new cinemas in suburban Belfast were eating into the box office revenues of city centre first-run cinemas.[25] Indeed, a newly-built provincial cinema was being sold because 'business in some of the country areas' declined in 1938.[26] According to the trade, experience had proven that only one cinema in a town of 5,000 people in Northern Ireland could just about pay.[27] By 1937, with new cinemas planned for Dundonald and Castlereagh Road, Belfast, 'all sections of the Trade' were 'agreed that for the time being at any rate the limit has already been reached.'[28] Even Northern Ireland's minister for finance, J.M. Andrews, concurred, declaring that 'the number of new kinemas appears to have reached a maximum for the present.'[29] Part of the problem from the perspective of established exhibitors, as it was analyzed in the 1940s, was that there were 'quite a number of people who have never been in the kinema business' opening halls in small places such as Fivemilestown, Co. Tyrone; Draperstown, Co. Derry; and Tobermore, also in Co. Derry.[30]

Some English magistrates, however, interpreting the Cinematograph Act 1909 as conferring onto them the devolved power from the local authorities to prohibit cinemas being built in some areas, were able to ameliorate existing exhibitors' fears of over-saturation. In the case of Darlington in 1936, where there were six cinemas within 300 yards of a proposed 2,000-seater, the new cinema was refused a licence. 'It must be assumed', Rachael Low writes, that the refusal was made on the grounds of 'protecting inferior cinemas', [31] though such resistance to new cinemas had faded away by the time of the outbreak of the Second World War, which anyway caused the suspension of cinema building altogether.

Mirroring other areas of Irish business life, there was only very limited investment between north and south film interests in the post-independence decades. The Curran circuit, for example, owned (or booked for) only one Free State cinema, Sligo's Savoy; W. O'Hanlon's circuit, based around Limavady and Dungiven, Co. Derry, had one in nearby Milford, Co. Donegal; and Dublin-based H.K. Campbell's five-cinema circuit with venues in Dundalk, Cork, and Waterford, had two cinemas in Northern Ireland, in Armagh and Portadown. Film distribution, by contrast, did not follow this pattern. It seems that distribution was organized mostly on an all-island basis, with Northern Ireland most often being dealt with either from the regional Dublin branch office, or directly from London. Consequently, British and American companies did not have branch offices in Belfast in the same numbers as they did in Dublin. General Film Distributors, owned by J. Arthur Rank by the early 1940s, had offices in both Dublin and Belfast, but in 1945 Rank's international sales arm, Eagle-Lion Distributors Ltd, transferred its Irish headquarters from Belfast to Dublin with Maurice Mitchell as manager. Like other distributors, it took offices in Abbey Street.[32] Perhaps reflecting the scale of the Irish market, 'a curiously anomalous situation' pertained whereby exhibitors were renters and *vice versa*. Belfast's Harry Wilton, who owned the Troxy, 194 Shore Road, which opened on 24 October 1936, was also Northern Ireland representative for the film production company British Lion Film Corporation,[33] while Louis Elliman of the premier film exhibition family was the company's agent in the south. While this was not uncommon in the early decades of cinema, with James T. Jameson for one occupying the dual position, by the 1930s, it was less common, with, perhaps, Walter McNally the only other person occupying the dual role of independent exhibitor and agent for a foreign distributor.

ECONOMIC NATIONALISM AND BRITISH EXHIBITION: 'ALIEN PENETRATION'
IN THE 1930S

If the opening by Associated British Pictures of the Savoy Cinema, Dublin, in November 1929 indicated a renewed interest in Irish film exhibition by British companies, its ceremonial opening by President William T. Cosgrave was a clear signal from the Irish Free State government that such an investment was welcomed. Nevertheless, the experience, for many, of being in the British-owned, if, largely Irish-built and Irish-staffed Savoy must have carried bitterly ironic resonances given that the site on which the cinema had been built had been derelict since the civil war when the hotels located there had been destroyed, and that the General Post Office, headquarters of the 1916 Rising in which many of that night's audience had fought, was only a short distance away.[34] Indeed, ABC's Savoy implicitly suggested that post-war reconstruction required the economic power of the old enemy, thus maintaining Ireland's dependency, but in another form. While this postcolonial contradiction was not so obviously felt by Cumann na nGaedheal, since its social class and institutional allegiances remained close to the British establishment, it was acutely experienced by Fianna Fáil after that party came to power in 1932.

Competing nearby cinemas, of which there were fifteen in central Dublin all of which offered a less salubrious experience than the Savoy, could hardly have welcomed the new cinema. However, the Savoy's pricing policy of 1s. to 5s., inclusive of entertainments tax – the dearest cinema seats in the city – clearly precluded the majority of regular cinemagoers in favour of a more elite prosperous audience. Nevertheless, such an audience became increasingly thin in the context of the Great Depression, which followed in the wake of the Wall Street Crash that happened exactly a month before the Savoy's opening night on 29 November 1929. Within two years Ireland was in the midst of a serious economic crisis. With Fianna Fáil's accession to power in March 1932, Irish economic policy, reflecting a more generalized international trend, embraced what during the 1920s had been a minor feature of Cumann na nGaedheal's approach to the economy – protectionism.

Despite the fact that Fianna Fáil's power base has often been understood as being largely rooted within the rural and small farmer community, the urban polices which Fianna Fáil pursued during the 1930s secured their support among the urban working classes and proved crucial to the party's success. While the most obvious and visible pro-urban policy was their urban house building programme, designed to help to eliminate slums,[35] the macro-economic policy of protectionism, and development of industry, also favoured the urban classes, given that it allowed for a shift in resources away from the countryside. Though protectionism was part of the 'economic war' (July 1932–March 1938) with Britain, which began with the Irish government's withholding from Britain the annual land annuities payments,[36] it was nonetheless ideologically and conceptually independent of the conflict between the two countries, and found articulation though the finance acts, which imposed import tariffs on foreign (mostly British) goods, and the Control of Manufacturers Acts 1932–4. Within the context of this study, the Control of Manufacturers Acts are particularly relevant as they set down the condition that at least 51 per cent of a company had to be Irish-owned in order for it to be established. It was believed that such a strategy would help develop an indigenous industrial base, and hence increase employment. That Fianna Fáil managed not only to survive but consolidate its power at a time when, as a result of the economic war with Britain, there was profound poverty, particularly among the rural and farming community, with unemployment rising from 29,000 in 1931 to 138,000 in 1935 (a 475 per cent increase),[37] was as much the result of the construction of the struggle for economic independence in ideological terms as any large scale or long term net benefits that flowed from the policy itself. In this political and economic environment the disruption caused by sound cinema could not be ignored.

Live musical accompaniment of one form or another had been a feature of cinema since its beginnings. While smaller and rural cinemas were unlikely to employ more than a single pianist on an upright piano, in the first-run and larger cinemas, small orchestras, such as the type in the Rotunda during the early 1900s, were the norm, and featured prominently in advertising. Moreover, it was the case that the musical director could be paid more than the cinema manager, while the other musicians could be paid as much as, or even more than, the chief operator, or main projectionist. Evidence from the wages' book of the Stella Cinema, Rathmines, confirms this. Of the gross wages of £53 0s. 5d. paid to the cinema's twenty staff for the week ending 4 December 1926, the highest single wage, £6 17s. 6d., was paid to the musical director, Mr Moody, while only £6 went to the manager,[38] the same figure as that paid to the cellist (Mr Schofish). With the organist (Miss Gray) and pianist (Miss O'Neill) both receiving £4 10s., and the other instrumentalists receiving £3 5s. (Mr Moody Jnr) and £1 15s. (Miss Naylor), the total amount paid to the musicians was £26 17s. 6d., or approximately half of the weekly wage bill. By contrast, the first or chief operator received only £3 14s., less than all but one of the musicians, with the second and third/trainee operators receiving £2 9s. 3d. and 11s., respectively; other staff payments were £1. 3s. (cashier Miss Brennan); £2 12s. 6d. to £2 8s.6d. (doorman P. Fitzsimons); 14s. 6d. (page); 17s. (curtain duties, paid to two employees). The Stella Cinema's gross weekly wage bill for the week ending 14 January 1928, just over a year later, shows the continuing powerful position of the musicians. From a total of £68 2s. 9d., the manager was now being paid £7, an increase of 16.5 per cent on the December 1926 figure, while the musical director was paid 45 per cent more than the manager – £10 3s. 6d. – an increase of 48 per cent on his December 1926 wage. Altogether, the musicians were being paid £38 8s. 6d. or 56 per cent of the total wage bill, an increase of 6 per cent.[39]

Notwithstanding the capital costs of installing sound equipment, we can see how attractive sound cinema must have become for many cinemas, particularly in the context of the actual film hire costs which, as is clear from the Stella's records for 1931 and 1932, was generally no more than the total wage bill, even when there were two film programmes screened. While in this period most feature films were priced at £15 to £20 per screening run per week (or less), many well known titles or ones with popular stars were as much as £30, with a small number of films even more expensive.[40] For example, Paramount Famous Lasky's *The Vagabond King* (Ludwig Berger, 1930; shown February 1931) was £75 or 40 per cent of the gross box office take; the musical revue *Paramount on Parade* (Dorothy Arzner et al, 1930; shown from 1 March 1931) cost £75 or 33.3 per cent of the gross box office take; Ernest Lubitsch's musical comedy *Monte Carlo* (1930; shown November 1931) was £60; while *City Lights*

(Charles Chaplin, 1931; shown from 3 January 1932) was £100, the most expensive title listed during 1931–2 for which records survive.[41] The other items that made up the programme, such as shorts and newsreels, cost between £1 and £9 each.[42]

Anticipating the inevitable consequences sound cinema would have on their relatively lucrative livelihood, the Belfast local musicians' union initiated a handbill campaign targeted at cinemagoers in an attempt to stop the advent of sound.[43] While the Stella employed only seven musicians, in Belfast the prestigious Belfast Picture House, Royal Avenue, under musical director J. Gold, employed forty musicians; the Classic, Castle Lane, had a thirty-person orchestra under conductor T.S. Clark-Brown; and the imposing suburban cinema the Clonard, Falls Road, had twelve musicians in its silent cinema heyday, though this was later reduced to just one pianist, who became redundant in 1931 with the introduction of sound.[44] In those rare instances when a Wurlitzer organ had been installed for interval music, such as at the Classic in 1927, or a Compton at the Ritz in 1936, a single organist sufficed.[45] While the change to sound may not have been as rapid in Ireland as it had been in other countries with *Bioscope* stating in May 1931 that Northern Ireland was 'very slow' to fully convert to sound cinema,[46] nevertheless, by May 1932, following the conversion of Belfast's Kelvin Cinema, all Belfast cinemas had installed sound.[47]

While the redundant Belfast musicians initiated orchestral concerts,[48] and later, in 1934, more formally, co-operative Sunday evening concerts were arranged, with proceeds (after expenses) shared,[49] these could not offer either the money or the security provided by a cinema position. Unsurprisingly then, sound cinema with its 'canned music' was described at the 1934 annual dinner of the Society of Professional Musicians in Ulster as 'a menace of the music teacher and the music maker'.[50] Following the introduction of sound, approximately 500 musicians were displaced in Ireland, north and south of the border (compared to 12,000 in England). What once had been the stronghold of the professional musician now gave employment to only a handful of musicians, one of whom was Philip Dore, a Cambridge MA graduate with diplomas in music who had been appointed at the Savoy, Dublin, as soloist to play the Compton organ from 1 January 1932.[51] Indeed, novelist May Nevin in *Over the hills*, published in 1935, has one of her characters, violinist Betty, the 'Irish Cinderella', note that 'the advent of the "talkies" had left many musicians on the list of the unemployed, in spite of the many dance bands needed'.[52]

Both the Cumann na nGaedheal and Fianna Fáil governments in the south took action to alleviate the plight of the musicians. In an attempt to aid their re-employment, the 1931 Finance Act abolished entertainments tax where personal performances, or variety, consisted of more than 50 per cent of the show. It was not until 1 July 1936 that the cine-variety concession, which had resulted in 'an exceptionally severe type of competition' for the regular Dublin cinemas in particular,[53] was modified upwards to 75 per cent, while those shows with personal performances of between 50 and 75 per cent could claim a tax rebate of 50 per cent.

To help restore the consequential loss of exchequer revenue caused by sound cinema, and perhaps in part to slow down the introduction of sound, the 1931 Finance

Act trebled the excise duty on imported sound films from 1*d*. to 3*d*. per foot. Though this had been designed to penalize the predominantly foreign film renters and film producers in order 'to compensate for the dislocation in the economic life of the State which the introduction of the [sound] films has produced',[54] the tax was later passed on as a special surcharge to the exhibitors, who from the outset resented this, at times, crippling charge, not least as it was greater than the import duty demanded by the government.[55] In turn, some of the exhibitors, enabled by an amendment to the act,[56] passed it on to cinemagoers. Thus, as predicated by opposition spokesman on finance, Fianna Fáil's Seán MacEntee, during the Dáil debate on the act, it ultimately served as another tax on cinema admissions.[57]

According to *Kine Weekly* in 1932 there was already a 'crisis' in Free State exhibition due to the heavy film duty, with rumours of cinemas closing down and 'bad business' in the suburbs and country districts. A delegation from the Irish Theatre and Cinema Association went to London seeking to renegotiate rental terms with the Kinematograph Renters Society, but, despite their explaining the current circumstances, which, if left unchecked, would lead to staff reductions and/or cinema closures, the KRS remained unmoved. Another delegation, consisting of Maurice Elliman, D. O'Brien, Nathan Karmel, George Nesbitt, George O'Connor, P.J. Munden, P.J. O'Toole and John J. Farrell, met the minister for finance, Seán MacEntee, in advance of the 1932 budget. Although they pointed to the irony whereby variety houses, which 'largely employed foreign artists',[58] benefited from the new entertainments tax, while native Irish exhibitors (and cinema patrons) suffered, no substantial change in import duty or entertainments tax rates was affected. While, following the meeting, the lowest priced seats saw a marginal decrease in entertainment duty, having already been reduced slightly in 1931, the tax on the higher priced tickets was increased by about 50 per cent from 1 October 1932. Thus, a ticket costing more than 1*s*. 8*d*. carried an additional tax penalty of 6*d*., while those exceeding 2*s*. had a tax of 9*d*. added to the price of the ticket. Furthermore, and despite the pleas of the industry, three years later, in 1935, all but the lowest priced tickets were increased. While entertainment duty amounted to approximately 20 per cent of gross box office receipts before the increase, the 1935 changes raised this to nearly 30 per cent of gross receipts. On this occasion renters and exhibitors combined to press MacEntee for some relief as they feared 'a heavy fall in box office returns'.[59] They were right to be fearful as during the first two months of the new rates being in operation, there was, even according to MacEntee, 'a very considerable falling off' in cinema attendances,[60] while a cinema in Bagnalstown, Co. Carlow, suffered a boycott by locals when its prices increased from 3*d*. to 7*d*. (not all of which was due to the tax).[61] Notwithstanding the partial recovery later in the year, the minister acknowledged that 'the adverse effect was much greater in the case of working-class Cinemas, where the top inclusive price [was] 1*s*. or less.'[62]

That the entertainments tax was more about maximizing state revenue than supporting live (musical) performances can by seen in relation to the total income accruing from the entertainments tax which mostly came from cinemas. In 1935–36 entertainments tax amounted to £255,291, an increase of nearly £89,882, or 54.3 per cent, on the 1931–32 figure.[63] By 1936, however, MacEntee had accepted that 'a 3.5*d*. tax in respect of an inclusive price of 1*s*. [was] excessive' and reduced both this tax rate and the lower one of 1.5*d*. pertaining to 6*d*.–8*d*. tickets, by 0.5*d*. While tickets costing less than 6*d*. were exempt from tax, there were no reductions on seats priced above 1*s*. inclusive of tax.

It is also clear that during this period, marked as it was by the legacy of the global economic depression and the continuing economic war with Britain – what MacEntee described as 'the existing peculiar circumstances'[64] – even marginal changes of as little as 0.5*d*. on cinema admission prices could adversely impact on attendances in working-class areas. Indeed, such must also have been the case for ostensibly more prosperous cinemas given that the organized section of the trade called on the minister to make the installation of automatic ticket machines in every cinema compulsory. In a unique acknowledgement of tax evasion within the sector, they argued that such a move would force 'all exhibitors [to] pay their rightful share' and result in additional state revenue of £50,000.[65] Of course, those distributors being paid by exhibitors on a percentage basis rather than a flat film rental hire charge would also benefit from such a system.

Thekla Beere's profile of Irish exhibition for 1934–5 starkly outlined the problems being experienced by small Irish film exhibitors, the vast majority of the country's cinema-owners. While the introduction of sound which 'required considerable capital expenditure' on equipment, 'told heavily on the small Cinema', additional pressure came from 'the keen competition of the new houses, both as regards variety of programme and the provision of more comfortable surroundings, together with the increased burden of Entertainments Tax.' Consequently, 'signs of prosperity [were] noticeably lacking' in such venues.[66] Similarly lacking, though in the sector more generally, were 'signs of co-operation':

> the interests of the large and small houses are often dissimilar if not actually conflicting, while between houses of a like size and situation there appears to exist an almost aggressive competitiveness.[67]

Such aggressiveness subsequently manifested itself in a cinema admissions' price war in 1936, during which even first-run Dublin cinemas, including the Metropole, felt obliged to cut prices.[68] Nevertheless, while intense competition for audiences remained a feature of Irish exhibition, later in the 1930s, the interests of both large and small Irish exhibitors did co-join, at least for a time, against the threat posed by 'alien penetration' of the industry.

Disproving 'the oft-repeated assertion that the Irish, especially in Dublin, are the greatest Cinema-going public in the world',[69] Beere revealed that while Great Britain had twenty-two cinema admissions per head of population per annum, the Free State, which had few significant large urban centres beyond its capital city Dublin, had only six. Dublin, based on the calculation that it had 11 million cinema admissions annually, rather than the 'commonly quoted estimate' of 300,000 per week, or 15.5 million

annually, which Beere deemed 'a gross exaggeration',[70] had twenty-three admissions
per person per annum. This was considerably smaller than many non-capital cities such
as Liverpool and Vancouver which registered thirty-five and thirty-one admissions per
head, respectively.[71] In commenting on the famous Dublin queue, Beere explained that

> there may often be a queue outside and many empty seats inside. It is proba-
> ble, indeed, that the increased admission prices tended to lengthen the Cinema
> queues, as many people were obliged to seek a less favourable part of the house
> than that which they had previously been accustomed to patronise. Further, it
> must be remembered that while there are queues waiting at the two or three
> houses showing the most popular films of the week, other houses with less
> attractive programmes may be left with many vacant seats.[72]

A more complete understanding of Beere's findings is facilitated by reference to
Simon Rowson's contemporaneous authoritative statistical survey of British distribution and exhibition, which, similar to Beere's, was that country's first national analysis of the sector.[73] Most starkly, such a comparison establishes the Irish market (in numbers at least) as being about 1.9 per cent of the British market. While in 1934, Britain
registered 963 million cinema admissions to its 4,305 cinemas with 3,872,000 seats,
in the Free State, which had 190 cinemas with 111,438 seats[74] (or one cinema per
16,000 persons compared to the USA's one per 5,500),[75] the 1934–5 annual cinema
admission figure was 18.25 million, or *less than* the *weekly* British total of 18.5 million. Furthermore, seat occupancy in the Free State was somewhat less than in Britain.
Whereas Britain had 247 admissions per cinema seat per year, the Free State had only
167 admissions per cinema seat per year, or just over two-thirds the British rate. Despite
the low national average for seat occupancy, Dublin, with 361 admissions per cinema
seat in 1934, was, with the exception of Liverpool with 416 admissions per seat, ahead
of such cities as Vancouver, Toronto, Munich, Prague and Warsaw.[76]

A further comparison can be made in relation to admission charges for 1934. While
nearly 80 per cent of British cinema patrons paid 1s. or less, with 43 per cent paying
6d. or under, in the Free State where the average admission price (inclusive of entertainment tax of 2.3d.) was 11.76d., only 47 per cent paid 1s. or less, of whom only 19
per cent paid less than 6d.[77] Not only were Irish people going less frequently to the
cinema than their British counterparts, but they were paying on average more, though
the imbalance created by the dominance of Dublin in the figures belies the low admission prices in provincial and second-run urban cinemas.

Although the Irish gross box office for 1934–5 calculated at £895,000 and of which
£550,000, or 61 per cent, emphasizing the national imbalance, was estimated to have
been taken in Dublin cinemas (including those of Dún Laoghaire), represented 2.17
per cent of Britain's 1934 gross box office take of £41,120,000; a more disturbing contrast is seen in relation to the respective entertainment duties payable out of the gross
figure. While in Britain this amounted to £6,800,000 or 16.5 per cent of the total, in
Ireland, the figure averaged £200,886, or 22.4 per cent of gross box office, which rose

in 1936 to £255,291, or about 28.5 per cent.[78] Nationally, the net amount in the Free State after distributors' percentage (approximately 30 per cent of gross box office), and entertainments' tax (approximately 20 per cent of gross box office before increases in the tax to about 30 per cent in 1935) was perhaps less than £500,000 out of which wages and overheads had to be paid.

Consequently, film exhibition in the Free State, despite having had investments of, perhaps, as much as three million pounds, was not a particularly lucrative business.[79] Evidence suggests that the small exhibitor's turnover was similar to that generated by a pub or grocery store, or at best a small provincial hotel. Indeed, a TD told the Dáil in 1931 that even though cinema was 'the only [commercial] entertainment' available to many people, particularly in non-urban areas, a full house in a country cinema could only take £5 or £6.[80] The records of Horgan's Picture Theatre, Youghal, Co. Cork, later in the decade suggests that a small town cinema show could take anything from £3 to £21 gross, depending on the popularity of the film and the day on which it was shown.

As recorded in the previous chapter, the only cinema for which box office data is available in the 1910s is Horgan's Picture Theatre. The same is true for the 1930s after the cinema had been restored following a fire in August 1935 that destroyed the adjoining Hurst Picture Palace and 'considerably damaged' the Horgan cinema.[81] Between 2 January 1936 and 8 October 1936, a total of forty weeks, the cinema took a total of £1,450 8s. 10d. at the box office. While the average weekly gross box office income was approximately £36 5s., this varied from a low of £20 12s. in the first week of October to a high of £51 16s. 3d. in the week immediately after Easter, following the cinema being closed for a number of days due to religious observance, and the return of those patrons who had absented themselves from the cinema during Lent. Though the second-highest week with £51 14s. 7d. was during Lent, it was specifically the week to 19 March and as such included St Patrick's Day, traditionally regarded as a day when Lenten abstinences could be suspended. In fact these two weeks were the only ones (of the forty for which data is available) where the gross weekly takings exceeded £50, though importantly, the lucrative Christmas period is not included. The slackest period was the summer. Thus, the first four months of 1936 (seventeen weeks) accounted for £689 10s. 1d. or an average of £171 2s. 6d. per month, while the May to August 1936 period (also seventeen weeks) totalled £577 11s. 6d., or an average of £144 2s. 10.5d. per month, which was about 16 per cent less than the first four months of the year. Apart from the good weather and bright evenings, which may have served as a disincentive to cinema-going, it should be noted that August saw the opening of Hurst's new cinema, located on the same street as Horgan's.

Data from June to August 1937 gives a profile of the running costs of the Horgan cinema, with the breakdown in the seven categories of expenditure as follows: film hire, by far the biggest cost for the cinema, being £169 8s. 3d. for the three-month period; entertainments tax, £76 11s. 6.5d.; wages, £63 9s. 5d.; carriage for films, £27 4s. 1d.; sundries (such as projector lamps, maintenance), £23 11s. 3d.; printing, £2 19s. 6d.; and postage, 18s. 2d. The account books also offer an insight into the distribution of box office income of individual titles between the exhibitor and distributor. In the case of the successful Irish War of Independence drama, *The Dawn* (released in May 1936), it was screened in the cinema in early December 1936 for a five-day run (Wednesday to Sunday). Given that the cinema usually ran programmes for two or three days, this was an unusually long period. Box office receipts from the film's six showings were £74 1s. 3d., with £34 18s. 5d., or 47 per cent, of the total taken on Sunday, split between the matinee (£13 11s. 3d.) and night (£21 7s. 2d.) presentations, when 799 of the 1,666 patrons who saw the film attended. Such figures confirm the long-held view by exhibitors of the importance of Sunday box office income to the viability of a cinema. Of the £74 1s. 3d. taken at the box office, it seems as if £38 1s. 0.5d., or 51 per cent, went to the film's distributor, exhibitor Tom Cooper, who was also the film's director. Notwithstanding that December was a good month for entertainments, the exceptional nature of the film should be emphasized. *The Dawn* proved to be extraordinarily popular in Ireland, and, as was the case sixty years later when another Irish War of Independence drama was released – Neil Jordan's *Michael Collins* – it succeeded in bringing people who were not regular or even occasional cinemagoers to the cinema. Therefore, a more typical film might be one such as *Song of Freedom* (J. Elder Wills, 1936, GB) with African-American singer Paul Robeson, which was shown at the cinema from 19 June to 21 June 1937. For this film, over its three screenings (complemented by shorts) only 380 tickets were sold (with an additional fourteen tickets given as comps, no doubt to shop and pub owners and others for putting the cinema's programme on display in the windows of their premises). While the gross income was £14 4s. 11d., the exhibitor's net, after entertainment tax of £3 5s. 10d., was only £10 19s. 1d., out which would have come the distributor's flat rate rental charge (possibly 35 per cent, rather than the *Dawn*'s 51 per cent), thus reducing the cinema owner's net before paying wages and other expenses to just over £7 for three days of screenings.[82]

It seems, therefore, that any significant profits were taken by a select number of Dublin exhibitors, not least the Elliman and Farrell families and the British ABC chain. Notwithstanding that Dublin had only 15 per cent of the population, through its thirty-six cinemas incorporating 30 per cent of the country's cinema seats and representing 20 per cent of the country's cinemas, it registered almost four times the national average of cinema admissions, while its exhibitors took more than 60 per cent of the gross box office income. Together with the three next major urban centres – Cork, Limerick and Waterford – these four cities accounted for no less than fifty-five cinemas or just over a quarter of the country's cinemas; more tellingly, with a combined total of 48,045 seats, the four centres had 43 per cent of the national total of cinema seats. Despite the regional imbalances, cinema, nevertheless, consumed a significant share of national expenditure, perhaps as much as 4 per cent.[83]

Given that T.J. Beere's statistical analysis was published at a time when there was heightened activity in the Catholic-nationalist campaign against the cinema and more generally an increased cultural awareness of and focus on the effects of cinema, unsurprisingly, various interested parties sought to use her findings to support their particular agendas. What the report highlighted for a great many commentators, ranging from Liam O'Leary of the Irish Film Society, on the left, who was seeking the development of an indigenous Irish-produced cinema (see chapter 6), to Fr Richard Devane, on the right, who was crusading for an Irish (Catholic) Film Institute (see chapter 7), was Ireland's dependency on foreign cinema and consequent economic and cultural vulnerability. However, two months prior to Beere's review being published in May 1936, Joseph A. Power in his 'Stage and Screen' column in *The Standard* had already revealed how beholden Irish exhibitors were to foreigners when he reported the 'black listing' by the major British-based organization representing the interests of foreign distributors in Ireland, the Kinematograph Renters' Society, of a number of exhibitors active in Cork, Kerry and Tipperary. Having 'revolted against the dictation' of (foreign) renters' groups, these Munster exhibitors formed the Kinematograph Exhibitors' Society with the 'principle objective' of securing 'the booking of films at a fixed price instead of a sharing [that is, a percentage] basis.'[84] Complaining about the lack of support the new body was receiving from other exhibitors, Power concluded that the only hope for the exhibitors' society could come from the very few independent renters, but these did not control high earning first-run product. A week later, Power reported that 'a big English combine' was coming to Ireland to build new cinemas and to acquire sites for other ones.[85]

Such 'scare' stories resurfaced with regularity throughout the year, and, playing as they did on the grim reality of the economic insecurity within the sector, were regarded as sufficiently authoritative that the main Irish exhibitors' organization, the Irish Theatre and Cinema Association,[86] set about the defensive action of building an alliance with the National Agricultural and Industrial Development Association (NAIDA). Closely aligned with Fianna Fáil and exerting particular influence on that party's economic policy, the NAIDA was the main propagandist body for economic protectionism and self-sufficiency. Nevertheless, the irony of reserving for Irish people the privilege of promoting *foreign* made cinema in Ireland seems to have been missed by all, which is particularly surprising given that the membership of NAIDA included many economic and cultural nationalists. Indeed, at an annual event NAIDA secretary Erskine Childers,[87] when introducing Padraig O'Keefe, secretary of the Gaelic Athletic Association, to the organization,[88] declared that 'in proceeding towards national reconstruction ... we must also beware of influences which would go far to nullify them – demoralising and unsettling exhibitions on stage and screen.'[89] In any case, given that Irish exhibitors, unlike farmers or industrial manufacturers, had no control over either the production or distribution of the product they were retailing, no matter what action they took against distributors, they ultimately had to accept the limited power available to them within the sector.

Following an approach to NAIDA by the Irish Theatre and Cinema Association, a special NAIDA/ITCA committee was established in late 1936 'to discuss the various attempts by foreign chain-cinema organisations to obtain a hold in the Irish Free State', where such investment was estimated at three million pounds.[90] Subsequently, a NAIDA/ITCA delegation (whose members included NAIDA president, J.J. Holloway; Mr F.M. Summerfield; Padraig O'Keefe; NAIDA council members, N.J. Ffrench and George J. Nesbitt, also a director of the Elliman-owned Metropole cinema group; Mr

H. Margey of Irish Cinemas Ltd; and Tommy Gogan of the Pavilion Cinema, Dún Laoghaire) met the minister for industry and commerce, Seán Lemass, on 18 December to discuss the 'alien penetration' of Irish exhibition by foreigners. As a means of stopping 'British combines' from getting 'a foothold in the country' they proposed that a system of state-controlled cinema licences and film bookings be established.[91]

Recommending the licensing of all cinemas in the Free State, the NAIDA/ITCA committee decreed that cinemas under construction and those for which plans had been submitted should not be granted a licence unless the capital involved was, or would be, 'entirely Irish' and its operation would be by Irish nationals. A further condition was also proposed to ensure that unfair advantage in booking films was not accorded to some cinemas because of connections a cinema might have with foreign distributors. Finally, it was suggested that a licence could be revoked if a cinema was leased to a foreign exhibitor. While Lemass agreed to consider their suggestions,[92] the exhibitors' campaign was fortified further when, at a meeting of the joint committee on 13 January 1937, Childers reported that NAIDA's council was prepared to give the exhibitors all the assistance they might require.[93]

Agitating both the ITCA and NAIDA at this time was the development plan by a consortium to build a cinema on the Plaza building site at Middle Abbey Street, just off O'Connell Street, Dublin, which prior to a fire two years earlier in 1935 had housed the offices of the highly successful Irish Hospitals' Sweepstakes' organization.[94] It was not the cinema itself that was problematic, but the fact that the consortium's directors included Associated British Cinemas' John Maxwell.[95] The other directors were William H. Freeman,[96] a member of one of the important sweepstakes' families;[97] and William M. Middleton, of Adelphi Ltd. Since building Dublin's Savoy Cinema and disposing of it five years later, Maxwell had greatly expanded his holding company, Associated British Pictures Corporation, such that by 1937, through its integrated corporate structure of production and distribution companies, together with its network of 450 cinemas,[98] it had attained dominance within British film. (J. Arthur Rank's growing film interests only later superseded ABC.) Given that the Control of Manufacturers' Act was, as acknowledged by ITCA, 'useless in itself' in controlling such developments as the one proposed for the Plaza site,[99] ITCA was fearful that a foreign exhibitor/distributor, even with a 10 per cent holding in a cinema, could exclusively channel its own product into its Irish operation, thereby not allowing other Irish exhibitors the possibility of bidding for certain films. Unfortunately, from ITCA's perspective, their concern was later justified.

As the new cinema neared completion, 'strong rumours' surfaced that local exhibitors would 'stage another big anti-combine drive' to pressure the minister for industry and commerce to introduce regulations on foreign ownership of cinemas,[1] but the government did not act. In January 1939, the 2,325-seat Adelphi, described by one report as 'an Irish concern' but 'London-controlled and with English Nationals [presumably of ABC] holding a large block of shares',[2] opened on the Sweepstakes/Plaza site.[3] Unchecked by the introduction of any new legislation on foreign involvement within Irish film, an indication that cinema was too important a source of government revenue to be tampered with, something made explicit by the department of finance when Fr Richard Devane proposed that Irish film be encouraged and protected by a quota system,[4] ABC made further investments in Ireland. In 1948, it built the 1,601-seat Adelphi, 40–2 Upper George's Street, Dún Laoghaire, while in 1959 it took over the independently owned first-run Carlton, O'Connell Street. In all of these cinemas, it screened films from particular distribution groups, a pattern no different to other native and foreign exhibitors.

At the height of the campaign against British exhibition 'combines' in late 1936 and early 1937 the British film trade newspaper *To-day's Cinema* displayed perhaps the most astute understanding of the concerns of Irish exhibitors, while also pointing up the Irish Free State's financial interest in the sector,

> The cinema business in the Irish Free State if it ever had been was no longer a gold mine. It was already intensely competitive and offered a very modest return on capital invested chiefly owing to the heavy taxation it had to bear.

Additionally, it noted that, according to the NAIDA/ITCA committee, in comparison with Britain, Irish cinemas were not understaffed and Irish cinema wages were 50 to 100 per cent higher than in English cinemas, though no figures were offered for comparison.[5]

In February 1937 the NAIDA council agreed that since sixty of the seventy members of ITCA were Irish nationals, they were eligible for election to NAIDA. Among these were the chair of ITCA, Patrick Farrell, son of John J., and whose family exhibition interests extended by the early 1940s to nine cinemas, including one of Dublin's five 'supers', the Capitol;[6] and Maurice Elliman who in 1944 was described by *Kine Weekly*[7] as the 'Grand Mogul' of Irish exhibition, controlling as he did, directly, or indirectly through directorships, a total of twelve cinemas, seven of which were in Dublin.[8] Notwithstanding the relatively small number of Dublin first-run exhibitors, the Farrells and Ellimans were unrivalled within the Irish context where the majority of exhibitors, most especially those outside of the major urban centres, operated as part-time cinema owners often coupling their exhibition interests with other business or retailing activities such as pubs, grocery shops, hotels, newspaper publishers, printers, shoe manufacturers, or were politicians, schoolteachers or clerics.[9] Consequently, the economic gulf between these small, often part-time exhibitors, on the one hand, and the Ellimans, Farrells and other Dublin quality exhibitors, on the other, must have been remarkably acute within the ranks of the all-embracing Irish Theatre and Cinema Association. It is hardly surprising, therefore, that a new organization, the Association of Provincial Exhibitors (APE), was formed to represent the small and independent cinemas outside Dublin.

Following a meeting of 'a large number' of cinema owners in Dublin in March 1939, at which APE was established, a delegation was appointed to meet the government committee charged with investigating all aspects of film in Ireland (discussed below). The delegation members were Revd J. O'Doherty CC, Balbriggan, perhaps a member of the Town Hall cinema committee formed in 1934;[10] J.M. Stanley, whose company, Boyne Cinemas Ltd, owned, then or later, Dundalk's Oriel Cinema, Drogheda's Boyne Cinema, Co. Cavan's St Michael's Cinema in Cootehill, and Cavan's Town Hall Cinema; P. Delahunty of New Cinema, Thurles, and the Rock Cinema, Cashel, Co. Tipperary; C. Dann, Longford; Chris Sylvester, a pioneer exhibitor with cinemas in Navan and Armagh; J.G. Murphy, Abbey Cinema, Drogheda; T. Doyle, Astor Cinema, Enniscorthy, Co. Wexford; W.J. Barry, secretary of the Temperance Hall, Roscrea; and P.J. Mulligan, Ballina.[11] Though an eclectic mix complete with a Catholic cleric and a temperance campaigner, it, nonetheless, represented the typical small provincial cinema circuit. However, unlike ICTA, which represented large Irish exhibitors, APE (itself an unfortunate acronym) confused its defence of local small business interests with the anti-cinema moral campaigning of the churches. Whatever moral strictures were affecting southern exhibition through the strict policies of the official film censor, cinemas in the south, unlike in Northern Ireland, at least did not have to contend with some of the divisive issues manifest in Northern Ireland.

NORTHERN IRELAND'S EXHIBITION WARS IN THE 1930S AND 1940S

(a) Siting of cinemas
Described on his death as 'the father' of Northern Ireland's film industry,[12] Will White's importance within the sector owed less to his 'extremely attractive and very large' Duncairn Picture Theatre, Belfast, which, boasting an 'exceptional quality' and 'originality of … design',[13] incorporated retail outlets on its ground floor and a tea lounge on its upper floor from where it was possible to view the cinema screen, than to his establishing the White Cinema Club in the early 1920s. Envisaged as a trade association to promote the interests of Northern Ireland-based exhibitors, by 1935, it had seventy-seven members, including more or less all of the province's exhibitors.[14] One of the first major activities of the benevolent, campaigning body was a one-day, high profile visit to Dublin in June 1925 to meet with Free State colleagues. A year after the civil war had ended, the event, which included most of the prominent exhibitors, north and south, represented largely by Belfast and Dublin, seems to have reinvigorated a bond between the two jurisdictions. While not seeking to deny the border (in political terms), the two groups deemed their business to be sufficiently transnational (and their product not at all Irish-originating) so as to enable them transcend ideological differences.[15] During the following decades a regular traffic of communication and personnel was maintained between Belfast and Dublin.

While the White Cinema Club expended considerable energy, as did their southern counterparts, in raising money for its industry benevolent fund,[16] including initiating in Belfast in 1929 an annual ball that became one of the city's leading social events,[17] in order to protect and enhance the economic and political power of exhibitors, it also engaged in other less culturally benign activities. In the interwar period, for example, it (unsuccessfully) attempted to have entertainments' tax reduced.[18] More explicitly political was its attempt to influence local councils by having its (exhibitor) members elected. In one instance in 1933 when councillor George Gray JP was refused his party's nomination for re-election, the White Cinema Club put him on their ticket and he was returned unopposed. Other exhibitors put forward by the club, and similarly elected unopposed, included councillor Jimmy Boyle (Arcadian Cinema, Belfast), and councillor T.R. Dunseith (Picture House, Portrush).[19] The most important such exhibitor-politician, however, was Sir Crawford McCullagh, an MP and DL. A director from its opening in 1923 of Belfast's prestigious Classic Cinema, he was elected mayor of Belfast in 1927. Surpassing Dublin's contemporaneously famous cinema-associated lord mayor, the independent Alfie Byrne, McCullagh was re-elected for the thirteenth time in 1940, his tenth successive year in office.[20] It seems that, reflecting his political astuteness, he remained somewhat aloof from the often vitriolic battles in Belfast during the 1930s regarding cinema and censorship.[21] Despite the push by anti-cinema campaigners, particularly Protestant church groups, to have the more stringent film censorship policies of the Irish Free State adopted in Northern Ireland, with some activists even citing local cinemas to the police when they showed a film banned in the south,[22] there was no influential political support for doing so. Indeed, the minister of home affairs, Dawson Bates, told one such lobbying delegation, the Belfast film committee of churches, that he would need convincing on the matter of altering the certification system made by the British Board of Film Censors.[23] While lobbying persisted, no change was made to the existing system. Consequently, as in all other UK regions, Northern Ireland was bound by the 1909 Cinematograph Act, which in the case of the influential Belfast corporation was administered by its police committee, a body somewhat akin to Dublin corporation's public health committee, which became redundant with regard to policing content following the introduction of the 1923 Censorship of Films Act. A product of Irish independence, the 1923 act established national censorship and removed the power of local authorities in the twenty-six counties to censor films. Northern Ireland exhibitors, though, had two other areas of related concern with which to contend: the siting of cinemas and Sunday opening.

Given that church opposition to building new cinemas in Belfast appeared to be, according to *Kine Weekly*'s opening comment on a siting of cinemas controversy, which was to last six months, 'more effective than any trade arguments concerning redundancy'[24] and the oversupply of cinemas, exhibitors became suspicious that challenges on the basis of a proposed cinema's proximity to a church was the thin end of the wedge through which to contain and suppress cinema, and, as such, part of the anti-cinema campaign. Following objection by would-be neighbouring Presbyterian churches, Belfast corporation's improvement committee refused planning applications for cinemas by Messrs Winters and Crawford at Ulsterville Avenue and by James Gaston at Lisburn Road. However, as one of the committee members pointed out, church opposition did not always hold sway, as plans for five other cinemas, also close to churches, were approved. These included a city centre super cinema opposite Church House, headquarters of the Presbyterian church in Ireland.[25] It seems, therefore, that the strength of local opposition varied depending on the particular church involved and the proposed location. Furthermore, while the improvement committee took an increasingly strict approach, the full corporation, which had to approve the committee's decisions, was somewhat more tolerant. Thus, two months later, the corporation accepted the plans for Gaston's Majestic Cinema, Lisburn Road.[26]

The following September, the corporation's improvement committee once again rejected plans for a proposed cinema because of its nearness to a church, 'a precedent', *Kine Weekly* warned, that would 'be challenged by the Northern Ireland trade'. In this case, the developers of the proposed Shankill Road cinema, Irish Theatres Ltd, and the objectors, the Shankill Baptist Tabernacle, Shankill Road, presented their arguments to the full corporation before the body voted on the subcommittee's judgment. While Irish Theatres' general manager Ferris Pounds, its chairman J.Y. Moore, and Murray Bass focused on practical issues pertaining to the cinema, including the fact that the cinema would be fully soundproofed and that the £15,000 spent on the building 'would give a large amount of much needed employment in the city', Pastor Ravey, representing the Baptists, made a generalized attack on cinema. Similar to other church contributions in the south of Ireland,[27] he declared that cinema

> excited the imaginations, aroused the passions and appealed to the lowest and basest in men. It was not seemly that people passing to church should be called upon to see such things, which were opposed to all that was highest, noblest and best in life. ... In the name of God, in the name of religious liberty, and in the name of the city, ... confirm the decision of the Improvement Committee and ... settle once and for all the policy that no picture house could be erected next door to any church in the city.

Reflecting the anti-cinema bias of the corporation, often divided along majority unionist and minority nationalist lines, it voted twenty-six to thirteen to confirm the improvement committee's negative decision.[28] As *Kine Weekly* so aptly put it two weeks later, this move initiated a 'new phase of church war' whereby a 'concerted policy of opposition' to the building of new cinemas was adopted by the (Protestant) churches with the nearest church to a proposed cinema charged with the lodging of an objection. The first test of the new regime was when the corporation's improvement committee approved plans by D.D. Young of Belfast's Lyric Cinema for a cinema on Cregagh Road. The local Methodist church objected on the grounds that the venue would interfere with the work of the church, but they were in the somewhat dubious position of screening films on Friday and Saturday in their own city centre Grosvenor Hall in competition with regular cinemas and at lower prices. Perhaps as a result, the improvement committee rejected their application, but, as likely, the corporation might have come to realize that they had no legal authority to refuse a cinema on such grounds, since to do so would make its members potentially liable to compensation claims from disgruntled exhibitors.[29]

The debate quickly shifted to the legal terrain, and within a week of the Cregagh Road decision, it was being confidently reported that Belfast corporation 'had no alternative but to pass plans conforming to regulations.' Consequently, Irish Theatres Ltd sought a reversal of the Shankill Road/Tennent Street decision. Following the corporation's solicitor's advice that if referred 'to the King's Bench Division, the Corporation would not win the action, and would be compelled to pass the plans', the improvement committee decided that it would move a resolution at its next meeting rescinding the corporation's and committee's ban on the proposed cinema and pass the plans. At the same meeting the committee also approved plans for new cinemas on the Albert Bridge Road, and at the corner of Oldpark Road and Torrens Avenue, which was opposite a Moravian church and beside a site proposed for a new church.[30]

While church groups began to consider parliamentary action and the possibility of promoting a private member's bill stipulating the number and the permissible location of cinemas, a potentially more effective legal instrument, the Town Planning Act 1931, was already a statute. At its next meeting, the improvement committee voted, after an intense and heated debate, by a majority of two to amend the regulations governing the 1931 act and prevent the erection of a cinema within 100 yards (300ft) of any church. As a result, the Oldpark Road/Torrens Avenue cinema was approved, but the Shankill Road one was rejected.[31] Following further representations from the Oldpark Ratepayers' Association and local churches, who wanted the distance increased to 200 yards (600ft), the full council voted by twenty-two to eleven to set the distance at 120 yards (360ft),[32] a sufficient distance to ensure that the Oldpark Road cinema could not be built.[33] Perhaps, unsurprisingly, the cinema's promoters, Shankill Stadium Co., appealed the decision and in April 1936, the minister of home affairs, Dawson Bates, gave a definitive ruling on the issue stating that to refuse a cinema based on its close proximity to a place of worship was *ultra vires* (that is, beyond any council's legal power or authority under the act). Hence, the banning resolution was withdrawn without a dissenting vote,[34] while a censure motion was defeated by twenty-two votes to four.[35] Although the possibility of placing restrictions on the siting of a cinema had ended, exhibitors faced an even bigger struggle against anti-cinema campaigners in the battle over Sunday opening.

(b) Sunday opening

Though calls for Sunday closure of cinemas, often decrying cinema's 'demoralizing' and 'baneful influence',[36] were made periodically in the Irish Free State, with action occasionally being taken by local authorities to restrict or ban Sunday opening,[37] generally, annual cinema licences stipulated closure only during evening devotions, usually from 6.30p.m. to 8.30p.m., thus allowing most southern cinemas to operate a two-show policy on Sundays. Apart from the issue of Sunday prohibitions, which for the most part began to fall away in the mid-1940s, there were four days in the south on which cinemas were forbidden to open: Christmas Day and the three consecutive days prior to Easter Sunday (Holy Thursday, Good Friday and Saturday). Strangely, perhaps, when we consider the nature of the debate on Sunday opening, cinemas in Northern Ireland, including within the intensely Sabbatarian Belfast corporation area, were allowed to open on Christmas Day and, at the 'discretion' of the exhibitor, on Good Friday. Some, treating the day as a public holiday, opened earlier than usual, while others, closing for up to three days preceding it, remained shut.[38]

Until 1931, some licensing authorities in England did not object to Sunday opening, usually, but not always, on the grounds that all or part of the profit was donated to charity, but in 1931 this practice was challenged in the courts. Consequently, Sunday opening became temporarily regularized through the Sunday Performance (Temporary Regulations) Act 1931, which stated that where, within one year before the passing of the act, a cinema had opened on Sundays for film screenings, the local authorities could allow these activities to continue. In 1932, this was replaced with the Sunday Entertainment Act, which, excluding Northern Ireland and Scotland, gave local authorities in England and Wales the right to permit Sunday cinema opening, though it stopped short of granting exhibitors an automatic right to such permission.[39] During the rest of the 1930s and 1940s, a series of battles, often backed by local referenda, gradually eroded the opposition to Sunday cinema opening in England and Wales, such that half of the 300-plus places where Sunday opening had been established prior to 1930, had been secured in 1946.[40]

The question of Sunday opening in Northern Ireland, as *Bioscope* commented in 1929, 'is a peculiar one. In some parts it is permitted, but in others the very mention of an application is sufficient to cause a riot.' Surprisingly, it reported that 'on the whole exhibitors are against Sunday opening.'[41] In certain districts, Sunday opening had been allowed to develop during the 1920s without any controversy, but by the 1930s, perhaps coinciding with a greater assertion of Protestant/unionist majoritarian political culture, determined attempts were made to row back on such policies. In 1931, for example, two cinemas in Armagh that opened on Sundays led to a protest from the Orange Order, while the Loyalty League wrote to the Northern Ireland prime minister complaining that 'more cinemas than ever' were opening on Sundays.[42] Nevertheless, the following year, Enniskillen local council gave permission for a Sunday screening of a religious film provided there was no admission charge.[43] The council continued to allow Sunday screenings, providing the films were religious, but it retained its right of veto which it exercised against the Regal Cinema when in December 1938 a local (Catholic) curate applied to show *The Angelus*, a Catholic rather than a Protestant prayer.[44]

Belfast was one of the few places, including Bangor, Co. Down, which did not permit Sunday opening, even if the programme was religious and was provided free.[45] In other districts, campaigns got underway in 1933 to impose a regulation making charity contributions obligatory with a suggestion, rejected by exhibitors, that 7.5 per cent of Sunday takings be given to charity. Meanwhile, the Pallidrome, Strabane, Co. Tyrone, offered one-night's takings to charity which the Strabane local council gratefully accepted.[46] The following year, despite opposition by clergy of all denominations, the same council voted five to three to allow Sunday opening.[47] However, even when Sunday opening had been won, many exhibitors continued to feel vulnerable. In 1934, for example, a Ballycastle, Co. Antrim exhibitor decided not to exercise his right to open on Sundays when a local councillor proposed a resolution threatening change.[48]

The battle heated up when Armagh's civic commissioner, George B. Hanna, declared that Sunday opening, which had been in the town since 1924, should cease as of 31 March 1935.[49] In addition, he was considering banning Saturday matinees and imposed 'a clerical film censorship' whereby two local clergy were appointed censors. They, in turn, appointed a further two censors from within the lay community. As might be expected, this alarmed locals who then demanded a vote on the matter. While exhibitors sent a deputation to the ministry of home affairs, the White Cinema Club embarked on an investigation of the issue.[50] In the meantime, the local censorship committee, chaired by the town clerk, was expanded to include two representatives from each of the two local cinemas and the referendum on Sunday opening was set for 14 March, though the threat to Saturday matinees was withdrawn.[51] The plebiscite campaign, reflecting the pertaining power structures and the fact that Hanna had initially only consulted with the Protestant churches, though he did receive a communication from the Catholic church prior to announcing the proposed ban, predictably, had a sectarian dimension. The advice given to Catholics during their religious services, just a few days before the vote, was that they should abstain from voting and boycott the two cinemas 'until [the cinemas] made an effort to exhibit clean films only'. With Catholics largely abstaining, the turn out was about 20 per cent, 'the great majority' of which were Protestant. Despite the comprehensive result of 302 in favour of Sunday closing, with only 219 against,[52] Hanna met with local exhibitors and a compromise was brokered. Though Hanna relented and permitted cinemas to continue as before on account of the fact that they had borne the cost of the plebiscite (and should therefore be permitted to recoup the losses), it seems that cinemas opted to close 'voluntarily' on Sundays.[53] Hanna also abolished the censorship committee in early April and appointed the town clerk as sole censor. Thus, when *Tarzan and His Mate* (Cedric Gibbons, 1934) was shown at the Market Street Picture House, the Catholic clergy attacked the screening from the pulpit as the film had not been passed by the censorship committee.[54]

The same year, 1935, also saw an important interpretation regarding the right of appeal against conditions in the annual cinema licence following the successful appeal to the Armagh county court by Lough Neagh Hotel, Lurgan, Co. Armagh, against Lurgan council's decision to ban all Sunday entertainments. The hotel had taken the case on the basis that Sunday entertainments, especially dancing, were essential for summer tourists. Though the ruling clearly established the right of licensees to appeal against onerous conditions imposed by the local authority and opened up a path for cinema owners to seek similar concessions,[55] imposition of Sunday restrictions continued. By the end of the year, a worried trade was concerned to protect those districts where Sunday opening was practiced, but as is plain in the decision by Lurgan council, cinema was not uniquely vulnerable. Indeed, at this time, there was a growing drive by Sabbatarians to have, by way of parliamentary legislation, *all* entertainments banned or, at the very least, severely restricted on Sundays throughout Northern Ireland, though the pressure was felt more keenly in some areas, including Belfast and the seaside town of Portrush, Co. Antrim. Nevertheless, in a point repeatedly made by disgruntled exhibitors, it remained the case that even in Belfast, a range of entertainments, including dancing, variety shows, stage plays, and even church-run whist drives were permitted on Sundays.[56]

Outside Belfast the approach to Sunday opening was uneven; even contradictory. In Dungannon, Co. Tryone, one cinema was awarded a seven-day licence, while another was only given a six-day one.[57] In the case of Newry, Co. Down, following a letter of complaint from a local Catholic priest, a motion seeking to restrict cinemas opening until after 8.45p.m. on Sundays pending a full debate on the issue was passed in December 1935,[58] while Omagh rural council, Co. Tyrone, was just one of the councils against which exhibitors successfully appealed to the county courts in order to maintain Sunday opening in their new licences which fell due in January 1936.[59] The decision that a county court judge could approve applications for Sunday licences following refusal by a local council was endorsed by the high court and led at this time to the confirmation of nine other licences.[60]

The campaign against Sunday opening went beyond the established opposition of the Protestant churches and by 1936 fully incorporated the Orange Order, perhaps the province's most powerful lay body. At its annual 12 July demonstrations, the first attacks on cinema for many years were made with opposition expressed in relation to the granting of Sunday inclusive cinema and other entertainment licences.[61] However, as *Kine Weekly* reported, 'quite a number of local councils are point blank refusing to abolish all Sunday entertainments, and are declaring that the matter is being taken too far.'[62] Other councils were dogmatic on the policy, with John Brady, owner of the only cinema in Aughnacloy, Co. Tyrone, being refused Sunday opening on three separate occasions in 1938.[63]

As might be expected, concern over cinema opening was not confined to the issue of Sunday trading or bound by religious argument. With regard to Christmas Day opening, as noted, there were no restrictions in Belfast,[64] but some exhibitors, perhaps motivated by the fact that employees received double pay and a day off in lieu, chose to close. Nevertheless, following pressure from the cinema workers' trade union, NATKE, which, working with the CEA, had negotiated Christmas Day cinema closure in England and Wales in 1946, a concerted effort was made to shut all union houses in Northern Ireland on that day.[65] The opening of cinemas on Good Friday, despite calls in the 1930s by religious reformers for their closure and the closure of businesses generally,[66] was similarly left to the discretion of individual exhibitors, though, as with Christmas Day, many chose not to open,[67] and, indeed, followed the pattern in the south of also closing on the Thursday, Friday and Saturday before Easter Sunday. In any case, more generally, there was a slump in cinema attendances in the period leading up to Easter Sunday, due, in the first instance, to the predominantly Catholic Lenten practice of abstinence and denial of pleasurable activities, and in the second, to the annual church missions which took place during the second half of Lent.[68] During the summer months, especially outside the main urban areas, when seaside and other outdoor counter-attractions diluted audiences, industry-induced closings affected one-third of all country cinemas. In some areas, cinemas closed completely, while elsewhere, they shut for shorter holiday periods,[69] though attempts were made to have adjoining cinemas synchronize their closing for particular periods during the summer.[70]

While the outbreak of war in September 1939 necessarily impacted on cinema-going, the most persistent and contentious issue during the war centred on Sunday opening. The White Cinema Club, representing exhibitors' interests, sought to open a chink in the Sabbatarians' opposition to Sunday opening by championing screenings for members of the armed forces, and even offering cinemas as a venue for live shows and concerts. Notwithstanding that outside Belfast and Derry some local councils permitted limited Sunday opening for armed forces' personnel, at times even allowing a civilian to accompany a soldier to the entertainment,[71] by May 1940, 'the big battle', as *Kine Weekly* called it, was 'reaching boiling point' with fourteen town councils due to vote on the issue.[72] At Bangor, one cinema was allowed to open on Sundays for the benefit of the troops,[73] though later in 1940, reflecting the generalized inconsistencies within council policy, a similar request for a variety concert at the Tonic Cinema in aid of the War Comforts Fund was rejected by one vote by the finance and law committee of the council.[74] Nevertheless, in September 1940 Newtownards voted nine to five to grant a licence to the Regent Cinema for stage shows on Sundays after church services, or from 8.30p.m. (The cinema, which had been approached by the military, was being supplied free of charge while the programme was entirely provided by the military.)[75] Portstewart voted unanimously to grant the local cinema Sunday opening, no doubt helped by the fact that the chairman of the council, John Hunter, owned the local cinemas.[76] Similarly, Kilkeel granted the military's application for Sunday cinema for troops 'at once';[77] while in contrast, Coleraine,[78] Ballymena[79] and Newcastle[80] councils rejected Sunday opening applications. Even when permission was granted, local opposition often intensified. Thus, though Derry council, following 'a heated debate', voted by a majority of one to grant a request from the chaplain of the armed forces for the Strand Cinema to open on Sundays,[81] the military authorities decided not to avail of the licence even though the move to try to rescind the licence had been 'definitely abandoned'.[82] In Bangor, despite having had advance approval, the Northern Ireland command entertainments' officer's application for a Sunday licence was rejected because 'local clergy turned out in force to object to the idea.'[83] Further requests for Sunday opening were made into 1942. Cookstown approved military-only events provided admission was free; Ballymoney council rejected an application from the officer commanding to use a cinema for the purpose of running gramophone record concerts; while the normally Sabbatarian Larne gave permission for training films to be screened on Sundays for the Home Guard.[84]

It was not just the councils that prevaricated and allowed the issue of Sunday opening to remain unresolved, exhibitors as a body were certainly divided and ambivalent, such that exhibitor George Gray who was also a Belfast councillor and member of the stringent police committee, had to consult the trade for guidance concerning the sector's attitude to Sunday opening. Though, as reported by *Kine Weekly*, Sunday opening was 'not favoured' by the Ulster trade, nevertheless, exhibitors stated that if the military authorities secured permission for Sunday opening, they would help in providing Sunday shows.[85] The military authorities, however, left the matter entirely with the civic authorities to deal with, though they did request that one cinema in each of the province's principal towns should be opened on Sundays for them. In December 1940 Belfast corporation voted by twenty-five to twelve to refuse this request,[86] but just over a year later in January 1942, it made a concession permitting Sunday shows for the home guards and the air raid precautions' wardens.[87] Two months later, the corporation again voted, this time by twenty-two to seventeen, 'the narrowest [vote] in the history of the Belfast Sunday opening fight', to refuse Sunday screenings.[88]

Adopting a more pro-active role, exhibitors offered two cinemas to the military for Sunday ENSA concerts. When the application came before Belfast corporation, Sabbatarians, not seeking to set any precedents, argued that if the armed services wanted Sunday shows, they should requisition cinemas, to which the military response was that it only needed such venues for one day a week.[89] The month following the corporation's refusal of Sunday ENSA concerts at the Hippodrome,[90] the military pulled rank and issued an order[91] to the Hippodrome which then ran a series of ten free Sunday night concerts for 25,000 members of the armed forces. Before issuing the order to the venue's sympathetic management, the war office had cleared it with the Northern Ireland government, which pronounced itself in favour of Sunday opening for troops.[92] In line with the Cinematograph Exhibitors' Association policy that Sunday opening should be for everybody and not just troops, film exhibitors in general were unhappy with what had happened. Consequently, by way of protest, two of Belfast's premier cinemas, ABC's Classic and the Ritz, were not offered to the military, while it seems from military complaints that film renters refused to supply films for the Hippodrome shows following CEA objections.

These issues were taken up by the Northern Ireland branch of the CEA, which, following a vote in November 1941 by the White Cinema Club to affiliate with the CEA, had been established with effect from January 1942.[93] Thereafter, the White Cinema Club reverted to its original object of social work and charitable effort on behalf of the film trade,[94] while the new body, charged with looking after business affairs, passed a resolution setting forth the terms under which cinemas would be available to the military on Sundays. Including the offer of one city and one suburban cinema, it also set out minimum admission prices and advised that films would form the major part of the entertainment.[95] In Belfast, exhibitors offered the military fourteen cinemas, of which four – the Imperial,[96] Picture House, Kelvin and Regal – were selected only after the police committee had refused a Sunday cinema show at the Ritz even though it was in aid of the RAF benevolent fund.[97] It was stipulated that any screenings there would be restricted to uniformed British and American armed forces and members of the merchant navy.[98] While other councils at times voted to deny Sunday screenings or concerts for the military, when the military requested that the troops could be accompanied by civilians, with the clear implication of girlfriends, the refusal was even more certain as was the case in Derry.[99] Councils in Fermanagh[1] and Coleraine also refused to allow civilians attend armed forces' entertainment, even though exhibitor Raymond Stross told Coleraine borough council that three of his other cinemas were given such permission.[2] Portrush council, however, went even further in the attempt to deny sexual desire on the Sabbath by stipulating that no 'females in uniform or civilian clothing shall be admitted.'[3]

Belfast's police committee found itself in a serious dilemma in August 1944 when a request was made to screen at the Ritz Cinema on three Sundays for war workers, two propaganda films, the *Why We Fight* series and *Divide and Conquer*, which, pre-pared by the ministry of information, had been presented to the Northern Ireland Prime Minister Basil Brooke by British Prime Minister Winston Churchill. A casting vote by the police committee chairman passed the application[4] and this was subsequently uniquely approved by the full corporation. While a request for a further four shows of the films was also approved by the police committee (though also only on the cast-ing vote of the chairman), this time the council, regretting its earlier action, rejected the recommendation by nineteen votes to twelve, even though, as *To-Day's Cinema* pointed out, it had licensed other halls for variety shows, dances and whist drives on the Sabbath.[5] The Northern Ireland war production council of the Electrical Trades Union responded by sending a delegation that argued that if showing films on Sundays desecrated the Sabbath, so, too, did their work and, therefore, if the decision was not reversed they would have to consider stopping work on Sundays.[6] Belfast's *Evening Telegraph* declared in support of the Ritz: 'Let the people see these films.'[7] The cor-poration was not for turning, and, following the appearance before it in early November of a delegation from the war production council and the Electrical Trades Union seeking the withdrawal of the ban on Sunday screenings for war workers, coun-cillors voted by twenty-three to fourteen to maintain the prohibition on all Sunday film screenings.[8]

If anything, the resolution of Protestant Sabbatarians intensified in 1945. The first case was when G.L. Birch, owner of the Hippodrome, was charged by the police com-mittee for running a Sunday charity show for the Belfast railway disaster relief fund without a licence, but, as *Kine Weekly* highlighted, about fifteen entertainment halls and night clubs, against which no action was taken, were also in breach of the six-day licence.[9] In the end, the corporation accepted Birch's apology and did not prosecute.[10] Almost simultaneously, the Sunday opening controversy became even more unpleas-ant as sectarianism on the part of Belfast corporation's police committee, reported by *Kine Weekly*, became explicit. The committee voted nine to three disallowing two Catholic halls to run Sunday shows for charities and religious purposes. One of the venues, St Mary's, had been holding such shows for sixty years, while the other, in Ardoyne, also had been holding, for some time, entertainments in aid of parochial funds. While twenty Catholic parochial organizations had supported the application, a delegation of 150 people, representing twenty-six Sabbatarian Protestant organiza-tions, had opposed it.[11] To the annoyance of Sabbatarians, the two churches success-fully appealed the decision to the Belfast recorder, though it was not long before the issue was raised in the Northern Ireland house of commons. The minister of home affairs, J.E. (Edmond) Warnock, affirmed that 'under no circumstances would he con-sider restoring the jurisdiction', stating that it was only in 'rare cases' that the county court judges reversed local authority decisions. He added that his inclination would be to extend rather than curtail the powers of local authorities in this respect.[12] Regardless, the Sabbatarians pressed for a change in the law to close off the right of appeal.[13] While the extreme Sabbartarian views as expressed through the decision of Belfast's police committee and the corporation more generally may have been out of favour with elements of the Northern Ireland government and, indeed, contrasted with the practices in England and Wales, where in the immediate post-war period, Sunday restrictions were being eroded, they continued to dominate in Belfast and to a lesser extent throughout Northern Ireland.[14]

Even outside Belfast, Protestant and Orange Order pressure, occasionally of a violent kind, resulted in Sunday closures, with Derry county council, for example, revoking all Sunday cinema licences in May 1946. Sunday shows had begun at the Kilrea Cinema six months earlier, on 17 March 1946, but 'hostility became so violent' that, following police advice, the cinema stopped the Sunday programme.[15] Such religious intolerance, which was no less evident in housing policy and the gerrymandering of local government representation, and which served to maintain a deep-seated resentment among the minority community in Northern Ireland, finally erupted on the Irish national and international stages twenty years later. Commenting in 1958 on the then crisis facing Northern Ireland exhibitors, *Kine Weekly* and *Belfast Telegraph* correspondent Gordon Duffield pointed out that 'it must be remembered that the cinema trade is not simply trying to repair a broken economy – it is fighting a social revolution.' He added that it would be helped to a certain extent if Sunday opening was allowed, since, he reminded readers, 'films [were already] being shown in the majority of homes – through TV – on Sunday night.'[16]

The Northern Ireland government finally acted to reform the sector with the introduction of a cinematograph bill that was given its second reading in October 1959.[17] Designed to ensure the protection of children from unsuitable films, the use of BBFC certificates, and allow for non-commercial exhibitors' exemptions from local authority restrictions, the bill also granted exhibitors the right of appeal to the courts against local authority decisions, including those pertaining to Sunday opening. Eventually, in 1965, the law was enacted by the Northern Ireland parliament and an appeals' mechanism against a local authority's refusal to permit Sunday cinema opening was formally introduced.[18]

OTHER EFFECTS OF WAR ON IRISH EXHIBITION NORTH AND SOUTH

The outbreak of war in September 1939, with its consequent impact on national priorities, particularly in Northern Ireland, and the restrictions placed on the use of building materials, put a stop to the decade-long expansion of Irish film exhibition.[19] Additionally, many northern cinemas were destroyed: German bombs flattened Belfast's Midland Picture House, Canning Street; the Queen's, York Road (both on 15 April 1941); and the Lyric, High Street (on 5 May 1941); while fires ravaged the Opera House, Carlisle Road, Derry; the Gardens, Warrenpoint; Maypole, Holywood; the Picture House, Omagh; and the Palace, Bangor. As a result, with the ending of the war in sight, in March 1945 the Northern Ireland branch of the CEA sought the granting of licences for the rebuilding of cinemas by the ministry of commerce, and with priority going to 'blitzed' cinemas in any rebuilding scheme.[20]

More mundane day-to-day business activity was also affected by the war, including the problem in the south of accessing spare parts for projectors. Eventually, however, Southern Irish exhibitors were included in the British carbon pool, which helped to eliminate the problem, but supplies of commodities for making the repair solution for broken films remained in short supply as late as 1944.[21] Some renters, 20th Century-Fox in particular, sought to gain advantage with Sunday screenings by imposing on exhibitors four- and seven-day bookings instead of three- and six-day bookings whereby the one-off Sunday show could be treated as a single fixed price rental. The Cinema Exhibitors' Association, supported by the southern-based Irish Theatre and Cinema Association, regarded this as 'part of a general drive by the renters to obtain increased rentals from exhibitors.'[22] At a meeting of northern exhibitors it was even suggested that 'a booking holiday', or boycott, of Fox should be considered.[23] In the south, too, Fox in late 1945 became the centre of a dispute having employed five non-union women cleaners. The 1,500-member cinema branch of the ITGWU, which sought to impose a closed shop in all film renting offices, threatened a strike,[24] even though the industry had rarely engaged in such action,[25] but a closed shop agreement was reached with effect from 1 January 1946.[26]

One of the foremost difficulties for exhibitors in the south during the war was the banning of all war films, fiction and non-fiction. This added to a product shortage as 265 films were banned under emergency powers' legislation during 1939 to 1945.[27] As a result, Irish exhibitors relied on renters importing reissues to fill the gap in product. Due to the shortage, many films that had been in the flat rate category before the war were being charged at 33.3 per cent of box office, while those previously rated at 33.3 per cent had risen to 50 per cent. While such increases might have been absorbed by an increase in admission charges, this was not possible as the government had introduced a 'standstill' order on prices for the duration of the war. The quality of film prints also deteriorated as renters – north and south – were only importing one copy of each film into the country, therefore, by the time a film reached provincial or second-run houses it was often in a very poor state.[28] According to Maurice Baum, costs were anything from 20 per cent to 200 per cent above pre-war levels. Of course, by the second half of 1945 there was an avalanche of product when the wartime restrictions were lifted. Nevertheless, people were tired of war films by the end of 1945, and there was a discernible downward trend in admissions.[29]

On top of this, the south's exhibitors were faced with cuts in electricity supplies for most of the war period. Based on a percentage of the units consumed in 1941, cinemas had to operate within the electricity quota, usually 40 per cent of normal. When, in 1944, there was an unprecedented water drought coupled with a coal shortage for electricity power stations, the already reduced cinema opening times were further cut. Central Dublin cinemas, which had been cut from three to two programmes with cinemas usually opening at 6.30p.m., were now reduced to one show on weekdays and two on Saturdays, while provincial and suburban Dublin cinemas, cut from six shows weekly in the pre-war period to four, were now obliged to close for three or four days of the week. Additionally, with Dublin city bus and train services ending at 9.30p.m., suburban patrons were discouraged from attending evening cinema shows.[30] Furthermore, with only one train or bus daily to provincial centres, transport of film prints was also a problem, especially because of the absence of private motoring. Of course, Northern Ireland, Belfast especially, unlike Dublin, had the extra inconvenience of having to adhere to a blackout policy for the duration of the war.

THE NATURE OF COMPETITION: EXHIBITION

While in Northern Ireland, the Sabbatarian or Protestant agenda, which adversely affected exhibitors' income, predominated, in the south, following the *Irish Press*' short-lived conflict with Dublin's major exhibitors in 1935, a more constructive Catholic campaign led by Fr Richard Devane SJ was launched. The most persistent Catholic activist of the period for Irish cinema reform, Devane sought the establishment of a government inquiry into all aspects of film in Ireland and the subsequent formation of a broad-based film institute (see chapters 7 and 8). In part because of Devane's pressure, his using of his friendship with head of government Éamon de Valera and his having garnered the support of civil servants, and, in part because of the government's wish to manage concerns within and beyond the film industry (namely with regard to the exhibitors' anxiety over 'alien penetration' and extreme Catholics who deemed the film censorship regime to be inadequate), but also in order to maintain the status quo within the sector given that the government had received some native and foreign proposals seeking the establishment of an Irish film studio, on 17 February 1938 the government set up an inter-departmental committee on the film industry. Unsurprisingly, its brief included provision for an examination of 'the extent to which it is desirable to limit the ownership and control of cinemas ... by non-national persons or bodies [and] to control the exhibition of films in Éire in the interests of moral, national and cultural development.'[31] In early 1939, the committee, which was under the aegis of the department of industry and commerce and whose membership was confined to civil servants, invited representations from the film trade and other interested groups to discuss a broad spectrum of issues relating to film in Ireland, especially proposals for the establishment of an Irish film industry.

Various bodies, including ITCA, the KRS, and the two main organizations promoting native industry, the Federation of Irish Manufacturers and NAIDA, both of which supported the government's plans for a film industry, were consulted and provided data. The federation and NAIDA favoured a quota of Irish films, suggesting that half of all newsreels exhibited should be Irish-produced. In addition, they proposed the introduction of a compulsory minimum of 400 feet per programme of short films dealing with Irish industries, culture, sport, music or agriculture, and recommended the promotion of Irish language films.[32] The committee also held meetings with a wide range of individuals, including Devane (who was later singled out for praise in the report) though, surprisingly, Thekla Beere, author of the 1936 study on cinema in Ireland, and who subsequently played an important role in government policy,[33] seems not to have contributed to the committee's work, though the lack of a credit may simply reflect the fact that she was a civil servant.

Though the committee's findings were completed by March 1942, the resulting fifty-five page *Report of the inter-departmental committee on the film industry* focused on production (9 pages) and including sections on exhibition (5 pages), distribution (6 pages), censorship (to which no significant change was recommended;[34] 12 pages) and 'direction and control' of the cinema (13 pages),[35] was never published as its contents were deemed to be confidential.[36] However, given that no confidential data relating to either individual film titles or companies was included,[37] it is more likely that it was not published because the proposals for an Irish film industry did not conform to the evolving views of the minister for industry and commerce, Seán Lemass, under whose remit this fell.[38]

According to the committee, which seems to have collected most of its exhibition and distribution data during 1939–41, by 1939 there were 220 cinemas with 140,000 seats in 'regular operation' in the south. Forty-seven of these, representing 52,350 seats, were in Dublin and the adjoining borough of Dún Laoghaire; twenty-one with a total of 17,350 seats were in the county boroughs of Cork, Limerick and Waterford; twenty-three, but with only 15,000 seats, were in Bray, Drogheda, Dundalk, Galway, Kilkenny, Sligo, Tralee and Wexford, while the remaining 129 cinemas with 55,300 seats were situated in the rest of the country. While city cinemas and those in larger towns usually opened from early afternoon until 11.00p.m., allowing for three shows daily with the exception of Sunday when, due to local authority restrictions, only two shows were possible, cinemas in provincial towns usually only had two evening performances. In smaller towns, cinemas generally opened only two or three times per week, mostly for one screening, while many actually closed during the summer months. Nationally, the annual estimated admission figure for 1939 was 28 million. Box office receipts were 'calculated to have been well over' £1 million, while entertainment tax collected from cinemas was approximately £287,000 (1940).[39] What immediately emerges from this profile of Irish exhibition is that either there was a significant improvement in the sector in the five years since Thekla Beere had collected her data during 1934–5, or, more likely, the resources available to the committee allowed for a more complete survey of the sector to be undertaken, thus revising upwards many of Beere's figures.

Dublin exhibitors, where one-third of the country's cinemas seats were located, informed the committee that the business, especially in the city centre, had 'reached saturation point' and that building further cinemas would result in the closing of existing ones. They requested that as Dublin corporation (or indeed any council) could not refuse a licence for the construction of a new cinema on the basis of adequate or over supply,[40] the committee should consider a new licensing scheme whereby a new cinema could not be approved by a local authority until a licence to build it had been granted by the minister for industry and commerce. In deciding on a licence it was envisaged that the minister would take into account the number of existing cinemas in the district. Though the committee rejected this anti-competitive proposal, which would set a precedent for other enterprises,[41] it did go on to recommend a licensing system which it hoped could be used to indirectly influence cinema-building and control the actions of combines.

Noting the cut-throat rivalry for first-run product in central Dublin, the committee stated that the competition 'was so severe that rental charges ... were forced to an abnormally high level', adding that similar competition arose over second-run product. The report explained that as a result of this, and in order to reduce competition and to secure greater bargaining power with the renters, many exhibitors had formed a number of combines and circuits. Thus in Dublin, of the forty-seven cinemas (comprising 52,350 seats), twenty-seven of them (comprising 30,000 seats), including almost all first-run cinemas, were controlled by just six groups. While some of these were single companies owning a number of cinemas, others, while nominally distinct companies, each owning one or more cinemas, were in fact associated with each other through interlocking directorships. (The most complex of such entities in the post-war period – the Ward Anderson group – is examined in chapter 4.) Registering the increasing activity of Dublin-based cinema groups in provincial areas, it cited one unnamed company, almost certainly the Elliman chain, which had eight cinemas in Dublin incorporating 12,360 seats, as well as a large cinema in Cork and in Limerick, bringing the group's aggregate number of seats to 16,000. Also mentioned was another circuit, probably that of the Farrells, which had 6,000 seats distributed among cinemas in Dublin, Cork, Waterford and Galway. In addition to the Dublin-based combines, other circuits with common directorships were based in the nearby counties of Wexford and Kilkenny; Dundalk and Drogheda; and Athlone, Carlow and Clonmel; while numerous small circuits existed in smaller provincial towns, with individuals usually controlling two or three cinemas situated in adjoining districts.[42]

The committee, presaging allegations made during the consolidation of film exhibition from the late 1960s onwards, outlined the tactics of a combine's agent in relation to an independent exhibitor in a provincial location. If an independent refused to sell his/her cinema to the combine, the independent would be informed that a rival cinema, capable of screening more recent releases for a lower admission price, would be built in the neighbourhood, with the threat backed up by the agent having already secured an option on a nearby site for the proposed venue. If the cinema owner still refused, the new cinema would be built eventually forcing the old cinema out of business. The report adds that even when such pressure was not applied, the superior bargaining power of a combine enabled it not only to secure the best pictures, but earlier and on better terms than independent cinemas. Thus, independents, especially the smaller ones, had to accept less attractive or previously screened films. It was because of this that the committee proposed the introduction of a licensing system under which a limit could be set on the number of seats that an exhibitor or group of exhibitors might control.[43]

After analyzing the company ownership structure of ninety-five cinemas comprising of 82,500 seats, it concluded that less than 15 per cent of the issued share capital of £1.25 million was held by non-nationals. The bulk of the investment by non-nationals was found to be in the larger Dublin cinemas, with very little in smaller towns.

While the report stated that 'penetration ... by outside interests has so far not been serious', it went on to state that there was 'nothing to prevent foreign interests from securing control of the cinema industry' in Ireland. In an indirect reference to ABC's ownership of the Adelphi, it said that it may be 'the first of a chain of cinemas which will be used to provide an assured market' for its film production arm. As a result, other (presumably Irish-owned) first-run cinemas felt that 'their interests [were] being seriously threatened.' In reviewing the more than 50 per cent Irish ownership and the two-thirds issued share capital clauses in the Control of Manufacturing Acts 1932–4, the committee felt that 'a more stringent measure of control would be necessary' for the cinema. While it recognized that it was hardly expedient to refuse licences to cinemas already in the hands of non-nationals, it, nonetheless, suggested, though without offering policy proposals, that licensing conditions could be devised so as to confine ownership within existing limits by such interests.[44]

With the reality of the commercial (and ideological) threat presented by British combines challenged, the report concluded its section on exhibition with a wide-ranging paranoid attack on the Jewish influence in the cinema. Taking its lead from some of the representations made to the committee, the report states that it 'was considered undesirable' that the cinema, which 'plays so large a part in the social and cultural life of the community, should be controlled to such an extent' by persons 'whose ideas and general outlook are alien to those of the majority of our people.' To allow Jews to be 'free to prescribe cinema programmes', it argued, 'was to allow them too important a measure of influence over the minds, culture and social habits of our people, and was tantamount to giving them partial control of our public education.'[45] Nevertheless, the committee decided that while certain measures could be adopted 'against foreign interests in general', legislation could not be introduced 'which would be directed, surreptitiously or otherwise, against Jews in particular.' Having raised the hare of anti-Semitism, it pointed out that many Jews, such as the Ellimans, were Irish nationals, and that 'the Constitution does not recognize any racial discrimination between citizens.'[46] The report's authors, however, did not (want to?) draw the obvious conclusion: support the development of an indigenous film industry as a means of countering the dominance of non-Irish product in Irish cinemas.

THE NATURE OF COMPETITION: DISTRIBUTION

'This country', the report's opening sentence on distribution bluntly states, 'is dependent for its supplies of films on outside sources' because native productions are 'so rare that they cannot be counted as a factor affecting the normal supply.'[47] Even in the matter of the availability of film prints, the report deemed Ireland to be at a disadvantage with the majority of films screened in Ireland printed in Britain.[48] Indeed, for purposes of distribution, Ireland, reliant as it was on Anglo-American product,[49] was considered by British and American companies 'as a part of the United Kingdom [with] Dublin being treated as a branch like Glasgow, Cardiff or Belfast.'[50] Apart from the subsidiary local offices of the various British and American companies, which enjoyed 'a virtual monopoly of supplies', there were a number of 'relatively unimportant' small independent distribution agencies whose titles were confined to independently-produced American or British films, continental productions with a general appeal, and infrequently-made Irish films. One such company, a specialist in films made in Ireland, was Tommy Hanlon's Irish International Film Agency, which had been established in 1935.[51] His 'phenomenal successes' with *The Luck of the Irish* (Donovan Pedelty, 1935); *The Dawn* (Tom Cooper, 1936); and *The Early Bird* (Donovan Pedelty, 1936) 'astounded' the Irish film trade,[52] while the company's documentary *Star of Ulster* (1938) was distributed to no less than forty-five cinemas in Northern Ireland alone.[53]

As might be expected, since Ireland was forced into such an inequitable relationship with foreign distributors there were many undesirable effects ranging from the cultural (and issues around representation and ideology) to those centred on the economy. Not only did the agency system of branch offices hinder 'the growth of an independent or domestic film renting industry',[54] it afforded 'little benefit' by way of local employment or in terms of revenue.[55] The majority of film hire contracts, prepared as they were in the London head offices, were validated by British revenue stamps, while foreign renters incorporated in Britain, were, under reciprocal fiscal arrangements between the two countries, not subject to Irish tax.[56] As a result, apart from fees chargeable for formal registration under Irish company law, the only money collected from foreign renters was in respect of censorship fees, which were non-profit based and accrued no advantage to the exchequer, and customs' duty, which was being passed on by the renters to the exhibitors by way of, an at times profiteering, surcharge. The rate charged on a film's first week's rental was initially set at 10 per cent for American films and 6.66 per cent for British films, no matter how much the exhibitor paid for the film and regardless of whether the sum exceeded the duty.

Recognizing the imbalance of foreign renters being 'subject to very little control, financial or otherwise', on the one hand, and, on the other, being able to enjoy 'a virtual monopoly of supplies' through which they dominated the film trade in Ireland, often with recourse, it was alleged, to imposing 'burdensome and unfair' conditions on native exhibitors,[57] the committee, seeking to bring the foreign renters 'under control', made two proposals. One of these, following the lead of other countries, offered a generalized form of redress through the introduction of a state-controlled licence. This was envisaged to give 'special regard' to native renters, and which could be revoked should a renter fail to comply with the conditions as set forth by the statutory body. The other proposal pertained to the practice whereby renters passed on the customs' duty to the exhibitors.

The renters informed the committee that not only did they seek to recoup the duty ('the only contribution of any consequence that foreign renters are called upon to make in return for the profits they derive from this country') through the surcharge, but that 'they would not suffer their income from [Ireland] to be diminished' by such a tax and 'that any further taxation that might be imposed on them would also be passed on to exhibitors.'[58] Though the committee recognized that any attempts to control film rentals so that renters bore 'the full weight of taxation' might lead the large distributors 'to retaliate by withholding film supplies in the hope that the resultant dislocation of the Irish cinema trade would ultimately induce the Government to re-consider its decision', it nonetheless concluded that the possibility of such action[59] should not prevent the adoption of 'a reasonably firm attitude'. The Irish market, 'though admittedly small, is nevertheless of sufficient importance to be worthy of consideration'.[60] It suggested that the customs' duty should be replaced by a 'film hire tax', which could not so readily be passed on to exhibitors. Noting the undifferentiated per foot tax on imported film irrespective of its box office value, the film hire tax would be imposed *after* the film had finished its run, a system in operation in New Zealand and Sweden.[61] The committee argued this would prove of particular advantage to small independent renters who would be able to import films 'as a speculation, thereby making for a freer market and creating for Irish nationals an important distributive trade' which could not be built up under the current import duty regime. Such a speculative importation arrangement could be used to help the emergence of a cultural cinema by enabling many productions 'of merit' to reach Ireland which otherwise would not be brought in due to their limited appeal.[62] Not only would the film hire tax compensate for the import duty, but, according to the committee, in a first and rare Irish voicing of a levy system, it would 'provide a surplus which might be used for developing the production of films in this country.'[63]

Nevertheless, the committee concluded that even if all their proposals were acted upon, 'it is evident that we cannot alter fundamentally the manner of film distribution'. While acknowledging Ireland's dependency on Britain and America, the report noted that it was not peculiar to the film sector as Ireland was 'obliged to accept' many goods and services 'through channels not under its control'. It also stated that there was

> little use condemning on cultural grounds the existing system of distribution of films, since even if we acquired control of distribution we should still be in the hands of alien producers. Cultural control could not be attained unless we were in a position to produce sufficient films to meet our main requirements.[64]

And, even then, though not stated in the report, it would rely on exhibitors choosing to show the native product. Sadly, most distributors and exhibitors throughout the history of film exhibition in Ireland, whether native or foreign, have made that choice, or have not shown significant commitment to indigenous Irish cinema, at least until the 1990s. Similarly, prior to the 1990s, the Irish state itself had allocated very little investment to Irish cinema.

In the absence then of an Irish product, the only other possibility open to countering the reliance on Britain was the direct importation of films from the USA. However, the committee noted that while the annual net outflow of £200,000 by the renters was 'a considerable sum' in Irish terms, 'it is small in comparison with the amount which American producers derive from the British market,[65] and is an *unim-*

portant fraction of the proceeds from American films throughout the world as a whole'[66] [emphasis added]. Consequently, it reasoned that American companies were unlikely to set up separate organizations to deal with direct imports. Furthermore, there were no facilities for printing films in Ireland, nor could they be justified for the sole purpose of printing imported films due to the small size of the Irish market.

Nevertheless, the report also suggests how certain booking and other practices designed to serve distributors could be modified through the introduction of a standard film-renting contract. Such a contract, which already existed in New South Wales and New Zealand, the report advised, could eliminate the 'friction' between exhibitors and distributors, caused in part because current contracts seemed to favour distributors. The committee had received complaints that (unspecified) additional conditions were often imposed, while 'special unwritten conditions may be imposed on individual exhibitors.' In order to ensure compliance with these extra conditions, renters cooperated with each other through the KRS. In this body, information was alleged to have been exchanged about exhibitors who failed to comply with distributors' demands, and a 'black-list' existed of such exhibitors. An exhibitor 'who gives offence' to a particular renter was liable to have films or credit withdrawn not only by that renter, but also by other members of the KRS. The report stated that smaller exhibitors were 'especially susceptible to the threat of penalisation in this way', adding that 'such methods do not make for amicable relations between renters and exhibitors generally.'[67]

While the report's section on booking outlines such established practices as renting on a percentage basis of the gross takings less entertainment tax,[68] and of debarring during a specified period other districts or cinemas from showing a film being screened in a particular cinema,[69] it largely comprises of a consideration of 'block', 'blind' and 'advance' booking. Under such forms of booking, exhibitors, even if seeking a 'good-class feature film' only, were 'invariably obliged' to contract for a number of films (including the company's newsreel), often unseen, and usually for up to between twelve and fifteen months in advance. As a result, an exhibitor might find it difficult to provide a screening for an Irish-made film that became available. While not proposing to ban 'block booking', the committee suggested that exhibitors be given the right to reject a certain proportion of films when offered *en bloc*. (Of course, from the perspective of the renter, block booking ensured that less attractive films were taken along with first-run or commercially-viable bigger films.) To further the exhibitor's control, the report also recommended that contracts between renters and exhibitors should be limited to nine months. Though it noted that 'blind booking' was outlawed in some countries, given the British context of compulsory trade shows, which allowed exhibitors the opportunity to see all films before booking them, such a ban was deemed unnecessary. Nevertheless, it did state that the trade showing in Ireland of films should be encouraged, though such shows, when they occurred were usually confined to those organized (and paid for) by small independents and featured the smaller, more vulnerable renters.[70]

CHAPTER 3

Dividing the Spoils: British and American Film Interests in Ireland after the Second World War

'The cinema is a fleeting thing. One is always looking forward to next week's show.'[1]

J. ARTHUR RANK'S CINEMA EMPIRE

(a) Rank's beginnings

In the Strand Cinema's souvenir programme of 16 March 1945, marking its reopening following a complete reconstruction, managing director Leonard Ging wrote that the company's directors,

> each of whom is an *Irish born* Citizen, take special pride in the fact that a combination of *Irish* Capital, Enterprise, and Labour has been responsible for the provision of a Cinema and Theatre worthy of this great district – one of the most important and populous in the Dublin area. [Emphasis added.][2]

Such an assertion of Irishness had a particular resonance given the growing anxiety over foreign investment within the industry, which was realized ten months later when J. Arthur Rank, in the most momentous transformation of Irish film exhibition thus far, entered the Irish market. Four years later, Ging sold all but one of his five cinemas to Rank whose investment in Irish exhibition remained by far the most significant foreign investment in the sector until the development of multiplexes from the late-1980s onwards.

At 17 years old, Joseph Arthur Rank (born 1888), the youngest son of Joseph Rank, who ran a significant flour milling operation in Britain and Ireland, including a plant in Limerick, entered the family business and became in 1933 managing director of Joseph Rank Ltd. As a Methodist who taught Sunday school, Joseph Arthur was dissatisfied with the quality of religious films and founded the Religious Film Society, through which he commissioned two short films in 1933–4. In October 1934, in partnership with wealthy widow Lady Yule he established British National Films, whose first film was *Turn of the Tide* (Norman Walker, 1935).[3] Made at Elstree film studios, the film, an adaptation of a novel about two feuding Yorkshire fishing families that ends in marriage, was designed to promote Christian values under the guise of entertainment. Unconvinced by the interest, and hence ability, of distributors in promoting such a film, Rank joined forces with experienced distributor C.M. Woolf, who, in mid-1935, having left Gaumont-British, where he had been joint managing director, was determined to start a distribution company of his own. With backing from international banker Paul Lindenburg, they set up General Film Distributors (GFD) which, registered in June 1935,[4] began operations the following November.

The next year, Rank helped to establish General Cinema Finance Corporation (GCFC),[5] a company registered in 1936 to take over 90 per cent of GFD's share capital, and with capital of £1,225,000 for production and distribution. In April 1938, Rank, succeeding paper manufacturer Lord Portal, became its chairman. Following its investment in the ailing American studio Universal, GFD acquired the British distribution rights to Universal's films and took over its British newsreel, while Universal agreed to distribute some of GFD's films in America. Meanwhile, Rank also became involved in studio ownership by way of an association with Sheffield building and engineering tycoon Sir Charles Boot who had purchased a large site in May 1935 at Pinewood, Buckinghamshire. Registered as Pinewood Studios in August 1935, the impressive facility was completed with Lady Yule's support and in September 1936 opened with five sound stages. When in early 1937 Rank and Yule ended their partnership she sold her Pinewood shares to Rank and he became the studio's chairman. Rank, however, resigned from production company British National, thus leaving Yule and John Cornfield in charge there.

Realizing the importance of controlling exhibition venues both in terms of ensuring screenings of his own films and to secure a lucrative business, Rank used GCFC as a vehicle to acquire cinemas, including in 1937 London's Leicester Square Theatre, and circuits in London, the west of England, Wales, and elsewhere. In 1939, he invested in one of the three big British circuits, Oscar Deutsch's Odeon group, which was synonymous with comfort and luxury, while in 1941 GCFC took control of the second circuit, Gaumont-British Picture Corporation, which included exhibition subsidiaries Provincial Cinematograph Theatres and General Theatres Corporation. Less than six weeks later in December 1941, Deutsch's widow sold Odeon Theatres to Rank, thus leaving only the ABC circuit independent of Rank. In 1942, Rank's Odeon, having experienced 'a boom period' during 1941–2 with record profits of over one-and-a-half million pounds, more than twice that of the previous year, allowing payment of a dividend to shareholders of 10 per cent, re-entered negotiations with Paramount to acquire leases on Paramount's remaining first-run prestigious, large and lucrative city centre cinemas which were located in Birmingham, Glasgow, Liverpool and on London's Tottenham Court Road.[6] In August 1942, Rank secured the cinemas, whose names were promptly changed to Odeon. Having left the American company with only two West End venues, Rank became the preferred distributor of Paramount films[7] and the new Odeon cinemas continued to show British Paramount News. Although such a con-centration of ownership led to tension between the British government and Rank, fol-lowing the government's extraction of a promise from Rank (and from ABC) that their circuit would not exceed 607 cinemas,[8] they did not attempt to stop the Paramount-Rank deal.

Given that building permits were unavailable during and after the war, and the gov-ernment had placed restrictions on ownership of British cinemas, Rank, seeking to create a distribution and exhibition network for British films to rival the dominant American firms, unsurprisingly, began to invest outside of Britain. In 1944 Rank sent close aide John Davis to Canada where he bought a 50 per cent stake of a 102-cinema circuit; the following year, Rank took a half share of an Australian 72-cinema circuit; while three months later, in January 1946, Rank acquired an interest in Irish Cinemas Ltd, soon afterwards taking full control of the company and renaming it Odeon (Ireland) Ltd. By the late 1940s, Rank controlled exhibition circuits in South Africa, Jamaica, Malaya, Holland, and New Zealand, and had built cinemas in Cairo and Lisbon. Due to British government directives Rank had been prevented from buying into the USA market, nevertheless, during 1945–8 the company leased the United Artists'-owned Winter Gardens, New York City, in order to showcase Rank's British films. While the number of Rank productions increased dramatically during 1947–8, the expansion was financially disastrous, with Rank's debt in 1948 more than £16 mil-lion. This was largely caused by the government's revoking of the penal *ad valorem* tax of 75 per cent on foreign films in 1948, which led to the re-entering into the British market of American companies following their eight-month boycott.[9] Though Rank was forced into severe cost-cutting and abandoned the type of prestige productions, such as those by David Lean, and Michael Powell and Emeric Pressburger, with which it had been associated, it recovered and continued its involvement in production, most particularly through Ealing Studios, remaining an important film producer during the 1950s.[10] Nevertheless, its roles as distributor and exhibitor were the most important and served to support its role as a producer. (By 1954, half of the income generated by Rank's own productions came from abroad.)[11]

(b) Rank in Ireland
In Ireland, the Second World War had seen an intensification of the commercial rivalry between the USA and Britain. At the outbreak of the war, America supplied only 11.4 per cent of Irish imports, while Britain supplied 72 per cent, and in turn bought 90 per cent of Irish exports, which were, in the main, agricultural. Though some officials at the American embassy in Dublin sought to weaken British business connections in Ireland, they were restrained from doing so by policy-makers in Washington.[12] Despite there being ample opportunity, American manufacturers, perhaps following their gov-ernment's policy, did not expand their interests in the Irish market, similarly USA film exhibitors largely remained outside Ireland (though, as is clear from the brief discus-sion of Paramount, they entered Europe and elsewhere). By contrast, Rank, the largest integrated British film production, distribution and exhibition group, was keen to

acquire a stake in Irish exhibition, which, at the end of 1945, comprised of a total of 109 limited companies of which 105 were private and four public. While their combined share capital was £2,206,140 with a total paid-up share capital of £1,417,000, the four public companies, one of which was the Elliman-controlled Irish Cinemas Ltd, had a total nominal share capital of £573,000, of which £548,134 was paid up.[13]

Perhaps in anticipation of a deal with the Ellimans, Rank committed to the Elliman-owned Regal Cinema as a first-run venue (even though previously it had served as second-run to the Savoy) by releasing *Henry V* (Laurence Olivier, 1944) there in August 1945. (Later, *The Life and Death of Colonel Blimp* [Michael Powell, Emeric Pressburger, 1942] and *Blithe Spirit* [David Lean, 1944] were released at Elliman's Theatre Royal.)[14] Speaking in Dublin at the time of the screening of *Henry V*, and perhaps, by way of a further softening up process prior to Rank making a formal move to take over the Elliman circuit, Rank's Clayton Hutton said that Rank was considering establishing a film studio in Ireland.[15] Shortly before Christmas 1945, the *Irish Times* restated the possibility of such a venture and reported that Rank had purchased a site for a central Dublin cinema in which 'to exhibit his own productions exclusively', and that he was considering acquiring an interest in a cinema circuit as he had done in Australia[16] and in some European countries.[17] On 18 January 1946, confirming the rumours of a deal between the Ellimans and the Odeon circuit, Rank announced his investment at a dinner at London's Dorchester hotel attended by a number of Irish film correspondents whom Rank had invited to London to visit his Denham Film Studios.[18]

Under the Elliman-Rank agreement, the Odeon circuit acquired an interest in ten Elliman properties with a total seating capacity of 15,100. While five of these were owned directly or indirectly[19] by Irish Cinemas – the Savoys in Dublin, Cork and Limerick, and the Theatre Royal and Regal Rooms, Dublin – the remaining five – the Metropole, Corinthian, Theatre de Luxe, Queen's Theatre and the Picture House, Phibsboro – all in Dublin, were owned by Metropole and Allied Cinemas, which itself held a controlling interest in Irish Cinemas Ltd. Though the ten venues constituted only about 12 per cent of Irish cinema seats, given that they represented some of the country's most prestigious cinemas, they took as much as 25 per cent of Irish box office income. Though the cost to Rank was not disclosed, the figure of £1.25 million was mentioned. Nevertheless, this was denied by Louis Elliman, who wrote to *Kine Weekly* stating that the family had received less than a million pounds[20] from Rank which at the time of the investment did not take a controlling interest in the companies. Indeed, as Rank's John Davis told *Daily Film Renter*, there would be 'no alterations whatever in the management of the theatres', which would be operated 'as at present'.[21]

Although there was a 'persistent demand' for shares in Irish Cinemas Ltd which, under the new order, was chaired by Rank with Maurice Elliman as vice chairman, and Geoffrey Elliman, Abe Elliman (controller of cinemas), Jack Elliman (publicity), Gerald Ellis (accounts) and Mr Margery (catering) serving as executive assistants, the *Irish Times* commented that 'on the present dividend, and even allowing for the promising outlook for this industry, the shares would appear too high.'[22] Indeed, the shares, valued as low as 1s. 3d. in 1941,[23] had risen in anticipation of Rank's investment from their 1945 low of 5s. to 12s. 6d. on the day of the announcement, a rise of 150 per cent in a month. With the feeling persisting that Rank would increase its stake in the company, in early February the shares were at 10s. and a 5 per cent dividend 'fully valued' the company,[24] but by the end of March 1946 they had returned to their earlier high value.

Although the Elliman-Rank deal was reported neutrally by the press, T.J.M. Sheehy, through his column in the *Irish Catholic*, sought to generate a negative campaign. Two weeks prior to the announcement of Rank's investment[25] Sheehy had attempted to alert his readers to the imminent expansion of Rank into Ireland and warned how elsewhere, such as in Norway, Portugal and Spain, the company had used native film companies to enlarge its 'empire'. Later, in an ideologically loaded historical reference, Sheehy represented Rank as 'Ireland's absentee film landlord'.

> Absentee landlordism is an old evil which seems to be taking on a newer and more potent form ... Rank's monopoly control of to-day can easily be sold again to-morrow to the Aga Khan, to Joe Stalin, or M. Molotov, or whoever can bid sufficiently high for it.[26]

While Sheehy's attack on Rank was regarded as 'vicious' by *Kine Weekly*,[27] the regional newspaper *Wicklow People*, following Sheehy, focused further on the potential moral-cultural consequences of the transformation of Irish film exhibition whereby the ownership of all of the principal cinemas was no longer predominantly Irish. The paper suggested that the only way to ensure some protection against the foreign produced and distributed films, which 'for the most part [were] more or less objectionable', was to insist on majority Irish interest in cinema ownership. If this was the case, renters and producers would be forced, as had been the case prior to Rank's investment, to consider 'Irish susceptibilities'.[28] Despite Sheehy's stance against Rank which was motivated by 'national principle',[29] he was impressed, nonetheless, by Rank's character[30] and aspects of his film programme such as the importation into Britain of French films following his acquisition of British exhibition interests,[31] and especially his proposal to extend his Children's Cinema Clubs to Ireland.[32]

In March 1946 Fianna Fáil TD J.S. O'Connor, recognizing that Rank's entry into the Irish market had resulted in 'disturbing various intensely nationalistic interests',[33] particularly exhibitors, who were annoyed at the government's *laissez-faire* attitude, asked in the Dáil if the minister for industry and commerce, Seán Lemass, would consider introducing legislation to amend the Control of Manufacturers' Acts and extend its restrictive provisions to the ownership of theatres, cinemas and other places of public entertainment. However, the minister's parliamentary secretary, replying on Lemass's behalf, in a clear denunciation of what had heretofore been the main plank of Fianna Fáil's industrial policy since it took power in 1932, that of economic protectionism, rejected this potentially effective method of restricting Rank stating that such a move was not being contemplated, though it would be kept under review.[34] As Paul Bew and Henry Patterson observe,

It is certain that by 1945, at least, Lemass personally had made the intellectual break with the narrow type of economic nationalism which had characterised his views in the 1930s. This break was not simply confined to a matter of protectionism. It applied also to the hallowed principle of Irish ownership of Irish resources.[35]

Unsurprisingly, then, when in 1948 Rank took a stake in Associated Pictures' Houses (1944) Ltd,[36] which comprised of six cinemas located in or near Dublin – the 600-seat Regent, Blackrock; the 1,320-seat Pavilion, Dún Laoghaire; the 500-seat Picture House, Dún Laoghaire; the 650-seat Broadway, Manor Street; the 927-seat Royal Bray; and the 360-seat Camden Picture House – no action was taken. However, while Lemass had told Rank that it was his 'personal view' that the acquisition of the Elliman cinemas did not create a situation in which the government might deem it necessary to introduce legislation 'to exercise control', when the cinemas were bought, 'it was made clear' to Rank by Lemass that nothing which he had said previously 'should be interpreted as an assurance that the Government might not consider it necessary' to introduce some form of state control with regard to cinema ownership.[37] Though the Associated Picture Houses (1944) Ltd deal brought Rank's Irish cinema seats to just under 20,000 (19,457) spread across sixteen venues, on 28 August 1948 Odeon (Ireland) Ltd closed down the small Camden Picture House,[38] which was near its Theatre de Luxe, while the 1,200-seat Queen's, which showed films only on Sundays, reverted to the Ellimans shortly before it became from 1951 to 1966 home to the Abbey theatre whose own venue was destroyed in a fire.

Despite the government's inaction, but chastened in the ways of Irish politics, when Rank was considering acquiring a further four cinemas, the company's Irish subsidiary, Irish Cinemas Ltd, sought a meeting with the coalition government's minister for industry and commerce, Daniel Morrissey. In March 1949 Morrissey's parliamentary secretary met with the three Irish Cinemas' representatives who were advised that 'while the Minister had no power to prevent the acquisition of cinemas by any group, he did not look favourably on the extension of [their] activities.' The directors of Irish Cinemas responded by pointing out that the cinemas in question had to be sold as a block and that their company was the only Irish group in a position to make the purchase. Nevertheless, they added that they would not proceed without 'at least the tacit approval of the Minister'. While they were informed that, given the circumstances, 'the Minister offered no objection', once again this was 'without prejudice to the Minister's attitude in the event of there being any further acquisitions by the group'.[39] Rank's purchase of these four cinemas – the 1,400-seat Fairview Grand; the 1,200-seat Grand Cinema, Drumcondra; the 1,100-seat Strand Cinema, and the 1,634-seat Cabra Grand, which was only completed shortly after Rank's purchase and opened on 16 April 1949 – which were previously owned by Leonard Ging, was received neutrally by the press except for a predictable barrage against Rank from the *Irish Catholic*.[40] Speaking in the Dáil, Fianna Fáil's opposition spokesman on industry and commerce, Seán Lemass, simply enquired whether the minister had objected to Rank's expansion. When told that he had not, Lemass did not pursue the matter or attempt to score ideological points, though his colleague Frank Aiken did by taking a swipe at Clann na Poblachta's acquiescence to the deal, even implying that they might have made representations to the minister to the effect 'that it was right to allow these British organisations to come in and buy up' cinemas.[41] By this time, Rank, which owned almost twenty cinemas in the Republic, had combined the Odeon and Gaumont circuits under a new umbrella, Circuits Managements' Association Ltd (CMA). In 1948, this company had about 564 cinemas operating in Britain, including one Gaumont in Northern Ireland, the Classic, Castle Lane, which had been taken over as part of its purchase of the Gaumont circuit in 1941, and which was renamed the Gaumont in July 1950.

In August 1950, a memorandum on the ownership of Irish cinemas was circulated to the inter-party, or coalition, government prior to a cabinet meeting on 15 September 1950. Prepared largely by the department of industry and commerce for the inter-party government following a request from the department of the taoiseach, the document outlined Rank's recent Irish acquisitions and highlighted the fact that cinemas, both in cities and larger provincial towns, were being increasingly amalgamated into combines that were controlled by both foreign and native companies. The minister was of the opinion that

> the possibility cannot be ruled out of the formation ultimately of an organisation with sufficient control over the distribution and exhibition of films to eliminate competition by individual cinema owners and so to stifle private enterprise in the industry.[42]

Consequently, it endorsed as having contemporary relevance the recommendation of the 1938–42 interdepartmental committee on the film industry that

> The growth of large cinema circuits should be restricted ... measures should be taken to check penetration of the cinema industry by alien interests, and ... the existing methods for the distribution of films should be revised.[43]

Apart from Rank's Irish Cinemas and Odeon (Ireland) Ltd, which controlled eighteen cinemas (mostly first-run Dublin city centre venues or the most attractive suburban cinemas, as well as the two premier houses in Cork and Limerick), the document noted that the British company Associated Cinema Properties Ltd, an ABC subsidiary, owned a controlling interest in the Adelphi Cinemas, Dublin and Dún Laoghaire, while it stated that 'a British national' operated three provincial cinemas. Though the 'British national' was unnamed, it was most likely Maurice Baum who had moved to Ireland in the 1930s, and set up National Film Distributors in 1943. Baum's exhibition interests included two cinemas in Bray – the Picture House and Roxy, the latter, it seems, only for a few years – and the Rialtos in Dublin and Wicklow (see previous chapter). The memo also pointed out that there were five or six circuits operated by Irish groups. However, in fact, if excluding Baum's, which de facto was an Irish circuit, there were about twelve reasonably important Irish circuits in the mid- to late-1940s, many of them regionally-based. These Irish groups can be identified as those of the Farrells, who, in addition to operating the Electric, Plaza, Phoenix (all in secondary locations in Dublin), and Rotunda, retained control of one of the two non-British-owned first-run Dublin cinemas, the Capitol; Jack Ellis, who owned the first-run Carlton and the Grafton cinemas, Dublin; Dan McAllister, who had four Dublin cinemas: the Leinster, Tivoli, Lyric and Stephen's Green, the latter the most important cinema on the south side of the Liffey; Harry Culleton's Amalgamated Cinemas (Ireland) Ltd, which controlled nine provincial cinemas: the Savoys in Waterford, Galway, Portarlington, Athy, Kiltimagh and Edenderry, the Castle in Oldcastle, and the Town Hall and Gaiety cinemas in Ennis; M.J. Deasy whose Ritzes were located in Clonmel, Athlone, and Carlow, while his Ormond was in Nenagh; Gerry Kirkham and Joe Riley whose circuit comprised of two Dublin suburban cinemas (the Odeon, Dundrum, and Cinema, Inchicore), and two provincial ones (the Odeons in Tuam and Longford); John Egan, who controlled eight cinemas in Maryborough (Portlaoise), Nass, Mountrath, Abbeyleix, Portumna, Moville and Carlow; Tom Cooper, director of *The Dawn* (1936), who ran four cinemas, all named Casino, in Killarney (Co. Kerry), Rathmore (Co. Kerry), Tramore (Co. Waterford) and Doneraile (Co. Cork); and James J. Kavanagh, Martin Breen, and H.K. Campbell, all of whom, as already discussed, had small circuits north and south of the border.[44]

By way of conclusion, the document reported that it was the minister's intention to establish an interdepartmental committee with representatives from the departments of finance, education, justice, external affairs, and any other departments that might be concerned with film exhibition and distribution, to examine cinema ownership in Ireland and the control of film distribution in the country. It was also envisaged that the committee would recommend the controls, if any, which might be imposed on the film trade.

The revived interest in the ownership and control of Irish exhibition one year after Rank's most recent cinema acquisitions was not prompted solely by the department of industry and commerce seeking to apply some undefined anti-monopoly competition laws to the film business, but by clerical pressure on the government to act decisively against non-Catholic foreign business interests. Following a discussion by the Catholic hierarchy on foreign ownership of cinemas, the joint secretary to the Catholic hierarchy, James Staunton, bishop of Ferns, wrote to the taoiseach, John A. Costello, on 21 April 1950 reporting that the bishops were 'grave[ly] concern[ed]' at the increasing control of Irish cinemas by monopolies.

> They are especially concerned at the fact that these monopolies, which exercise so great an influence over the minds of the youth, forming the outlook of very many, are in the hands of persons who are not Irish nationals and of persons whose outlook is entirely alien to the religious and moral convictions of the Irish people.[45]

The taoiseach, having assured Bishop Staunton on 25 April that 'the matter [would] receive full consideration',[46] referred the letter four weeks later to the department of industry and commerce[47] for comment. On 16 June, industry and commerce replied to the department of the taoiseach in a memorandum, which detailed the extent of foreign ownership of Irish cinemas and reported that the Irish Provincial Cinema Owners' Association (the new name for the Association of Provincial Exhibitors) and others had complained to the minister regarding 'the formation of combines to control cinema circuits.' The complaint was not just against Rank's Irish exhibition interests, but Rank's distribution interests that gave the company control over films from five of the principal foreign film production companies. Though these companies were not specified, they would have included Universal Studios in which Rank had a stake and whose productions were usually released on the Rank circuits; 20th Century-Fox with which Rank had close ties and, of course, Rank's own production units which distributed overseas through Eagle-Lion Distributors Ltd. As a result of Rank's control of distribution, Irish independent renters complained that it was 'very difficult for [them] to secure the patronage of a large number of exhibitors.'

Referring directly to Bishop Staunton's letter, industry and commerce highlighted the absence of concern by the clergy regarding the impact that the increasing monopolization within the sector would have on Irish trading and commerce. However, it went on to observe that if the clergy's ultimate interest lay in film content and censorship, no 'specific complaint [had been made] about the character or quality of the films exhibited', nor any suggestion made concerning the issue.[48] Though not commented upon within the document, the letter is marked by a curious and logically unsound perspective that deems foreign ownership of Irish cinemas problematic even though the films, which non-nationals screened, were similar to those being shown in Irish-owned venues. While this might indicate a naive belief that Irish exhibition, if undiluted by foreigners, could affect the product via booking and programming patterns, it might also point to the deliberate blindness regarding the cultural and ideological importance of the films themselves given that Ireland, unlike Britain, or, indeed, any number of European countries did not even attempt to create a product to rival American cinema. Interestingly, at no point does the letter address the question of what should be shown in Irish cinemas. Indeed, had the focus switched to the films themselves, and the clergy actually influenced a prohibition on morally corrupting or non-Catholic films, undoubtedly, the issue of cinema ownership would have been replaced by falling admission figures and cinema closures. The eight-month American boycott of British exhibition in protest against the 1947–8 penal tax on film imports provides a useful context. Taking the benchmark of the 1946 figure for cinema admissions, the figure for 1947 dropped by 173 million, or almost 10 per cent, on 1946, to the lowest level in six years.[49]

In any case, the matter was academic as following the cabinet's consideration of the industry and commerce memo on 15 September 1950, no action was taken in respect of film distribution and exhibition, or, for that matter, with regard to Bishop Staunton's letter, other than the decision, for the time being, not to reply to it. Within a few months, the inter-party government was breaking up and Fianna Fáil returned to power following the general election of May 1951. Though a coalition government similar to that of 1948–51 was in power again during 1954–7, no intervention in the film exhibition or distribution markets was contemplated, except that, by now, a decade after Britain, Irish cinema audiences began to decline from 1956 onwards. By then, Rank, which had augmented to nineteen its southern Irish cinema portfolio with the opening in 1954 of the Grand Cinema, Whitehall[50] – its first designed and built cinema in the country – had become active in Northern Ireland.

In the wake of the decline in cinema admissions in Britain, by 1953 Rank had reduced its cinemas to 550, 57 cinemas below what it was legally permitted to control, but its overseas' cinema portfolio had increased dramatically to include 642 foreign cinemas of which 18 were located in the Irish Republic (though by the end of July 1954 this had increased to 19); 136 in South Africa; 133 in Australia; 120 in New Zealand; 103 in Canada; 66 in Ceylon; 31 in the West Indies; 17 in Holland; 17 in Malaya and Singapore; and one in Portugal. In 1955–56 through its umbrella company CMA Rank 'embarked on a buying spree of ... existing cinemas on a scale not seen since the war years.'[51] Part of this expansion was into Northern Ireland, where the company established Odeon (Northern Ireland) Ltd in February 1955 to purchase the twelve cinemas operated under Irish Theatres Ltd and owned by George Lodge, who subsequently stayed on as Rank's managing director. Seven of the cinemas were in Belfast; these included the 800-seat Alhambra; 900-seat Coliseum;[52] 1,250-seat Forum; 808-seat New Princess; 1,000-seat Mount Pottinger Picturedrome; 1,400-seat Stadium; and 1,000-seat Tivoli (renamed the Gaumont in 1961), Finaghy, which was in the process of being built and opened on 17 June 1955. The provincial cinemas were the 950-seat Palladium, Coleraine; 800-seat Regal, Enniskillen; 900-seat Regal, Larne; 650-seat Picture House, Lisburn, and 409-seat Palladium, Portstewart.[53] In December 1956, Rank took a majority shareholding in Curran Theatres, the province's most important circuit, buying eleven of its twelve cinemas. (The twelfth – the 800-seat Frontier, Newry – reverted, according to its lease, to Irish National Foresters in 1957.) Four of these cinemas were provincial venues located in Bangor (2,001-seat Tonic), Portrush (700-seat Majestic), and Derry (1,077-seat Strand, renamed the Odeon in 1958, and 850-seat Midland Cinema), while the remaining seven were in Belfast and included the 900-seat Apollo; 1,275-seat Astoria; 1,380-seat Broadway; 1,000-seat Capitol; 950-seat Lyceum; 1,380-seat Regal; and the first-run 850-seat Regent (from 1947; formerly Belfast Picture House, Royal Avenue) which Rank had attempted to buy from Sydney Smyllie's Barrow Trust Ltd for a six-figure sum in July 1946.[54] Though a price of £500,000 was put on the Curran deal, a value similar to that paid for the Lodge cinemas, given that Rank was planning to sell back to the company 'a number of [unspecified] associated interests', in real terms, the sum was significantly reduced.[55]

The acquisition of the Curran venues, which brought Rank's Northern Ireland cinema seat total from a low in 1949 of only 1,807 seats in one cinema[56] to 25,037 across twenty-four cinemas, secured Rank's position as the province's dominant exhibitor. It also served, if somewhat belatedly, to confirm northern Irish exhibitors' fears of a foreign invasion of the sector which had come to the fore following Rank's investment in the Elliman chain in 1946. In language not dissimilar to that employed in the south, *Kine Weekly* had reported that northern exhibitors were

> preparing a secret plan of campaign to combat possible infiltration tactics by cross-channel invaders. What with this concerted opposition and the difficulties in obtaining building permits, it is anticipated they will be able to cope with prospective buyers, either of kinemas or sites.[57]

Clearly, they were not able to cope and perhaps were even more marginalized than their Dublin (and Irish Republic) counterparts. By the end of 1961, Rank, which by this time had added Belfast's Royal Hippodrome (renamed the Odeon) to its portfolio,[58] together with ABC, which owned seven cinemas, had a total of 34,377 seats, many of which were in the most lucrative cinemas. Indeed ABC's assets included Belfast's 2,219-seat Ritz, the province's premier cinema. ABC's other cinemas were located in Belfast (the 1,369-seat Majestic and 1,141-seat Strand); Derry (the 800-seat Palace and 800-seat Rialto, which was rebuilt as the 1,166-seat ABC in 1960); Armagh town (the 782-seat Ritz); and Newtownards, Co. Down (the 713-seat Ritz). In the Republic also, these two groups represented a significant proportion of the exhibition market having as they did a combined total of twenty-two cinemas (or just under 30,000 seats). In addition to the Rank and ABC deals already discussed, in 1959 ABC took over Dublin's 1,996-seat Carlton thus establishing the Adelphi-Carlton group of cinemas. The Carlton not only gave ABC a second city-centre first-run outlet, but also considerably raised the total of its southern Irish cinema seats to 5,893. Though the value of all these, often first-run, cinemas is impossible to quantify because of an absence of data, the two groups, as early as the mid-1950s, probably accounted for over half the all-Ireland exhibition market. It was an unassailable position that would only be weakened when the decline in cinema audiences transformed both companies in the 1960s.

CINEMA TAXATION

The first United Kingdom taxation on cinema films was introduced in September 1915 through the Finance (New Duties) Act, whereby an import duty of 1*d*. per foot[59] was charged to distributors, who invariably passed some or all of this cost on to the exhibitors. Since the British produced so little film,[60] exhibitors had no option but to rely on imported, predominantly American film, and incur the extra expense.[61] When Ireland became a separate entity for taxation in 1922, the Irish Free State government retained the import tax on an annually renewed basis until it was established as a permanent duty in the 1932 Finance Act, though from 1925 educational films were exempted from the tax. In the Finance Act of 1931 the 1*d*. per foot rate was trebled for sound films, though news films, silent films, and films 7/10 inch/16mm or less in width (also known as substandard film), remained at 1*d*. per foot. Unsurprisingly, the amount collected in 1932, a transition year to sound films, was double that of 1931, while by 1936, when the amount had risen to £60,408, it was three times the early 1930s figure. As noted, this duty, except in the case of news film, was passed on by distributors to exhibitors by way of a surcharge on a film's first week's box office income (10 per cent on American films and 6.66 per cent on British films).[62] While the 1939 Finance Act excluded from duty films imported for screening by the Irish Film Society, a further concession was introduced in 1946 whereby a second copy (though only a second, and not subsequent prints), could be imported at half the rate charged, presumably as a means of more quickly exploiting a film, but also, perhaps, a recognition that the physical quality of a single print would be very poor by the time it was shown countrywide. In response to the exhibitors' and distributors' anti-cinema tax campaigns in the 1950s, the duty was abolished in the 1958 Finance Act and, consequently, the distributors' surcharge to exhibitors, which was then 7.5 per cent, was abolished with effect from 8 May 1958.

As discussed in chapter 1, in 1916, entertainments tax (ET), which set a tax on admission prices to public entertainments, was introduced as another wartime revenue-generating measure by the Westminster parliament, though it was to remain in place for more than forty years. Even though the tax served to magnify the financial difficulties of British exhibitors, some of whom were forced to cease trading, the government, while maintaining it after the war, finally succumbed to lobbying pressure by the British Entertainments Tax Abolition League and reduced the rate on the cheapest seats, such that in 1924 the earlier 2d. tax free rate was increased to 6d. tax free, while duty on payments over that amount up to and including 1s. 3d. was reduced.[63]

Just as the Irish Free State government had adopted the British customs duty on film, so, too, did it retain ET, but without modifying it downward, as happened in 1924 in Britain. Northern Ireland's parliament, which had limited revenue-gathering functions, also implemented the entertainment tax and though it pledged that its taxation would be the same as Britain's, it did not follow the British Labour government's adjustment. Finance Minister Hugh Pollock said that to introduce equivalent relief in the province would involve a loss of revenue of approximately £45,000 per annum, and while he would have liked to follow the lead of the British chancellor of the exchequer, 'owing to the financial position in which we stand at present by reason of the uncertainty regarding our commitments in connection with the Special Constabulary, we do not propose to grant the remission in Northern Ireland.'[64] James Augustine Duff, an MP for the ruling Ulster Unionist Party in working-class East Belfast, responded by declaring that it was 'a little bit unfortunate that the first sacrifice that has been demanded' from the Northern Ireland parliament was 'going to fall on the lowest standard' in the province. He went on to point out that those who, like himself, knew Belfast, 'know that the great masses of our industrial people go to entertainments that do not reach a higher figure than sixpence.'[65] MP and cinema director Sir Crawford McCullagh added that 'the matter has caused widespread dissatisfaction.'[66]

The differentiation was spelt out in the Northern Ireland parliament the following year when Pollock rejected an amendment, defeated twenty-two to eight, to the finance bill to bring Northern Ireland's rates into line with those in Britain. At that time, in Britain, there was no tax up to and including 6*d.*, whereas in Northern Ireland, a 2.5*d.* ticket had 0.5*d.* added in tax; a 3*d.* to 4*d.* ticket attracted 1*d.* tax; and 4.5*d.* to 5*d.* had 1.5*d.* added in tax. While seats costing 7*d.* to 1*s.* in Britain had 2*d.* tax added, in Northern Ireland, such seats had a 3*d.* tax rate. With regard to the 1*s.* to 1*s.* 3*d.* ticket price range, Britain applied 3*d.* in tax, whereas the Northern Ireland administration added 4*d.* Warning that cinema employment would become seasonal – with the summer months particularly vulnerable during good weather – Belfast North MP for the Northern Ireland Labour Party, Samuel Kyle,[67] sought concessions for both cinemas and football clubs. Indeed, a theme of debates on ET during the 1920s and 1930s was the disproportionate burden of such taxation on working class patrons of entertainments and sport. Kyle was supported by veteran politician and leader of the Nationalist Party of Northern Ireland, the MP for West Belfast, Joseph Devlin, who had abstained from the Stormont parliament until the 1925 general election held five weeks earlier. In a dispiriting time for northern nationalist politicians and their constituents, Devlin largely confined himself to promoting the interests of working-class Catholics, something reflected in his comments on the role of the cinema and football in the community:

> I have a sneaking regard for these picture houses and I am anxious to see them encouraged. As football is the sport of the working classes so the picture houses are the centres of joy and amusement for the poorer classes. I see women with shawls, who would not for the world go to the centre of the city to attend a theatre, going to them, and I see little barefooted children getting in for 2*d.* or 3*d.*, and sometimes for 1*d.* In their grey and grim lives they witness very little joy and for this reason some of them go to these places and enjoy a couple of hours seeing a good story …

> Many of these picture houses are centres of a very educative character, educative in the sense that those who go there see foreign countries and witness representations of scenes that would never otherwise come before their eyes. The pictures lift them … out of the grim and grey existence which they are called upon to live in the squalid and wretched homes which are so blighting an influence upon the character and virtue of otherwise good and kindly people. What sort of mean taxation is it that makes these people out of their inadequate wage, out of their dole, pay this penny upon an entrance fee of 4*d.*? I do not think it can be justified.[68]

If there should be a tax, Devlin argued, it should be a tax on profits and not a tax on entrance, adding that 'if a poor woman' goes to a cinema in Belfast she should pay precisely what she would pay in Manchester, Liverpool, London, or Glasgow, because 'if England was generous, Belfast Britons would be put in the same position as British Britons.'[69]

Pollock replied by declaring that although he had never given any undertaking to a trade delegation to align Northern Ireland's ET with that of Britain, he was 'perfectly willingly' to make all Northern Ireland's services the same as Britain's but 'within the limits of [the North's] financial resources.'[70] To make all entrance fees under 6*d.* free of tax would cost £22,000, while to fully align Northern Ireland rates with those in Britain would cost £45,000. The minister went on to explain that even if the £45,000 was rebated, cinema patrons would not actually benefit because, as he had been told 'perfectly straightforward[ly]' by the exhibitors, it was their intention in the event of a tax reduction not to pass on any savings but to keep the money which they felt justified in doing given the 'parlous condition' of their sector in which 'too many picture houses … [were] not making money.' Indeed, where relief had been given in Britain it had been taken as 'a subsidy' by exhibitors and did not benefit cinemagoers.[71] Pollock continued to reject any ET concessions in 1926 because of the 'graver conditions' existing in Northern Ireland, and 'our extreme [financial] necessities'.[72]

Though the White Cinema Club continued to agitate for tax parity with Britain, it was not until 1927 that exhibitors in Northern Ireland finally benefited from the ET concessions granted by the British government in 1924, though an attempt to extend the concessions in the British house of commons had been defeated in 1926. In the 1927 Northern Ireland budget Pollock abolished ET on tickets priced 6*d.* or less, at a cost to the exchequer of £28,000 in 1927 (or £35,000 in a full year).[73] The motivation for this was that due to the 'internecine competition' in Belfast in particular where there were 'too many cinemas', and the fact that small cinemas in the poorer parts of Northern Ireland's cities and those that catered for workers in the country were 'beyond question going through a difficult time', with 'most of them' not able to 'make ends meet'.[74] He added that exhibitors 'have to pay so much for their films, [it was] out of all proportion to the receipts they get.'[75] Nevertheless, Pollock defended ET as 'one of the fairest taxes that has ever been devised' on the basis that it was a 'universal tax' which was to be found throughout Europe and America. He went on to state that it was a tax on those 'who seek amusement', and, betraying a puritan streak, added that 'as such [it] is justifiable on every ground.'

Pollock proposed that ET 'should not be placed on the healthy outdoor instincts of our people', but the concession he offered in this area was narrow and class-based, as it excluded outdoor sports that involved horses, dogs or other animals, or mechanically propelled vehicles. Thus, one of the main beneficiaries of the dispensation was the predominantly middle-class game of rugby, which, according to the minister, a man attends not 'so much for amusement as to cheer his friends and encourage his team to victory.'[76] This social bias was seized on by Joseph Devlin, who regarded it as 'a most damaging attack on footballers' since the minister drew a distinction between one class of footballers and another, adding that 'as long as the common people follow what is known as Soccer no consideration ought to be given to them, but when people engaged in Rugby, the physical exercise of the aristocracy, then the conscience of [Pollock] is touched.'[77] Devlin was, perhaps, a surprising champion of exhibitors when he continued to argue in 1928 for the abolition of ET on both cinemas and theatres because competition was 'so great that hardly any of them are able to make ends meet.'

1 Irish film exhibitors gathered at Dublin's Gresham Hotel on the occassion of the visit on 26 January 1939 of Adolph Zukor, president of Paramount Films, during which gifts were presented to him by Leonard Ging, president of ITCA. The picture includes left to right *front row*: Chris Sylvester (Curragh Camp cinema), P.J. Whelan (Associated Pictures Houses Ltd), David Rose (managing director, Paramount, Great Britain), Adolph Zukor, Leonard Ging, Maurice Elliman (Metropole & Allied Cinemas), J. Cloran, John J. Farrell (Dublin Kinematograph Co. [1920], Ltd); *second row*: J.M. Putapish, Patrick Farrell (secretary, Dublin Kinematograph Co.), F.J. McDonnell (chairman and managing director, Green Cinema), P.G. O'Toole, Kevin C. McCourt (secretary, TCA), C.W. Chambers, Abe Elliman (manager, Metropole, Dublin), Walter McNally (manager, RKO Pictures, Dublin), J. McGrath (manager, Theatre Royal), G. Rithie [Richie?] (manager, Paramount, Dublin); *back row*: J.R. Pearse [J.E. Pearce?] (Irish Cinemas Ltd), T.J. Cogan (manager, Carlton, Dublin), F. Farrell, J. Pilis, Max Elliman (manager, Corinthian). (Photo and list from Liam O'Leary collection, NLI. Note that some have not been identified while the status of others is unknown.)

2 Film exhibitor Frank W. Chambers who was one of the co-founders with George Peter Fleming of both the Carlton, Upper Sackville/O'Connell Street, which opened at the end of December 1915, and La Scala Theatre and Opera House, Princes Street, which opened in August 1920. An entertainment entrepreneur, previously, he was the lessee of the Skating Rink, Rotunda Gardens, and owner of several billiard rooms.

3 Northern Ireland distributor John Yeats Moore (*left*) delivering films by car *c*.1913. Not only did he screen films from 1908 at Belfast's St George's Hall, High Street, but co-owned through Irish Electric Palaces Ltd, the Regal Cinema, Larne, and later became chairman of Irish Theatres Ltd, which vied with Michael Curran's cinemas as the province's largest local circuit.

4 Photograph of English-born Norman Whitten who came to Ireland in 1912 and subsequently established General Film Supply, the only integrated production and distribution company in Ireland in the pre-sound era. In addition to producing Irish newsreel material, notably through its *Irish Events* newsreel series (1917–20), the company made innovative documentaries, Ireland's first animated film (*Ten Days Leave*, 1917), and in 1920 Whitten's own feature film, *In the Days of St Patrick*. He returned to England in the late 1920s.

5 Michael J. Tighe, manager of Cork's first custom-built cinema, the Coliseum, from its opening in 1913 to c.1925, seen here filming local events in Cork, 1920. Previous to managing the Coliseum he had been in charge of Cobh's Imperial Cinema.

Early film exhibitors in Ireland as illustrated in the first Irish trade publication *Irish Limelight* during 1917 and 1918. These are Izidore Isaac Bradlaw, Princess Cinema, Rathmines, Dublin (6); J.J. King, Phibsboro' Picture House, Dublin (7); Frederick A. Sparling, Bohemian Cinema, Phibsborough, Dublin (8); Cathal McGarvey, manager, Phoenix Picture Palace, Ellis Quay, Dublin (9); Alex McEwan who had cinemas in Cork, Limerick and Waterford (10); and J.E. MacDermott, proprietor, The Picture House, Quinsboro' Road, Bray, Co. Wicklow (11).

12 James T. Jameson, through his Irish Animated Picture Company, established film exhibition as a popular entertainment at Dublin's Rotunda during the 1900s and 1910s. This cartoon was featured in the British film trade journal *Bioscope* in 1912.

13 Michael Curran (*c*.1872–1940) was the principal figure in Curran Theatres Ltd, which, established in 1934, was the second most important indigenous circuit in Northern Ireland. By the time of his death in 1940 Curran Theatres had ten cinemas, six of which were in Belfast. The circuit, which included Bangor's *Tonic*, one of the island's largest cinemas, and Belfast's Lyceum, the first Northern Ireland cinema to show fully synchronous sound films, was noted for its quality cinemas and mostly catered to a (lower) middle-class suburban audience.

14 A.D. Coon, prioprietor of Coon's Travelling Cinema, one of the many travelling exhibitors that toured Ireland up to and including the 1950s. Apart from James T. Jameson's Irish Animated Picture Co., which began its tours in the early 1900s, other important exhibitors included the Ormonde family from Kilkenny, while in the north and northwest of the country the Daniels family was active. From the late 1910s to at least the mid-1920s, Coon owned and managed the *Picture House* in Letterkenny, Co. Donegal.

15 James Horgan with his son Joseph are pictured beside a lantern-cum-cinematograph projector in *Horgan's Picture Theatre*, Friar Street, Youghal, Co. Cork, which was opened on 23 December 1917 by James Horgan with his brothers Thomas and Philip.

16 In the pre-sound era, live musical accompaniment in cinemas was the norm and ranged from the single pianist in smaller and regional cinemas to substantial orchestras in large urban first-run venues. Often the musical director and some performers were paid the same or more than senior cinema staff, including the manager and chief projectionist. Horgan's small orchestral group would have been typical of most mid-sized cinemas. Following the introduction of sound, approximately 500 musicians were displaced in Ireland, though many of the larger cinemas retained an organist.

17 Staff outside the Dorset Picture Hall, 1910s. Note the military-style braided uniforms of the commission-aires complete with peaked caps and epaulettes. Other staff such as managers, ticket sellers and page boys generally did not wear uniforms, though in most cinemas ushers often did. The posters in the background highlight the twice-weekly change of programme and the cinema's 'popular' (or cheap) pricing policy.

18 Cinema queue outside Dublin's Corinthian, Eden Quay, for Fritz Lang's *Metropolis* (1927). Notwithstanding the crowds, the end of the 1920s saw the cinema (designed by Thomas MacNamara), trade at a loss. It was sold in 1930 to Maurice Elliman, George Nesbitt and P.A. Corrigan who redecorated it and installed sound. It closed in 1993.

19 Cinema queue outside the Metropole, O'Connell Street, opened in February 1922 by Maurice Elliman and partners. *The Sheik Steps Out* (Irving Pichel, 1937) starred Mexican sex symbol Ramon Novarro and Lola Lane. Despite the famous Dublin queue, as statistician Thekla Beere explained in the 1930s, it was generally for the cheaper seats only, given that the depressed incomes of many Dubliners would not have stretched to the expensive seats which often remained empty. She estimated annual admissions across the country's 190 cinemas at 18.25 million, with Dublin accounting for about 60 per cent of the southern Irish box office.

20 Dr John Charles McQuaid, archbishop of Dublin from 1941 to 1972. He played a pivotal role in establishing the National Film Institute of Ireland during 1943–45 as an exclusively Catholic organization with its terms of reference informed by the 1936 papal encyclical on the cinema, *Vigilanti cura*. He became patron of the institute in 1947, a position he retained until his death in 1973.

21 Limerick-born Jesuit Fr Richard S. Devane was the most consistent Catholic cleric, who, despite his agitation for stricter standards of censorship, promoted the potentionally positive role which cinema could play in Ireland and in the 1930s and 1940s campaigned for the establishment of a national film institute. Influenced by the papal policy of vocationalism as expressed in the 1931 encyclical *Rerum novarum,* he imagined such an organization as being state supported and interdominational, but Catholic led.

22 Meeting of the council, or board, of the National Film Insitute of Ireland, in 1954 on the occassion of the first annual general meeting to be held at their new premises, 65 Harcourt Street, Dublin. *Left to right*: Áine Ní Chanainn, Patrick J. O'Hagan, Dermot O'Flynn, Joseph Murphy (vice-chair), James C. Fagan (chair), Francis B. Ryan (secretary), Pádraig Ó Nualláin, H.J. Healy, and J.J. Jennings.

23 Members of the Irish Film Society in 1937. Front: Denis Johnston, May Carey, Roisin Walsh, Sean O Meadhra. Back: P.J. Fitzsimons, Liam O'Leary, Geoffrey Dalton. Though initially established with the aim of screening aesthetical rich non-mainstream films, its activities expanded during the 1940s with the establishment of a school of film technique, a children's film committee and the publication of the journal *Scannán*. In 1977 the society was reformed as the Federation of Irish Film Societies, which in turn was reformed in 2001 as access>CINEMA.

24 A 1990 photograph of Michael Hannigan (*left*, then co-director of the Cork Film Festival and later founder of the *Kino* art cinema, Cork) and David Kavanagh (*right*, then director of the Irish Film Institute) with Liam O'Leary (*centre*). Born in Youghal, Co. Cork O'Leary (1910–92) not only co-founded the Irish Film Society in 1936 and was central to promoting a viable alternative film culture in Ireland, but also contributed greatly to the preservation of Irish film material through his archival activities.

25 Author Kevin Rockett (then chairman of the Irish Film Institute) with statistician, public servant and film society activist Thekla Beere, photographed outside the Light House Cinema, Abbey Street, Dublin, in 1990, on the occasion of Liam O'Leary's eightieth birthday. Beere was responsible for the first authoritative study of Irish film exhibition and distribution which was carried out during 1934–5.

26 In 1956 Dermot Breen, manager of Cork's Palace Theatre from 1956 and Ireland's film censor from 1972 to his death in 1978, instigated the Cork Film Festival, Ireland's first such festival, as a means of generating tourism. The appointment in 1986 of Michael Hannigan and Theo Dorgan as co-directors of the festival transformed it into a culturally important event within both the national and international film calendar.

27 Michael Dwyer's contribution to film in Ireland began with his developement of the Tralee Film Society and his subsequent efforts in establishing, from 1977, the new Federation of Irish Film Societies. In 1985, by then a journalist writing on film for the *Irish Times*, he co-founded Dublin's first film festival, which he programmed until 1991. Following its demise in 2001, in 2003 Dwyer established another successful non-competitive festival, the Dublin International Film Festival. He died in 2010.

28 The crowd outside Cork's Savoy Cinema during the inaugural 1956 Cork Film Festival gives a clear indication of the popularity of the event at which the attendance of film stars became a particular attraction for locals and the media.

29 Dublin-born actor Colin Farrell meeting the press at the 2010 Dublin International Film Festival on the occassion of the screening of Neil Jordan's *Ondine* in which he stars. Gráinne Humphreys took over as festival director from Michael Dwyer in 2008.

30 Galway Film Fleadh (gaelic for festival) began in 1989 and was the result of the combined efforts of local film activists Lelia Doolan and Miriam Allen supported by filmmaker Bob Quinn, animator Steve Woods, and Galway Film Society's Joe McMahon. Unlike most large festivals, it has an intimate and convivial atmosphere which facilities the easy mixing of film industry personnel and audiences. It has become an important showcase for young film-makers and animators, particularly from Ireland, and since its beginning has included discussion and workshop strands. The locating of the re-established Irish Film Board to Galway in 1993 has added to the festival's relevance.

31 Leo Ward being presented with a Dublin International Film Festival Volta award in 2008 by James Morris, chair of the Irish Film Board, in recognition of his work in Irish film exhibition and distribution since the 1940s. Together with his business partner, half brother Kevin Anderson, and subsequently both of their families, he has been the dominant film exhibitor in Ireland since the 1960s.

32 Film and theatrical impresario Louis Elliman with film director Cecil B. De Mille (*left*) during a trip to Hollywood. Son of pioneering film exhibitor in Ireland, Maurice Elliman, not only was Louis behind the opening of two of Ireland's architecturally most important modern cinemas, the Ritzes in Athlone and Clonmel, but he was also one of the investors in the establishment of Ardmore Studios in 1958.

33 Kevin Anderson pictured in 2004 outside Dublin's priemer cinema, the Savoy, which is owned by the Ward Anderson group. Kevin Anderson and his half brother Leo Ward entered the film business in the 1940s and have since established themselves and their respective familes, now including a third generation of exhibitors, as the dominant film exhibition group in Ireland and, through the Empire chain, the fifth largest in Britain.

34 Independent exhibitor Albert Kelly outside his Classic, Harold's Cross, Dublin, a venue which became famous for screening the cult film *The Rocky Horror Picture Show* (1975) every Friday night for twenty-three years from 1980 to 2003.

35 Exhibitor Paul Ward, son of Leo Ward, has been central to developing the family's Irish Multiplex Cinemas (IMC) brand.

36 Exhibitor Paul Anderson, son of Kevin Anderson, has developed the second main Ward Anderson brand, the Omniplex circuit. In the latter part of the 2000s, a third Ward Anderson brand, the Empire, was developed in Britain and Northern Ireland following the purchase of London's Leicester Square Empire.

37 Veteran independent exhibitors Ossie Spurling (*left*) and Andrew O'Gorman joined forces to establish the high quality Movies@ chain with multiplexes in the Dublin suburb of Dundrum (2005) and at Swords, Co. Dublin (2006).

38 Northern Ireland independent exhibitor Michael McAdam, who in 1990 founded the Movie House chain, with the north's first multiplex. By 2010 the company had thirty-nine screens across five multiplexes located at Belfast (Dublin Road and City Side/Yorkgate), Glengormley, Maghera and Coleraine; employed over 200 people; and had a turnover of over £10 million.

39 A window display of tie-in items to Al Jolson's *The Singing Fool* (1928) which was playing at Dublin's Capitol from 22 April 1929, and opened at Belfast's Picture House a week later. A popular success that helped to establish the new sound medium, the part-talkie with musical interludes attracted 100,000 patrons during its first two weeks at the Capitol, while 12,000 attended during its first five days at Cork's Pavilion, which was the city's first cinema adapted for sound.

40 Reflecting the development of a more informed film culture, the Irish Film Institute included a specialist film and media book and DVD shop in its Eustace Street premises which opened in 1992. With the redevelopment of the complex in 2010, when an extra screening room was added, the shop was enlarged and moved to its current position.

Furthermore, 'in this period of trade depression', and with people living in 'wretched slums', cinemas were 'of tremendous value to the public'.[78] Despite Devlin's entreaties, Pollock justified the continuation of the tax because of 'our necessities'.[79]

In 1929 in an exchange of correspondence with Northern Ireland Prime Minister Viscount Craigavon, the White Cinema Club, which was seeking parity with Britain with regard to ET rates, was told that no further concessions would be entertained as the present rate was based on the exigencies of the Northern Ireland economy, and, anyway, the exhibitors were passing on the tax to their patrons, a view also expressed by the minister for finance.[80] Despite this rebuff, the organization continued to press for a compromise, seeking the abolition of ET on admissions up to 1s. or at least its reduction to the British level. To this end, it held a meeting in March 1930 with the finance minister, Pollock, ahead of that year's budget.[81] However, by 1931, given that the minister was 'reaping such a rich harvest' from cinemas, the exhibitors decided it 'would be a waste of time and energy to pursue the matter' until the economy improved.[82] They were already concerned that Pollock might follow the Free State's example and introduce even more penal cinema taxes, something that did not occur.[83] Even though British ET rates increased in 1931, the Northern Ireland ET tax on a 1s. seat was still 0.5d. more than the British rate.[84]

Prompted by the 1924 success of the British anti-ET campaign, Irish Free State exhibitors pressed to have ET reduced. In March 1926 a delegation of exhibitors consisting of P.J. Munden, Fountain Picture House; Eric Nolan, Corinthian Picture Palace; George Kay, Rotunda; I.I. Bradlaw, Olympia; and Mr Kennedy, secretary of ITCA, met the minister for finance, Ernest Blythe, and argued that a reduction in the cheaper rates would not adversely affect government revenue as an increase in audience numbers following such a tax reduction (as had happened in Britain in 1924), would compensate. They unfavourably compared the Irish Free State's ET rates, whereby 1d. to 2.5d. seats attracted a 0.5d. tax; 3d. to 4d. seats, a 1d. tax; 4.5d. seats, a 1.5d. tax; and 5d. to 6d. seats a 2d. tax,[85] to Northern Ireland, where, as noted above, seats below 6d. were taxed, but not quite as high as in the Free State, and Britain where seats of 6d. and less incurred no tax at all. Rates only aligned between the three jurisdictions on seats of 1s. 3d. to 1s. 6d. when tax was set at 4d. When Blythe, who, according to *Bioscope*, believed there were already too many people engaged in the industry, did not respond sympathetically, the exhibitors threatened to use their screens to agitate against the tax, something which did not occur until 1948. Recognizing that the delegation did not include any of the major Irish first-run exhibitors, such as J.J. Farrell or the Ellimans, *Bioscope* called on exhibitors to mount a similar campaign to that employed by their British counterparts, advising that

> If the exhibitors of the Free State have the strength and pluck to utilise the screens throughout the country as a medium for educating their audiences to the true facts of the case, [then] it will probably not take officialdom very long to realise the fact that, where there are legitimate and glaring grievances of this sort, it is highly advisable to do something to lessen them.[86]

The independent Irish government finally abolished tax on tickets costing 4*d.* or less from 17 July 1928, and though this led in 1929 to a reduction in ET revenue of £15,855, approximately a 10 per fall on the previous year, such that 1929 represented the lowest figure ever, by the following year, it recovered to just under the amount raised in 1927. Despite this and the fact that small reductions on other priced seats were made in October 1931,[87] the first half of the 1930s saw ET being used as an increasingly important source of exchequer revenue with the amendments of 1935, operational from August of that year, seeing nearly all rates increase on seats priced 6.5*d.* and higher. Such were the increases, which ranged from 50 per cent – the mean increase – to as much as 125 per cent,[88] that a reduction in rates had to be made the following year in order to combat the decline in audience numbers.[89] Nevertheless, the upward trend of revenue extracted continued throughout the decade with marked rises in 1936 and 1937.[90]

By July 1936, following the most recent ET adjustments (in October 1935 and July 1936), significant differences existed between the Free State and Northern Ireland. For example, in Northern Ireland no tax was charged on seats priced 6*d.* and under, while in the Free State, only seats 4*d.* and under were exempt from tax with seats priced 4.5*d.* to 6*d.* all carrying a 1.5*d.* tax; there was no difference on a 9*d.* seat which attracted a 3*d.* tax in both jurisdictions; a 1*s.* seat in Northern Ireland had a 3*d.* tax, but in the Free State it had a 6*d.* tax; while the contrast in the tax between north and south became even more pronounced with regard to the more expensive seats. Despite this advantage over the south, Northern Ireland exhibitors continued to agitate to be put on a par with their British counterparts, who enjoyed even lower rates of ET,[91] and in 1940, following the outbreak of the Second World War, this finally happened. However, it was far from the hoped-for reductions; indeed, it was very much the contrary.

In July 1940, the British chancellor of the exchequer increased ET rates such that 3*d.* to 5*d.* tickets attracted a 0.5*d.* tax; and those priced 5*d.* to 6.25*d.*, had 0.75*d.* tax added.[92] Within two weeks, Northern Ireland's minister for finance, J.M. Andrews, had adopted the new rates with effect from 6 October 1940. This decision resulted in the amount collected from ET increasing from £77,286 in 1940[93] to over £150,000 in 1941. Less than two years later, the British chancellor, once again adjusted rates upward raising a further £14 million in a full year, 90 per cent of which was from the cinema.[94] Though the Northern Ireland rates did not follow this lead, when the British chancellor turned again in April 1943 to cinema patrons to extract more tax,[95] the Northern Ireland government copied the rates.[96] The result was that a seat at the popular price of 8*d.* attracted a 3.5*d.*, or 43.75 per cent, tax, with the more expensive seat prices being more heavily taxed. Consequently, the amount collected from ET in Northern Ireland grew five-fold during 1941 to 1945, by which time ET revenue was £751,790. While 1945 remained the high point for ET revenue, even as late as 1957, five years before the tax was abolished, the amount collected was still a considerable £675,957.

Though the significant increases in southern Irish ET rates in 1935 magnified further the tax inequities between Irish Free State exhibitors and those in Britain and, to a lesser extent, Northern Ireland, one of the justifications that the Irish government put forward in relation to their taxation policy was that southern exhibitors did not have to contribute a percentage of Sunday box office income to charity as was the case in the neighbouring jurisdictions, especially in Britain since the reform of Sunday opening in 1932.[97] Nevertheless, the southern government introduced in the 1943 Finance Act a provision exempting from ET events that were devoted to promoting the use of the Irish language providing that their administration costs were less than 30 per cent. However, it was the concessions in relation to 'personal performances' that proved most significant.

As early as 1931 theatres, concert venues, and music halls, including cine-variety, were exempted from ET if more than half the programme comprised of 'personal performances' as such performances were likely to employ Irish artistes. Due to the severe competition it caused in relation to regular cinemas, this concession was amended in the 1936 Finance Act, which limited a full ET exemption to shows featuring 75 per cent or more personal performances, and introduced a half exemption for events comprising of between 35 and 75 per cent personal performances. In the May 1947 budget, in response to the serious economic crisis facing the government and the need to raise extra revenue, ET rates were increased to get an additional £260,000 that year and £400,000 in a full year. In addition, the exemption rate for 'personal performances' was reduced from 50 per cent exemption to 30 per cent, the changes taking effect from 15 August.[98] Five months later, in October 1947, the minister for finance, Frank Aiken, brought in a supplementary budget that further increased ET rates and reduced to 15 per cent the exemption limit for personal performances from 16 January 1948, only a few weeks before a general election.

Aiken claimed during the debate on the 1947 supplementary budget that the new ET scale started at 37.5 per cent tax and increased to 60 per cent tax for the more expensive seats, though this was clearly not the case.[99] When the new 1947 rates are compared to what pertained during 1936–46, the contrast becomes stark. In the case of lower admission prices, a ticket costing less than 4*d.*, which had been exempt from tax since 1928, remained tax-free, but with the second budget in 1947 those costing 4*d.* to 5*d.* had 3*d.* tax added (double the ET rate of 1.5*d.* for the 4*d.* ticket, which had been in place since 1936, including in the first 1947 budget), while the 5*d.* to 6*d.* ticket attracted a 4*d.* tax. At the other end of the scale, a 2*s.* ticket, which attracted a 1*s.* 1.5*d.* tax during 1936 to 1946, following the second 1947 budget had a tax of 4*s.* 6*d.* (or 225 per cent) added to the price of the ticket.[1]

Opposition attacks on the measures focused on how the extra tax would impact on the lives of poor people in both urban and rural areas. 'I have met old people', the leader of the National Labour Party, James Everett, a TD for Wicklow, told Aiken, 'who often go to the 4*d.* seats on a Sunday night simply and solely because they have no fire or light and they are saved that amount of hardship'.[2] Fine Gael (and former Labour) TD Daniel Morrissey, argued that proportionately the tax 'will bear more heavily on those who are forced to occupy the cheapest seats.' He went on to say 'that after labouring, in a working-class home from [7a.m. to midnight], struggling to rear a family on a wage that cannot keep pace with the cost of living, a woman's sole relaxation is perhaps one visit, or two at the outside, to the local cinema each week.' Unless 'the very poor ... are to be deprived entirely of any little enjoyment', then the ET increases should not be introduced.[3]

One political consequence of the 1947 adjustments of ET was the decision by over 100 exhibitors to screen in January and February of 1948 the anti-government ten-minute party political film, Ireland's first, *Our Country* (1948). Made in support of the socially radical republican party, Clann na Poblachta, the film offered a sustained attack on Fianna Fáil's economic and social polices including those on emigration and housing, though no reference was made to ET.[4] Exhibitors, nevertheless, made audiences aware of ET through notices on their screens informing patrons of the amount of tax paid on each seat price. In addition, the Irish Cinema Association placed advertisements in national newspapers urging people to lobby parliamentary representatives for lower ET rates, while cinemas also distributed petitions pressing the minister for finance to reduce the tax in the next budget. In a February 1948 article on the issue, *Daily Film Renter* reported that O'Connell Street, 'noted for its cinema queues', only had them for the cheapest seats, since 'all higher priced seats are boycotted'.[5]

The increases in ET led to extensive tax evasion with a drop in revenue of £45,701 over the previous year in a period of rising audience levels as exhibitors took advantage of the cine-variety concessions. While prior to the 1947 budgets only 11 out of 360 exhibitors and cine-variety houses (16mm as well as 35mm venues) availed of the personal performance rebate, this jumped to 248 by 1948. In presenting his first finance bill in June 1948, the coalition government finance minister, Patrick McGilligan, described the methods used by exhibitors to achieve this 'very big evasion'. He reported that in the majority of cases the method adopted was to augment the regular cinema show with a pseudo live performance of little or no merit. Though the cinema show would be advertised from 8p.m. to 10p.m., the house would open at 6p.m. from which time until the film was screened someone would strum a banjo or play a piano, usually local amateurs as there were few professional musicians outside the main urban areas. This live portion of the non-integrated show, which would last ten minutes more than the screening time, had a low audience count, and in an instance detailed by McGilligan the audience varied from nil to thirteen while the film show was attended by 120.[6] While with effect from 1 June 1948 McGilligan returned most of the ET rates and personal performance rebates to those introduced in the first budget of 1947 (the exceptions were in the 1s. 4d. to 2s. range as he added 2d. to 3d. extra to the rates introduced in the first 1947 budget), nevertheless, the revenue generated by cinema ET jumped from £524,100 in 1947 (81.7 per cent of total ET) to £791,154 (89.2 per cent of total ET) in 1948, an increase of £267,054, or just under 51 per cent. Reflecting the continuing expansion of cinema audiences during the first half of the 1950s and the impact the 1947 increases continued to have, cinema ET climbed to the high point of £1,397,086 in 1957, by which time cinema ET accounted for 86.9 per cent of the total ET, though in 1954 it reached 97.7 per cent of total ET.[7]

The restoration of the *status quo ante* in June 1948 and the subsequent move away from the quasi-cine-variety format, 'brought a virtual boom of business' for the country's 16mm exhibitors of which there were approximately 300,[8] with several such exhibitors who had closed down because of the effects of the tax, recommencing business. By 1949, many 16mm halls and circuits were reopening, and at least one circuit with five halls was added in Co. Galway.[9] Indeed, in great part, the sector also built on the considerable expansion internationally in the post-war period when 16mm projection equipment and a greater number of feature films in the format became more widely available (and for a fraction of the cost of standard 35mm). One supplier of 16mm equipment, Atlas Cine Supply Co., 50 Lower O'Connell Street, Dublin, advertised the benefits of parish hall cinemas using 16mm because they were 'Free of Tax';[10] there was a ready supply of 'first-class' films; an operator could be trained in a few days; and generators could be used where no electricity existed (as this period predated the installation of electricity throughout rural Ireland). With the decline in box office north and south by the end of the 1950s, such 16mm exhibitors were seen as a threat to full-time regular (35mm) cinemas.[11]

Meanwhile, in April 1948, the British chancellor of the exchequer, responding to the decline in British cinema audiences, and recognizing the role of entertainments in agricultural communities as an aid in stemming the depopulation of the countryside, made the radical step of exempting from ET all entertainment venues in rural areas where the population was under 2,000 and the seating capacity of the building was no more than 200.[12] Unsurprisingly, this demographic-based concession quickly influenced ET policy in Ireland. A month later, the Northern Ireland minister for finance, Major M.T. Sinclair, similarly exempted rural entertainment venues with seating capacities of 200 or less, but rather than using a population measure, it defined rural as situated over two miles 'as the crow flies' from the nearest town boundary. (This was claimed to be more inclusive than the British approach.) Nevertheless, it was aimed less at the cinema than at church concerts, young farmers' clubs, women's institutes, and the like.[13] Sinclair also reported that following a meeting with a film trade delegation in 1948, he undertook to review the 'complicated subject' of the tax structure applicable to cinemas, but resisted any attempts to introduce changes to ET until the whole question had been 'thoroughly examined'.[14]

By the end of 1948, demands for similar concessions to those granted in Britain and Northern Ireland were being voiced in the Dáil. Thus, Farmers' Party deputy Patrick Cogan declared that there was 'an unanswerable case for a differentiation as between rural cinemas and the cinemas in large urban areas.' He added that due to high overheads and a small population, 80 per cent of the cinemas in rural areas were losing money.[15] Such pleas were at least partly answered when from 1 June 1949 ET was charged only in respect of cinemas in, or within three miles of, towns populated by more than 500.[16] However, a month earlier, Northern Ireland exhibitors had won even greater dispensations. Not only were venues in towns with populations of under 2,000 exempted from ET, but the general exemption rate of 3d. was raised to 5d. tickets, with minor adjustments to other rates.[17] Even so, and despite further adjustments in 1951 following a meeting with exhibitors, the Northern Ireland finance minister, Sinclair, expected to get an 'increased yield' from the tax.[18] Subsequent to another meeting with the film trade, Sinclair once again altered ET rates, including increasing the exemption rate to tickets priced less than 7*d*. but by way of compensation to the exchequer increasing ET rates on higher admission prices, such that Northern Ireland rates were made 'more closely approximate [to] those current in Great Britain'.[19] The trend was continued in 1954 when ET rates were further tweaked;[20] however, in 1955, the minister for finance, Brian Maginnis, called a halt to the concessions, claiming that attendance during the previous year had not only been 'well maintained' but that there had been 'a slight increase', and that several new cinemas had been opened or were planned.[21] His successor to the post, G.B. (George Boyle) Hanna, declared his 'considerable reluctance' not to propose any change to ET rates in 1956.[22]

Meanwhile, as might be expected, further pressure had been mounted on the southern Irish minister for finance when in 1953 a delegation from the rural-based Irish Cinema Association met him and agreed to provide detailed accounts of twenty-two cinemas in order to demonstrate the financial strains that such exhibitors were under.[23] As *To-day's Cinema* reported, while the receipts from such cinemas had been 'fairly constant' during the previous decade, and a 1951 order requiring exhibitors to receive ministerial approval before raising admission prices had been lifted in January 1953,[24] their costs had 'risen sharply' such that the film carriage bill for many, where there were four or five changes of programme each week, was up to £400 per annum.[25] In this context of unregulated seat prices and rising costs, the minister for finance, Seán MacEntee, who 'had repeated representations' from exhibitors during the previous two years, raised ET rates for higher priced tickets though he provided 'some relief at the lower levels of admission charges',[26] an announcement which was welcomed by provincial exhibitors 'where low admission is the rule.' However, the manager of a major Dublin cinema told *To-day's Cinema* that 'it will prove a most unpopular move' with the film trade in the capital. According to the manager, the previous increase in ET, which saw a 3*s*. 6*d*. seat go up to 4*s*. 3*d*. resulted in 'a very heavy box-office falling off. Moreover [such increases] hit [...] the people who are most hit by the budget – the white-collar workers.'[27]

The 1953 Finance Act also introduced an additional amendment through its extension of the 1943 rebate on events encouraging the use of Irish.[28] However, as had happened in relation to the live-performance provision, this was used by some exhibitors as a means through which to evade tax. Indeed, by 1958 the finance minister, James Ryan, had discovered 'gross abuse' of the concession, which allowed for a 50 per cent rebate if one-third of a film's soundtrack was in Irish. He reported how an unnamed proprietor had begun showing Irish language films in two of his cinemas for about 1.5 hours either before or after the usual English language films that ran from 8p.m. to 10.30p.m. After this exhibitor had successfully claimed his entitlement to an entertainment duty rebate, he extended the practice to five other cinemas and was followed in the process by other cinema owners, such that in March 1958, the reduction was being claimed by thirty-six houses altogether. The way in which the Irish language films were shown in these houses 'left no doubt' that it was used merely as 'a legal device' to get remission from entertainments tax.[29] Ryan also pointed out that the Irish language films screened had received no publicity and in many cases a single short film was shown repeatedly until the required amount of time for ET rebate had been completed. (As an aside, the 1956 Finance Act included an exemption for films with an exclusively Irish language soundtrack, even though it was not until 1959, with the release of George Morrison's *Mise Éire*, that a feature-length Irish language film became available.)[30]

With effect from 1 September 1954, the population limit under which a rural venue was exempt from Irish Republic ET was raised from the 1949 figure of 500 to 1,000, while cinemas within a three-mile radius of towns of up to 2,000 persons were given a 50 per cent ET rebate. The cost of these additional dispensations was estimated at £35,000 in 1954, or 2.7 per cent of the amount collected in 1954.[31] Given that these reductions probably amounted to less than 10 per cent of total cinema ET in a full year, the Irish Cinema Association sought further modification of ET rules, but the minister for finance, who introduced a new duty scale from 1 August 1957, declared that he was 'unable to agree to any concession which would involve loss to the Exchequer.'[32] The following year, the ICA demanded that the population limit of a town within a three-mile radius of a cinema required to qualify for a full ET exemption be increased to 3,000. Additionally, it proposed a 50 per cent rebate for cinemas within a three-mile radius of towns of 3,000 to 10,000 persons and a 33 per cent rebate in respect of cinemas within centres populated by between 10,000 and 20,000 persons.[33] Indeed, the minister for finance, James Ryan, acknowledged during the 1958 budget debate that, having met provincial exhibitors, he accepted that they were 'certainly in a bad way' and were finding 'it very hard to carry on', though the Labour Party's Brendan Corish quipped that 'they did very well in the past 15 years', a point, Ryan reported, that was accepted by exhibitors.[34] The concessions sought were not granted that year, but a threat by the Rank Organization,[35] the only large exhibitor offering cine-variety, to end their variety programme at the Theatre Royal, thus making Irish artistes redundant, helped lead Ryan to modify the concession regarding cine-variety in the 1958 Finance Act, at which time the ET rebate was altered from 30 to 50 per cent.[36] The following year, in 1959, the rebate was further raised, this time by 50 per cent from 50 to 75 per cent at a cost of £10,000.[37] In an additional cost to the exchequer of £150,000, the minister also introduced new ET rates, which included an exemption on tickets priced 8d. and under, an increase on the 1957 amendment of 4d. to 5d.; a reduction of 1d. in the duty element in inclusive prices up to 1s. 9d.; a reduction of 1.5d. at prices between 2s. and 2s. 7d.; and a reduction of 2d. at prices from 2s. 9d.[38] The new rates were designed to balance the needs of the cinema industry,[39] which was deemed to be in a 'parlous state'[40] as a result of falling attendances (which, as Maxwell Sweeney noted in relation to the fall-off in second-run or working-class central Dublin cinemas, was contributable in part to the government's major public housing programme and 'the resettlement of the former populations in new housing estates [away from cinemas] on the outskirts of the city'),[41] against the needs of the state and the 'very big [and ultimately unaffordable] loss of revenue' that would be caused by adjusting Irish ET rates downward to match British ones.

This tinkering with Irish ET rates (mostly in the form of redistributing amounts from the lower to higher priced tickets rather than impacting on the total tax col-

lected),[42] which had been a feature of taxation policy from 1953 onwards, continued
with the 1960 Finance Act. Despite the increasing difficulties within the cinema exhibition sector, manifest in the reduction in gross box office receipts (from a high of
£4,367,000 in 1956 to £,3,930,000 in 1960),[43] the fall in admissions (of 10 million
compared to the peak year of 1954), and a decrease in film rentals (from £924,000 in
1957 to £841,000),[44] Ryan remained committed to ET as an important source of government revenue, even though the tax came under scrutiny during the oireachtas debate
on the proposed new Irish television service in 1960, just prior to the passage of the
finance act.[45] Indeed, as reported in early 1960, the BBC and UTV were already eroding the cinema audience not just in Northern Ireland, but also to a degree in the
Republic given that many southerners as far south as Dublin were able to receive 'spill-
over' transmission signals.[46] By October 1960, it was estimated that there were as many
as up to 60,000 television sets in the Irish Republic getting fringe reception from
Northern Ireland,[47] and almost double that number, 118,409, by October 1962.[48] By
then, of course, Ireland's own television service had been launched. Inaugurated on 31
December 1961,[49] the new service was only extended to remote areas such as the south-
west in 1963, thus delaying cinema's decline in those areas. However, by 1963 the
number of households with televisions in the Republic had risen to 237,000. This was
divided in a 57.4 per cent to 42.6 per cent ratio, urban to rural,[50] with 52 per cent of
the total receiving the single Irish channel – (R)TÉ/Telefís Éireann – only. The following year, over half the homes in the Dublin region had a television set, while nationally there were 250,000 sets.[51] Ironically, the advent of television brought at least one
innovation to cinema exhibition in Britain and Ireland: the conversion of cinemas that
would have normally shown feature films to news cinemas. In December 1958, specialist company Capitol and Provincial News Theatre[52] took over Belfast's Mayfair,
College Square, and reopened it as Ireland's first news cinema.[53] (Nevertheless, a small
and short-lived news and cartoon cinema had already opened in Dún Laoghaire, Co.
Dublin, in January 1950. Situated on Georges Street, the Tatler replaced the Kingstown
Picture House, which had opened in 1911.)[54] Nine months later, Capitol and Provincial
opened their fifty-ninth such theatre; this was Dublin's Grafton News and Cartoon
Cinema, which had been previously known as the Grafton Cinema.[55]

Although the 1960 Finance Act did not submit to the demand from, among others,
the Irish Theatre and Cinema Association to abolish ET, nevertheless, cinemas in towns
with fewer than 2,000 persons were exempted from the tax completely. (Prior to this
such cinemas had been rebated half the ET tax since 1954.) Additionally, all other
cinemas were to receive an ET rebate of 20 per cent, plus the balance of the duty, or
£10, whichever was the smaller. The total loss to the exchequer as a result of these
relaxations was only £300,000, or about one-fifth of the amount collected in 1959.[56]
These piecemeal reforms of ET led ITCA, which feared that the concessions would
be insufficient to enable many cinemas to operate economically within a context of
the increasing availability of television, to point out that concessions would not lead
to any reduction in cinema admission prices, as the money would be used for essential
maintenance work postponed due to the financial demands made by the tax.[57]

Maintaining pressure for its complete abolition, ITCA and ICA held a joint meeting in Sligo in February 1961 at which it was stated that the tax still represented 22 per cent of the gross turnover of cinemas.⁵⁸ The following month, James Walls, chairman of ITCA and secretary of Irish Cinemas Ltd, in his paper 'The cinema as a business' highlighted the grave state of the industry. According to him, admissions had dropped by 16 per cent between 1956 and 1959, while gross cinema receipts were down to about £3,500,000 per annum.⁵⁹ Yet to the dismay of the industry, no further concessions were made in 1961.⁶⁰

Exhibitors faced further difficulties when, on 14 May 1961, a lengthy strike by 1,400 ITGWU cinema workers broke out. As well as issues over weekend work, they were demanding a change in their holiday entitlement, from two to three weeks, and a reduction in the working week. Of the more than sixty cinemas in Dublin city and suburbs, only five suburban cinemas succeeded in reaching an agreement with the union and remained open.⁶¹ Though, when giving evidence at the labour court just as the strike was entering its fourth week, Walls claimed that Dublin wage rates were higher in every grade than London's,⁶² by the sixth week, ITCA had conceded to a number of demands. These included a reduction in the working week from 48 to 44 hours in class A and class B houses; pay rises of 15s. per week for all adult males in A and B houses and 12s. in C houses, with scaled increases for females and juniors; an extra 5s. per week for cashiers; and financial compensation for C house employees who worked a 36-hour week. The strike, the first protracted industrial action over pay and working hours by unionized labour in the history of Irish cinemas,⁶³ finally ended on 23 June,⁶⁴ but it led to a hike in seat prices by between 1d. and 3d. in Dublin and Cork.⁶⁵ Unsurprisingly, attendances continued to drop, with a further 3.7 million (or almost 9 per cent), lost in 1961 compared to the previous year, though, in comparison to 1959, it was a loss of 6.3 million (or 14 per cent).⁶⁶ Nevertheless, due to inflated admission prices, gross receipts in 1961 only dropped, in relation to 1960, by £199,000 (or 5 per cent). Despite the abolition of ET, effective from 1 October 1962,⁶⁷ exhibitors still had to deal with the continuing reality of declining audience numbers. Despite this, in 1964, perhaps in order to stave off any potential worker unrest, exhibitors still found it possible to give the 1,500 cinema workers in Dublin city and suburbs a 12 per cent pay rise while simultaneously reducing their weekly working hours from 44 to 43. Admission charges were increased by a maximum of 2d. to cover the cost.⁶⁸

By this time, however, Rank, concerned at the reduction in both first-run product and audience numbers, and despite the government's relaxation of the cine-variety concession in 1959, had already closed the Theatre Royal and Regal Cinema, which had a combined seat total of 4,310 (3,410 and 900, respectively) and a staff of 167. Of all the cinema closures, it is perhaps the closure in June 1962 of this complex which is most often and nostalgically recalled, with frequent references made to the Theatre Royal's unique character; the variety acts, such as Tom Mix, Judy Garland, Bob Hope, and Bing Crosby, and other such live performers and stars, often on European tours; and the Sunday night film shows. In its place, Rank built a multi-storey office, one of Dublin's most ugly brutalist buildings, in a period when many such 'modern' constructions were put up at the expense of 'inefficient' older, if architecturally richer build-ings.[69] Nevertheless, another cinema, the New Metropole, was eventually built on part of the site in 1972.[70] Meanwhile, Rank, which was no doubt confident that its premier cinema in Ireland – the 2,300-seat Savoy – would survive the current crisis, continued to invest in other Dublin cinemas, giving 'face-lifts' to both the Corinthian and Fairview Grand in 1964.[71]

Between the years 1964–5 and 1972–3 turnover tax, introduced in 1963 as a levy of 6 per cent on retail sales and services, was applied to entertainments, including cin-emas, though the amounts collected *in toto* were very small. Excluding dances, on which the rate was adjusted to 10 per cent in 1967, the amount extracted from enter-tainments never exceeded £350,000 and in 1966–7 was as low as £136,399 when 530 places of entertainment (excluding dance halls), were registered for the tax.[72] No sep-arate information is published for cinemas in the official statistics. Turnover tax was superseded by value added tax (VAT) which was introduced during 1973–4. However, perhaps in recognition of the fact that the cinema industry was facing difficulties with poor audience figures, VAT on cinema tickets was only introduced from 1 September 1982 at a time of extreme strain on the public finances; though during that decade the rate was as high as 23 per cent. Although no separate figures have been published by the revenue commissioners of the amounts collected from VAT on cinema admissions (or entertainments in general), distributor and exhibitor Leo Ward suggested that in the years 1983 and 1984, the VAT on cinema admissions was £3 million and £2.5 mil-lion, respectively, while in 1985, the figure was estimated by the ICA to be 'over' £2 million. Unsurprisingly, Ward and the ICA called for the VAT rate to be reduced from 23 per cent to 10 per cent.[73] Later, the VAT rate was dropped to the 12.5 per cent reduced services rate, but, in line with the general increase, rose to 13.5 per cent, the rate it remained at in 2010.

The exhibition crisis in Northern Ireland was no less acute, and the campaign by the local branch of the Cinema Exhibitors' Association, strongly supported by the Northern Ireland branch of NATKE, against ET sought the complete abolition of the tax from the early 1950s. Recognizing that the threat to Northern Ireland's cinemas was very real, in 1957, the province's minister for finance, Captain Terence O'Neill, brought in a lower scale of ET for cinemas which was designed to half the amount of tax paid on admissions over 9*d*., leading to a total reduction in ET of 18 per cent. In addition, the population limit for ET exemption was increased from 2,000 to 3,000 for cinemas with 400 seats or less. Seeing a loss of revenue of £162,000 in a full year, O'Neill proposed a new £1 excise duty on television licences, which would raise £64,000 annually.[74] Even though the shutting down of the Belfast Central in March 1958 was the second cinema closure in the city in twelve months,[75] when O'Neill made a statement to parliament the following month to the effect that the impact of televi-sion was not as great in Northern Ireland as in Britain, the local CEA became 'alarmed'[76] and requested a meeting with him. A deputation consisting of George Lodge, Victor Powell, Noel Donaghy, and Albert Dougan from the Northern Ireland branch of the Cinema Exhibitors' Association met O'Neill in May 1958 and pressed the case for relief, especially in light of the imminent extension of ITV (Independent Television established in 1955) to Northern Ireland.[77] (This happened in 1959 through local operator Ulster Television.)

Two weeks later, while O'Neill admitted to parliament that dutiable admissions were down 7.7 per cent in 1957 compared with the previous year, he noted that the drop in Britain was 18 per cent. Furthermore, he stated that though five 'taxpaying' cinemas in Northern Ireland had closed in the previous four years, ten new ones had opened, while in Britain in the same period 440 cinemas had shut. Given the differing admission price structure in Northern Ireland and Britain, he explained that if Northern Ireland attempted comparable reductions in ET to those made by the British chancellor, who reduced the rate of duty to one half of the admission price exceeding 11*d.*, and to one-third of the price, including duty, over 1*s.* 6*d.* at a cost of 58 per cent of the tax in a full year, then it would cut 87 per cent from Northern Ireland's ET income. As a result, from 9 June 1958, O'Neill set ET rates as chargeable 'equal to one-half of the amount (if any) by which the amount of the payment, excluding the amount of the duty, exceeds' 1*s.* 1*d.*, a change from the previous 50 per cent charge for admissions exceeding 9*d.*, including duty. The cost of this reduction was £255,000 in 1957 and £285,000 in a full year, a reduction of 63 per cent. From then on, nearly one-quarter of total admissions that had been liable for tax became duty free.[78]

As noted, television made an impact in Northern Ireland before the Irish Republic. In spring 1953, just prior to the coronation in June of Elizabeth II, which, it was thought, would stimulate the sales of television sets and licences, a temporary low-powered transmitter relayed the BBC service.[79] In July 1955, a permanent transmitter, located on Divis Mountain overlooking Belfast, dramatically boosted the signal such that it covered 80 per cent of Northern Ireland, or two-thirds of the population and allowed for the emergence of a mass audience.[80] The Divis Mountain signal was subsequently extended through a series of supplementary transmitters such that by the end of 1957, 96 per cent of Northern Ireland could receive the BBC. In 1959 when UTV[81] came on stream the number of television sets in use in Northern Ireland was 97,000, while by mid-1963, the year in which BBC Belfast extended its television facilities,[82] the number had more than doubled to 206,000.[83] Given the increasing importance of television as a visual medium, the appointment of the regional controller of Rank's advertising arm – Rank Screen Services, Ltd – as Northern Ireland advertisement sales manager for UTV in April 1959, six months before the service began,[84] must have caused further concern over the future of commercial cinema in Northern Ireland. This fear was made all the more real with the closure by Odeon (Northern Ireland) Ltd of their Alhambra, North Street, in late 1959, and that of another Belfast venue, New Princess Cinema, Newtownards Road, in April 1960, just ahead of the Northern Ireland budget. Consequently, much pressure was placed on the minister for finance, Terence O'Neill, not least by the Northern Ireland CEA, to introduce further tax relief on cinemas.[85] Though he delivered concessions worth £64,000 in a full year, which amounted to an average of £1,040 for the bigger cinemas, Northern Ireland's exhibitors led by local CEA chairman George Lodge who had claimed that ten cinemas had closed with the loss of 300 jobs between January 1956 and December 1959,[86] were 'bitter' at the government's failure to emulate Westminster's abolition of the tax in the 1960 budget.[87] O'Neill's budget decreed that the first £20 of tax in any week would be remitted, while smaller cinemas, which did not reach £20 tax in a week, would pay no tax.[88] After the concessions, the tax take was still a considerable annual figure of £200,000,[89] though the sum dropped to £140,000 in 1961. Despite these difficulties, ABC continued to show confidence in the Northern Ireland cinema market, and in June 1960 opened the 1,200-seat ABC Derry, the seventh new cinema in Northern Ireland since the war.[90]

However small the concessions were, renters nevertheless sought to accrue some benefit and demanded the exhibitors share the tax concessions with them. Following CEA-KRS meetings, it was decided that the first £500 gained from the relief in any one year would be retained by the exhibitor, but on savings of £500 to £750 only half would be retained by the exhibitor while the other half would be subject to whatever percentage agreement was in force between the exhibitor and the renter, usually 35 per cent.[91] Shortly afterwards in August 1960, representatives of the KRS visited Dublin to meet with the ITCA in order to similarly amend rental terms following that year's Irish government ET concessions.[92] The following year, with pressure against ET maintained,[93] the Northern Irish government fully abolished the tax effective from 27 May 1961, a few days after the finance minister, O'Neill, delivered his budget speech, and more than sixteen months ahead of its abolition in the Irish Republic. During the speech, O'Neill acknowledged the fragile state of the cinema industry which was 'still facing difficult times' and noted that attendances had not yet 'stabilised at the probable long-term level'.[94]

Regardless of the abolition of entertainments tax, Supreme Cinemas' Whitehead Cinema closed down in October 1961, as it had been losing money for some time 'due to lack of support'.[95] Seeking to hold back the decline in suburban audiences, ABC introduced occasional Belfast suburban first-run films, beginning with the March 1962 release to the Strand and Majestic of British Lion's *Weekend with Lulu* (John Paddy Carstairs, 1961, GB) and *Rag Doll* (Lance Comfort, 1960, GB).[96] Nevertheless, even ABC was succumbing to the decline in exhibition with plans to open Northern Ireland's first bowling centre on its Strand Cinema site, Holywood Road, but this proposal was turned down by the corporation.[97] While bowling was already well established in Britain, it was not until December 1963 that the Irish Republic opened its first twenty-four-lane bowling centre at Stillorgan, Co. Dublin, shortly before the country's first shopping centre opened on a nine-acre site across the road.[98] The historical cycle that had seen cinemas replace skating rinks in the early 1910s, now saw another participative sport, bowling, take cinema's place as the 1960s progressed.

THE POST-WAR AUDIENCE

Though the comprehensive data available regarding film exhibition in the Irish Republic in the 1930s is absent for the 1940s, commentators agree that a gradual increase in both box office income and cinema attendances took place. While in 1944 *Kine Weekly* estimated box office income in the Republic as being worth £2.6 million,[99] the USA's inquiry reference service put cinema attendance there at 21 million per annum.[1] Other surveys give a more complete account of the Irish exhibition market. According to a 1950 USA government department of commerce report the gross annual box office receipts in the Republic totalled about £2.85 million, roughly divided between the principal territories: 75 per cent American and 25 per cent British.[2] Two years later, Cinema and General Publicity Ltd, the major supplier of advertisements to cinemas,[3] commissioned a report on the Irish cinema market.

Entitled *The Irish audience for screen advertising* (1953), the document, which in part was based on interviews with a cross section of 2,400 adults conducted by Research Services Ltd during late 1952/early 1953, revealed that in 1952, taking account of the country's 283 full-time (commercial) cinemas, the average cinema sold 3,400 seats each week, while the national weekly figure of cinema admissions was 965,000. This figure, 33 per cent of the total population of 2,950,000, represented 41 per cent of the seating capacity. The annual national box office take was estimated at £3.5 million, with two-thirds of the tickets purchased priced between 1s. and 1s. 8d., inclusive of entertainments tax.

In terms of audience profile, the report noted that a total of 750,000 over-16s (or a quarter of the population) went to the cinema regularly, with 31 per cent of this group attending weekly and 36 per cent attending fortnightly; in greater Dublin, 46 per cent were regular cinemagoers; while in the rest of the country only 41 per cent went regularly. Within the agricultural community, less than 20 per cent of adults went to the cinema weekly, while within the non-agricultural sectors, 42 per cent went weekly. The gender divide of cinema patrons was 58 per cent male and 42 per cent female.[4]

Although the regular trade report on Ireland compiled in 1950 by the USA department of commerce stated that 'in order that preference might be given to construction to alleviate the critical housing shortage, the government has consistently refused to grant licenses to exhibitors desiring to build new theatres',[5] it was the case that from the late 1940s there was cinema building in the south of Ireland. In Dublin, for example, the Adelphi, Dún Laoghaire, and suburban Cabra Grand began trading in 1947 and 1949, respectively.[6] By contrast, in Northern Ireland, it was not until the mid-1950s that new opportunities for cinema construction emerged following the lifting of war-time restrictions on building materials. The first new post-war cinema to be erected there was the 1,025-seat Lido, Greencastle, overlooking Belfast Lough.[7] Opened in April 1955, and including CinemaScope, it was built by Troxy Cinemas (Belfast) Ltd, a major investor in the Duncairn Cinema.[8] Within two years, five further cinemas had been built. These were the Tivoli, Finaghy (June 1955), the only cinema to be built by Rank in Northern Ireland; two similar sized 1,000-seat cinemas in Dundonald (the Metro) and Ballyclare (the New Reo) which, opening within weeks of each other in September 1955, were controlled by the Supreme Group;[9] and the Alpha, Rathcoole, which opened on 1 April 1957[10] and was designed by innovative modernist architect John McBride Neill, who also had designed the Lido.[11] By the end of the year, another cinema to cater for Belfast's burgeoning housing estates opened, the 400-seat Comber (Cinema) in south-east Belfast. The fourth cinema in the Solar Group, the Comber was built to augment Solar's Comber Picture House situated on an adjacent site.[12] The following summer, at a cost of £27,000, Joseph Barr and James McGrogan launched their 400-seat New Antrim Cinema, Castle Street, to replace the Antrim Cinema across the road.[13]

Meanwhile, cinema building in the Republic remained buoyant. During the 1950s a number of cinemas opened, including in 1950 the 1,300-seat Killester Cinema, Collins Avenue, Killester, which was opened by Metropolitan Cinemas Ltd, a subsidiary of Stephen's Green Cinema Company, owners of the Green Cinema. In 1953, three cinemas opened: the large Dublin suburban 1,750-seat Star Cinema in Crumlin, designed by architects Jones and Kelly, which took over a year to complete and included a stage; the small 313-seat Astor in Dublin city centre, which specialized in continental European films; and the 1,115-seat stadium-style Kenilworth Cinema in Dublin's Harold's Cross designed by Peter D. Kavanagh. The following year three further cinemas opened in Dublin:[14] the 1,400-seat State, publicized as the 'first CinemaScope cinema to be built in Europe',[15] replaced the Odeon's run-down Phibsboro Cinema which, originally opened in 1914 and remodelled in 1938, had been demolished shortly after it closed in 1951; the 900-seat Ormonde Cinema, Stillorgan, complete with the most modern Zeiss-Ikon projection equipment and large (33ft high x 34ft wide) CinemaScope screen; and Irish Cinemas' 1,088-seat Whitehall Grand, which was officially opened by tánaiste (deputy prime minister) William Norton. In 1955, four more Dublin cinemas were established: the 1,000-seat Stella, Mount Merrion, which had been built against much local opposition from those concerned that the cinema would lower the tone of their neighbourhood; two of the largest suburban cinemas to be built, the 1,850-seat Gala, Ballyfermot, designed by J.F. McCormack, which was controlled by Republic Pictures, and the 1,910-seat Casino, Finglas, which was a subsidiary of the Stephen's Green Cinema Company; and the 900-seat Landscape Cinema, Landscape Road, Churchtown, built by developer James Brophy to serve the burgeoning housing developments in the area. In April 1957 the Breen circuit opened Waterford city's fourth cinema, the Regina, at a cost of £6,000 to replace the Theatre Royal which had closed a year earlier.[16] Other smaller regional cinemas started up throughout the country such as at Derrybeg and Falcarragh, Co. Donegal, in 1958.[17]

Throughout the 1940s there was a rise in the amounts taken in entertainments tax and the sums repatriated as profits by foreign exhibitors and distributors as there seems to have been a sustained surge in cinema-going in this period. Notwithstanding the fact that ET rates had not changed since July 1936, from 1940 to 1946 the exchequer income from ET on cinemas doubled (see appendix, table 7), while the increase in repatriated profits during the same period was 74 per cent. This latter figure rose sharply in 1948 when it was 2.7 times that of the 1940 amount (see appendix, table 9). A similar, but more pronounced, pattern of increased cinema admissions to that of the mid and late 1940s also marked the first half of the 1950s, with the most complete set of statistics for Irish exhibition, those prepared by the central statistics office from entertainments tax returns for the decade 1950–60, revealing a trend contrary to that experienced in most other European countries.[18] As can be seen in tables 4 and 5 of the appendix gross box office receipts continued to increase until 1956, though cinema admissions increased only until 1954.[19] By 1958 admissions had fallen back to a similar level to that of 1950. With the decline continuing throughout the 1960s and 1970s, by 1976 the cinema admission figure was only 5.4 million, or 10 per cent of its 1954 high.

The explanation for the post-war expansion of the Irish audience and, indeed, its subsequent, though relatively late decline, is complex. Prior to the war, the low audience level owed largely to the fact that the 1920s and 1930s had been periods of relative economic depression in Ireland, with the Great Depression combining with the economic war with Britain in the 1930s to negatively impact on the real wages of industrial workers, agricultural employees and proprietors alike. Even though, between 1926 and 1936, due to the attempt by the urban middle classes (behind the barrier of trade protectionism), to shift a proportion of economic wealth from the countryside to the city, non-agricultural productive industrial employment, based in the cities – the major catchment area for cinemas – increased by 25.3 per cent. Nevertheless this still represented only 16.6 per cent of those at work. (Agriculture still employed 49.3 per cent while the remainder were in professions such as finance and transport.) Furthermore, as these wages were not particularly high, the surplus spending power for leisure pursuits of the urban working class did not significantly increase during that decade. The onset of war and the restrictions on wage rates under the Emergency Powers Order, which prohibited increases for anyone earning more than £3 per week, unsurprisingly, had an effect on cinema income. As a result, there was upward pressure on wages in the post-war period, resulting in the relatively successful film exhibition business conceding significant salary increases (from 6s. to over 50s. per week) to the 1,000 or so unionized workers in 1947.[20]

After the war, a series of crises, including severe fuel shortages and adverse weather conditions, which reduced agricultural production, continued to impact on the Irish economy, while migration, a barometer of the economy, rose to a level higher than in any period since the 1880s. During 1941–50 there was net migration of 267,000 people, while from 1951 to 1961, as other European economies were recovering from the war, net migration was 408,800. Consequently, in these two decades net migration from Ireland was 675,800.[21] Furthermore, it should be noted that the majority of those leaving Ireland would have come from the cinema-going age group (15 to 34 years) with by far the largest proportion of emigrants in the 15- to 24-year-old age group coming from rural areas. Between 1943 and 1951, for example, the number of those aged 15 to 34 years who emigrated represented 78 per cent of females and 90.6 per cent of males of all those who emigrated.[22] The period 1951 to 1961 saw a further decline within this age bracket through migration of 286,900 people.[23] In terms of gender ratio, it seems that marginally more males migrated. Between 1936 and 1946 there was a 9.4 per cent drop in males aged 15 to 29 years, compared to 3.6 per cent for similar aged females; while in 1946–51 there was a further 5.5 per cent decline in males, compared to 8.8 per cent in females. Therefore, it should be no surprise to discover that Ireland's proportion of 15 to 44 year olds in 1951, 41 per cent, was lower than England, Wales, Scotland (all 42.7 per cent), USA (44.6 per cent) and Australia (45.5 per cent), while in a comment on the structure of emigration, the commission on emigration[24] observed that 'in a list of 25 countries, the 26 Counties has the lowest proportion in the "young active" group, 15–24.'

Nevertheless, cinema-going increased in Ireland such that by 1950 the cinema admission figure of 46.1 million was more than twice that of the 21 million of 1944, while the peak of 54.1 million in 1954 was two-and-half-times the 1944 figure. In part this was a reflection of the delay in Ireland embracing the social and technological changes that were being experienced elsewhere and were contributing to a decline in cinema attendance. Thus, Irish film exhibitors, unlike their British and American counterparts, did not have to face competition from television or cope with the financial consequences of their (working class) patrons migrating from centre city areas to developing suburbs until the late 1950s/1960s.

Additionally, while Ireland remained throughout the 1940s and 1950s a largely agricultural society, the 1951 census of population recorded for the first time a majority, 51.6 per cent of people, living in towns and villages where cinemas were typically located. Notwithstanding that Dublin and its environs, and the cities of Cork, Limerick and Waterford and their suburbs, still contained only 27.9 per cent of the population, the move towards urbanization clearly benefited cinema exhibitors, even though despite this, within a decade, all these cities were to experience a rapid decline in cinema admissions, in part due to the continuing drop in the number of young adults in the population. (In Dublin alone, it is estimated that one per cent per annum migrated during the 1950s.)[25] In any case, between 1936 and 1951 rural areas declined by 180,000, or 9.4 per cent, while Dublin county and Dún Laoghaire increased its population in the same period by almost double that percentage figure – 8.4 per cent between 1936 and 1946 and a further 8.9 per cent during 1946 to 1951, such that by 1951 it comprised 21.4 per cent of the total population.

Furthermore, perhaps counterbalancing the relatively high level of migration, particularly from those most likely to attend cinema regularly, there was a continuing relatively high proportion of unmarrieds in the population which helped maintain cinema box office revenue, especially in the absence of alternative (organized) leisure activities outside the (male-dominated) public house. While the average age of marriage in Ireland during 1945 to 1946 was 33.1 years for men and 28 years for women, in England and Wales, albeit for 1951, the average marriage age was 29.7 years for men and 26.6 years for women. When the Irish figures for unmarried men are compared with other territories Ireland's continuing high incidence of bachelors remains striking. In the 30- to 34-year-old age group, 57.9 per cent of Irish men in 1951 were single, compared to 24.8 per cent in Scotland, 18.6 per cent in England and Wales and 13.2 per cent (though for the year previous) in the USA. Northern Ireland was also much lower than the Irish Republic with only 43.8 per cent unattached men in 1937. Unsurprisingly, given traditional practices around inheritance and marriage, the ratio of unmarrieds to married couples in rural areas was considerably higher than in urban areas. In 1951, for example, 75.9 per cent of men and 45 per cent of women in the 25-to 34-year-old-age group were single in rural areas while in Dublin and Dún Laoghaire this figure was 53.7 per cent men and 47.3 per cent women. In all other towns above 1,500 persons, unmarried men and women never exceeded 59.1 per cent and 47.3 per cent, respectively. Given that young married people, especially if they have children, cease going to the cinema, or at best go less frequently, until the children have grown up, at which time a small proportion of them return to being regular cinemagoers, it was a significant dynamic in the expansion of audience numbers that so many young Irish men and women were unmarried and free to attend cinema regularly.

An additional, perhaps not insignificant, factor in maintaining Irish admissions might have been the loosening up of religious observance. Though the first signs of secularization only became apparent in the late 1950s and early 1960s, it had clearly begun somewhat earlier as is evident from a comment in 1959 by *Kine Weekly's* Irish correspondent, Maxwell Sweeney. Following discussions with cinema managers he reported that while 'the period immediately after Easter invariably shows an upswing in Irish cinemas, [with] many people voluntarily restraining from picture-going during the Lent season', managers had told him that such a variation was 'not so sharp' as it had been ten or fifteen years earlier.[26]

The highest national figure for Irish cinema-going, in excess of 54 million in 1954, or eighteen cinema visits per person, needs to be set in a wider context, not least the fact that historically, as Beere's study revealed, Ireland had a relatively low level of visits per capita. In 1936, she estimated that the average number of visits per head of population annually was only six. While the 1954 figure is somewhat greater than that recorded in other European countries, as can be seen with comparable figures for 1951 when Ireland had sixteen visits per head in contrast to Italy's and Belgium's fourteen; Denmark's twelve; West Germany's eleven; and France's and Norway's nine admissions, nevertheless, Ireland's rate was much less than Britain's and America's, the countries which have tended to be seen as most culturally relevant to Irish society and the economy. While a cursory look at cinema visits per person per year in Britain in the years 1935 (twenty-two visits),[27] 1945 (thirty-two visits),[28] 1955 (twenty-four visits),[29] and 1960 (ten visits,[30] considerably lower than the Irish figure[31] and explainable in part due to the rise in television and the fact that there were more than 10 million television licences)[32] reveals a dramatic picture, perhaps a more useful frame of reference is provided by a major study of cinemas and cinema-going in Britain published in 1954. It shows that in 1950–1 Britain had an average of twenty-eight admissions per person, the USA (in 1949) had twenty-three, New Zealand (also in 1949) had nineteen, while Canada (in 1950) and Australia (in 1948) both had seventeen admissions per year.

Three censuses of distribution for 1951–4, 1956–9, and 1966, give further clues as to the nature and organization of Irish film exhibition nationwide. Among the points illustrated in the 1951–4 survey of 219[33] commercial cinema and cine-variety establishments was that besides the £3.1 million taken in box office receipts, there were receipts of £0.5 million or 14.4 per cent additional earnings from the sales of meals and refreshments. Annual wages and salaries were £0.7 million or 18.7 per cent of total receipts.[34] Though only about 20 per cent of the establishments were in Dublin city and suburbs, 45.3 per cent of those who were employed nationally in the sector worked in Dublin, while 55 per cent of total receipts were generated there. This figure can be compared to Beere's 1934–5 estimate that 61 per cent of the box office came from Dublin and Dún Laoghaire. The percentage breakdown of box office receipts across the provinces was: Leinster, 73.5 per cent (45.1 per cent of the population in 1951); Munster, 20 per cent (30.4 per cent of the population); Connacht, 4.7 per cent (15.9 per cent population), and the three Irish Republic counties of Ulster, 1.8 per cent (8.6 per cent of the population). Although 99 per cent of total receipts came from 82.5 per cent of all establishments (the term used, but mostly referring to cinemas) where average receipts were greater than £2,500, 20 per cent or £736,000 of this had been generated by only four establishments where average receipts exceeded £100,000; 26.4 per cent by fifteen cinemas with average receipts between £50,000 and £100,000; and 37.5 per cent by sixty-two establishments with average receipts between £10,000 and £50,000. Of the 219 establishments surveyed, 135 were in sole ownership; twenty-nine were accounted for by those who had two establishments; four who had three; seven where the chain stretched to four cinemas; fifteen of the cinemas were in chains of five; and twenty-nine cinemas were represented by those in chains of six and over, which contributed 48 per cent of total receipts.[35]

Though the 1956–9 census of distribution survey is not strictly comparable to the earlier survey, in that theatres were included, nevertheless, it gives greater insight into the state of the cinema industry in Ireland, not least the dominance of Leinster and Munster, but particularly Dublin within the market. Of the 341 cinemas and theatres nationally, the survey looked at 286 venues, which combined had 185,654 seats; 53,765,000 paid admissions annually;[36] and generated £4,429,000 in box office receipts, with an additional £584,000 taken by kiosks during performances and from other sales, perhaps including programmes, making a total of £5,013,000.[37] Annual wages and salaries came to £856,000 or 17 per cent of gross income,[38] while the cost of film hire amounted to £805,000, or 16 per cent of gross income (while this figure seems somewhat low,[39] it should be remembered that the survey also included theatres).

The aggregate gross box office receipts of the forty-five establishments surveyed in Dublin city and suburbs (but excluding Dún Laoghaire) out of a total of fifty-two venues was £2,234,000 or 50 per cent of national box office. Establishments in Dún Laoghaire (part of the greater Dublin area) and in the cities and suburbs of Cork, Limerick and Waterford, of which there had been twenty-four of twenty-seven surveyed, accounted for a further £701,000 of gross box office, or 15.8 per cent of the national box office income. Leinster (including Dublin) took 69.5 per cent of the box office, yet it accounted for only 46.2 per cent of the population; Munster took 22 per cent of box office, and had 30.3 per cent of the population; Connacht took only 5.7 per cent of box office, but had 15.4 per cent of the population; while the three counties of Ulster in the Republic accounted for only 2.6 per cent of box office receipts and had 8.1 per cent of the population.[40]

Thus the profile of the regional distribution of box office in both census of distribution surveys emphatically debunks the myth of the Irish as frequent cinemagoers. It seems that cinema-going was largely an urban based activity and, even then, most especially in the greater Dublin area where it had three to four times the national average of cinema admissions per capita. Nevertheless, as we have seen, Dublin, historically speaking, was not remarkable as a cinema-going community except in the period of cinema decline in other European countries. In any case, in 1951 Dublin considerably out-performed London in terms of annual visits to the cinema where there were approximately thirty-four visits per annum; however, nationally, the rate of cinema attendance in Britain, where there were twenty-eight admissions per head in 1950, five more than the USA figure, and eight more than any other country,[41] remained far higher than Ireland's.[42]

Though Dublin had a disproportionate amount of the Irish cinema audience, roughly 60 per cent of the national audience figure, from 1935 to 1950 it had only 30 per cent of the seats. London, by contrast, which had 8.25 per cent of national admissions, had 6.76 per cent of Britain's cinema seats. Dubliners, therefore, with less seats per head than their rural compatriots or their British neighbours, had no doubt more competition in accessing the seats, particularly the cheaper ones, and hence the famous image of the Dublin cinema queue. The Cinema and General Publicity analysis of exhibition in Ireland in 1952–3 quoted above would seem to bear out a view of high cinema seat occupancy. Though, according to the report,[43] only 41 per cent of all Irish cinema seats were sold nationally, this is significantly higher than in Britain where only 33.3 per cent of capacity was filled in 1950–1.[44] It must be remembered, however, that by 1951 Britain had already lost 270 million admissions since 1946, 20 per cent of its 1951 admissions.[45]

The decline in Irish cinema-going can be traced from 1954 (see appendix, table 4), but as the censuses of distribution illustrate this was not fully reflected in a drop in cinema receipts for a number of years, not least because of increases in seat prices. While cinema admissions fell by 22.2 per cent between 1954 and 1960, gross box office receipts actually reached their peak in 1956 and thereafter declined only by 10 per cent to just under £5 million in 1960 (£4,974,680), which was still 7.8 per cent more than the 1953 figure of £4,584,810. Nevertheless, the strategy of increasing seat price was two-edged. If cinema prices rose too rapidly, further and, perhaps, more significant falls in cinema attendances could result. This was indirectly acknowledged by Rank's chairman, John Davis, in the 1968 annual report of Rank's Irish subsidiary, Irish Cinemas Ltd, who reported that while British cinema admissions prices had increased 127 per cent during the previous decade, Dublin city centre prices had only risen by 50 per cent.[46]

While it was reported in the 1956–9 census of distribution that box office was down 10 per cent in 1957 compared with the previous year, with rural exhibitors claiming a 15 per cent fall in box office, clearly a result of migration both to Dublin and elsewhere, particularly to London,[47] not all was gloom. When the Dublin-based feature *Rooney* (George Pollock, 1958) was screened in March 1958 in the Savoy, Dublin, it had 30,000 admissions in its first four days following its world premiere at the cinema and broke the Savoy's one-day house record with 10,000 admissions.[48] Nevertheless, the 1966 census of distribution and services of cinemas and theatres gives supplementary detailed evidence of the downward trend. From a total of 196 of the 267 establishments surveyed, and of which cinemas as the main form of public entertainment dominated, gross box office receipts of £3,233,000 were generated. This was 27 per cent down on the 1956–9 figures. Paid admissions, estimated at 21,920,000, were 59.2 per cent less than the figure quoted in the 1956–9 census of distribution and even if one makes adjustments in relation to the seating capacity which at 126,456 was 32 per cent less than in the 1956–9 survey, there is still an admission drop of 40 per cent. Even with the inclusion of theatres, though such could compensate for the absence of some cinemas, there was a drop of 46.8 per cent in relation to the 1960 cinema admissions figure and 26.9 per cent with regard to the 1965 figure, both given in table 4 of the appendix. This time it was the main urban areas that saw a greater decline in audience numbers. While Dublin city and suburbs and Dún Laoghaire, as well as the cities and suburbs of Cork, Waterford and Limerick, accounted for 13,171,000 admissions, or 60 per cent of the total in 1966, in the 1956–9 survey they had represented 64.2 per cent of national admissions. More staggeringly, the percentage drop in admission figures within these urban centres between these dates was 62 per cent. Nevertheless, kiosk sales and sales during performances amounted to £685,000, and unspecified 'other receipts' were worth another one million pounds, and, thus, these additional areas of income showed a marked increase of 288 per cent in relation to the sales/other receipts reported in the 1956–59 census. Indeed, the ratio of box office takings to other sales within the 1956–59 survey had been 88.36 per cent to 11.64 per cent, but by 1966 this was 65.7 per cent to 34.3 per cent. Aiding the continued existence of cinemas was the fact that in 1966 film hire expenses had only risen 12 per cent to £991,000 since the previous survey, though wages and salaries for the 2,916 persons employees amounted to £1,168,000, an increase of 36 per cent.[49]

The slump in audience numbers continued unabated through to the mid-1970s. A reliable estimate for the mid-1970s is the one offered by the restrictive practices commission, which declared that it was 'widely accepted' that total cinema attendance in 1976 was only 10 per cent of its 1954 level. Given that the revenue commissioners estimated that cinema attendances in 1954 were 54.1 million, their highest ever total, admissions in 1976 were about 5.4 million.[50] Two years later, Rank reported that its Irish cinema admissions were only 1.1 million compared with 10.5 million in 1956.[51] Of course, in the meantime Rank had closed many of its provincial and Dublin suburban cinemas, such that the trading profit of one of the companies through which it operated, Irish Cinemas Ltd, had declined in 1967 to an all-time low of £6,226, though Irish Cinemas' 'parent' subsidiary Odeon (Ireland) Ltd had profits, before tax, of £389,197 the same year and continued to earn significant profits throughout the 1960s, though by 1975 it, too, had declined dramatically with a recorded profit of only £36,583.[52] When put in the context of the Rank organization's total profit before tax of over £50 million in 1972, £68 million in 1973, and £62 million in 1974, its Irish exhibition business had become quite marginal.[53]

In 1980 the Irish audience admission figure almost doubled by comparison with 1976, and, based on the figure of £4.2 million for repatriated profits given by the revenue commissioners, the last such to be recorded (see appendix, table 9), the box office for that year was in the region of £15–20 million (see appendix, table 5a). While box office receipts continued to increase such that by 1984 it was being claimed that £20 million was being repatriated annually by transnational distribution companies,[54] though the figure was more likely to have been less than half of this,[55] by 1985 audience admissions had dipped once again to the even lower figure of 4.5 million. Nevertheless, with few exceptions, it has risen annually since then, though the figure for 2007 of 18.4 million was still only one-third that of 1954. (See appendix, table 4.)

While exhibitors and distributors looked to the state to reduce film taxation and relax the strict censorship regime, they were much slower in seeking out new audiences or adapting their cinemas to the changing circumstances, though, as in the past, large-scale foreign capital, as will be seen in the next section, seemed to adapt more rapidly to the changing environment. Perhaps the complacency displayed by many Irish exhibitors owes to the fact that the decline in southern Irish cinema admissions was more gradual and less dramatic than in Britain and Northern Ireland. While in 1962 Belfast's Troxy Cinema, seeking to compete against the new leisure activities, most particularly television, discos, singing pubs and bingo, which were eroding the cinema's audience, flirted with soft pornography and tested the patience of the police committee by screening nudist camp films,[56] though the demand for these (and other 'X' rated or sensational films) was already waning, the Irish Republic only indulged in such transgressive material in the 1970s. Such was the migration away from cinema that the film trade paper *Kine Weekly* sympathetically quoted Dr John H. Davy, moderator of the Presbyterian general assembly, someone who would have normally been on the other side of the popular culture moral plane, who described bingo as 'an evil in society, destroying the bodies, minds and souls of the people', a comment prompted perhaps by bingo's (modest) gambling stakes.[57] Despite making such allies, the tide of change continued and, within a few years, suburban and provincial cinemas in particular began to close and were converted to supermarkets, bingo halls and carpet salesrooms, or were demolished for redevelopment as offices or department stores, developments which helped pave the way for the consumerist frenzy of the Celtic Tiger years.

INNOVATION, RETRENCHMENT AND REORGANIZATION

One of the first technological gimmicks to entice audiences back to the cinema was 3D, an effect which created the illusion of a three dimensional image. The technique was not new, but dated back to the stereoscopic photographs (and viewing devices) of the nineteenth century in which two images were combined or overlaid on each other through a special lens.[58] While there had been sporadic interest in the effect, particular from the early 1920s when audiences in Ireland such as at the Bohemian[59] and the

Metropole,[60] both in Dublin, and internationally, enjoyed plastigrams in which 'players always seem[ed] to be marching straight up to each member of the audience!'[61] or 'in the most startling fashion'[62] threatening them with objects 'which stretch[ed] further and further till [they] threaten[ed] to enter the eyes of the onlookers–then disappear[ed] at the psychological moment, to the general relief and amusement',[63] the industry never fully developed the process. In part, this was due to the fact that until the end of the 1940s/early 1950s[64] such technical innovations were not needed to maintain the strong audience base, but also because the industry had deemed that the wearing of spectacles, essential to creating the 3D experience, would not catch on with audiences.[65]

This did not deter radio personality and independent producer Arch Oboler from making the first full-length commercially released 3D colour film, the African jungle adventure melodrama, *Bwana Devil*. Set at the turn of the century, it featured two man-eating lions and naked savages throwing spears at the audience.[66] Premiered in Hollywood in November 1952, it was cheaply made using Polaroid filters (rather than the anaglyphic format),[67] and was otherwise unremarkable. Though a few 3D films, such as Warner Bros' *House of Wax* (André de Toth, 1953), the highpoint of 3D filmed horror[68] and also the first such film with stereophonic sound, proved popular, encouraging other studios including Disney and Universal-International to use the technology, the medium soon came to be largely associated with exploitation genres, no doubt as it was a relatively inexpensive process and lent itself to the potential viserality of such genres.[69] Consequently, 3D never fully caught on and the phenomenon was short-lived. By spring 1954, 3D had almost disappeared[70] as more user-friendly,[71] more comfortable and more immersive rather than assaulting viewing experiences, such as those offered by Cinerama and CinemaScope, asserted themselves within the market.

These widescreen processes, however, even though they did not rely on '"true" (binocular) stereo photography',[72] were often referred to as 3D in order to distinguish them from the previous standard of 1.33/7:1 which was regarded as flat or 2D, to emphasize that the image gave audiences an enhanced illusion of depth and of participation, but also, in the initial period of the golden age of genuine 3D, to take advantage of the 3D craze. In any case, 3D films even in the golden age were mostly shown 'flat' (without the 3D effects) as many cinemas were not equipped with the two projectors required to run simultaneously;[73] the special silvered-coated screen; or the stereoscopic viewing glasses for patrons.[74] Nevertheless, in Dublin, the Theatre Royal seems to have been one of the few cinemas where 3D films could be fully experienced.[75]

Perhaps the greatest technical surprise of the late 2000s was the rapid comeback of 3D cinema[76] with films such as Irish band U2's concert film *U2 3D* (2007),[77] which tried to show the immersive and emotional potential of the medium rather than just the assaultive 'pop-out of screen' effects,[78] and *Beowulf* (2007) leading the way. However, at the time of *Beowulf*'s release the only Dublin cinema complex that could show 3D films was Movies@Dundrum.[79] Given the dramatic increase in the production of 3D features (from 2007 when only two such films were widely released,[80] to spring 2010, when ninety-nine new 3D movies, planned to be competed by 2012, were in production[81]), an expansion consolidated beyond all expectations with the release in December 2009 of James Cameron's multi-Oscar winning *Avatar*,[82] which quickly became the most successful box office hit of all time in many countries (though, in Ireland, it remains number 2 to Cameron's earlier *Titanic*), and that of Tim Burton's *Alice in Wonderland* in early 2010, Irish exhibitors, following American and international trends, scrambled to install 3D which came to be regarded as the 'blazing bright spot'[83] for the industry, not least as it cannot (yet) be pirated. Indeed, as evidenced in the fact that four of the ten major 3D movies released in 2009 were in the top ten highest grossing films at the global box office, that the number of European digital screens tripled in the same year, and that the European gross box office increased by 12 per cent to a new record high largely due to the premium prices for 3D screenings,[84] 'the possibility of a wholesale shift to 3D by Hollywood has never seemed more technically, economically or aesthetically feasible.'[85] Confirming this possibility, in 2009, IMC, part of the Ward Anderson group of companies, announced a partnership with 3D outfitter RealD to install 3D capabilities in fourteen screens covering all of its Irish multiplex network ahead of the release of DreamWorks' *Monsters vs. Aliens*.[86] Shortly afterwards, IMC's sister company, Omniplex, announced it was installing, at a cost of €1 million, digital 3D at four of its complexes (at Galway, Limerick, Newry and Santry), following the installation already at its outlets in Cork, Wexford, Armagh, Lisburn and Dundonald.[87] By March 2010, approximately 15 per cent of screens in Ireland, or more than one in seven, were 3D,[88] though reflecting the pattern elsewhere the screens have tended to be concentrated in terms of exhibition companies. By then, the next 3D technological leap was well underway as 3D retail television sets became available in 2010,[89] with the estimate that by 2011, one in ten sets sold would be 3D-ready,[90] with the sports market already marked as significant.[91] Furthermore, the making of 3D versions of standard 2D films was also underway.

Returning to the 1950s, Cinerama, which promised audiences that they wouldn't be just gazing at a movie screen, but that they'd be 'swept right into the picture, surrounded by sight and sound', found a huge audience when it was introduced in September 1952.[92] Developed outside the film industry by American inventor Fred Waller, it entailed three interlocking 35mm cameras fitted with wide angle lenses to film the action, and three similarly interlocked projectors in three booths to project the three strips of film onto a large deeply curved screen that was designed to play on the viewers' peripheral vision so as to enhance the sense of being enveloped by the screen. *This is Cinerama*, the first feature to use Cinerama, was hugely successful, running for 122 weeks in New York, where it took $4.7 million. The film, which cost just $1 million, yet grossed over $32 million at the box office, traded on early cinema's interest in the travelogue. This was because the process, ideally suited to spectacle, required flat lighting and was unable to achieve the close-up or intimate shot[93] that was central to the story-telling process and audience identification of Hollywood classical narrative;[94] indeed, the medium also struggled with panning shots. Regardless of its limitations, most critics and commentators heralded Cinerama as 'the most important step in motion picture history since sound.'[95] Nevertheless, the first five Cinerama films (all travelogues), were only shown in twenty-two cinemas (though they grossed

an impressive $82 million).[96] Even by the mid-1960s, by which time the process had
been extended to fiction features with MGM's at times spectacular, but ultimately nar-
ratively poor and disjointed, epic *How the West Was Won* (Henry Hathaway, John
Ford, George Marshall, 1962) and the less than wonderful, *The Wonderful World of
the Brothers Grimm* (Henry Levin, George Pal, 1962) – (in)complete with three of the
Grimm stories – there were still only ninety-five Cinerama theatres worldwide. One of
these was the Dublin Cinerama Theatre, Talbot Street.

Formerly the 1,500-seat New Electric, the Dublin Cinerama Theatre had been leased
from Capitol and Allied Theatres by Bertie McNally and Charles Regan who converted
it into the 1,000-seat Cinerama Theatre. Equipped with a Todd-AO 70mm system
(described below) modified with a Cinerama lens that could project a film image onto
a Cinerama screen, the cinema opened with *This is Cinerama* on 14 April 1963, which
it proudly declared in its publicity material 'will not and cannot be shown at any other
theatre in Ireland!'[97] With prices from 4s. 6d. to 10s. 6d., the seats were probably the
most expensive ones in Dublin at the time.[98] The film, which ran for three months, was
followed by *Seven Wonders of the World* (Tay Garnett, Paul Mantz, Andrew Marton,
Ted Tetzlaff, Walter Thompson, 1956), though the first major narrative film to be
screened there was *The Sound of Music* (Robert Wise, 1965). Filmed using Todd-AO
(rather than Cinerama, though screened as Cinerama) it ran for two years, while other
wide-screen format films, including Stanley Kramer's slapstick *It's a Mad, Mad, Mad,
Mad World* (1963, Ultra Panavision 70) and John Frankenheimer's *Grand Prix* (1966,
Super Panavision) were also screened there. Indeed, by the end of 1963 three-strip
Cinerama had been replaced by Ultra Panavision, which succeed in replicating
Cinerama's aspect ratio of 2.77 : 1 (width : height) with a single 70mm camera.

Seeing the success of the Talbot Street Cinerama, the Cinerama Group decided to
open their own venue and to this end converted the Plaza Cinema, off Parnell Square
at the corner of Granby Row, which had closed in October 1966, into a 754-seater
with a 60ft curved screen. Redesigned by Stephenson Gibney and Associates with Ernest
Muncer at a cost of £75,000, the new Plaza Cinema opened on 28 September 1967
with *Grand Prix*. However, it closed fourteen years later and, subsequently, in what
can be regarded as a reversion to a pre-cinema entertainment environment epitomized
by the World's Fair, Henry Street, where some of the first films shown in Ireland had
been screened in 1896, the building became home to the National Wax Museum from
26 October 1983 to 26 June 2005.[99] Meanwhile, the Talbot Street cinema had its
Cinerama franchise terminated and was renamed the Superama overnight on 1–2
August 1968. In 1971 under the management of owners Capitol and Allied Theatres,
it reverted to a more conventional cinema format. Despite an investment of £20,000
for decoration and seating, which was reduced from 930 to 850,[1] and its rebranding
as the New Capitol following the closure of the Princes Street Capitol in March 1972,
the cinema closed permanently on 29 August 1974. From the Electric in 1911 to the
New Capitol, the site had been in use as a cinema for sixty-three years, making it one
of Dublin's longest continuously-used cinema sites.[2] Perhaps only the Rotunda, by then
known as Capitol and Allied's Ambassador, could claim such longevity, though the

latter had only a few more years as a cinema venue. While Cinerama remained an expensive and technologically complex system whose films could only be shown in specially-adapted cinemas, other widescreen formats, especially 20th Century-Fox's CinemaScope, what John Belton has called the 'poor man's Cinerama',[3] came to colonize the mass market and indeed helped cinema to distinguish itself through image size and composition from television which had copied cinema's aspect ratio.

The first time such a widescreen format was presented in Britain was at the Odeon, Leicester Square, on 14 May 1953,[4] when *Tonight We Sing* (Mitchell Leisen, 1953) was screened in a 1.66:1 aspect ratio as opposed to the then standard of 1.33:1. While other cinemas soon followed, this format paled in comparison with Fox's CinemaScope, which, compressing a wide angle of view onto 35mm film, had an aspect ratio of 2.55:1 (though when an optical stereoscopic sound-track was added in 1954 this was reduced to 2.35:1). Launched in September 1953 with the hugely successful release in New York of the biblical epic *The Robe* (Henry Koster, 1953),[5] by the end of 1954 the process was adopted by every studio except Paramount.[6] Within a year, 13,500 American cinemas had installed CinemaScope, while by September 1957, 17,644 of a total of 20,971 theatres in the USA and Canada had done so.[7] Worldwide, by then, the phenomenon was replicated with 46,544 cinemas installing the requisite equipment, though many of these did not install stereo sound.[8]

In Britain, Fox liased with Rank and, following an impressive trade demonstration of CinemaScope in Rank's Odeon, Tottenham Court Road, on 30 June 1953 on a 53ft by 21ft screen with a 3ft deep curve, it was agreed that *The Robe* would be given a full Odeon circuit release, and *How to Marry a Millionaire* (Jean Negulesco, 1953), the second CinemaScope feature, a Gaumont circuit release. On 19 November 1953, *The Robe* finally had its British, and, indeed, European, premiere at the Odeon, Leicester Square, complete with the imported 'miracle mirror'[9] screen (52ft by 27ft masked down to 50ft by 20ft) where it ran for three months, but despite Rank's initial interest, evident in its conversion of over sixty of its 550 cinemas to CinemaScope, relations with Fox began to break down, not least because of Rank's decision in early February 1954 not to install any more of its cinemas with stereo sound which cost more than CinemaScope itself, and Rank's reluctance to break with their regular programming in order to accommodate the extended runs preferred by Fox.[10] As a consequence of this, Fox sought to develop a fourth British circuit using its own London cinemas and those controlled by independents and withdrew its films from Rank whose seventy installations of CinemaScope and stereophonic sound sat idle.

Nevertheless, by this time, Rank had committed to installing CinemaScope in Dublin's Savoy, which became, on 23 April 1954 with the screening of *The Robe*,[11] the first cinema in the Republic with Cinemascope. (One had opened in Belfast in January 1954.) Additionally, as Rank was rebuilding from 1953 the Phibsborough Picture House, which had closed in 1951, the new cinema, renamed the State, became one of the first cinemas anywhere in the world in which the CinemaScope format was incorporated into the design brief. Thus, one of the State's walls roughly approximated the dimensions of a CinemaScope screen (50ft wide by 20ft high).[12] Given that the screen and auditorium formed one unit, an *Irish Times* writer commented, 'the general effect ... [was to] give the impression to the patron that he is viewing an actual screen as distinct from looking at a heavily-framed photograph.'[13] Indeed, conversion to CinemaScope of venues with relatively small proscenium arches, particularly prevalent in venues built before the First World War, was problematic: screens had to be masked down giving a letterboxing effect and undermining the dramatic illusion, or were replaced with new widescreens built in front of the proscenium.[14] The new 1,300-seat State Cinema, built at a cost of £100,000, opened on 24 April 1954, but given that *The Robe* was running at the Savoy, it was forced to screen a non-CinemaScope production, Harry Watt's Technicolor sequel to his *Where No Vultures Fly* (1952), *West of Zanzibar* (1954, GB), filmed in Africa. Thereafter, the State screened Rank's second-run CinemaScope films (or, in other words, films which had already been shown in the Savoy), including *How to Marry a Millionaire* which had followed the four-week run of *The Robe* at the Savoy, and the unremarkable North-West Frontier adventure *King of the Khyber Rifles* (Henry King, 1954). In 1962, the State was awarded first-run status, but it closed down in 1974, and was later reinvented as the Silver Skate ice rink.[15]

Despite the success of CinemaScope, by 1967 Fox had discarded the process and was using Panavision (based on the CinemaScope process), for 35mm films and Todd-AO for its widescreen ones. While CinemaScope, its clones, and rival 35mm Vista Vision came to be shown without stereo sound[16] or in incorrect aspect ratios within regular cinemas, Todd-AO (named after entrepreneur Mike Todd and engineering company American Optical) became associated with the upper end of the theatrical market and led the way for other 65/70mm processes. ABC, which had shown considerably more enthusiasm than Rank with regard to both 3D and CinemaScope, installed the technically sophisticated Todd-AO system in its most prestigious cinemas. As John Belton notes, 'by associating itself with prestigious theatres and exceptional motion picture productions, Todd-AO established itself, at the height of the widescreen revolution in the mid- and late 1950s, as the premiere widescreen process.'[17] In effect, it duplicated Cinerama, complete with a deeply curved screen, but with one, not three projectors. Unlike Cinerama, which was only suited to spectacle, the Todd-AO camera, which also incorporated six-track stereo magnetic sound, had a number of lenses ranging from a 128 degree bug-eye lens which approximated that of Cinerama, through to a 68, a 48 and a 37 degree lens, which, with narrower angles, could be used for more intimate shots. As Fred Zinnemann, director of *Oklahoma!* (1955),[18] the first production to use the process said, 'there is nothing you cannot do with this medium. This includes the use of close-ups and complete mobility of the camera as regards pan shots, dolly shots, etc.'[19] Whereas by the end of 1957 there were only sixty cinemas equipped with Todd-AO systems, compared to over 46,500 cinemas equipped with CinemaScope,[20] by the end of 1961, this had risen to 606.[21] Despite its superiority, only fifteen Todd-AO feature films were made in its first fifteen years, by which time generic 70mm films began to appear, though these were often just 35mm films blown up to the larger format.

In Ireland, ABC installed two Todd-AO projection systems: one at the Ritz, Belfast, where it cost £25,000, and the other at the Adelphi, Dublin. Opening within a day of each other, Christmas day,[22] traditionally a closed day in the Irish Republic, and St Stephen's day, 26 December,[23] both cinemas presented the new technology by screening Joshua Logan's version of Richard Rogers and Oscar Hammerstein's musical *South Pacific* (1958). The original Todd-AO production of *Oklahoma!* was screened eventually at the Adelphi in April 1960 with the top price raised to 7s. 6d. The same month, Rank finally installed 70mm in Dublin's Savoy,[24] though it had put Technirama-70, a system released in 1957 designed to emulate Todd-AO, into the Theatre Royal, Dublin, ahead of the opening on 18 December 1959 of Walt Disney's CinemaScope feature animation *Sleeping Beauty* (Clyde Geronomi, 1959).[25]

Installing the latest widescreen format was not the only way cinema companies sought to protect their assets or their shareholders' dividends. In Britain, Rank, which attributed 10 per cent of the fall in cinema admissions to the arrival of ITV alone,[26] invested in ITV's franchise for Southern Television. Similarly, other cinema companies, including ABC and Granada, also became involved in other ITV regions. According to the Rank organization, it was not just television that was negatively impacting on the film exhibition industry, but also the excessive burden of entertainments tax. In 1953, of Rank's 550 cinemas, 236 were operating at a loss of £725,000 even though at the same time these theatres were paying £3,449,000 in ET. Though little changed over the following years, few cinemas actually closed. However, in August 1956, Rank issued a statement publicizing the closure of forty cinemas, which it presented as a 'logical consequence of the [British] Chancellor's refusal to reduce tax.'[27] A month later, the closure of thirty-nine further cinemas was announced. Though only fifty-nine cinemas actually closed, most of which were run-down, off-circuit or secondary Gaumont establishments, an additional sixteen cinemas ceased trading by the end of 1957, followed by a small number in 1958, mostly Gaumont halls. When these were sold, it was generally stipulated in the contracts that the properties would not be reopened as cinemas.[28]

Additionally, Rank diversified into other areas of the entertainment industry, such that by as early as 1956, 30 per cent of its profits were coming from manufacturing radios, televisions and optical equipment. Most radically, Rank invested one million pounds in the development of a photocopying process that became known as Rank Xerox. Furthermore, one of its subsidiaries, RenTel Ltd, opened television leasing businesses in shops beside both the Savoy and State cinemas in Dublin in late 1959/early 1960, a year before Irish television went on air.[29] As Rank correctly predicted in 1959, non-cinema investments would soon exceed those from cinema activities.[30] To reflect this increasing diversification, Odeon Theatres Ltd was renamed the Rank Organization Ltd in 1955. While in 1958–9, Rank's UK cinemas contributed 40 per cent of sales and almost 60 per cent of profits, by 1964–5 this had collapsed to 22 per cent of both sales and profits, just ahead of the contribution from Rank Xerox and other manufacturing activities.[31]

Rank's Irish exhibition experience, if ultimately no different to that in Britain, at least saw a delay in the collapse of its business. Rank's two Republic of Ireland subsidiaries, Irish Cinemas Ltd and Odeon (Ireland) Ltd, maintained profitability well into the 1960s and consistently paid annual dividends of 17.5 per cent to 27.5 per cent.

Nevertheless, by the 1970s this had changed such that at the Irish Cinemas' annual general meeting in Dublin in March 1974, chairman John Davis acknowledged that the company was making 'very little' from its cinemas. This was in sharp contrast to the fortunes of the Green Group, which was forecasting a profit in 1974 of £92,000 from cinemas alone. Irish Cinemas annual general meeting lasted only ten minutes, and afterwards, when questioned by an *Irish Times* financial journalist on the company's position, Davis declared that 'we never elaborate' on such issues. While the company's profits had fallen 77 per cent, from £122,133 to £28,026 during 1973, Rank's hotel, restaurant and television interests made up for any decline in box office revenue; indeed, the accrued profits from associated companies rose by 41 per cent, from £78,747 to £111,392. As Irish Cinemas Ltd held a 50 per cent share of both RenTel Ltd and Commercial and Industrial Property, the company which owned the properties built on the Theatre Royal/Regal Cinema site, including the Hawkins House and College House office blocks, as well as the New Metropole, which was let to Odeon (Ireland) Ltd, the income from such investments alone far exceeded that generated by film exhibition.[32] In 1975 Irish Cinemas Ltd sold all but its central Dublin cinemas as well as its catering interests except for the public house '19 O'Connell'. From these sales the company netted £510,503.[33]

While during the late 1950s and early 1960s in particular, exhibitors and distributors, both native and foreign, were not proactive in the redefining of their businesses to meet the changing circumstances and seemed almost to be paralysed by the new entertainment environment, one local company, Amalgamated Cinemas, began to diversify by developing its catering interests and planned to build a hotel in Arklow.[34] Nevertheless, a greater and more rapid level of adaptation seemed to come from large-scale foreign capital with many of them who had Irish offices cutting overheads, including through staff redundancies and resisting wage demands. British Lion, for example, one of the few renters with offices in both Dublin and Belfast, closed its Belfast outlet in March 1958 and centralized Irish distribution through Dublin,[35] while the following month, RKO closed its Dublin office and transferred its salesman to the Paramount office, with film handling centralized through JARFID. Twentieth Century-Fox 'imposed a severe staff cut' in Dublin; Columbia divested itself of its 16mm division through Irish company Sight and Sound Ltd, a specialist 16mm distributor, one of the largest in the country;[36] and in 1970, Paramount and Universal formed Cinema International Corporation (CIC) as their joint distribution arm for non-American business, an arrangement that continued until 2006.[37]

The extent of the transformation of the Irish cinema industry in the face of the encroachment of new leisure activities, particularly television, but also bingo, dancing and singing pubs, as well as the shift towards suburban living, is most starkly illustrated by tracking the number of cinemas operating in Dublin from 1960 onwards. While in 1960, there were forty-three cinemas in Dublin city and suburbs, including Dún Laoghaire, at which time the population was 663,389 (1961 census of population), and fourteen cinemas in the rest of the county with three in the nearby town of Bray, Co. Wicklow, by 1978, when the population of the same Dublin areas had grown to 778,127 (1971 census of population), forty of these greater Dublin area cinemas had been closed down. By 1989, Dublin (city and county) and Bray, by then an area with a population of more than one million people, had only fourteen cinemas with a total of thirty-five screens. Even more revealing of the industry's decline[38] was the collapse of Rank's Irish cinema interests from the late 1960s onwards, from which time it pursued a twin policy of reducing both staff numbers and the size of its central Dublin cinemas. This is most evident in a comparison of Rank's Irish cinema interests in 1956 and in 1976.

In 1956 Rank's Odeon group owned eighteen Irish cinemas (25,117 seats), all of which, with the exception of the Savoys in Cork (2,242 seats) and Limerick (1,483) were located in Dublin city centre and suburbs. In that year, total admissions to Rank cinemas were 10.5 million.[39] Though this represented approximately 20 per cent of the country's cinema audience, it might have generated 40 per cent of national box office revenue as many seats within their centre city cinemas would have commanded higher than average prices. However, by 1976 Odeon Ireland was selling only 1.1 million tickets, or 10.4 per cent of its 1956 figure,[40] and was left with six screens and 3,473 seats across just three central Dublin cinemas – the Savoy, Corinthian and Metropole – all of which had been remodelled. In 1969, at a cost of £400,000, the Savoy had been converted into a twin cinema.[41] It was subsequently converted in 1975 to a triple-screen, and later to a five-screen venue. The Corinthian, renamed the Odeon, was similarly converted to a twin in 1975, and though the O'Connell Street Metropole closed in March 1972 and was sold to British Home Stores, which also purchased the adjoining Capitol Cinema, to construct its only Irish store,[42] the same month a new single screen Metropole with 878 seats opened. Built on part of the site of the Theatre Royal, which had been closed in 1962, it, too, was later converted to a triple-screen complex.

The other major British exhibition company in Ireland, ABC, which was taken over by EMI in 1969, fared no better. Shortly after its takeover it converted the Adelphi, at a cost of £300,000,[43] into Dublin's first triple cinema – 711 seats in cinema one; 234 seats in cinema two; and 375 seats in the new cinema three in its former Hideout restaurant – which opened in October 1970. However, the following year, the company closed its Dún Laoghaire Adelphi, one of the country's largest cinemas. In 1973, the Adelphi, Dublin, was again converted, this time to a four-screen complex when Adelphi 2 was subdivided into two screens. In 1976, its other cinema, the Carlton, was remodelled as a three-screen venue with a loss of nearly 700 seats, though the conversion of the restaurant to a 126-seat fourth screen compensated somewhat. Adelphi-Carlton became part of the Thorn-EMI group, which sold its two Dublin cinemas to the Cannon Group, which in turn was taken over by MGM.

Despite the 50 per cent drop in audience figures during the decade from the mid-1950s to the mid-1960s, and further decline during the following decade,[44] which led to and fed the downturn trend within the industry (evident in the reduction of the number of cinemas and the costs incurred through the conversion and modernization of cinemas), foreign exhibition and distribution companies remained profitable. That this was the case is illustrated by the net amounts repatriated as profits by foreign film interests in Ireland (see appendix, table 9). While during the 1960s there was an erratic pattern to the amounts repatriated, nevertheless, it rarely fell below one million pounds, and from 1970 until such figures were no longer published a decade later, there was a steady, even a dramatic, increase in repatriated profits. Even allowing for inflation, the increase in profits sent out of Ireland back to offshore corporate headquarters from £1.2 million in 1970 to £2.1 million in 1974, £2.2 million in 1976, and £4.2 million in 1980 (the last year such figures were published by the revenue commissioners), indicates that there were healthy returns for foreign distributors and exhibitors in Ireland.[45] In 1983 this figure might have been between £6.6 million and £9 million,[46] while a late 1980s estimate unofficially put the amount at £10 million.[47]

Irish exhibitors could not hope to compete either with Rank or ABC in the provision of more luxurious cinemas or in gaining access to blockbuster first-run product. Not only did Rank and ABC own most of the capital's premier cinemas, but through their long-standing relationships with distribution companies, they were also more assured of a steady supply of first-run product than independent Irish exhibitors. Nevertheless, Irish exhibitors proved to be very tardy, even lazy, in developing new ideas to win back cinema audiences or adapting to the changing film demands of a new generation. Many Irish exhibitors followed the route taken by Rank and closed suburban and provincial cinemas, while others merely relied on reissues. There is though one important exception. While the Elliman and Farrell families were continuing their disengagement from the film business in the 1960s (Abe Elliman died in 1962 and his brother Louis in 1965) and the 1970s, symbolically, it was the sale of the Farrells' Capitol and Allied Cinemas to two established independent film distributors and exhibitors, Leo Ward and Kevin Anderson, in 1977, and, as importantly, their purchase of Rank's remaining Irish cinemas, the Savoy, New Metropole and Corinthian/Odeon in 1983, which heralded the next significant change in Irish exhibition.

The Emergence of Ward Anderson and the Challenge from New Distribution Technologies

'I've never known how many cinemas we [Ward and Anderson] own. I've lost count – we have them all over the place.'

Kevin Anderson, 2004[1]

THE WARD ANDERSON COMPANIES

Though Leo Ward (1919–) first entered the film business in 1939,[2] within three months he had become a professional footballer with Manchester City, the then pre-eminent team in Manchester. His football career, however, was cut short by the outbreak of the Second World War, whereupon, for the duration of the war, the club suspended all players' contracts. Ward returned to Ireland and while continuing his football career with Dublin team Drumcondra,[3] he resumed his involvement with film as a clerk in John Hanlon's Irish International Film Agency, the first specialist Irish distributor in the sound era of Irish and European, particularly German, films. The company also supplied 16mm films and projection equipment to educational institutions and for private parties. Within a short period, he and his half brother Kevin Anderson (1915–),[4] who also had been involved in film distribution and had acted as Leo's replacement in the agency when Leo had left to go to Manchester,[5] established a new film distribution company, Abbey Films Ltd, which was based initially on Dublin's Mary Street and subsequently on Middle Abbey Street. Though not actually registered until 1954, the company was certainly making its presence felt from at least 1948,[6] having received a large injection of capital following Leo's 1946 testimonial match[7] which marked his retirement from football, while 'a few bob' also came from Anderson.[8]

Although in its early years Abbey Films produced a number of documentaries, including *Who Fears to Speak of '98?* (Kevin Anderson, 1948) narrated by Cyril Cusack, which tied in with the 150th anniversary commemoration events of the 1798 Rising,[9] it was as an independent distributor and later as an exhibitor that the company became best known. However, without the scale, power and product quality of the American majors who could offer attractive packages of films to exhibitors, and within a market that already had too many films for the number of screens available, it was forced to survive on distributing 'B' productions. These included the six films bought from Butcher Films, London,[10] the most important perhaps of which were the romantic melodrama musical *The Hills of Donegal* (John Argyle, 1947),[11] which did particularly well in Cork and allowed them to forge important contacts,[12] and the British National Films' *Old Mother Riley* series (1937–52) featuring the comic characters Arthur Lucan and Kitty McShane as Mrs Riley and Kitty Riley. Other films in their catalogue were those made by Irish boxer Jack Doyle,[13] one of which Anderson bought for £50 while working with Hanlon's agency when Ward was in Manchester[14]; the successful *Danny Boy* (Oswald Mitchell, 1941)[15] and *Rose of Tralee*,[16] both of which helped to establish Ward and Anderson's credentials;[17] and films of the All-Ireland hurling and gaelic football finals. Nevertheless, it was not until the early 1950s that the pair got their first real break in distribution when Anglo-Amalgamated Film Distributors[18] appointed them as agents, including for the very lucrative *Carry On* films, on which they made their money 'ten times over'.[19] Despite having succeeded to an extent in breaking the stranglehold of the established cartels, they decided, against a backdrop of the contraction of the film business and the rationalization of the major distribution houses, to expand into film exhibition.

Ward, 'the one who loved films',[20] continued to look after the film side of things, while Anderson remained in charge of the company's finances. Indeed, though it was Ward's contacts within the business and his reputation among independent exhibitors such as Mrs Murphy (for whom he part-time oversaw the management of her cinema, the Pavilion in Cork),[21] which provided them with the opportunity of taking over or being offered an option of buying into an existing cinema, it was Anderson's shrewd investments[22] in the stock market which provided the much needed finance, particularly given that it was company policy never to borrow, but to expand on the basis of retained profits. As Anderson later recalled, 'we never owed the bank money, never.'[23] In the late 1970s this practice of accumulating with an eye to future investments caused them some difficulty when a small number of disgruntled shareholders in a public company, the Green Group Ltd, with which Ward Anderson had become involved, pushed to have a share of the company's rich liquidity distributed to them.

It should be noted, however, that Leo Ward's skill as a tough negotiator,[24] always demanding the best deal from distributors, was also pivotal to their success as exhibitors. Indeed, as recent as 2005 Ward, by then aged 86, was described by one distributor as the 'glue that holds it all together.'[25] He is the person who makes it a group, rather than two different chains'[26] operating either complementary or, as is the case in Limerick, in competition with each other. At that stage, Paul Ward, Leo's son, was running the IMC cinema chain, while Paul Anderson, Kevin's son, was managing the Omniplex chain, the two major Ward Anderson designations.[27] There are, however, more than just these brands within the Ward Anderson film group which by 2010 owned almost half the screens in Ireland. In fact, there is no single company known as

Ward Anderson, but instead a myriad of over fifty inter-related companies jointly or independently owned or controlled by the two families.

Rather than compete with first-run Dublin companies, such as Rank, ABC, and the Farrells, Ward and Anderson used their knowledge of, and within their distribution base, to focus their exhibition interests outside Dublin's city centre. However, as Leo Ward recalled in 1985, 'It wasn't so much a predatory expansion policy'

> as an attempt to bolster the distribution side of our business. Many small-town cinemas were owned by the local grocer-publican-undertaker cum half-a-dozen other things. He hadn't time or expertise enough to attend to his cinema business properly, with the result that many [such cinemas] were closing down. If they closed we lost a customer so we bought some over the years ... in Cork, Limerick, Galway, Waterford, Tullamore and elsewhere.[28]

In a 1968 article, 'Enterprise in the provinces', Ward highlighted 'a recurring failure' on the part of many 'very courageous' provincial exhibitors and their local bankers, who provided the funds for buildings and furnishings, 'to estimate the cost of the complete cinema.' Instead of understanding that the builder's estimate was only part of the cost, 'many potential exhibitors were more than surprised to discover that the furnishing and equipping of a cinema also required considerable capital and further financing to provide maintenance and replacement during the operating years', including entertainments tax, which had been 'an excessive burden' on many small town exhibitors and had contributed to the closure of some cinemas.[29] (The new 'crucifying' burden potentially facing small independent cinemas is the revised proposed royalty charges payable to the Irish Music Rights Organization, IMRO.)[30] While Ward's observation throws into relief the contrast between his experienced business focus and many of those involved in small-scale film exhibition, it also reveals how naïve many independents were when it came to the film business. Though he does not provide any sample figures, it was probably the case that the cost of a basic, almost-barn-like small provincial town cinema building was less than the equipment and furnishings inside it. It is not surprising, therefore, as the exhibition business became tougher from the mid-1950s onwards that many such exhibitors turned to Ward and Anderson as partners, but also as a source of help and advice both in terms of programming and in maximizing turnover (which, moreover, was realized through the creation of smaller multiple units).[31]

Additional pressure on small exhibitors came in the 1960s, not least from television, but also as a result of the availability of personal and public transport that allowed audiences to go to larger urban venues. Other factors impacting on exhibitors included the costs involved in showing widescreen and CinemaScope presentations; the fact that many new releases were produced for adult audiences, thus resulting in a decreased number of family or universal films, the dominant fare of local cinemas;[32] and the business arrangement with suppliers who were forcing exhibitors into longer runs, thereby disturbing the 'long established pattern of presentation' and 'cinema-going habits'.[33] As Kevin Anderson pointed out, this caused further cinemas to close and 'because they were closing you could buy them quite cheaply so long as you could keep them open.'[34] Dublin suburban cinemas also showed a marked decline in this period with the closure of the Regent, Blackrock in 1961; the Astoria, Glasthule, in 1962; the Sutton Grand in 1967; and the Drumcondra Grand in 1968. As might have been predicted given their move towards exhibition, the two men became active in the provincial exhibitors' Irish Cinema Association, and as early as 1961 the pair were listed on the organization's committee, Leo Ward as a Mullingar exhibitor and Kevin Anderson as a Lucan exhibitor.[35]

The first such cinema they took over was a small suburban 300-seater in Lucan, Co. Dublin, the Premier, in 1955. The cinema, for which they paid £18,000,[36] had a substantial overdraft, and was subsequently run by the Andersons and their four children.[37] Completely renovated by Paul Anderson at the end of the 1960s, by 1970 it had been expanded to more than twice its original capacity to 750 seats and was renamed the Grove.[38] In 1968, *Showcase*[39] reported that Ward and Anderson owned thirty-eight cinemas in Dublin (the most important of which was the Green Cinema, St Stephen's Green)[40] and the provinces, where, for example, they owned most of the cinemas in Cork city, having initially bought into the Lee[41] and Pavilion[42] cinemas in the 1950s, and in Waterford, where they were involved with the Breens, who, as discussed in chapters 2 and 3, had a cinema chain in the south-east of the country. After the Breens extended their hotel interests into the local Ardree hotel, Ward and Anderson bought the Breens' remaining cinema shareholdings.

More often than not Ward and Anderson did not assume full control of a cinema but began a systematic programme of partnerships, usually on a 50/50 basis, with the local operator. Generally, the original owner continued to run the cinema, but Ward and Anderson provided the expertise to do so, as well as delivering the further much needed investment and modernization, which later often involved the twinning of the cinema. It was only when an operator wished to get out of the business, perhaps to retire, that the pair would then buy the remaining 50 per cent. Most of the cinemas, though, remained on a 50/50 ownership basis, with their interests eventually becoming dominant only in the major provincial cities and towns such as Cork, Galway and Limerick.[43] Of course, a side effect of this style of merger, as happened in many locations including Killarney and Waterford, was the proliferation of Ward Anderson companies as each cinema or small circuit had a deal made specific to that location often with a separate company registered or established. Consequently, retrospectively establishing the cinemas with which they were involved or controlled is difficult as neither of their names is included as being registered proprietors, instead a company name, usually one incorporating the cinema's name, is listed as is the case in the *Kinematograph and Television Year* annuals. Nevertheless, from the late 1960s onwards things become more transparent as the names of Ward and Anderson became interchangeable with the Green Group.

In 1967, Ward and Anderson, having acquired a considerable number of shares in the Green Group, which took its name from the Green Cinema, joined the company's board of directors.[44] As the Green Cinema was not profitable, one of the directors, Mr

McAllister, asked Ward Anderson to look after the booking of its films. Leo Ward reprogrammed it as a successful reissue house, first screening a series of James Bond films[45] for which he had bought the distribution rights and which proved very profitable. This he followed with *Carry On* and Bruce Lee films as well as screenings of popular films such as *Madame X* (David Lowell Rich, 1965) and Douglas Sirk's melodrama *Imitation of Life* (1959), both starring Lana Turner. In 1972 they converted the Green Cinema into a twin screen, with 340 and 377 seats, and, more generally, the 1970s saw a considerable expansion of the number of screens they controlled. Apart from their interests in exhibition they were also involved in 16mm distribution through General Film Distributors; cinema publicity through a 50 per cent share in Cinema and General Publicity; cinema equipment supply through National Electric and Cinema Equipment Co.; as well as, of course, 35mm distribution through Abbey Films, which was agent for five companies, including EMI Film Distributors, and through an association with Impact Films, distributing for Brent Walker.

For the year ending 31 October 1976 the Green Group and its associated companies under the directorship of Paul Ward,[46] had pre-tax profits of £341,249, rising to £432,893 in 1977, compared with only £75,027 in 1972.[47] As the *Irish Times* commented after the release of the company's 1976 accounts, 'the Green Group is in an exceptionally strong financial position', adding that its 'bearings' or liabilities were nil and that it had £950,000 on deposit. While the return on capital employed apparently dropped from 52.3 per cent to 36.3 per cent between 1975 and 1976, this disguised the fact that the company earned a substantial £62,751 from deposit interest; £57,287 from investment income; and £7,526 from rental income, suggesting that box office income was being supplemented by less tangible sources of revenue. The shares had risen from 33p to 42p and were considered 'high enough for the moment'.[48] Nevertheless, within less than a year, in March 1978, its shares had been suspended from the Irish stock market, something which accelerated its change from being a public to a private company.

The change in status from public to private arose following a dispute with the Irish stock exchange when the Green Group sold its 500,000 shares in British poster and advertising company Mills & Allen, which was about to be amalgamated with majority shareholding company J.H. Vavasseur. Despite the financial health of the company, the Green Group took this action to avoid being locked into the company as a minority shareholder with no quotation, or end up as a Vavasseur shareholder. Though the group made a net profit of £160,000 through the sale, had it waited, it might, if it proved possible to sell at that stage, have netted a further half a million pounds.[49] While there was nothing untoward in the transaction, the fact that the Green Group failed to provide the stock exchange with a class one document explaining how it might invest this money, not least because more than half its net assets were in cash, the stock exchange suspended the company's shares. Even when the company's accounts were published, much to the annoyance of many of the group's shareholders, the information was deemed to be inadequate and the shares remained suspended,[50] thus leaving the company 'rather in the lurch'.[51] Nevertheless, during the company's previous few annual general meetings, a number of minority shareholders had already been calling for the 'embarrassment of riches' to be distributed to them, and for the board to be relieved 'of the burden of investing the cash', which, in 1977, amounted to £722,806 on deposit and £305,822 in investments,[52] but Ward and Anderson took a different view as to how the company's capital should be used.

Only five weeks after the Green Group's 1978 annual general meeting, the directors, including the dominant duo of Ward and Anderson who individually and through associated companies controlled 54 per cent of the company's equity, bid £800,000 for the outstanding shares. Rather than seek a relisting on the stock exchange (something which Kevin Anderson had stated in August that the board was keen to do, and to that end had engaged in talks with the stock exchange, the take-over panel and the Bank of England),[53] the directors used a private company controlled by them – Torgyle Holdings – to present shareholders with a buy-out document. They offered to buy ordinary shares for 77p (which compared with the last quoted price of 62p), and preference shares for 60p (which compared with the last price of 45p).[54] Though the *Irish Times'* Bill Murdoch in analyzing the bid, mused, as did many shareholders, why the company, which had 57.8 per cent of its net assets in cash, amounting to 47p per share, did not distribute at least some of the cash, arguing that shareholders 'could still retain a holding in what would then be a cinema operator',[55] he pointed out that even though the net asset value per share was only 4.5p above the bid price and that value was 'likely to be higher because of retained earnings', the terms were 'not unreasonable', particularly given the activity within the stock market. He also drew attention to the fact that chartered accountants Bastow, Charleton and Co., as quoted in the offer document, had considered the terms 'fair and reasonable'.[56] However, as later emerged, the letter from which Bastow, Charleton, and Co. had been quoted in the Torgyle offer document had also stated that their opinion was based *only* on information supplied by the Green Group's directors and importantly this information had not included an updating of the value of the assets to current market value, some of which had not been revalued since the early 1970s. Perhaps, unsurprising, according to some stockbrokers, the offer document 'would not have been acceptable to the Stock Exchange had Torgyle been bidding for shares that still had a quotation.'[57] Indeed, although Murdoch had suggested that shareholders 'should consider retaining part or all of their holdings' a drawback could be that if they subsequently wished to sell their shares this might prove 'difficult' without a listing on the stock exchange.[58]

In February 1979, when the offer for the outstanding shares closed, the directors controlled more than 80 per cent of the equity. Under company law,[59] they could then compulsorily acquire the remainder of the ordinary shares. At that stage, some shareholders, in an unprecedented action, applied to the high court to determine a fair value for their shares. As Eoin McVey, writing in the *Irish Times*, pointed out, considering shareholders funds were only £2.1 million, the last published balance sheet for the group showed it in the 'enviable position' of having more than £1.1 million on deposit and £0.75 million in investments, but 'what might disturb shareholders most' was the fact that no property revaluation had been undertaken.[60] The high court challenge fizzled out and the company retreated to secrecy. As it went private, the Green Group was one of Ireland's most profitable companies with the fourth-best return on capital employed at 37.6 per cent of any publicly quoted company. With only 114 employees, it was also the fourth-smallest employer of labour of all Irish publicly quoted companies.[61]

The extent of the Green Group's liquidity put it in an exceptionally powerful position with regard to acquiring assets, in particular cinemas, during the 1970s and 1980s, and with the disengagement of both foreign and independent native exhibitors from the sector, Ward Anderson companies were usually the only bidders for cinemas as going concerns. Thus, by 1977 in Dublin, mainly through the Green Group, they controlled or had interests in four cinemas in the city – the two-screen Green, along with what had been Capitol and Allied's remaining cinemas[62] (the 1,100-seat Ambassador, the 369-seat Regent and the 634-seat Academy) – and a further five in the suburbs and county – Pullman, Inichore; Grove, later Panorama, Lucan; Gala, Ballyfermot; Star, Crumlin; and Stella, Rathmines[63] – while outside of the capital, through a myriad of other companies, they controlled many times that number, even though they had recently sold the Rialto, Nenagh (for a sum in excess of its book value) and the Ritz, New Ross. In Cork, they owned four of the city's six cinemas: the Pavilion, Lee, Palace and Capitol whose second screen was known as the mini Capitol. (The remaining two cinemas, the Classic and Cameo, were independently owned by Seamus Quinn, though in 1979 Quinn sold the Classic to Abbey Films, while the Cameo was converted to a disco in 1983, though films continued to be shown there occasionally until 1985.)[64] In Cork county they booked at least four cinemas, including the Ormondes in Fermoy, Cobh and Midleton, and the Abbey in Youghal. They had a complete monopoly in Limerick, owning the city's four cinemas – the Royal, Cecil Street; Central Studio, Bedford Row; Carlton; Roxboro Twin Theatres/Movieland (two screens)[65] – and in Galway where they controlled the Town Hall, Claddagh Palace and the Savoy. In Tipperary, they had five, or more than half of the county's, cinemas – the Capitol and the New Cinema, Thurles; Rock, Cashel; and the Regal and Ritz in Clonmel. In Waterford, they had a three-screen complex – the Regina – as well as the Dungarvan Ormonde; in Kerry they booked almost half of the county's cinemas, the Picturedrome and Royal in Tralee, the Astor in Listowel and the Lakes in Killarney; while in Louth they controlled the Abbey, Drogheda, and the Casino (two screens) and Adelphi, Dundalk. Other Ward Anderson cinemas included the Coliseum, Carlow; Magnet, Cavan; Grove, Athy; Regent, Kilkenny; Ideal, Westport; Hibernian, Mullingar; and Abbeys in Wexford and Wicklow. In the country as a whole, according to this survey prepared by the restrictive practices commission, by 1978, Ward Anderson owned or co-owned more than forty cinemas, or a quarter of all cinemas in the Republic, while in the period 1974 to 1977, Leo Ward acted as booker of films for more than fifty, or just under a third of cinemas.[66] Nevertheless, there were a number of locations such as in the north-west – Roscommon, Sligo and Donegal – among other areas, where they were not active.

In terms of the wider context of declining screens, in all, between 1962 and 1978, forty-seven cinemas had been closed in towns where only one cinema had existed. More generally, in the period 1962 to 1977, it was estimated that 190 cinemas had been closed, eighty-seven of them between 1971 and 1977, with thirty closing in 1976 alone. Notwithstanding the addition of forty-three new screens through twining (or the dividing of cinemas across two or more screens) or the opening of new cinemas, by mid-1977 there were only 177 screens compared with 324 screens in 1962.[67] This large reduction reflected the even more dramatic decline in cinema audiences, with cinema attendances in 1976 only 10 per cent of those in 1954. While the reasons for this decline owe largely to cultural and demographic shifts within the Irish population, other difficulties facing the distributor were more industry based. In his 1968 *Showcase* article quoted above, Leo Ward, commenting more as a distributor than as an exhibitor, lamented the dwindling supply of films suitable for family audiences, a familiar refrain from all exhibitors within a few years of the widespread issuing of limited certificates by film censors from 1965 onwards. He also complained about the burden being placed on the provincial exhibitor by major distributors who were demanding extended runs of films both in the larger population centers, which were increasingly drawing local audiences away from the smaller venues, and in provincial areas which not only augmented costs for the exhibitor, but interrupted the pattern of presentation whereby programmes were changed on a weekly or twice weekly basis, thus 'interfering with the cinema-going habits of his patrons.' In an ironically prophetic comment, Ward concluded that the time was coming when the provincial cinema owner, who was 'becoming more perturbed with recent trends', must 'seek for enquiry to be made regarding the amount of control which the Government should exercise over his suppliers in the present circumstances'.[68]

Such a time eventually came when the remaining independent exhibitors sought redress from the state. However, it was the interests of Ward Anderson that were a primary focus of the independents' complaints. Among other things, the independents argued that members of the Kinematograph Renters' Society, representing the main film distributors, gave Ward Anderson preferential access to films. It was to be a long and involved process that ultimately vindicated the dominant Ward Anderson group whose position in the market continued to grow.

INVESTIGATING MONOPOLY PRACTICES

In January 1970, the fair trade commission, having received a number of allegations from independent exhibitors about unfair restrictive practices in the distribution of cinema films, held a series of meetings with exhibitors and distributors. These meetings culminated in the formation of a cinema trade complaints' committee (CTCC) whose terms were defined in May 1970. Subject to review by the fair trade commission, the voluntary committee was to include equal representation from the Kinematograph Renters' Society (KRS); the Irish Theatre and Cinema Association (ITCA); and the Irish Cinemas Association (ICA), whose membership was confined to exhibitors operating in towns with under 10,000 inhabitants. The CTCC's function was to consider complaints relating to the supply and distribution of films, but its decisions, which had to be unanimous, were not lawfully binding and, therefore, to be effective, had to rely on goodwill within the trade.

The first complaint came in July 1970 from a Co. Cork exhibitor Mr R. Cogan who alleged that 'major renting companies' treated him unfairly by not allocating films to his Oakwood Cinema at Carrigaline within a comparable timeframe to that of similar venues. He also declared that he was forced to follow the dates of the Lee Cinema, Cork city, which was under the management of Leo Ward. Consequently, Cogan won parity with similar Cork cinemas and withdrew his allegation against Ward and KRS members. Nevertheless, in January 1971 Cogan once again contacted the CTCC, this time complaining that neither United Artists nor Columbia were abiding by the agreement, but by 18 February, Cogan had written to the committee thanking them for their successful intervention on his behalf. Ward became the subject of another complaint in September 1970 when Mr H. Hurst of the Regal Cinema, Youghal, argued that unfair advantage was being given to Youghal's other cinema, Horgan's Theatre, since Ward had taken over its management in 1966, but, in this case, the committee, after careful consideration, rejected the allegation. No further complaints were received by the committee between mid-1971 and early 1975.[69] However, this did not indicate greater commercial film opportunities for the independents, but rather reflected their lack of confidence in the CTCC's ability to effect any fundamental alteration in the patterns of distribution. Such a view was confirmed during 1975 and 1976 when the increasingly embattled Dublin city centre independent exhibitors and Dublin suburban operators sought quicker access to box office hits.

In February 1975 four suburban Dublin exhibitors – Albert Kelly of the Kenilworth, later the Classic, Harold's Cross; Anthony (Tony) O'Grady, the Stella, Mount Merrion; Andrew O'Gorman, the Ormonde, Stillorgan; and Barney O'Reilly, the Forum, Dún Laoghaire – complained about Columbia-Warner's non-compliance with an agreement whereby films were to be made available to them four weeks following their first-run providing the films had not been picked up within that period by a city centre cinema. Harry Crofton of Columbia-Warner agreed that, for a trial period of six months, films would be made available to the suburban cinemas immediately on the conclusion of their centre city engagement.[70] It was clear that all three sectors of independent cinema exhibition – central Dublin, suburban Dublin and provincial – were dissatisfied with the piecemeal way they were extracting concessions from the KRS. As a result, in January 1976, two independents bypassed the CTCC and complained directly to the examiner of restrictive practices, alleging that the large exhibitors were 'us[ing] their muscle to obtain the cream of the releases from the film distributors.'[71]

The same month, both the *Irish Times* and the *Evening Herald* highlighted the plight of independent exhibitors. The former, seeking to save independent cinemas, called for a legally backed 'urgent investigation' into the country's 'whole distribution system', suggesting that 'the possibility of a monopoly situation, or at least of restrictive practice', be examined by the 'appropriate commission'.[72] The *Evening Herald*,[73] on the other hand, reported claims by provincial exhibitors of being 'muscled out' of the business by the bigger cinema chains, and by suburban exhibitors, who maintained that bigger city centre cinemas were holding on to top grade movies for so long that by the time a film had its first and second showings in the city centre it was no longer profitable. The following month, the examiner met the chairman of the CTCC, who, while acknowledging that such allegations of 'unfairness' were recurring, pointed out that the two new organizations representing independent exhibitors had refused to participate in the CTCC.[74] These were the Society of Cinema Exhibitors (SCE), which was a reconstitution of the Irish Theatre and Cinema Association, one of the committee's original three organizations and whose membership of about 160 in 1978 considerably overlapped with the ICA; and the recently-formed Independent Film Renters' Association (IFRA). Chaired by Kevin Anderson, IFRA's members included Independent Film Distributors Ltd; Impact Films Ltd; National Film Distributors Ltd; and Abbey Films Ltd. (It had also included Elliman Films Ltd until it ceased trading in 1976.)[75] Both these groups, carrying within them the historical contradictions between large- and small-scale Irish exhibitors' and distributors' bodies, included as members Ward Anderson companies, thus allowing Kevin Anderson to give evidence to the public enquiry on behalf of the two organizations. With the increasing volume of complaints being directed to the examiner of restrictive practices, the examiner concluded that the CTCC's terms of reference as laid out in May 1970 were no longer adequate and that, from April 1976, he would assume full responsibility of investigation.

The following month the examiner met with the Irish Cinemas' Association, which represented provincial and, more latterly, suburban and central Dublin independent exhibitors. With a membership base of twenty-eight exhibitors operating a combined total of fifty-one cinemas, their concern focused on the limited access to 'worthwhile' product by both provincial and suburban Dublin cinemas. As a consequence of this, the Classic and Kenilworth cinemas, both in the Dublin suburbs (Terenure and Harold's Cross, respectively), had been forced to close. According to the ICA, notwithstanding the efforts of the CTCC, which resulted in sporadic periods of harmony between exhibitors and distributors, the CTCC had proved incapable of forcing distributors to make any lasting changes such that suburban cinemas, depending on the rating of a film, were made to wait between two and fourteen months for films. The ICA attributed this delay to the preferential status being given to the Ward Anderson-owned Green Cinema which got films immediately following their city centre first-run. Not content with this advantage, Ward Anderson continued to run the film 'as long as they were getting packed houses.' Only after fully exploiting its commercial value was it made available to suburban cinemas with 'the result ... that the suburban exhibitors were being gradually edged out of business.'[76]

According to the ICA's provincial exhibitors, a similar situation pertained outside the capital with the forty plus cinemas operated by the thirty-five Ward Anderson controlled companies,[77] getting all the first-runs (outside Dublin) 'even while [the films] were playing first-run in Dublin.'[78] As a result of poor product supply, many provincial cinemas closed, some of which, ironically, were taken over by Ward Anderson, who have always maintained[79] that their involvement in exhibition was motivated, in the first instance, by the desire to boost their 'easier'[80] and preferred business of film renting. Furthermore, Ward Anderson pointed out to the enquiry that they had not initiated these acquisitions, but had only responded to approaches made by exhibitors who had found themselves in difficulties. This, perhaps somewhat disingenuous, response was in part designed to maintain the shroud of secrecy surrounding their operations. Indeed, such was their lack of cooperation with the examiner that Ward Anderson would not divulge which company operated which cinema(s). Indeed, Abbey Films refused the examiner's representatives access to relevant files and the company subsequently challenged in the high court the constitutionality of the power under which the officers were acting.[81]

During the 1977 public enquiry Ward Anderson defended their position by arguing that any trading advantage they might have was attributable to their expertise in booking and exhibiting films as well as their investment in the modernizing of their cinemas. This was backed up by the KRS, which claimed that the Green Group was supplied with films because they 'catered for the public needs by having first class, comfortable and attractive premises and a high standard of presentation of product.'[82] Similarly, in 1978 the restrictive practices commission's *Report of enquiry into the supply and distribution of cinema films* noted that investment in renovation, refurbishment and equipment, such as that carried out by Ward Anderson, Adelphi-Carlton (EMI), and Odeon (Rank), which, combined, amounted to £2 million, had been a significant factor in their success. It went on to state that where no such investment occurred, cinemas 'have gone out of business or have barely survived in recent years'.[83] The ICA, however, refusing to accept such simplified explanations, argued that there were 'many examples ... where exhibitors ... up-dated and modernised, ... [but] were forced to close because there was no improvement in the supply of product.' Furthermore, the association blamed the reluctance of others to invest on the fact that 'there was nothing to suggest that viable product would be made available to them' if they did. [84] The ICA went on to argue that 'if an equitable system of distribution' could be established, it would result in a widespread raising of standards with regard to comfort, attractiveness of premises, presentation of product and equipment.[85]

In a more generalized comment on the state of exhibition, Ward Anderson, referring to a study that they had undertaken regarding Irish cinema-going in which had been revealed that adults made twelve visits to the cinema per year, stated that there were too many cinema seats in the country and that all towns had more cinema seats than were justified.[86] Consequently, they reasoned that 'if the available product was split between two cinemas [in a provincial town] then [as was often the case] the result would be that both cinemas would do bad business and not just one.' In these circumstances, Ward Anderson argued that 'no intervention in the market was desirable.'[87] The decline of the independent exhibition sector was thus in the interests of the Ward Anderson companies. Indeed, this is quite clearly what occurred. While the ICA's membership in 1968 was 104, by 1976 it had shrunk to thirty-three. In an attempt to protect its much-depleted membership from the expansionist designs of Ward Anderson, the association made proposals regarding the allocation of film to suburban and provincial cinemas to the Irish advisory committee (IAC) of the KRS, an organization, which, in 1979, metamorphosed into the Society of Film Distributors (SFD). Following discussions with the examiner of restrictive practices, Austin Keenan, and with exhibitors' bodies, the KRS, hoping to placate the increasingly hostile attitude being adopted by Keenan, introduced a more equitable product allocation scheme for provincial exhibitors akin to the UK model. Effective from January 1977, disputes were to be resolved locally between exhibitors, and, if no resolution ensued, then the IAC's product allocation committee (PAC), comprising of two distributors' representatives (from the KRS and IFRA), two exhibitors' representatives (from the ICA and SCE), and with an independent chairperson, would hear the case. The ICA was dissatisfied that the final decision lay with the KRS, but an appeal tribunal was also formed and sanctioned by the public enquiry.[88] The appeal tribunal, which had to be contacted within two weeks of the PAC's decision, consisted of an independent chairperson, appointed by representative members, whose decision was final, and not more than two distributors' representatives and an equal number of exhibitors' representatives not present at the time of the original PAC hearing, who were to act in an advisory-only capacity.[89]

By the time of the public enquiry, the ICA acknowledged that the scheme had led to a considerable improvement in provincial exhibition.[90] Meanwhile, in early 1977, the KRS also introduced a scheme for Dublin suburban cinemas whereby a film had to be available for screening not later than the beginning of the thirteenth week following its city centre release (four weeks later than had been hoped for by the suburbans),[91] though in the case of the Green Cinema, this was set not later than the beginning of the eleventh week. Under the system, regarded by the exhibitors as 'a considerable improvement' on what pertained hitherto,[92] films would be made available earlier if the first-run period was less than twelve weeks. According to the commission's fair practice rules it was to be not later than the day following the end of the first-run exhibition in a Dublin city centre cinema. The new schemes did not, however, attempt to alter distribution in central Dublin or in the scores of small towns throughout the country.[93]

Despite the KRS's introduction of these schemes, the ICA remained wary of what might occur once the restrictive practices commission turned its attention away from film distribution and exhibition and remained suspicious as to whether the KRS would continue to give its backing to the allocation committee, or abandon it. In particular, they were concerned at the power of the Ward Anderson interests, though it should be noted that Ward Anderson was not the only large circuit operating in Ireland at that time. Louis O'Sullivan, Patrick ('Paddy') Melia, Colman Conroy,[94] and Fionnuala O'Sullivan, for example, were directors of nine companies[95] which operated twelve cinemas in Naas, Ennis, Ballinasloe, Tipperary, Kells, Newbridge, Athlone, Birr, Roscrea, Portarlington, Portlaoise and Carrick-on-Suir;[96] while Geoffrey and Edward Elliman of the famous film exhibition family, Walter McNally, and Peter Roughneen, as directors of no fewer than fifteen companies,[97] operated cinemas in Athlone, Ballina and Dublin.[98] Unsurprisingly, when the examiner, sharing the independents' concerns, rejected the new allocation schemes, the relationship between him and the KRS became even more strained.

For nine months prior to the introduction of the film allocation schemes the examiner had been compiling information on distribution and exhibition in Ireland, including establishing, with regard to seventeen specific films, the various terms and rental percentages demanded of exhibitors by renters. This information went on to form a substantial part of his subsequent 226 page *Report of the investigation into the distribution of cinema films*, which was completed in March 1977. Restricted primarily to 'unfair practices' but without questioning whether exhibitors had 'equal opportunit[ies]' to bid for a film, the report made no attempt to analyze in any detail the economic structure of distribution and exhibition or the relative strength of companies in terms of assets and profits. Nevertheless, it did include a list of the principal complaints made by the seventy-five independent cinema owners and managers interviewed during the course of the examiner's investigation. The interval between a film's first-run and its appearance at subsequent cinemas was deemed too long; the 'bar' system that prevented a film being shown before it appeared in specified towns was regarded as discriminatory; the rent charged for films that had already been shown throughout the country was regarded as being excessively high; the number of film prints available was judged to be inadequate and as such was considered as limiting potential box-office income; while many independents argued that the setting of minimum rental periods, usually between five and thirteen days, was too high given the size of their audience and the fact that screenings of the same film in adjacent towns reduced the film's commercial worth. As a result of the latter, independent exhibitors claimed that they were restricted to showing second-rate films or old box-office hits as these were the only products available to them for one or two-day screenings. They also alleged that when Ward Anderson opened a cinema in a town it 'invariably' received first-run films and, consequently, the independents could not continue to operate even at 'a modest profit' in such circumstances.[99]

In the section entitled 'Agreements and monopolies' the report declared that agreements allowing monopolies to exist were in place, and, according to the examiner, the existence of these 'was acknowledged by all parties'.[1] The report alleged that while in the centre of Dublin EMI subsidiary Adelphi-Carlton had a monopoly of first-run films from Cinema International Corporation (CIC) and Columbia-Warner, Rank's Odeon (Ireland) Ltd had a similar monopoly over films not only from Rank Film Distributors as might be expected, but also 20th Century-Fox and United Artists. Outside of Dublin 'these five renters in addition to Scotia-Barber Distributors established the Green Group [that is, Ward Anderson] in a monopoly position throughout the country.' Correspondence between renters and exhibitors, reproduced in the report, as well as the booking dates and rental charges for individual films, including *The Sting* (George Roy Hill, 1973), *Earthquake* (Mark Robson, 1974) *Enter the Dragon* (Robert Clouse, 1973), *Barry Lyndon* (Stanley Kubrick, 1975, GB), and *The Happy Hooker* (Nicholas Sgarro, 1975), 'bears witness'[2] to such agreements. 'Wholesale discrimination',[3] as evidenced in the different rental fees charged to different exhibitors, could be seen in relation to many of the films. With regard to *The Sting*, for example, one independent at Killorgan, Co. Kerry, was charged 55 per cent, or 10 per cent more than the Adelphi-

Carlton's 50 per cent despite the fact that there was a twenty-two month differential and that it was no longer a first-run film. Even admitting that the Adelphi cinema, Dublin, was charged 90 per cent in excess of £2,850 two months earlier, Clonmel's Regal, which was booked by Leo Ward, was only charged 30 per cent of box office income.[4] For the examiner, 'the conclusion [was] inescapable that the rentals charged amount[ed] to discrimination in favour of the monopoly groups whose position has been thereby further strengthened. The obverse of the coin has been further erosion of the ability of independent cinemas to compete.'[5] It was also reported that the members of the Independent Film Renters Association, which included the Ward Anderson 35mm distribution company Abbey Films, also showed discrimination in favour of their own cinemas, though not to the degree exercised by the major renters, though this may simply have been the result of having a less commercially viable product.

Despite the examiner's growing body of evidence against the KRS, during a meeting with the examiner in June 1976 the society, whose members at that stage were CIC (UK), Columbia-Warner Distributors Ltd, Rank Film Distributors Ltd, Scotia-Barber Distributors Ltd, 20th Century-Fox Ltd, and United Artists' Corporation Ltd, denied acting with partiality. Arguing that many of the disgruntled exhibitors had failed to make the necessary capital investment in updating equipment and modernizing of their venues, they requested the reactivation of the cinema trade complaints' committee. When the examiner refused, pointing out that over a period of five years the committee had failed to satisfy the independents, the KRS then attempted to shift the responsibility for product allocation directly onto the exhibitors by proposing that the ICA and Ward Anderson work out distribution arrangements between themselves. Adamant that 'the onus was squarely on the renters to distribute cinema films in a fair manner', the examiner informed the association that either each renter adopt 'a fair and equitable system of distribution based on objective criteria or, alternatively, the Examiner would recommend that the restrictive practices commission should hold a public enquiry.'[6]

It was in this context that the KRS had devised its allocation schemes. Nevertheless, the examiner rejected them and proposed an alternative means of film allocation whereby each cinema in each county would have, in turn, the right to choose a first-run film. The first-run period was to be no more than one month, while maximum subsequent runs, until all cinemas had shown the film, would be a fortnight.[7] As was pointed out at the time,[8] this meant that blockbuster films such as *Jaws* (Steven Spielberg, 1975) or *A Bridge Too Far* (Richard Attenborough, 1977) could open in suburban cinemas rather than first-run city centre venues. While the examiner noted that reasonable conditions relating to a cinema's standards of furnishing, facilities and equipment would need to be observed, he failed to appreciate the economic implications, not least that first-run city cinemas required more capital investment than suburban and provincial ones and generated much greater returns for the distributor. Indeed, even independent exhibitors would acknowledge that they benefited from the publicity and advertising associated with first-run centre city releases. The KRS responded tersely, informing the examiner that his proposals were

... contrary to the accepted principles of distribution world-wide. They are completely unrealistic and impracticable, would cause a state of chaos and unwarranted delays and would undoubtedly lead to the closure of more cinemas, both in cities and provinces, with consequent loss of employment and damage to the public interest. Furthermore they would be to the detriment of the very cinemas you are seeking to help.

Deeming it 'palpably obvious that [he was] not conversant with the operations of the film industry with its many complications', and being 'just as concerned as [he was] for the welfare of independent exhibitors and the public interest',[9] they announced that, though they had withdrawn their proposals, they would be introducing them without delay. A breakdown between the two parties ensued, and in March 1977 it was announced that a public enquiry would be held to investigate the supply and distribution of films. In his report prepared for the restrictive practices commission, the examiner suggested that renters should be required by legislation to abide by systems of distribution based on objective criteria that were fair to all parties and to adopt terms and conditions that were both reasonable and equitably applied to all exhibitors.[10]

The public enquiry, which took evidence from twenty-one witnesses, including the examiner who had managed to survey fifty-two exhibitors[11] on matters of ownership, seating capacity, projection equipment, admission charges, major capital expenditure and competitor details, began on 23 June 1977. In April 1978, five months after the sixteen days of hearings ended on 4 November 1977, its findings were published as the restrictive practices commission's *Report of enquiry into the supply and distribution of cinema films*. In more detail than the investigation report, the document outlines the structure of the cinema trade in Ireland and internationally, pointing out that 'to a great extent, Ireland has always been regarded as part of the UK film distribution network, whether the films were produced in the U.K. or elsewhere.'[12] In the section on the Irish advisory committee (IAC) of the KRS, it states that the committee, formed in 1917 as an advisory body with subsidiary provincial status following the KRS's establishment,

> deals with any problems arising within the industry or with any day to day matters of common concern for their members, and advises the [London-based] Council of the KRS on any matters pertaining to the Irish situation.[13]

Thus, no attempt was made to suggest that the IAC operated independently, except in minor local matters, even though IAC members had asserted to the enquiry that Dublin branch managers 'enjoyed considerable autonomy in Ireland'.[14]

Witnesses for both the KRS and IFRA denied, under oath, that any agreements or understandings conferring monopolies on groups of exhibitors, as alleged by the examiner, were in place, and adamantly rejected the examiner's statement that the evidence of these 'was acknowledged by all Parties.' From the renters' perspective their relationships with exhibitors conformed to 'normal and traditional' patterns of trading.

There were no prior arrangements whereby their firms were committed to [specific Dublin city centre] cinemas, nor had these cinemas any obligation to take any films from them. They denied that there was any collusive action by members of the KRS or the IAC and stated that distribution policies were never discussed at KRS or IAC meetings.[15]

The examiner argued that de facto 'an agreement, whether it was written or tacit, whether just a gentleman's arrangement or an understanding' existed in the distribution pattern of the seventeen films listed in his investigation report. With reference to an authority on European Economic Community competition law, he pointed out that it was internationally accepted that when collusion could be inferred through conduct and concerted practice, 'it is unnecessary to prove the existence of an agreement.'[16] A much narrower view of restrictive practices, however, was assumed by the three enquiry judges: labour historian and later head of business studies, Trinity College Dublin, Charles McCarty; Trinity College lecturer in statistics, Patrick Lyons; and the commission chairman, John Walsh. While the report acknowledged that the independent exhibitors, who had given information to the enquiry, had 'voiced strong suspicions that there must be some type of agreement', given that the pattern of release could not be explained solely by renters acting in their 'best commercial interests', the report starkly stated that none of them 'could substantiate the allegation'.[17] While the enquiry noted that cross-ownership of cinemas made distribution easier (something that distributors acknowledged in relation to Ward Anderson),[18] it maintained that there were no monopolies in place within the Irish film trade. It also stated that there was no evidence to conclude that rental terms were 'unfairly discriminatory',[19] or an agreement existed between renters and Ward Anderson.[20] Nevertheless, in a somewhat self-undermining observation, it highlighted a lack of transparency within the system that could lead 'to some abuse which would be difficult if not impossible to isolate.'[21]

It was the commission's opinion that many cinemas would have closed in recent decades regardless of the distribution system adopted, but reflecting, perhaps, the changes already well underway in Irish business in general, the *Report of enquiry* stated that

> a strong cinema circuit is to the advantage of the public, in ensuring investment in facilities, and in providing a degree of countervailing power to the renters in what has become a seller's market.[22]

Regarding statutory controls of film distribution as 'too rigid and inflexible to serve as an effective means of ensuring equity' in the variety of circumstances which made up the film business,[23] particularly given the fact that the industry had been deemed to be relatively fair, the commission made recommendations for a more transparently equitable distribution of films. This was to be achieved through a voluntary adherence by exhibitors and distributors to fair practice rules, which included details of the functions and mechanism of the product allocation committee and the appeals' tribunal.

The film allocation proposals devised by the KRS, but slightly amended during the course of the public enquiry, were accepted. Although these 'fair, equitable and fool-proof'(at least according to the KRS)[24] schemes nominally satisfied the main groups of complainants, the arrangements with regard to the Dublin suburban cinemas had the potential to damage the Dublin city centre independents (including Ward Anderson) who were excluded from the scheme. Consequently, these exhibitors, who unsurprisingly favoured concurrencies with first-run cinemas (notably, the Adelphi-Carlton and Odeon), strenuously objected to the new arrangements. Although the commission noted that it might appear 'harsh that some of the city centre cinemas fare considerable worse than suburban cinemas in the matter of the timing of product supply', it also pointed out that there could be 'grave financial consequences' in the arbitrary division of first-runs, particularly given the overcapacity within the city centre. It weakly recommended therefore that city centre independents could refer complaints to the product allocation committee and the appeals' tribunal, but, indirectly confirming the international hierarchical pattern of film distribution, warned that their complaints be limited to specific disputes and not to systematic allocation of product. It also recommended that renters might be encouraged to experiment with concurrencies, particularly 'where there is a move-over', and that city centre independents, on request, achieve second-run status at least on a par with suburban cinemas.[25] In its concluding remarks, the commission hoped that the 'somewhat intractable problems' of Dublin city centre would be eased by the changes.[26]

As well as determining the sequence in which cinemas outside Dublin got films following their Dublin city centre first-run, and resolving disputes regarding the allocation of product, including issues relating to barring and splitting, the product allocation committee[27] was to encourage and give assurances to provincial exhibitors who were considering modernizing their cinemas. With the power to confirm and make binding on KRS members any agreement reached by the committee, the PAC could thus instruct a KRS member to allocate a certain proportion or type of film to a particular provincial exhibitor on an exhibitor's investing in a cinema's modernization so as to ensure a reasonable chance of recouping, with profit, all costs incurred. Nevertheless, by this time, outside of Dublin, Ward Anderson interests had become so dominant throughout the country that few exhibitors remained to take advantage of the new competitive opportunities. The future of Dublin city centre independent exhibitors was perhaps even bleaker.

FURTHER DECLINE IN THE 1980s

Within fourteen months of the publication of the restrictive practices commission report, Dublin city centre independents, most notably Michael Butler of the Film Centre, O'Connell Bridge House, and the Cameo, Middle Abbey Street, and Michael Collins of the Curzon, Middle Abbey Street, were complaining about being 'starved' of first-run films by 'the big groups' to the point where they were facing imminent closure. According to Butler, who claimed that he had been 'reduced to showing either rubbish or re-runs', the commission investigation 'had [only] helped the country and suburban cinemas but [had done] nothing' for the city centre exhibitors. He said that although they had gone to the KRS again and again and the IAC had given them a courteous reception, the organization was unable to help them as distribution decisions were being made in London. He also pointed out that it was not a simple issue of too many screens for too little product, as the Savoy was in the process of adding two extra screens because they did not have 'enough outlets for the available product. We have established screens but can't get the product.' Indeed while big cinema groups (such as the Odeon or Adelphi-Carlton) could have bookings up to a year in advance, he did not know what he would be showing the following week. He declared that he had no choice but to go back to the restrictive practices commission to seek assistance,[28] but, despite his and Collins' complaints, no further action was taken by the commission. In 1984 following further representations from the independents, the minister for industry and commerce, John Bruton, threatened to legislate if the distributors did not sort out central Dublin's independents who were seeking the same access to first-run films as Dublin suburban cinemas, which at this time was from the film's fifth week of release, but, as Philip Molloy commented, it would have suited the cinema chains if the independents were 'driven out'[29] since central Dublin with twenty screens was regarded as being 'overseated'. This is what effectively happened, despite the government's attempt to introduce an agreement similar to one in Britain, whereby in a year-long experiment, city centre independents in Glasgow and Liverpool were given access to films four weeks after their first-run release in order to test whether allowing such access 'would substantially harm' the chains.[30] Such measures were too late for Dublin city centre independents. The die had been cast, and, by the end of 1987, following the closures of the Film Centre and the Astor in 1984, and the Curzon in 1987, the only remaining central Dublin independent cinema was Butler's twin-screen Cameo.[31] The situation was even grimmer in Cork city, where in 1984, the last surviving independent cinema, the Cameo was put up for sale.[32]

By contrast, both Ward Anderson and suburban Dublin exhibitors emerged from the restrictive practices enquiry with enhanced positions. In terms of Ward Anderson, not only had the independents' allegations against them not stuck, but the Green Cinema was guaranteed access to first-run product eleven weeks after city centre first-run opening and, crucially, two weeks ahead of suburban Dublin cinemas, while not only did suburban Dublin cinemas continue to be profitable in the wake of the enquiry but in the period between 1976 and mid-1984, investment in such cinemas increased with the number of screens rising from six to ten. In 1978, for example, two years after Anthony O'Grady had closed the Stella, Mount Merrion, he reopened the Stella, Rathmines, which had been opened initially in 1923 by his grandfather after whom he had been named. While the original cinema had about 1,000 seats, the new venue had only 330 'luxury' seats on the ground floor.[33] The same year, Albert Kelly reopened the Kenilworth, Harold's Cross, which, along with the Classic, Terenure, had been closed by Sundrive Cinemas Ltd[34] in 1976. Two years later, he twinned the venue, which he had renamed from its reopening as the Classic, such that there were now an additional ten seats spread across the 300-seat and 190-seat auditoria. He continued to run it as a successful independent cinema until his retirement in August 2003, by which time it had become known for its late-night screenings of *The Rocky Horror Picture Show* (Jim Sharman, 1975).[35] The Forum, Glasthule, which remained operational until 1999, was also twinned in the early 1980s.[36] Thus, the post-enquiry environment for independent cinemas was mixed, but optimistic. Indeed, in 1983, Albert Kelly, the chairman of the all-embracing Independent Cinemas' Association of Ireland (ICAI), which seems to have superceded by, or was the renamed, Irish Cinema Association, could report that the organization represented fifty-five members with eighty-four screens throughout the country, following the recent successful opening by Andrew O'Gorman of the triple-screen Ormonde, Stillorgan.[37]

Ultimately, the relevance of the commission was superseded by the dramatic transformation of exhibition in the 1980s, particularly in Dublin where the real loser proved to be Rank. By 1980, through its Irish subsidiary, Odeon (Ireland) Ltd, Rank controlled Dublin's premier cinema, the Savoy, which had been remodelled as a five-screen complex and reopened in July 1979 with 2,100 seats; Odeon, Eden Quay, which had opened in October 1975 as a twinned and renovated version of their single screen Corinthian; and the Metropole, on the corner of Townsend Street and Hawkins Street, which had opened in 1972 as the New Metropole, and for which a triple screen conversion with 256, 222 and 243 seats was completed in December 1980. Yet, in September 1982 Rank announced its intention to sell these three cinemas with ten screens and 3,304 seats. Though a settlement was reached a year later with Ward Anderson agreeing to purchase them for £2.25 million, it was not until June 1984 that the deal, sanctioned by the minister for industry, trade, commerce and tourism, and which brought the group's portfolio to over sixty cinemas, went ahead. The delay was caused by an investigation into Ward Anderson by the examiner of restrictive practices, J.C. Caldwell, following complaints from other exhibitors. True to form, Ward Anderson paid in cash,[38] though their 're-sale' of '19 O'Connell' (a public house, situated beside the Savoy, which was part of the deal) to Madigan's pub chain, reduced the price somewhat.

Ward Anderson was not just the highest bidder, but also the only one that 'wished to retain [the properties] as cinemas';[39] all the others were developers.[40] According to Ward Anderson, who renamed the Odeon and Metropole as the Screen at O'Connell Bridge and the Screen at College Street, respectively, Rank's failure in Ireland had been due to its expensive Irish head office, which cost £1 million a year. In any case, the acquisitions from Rank brought Ward Anderson's total number of central Dublin screens to fifteen across seven cinemas.[41] Given the high proportion of screens that this represented in Dublin, other cinema owners, fearing that Ward Anderson would have a monopoly, contacted the monopolies commission, which sanctioned the purchase.[42] But then, according to Ward, such complaints typified the moaning and begrudging attitudes of their competitors. Suburban cinema-owners were constantly sniping at the length of Ward Anderson's exclusive runs even though Ward Anderson, with its more expensive overheads, had the cost of launching, publicizing and testing films, as well as the additional problem of enticing people into the city[43] at a time when cinema, reflecting the relative weakness of the Irish economy and high unemployment, 'was at a low point'.[44]

To celebrate the Savoy's coming into Irish hands, for one day Ward Anderson sold all tickets for £1. This not only led to long queues, but also resulted in sales greater than the total sales for the previous two weeks.[45] Thereafter, a reduced staple afternoon seat price of £1.50 was introduced which proved very popular in the recessionary 1980s. In the Screen at College Street their principal innovation was the screening of quality mainstream non-Hollywood independent productions (as opposed to challenging art films) such as *Paris, Texas* (Wim Wenders, 1984, West Germany/France) and *Another Country* (Marek Kanievska, 1984, GB). Its programming policy, partly modeled on London's Screen on the Hill, and affirmed with the advent of the Dublin Film Festival in 1986, established the Screen as an alternative, if not necessarily, a consistently art-house cinema. It retained this status throughout the 1990s and 2000s under the direct guidance of Paul Ward, who, like his father, might be described as having a 'genuine interest in film'.[46] In 1999, for example, the cinema screened what became the Irish all-time foreign language hit, Roberto Benigni's at times comic film about the resilience of the human spirit against the backdrop of the Holocaust, *Life is Beautiful* (*La vita è bella*, 1997, Italy), which grossed over £200,000 at the box office and was still taking £4,000 per week after six months.[47] Nevertheless, the plan, announced in June 1997, to expand the cinema from three to five screens, which was both recognition of the 'lack of screen space' in Dublin for art house product as highlighted by Paul Ward, and an index of Ward Anderson's faith in the growth of art cinema within the city centre, never materialized. Within a week of its being reported, the public was informed that the cinema would remain open 'until further notice'.[48] Similarly, in 1985, a much earlier plan, but for a health food restaurant, envisaged as a replacement of the 'Metro' burger bar, had also been dropped; it was, it seems, an alternative too far![49]

During the 1980s many of Ward Anderson's other Dublin cinemas were closed or sold. The most interesting transactions centred on the Green Cinema, which was unsuccessfully sought by the Salzenger family, who assembled the large valuable site on which later was built the St Stephen's Green shopping centre. In 1974, although Ward Anderson sold the cinema to developer Patrick Gallagher for a record price of £1 million cash, a particularly impressive sum in a period prior to the introduction of capital gains' tax, they managed not only to get an option on the two new cinemas in the proposed development (which in the end were never built), but also to retain use of the cinema for a further three years. They were still running the cinema in the early 1980s, and when Gallagher went bust, Anderson bought the cinema back from the liquidator in 1982 for about the same amount as he had sold it eight years earlier. Within two years, though denying their status as property developers, they had acquired also through the Green Group (of which Ward controlled 50 per cent, Anderson 45 per cent and Andrew Ryan 5 per cent, while Paul Anderson was an executive director) the whole site from the Green Cinema to the College of Surgeons. As Gary Culliton commented in his 1984 profile of Kevin Anderson, 'if property is just an extraneous interest for [him], a lot of people would hate to see him take it up seriously.' But then, as

Anderson pointed out, 'we couldn't be left out of what [was] going to happen' in the area, and, as it was a 'bad time' for selling offices, they were continuing to operate the cinema, although it was envisaged that when they would redevelop the site the office block would contain a modern cinema.[50] In October 1987[51] hotelier P.V. Doyle bought the cinema and adjoining site for 'a substantial seven-figure sum' in order to prevent a hotel being built in competition with the nearby Westbury hotel owned by members of his family. Planning permission to develop the Green Cinema site as an office block was not granted until 2002, by which time the site had become 'an eyesore'. Ironically, an adjacent site at this time was occupied by the up-market Fitzwilton Hotel, a competitor of the Westbury.[52] While the early 2000s would become a byword for dealings of excess in Dublin's commercial property world, this tale is a reminder that such shenanigans were played out during every decade since the 1960s.[53] In any case, it was not until 2010 that expectations of a new (Ward) Anderson cinema located on Stephen's Green became a reality when, as noted in **chapter** 5, plans were announced to build a twelve screen multiplex, the first such venue on the inner city's southside, on the top deck of the car park of the St Stephen's Green shopping centre.[54]

In October 1988, almost a full year after the Green Cinema had closed, the Ambassador also closed to become a financial centre.[55] The project foundered and in 1994 the building returned to being an occasional venue for live events and screenings as it had been in the early twentieth century, and though in 2007 it was announced that the public library in the nearby ILAC shopping centre was to be relocated there,[56] it has remained an entertainment space and even presented the controversial international *Bodies* exhibition in 2009, itself a throwback to eighteenth century forms of shocking educo-entertainments.[57] The other two cinemas Ward Anderson had acquired from Capitol and Allied had similar fates. The Regent had already closed in March 1985, while the Academy, despite closing as a full-time cinema at the end of 1981, continued to be used periodically for both screenings and theatrical performances until the early 1990s. Destroyed by fire in 1994, Ward Anderson finally transformed it into a large extended office building during 2004 to 2006, though it restored the original Antient Concert Rooms auditorium as part of the redevelopment. Meanwhile in 2002, their Screen at O'Connell Bridge, which had closed in 1993, together with the neighbouring cinema, the Astor,[58] which had closed in June 1984 after they had acquired it from Vogue McNally, Bertie McNally's widow, was redeveloped as an apartment building and live entertainment venue, confirmation that the group was as interested in maximizing the potential from their property assets as it was in developing film exhibition interests.[59]

THE CHALLENGE FROM NEW DISTRIBUTION TECHNOLOGIES

It is of note that during the 1990s the foyer of what had been the Astor Cinema, Eden Quay, was used as a video tape retail outlet (with viewing facilities), as it was video, which made its presence felt from the early 1980s, that contributed to the major transformation of cinema exhibition and indeed led to the redefinition of the cinema venue from a single or even triple screen complex to a building with multiple screens. Pressure on all exhibitors came not so much from the explosion of video within the home, though that clearly had an increasing impact, but from the short-lived phenomenon of the early to mid-1980s whereby public houses, hotels and other such establishments pre-empted or mimicked cinemas, by showing large screen presentations of unreleased and, at times, even pirated copies of recent feature films. Abbey Films claimed that 1980 box office takings were down 20 per cent on the previous year, though the 'biting recession' of the period was as much responsible for the fall-off in income as anything else, including video. Full-time cinema staff had been halved to 350 during the 1970s, or one-quarter of what they had been at the height of cinema-going.[60] Indeed, one independent, Aidan Daly of the Oscar Cinema, Carrickmacross, Co. Monaghan, said in 1981 that he abandoned plans for a £150,000 cinema investment in Monaghan town due to the 'video explosion'.[61]

The decline in audiences continued into 1982, with reports of a 15 to 25 per cent drop in Dublin admissions, or 20 per cent in real terms. Harry Band, UIP's Irish manager, described it as 'a very, very bad phase in the cinema business.'[62] By 1985 Leo Ward was admitting that admission prices were 'too high', but he also pointed out that 'with overheads as they are and VAT at 23 per cent [raised from 18 per cent in 1983] there is little scope for reduction.'[63] Indeed, from a box office income that year of £16 million, the taxman's take was the same as the renters, £3.5 million.[64] Nevertheless, Ward Anderson did manage to offer concessionary prices, particularly for afternoon shows, in an attempt to bolster attendance. (Indeed such practices came to the fore once again in the context of the late 2000s recession, with the IMC Dún Laoghaire for example offering unemployed patrons admission of €4 before 5p.m. Monday to Friday, with a supplement of €1 on 3D films.) With the rise of suburban living, many were not coming into Dublin city centre, not least because, as Ray Comiskey observed, it had become negatively associated with dirt, car theft, violence and poor public transport and was increasingly regarded as an unattractive place to visit;[65] others were simply 'short of money'; and tourism was down. Immediately after the 1984 budget, when the VAT rate on cinema tickets was not reduced from 23 per cent, the Independent Cinemas Association of Ireland started an anti-VAT campaign. In a letter to TDs, senators, and county councillors outlining the difficulties that continued to face their members, including tourist fall off, video and video piracy, and lack of access to new product, they declared that VAT was most devastating to their business and blamed it on the closure of upwards of thirty halls in the previous twelve months, including the Grand Central twin-screen cinema in Tramore, Co. Waterford,[66] which had opened in 1981, and four Dublin cinemas. The letter also noted that they had requested the minister for finance, Alan Dukes, to make cinemas exempt from VAT, but he did not do this even though VAT on theatres had been reduced in the previous two budgets, and by then was only 5 per cent. Leo Ward, though usually and increasingly at odds with the independents, particularly given that suburban exhibitors were now getting films after only five weeks of their release in the city centre which had declined as a hub for entertainment, not only backed the ICAI but claimed that the minister was putting

2,000 jobs at risk. Nevertheless, Michael Algar, chief executive of the Irish Film Board, had little sympathy for the exhibitors. He argued that by importing and screening foreign films they were, unlike theatres, which employed local talent, in the business of exporting profits. He suggested that they would have 'power to alter the Minister's mind on VAT by putting funds into Irish film-making, and thereby justifying a reduction on VAT.'[67] In any case, by 1991, the VAT rate for cinemas had been reduced to 12 per cent,[68] and remained at this or the 12.5 per cent rate until it was increased to 13.5 per cent in 2003, the rate at which it has remained. (By comparison, exempting the period from January 2001 to March 2002 when the standard VAT rate was 20 per cent, the standard VAT rate from March 1991 to 1 January 2010 was 21 per cent, after which it was increased to 21.5 per cent.)

This was, undoubtedly, the nadir of Irish cinema box office, and by the end of the 1980s, a steady increase in cinema income was evident. The stemming of the thirty-year long decline in Irish exhibition owed to a number of factors, foremost among them were the emergence of a new concept in cinema exhibition, the multiplex (discussed in the next chapter), which first made its home in the suburbs, moreover within a shopping centre; and the huge social and economic transformation of Irish society during the 1990s and 2000s. Additionally, resurgence in Irish filmmaking, heralded by the Oscar success of Jim Sheridan's *My Left Foot* (1989), helped to grow audiences and increase interest in cinema more generally. Unsurprisingly, mainstream films with an Irish content, or films made by Irish directors or featuring leading Irish actors, attract large home audiences. *The Commitments* (Alan Parker, 1991), for example, based on Roddy Doyle's book about a Dublin-based soul band, had full houses during its three-month run at the Savoy and grossed over £2 million, a fifteenth of the total Irish box office take of 1991, while Irish director Neil Jordan's *Michael Collins* (1996), took more than twice that figure at the Irish box office. In 2003 three Irish films – *Veronica Guerin* (Joel Schumacher), the year's top Irish box office film; *Intermission* (John Crowley), the top grossing Irish Film Board film at the Irish box office;[69] and Jim Sheridan's *In America* – combined to account for 12 per cent of that year's €97.4 million box-office takings.[70] Other Irish top grossing films in the years since have included *Man About Dog* (Paddy Breathnach, 2004, number 11 in the annual box office hits) which took €2.1 million;[71] *The Wind that Shakes the Barley* (Ken Loach, 2006, number 3) which took €4.1 million; and *In Bruges* (Martin MacDonagh, 2008, number 7) which took €3 million.[72] Nevertheless, to place this in perspective, it must be remembered that most Irish-made films, in keeping with all regional films, are not generally big budget, and, as the appendix (tables 13a–d) reveals, they often fail to be released across a significant number of screens and/or do poorly at the box office compared with Hollywood product; are manifestly different to mainstream American product in content if not in form; do not fit (as easily as American big budget films) the conventional modes of distribution, not least due to the costs involved in marketing and promotion; and are often financially and otherwise muscled out by the stranglehold of multinational distributors. As managing director of Buena Vista International Ireland Brendan McCaul said in 2001, 'distributing any more than three Irish films a year just isn't feasible for us.'[73] Screening

Irish films abroad is even more problematic, particularly in America, where distributors and exhibitors tend to be ideological and cultural isolationists, with the result that those few Irish films which are screened are very often seen only in the limited contexts of festivals, art cinemas, or (Irish) ethnic environments.

Despite the upturn of cinema attendance there remained in the twenty-six counties, in contrast to Northern Ireland, a problem of film print availability. According to Irish exhibitors, an insufficient number of prints is made available for each release in relation to the size of the market. While some have regarded this as a result of American distribution policy, many of the smaller independents, which, as a body, have been more affected by the shortage of product, and thus were either struggling or being forced to close, displaced the blame from the distributors to the larger exhibitors. In any case, as one disgruntled independent starkly stated in 1992, 'cinemas are closing down, and it's not because there is no business it is because there is no product.'[74] Speaking five years later, Diarmuid O'Shea, owner of the single-screen Oisín Cinema in Killorglin, Co. Kerry, explained the plight of the independent more fully. People, particularly in the context of video, 'want to see films straight away ... I got *Titanic* five weeks after its release and it was a complete flop. I had to take it off after the third week.'[75] By the end of 2001, the Oisín, following the fate of countless small cinemas, had closed, but although this left many areas without a local cinema, the improvements in road building, and the location of many multiplexes on or near motorways, has meant that the absence is less real than might be apparent. However, closure of such cinemas, which continued throughout the 2000s, most publicly in relation to the Greenes' Ormonde, Midleton, Cork, in 2006,[76] should not be simply seen as the direct result of competing technologies, multiplexes and distribution practice, but also in terms of property development, particularly in the context of cinemas located in city centre sites. Furthermore, it was not just independent cinemas that closed, but several cinemas owned by Ward Anderson, who had come to understand that modernizing old cinemas did not (re)generate the audience to the degree that investing in a new purpose-built cinema would. Investment in such new spaces during the 1990s and 2000s, not least by transnationals, which led the way, resulted in a huge expansion in the number of screens, as is discussed in chapter 5.

Given that considerable pressure was put on smaller second-run or independent cinemas by the release of films on video within an increasingly short period of their original theatrical release date, it is important to outline, even if only cursorily, the video retailing and rental sector in Ireland. Ironically, however, the threat of the simultaneous theatrical and DVD/video release of films, imminent by the early 2000s, led to exhibitors such as at Dublin's Dundrum multiplex to try to recreate 'cinema-going as an event and embellishing the social aspect' through enhancing the design and comfort of the cinema space and the cinema experience.[77] Its postmodern design, incorporating the art deco glory of cinema, which was to the fore in the redesigned Strand, Belfast, when it reopened in 1999 following extensive renovation in order to distinguish itself from the 'square box' multiplexes,[78] offers a fantasy space far removed from home-cinema. However, in a display of confidence in the cinema as a wholly-different, if related, product to DVDs and games, and recognizing the economic importance of DVD online rental, since summer 2010, the Dundrum cinema website has been offering (through the services of Irish-owned, and relatively small Online DVD rental), films and games for rent.

The experience of Xtra-vision, the dominant Irish video retailing group, is of interest not least as it shows, yet again, a market being identified and cultivated by an independent Irish business, but consolidated and expanded by a large-scale transnational. Founded by former motorcycle courier Richard Murphy in 1982, Xtra-vision expanded rapidly until 1989 when it was floated on the Irish stock exchange and became, according to the *Irish Times*' Brendan McGrath, 'a classic "boom and bust" stock'.[79] While its stock market listing led to 'an aggressive expansion' in Ireland, Britain and the USA, funded by share issues of £22 million, within a year, the company had accrued debts of £18.3 million and losses of £20.3 million. At that point, Cambridge, a fast-growing financial services group, acquired 61 per cent of the company and Murphy was replaced as chief executive by the head of Xtra-vision's US operations, Sal Perisano. However, in September 1993 Cambridge, whose shares in the company had already been reduced to 48.1 per cent following share issues in 1992, went into receivership. As a consequence, Xtra-vision, which was in default by £11.8 million to a banking syndicate, had its shares suspended at 1.625p and the Irish high court appointed an examiner, accountant Brendan Somers. By July 1994, two British venture capital groups, 3i and HSBC Private Equity, had bought the company out of examinership.[80] At this time, NCB corporate finance director, Peter O'Grady Walshe, who had been pivotal to the deal, was appointed managing director, and ordinary shareholders were offered 0.125p for their shares, a fraction of their high of 108p. The company refocused its market away from America, selling its US interests for $2 million and repurchasing in 1995 the Northern Ireland stores, such that by January 1996 it owned 225 stores (all Irish), employed 1,000 people, and was debt free.[81] By way of context, it is interesting to note that according to a 1994 estimate, only three times this number were employed across the *entire* Irish film distribution and exhibition sector, which at this period was spread across 184 screens in seventy cinemas.[82]

Unsurprisingly, Xtra-vision's leading position within the Irish market attracted international attention, and in October 1996 the video rental group was bought for an undisclosed sum, probably in the region of £20 million,[83] by video retail giant Blockbuster, a subsidiary of the American entertainment group Viacom[84] which already owned 5,300 such stores worldwide, 700 of which were in Britain where it controlled 21 per cent of the video rental market. At this time, Xtra-vision sales were roughly £25 million, £18 million of which came from the Irish Republic and the remainder from Northern Ireland, and combined profits were £3.7 million, of which £3.2 million was generated in the south. Commenting on the Irish acquisition, Blockbuster's chairman Bill Fields said that the combination of Ireland's high VCR penetration at 72 per cent compared with Britain's 79 per cent and the quality customer base established by Xtra-vision made Ireland 'a great place' for Blockbuster, adding that the company intended to locate its 'successful entertainment retailing concept in both established and developing markets worldwide.'[85] In its first full year of trading in Ireland, 1997, Blockbuster Entertainment (Ireland) Ltd had £25.4 million in sales; by 2000 the company controlled roughly 55 per cent of the Northern Irish market, and slightly less of the Irish Republic's.[86] Despite suffering a series of high-profile management defections during 1996 to 2000, and the number of outlets dropping to 217, eight fewer than when Blockbuster had acquired the company,[87] nevertheless, by 2002, Xtra-vision had £6 million profit on turnover of £70 million.

Of more consequence for cinemas, however, has been the threat from new technologies, including the internet, cable tv, video-on-demand, and even earlier access to feature films on film channels such as Sky Movies, particularly given that the video rental market experienced a decline from the late 1990s. While this decline, in part, was a result of the expansion within the cinema theatrical market, it was no less due to the almost simultaneous release of rental and retail videos, and the fact that studios were making films available at relatively low costs, thus encouraging consumers to buy rather than to rent. Indeed, such encouragement is also seen in the issuing of collectors' editions, limited box sets and pre-packed grouped films such as a trio of action or horror films, and, in terms of DVDs, the addition of bonus features that might include an alternative version(s) of the film; deleted scenes; short documentaries on the various aspects of a film's production or history, something particularly important in special effects' movies; commentaries by the directors and/or cast and crew; interviews with cast and directors; and, for children's titles, also games, sing/read-alongs, and complementary cartoons. Notwithstanding that Ireland lagged behind other European countries in terms of VCR ownership, Irish buying of films increased by 23 per cent in the period 1993 to 1994, and a further 15 per cent from 1994 to 1995, bringing the value of the sell-through market to £12 million compared with the rental market which was worth £45 million.[88] The VCR market, which continued to grow dramatically in Ireland throughout the 1990s, has largely been superseded by the more versatile DVD which not only is compatible with other technologies, including computers and gaming machines, but, as a digital rather than analogue technology, offers better picture and sound quality: it can store more information; does not degrade (to the same extent) as video and so is more suited to permanent collection; is cheaper to produce; and is easier to store both in terms of space and conditions. (The establishment of the superior higher-definition Blu-Ray format, compatible with gaming consoles, as equivalent to or more popular than DVD, has been thwarted somewhat by the global economic difficulties of the late 2000s.)

While the DVD entered the market in 1997, it was not until the early 2000s that it reached the same penetration levels as the VCR,[89] though with even multi-region DVD players available for as little as €30 by the mid- to late 2000s, it is not the cost of the hardware, but the software, the films themselves, which remained higher in Ireland than most other countries in Europe. In a 2010 survey of twenty-two European countries by *Screen Digest* for the European Audiovisual Observatory, Irish consumers were said to pay the highest prices for renting and purchasing DVDs. On average, DVDs cost €4.60 to rent, 48 per cent higher than the European norm of €3.10, while the average purchase cost of a DVD in Ireland was €14.00, 25 per cent higher than the European average of €11.20. Ireland was third highest for renting after Denmark and Norway, while retail costs put Ireland at the fourth highest in Europe. Similar to per capita cinema-going, Irish people rent and buy more films than anyone else except Icelanders, renting on average 11.6 films per year (compared with France's two), and buying eleven films a year. One explanation for Ireland's higher prices is that unlike elsewhere in Europe where most DVDs are sold through supermarkets and consumer electronic specialists, a large portion of the Irish market is serviced by specialists such as HMV and Xtra-vision, which had 84 per cent of the Irish rental market in 2009. Nevertheless, the cost of buying DVDs in Ireland dropped during 2009, in large part due to an aggressive pricing policy by supermarket giant Tesco, but, even this retailer charged much more for DVDs in Ireland than in its British outlets, though it chose to blame distributors' pricing policies for the differential between the two territories.[90] That said, there is an increasing number of non-chart, though recent and mainstream, DVDs available to buy for between €5 and €10.

The issue of the simultaneous release of films for retail and rental led to a dispute in 2003 between Blockbuster and Warner Bros which resulted in Warner Bros withdrawing their supplies from Xtra-vision.[91] Seemingly undaunted, Blockbuster/Xtra-vision's response to these challenges was to offer 'the complete entertainment package'. In 2005, it committed to spending £5 million on remodeling sixty-five of its shops, increasing the size of the shops and upgraded the facilities in an era of media convergence to include DVDs, video games, compact discs, and mobile phones.[92] Nevertheless, Blockbuster, whose largest shareholder was activist investor Carl Icahn, was a giant in decline. From 2006 onwards, when it reported a drop in profits in Ireland from €9.6 million in 2005 to €8.4 million, speculation was rife that it would withdraw from non-USA markets. By 2008, Irish profits had dropped by a further 26 per cent to €6.2 million. Indeed, in early 2007, it sold its UK arm, Gamestation, to Game Group Corporation, and it was expected that the sale of Xtra-vision would soon follow.[93] By early 2009, concern that Blockbuster's diversification into DVD-by-mail and download video was not stemming the company's losses, led to further store closures and disposals, including of Xtra-vision, which was sold in August 2009 in a deal potentially worth €32 million, though subsequently realized at only €20 million[94] to a conglomerate comprising of Pageant Holdings with principals Peter O'Grady Walshe[95] and Nicky Furlong,[96] NCB Stock-brokers' Ventures fund with 50 per cent of the chain, and the chain's management with a 10 per cent stake. Operating through a new Irish company, Birchhall Investments, the chain's 186 stores and 1,400 staff in Ireland, had a new chief executive, Tony Keating, previously the finance director of the former company.[97] The Xtra-vision story is somewhat unique in Irish terms in the sense that the company started as a small business, and then went through a series of foreign owners before returning to Irish control. (Of course, almost all the products in Xtra-vision stores are imported.) By the end of October 2010, by which time it was operating 184 outlets in Ireland, it was in talks with the troubled Chartbusters concerning a takeover of 'two or three' of its shops, any more would be 'pointless' as most were near their own outlets.[98]

Chartbusters was established by Richard Murphy in 1993 as a modest, video retailing and rental chain, with initial stores in Blanchardstown and the Square, Tallaght. By September 1996 it had eighteen stores, with another eight or nine planned, most of which were in large outlets with an average of 12,000 videos and some were open twenty-four hours. Pioneering in the Irish environment, the shops also offered for sale other home entertainment goods such as Sony's PlayStation, while also leasing store space to a phone retailer. Additionally, between 2000 and 2002 Chartbusters opened more than forty 'Tan.ie' outlets at its video shops.[99] In an interview in 1996, Murphy stated that profit margins were 'way in excess' of 17 per cent and the stores were 'making really good money'. He also pointed out that the business was run without recourse to long-term financing, but operated only with a 'small overdraft'. Interestingly, the shareholders of Chartbusters were mainly property developers – Paddy Kelly, John Walsh, Jarleth Sweeney and John McCabe – whose long-term interests, at least from the perspective of the mid-1990s to the mid-2000s, probably lay as much in the stores' site values as their videos.[1] By 2002 it had fifty stores with a gross profit of €11 million, rising to €17.5 million two years later.[2] However, shareholder Kelly became one of the most high profile casualties of the property crash when in 2009 he found himself before the courts in both Ireland and the USA as creditors sought repayment of outstanding or non-performing loans.[3] By then, the commercial property house of cards had collapsed as the Irish state took responsibility for over €70 billion worth of 'toxic' bank loans made to property speculators/developers which were heavily discounted to reflect the dramatic fall in asset prices in the late 2000s' recession.[4]

While video and DVD renters and retailers in Ireland, including the chains Xtra-vision, Chartbusters, Advance Vision, and Movie Magic (which had sixteen outlets in 2007 and nineteen stores by 2010),[5] sought to counteract the new entertainment-based threats[6] to their business by in part incorporating them, as much as possible, and diversifying into music/movie/ computer game[7] and other related sales, and in some instances, particularly small independents, establishing internet access points, by the mid-2000s it had become clear that the golden days of traditional rental had disappeared. In central Dún Laoghaire, for example, by 2008 there was no longer a large specialized video/DVD rental outlet, but more dramatically, family business Advance Vision, which had ten outlets in 2007 had been reduced to only two, while in 2008 Xtra-vision held talks with retail giant Tesco with a view to offloading a large number of its 200 stores around the country.[8] Although Xtra-vision, with its integrated movie, games, music and electronic items, has remained the dominant entertainment store and as of December 2010 employed 1,400 staff, had 186 shops (with almost fifty of these in county Dublin), and listed on its website its association with the Irish Film Board, financial difficulties, largely resulting from high rents led the company to seek a high court examinership in early 2011.[9]

The route of examinership had already been taken by Richard Murphy in relationship to Chartbusters in early 2009 at which time the company, having shed thirteen of its stores since 2002, had thirty-seven 'home entertainment' outlets (nineteen in Dublin and eighteen elsewhere in the state); employed 267 workers; and carried debts of €20 million. Twenty of the stores were operating profitably, though group turnover had dropped to €12.2 million in the year to 30 April 2008, while extra costs, especially rent, had eroded profits. As a result of its difficulties, an examiner was appointed to the company by the high court, though this was opposed by two of the group's creditors, Lombard Ireland Bank and Winchurch Investments Ltd, who argued that the core DVD business was 'dead', and declared they had lost faith in the group's management.[10] Nevertheless, the court, though accusing Murphy of engaging in 'sharp practice' and 'sleveenism' in his treatment of Winchurch,[11] gave protection to the company, subject to conditions, including the closure of seventeen of its thirty-seven shops.[12] Though the slimmed down Chartbusters with twenty-eight stores and 170 employees emerged out of court examinership in April 2010 after its creditors accepted a maximum of 10 per cent of what they were owed, and the company continued to operate with John McCabe of McCabe Builders brought on board as a director, its future was put in doubt again when a wind-up petition was presented to the courts in July 2010.[13] Its long slide to liquidation continued until October 2010, when its remaining sixteen outlets in the Republic closed, with the loss of twenty-two full-time and sixty-five part-time jobs.[14]

In 2006, adding to the ever-increasing modes of distribution of films, DVDs became available in Ireland through vending machines. These could hold up to 1,500 DVDs, needed no staff in attendance, and could fit in a space of two square meters. The innovative company, Original Video, the first and only UK and Ireland manufacturer of automated DVD rental vending machines, hoped to replicate the vending machine's success in Spain where Blockbuster, in response to the competition, was forced into bankruptcy and closed all its branches, but, despite limited success in Ireland and Britain, which led the company to open a manufacturing plant in Mexico,[15] the concept failed to take off. The first Irish outlet was in the convenience store Supervalu, Eden Quay, Dublin, in spring 2006.[16] This was followed by one in Maynooth, Co. Kildare, in August 2006, where the machine was installed in an off-licence, and within eight months had 900 members renting up to 1,900 DVDs per month at a cost of €3 per film per night.[17] The same month, a store was opened at Wood Quay, Ennis, Co. Clare, where 1,000 members were renting 3,000 videos per month by April 2007.[18] Original Video's fourth DVD machine was installed at 24/7 DVD, Nenagh, Co. Tipperary,[19] though the progress of the concept thereafter remained limited with Original Video's apparently unrevised (since 2007) website identifying only six current locations in Ireland with four due to open 'soon', a number not dissimilar to that in Britain where eight were open with a further eight expected.[20] It was yet another apparently good business model, which used the internet for stock control and maintenance, but which could not offer the internet's increasing availability of movies, music and games, whether legally or illegally.

Nevertheless, one of the most feared rivals of the video rental market, the online video/DVD retailer, has not been without causalities, with once again, an Irish company succumbing to the might of global capitalism. Belfast-based Blackstar Films, which set up the first British or Irish online video and DVD sales company in 1997, expanded quickly. Its founders – film producer Darryl Collins, technology expert Tony

Bowden and designer Jeremy Glover – who raised over GB£10 million from investors, including from venture capitalists TPG (owned by American David Bondermann, chairman of Irish airline Ryanair), Tarrant Venture Capital, Atlas Venture, and Pilton company founder Nicky Furlong, succeeded in talking its value up to £200 million. However, the company's stock market flotation and planned expansion into Europe was stymied with the collapse of the dot.com bubble in 2001. While claiming in 2000 to have grown by 800 per cent in 1999, and having 100,000 customers, 130 employees,[21] and a stock of 50,000 titles, compared with the average 'real-life' outlet of 2,000–3,000 titles,[22] it had little that was unique and found itself rudderless in the post-9/11 downturn. By then, online bookseller Amazon.com had already established a British offshoot by buying in 1998 the IMDb movie information website, which had sold videos since 1996.[23] Amazon's entry into the market in Britain where Blackstar had 80 per cent of its sales, effectively sounded the death knell for Blackstar by obliterating its only major advantage over the Americans – the ability to supply European format videos and DVDs. Indeed, titles not yet released in Ireland were becoming available on Amazon,[24] but as a means both of thwarting pirates and ensuring maximum theatrical revenues, by the early 2000s major productions were being released simultaneously worldwide. By then, Blackstar, which had begun to ship from Jersey in 2003 as a means of avoiding VAT on items less than GB£18,[25] had been reinvented as sendit.com and was owned by video distribution group Pilton, which in turn was bought by DCC in 2005.[26] In 2008, Sendit was trading well with net profits rising from GB£613,000 for the fourteen months ending 31 March 2006 to GB£698,000 for the year ending 31 March 2007. However, the increased profits had come largely as a result of staff cuts and its actual turnover in the same period had fallen from GB£9 million to GB£5.8 million.[27] Speaking in the wake of the published accounts, the company's directors stated that though they would continue to look for opportunities to expand turnover and profits, 'the principal risks facing the company [were] … the advent of new technological developments in downloading and new viewing platforms.'[28] While Blackstar had tried to build an online business out of Ireland, the small size of the domestic market not only required it to grow overseas, but such Irish online operators would be vulnerable to larger scale foreign, especially British and American, rivals, a story familiar to commercial entertainments in Ireland since Dan Lowrey's was sold to Moss & Thornton in the 1890s, as discussed in the companion volume.

Since 2001 the availability of online DVD rental has become a reality in Ireland. While online rental – whereby for a fixed fee[29] a consumer can order a film, have it delivered and returned by free post, and immediately replaced by another – has made a significant impact in America not least through Netflix, which had 9.39 million customers by the end of 2008, having surpassed Blockbuster two years earlier, a reporter, backed up by traditional video rental operators, was predicting that it was unlikely to pose a serious threat to the Irish rental market due to issues around scale.[30] Nevertheless, a former IT manager, Frank O'Grady, sought to emulate the Netflix formula in Ireland by establishing dvdrentals.ie, which was rebranded as Screenclick.com shortly afterwards, and was offering 650 titles by mid-2002.[31] However, as Niall

Kearney, a director of video store Advance Vision, Bray, pointed out in 2006, DVD rental by mail 'suits countries where you have vast distances, like the US and Australia.'[32] Despite this, a number of other Irish online rental companies, including, among others,[33] Moviestar.ie, founded in August 2006, grew, while, notwithstanding Xtra-vision's continued and considerable, if diminished presence, traditional rental outlets have declined, such that Brian O'Connell in an article entitled 'What will no longer be here by 2020?' wrote in 2010, 'it's hard to see how video and DVD rental shops will survive the next decade' given that most independent small video shops have been forced to shut.[34] (Of course, the days of video or the VHS format have been already clearly numbered with few shops actually stocking VHS tapes.)

Moviestar.ie, established by Dublin brothers Gavin and Iain McConnon whose previous business practices attracted negative attention,[35] remained 'independent' for just over two years. Given the McConnon's history, it is perhaps unsurprising that their video online business almost immediately became mired in controversy when, within a few weeks of starting, they were deemed to breach film copyright by renting retail 'sell through' DVDs rather than rental DVDs, which cost three times the price of retail DVDs.[36] Competitor Screenclick.com (taken over by major British online rental company LoveFilm International Ltd for €3 million in 2005, but with Frank O'Grady still in charge, at which time it claimed 70,000 registered Irish users)[37] reported Moviestar.ie to American corporations Miramax and Disney for copyright breaches. Yet despite its questionable beginnings, and indeed the hostile comments on internet blogs concerning their former activities, by 2008 Moviestar.ie was claiming to have €1.2 million turnover and 15,000 customers,[38] which it was hoped would grow to over 40,000 by mid-2008 following the launch in May 2008 of a digital video-on-demand download service. (Crucially, this service did not include American feature films, but was largely confined to television content.)[39] The McConnon brothers predicted that by 2013 the Irish online rental market would have in excess of 200,000 subscribers and would be worth €35 million per annum.[40] However, Moviestar.ie's owners followed the tradition of Irish entrepreneurs becoming established in the local market and selling out at a profit to a transnational corporation, in their case, in January 2009, to the dominant British and Irish online service provider, Screenclick.com/LoveFilm.

LoveFilm's dominant position in the British, Irish and other markets emerged out of a series of mergers and acquisitions during 2002 to 2008 following the establishment of Online Rentals Ltd in May 2002 in Harlow, Essex, and the launch in September 2003 of two London online companies, ScreenSelect and Video Island. By the end of 2004, LoveFilm had 50,000 subscribers, while in March 2005 it was claiming that it was shipping 700,000 rental units per month. This scale of operations was somewhat similar to ScreenSelect, which merged with Video Island in September 2004, and with LoveFilm in April 2006. Two years later, in February 2008, LoveFilm took over Amazon.com's UK and German DVD rental business, though in the process Amazon became LoveFilm's largest shareholder. A complaint against LoveFilm/Amazon/Screenclick familiar from the history of film exhibition is that such a dominant online DVD rental company squeezes out independent operators.[41]

LoveFilm operates a DVD service of rentals, resale, console games and online film viewing in the UK, Republic of Ireland, Germany and Scandanavia. In January 2009, LoveFilm claimed to have one million members and over 65,000 titles, with over 4 million rentals per month across the five countries in which it operated. The company's growth comes in part from a large number of partner companies, which are separately branded versions of the main company, and to which LoveFilm provides the website and the services. These partners, which bring in large customer bases otherwise unavailable to LoveFilm, include supermarket chains and newspapers. The *Irish Times* is one such media company that has branched out beyond its traditional core print business to acquire not only the property website myhome.ie, as it seeks alternative revenue streams as newspaper publishing declines in the digital age, but also a DVD rental service boasting 'the biggest selection of DVDs in Ireland.' While all such DVD rental services may be provided, ultimately, by LoveFilm, the presentation and pricing structure may vary from one partner to another, though in the case of the *Irish Times*, not only does it have an identical pricing structure to Screenclick, and even uses its graphics, if slightly rearranged, but announces that the website is 'powered by Screenclick, Inc.'; the contact phone number is even the same for both websites. The Screenclick/LoveFilm/*Irish Times* sites offered in early 2010, one DVD for €12.99 (bronze unlimited); two at a time for €17.99 (silver unlimited); three at a time for €24.99 (gold unlimited); and four at a time €31.99 (platinum unlimited), with no late fees, no postage charge, and no contracts.[42] Such prices are similar, though slightly more expensive than those offered by the smaller Irish owned company onlineDVDrental.ie, where each package, excepting the platinum bundle priced identically by the two companies, is €2.00 less.

Notwithstanding the fact there is no weekend post in Ireland, from the perspective of the customer, online rental makes a lot of economic sense not least because it gets rid of late fee charges as a film may be kept for as long as a customer wants. Similarly, from the point of view of the online renter, not only does the operator get a fixed sum of money in advance, facilitating more accurate financial and management planning, but also there is the additional advantage of smaller overheads with regard to buying/renting, servicing and staffing shop space. As Peter O'Mahony, managing director of Busy Bee DVD, noted in 2006, at any one time, 85 per cent of Netflix's stock was in transit.[43] Such a distribution system, whereby storage is considerably reduced, also allows these companies to offer a greater range of titles. In 2006, Busy Bee, launched the previous year, was reporting that they had 12,000 of the 24,000 movies available in Ireland on DVD, compared with the 2,000–3,000 films of the typical non-virtual renter; Screenclick.com, which took over Busy Bee DVD (its main rival) in 2007, stated it had over 15,000 titles available in 2010. The development of home cinema as a concept from the late 1990s has been central to the growth of such online operations. This idea of radically renovating the home to incorporate a large plasma screen and home cinema sound system was used in 2008 in a national radio advertising campaign for supermarket Daybreak, which was offering prizes of a year's rental supply of DVDs to customers. While DVD rental distribution through a local store, vending machine or via the post have ensured all customers are catered for, nevertheless, all of these would be seen as traditional distribution patterns which are coming under increasing strain from online delivery via the internet to home or office computers, and even to palm devices such as smart phones.

By 2007, one such challenge was being mounted by Apple Corp. through iTunes as it began to make television material available online for downloading. By that stage, the internet, a reality only since 1993, was already becoming increasingly used by film-makers, mostly with regard to short independent films, as a means of direct exhibition, either in order to bypass conventional modes of distribution including off-line film festivals, or in an attempt to attract the attention of distributors in order to win a theatrical release, thus redefining the web as an 'another layer of gatekeeping [in] the [distribution] system'.[44] (Major studios similarly use the web for promotional purposes by issuing trailers of forthcoming films.) In 1999 alone, around thirty sites had been launched, including iFilm.net and Atomfilms, the largest and most recognized web film sites, and by 2000 it was estimated that there were roughly 100 sites, with the short e-film considered 'one of the hottest business on the Web'.[45] The 'penetration of streaming video players and broadband technologies into the consumer market ... made watching media on the Web not only increasingly feasible but also increasingly attractive',[46] with the result that the short, increasingly cheap and easy to make digital video has become ubiquitous on the web, not least on You-Tube, but it should be remembered that, generally, filmmakers who post their films do not get paid directly. In May 2008, Apple extended for its American customers only its material available on iTunes to include, from the same day as their DVD release, new films from major studios, including 20th Century-Fox, Walt Disney, Warner Bros, Paramount, Universal and Sony. The films, which could be downloaded at a cost of $14.99 for recent releases or $9.99 for older titles, can then be replayed on video iPods, iPhones and Mac or Windows computers.[47]

While, as of summer 2010, this remained unavailable to Irish consumers, it is only a matter of time before subscribers to broadband providers will be able to access such services. Indeed, broadband provider HomeVision was offering downloads, for rent of €1 to €2.50, of a number of films and television broadcasts, mainly from the BBC, while, as noted, a greater range of such material was available from May 2008 from Movie.star,[48] a process that may accelerate given that transnational Screenclick/LoveFilm now owns the company. While online rental will not come fully of age until feature films are routinely available for download, such new home entertainment technologies have come in the wake of the most momentous transformation of film exhibition globally since the introduction of sound in the 1920s/1930s, or the investment in multiplexes largely from the 1980s. It is, of course, in such a context that 3D cinema has particular appeal for Hollywood, but then even if, as Kevin Anderson says, people no longer go to the cinema as an outing in and of itself the way many Irish people did in the past, but only in order 'to see a film which happens to be in a cinema',[49] as Graham Spurling, a principal figure in Movies@, has argued, 'if you're genuinely interested in watching film, a computer screen is nothing like a 40- or 50-feet-wide screen and being surrounded by 300 or 400 people enjoying the atmosphere.'[50] It is then perhaps fair to state that cinema, which has been relatively resilient to wars, recessions and other disasters, and has survived competition from other cultural forms, will no doubt survive the new means of accessing film, whether through downloading or online rental, not least as, ultimately, these can be regarded as complementary to cinema exhibition rather than just competing with it.

CHAPTER 5

Multiplexes and the Renewal of Irish Exhibition

'The reasons which lay behind our desire to build multiplexes in Europe had to do principally with the synergies which they can generate ... in [shopping and Leisure] complexes with many bars and restaurants offering a range of after-show attractions.'

Europe president of AMC, the group behind Ireland's first multiplex in Tallaght.[1]

DEFINING THE MULTIPLEX

From the 1960s onwards, many Irish exhibitors, large and small, adapted to the changes in film-going practice brought about by the transformation of Irish culture and society, by twining and further subdividing existing cinemas. While such renovations and refurbishments invariably increased a cinema's viability, more often than not it also resulted in an inferior viewing experience for the cinemagoer, just as had happened in America in the 1960s when multiplex cinemas, mostly situated in shopping malls – hence their popular name as mall cinemas – began to emerge. Although it could be argued that in the 1960s and 1970s many of these American cinemas with their paper thin walls, sticky floors, cramped seating, noisy patrons, and projection booths that rarely lined up with the (small) screens, presented worse conditions than many Irish cinemas of the same period, the (refurbished) Irish cinemas were also less than ideal. Firstly, too many seats, generally inadequately raked and not of a high quality in terms of comfort or legroom were often packed into the new smaller auditoria which often led to bad lines of sight; secondly, screens were small, with some, including those of non-adapted cinemas, dirty and even suffering from poor illumination of the film image as exhibitors pared back on cleaning and maintenance costs; and thirdly, poor soundproofing meant that, at times, there was considerable noise 'bleed' from one screen to another. However, with regard to the last point, as Douglas Gomery, writing in the context of American mall cinemas, notes, noise bleed was also a by-product of better sound systems that had been developed largely in response to television.[2]

While cinema exhibition internationally, particularly in America, Australia and Britain, underwent a radical shift in the early 1980s, marked by the opening in Toronto of the eighteen-screen Cineplex Odeon in 1979, which ushered in a new era of custom-built, comfortable, stadium seated, large-screen multiplexes, Irish exhibitors continued well into the 1980s to convert rather than to radically rethink exhibition venues. For example, as late as 1987 and 1988 Ward Anderson, which at this time was planning to build a series of mini- and multiplexes in the major provincial centres with the intention of providing a more viable exhibition system, reopened, respectively, the Abbey, George's Street, Wexford town, and the Regal, Clonmel, as only three-screen venues.[3] By the early 1990s, however, notwithstanding their £1.75 million conversion of the Capitol, Cork, in 1989, into 'the most modern cinema in the British Isles at the time',[4] the success of which helped lead to other multiplexes opening around the city throughout the 1990s, such piecemeal attempts at multiplexing became outmoded in the wake of the spectacular successes of a number of multiplex developments in Dublin.

Usually defined as having five or more screens,[5] multiplexes tend to be purpose-built structures on green- or brownfield sites. In comparison to the auratic picture palaces of the earlier period they are mostly bland functional buildings with bright interchangeable features, akin to modern fast food outlets or large warehouse-style retail units. Though this was especially true of the earlier multiplexes, which had prioritized the ability to convert the space to other uses should the cinema fail, increasingly, multiplex design, particularly with regard to its interior styling, has been less obviously international modern, and, indicative of a future direction, already apparent by 1990, has moved towards embracing fantasy and postmodern lavishness. While this could be seen in the mid-1990s in twinkling star lights set against the navy blue ceiling in the Virgin multiplex at Parnell Street, Dublin, and in the restoration in 1999 of Belfast's Strand Cinema's original art-deco design, it is perhaps epitomized best by the Dundrum cinema, Dublin.[6]

In terms of space and form, and the attempt to create architecture specific to the cinema, those cinemas that have moved away from the single level, room-off-corridor, mall model are of most interest. In that regard, UGC (now Cineworld) lead the way, both in Dublin through its seventeen-screen redevelopment of the Parnell complex (2003) and elsewhere including in Glasgow where in 2001 their Renfrew Street eighteen-screen cinema, the tallest cinema in Europe at over twelve storeys and 200ft, opened. Nevertheless, the new Light House Cinema, which opened in Dublin's Smithfield in May 2008 though closed three years later, deserves note given that it offered a dramatic play with space, light and shade, while also opting for clean contours, bold profiles and modern materials. To quote architect Colin Mackay of DTA Architects, the screening rooms were organized and distributed in a way that 'allowed patrons to walk over, under and around the forms, affording an alternative and dramatic cinema experience', and creating an almost haptic or visceral architecture, which played with the idea of the labyrinth and thus interiority and desire.[7] Nevertheless, despite some exceptions, the predominant look of Irish multiplexes, notwithstanding the plush furnishings in many foyers and attention to art and design, such as the tile floor and mural mosaics in Dún Laoghaire's IMC complex beside Bloomfield's shopping centre, is clean, contemporary and is more futuristic than nostalgic, with the corporate or brand look important for the identity of cinema chains.

In order to maximize the potential audience, which from the 1960s was becoming increasingly mobile, generally speaking, multiplexes are sited, with a high degree of visibility, near established centres of populations, on or near motorways, and more-over, within, or in very close proximity to, a shopping centre or retail park. While ded-icated (mostly free) car-parking, often with surveillance, has clear convenience and safety benefits, which was particularly relevant at a moment when city centres were being regarded as dangerous un(der)regulated environments, the integration of the cinema within a broader cultural geography of consumption, where the aesthetics of duration and function are replaced by ephemerality and pleasure, allowed for multi-plex exhibitors to 're-articulate the cinema as but one part, albeit the central part, of a total leisure package set around the notion of a "whole night out" or even a "whole day out".'[8] Indeed, in 2003, Nigel Drake, general manager of Ster Century (now Vue), which is located in the Liffey Valley shopping centre, Lucan, Co. Dublin, explained that the placement of the multiplex within the shopping arena has made going to the cinema in the suburbs 'far more of an event' as it allows people to go shopping and then go to the cinema.[9] This reimagining of cinema-going was central to the develop-ment of the multiplex. Europe president of American Multi-Cinema (AMC), the com-pany which built Britain's first multiplex in Milton Keynes in 1985 and started the Irish multiplex revolution in 1990 with the development of the Tallaght complex, fol-lowed closely by one in Coolock, stated that

> the reasons which lay behind our desire to build multiplexes in Europe had to do principally with the synergies which they can generate ... We thus tried to position ourselves in the leisure industry, with plans to open big cinema the-atres that would create major audience flows: all these people would be cus-tomers not only inside, but also outside theatres, in complexes with many bars and restaurants offering a range of after-show attractions.[10]

In effect, such a strategy, evident in all the current proposed cinemas expected to open in Dublin by 2012,[11] offers a return to the film environment of the 1920s and 1930s when cinema-going was not just confined to viewing a film, but was part of a more complex social event. This time, however, as a result of the cinema's location within the shopping centre/leisure complex/retail park (which 'increase[s] the dwell-time of shoppers')[12] and thus the merging of the conventions and aesthetics of cinema with those of the mall/commodity culture, the experience is more uniformly repeatable. Furthermore, the experience is safer as the cinema-consumer is insulated against the range of blights and realities affecting public urban space. These might range from traffic, violence, the presence of beggars or other classes of individuals or groups perceived as anti-social, and inclement weather, to time itself, as even light and dark can be controlled. Unsurprisingly, then, a survey, albeit based in Singapore, found that cinema patrons prefer to watch movies at a cineplex located in shopping centres,[13] while in 2007 a spokesman for the Irish competition authority summed it up thus: 'Consumers like the convenience of parking and combining a movie with shopping or eating out'.[14]

Additionally, given the number of films (potentially) available in each complex, the experience is also more driven by impulsive desire. Although, with the increasing availability of more tailored television (for example through Sky TV recorders) more akin to the VCR in its time-shifting aspect, and easier access to films through multiple channels, a cinema's success ultimately relies on its access to good (or great) films rather than on average ones for which most people will happily wait the three or so months for their second-life release. In any case, just as the mall-shopper is offered a 'vast array of merchandise'[15] and is invited to browse and make impulse purchases, so, too, is the multiplex patron presented with a potentially wide range of titles from the dominant American mainstream films to the more occasional specialist art or independent films. Therefore, in similar ways the multiplex and the shopping mall can be seen as facilitating the spectator-shopper's trying on different identities and engaging with a 'kind of identity bulimia. Leaving the [cinema] theatre, one abandons the garment, and takes only the memory of having worn it for a few hours – or having been worn by it.'[16] That said, while it is theoretically possible for all members of a family to attend a multiplex and view different films, the dictates of profits often mean that the range is not as great as it might be as the same title is often simultaneously shown, though at different times, in a number of screening rooms. Indeed, multiplexes with their many screens are designed precisely to be able to accommodate a high earning film, and once this is done, the exhibitor can then maximize the audience by showing the box office hit in the largest room and simultaneously in other screens, thereby increasing profit for exhibitor, distributor and producer alike. A multiplex with nine or twelve screens is three or four times more likely to hit on a blockbuster than a three-screen venue.

While it is the case that the excessive cost of marketing a film, which first began in earnest with the extensive advertising of *Jaws* (1975), only makes economic sense if a film receives saturation screenings,[17] the sharing of this cost over more and more cinemas means that the costs per cinema remain manageable. Nevertheless, the downside of this, from the consumers' perspective, is that the same (limited if popular) selection of films, from the same major distributors, might be screening in all the nearby multiplexes. It seems that more screens, while opening up greater possibilities for longer runs, do not necessarily guarantee a greater range of choice.[18] In 2001, it was argued in *Film Ireland* that the screening space for indigenous Irish films and foreign language films was being eroded by the multiplex phenomenon, not least because such films require distributors to spend a 'tremendous amount' of work and money, since without the benefit of the Hollywood packaging, they 'have to do all the marketing entirely from scratch.'[19] As a result, many exhibitors refuse to screen alternative or non-commercial mainstream films given the increased risk of these failing to break even in terms of print/screening outlay. Furthermore, such films are seen as potentially impacting negatively on both snack or kiosk sales and audience loyalty.

Nevertheless, the managing director of Parnell Street's UGC, speaking after its transformation into a seventeen-screen megaplex, stated that at the heart of UGC's philosophy is giving equal billing, not only [to] the main-stream-blockbuster-Hollywood-type products, but also to indigenous product, independent filmmakers, films from across the globe. We believe that any cinema that limits its products, limits its audience.[20]

Some years earlier, Matt Connolly, the then manager of the complex, had admitted that they would like to offer 'more independent and international films', but blamed the public, who he said, 'prefer the blockbusters', on their lack of range.[21] Although the concept of the dual-identity multiplex as explored in Australia whereby a multiplex is clearly divided between the two types of cinema,[22] has yet to be embraced in Ireland, Dublin, briefly, boasted the four-screen Light House, which, as a reincarnation of the two-screen Light House that closed in 1996, was devoted to non-mainstream product, yet in terms of design, space, comfort and screen size, out-multiplexed most conventional multiplexes, while Galway's Eye multiplex cinema regularly features art-house product.

Whatever the variety of titles, staggered commencement times mean that films are almost always available. This becomes particularly relevant given that the practice of patrons entering a cinema in the middle of its screening is no longer acceptable. Indeed, Cineplex Odeon, which, as noted, began in Toronto in 1979 and had become by the 1990s the model for the industry generally, initiated from the onset, in an attempt to go beyond the mall cinema, a practice whereby screening times were staggered in fifteen-minute intervals with 'no tickets sold after the start of the show in order to prevent latecomers from disturbing the audience.'[23] Despite this, it seems that noisy disruptive audiences have not entirely been consigned to history. Leo Ward was complaining in 2001 that while contemporary audiences are looking for better standards of comfort and presentation, 'nowadays cinemas are abused, seating is torn, and covered in graffiti. It didn't happen years ago. You see grown men with their feet up on the backs of seats.'[24] Others have highlighted the rise in distracted and restless viewers,[25] at one level something that could be explained by the absence of the controlling usher and a (negative) change more generally in social values and respectful behaviour, but at another can be seen as a result of the transformation in the relationship many have with screen entertainments, which have been increasingly integrated into the home. Arguably the cover of darkness coupled with (a) the familiarity with advertisements and trailers (which allows viewers to treat such material as background and not worthy of full attention, or at least the distracted attention normally associated with television viewing); (b) the higher screen noise levels;[26] (c) the social aspect of cinema-going, particularly in relation to groups of teens attending certain films especially at the weekend; (d) more causal parenting whereby young children are permitted to treat the at times significantly under-occupied space as a place to explore; and (e) the ritual of eating; seem to give a licence to patrons not to accept the cinema space as equivalent to that of the legitimate theatre or (classical) concert hall,[27] a throwback, perhaps, to early's cinema communal and interactive exhibition experience. Indeed, in 2003 foremost among the reasons one journalist gave for hiring out Dublin's plush and intimate Denzille Private Cinema was precisely because one might be 'sick of movie audiences behaving like noisy, grunting, endlessly-eating pigs? Tempted to set about them with a meat cleaver? Avoid troublesome murder convictions by hiring your own cinema and filling it full of your well-behaved friends.'[28]

That said, in general, and notwithstanding some problems with mobile phone etiquette, it would be inaccurate to characterize audience behaviour within Irish cinemas and multiplexes since the 1980s as unruly and disruptive. While some cinemas, such as Ward Anderson's Savoy, Dublin, temporarily resorted (from the end of 2002) to using a mobile phone blocker to jam signals, justifying their action, not least on health and safety grounds as fights were breaking out because someone was talking (or receiving texts) on their mobile,[29] this problem, which has not been fully addressed, has been considerably ameliorated, perhaps in part due to the screening by most cinemas of a health and safety advertisement, produced by Vodafone, reminding people to switch off their mobile phones 'completely'. Nevertheless, many exhibitors believe that mobile phones continue to be a source of irritation for their patrons with Mark Anderson stating in 2006 that 'it's certainly a problem for us'.[30] The Vodafone advertisement also advises patrons to locate the exits, and not to smoke in the building. While a blanket ban of smoking in work places was introduced in Ireland in March 2004, smoking in cinema auditoria and other palaces of entertainment was prohibited from the mid-1980s.

Other features that are regarded as defining the modern multiplex are its superior technological features; its enhanced presentation of film image and film sound; and its increasingly high degree of comfort and personal space. This latter feature manifests itself in a number of areas, including most obviously, in the luxurious stadium style seating with cup holders and generous leg room (sometimes available on a reserved seating basis);[31] advanced ticket sales and computerized ticketing available online; automated telephone booking and automatic ticket machines, which were developed in 1990 by AMC,[32] and/or numerous points of ticket sales thereby minimizing the need to queue, as one Irish multiplex chain IMC was informing its customers in the mid-2000s, 'Q is their least favourite letter'; and the large lobby area, which not only reduces contact with other patrons, but in addition has a better and extended range of concessions. Nevertheless, the same IMC Dún Laoghaire, reflecting international trends, closed its dedicated ticket sales windows in 2008 and combined ticket sales with popcorn/candy/drinks as a means, presumably, not only of making savings on staff costs, but also of encouraging patrons to purchase the food in front of them.

Given that popcorn has become 'such a part of the moviegoing experience',[33] it is hard to imagine a time when concession stands were not a feature of cinemas, yet during the 1920s movie palaces had steadfastly refused to sell food, leaving it to the nearby shops.[34] This only changed in the 1930s when cinema theatre owners, struggling in the wake of the Great Depression, saw candy sales as a way to supplement their income. Towards the end of the 1930s the sale of popcorn became widespread within cinema foyers, while its popularity was further enhanced during the war when sugar was rationed. Following the end of the war, Coke, in conjunction with the thirst-making Morton's salt sprinkled on the popcorn, aggressively entered the cinema concession market, and exhibitors, seeing that the income from non-film sales was the source of real profit, not least as it did not have to be shared with the distributor, began to promote intermissions to allow their patrons visit the concession stand, while drive-ins which extended the menu to hot dogs and fries further enshrined the coupling of food and film. By the 1980s, Cineplex Odeon's concession areas had become 'the size of basketball arenas',[35] while the 1987 exhibitors' trade fair ShoWest focused on the increasing importance of concessions and revealed trends towards 'bite-size candies, including M&Ms and Gummi Bears and other more "upscale" offerings.'[36] Whatever about bite-sized, the trend is most definitely towards super-sized portions with the servings of popcorn up to thirty times the size of recommended portions; indeed, the average Irish cinema bucket of popcorn contains 100 calories and 76 grams of fat, the same as six McDonald cheeseburgers,[37] while even child portions, introduced by UCI in recognition of the growing problem of obesity,[38] are seven times the size of the recommended adult portion.[39] However, in a much-delayed response to rising concerns over obesity, an issue raised in the film *Super Size Me* (Morgan Spurlock, 2004, Canada), Sony Pictures chairman Michael Lynton, speaking in 2010 at a convention in Las Vegas of cinema owners, was adamant that healthy alternatives to the usual cinema concession fare of popcorn, sweets, ice cream and fizzy drinks should be made available. Nevertheless, he added that he was 'just talking about *adding some healthier* items', and not advocating a wholesale abandoning of junk food. 'I don't think giant tubs of spinach or broccoli is a good idea ... And nobody wants to eat cauliflower or drink a 40 ounce cup of prune juice while watching *Spider-Man*.'[40]

In Ireland, non-box office income in the 1950s was estimated at nearly 15 per cent of turnover (see chapter 3), while a survey in the 1970s showed that sales at kiosks during performances at cinemas and theatres were 21.8 per cent of box office takings, or 13.92 per cent of total receipts.[41] By 1992, it was suggested that sales of foodstuffs were 'probably' adding as much as 30 to 40 per cent to cinema revenue,[42] though a more conservative estimate in 1996 proposed that sales from popcorn, sweets and soft drinks could represent up to quarter of a cinema's takings.[43] In 1998, reflecting the 'pricey, high margin',[44] it was being suggested that up to 40 percent of UCI's profits derived from food, merchandize and other sales, with each customer spending at least £1 on refreshments.[45] According to UCI's regional manager, Karl Milne, the greater emphasis on non-ticket revenue has resulted from more competition and therefore such sales represent 'an extremely important part of the business'. Nevertheless, Milne, like other exhibitors, in an attempt to displace notions around profit or perhaps profiteering, has also foregrounded the importance of tradition and ritual with respect to cinema goodies, pointing out that they 'have become part of the cinema experience.'[46] As one commentator wrote in 2001, 'cinemagoing, in the bold new multiplex era, has become as much about drinks 'n' snax as about watching a movie.'[47] Similarly, Paul Ward, speaking in 1995, perhaps somewhat disingenuously, told a reporter that there was 'no price resistance' to concessions.[48]

From 1998 to 2003, net revenue from concessions grew by 82 per cent from €17.4 million to €31.7 million,[49] while in 2003, when cinema admissions were 17.4 million and gross box office was €97.5 million[50] (a figure similar to 2004),[51] and with average film rental rising from 39 per cent of gross in 1998 to 42 per cent in 2003,[52] such retail revenues amounted to over 20 per cent of the overall turnover of a multiplex.[53] However, given that any profit arising from food and drink is neither shared with distributors[54] nor subject to value added tax (as is the case with revenue from ticket sales), and that profit margins on concessions, sometimes as high as 80 per cent,[55] 'are far greater than on tickets',[56] when adjusted, the net profit from such sales is nearer to 30 per cent, the figure anticipated in 1999 by Ster's managing director Mike Ross.[57] Nevertheless, in an echo of earlier estimates from within the trade, suggesting that, as a percentage of total revenue, sales of popcorn and other food/drink amounts to anything from 25 per cent to 50 per cent,[58] one journalist made the claim in 2003 that the total spend at Irish cinemas was double that of the box office receipts.[59] In relation to the UK, whose market is about ten times the size of Ireland's,[60] Dodona Research has reported that net concession revenue in 2006 was GB£213 million, while total UK box office revenue for the year was GB£770 million.[61] Concession income rose to £302 million in 2009, with a further £195 million earned from cinema adverts. By then, gross box office revenue for the UK and Ireland had risen to £1,127 million, an increase of 21 per cent on 2008, making concession income worth 26.7 per cent of box office income, a figure slightly below 2006's 27.6 per cent.[62]

Not only are these goods retailed at extortionate prices, often between two and three times their supermarket price, to a captive audience, but also, in general, cinema patrons are not allowed to consume food or drink in the cinema that is not purchased in the cinema, thus making concessions even more lucrative to the industry.[63] Most multiplexes prominently display signs forbidding on *health and safety* grounds the bringing of food and refreshments not bought in the cinema's foyer into the auditoria. While staff stop short of frisking patrons, and turn a blind eye to the many patrons who might have a drink or small item in their pockets, they do not allow patrons to bring large bags into the auditoria and operate a policy of searching bags for food stuff and/or recording equipment. Those found with 'offending material' are asked to leave it with staff for collection after the film, or to leave themselves with a full refund of their admission ticket. In 2008, the *Daily Mail* carried a report of one man being thrown out of a Cineworld cinema in Stockport, Cheshire, England, for buying his own 'much cheaper' sweets elsewhere.[64] A spokesman for the cinema stated that it searches bags for recording equipment, and if food is found, it enforces its no-food policy: 'Cineworld terms and conditions outline that all food consumed on the premises must be purchased at one of our concessions, which is in line with most cinema chain policies',[65] as such it is hardly surprising then that even during the recession, the group's retail sales in 2009 increased by 9.6 per cent.[66] Nearer to home, and more recently, the *Nationalist* reported on a young teenager who was forced to dump his sweets in a bin before entering a screen in Carlow's Cineplex even though he had already bought popcorn from the concession stand.[67]

Besides large concession areas, a number of which are becoming self-service, thereby reducing staff costs further, another manifestation of the maximizing of non-cinema ticket revenue which includes cinema advertising, of which about €10 million was spent in 2004,[68] and which represents in Ireland about 3.5 per cent of turnover, is the space given to café and bar areas, as well as small entertainment areas featuring video games, and kids' party room(s). In this regard, the most impressive is the 'spectacular art-deco centre-piece'[69] bar in Dublin's UGC, Parnell Street, which, according to Margaret Taylor, managing director of UGC for the UK and Ireland, was driven by the desire to give customers 'what they want' rather than as another way to generate profit. 'We like to encourage people to dwell and talk about the movie they've just seen. ... It's all about making film as accessible and visible as possible.'[70] Although the bar in the Eye Cinema in Galway, situated on the second level, is not as dramatic, the seating area with floor-to-ceiling windows and which curves around the screens, allows for spectacular views of Galway Bay. It is perhaps of note that both of these venues have a non-mainstream/art house strain within their programming, thereby confirming the bias with regard to concessions in different types of cinemas. Art house, exemplified best by Dublin's independent cinema the IFI, tends to be more coffee, wine and beer and real food (it has a full bar and restaurant), while commercial movie houses tend towards sweets, popcorn and fast food. Indeed, one of the shorthand, if, perhaps, crude and, ultimately, limiting definitions of the art house or cultural film is that it is not a 'popcorn movie'. By 2010, such attempts to offer seated refreshments' docks by a number of multiplexes had been discontinued, perhaps a reflection of the economic downturn, the staffing costs, or competition from nearby bars and cafes and the fact that these refreshment areas failed to deliver either a quality or sumptuous experience for the customer or a high profit return on the space for the owners. The IMC Dún Laoghaire 'bar area', for example, became a games' space before finally being converted in July 2010 into a small cinema (no. 13).

THE MULTIPLEX IN IRELAND

While strictly speaking the multiplex can be traced back to 1963 and the opening by Stanley H. Durwood, founder of American Multi-Cinema Corporation, of a small duplex in a shopping centre in Kansas City, Missouri,[71] the multiplexes of the 1960s and 1970s bear little relation to the modern comfortable multiplexes which developed from 1979 with Canadian company Cineplex Odeon. Nevertheless, the founding idea of the merging of two or more screens under one complex, thus saving on staffing and projection costs, and the importance of being (centrally) located within a shopping complex, which already had been happening before 1963 with *Box Office* announcing in 1961 that 'a new star in the motion picture firmament is the shopping center theatre',[72] proved central to the success of the multiplex. By the mid-1980s, the (refigured) multiplex explosion had already transformed American exhibition and pushed up admission figures; however, Europe lagged behind.

Seeking to increase market share for their own/American product, and to create bigger and better outlets, American exhibition companies, many of which were vertically integrated with major distributors,[73] and all with considerable financial resources to enable them to compete aggressively in the market, entered Europe. A spokesman for one such group, MCA (Music Corporation of America),[74] the parent company of Universal (partner, from 1986, to Cineplex Odeon having bought a half interest in the theatre chain, and among the largest producers of films, television programmes and recorded music),[75] claimed that 'the multiplexing of Europe [would] enable [them] to release twice as many movies.'[76] Other American exhibitors included Warner Bros International Theatres; Cinema International Corporation (CIC), which was reconfigured as United Cinemas International (UCI); American Multi-Screen (AMC); and National Amusements.[77]

In part this would be helped by the consolidation of European exhibition, which in real terms would mean fewer exhibitors, and, as such, would enable US distributors to more easily control release patterns. Indeed, in the period 1986 to 1991, following the opening of hundreds of multiplexes in Europe and particularly in Britain, where roughly 500 new multiplex screens opened, film revenue for US companies from foreign sales increased by 267 per cent from $2,355 million to $6,286 million, compared to growth of only 163 per cent in the domestic market from $4,366 million to $7,132 million.[78] Confirming the statistics, the head of Warner Bros international division reported that by the early 1990s, 'business ha[d] improved tremendously. Before, you'd be in line to get your films into the two theatres in town. Now you can get them out much earlier and feed off a lot of the publicity coming out of the United States.'[79] Given such expansion, it is hardly surprising that multiplexes led to a rise in European admissions, the first growth since the Second World War. Whereas in 1990 there were 610 million admissions, by 1994 this had risen to 690 million, rising to 850 million by 1998.[80] As the multiplex building boom in Europe had been fuelled by American capital, as might be expected then, it was American companies that largely benefited from the improved box office receipts. By 1991, American films accounted for 50 per cent of European box office, with the share rising to over 70 per cent in Britain and Germany,[81] and, it could be added, Ireland, too.

Britain, which, as a result of declining audiences, was on the verge of being regulated to the status of a Third World cinema region, with releases 'handled through local intermediaries from offices in Paris or Los Angeles',[82] became the primary focus of America's European invasion. Nevertheless, the US majors had not wished to become the 'backbones of local exhibition markets' but had 'originally conceived strategies' through which they might become 'catalysts' by forcing a shake up of local markets and in this way encouraging or compelling exhibitors to invest in modernizing their facilities.[83] Despite the apparent poor state of exhibition in Britain, which was controlled by a duopoly of Rank and ABC, the political and social conditions there were ideally suited to the development of multiplex cinemas and to foreign investment,[84] not least because out-of-town shopping centres – the spiritual home of the multiplex – were being promoted as a key element within regional regeneration developments. AMC, which had begun to research British exhibition as early as 1979, was the first American exhibitor to realize a multiplex project in Britain. While this finally came to fruition in 1985 in the Point, Milton Keynes, situated north of London, it was followed quickly by other American-based exhibitors, but also by Britain's own ABC. However, by the time the ABC/Thorn-EMI eight-screen Manchester multiplex opened in 1986, ABC had been taken over by Cannon, which then became the largest exhibitor in Britain. Later, Cannon also bought out Cineplex Odeon whose British interests developed in 1988 through their Gallery and Maybox chains.

Given the historical linking of Irish and British distribution and thus exhibition, it is unsurprising that American interests quickly turned to Ireland. In 1987 reports surfaced that AMC, which by this stage had over 1,400 screens in the USA and ten in Britain (through the Milton Keynes complex) with a further ninety screens planned which would be evenly divided over nine complexes, was interested in taking over the prosposed 2,500-seat, ten-screen multiplex in (west) Dublin's Blanchardstown shopping centre owned by Green Property (an entity not to be confused with Ward Anderson's Green Group Ltd). In reviewing the possibility, Damien Kiberd welcomed the development as it would provide a 'major shake-up' of the Dublin city oligopoly of Adelphi-Carlton and Ward Anderson. By contrast, Leo Ward, who considered the 'basic principle' of the multiplex premature in Ireland, threw cold water on the proposal – 'I think they are a bit crazy, with the economy in such a terrible state, the business is simply not there … [you] would have to fill at least half of the seats to make [a multiplex] pay' – while Adelphi-Carlton also cast doubt on the viability of the complex.[85]

A year later in an *Irish Times*' report on CIC's six-screen High Wycombe multiplex, north-west of London, Ray Comiskey, echoing Kiberd, argued that the Irish public 'could do with … more, much more, competition to shake the comfortable powers-that-be in the industry out of their cosy ways.' While he believed that Irish cinemagoers deserved a 'much better service', he concluded that, 'accustomed' as they were

> – even in some first-run Dublin cinemas – to dirty screens, less than optimum projection standards, uncomfortable seating, badly designed auditoria, [which were] understaffed … by people poorly paid and with little say in how the cinema is run, and outmoded approaches to serving the public, all this must seem slightly unreal.[86]

The next day, the *Irish Times* reported that Monarch Properties Ltd intended to build a multi-screen cinema and entertainment complex in the established north Dublin working-class suburb of Coolock, about four miles from the city centre, at a reported cost, including the site, of just over £3.55 million,[87] and a ten-screen cinema in the south-west Dublin suburb of Tallaght at an estimated cost of £20 million.[88] Seven months later, in a deal valued at £10 million, AMC signed an agreement with Monarch Properties, developers of Tallaght's major shopping centre, The Square, to invest in the centre's sixteen-screen (later reduced to twelve-screens and 3,200 seats) multiplex, and in a ten-screen complex in Coolock. There was no existing cinema in either area, and it was envisaged that the new complexes, which were set to employ seventy-five people each, would share concurrencies with Dublin city centre,[89] thus, effectively signaling the end of the long-running release delays between city centre and suburban cinemas.

Tallaght, a new fast growing suburb with a predominantly young working-class constituency,[90] lacked many basic community amenities until the opening in 1990 of what was then Ireland's largest shopping centre and first proper town centre.[91] Though shopping centres in Ireland had developed in the 1960s with the opening of Newtownbreda, Belfast (1964) and Stillorgan, Dublin (1966), and had grown in popularity during the 1970s and 1980s when centres such as Dublin's ILAC in the city centre and Nutgrove in the south-Dublin suburb of Rathfarmham were established, it was only from 1990 that shopping centres made a significant impact on the Irish retailing landscape. Not only did they grow in number, such that in 2001 it was estimated that there had been a 35 per cent increase in large-scale shopping development space in Dublin over the previous five years following the opening of thirteen new shopping centres and retail parks, but also they increased dramatically in size, with an average expansion of roughly 50 per cent over complexes developed prior to 1997 evident in the fact that by 2001 nine of the ten largest purpose-built developments in Dublin had opened after 1990.[92] More importantly in the context of this study is that echoing patterns elsewhere, and as exemplified in Tallaght, these shopping centres began to incorporate leisure facilities, notably a multiplex cinema, as was (or would be) the case at Coolock, Blanchardstown, Swords, Liffey Valley and Dundrum, as well as increasingly developing on their edges retail parks such as at Blanchardstown and Liffey Valley.

At the time of its opening, Tallaght's centre, The Square, which spearheaded the town's development throughout the early 1990s, boasted, among other features, an impressive scale comprising as it did of twenty-eight acres; five major stores; 135 shops and financial institutions; a crèche; a radio studio; stage areas; nine restaurants; a massive free and supervised carpark with over 2,000 spaces; and a twelve-screen cinema, which was officially opened by the Irish president, Mary Robinson at the end of November 1990.[93] Interestingly, and in keeping with the cultural trend to move away from public space proper in favour of a safe cocoon of private space masquerading as public and bound by surveillance and control, the publicity for the distinctive pyramid shaped, glass-clad, three-level, enclosed complex (developed by Monarch Properties/GRE Properties and designed by Burke Kennedy Doyle), highlighted its safety and comfort aspects, reporting that 'security is all important.' In addition to the patrolling staff of the specially formed security team, Allsecure Ltd, identifiable by their black uniforms, there were sixty high-tech cameras, which cost £0.5million, in operation 'all day everyday'.[94] Anticipating that the £85 million shopping centre would attract many from outside the immediate area, Dublin county council working with the developers, spent hundreds of thousands of pounds improving road networks around it, so that 'whether you're coming from the North, East, South, West or the City, there's a major road to provide you with quick access to the centre.'[95] The complex, like those developed in Britain under the conservative government's Enterprise Zone projects from the early 1980s,[96] benefited from a special tax designation, which meant that those trading within The Square did not have to pay full business rates for ten years. Other multiplexes, including the Parnell Street complex, would benefit similarly from rates exemptions (for ten years) and capital tax allowances such as accelerated capital write offs and/or double rent allowances.

By the opening of the Tallaght multiplex (which offered up to fifteen films a week and was complete with the latest screens and sound technology, and comfortable 100 per cent sound-proofed auditoria) AMC's British and Irish operations had been taken over by CIC/United Artists. This was then grouped with UCI (United Cinemas International), a company formed by Paramount and Universal Pictures. By 1990 UCI had an annual turnover in the UK of over GB£55 million from its seventeen multiplexes, while it was hoped that turnover from the Tallaght and Coolock UCI multiplexes would reach £2 million per annum, although reflecting the importance of ancillary sales within contemporary film exhibition, UCI's UK managing director, Ian Richies, was predicating that 'a sizeable proportion' of this would come from sales of own brand ice cream, hotdogs and popcorn. Given that the company had its own central booking office based in London, *Business and Finance*'s John McGee commented that UCI Tallaght 'will nearly always bypass the Dublin-based distributors.' More worrying from Adelphi-Carlton's perspective was the fact that UCI's relationship with founding companies Paramount and Universal would impact on the long-standing film release arrangements they had with Paramount and Universal, though according to Richies, UCI's relationship with these was 'very much an arm's length one'.[97]

More generally, UCI's entry into the Irish market was a source of fear for Irish exhibitors, most particularly the two dominant players, Adelphi-Carlton and Ward Anderson. While Adelphi-Carlton, owned by Metro-Goldwyn-Meyer, Inc. following MGM's purchase of the Cannon Group in 1990, had a turnover of about £2 million, Ward Anderson had an all-Ireland turnover of about £12 million, £8 million of which was generated in the Republic, representing a third of the Irish Republic's cinema market. Furthermore, from the late 1980s through to early 1990 Ward Anderson, which controlled forty cinemas (some perhaps still co-owned) comprising of fourteen of Dublin's twenty-eight screens and seventy provincial screens, had spent about £12 million on developing and acquiring cinemas, including, as noted, redeveloping Cork's Capitol as a six-screen complex and the Savoy complex in Limerick at a cost of £2 million, and opening a £2 million leisure centre in Lurgan, Co. Antrim, which included four screens.[98]

Nevertheless, and notwithstanding that UCI Tallaght, from its opening on 30 November 1990 to the opening of UCI's second Dublin multiplex at Malahide Road, Coolock, on 30 July 1991, had managed to sell 600,000 tickets, cinema admissions to established venues did not fall, but, mirroring trends elsewhere, actually rose. Although independent exhibitor Albert Kelly, also chair of the much-depleted Independent Cinemas Association,[99] was aggrieved that he had to wait four weeks for releases while UCI was given parity with city centre cinemas, nonetheless, he accepted that his business had not been reduced by the opening of UCI Tallaght even though his sole cinema, the twin-screen Classic, Harold's Cross, was geographical the closest to the new multiplex.[1] Leo Ward reported that it was 'one of the best years' the company ever had with the Savoy's business in particular 'way up'. In part, as UCI's marketing manager, Ian Grey, pointed out, this was perhaps as a result of the extra publicity generated by the multiplex having a positive spin-off for existing cinemas. Indeed, in 1991 UCI's managing director estimated that roughly 'seventy-five per cent of total admissions to each new cinema was new business',[2] while by June 1992 one cinema owner was reckoning that the established operators had only taken a 5 to 10 per cent hit in box-office revenue from the newcomers.[3] Six years later, it still remained the opinion of many within the industry that 'multiplexes don't take audiences away from existing cinemas. They build new audiences instead.'[4] In 1998 Leo Ward explicitly acknowledged that such cinemas stimulate audience demand and lead to increased admission figures when he stated that 'where we might have taken £3,000 on a film in our old cinema in Killarney, now [in the new multiplex] we would take £12,000.'[5] Nevertheless, with a four-screen multiplex costing between £2.1 and £2.3 million, the investment was 'huge', especially if money had to be borrowed at the then rate of 8 per cent, something, of course, Ward Anderson generally avoided.

In their first year of trading UCI Tallaght had 1.7 million admissions, while UCI Coolock had 800,000. The combined figure of 2.5 million plus admissions for the two cinemas was maintained into the mid-1990s.[6] Though UCI recorded a loss of £320,000 in 1992, the following year it posted a surplus of £670,000 and had operating profits of £2.1 million on turnover of £8.6 million, a figure way above original projections, and helped to give the two UCIs about 20 per cent of Irish box office revenue estimated at between £36 and £40 million. UCI was 'clearly running a tight ship' as staff costs of £1.4 million averaged out at £12,500 per employee, an amount close to the average annual salary of £12,715 in the distribution sector, in which cinema would have been counted.[7] Despite the fact that discussions regarding a cinema in Blanchardstown began as early as 1987, it was not until December 1996 that this materialized when UCI opened its third Dublin multiplex there as part of the new west Dublin Blancharstown shopping centre. The £9 million, 2,500-seat, nine-screen cinema, opened by actress Patsy Kensit, had the biggest first week's box office ever of any UCI cinema in Ireland or Britain.[8] By then, Britain, with about 40 per cent of its screens in multiplexes, and Ireland, had the two most developed multiplex markets in Europe.[9]

As might be expected, despite the relative resistance cinema shows to economic recessions and even wars, the continuously troubled political climate of Northern Ireland contributed to a culling of Belfast's cinemas. In contrast to the twenty cinemas operating at the end of the 1960s, by the early 1980s, following the closure of the Belfast Picture House, Royal Avenue, in 1983, only four cinemas remained. At the beginning of 1991, cinema exhibition in Belfast, at least with regard to the number of cinemas and screens, had changed little. At that time, the Belfast city centre cinemas operational were the small single-screen specialist Queen's Film Theatre (though a lecture room provided a second screen); the four-screen Cannon, Fisherwick Place (formerly ABC Film Centre and the Ritz) with almost 1,500 seats; the Strand (formerly an ABC), Holywood Road, also four screens, having been split from a single screen in 1984; and the Curzon, Ormeau Road, which had been converted into a three-screen venue in 1981. On 11 May 1991, however, these four cinemas were joined by Belfast's first purpose-built five-screen multiplex.

Situated in the Kennedy Centre shopping centre, Falls Road, the 1,011-seat cinema was initially operated by the independent Curley's Cinemas, though by the end of the decade it had become part of Ward Anderson's Cineplex circuit. Each of the screens was named after former West Belfast cinemas: Clonard, Broadway, Arcadian, Coliseum and Diamond. Fifteen months later, an eight-screen, 1,450-seat, €6.5 million multiplex opened in Belfast's Co-Op Wholesale Society Yorkgate leisure and retail complex (now known as City Side retail park, York Street). Although UCI and Warner Bros had been approached to develop the multiplex, both refused, as it was their 'policy not to trade in Northern Ireland' in the context of continuing civil conflict. This was despite the fact that the site was regarded as being in 'a neutral area', and located at the intersection of two motorways, would have served both Catholics and Protestants equally. Consequently, it was run by Film Network, founded in 1987 with the intention of developing high-quality cinemas.[10] Subsequently, the complex became part of the small but high quality Movie House circuit operated by Michael McAdam, who, around 2000, expanded it from eight screens to fourteen. That the cinema had 1,400 car parking spaces, the then real fear in the early 1990s of having one's car stolen for purposes of 'joy-riding' was somewhat alleviated.[11] (Such a fear remained even as late as the early 2000s as evident in Vinny Murphy's *Accelerator* [2001] which takes as a theme joyriding and multiple car theft [from a Belfast car-park].) The third Belfast multiplex to open was at 14 Dublin Road, close to Shaftsbury Square in Belfast's city centre, on 18 July 1993. Developed by the Sheridan Group, it had been envisaged that the ten-screen, 2,501-seat facility would be run by Cannon; however, in early 1990 Cannon was taken over by MGM, which then gave its full support to the cinema. It was subsequently run by Virgin (from 1995) and by UGC (from 1999), before it became part of the Movie House chain in January 2004. Like other purpose-built multiplexes, it was designed as part of a leisure centre, which included leading food franchises and 520 car spaces.[12]

Meanwhile, and indeed central to the development of cinema exhibition and, more generally, the restoration of business confidence, Northern Ireland's political landscape was changing. In 1998, following moves towards a comprehensive political settlement in the wake of the 1994 IRA ceasefire, the Good Friday (peace) agreement was decided. By then, in terms of the Republic, exhibition within Dublin's city centre had also been radically transformed. Not only had the Carlton and its sister cinema the Adelphi, controlled since 1992 by French bank Credit Lyonnais, closed in October 1994 and November 1995,[13] respectively, but the multiplex had found its way from suburbia into the city centre with the launch in November 1995 of Virgin's nine-screen multiplex.[14] Although it was opposite the large ILAC shopping centre, which had opened in 1981, and was only 200m from the two major shopping thoroughfares of Henry Street and O'Connell Street, the area was decidedly unfashionable, even dangerous, particularly after dark, and, as such, the choice of location might have seemed an unlikely one. However, firstly, the cinema had been designed to be part of an all-encompassing complex where the visitor could safely park the car, go to the cinema, and have something to eat and drink, without having to experience the city's streets; secondly, it made financial sense given that the (just under) four-acre site had a low purchase price of only £2.5 million; and, thirdly, perhaps most importantly, the cinema's developer, Belfast-based Sheridan Group, had already successfully opened, in a similarly depressed area, Belfast's Dublin Road multiplex.[15] While the intended operator of the cinema was to be MGM (the company which not only came on board with regard to the Dublin Road cinema in Belfast, but also actually proposed the new complex in Dublin and had envisaged it as an eight-screen venue), by the time the Parnell complex had been completed, the troubled bank Credit Lyonnais had sold its 450 MGM cinema screens in Ireland, Britain, the Netherlands and Denmark. Consequently, the new complex opened as Virgin Cinemas, with Virgin, a company more associated with air travel and music than with cinema entertainment, having bought MGM's British and Irish interests.[16] At the time, the rent was set (for five years) at £350,000 per annum.[17] Four years later, in October 1999, French cinema group Union Générale Cinématographique (UGC) paid GB£215 million for the thirty-four Virgin multiplexes in Britain and Ireland,[18] though in December 2004, reflecting a certain consolidation within the industry, the major American private-equity group Blackstone, which had acquired the Cine-UK chain three months earlier, bought all forty-two British and Irish UGCs for about €200 million, thus becoming the second-largest British exhibitor.[19] In 2005, in line with the other cinemas of the group, the Parnell complex, the only Irish venue, was rebranded as Cineworld.[20] The Belfast multiplex on the Dublin Road, previously owned by UGC, had already been sold and in January had been incorporated into Michael McAdam's Movie House circuit.

Founded in 1990 with a cinema in Glengormley, by 2010 the independent Movie House chain comprised of five multiplexes. In addition to the Glengormley six-screen venue and the ten-screen Dublin Road cinema – Movie House's flagship property – the list included the fourteen-screen multiplex at Belfast's City Side retail complex; the three-screen Maghera cinema, Co. Derry; and the six-screen Jet Centre cinema, Coleraine, Co. Derry; however, in 2007 McAdam also took a short-term lease on the small one-screen Portrush Playhouse, where he had begun his career as an exhibitor in 1987, having left his job as a vision mixer with Ulster Television. Notably, in 2009 McAdam, in keeping with his trademark promotion of 'Crazy Tuesdays' and heavily reduced ticket prices, was the first exhibitor in Ireland or the UK to do away with the premium charge on 3D films; while in 2002 Movie House at Yorkgate (now City Side, York Street) hosted the first Irish trial of a system designed for deaf and blind people.[21] As McAdam told reporters at the time, 'it is part of our company philosophy to make movie going as accessible and enjoyable to as many members of the public as we can'.[22] While such an inclusive policy has been less than urgently pursued by other Irish exhibitors,[23] nevertheless, in April 2010 the Irish Deaf Society was able to commend twelve cinemas in the Republic for providing subtitled access to (current) mainstream films,[24] following Tom O'Connor's innovative screening in March 2010 of Tim Burton's *Alice in Wonderland* with English subtitles at his cinema in Blackpool, Co. Cork.[25] As one commentator wrote, 'if Hollywood has any sense it will automatically produce future films with English subtitles and award Mr O'Connor an Oscar for showing the way.'[26]

Another newcomer to Irish film exhibition in the 1990s was the South African corporation, Ster Kinekor, which, operating as Ster Century, emerged in 1999 as the tenant of the new £10 million, fourteen-screen, 3,477-seat multiplex at Liffey Valley, Clondalkin, Co. Dublin, yet another out-of-town shopping centre. That the company chose Dublin as a location for European expansion is perhaps unsurprising given that in an industry measurement of cinema use in relation to population in which two is awarded to 'better' locations, Dublin as a city came out at almost three, pushing the country's average much higher than the European average.[27] Nevertheless, Liffey Valley remained their only cinema in Dublin and, indeed, in the Republic, as the sixteen-screen, 3,400-seat multiplex, which they had planned to open in 2000 near Santry, north Dublin, did not materialize.[28] Like the UCIs in Tallaght and Blanchardstown in particular, the Liffey Valley cinema is very well serviced by motorways which considerably expand the potential catchment area as it allows patrons to travel there by motor car rather than by the often inadequate public transport system which in 2008 was serving only 20 per cent of the population. But then, as David Clerkin wrote in 2006,

> Anyone interested in the cinema equivalent of a pub crawl can use the M50 as a handy guide. Starting in the north of the city at Coolock's UCI complex and hitting the motorway near the Omniplex in Santry, cinema fans who don't mind traffic will pass the UCI in Blanchardstown, the former Ster Century (now Vue) at Liffey Valley, another UCI at the Square in Tallaght and the new Movies@Dundrum in the Dundrum Town Centre before reaching the end of the road near Dún Laoghaire, where an IMC complex awaits.[29]

Another feature of Ster's Dublin cinema was that one of its screens, at 20m by 10m, was the largest in Britain or Ireland, while four of the screens were in the top ten. All of this helped to give Ster Century 'a staggering' 17 per cent share of the Irish market in its first full year, 2000, with 1.2 million admissions.[30] As a result of the development of the multiplex phenomenon in Dublin, the number of cinema seats had increased to 24,276 by the end of 1999,[31] by which time Dublin had seven large multiplexes, five of which had been established with foreign capital – Tallaght (twelve screens), Coolock (ten screens), Blanchardstown (nine screens), Parnell Street (nine screens) and Liffey Valley (fourteen screens) – while only two were Irish-owned. These were Ward Anderson's Santry Omniplex (ten screens), which had opened in March 1992 in the almost-new shopping and leisure centre that had started trading the previous October; and their IMC, Dún Laoghaire (twelve screens), which had opened in November 1999, beside the new Bloomfield shopping centre, situated just off the main shopping street. More telling, perhaps, is the increase from sixty-six screens in Dublin in 1992 to 117 by 2006, while nationally, in the same period, the number of cinema seats increased from 40,176 with an average of 234 seats per screen and 20,389 inhabitants per screen, to 66,786 seats with 178 seats per screen and 10,500 inhabitants per screen. It was a dramatic transformation, though the number of seats was still less than half the 1939 figure. (See appendix, table 2.) Notwithstanding that Ward Anderson historically had focused their exhibition interests largely outside of Dublin, it was clear from the early 1990s and the arrival of UCI that if it was to maintain a dominant presence within the Irish market, the group had to invest or face decline. Though the latter scenario seemed an unlikely one, given that they owned a number of highly profitable companies, their reluctance to borrow, coupled with their traditional notions of Irish exhibition, may have served as an impediment to any rapid expansion, particularly within the Dublin market.

WARD ANDERSON AND THE MULTIPLEX

Making sense of Ward Anderson's corporate empire is, as is evident in chapter 4, far from easy. While the large number of Ward Anderson companies identified by the examiner of restrictive practices in 1977 was relatively simple to understand, especially given that Ward Anderson's main activity was film distribution and exhibition, by the 1990s, share dealing (important to the group since the 1950s), property transactions and the myriad of inter-company loans, made any unravelling of its corporate governance extremely difficult. A 1992 article by Daire O'Brien estimating Ward Anderson's turnover as about £15 million per annum with total profits 'probably comfortably in excess of' £4 million, states that 'to describe the corporate structure [of Ward Anderson] as opaque would be an understatement.'[32] Other attempts to quantify Ward Anderson's business interests similarly concluded that 'trying to get a definite fix on the group's financial performance is made hugely difficult by a labyrinth of stand-alone companies, cross shareholdings and shareholder trusts.' For Brian Carey the 'complexities really begin' with the 'plethora' of investment companies such as the key vehicle Torgyle Holdings which, in 1997, had a large minority stake in another company, Mayfair Entertainment, as well as four subsidiaries, one of which, the Green Group Ltd, had a further five separate investment holdings subsidiaries. He also noted how 'the business throws up buckets of cash' with Dublin Cinema Group having £3.5 million in cash or bonds and earning over 20 per cent of its profits from interest in the year to 31 October 1995. Estimating the number of Ward Anderson screens in 1997 as 141 across thirty-three sites in twenty-nine towns in the Irish Republic with an additional forty-four screens at eleven sites in Northern Ireland, Carey speculated that if Ward Anderson was able to translate screen share to admission share then it could have had net profits from cinema admissions of £9 million, compared with UCI's operating profit of £2 million on gross sales of £9.5 million in 1994 from twenty-two screens. While this was something of a facile exercise given the many second-run and secondary location screens within Ward Anderson's portfolio, earnings from cash on deposit and stock market dealings, not to mention property transactions, would have put it on a par with the transnationals.[33] Two years later, Carey reassessed the group's cinema holdings, north and south, as 186 screens spread over thirty-four separate sites, once again observing how the '70-odd' Ward Anderson companies[34] constituted 'one of the most complex corporate structures in Ireland.' Even when this had been reduced, following voluntary liquidations from 2002 onwards, to forty-five companies and trusts, by 2005, Ian Kehoe came to the conclusion that 'trying to work out just how well the company is performing is like trying to pick up mercury with a fork. There is no such company as Ward Anderson [but an] intricate web of related companies, cross-investments, trust companies and inter-company loans.'[35] It is not perhaps surprising then that even Kevin Anderson admits to not be fully conversant with company details: 'I've never known how many cinemas we own. I've lost count – we have them all over the place.'[36]

Carey's 1999 article also highlighted one of the trademarks of Ward Anderson companies, the 'almost complete absence of bank debt' and the fact that many of the companies had substantial cash. Dublin Cinema Group, for example, had at that time £4.4 million; Abbey Films, £1.1 million; Green Group, £1.5 million; Omniplex Holdings, £900,000; while a further £1 million was spread between Torgyle Holdings, Fairfax, and Paramount Enterprises.[37] The same year it was reported that Ward Anderson through their 112 screens in the Republic, worth an estimated £85 million, controlled 43 per cent of the cinema market,[38] though by the end of 2006 this had increased to over 50 per cent of the market. By then they had roughly twenty-four cinemas with 140 screens in the Republic and a further twelve cinemas with 80 screens in Northern Ireland. In 2001, the *Sunday Tribune*'s 'Ireland's richest 100' list placed the Ward Anderson families at number 59, a slight drop from the previous year's 55, and valued their cinema and investment assets at a 'conservative' £105 million.[39] By 2003, having dropped from number 62 in 2002 to 69, the Ward Anderson families were thought to be worth €95 million,[40] but the following year, while still in 69th place, they were said to be worth €123 million.[41] By 2006 the *Times* estimated Leo Ward and Kevin Anderson to be worth €59 million each (or combined €118 million);[42] while the following year they were worth €85 million each, and individually ranked, came in at joint-162nd place (up ten places).[43] These estimates are likely to have undervalued the property assets of the company, which by the mid-2000s could very well have been in excess of €200 million, though the collapse in Irish commercial property prices from 2007 onwards, with 2010 property values similar to those of 1999,[44] would have substantially reduced their value. Nevertheless, the key investment weapon in a recession is cash, and the collapse in asset prices gave Ward Anderson's cash-rich companies unrivalled opportunities in the twentieth-first century's first recession.

Ward Anderson's cautious and somewhat delayed approach in entering the multiplex market was rewarded when a developer appeared who was willing to carry most of the cinema's capital cost. Not accepting the risk of investing £3 million in the ten-screen cinema which was to be part of a shopping centre in Santry, north Dublin, they entered into a deal whereby the builder would supply the cinema, they would equip it, and the takings would be split on a 50/50 basis, an arrangement which was still in place at least until 1996.[45] While this typified Ward Anderson's conservative approach to borrowing and risk-taking, very many early multiplex developers, as Stuart Hanson points out, 'were keen to minimize potential risks by not owning the building in which the multiplex was housed'.[46] AMC, for example, sold their buildings and then leased them back. Nevertheless, Paul Ward, speaking in 2005, revealed that their 'preference is to buy rather than lease', but 'developers invariably prefer to hold on to the freehold of properties.'[47] Of course, the general design of multiplexes, as noted, had been, from the outset, dictated by the requirement that they could be easily reconfigured as non-cinema spaces, such as supermarkets, warehouses or large retail outlets, hence the shed-like look of many such complexes.

The first Ward Anderson multiplex in its Omniplex brand, the Omniplex, Santry, opened in March 1992. Like its nearest competitor, UCI Coolock, it achieved a capacity only in the region of 30 to 40 per cent, though the much smaller investment of only £1.8 million by Ward Anderson in Santry can be compared with the £3.55 million spent by UCI in Coolock. Throughout the rest of the 1990s, Ward Anderson invested heavily, and, in the five years preceding the opening of their £9.5 million IMC (Irish Multiplex Cinemas) in Dún Laoghaire at the end of 1999, Paul Ward estimated that the group had invested £50 million in cinemas, giving them a total of 183 screens across thirty-five complexes. While these were mostly in the Republic (125 screens in fifty-eighty complexes), with a significant number in Northern Ireland (fifty-eight screens in nine complexes), no less than 35 per cent of their business was in the Dublin area.[48] By August 2003, Ward Anderson owned and operated twenty-three cinemas with 131 screens[49] (increased to 135 screens by 2004) in the Republic, and a further twelve complexes with seventy-nine screens in Northern Ireland.

Perhaps the most obvious measurement of the growth of the Ward Anderson group is the development of the Omniplex brand under the management of Paul Anderson, which according to son Mark, the third generation to enter the business, owes to their catering to audience demands. In 2008 he described their target patron as the 'more discerning, movie-going audience who want to see a wide choice of films in comfort, who want to be able to book on the internet and enjoy fresh popcorn and chilled drinks.'[50] Indeed, in spring 2005, within a time span of just two weeks, the chain opened two Omniplexes in Cork and Galway. The first of these was a thirteen-screen cinema (with over 2,600 seats, wall-to-wall screens and Dolby sound in each room) located at a new shopping complex, Mahon Point, in the Cork city suburbs, while the second was a seven-screen, 1,400-seat facility, for the same cost of €10 million, sited at the €20 million City Lights Leisureplex in Oranmore, on the west side of Galway city, 10km from the city centre, but which, in contrast to the Cork cinema, they had been able to buy outright.[51]

Like its sister IMC chain, the Omniplex brand seems to have been set up with borrowings from one of Ward Anderson companies, Grokenda Holdings, and increased its presence dramatically throughout Ireland during the 1990s and 2000s. Omniplex Holdings, the company which operates the chain as well as those cinemas carrying the Cineplex identity (created subsequently and apparently reserved for smaller multiplexes of six or fewer screens) was valued in 2007 in excess of a staggering €56 million. The same year the company registered a profit of €2.9 million, bringing retained profits to €10.7 million.[52] While a number of the cinemas have used both identities it seems that by the end of 2010 only two cinemas were being grouped as Cineplexes. These were the Ballina Cineplex (six screens, which replaced the two-screen cinema that closed in 2001 due to competition from Castlebar's seven-screen multiplex, leaving the area with no cinema); and the Killarney Cineplex (five screens). Consequently, twenty-six cinemas with 191 screens remain under the Omniplex umbrella proper, even if some retain the Cineplex name[53] and others carry unique designations, as is the case with three Dublin cinemas (the Swan Centre, the Savoy and Screen at College Street). Among these twenty-six cinemas are ten cinemas in Northern Ireland – Armagh (four screens); Bangor (seven screens, expanded from original four); Carrickfergus, Co. Antrim (six screens); Derry (built on the site of the Strand Cinema; seven screens); Dundonald (eight screens); Enniskillen (seven screens); Lisburn, Co. Antrim (fourteen screens); Newry (nine screens); Belfast's Kennedy Centre (eight screens), Larne (eight screens) – the three Dublin cinemas not named Omniplex or Cineplex listed above (twelve screens); and thirteen Omniplexes in the Irish Republic – Carlow (eight screens);[54] Clonmel (five screens); Mahon Point, Cork (originally seven screens, later expanded to thirteen screens);[55] Abbey Centre, Drogheda (six screens); Santry, Dublin (eleven screens); Galway, Headford Road (ten screens) and at City Limits entertainment centre, Oranmore, Galway (six screens); Kilkenny (four screens); Limerick (twelve screens);[56] Longford (four screens); Tralee (eight screens);[57] Tullamore (six screens); and in Drinagh, Wexford (eight screens). The new Stephen's Green multiplex, due to open in 2011, will also fall under the Omniplex brand.[58]

Meanwhile the IMC chain, founded in 1998, and run independently by Paul Ward, who also is responsible for the less mainstream, more art house dominated Screen, Dublin, has continued to grow, but somewhat less dramatically. According to their website, IMC, 'one of Ireland's leading innovators in the film entertainment business', is committed to 'bringing great cinema to local communities with a commitment to high quality and friendly service.' By the end of 2010 it had six Irish multiplexes, one of which was in Northern Ireland at Ballymena (seven screens). The remaining five in the Irish Republic were located in Athlone (six screens); Dundalk (seven screens); Mullingar (six screens); Thurles (five screens); and, having won out over both UCI and Virgin who were initially interested in the site, Dún Laoghaire (thirteen screens). Thus, by 2010's end, the Ward Anderson families controlled about 235 screens, and had interests in at least three other screens.

Chief among these screens, however, are those located in their flagship cinema, the capital's six-screen Savoy, which, though grouped as an Omniplex cinema, is, nevertheless, in its scale, grandeur and history, a cinema apart from other more regular multiplexes over which it 'still scores' particularly 'when it comes to capacity for a premiere and the size of the screen.'[59] In order to maintain the cinema's high standards it has undergone no less than five renovations and refurbishments in the last quarter of a century, with the most recent in 2003, which cost €2 million and largely focused on the foyer areas, staircases and cash desks,[60] and in 2005.[61] Even though the current crop of multiplexes such as Dún Laoghaire's IMC should 'hold good for another 25 to 30 years regardless of how film projection is likely to change',[62] most will be renovated to some degree within ten to fifteen years of their opening as indeed has been the case with the Tallaght complex which was refurbished in stages in 2005 and 2006,[63] though despite this when it closed in March 2010, it was regarded by many as having been let run down.

THE MEGAPLEX

By the mid-1990s, multiplexes had transformed Irish, as much as they had, European exhibition. At the end of 1995 there were 328 multiplex cinemas in western Europe with a total of 2,700 screens, twice as many as in 1990. In 1995, multiplexes accounted for 13 per cent of the market as they squeezed out 'old style' cinemas. Despite this growth, there were only two pan-European multiplex companies; both were American – UCI and Warner Bros International Theatres – though Warners did not invest in the Irish Republic.[64] At the beginning of 1999 there were 401 multiplexes operating in Europe, with a total of 4,230 screens,[65] while, by 2005, according to the Irish Competition Authority, in Ireland there were seventy cinemas of which thirty-seven were multiplexes; this latter venue type, comprised 308 of the total 385 screens, and three-quarters of the 71,000 seats.[66] By this time, however, a new concept, the megaplex, had entered the lexicon. Usually reserved for cinemas with sixteen or more screens, though sometimes there can be as little as fourteen screens, megaplexes have been char-acterized by 'new exhibition technologies, expanded leisure and entertainment offer-ings [such as the availability of new film formats like IMAX or in the period prior to the explosion from 2009 of 3D, 3D, as well as video games and virtual reality tech-nologies], large screens, plentiful seats, and a model of customer service.'[67] Furthermore, unlike multiplexes in which the synergy between shopping and cinema is maximized, a feature of the megaplex is that, in general, they are not integrated within a dedicated mainstream shopping precinct.[68] While the first megaplex in Europe was established in Belgium in 1988 by the Kinepolis group, which also opened a twenty-five-screen cinema in Madrid, and the first megaplex in Britain, situated in London's Battersea Power Station complex, opened in 1997,[69] Ireland did not go megaplex until 2000, and even at the close of 2010, the Republic could still only claim this single megaplex. Nevertheless, the close of the decade saw, if also belatedly, another 'mega'-based inno-vation finally come to Ireland, when the country's first drive-in cinema, Movie Junction, opened on 19 November 2010 in Fota Retail Park, Carrigtwohill, Co. Cork, with accommodation initially for 100 cars, potentially rising to 370 cars, and with a 17m high by 20m long (approx. 2,500 square feet) screen. The admission cost per vehicle was €16, with three shows nightly from 6.30p.m. to 12.30a.m.[70]

Following the commercial failure and closing in October 2000 of the 370-seat IMAX theatre in the Parnell Street cinema and leisure complex, the opportunity arose for UGC to extend their nine-screen multiplex to megaplex size. When the £7 million IMAX theatre opened in June 1998 it was hoped that, as the first such theatre in both Ireland and Britain,[71] it would attract 500,000 patrons in its first year.[72] However, despite boasting an eight-storey high, 62ft by 82ft screen and state-of-the-art sound system, it failed to entice repeat custom. Even its change of programming in 2000 away from wild life and traditional documentary in favour of animated films targeted at 'the lucrative family cinema market'[73] was not enough to save the cinema. While there are a number of reasons why it failed, a key factor was, no doubt, its undesirable location. Even though the complex's developer, Peter Curistan, managing director of the Sheridan Group, stated that 'the stain of northside inner city' had been 'killed' as early as the mid-1990s,[74] one real estate agent was quoted as saying 'the Dublin consumer has yet to be convinced about socialising in the Parnell Square area. The idea of entertainment after dark has not taken off in the area.'[75] In any case, its closure afforded UGC the opportunity to increase its screens to seventeen, thus bringing the number of city centre screens to twenty-eight, spread over UGC, the Savoy (six screens), Screen (three screens) and Irish Film Institute (two screens). The Sheridan group,[76] who retained control of an amusement arcade, Century City, within the Parnell complex, opened another IMAX cinema in November 2001 in Belfast's main post-ceasefire rejuvenation entertainment and sports complex, the GB£100 million Odyssey Centre.[77] Although this was one of the flagship projects of the new Belfast, from the end of the 1990s there had been a myriad of small and large developments in the city ranging from the pedestrianization of streets to the development of a sidewalk café culture. These not only allowed Belfast to cater for the short-stay and weekend tourist, but also suggested to cautious transnational cinema exhibition companies that the city, which was 'underscreened', was a safe environment in which to generate profits. Indeed in 2001, for example, Warner Bros opened a multiplex on Belfast's Dublin Road, though this, along with Warner's other UK cinemas, was taken-over two years later by Vue Entertainment.[78]

Given that the nine-screen Parnell Street UGC cinema was recording high occupancy rates – in 2002 it had one million admissions with higher occupancy than any of the company's British multiplexes – and was not restricted in its physical growth by being part of a shopping centre proper (though of course it was in close proximity to shopping districts and a major shopping mall), it was not surprising that UGC took the decision to extend into the adjoining IMAX building. Despite there having been considerable investment in suburbs and new towns outside Dublin city centre, there had been no major investment in cinemas in Dublin city since the original opening in 1995 of the Parnell complex, even though the numbers living in or near to the centre, encouraged by tax incentives for developers, investors and residents, had increased considerably. As the managing director of UGC, Margaret Taylor, pointed out in an interview in 2004, in which she suggested that the cinema had played an important role in the regeneration of the surrounding area, 'there are almost as many people living and working in the centre as there are in the suburbs'.[79] Furthermore, with at least 8,000 cinema seats lost in the O'Connell Street area during the 1970s and 1980s, it was widely considered within the industry that Dublin was under-seated, such that, according to Emer McEvoy, marketing manager of UGC Ireland, 'distributors are always saying that their films are not kept for long enough.'[80] Indeed, it was in the context of the insufficient number of screens in Dublin that long-drawn out negotiations for the redevelopment of the Carlton Cinema site (opposite the Savoy) O'Connell Street, were explored. While UCI expressed interest in operating a multiplex there, all such plans remained frozen as legal and other difficulties thwarted the project. Eventually, planning permission was granted in 2010 for the 5.5 acre site with 800,000 square feet of development at a construction cost of €900 million, and while there will not be a multiplex included in the massive development, it has been decided that the art deco façade of the Carlton Cinema will be retained, albeit, moved 50m further up the street![81]

As UGC continued to trade throughout the extension and renovation of the existing screens and foyer area, the megaplex – designed over different levels as opposed to the more traditional mall model of screens off long corridors – opened in two phases in September and November 2003 at a cost €13 million. While the auditoria, or rooms, varying in size from 92 to 404 seats, were finished with 'fourth wall' screens (whereby the screen covered all wall space) and stadium seating, to deal with the complex's lack of streetscape presence the largely glass exterior was also given a 'face-lift' through strong exterior lighting and the addition of an enormous four storey high canopy: a 19m by 12m advertising banner. Other innovations and features of the cinema included, in a reflection of UGC's roots within a strong French cultural tradition, a broader programming policy, though they did not intend to displace alternative cinemas, but, by devoting between a quarter and a half of their screens to 'smaller' films, they sought to grow, sometimes in partnership with local film centres or film festivals,[82] a 'bigger cinema-going audience that watches more than just mainstream films';[83] a children's party room where kids could be brought, fed and entertained before watching a movie; and the possibility of seeing any number of films for a fixed monthly charge. Though this latter scheme, which UGC found encouraged patrons to 'take the risk of going to a film they wouldn't usually watch',[84] was deemed successful enough to be adopted by the new owners Blackstone (who acquired the cinema from UGC in December 2004 and rebranded it Cineworld) and remains as of end of 2010,[85] it, nevertheless, has a downside in that it has also served to encourage less respectful or more casual television-like viewing whereby audience members can disturb other patrons not least by leaving mid-way through the movie. At another level, some distributors have regarded it as income reducing. Distributor United International Pictures (UIP), for example, felt their revenues declined as a result of it and they withdrew temporarily their films from the UGC network.[86] This is not an isolated case of a distributor-exhibitor dispute in 2006. It was reported that London-based Entertainment Film Distributors (EFD), without giving a reason it seemed, were refusing prints of the gay western *Brokeback Mountain* (Ang Lee, 2005) to Ward Anderson.[87] The disagreement between EFD and Ward Anderson, agents for the company since 1971, began in 2005 and remained unresolved in 2008 with EFD refusing Ward Anderson prints of *Sex in the City* (Michael Patrick King, 2008), thereby leaving many cities and towns in which Ward Anderson is the only exhibitor, such as Athlone, Mullingar, Dundalk, Tullamore, Tralee and Killarney, without the much-hyped film.[88] However, even without there being any dispute, and despite the increasing size of the Irish cinema market, many films with Irish distribution rights continue to be passed over for theatrical release.[89]

While in 2002 and 2003 the Parnell cinema made losses of €400,000 and €1.2 million, respectively,[90] which starkly contrasts the performance in 2002 of the three

Dublin UCIs, which, exactly reflecting the growth in the Irish box office, increased turnover by 8 per cent and made pre-tax profits of €4.5 million,[91] the cinema's actual turnover in 2003 increased by 40 per cent from €6.3 million in 2002 to €8.7 million. Also on the positive side, UGC Cinema Holdings, the parent company for Irish and British operations, made an overall profit in 2003 of €3.62 million, up dramatically on the loss of €44 million in 2002.[92] Despite a 1 per cent fall off in admission in 2005 compared to 2004, the Parnell Street complex, by now owned by Cineworld, saw its operating profits, as a result of a 4 per cent increase in spend per head, double from €708,000 to €1.4 million, while pre-tax profits jumped to €1.2 million. The turnover for 2005 was €15.3 million, compared to €14.7 million for 2004.[93] By 2006, its pre-tax profits doubled to €3.3 million over the previous year on turnover of €15.9 million and a wage bill of €1.9 million.[94]

One controversial transformation of the Parnell Centre complex as it is known, and potentially commercially-damaging to the cinema, was the decision to replace the adjoining sports-themed restaurant and bar, Shooters, with Peter Stringfellow's first Irish lapdancing club. Though this had the power to transform, by osmosis or association, the quality of the experience in the adjoining cinemas, in the end, the club only lasted less than six months and closed in July 2006. The club's failure was not so much due to its lack of a market as its inability to withstand the continuous picketing by hostile residents and women's groups. Of course, even prior to the club's opening, the area, as noted, was already less than fashionable. Indeed, directly opposite was a low-priced LIDL supermarket, while more generally, the street itself had become synonymous with multi-ethic, mostly African, migrants, such that city planners were expressing concern about the creation of a possible immigrant ghetto in the area. Seeking to restore his original vision for the area, in 2009 Sheridan's Peter Curistan acquired the vacant Stringfellow's for €4 million from accountant Alan McEvoy and businessman Tom Butler and in 2010 bought out the Parnell Centre's outlets from the Parnell Partnership (including John, Deirdre and Ian Murphy, and Michael O'Sullivan) for about €6 million.[95] With complete ownership of the Parnell Centre, Curistan then announced his intention to redevelop the centre 'significantly ... despite the recession', since the Parnell Street area was emerging as 'one of the busiest shopping and commercial areas in Dublin and the multiplex which our units complement is the busiest on these islands.'[96]

OTHER DEVELOPMENTS IN IRISH EXHIBITION FROM THE LATE 1990S

Even before the opening of UCI Blanchardstown, 1996 – the first year proper of the massive expansion of the Irish economy, or of what would become known as the Celtic Tiger – had seen a 20 per cent increase in national admissions, to almost 11.5 million, up from the 1994 record year of just over 10.4 million admissions. By early 1997, UCI had 45 per cent of the Dublin market, with its Tallaght complex ranked fourth in Britain and Ireland, while the addition by Ward Anderson of twenty new screens in 1996, had increased the number of screens in Ireland by 50 per cent in ten years.[97]

Despite a temporary slump in the early 2000s, as a response to 9/11 [2001] and the dot.com bubble, the years following 1996 to the mid-2000s maintained steady growth rates such that Ireland had the fastest growing economy in the OECD for many years. Employment figures doubled to more than two million, and with taxes reduced, net take home pay went up for many workers, though the cost of housing dramatically increased such that by the early 2000s affordability by even professional workers had become an issue. Therefore, the sharp 'contraction' in the housing market from 2007 onwards which saw prices tumble by 50 per cent or more, gave little comfort to those who had borrowed many more multiples of their salaries for residential property than their predecessors, and found it a struggle to pay their mortgages even if they maintained their jobs as unemployment rose to more than 13 per cent of the workforce. By 2010, the full impact of the global crisis, magnified in Ireland's case by the legacy of poor regulation of the banking system at a time of access to low interest loans following the introduction of the euro, and the government provision of the 2008 blanket bank guarantee, was being felt. A four-year economic plan,[98] followed by one of the most austere budgets in Irish history, provided the backdrop to the loan in 2010 of €85 billion from the International Monetary Fund and the European Union, and while unemployment stabilized at around 450,000, many believe, as has been the case at various points in Irish history, that at least part of the solution to the country's economic difficulties lies in emigration. The social and cultural consequences of the dramatic rise and traumatic fall of the 'Celtic Tiger' economy may take decades to be fully experienced and understood.

In terms of cinema attendance, by the end of the 1990s, a Eurostat survey suggested Ireland had the highest admission figures of all European Union countries with an average of 3.2 tickets sold per capita each year. This compared with Britain's 2.1 tickets and France's 2.3. Of all western countries, the USA continued to have the highest average with 4.6 visits to the cinema per person per year.[99] By 2002, when the European Union's twenty-five states recorded one billion admissions, Ireland had the second-highest per capita cinema attendance in Europe, with 4.4 visits to the cinema (only Iceland with 5.5 visits per year surpassed Ireland), with Dubliners attending on average 8.8 times. This compares with France's average of 3.06 and the UK's 2.99 visits to the cinema per annum. Cinema-going had more than doubled in Ireland during the previous decade compared with Europe's average of 60 per cent.[1] While in 1991, there were 8.08 million admissions in the Republic of Ireland, in 2002 there were 17.3 million, with box office income of €93.5 million compared with 1991 when box office income was €26,157,000 (*c.* £20 million),[2] with a peak of 18.365 million admissions reached in 2007. During the subsequent two years as the economic recession took hold, admissions dropped to 18.229 million in 2008, and, following a more significant tumble of 575,000, to 17.654 million in 2009, though the gross box office figures continued to climb from €112 million in 2007 to nearly €124 million in 2009.[3]

In this environment, the multiplexes continued to record healthy profits, with UCI, in line with the industry generally, increasing its Irish box office turnover and other revenue, including confectionary sales. Whereas its pre-tax profits of £1.3 (€1.65) million in 1994 was double that for 1993, its 1994 turnover on sales of £9.6 (€12.15) million[4] had risen by 2001 to €19 million (or 16 per cent of the national box office total of €83 million), with pre-tax profit of €4.54 million, at which point its then three Dublin suburban complexes recorded more than two million admissions.[5] The following year revenue was up by 8 per cent to €21.5 million, when pre-tax profits were €4.87 million, and another €5 million was paid by way of dividend to its parent.[6] In 2003 profits rose to nearly €5.6 million, a 14 per cent increase, on turnover of €21.34 million, and which allowed it to pay a further €5 million dividend to UCI Multiplex.[7] Similarly, Ster Century's screens at Liffey Valley, which accounted for 20 per cent of Dublin's admissions in 2001, or 10 per cent of the Irish total,[8] was enjoying a period of growth. With 1.7 million admissions in 2001, compared with one million in 1999, not only was it the group's busiest cinema, but also, it was the third-busiest complex in Britain and Ireland.[9] While such levels of growth continued as a feature of the market throughout the early and mid-2000s, as noted, the last years of the decade experienced a slight fall on 2006 and 2007 figures.

Inevitably, and increasingly from the late 1990s, concern was raised about saturation in the Dublin market in particular, as had been the case in the UK and American markets.[10] In 1998, Leo Ward reported that while he was in the process of building a six-screen cinema in Castlebar, Co. Mayo, which had a population of only 10,000–12,000, some English cities with populations of 500,000 had only a two-screen complex. The ratio of cinemas per head of population was even more dramatic in Dublin where it seemed they were 'being put up at random'. Karl Milne, regional manager of UCI, who agreed with such a view, suggested that Dublin had already entered a new stage of development, 'where cinemas begin to cannibalize each other.' He predicted that in a couple of years cinemas would not be as big or as profitable as they currently were.[11] Nevertheless, three years later, in 2001, by which time Dublin had ninety-eight screens, with further multiplexes planned,[12] one commentator was declaring that there was still scope for smaller suburban 'infill developments' with five or six screens.[13] Additionally, Milne pointed out that further screens in carefully chosen locations would act to stimulate audience growth rather than divide or scatter it, and thus affirmed that there were many 'potentially successful development sites [available] in Dublin' particularly in the south-east of the city, but also in the city centre.[14] Nevertheless, by 2006 only the Dundrum complex had been opened, but then in 2005 Paul Ward had been reported as stating that Dublin had already reached saturation point and that the 'the main prospect for growth' was limited to regional centres such as their thirteen-screen Omniplex at Mahon Point, Cork, which opened in March 2005.[15]

Notwithstanding Ward's stated position, the group planned further expansion in Dublin through its Dublin vehicle, Dublin Cinema Group (DCG), the holding company for the group's operations in the capital. In 2003, DCG acquired the Stella, Rathmines,[16] but, with a view towards a much bigger project nearby, closed the cinema. In 1999 DCG sought unsuccessfully to gain planning permission for a seven-screen multiplex in the Rathmines Swan shopping centre. Following the rejection, DCG then bought the centre outright for £13 million from British property company British Land, which, by 2004, with tenants including Dunnes Stores and McDonalds, was valued at €40 million.[17] In early 2005 another Ward Anderson company, Sawbridge Ltd, sought planning permission to build a nine-screen, 1,719-seat complex there.[18] In summer 2007, once again through Sawbridge, a planning application was lodged but for a three-screen cinema.[19] This time it was successful and the project was approved in April 2008,[20] with the €3 million, three-screen, 571-seat complex opening in December 2009, with some of the first custom-designed rooms for digital cinema projection in Ireland. As befits a predominantly middle-class area, plans were announced to transmit in the cinemas live opera, though this highbrow ambition was tempered by a desire to show the more down-market Formula One races live.[21] Not accepting that Dublin might have enough screens, in 2010 Omniplex Holdings announced an agreement with the Stephen's Green shopping centre, no more than two miles from the Swan Cinemas, to build a twelve-screen complex on the top deck of the centre's carpark.[22] While nostalgically this could be seen as a return to the area where the Green Group started with the Green Cinema, more prosaically, a deciding factor is not just the fact that the area, just off the still fashionable Grafton Street, enjoys a steady footfall during the day and has a vibrancy at night, but that the LUAS light railway terminal is located just outside the shopping centre, thereby allowing easy access to the new complex from south Dublin's middle-class suburbs. The decision to open a food court on the shopping centre's top floor will no doubt add to the attraction of the cinema, which is expected to open by the end of 2011 when it will become the first multiplex on the southside of the city centre. It was reported that the Andersons will be paying an initial annual rent of around €1 million.[23]

In 2000, according to Carlton Screen Advertising, twice as many were going to the cinema as a decade earlier, while the number of screens had risen by 83 per cent. This had also led to an increase in the number of films released from 136 in 1995 to 175 in 1999. By 2000, admissions had increased to 14.9 million in the Irish Republic, with 7.2 million, or just under half the total, in Dublin. There were 4.5 million admissions in Northern Ireland the same year. The profile of the cinema audience corresponded to international patterns, with half in the 15 to 24 age group, and a third aged 25-to-34 years. During 1995 to 2001 profitability also grew when average ticket prices almost doubled from £2.60 to over £5. From January 2000 to January 2008 adult ticket prices before 6p.m. increased by 47 per cent to €7.00, while those after 6p.m. rose by 34 per cent to €9.00, with similar increases of 32 and 35 per cent affecting children and dedicated Saturday and Sunday early shows, though student and OAP tickets increased by only 16 per cent to €5.50.[24] In the period between 2003, when Dodona Research considered Irish ticket prices 'still low',[25] and 2006, ticket prices increased on average by 14 per cent with some cinemas putting up their prices by more than 20 per cent. Nevertheless, according to the Competition Authority such increases were 'below the level of inflation and are not high by international standards.' A spokesman for the organization went on to explain that 'ticket prices have risen by 4.1 per cent [during October 2005 to October 2006], compared to an overall inflation rate of 4.9 per cent. The price of a cinema ticket in Ireland compares favourably with other EU countries and is cheaper than in the US.' Furthermore, many cinemas including Cineworld and

IMC offer regular cinemagoers special monthly prices (roughly €20) for unlimited access to films,[26] as well as family discounted tickets, while all cinemas offer off-peak prices which are on average 20 to 25 per cent less than those for prime-time shows. Even so, cinema was a 'costly treat' for many families, particularly given the additional costs of parking at some cinemas or other travel expenses; the surcharges incurred, often on a per ticket basis rather than as a single transaction fee, when booking online or with credit card over the phone;[27] and over-priced popcorn, sweets and ice-cream.[28] Indeed, while a substantial source of cinema income is, as might be expected, from ticket sales, with bigger chains increasingly getting significant revenue from advertising,[29] concession sales, as already discussed, can represent anything from twenty up to forty per cent of a cinema's profits.

From 2003 onwards, though largely ending in 2005, there was an 'unprecedented level of corporate activity'[30] in the sale and ownership of the large multiplexes in Britain and Ireland, as rival venture capitalists, attracted by the healthy cash flow of the multiplexes, entered the market. In July 2003, less than four years after opening, Ster sold its Liffey Valley cinema, as well as its six complexes in Britain, amounting to almost ninety screens, to a private equity group, Inflexion, backers of Aurora Cinemas, for the modest sum of GB£16.9 million, in what was considered 'an embarrassing exit' for South African owners Primedia. Primedia, which had other cinemas in eastern European and Spain, had been trying unsuccessfully to sell its cinemas for two years, and lost over €70 million in the venture.[31] A year later ownership of the Liffey Valley complex changed hands again when it was bought by specialist debt provider Hutton Collins for an estimated GB£32million, almost two times the price Inflexion paid.[32] The same year, UCI, established in 1986, was put up for sale by owners US film and television production and distribution giant Viacom and Vivendi Universal Studios, which had acquired it in 1989 through Merrill Lynch for €740 million. By then, it had 1,000 screens at 106 sites worldwide and employed 6,500 people, 124 of them in Ireland. It had thirty-five complexes in the UK and three in Ireland. While interested parties included HgCapital, Vue Entertainment, Cine-UK,[33] and Iranian property developer Robert Tchenguiz (who sought to merge it with Odeon cinemas in which he was a minority shareholder),[34] it was financier Guy Hands' venture capital company, Terra Firma Capital Partners, founded in March 2002, that proved successful and in October 2004 bought the Irish, British and continental European divisions of the UCI chain for €260 million.[35] Already, Terra Firma had beaten off thirteen rivals to take over Odeon, Britain's largest chain,[36] in August 2004, which had been put up for sale two months earlier. Next to change hands was UGC Cinema Holdings, the parent company for Irish and British operations, and, as noted above, sold out in December 2004 to American venture capital company Blackstone, which had acquired the Cineworld UK chain two months earlier,[37] making Blackstone's Cineworld chain the largest in Britain and Ireland, with 23 per cent of cinema screens in Britain in addition to its highly successful seventeen-screen Dublin complex, which was renamed Cineworld, Dublin.[38] Four months later, in April 2005, yet another venture capital company, Vue Entertainment, formed in 2003 with the merger of the Warner Village chain in the UK (including the Belfast complex at the Odyssey) and SBC International, bought Ster Century's British and Irish multiplexes and rebranded them under the Vue name. At that stage the Ster Century in Dublin along with Dublin's UGC had the highest admissions of all cinema complexes in Britain and Ireland.[39] The purchase of the Ster cinemas brought Vue, which had been backed by private-equity groups Boston Ventures, Clarity Partners and L&G Ventures, to almost 500 screens across forty-nine sites[40] and positioned it as the third-largest exhibitor in Britain.

Though the ownership changes of 2003 to 2005 affected the lucrative Dublin and Belfast markets and brought the Irish-owned subsidiaries of American, French and South African exhibitors under British and American private equity control, most activity within Irish exhibition in this period, and, indeed, subsequently, has been from established Irish exhibitors as well as new Irish entrants to the market. By early 2005, Dublin was registering 743,000 cinema admission per month, an increase of 10.5 per cent on February 2004. Nationally, cinema admissions were 1.5 million in February 2005, up 15.8 per cent on the same month in 2004. With per capita admissions of over four, the possibility was being discussed that Ireland could be on a par with the USA within a few years.[41] That, however, has failed to materialize. Irish admissions, though, need to be put in a wider context.

While there were 17,261,900 ticket sales in the Republic of Ireland in 2004, Britain, including Northern Ireland (which roughly represents 3 per cent of the total), recorded almost ten times that number, 171.3 million with revenue of £770 million,[42] compared with €100.9 million (approximately 10 per cent of the British figure) in Ireland in 2004. (Interesting, in 2009, despite the recession, Irish Republic gross box office climbed to €124.6 million, almost 25 per cent more than 2004's figure, though the number of tickets sold rose by only 392,100, or 2.27 per cent, suggesting a considerable increase in ticket prices, perhaps in part explained by premium charges for 3D films.) Furthermore, as table 13c of the appendix records for this snap shot year, in 2004 the top ten box office hits (which took €38,223,125 of the total box office for the island of Ireland of €123–31 million)[43] were all American or British productions.[44] As such, it should be clear that the benefits that commercial film distribution and exhibition make to the Irish economy, or, more specifically, to the Irish film industry, are extremely limited.

Nevertheless, confirming the strength of Irish business, when the new twelve-screen postmodern 'multiplex palace' opened in August 2005 as part of the up-market Dundrum suburban shopping centre, the tenants were not a foreign corporation, but a joint venture company involving two Irish independent exhibitor families – the O'Gormans and Spurlings – both of which made a decisive leap in scale. The O'Gorman family had been long-time operators of the twin-screen Forum, Glasthule, which closed on 3 September 1999, and the Ormonde Cinema, Stillorgan, a few miles from Dundrum, which, though purpose-built in 1983 as a three-screen venue was extended in 1997, at a cost of £2 million, to seven screens[45] and had around 500,000 admissions annually in the late 1990s, though it closed in April 2011.[46] The Spurlings, on the other hand, who were associated with Ward Anderson from the late 1970s to the mid-1990s,[47] have, since becoming independent exhibitors, operated both outside and within Dublin. While prior to the mid 2000s, the Spurlings confined their activity to areas outside of Dublin, where their interests include Mayo Movie World (Castlebar), the SGC Enniscorthy (aka Slaney Plaza Cinema, Co. Wexford) SGC Dungarvan (Co. Waterford), and the seven-screen, fully digital and 3D-capable cinema in Gorey (Co. Wexford) that opened in June 2010, the decade saw the family, along with partners O'Gormans, become major players in Dublin exhibition through the establishment of the Movies@Cinemas group which agreed a twenty-five year lease for the 51,666 square feet (4,800 square meters) Dundrum multiplex at an annual rent of €1.2 million.[48] A year later, in May 2006 the group signed another agreement to take over the eleven-screen, 2,000-seat cinema planned as part of the €40 million second phase of the Pavillions shopping centre, Swords, in north county Dublin, which opened in December 2006 and considerably increased the number of visitors to the shopping centre.[49] Both cinemas have proved profitable, with Dundrum's success prompting the closure in July 2007 of Spurling's Wicklow cinema, the Screen by the Sea, Greystones. While Dundrum recorded a pre-tax profit of just under €1 million for the year ending August 2009 despite the recession (though reflecting the economic downturn the figure is almost 50 per cent down on the previous year's €1.85 million),[50] less dramatically, Swords made €38,000 in the same period (down almost 80 per cent from the previous year's recorded pre-tax profit of €184,000). Both cinemas by autumn 2010, in line with Spurlings' other screens, were upgraded to being fully digital. Though the plans to open a ten-screen complex at Salthill, a Galway city suburb without a cinema, were stymied by planning objections, a similar sized all digital cinema with 1,600 seats, beside the Ice Dome in Dundalk Retail Park, Movies@Dundalk, was announced in 2009.[51] Perhaps to stave off the recession or any dip as a result of the saturation of cinemas (particularly on the east coast), in July 2010, Movies@ expanded its business to include the rental of DVDs and games through its website.[52]

Though Dundrum was Ireland's first cinema with digital projection facilities installed in a number of its screens from its beginning, by May 2006, when *Prime* (Ben Younger, 2005) was the first film to be released in digital format in Ireland, eleven of the fifty-nine cinemas where the film was screened could show it digitally. Besides Dundrum, the others were at the Gate, Cork city, opened by Cado Ltd[53] in 1998; Reel Pictures, Blackpool, Co. Cork; UCI Blanchardstown, Dublin; the Eye, Galway; Gaiety, Sligo, which when it opened in December 2002 at twelve screens was the biggest cinema outside Dublin;[54] Clonmel Omniplex; Capitol, Thurles; SGC Dungarvan; Slaney Plaza, Enniscorty; and Storm, Portlaoise.[55] By the end of 2006, Storm opened Ireland's first fully digital complex, the five-screen cinema[56] in Naas, Co. Kildare, though Kildare's Newbridge multiplex, which had been in the offing from 2002, to the anger and frustration of the residents, remained unrealized. In January 2008 the planning permission to build the cinema, envisaged as part of the Whitewater shopping centre that opened in April 2006, expired, thus in effect releasing the developers from their commitment to the town.[57] Nevertheless, a six-screen multiplex was eventually built as part of the shopping centre, and was opened on 16 December 2009 by operators UCI.[58]

In the meantime, an independent Irish company, Digital Cinema Ltd (DCL), of which DTS (Digital Theatre Systems, the worldwide supplier of digital sound systems for cinemas and home use) held a 25 per cent stake, announced in 2005 that it would launch a scheme to provide digital cinema equipment to all cinema screens in Ireland. By early 2008 they had installed thirty-three such systems at thirteen cinema sites, including ten at Dundrum, with most cinema complexes having two systems installed. The DCL business model is based around projector costs of about €50,000 payable through a virtual print fee by film distributors and screen advertising companies, while exhibitors are obliged to commit to an exclusive rental contract for the equipment, as well as service and maintenance charges. In the USA, as well as in Ireland and the UK, exhibitors have expressed concern about how the data generated through the digital projection equipment such as film start times could give supplier-shareholders or competitors access to sensitive business information. However, not all Irish cinemas were offered the deal, as DCL identified approximately forty cinema screens, among them the country's independent art cinemas, where DCL did not think the virtual print fee would generate sufficient return for the company. In response to this problem, the Arts Council and the Irish Film Board through the Cultural Cinema Consortium, announced in January 2009 a total of €750,000 in grants to seven cinemas to purchase and install digital projection equipment. The largest grants were made to the Light House Cinema (€200,000), Irish Film Institute (€150,000), and Screen Cinema (€110,000). The other awards went to Cinema North West; Cinemobile; Mermaid Wicklow Arts Centre; and Town Hall Theatre, Galway.[59]

It has been estimated that should DCL succeed in its plan to convert the 500 or so screens in Ireland to digital projection, the total investment would need to be €30–35 million.[60] Of course, while the onset of the recession scuppered the ambition to have this target reached by 2009, it is undoubtedly the case that by the mid-2010s there will be few cinema complexes in Ireland, if not necessarily cinema screens, without digital projection. It should be recalled that sound cinema arrived during the last great recession and considerable investment was required even by small exhibitors (see chapter 2), yet, the cost savings through not employing musicians, as well as the elimination of silent films from distribution, made it imperative to switch to sound, such that by the mid-1930s few Irish cinemas even in remote areas had not converted to the new format. Similarly, taking into account transport, distribution and staff savings[61] and the fact that many films in the future will probably be available on digital only, particularly in the context of 3D as an emerging and increasingly favoured format, especially with regard to children's films, exhibitors and distributors alike may find it necessary to shift to the new distribution format. Furthermore, it should be remembered that digital film, stored as it is on a computer hard drive, unlike (analogue) celluloid prints, which never have the same high quality as the master version, do not deteriorate with each viewing.

Meanwhile, further exhibition activity was taking place outside of Dublin. Tom O'Connor of the Reel Cinema group, who already had a complex in Ballincollig, Co. Cork, which posted a profit of €230,000 in the year to the end of August 2003, opened the seven-screen Reel Picture complex in the Cork city suburb of Blackpool in March 2005. The same month, Gerry Barrett's Edward Holdings, developer of a number of distinctive hotels in Ireland and Britain, built Galway city's second complex, the luxurious multi-purpose nine-screen, 1,200-seat, Eye Cinema, as part of their €75 million Wellpark retail park on the Dublin Road, about two kilometres from Galway city centre.[62] Within a month, Ward Anderson opened another multiplex in Oranmore, Co. Galway. Reflecting the growth within Irish business, more multiplex buyouts occurred from 2006 that saw Irish groups gain control of a number of large multiplexes. In May 2006, the independent cinema chain Storm cinemas, which at that stage had multiplexes in Limerick (eight screens),[63] Cavan (four screens), and Portlaoise (five screens), took over from Vue, at an estimated cost of €7 million, Belfast's biggest cinema, the twelve-screen Warner Village complex at the Odyssey Pavilion. At the time, Storm director Patrick O'Sullivan, who anticipated growing the admission figures, was reported as saying that the cinema, which had opened in 2001, was to be rebranded as Storm over the summer of 2006, and 'would benefit from having local management, instead of being run from Britain.'[64] Continuing to expand, in June 2007 having identified a 'gap' in the Waterford area in which only one Ward Anderson-controlled cinema, the Regina, Patrick Street (now closed), operated, the company opened their purpose-built, eight-screen, 1,112-seat cinema (on four levels) at Waterford's Railway Square mixed-use urban development.[65]

In response, Ward Anderson announced a 'major multi-million' face-lift of the Regina, though this had not happened by the close of 2010, and confirmed that they were '"seriously" looking at opening a new facility on the outskirts of the city (as part of the development proposed for Ballinaneeshagh's Waterford Crystal sports grounds on the opposite side of the city to Storm's complex) which 'they [felt] there's most definitely a demand for.'[66] The project, for which planning permission has been secured, was expected to start, despite the recession, in 2010, though this had not proceeded by the end of the year.[67] In any case, by the end of 2008 Storm itself had been substantially swallowed up with five of its six cinemas (Limerick, Portlaoise, Castletroy, Naas and Cavan) having been bought by Ciárán and Colum Butler[68] through their Entertainment Enterprises Group (which owned Leisureplex, Stillorgan, before it was sold to major developer Treasury Holdings). Entertainment Enterprises then entered a deal with Odeon-UCI under which the cinemas would be operated.

Given that the Butlers now controlled a total of sixty-one screens across eight Irish sites,[69] this was clearly not their first major acquisition. Previously, in autumn 2006, in a deal estimated at €90 million, they not only acquired the three Dublin UCIs at Tallaght, Coolock and Blanchardstown from the UK-based Odeon chain controlled by Terra Firma,[70] but also made a similar deal with Odeon-UCI, whereby it was agreed that the British-based company would continue to operate the cinemas.[71] (With Leisureplex units in close proximity to the Coolock and Blanchardstown multiplexes it is possible that these sites will be redeveloped as new leisure complexes.) As of 2010, both Storm and UCI chains retain their independent identities, though the word 'Odeon' appears on some UCI promotional material drawn from Odeon UK.

Meanwhile, Liam Carroll, one of the country's wealthiest men until the property crash of the late 2000s, sued the Butlers following a dispute over the sale of UCI

Tallaght claiming that he had a contract to buy it from them but that it was later sold (in 2007 for an estimated €50 million) to Noel Smyth, a solicitor and rival developer who planned to incorporate it into the €300–500 million redevelopment of The Square shopping centre and adjoining land.[72] Following much legal wrangling and shifting of economic fortunes, the Tallaght cinema closed for business on 8 March 2010 with landlords Alburn (one of Smyth's companies) stating that the lease for the cinema had expired and would not be renewed.[73] Despite sadness at the loss of fifty jobs, most of the comments posted online in the wake of the closure gave less than a flattering picture of the cinema, which seems to have become run-down and offered less facilities than other Dublin cinemas, including charging for parking. That few mourned its loss was perhaps due to the expectation that a new cinema and shopping complex would be developed on an adjacent site. Indeed by summer 2010, UCI[74]/ Leisureplex had already committed to a twenty-five year lease to occupy 145,000 sq ft, or 56 per cent, of this new proposed complex whose completion date was set by another embattled developer, Bernard McNamara, for 2012.[75] Meanwhile, Smyth was in negotiations with a number of parties, of which Ward Anderson was rumoured as one, to operate (perhaps only on a short-term lease) the cinemas vacated by UCI/Odeon.[76]

Ward Anderson's strategy of retained profits has not only allowed the company to expand in Ireland in the manner of these other exhibitors, but also, reversing earlier trends, to establish itself in the British market. As already noted, their company DCG, a holding company for the group's various operations in the capital, has been a highly profitable operation. In 2001 it had pre-tax profits of €1.7 million and although pre-tax profits halved in 2002, retained profits were up.[77] In the year to end of November 2003, recorded pre-tax profits were more than €1.3 million,[78] while retained profits reached €17.4 million.[79] The following year, 2004, saw pre-tax profits slump to only €288,000, but it was in the context of having given the Savoy a €2 million face-lift and buying the Stella, Rathmines, and though they made an operating loss of €113,396, investment income and bank interest kept it in the black.[80] In the year to the end of October 2005, after heavy cost cutting, and despite a drop in admissions because of competition, the company returned to an operating profit of more than €250,000 and had retained profits of just under €18 million,[81] a similar figure to that retained in 2006.[82] In the year ending October 2007, despite the lack of major blockbuster films that year, the company made a pre-tax profit of €1.05 million, up 11.7 per cent on the 2006 figure, and had retained profits of €19.4 million. Interestingly, while other companies at this time were suffering from increased wage bills given Irish inflation and growth figures, DCG's wage bill for its seventy-eight workers actually declined by just over 5 per cent or almost €80,000 on its 2006 figures to €1.4 million.[83] Also of note was the fact that founders Leo Ward and Kevin Anderson both resigned from the board of directors, something unsurprising given their ages (87 and 91, respectively). Meanwhile, in 2004, holding company Torgyle Holdings had €25 million in cash; after-tax profits of €13.5 million from its subsidiaries; accumulated profits of €3.2 million; general reserves of €7.2 million; and had debts to group undertakings of €24.4 million.[84] Two years later, it had combined reserves of €34.5 million and made a total profit of €5.5 million in 2005.[85] Outside Dublin, the Ward Anderson cinemas were also very profitable, with its Galway city Omniplex alone posting pre-tax profits of €2 million in 2002.[86] Nevertheless, reflecting the decline in the economy in the late 2000s, profit from the renamed Galway Multiplex Ltd dropped in 2009 to only €712,795 (17 per cent down on the 2008 figure), although Ward Anderson still managed to take a €300,000 dividend, the same figure as the year previous.[87] Such an obvious dip led one reporter to ask, 'after years of stellar growth, is this the first tentative sign of a softening in Irish cinema attendances?'[88] That said, despite the fall (relative to immediately previous years), attendances totalling 17.7 million were still 20 per cent higher than a decade earlier and Ireland remained in 2010 the second highest cinema-going country in Europe after Iceland.[89]

As was the case with the expansion overseas of American exhibition companies when 'the internationalization of exhibition followed the saturation of the domestic market',[90] so, too, with Ward Anderson as their all-Ireland reach was (almost) complete, the logical move was into Britain. Such a direction also makes sense not just in terms of their assets and cash, but also in the context of Irish business activity from the 1980s into the 2000s, which saw a trend in overseas expansion such that the value of Irish business investment abroad expanded exponentially until the deflation of the commercial property bubble in the late 2000s wiped out much of the capital gains on such assets as they sank under a mountain of debt. However, unlike speculative developers, the Ward Anderson business model has been built since the 1950s on minimizing bank borrowings. Just as important is how the company has benefited from the activities of venture capitalists and anti-monopoly legislation in Britain.

Ward Anderson's first entry into the British market was through Paul Anderson's Omniplex chain, which became owners of two multiplexes in the south of England,[91] though one of these, a four-screen complex in Hertfordshire, in which €600,000 had been invested, proved unsuccessful.[92] Undeterred, Anderson sought bigger cinema investments, and in October 2005 it was announced that through Cinema Holdings Ltd, a joint venture between Ward Anderson and Thomas Anderson, one of the group's top executives and brother of Paul Anderson, the Ward Anderson group had bought eleven cinemas in Britain for about €80 million.[93] These cinemas represented sites where UCI and Odeon overlapped and it was a condition set by the British government's competition authority, the Office of Fair Trade (OFT), on venture capital group Terra Firma's £580 million acquisition of the UCI and Odeon chains in Britain that it had to dispose of them.[94] By the end of January 2006 Ward Anderson once again were the beneficiaries of an OFT ruling and, in a deal worth about €40 million, they acquired from Cineworld following its €300 million takeover of UGC, six cinemas in areas where the chains' interests were duplicated.[95] Following these acquisitions, Cinema Holdings Ltd was the fifth largest exhibitor in the UK cinema market (including Northern Ireland) with 142 screens by the end of 2006, rising to 213 screens at twenty-five sites three years later, giving Ward Anderson 5.8 per cent of the UK's 3,651 screens in 2009, and making it one quarter the size in terms of screens of largest exhibitor Odeon.[96] With a presence in London, Glasgow, Birmingham and Newcastle, Cinema

Holdings Ltd/Ward Anderson, in a reference to their high-profile Empire cinema in London's Leicester Square (previously owned by UCI), began to rebrand their British cinemas under the Empire name.[97] If this can be seen as a return of the repressed as the Empire was the despised name given to Dan Lowrey's Star of Erin Music Hall in 1897 when it was taken over by Moss and Thornton's Empire of Empires' chain shortly after the first films were shown at Lowrey's in 1896, it also necessarily carries the historical reference to Irish-born Robert Barker who established in London's Leicester Square from 1791 the first major commercially successful public entertainment, the panorama. Ward Anderson's British expansion also represents, however, a continuation of the Irish tradition established over the last two centuries in which most Irish entertainment entrepreneurs, managers and performers working in London have had little control over the production (and thus content) of the entertainment offered. In that regard, the activities of Ward Anderson, while a success story in terms of an Irish film exhibition family, remain largely irrelevant to the Irish film industry as a whole and can neither be taken as a microcosm of Irish exhibition, nor as a means in itself through which it may be possible to alter patterns within film exhibition in Ireland.[98]

CHAPTER 6

Alternative Exhibition

'A film festival is not something that comes naturally to the [Cork] proletariat, who now [in 1970] accepts it as a week-long series of publicity glimpses of eye-catching, breath-stopping women who turn out to be absolutely no one they ever heard of.'[1]

IRISH FILM SOCIETY/CUMANN NA SCANNÁN

In January 1930 Mary Manning, secretary of the recently formed Dublin Film Society, wrote to the *Irish Statesman*, a fortnightly of which she was film critic, to announce the society's establishment. In the piece, she revealed that its first season would comprise of a programme of twelve films. Among these were to be one of the most celebrated city films, the cubist-styled *Berlin: Symphony of a Great City* (*Berlin: die Symfonie der größstadt*, Walter Ruttmann, 1927, Germany); Sergei Eisenstein's cinematic masterpiece of montage, *The Battleship Potemkin* (*Bronenosets Potyomkin*, 1925, USSR) about the 1905 abortive revolution; Danish filmmaker Carl Dreyer's critically acclaimed *The Passion of Joan of Arc* (*La Passion de Jeanne d'Arc*, 1928, France), and an Egyptian film, *Soada*.[2] For a charge of 25s. for the season, she invited the public to become members of what was the first organization of its kind in Ireland.[3] An *Irish Statesman* editorial welcomed the proposed formation of the film society, but used the occasion to launch a strong attack on sound cinema:

> To sit through one of these performances is like having carbonic gas blown into the soul to bring about its dissolution ... At present if the universe spirit awarded justice as it did on Sodom and Gomorrah, Dublin, for its meek acceptance of these talking films, ought to be buried under a Dead Sea. Perhaps it is spiritually and we don't know it.[4]

Since the editorial's tone is in keeping with Mary Manning's response to early sound cinema, it is possible that she wrote the piece.

Regardless, the proposed films, all silent, established for many years the dominant pattern of programming for the eventual film society movement in Ireland, whereby

European and Soviet films were favoured over the more dominant Anglo-American ones. Given the links between aesthetics, politics and ideology, or, in other words, between form and content (evident in the fact that it can be demonstrated that a film's formal aspect carries, intentionally or otherwise, political or ideological meaning, inde-pendent of the film's overt narrative content),[5] it is perhaps unsurprising that when the Dublin Film Society came to the attention of the authorities it was treated with deep suspicion and its promoters became the subject of a police investigation. Nevertheless, it seems that, in the first instance, the state's fear was not predicated on an apprecia-tion of the finer subtleties of critical and artistic discourse, but simply on difference and cultural prejudice. Ironically, just over a year later, a prominent Fianna Fáil TD, Seán MacEntee,[6] in a Dáil speech, promoted the distribution in Ireland of Soviet films, including *Storm Over Asia* (*Potomok Chingis-Khana/The Heir to Genghis Khan*, Vsevolod Pudovkin, 1928), one of the society's proposed films and which was being shown in a Dublin cinema, as a counter-attraction to Anglo-American cinema.[7]

Following on from the nascent film society's January announcement, the society wrote to James MacNeill, the governor-general of Ireland – a sort of native lord lieu-tenancy that Éamon de Valera effectively abolished within a couple of years – to enquire whether he would give the organization his 'personal influence and support' and become a sponsor, in line with how London's Film Society had been established in 1925 with influential, even aristocratic, sponsors. MacNeill's secretary, Ms E.M. Coulson, seeking advice on the matter, wrote to Diarmuid O'Hegarty, executive secretary at the department of the president of the executive council since 1922,[8] who, in turn, instructed H. O'Friel to seek information on the society from the special branch of the Garda Síochána and suggested that he contact the official film censor, James Montgomery.[9]

Eight days later, on 19 February 1930, O'Hegarty forwarded to MacNeill's secre-tary a distillation of both the police report and his own investigation of the matter. Stating, perhaps somewhat patronizingly, that 'the Society has as its promoters a group of persons *who regard themselves* as "intellectuals"' (emphasis added), he pointed out that Mary Manning, in addition to her role as film critic for the *Irish Statesman*, was an occasional writer on fashion for the London *Times*, one of whose writers, Ivor Montagu, incidentally, had been central in the setting up of the London Film Society. Notwithstanding that Manning was seen as a supporter of the Cosgrave government, the police report, rather surprisingly, concluded that she was 'never known to take any interest in politics.' All but one of the other founders of the society were similarly deemed never to have had an interest in Irish politics, even though this seemed to be in conflict with the fact that each of them was characterized as having a particular political sympathy. Harold Douglas was Senator Douglas' son; Lilian Dalton, who worked in the Belgian consul's office and whose father was a civil servant at the depart-ment of education was an 'imperialist'; and George E. Cowell, a relative of Dalton's and a student at Trinity College, was 'a supporter of the British Government'. No such contradictory assessment was arrived at in relation to Paul O'Farrell, who was regarded as the only film committee member to be interested in Irish politics. Described by the police as a 're-instated' civil servant with 'artistic leanings', it stated that O'Farrell had approached Jim Larkin, the legendary labour leader (and currently leader of the Workers Union of Ireland and a member of the Dáil), in an attempt 'to get Russia to supply finance to purchase a Theatre in Dublin for the purpose of showing Russian films.' The 'most reliable source', who had informed the police of this, also pointed out that O'Farrell believed that the society could purchase the Tivoli Theatre quite cheaply from Fianna Fáil given that the venue had not proved suitable for the production of the party's proposed newspaper.[10]

The references in the police report to politics and 'Russia' were sufficient to agitate the governor-general's advisers in the department of the president, with the result that it was decided that the contents of the film society's planned programme were 'disturbing'. *The Battleship Potemkin*, which the society had hoped to show on the first Sunday of March at the Grafton Cinema as their first film, was judged 'largely Bolshevist propaganda', as were Vsevolod Pudovkin's formally very different *Mother* (*Mat*, 1926, USSR), based on Maxim Gorky's novel, and the visually stunning *Storm Over Asia*, his last silent film, which began to position him beyond the ideological parameters of the Communist Party. In a prophetic statement as to how alternative exhibition came to be viewed in some quarters, O'Hegarty wrote to the governor-general's secretary stating that

> We have some reason to fear, and this fear is not dictated by reference to the personnel of the Society, that Bolshevist propaganda agents look to this Society as a medium for the dissemination of films which would otherwise fail to secure publicity here. Apart from this I am somewhat nervous of the 'Cinema as an Art Medium' in the hands of a Society such as the present.

Consequently, the governor-general was gently cautioned that 'it was not a project in which he would care to be prominently associated.'[11] However, this proved to be irrelevant, as the Dublin Film Society was unable to proceed with their inaugural programme due to lack of money. Indeed, the police detective who prepared the report for O'Hegarty took comfort from the fact that the promoters of the society 'are known to have very little financial backing ... Their financial resources are so weak that they are unable to pay in advance for any decent cinema for a Sunday afternoon.'[12] Even though as a private society operating under club conditions they were immune from the process of censorship and the related fees, they were, nonetheless, liable for import duty, which was charged at 1*d.* per foot of imported film.[13] As a result of such cost, and the expenses incurred in relation to insurance, film transportation, publicity and rent for the Grafton Cinema, the society calculated that in order for the season to be viable it would have to charge 500 members 30*s.* each or a total of £750 for eight films. The revised fee, almost double or 1.8 times the original fee of 25*s.* for twelve films, worked out at 3*s.* 6*d.* per film, of which 1*s.* was the cost of import duty, and significantly contrasted with the average cinema ticket price of just under 1*s.*, or top prices of 2*s.* to 3*s.*

Contemporaneously, a more overtly political body, the Workers' Film Guild (WFG), was established in Belfast in December 1929 with the aim of presenting films of a 'definitely working-class character' that were generally unavailable in Ireland.[14] It seems that not only did it follow in the wake of the British Federation of Workers' Film Societies, set-up in autumn 1929 and complete with its own distribution arm, Atlas Film Company, but also that the Belfast group was most probably in touch with the London guild, a relationship suggested in the fact that on 13 December 1929 the WFG screened Georgi Stabovoi's film of the Russian civil war, *Two Days* (1927, Ukraine), which, less than a month earlier, had been shown in a co-op hall by the London Workers' Film Society following London county council's decision to forbid its screening in a cinema.[15] While the Belfast body planned to show both Eisenstein's *Potemkin*, shown by London's film society on 10 November 1929, despite it having been banned by the British Board of Film Censors (BBFC) in 1926,[16] and *October* (aka *Ten Days that Shook the World*, 1928, USSR), there was unlikely to be any official tolerance of such 'subversive' films in the highly volatile post-partition Northern Ireland. This was clear in October 1930 when the Belfast corporation's censorship body, the police committee, refused Atlas Film permission to show Pudovkin's *Mother*. The committee, unanimously confirming the BBFC 1928 ban on the film, deemed it 'subversive to discipline' as it 'placed mob rule on a pedestal'.[17] As it was the case in Northern Ireland (unlike in England) that such films could not be seized by warrant under current legislation, regulation 26 of Northern Ireland's Special Powers Act covering newspaper censorship was extended to include 'undesirable films'. In contrast to the British legislation (invoked only once in March 1928 in relation to Jim Larkin's importation of films into England following a trip to the Soviet Union), the amended Northern Ireland Special Powers Act allowed the government to 'detain a film *indefinitely*' (emphasis added). Though the extension of the act proved effective in preventing the screening of films dealing with the Irish War of Independence,[18] as John Hill outlines no Soviet film was ever banned in Northern Ireland under the regulation as the British film trade, which had previously sought to circumvent the ban on Soviet films by making these and other 'subversive' films available through the workers' film society networks, chose, in the context of the additional legislative powers, 'the lesser of two evils and opted for a ban on Soviet films in Ulster'.[19] Therefore, the announcement of the formation of the Dublin Film Society, even if it was to promote 'film as art' rather than a more explicitly political propagandist agenda, was likely to unsettle such a conservative and long-serving senior civil servant as Diarmuid O'Hegarty. In any case, it was another five years before another group of 'film as art' promoters took up the Dublin Film Society project, and yet again *Potemkin* featured prominently in its plans.

Operating from the same cultural and artistic perspective as the proposed Dublin Film Society, the Dublin Little Theatre Guild was a 'non-political and non-sectarian'[20] amateur group. Though primarily interested in Irish theatre and European avant-garde drama, many of its members, including Liam O'Leary,[21] were also interested in cinema, and following the screening in 1935 of the German Expressionist classic, *The Cabinet of Dr Caligari* (*Das Kabinett des Dr Caligari*, Robert Wiene, 1919, Germany), it was decided that the guild would screen more films in 1936 using the substandard 16mm film gauge, though the first films seem to have been shown on the even more inferior 'amateur' 9.5mm film gauge.[22] Such substandard gauges had the advantage over the commercial exhibition standard of 35mm not only in terms of relative cost, ease of use, and the non-requirement of a specialized theatrical space, but more importantly, the fact that such films were not subject to import duty, which, as noted, had proved to be the final nail in the coffin of the Dublin Film Society.

The first season included Fritz Lang's visually exciting *Spione* (*Spies*, 1928, Germany) about a master criminal intent on ruling the world; the comedy *The Italian Straw Hat* (*Un Chapeau de Paille D'Italie*, France, 1927) by René Clair who was to become one of the society's favourite directors; and *Battleship Potemkin*, 'the classic film par excellence', for which they envisaged its first Irish Free State screening. Though distributed extensively outside the USSR following its European and American premieres in 1926,[23] the film continued to be dogged by censorship difficulties and generated much suspicion.[24] Indeed, though it was shown in France through film clubs to tens of thousands, it remained banned there until 1953, a year before the BBFC reversed their ban of the film imposed in 1926. In the meantime, official and unofficial harassment of those screening Soviet films continued in Britain throughout the 1930s through such means as checks on club membership lists, threats to prosecute exhibitors even for private screenings, and government circulars to film laboratories demanding that they stop the making of prints of such films, and as *Potemkin* was the most infamous of the period, it gained 'widespread notoriety' which added 'greatly to the film's subsequent popularity'.[25]

Notwithstanding the international responses to the film, which would have been well known to the Irish authorities and opinion-makers, not least through the mainstream British press, it seems that the Irish Free State premiere of the film by the guild on 21 February 1936 passed off without any controversy.[26] According to Liam O'Leary[27] the audience attending the screening consisted of

> Dublin Little Theatre Guild aesthetes, members of Legion of Mary in the role of culture vultures, proletariat from the Workers' College, a distinguished Jesuit, and a popular District Justice who promised to let the sponsors off lightly if they were brought before him in the morning, on condition of course that he and his wife were left in to see the film. Outside the street was blocked with diplomatic cars whose owners clamoured for admittance while police tried to regulate the crowds. Strange to relate amongst the audience was – a sailor[28] from the Battleship Potemkin.

Despite the success of this first night, a subsequent showing of *Potemkin* the following night in the Little Theatre, St Stephen's Green, was stopped just prior to its screening. The audience were informed that the film censor's office had reasoned that as the spectators had been charged an admission fee, such a screening could not be considered as a private showing and thus was subject to the Censorship of Films Act 1923.

Though it was hoped that the film could be shown once the Little Theatre Guild made representations to the censor, this did not happen.[29] Although later O'Leary claimed the guild withdrew the film 'on [their] own initiative', it was clear that the society did so only in response to the department of justice and the censor's highlighting their breech of the act, something O'Leary subsequently acknowledged.[30]

Notwithstanding this *de facto* ban, both the *Irish Independent* and the *Irish Times* were positive in their appraisal of the film. While the *Times* in its regular weekly film review congratulated the guild for screening the 'film classic' and encouraged them to import more films and to give frequent shows,[31] the *Independent* in its erroneously titled review, 'Einstein's [sic] Potemkin' (a misnomer repeated in the article), largely concentrated on praising the film's revolutionary technique, but also implicitly endorsed its anti-statist politics:

> few scenes in sound films can equal the suspense when the Imperial Fleet steams in to shell the rebel battleship – and suddenly the anxiously waiting rebels see the red flag hoisted on the masts of the attacking ships. The battleship 'Potemkin' steams slowly out to sea to the salutes of their fellow seamen who have taken command of the Imperial Fleet.[32]

The Catholic Church, however, was not similarly impressed.

Nearly four months after the single screening of the film, the church's key organ, the *Irish Catholic*, launched a virulent attack on the film and the context of its showing. Under the unambiguous headline 'SPREADING SOVIET POISON First Soviet Propaganda Film in Ireland; Subtle Subversive Manoeuvres Exposed; A Call for Government Action', J.V. Hallessy (signed J.V.H.) argued that such a screening represented the 'thin end of the wedge, preparatory to the introduction of more advanced Communistic doctrine by film.' Understanding perhaps better than most critics of the film, he pointed out that the idea that such a film 'would be harmless to the Irish because we have no navy', was 'altogether false and misleading' given that 'the ideology of the film covers a much wider sphere':

> The Navy was used merely as a vehicle to carry the poisonous doctrine of the alleged glory and necessity of revolt by the masses against lawful authority, and because the suggestion is so subtly wrapped up in Art it is all the more effective and lasting.

Without fully understanding the powers granted to the Irish film censor under the 1923 act, he stated that 'had the promoters of the recent exhibition submitted the film to the Censor he would have been bound to pass it for general exhibition' given that he could not 'legally reject films suggestive of Communistic doctrine'. Consequently, Hallessy went on to declare that to insure the supply of 'Soviet poison ... be cut off' the law 'needs immediate change', unless, he reminded his pro-Franco readers, 'Irish Catholics want to see their country follow the example of Mexico and Spain.'[33] Of course, such films, and indeed those of a leftist tendency more generally, could be and were censored under the act's provision dealing with material deemed 'contrary to public morality.'³⁴ In any case, other writers, including two English Catholics – Fr Ferdinand Valentine OP, chairman of London's Catholic film society,³⁵ and James Walton, who affirmed that 'the only protection against the Russian film is to crush it every time it shows its head'³⁶ – supported Hallessy's call for the state to intervene on the matter of Soviet films.

In the next issue of the *Irish Catholic*, Hallessy was no less subtle in his attack on O'Leary stating that those 'exhibiting Soviet films become, *ipso facto*, Soviet agents.' While O'Leary sought to extricate the society from accusations of it having communist sympathies by highlighting the guild's interest in art, Hallessy cautioned that many Soviet films contained an 'advanced form of technique' and 'must not be confused with Art', given that 'Genuine Art always mirrors in some way the Divine beauty of which all forms of earthly beauty are but faint reflections.'³⁷ Having reiterated that the society was free as an independent, non-sectarian body to choose films from any nation, including the USSR, in which country the cinema 'represented a manifestation of human activity in which the Guild was interested – namely, the Art of the Film',³⁸ epitomized by such directors as the 'great visual poet' Pudovkin whose 'humanity', according to O'Leary, 'transcends his Communism',³⁹ O'Leary returned the following week to a defence of *Potemkin*.⁴⁰ This time, notwithstanding his view of himself as an 'internationalist', or at least a European interested in art and form, he reground the debate in metaphysical/Catholic or spiritual terms, perhaps motivated by a desire to find some point of reconciliation with Hallessy. He stated that he, too, believed 'Art mirror[s] the Divine Beauty', and, asserting his own Catholicism, added that 'paradoxical as it may seem, it is only a Catholic [who] can fully appreciate that fact, especially in relation to a Russian film.'

The often-abusive charge and counter-charge between Hallessy and O'Leary in the *Irish Catholic* continued over six weeks, during which time Hallessy gradually shifted the debate from the screening of *Potemkin* to a more generalized attack on films that infringed Catholic theological concerns. In the final installment of the controversy, Hallessy declared that O'Leary was

> obsessed by the delusion that Art – in which category he includes Soviet film technique – is a power above, or at least equal to Christianity and moral law, therefore, nothing that might hinder its development, or free expression, should be tolerated. Comment on the point would be superfluous, as the penny Catechism adequately refutes the fallacy.⁴¹

With such a dogmatic stance being adopted by Hallessy, who two years later emerged as the director of the Catholic Film Society of Ireland (CFSI), an organization that won some episcopal approval,⁴² there was little point in any further debate. In any case, an alternative direction in the religion-cinema debate was signaled in the editorial of the same edition of the *Irish Catholic*. The piece welcomed the recent publication of the papal encyclical on the cinema, *Vigilanti cura*, and called for the establishment of a Catholic film library. As is discussed in chapters 7 and 8, these were two of the main planks of Catholic film policy during the following decade and beyond.

Meanwhile, O'Leary and his colleagues sought to return to the calmer waters of 'art' cinema and, to this end, based on the interest shown in the Theatre Guild film screenings, even of abbreviated versions of classical films as part of their theatre work-shop programme, guild directors O'Leary, Seán O Meadhra and Patrick J. Fitzsimons, along with Edward Toner of Queen's University, Belfast, decided to form a film soci-ety independent of the Theatre Guild. Thus, in autumn 1936, the Irish Film Society (IFS), which began with forty members who paid 5s. each for two films and a lecture, had their inaugural screening in the Guild Theatre on 15 November 1936. As O'Leary recalled a decade later, they 'worked on substandard gauge in austere obscurity'[43] and regularly showed Soviet films but without the same attention being accorded to them by anti-communist groups as had been the case in relation to *The Battleship Potemkin*.

Formed with the two declared aims of showing the best contemporary films from all countries not otherwise available to Irish film-goers and reviving silent as well as sound films which were outstanding in the history of cinema, it is fair to say that the IFS had a certain proselytizing view of itself. In its 1938 programme it declared that when such films had been brought into Ireland 'public indifference and lack of appreciation ... resulted in financial failure at the expense of those with the courage to experiment', but they hoped 'to overcome [this] and make the showing of worthwhile and unusual films a sound business proposition for the exhibitor.' The society would 'serve as the creator of audiences for such films and as propagandist for a more varied and less stereotyped cinema programme.' Following its modest beginnings in 1936, during the next two seasons the society attracted 100 members, each paying a guinea (21s.). By 1938 it had moved its screenings, which took place on Sunday evenings, to the Oak Room of the Mansion House. Its 1938 season included two films by G.W. Pabst, who was one of the many who chose to or was forced to leave Germany following the Nazis' rise to power in 1933. These were the politically charged *Kameradschaft* (*Comradeship/La Tragédie de la Mine*, 1931, Germany/France), which calls for solidarity of all workers regardless of national allegiance, and his unrelenting anti-war film, *Westfront 1918* (1930, Germany). Given that they were presented under the lamenting title of 'G.W. Pabst: Artist in Exile', it is somewhat curious that Leni Riefenstahl's *The Blue Light* (1932, Germany) was also screened, not so much because Riefenstahl's celebration of the rugged mountain landscape of Germany was a key motif of Nazi propaganda, but because her *Triumph of the Will* (*Triumph des Willens*, 1936), already well known, was a celebratory hymn to the Nazi Party. The other films shown were Luis Buñuel's documentary *Land Without Bread* (*Las Hurdes*, 1932, Spain), a powerful indictment of rural poverty in Spain; and Viktor Turin's *Turksib* on the building of the Turkestan-Siberian railway, an influential Soviet documentary made in 1928. By this time the society was already holding lectures and discussions on such topics as 'The child and the film'; 'The making of a film'; and 'The film, the trade and the people'. It was also, rather ambitiously, planning to subtitle three films in Irish: Charlie Chaplin's *Easy Street* (1917), Jacques Feyder's *Visages d'Enfants* (*Faces of the Children*, 1925, Switzerland), and *The Chess Player* (*Le Joueur d'Echecs*, Jean Dreville, 1938, France). It was intended to use this project to introduce the films to schoolchildren, but it was not realized due to obvious copyright and logistical problems. (Nevertheless, in the 1940s and 1950s the National Film Institute of Ireland titled and dubbed some foreign English-language films into Irish, though this project was confined to instructional films.) The society's interest in production, however, proved more successful and in 1939 its filmmaking arm got underway with the making of a short drama, *Foolsmate* (Brendan Stafford, 1940), set during the War of Independence, and featuring a love triangle in which a husband accidentally shoots his wife who has cheated on him with an IRA soldier.

By the end of 1938 the Irish Film Society was on the brink of disbanding due to the 'shortage of sub-standard film supply', the only format that they could afford to import due to the absence of a duty charge. For a year they had been making 'strong representations' to the department of finance seeking to 'secure special recognition for the Society as a body of cultural importance' and pressing for exemption from excise duty on imported 35mm films, as had been introduced in other countries. 'At the very moment' the society was about to dissolve, they received a letter from the department of finance (where the sympathetic Seán MacEntee was minister) saying that the 1939 Finance Act would contain a clause to meet their requirements.[44] A key player in this decision was a department of finance official who was also an IFS member, William D. Carey, whose wife May (sometimes Mai), a Gate Theatre actress, featured in the IFS's 1944 film *Mannon's Acre*, and whose son, Patrick, would become a distinguished documentary filmmaker.[45]

Section 12, part 2, of the Finance Act 1939, defined for the only time in Irish law the conditions under which a film society or club could be exempt from regulations and charges applied to 'public' events. These stipulated that the organization is conducted wholly or mainly for 'the purpose of the study of film technique by the members thereof and is not ... for profit'; that positive cinematograph film imported is done so on behalf of the said non-profit organization only; that film may be exhibited to members 'and persons invited to such exhibition by a member of such organisation' only; that no payment 'will be made by or taken from any person for admission to any exhibition of such films other than the annual subscription or other periodical subscription'; and that following a film's screening, the film must be exported. These conditions in law fitted exactly the operation of the IFS, and while they were never tested in the courts in relation to other groups, they have formed the only legal basis on which film clubs and film festivals operate to this day, as will be discussed below. Indeed, the voluntary, educational and ethical practices of the IFS from the 1930s until its demise in the 1970s are the bedrock on which modern alternative film exhibition events are permitted to operate by the Irish state.

Freed from the onerous cost of film import duty, as well as being able to bypass costly (and ideologically conservative) film censorship due to its 'private' status, the society embarked upon a fourth season in 1939 with renewed enthusiasm. Not only did it adopt the 35mm format and move to a conventional cinema, the Dublin suburban Classic, Terenure, but it also set up a permanent headquarters at 5 North Earl Street with a paid secretary in attendance. The features during its first season at the Classic were two French comedies, *La Kermesse Héroïque* (*Carnival in Flanders*, Jacques Feyder, 1935) set in sixteenth-century Flanders with Louis Jouvet, and the inventive *The Story of a Cheat* (*Le Roman d'un Tricheur/The Tale of a Trickster*, Sacha Guitry, 1936); one of the supreme examples of poetic realism, *Le Quai des Brumes* (*Port of Shadows*, Marcel Carné, 1938, France) with Jean Gabin; the anti-war film *La Grande Illusion* (*Grand illusion*, Jean Renoir, 1937, France); a critically acclaimed curiosity about a doctor's attempt to cure meningitis and in which schizophrenia is cinematically visualized, *Die Ewige Maske* (*The Eternal Mask*, Werner Hockbaum, 1935, Austria/Switzerland); one of Pare Lorentz's landmark (short) documentaries supporting Franklin D. Roosevelt's New Deal, *The River* (1937); the folk ballad, Robin Hood-like, *Jáno sík* (Martin Friç, 1936, Czechoslovakia); and Lotte Reiniger's silhouette animation films, most of which were based on fairy tales and operas. Such an eight-feature film programme with its 'embarras des riches', as O'Leary termed the new dispensation, resulted in the society's membership jumping from 100 to 500.

The IFS's membership continued to grow throughout the next decade despite difficulties during the Second World War,[46] such that by the end of the 1940s the society had more than 2,000 annual subscribers to its main season. Also, it had begun by this time to develop a network of affiliated film societies both in Dublin (at Trinity College, University College and Guinness' Brewery at St James' Gate), and in the main provincial cities. A restriction on the independence of provincial and university film societies was imposed by the revenue commissioners, which refused in 1945 to grant permission under the 1939 Finance Act provisions to allow for the establishment of separate societies,[47] thus confirming the dominant position of the Dublin-based organization, something which would have repercussions in the 1970s, as is discussed below. Anyway, many of the provincial societies, often established with a flourish of enthusiasm in a local cinema, quickly succumbed to financial strain given that by the end of the 1930s a single showing of a print cost £20,[48] a cost magnified by the much smaller membership constituency of the regional societies. As a consequence of the expenditure involved in 35mm, some provincial branches confined themselves to 16mm screenings in local halls, even though many such premises were not always readily available or entirely suitable.[49] In any case, branches were established in Cork, Waterford, Limerick, Sligo, Kilkenny, Drogheda and Portlaoghaise, with the latter chapter particularly active. Founded in 1944, within a year it had established its own professionally produced film journal, *Scannán*, edited by Richard Delaney, and from late 1946 was produced independently of the society.

In the post-war years film rentals not only continued to climb from £10 in the late 1930s towards £15 to £20 per showing, but also British film renters, from whom most of the society's films were hired, were 'not very keen' to send films to Ireland because increased transport time meant that they might lose out on further bookings from the mushrooming British film society movement.[50] Such problems with British distributors of both 35mm and 16mm 'art' films has been a recurring feature of all Irish attempts to develop alternative exhibition. The British Film Institute, which had provided a booking service to the IFS, ceased to do so, and, as a result, the society found it difficult to book films through individual distributors who, unsurprisingly, were reluctant to send 'attractive films for short bookings'. When negotiations with distributors proved 'lengthy and fruitless', the society was obliged to change its programme, often at short notice, and, consequently, membership dropped from 1,000 in 1947 to 720 in 1948, though other factors, such as the continuation of the post-war economic crisis, may have impacted on membership also.[51] However, film supply improved in the 1950s as more British independent distributors emerged and the IFS's national membership rose to an impressive 3,000.

During the 1940s the society initiated other developments, most especially with regard to children. These included the promotion of a policy of informing viewers of suitable films for children; and more specifically, weekend events on 'The child and the film' in 1940, and the establishment of a dedicated children's film committee in 1942. By then, a teachers' group had already been set up and from this a joint council with the Irish Theatre and Cinema Association was formed with the aim of presenting special matinees to children and cooperating with cinema managers in the promotion of them. The group subsequently formed the Educational Film Programme Group and made several teaching films.[52] As noted, filmmaking had already been incorporated into the society's remit and in 1940 the organization had even established a training facility, the Irish School of Film Technique/Irish Film School. This not only presented a series of lectures by filmmakers, such as Liam O'Leary and Geoffrey Dalton, and by distributors, but also facilitated the making of a number of films. Among the titles thus produced were a number by O'Leary – *Aiseirghe* (1941, co-directed with Fergus O'Ciarbhain) about the eponymous Gaelic revivalist organization (Craobh na L'Aiseirghe); a short documentary depicting the activities of a Boy Scouts' encampment, *Campa* (co-directed with Caoimhín O'Ceallaigh [Kevin O'Kelly], 1942); and *Dance School* (1946), a portrait of Erina Brady's Dublin Dance School – and by Peter Sherry – two fishing documentaries, *Fishing Village* (1940) and *They Live by the Sea* (1942); the short film *Tibradden* (1943) with a menacing atmosphere; and *Mannon's Acre* (1944), which sets up the binary of farm and family against girlfriend and city.[53] By the end of the 1940s, production activities largely ceased as a result, not so much, of the limited technical and financial resources, but the unavailability of teachers, who had become busy with their own careers, many becoming professionals in the film industry. Consequently, *These are the Times*, made in 1949 about the housing crisis, was the last significant film thus produced, though the same year the Trinity College branch of the society made *Asylum*, which was highly commended at the Amateur Cine World competition; adapted a short story by Ambrose Bierce, *A Horseman in the Sky*; and produced a newsreel of Trinity Week events.[54]

Writing in 1947, O'Leary characterized the voluntary task on the part of the society's members as being carried on out of a 'sense of social service'. At that time he gave the most complete defence of the society's policy of showing European rather than Anglo-American films, while maintaining, as many other members of the society did, that antipathy to Hollywood did not feature in the decision-making process. American films, given their virtual monopoly within ordinary cinemas, he declared, were well able to look after themselves. In an assertion very difficult to defend, he stated that 'very few masterpieces [were] lost by the censor's intervention' and that any American film of merit was likely to gain an Irish release.[55] In truth, however, not only did literally hundreds of films go unreleased in Ireland as a direct result of banning by Ireland's official film censors – James Montgomery (1923–40), who used the Ten Commandments as his guide, and the equally conservative incumbent, Dr Richard Hayes (1940–54), whom O'Leary deputized for during holiday periods in the 1940s – but also many were not even submitted because of the dogmatic policy of assessing films according to strict traditional Christian moral law and the dominant ideology of the sanctity of the family, while those films that were passed often had been severely cut.[56]

According to O'Leary given that American films were 'designed for mass-consumption and international markets', their necessarily 'arbitrary and artificial approach ... lowers [their] whole artistic value.' For him, while the international (American) formula picture was 'fundamentally insincere and [was] almost identical with the preposterous star-vehicle', films from Europe, with their smaller scale of production, allowed the individual artist to keep a closer contact with, and, thereby, reflect, 'the true life of the milieu in which he lives'. It was 'precisely' this 'national element' within European cinema, moreover 'sadly lacking when Hollywood inveigles European directors to its services with the bait of financial success', which gave European national cinemas their strength and their 'true international significance'.[57] Working from such a premise, the society's selection of American film titles makes most sense when understood in terms of auteurism and the director's personal vision or artistic sensibility, particularly when the director was of European origin, rather than in relation to genre or, more generally, film form and narrative content.

By 1947, the pattern of IFS programming was well established with European cinema, especially French, and to a lesser extent Italian, featuring prominently in the society's programmes. The IFS's 'A' or main programme of 35mm screenings in a rented commercial cinema (the Theatre de Luxe by the late 1940s, and, later, the State, Phibsboro), normally consisted of an annual season of eight features. During the twenty-three seasons from 1947/8 to 1974/5, for which complete details are available (the five seasons from 1962/3 to 1966/7 are not included), of the 187 features shown, France accounted for sixty-nine, or 37 per cent, while Italy had thirty-eight, or 20 per cent, of the films in the programme. Even allowing for a certain amount of duplication due to a number of French/Italian co-productions included here, these two countries accounted for more than half of the main features screened. Next were the USA with twenty-two films; USSR with eleven; West Germany with ten; Sweden with nine; Japan with eight and Britain with three. While many of the non-Anglo/American films would never have been submitted to the Irish film censor, a number of the films screened by the society, including American and British ones, had been banned in Ireland for public release. These included *The Rose Tattoo* (Daniel Mann, 1955, USA)[58] and *La Strada* (*The Road*, Federico Fellini, 1954, Italy),[59] which were screened during the 1956/7 season; *Theorem* (*Teorema*, Pier Paola Pasolini, 1968, Italy)[60] during the 1970/1 season; and *Brief Encounter* (David Lean, 1945, GB), which was screened during the 1948/9 season as part of the separate 16mm programme that usually included 'classics', especially from the 1920s and 1930s.[61] At the time of its banning, censor Richard Hayes drew attention to the fact that not only were 'moral considerations ... completely ignored right through the picture', but also that 'the intriguing pair as presented tend to arouse a certain sympathy in their amorous relationship.'[62]

During some seasons the society, directly, or through its Junior Film Society (a new version of the original children's cinema committee), ran more specialized events, including a documentary programme, and a wide range of lectures and film study sessions. In 1950/1, for example, topics, indicating the socially progressive nature of the society's members, including 'The welfare state', 'The colonial question', and 'Science and progress', were discussed following the screening of documentaries on these subjects, while the following year debate was focused on 'Women and society', 'Labour organizations', and 'Town and country planning'. As the context suggests, the programme was orientated more towards discussion of the subject rather than the film. Nevertheless, in 1951/2 the subject of film studies itself featured with an assembly devoted to 'The structure of the film'. Two years later, Colm Ó Laoghaire presented a series of lectures on film appreciation; this was repeated the subsequent year with a series on 'The theory of the film'. In the 1960s these events were extended and there was a general expansion in the society's range of activities including support for film publications, such as *Take 1* (a broadsheet of news and comment on the cinema) and *Scannán* (a forum for serious writing on the cinema), and through their maintaining of a film book library, which already had 153 books by 1947. Outside Dublin, such book collections were developed in local libraries, with the Longford-Westmeath county librarian, who was also vice-chairman of the Mullingar branch of the IFS, which had 200 members, able to acquire forty books on the cinema for the local library.[63]

During the 1950s and 1960s membership of the IFS grew steadily. At the time of its twentieth season in 1955/6 the society had more than 2,500 members across its eight branches. In addition to the main Dublin Film Society there were chapters located at Trinity College Dublin, St James' Gate (Guinness', Dublin), Cork, Arklow, Carlow, Mullingar and Naas. By the beginning of the 1960s membership exceed 4,000 and by the end of that decade this rose to almost 5,000 members across eighteen branches (inclusive of the main Dublin one). However, in the early 1970s, membership began to drop, perhaps as a result of the easier availability of continental European films in Dublin's commercial cinemas, especially the Academy, International Film Theatre, Curzon, Astor and Adelphi 3, as well as on television, including RTÉ's Cineclub slot. Whereas the 'A' programme had attracted 1,701 persons in 1966, five years later, in 1971, only 993 such memberships were sold. At the same time, the total membership of the other branches in the provinces and universities dropped from 3,160 to 2,154.[64]

By 1972/3, the Dublin Film Society (DFS) had 1,350 members, while the other Dublin-based branches, of which the majority were at third-level colleges, accounted for almost 1,150,[65] leaving only around 950 members outside the capital (in branches in Cork, Galway, Clare, Tralee, and University College Cork). The following year,

1973/4, while the Dublin Film Society membership dropped by almost 38 per cent to only 839 members,[66] causing the society to place further emphasis on its educational aspect,[67] membership of Dublin branches rose slightly to around 1,200. (The non-operation of both the 200-strong branch at Guinness' and the smaller twenty-five-member Milltown Park chapter had been more than compensated for by the establishment of a society at St Patrick's Training College, Drumcondra [300 members]). As a result of new societies being established at Carrickmacross (174 members) and Dundalk Regional Technical College (100 members) and the reactivation of the Kilkenny branch (53 members), the organization's membership outside the capital rose to approximately 1,150. Despite the substantial increase of over 21 per cent, this represented just a little over a third, or 36 per cent, of the organization's total membership base of 3,186, which itself had fallen by just over 7 per cent from the previous season's total of 3,441.[68] Nevertheless, membership during 1974/5 improved and, at 3,572, represented a marginal increase on the 1972/3 season.[69] Importantly, the DFS decline was reversed with the addition of 311 members (total 1,150(e) members), though the branches at University Halls and Clare joined the status of those at Guinness' and Milltown Park as non-operational. While the overall membership level was more or less maintained the following season, that total branches' membership reached roughly 2,800 meant that membership of the DFS must have once more fallen, this time to under 900.[70]

From this period, certain divisions became manifest both within the Dublin Film Society where some members were seeking to transform its seasonal activities into a permanent national film theatre[71] (a somewhat unrealistic aspiration given the absence of any substantial state resources being allocated to film, even though the Oireachtas had finally in 1973 recognized film as an art), and between the DFS and the other branches. Notwithstanding that individual societies could choose (from an overall list) whatever films they wanted, IFS members outside the DFS had long resented the lack of democratic control over programming policy, which was determined largely by the centralized leadership of the DFS. More generally, there was an overwhelming informational and economic imbalance favouring Dublin, not least evident in the fact that the IFS library was located in Dublin, but most obviously in that DFS members, unique within the IFS, had a vote each in contrast to one vote per branch.[72] Belatedly, the IFS's fortieth season report for 1975/6 finally recognized that its council was 'unrepresentative' and it was proposed to give representation on the council to the branches.[73] It was too little, too late, and as a result of the growing provincial dissatisfaction with the DFS, two new bodies were formed with Arts Council assistance. One, a full-time film club, the Irish Film Theatre, which incorporated some of the then-divided Dublin Film Society, and the other, the Federation of Irish Film Societies (FIFS).

FEDERATION OF IRISH FILM SOCIETIES/ACCESS>CINEMA

The Federation of Irish Film Societies was established in August 1977 when Michael Dwyer, the main force behind the hugely successful Tralee Film Society, which had grown from fifty members in 1972/3 to 700 members by 1977,[74] was appointed its full-time administrator. Providing a national framework in which local film societies could develop, the new organization offered a combination of advice, and, acting as a facilitator between societies and the film trade, a wide choice of films at competitive prices allowing each society to create its own programme. Under the energetic leadership of Dwyer, later the *Irish Times'* film reviewer and recipient in 2006 from the French government of a *Chevalier des Arts et des Lettres*,[75] the federation grew from seven societies in August 1977[76] to seventeen during its first year. By November 1978, it had twenty-six member societies with three more in the pipeline;[77] by the 1979/80 season, it had expanded to thirty-nine,[78] while the 1981/2 season had forty-nine chapter members.[79] However, it was not just the number of societies that increased apace, but the membership within each branch, with, for example, Galway jumping from sixty in 1977 (down from 260 in 1972/3 and 200 in 1973/4), to 350 members by September 1978.[80] As Dwyer commented in 1989, the film society movement remained strong because films from outside the Hollywood mainstream such as *Au Revoir, les Enfant*s (*Goodbye, Children*, Louis Malle, 1987, France)[81] shown by twenty of the FIFS's twenty-seven societies, rarely got a screening outside Dublin, and even in Dublin only seven of the 100 films released during the first eight months of 1989 were non-English language films.[82] Nevertheless, the viability of some of the new societies was in doubt in the recessionary 1980s.

Notwithstanding Dwyer's important and successful initiative during the 1979/80 season of annual 'screening sessions',[83] which included a selection of the titles that would be available to societies during the following season and which helped to consolidate the organization,[84] by the time of the 1982/3 season, the number of member societies had dropped back to its 1980 figure of thirty-nine societies with a total membership of about 7,000, an indication that the FIFS was suffering from the same recessionary woes that led to the demise in 1983 of the full-time film club established at the same time as the FIFS, the Irish Film Theatre (discussed below). By 1988/9 the decline continued with membership estimated at 4,500 across twenty-seven societies, which offered 180 films and 500 screenings.[85] During 1992/3 to 1996/7 this remained the typical number of societies, while average annual membership for the whole organization was 3,729, less than half of the members in 1980 when there were 'over' 8,000. In this same five-year period, the average number of titles screened each year was 125 (half the 1980 figure of 'over' 250) films; the number of film presentations averaged 406 per annum; and the average annual admission figure was 38,602.[86]

As the FIFS's own 1997 report acknowledged, they were operating in 'a much tougher' social and cultural climate than had been the case when they had first set up. Part of the difficulty was that London independent distributors were releasing fewer films on 16mm, due, in some measure, to declining sales as a result of television.[87] In this context, the two major outlets for 16mm prints were the major distributors' centralized company, Filmbank, and the British Film Institute, on which the FIFS was 'hugely reliant'.[88] The stark reality facing the federation was that either it had to shift gear to 35mm, as the original film society did in 1939, or continue to decline because of product shortage. Furthermore, as consumers became more used to high quality home video, and from the 1990s onwards, digital versatile disk (DVD) systems, the often poor viewing experience with old 16mm projection systems also inevitably led to a falling off of audience numbers. Nevertheless, local societies placed great importance on the social and community aspects of the local body even when screenings took place in less than ideal surroundings, such as in pubs, hotels or community halls. In any case, the situation was becoming academic, as even the film stock on which 16mm reduction prints were struck was no longer being manufactured by 1997, making it necessary even for the BFI to access negative stock in the USA. Clearly, the writing was on the wall marking the end of this type of screening activity and if film societies anywhere were to survive they had to move to 35mm or to the new quality home technology of DVD. Indeed, as part of its submission to the Arts Council – the long-standing grant source for the FIFS – the federation proposed that a capital grant of £30,000 be made available for the purchase of portable 35mm equipment as it recognized that most societies did not have permanent venues.[89] However, one such move to 35mm happened as part of the redevelopment of Galway's Town Hall Theatre,[90] traditionally also a film venue, when 35mm as well as 16mm equipment was installed for film society use. Not only did this allow the space to become home to the Galway Film Society, whose attendance increased dramatically from what it had been when it had been located at Galway's university campus, but also it enabled it to become a major venue for the annual Galway Film Fleadh. Less successful was the installation of 35mm equipment at Garter Lane Arts Centre, Waterford, due to the centre's unsuitable three-sided theatre space.[91]

In 1998, the FIFS put forward proposals not just for the technical upgrading of its screenings, but also for the restructuring of the organization. At this stage there were thirty-three film societies, eight of which were using 35mm; twenty-four using 16mm; with five operating video, sometimes in combination with 16mm. The seven third-level colleges used lecture theatre venues, and, while five pubs and four hotels were also employed by the organization, most of the other societies were based in custom-built arts centres.[92] Following on from this intense examination of its role and structure, and the overarching concern with new technology, in October 2001 the organization, which at this point had twenty branch-members,[93] took the step of renaming itself access>CINEMA. The body's reorientation, as the recently-appointed director, Maretta Dillon, previously of the Light House Cinema (closed in 1996) and co-author with Neil Connolly of the *Developing cultural cinema in Ireland* report,[94] put it, was to express the 'aspiration to be a resource organization for anyone or body interested in regional cultural cinema exhibition in Ireland.' Chairman Frank Ryan added that links with arts centers (already a reality for many film societies) and local authorities would allow for 'a more integrated approach' with regard to their activities.[95]

By the early 2000s, 16mm had finally disappeared and had been replaced by 35mm and DVD, the format in which almost all films, theatrical and non-theatrical, were being released. By 2003, access>CINEMA had twenty-six members, half of which showed films on 35mm, the other half on DVD, while twelve of the societies were located in areas where there were no cinema facilities whatever.[96] By the organization's thirtieth year, no less than forty-seven film clubs and arts centres[97] were receiving the organization's support in such areas as programming (extended to the development of repertory classics with each member society 'encouraged' to show 'at least one classic film per season');[98] technical advice on formats and film technology (in some measure designed to promote high presentation standards); as well as support in relation to marketing and audience development (most often done through the provision of pro-motional/support material and training seminars).[99] As Dillon pointed out, this latter function was particularly important given that showing films 'as a "one-off" means you don't get the build-up of word of mouth.'[1]

Access>CINEMA's roots remain firmly in foreign-language cinema, with the only English-language film shown at the 2006 viewing sessions, Irish director Cathal Black's *Love and Rage* (1999), with other titles from eastern and western Europe, Mexico, Thailand and Japan. The 2010 viewing sessions, which took place in the recently con-verted to digital Mermaid Arts Centre, Bray, included among its thirteen feature titles two Irish films (the same number as screened during the 2009 Letterkenny viewing ses-sions): the deceptively-simple documentary *His & Hers* (Ken Wardrop, 2009), which won the Galway Film Fleadh's award for best Irish feature and was the best perform-ing Irish-made film in 2010 (€325,000 at the box office), and Conor Horgan's debut feature, *One Hundred Mornings* (2009). The other 2010 films were from Iran, Australia, Slovakia, Greece, Israel (co-produced with France and Germany), Austria, Romania (co-produced with the Netherlands), Italy and Sri Lanka (co-produced with Italy and Germany), Russia, and the UK (an archival screening of Muriel Box's *This Other Eden*, 1959).

While film society screenings are normally confined to over-18s, since 2005, through an access>CINEMA initiative, ZOOM, a number of screenings have been targeted at 15-to-18-year-olds. Designed to provide a more diverse range of films for this age group than normally available at the local multiplex,[2] the titles offered in 2005 by this inter-national extracurricular film programme included a high-speed romantic thriller set in a labyrinthine netherworld in the Budapest subway system, *Kontroll* (Nimród Antal, 2003, Hungary); a coming-of-age story set against the run up to the 1973 military coup in Chile, *Machuca* (Andrés Wood, 2004, Chile/Spain/UK/France); an exploration of what it means to be Asian, Muslim and British, *Yasmin* (Kenneth Glenaan, 2004, UK/Germany); a kidnap crime drama, marked by young idealism and shot with a hand-held style, *The Edukators* (*Die Fetten Jahre sind vorbei*, Hans Weingartner, 2004, Germany/Austria); and the James Dean classic *Rebel Without a Cause* (Nicholas Ray, 1955, USA); while in 2007 the films included *Echo Park LA* (*Quinceañera*, Richard Glatzer, Wash Westmoreland, 2006, USA) in which a teenager discovers she is preg-nant; the real life Irish gangster film *The General*, John Boorman, 1998, Ireland); a comic horror with the tagline, 'It is lurking behind you', *The Host* (*Gwoemul*, Joon-ho Bong, 2006, South Korea); and a fantasy world set against a backdrop of fascist Spain in 1944, *Pan's Labyrinth* (*El Laberinto del Fauno*, Guillermo del Toro, 2006, Mexico/Spain/USA).

That year, 2007, also saw a change of director as Maretta Dillon left to rejoin Neil Connolly in order to run the new Light House Cinema in Dublin's Smithfield. The new incumbent as of July 2007 was Maeve Cooke, who since 2006 had been the programme manager of the organization, which at that stage was working with over forty-seven film societies, arts centres and festivals. Since then not only has the work of access>CINEMA received international recognition when it and the Light House Cinema were awarded the Europa Cinema's prize of Best Entrepreneur 2008,[3] but echoing the rise in the popularity of the book club during the 2000s, the number of affiliated societies and clubs has risen dramatically with seventy-two such groups listed in spring of 2010, seventy-six in summer 2010, and eighty-two in autumn 2010.[4]

CULTURAL CINEMA IN NORTHERN IRELAND

Northern Ireland developed parallel film society and art cinema organizations to those in the south. The first of these was announced in January 1929 when an advertisement appeared in Belfast's *Northern Whig* newspaper declaring the formation of the Provincial Film Society of Ireland. The principal figure behind the venture was Louis Morrison, brother of painter Boyd Morrison. Unlike the contemporaneous proposal to establish the Dublin Film Society, the Northern body was also designed to produce 'Film Plays of Ulster, Irish, and general interest' using 'local talent and ability', the first of which would be a series of Ulster comedies. The *Northern Whig* advertisement went on to report that as well as acquiring suitable studio premises, the founders had cine equipment and projectors for making professional 16mm (or substandard) films, and were intent on 'show[ing] the film world what can be done in Ulster by Ulster people'.[5] Nine days later, *Bioscope* reported not just on this new body, but also on another proposed film production organization, the Belfast Film Society, which had already met, but decided upon joining forces with the Provincial Film Society.[6] Following a general meeting three months later, a committee charged with overseeing the new society was formed. It comprised of Charles Haig (chairman), Mr Graham (treasurer and honorary secretary), Mr Beattie (honorary secretary), Clifford Carter, H. Devlin, Dr Foster, C. Kerr, W.H. Leech, J.G. Smyth, and H. Weir. While the group's first film, *Easter Amusements in Ulster*, failed to impress *Bioscope*, which judged it a 'very poor topical news film' with 'poor photography [and] dull scenery' that 'conveys the impression that Ulster is a most dismal place',[7] a more ambitious production, *Kitty from Coleraine*, seems not to have been made at all.[8] Though the organization remained in existence as the Film Society of Northern Ireland until, at least, 1930, the initiative fizzled out, especially when a general call for members included the request for financial contributions towards productions.[9]

It was not until 1934 that the first proper initiative for cultural or art cinema in Northern Ireland came about, when a Northern Ireland branch of the British Film Institute (BFI) founded in 1933, was formed.[10] Among those on the high-powered, establishment committee were the duke of Sutherland KT, who acted as chair; the marquis of Dufferin and Ava who assumed the role of president; Lord Charlemont; Lady Moore; Lady Brooke; MP J. Milne Barbour, Northern Ireland's minister for commerce; and Major Rupert Stanley. It was argued that since 100,000 went to the cinema in Belfast,[11] a demand should exist for a cinema with a more educational appeal. As J. Crossley Clitheroe, writing in 1936 in the capacity of editor of the branch's journal *Bulletin*, first published in December 1934, stated:

> Many of the public would flock to see the execution of criminals if this were done publicly, and because gruesome and vulgar pictures command full houses that is no reason for their exhibition. Our aim is to bring a body of opinion gradually to bear on the question that will effectively banish the vulgar and horrible from film shows, and we appeal to all lovers of the cinema art to join our ranks and to spread out influence as a much-needed social work.[12]

Such a plea for an educational or morally uplifting cinema was unlikely to appeal to those who enjoyed the viscerality and narrative excitement (if also predictability) of commercial cinema. As a result, by October 1936, concern was being expressed about the future of the branch, which was at this time seeking to attract more members with a proposal for monthly film screenings.[13] However, when one such screening occurred in December 1936 it was poorly supported,[14] and, by then, a film society for Belfast, independent of the BFI, was being anticipated.

The Belfast Film Society (BFS), formed in January 1937 with Professor Montrose as its chairman, was, like its recently formed Dublin counterpart, designed to show films not typically seen in cinemas.[15] It began its first season on 5 March 1937 when it used St Mary's Hall in the city centre,[16] and though it was 'greatly oversubscribed' with 420 members, it was well below the expected 1,000 members.[17] Among the films shown in the first season were *Night Mail* (Harry Watt, Basil Wright, 1936, UK), one of the finest documentaries of John Grierson's GPO unit, and the first Soviet sound film, *The Road to Life* (*Putyovka v Zhizn*, Nikolai Ekk, 1931, USSR).[18] By its second season, 1938/9, it had 500 to 600 members and was using the Apollo Cinema, Ormeau Road, Belfast, where it screened the poetic realist colonial tale *La Bandera* (Julien Duvivier, 1935, France) and the New Deal documentary *The Plow that Broke the Plains* (Pare Lorentz, 1936, USA).[19] From the beginning, the BFI's Northern Ireland branch cooperated with the BFS, and in recognition of the new dispensation, in October 1937 the BFI Northern Ireland chapter renamed its *Bulletin* the *Belfast Film Review*, while in 1939 it formally merged with the new organization, creating a new body, the Belfast Film Institute Society (BFIS). However, as John Hill notes, while the two groups shared a common purpose in promoting 'the art of the cinema', there remained 'a degree of tension' between them as to how they could achieve this.[20] Furthermore, the problem of a venue returned when the owner of the Apollo Cinema died.

Though the BFIS was hampered, as were mainstream exhibitors more generally, during the Second World War with product shortages and other difficulties, it still managed to offer occasional film seasons during the war. Its 1941/2 season had eight shows, including screenings of the Popular Front-themed *La Marseillaise* (Jean Renoir, 1937) about the 1789 French Revolution; the Soviet socialist realist *Chapayev* (*Chapaev*, Georgi Vasilyev, Sergei Vasilyev, 1934) about the eponymous Red Army commander; and *Musical Story* (*Muzykalnaya Istoriya*, Alexander V. Ivanovsky, 1940) which was the first Soviet sound film to be set in the world of grand opera. Its most popular film was Marcel Pagnol's drama of a cuckolded baker set in Provence, *La Femme du Boulanger* (*The Baker's Wife*, 1938) starring Raimu, a film which had its censorship problems in the south,[21] while its 'most unusual' programme was the double bill of *Zéro de Conduite: Jeunes Diables au College* (Jean Vigo, 1933), a critique of the author-itarian adult world set in a French boarding school, and the equally, but differently, subversive Marx Brothers' *Monkey Business* (Norman Z. McLeod, 1931) in which the zany comics get up to their usual anarchic antics during a transatlantic crossing.

Though membership was 'on the small side', 'many guests' from the British and American armed forces supplemented numbers during the war.[22] Nevertheless, the orga-nization's existence remained precarious. Despite continuing efforts to protect and expand their constituency, including producing bulletins with a guide to current films (nine monthly editions of which were issued during the 1941/2 season) and encour-aging Belfast corporation to purchase fourteen 16mm projectors for use in educational establishments throughout the city, its 1942/3 season was only possible because com-mittee members gave a financial guarantee for the organization's expenses, but, even then, the society had to abandon the comfort of a suburban cinema on Sunday after-noons in favour of the Wednesday evening screenings at the 'austere' Grosvenor Hall, the body's original home. The season included the historical comedy *Remontons les Champs-Élysées* (Robert Bibal, Sacha Guitry, 1938), in which the history of the famous Parisian thoroughfare is presented with Guitry playing five roles, including Louis XV and Napoleon III; *We from Kronstadt* (*My iz Kronshtadta*, Efim Dzigan, 1936, USSR), which, about the 1919 victory of the Red forces over the White Russian army, won its director international acclaim; the thinly disguised anti-Nazi film *The Testament of Dr Mabuse* (Fritz Lang, 1933, Germany) in which incarcerated criminal mastermind Mabuse controls an underworld empire; the slick Russian comedy *The New Teacher* (*Uchitel*, Sergei Gerasimov, 1939); and Carné's *Quai des Brumes*.[23]

Notwithstanding that the BFIS 'took on a new lease of life' when it became affili-ated to the British Film Institute as part of its regional network of film societies,[24] the lack of a suitable venue together with falling membership seems to have led to its demise in 1946.[25] It was not until a renewed awareness of an alternative or a critical cinema culture was reinvigorated in the 1960s that Belfast again had the possibility of access to cinema beyond the dominant Anglo-American product, though by that stage Queen's University already possessed an active film society.

In 1966, somewhat earlier than its southern counterpart, the Arts Council of Northern Ireland (ACNI) declared an interest in specialist film programming.[26] Simultaneously, the British Film Institute sought to promote the development of regional film theatres, expanding from its successful London venues. In this context, the ACNI provided a capital grant for the conversion and equipping of a dedicated Queen's Film

Theatre (QFT) to replace the university's film society. Founded by Michael Emmerson and Michael Barnes, both former directors of the Belfast (Arts) Festival, the theatre opened in October 1968, but while the BFI sought to support the new cinema, it was precluded by statute from funding activities in Northern Ireland. Consequently, QFT found it difficult to sustain itself, and after three years of operation, and having accrued a small financial deficit it closed in 1972. The closure was brief and in October of the same year it reopened and has operated continuously ever since, receiving ACNI support from the late 1970s onwards. By then, Michael Open had been appointed director of QFT, a position he retained until 2004 with only a brief period in the mid-late 1970s when Robert Caldicott was director. From its reopening, Open pursued a popular art cinema repertoire, and even developed the QFT bulletin into a news and auteurist-style film magazine, *Film Directions*. However, in its failure to critically engage with an evolving Irish film culture, the publication never realized its potential as a significant Irish film cultural journal, but retreated to being the cinema's in-house paper.

Although the growth of multiplexes and new levels of comfort within cinemas negatively impacted on the QFT, their 1996 season marking the centenary of the cinema stemmed any decline and served to relaunch the cinema, which remains the only cinema in Belfast to screen repertory films alongside new, often alternative and independent cinema. In the mid-2000s, following a major refurbishment of its 220-seat auditorium, and the addition of a new purpose-built 90-seat cinema and a spacious bar and lounge area, it became part of the new Centre for Drama and Film, while also serving as a venue for the Belfast Film Festival. In September 2005, by which time Graeme Farrow had taken over as director, it announced a three-year creative association with lager brand Stella Artois, after which cinema one was renamed, while in 2007, thanks to a grant from the UK Film Council and support from the Northern Ireland Film and Television Commission, it was the first Northern Ireland cinema to go digital.[27] One of the core activities of QFT continues to be in education and as such it regularly features events and screenings that support the national curriculum as well as programming out-of-school and summertime activities for young people.

COMMERCIAL ART CINEMA IN THE IRISH REPUBLIC

Before the 1960s, apart from the activities of the Dublin Little Theatre Guild and the Irish Film Society, occasional non-Anglo/American films were shown commercially in a few Dublin cinemas. These films were distributed by the Irish International Film Agency, the only such distributor in the middle years of the century, and for which, as noted, both Leo Ward and Kevin Anderson worked. Nevertheless, the number and condition of the agency's films was heavily circumscribed by the activities of zealous Irish film censors. Indeed, as already outlined, the Irish Film Society, especially through its annual eight-film 'A' programme, imported a number of films that otherwise were unlikely ever to be released in Ireland, either due to a lack of commercial interest in them or, moreover, because of censorship and the then policy of not issuing age limitation certificates in favour of banning or cutting films to suit a universal or Catholic family audience. For example, films such as *Rashomon* (*In the Woods*, Akira Kurosawa, 1950, Japan), a rape-murder narrative told from four different perspectives, shown as part of the IFS's 1951/2 season, was not commercially released in Ireland until 1957 when it was passed with cuts;[28] *La Strada*, shown in the 1956/7 season, was banned in 1955, though eventually was passed with cuts in 1960; while the neo-realist inspired *Pather Panchali* (*Song of the Little Road*, Satyajit Ray, 1955, India), a study of a poverty-stricken family in Bengal, shown in the 1958/9 season, was unlikely even to have been submitted for a censor's certificate given its minority interest.

In the changing commercial cinema environment of the 1960s when exhibitors were desperately trying to maintain their audiences, some began to look to the ready-made constituency of the Dublin Film Society. Already, the 313-seat Astor Cinema, Dublin, whose opening film in March 1953 was none other than Vittorio de Sica's deceptively simple[29] and moving neo-realist classic *Bicycle Thieves* (*Ladri di Biciclette*, 1948, Italy), had developed a reputation as a provider of occasional foreign language films as well as periodically facilitating the film society with screenings at its cinema. Owned by Bertie McNally, it was one of the few Irish outlets for such product, and, under manager Tommy Gogan, had a major success when it recorded 50,000 admissions in eleven weeks for the sensuous film noir *The Face of the Cat* (*La Chatte*, Henri Decoin, 1958, France), the popularity of which helped to spawn a sequel two years later.[30] By the time Gogan died in 1961, it had 'built up a profitable business for continental films',[31] but by the early 1960s their foreign film policy had largely ceased, such that in 1962 the *Irish Times* observed that

> since the virtual cutting off of the supply of Continental films to Dublin, due either to the indifference or ineptitude of local cinema managements, there have been few pictures of either depth or sensitivity shown here on which to comment.[32]

A few months later in February 1963 the Fine Arts Cinema Club began at Busarus' Eblana Theatre with a Sunday night screening of Polish director Andrzej Wajda's first feature, *A Generation* (1954), whose focus is a group of young people living under Nazi occupation. The cinema's name, notwithstanding the *Irish Times'* comment that it was more suggestive of 'antique furniture' than of film,[33] indicated its attempt to attract a middle-class high art audience, a major part of the film society's constituency. However, the club confined itself to reissues, obviously due to (a) the relatively high cost of censoring films, (b) its irregular screenings and (c) its potentially small audience. Thus, in 1964, newspaper critic Fergus Linehan was once again complaining that 'the supply of films from non-English speaking countries has virtually dried up.' He blamed 'pretty meagre' film product, rather than television, for the drop in attendances:

> Who can blame [audiences] for not supporting gimcrack Italian epics, horror films made on the cheap, or formula comedies, supported, as often as not, by an ancient travelogue, a cretinous cartoon and/or a newsreel showing events

which television covered a week before? Yet this is the sort of thing which is served up week after week as an alternative to the smaller screen.[34]

While acknowledging the difficulties in getting some non-English-language films passed by film censor Christopher Macken, Linehan believed that it would still be possible to identify some twenty to thirty such films that even Macken would approve of and that would be commercially worthwhile. 'One is forced to conclude sadly', Linehan commented, 'that the managements of cinemas suitable for this kind of thing can't be bothered to take the extra trouble which getting such pictures would entail, as long as they can easily lay their hands on reissues.'[35] Indeed, as is clear from the film censor's identification of the nationality of films submitted to him, particularly during the 1950s, only a relatively small number of foreign films were even presented for certification. Given that many of these films were then cut or banned, only a very small proportion of the non-Anglo-American films released in Britain was released in Ireland.[36] In the 1960s, however, especially from 1965 onwards following the systematic issuing of limited certificates, this began to change when there developed an awareness among some exhibitors that there were different audiences, one of which, identified with the Irish film society movement, was cultural and/or adult, and that specialized markets existed. Thus, in June 1966, the founder of the Fine Arts Cinema Club, Michael Collins, moved to a full-time commercial cinema, the 240-seat International Film Theatre, which was situated near the main buildings of University College, Dublin at Earlsfort Terrace. There, French, Swedish and Italian films, adult American and British films, as well as a four-month run of the controversial documentary *The Rocky Road to Dublin* (Peter Lennon, 1968) in 1968/9, established it as Dublin's main alternative cinema.[37] It remained open until October 1976, though another cinema, the Irish Film Theatre, was established there the following year which ran until May 1984.

The other venue to establish a distinctive adult programming policy was the Academy, Pearse Street. Located in close proximity to Trinity College, the 640-seat Academy had been remodelled from the Embassy, which in turn, had been the Antient Concert Rooms. The Academy 'built a reputation for adult Films' with such titles as Joseph Losey's anti-war art film *King and Country* (1964, GB),[38] and Losey's second collaboration with Harold Pinter, *Accident* (Losey, 1967, GB),[39] a visually striking film about two Oxford dons and the girl who comes between them; the sharp and witty comedy *Divorce American Style* (Bud Yorkin 1967); and the popular romantic melodrama *Un Homme et une Femme* (*A Man and a Woman*, Claude Lelouch, 1966, France).[40] The other independent cinemas operating in central Dublin in this period were the Film Centre which opened in 1966 on the south side of O'Connell Bridge, almost directly across from the Astor with which it shared a similar interest in an Irish version of 'soft porn', a category of film that could hardly be compared to its much more explicit British counterpart due to the activities of the Irish film censor; the Cameo, Middle Abbey Street, which had its inaugural screening in 1976, and like the Film Centre was owned by Michael Butler; Michael Collins' Curzon which, sited opposite the Cameo, opened in 1968; and the Regent, Findlater Place (just off Upper O'Connell Street), which was operational from 1967. However, with the general decline in Irish exhibition in the 1970s and 1980s, all these venues either closed or became marginalized as they began to rely on reruns of commercial films or did not maintain a consistent art cinema policy. The art cinema void then became filled, north and south, by a variety of film clubs.

PROJECT CINEMA CLUB

The legal basis of a film club has never been tested in the Irish courts, but essentially it is similar to that of a film society. Only members of a *private* club or society, with one or, perhaps, two guests, may attend a film that has not received a certificate from the official film censor. While members of film societies pay for a complete season of films in advance, film clubs like commercial cinemas sell tickets at the point of entry, but like societies, insist on membership, though the conditions of such memberships varies across the clubs. For example, while the Irish Film Theatre (IFT), founded in February 1977, sold membership during office hours only, the Project Cinema Club (PCC) established in September 1976 as part of Project Arts Centre did so just prior to patrons entering the cinema. That no legal sanction was taken against Project for this practice may be due to the fact that the venue had only eighty seats and its membership was not much more than 1,000, while at the height of its success the IFT had more than ten times that number of members. In addition, the two organizations pursued very different programming policies.

The 16mm Project Cinema Club (PCC), during the two years in which it operated, was largely programmed by the author Kevin Rockett, who placed particular emphasis on presenting contextualized film seasons. These events, often featuring independent films that otherwise would not have received an Irish screening and seminars or weekend conferences, focused on areas such as new German cinema, Brecht and the cinema, Japanese cinema, feminism and film, and the avant-garde. At the time, the PCC's policy was described in an issue of the cinema's quarterly bulletin as being motivated by an attempt to break away from films as mere objects for consumption to films as a means through which to explore and assess 'culture' and society and allow audiences to move towards a more developed critical awareness of film and of their own position as producers of meaning.[41]

Perhaps the most enduring film event held by the PCC was a ten-week 'Film and Ireland' season in summer 1978. Described by *Irish Times* reviewer Ray Comiskey as 'quite different from anything attempted previously' it screened over 100 films in ten categories including 'The family', 'The north', 'Depiction of class/work', 'The construction of Irish history', and 'The politics of representation'. Comiskey went on to observe that

> the approach adopted by the organisers is essentially analytical, examining films from the point of view of stylistic function, formal structure, and the conscious or unconscious assumptions that underlie the selectivity involved in their

making. They intend to place each film, as far as possible, within the social and artistic context it reflects, and to use contrasts, sometimes violent, to stimulate thought about the films being shown. By these means it is hoped to open up new ways of looking at film, especially Irish work or work that may be relevant to this country.[42]

Despite the critical endorsement of the Project Cinema Club's activities, the combination of poor physical facilities and the undeveloped film cultural environment in Ireland ultimately served to marginalize it.[43] Perhaps, there was a necessary stage yet to be gone through: the establishment of a more conventional art or independent film theatre.

IRISH FILM THEATRE

A by-product of the establishment of the Federation of Irish Film Societies was a clearing of the decks for the upgrading of the Dublin Film Society to a fully-fledged public 'art' cinema. While some DFS members did not agree to their own dissolution as a corporate body and held occasional film events for a few years, others, including some of its most active members, joined with the Arts Council to form the Irish Film Theatre. In early 1976 the Arts Council's first film officer, David Collins, organized a successful 'European Film Fortnight', which demonstrated that there was an audience beyond the film society cohort available for non-Anglo/American mainstream product. Within a year, the Arts Council, after failing to secure a managerial-only arrangement with the operators of the International Film Theatre, Earlsfort Terrace, entered into a deal with the owner of the cinema building, the Irish Sugar Company, to lease the cinema (closed since October 1976) through Irish Film Theatre Ltd, a specially formed private company incorporated on 25 May 1977. Dublin Film Society member Ronnie Saunders[44] was appointed administrator of the new body, while Irish Film Society founder members Liam O'Leary and Edward Toner, and former DFS council members Joan Byrne, Gerry Daly, Christina Albertini and Alf MacLochlainn (the director of the National Library of Ireland), were appointed to the Film Theatre's board.[45] The Irish Film Theatre opened on 8 March 1977.

At its first meeting, the IFT board agreed that admission to the cinema would be limited to members and their guests, and 'as a consequence the operation could be termed private within the meaning of the law and [as such] the Board held the opinion that the IFT need not submit films for censorship.'[46] To assess what the legal response would be to such a position, a delegation from the IFT met with officials of the department of justice. In its formal reply justice reiterated the relevant clause of the Censorship of Films Act 1923, which forbade uncensored films being shown 'in public'. It refused to comment on 'the legal aspect' of the IFT's proposals and warned that

The exhibition daily of uncensored films in a full-size cinema to *large numbers of persons* enrolled as members of a club would be something quite different

from the practice of any film society that has functioned hitherto and its implications would almost certainly have to be considered by the Gardaí and the
Law Officers. One such venture in itself, assuming that it was held to be within
the law, might oblige the Minister to consider whether the law needed amendment: the venture if followed by others would almost certainly lead to the introduction of amending legislation to prevent the by-passing of the Censor.[47]
(Emphasis added.)

Though the IFT board noted in 1980 that neither had it submitted any films for censorship, nor had it had any representation from the department of justice, it reported
that it believed 'spot checks' were being made 'from time to time to see if IFT is enforc-
ing its membership rules rigidly.'[48] (Such unannounced inspections were also thought
to have been carried out at the PCC.) What seems to have concerned justice most was
not that middle class cineastes were seeing representations of a type that were being
routinely cut or banned by the film censor, but that the notion of a film club and its
potentially dangerous or non-ideologically conforming films might percolate through
to the commercial cinema sector, thus undermining the containment of mainstream
adult cinema, or even lead to 'pornography' being shown in Ireland.[49]

    With the cost and inconvenience of film censorship dispensed with, the Irish Film
Theatre, which seated 240, became an immediate and dramatic public success. Though
initially the membership ceiling was set at 3,000, very quickly this was revised upward
to 7,000 and subsequently to 9,000, which was considered the optimum if 'excessive
numbers' were not to be turned away from popular films, but in the early 1980s, it
further increased by more than 2,000. Seat occupancy in the first two years – at least
with regard to the main five-day run programmes – was a highly creditable 52 per cent,
with a total of 158,008 admissions recorded over the 125 'five-day/ten screenings' in
the period 1977–9, or an average of 1,264 persons per film. These five-day, two-screen-
ings per day, runs of the most popular and often diverse films, were complemented
with special seasons on Mondays and Tuesdays, which included the work of directors
such as Orson Welles, Luis Buñuel, Miklós Jancsó, Federico Fellini, Bernardo Bertolucci
and Ken Russell. In addition, it offered periodic national film weeks highlighting the
recent work from various countries, which during 1977–9 included Spain, USSR, India,
Poland, France and Denmark.

    The top films in the five-day runs included in 1977 *Lenny* (Bob Fosse, 1974; 2,140
admissions), described by the Irish censor two years later when he banned it because
of its corrupting and obscene dialogue as 'a compelling account of the life and times
of Lennie [sic] Bruce, a satirical comedian';[50] *Everything you Always Wanted to Know
About Sex ...* (Woody Allen, 1972; 2,091 admissions), banned in 1973, but passed in
1980 with cuts for over-18s;[51] and the adaptation of Hermann Hess' novel *Siddharta*
(Conrad Rooks, 1972; 2,026 admissions) which follows a young Indian's search for
the meaning of existence and had been passed but with almost three minutes cut.[52] In
1978, the top three IFT films were Federico Fellini's interpretation of the Latin lover,
Casanova (1974, Italy; 2,400 admissions), which was banned, but passed with cuts in

1982;[53] the bizarre *Private Vices & Public Virtues* (*Vizi Privati, Pubbliche Virtù*, Miklós Jancsó, 1976, Italy/Yugoslavia; 2,400 admissions); and Paolo and Vittorio Taviani's best-known film *Padre Padrone* (*Father Master*, 1977, Italy; 2,281 admissions), which explores an oppressive father-son relationship in which the son is victorious. In 1979, the top three were the gritty gangster film noir *The Killing of a Chinese Bookie* (John Cassavetes, 1976; 2,388 admissions), which centres on a strip club owner and the mob while offering an exploration of masculine identity; *The Lacemaker* (*La Dentellière*, Claude Goretta, 1977, France/Switzerland/West Germany; 2,363 admissions), a love story that deals with issues around class; and Ken Russell's extreme medieval sexually explicit and violent black comic horror drama *The Devils* (1971, GB; 2,108 admissions) centered on witchcraft and politics, which had been banned in 1972.[54]

As might be seen from these top threes, a great many of the most popular films shown at the IFT either had been banned or never submitted to the Irish censor as they were considered not commercial or sexually too explicit. Indeed, a more inclusive list of other films shown confirms this. For example, *Les Valseuses* (*Getting It Up/Going Places*, Bertrand Blier, 1974, France) has two amoral thugs rape, murder, steal and charm, a little bit like in *A Clockwork Orange*; *Sebastiane* (Derek Jarman, 1976, GB), offers a homoerotic portrait of the saint; *Sunday Bloody Sunday* (John Schlesinger, 1971, GB) presents a love triangle involving a bisexual man and was one of the first widely distributed mainstream films to show two men making love;[55] Pier Paolo Pasolini's medieval inspired trilogy of films predominantly focuses on sex and exoticism, rather than on social comment (the films include the portmanteau-structured *The Decameron* [*Il Decamerone*, 1971, Italy/France/West Germany], which, according to the Irish censor, not only featured 'male and female pubic hair, vulgar expressions and suggestive conversations and dialogue', but also contained within the octet of tales, stories that were 'completely objectionable and would have to be entirely removed',[56] *Canterbury Tales* [*I Racconti di Canterbury*, 1972, Italy/France],[57] and *Arabian Nights* [*Il Fiore Delle Mille e Una Notte*, 1974, Italy/France], shot on location in Iran);[58] the socially chilling *Stepford Wives* (Bryan Forbes, 1974); *That Obscure Object of Desire* (*Cet Obscur Objet du Désir*, Luis Buñuel, 1977, France/Spain) explores sexual obsession; Bernardo Bertolucci's notorious and sexually explicit *Last Tango in Paris* (*Ultimo Tango a Parigi*, 1972, Italy/France) passed in Ireland for adult-only audiences as late as 2009, uses sex as a 'power motivation and narrative device';[59] *Empire of Passion* (*Ai No Borei*, Nagisa Oshima, 1978, Japan/France), not to be confused with the director's *Empire of the Senses* (*In the Realm of the Senses/Ai No Corrida*) made two years earlier and for which he is perhaps best known in the west, has two lovers murder the cuckolded husband; the Wagnerian *The Damned* (*La Caduta Degli Dei*, Luchino Visconti, 1969, Italy/Switzerland),[60] which, marrying politics and opera, charts the (mis)fortunes of the Krupp family whose steel empire supported Hitler's rise to power; and *Ulysses* (Joseph Strick, 1967, USA/GB), which, surely, needs no comment.[61]

As a result of this twin policy of screening banned films and showing risqué European cinema, the IFT developed a certain reputation, not least through its promotional literature's use of female nudity, of encouraging voyeurism, or at least titillation as a marketing ploy behind the rubric of 'art' cinema. Indeed, it was not the only cinema to engage in such titillation. Seamus Quinn of Cork's Cameo, which specialized in the late 1960s and 1970s in foreign/adult films, though which, as a commercial cinema, could only show films that had been approved by the censor, is quoted by John McSweeney as saying, 'I spiced up the ads ... I used to put illustrations around them – bras and knickers and things like that.'[62]

As well as offering regular programmes and special events, in 1977 the IFT also organized a Christmas festival. Although this was not particularly successful, the following year it started a series of 'Winter Festivals', which took place during the first fortnight of December and drew on films available at that time for the London Film Festival. Dubbed as 'Dublin's film festival', the initiative proved extremely popular and it was only as a result of the restraint of the Arts Council (perhaps in deference to the declining Cork Film Festival discussed later) that it did not develop into a full-scale Dublin film festival. By the early 1980s, though, the IFT's future was no longer certain.

Even during its highly successful first three years, the relationship between the IFT's income and its expenditure was very tight. In 1977, it recorded a deficit of £4,584 (on expenditure of £63,918); a small surplus of £2,204 (in relation to expenditure of £112,994) the following year; while in 1979 it once again was in deficit to the sum of £4,054 (with expenditure £130,309). By 1980, reflecting a significant rise in expenditure of £187,507, losses reached £10,305, but defying the trend, a profit of £22,326 (on expenditure of £236,960) was made in 1981.[63] Even if the 1981 figure was correct, such figures did not suggest grounds for expansion, but, nevertheless, this is what happened, and as costs began to spiral upwards, its audience actually declined. In part this was due to the fact that many of its members became disillusioned by their inability to gain admittance to the cinema, even though a second small screen was later carved out of the Sugar company's adjoining restaurant.

Other developments largely outside the control of the IFT also contributed to an impending crisis and highlighted the IFT's poor managerial planning. Firstly, the nearby University College, Dublin complex at Earlsfort Terrace had more or less completely moved to its suburban Belfield campus by the early 1980s, thus depriving the IFT of a ready-made local audience whose constituency would naturally be attracted to an adult alternative cinema; secondly, by 1981 a lengthy depression in the Irish economy began to bite into the disposable income of even the middle-class clientele of the IFT; thirdly, and compounding the move away from cinemas was the home video recorder boom which began to make it much cheaper for individuals, not to mention married couples, to view films at home rather than at cinemas; and finally, if a less important factor, was the arrival in 1982 of Britain's Channel Four television station which from the outset regularly broadcast a wide range of non-mainstream cinema. Possibly, a further issue relates to the demographic profile of the IFT's audience. While students are always important to non-mainstream, or 'art', cinemas such as the IFT, the 1960s generation of 'art' cinemagoers, who were prominent in the IFT's audience, by the 1980s were moving into their thirties and forties, when generally cinema attendance begins to fall-off because of life-stage choices and family. (Despite findings by Cinema and Video Industries Audience Research [CAVIAR] in 1999 suggesting that the significant proportion of art cinema patrons are in the over 45-year-old category, other research gathered by the BFI, and which in the 2000s was seen as more closely approximating the Irish experience has found that the 'age profile is actually spread more evenly' with only 20 per cent in the plus 45-year-old set.)[64] Incredibly, as their audience base was declining, the IFT, led by its director Ronnie Saunders, though, of course, approved by its board, embarked on an ill-fated policy of regional expansion that sought to bring full-time film theatres to Cork, Limerick and Galway.

The first of these ventures was IFT Limerick, which opened in July 1980 and used a screen in a Ward Anderson complex, Roxboro Twin Theatres/Movieland. Six months later, the IFT reported that membership at Limerick stood at 1,000 with about 500 admissions per week, but with only a few attending the early evening screenings these had to be discontinued, thus reducing the programme to one screening each evening with two on Sundays.[65] Poor attendance, however, was not limited to early screenings. With a film run capacity of 1,218 seats, only two films in 1980 – *Last Tango in Paris* (with 817 admissions) and the internationally successful ribald comedy *Get out your Handkerchiefs* (*Préparez vos Mouchoirs*, Bertrand Blier, 1978, France/Belgium; 731 admissions) – achieved more than 50 per cent capacity, while nineteen of the thirty films shown got less than 30 per cent capacity, with five of these not even registering as 'much' as 20 per cent.[66] Less than a year-and-a-half after the Limerick operation opened, during which time it had to endure problems with the cinema's sound-proofing and technical standards, as well as being 'subjected to business practices by its landlords [Ward Anderson], which [the IFT's board of directors deemed] totally unacceptable',[67] on 20 December 1981, with membership having dropped from a high of 2,000 to 1,200, insufficient to sustain a profitable operation, IFT Limerick ceased business. Though it planned to move within a few months to a full-fledged IFT cinema at a new development, the Granary, Michael Street, this did not materialize, as by autumn 1982 IFT Dublin, which in effect had been subsidizing Limerick, were experiencing a rapid deterioration in their own finances. It was only in July 2003 when the Limerick Filmhouse Centre, located at the Belltable Arts Centre, was awarded funding of €750,000 through a cultural cinema initiative, that the city began to see again the possibility of a full-time alternative film theatre.[68] Nevertheless by the end of 2010 it remained the case that while the Belltable was home to the Fresh Film Festival (see below) and the Limerick Film Forum, alternative cinema screenings were still limited to one-night per week given that the arts centre's auditorium, as in similar centres, has to accommodate other events including theatre and music. Perhaps more surprising than Limerick city centre not having a dedicated alternative cinema screen is the fact that it does not have a regular commercial cinema.

Meanwhile, in Cork, protracted discussions with the Cork Film Festival (CFF) regarding a possible IFT in the city, led in November 1982 to a week-long 'Festival of Film Cork', jointly programmed by Saunders and CFF director, Robin O'Sullivan. It was a stopgap measure for the crisis-ridden CFF (see below), whose £41,000 debt had just been cleared by the Arts Council, and which had received from the Irish Film Board a guarantee of up to £5,000 against potential losses on an event budgeted at a modest £10,000–£12,000 (this can be compared to the 1981 festival's expenditure of £85,000).[69] Though the Festival of Film Cork programme announced that an IFT Cork was to be established, it was somewhat premature, as no venue had been acquired. As it turned out, it was not until 1996 that Cork got its first full-time art cinema when the Kino was opened by Michael Hannigan, who with Theo Dorgan, from their appointment as co-directors of the CFF in 1986, had managed to revive the festival, which had been 'limp[ing] dismally along'.[70] What is most ironic about the ambition of O'Sullivan (also a member of the IFT board)[71] and Saunders is that a week before the opening of the 1982 Cork event, Saunders warned the board that the IFT 'would be insolvent' by February 1983 if IFT's finances continued to deteriorate. In his report to the board, Saunders declared that 1983 would be the organization's final year 'unless there is a dramatic turn-around in its fortunes.' 1982 had been 'nothing short of a disaster' with membership down 45 per cent as a result of members not renewing and with few new members, and attendance down 30 per cent. With losses of £33,000 predicted for 1982 and £69,000 for 1983, IFT was 'rapidly approaching insolvency'. Part of the problem was that fewer mainstream art films were becoming available from London distributors, and even these were finding their way to the Curzon where open-ended runs were more lucrative from distributors' points of view, symbolically and actually reflected in the Curzon's success in securing *Diva* (Jean-Jacques Beineix, 1981), which ran there for fifteen months from December 1982. Saunders' solution to the chronic state of IFT finances was that it should go 'public', that is, show censor-approved films (though none that had been subject to cuts), as a means of providing open-ended runs in a venue more attractive to distributors than the Curzon, while retaining a membership content, such as priority booking, reduced admissions charges, and 'members-only' screenings. It was hoped that such a policy would generate at least 1,800 admissions per week.[72]

By early 1983, Tiernan MacBride, IFT chair and member of the first board, was predicting that the IFT would close down if attendances did not 'improve significantly'. This prediction followed in the wake of the losses in both Dublin and Limerick, and a fall in the Dublin membership to only 6,000 (from a high of over 11,000) when annual attendances per member dropped from an average of nine per person to five. In an attempt to halt the slide at the IFT, the cinema went 'public' and introduced open-ended runs of certified films to which non-members could attend.[73] At a board meeting on 10 January 1983 concern over the financial situation[74] led to a meeting with the Arts Council. The council subsequently provided an immediate interest-free loan of £6,000, with a further £14,000 to follow.[75] By April, 'the question', the IFT minutes record, 'was whether the Theatre should close immediately or whether the [Arts] Council should have confidence in a rectification in the long term.'[76]

By then, the accumulated losses to the end of 1982 were calculated at £47,000, and 'the situation had deteriorated' with board members 'express[ing] grave concern' about the company's financial position. After asking Saunders and his assistant to leave the meeting, they were invited back after the board had decided to make all staff redundant by the end of April and to close the cinema at the end of June by which time contracts for films would have been honoured. After adjourning the meeting for two weeks to 25 April, the reconvened board heard that the 'peasant fresco' *Night of San Lorenzo* (*La Notte di San Lorenzo/The Night of the Shooting Stars*, Paolo Taviani, Vittorio Taviani, 1982, Italy), about the struggle against fascism, and *Another Way* (*Egymásra Nézve*, Károly Makk, János Xantus, 1982, Hungary), an exploration of political and sexual repression in Hungary, had only averaged 915 admissions per week, a level of attendance which 'would make it impossible to break even in the cinema' as it was estimated that admissions of 1,400 per week were required to ensure that the deficit would not increase.[77] Two weeks later, on 9 May 1983, at another board meeting the full extent of the IFT deficit was finally revealed. By now, 'actual liabilities' were calculated at a massive £65,591, though the Arts Council, which decided to cover all the company's debts including redundancies, felt it necessary to set aside £81,391. The Arts Council also decided that the board would not be dissolved and appointed Arts Council employee Phelim Donlon as company secretary with a free hand to run the operation. Arts Council director, Colm O'Briain, who was furious with the whole debacle, blamed Saunders, something acknowledged in the board minutes though some board members sought to change the perception that he or the board 'were at fault'. Indeed, Saunders extracted an agreement whereby in return for his resigning as company secretary, his resignation would not appear in any publicity nor would it affect his redundancy claim.[78] This did not stop him from writing to the Arts Council chairman, James Whyte, three months later expressing concern at 'the level of opprobrium with which the Arts Council apparently view the contribution' he made to the IFT.[79] The final act in the drama for those involved in the original IFT came on 5 December 1983 when following an annual general meeting their services were summarily dispensed with by the Arts Council.

What is ironic about the Arts Council's role in the IFT saga is that had it intervened earlier with even modest financial support it could have steered the cinema through the recession and it would have had greater leverage in dissuading the company from the expansion into Limerick at that particular time and into the ill-suited venue. Nevertheless, the Arts Council wanted to keep the IFT open and to this end approached the Irish Film Institute (IFI), which held an extraordinary board meeting on 27 April 1983 to discuss the IFT crisis. Echoing the IFT's own analysis, the IFI's director from early 1983, David Kavanagh, who had left his job as the Arts Council's film officer to take up the post, concluded that while overheads could be reduced, the IFT could not be made viable unless there was an increase in average seat occupancy of a minimum of 300–400 per week. The consensus was that while every effort should be made to assist the continuation of the IFT, no risk should accrue to IFI.[80] At another IFI board meeting two weeks later, the board approved an arrangement whereby, for a fee from the Arts Council, and with no liability to the IFI's assets or balance sheet, the IFI would, in the short term, programme and promote the IFT.[81] A year later in April 1984, Neil Connolly, who had been engaged by the IFI to operate the IFT, reported to the IFI

board that there was 'a disappointing level of business',[82] with average weekly attendance for the evening screenings during the first fifteen weeks of 1984 having declined
from 634 in early January to 578 by April.[83] Bearing in mind the IFT estimate in 1983
that 1,400 admissions were necessary to break even, such poor admissions, only 40
per cent of the IFT's minimum to maintain an independent existence, clearly indicated
that the decline was terminal. In a decision regretted by the IFI board, the Arts Council
closed down the cinema on 31 May 1984, when the final film, *Forbidden Relations*
(*Visszaesök*, Zsolt Kézdi-Kovács, 1983, Hungary), a love-incest story between a brother
and sister, was open to non-members. While some hope was held out that the IFT
would reopen, the IFI was already looking towards a far more ambitious project than
merely running an art cinema. This was the beginning of a long period of radical transformation of Irish film culture, which culminated in 1992 with the opening of the Irish
Film Centre. In the interim, another short-term measure emerged between the IFI and
Neil Connolly.

IRISH FILM INSTITUTE CINEMAS
(INCLUDING THE LIGHT HOUSE CINEMA, ABBEY STREET)

In 1984–5, the Irish Film Institute, under the joint leadership of David Kavanagh as
director (1984–96) and principal author of this study Kevin Rockett as chair (1984–
91), adopted an ambitious plan to develop not just cinemas for screening art house or
minority product, but sought to establish a national centre for film. While this idea of
a centre was being realized, in 1988 the IFI entered into a 50/50 partnership with Neil
Connolly, by then the executive-director of the Dublin Film Festival, which had begun
in 1985, to lease and run the former two-screen Curzon Cinema, Middle Abbey Street,
as the Light House Cinema. Having adopted a programme of specialist art cinema and
independent commercial films without club conditions and, as such, films subject to
censorship, the Light House's early success showed, what the new Dublin Film Festival
and other art screenings had suggested, that there *was* an audience for films outside
those of mainstream commercial cinemas. More importantly, Connolly understood
that this audience had to be carefully cultivated through targeted advertising and consistent programming (rather than the strictly limited or regulated sort as at the old IFT)
that would balance the need 'to keep a good film if [it was] going well' with the need
to offer a variety of titles to sustain a regular audience. In this regard it is worth noting
that one of the factors that led to the Curzon's decline was that, notwithstanding its
considerable successes with the cult films *Diva* and *Rumble Fish* (Francis Coppola,
1983), it not only failed to nurture the art-cinema audience, but also abandoned it by
the screening of mainstream commercial films, many of which were second-rate.
Though prior to the opening of the Light House, the art house or cultural film audience was being served to some degree by the Ward Anderson owned Screen at College
Street, which had developed a partial art cinema policy, consolidated in 1985 when it
became the venue of the first Dublin Film Festival, it is fair to say that independent

Irish exhibitors have rarely shown the imagination and flair, particularly with regard to broadening the range of films available, which would have fully satisfied such an audience, or created new ones.

The Light House's first twelve weeks (11 November 1988–2 February 1989) saw a total of 11,575 admissions in the 280-seat cinema one and 6,608 to the smaller 80-seat cinema two, or a total of 18,183 admissions – 1,515 per week – for the two screens, taking a net after distributors' share and VAT of £32,375, or £1.80 net per admission. With wages and salaries accounting for 45 per cent of costs, and rent and advertising, £10,299, or 32 per cent of net income, it is surprising perhaps that the cinemas ran only a very minor loss during its first three months in operation, particularly in light of the cost of censorship and competition from existing exhibitors, as Connolly explained a month into the operation, 'films that we are interested in are attracting sudden interest from the city's larger exhibitors.'[84] While the opening films were veteran French filmmaker Eric Rohmer's *4 Adventures of Reinette & Mirabelle* (1987) and Pedro Almodóvar's critically acclaimed homoerotic *Law of Desire* (*La Ley del Deseo*, 1987, Spain), seen by many as the future of Spanish cinema, the three main films shown during its opening quarter, all international successes, were *Law of Desire* which had 2,714 admissions over four weeks in cinema 1 and a further 1,450 in cinema 2 over four weeks; Terence Davies' super-realist and lyrical autobiographical film, *Distant Voices, Still Lives* (1988, GB), set in 1940s/1950s England, had 5,262 admissions over six weeks in cinema 1 and a further 1,516 over two weeks in cinema 2; and one of the Light House's most successful films, Peter Greenaway's *Drowning by Numbers* (1988, UK/Netherlands) which had attendances of 3,599 during its first two weeks, a figure which compared favourably with its London release.[85]

When the IFI board had approved the organization's involvement in the Light House project, 'a fundamental issue was that the cinema did not incur losses'.[86] Indeed, by February 1989 the IFI board was congratulating Connolly for 'a more than creditable achievement' in making the venture a success.[87] Unlike the context in which the IFT found itself in 1982–3 as a deep and long recession took hold in Ireland, by the end of the decade a degree of economic light was evident. Also, Connolly's nurturing of the Light House's audience gave patrons a feeling of ownership of the cinema, which the more aloof IFT never achieved, despite it being a successful cinema in its first four years. While the Light House also experienced ups and downs depending on film availability, it, nevertheless, retained average weekly attendances of about 1,600 admissions in 1990,[88] and by the end of the year, the annualized figure had risen to 97,000 admissions (averaging at 1,865 admissions per week), with a turnover of £300,000,[89] a figure not far below the 108,000 admissions achieved by the four-screen Light House, Smithfield, in its first year, 2008–9. A significant aspect of the Light House's policy was its open-ended runs of well-known independent or art cinema product in its main auditorium, such as its 1993 screening of Sally Potter's visually rich *Orlando* (1992, UK/Russia/France/Italy/Netherlands) inspired by Virginia Woolf's complex interweaving of history, gender and identity, which attracted an impressive 16,000 admissions.[90]

In September 1992, the IFI, intent on maximizing the number of non-mainstream films shown in Ireland, finally opened their own £2.2 million, twin-screen Irish Film Centre at 6 Eustace Street, Temple Bar, a property acquired from the Quakers in 1987.[91] As a result, IFI sold its half share in Light House Cinema Exhibition and Distribution Co. Ltd. to Neil Connolly, who continued to operate the cinemas with such successes as Krzysztof Kieslowski's *Three Colours* trilogy (*Blue* in 1993, *Red* in 1994 and *White* in 1994) and *December Bride* (Thaddeus O'Sullivan, 1990), as well as re-releases of classics such as *L'Atalante* (Jean Vigo, 1934, France) and *Smiles of a Summer Night* (*Sommarnattens Leende*, Ingmar Bergman, 1955, Sweden) until its closure on 26 September 1996. This was brought about because Arnotts' department store, the owners of the cinema building as well as of the adjoining Adelphi Cinema site, would not renew the cinema lease as they had decided to expand their already large retail store into the space forming a link between Middle Abbey Street and Henry Street. Although there was a vague statement in Arnotts' planning application that cinemas 'may be provided' in a basement area, no such cinema was incorporated into the new store even though Connolly forced a public hearing on the matter.[92] (As it turned out, it was the first of many such [successful] attempts by developers, with Newbridge's Whitewater shopping centre, mentioned in chapter 5, perhaps the most notorious example, to use an empty promise of providing a cinema, or some form of social and cultural amenity, as a means to persuade planners to approve a large retail development.) Despite this considerable setback, Connolly and business partner Maretta Dillon finally succeeded in May 2008 in opening a new Light House. Located in one of Dublin's regeneration areas, Smithfield, the four-screen cinema (with 277, 153, 116 and 68 seats), with a focus on the best of Irish, independent, foreign-language, art house and classic cinema, unsurprisingly, aimed to pursue the original Light House's 'ambitious and adventurous programming',[93] which had been described as consistently and commendably thoughtful.[94] According to its mission statement, the cinema, which has since closed down, was

> committed to championing films of quality from *original, creative film makers.* We passionately support cultural diversity and personal expression in world cinema. Our aim is to firmly establish [it] as a springboard for wider distribution of independent, world cinema in Ireland.[95] [Emphasis added.]

The opening of the twin Irish Film Institute cinemas – with 258 and 106 seats[96] – which were opened by Taoiseach Albert Reynolds, not only kick-started in a material way what the Temple Bar Renewal and Development Act set forth in 1991, but also, more importantly, in the context of this study, transformed alternative film exhibition in Dublin with 150 additional art cinema titles screened in its first year alone. The number of members it attracted in the same period was, remarkably, one hundred times this (15,000). While such a membership base provided a considerable revenue stream, it was the means by which the IFI avoided submitting films for the costly business of certification. Actual admissions were similarly healthy at 130,000 in the first year.[97]

Such a figure is just over 20 per cent higher than that recorded for the new four-screen Light House in its first year (108,000). However, not only was the new Light House located in a more remote part of town in an area which failed to become a fully renewed urban (middle-class) district, but the cinema also had the misfortune to open just as the recession was leading to a downward spiral in the spending by consumers of discretionary income.

Michael (Mick) Hannigan, a board member of IFI in the years before the opening of the IFC, was the IFI cinemas' first programmer, but two years later he returned to his native Cork to resume his role as director of the Cork Film Festival.[98] In his place, Peter (Pete) Walsh, who had over twenty years experience of art house programming for cinemas and festivals, including as programmer of Birmingham Film Festival, was appointed in November 1994, a position he still holds.[99] While the first year was financially successful, a rocky period followed during which the cinemas sustained losses, and the IFI itself went through a financial crisis which was resolved with five staff redundancies and an increase of 83 per cent in its Arts Council's grant to £330,000 announced in August 1994.[1] Nevertheless, the cinemas had to operate without subsidy. In a review of the cinemas fifteen months later for IFI's forty-sixth annual general meeting in November 1995, IFI director Sheila Pratschke commented that the cinemas, which in the year ending August 1995, had screened 200 features and generated over 90,000 admissions and box office revenue of £329,398 (€416,959) were operating in a difficult, competitive and constantly changing environment.[2] According to the IFI chair at the time, the task of 'reflecting the breadth and quality of international cinema in all its diversity, without subsidy' was 'in commercial terms, attempting the impossible'.[3] Notwithstanding this, the IFI board policy remained that the cinemas should break even, and over the following decade this proved to be the case with box office revenue continuing to improve in the environment of the 'Celtic Tiger' economy, such that its box office revenue in 2007 was €1,132,685, though total cinema income was €1,550,890 when club membership, cinema hire, advertising, grants and sponsorship are included. When direct charges (distributors costs and running of the cinemas) of €1,202,284 are taken into account, the cinemas generated a surplus of €348,606, considerably up on the previous year's €257,602.[4] Furthermore, and despite the recession and the competition from the new art house venue, the Light House, Smithfield, IFI cinemas continued to attract an average of 14,000 patrons per month during the first nine months of 2008.[5]

Regardless of the IFI's relative success, it has failed to fully resolve the tension, highlighted in a 1995 policy document, between being a commercial cinema and a cinémateque. The imperative to maintain a break-even budget while offering a full range of contemporary and archival screenings and associated events is one which has fluctuated as much through the availability of attractive titles as through a commitment to such a programming strategy. The *realpolitque* of distribution even of art house product was noted when the 1995 report commented that it was 'pointless' to attempt to forge 'special relationships' with certain distributors as they would offer their 'large' titles to other cinemas and attempt to have IFI take 'unattractive or smaller titles'.

Indeed, as 'a small player' IFI was not in a position to compete with its main rivals for either commercial or art house titles. Given that the Light House and Ward Anderson's Screen at College Street favoured open-ended runs for successful films over the maximizing of the number of titles screened, a feature evident in the IFI cinemas' screening policy, and that Ward Anderson, through its associated company Abbey Films, could offer its network of provincial cinemas to distributors, both the Light House and the Screen were able to offer 'the all-powerful distributors far better deals' than IFI. Even if the IFI wished to compete or gain advantage by screening more explicitly commercial films with open-ended runs, it would then have to set aside a budget to cover costs of film censorship and additional marketing. As a result, IFI's own analysis acknowledged that it could only operate as a fully-fledged commercial art cinema if investment was made, or as a full-time cinémateque with subsidy. Unsurprisingly, the analysis came down in favour of a cultural cinema policy with film programming seen as only one element and where complementary presentations and special events would also be programmed.[6] As part of its cultural remit, IFI cinemas have programmed or facilitated national cinema weeks, such as the especially successful annual French Film Festival (from 2000);[7] an annual Gay and Lesbian Film Festival (from 1993) now known as GAZE, but which in 2010 moved to the Light House;[8] the Junior Dublin Film Festival (from 1990 to 2000); the Halloween Horrorthon (from 1998);[9] and the Stranger than Fiction Documentary Film Festival (from 2002), which, complete with a documentary film market, is the largest dedicated non-fiction film event in Ireland.[10]

By the time of its tenth anniversary in 2002 the IFI cinemas were screening a combined 400 films each year, with audience numbers doubling between its fifth and tenth years, and with one million tickets sold before the end of the 1990s. The hit titles during that decade were the inspiring documentary about Muhammad Ali's legendary 1974 fight with George Forman, *When We Were Kings* (Leon Gast, 1996, USA); another documentary, *The Buena Vista Social Club* (Wim Wenders, 1999, USA/Germany/France/Cuba) following the 'lost' Cuban musicians who were brought together by Ry Cooder in order to record what became a million-selling album; stylish, fast-paced hyper-postmodernist *Run Lola Run* (*Lola Rennt*, Tom Tykwer, 1998, Germany) in which three possible scenarios, all variations of each other, are played out; and the *wuxia pian* or martial arts chivalry film, the spectacular *Crouching Tiger, Hidden Dragon* (Ang Lee, 2000, Hong Kong/Taiwan/USA), all of which established new box office records.[11]

By 2008, IFI had become a major business with fifty-seven employees and income of €4.426 million, only 20 per cent of which came from Arts Council grant aid, surely the Irish arts organization least dependent on the state for revenue funding. That year, the bar and bookshop contributed €1.479 million, or 33 per cent, to turnover, while cinema box office and membership were the next major contributors with €1.222 million, or almost 28 per cent, of turnover. Despite a sudden downturn with the onset of the recession in the latter part of 2008, IFI still posted an operating surplus of €70,054, allowing it to look with some confidence to being able to ride out the economic collapse under the guidance of the new director, Sarah Glennie.[12] In addition, the IFI has undergone physical transformation, the most radical of which occurred in 2009 when a third (digital and 16mm) fifty-eight-seat 'studio' cinema was created out of an upstairs conference room. In addition, the inadequate toilet facilities were greatly improved, a more spacious and attractive bookshop was opened, new film archival research facilities were provided, and the bar and restaurant were revamped, at the cost of €1.9 million, more than two-thirds the cost of IFI's original renovations. By its seventeenth year, 2009, the IFI could claim to have hosted 42,500 screenings with over 2 million viewers; put 170,000 school children through its education programme; preserved 25,000 cans of films, 5,000 tapes, 10,000 images, and 20,000 documents; attracted 500 donors to entrust their films to the Irish Film Archive's care; and supplied through the archive, footage to over 1,000 documentaries.[13] Irish film culture had indeed come a long way in twenty-five years since the possibility of such a national film centre was first imagined.

DEDICATED FULL-TIME ART CINEMAS OUTSIDE THE CAPITAL

The bringing of a more cultural, less mainstream, moreover often artistically and intellectually challenging cinema to a wider audience throughout Ireland, has been a long-term aspiration of the Arts Council. This found articulation in their *Arts plan, 1995–97*, which, prepared at the request of the government and published in 1994, proposed that facilities for an art house cinema outside of Dublin were needed in order to expand and create a more discerning Irish audience. It was affirmed again in their 1998 report, *Film in Ireland: the role of the Arts Council*, which, seeking to encourage the creation of an art house cinema circuit, promoted the idea of a 'project fund' that would provide a subsidy for every occupied cinema seat at a venue showing non-mainstream commercial films;[14] and also in their 2001 report *Developing cultural cinema in Ireland*, published in cooperation with the Arts Council of Northern Ireland and in association with the Irish Film Board. The practical task of realizing this aspiration has been largely guided by the now all-Ireland, resource organization, access>CINEMA, whose central activity remains the booking and distribution of films on behalf of its member film societies. By September 2010, access>CINEMA had eighty-two such affiliates with eleven of these based in Dublin, four in Northern Ireland, and twenty with 35mm screening facilities.[15] Such work by access>CINEMA has been complemented by the IFI which, in common with the Irish Film Theatre before it, has included within its remit a commitment to help to develop a regional art cinema network with titles screened in their cinemas subsequently being distributed to cinema sites nationwide, but mostly in larger contexts in places such as Galway's Eye multiplex cinema, thus reducing the overall cost.

Such activity by access>CINEMA and the IFI, often working in conjunction with each other,[16] coupled with: (a) a rise in a more generalized awareness of film as a cultural form, in part, the result of the incorporation of film studies into the educational curriculum,[17] and evident in the rise of film festivals and clubs;[18] (b) the growth of the home-cinema experience and the increasing availability on DVD, at a relatively low cost, of a greater range of recent, classic, and silent, independent, cultural or non-mainstream films than had been the case previously (even as late as the 1990s); and (c) a shift in commercial exhibition patterns discernible since the 1990s whereby a number of mainstream cinemas, both within and beyond the capital, have recognized, and, indeed, contributed to, a wider audience for more minority or cultural films; has meant that Irish audiences at the end of 2010 have never been so well served in terms of access to cultural or minority-interest film. In Dublin, for example, this trend towards a more inclusive and diverse programming within commercial cinemas can be seen with regard to Cineworld, but also, among others, Movies@, IMC Dún Laoghaire and the Swan Cinema, Rathmines, which was host in summer 2010 to Ireland's first major Indian film festival, envisaged as an annual event.[19] Outside the capital, at least two venues may be singled out for special recognition. These are Co. Kerry's Listowel Classic Movieplex, owned by Kieran Gleeson who established a weekly alternative film club there in 2005,[20] and Galway's Eye Cinema. Indeed, shortly after the Eye opened, it launched its 'Cinema within a Cinema' concept through which it has presented (at times under club conditions) first-run, non-mainstream films, as well as cult and classic (foreign and Irish) films. In addition to such regular alternative screenings, the cinema in association with the Irish Film Institute showcases a number of special screenings, including films from the Irish film archive, and festivals such as the 'Stranger than Fiction' documentary film festival and Campo Viejo Spanish Film Festival. Complementing the work of these 'regular' cinemas has been a number of cinemobiles.

The first of these, a 100-seat mobile cinema, was imported from France for ten days in October 1996 with the support of the Irish Film Board and the Northern Ireland Film Council at a cost of £30,000, as part of the celebrations of cinema's centenary,[21] and used to screen special films as well as mainstream programmes particularly in areas not served by an existing cinema. With funds from the Millennium Committee, IFI subsidiary Fís na Milaois Teo launched Ireland's own Cinemobile 2000. Able to convert in forty-five minutes from a truck into an air-conditioned, fully-heated, state-of-the-art, Dolby surround sound, 100-seat 35mm cinema, it tours the country, visiting towns not serviced by cinemas, trying to return to each place at least twice a year.[22] By 2009, more than 100,000 people had seen films in the Cinemobile.[23] Ireland has a second, similarly furnished, cinemobile, another millennium project, which was the initiative of Leitrim county council. Known as the Aisling Gheal Liatroma or more simply, the Leitrim Cinemobile, it was relaunched in 2007 under the name Cinema North-West as a dedicated alternative 'cinema with focus on World Cinema, Independent and Irish feature films.[24] In addition to curating small film festivals such as the annual Adaptation[25] and Lightbox Animation[26] festivals, Cinema North-West, owned and run by 'filmmakers and film lovers', has recently begun to offer distribution of Irish feature films including Sligo-based Conor McDermottroe's debut feature *Swansong: The Story of Occi Byrne* (2009).[27]

Nevertheless, despite such activity within the non-mainstream film exhibition market in Ireland, the somewhat disturbing position as of May 2011 was that, in contrast to the capital's two dedicated whole-time cultural cinemas with a combined total of six screens – three at both the IFI and the Screen – the rest of the country had only a single such venue, Belfast's three-screen QFT, thus leaving the Republic outside Dublin with no alternative cinema venue, other than, of course, the travelling cinemobiles. This has been the situation since the closure in November 2009 of the one-screen Kino in Cork, and although it was anticipated at that time that a new three-screen art cinema would open in Galway city in 2011, since early 2011 it has been clear that the cinema might take years to be built. Ironically, the Kino's demise ultimately resulted not so much from a lack of state intervention (which, as noted, is necessary for any such cinema with an experimental or cultural programming policy to flourish), or even a lack or decline in audience attendance, but as a consequence of an inadequate state policy with regard to encouraging regional art cinema development, coupled with a more ambitious project whereby redevelopment costs were allowed to rise from a projected €1.5 million to over €4 million.

Though the Kino[28] received an initial grant of £100,000 through the European Union cultural development incentive scheme (administered through the department of arts, heritage, Gaeltacht and the islands), from its beginnings on 29 November 1996 the cinema, run by Michael Hannigan, the IFI's first programmer and director of the Cork Film Festival, was privately financed with no on-going public funding. Following the publication of the Arts Council report, *Developing cultural cinema in Ireland*, which concluded that 'establishing a network of art house cinemas will only become feasible if underlying infrastructural deficiencies are addressed',[29] an initiative known as the Cultural Cinema Consortium was set up to provide capital funding for new art cinema projects.[30] Unsurprisingly, the pioneering Kino, which the authors of the Arts Council report, Neil Connolly and Maretta Dillon, had recommended could be conceivably upgraded not just to a two-screen but a three-screen venue, not least based on the city's demographics,[31] was offered capital funding of €750,000 in 2003. (A similar award was made to Limerick's Filmhouse in order to allow it to be developed through the city's Belltable Arts Centre, though this has not happened.)[32]

At that time, Hannigan, who paid tribute to the city council and Cork enterprise board for the funding of a feasibility study for the expansion, stated that 'the funding is roughly 50 per cent of the overall development budget, ... the remainder [of which] we must raise ourselves.'[33] Though work was planned to begin in early 2004 with an extended and refurbished two-screen Kino, complete with a café-bar, due to open in early 2005 in time for Cork's year as European Capital of Culture, this did not happen. By 2004, reflecting the excesses of the Celtic Tiger not only had costs increased from €1.5 million to €2.5 million, but the decision had been taken to opt for an entire rebuild with three screens. The budget continued to rise and by 2009, due to the €100,000 debts incurred in preparing plans through employing architects and other professionals, which could not be cleared with the Cultural Cinema Consortium allocation or any other funds raised as building capital, the cinema's future was in jeopardy. The final straw was architects Dennehy and Dennehy Designs Ltd suing Mick Hannigan for unpaid work totaling just over €50,000, but even without that there was the not-inconsiderable longer-term problem of making the cinema financially viable. Indeed, the precarious economics of running an art cinema are reflected in the fact that throughout its life, the Kino merely broke even, and that was without Hannigan taking a salary for his work in the cinema.[34] Despite public outcry at the closure of the cinema and a campaign (with a Facebook group, 'Save the Kino', of over 8,000 people) to save it, the cinema has remained shut, though the Cork Opera House has offered its 150-seat Half Moon Theatre for occasional art-film screenings.[35]

One of the many problems the demise of the Kino highlights is the inadequacy of such limited state grant-aid which invariably leaves the project struggling to raise the rest of the financing, usually many multiples of the amount offered by the Arts Council. The differential involved was no less evident in the Light House, Smithfield, which also was awarded a Cultural Cinema Consortium grant of €0.75 million. While total state grant aid amounted to €1.75 million, the actual building costs of the Light House were about €5.5 million, leaving a shortfall of €3.75 million, which, in the end, was provided by developers Fusano Properties who were required by Dublin city council's strategic planning guidelines to provide 80,000 square feet of cultural space within their Smithfield development.[36] Even with all this money, the extra expense of going digital, which for all four screens would have cost around €300,000, proved a financial bridge too far.[37] (Nevertheless, this decision against digital was also influenced by other factors, not least the issue of access to back [non-digitalized] catalogues. However, as noted in chapter 5, in 2009 they were awarded a digital conversion grant of €200,000.)[38] That 'any art cinema is always going to be fragile' and that 'venture capitalists are looking for future profits at a high level [but] art house cinemas are largely showing films that have been defined as "minority interest",'[39] only magnifies the problem of state-under-resourcing.

A further later grant awarded by the Cultural Cinema Consortium, it is hoped, might be more fruitful: this was made in relation to the Galway cinema, Solas (Irish for light), which, set to cost €6.36 million, was, in 2009, due for completion in 2011, with Labour Party president and former arts minister, Michael D. Higgins, having 'turned the sod' in early July 2009. However, as noted above, the project has floundered and may not be completed for a number of years. In any case, the project (led by Lelia Doolan, co-founder of the Film Fleadh, and initiated in partnership with the Galway Film Society, Galway Film Fleadh, Galway Film Centre and Galway Arts Centre),[40] has received state financial aid through the department of tourism, culture, and sport's arts and culture capital enhancement support scheme (ACCESS), and has benefited from city council support in the form of €1.96 million and the donation of the cinema's site at 15 Lower Merchants Road. (Similar, if not as generous, support by Cork's city's council was promised to Kino.)

Solas' location is not accidental, as in May 2008 Galway councillors unanimously agreed to develop the area as Galway's cultural quarter in which would be included the Galway City Museum, Spanish Arch, and the soon to be refurbished Druid Theatre.[41] Of course, more generally that Galway should have the Republic's only art cinema outside the capital, may, on the surface at least, seem strange. Firstly, based on the findings of the 1997 London Economic and Dodona Research study of specialist cinema,[42] the city can hardly justify even one full-time cultural cinema screen; and secondly, the fact that Cork, with a larger population (119,418, compared to Galway's 72,414)[43] and with an established historical relationship to art cinema through the Cork Film Festival and the more regular screenings of the Kino and the Cinematek at Triskel Arts Centre, is without a single full-time screen. Nevertheless, as Connolly and Dillon clearly demonstrated in their 2001 Arts Council report, specific demographic factors, including education, wealth or cultural tradition can considerably 'drive performance above the average [and result in] significantly higher than average admissions'.[44] In this context then it should be remembered that not only is Galway a vibrant university city, but it has, perhaps, a unique association with the arts, expressed not least through the street theatre group Macnas, whose spectacular shows have drawn on Irish mythology, and also in its annual arts festival every July; its annual film fleadh, also in July; and the location of the Irish Film Board in the city.

Though the cinema, which will incorporate three screens over four storeys, approximately 350 seats, 35mm and digital projection, a café and bar area, a film book and DVD shop, and offer online cinema resources,[45] has been greeted as a positive addition to the cultural life of the city, it has not been without its critics. Independent Galway City West candidate A.J. Cahill, for example, has stated that in the current climate in which 'Galway has had a 74 per cent increase in unemployment', 'Knocknacarra is still without a community centre or sufficient schools after years of waiting', housing lists have grown, and there is a lack of funds for school books, special needs' teachers and new businesses, such a project is inappropriate as it 'prioritises film buffs ahead of families and children'.[46]

Whatever about the argument vis-à-vis the relative value of culture in a society, Cahill clearly articulates the perception that culture is not for families or children. While it is true that the typical constituency of art cinema tends to be well educated or culturally informed and, as such, conjures images of (radical) students and middle-aged, middle-class patrons who use art as a cultural weapon rather than a means of visceral enjoyment (or even at the other end of the spectrum, shower-proof coat wearing dirty old men who find titillation in the fantasies of European directors), such an image is far from accurate. Indeed, from the beginnings of the establishment of a non-mainstream cinema exhibition in Ireland in the 1930s and 1940s, children and education has been a central focus. Although the IFI is without doubt the leader in film education, albeit largely for secondary schools rather than young children or pre-teens (though it has initiated in conjunction with Temple Bar Cultural Trust the Irish Film Institute Family Festival),[47] other art house venues including the cinemobiles, moreover working with access>CINEMA, actively engage with young people. Indeed, a list of exemplary events might take in Cinemagic and Filmclub[48] in Northern Ireland; the Junior Film Festival in Dublin; Fresh in Limerick; or the Lightbox Animation Festival, whose summer 2010 programme included family friendly fare such as the award-winning *Ponyo* (Hayao Miyazaki, 2008, Japan) from the renowned Studio Ghibli,[49] *Lost and Found* (Philip Hunt, 2008, UK), based on Oliver Jeffers' best-selling picture book, and the Oscar-nominated and multi-award winning *The Secret of Kells* (Tomm Moore, Nora Twomey, 2009, Ire), given its Irish premiere at the 2009 (February) Jameson Dublin International Film Festival and subsequently screened at the Light House, Smithfield (as well as at commercial venues). Furthermore, the Light House, following the trend of parent and baby screenings in a number of commercial cinemas, set up in 2010 a similar Babes in Arms programme (though as Maretta Dillon has pointed out, from the outset they tried to avoid subtitled films as the adults might not be able to always have their eyes on the screen!).[50] Given the more inclusive nature of art cinema than is often presented in the media, it is perhaps unsurprising that Solas' proposed programming places 'special emphasis' on 'educational screenings and matinee opportunities for diverse audiences'.[51]

FILM FESTIVALS IN CORK, DUBLIN, GALWAY, DERRY, BELFAST AND
ELSEWHERE

Film festivals, which have been proliferating at a considerable pace since the late 1990s, continue to offer the most concentrated offerings of alternative cinema. Below is included both the major regional film festivals and the smaller or newer festivals, some, such as Darklight, which go beyond the boundaries of film itself to embrace new media technology.

(a) Major film festivals in Ireland

Cork Film Festival (1956–)
In 1953, as a means of giving an early start to the tourist season, the Irish government supported an initiative known as An Tóstal (Irish for pageant or parade) but also referred to by its English language name, 'Ireland at home'. This cultural spring festival, aimed not least at American tourists, officially launched by Seán T. O'Kelly on Easter Sunday 1953, was envisaged as 'an expression of Ireland's national life, presenting an opportunity to project widely "our spiritual and cultural place in the modern world".'[52] It was not, however, an immediate success, with its opening ceremony descending into a riotous farce and with tourist numbers actually down in 1953. By the end of the 1950s, by which time it had been extended to April through to September, it was no longer a cohesive national event and slowly disappeared. Nevertheless, in addition to foregrounding the importance of tourism to the national economy, and the arts in general, particularly theatre which flourished as a result of the Tóstal festival,[53] it spawned a number of cultural festivals including the Drumshanbo traditional music festival (Co. Leitrim); the Dublin theatre festival, inaugurated in 1957; the Waterford light opera festival; the Cork choral festival; and the Cork film festival, all of which have achieved international recognition.

The idea of a Cork film festival had been first suggested by Dermot Breen, a member of the Cork Tóstal committee in 1954 and on 22 May 1956, the first such event took place, at which time, the principal European film festivals were at Cannes,

Venice and Berlin. The local response was immediate and enthusiastic, with 1,900 season tickets sold on the day the box office opened. The inaugural film was the Second World War drama *A Town like Alice* (Joseph Jack Lee, 1956, GB) in which a group of women are made to march to a Japanese camp, while the first awards were given to *Les Assassins du Dimanche* (*Sunday's killers*; *Every Second Counts*, Alex Joffé, 1956, France) in which, much to the distress of the mechanic, a car becomes a potential lethal weapon as it has not been repaired correctly, and to Yves Massard for his role in *Un Missionnaire* (Maurice Cloche, 1955, France). A feature of Cork's first and many subsequent festivals was the use of stars and directors to create a frisson suggestive of movieland. Thus, hundreds lined the platform of Cork's railway station to greet the 'Star Express' which brought to the festival actors such as Peter Finch, who appears in *A Town like Alice*; John Gregson (1919–75), who starred in the recently-made Northern Irish story *Jacqueline* (Roy Ward Baker, 1956, UK); and Dublin-born character actor Noel Purcell (1900–85), also in *Jacqueline*.[54] In the early period through to the end of the 1960s, such star attractions (at times of the starlet variety) often received more newspaper coverage than the films being shown. Most notoriously, in 1957 British-born actress Dawn Adams, whose mother, Ethel Mary Hichie, hailed from Cork, asked for a milk bath in her hotel but was refused. She was told by festival director Dermot Breen that such a request was 'in poor taste', but, trading on the publicity, the required twenty gallons of cold Jersey milk, at a cost of £3, was later supplied by a Dublin hotel, an event that was even raised in the Dáil.[55] Whatever titillation the fantasy of Adams in a bath of milk may have generated, a more pressing issue for the festival's organizers was how to deal with film censorship.

Though the committee[56] was very well connected politically, especially with Fianna Fáil, something which remained true of subsequent committees, it nevertheless had to contend with the problem of screening uncensored films in public, which was forbidden under the Censorship of Films Act 1923. From the outset, the decision facing the committee was whether they would require audiences to become club/society members or whether they would defy the law. Though Breen was unsure how to proceed, in the end, he chose to ignore the film censorship regime. This approach was subsequently highlighted in an (English Sunday) newspaper article that stated that the festival's twelve-person committee, including Cork's lord mayor, might be jailed for defying the law by showing twenty-five uncensored films. Breen's response was both dismissive and defensive: 'It's beneath contempt.'[57] When the minister for justice, Jim Everett, a Labour Party member of the 1954–7 coalition government with Fine Gael, was alerted to the issue, he sought the opinion of the attorney general, Paddy McGilligan. Although the CFF was deemed, according to advice from the film censor's office and the gardaí, to be acting illegally, given the festival's success and its endorsement by President Seán T. O'Kelly, a Fianna Fáiler, who attended the first festival's closing film in May 1956, the government did not interfere.[58]

Notwithstanding the CFF's defiance of the film censor, and the observation by some commentators that at least one film shown at the first festival – the Japanese film *I am on Trial* (*Kamisaka Shirô no Hanzai*, Seiji Hisamatsu, 1956) – would not have passed the Irish film censor, the festival organizers were sufficiently attuned politically (and no doubt morally conservative) to ensure that a major censorship controversy would not arise. As a result, the Danish film *A Stranger Knocks* (*En Fremmed Banker På*, Johan Jacobson, 1959, Denmark) was withdrawn from the 1959 programme because of its 'intimate scenes' and replaced by the very safe film *Fanfare* (Bert Haanstra, 1958, Netherlands) about a (brass band) fanfare competition made by a director celebrated for his documentaries rather than his occasional features.[59] Nevertheless, later that year, Breen made it clear that the festival would accept films that might not be suitable for general distribution, 'provided they were of artistic merit', but in a reference to the withdrawal of *A Stranger Knocks*, he said that if foreign festivals were able to reject films on political grounds, then Cork had 'the same right, and intend[ed] to use it, to reject films on moral grounds.'[60] Eight years later, amid hisses and boos, the British film *Separation* (Jack Bond, 1968) was also cancelled at the last minute. While this, no doubt, was because of the film's sexual content, the committee justified their action by stating that the film, which had been chosen by Breen on the basis of a rough cut only, was not up to the 'required standard'. By the time the replacement film – a USA horror, *Incubus* (Leslie Stevens, 1965) – had ended, the cinema was nearly empty.[61] Although the festival stood aloof from overtly political activities, in 1968, following the Soviet invasion of Czechoslovakia, it excluded Russian films,[62] a decision which led to the resignation of CFF council member Seán Henrick,[63] while in 1970 two Sinn Féin members threw a petrol bomb at a cinema screen during a British film night. The last (publicly) known 'banning' of a film by the festival was the pulling in 1979 of innovative documentarist and cinematographer John T. Davis' Northern Ireland punk rock film, *Shellshock Rock* (1979), just three days before it was due to be screened as it had been deemed not 'up to standard'. However, after Davis organized screenings of his film in Cork, the conclusion was drawn that it was not so much the film that had not been 'up to standard' as the festival itself, with the new CFF director Robin O'Sullivan seen as defending the indefensible.[64]

Only very occasionally, Cork showed films that generated controversy. Most famously, one such instance was the screening on 13 September 1969 of *I Can't, I Can't* (Piers Haggard, 1969, Ireland) as the opening film, the first time an Irish fiction film was so privileged. Following its screening, the bishop of Cork, Dr Cornelius Lucey, who had written to the festival seeking the film's withdrawal, publicly criticized the event on the basis that *I Can't, I Can't* dealt with birth control and contained nude or semi-nude scenes that might lead to 'immodest thoughts, looks and words',[65] even though two-and-a-half years later, under the new title *Wedding Night*, it was approved with cuts by the Irish film censor.[66] Ironically, by then not only was Breen a member of the censorship of films appeal board, but within two weeks, on 21 June 1972, he would become Ireland's official film censor, the sixth incumbent in the post which he retained until his death in October 1978. Other films to generate debate were Peter Bogdanovich's *The Last Picture Show* (1971), a study of 1950s Texas, which, screened in 1972, came under fire from Cork's lord mayor even though it had been passed by the censor in May 1971, albeit with three cuts and an over-18s certificate;[67] an antiabortion drama *Thou Shalt Not Kill* (*No Matarás*, César Fernández Ardavín, 1975 Spain), which led to audience walk-outs in 1975;[68] Jean-Luc Godard's *Je Vous Salue Marie* (*Hail Mary*, 1983, France), about a modern Blessed Virgin married to a taxi driver, which was shown in 1985; and Martin Scorsese's *The Last Temptation of Christ* (1988) which was part of the 1988 programme.[69] During the extended protest on the night of *The Last Temptation...* screening irreverent local university and art college students, parading under the banner of 'The acolytes of Our Lady of Ballinspittle' (a reference to the contemporaneous 'moving statue' phenomenon in the eponymous Co. Cork village), and bearing placards declaring that 'Jesus was nailed, not screwed', 'Mary Mag was a hag' and 'They've got the guns, but we've got the nuns. US culture out of Ireland', joined in the official protest. Unsurprisingly, this 'devastatingly subversive' move by the students led to scuffles.[70]

Seeking to carve out its own niche, and recognizing that its provincial status was unlikely to allow it to compete against the major international festivals for feature film presentations and awards, CFF quickly focused on both documentary and short films. Films from fourteen countries were screened at the second festival when awards were made in the categories of documentary, educational short, general interest film, and cartoon short; while in 1958 the number of countries represented rose to twenty-four. A commitment to Irish cinema was reflected in the world premiere in 1958 of *Sally's Irish Rogue* (George Pollock, 1958), the first feature film made at Ardmore Studios, while the following year saw the premiere of *Mise Éire* (*I am Ireland*, George Morrison, 1959) about the struggle for Irish independence, and two years later, its companion feature, *Saoirse?* (*Freedom?* George Morrison, 1961) opened the somewhat slimmed down festival given that only fifty-nine shorts were shown, forty-three less than in 1959. The 1962 event saw the first Irish winner with Colm Ó Laoghaire's *Water Wisdom* (*Fíor Uisce*, 1962), a government-supported film in which the setting up of group water schemes is encouraged, being given best educational film. While the following decade, George Morrison's *Uisce Beatha* (*Water of Life*, 1972), which explores the tradition of Irish whiskey manufacture and marketing, was the first Irish short to be recognized, it was not until the 1990s, following the expansion within Irish film production, that Irish films began to feature regularly among the prize-winners.

Countering the downturn evident in the early 1960s, the festival received renewed impetus in 1963 when its programme, drawn from thirty countries and including twenty feature films, achieved the fastest ticket sales ever, while in 1965 it achieved record attendances. In part this was due to the help of the Irish Tourist Board/Bord Fáilte, which, in the absence of the availability of dedicated funding for Irish film exhibition during the 1960s, largely funded the CFF. However, the tourist board's commitment to the event was measured by the number of foreign tourists it could attract, and this inevitably led to doubts over its continued involvement and the future of CFF. Nevertheless, the number of European journalists attending the festival increased, as did the number of non-nationals, with a large number coming from British film societies on package tours. This momentum continued the following year with most tickets sold out six weeks prior to the event which included films from thirty countries, while in 1967, 600 delegates from thirty countries attended the festival in which twenty-three feature films were shown. Importantly, even though the International Federation of Film Producers reduced the number of competitive festivals to seventeen, Cork managed to retain its status as a competitive festival but its awards were confined to short films. That year, Taoiseach and local TD Jack Lynch praised the festival for the role it played in putting Ireland on the world's cultural map. The converse of this was that it put the world on Cork's map. Indeed, as Cork poet Theo Dorgan has argued, through the festival Dermot Breen 'opened a gap and let the greater world into the minds and hearts of Cork people. He widened our cultural horizon.'[71] At a more local level, however, the festival could also be accused of serving an excluding role as its attendant social events and festival club with its black-tie requirement,[72] were dominated by the local bourgeoisie and business community, who made little financial contribution to the festival, yet gained considerably by it.

Throughout the 1970s the festival was under financial strain, with only a late grant from Bord Fáilte of £11,000 saving the event in 1974. The following year it declared that it was in danger of 'extinction' unless it received additional funding, and, indicating its increasing marginalization as new festivals were being launched internationally, complained about the quality of feature films being offered to it. Yet in 1978, just as the Arts Council was seeking to encourage the festival to become more professional in its approach, festival director Dermot Breen insisted that CFF would remain under the control of 'amateurs', arguing that 'the day that professionals come in is the day the festival will die.'[73] That year he himself died and was replaced for the 1979 festival by a marketing executive, Robin O'Sullivan. While that year's programme included thirty features and 100 shorts, it also saw Cork's opera house transform into a cinema for the duration of the festival. However, in 1981 indicating a continuing crisis, Cork, for the first time, became non-competitive, with the 1982 event similarly cast. Though, as noted above, CFF's difficulties were somewhat ameliorated by the Arts Council's injection of a debt-clearing £41,000, the 1982 festival was pared back to screening eighteen feature films only, but it broke even. Reflecting its more modest scale, it changed its name from the Cork International Film Festival to Festival of Film Cork. The 1983 festival, under co-directors Robin O'Sullivan and Ronnie Saunders, also remained modest, but the shorts' film programme was restored while a working group was established to restore the festival's full international status. Importantly, with box office receipts of £9,000, it finally succeeded in generating a profit. As part of the process of renewal, the 1984 affair ran for an unprecedented nine days, and screened fifty-two feature films and twelve shorts from a total of twenty-seven countries.

With the appointment in 1986 of Michael Hannigan and Theo Dorgan as co-directors, in the wake of O'Sulllivan's 1985 departure, the festival took a decisive and positive shift away from its amateur/non-specialist identity, which at times had displayed a greater interest in the festival's social aspect and the need to put on more mainstream films in order to fill the large Savoy Cinema, than in cultural or alternative films or in film culture more generally. This repositioning led to a rise in attendances. In 1991, in a clear signal that Ireland was changing and that a different politics was to the fore at the CFF, Ireland's first ever Lesbian and Gay Film Festival was opened by journalist Nell McCafferty during the middle of the festival as a complementary event. However, just as Irish cinema was beginning to find a more mainstream audience, in 1994 the jury for best Irish short film caused controversy when it failed to make an award, stating that there was 'nothing exceptional' among that year's entries.[74] That year the talented young filmmaker Claire Lynch died in a fire while attending the festival and from 1995 an award for best first film has been made in her name, the first winner of which was Seán Hinds for his Belfast-based bizarre comedy, *The Pan Loaf* (1994).

By 1999, such had been the success and expansion of the festival that four venues were in use, including the Cork Opera House, the Kino, the Triskel Arts Centre, and, for the first time, the Gate multiplex. Despite the dramatic rise in attendance at Cork (and indeed, at other festivals elsewhere in Ireland), festival admissions still represent only a minor part of Irish box office income. For example, though 1997 was Cork's 'record-breaking' year with £54,000 taken at the box office, a figure that was slightly bettered in 1998,[75] the Republic of Ireland's gross box office for 1997 was in excess of £40 million. Reflecting the increasing output of Irish-themed films, the festival's opening or closing gala events have included, since the late 1990s, such films as *Trojan Eddie* (Gillies MacKinnon, 1996, Ireland), *Divorcing Jack* (David Caffrey, 1998, GB), *The Magdalene Sisters* (Peter Mullen, 2003, Ireland), *Song for a Raggy Boy* (Aisling Walsh, 2003, Ireland) and *Inside I'm Dancing* (Damien O'Donnell, 2004, Ireland), though such prominent positioning has not been the case since 2005. In 2006, the festival, sponsored by drink's company Corona (who took over from Murphy's, another producer of beer), celebrated its fiftieth anniversary, but while by then it may have been the oldest film festival in Ireland, and had established itself as a major showcase for Irish film production, particularly in the area of shorts, it was by no means unique, with Dublin, for example, enjoying its second film festival, established, as was the first (1985–2001), by the energetic Michael Dwyer. In any case, the Corona Cork Film Festival remains a vibrant force within the Irish and international film festival scene,[76] complete with its complementary Cork Super 8 film festival – Silent Light – which made its first appearance during the 2005 festival when Cork was European Capital of Culture. The one-day film event has the distinction of being the first fringe event of the official Cork Film Festival and the first such event in Ireland. Three years later, in 2008, the fifty-third festival screened over 300 films, opening with the Coen Brothers' *Burn After Reading*, and featured veteran filmmaker Peter Greenaway who delivered the inaugural lecture in memory of Donal Sheehan, who was festival director for the period 1990–3. In 2009 the festival moved from its traditional place in the arts calendar to November and showcased 'one of the most crowd-pleasing line-ups in recent years' including a special GAA 125th anniversary programme presented by the Irish Film Archive. Though it exceeded box office expectations, within the month it and Cork lost the Kino as a cultural cinema venue.[77] Nevertheless, the 2010 event, which was offered over 3,000 films, to some small degree compensated for that loss,[78] and while the event's reputation was built on its focus on short films, festival director Mick Hannigan sought to avoid being so pigeon-holed and remained committed to showing a broad spectrum of cinema.[79]

Dublin Film Festival (1985–2001)

It was not until 1985 and the combined efforts of Michael Dwyer and RTÉ radio's Myles Dungan that Dublin finally had its first film festival, though as noted above, in the early 1980s the Arts Council had discouraged the Irish Film Theatre, largely in deference to the CFF, from developing such an event. With very modest resources available – some help from the Dublin Theatre Festival and two department of labour employees under the 'Teamwork' scheme, and sponsorship from International Youth Year Committee and Shell Ireland – Dwyer and Dungan convinced the Ward Anderson group to make available to them their three-screen Screen at College Street for the inaugural event. Over eight days, fifty-seven feature films were shown, along with Edgar Reitz's complete fifteen-hour *Heimat* series (1979–84, Germany), in which a counter to depictions of Nazi Germany and the Holocaust is offered through its chronicle of life in a fictitious provincial German village from 1919 to 1982; and, in recognition of the struggling Irish film industry, a selection of five shorts under the title 'New Irish Cinema'.[80]

One consequence of the link forged by Dwyer and Dungan with the theatre festival apart, that is from what is clearly visible in its programme,[81] was that the theatre festival's director at the time, Lewis Clohessy, who had no obvious background in film, became chairman of the board of the film festival. Besides Clohessy, Dwyer (programming director) and Dungan (administrative director), the other board members were film producer David Collins, media lawyer James Hickey, and Dr Dietrich Kreplin of the Goethe Institute, though by 1987 community art activist Sandy Fitzgerald (of Grapevine Arts Centre, Dublin) and solicitor Pat McCartan TD (later a judge) had also joined. Although in order to ensure its commercial viability, the festival, in a decision frequently criticized and mirroring the CFF, particularly prior to its take over by Hannigan and Dorgan, screened mainstream Hollywood films, often shortly before their commercial release, the Dublin programme, nevertheless, also contained a wide diversity of product, with, for example, the 1986 festival, which screened an impressive ninety-six feature films and twenty-two shorts, including a season of Margarethe von Trotta films with the director in attendance.

By its third year, the finances of the DFF had grown only marginally from its second year, by which time, in contrast to its modest first year, it had secured grant aid from the Irish Film Board and Dublin corporation as well as a number of sponsors and had a budget of £40,000. Though in 1987 Dungan was still bemoaning the fact that the festival was 'largely unembarrassed with sponsorship riches',[82] the grant aid (£10,000 from the Irish Film Board and £3,000 from Dublin corporation), combined with sponsorship[83] and advertising revenue of £13,000 (£5,000 of which came from RTÉ), along with £47,000 in box office receipts allowed the festival to cover its costs. With over 5,000 members, a seat occupancy rate of 89 percent (of over 20,000 available seats) and with no less than forty-six of the seventy-seven screenings sold out, the festival, which included retrospectives of the films of Francesco Rosi – the political and social conscience of Italian cinema – and the controversial *enfant terrible* of British cinema, Ken Russell, both of whom gave public interviews at the festival, became firmly established within the Irish arts' scene.

However, 1987 was a bleak year for Irish film with the Irish Film Board abolished and the Arts Council's budget cut by £2.2 million as part of the 'Mac the Knife' cutbacks in the government's finances. It was more bitterly ironic that the DFF should be concerned with its future given that 1988 was being heralded as a year for celebrating Dublin's millennium.[84] In the end with funding from the National Lottery (£15,000), Dublin corporation and RTÉ, the 1988 event took place, though without the participation of Dungan. Opening with an Irish made film,[85] *High Spirits* (1988, UK/USA), directed by the 'uniquely talented' Neil Jordan,[86] it screened eighty-seven feature films, including an eight-film retrospective of director and screenwriter Paul Schrader,[87] who also gave a public interview as part of the festival, as well as many shorts, including three Irish cinema programmes. The next festival, which moved from the crowded October–November cultural calendar to the following February–March 1990, maintained the high audience attendances and eclectic mix of programmes evident since the first festival. The international mix was similarly apparent in 1991 when, as the first major event of Dublin's year as European City of Culture, it showed films from twenty-four different countries, and presented two retrospectives: one, devoted to German-born Fritz Lang, the other to Italian director Ettore Scola, who attended the festival. The 1991 event, which included sponsorship from ACC Bank, whose name was formally attached to the festival from 1995, was also Michael Dwyer's swansong, as Martin Mahon, who had joined the board of directors in 1990 along with David McLoughlin and Liam Miller, took over the role of programme director from 1992.

If anything, the 1992 festival was even bigger than its six predecessors, with 118 films from twenty-five countries shown. The number of titles screened grew to 143 films from thirty-nine countries in 1993 when a season of African films was programmed. By then, David Collins was chairman, with film director John Boorman, Dublin Business Association's Tom Cox, RTÉ executive Liam Miller and broadcaster Doireann Ní Bhriain serving on the board of directors along with Clohessy, Hickey and McCartan. The drive towards a greater number and greater representation of countries was to the fore in the following years. The 1994 event, for example, screened over ten days 151 films (including a Latin-American season) selected from forty countries; the tenth festival in 1995, showed over eleven days an even more impressive number and range of films, and included a 'distant horizons' event focused on Far Eastern cinema, a Cuban night, and French and New Zealand shorts' programmes; while the eleventh festival, which offered over 200 films, incorporated a special season entitled 'Phileas Fogg cinema of three continents', which highlighted cinema from Africa, Latin-America, and the Far East (China, Taiwan, Korea and Japan) with a mini-season of five films from Iran. Reflecting the new surge in Irish film production, films from Ireland became more prominent such that the 1996 event opened with Martin Duffy's *The Boy from Mercury* (1996) while the 1997 programme, which featured a retrospective[88] on Irish-born Pat O'Connor, opened with *A Further Gesture* (Robert Dornhelm, 1997, Ireland, UK, Germany, Japan), an Irish/New York story about Irish and Guatemalan political activists featuring Stephen Rea. However, the seeds of change, or of decline as Michael Dwyer put it five years later, were sown when Collins resigned as chairman of the board, Clohessy resumed his former role, and Mahon left as programme director. At that point, in 1997, Áine O'Halloran, formerly of the British Film Institute and programme director of the West Belfast Film Festival, 1994–97, took over as the festival's programmer,[89] though her tenure was short-lived.

In March 1998, the festival received a further blow when it lost the exclusive use of what had been its main venue, the Screen at College Street, forcing the event to bi-locate with the Ambassador, which reduced both the special festival atmosphere at the Screen and the number of nightly screenings by two over the eight days.[90] By October 1998, Maretta Dillon, who had worked as festival manager in the early 1990s as well as running the Light House Cinema with Neil Connolly until it closed in September 1996, was programme director, but O'Halloran remained to the fore, occupying the post of development manager, which was also described as sponsorship and marketing manager.[91] The April 1999 festival, dubbed as 'a stabilizing operation' by Dillon,[92] who had sought to shift its emphasis away from commercial cinema towards European and world cinema,[93] was mainly based at the Virgin multiplex, Parnell Street. However, the festival's future was uncertain not least as it suffered a 20 per cent drop in box office receipts compared with 1998,[94] while in September 1999 Dillon left the festival citing 'irreconcilable differences', especially demarcation disputes with O'Halloran as her reason for doing so. In addition further resignations came from board members David Collins and James Hickey, both of whom had been with the festival since the beginning in 1985, and Alan Robinson.[95]

With only seven months to the fifteenth Dublin Film Festival, Paul Taylor, formerly of the British Film Institute, was appointed programme director.[96] He not only had to face the fact that the festival was drifting dangerously close to the Cannes Film Festival, thus reducing its access to many titles, but also that as a result of the exponential growth in film festivals worldwide from the 1990s, the securing of an available film print (rather than simply the permission of the director or producer[s]) became a real issue.[97] A further problem was, of course, Taylor's lack of understanding and engagement with Irish film culture. This was highlighted in reviews of the 2000 event, most of which were overwhelmingly negative.[98] According to Philip Molloy the event had lost its focus during the late 1990s,[99] while, after the festival ended, Michael Dwyer wrote an understandably angry piece.[1]

Though the 2000 festival, which carried the prefix of the principal sponsor's name, beer company Miller, continued to show an eclectic mix of films, it made the disastrous decision to abandon the Screen at College Street in favour of a dual city location at the Irish Film Centre and the UGC multiplex at Parnell Street, as well as offering screenings in the suburban UCI multiplexes at Blanchardstown, Coolock and Tallaght. Though the Screen was undeniably shabby and in need of refurbishment, nevertheless, it had the intimacy and scale needed for such an event and allowed for a real sense of community and audience ownership. That the festival had use of only a small number of the UGC's screens meant that the identity of the festival audience was lost, while the (relatively) long trek from Parnell Street to Eustace Street militated against the sense of community which is an important feature of most such festivals, including the early years at Dublin and those at Cork and Galway. As a result, this dissipation led to a decline in attendances with the consequence that the viability of the festival was put in doubt. When the sixteenth Dublin Film Festival in April 2001 proved to be the last, Michael Dwyer was withering in his criticism of the event's decline. Expressing 'deep disappointment', he noted that the appointment of so many programme directors in such a short space of time had served to 'undermin[e] the consistency and continuity a festival needs.'[2]

Dublin International Film Festival (2003–)

Another festival stalwart, David McLoughlin, formerly a DFF manager, a film producer, and later administrative director of Wexford Opera Festival, approached Dwyer about starting another festival in Dublin, noting that many cities in addition to having a vibrant all-year round alternative cinema culture, such as that found in Dublin through the IFI cinemas, have major film festivals. Taking his cue from Toronto, his favourite film festival, Dwyer subsequently set about re-establishing another non-competitive event in Dublin.[3] With a new name, Dublin International Film Festival, or DIFF, which lent itself to the slogan 'It's different', a new sponsor in Jameson whiskey, yet another alcohol drinks' company,[4] and a new board of directors with McLoughlin as chair,[5] the first festival ran from 6 to 13 March 2003 and included sixty-seven films from thirty-two countries, with a strong Asian and Spanish-language presence. The Screen at College Street was re-established as a festival venue as was the IFI (where eleven films were screened) and the Savoy 1 (where seven films were screened).[6] Of the festival's budget of €350,000/€400,000, less than 10 per cent of the total came from Dublin corporation and the Arts Council, with the latter's €25,000 contribution amounting to less than one-fifth of what it had given to Cork or Galway in 2004. The following year, though, the Arts Council increased its contribution to €38,000, which represented 8 per cent of the festival's budget, this was still only a fifth of what it gave to the CFF (€190,000), or two-ninths of the Galway Film Fleadh's award of €170,00, and led DIFF's chief executive Rory Concannon to question the criteria by which the Arts Council made such awards.[7] Nevertheless, the 2004 festival, which included a retrospective on the work of little-known director Julio Medem,[8] was a success and saw a 60 per cent increase in admissions over the inaugural event.[9] In February 2005, ninety-five features from thirty-four countries were screened, which included special seasons on new Irish cinema, Canadian cinema, new Danish cinema, independent filmmakers, documentary, Asian cinema and a retrospective on Italian Gianni Amelio whose work is marked by an interest in human relations under stressful and painful circumstances. The following year in 2006, over 100 films from thirty-four countries were presented with special seasons on documentary, world cinema, Canadian cinema, Irish films, American independents and even football films, as well as offering talk shops for emerging filmmakers with debates on Irish film policy. Shortly after the 2006 festival, Michael Dwyer announced that the 2007 festival would be his last as programme director, though he promised to continue to play a prominent role as chairman of the festival's board. In January 2007[10] former IFI assistant director Gráinne Humphreys joined DIFF as director-designate and in 2008 programmed the sixth DIFF, which in terms of number of titles topped the 2007 record of 107 films with over 120 films and included a special presentation of G.W. Pabst's *Pandora's Box* (1929) and a season on experimental filmmaker Jonas Mekas,[11] while the following year, in 2009, influential avant-gardist filmmaker Chantal Akerman was the subject of a retrospective. The 2010 event, which featured, once again in excess of 100 films including nine Irish features, was overshadowed by the death on New Year's Day of double-Dublin film festival founder, and until his death, DIFF's chairman, Michael Dwyer, in whose honour the 2010 festival was dedicated.[12]

Galway Film Fleadh (1989–)

From its beginning in 1989, Galway Film Fleadh, or festival, which takes place in July just prior to the massive Galway Arts Festival,[13] has been distinguished by a number of distinctive characteristics. Not only is Galway many Irish people's favourite city (after their home place), but as a university town it has an immediacy, intimacy and sense of community that is perfectly suited to such an event. However, the fleadh started at a most inauspicious time for Irish film as not only had the Irish Film Board been closed down two years earlier but also there was no funding available for the type of committed indigenous production that was being promoted by those on the fleadh's organizing committee. At that time, the committee comprised of Lelia Doolan, a former actress, theatre and television director, and film producer, but above all a film activist who was formally recognized when the 2010 fleadh honoured her with a tribute; her festival co-director, Miriam Allen; pioneering filmmaker Bob Quinn (Quinn and Allen later married); animator Steve Woods, whose work is distinguished by political and historical concerns; and one of Galway Film Society's organizers, Joe McMahon. Based at the Ward Anderson owned Claddagh Palace twin cinemas in Lower Salthill, the five-day event was marked by an interest in and promotion of Irish filmmaking, and appropriately ended with a picnic on the Aran Islands. In all, during the first fleadh, eighty features and shorts, including twenty-four from emerging Irish filmmakers, were shown. The programme, which opened with the Orkneys' story *Venus Peter* (Ian Sellar, 1989, GB) featuring Irish actor Ray McAnally, included an archival retrospective on the late cinematographer Vincent Corcoran; a screening, attended by the director, of *Another Shore* (Charles Crichton, 1948, GB), which had been made in Ireland; a retrospective of the films of Joe Comerford, whose most recent film, *Reefer and the Model* (1988, Ireland) had been produced by Doolan; a strong Irish language filmmaking element with a retrospective selected by Quinn featuring the films of Louis Marcus, an approach that befitted an event held on the edge of the Galway Gaeltacht; and an eclectic selection of contemporary European and non-western cinemas. The films were complemented by a lively set of film related discussions including an exploration of the European Community's MEDIA '92 programme, especially its SCRIPT fund from which Irish writers and directors received an impressive 14 per cent of the fund's investments.[14]

The second fleadh in 1990, a six-day event, continued the policies of the first year with a showing of the controversial documentaries by Kenneth Griffith on the Irish War of Independence and others on the contemporary Troubles in Northern Ireland;

a retrospective of the work of Irish filmmaker Thaddeus O'Sullivan; a tribute to Rex Ingram with the attendance of Ingram's biographer Liam O'Leary; Irish language films, some of which emanated from development agency Údarás na Gaeltachta; short films by Irish directors; animation from Irish and European students; a programme of children's films; and a midnight-to-dawn selection of American B-movies from the 1940s. The public discussion was maintained with the focus on the present and future state of independent film and television in Ireland.

The fleadh quickly established itself as the premiere event where young Irish film-makers met and showed their films, a gathering that added to the conviviality and engaging environment of the festival. As Michael Dwyer put it in 1992,

> the fleadh has a special atmosphere, unusually relaxed and relaxing for a film event ... In four years it has made its mark as a very lively talking shop, as a showcase for young Irish film-makers and for animation, and as an outlet for first-time feature film-makers from around the world.[15]

By 1993, a newly self-confident Irish film production sector could celebrate the re-establishment of the Irish Film Board, with fleadh co-director Lelia Doolan appointed its chairperson and acting chief executive. Indeed, Galway had more to celebrate when the minister for the arts and Gaeltacht, local TD Michael D. Higgins, decided to relocate the Film Board to Galway. The following year, new Film Board chief executive Rod Stoneman opened the fleadh, which screened not only a selection of the original Film Board-supported productions from the 1980s, but also films from Europe, the USA, South Africa, Argentina, India, Tunisia, and Russia. The pattern continued in subsequent years, and although a relocation from the 'much lamented' Claddagh Palace was precipitated by its redevelopment as an apartment complex, two alternative venues presented themselves: the Town Hall Theatre, which had recently been redeveloped with 35mm screening facilities, and the Ward Anderson owned Omni multiplex, which was within a short walk of the Town Hall. Both venues remain the main sites used by the fleadh. Add to this, the nearby boat club as the festival club and all the old ingredients could continue to be experienced, but on an even more expanded scale. However, as the Town Hall was required for theatre productions during the arts festival, the fleadh shifted to the week before the main festival. By 1996, too, the festival had a new programme director, Antony Sellers. This position has since been occupied by Pat Collins (from 1999); Sally-Anne O'Reilly (from 2001); and since the 2006 fleadh, Felim McDermott, a writer and arts manager, who had previously worked with both the Cork Film Festival and Galway Film Fleadh.

By the time of the ninth fleadh in 1997, as Sellers put it, 'an artisan based movement [had] been industrialised', and, as a result the fleadh hosted presentations on marketing and distribution, as well as a film fair, at which filmmakers with film projects in development and/or completed films could engage with film distributors, producers and film financiers, the only such fair at an Irish film festival. It was a festival orientated more than any other Irish event towards filmmakers and their practical needs. The fleadh's focus on production rather than critical or historical enquiry has been apparent in its seminars on film financing and 'master-classes' or public interviews with various prominent players in the film business. Visiting actors have included Gabriel Byrne (1999), Woody Harrelson (2000), Colm Meaney (2001), Aidan Quinn (2002), Pierce Brosnan (2003), Maureen O'Hara and John Lynch (2004), Matt Dillon, Campbell Scott and Patricia Clarkson (2005), Kathy Bates (2006), Jeremy Irons (2007), Peter O'Toole and Jessica Lange (2008), Angelica Huston and Michael Fassbender (2009) and Brendan Gleeson (2010).[16] Among the recent directors have been Michael Winterbottom (1999), Stephen Frears (2000), Abbas Kiarostami (2001), Mira Nair (2002), Agnieszka Holland (2003), Stanley Tucci (2004), Luis Mandoki (2005), Nicholas Roeg (2006), Alex Gibney (2008) and Stephen Daldry (2010); while screenwriters have include Paul Laverty (2004), Paul Schrader (2005), Robert Towne (2006), Martin Daniel (2008), Christopher Hampton (2009) and Ronald Harwood (2010). Other aspects of filmmaking have also been covered, including low budget production (digital filmmaking) in 1999, set-decoration with the Irish Oscar-winner Josie MacAvin in 2004, and cinematography with Seamus Deasy in 2005. In addition, the 2003 festival featured a debate on 'the ethics and aesthetics of extreme cinema', while in 2007 an event entitled 'New media opportunities for filmmakers' was held. The fleadh's commitment to alternatives to mainstream commercial cinema is reflected in its selection each year of a particular European and World cinema country as a canvas for showing a group of films, with, for example, Germany and South Korea the focus of the 2003 event; New British cinema and Latin America in 2004, and Russia and France in 2005.

As the 2004 fleadh programme booklet put it, looking back sixteen years, the festival had 'promised to deliver a diverse and dynamic programme of "post colonial" film', and 'to champion the smaller, less visible film',[17] and without any doubt it can be judged to have achieved this goal. Of course more than that it has succeeded in a somewhat unique way in bringing filmmakers and practitioners (at all levels from students to established professionals on both sides of the camera), and audiences together in a most intimate and productive way. In July 2008, the festival, which featured an additional strand of 'music on film', its third season of Queer cinema, which continues to be a strand of the festival with the 2010 event including six screenings under the title of 'Out in Film', celebrated its twentieth anniversary. Under the direction of Miriam Allen (and programmer McDermott), the 2008 fleadh opened with *Fugitive Places* (Jeremy Podeswa, Canada/Greece, 2007), a film about loss and redemption during the Second World War, and screened over eighty features, 120 shorts and twenty-five documentaries. By the time of its twenty-first birthday in 2009, the week-long programme of world premieres, special tributes, Irish and international features, documentaries and shorts was well established as one of the country's most diverse film festivals. The 2010 event, which received a record number of shorts, screened eight world premieres, fifty-three Irish premieres (including eight Irish features), 100 feature films and 115 shorts, and to counter the current gloom, evident in many of the films, offered a mini season of five films on love.[18]

Foyle Film Festival, Derry (1987–)

Northern Ireland's Foyle Film Festival in Derry, which began in 1987, emerged as a community-based event in a manner not too dissimilar to Galway's Fleadh, though unlike other festivals it had links to the local university, the University of Ulster at Coleraine, whose lecturer in media studies, John Hill, was Foyle's first chairman.[19] From the beginning, the organization's mixture of academics, local filmmakers and cultural activists infused the event with an educational and discursive dimension. Thus, in 1987, the festival included an all-day event focused on 'Images of Derry – the insider and outsider view' which presented over twenty films and television programmes featuring the city, and was complemented by a debate on 'Culture, identity and Derry' featuring four locals: filmmaker and academic Desmond Bell; academic Martin McLoone; poet and academic Seamus Deane, and journalist Nell McCafferty. Furthermore, a 'neighbourhood event' emphasized Foyle's links with the local community. In addition, Irish archival films were screened, as were recently released films.

Like the Galway festival, the Foyle event took on a campaigning aspect. For example, in its third year – 1989 – it hosted an international forum on censorship in the context of the British government's broadcasting ban (on paramilitaries and their spokespeople), which had been introduced the previous year. Screenings of films that had been banned or were otherwise controversial, especially those displaying Irish republican sympathies, were shown. By then, the festival had become part of Foyle Film Projects, an organization established that year to promote the understanding, exhibition and production of film and video within a community context.[20] By the time of the sixth festival in 1992, Foyle Film Projects, which had received £25,000 from Channel Four television to equip its training unit at the Nerve Centre,[21] had expanded its filmmaking activities, while a year-round film club had been established in the wake of the festival's success. With the theme of the 1992 event 'The Irish abroad', screenings that year included key feature films about the Irish made in the USA and Britain as well as a selection of new Irish shorts; the productions of Northern Visions, formerly Belfast Independent Video; American independent films; a John T. Davis retrospective; and a seminar with screenings on 'Images of Protestant identity'.

The tenth festival, which ran for nine days in November 1996 at the Orchard and Strand cinemas, took as its theme the relationship between literature and film. A forum chaired by local filmmaker Margo Harkin and including writers Roddy Doyle and Ronan Bennett explored whether Irish cinema was too dependent on literary adaptations and the word more generally rather than on the image. One of Foyle's distinguishing features has been its low admission prices, something that has encouraged young people to attend, while its lectures and workshops are free. Its approach has always been to cater for the local audience first without seeking to establish itself on the international film festival circuit. Attendances grew 50 per cent in 1996, with 9,632 admissions. Like other Irish cities outside Belfast and Dublin, Derry does not have a full-time exclusive venue for showing non-mainstream films, so the festival provides the community with an opportunity to see films otherwise unavailable.[22] As the *Irish Times'* Hugh Linehan argued in his report of the 1998 festival, which ran during late April/early May, the event that year explored the relationship between films and their audiences and, in so doing, 'threw up some provocative and timely observations', and, thus, puts many of the larger Irish contemporary festivals 'to shame for imaginative programming, thematic strands, seminars and educational workshops.' Pointing out that the festival's name locates it in the middle of a river, rather than on land as would be the case if it were called the Derry Film Festival, or even Londonderry Film Festival if it was 'owned' by those on the other side of the political divide, Linehan suggested that it be rebranded as the Northern Ireland Film Festival, 'which is what it has become'.[23]

While its name has remained unchanged over the years, its orientation in the context of the growth within film production in Northern Ireland from 1997 onwards has, however, shifted. By the time the sixteenth festival was held over ten days in November 2003, the event, which had become Oscar affiliated in 1999, had expanded to show 139 films, including twenty-three Irish and British premieres. Furthermore, a series of nine awards were introduced, including for best feature film, documentary, animation, and short film. Reflecting perhaps the transformation in local filmmaking practice, a master-class in special effects was given by Industrial Light & Magic's Colin Flavin, while an outreach programme to local schools brought filmmaking into the classroom, itself a indication of the Nerve Centre's continuing commitment to film education and training.[24] The 2005 festival[25] celebrated its twentieth anniversary and introduced the Stella Artois Film Awards in five categories, while in November 2007, the festival, with the prefix of principal sponsor Seagate (also sponsors of the 2006 festival), included workshops and was regarded as a 'very creditable contribution to contemporary Irish exhibition practice.'[26] By then the Nerve Centre's Bernie McLaughlin had taken over as programme director.[27] The twenty-third annual festival took place in November 2010, and continued its policy of screening a broad range (classic, themed and new) of international as well as Irish films at a number of venues[28] and of bringing the top film and cinema industry professionals to Derry, alongside other events, including education and outreach programmes, and master-classes and workshops.[29]

Belfast Film Festival (2000–)

Belatedly in 2000 Belfast established a film festival, though its origins date back to 1995 and the West Belfast Community Arts Festival, and its offshoot, the West Belfast Film Festival. However, when the Belfast Film Festival started in 2000 it sought to ensure that it would reach beyond the republican constituency of west Belfast. While Belfast, like all film festivals, seeks to show a selection of well known recently made feature films, it has continually sought to highlight a distinctive strain of engagement that might feed into or complement the transformation of Northern Ireland in the context of the Good Friday agreement of 1998. Therefore, since its beginnings, the festival has presented a series of films exploring a political theme that could have relevance to the local situation, with topics including 'Reconciliation and divided societies' (2000); 'Ulster Protestant identity on film' (2001);[30] 'Irish women filmmakers'; 'Human rights on film' (2004);[31] 'Racism' (2005); 'Societies in transition: policing for the people' (2007); 'Memory, truth and transition' (2009); and 'Policing and the people' (2010).

This emphasis on 'politics and general socio-political issues' has given the festival 'an identity' according to festival director Michele Devlin, while its commitment to documentary practice, another distinguishing element of the festival, led it to name an award after the renowned American documentary filmmaker and cinematographer Albert Maysles. Following a serious setback when a fire destroyed its offices, 2005 saw the festival expand as a result of new capital from the European Union, the department of social development, and Arts Council of Northern Ireland, which enabled a move to new offices in the Cathedral Quarter and the launch of a fifty-seat digital studio cinema. With venues for the 130 events, in which more than twenty countries were represented, 'at all compass points in the city', the fear of political sectarianism was alleviated.[32] By the sixth festival, it had achieved 'a level of permanence' such that 'its growing international stature' gave it access to an increasing number of premieres,[33] while its seventh season in March–April 2007,[34] during which over 130 films were screened across almost a dozen venues, surpassed all of its previous efforts in terms of audience figures; indeed, less than half-way through the eleven-day event the total admissions record was broken. Noting that the Maysles' documentary competition and Jameson shorts' competition had become integral elements of the festival, Michael Open in his 2007 festival report commented that the overall programme quality was 'much higher' than previous years.[35] Nevertheless, the eighth Belfast Film Festival boasting 125 events and representation from thirty-two countries promised the 'most innovative and expansive programme to date'. In addition to screenings of Irish, UK and European premieres, Oscar-nominated films, local short films, and international documentary competitions, a wide range of special events, including the ever-popular drive-in movies, an evening of cinema and cuisine, workshops, master-classes and special guests, the programme also offered the web-based initiative Movieoke (where audiences bask in the spotlight), and Oska Bright, a film festival by and for people with learning disabilities.[36] By the time of its ninth festival in 2009, there were 130 screenings from thirty countries over ten days in March/April, indicating that Belfast had found its niche in the international film festival calendar,[37] while in 2010, when the festival celebrated its tenth birthday it was further extended to sixteen days during which no less than thirty UK/Irish premieres were screened. As a way of supporting filmmaking in Northern-Ireland a two-day seminar was held in conjunction with Northern Ireland Screen, 'Northern Exposure = Deal Closure'.[38]

There is, of course, a second festival in the city – the Belfast Festival at Queen's – which celebrated its forty-eighth event in October 2010. While it attracts 60,000 visitors annually, and incorporates music in all genres, film, theatre, dance, visual arts, talks and family events, in recent years, the importance of the film strand has become somewhat diluted and less significant.[39]

(b) Other film festivals, including youth, regional, thematic and new media.

Besides the major festivals at Cork, Dublin, Galway, Derry and Belfast, a plethora of other specialized film events sprang up in the 1990s and 2000s, many of which operated and continue to be operate at a modest local level and use video or DVD. The majority of these have been thematically or generically organized such as the many already mentioned run by the IFI and access>CINEMA, with the Cork French Film Festival run by the Alliance Française Cork and the Triskel Arts Centre, operational since 1990, the twenty-first of which was held in March 2010, exemplary. Many other such thematically or generically run events, including the animation festival Féile Beochan, which had its first event in Kilkenny in September 2005,[40] and Ireland's only maritime film festival held on Tory Island, Co. Donegal, which held its fourth annual festival in July 2008,[41] however, have proved not to be so long lasting.

Youth film festivals
A number of these other festivals have been age-specific in terms of the target audience and/or the age of the filmmakers. Since 1989, for example, Belfast has played host to Cinemagic,[42] 'the largest film and television event for young people [aged 4 to 25 years of age] in the UK and Ireland',[43] while during the 1990s Dublin presented the Dublin Junior Film Festival. Though this latter festival subsequently fizzled out, April 2008, saw the beginning of the Dublin Coca-Cola Cinemagic Film and Television Festival for Young People, a sister event to the Belfast festival held in November,[44] while in July 2008 the inaugural event of IFI's 'Lights Out!' National Film Festival for Young People (5-to-16 year-olds) took place in the capital, before travelling to six provincial venues.[45] Outside Dublin and Belfast, the Galway Junior Film Fleadh has operated since 1994, the seventeenth of which was held in November 2010;[46] while in an extension of the schools' video competition begun in 1997 as part of Limerick's Irish Film Festival, started in 1995,[47] the Fresh Film Festival, confined to filmmakers (including in the digital format) under-18 year-olds, was established in 1998. Screening up to 200 films, this competitive festival, like other film festivals aimed at under-18s, also offers a strong workshop and educational element with master-classes given by practitioners in various areas of filmmaking and scriptwriting and through the provision of study guides.[48] Another film festival – the FÍS film festival – though aimed at even younger filmmakers, developed from a government educational initiative, launched in March 2000. Designed to encourage primary school children (generally under-12 years-of-age) to make films, the department of education and science introduced a three-year pilot film-training programming, which was managed and delivered by the National Film School, Dún Laoghaire Institute of Art, Design and Technology. Following its success, the scheme under the control of the National Centre for Technology in Education in conjunction with NFS, DLIADT, was mainstreamed such that, in 2004, fifty schools participated, with a further twenty-five schools added in 2006, while in 2007 over 100 schools took part, a figure similar to that for 2009/10. In 2010, the Fís Film Festival went online (FFF10), although the annual screen exhibition venue of the Helix, Dublin City University, remained.[49]

Regional film festivals
New regional film festivals have been established in a number of counties, including in Clones, Co. Monaghan. Launched in 2001, the Clones Film Festival takes place

annually over the October public holiday and has continued to grow with its educational and interactive workshop aspects further expanded in 2010.[50] An important part of this festival, which also caters to children and uses the Cinemobile, is its Scanbitz short film challenge whereby practitioners are invited to make a short film over the duration of the festival. The same year as Clones established its festival, described by one of the festival's directors as having a 'great buzz' not dissimilar to Galway twenty years ago,[51] Laois also inaugurated their highly successful annual arts festival (including film, music, theatre, dance, exhibitions and workshops).[52] Waterford followed soon after and in November 2007 presented its first dedicated and competitive Waterford Film Festival when over seventy films were screened and over 80 per cent of the featured filmmakers from Ireland, the UK, Spain and New York attended.[53] (Prior to 2007, as part of the Waterford Arts Festival, which celebrated its fifth year in 2007, films had been shown in a festival context under the banner of Imagine.)[54] Also in 2007, Limerick saw the launch of a new annual festival for Irish film – the Tiger's Eye Film Festival – based at the University of Limerick,[55] the success of which was repeated in March–April 2008, when winning entrants of the Fresh Film Festival were screened. By then, Kerry had also established its own festival.

This latter festival, which has proven to be a more substantial affair, was founded in 1999 by Maurice Galway as a collaborative venture between An Samhlaíocht, an arts promotion organization, the Rose of Tralee Festival and Kerry county council. After the 2000 event was positively received, the festival was expanded throughout the county, often using the Cinemobile to visit locations without a cinema.[56] (Its sixth festival in 2005, for example, used eight locations, including Killarney, Listowel, Tralee and Dingle.[57] On that occasion it screened 200 short films from no less than eighteen countries with five Palestinian filmmakers in attendance.) Now known as the Samhlaíocht Kerry Film Festival and held in October/November, the festival has distinguished itself through showing much non-western cinema in its programme and by focusing on young filmmakers seeking greater exposure for their work. Its eight festival in 2007 under new management with Jason O'Mahony, previously of the Sundance and San Francisco film festivals, as artistic manager, saw admission figures double in relation to 2006,[58] while the number of entrants for its short film competition for young filmmakers continued to rise. In 2008 it attracted 400 entries, more than double that of previous years; in 2009 this rose to close on 500, while in 2010 there were over 500 hopefuls. The competition's adjudicators have included Mike Leigh, Jim Sheridan, Gabriel Byrne, John Carney, Liam Neeson, Kirstin Sherian, Jeremy Irons, Michael Fassbender, Simon Brown, and James Christopher.[59] In 2008 it launched its Maureen O'Hara award for women who have excelled in film, with the winners including Brenda Fricker (2008), Rebecca Miller (2009) and Juilette Binoche (2010). On the occasion of its tenth event in 2009 Rebecca Kemp in *Film Ireland* commented that not only did it continue to 'hold its own with an impressive short film programme' and succeed in 'securing the participation of movie heavyweights', but also it 'remain[ed] one of the few local festivals that embraces venues throughout the county, and successfully marries a conventional film programme with experimental cultural events.'[60] According to artistic director O'Mahony, 'after the 3 big festivals in Galway, Cork and Dublin, we like to think of ourselves as being the biggest on the next tier, in terms of the audience that comes.'[61]

Meanwhile, in September 2007, Dingle itself held a festival independent of the Kerry Film Festival using venues that ranged from the traditional cinema (the Phoenix) to the local church. Organized by Maurice Galway (director) and Tom Hogan (festival coordinator), the event, which featured a short film competition, was deemed to have successfully 'held its weight with a strong programme and exceptional special guests', including Alan Parker and Sarah Miles.[62] The guests at the 2008 Dingle Film Festival were Cecilia Peck, whose father, the Oscar-winning Gregory Peck (who had family connections with Dingle) was been honoured, and Ireland's Gabriel Byrne. The festival's special (Gregory Peck) award in 2009 went to Irish director Jim Sheridan, while in 2010, when the festival's special guest was actor Cillian Murphy, the award was given to Stephen Frears.[63] Motivated by the fact that its September date had clashed with Toronto, something which made the securing of Irish prints difficult, the 2010 event took place in March, a move which seems to have positively impacted on the box office, as its takings doubled in relation to September 2009. In any case, the festival, which presents both new and archival film from Ireland and around the world, aims to be the only film festival in Ireland to be led by its workshop programme, which features experts from the film industry.[64]

Other regional festivals include the non-competitive Mid-Ulster Film Festival, which began at An Creagán Centre, near Omagh, Co. Tyrone, in 2004 and is devoted to independent cinema and showcases a diverse programmes of features, documentaries, shorts, animation, workshops and seminars, though the 2010 event was cancelled due to lack of funding;[65] the Sound + Vision festival, Ballina, Co. Mayo, whose 2006 event included films on rock band Velvet Underground and a workshop on making music videos, while the 2009 event focused on Bob Dylan;[66] and the Guth Gafa Documentary Film Festival, Gortahork, in west Donegal, which, began in 2006 and unusually stipulates that directors must attend and be available for post-screening discussion. In June 2010, this latter festival enjoyed sell out screenings for nine of its thirty-five films and an average attendance of no less than 70 per cent capacity.[67] Several other festivals have operated, including the Navan Film Festival, which, established in August 2005, seems to have disappeared by 2007.[68] Similarly, the Temple Bar Film Festival, which began in 2006, when it featured Irish-made features, shorts and documentaries, and Dundalk's Cinergy Film Festival, organized by the Louth, Newry and Mourne Film Commission, which took place in February 2007,[69] also appear to have been unable to realize their ambitions to become a permanent fixture on the arts calendar.[70]

Short film festivals

Festivals dedicated exclusively to shorts have also developed, though many of these proved to be transitory. For example, Ireland's first digital short film festival, the Sligo Short Film Festival, the first of which was held in September 2005,[71] seems to have quickly vanished as an independent festival almost as soon as it arrived, but in any case by 2010 the county was being served in that regard by the Lightbox (animation

41 The Volta Cinema, 45 Mary Street, Dublin, opened on 20 December 1909 and is regarded as Ireland's first full-time cinema. Interest in the Volta has been fuelled by the involvement of writer James Joyce in the project. However, ten days after the cinema's opening Joyce returned to his home in Trieste and, it would seem, played no subsequent role in the cinema's programming.

42 On 20 December 1910, exactly a year after the opening of the Volta, Belfast's Kelvin Picture Palace, College Square East, opened. Its name was taken from the original owner of the converted premises, engineer and physicist Lord Kelvin (William Thomson) whose name is also remembered as a unit measurement of temperature. This is the earliest known photograph of a Belfast cinema and can be dated from the advertised film, the one-reel 1798 rebel story, Sidney Olcott's *Rory O'More*, which was shot in Kerry in 1911.

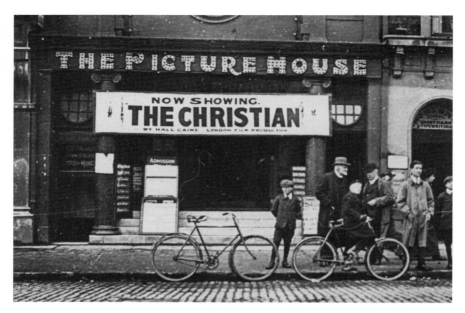

43 The Picture House, 51 Lower O'Connell Street, Dublin, was the first cinema to be located on what would become the premier street for cinemas. It was opened in 1910 by the British company Provincial Cinematograph Theatres and catered to a middle-class audience. The film, *The Christian*, an adaptation of Hall Caine's novel, dates the photograph to 1915.

44 Larne Electric Theatre, *c.*1913, with advertisement for *The Redemption of White Hawk* (1912). Visible in the car in front of the cinema, designed by John McBride Neill, are Belfast film distributor and exhibitor John Yeats Moore and Michael Curran, who would emerge by the 1930s as the province's principal exhibitor.

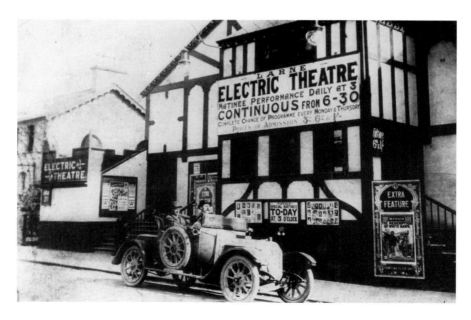

45 Dublin's 372-seat Pillar Picture House occupied a narrow four storey building opposite Nelson's Pillar. Opened on 2 December 1912, it was owned by alderman and former lord mayor John J. Farrell and was designed by Audrey V. O'Rourke, an architect who designed a number of early cinemas.

46 A middle-class venue on fashionable Grafton Street, the Grafton Picture House was opened on 17 April 1911 by the major British film exhibition company, Provincial Cinematograph Theatres, which had already opened the O'Connell Street cinema. The coach and horses were being used to promote a highwayman story set in France, *The Lyons Mail* (1931), adapted from Charles Reade's play.

47 Opened by the three Horgan brothers on 23 December 1917, Horgan's Picture Theatre, Friar Street, Youghal, Co. Cork, was typical of Irish small town cinemas and could almost be mistaken from the outside as just another shop. The cinema is seen here after having been rebuilt following a fire in 1935 which destroyed the adjoining cinema, Hurst's Picture Palace.

48 Though the paintings and decoration of Horgan's Picture Theatre pale in comparison with the highly ornate first-run urban cinemas, nonetheless they offered a degree of opulence when much of Irish society was marked by a sparseness. The cinema could accomodate about 600 patrons.

49 The sumptuous interiors, referred to as 'atmospherics', in the Savoys in Dublin (1929), Cork (1932) and Limerick (1935) were among the most luxurious and exotic in the country. This image shows Cork's Savoy, which had a Venetian theme, included a painted safety curtain and frescos on the walls, while the proscenium arch was imagined as a Venetian bridge complete with 'Romeo and Juliet' balcony. (It had an art-deco exterior.)

50 Built on the derelict site of the Metropole hotel, O'Connell Street, destroyed during the 1916 Rising, the Metropole, opened on 11 February 1922 with the design by Audrey V. O'Rourke, who also designed the Pillar and Phibsborough Picture Houses. Its domed ceiling was decorated with scenes from William Shakespeare's plays. The Metropole had a restaurant (first floor), a ballroom (second floor) and employed a full orchestra.

51 Slick exterior of the *c.*1,000-seat Regal, Bridge Street, Portadown, with long vertical windows, one of the many cinemas built in Northern Ireland in the 1930s, most of which were in the International Style. The cinema continued for over fifty years.

52 Comfortable interior of the Regal, Portadown, with the walls decorated with pastoral scenes. Such paintings, and indeed the more luxurious atmospherics, fell out of fashion in the 1950s. While imitative of Italian frescos, they also carry a reference to the pre-cinema entertainment of the panorama, invented by Irish-born Robert Barker.

53 Exterior of the ultra-modern Ritz, Belfast. Opened on 9 November 1936 and designed by London-based Leslie H. Kemp and F.E. Tasker, it was not only the largest cinema in Ireland, but quickly became known as Ireland's Wonder Cinema. In common with cinemas internationally, it was subdivided into four screens in the 1980s, but eventually closed in 1993 as the multiplex phenomenon took hold.

54 The interior of the Ritz, Belfast, was fitted with 2,219 seats, featured a Compton organ, a café on the first floor, and a large restaurant complete with a maple floor that could be used for dancing.

55 Interior of the Jones and Kelly-designed Green Cinema, St Stephen's Green, Dublin, which opened on 18 December 1935. The impressive pure art deco style provided a sharp contrast to the sensuous 'atmospheric' design of other cinemas, notably the Savoys.

56 Art deco curved lines can be seen in the lobby of the Stadium, Shankill Road, Belfast, which opened on 16 October 1937. With a 180ft auditorium it had the longest cinema auditorium in Belfast.

57 Cafes and restaurants were an attractive feature of first run and better equipped cinemas from the beginning. This is the cafe area of the Pavilion Cinema, Cork, in the 1950s. By the end of the 1960s such areas had largely disappeared. One of the few contemporary cinemas with a bar-restaurant is Dublin's IFI complex.

58 The interior of the Cameo Cinema, Military Road, Cork (formerly the Bellevue Cinema, and Gaiety Ballroom) which could double as a dancing venue. It was the first Cork cinema to introduce late night screenings, but a lack of attractive films forced owner Seamus Quinn to convert the venue into a disco in 1983 before fully closing it in 1985.

59 The 'cinema' fire in Co. Limerick's Drumcollogher on 5 September 1926 caused the deaths of forty-eight people. The accident occurred when nitrate film caught fire during a film show in an unlicensed room on the upper floor of a two-storey wooden shed on Church Street, the ground floor of which was used as a store for timber and glass. The photograph shows the aftermath of the fire with rows of coffins lining the walls of the burnt out building.

60 While the Drumcollogher fire was the only cinema fire in Ireland to have resulted in fatalities, a great many cinemas were damaged or destroyed by fire even after the highly combustible nitrate film ceased to be used. In this case, a fire brigade, having done its job, remains on duty outside the Park Street Cinema, Dundalk, after it was gutted on 21 February 1961.

61 With the decline in cinema-going from the late 1950s onwards, a great many cinemas were converted to other uses, notably large retail outlets such as supermarkets, carpet showrooms and furniture stores. Others were pulled down to make way for new buildings, such as the Capitol, O'Connell Street, Dublin, above, which having closed in March 1972, was torn down along with the adjoining Metropole Cinema to make way for a department store.

62 In 1999, Athlone's Ritz Cinema, perhaps the finest cinema outside Dublin in the international modern style and which operated from 1940 to 1984, was knocked down to make way for an apartment block and other facilities.

63 Meeting House Square, Temple Bar, described as Dublin's 'first truly modern square', being used to screen late-night movies. The square is bounded by institutions devoted to still and motion picture archiving and presentation including the Irish Film Institute and its archive, the Gallery of Photography, and the National Photographic Archive.

64 Movie Junction, Fota retail park, Cork, opened in November 2010, as Ireland's first such permanent venture. Though the hey-day of (American) drive-in cinemas past almost fifty years ago, Movie Junction with its sloping site, allowing each car an unobstructed view of the 17m x 20m screen, offers a perfected drive-in experience suited to Irish weather: an in-car heater in each of the hundred parking bays, all of which are complete with an individual canopy to protect the car's windscreen from rain.

65 The Irish Film Institute transformed the Society of Friends/Quakers' Meeting House at 6 Eustace Street, Temple Bar, Dublin, into the national centre for film culture in Ireland. Opened in September 1992, the complex currently includes three cinemas – the larger of which (above) was adapted from the Quaker Meeting Room – the Irish film archive, a library, a film book/DVD shop, a restaurant and a bar.

66 The sumptuous postmodern nine-screen Eye Cinema, Galway, opened in 2005. Locally owned and operated, the cinema's design incorporates a 100 metre curved glass wall which in effect becomes a kind of reality screen for those outside. While offering the usual multiplex fare, it has also created the notion of a cinema within a cinema through its 'art house screen' dedicated to alternative non-mainstream films. As well as bar and café areas, it has an ice cream parlour.

67 Given that the sale of over-priced sweets and over-sized portions of popcorn and soft drinks accounts for as much as one quarter of cinemas' revenue, unsurprisingly concession areas have increased in size with a recent trend emerging whereby manned dedicated ticket sales areas have been abolished in favour of combining ticket sales with food sales, no doubt to cut staff costs while also encouraging the sale of over-sized unhealthy foods. This large tiled ornate lobby area is located at the fourteen-screen Vue multiplex, Liffey Valley, Dublin, which opened in 1999.

68 A stairway at the postmodern and lavishly designed multiplex, Movies@Dundrum, Dublin, complete with art deco elements, as seen in the mirror and surround, which opened in 2005. Designed by McNally Design International (MDI), it looks back to the opulence of the old cinema palaces and, combining modern features such as hard sparkling tiles with cushioned more traditional patterned carpets which feature the cinema's logo, has an overall palatte of dramatic red complemented with black and gold/yellow. It was the first cinema in Ireland to offer unique VIP and Children's Zones.

69 In 2003 UGC combined Dublin's Parnell Street multiplex, originally opened in 1995 by Virgin Cinemas as a nine-screen cinema, and the adjoining IMAX cinema, opened in 1998 and shut in 2000, and converted them into Ireland's first and only megaplex with seventeen screens/3,348 seats. It was rebranded as Cineworld in 2005 following another change of ownership.

70 Exterior of the sucessful fourteen-screen Movie House multiplex at the City Side complex, York Street, Belfast. Operated by independent exhibitor Michael McAdam since its opening in 1992, at which point it was an eight-screen venue, the cinema is part of the five-cinema strong Movie House chain.

71 Outside the main urban areas many people's experience of cinema during the first half of the twentieth century was through the periodic visits of travelling cinemas to their region. Some of these exhibitors came as part of circuses or other shows, while others, such as Dublin's Irish Animated Picture Company, Kilkenny's Ormonde family or in the northwest, Coon's (based at Letterkenny, Co. Donegal), visited towns and villages without permanent cinemas, and often used municipal and religious-owned buildings such as town and parish halls. The hazards for travelling exhibitors are reflected by an incident in April 1910 in Toomebridge, Co. Antrim, when an exhibitor showing films at a charity bazaar had his screen destroyed by audience members who objected to a religious film. It was reported that an attack on his van was narrowly averted.

72 A modern version of the travelling cinema is the Cinemobile, an import from France, two of which operate in Ireland. The cinema-truck converts in less than one hour to a 100-seat air-conditioned cinema.

short) festival. The Minicinefest short film competition, run in conjunction with the Ranelagh Arts Festival (Dublin), ran from 2006 to at least 2008, though the Ranelagh Arts Festival continues to feature a cinema strand which presents Irish made films (including shorts) while in August 2010, the Uppercross House Hotel, 30 Upper Rathmines Road, played host to the original 'café cinema' experiment, which in its third year, presented free screenings of shorts (including Irish films).[72] Similarly, the PintSize Film Festival, the first of which was held in March 2007 and in which films, in keeping with the average price of a pint €4.40, were limited to 4 minutes 40 seconds appears not to have continued beyond its first year. (Fittingly, the venue for this smallest of small film festivals was Dublin's smallest bar, the Dawson Lounge.) A film festival dedicated to even shorter shorts of exactly twenty-five seconds in length (with five seconds given over to the opening credits, fifteen to the main film and five to the closing sequence) was imagined in Northern Ireland as the 15 Second Film Festival (the cinema of distraction) which tours film, arts and music festivals in Ireland, Britain and Europe. In 2009 this traveling microfilm festival received £50,000 from the creative industries innovation fund and a further £25,000 (towards a touring vehicle, a two-seater art deco picture palace, the 'mini-mogul') under the equipment grant scheme, administered by the Northern Ireland Arts Council and department of culture, arts and leisure.[73] Finally, one of the youngest of the short-based festivals is the Corona Fastnet Short Festival, Schull, Cork, the first of which took place in May 2009. Like other such festivals it has placed an emphasis not just on the competitive aspect and the showing of an impressive number of films (over 200 in 2010), but also on encouraging the participants to take part in the various workshops and audiences with invited directors, scriptwriters and others involved in the film industry. (Past guests have included Jim Sheridan, Gerry Stembridge and Steve Coogan.)[74]

Ethnic film festivals
Festivals, however, have not just been informed by formal or generic parameters; indeed, quite a few festivals have emerged to reflect the changing constituency and cultural diversity of Ireland's citizens. Cavan had its first such event in September/October 2007 with the Ramor Film Festival, which had as its focus social change as depicted in Irish film, with particular emphasis on emigration and immigration, and, alongside screenings of germinal and recent films, featured workshops in critical analysis, the Irish language on film, scriptwriting, filmmaking and animation.[75] At the beginning of 2008, Limerick's Belltable Arts Centre and Doras Luimní, a support group for asylum seekers, refugees and migrant workers, presented the first World Witness Film Festival which showed over four days a selection of international films inspired by human rights issues; while, in June 2008, Galway One World Centre, Galway Film Society and the Huston School of Film and Digital Media held Galway's first ever African Film Festival, which, funded by Irish Aid, was free of charge to all and took place in the Town Hall Theatre. While previously a Dublin African Film Festival (DAFF) had been established with screenings in Cineword,[76] the distinction of being the first African film festival in Ireland lies with the Carlow African Film Festival, founded in September 2005 by Ade

Oke, and supported by access>CINEMA and the Arts Council. Promoting social cohesion and integration, it has offered screenings (35mm since 2006 of around five to seven feature films); symposia (since 2007 on such topics as 'Imagining an African Irish cinema' in 2007 and 'Africa and African diasporic cinema' in 2008); workshops (since 2008, when the programme included a session on African storytelling); and has featured over the years a host of eminent African filmmakers, actors and academics.[77] Additionally, in September 2008, the first Kinofest, with exclusive access to the films shown at the Czech Republic's prestigious 42nd Karlovy Vary International Film Festival, took place in Westport, Co. Mayo, an area in which roughly 800 eastern Europeans are resident;[78] while in October 2010, Carrick-on-Shannon, home to a small Kurdish community, hosted Ireland's first Kurdish film festival, which was curated by Mustafa Gundogdu (one of the founders and organizers of the Kurdish Film Festival in London and New York) and funded by the Peace III programme through the European Union's regional development fund.[79]

Beyond film (including Darklight and Celtic Media Festival)
Dublin's Darklight Festival, which began in 1999, is quite different to the other, more conventional events.[80] Darklight's remit is to explore 'the convergence of art, film and technology', as its website puts it, with an emphasis on filmmakers, animators and artists. As a result, digital filmmaking in general, and animation in particular, are central to the annual event, with the selection favouring work that 'pushes technological boundaries and displays creative excellence.' As part of its rejection of traditional production and exhibition practices, it abandoned the conventional cinema setting in 2002 and took over a 20,000 square foot warehouse located in Dublin's Digital Hub. There, two cinemas, an art gallery and a lounge area hosting music, discussions and refreshments allowed for a more fluid exhibition experience and one which is as much aligned with the gallery as it is with the cinema. Nevertheless, the IFI cinemas continued to be used for screenings, and within a few years the festival had moved completely from Thomas Street's Digital Hub, favouring instead various venues around or near Temple Bar, such as, in 2008, for example when the festival was under the direction of new programme director Derek O'Connor,[81] IFI, Filmbase (near to IFI), the new Light House in Smithfield and in Dublin's 'first truly modern square', Meeting House Square (at the back of the IFI).[82] (Given that this square, with a scale very different to 'the great Georgian set-pieces', is accessible from three sides, including a connecting passageway from the IFI buildings, and has a proscenium arch stage and a retractable large screen, it essentially becomes 'an outdoor [performance] room'.)[83] In October 2010, the twelfth festival under the direction of Nicky Gogan, took as its theme 'Heroes' whereby some of the key figures associated with the festival over the previous eleven years were invited to contribute programmes, including animator David O'Reilly; art/music/technology collective Synth Eastwood; independent music promoters and producers Skinny Wolves; and film and animation history lecturer and musician Michael Connerty; documentary filmmaker and digital rights expert Caroline Campbell; and producer Katie Holly.[84] Lance Weiler, whose $900 budget horror feature film *The Last Broadcast* (co-directed

by Stefan Avalos, 1998) was screened by Darklight in 1999 and for which he was singled out by *Wired* as one of the twenty-five people reinventing entertainment, provided
the 2010 festival's keynote.[85] Elements of this eclectic mixture were included in the
Capital Irish Film Festival held in Washington DC in December 2010.

There is one further festival that should be noted: the Celtic Film & Television
Festival, originally known as the International Festival of Celtic Film (1980–1), and
renamed in 2007 as the Celtic Media Festival.[86] Established in 1980 to provide an
annual competitive environment in which films from Scotland, Ireland, Wales, Cornwall
and Brittany would be showcased, its first event was held in Scotland, while its first
Irish festival was held in Wexford in April 1982, with other Irish hostings in Newcastle,
Co. Down in 1986; Gweedore, Co. Donegal in 1990; Derry in 1994; Tralee in 1998;
Belfast in 2003, Galway in 2008 and Newry in 2010. Though the three-day festivals
screened both television material and independent productions, very quickly it became
apparent that the film cultural projects of independent filmmakers did not rest easily
with the agendas being set by television executives, especially as the latter provided
most of the funding. As a result, within a short time, the Celtic festivals came to serve
as an annual gathering of television personnel, with independents being marginalized.
Indeed, given that the events have often taken place within hotel environments rather
than cinemas has, while demonstrating to cinephiles in particular that cinema and television are two very different media, served to dilute somewhat its status as a film festival. Nevertheless, the festival provides an important platform for films and television
programmes made in the Celtic languages.

An increasing relevant issue for all film festivals, as well as cultural cinema programming more generally, is the relationship to the market, and even to the 'mundane'
issue of job creation within the 'culture industries'. As Graeme Farrow, festival director of the Ulster Bank Belfast Festival at Queen's, said about his own festival,

> the overall benefits of such a successful festival to the city from a tourism point
> of view are obvious. But perhaps more importantly [it] and the arts sector as a
> whole contribute positively to an image of Belfast as a vibrant cultural and eco-
> nomic capital, as a place that has a good quality of life and a place in which it
> is *a pleasure to do business*. Hopefully [it] prompts a little glimmer of civic
> pride. [Emphasis added.][87]

Similarly instructive in that regard is Foyle Film Festival's transformation from an event
with roots in the local and academic communities to its later configuration as part of
Ireland's North West economic strategy, whereby the Northern Ireland Business
Innovation Centre views the festival as a base from which to develop 'a recognised
world class centre for the digital multimedia industry'. This cross-border initiative,
known as Cluster.net, seeks to use the festival as part of its attempt to form a creative
industries cluster with national and international connections. The visit to the 2005
festival by special effect expert Rob Coleman, who worked on the *Star Wars* films, and
of Caroline Anderson, who was setting up a computer gaming company in the north-

west, are indicative of this change. This dilution of the cinema experience, or, for others, its broadening to encompass a range of related media, has marginalized the critical and educational role of cinema. Or, as the case is with the outreach educational programmes that have become a feature of many regional festivals, this is often confined to the technical (especially special effects) aspects of film and digital production, with little or no exploration of the film text as a creative and critical object. Nevertheless, film festivals continue to proliferate, and with at least thirty each year in Ireland, it is still only a fraction of the worldwide total, which, of course, has invaded the world of the internet and cyberspace. While in 1999 the *Irish Times* was already asking whether there were far too many film festivals in the world and even too many in Ireland, a country, which had only one film festival prior to 1985,[88] in 2007 Donald Clarke celebrated the feast of festivals noting that 'film enthusiasts in Moate, Athlone and all other midland locales will be faced with a difficult decision this weekend. Four separate festivals in four separate corners of the Republic take place over the next few days, and the choice of movies in each is notably enticing.'[89]

CHAPTER 7

Irish Catholic Film Policies in the 1920s and 1930s

'Teachers can tell the child who frequents the cinema because its imagination is so quickened that concentration at school becomes almost impossible. Therefore, on educational grounds, school children should be excluded from night shows as much as possible.'[1]

THE CATHOLIC HIERARCHY AND THE IMMORALITY OF IMPORTED POPULAR CULTURE

While it is generally accepted that the dominant figure in Irish Catholicism in the immediate post-Famine period was Cardinal Paul Cullen who, as archbishop of Armagh (1850–52) and subsequently of Dublin (1852–78), consolidated a policy of ultramontanism, whereby the centralized authority of the pope was emphasized,[2] there is less consensus as to the theological and moral influences on the Irish church, which, in turn, clearly impacted on the church's relationship with popular culture during the late nineteenth and early twentieth centuries. Some writers have highlighted Augustinianism, derived from the writing of the fourth/fifth century Augustine of Hippo, which proclaimed the essential sinfulness of man and the innate corruption of human nature,[3] as one such influence, while others have pointed to Jansenism, named after the Dutch Roman Catholic theologian Cornelius Jansen (1585–1638), who also drew his inspiration from Augustine in his major work, *Augustus* (1640).[4] Marked by a strict discipline and asceticism, Jansenism foregrounds the importance of God's Grace in the belief that it was gifted to an elect number and without which salvation cannot be achieved. Although this anti-Jesuit, largely French movement had effectively died out following the French Revolution, it continued to hold sway in some circles, including at the Catholic seminary at Maynooth where there had been a influx of French teachers following the revolution. Nevertheless, it seems that at Maynooth, Jansenism was in part confused or conflated with an institutional adaptation of its philosophy – rigorism – which has been described as 'the moral system of those who draw too tightly the reins of law in restraining man's liberty of action: those who are inclined to make precepts out of counsels and mortal sins out of venial sins.'[5]

Overarching both of these philosophies, however, was the Irish Catholic church's attitude to Protestantism. In a manner analogous to Irish nationalism's relationship to Britain, Irish Catholicism defined itself in relation to the changes within Christendom since the Reformation and the moment in the 1530s when Henry VIII renounced allegiance to the pope and he and his successors tried to force (not always successfully) those parts of Ireland under English rule to follow suit. (The whole island of Ireland only became subject to the British crown following the victories by William of Orange's forces at the battle of the Boyne (1690) and elsewhere after which more wholesale confiscation of property owned by Roman Catholics took place such that by the early eighteenth century close to 90 per cent of Irish land was owned by Protestants, though, of course, to this day only about one-quarter of the island's population is Protestant.) It is in this context that the embracing of Thomist theology and its institutional formulations in the Irish church should be understood.

While the contribution to western theology by the thirteenth century's St Thomas Aquinas largely rests on his reconciliation of Christian doctrine with the philosophy of Aristotle,[6] or the balancing of faith and reason, the neo-Thomist revival, promoted by such figures as Pope Leo XIII (1878–1903), who 'effectively' declared Thomas Aquinas 'the official theologian of the Roman Catholic Church',[7] and Pius X (1903–14), who lamented the fragmentation of the church brought about by the Reformation and decried the 'corrosive effects of Enlightenment rationalism',[8] came to be defined by an anti-rationalist hostility towards modernism. In Ireland, several influential Irish Catholic intellectuals adopted Thomism. These included a number of key figures involved in film policy such as Monsignor Michael Cronin,[9] a member of the censorship of films appeal board in the 1920s and 1930s; Limerick-born Fr Richard Stanislaus Devane SJ, who was particularly active in the 1930s and 1940s; and, not least, Dr John Charles McQuaid CSSp, who, as might be expected of a student of Fr Denis Fahey CSSp, himself a pupil of the influential proponent of the related philosophy of integralism, Fr Louis Billot,[10] and author of *The kingship of Christ, according to the principles of Saint Thomas Aquinas* (1931)[11] for which McQuaid provided a 'eulogistic' forward, considered Thomas Aquinas, as Fahey did, 'the apostle of modern times'. Indeed for these men, the thirteenth-century Dominican theologian's integration of intellectual and spiritual life in his *Summa theologica* 'provided Irish youth with an antidote to the anti-religious naturalism' arising from Martin Luther's sixteenth century-revolt against Rome.[12] Fr Devane in his book *The failure of individualism* (1948) similarly called for a return to the 'organic' Christian church of the pre-Reformation. However, as McQuaid's biographer John Feeney observes in relation to Fahey's *The kingship of Christ*, such a notion of a 'mythic Christiandom' whereby 'the social order willed by Almighty God was almost achieved in the thirteenth century – at the time St Thomas was writing' was one which inspired not just Irish Catholics but also all Catholic historians of the time.[13]

Importantly, within an Irish political and social context, such a rejection of all secular intellectual and institutional developments since the Reformation necessarily cast deep suspicion over the 'hybrid democracy' established in Ireland in 1922, given that this was seen as deriving from John Locke and Jean-Jacques Rousseau and hence tainted by English and French secular influences.[14] Thus, while the advent of independence ought, perhaps, to have been a period of triumph for the Irish Catholic church, not least in that finally the alien religion was displaced, in fact it brought unexpected doubts and new challenges to the Catholic hierarchy. Furthermore, while the church no doubt looked with confidence to a harmonious relationship with the new Free State, especially with regard to education (about which so many battles had been fought with British administrations during the nineteenth and early twentieth centuries), the Free State government did not prove as deferential to the hierarchy as might have been expected.[15] More critically, just as the church was formulating its new position and seeking to consolidate its ideological hold over its 'flock', the nation itself became fractured with the outbreak of civil war proper on 28 June 1922.

Having already supported the 1921 Anglo-Irish treaty, the Catholic hierarchy not only threw its weight behind the provisional government, which feared the possibility of an anarchic breakdown of social institutions, but also virulently attacked, even excommunicated, the anti-treaty IRA. Unsurprisingly, this had a disastrous effect on the power and unity of the church, and, as IRA activist Dan Breen remarked, ultimately served to 'save' the Irish 'from the Government of Maynooth'.

> The people were split on the issue of the Treaty but the Hierarchy went out and attacked the Republic, threw bell, book and candle at it in every pulpit in the country. And they drove one half of the people against them with the result that they never regained the power they once had.[16]

Although the church had condemned earlier groups of Irish revolutionaries, such as the republican Fenians, or the agrarian secret societies, generally those critiques had been largely limited to denouncing the methods used by such organizations or their secret nature (which was seen as an implicit challenge to the authority and importance of the church or the local priest), and not an all out attack on their objectives. Indeed, it was not uncommon for the Catholic clergy to promote alternative constitutionally based strategies through which to achieve Irish self-determination. (This found expression in early cinema in the character of the priest as represented in narratives set during 1798–1803. It can be argued that in films such as *Rory O'More* [1911], in which the priest 'sacrifices' himself to save the rebel from the scaffold, and *For Ireland's Sake* [1912], in which the priest helps to free a rebel from jail and subsequently aids his passage to America, the priest emerges as a more effective figure than the Irish rebel.)[17] Now, however, the Catholic hierarchy found itself in confrontation with the very people who had helped to secure the Catholic nationalist state, and for the first time, Irish people, rather than (exclusively) the Protestant English enemy, were responsible for Ireland's political and social disharmony, even destruction.

Against this backdrop, senior Irish Catholic leaders, clerical and lay, embraced Pius XI's 1925 papal encyclical, *Quas primas*, which fixed the last Sunday of October as the day on which Catholics were to reaffirm their commitment to the 'Kingship of

Christ on Earth', and reminded Catholics that papal teaching provided the principles on which a just social order could be built; indeed, the 1931 encyclical, *Quadragesimo anno*, focused entirely on social problems and suggested a reconstruction of the social order.[18] In response, An Ríoghacht (The League of the Kingship of Christ), a federation of Catholic study circles,[19] was formed to build up the independent Irish state 'on the lines of the Catholic national tradition but suited to modern circumstances.'[20] Founded by no less than forty members, including Éamon de Valera,[21] its programme not only included policies on economic development, the promotion of Catholic rather than state education, and the training of young people as lay defenders of the Catholic faith against communism, but also called for strict censorship with regard to the media and popular entertainment; the control of newspaper imports from Britain; and the regulation of the recently established national radio station 2RN (later RTÉ), cinemas, ballrooms and race meetings.

Under the leadership of Fr Edward Cahill SJ and by arrangement of Dr John Charles McQuaid, dean of studies[22] at Blackrock College (a private, Catholic, all boys, secondary school), the organization's first feast-day was held at Blackrock College on 31 October 1926. The congregation was addressed by Fahey, professor of moral theology at the school since 1912,[23] and by Cahill, professor of church history and lecturer in sociology at the Jesuit education centre, Milltown, Co. Dublin. A keen advocate of 'Catholic protectionism', Cahill not only promoted the idea that a conspiracy of Freemasons and Jews existed against the Catholic church,[24] but regarded film and popular culture in a similarly negative light. Indeed, in his pamphlet *Ireland's peril* published the following year, Cahill, in an echo of Fr Devane's complaints against the cinema, blamed cinema for weaning spectators away from 'the old Christian outlook and tradition'.[25] (Dr McQuaid, on the other hand, who, though in an endorsement of Cahill wrote the introduction for Cahill's *Freemasonry and the anti-Christian movement*, went on to play a central role in establishing the Catholic-controlled film institute, discussed below.)

While papal encyclicals such as *Quas primas* were addressed to the 'universal' church, bishops could articulate more parochial concerns through their annual Lenten pastorals. Moreover, these amounted to rather severe good-conduct guides and were often coloured with bombastic rhetoric and threats of damnation. In accordance with the hierarchy's rigorist morality and a pre-Reformation view of itself and its members, it was understood that these moral directives should be obeyed absolutely. Hostile to secularist and even intellectual ideas, the hierarchy regarded its 'flock' as children who needed to be guided by the church away from the potential and ever-present evils, including the anarchy of the anti-treaty forces. However, not wishing to recognize that it had been the internal divisions within the Irish Catholic nation which had fuelled the civil war, the church shifted the ground markedly from the conflict itself to an overbearing concern with 'immorality'. Thus, in 1925 the editor of the *Irish Catholic directory* summarized that 'chief among' the abuses attacked by the bishops in their Lenten pastorals of the previous year were 'women's immodest fashions in dress, indecent dances, unwholesome theatrical performances and cinema exhibitions, evil literature and drink, strikes and lock-outs'.[26] Indeed, according to the head of the Irish church, Cardinal Logue of Armagh, 'the dress, or rather the want of dress of women at the present day is a crying scandal',[27] while Bishop O'Doherty of Galway, was more general in his critique and clearly laid the blame on external influences:

> The dances indulged in were not the clean, healthy, National Irish dances. They were, on the contrary, importations from the vilest dens of London, Paris and New York – direct and unmistakable incitements to evil thoughts, evil desires and grossest acts of impurity. For the average individual these fast dances were immediate occasions of sin.[28]

Although such views were not unknown in the pre-independence period, in the wake of the establishment of the Free State, the church was desperately in need of a foil in order to better define and control its community and it was the diffuse notion of the 'immorality' of imported pastimes – dancing, reading, and the cinema in particular – which proved most convenient and effective. As such, the contrast between Irish-Irelander culture and foreign pastimes in Bishop O'Doherty's pastoral became an increasingly common feature of the bishops' pronouncements as the decade progressed. Dr James McNamee, bishop of Ardagh and Clonmacnoise, in his very first pastoral in 1927, for example, declared that

> the danger to our national characteristics was greater now than ever. The foreign Press was more widely diffused amongst us; the cinema brought very vivid representations of foreign manners and customs; and the radio would bring foreign music and the propagation of foreign ideals. Those new inventions had their uses, but they had also their disadvantages, being new and powerful agencies of *anti-nationalism* and perhaps of *denationalisation*. [Emphasis added.][29]

Dr McNamee recommended that 'a powerful antidote to the pleasure-seeking spirit of the time' lay with the 'Gaelic movement' and its ideals, which he argued 'exercised an elevating influence on the young people.' Similarly, a joint statement from the bishops in 1925 had commended as a form of healthy entertainment Irish dances noting that they 'cannot be danced for long hours'.[30] Not only would such vigorous, physically-exhausting dancing presumably ensure an early end to the night's entertainment, but also unlike many other forms of popular dance, Irish dancing was more open to family or cross-generational engagement, offered less sexualized or erotic display of the body, and allowed for little interplay or physical intimacy between the sexes. Nevertheless, Dr McNamee and the other bishops were indulging in wishful thinking if they thought that imported pleasures would be given up voluntarily.

No matter how often they denounced imported mass media and entertainments, even if they increasingly shifted the emphasis towards issues around nationalism, their advice was largely ignored. The failure of their exhortations was starkly revealed in the joint pastoral read in all churches on 2 October 1927. Though the pastoral, issued in the wake of the Maynooth synod of August 1927, which had been devoted to twenty-five years of 'spiritual stock-taking', looked forward to the day when 'Irish standards [would] be adopted in apparel and in amusement' it cautioned that

> The evil one is ever setting its snares for unwary feet. At the moment, his traps for the innocent are chiefly the dance hall, the bad book, the indecent paper, the motion picture, and the immodest fashion in female dress – all of which tend to destroy the virtues characteristic of our race.[31]

According to the bishops, these temptations had been allowed to grow because of 'a loosening of the bonds of parental authority, a disregard for the discipline of the home, and a general impatience under restraint that drives youth to neglect the sacred claims of authority and follow its capricious way.'[32]

In the same month in which the Maynooth synod had convened, Dr Thomas Gilmartin, archbishop of Tuam since 1910, presented a more insidious account of Ireland's transformation when he spoke at the opening of the Mayo Féis (or festival) at Westport. Extending the discourse beyond the much rehearsed, ultimately unproductive and ever more desperate attacks on imported entertainment and fashion, which more-over incoherently mixed plaintive tones with threatening demands, he included in his critique, a consideration of the everyday, increasingly marked by technology and a move away from the private to the public sphere. In so doing, he struck at the roots of moder-nity, making visible through a series of antimonies, the pull of the desire-filled, secular body electric.

> [C]heap foreign products of machinery have taken the place of the solid and lasting work of the Irish hand. Instead of milk and porridge, we have repeated doses of strong tea and white bread. Instead of socks and stockings made of Irish wool, we have foreign importations of imitation silk to minister to the vanity of our girls. Instead of visiting and story-telling, there are cinemas and night-walking, often with disaster to virtue. Instead of Irish dances we have sensuous contortions of the body timed to a semi-barbaric music. Instead of hard, honest work there is the tendency to do little for big wages.[33]

Cardinal MacRory, writing three years later, expanded this anti-modernist tirade to take in bicycles and other means of transport that allowed boys and girls to travel 'great distances to dances, with the result that a dance in the quietest country parish may now be attended by undesirables from a distance'.[34] (It would appear that even 'nice' young men and women were liable to become 'undesirable' or free when not sub-ject to the necessarily limiting surveillance of the local village, and given outsiders often carry a level of attractiveness or a touch of the exotic, such visitors, potentially, were more threatening to the moral and social order than locals.) It would seem then that foreigners, or vectors of difference, which inevitably affect a modifying influence on a community and endanger its integrity or identity, no longer were defined as exclusively coming from abroad, particularly England or America, but might equally come from adjoining or nearby parishes. In the same year, 1931, Dr Daniel Mageean, bishop of Down and Connor, in more apocryphal language and using imagery similar to that found in contemporary horror films such as *Nosferatu*, refocused the threat to the more definable and ultimately less challenging, but ideologically loaded area of (imported) entertainment. He warned that 'immoral papers and magazines, seductive novels, pornographic literature, obscene pictures and plays, are emissaries of Satan, assassins sent out by the devil to take the supernatural life of the soul.'[35]

While such concern, voiced largely during the 1920s and 1930s, about the importation, if not production, of immoral popular culture, was not confined to Ireland as evidence from, for example, the 1923 thirty-five-nation conference on the international distribution of 'obscene' literature held at Geneva and the national restrictions elsewhere on dances, publications and the cinema, a number of factors coalesced to heighten the perception of Ireland's vulnerability to external influences. These included Ireland's status as an English-speaking country; its peripheral position in the English-speaking world; its historical, social and economic relationship to England and to America; and its relational or oppositional definition of itself in terms of its colonial past. Perhaps more important than any of these was the need by the Catholic clergy and others to identify or create an external enemy that would serve to displace the focus away from uncomfortable internal questions. Therefore, it hardly mattered to the Irish Catholic clergy that the alleged and much hyped 'descent' into a Godless materialism or consumerism did not accord with the reality. On the contrary, many people in Ireland, both in rural and in urban areas, lived an almost 'pre-modern' existence in terms of access to technology, wealth or leisure time, as was readily apparent in their dress and the relatively low per capita rate of cinema-going, which was considerably less than Britain's.

In other words, the condemnation of 'selfish' pleasure gratification and popular culture in general, was merely a vehicle for asserting a particular form of conservative Catholic thinking in Irish society at a time of uncertainty and instability. Though the issue of the immorality of popular culture abated somewhat in the 1930s when the themes of communism as an evil and support for Francoist Spain came to the fore, cinema and dancing continued to feature prominently in the bishops' pastorals during the decade. Throughout this time, and complementary to the rejection of imported mass popular commercial culture, the Irish Catholic hierarchy sought to promote the pastimes of the Gaelic Athletic Association (GAA) and other 'Irish national' organizations, which were often informed by the Irish-Irelander ideals of a pre-modern Irish pastoral nation. In this way the Irish bishops set the context through which further restrictions on popular culture were introduced into Irish society. It only remained for Catholic activists to take up the cause and, as the decade prior to independence had shown, there were many well-organized groups ready to respond to the challenge.

FATHER RICHARD DEVANE'S CRUSADE FOR AN IRISH FILM INSTITUTE

As acknowledged by Fr Devane, the most articulate and dynamic campaigner with regard to seeking restrictions on imported entertainments, the bishops' pronouncements, most especially their Lenten pastorals, provided the impetus for the renewal in the 1920s of the campaigns against foreign popular entertainments and the imported press in particular. Though Fr Devane's engagement with 'evil literature' dated back to 1911 and the original campaign in Limerick, it was not until some years after his joining of the Jesuits in 1918, or, for that matter Ireland's achieving of independence, that he came to national prominence. In 1925, the minister for justice, Kevin O'Higgins, who had already introduced national film censorship following a meeting with a group of interdenominational anti-cinema activists in February 1923, agreed to meet a two-person deputation from the Priests' Social Guild seeking legislative restrictions on imported newspapers and magazines.[36] While one of the 1925 delegates was Fr John Flanagan, a member of the successful 1923 deputation, the other was the articulate Fr Devane who, using the pronouncements of the hierarchy as his bedrock, tirelessly promoted publications' censorship in the Catholic intellectual press[37] while encouraging popular campaigns against imported media.

In 1926, responding to the agitation, the government established the committee of enquiry on evil literature. While the committee heard testimony from organizations such as the Irish Vigilance Association, the Catholic Truth Society and the Irish National Teachers' Organization (INTO), it also invited a contribution from Fr Devane as a private individual, the only person afforded such an honour. Though he advocated the prohibition of birth-control literature and an 'improvement' in the definition of 'indecency' (one of the criteria, along with obscenity and blasphemy, which had been incorporated into the Censorship of Films Act 1923), unlike many of the other contributors to the hearings, he opposed the regulation of (foreign) reporting on judicial proceedings (often fertile ground for the salacious treatment of [British] divorce and other ideologically contentious court cases), and the state licensing of booksellers. However, given that he had been part of the vigilante activities of seizing and burning newspapers in Limerick in 1911,[38] he was not opposed to these more strict policies *per se*. Rather, he recognized that for regulation to be successful it needed the unanimous compliance by booksellers, and as this could not be guaranteed, he proposed that a more effective means of control would be the imposing of heavy tariffs on imported magazines and newspapers.[39] This he argued would have the result of reducing the commercial viability and, hence, circulation and negative effect of such material, while simultaneously serving to generate an income stream that could be used to fund the publication of Irish manuscripts.

With a position at once repressive and sophisticated, evident in his appreciation of how international taxation precedents might be used to achieve a Catholic and cultural nationalist agenda, Fr Devane, in the words of one media academic, 'truly reflected the mood of the activists of the period'.[40] While it transpired that a tariff on the imported press was not included in the Censorship of Publications Act 1930, it was introduced shortly afterwards in the 1932 Finance Act, though its inclusion in the finance act meant that it was vulnerable to each year's budgetary and ideological fluctuations. Despite having achieved a measure of success, Devane continued to warn against the imbalance between the volume of imported publications and Irish publications. As is clear in his article, 'The menace of the British press combines', published in *Studies*[41] shortly after the government established the censorship of publications' board in 1930,[42] he was particularly disturbed by the potential dominating power of British 'combines', an issue that he returned to in his campaigns regarding the cinema.

In tandem with his interest in imported publications, he campaigned for restrictions on dance halls, a recurring concern of the bishops, and acted as an adviser to the hierarchy as they pressurized the government into passing the measures that were finally introduced in the Public Dance Halls Act 1935. By this time, with restrictions having been imposed on three main areas of concern – cinemas, publications and dance halls – Fr Devane, established as the leading Catholic intellectual interested in imported mass culture, and with a formidable reputation both as an activist with practical remedies for restrictions on the imported media and as an articulate and well-informed commentator, began to pay more attention to the potential for the 'positive' use of cinema in 'national life'. While such an appreciation of cinema was rare within Catholic circles during the inter-war years, an even earlier exception to the almost universal mainstream Catholic hostility to the cinema was the setting up of the Catholic Educational Cinema Company in late 1921 by Fred A. Jeffs, 3 College Green, Dublin. Though the extent of its activities has not been determined, it distributed films (presumably those of a Catholic orientation) to schools, convents, hospitals, and other institutions, as well as providing projection equipment and an operator.[43]

Fr Devane's first major foray into the area of cinema was in early 1935 when he somewhat successfully hijacked an anti-cinema controversy being mounted by the *Irish Press*, Fianna Fáil's national daily newspaper. The campaign, which in part had been motivated by Fianna Fáil's attempt to jettison its radical past and reinforce its fidelity and subservience to the Catholic church, apparent at least from June 1932 when the Eucharistic Congress took place in Dublin, began with an editorial on 23 January 1935. Prompted, perhaps, by a series of recent newspaper reports concerning a public hearing of the industrial schools' commission, a government enquiry, at which its chairman, Mr G.P. Cussen, a senior district court judge, blamed the increase in crime by boys as 'largely due to the pictures',[44] the editorial argued that the effects of the cinema were 'bad' given that films supplied 'representations of life which, from the point of view of morality and truth, were distorted, and from the point of view of taste and artistry, were deplorable.'

Although it went on to conclude that 'thorough and intelligently applied' film censorship as practiced in the Free State, in contrast to many countries, including Northern Ireland's six counties, 'performs a public service' that 'happily protect[s] against the grosser abuses of the cinema',[45] it nevertheless pressed for more stringent controls with regard to the attendance of children at the cinema. Yet, while it acknowledged that many films, though 'harmless' for adults, were unsuitable for juveniles, as the films retained, despite the censorship process, an 'underlying mentality',[46] the editorial failed to draw the obvious conclusion and call for a system of grading films through the issuing of limited, or age restrictive, certificates.[47] While the overall tone of the editorial was quite mild, especially when compared with the more vitriolic denunciations of

cinema regularly seen in the popular Catholic press and from some cultural nationalists, it provoked a response from some Dublin exhibitors which, no doubt in retrospect, they must have regretted.

On 6 February 1935, the newspaper led with the stark headline: 'AN ATTEMPT TO
SILENCE THE IRISH PRESS'. The article related how three Dublin exhibitors – the Savoy
group (control of which had passed from ABC's subsidiary Associated Irish Cinemas
Ltd the previous year to a new public company, Irish Cinemas Ltd), the Metropole
group (owned by Maurice Elliman and associates), and the Grafton Cinema (owned
by the Ellis family, a member of which was also involved in the new Savoy group) –
had withdrawn advertising from the paper in protest against the editorial.[48] The *Press*
declared that its 'readers will learn with astonishment ... of the attempt ... [by] certain
cinema companies in Dublin to silence criticism of the sort of film Hollywood and
other centres produce.' It added that while such action had little material or financial
impact on the paper, 'the principle involved could not be magnified. It is simply this:
whether certain interests in this country are to use their trading position here to endeavour *to influence the Irish attitude to moral and social questions*'[49] [emphasis added].

Seeking to steer a middle course between the two positions, the exhibitors' body,
the Irish Theatre and Cinema Association (ITCA), issued a statement, which was carried by the *Press* the following day. It declared that the organization would be taking
no action and that their members were 'very jealous of the good name of the cinema
trade in the Irish Free State, protected as it is by the strictest Film censorship in the
world'. Unimpressed, the *Irish Press* viewed the statement as 'implied approval' of the
action of the three cinemas.[50] Four days later, the paper reported that the south Dublin
city Fianna Fáil comhairle ceanntair, an assembly of representatives of all the party's
cumainn (or branches) in the area, had passed a resolution calling upon 'all citizens to
endorse the action' of the *Press* 'in advocating a clean cinema campaign' and instructed
'all Republicans of Dublin to discontinue their patronage' of the three cinemas 'until
such time as they cease their boycott of the *Irish Press*.'[51]

Whether centrally organized or not, over the following few weeks Fianna Fáil
branches nationwide, including from south Monaghan, west Connemara, and west
Wicklow, began to pass similar resolutions of support, such that, by the end of March,
more than one hundred had done so. Furthermore, several public bodies in which
Fianna Fáil had a dominant influence also came to the 'defence' of the *Press*. Limerick
county council and nearby Ennis urban district council passed resolutions of support,[52]
as did Kilkenny corporation; boards of health in Mayo, Clare and Offaly; and the
urban districts councils in Templemore, Athy and Kildare. However, interestingly not
one opposition party meeting is recorded by the paper as having passed a resolution
in its support of the paper. Indeed, domestic political tensions emerged when a Fianna
Fáil resolution in support of the paper was proposed to Dublin county council. The
chairman, Fine Gael TD Patrick Belton, described it as 'irrelevant' and ruled it out of
order declaring that if the film censor was approving unsuitable films he should be cen-
sured, while Mr Corr added that the motion was an attempt 'to bolster up' the *Press*.
Belton subsequently successfully proposed an alternative motion calling for the presi-

dent of the executive council, Éamon de Valera, to identify failings in film censorship.[53] Later, *An Phoblacht*, the Sinn Féin publication, offered a similar appraisal by characterizing the *Press*' approach to the issue as the 'manufacturing [of] one of those carefully calculated Indignation Campaigns',[54] while in the Dáil, James Dillon of the United Irish Party (later of Fine Gael), probably the sharpest-tongued parliamentarian of his generation, referred to the 'fraudulent ... agitation about indecent films' as 'hypocritical slush', the purpose of which was to get 'a little popular kudos' by 'ranging themselves on the side of the angels as super-purists', but actually 'prejudice[d] that highly respected public servant [James Montgomery] who ha[d] shown scrupulous zeal in the very delicate task entrusted to his care and implie[d] that he [was] an incompetent or negligent person.'[55]

By this time, civil war tensions had also entered the debate with independent TD (and later member of Fine Gael, a party formed in 1933 that incorporated Cumann na nGaedheal) James Coburn, offering a reminder of how Fianna Fáil members had behaved during the civil war 'when you and your associates tolerated murder in the country.' Coburn's comments drew a response from Fianna Fáil TD Michael J. Kennedy, who had been a member of the IRA during the war of independence. He declared that Coburn and the other four opponents of the pro-*Irish Press* motion were 'so blinded by political prejudices that they could not do the proper, the courageous, the manly thing' and support the resolution[56] that had congratulated the *Press* and had called for 'a stringent control of films ... in the interests of public decency and ... as a protection for the youth.'[57]

Meanwhile, on 16 February Fr Devane had entered the fray with a letter to the *Irish Press* in which he attempted to reposition the debate away from party politics, or from one manufactured as a political publicity stunt towards a meaningful intervention on film. Having noted that for all the 'much loud-throated and vigorous destructive criticism' there was 'very little' or 'practically none' of a 'constructive character', he identified what he regarded as the crucial weakness of the anti-cinema campaign: that cinema as a positive tool had not been explored within the Irish context.

> It is very difficult to understand how the obstructive and destructive influence of the cinema which impedes and negatives all our cultural efforts has never really engaged the serious attention of our national leaders, though this is one of the greatest, if not the greatest, obstacle in their way.[58]

He reported that Spain, Germany, Italy and the USSR were using cinema 'in a thoroughly organized manner, for national propagandist, educational and cultural purposes and their education authorities are in close touch and heartily co-operate with this movement'.

There was much more than 'propaganda' that attracted Devane to these particular national examples. The elevation by fascist Europe and Stalinist Russia of the pure, sculpted 'classical' body was the obverse side of those societies' repression of representations of the sexual body. Soviet socialist realism and nazi cinema had much more in common in this regard than may appear immediately obvious, while the particular brand of repressive Victorian sexuality to which Devane and other Catholic ideologues subscribed, was not dissimilar to those countries cited whose ideologies and political systems appeared, at least on the surface, to be so different. Echoing the organized sports of Germany and Russia, for Devane, the antidote to pleasure-seeking (working-class) Irish youth was exercise, specifically athletics.[59]

The timing of Devane's letter, which called on Dublin's lord mayor to convene, by way of initiating a debate on Irish film policy, an informal conference at the Mansion House, which he hoped would lead to a government commission of enquiry dealing with cinema's cultural and national aspects (a linkage he always sought to emphasize), was fortuitous. Two days earlier, the same paper published an interview with Revd Owen Dudley, founder of the public morality council in Britain, who was embarking on a nationwide Irish tour with a rally at Dublin's Mansion House. According to Dudley, despite the fact that 'Dublin never suffered from bad films to the same extent as London and other capitals, the general tone [of the films] in Dublin and elsewhere was pagan and not Christian.'[60] On 17 February, a day after Devane's letter appeared, Dudley explained why this should be the case by claiming, during his lecture at Dublin's Gaiety Theatre,[61] that the film industry was

> in wrong hands, in the hands of pagans, and therefore 90 per cent of the films they got from Hollywood and even from Britain were if not unclean, at least pagan in atmosphere.[62]

Though he contended that 'the real degradation' came 'with the advent of the talkies',[63] nevertheless, he also noted cinema's potential as an educative, propagandist weapon.[64]

A further welcoming context to Devane's letter was provided by Fr Cahill's engagement with the anti-cinema campaign through discussions at the Sacred Heart (women's) branch of An Ríoghacht. While these discussions eventually culminated in calling on An Ríoghacht to form a national association to deal with the cinema question and a resolution stating that 'the existing censorship system is at best only a palliative and does not touch the root of the question',[65] action was postponed by the organization's ard comhairle or high council until the outcome of the proposal led by Fr Devane in response to the *Press* campaign had been assessed.

Within two weeks of his letter having been published, Fr Devane had helped to organize a public meeting at the Mansion House attended by a wide spectrum of civic and religious leaders. The speakers at the meeting on 27 February besides Fr Devane were Alfie Byrne, a long time critic of the cinema and lord mayor of Dublin, 1930–39; Revd Dean Kennedy of Christ Church Cathedral; Padraig O'Keefe, secretary of the GAA and a strong advocate of national economic and cultural self-sufficiency; W.A. Scott, president of Dublin trades council; District Justice Cussen of the children's court; Dr Frank O'Reilly; Fianna Fáil TD Seamus Dobbyn; and Patrick J. O'Hagan of the Irish National Teachers' Organization (INTO)[66] who, in April 1935, went on to successfully move a resolution at the INTO annual conference calling for a meeting between ecclesiastical and educational authorities 'and others interested in the social welfare of children, with a view to hastening legislation to regulate the admission of children to cinemas.'[67] That the Mansion House gathering had already decided to seek a meeting with the government, O'Hagan's resolution was probably a means of reinforcing that demand.

Whatever transpired between these cinema campaigners and the government is not known, but from then on Fr Devane, often with allies such as the INTO's O'Hagan and John D. Sheridan (a prominent lay Catholic writer and editor of the INTO organ, *Irish School Weekly*, who proposed, following the approval of O'Hagan's motion, that Ireland should follow the German example and ban under-16s from cinemas),[68] became the public voice of the cinema campaign. Unlike earlier Catholic anti-cinema campaigns, the recent *Press* controversy, or even the negative controls being sought by the INTO, Fr Devane focused the issue in a quite different direction. In a lecture 'The cinema and nation', aired on 2RN a few months after the Mansion House meeting, Devane called for a government commission of enquiry into the cinema in Ireland, the ultimate purpose of which would be the establishment of a film institute.

The national press unanimously supported Fr Devane's proposal. Though the *Irish Times* observed that the advantages of a film institute were too obvious to be dwelt upon, it cautioned that 'there are very real dangers also' as there 'is no guarantee that [the government] will use its power wisely – a fact proved by several of the countries quoted by Father Devane.'[69] The *Irish Press* gave Fr Devane's call a predictable nationalist resonance:

> Our picture houses are completely dependent for the entertainment they provide on outside sources. The propaganda they put on their screens ... is all foreign. The ideas reflected are usually British or American and nearly always pagan as well.[70]

The *Irish Independent* also called for support for the proposal:

> It is high time that the importance of the cinema in relation to the national life, culture, and economic development of this country was investigated along the lines suggested by Father Devane.[71]

Similarly, the *Irish Catholic*, noting that 'the educational possibilities of the cinema have only been touched upon in Ireland', also endorsed the call for an enquiry. This pattern of support was repeated in other papers, including the *Catholic Standard*, which unfavourably compared Ireland to continental Europe where Catholic cinema makers thrived, and pointed out that 'we have let things slide';[72] the *Evening Mail*, which called for united church and political support, with 'earnest consideration' given to the question, 'not in grandmotherly spirit, but as practical men of the world';[73] and even the nationalist *Derry Journal*, which, citing the general thrust of economic policy in the 1930s, wrote that

The Government has already controlled industry, farm-produce, marketing, transport, yet it has left uncontrolled the cinema which is moulding the thoughts, the ideas, the minds of young and old on lines that irrespective of whatever else may be said of them, are certainly everything but Irish.[74]

Unsurprisingly, the film trade publications were not so generous in their appraisal of Devane and his aims. *To-Day's Cinema* in a sarcastic 'Open letter to Fr Devane' signed editorially as *To-Day's Cinema* was withering even in its opening line, 'You do mean well, don't you?' In dismissing the notion of a film institute with the comment 'will it be worth the bother?', it also took the opportunity to castigate the recently formed British Film Institute as ineffectual.[75] Though *The Cinema*, another British trade paper, concluded that 'there could be no possible objection to the setting up by the Government of a well-balanced committee ... to inquire into the matter in all its aspects', nevertheless, it also provided a shrewd and well-informed assessment of the likely response from the government. Without resorting to insult, it reported that while it was possible the government would be asked to appoint the commission of enquiry,

taking all things into account it may be taken for granted that the reply will be that in view of the present system being quite effective and the difficulties in the way of making changes or acting at once upon the findings of any commission appointed, the question of an inquiry or the establishment of the institute will have to be deferred for the time being.[76]

This is precisely what happened.

Meanwhile, the *Irish Press*, having achieved its objective of asserting its Catholic-nationalist credentials, had begun to withdrawn from the campaign by the early summer of 1935, having sustained a certain degree of ridicule from very different quarters suspicious of its agenda. Indeed, later in the year it even failed to give any editorial endorsement or encouragement to a number of campaigners who variously sought stricter censorship;[77] Sunday opening restrictions;[78] and the prohibiting of juveniles from attending cinema shows other than those approved by the minister for education.[79] Furthermore, in September 1935 Liam MacGabhainn began what can be regarded as the most committed and interesting film column in any Irish newspaper of the period. His presence at the *Press* allowed the paper to bury its conflict with the three cinemas. In his first column on 24 September he reviewed the films running at these cinemas in the same manner as those at other Dublin cinemas. When the agitation by exhibitors against the possibility of foreign investment in Irish exhibition began to emerge six months later, as is discussed in chapter 2, Fianna Fáil, through its newspaper, was able to rebuild its relationships with exhibitors who previously had been the object of its (ideological) ire. Unfortunately, from their perspective, the party's key economic strategist, Séan Lemass, was already moving away from the economic protectionist policies he had done so much to introduce in the 1930s.

THE STATE RESPONDS

By 1937, three different documents influenced Fr Devane's thinking on the cinema: *The film in national life*, a comprehensive look at film in all its aspects in Britain, which led, shortly after its publication in 1932,[80] to the establishment of the state-funded though relatively independent British Film Institute; the 1931 papal social encyclical *Quadragesimo anno*, which, published at the height of the worldwide economic depression on the fortieth anniversary of the first major social encyclical, *Rerum novarum*, emphasized for Fr Devane the importance of vocationalism; and the first papal encyclical on the cinema, *Vigilanti cura*, published in 1936, which provided a Catholic moral context for film. Encyclicals, though not infallible documents, were nonetheless understood as representing the 'official teaching of the Church' and, as such, all Catholics, according to Dr Cornelius Lucey, professor of ethics at Maynooth (and later bishop of Cork from 1952), were bound 'to abide by [them] loyally'.[81]

While Fr Devane advocated a film institute for Ireland similar to the British one, heavily influenced as he was by the Catholic ideology of vocationalism, fashionable, though certainly not dominant in Ireland in the wake of *Quadragesimo anno*,[82] Devane suggested that such an organization be under direct state control with representatives from a diverse number of other Irish bodies. Though *Quadragesimo anno*'s advocacy of social harmony, especially between the competing demands of capital and labour (which the encyclical proposed could be achieved by divesting the state of power in favour of local or intermediate assembles made up of 'corporatist' or vocationalist[83] groups), was welcomed by representatives of capital, in particular, as it was seen as a means of diluting or neutralizing trade union power, nevertheless, the Irish state's response was limited. Indeed, this can be clearly seen in the 1937 constitution of Ireland. While the constitution acknowledged the 'special position' of the Catholic Church in Ireland[84] and prohibited divorce,[85] it made only one concession to the promotion of vocationalism by proposing that forty-three of the sixty members of the senate or upper house would be elected along vocationalist lines. Although the senate operated in this manner for a short time, it quickly reverted to political party elections. Similarly, the recommendations of the government commissions on banking, currency and credit (1934–38), with its social Catholicism-inspired minority report, and on vocational organizations (1939–44) were not implemented, but quietly shelved. Writing on this issue with regard to the Irish Catholic hierarchy, Finín O Driscoll notes,

> the pursuit of a vocational order was in stark contrast to the conservative stance of the Irish hierarchy. The bishops concentrated more on the protection of the Catholic population against the evils of the decadent, modern world. Ireland was a Catholic state where the church had secured a privileged position during the first decade of its existence. The development of popular political Catholicism would only have undermined the power of the bishops.[86]

In July 1936, an English-language version of *Vigilanti cura* was published in London with the title *The use and misuse of films*. Divided into three sections, it also carried a preamble praising the Legion of Decency's pledge-signing campaign in the USA through which signatories committed to boycott a film deemed 'offensive to Catholic moral principles or proper standards of living.' The first section of the encyclical, 'Previous warnings recalled', complained that the agreement with the USA film industry in 1930 had not been adhered to. At that time, the encyclical reported, the industry had accepted the need 'to safeguard for the future the moral welfare of the patrons of the cinema', but yet, 'the parade of vice and crime' continued on the screen.[87] Only the campaign by the Legion of Decency could stop films 'calculated to inflame the passions and to arouse the lower instincts latent in the human heart'.[88]

In its second section, 'The power of the cinema', the popularity of the cinema among those 'who work under the fatiguing conditions of modern industry' was acknowledged. This paternal concern for the working classes was tempered by the papal view of how they spend their leisure-time:

> A people, who, in time of repose, give themselves to diversions which violate decency, honour, or morality, to recreations which, especially to the young, constitute occasions of sin, are in grave danger of losing their greatness and even their national power ... Even the crudest and most primitive minds which have neither the capacity nor the desire to make the efforts necessary for abstraction or deductive reasoning are captivated by the cinema.[89]

It contended that this power of the cinema is 'still greater' with sound cinema and where dances and variety acts 'serve to increase the stimulation of the passions.'[90] Only Catholic action, the encyclical asserted, could contain such passions.

In its third section, 'A work for Catholic action', *Vigilanti cura* rather weakly called for 'moral films'. To achieve this it proposed influencing Catholics already working in the film industry, and more specifically by insisting that its followers adhere to the yearly pledge of support for the Legion of Decency, and by establishing in each country a Catholic reviewing office under the auspices of the bishops. While it recommended that a national list of appropriate films should be published regularly for the whole nation, it added that more severe criteria might need to be applied depending on the character of the region.[91] Thus, for example, a version of a film approved by the Catholic reviewing office in the USA might not be suitable for Ireland, or even a film approved in Dublin might not be appropriate for rural Ireland. It also suggested that advice and information could be exchanged between countries and that the screening of films in parish halls could be used as economic leverage to force changes in the type of films being produced. Nevertheless, the programme of action, in a typically negative focus on controls, omitted specific proposals regarding film production. However, the parallel campaign by the Irish-American dominated Catholic church was successful in transforming Hollywood product through strengthening the industry's own self-regulatory censorship system and the strict enforcement of a detailed production code from 1934 onwards. The Production Code Administration, as the new regime was called, resulted, within a short time, in the abating of complaints, even by Irish film censors, against American films.[92]

In April 1937, two years after his 2RN lecture, Fr Devane wrote to the national newspapers (re)proposing an enquiry into the cinema in Ireland. He declared:

> We are one of the few European nations who regard the cinema as a mere play-thing or as a gift from the powers of evil, and as a consequence have done nothing positively and constructively to use it as we should. Censorship, though necessary is but a negative attitude.[93]

Once again the *Irish Times*[94] editorially endorsed Fr Devane's proposal, though it cautioned against the commission being too strictly confined, while the *Irish Press* published prominently on its editorial page an article entitled 'The cinema and the nation' by Devane.[95] Additional support for the enquiry came from the Gaelic League, which formed a subcommittee on sound films, and the Irish Film Society, operational since the previous year.[96]

Two weeks after his public statement, Fr Devane received a letter from Eóin P. Ó Caoimh of solicitors James Duffy & Co. who reported that Patrick J. Whelan, managing director of Associated Cinemas Ltd, had met with a Mr L. Harrison ('obviously a Jew'), who was in Ireland on behalf of a syndicate with the intention of purchasing forty-five cinemas. Although Whelan agreed to inform his board of the syndicate's designs on Associated Cinemas, he told Harrison that the cinemas were not for sale. On receiving this information Fr Devane wrote to President de Valera on behalf of a group, interviewed and organized by Devane during the previous weeks, which were seeking 'a governmental enquiry into the cinema and its many relations to national life.' He pointed out that due to the vulnerability of Ireland as a small country, 'a thorough enquiry [was] an absolute necessity ... if we are to derive real cultural advantage from the cinema and prevent ourselves [from] being exploited by outsiders.'[97] De Valera, who at the time was finalizing the new constitution, was too busy to meet with the proposed named delegation, which represented a highly influential cross section of religious, cultural, educational, sporting, and Irish-language bodies,[98] but his private secretary, P.S. Ó Muireadhaigh, replied to Devane suggesting that he put forward for consideration terms of reference for the proposed enquiry.[99]

A week later, Devane responded that the enquiry investigate,

> the problem of the cinema in its various relations to national life and ... examine how it can be best employed as a constructive instrument for the national moral and cultural development of the nation.[1]

Its terms of reference should be, he continued: (1) to enquire into 'the present baneful effects of the cinema on the public as a whole, with special reference to the young, and to suggest the most effective means of protection against its demoralising and dena-tion-alising influences'; (2) the potential value of the cinema in all areas of education; (3) the value of the cinema as a medium of popular education and propaganda in 'Nation Building'; (4) the production, importation, renting and booking, distribution, examination and censorship, and exhibition of films; (5) the most effective means of 'absolute control by Irish nationals of places of film entertainment, whether wholly or merely partly devoted to this object, with special reference to chain cinemas'; and (6) the advisability of setting up a national film institute, as in Belgium, France, Holland, Austria, Poland, and other countries, 'for the purpose of synthesising and coordinating all national activities in relation to the above issues.'[2]

Following de Valera's circulation on 4 June of Devane's proposals, the department of industry and commerce, perceiving a threat to its position as being centrally responsible for film production in Ireland, countered with a proposal for a small interdepartmental committee involving the departments of industry and commerce, education, finance, and justice, to investigate an Irish film production industry.[3] This informal body, it was suggested, would present a report to the minister for industry and commerce and consider whether, and to what extent, the state should usefully intervene for the purpose of introducing a film production industry. It was envisaged that the meetings of the committee would not make any serious demand on the official time of the members and that the report should be completed within a few weeks. It also indicated that it was primarily interested in film production and not the broader issues of economic control over distribution and exhibition, and the attendant moral and censorship questions that Fr Devane was keen on. Within a fortnight of outlining these alternative proposals, industry and commerce replied to the president's department concerning Devane's propositions by saying that they already had embarked on their enquiry and, thereby, implied that no further action should be taken.[4]

The department of justice, which administered film censorship and which took umbrage at the implication that film censorship needed to be examined, was more forthright in its rejection of Devane's agenda.[5] Justice reported that its minister, Paddy Ruttledge, did not wish to be represented on the enquiry, for which the terms of reference were deemed 'very general and vague'. Piqued at Devane's implied criticism of the film censor, it also stated that the few complaints that had been lodged in the nearly fourteen years of national film censorship had come, in the main, from the film trade and, as such, Ruttledge deemed that there was no need for an enquiry into this aspect of film in Ireland. As for the other points, he saw no special advantage in restricting control of the cinema industry in the Free State to Irish nationals:

> The average person engaged in the entertainment trade, whatever his nationality, is moved mainly by the desire to supply what his customers want, at the same time keeping within the law.

Similarly, the minister for finance, Seán MacEntee, was, according to J.J. McElligott, the department's secretary who replied on his behalf, unimpressed with the need for either an enquiry or a film production industry.[6] He thought that even with the production of fifty films per annum in Ireland it would only reduce by five per cent, or £10,000 per annum, the sum of £200,000, the estimated amount for film rentals. In addition, it was pointed out that if there were any restrictions on what could be imported or shown in Irish cinemas then the £230,000 in annual entertainments tax revenue would be impaired:

> The taste of the cinema-going public has over a long period been systematically developed to expect a certain type of entertainment for which no adequate substitute can be found here, and the inevitable result of failure to cater for that taste must be depleted attendances at cinemas, with consequential losses on entertainments tax. [While *The Dawn* (1936)] appealed to the National sentiment and was the first of its kind to depict with any degree of accuracy the period of Irish history it covered ... it seems unlikely that any subsequent films of a similar kind would attract the same patronage.

From an employment perspective, MacEntee maintained it could not be justified since all technicians would probably be non-nationals for many years to come. MacEntee also argued against further state intervention in film exhibition, as the current restrictions can only be justified 'on the strongest moral grounds'.

Meanwhile, the department of agriculture merely stated that it saw no actual or potential value in the use of commercial cinema for agricultural education,[7] while the department of local government and public health, equally narrow in its response, declared that public health films should only be shown under medical supervision.[8] In this largely hostile environment, on 21 August 1937 de Valera furnished his ministers with a memo, 'The cinema: suggested commission of enquiry'. Unenthusiastic about the proposal, executive council meetings on 24 August and 19 October 1937 decided to postpone any action regarding the cinema enquiry. Following his failure to convince his colleagues of the need for an enquiry, de Valera held two meetings with Devane, on 27 October and again a fortnight later. Despite a memo being circulated by the department of finance on 16 November 1937 in which both the need for an enquiry and the reformulation of Devane's terms of reference were comprehensively rejected,[9] three days later, de Valera declared himself in favour of setting up a small committee to explore issues relating to the cinema.[10]

Once more, the department of industry and commerce sought to take the lead and thwart Devane's more grandiose ambitions for the enquiry. As a result, at an executive council meeting on 21 December 1937 the minister for industry and commerce, Séan Lemass, stated his intention of setting up an interdepartmental committee with terms of reference 'which would cover substantially the points raised by Fr Devane'.[11] When the terms of reference were sent to the president's department a month later not only had Lemass highlighted film production as the primary item, but also had removed Fr Devane's more emotional language. Regardless, when shown to Fr Devane by de Valera, he declared himself satisfied and promised to send along any material that might be helpful to the committee.[12] The terms of reference of the interdepartmental committee on the film industry contained five sections covering the feasibility and cost of establishing a film industry; what financial supports should be given to such an industry as regards the use of film in education, agriculture, industry, tourism, culture and for 'general propaganda purposes'; whether there should be changes to the distribution of films in Ireland; whether ownership and control of cinemas in Ireland by non-national persons or bodies should be regulated; and whether further control of exhibition of films 'in the interests of moral, national and cultural development' was desirable, in other words, whether film censorship should be changed.[13]

The interdepartmental committee on the film industry consisted of Sean Forde, secretary of the department of industry and commerce, who was chairman; E.J.C. McEvoy, executive officer, industry and commerce, who was appointed secretary; Seoirse Mac Niocaill, general and chief inspector of secondary schools, who was nominated by education; and T.S. Kealy, assistant principal officer, who represented finance. In a move regretted by a mystified Fr Devane, justice declined to participate in the committee.[14] One of Forde's and McEvoy's first meetings was with Devane,[15] who provided the committee with reports and documents on film activities in other countries, as well as detailed proposals on what should be done in Ireland, and, as a result, was singled out in the (unpublished) report for the 'invaluable help' he gave the committee.[16] In one such memorandum to the interdepartmental committee, 'Official steps taken to control films in the National interest', probably complied in the first half of 1938, Fr Devane highlighted the film policies of a somewhat-strange selection of countries: Belgium, Bulgaria, France, Germany, Yugoslavia, Dominican Republic, Uruguay, Afghanistan, Japan and Turkey.[17] In this sixteen-point memorandum, which seems to have been circulated to sympathetic bishops ahead of a meeting of the Catholic hierarchy in June 1939,[18] and which was quoted in an article published in the *Irish Independent* in April 1939,[19] Fr Devane revealed the principal reforms he wished to see implemented. These were the establishment of a national film institute, with very wide powers, which he revealingly suggested should be named after the French National Cinema Control Board, so as not to imitate the 'English' body, that is, the British Film Institute; and a revamping of the terms under which films were censored. He also supported the establishment of an Irish film studio.[20]

Among the powers he envisaged for this new control board or institute were ones governing the regulation and distribution of all films in the country. The board would be funded by special duties on Sunday screenings, after the British model, and 'a heavy tariff' on renters' profits after a film had earned over a certain amount, 'say £400'. This drastic measure was only one of the restrictions he foresaw being imposed on renters, who were almost exclusively foreign, and non-Irish exhibitors. His concern about a 'British invasion' by exhibitors had been fuelled by the recent opening of the Adelphi, Dublin, in which John Maxwell's ABC had invested, as well as Ó Caoimh's letter, cited above, regarding the English 'jew'. To stem this tide, he proposed the introduction of cinema operating licences, a suggestion, incidentally, put forward by the Irish exhibitors in a meeting with Séan Lemass in 1936, as noted in chapter 2. Fr Devane stated that a condition of the licence, which would be issued by the film institute, should include a requirement that part of the programme be 'devoted to films of a national character'. In addition, he wanted to see the break-up of the systems of 'block-booking', 'circuit booking', 'restricted credit' and the 'barred system' and recommended that each cinema be accorded a single booking of each individual film as it would cut out 'circuit booking'.[21] He also thought it might be possible to centralize renting in the institute, or through curbing the renters. If renters did not comply, it should 'be treated as conspiracy' and result in a withdrawal of the licence or in the imposition of a fine.[22]

Besides these new institutional and legislative changes, Fr Devane sought reforms of the existing film censorship system. As outlined in an eight-page film censorship memo, 'Proposals for a censorship code in Éire', prepared for the interdepartmental committee on the film industry (and circulated to members of the Catholic bishops conference in June 1939[23]), Devane proposed that in place of the 1923 act's 'nebulous generalities about indecency, obscenity, blasphemy, and tending to inculcate principles contrary to public morality, subversive of morality',[24] Ireland introduce a version of the censorship codes that existed elsewhere, such as in America (namely, the USA Production Code, with its detailed exclusions and warnings), 'Protestant' South Africa, and 'Catholic' Quebec.[25] Such a code, he argued, would 'give absolute and detailed directions to our censors so that they can point to a specific head when they order the cutting or the rejection of a film.' Nevertheless, by way of a preamble to the code, he recommended the inclusion of 'a few general principles of censorship', including the absolute instruction that the social philosophy of life, that of the Christian faith, be held sacrosanct and most jealously guarded; that the protection of marriage and the family, as set forth in the 1937 Constitution, be observed; that the standard of censorship be fit for purpose of the 'normal Irish Christian family'; and that sympathy must never be forthcoming for violation of the moral law in any of its phases, which must always be held in respect and never deprecated.[26]

In more colloquial language, Fr Devane declared that he

> would strongly support that films in which marriage and family life is cheapened or ridiculed, or in which the merit and permanence of marriage is treated as a jest or attacked indirectly, or in which adultery and divorce are regarded as inoffensive and normal should be forbidden exhibition in this country, especially since the new Constitution has made the family the primary social cell of our society and the foundation of our state. To attack this foundation of our society and our state is anti-social and akin to the subversal [sic] of the state.

In common with film censor James Montgomery, he went on to assert that he did not believe in categorizing films for adults and children: 'I prefer a common standard, approaching somewhat the family standard.'[27] Besides the principles laid out above in relation to the family and sexuality, he gave explicit expression to deficiencies in the 1923 act identified by Montgomery in the 1920s relating to how 'national sentiments' were expressed in films. As a result, he suggested that clauses in the code should cover such issues as ensuring that nothing 'derogatory to the Irish people or the Irish character' must be shown; that 'the Stage Irishman or the setting of Irish family life in a sordid background or any scene or comment offensive to Irish national sentiment must be eliminated'; and that 'films which attack or are calculated to give offence to friendly foreign nations, or to the heads of friendly states, must not be shown.'[28]

Through two three-part series of articles published in the *Irish Independent* on film censorship (April 1939), and on the child and the cinema (May 1939, discussed in the next chapter), Fr Devane sought to elevate the public profile of his campaign and to exert pressure on two fronts. By publishing summaries of his own evidence to the inter-departmental committee he hoped to indirectly influence the government, while simul-taneously actively seeking the support of the Catholic hierarchy. The first set of arti-cles advocated six changes to film censorship. Through the introduction of a detailed code, on the Quebec model, he sought: (1) the protection of marriage, as the recent constitution transferred 'the whole basis of our social life and of our State from "the individual" to "the family" and has, moreover, imposed the obligation on the State to defend the sacred character of marriage';[29] (2) that crime, 'horrific' (after the recent changes in Britain categorizing horror films with an 'H' certificate) and cruelty films be the subject of a special clause; (3) that films calculated to lead to a breach of the peace be censored as would films that 'instruct in the methods of crime – such as lock-picking, cat-burglary, safe-breaking, counterfeiting, forgery etc.' as these lead to imi-tative behaviour; (4) political propaganda films of the 'new ideologies' (though in this clause Fr Devane seemed less concerned with communist or nazi films than with the 'anti-Fascist, anti-Nazi' 'films for democracy' being produced in the USA and else-where, which he deemed were 'camouflaged International Popular Front' propaganda and needed 'immediate action');[30] (5) the defence of national sentiment and prestige, and the need for restrictions on imported films with Irish depictions; and (6) the defence of religion. This last category sought to extend the blasphemy clause of the 1923 act with a more detailed one along the lines outlined above.

THE CATHOLIC HIERARCHY AND FILM POLICY

As noted, throughout the 1930s the Catholic hierarchy continued to regard the cinema as a source of evil, and in 1937 when Fr Devane was seeking to gain government accept-ance for a film enquiry, the bishops' pastorals, which blamed the cinema even for endemic social and economic problems in Ireland, provided a supportive context. One such pas-toral written by Bishop McNamee declared that not least among 'the sins of the cinema' was its 'breed[ing] a discontent that is anything but divine in the prosaic placidity of rural life'. Unsurprisingly then, he held cinema responsible for the emigration of Irish girls to Great Britain. These he suggested were 'lured perhaps, by the fascinations of the garish distractions of the city, and by the hectic life of the great world as displayed before their wondering eyes in the glamorous unrealities of the films'.[31]

While it is without doubt the case that the cinema provided a window, albeit one which was at times opaque, distorted or in someway contrived and deceiving, onto a world that contrasted or at the very least posed a challenge to the real and repressed life-styles of Catholic Irish men and women, it is no less true that many films of the period, even if moreover they ultimately opted for safe, speedy and improbable (non-realistic) resolutions, raised, if not always foregrounded, problematic issues around city life, capitalism and indeed the hearts or spirituality of their secular subjects. Therefore, perhaps had McNamee looked to the state of Ireland's economy, which was severely depressed with a significant minority not only property-less, but also unable to sustain, let alone reproduce, themselves materially, he may have come to appreciate that such a view was both simplistic and inaccurate..

In contrast to McNamee, most bishops tended to confine their criticisms of cinema to its effects on Catholic morality, religious observance and cinema's representations of an often-fraught nuclear family. According to Dr Mageean in his 1937 Lenten pastoral, the cinema, which, he argued, alternatively has ignored religion or been 'openly anti-Catholic', has 'for years been a danger to the faith and virtue of the young'.[32] Dr Patrick Collier, bishop of Ossory, reported that

> in town and village and country place such attractions as the cinema and dance hall have sadly broken in on the sacred union of the family evening and there are real dangers that through this the Irish tradition of the family Rosary will suffer.[33]

Two years later, the pastorals persisted in decrying 'the inordinate pursuit of pleasure' and the 'growing tendency to desert the rural areas for the towns and cities', two interlinked social evils.[34]

With such obvious unyielding support for any restrictions on the cinema Fr Devane renewed his efforts to effect changes in film censorship. In May 1939 he sent details of his proposals regarding cinema to all the bishops of Ireland, who were due to meet on 20 June, and, unsurprisingly, found within that cohort a receptive audience. Indeed, even prior to their gathering, at least seven of the twenty-seven bishops wrote to Devane asserting their agreement with his campaigns.[35] In a letter to Dr Patrick Lyons, bishop of Kilmore, with whom Fr Devane seems to have had a close friendship, he enclosed copies of the *Irish Independent* articles, and declared that parts of the American production codes could be introduced 'without changing a word'.[36] In an oblique critique of the vague and subjective wording of the Censorship of Films Act 1923, he pointed out, in what might be construed as a sectarian comment – 'there is every possibility that the next Censor will be a Protestant' – and belying his Catholic protectionist ideology, cautioned that 'we should have every Censorship safeguard we can and leave nothing to chance or mere generality.'

A week after the hierarchy met at Maynooth, the bishop of Achonry, Patrick Morrisroe, reported to Fr Devane that his submission on the cinema (and dance halls, another of his concerns) had received a 'good deal of attention',[37] with the bishops adopting a film censorship policy along the lines proposed by Fr Devane 'with but a few verbal changes', as Devane told Dr McQuaid shortly after McQuaid became archbishop of Dublin.[38] Additionally, during the course of the June 1939 meeting, Bishops Lyons and McNamee were delegated to accompany Devane to meetings with the minister for justice, Paddy Ruttledge, and with the film enquiry committee, in order to present their proposals on film censorship. Interesting, Bishop Lyons also wrote to Fr

Devane in the wake of the assembly seeking a summary of the points to be made to the interdepartmental committee, but reflecting the position adopted by the congregation of bishops, recommended that it appear 'as *our* requests, and as representing the hierarchy, *their* requests'.[39] He also reported that he was looking for an appointment with the minister for justice and the enquiry committee's secretary, E.J.C. McEvoy. As a result, Devane's indefatigable allies, Dr Lyons, and the nearby bishop of Ardagh, Dr McNamee, accompanied by Devane, made a 'formal and personal presentation' of the hierarchy's case for reform of film censorship to Ruttledge and officials in justice.[40]

By the time the bishops met again in June 1940, no response had been received from the justice department to their proposals. Consequently, the bishops sought a meeting with the new minister for justice, Gerald Boland, who had replaced Ruttledge, someone not in Devane's favour as he had refused to appoint a representative from justice to the interdepartmental enquiry. Not only did Bishop Lyons believe that Boland would be better-disposed to their cause than his predecessor, even though the previous month he had told Devane that there was 'not much use' in approaching Boland,[41] he also felt that Sean MacEntee, who had moved from finance to industry and commerce, the departmental home of the film enquiry, and whom he knew 'fairly well', would also be 'very sympathetic'.[42] However, there is no evidence to indicate whether either of these men promoted changes in government regulations in line with the hierarchy's policies. On the contrary, MacEntee, while at finance, had already argued that the existing film censorship arrangements were justified only on the strongest possible moral grounds. Though some hope was held out that the appointment of a new film censor in autumn 1940 would herald changes supportive to their policy,[43] this was clutching at straws, and in the end it transpired that there was hardly an iota of difference between James Montgomery's and Dr Richard Hayes' censorship policies.[44] It is then perhaps unsurprising that the second bishops' meeting at justice did not go well.

According to Fr Devane, due to 'an administrative error', Bishops Lyons and McNamee, once again accompanied by Devane, only met three senior justice officials, including the secretary and assistant secretary, but not the minister as requested, and then not until May 1941. The bishops found the officials unsympathetic. As Fr Devane told Dr McQuaid shortly afterwards:

> The proposals of their Lordships were all turned down and compromises made at the interview were also rejected ... The Minister considers the present censors' powers adequate and the standards of censorship satisfactory. In this he is supported by the two censors [that is, Richard Hayes and his continuing adviser, the former censor, James Montgomery], the Censorship [of Films] Appeal Board, and by the senior officials of the [department of justice: the secretary, Stephen A. Roche, an assistant secretary, and another official].

Though Devane favoured seeking 'a personal interview' with the minister, the two bishops 'thought it would serve no useful purpose'.[45]

Despite Devane's attempt to keep up pressure on the department of justice in particular through attempting to have film censorship placed on the agendas of the annual gathering of the bishops, the assembly predominantly focused on the war as reflected in its post-meeting statements. During the 1940–5 period such meetings together with the Lenten pastorals were dominated by the war, and although concern was still expressed regarding 'immorality', issues such as the potential loss of faith and morals of emigrants working in Britain's war economy or engaged in the armed forces had come centre-stage. In the context of world conflagration and Ireland's at times uncertain situation in relation to it, Fr Devane's concerns must have appeared to be of minor importance, not just with regard to the government, but also the hierarchy as well, with one correspondent informing Fr Devane even before the war began, in July 1939, that 'it is hard to get their Lordships to move.'[46]

In a personal letter to Fr Devane sent some two months before the formal meeting at justice in May 1941, S.A. Roche, secretary of the department during the 1930s and 1940s, displayed a certain sympathy toward the proposals, but, nonetheless, outlined the dilemma in refining the law, especially in relation to Devane's core criticism, cinematic representations of marriage:

> At our end, marriage is a Sacrament, and is also a civil contract of the greatest seriousness, which cannot be set aside, absolutely, even for the gravest reasons, and even if both parties so desire. In the U.S., – if the pictures are right – the big business man arranges with his typist for a civil marriage before a Justice of the Peace at 24 hours' notice, to be annulled after a month and to be merely formal in the meantime. What do we do about this? Do we refuse to show such a ceremony at all, or, if we show it, do we expect the parties to treat it as if it were a Catholic marriage? If you say 'Don't show it at all, what do we lose by not showing it?' I have a lot of sympathy with that attitude but the popular mind is an illogical kind of thing and Ministers and Deputies and officials have to be careful not to be too dictatorial with it.[47]

While the letter serves as an administrative expression of the limits of censorship, perhaps just as importantly, and notwithstanding Roche's lurid sexual fantasy regarding America and capitalist secular culture, it, nevertheless, makes a distinction between the USA and Irish experiences, and implies that Irish audiences would also make such a distinction. Furthermore, it highlights the cultural significance of policy needing to be in line with public opinion, or perhaps more correctly, being *seen* to be so. In practice, given the conservative Catholic ideology of the official film censors James Montgomery, incumbent from 1923 to 1940, and Dr Richard Hayes, from 1940 to 1954, the Censorship of Films Act despite its failure to rigorously set down precisely what was and was not acceptable, was potentially, and in fact, even more restrictive than what Fr Devane would have wished to replace it with. However, as no doubt Roche and others recognized, to codify or to make the regulations explicit and transparent, would necessarily make the act 'too dictatorial', although from an ideological perspective it would also make censorship immune to the vagaries of subjectivity and

aesthetics or to a future censor who did not espouse a traditional Catholic ethos, something which clearly Fr Devane thought might happen given the state's failure to recognize the Roman Catholic church exclusively in its constitution.

Despite the tone of Roche's engagement with Devane, prior to writing this he had
helped to steer his own minister, Paddy Ruttledge, away from supporting Fr Devane's
original proposals. In a memo to the minister dated 14 October 1937, Roche had
declared that the composition of the committee (or delegation) proposed by Devane
to see de Valera was too narrowly composed: though 'conscientious and well-mean-
ing persons', the three on the list he knew, aged between sixty-eight and seventy-five,
had no right 'to speak for the ordinary citizen and elector'. While he admitted that
such groups should be given an opportunity of explaining their schemes as 'it eases
friction and may occasionally do good', he did not consider the proposed commission
of enquiry as the way. Instead, he recommended the establishment of a cross-party
committee of Dáil deputies, 'who would really represent the viewpoint of the ordinary
decent citizen and who would discuss the matter between themselves without party
prejudice or hypocrisy.' Roche's concern was to keep the law 'roughly in conformity
with popular opinion on moral and social questions and of avoiding the two extremes
with which we are at present continually threatened by, rushing into puritanical legislation or – the other extreme – doing nothing at all, even when something ought to be
done.' Roche was concerned in his memo about 'how far the individual citizen ought
to be restricted and harassed – how far he is actually prepared to be restricted and
harassed – in the interests of public morality.'[48]

In February 1941, Devane, no doubt frustrated by his lack of success in influencing a new direction for film, wrote to Archbishop McQuaid seeking in him a new ally
in his film agitation project. He noted McQuaid's interest in 'youth' and suggested that
because of this he thought that McQuaid might be supportive in having the censorship code implemented.[49] In May 1941,[50] ahead of the bishops' June gathering, and
less than two months after Roche's discouraging letter, Devane once again contacted
McQuaid and outlined the history of the previous two years' campaigning on film censorship. Fr Devane hoped, one assumes, not just that Dr McQuaid would use his influence within the hierarchy to promote his ideas at its meeting on 24 June, but also that
he would use his friendship with the taoiseach, Éamon de Valera, to aid the cause. By
then, a formal reply had been received by the bishops regarding their proposals made
to the department of justice. This reply was due to be considered by the hierarchy on
24 June 1941. But, as Fr Devane informed Dr McQuaid, the minister for justice, Gerald
Boland, 'considers the present censors' powers adequate and the standards of censorship satisfactory.' In this, Fr Devane reported, Boland had the support, not just of the
censors, but also of his senior departmental officials. In reply to Devane a few days
before the assembly of hierarchy, Dr McQuaid was non-committal.[51] Although Fr
Devane also sought support from other bishops, especially his long-time allies Lyons,
McNamee and Dignan, in the lead up to the bishops' gathering, when this failed to
progress his film censorship programme, Devane's focus shifted back to his primary
institutional objective: the establishment of a film institute in Ireland.

CHAPTER 8

Establishing a Catholic-Sanctioned Film Culture in Ireland

'Of course you will say – thousands of people say – that there is a film censorship in Ireland and that he is a Catholic and that we can be assured, therefore,
that nothing contrary to Catholic moral principles gets into our cinemas. That
is what you *think*!'[1]

ESTABLISHING AN IRISH (CATHOLIC) FILM INSTITUTE

In October 1939, more than eighteen months after the interdepartmental government
enquiry committee on the film industry in Ireland had been formed, Fr Richard Devane
SJ, wrote to Taoiseach Éamon de Valera urging that an interim report be handed in to
government. Four days later, de Valera and Devane met. Subsequently, de Valera
requested an interim report from the department of industry and commerce, but cog-
nizant that the department regarded Devane's interest as interference, de Valera
instructed his departmental secretary not to mention Devane.[2] Industry and commerce
replied by stating in classic bureaucratic language designed to delay action that the
committee had 'decided to examine forthwith the advisability of preparing an interim
report' on distribution and exhibition. It also stated that further information was being
awaited from 'two important bodies' (perhaps the exhibitors' body, the Irish Theatre
and Cinema Association, and the transnational distributors' organization, the
Kinematograph Renters' Society), and that a planned trip to London the previous
September to obtain 'essential information' had been postponed due to the outbreak
of war.[3]

Much to Fr Devane's frustration, the committee seems to have convened only intermittently during the following years, with what was probably its last meeting occurring in September 1942 when the committee met with the director of the British Film
Institute, Oliver Bell, who also took the opportunity to liaise with de Valera and, of
course, Fr Devane. This meeting, and indeed any other gathering that might have taken
place after March 1942, was gratuitous as it transpired, given that by that date the
committee had already completed its report, which, at least in part agreed to some

extent with Fr Devane's proposals of establishing a national film board and a small film studio facility,[4] though it firmly ruled out any significant changes to the film censorship regime as this was 'operat[ing] efficiently and satisfactorily'.[5] (The report's distribution and exhibition aspects are outlined in chapter 2.) Despite its completion, it was not circulated to any other government department and when Seán Lemass, minister of industry and commerce under whose auspices the committee had convened, was questioned in the Dáil throughout 1943–4 about the film enquiry report, especially regarding its publication, he invariably replied that the enquiry had been set up 'to report upon certain matters for the confidential information of the Government' and that there was no question of the *Report of the inter-departmental committee on the film industry* being 'prepared for publication'.[6] On the basis of additional proposals brought to government, it seems likely that the real reason why the report remained secret was that its film production recommendations fell short of what Lemass wanted.[7]

Nevertheless, somewhat serendipitously for Devane, who must have recognized that Lemass had effectively stymied any immediate reconfiguring of film within Irish society, a new avenue of possibility emerged when a little-known, predominately clerical, film club, the Irish Cine Club, which had been involved in amateur ('substandard') filmmaking since its beginnings in 1931 and had accumulated equipment valued at £300, declared an interest in establishing a film institute. On 14 February 1943, Fr John Redmond CC, curate of Iona Road Catholic church, Glasnevin, and the club's founder, convened and chaired a meeting at 29 Dame Street, Dublin, to discuss the formation of what was initially called the Irish Cine Institute. Among the fifteen others in attendance were club members Fr Sebastian OFM; J. Cashman, a press photographer; Gearoid MacEoin BL, a journalist;[8] and P. Marshall, a railway clerk;[9] and 'visitors' Fr Devane; Revd Daniel Collier, OMI, superior, House of Retreat, Inchicore, who, based on thirty years of teaching experience and research on the Irish language, wrote the popular work *Irish without worry* (1943); Con Drum, president of the Catholic Young Men's Society (CYMS), with which the club was already cooperating; and librarian Brigid Redmond. She was not just Fr Redmond's sister, but also author of a number of books including *The story of Dublin* (c.1921); a 1928 series of literary readers for schools, such as *The golden age* and *The golden crest*; and *Our land in story*, a series on city and county histories (1931). Aimed at the general (Catholic) reader, books such as *The golden age* gives a mythic and celebratory account of Irish Christianity in the pre-Norman era, and lauds the role of Irish missionaries, who 'evangelised and civilised England, Scotland and Wales'.[10]

According to the meeting's minutes, while Fr Collier related his own involvement in film, including in the production of a documentary, *The Making of a Priest*[11] and in exhibition through film screenings in Inchicore, and other speakers advocated that the club extend its field of activity, Fr Devane proposed a clear course of action for the club, including the need for a director. Having expressed surprise at how relatively unknown the group was, he identified twelve 'tentative' objectives that the club assume. These covered training, film production and distribution, as well as educating public opinion as to 'the cultural value of the film in public life'. Although some of those present argued for immediate action, Devane was more considered. He cautioned on the need to get ecclesiastical sanction for an education programme as set out in Pope Pius XI's 1936 encyclical letter on motion pictures, *Vigilanti cura,* and recommended that Fr Redmond proceed with this objective.[12] As a result, Redmond wrote to Archbishop McQuaid stating that the Irish Cine Club had agreed to form an 'Irish Film Institute' that would (a) act as a coordinating body to the large number of small clubs such as their own, and the cine branches of other organizations such as CYMS (and similar youth movements), the St Vincent de Paul Society, and the Legion of Mary; (b) establish a film library for use by associated bodies, schools and institutions; and (c) help with technical advice. He concluded by asking McQuaid for his 'approval and perhaps Patronage' of the proposed institute, pointing out that without his 'sanction' they could 'do nothing'. By this time, however, Collier already had contacted three bishops, including his brother Patrick, the bishop of Ossory, who offered 'a substantial subscription' to the new body.[13]

Dr McQuaid's response was both immediate and positive. That said, given that McQuaid had never lent his support to any of Devane's various agitations regarding film reform, of which, undoubtedly, he would have been aware, it is fair to assume that McQuaid's motivation was not an interest in film per se, but a desire to bind film culture in Ireland to an exclusive Catholic agenda. To do this, McQuaid understood that the influence of the Irish Film Society, referred to by Redmond in his letter as an active and 'comparatively young non-Catholic Body' with 800 associate members in Dublin and 200 in Cork, had to be contained and minimized. Indeed, from the time of McQuaid's installation as archbishop of Dublin on 27 December 1940, in an intermingling of the then current 'xenophobic and ultra-nationalist notions', he had set about systematically reorganizing his diocese along exclusivist Catholic lines. In a two-pronged approach, he instigated a 'rapid purge of all interdenominational or non-religious organisations'[14] and set about the creation of a Catholic infrastructure, of which the founding in 1941 of the Catholic Social Service Conference was central. While this body sought to 'maximise the effectiveness of the social, educational and medical services at the Catholic's Church's disposal', in order to alleviate the conditions facing the city's poor,[15] another group, the Catholic Social Welfare Bureau, which he helped to set up in 1942, had as its chief activity the aiding of emigrants to Britain. In terms of culture and the arts, apart from the role he would play in the establishment of the National Film Institute of Ireland, McQuaid's intervention is remembered for the founding of Our Lady's Choral Society whose first performance was of Handel's *Messiah* in the Pro-Cathedral on 16 December 1945.

On receipt of Fr Redmond's letter, McQuaid immediately invited Redmond to see him and the two met on 19 February, only five days after the Irish Cine Club assembly. McQuaid noted that it 'was an excellent venture for Catholic Education' and undertook to send a personal letter to be read at the group's next gathering.[16] The following day McQuaid wrote to Redmond declaring that the aims of the institute were worthy of support, and congratulated him and his fellow-workers, laymen and clerics, whom he deemed to be 'fully in line with the direction of the Holy See in the matters of the cinema'. He urged them to develop the work through the appointment of 'a clear-headed Executive that [would] be practical, as well as idealistic', and offered to give 'all the help that' he could. With regard to a patron, he suggested that they look to *Virgo Potens* (the most powerful Virgin Mary) 'for only the limitless power of Our Blessed Lady can avail to defeat the particular evils that the Institute attempts to combat.'[17] A week later, the new organization under the name National Film Institute of Ireland (NFI), perhaps chosen as a means to distinguish it from its British counterpart, circulated its 'aims and objects', the Catholic tone of which was clearly heralded by the institute's motto, *Virgo potens, ora pro nobis* (Virgin most powerful, pray for us).

The objectives, twelve in number and most probably principally authored by Devane given that they correspond closely with his proposals of 14 February (and indeed, more generally of the previous decade), set out (1) to direct and encourage the use of the motion picture 'in the National and Cultural interests of the Irish People', following the teaching in *Vigilanti cura*; (2) to ensure a film censorship regime of 'films for family entertainment', and to promote special shows for children; (3) to educate popular taste in film appreciation, including the exhibition of films of a cultural and technical value not ordinarily screened in commercial cinemas; (4) to promote the educational and religious use of films; (5) to encourage the use of film in teaching Irish, and to support the production of films with Irish soundtracks or with Irish subtitles; (6) to coordinate the activities of groups and individuals interested in the institute's activities; (7) to establish a central film distribution library and to issue a catalogue of films available for lending, and to maintain a specialist film book library; (8) to produce educational and cultural films; to give practical courses in film production; and to prepare the way for the establishment of a fully-equipped film studio; (9) to advocate legislation for the inclusion of Irish-produced films as part of every commercial cinema programme; (10) to encourage government departments to use films for educational and propagandist purposes; (11) to secure and preserve films of national and historical interest; and (12) to lead to the establishment of a state-aided film board, such as existed in other European countries, 'which would control and direct films in the best interests of the Nation'.[18]

In late May 1943, less than three months after the inaugural meeting of the film institute, Redmond sent a four-page progress report to Dr McQuaid. According to this the NFI's executive committee consisted of Fr Redmond as chairman; Brigid Redmond as honorary secretary and treasurer; Fr Collier; Fr Sebastian; Revd C. MacMahon CSSp, a Holy Ghost priest like McQuaid; Dermot J. O'Flynn, director of Youth Training Centre; solicitor James Fagan; and F. Bernard, auditor to the department of local government. Additionally, its membership base had expanded to incorporate a number of influential figures including John D. Sheridan, editor, *Irish School Weekly*; Mr E.P. McCarron, a chartered accountant; and Joseph Murphy, assistant secretary, ports and docks board.[19] Though McQuaid advised that the posts of honorary secretary and treasurer be separated, 'most especially in this case where your own Sister is the person in question', in a second communication the following day, he not only complemented the 'remarkable progress ... in so short a time', but also enclosed a cheque for £250 towards building up the library of films.[20] At a subsequently meeting, in the absence of Fr Redmond, journalist Gearoid MacEoin, who had attended the initial meeting on 14 February, took the chair and 'foist[ed]' a friend, Mr Gallagher, a solicitor, into 'the key position' of treasurer. Following some form of revolt, Gallagher was 'encouraged' to resign shortly afterwards whereupon accountant E.P. McCarron of Reynolds, McCarron & Co. became treasurer.[21]

By the end of June, the NFI's list of patrons was impressive, including as it did three bishops (Patrick Collier, bishop of Ossory; John Dignan, bishop of Clonfert; and James Staunton, bishop of Ferns); the president of the high court, Justice Conor Maguire; the president of University College Dublin, Dr A.W. Conway; the president of the Medical Association of Ireland, Dr J.P. Shanley; Dublin city manager, P.J. Hernon; and Professor Michael Tierney of UCD, a prominent lay Catholic. Although the film library's expansion was being curtailed by British wartime restrictions, attempts were being made to import fifteen anti-tuberculosis films, while a range of other activities was in train. These included a primary teachers' group negotiating for special children's matinees in commercial cinemas, and a film production unit planning a series of documentaries on subjects as various as Lough Derg, a swimming contest in Blackrock, and the model farm at the Albert Agricultural College, Glasnevin.[22] Interestingly, it took until August 1943 for McQuaid to finally respond to the invitation to become one of the NFI's patrons, perhaps an indication that he did not wish to share the role with others, as would become clear when the organization was incorporated as a company in 1945,[23] and/or to the fact that there remained important differences between the approach being proposed for the institute by Fr Devane and what McQuaid eventually succeeded in imposing.

While McQuaid, who was not only suspicious of all inter- and non-religious contact, was hostile to 'state intervention in many diverse areas',[24] Fr Devane had an ambition for a film institute that was a state organization run on corporatist lines. Writing in the *Standard* in 1940 Devane had presented a comprehensive set of proposals for a vocationalist film institute which would 'be under ultimate Government control in a manner to be determined'[25] and have representatives from various bodies such as educational institutions, government departments, the Abbey and Gate theatres, the Gaelic League, the GAA, city managers, farming organizations, women's groups, the cinema trade and the Irish Film Society. When in July 1943 it was announced that the National Film Institute of Ireland was to be formed, notwithstanding the absence of representatives from the cultural bodies identified by Devane, it appeared that this corporatist approach was, at least in part, being achieved. Indeed, his continuing hope for a vocationalist body is clear in *Irish cinema handbook*, an anthology of over thirty articles on film in Ireland, which, conceived of by Devane and for which he acted as advisory editor, was published at the end of 1943. Not only did Devane include a self-authored piece on 'the film in national life' in which, without any reference to the papal encyclical on the cinema (though *Vigilanti cura* was treated by Gearoid MacEoin in the book's opening article), he outlined the NFI's aims, but he also incorporated articles by Liam O'Leary and Edward Toner, both of the secular Irish Film Society. (A further essay was provided by Brigid Redmond, Devane's closest lay associate in the NFI, who wrote on the educational use of cinema.)[26]

Nevertheless, during the second half of 1943, tensions between Devane's inclusive vocationalist vision and the purely Catholic approach were being played out behind the scenes in a three-way conflict involving the Irish Film Society, Muintir na Tíre (People of the land/countryside) and, of course, the NFI. This was due to the fact that both the IFS (involved as it was in exhibition and educational activities, especially in the provision of special screenings for children, as well as in film production) and the vocationalist-style voluntary rural development guild-based organization, Muintir na Tíre (established in Tipperary by Fr John Hayes in 1931, a week before the publication of Pius XI's encyclical *Quadragesimo anno*, which promoted guilds and local decision-making over centralized state control),[27] already had vested interests in an area of cultural life that was being defined by the NFI as exclusively subject to their Catholic authority.

Though the friction was ultimately precipitated by the British ministry of information's offer in summer 1943 to supply the NFI on a monthly basis with 3,000ft of unexposed film stock to be distributed to Irish film organizations, relations between the exclusively Catholic faction of the NFI and the IFS were already fractious as were those between McQuaid and Muintir na Tíre. In the case of the latter pair, difficulties emerged in the early 1940s when the organization, described by de Valera as 'the most valuable movement in the country',[28] sought to extend its activities into Dublin. McQuaid, angry or perhaps fearful of the potential encroachment on his Catholic Social Services Conference by Munitir, which, in contrast to McQuaid's patriarchal Catholicism, admitted to its membership both women and Protestants, refused to speak at one of their meetings at which both Taoiseach Éamon de Valera and opposition leader W.T. Cosgrave were speaking. Later, he made clear his objections when a Ballsbridge–Sandymount branch of Muintir was proposed in November 1941. A subsequent meeting between McQuaid and Hayes in May 1942 only worsened relations. As a result, when it became clear that McQuaid (with his sectarian agenda) was guiding the National Film Institute of Ireland, Muintir, which had initially welcomed its formation and offered support and full cooperation,[29] quickly distanced itself from the new film body and proceeded with its own film plans mostly through the Co-Operative Film Society. Established in 1942, the co-op was aimed at parish guilds, and had, within three years of its existence, presented 500 film shows with its two 16mm projectors.[30]

Chief among those who played a part in the bringing about of the British offer was Dr R. Chambers, secretary of the Irish Red Cross, an organization with which both the IFS and NFI worked as members of its anti-tuberculosis committee. Chambers, who appreciated that the NFI with its Catholic episcopal sanction could provide a gateway to schools, and that the IFS with its many influential members, including Ernest Blythe (its president)[31] and various government department senior executives, could rely on a strong united Protestant base,[32] advocated a linking of the two organizations. He argued that such a union would be of mutual benefit to both and serve as a means of strengthening their positions with the British. In any case, the NFI asked Chambers to act, while on a trip to London, on their behalf and secure health films from the

British ministry of information. To the 'amazement' of the NFI, the ministry responded with the promise, noted above, of 3,000ft of film per month, which, given wartime restrictions, was a somewhat generous undertaking. However, when this was reported to the anti-tuberculosis committee, alarm bells must have rung for the Irish Film Society in particular, but also for Muintir na Tíre, which also had film production ambitions, as it meant that potentially they could find themselves beholden to the NFI, not just a Catholic organization but also one with an explicit film censorship agenda, for raw film stock supplies.

When Redmond failed to get written confirmation from the British ministry regarding the film allocation, Chambers enquired on the NFI's behalf only to be told that letters of protest had been received. Disappointed, Chambers informed Redmond that it was 'your own people [who] betrayed you'.[33] That such hostility manifested itself was hardly surprisingly given the poor relations that the NFI had with both Muintir and the IFS. Indeed, the extent of these had been made explicit in summer 1942 by Joan Lynam, a British ministry of information official and secretary to British embassy press attaché John Betjamin, who was showing films in Limerick on behalf of the IFS at a Muintir rural week. She told Brigid Redmond in no uncertain terms that priests, or those who might impose a rigorous Catholic agenda, were not wanted as members in or as (controlling) affiliates to the IFS. (Though it seems that Lynam was an IFS member, even if this was not the case, at the very least, she would have had established relations with the society given that the ministry were supplying information films to them.) Not wanting to accept the withdrawal of the British offer, Redmond sought a meeting with Barry Walsh, organizing secretary of Muintir. Nevertheless, she was unsuccessful in this as Walsh, like Fr John Hayes, also distanced himself from the NFI probably after learning of McQuaid's involvement with the institute.

In early September 1943, at the request of the IFS, two NFI members, encouraged by Fr Devane, met with the IFS to discuss representation within the institute. The IFS delegation asked that the NFI be open to all persons, irrespective of creed; that no moral or ethical standard be raised as regards films shown; that only artistic merit, and not moral value, be used to determine selection; and that there would be no mention of a religious aim or object within the institute's programme.[34] Unsure as to how to proceed, the NFI, through Fr Redmond, sought the 'guidance and advice' of McQuaid, to whom he posed the question,

> Whether, in view of the facts that the majority of our people are Catholic, [that] the constitution of Éire [is] based on Catholic principles and [that the] Government [is] mainly Catholic, and with a view to securing Government aid at some future date, ... [it] would be necessary to include mention of the Encyclical 'Vigilanti Cura' in the statement of our Aims?

Pointing out that some members of the organization felt that its inclusion 'might give the non-Catholic minority and Leftist elements excuse to protest against Government aid for the Institute', Fr Redmond suggested that 'Catholic control' could be effected by a constitution 'expressly framed for that purpose'. He indicated that while policy, control and administration could be vested in a council of patrons, as at present, additional representatives from educational bodies such as the INTO and government departments concerned with cinema matters, such as industry and commerce, justice, and education, could be included. He proposed that the executive committee would continue as before, but non-voting advisory panels could be nominated by national and educational bodies. While he felt that the NFI was not sufficiently developed to give voting representation 'to elements that may be alien to our purposes', undoubtedly a reference to the 'non-Catholic' IFS, neither was the organization 'strong enough' to confront cinema trade interests. In addition, he reported that the institution had already secured the approval of Bishops Lyons, Staunton and Collier, but that Fathers Devane and Collier were urging the NFI to seek the support of the other bishops who, as a body, were due to meet in October 1943.[35]

While McQuaid, in his reply, supported the NFI approaching the hierarchy, he argued that given the NFI's aims were 'so well in line with the desire of Governments for the moral welfare of a people' no 'valid argument [could] be adduced against' the use of 'well chosen' quotations from *Vigilanti cura*. As regards broadening the NFI's representation, he counselled that they proceed 'very slowly' and retain, 'at least for the present', a system of control 'by a carefully chosen' executive committee, pointing out that assistance in specific spheres could be acquired through purely advisory committees.[36]

Following McQuaid's strictures, the NFI, in a holding tactic, told the IFS that its constitution was not completed but that it wished to remain on friendly terms. No further formal meeting seems to have taken place between the two organizations, and while the NFI continued its sectarian agenda, the IFS moved closer to developing a schools' programme even though it had no episcopal sanction for it. Nevertheless, Brigid Redmond blamed this final meeting of the NFI and IFS and the reporting of it by the IFS to Lynam and Chambers, now working in England, on the withdrawal by the British ministry of information of its raw film stock offer. (Clearly, despite Chambers' comment that it was 'your' people that brought a revision to the British proposal, she was unable to conceive the idea that the 'betrayal' was by Muintir founded as it was by a Catholic priest and in accordance with the spirit of *Quadragesimo anno*.)

Whatever group of persons had acted to scupper the raw stock deal, it was the British Film Institute, with which the IFS would have had regular contact, that informed the NFI that film supplies could only be obtained through industry and commerce, though, as is outlined below, they were not responsible for the change in British policy. With the NFI removed from importation and distribution, industry and commerce, which had 'several highly placed officers' who were IFS members,[37] resumed full responsibility for film imports. Nevertheless, through John Leyden, the chief civil servant in the wartime ministry of supplies, who was sympathetic to the Catholic organization, the NFI resumed its efforts in seeking film supplies from London. The IFS, aware of this development through its membership of the anti-tuberculosis committee, convened a conference at which a broad-based Irish Film Council was formed.

(The new body seems to have been originally called the Irish Film Board, but, as Liam O'Leary reported to the IFS, this was reconstituted as the Irish Film Council by January 1944.)[38] This council comprised of Ernest Blythe and Liam O'Leary (secretary), both representing the IFS; exhibitor J.M. Stanley, who with cinemas in Drogheda, Dundalk and Cootehill, represented provincial exhibitors; John Hanlon of Irish International Film Agency, who was representing Jack Sheehan, secretary of Irish Hospitals' Trust Films; Barry Walsh of Muintir na Tíre;[39] and solicitor Roger Greene, representing actor and singer Richard Hayward. It set forth a seven-point programme. It sought (1) to decide the allocation of raw film quota for Ireland; (2) to manage the national film studio and laboratory; (3) to provide suggestions of subjects urgently required; (4) to provide facilities for certain productions; (5) to promote the distribution of Irish films abroad; (6) to promote the use of the Irish language through the medium of the film;[40] and (7) to provide suitable films for educational purposes. In addition, it was envisaged that the council would seek government recognition to pursue these objectives and make recommendations to government. The council's memorandum incorporating these proposals, *National film requirements*, was sent to the minister for industry and commerce, although no official response to the memo seems to have been sent by this or any other government department.[41]

Meanwhile, on 27 November 1943, Brigid Redmond met with Muintir na Tíre's Barry Walsh and outlined the NFI's position. She stated that they wished for full cooperation from Muintir, but, in a word of caution, advised that they had 'declined full cooperation' with the IFS because it was 'in non-Catholic control' and had aims 'totally opposed' to those of the institute and 'Catholic and national policy'.[42] She was more explicitly sectarian regarding the IFS when she wrote to Muintir's president, Dr Lyons, bishop of Kilmore, a month later. Not only did she find objection to the fact that the 'financial and executive control [of the IFS was] in Protestant hands' and that its executive committee, which included 'an admitted Communist', Owen Sheehy-Skeffington, and civil servant Thekla Beere, who was 'notably hostile to Catholic and Nationalist interests', consisted of five Protestants (chief among them Ernest Blythe) and only three Catholics, but also that its teachers' committee was run by two Protestants, 'although they put a Catholic teacher [Áine Ní Chanainn, later the principal of St John the Baptist primary school, Clontarf] to the front when advertising'.[43]

She warned Walsh that Muintir's alignment with the IFS, manifest at the Mansion House, 'the most public place in Dublin', was regarded by her organization as displaying a 'hostile and inimical' attitude to the NFI. As the institute was 'a body sanctioned and supported by the Archbishop of Dublin' this 'was bound to have disastrous effects'. Walsh replied by stating that Muintir 'did not fear any ecclesiastical criticism' for associating with the society given that such an association made practical and business sense and that, in any case, the society's policies and its inclusion of Protestant or leftist elements were irrelevant. He went on to point out that they had not encountered from the hierarchy in Tipperary the kind of rigidity that he had heard characterized McQuaid's rule in Dublin. In what must have been a shocking revelation, he also informed her that it was he who protested to the British official against the allocation of film stock to the NFI as a distribution body for Éire.[44] No doubt Walsh felt further justified in this when he read Fr Devane's criticism in the *Irish cinema handbook* of Muintir as a voluntary parish council rather than a statutory one, though Devane's view would have been apparent already to Walsh and others. In any case, the meeting ended with a promise from Walsh that Muintir would offer their cooperation and that Fr Hayes would nominate a representative to the institute. As it transpired, however, no such representative was nominated to the NFI,[45] and on 2 December, Walsh cranked up tensions between Muintir and the NFI (and, ultimately, Archbishop McQuaid) by sending out a circular to the press recommending the IFS to Muintir's members. Writing in a type of interdenominational language which no longer could be used by activist Catholics in Dublin without incurring episcopal sanction, he held out the possibility that with the help of the IFS, Muintir would 'create in this country film standards worthy of our national and religious ideals'.[46]

Not only was such a move by Muintir a very public rejection of the NFI, one which made impossible any future prospect of collaboration between the two organizations, but also what it showed above all else was that not all areas of Catholic Ireland were ruled with the strictness and forensic surveillance McQuaid inflicted on Dublin. Muintir's president, Bishop Lyons, reflected an alternative form of Catholic authority when he responded to Redmond's somewhat sectarian letter cited above. In a supportive, yet resigned accepting manner, he advised her not to 'be discouraged' as 'every good work for God meets opposition, even from good Catholics'. He asked her to 'avoid a public quarrel', pointing out that though 'paid officials', such as Walsh, dictate the need for financial security and may even 'dominate' the working of such organizations, he offered her the consolation that the NFI had 'a tower of strength and wisdom in Dublin' in McQuaid, who would not let them down.[47]

Ironically, despite Brigid Redmond's committed Catholic perspective, which was in conformity with McQuaid's wishes, nevertheless, and perhaps in part in response to the fact that Walsh had highlighted McQuaid's rigidity as the reason he had scuppered the film deal with the British, she was also the agent for what were being perceived as dangerously vocationalist ideas contrary to McQuaid's diocesan agenda. While Fr Redmond, as chairman of the NFI, may have hinted at some of these issues in his letter to McQuaid on 10 September 1943, it is clear from correspondence and memos in McQuaid's papers that some of McQuaid's correspondents suspected that these ideas were being cultivated by Brigid Redmond, who, in turn, was influenced by Fr Devane, who, in line with his vocationalist ideas, wrote to de Valera shortly after the publication of *Irish cinema handbook*, seeking government intervention.

Describing the NFI as 'merely a provisional body preparing the way for an official Institute – State-aided, which it is hoped will eventually arise', Devane stated that 'nothing of any real value can be done except under Government patronage'.[48] Notwithstanding that such a position would have been an anathema to Archbishop McQuaid, Devane also partially reached an accommodation with McQuaid, by drawing de Valera's attention to a section in *Irish cinema handbook*, which he enclosed and in which was argued that the institute, following examples in South Africa, Britain,

Switzerland and Denmark, 'would be State-aided but not State-controlled'.[49] Ultimately, though the government had little to offer, on 31 December 1943, it established an inter-departmental subcommittee on educational films, which was instructed to report on the recommendations 'refer[ing] to Educational Films and Films in the Irish language' contained in the interdepartmental report on the film industry.[50]

Chaired by Dr Michael Quane of the department of education's primary schools' section, and including representatives from the departments of agriculture (J. Mahony), finance (T.S. Kealy), industry and commerce (E.J.C. McEvoy and R.C. Coyne), and local government and public health (Dr E.J.T. McWeeney), the subcommittee met an NFI delegation consisting of Fr Redmond, Fr Devane, and Brigid Redmond on 31 January 1944. From this meeting a memo emerged in which Dr Quane outlined six conditions under which government grant-in-aid might be given to the NFI. Firstly, it was determined that the institute's membership would have to be broad-based, and, as such, debarring clauses including those referring to 'special denomination or special types of persons' were not to be permitted in the institute's constitution; secondly, the NFI's executive committee was to include representatives of the chief teaching bodies – Irish National Teachers' Organization (INTO), Association of Secondary Teachers of Ireland (ASTI), and the Irish Technical Officers' Association; thirdly, there were to be representatives of three government departments (education, agriculture, and local government and public health); fourthly, government representatives would have the right to recommend the purchase, acquisition and distribution of films bought with the government grant; fifthly, the government would have priority in showing films acquired with state aid; and, finally, the institute was to be encouraged to raise funds for its own future expansion.[51] When this document was forwarded by Brigid Redmond to McQuaid on 20 March 1944, the archbishop was livid, not least because during the previous four years he had successfully resisted concessions to interdenominational activity and created purely Catholic bodies, but also because this serious challenge to his policy came from a government headed by de Valera to whom he had been a close advisor for almost two decades.

On 23 March, McQuaid responded, not to Brigid Redmond, who had sent the memo as her brother was ill, but to Fr Redmond.

> I understood from the start that your Institute was properly Catholic, in aim, function, and in membership. Accordingly, I cannot accept that the Administrative Council of the Institute should include representation of all the Teaching Bodies in the country ... [which would] include non-Catholic and non-Christian denominations, ... and of the Irish Film Society [which had no] affiliation with Christian teaching ... and Muintir na Tíre [which was] not a properly Catholic grouping.[52]

Nonetheless, he conceded that once it remained clear that the organization's governance was exclusively Catholic, not least given that the NFI was 'intimately concerned with education' and that 'education for Catholics must be *integrally* Catholic', collaboration with such groups could be viewed as 'lawful and feasible and useful'. If, however, the condition of receiving government aid for the purchase of films was the inclusion of such bodies, then, McQuaid advised, 'remain independent of such aid and continue to live on the alms of the interested Faithful'. He added that if the NFI was to become interdenominational, his name was to be removed from the list of patrons and warned that he considered it his 'duty to take up the matter with the Hierarchy'. He concluded by pointing out that it was illogical that a government grant could be withheld on the basis of the institute's exclusive Catholic remit given 'the accepted denominational basis of education' in Ireland, and that such a grant would be similar to the subsidies paid to Catholic schools in the country. Though the letter put an end to any lingering ambitions for a vocationalist institute that Fr Devane may have had, Brigid Redmond, despite expressions of loyalty to McQuaid, continued to fight an increasingly futile, rearguard action to retain a semblance of inclusiveness within the organization.

Though the letter was not read to either the executive committee or advisory council, as had been requested by McQuaid, Fr Redmond nevertheless sent a copy of it to Fr Collier who then wrote to McQuaid on 21 April claiming that due to Fr Redmond's illness, the NFI was 'in difficulties as to what action to take' in light of the demand from the interdepartmental committee that the organization needed to broaden its executive representation ahead of receiving a government grant. A second proposal had come from the interdepartmental committee a week earlier, which seemed to have accepted that only the teaching bodies needed to be included on the NFI's executive committee, and as such had dropped the demand that the IFS and Muintir na Tíre be represented.

Adding that he agreed whole-heartedly with McQuaid's stance vis-à-vis exclusive Catholic executive membership, Collier pointed out that since its foundation, he had 'fought against allowing any person except a Catholic' on the executive committee, while the organization had expelled already 'cunning chancers who endeavoured to change the whole aim, function and membership even in the hope of getting power'.[53] Collier was granted a meeting with McQuaid, who, obviously annoyed that the executive committee had not heard his letter in the intervening month, insisted (through Collier) that Brigid Redmond, who, as secretary, controlled the agenda, convene on 28 April at 18 Westland Row a special meeting to have the letter read. As is clear from a fourteen-page letter Brigid Redmond sent to McQuaid on 16 May outlining the recent history of the NFI from her perspective, it seems that McQuaid also wished that 'a new and reliable Executive' with Collier as chairman would be appointed at the special meeting.[54]

Ahead of the 28 April meeting, Collier, presumably to ensure his election, held a private meeting with the priests involved in the organization, which Redmond, invoking her role as honorary secretary, attempted to stop, not least because she believed that the 'strange body of people' were using the NFI's offices without either the archbishop's or executive committee's approval. Against Collier's wishes, she then sought an appointment with McQuaid, who advised her to contact Fr M.C. Troy. However, Troy, clearly in support of Collier (and McQuaid), refused to see her before the meeting, though she met with Collier.

On the night of the full official meeting, Collier, acting as chair, announced that the executive committee had been dissolved because 'an outside body', presumably a reference to the IFS, 'had tried unlawfully to appropriate the functions and work' of the NFI. In response, Brigid Redmond declared that no outside body had usurped the institute's function, and affirmed that the executive committee was not dissolved, and could not be dissolved, without a majority vote of the committee. After McQuaid's 23 March letter was read, Collier vacated the chair, and, obviously in a pre-arranged manner, Fr Troy and Fr D. Vaughan proposed John J. Piggott, Professor of Education at the Catholic Teacher Training Centre, St Patrick's, Drumcondra, as chairman. Troy then named a subcommittee comprising of Vaughan, T.J.M. (Morgan) Sheehy,[55] Mr Fitzpatrick and Prof. Piggott, with Redmond as honorary secretary, which was charged with drafting the institute's constitution. Following repeated challenges from Redmond, the new committee contradictorily explained that the original executive committee was not in fact disbanded but would continue the day-to-day work, while it, as designed by McQuaid, would act as an *investigating* committee charged with drafting the constitution and dictating policy. Reporting to McQuaid on the night of the meeting, Collier noted that Fathers Troy and Vaughan 'were brilliant and a tower of strength to me', while Brigid Redmond, though initially 'cool' and 'quarrelsome', 'became completely reconciled' to the new regime. By contrast, Fr Devane, who seems to have been informed of the emergency assembly by Redmond, remained 'completely silent'.[56]

Whatever about the tactics and lack of sympathy[57] employed by Collier, Troy and Vaughan in dealing with the Redmonds, the trio clearly not only had McQuaid's full support, but also were acting on his instructions. Indeed, to reinforce the new direction and to quell any dissent or potential split in the organization, something which Redmond in her 16 May letter to McQuaid had suggested could be the outcome if there was 'any ill-timed interference of misinformed or uninformed people',[58] McQuaid himself attended the 19 May NFI meeting.[59] In a memo to the meeting, McQuaid reinforced the message he had already conveyed through Collier. While the executive committee was to be 'exclusively Catholic', subcommittees 'may usefully contain non-Catholics', and, in an important expression of his approach to institutions, said that the organization can be helped by priests, but 'this is one of the spheres in which [lay people] can share in [the] apostolate of the church.'[60] While bishops and priests would determine the NFI's policy, lay people would run the organization.

The following week, Collier informed the archbishop that Brigid Redmond had been by-passed in the constitutional subcommittee, which was made up of Gabriel Fallon, a civil servant, drama critic and occasional writer on film issues; Morgan Sheehy; Dr Quinlan; and Fr Collier; with Dermot O'Flynn in the chair. He commented that he expected Ms Redmond to resign from the organization.[61] It seems that McQuaid and the new strict Catholic order had deemed her work for the organization complete, despite her attempts to affirm her importance and centrality to the organization while suggesting a distance between herself and Devane though simultaneously attempting to accommodate and contextualize his efforts.[62]

Ultimately, all these events had largely flowed from Dr Quane's request for an agreement to be reached regarding the governance of the NFI. This was required before Quane could finalize the interdepartmental committee's recommendation of giving government aid to the organization. Fr Collier had already informed McQuaid that Quane had come to him 'confidentially' on 26 April and related 'government anxiety' about the IFS and Muintir na Tíre's film activities. Quane suggested that the NFI could be given a £2,000 annual grant for the film library, but 'the only snag' was that they would be expected to include a government representative on the executive council, 'not a member having a voice in policy, but with a watching brief in their interests only'. Collier, instead of embracing what was a relative victory, responded by stating that 'such an important decision' would have to be discussed by the NFI's executive committee.[63] On 30 May in advance of a final meeting on 1 June between the interdepartmental subcommittee on educational films and the NFI Quane met with Brigid Redmond. He reported that there was grant-in-aid available to the NFI from the departments of education, and industry and commerce (something which did not happen), and that the formulation for the appointment of a government representative to the NFI executive had been further diluted with the mandatory 'shall' appoint being replaced with 'may' appoint, 'thus changing a mandatory form to an optative form', as Brigid Redmond put it in a letter to McQuaid the same day. The interdepartmental subcommittee also accepted the NFI's position that representatives of teaching and other bodies would be confined to advisory committees. Indeed, Quane even said that the NFI's constitution could be 'framed as to exclude non-Catholics from the Administrative Council', thereby embedding sectarianism in a body receiving a government grant. If, however, the NFI did not accept the grant-in-aid, the government committee was sufficiently impressed by the Irish Film Council, made up primarily of IFS and Muintir personnel, to recommend the council for a grant.[64] Though Brigid Redmond attended the 1 June meeting along with Troy, Quinlan and Fallon, tensions between her and Troy were such that McQuaid felt the need to write to Ms Redmond asking her '*again* ... to put no obstacle in the way of reorganisation'.[65]

Despite the continuing infighting, two weeks later, on 15 June, the interdepartmental committee reported positively on the NFI to the minister for education, Thomas Derrig. The committee recommended the development of a library of educational films and the production of a small number of information films for government departments, but deferred the production of entertainment films in the Irish language 'until ample studio facilities, equipment, etc. become available'. Though it considered whether a government department could undertake such activities, it concluded that the 'nucleus' of a suitable organization already existed in the NFI, which not only had an educational film unit in place, but enjoyed a 'wide and influential membership' and 'the good will and active co-operation' of such bodies as the INTO, ASTI, Comhairle le Leas Óige, Irish Red Cross, GAA, and Comhdháil Náisiúnta na Gaedhilge [Gaeilge]. In a dismissal of the unnamed Irish Film Society, the Irish Film Council and even Muintir na Tíre, the report reasoned that as 'none of the other bodies interested in film matters possess all of the foregoing characteristics', then it was fitting that the NFI be entrusted with the task of both building up the library and arranging the production and distribution of educational and propaganda films for government departments, and for which they should be awarded a grant-in-aid of up to £2,000 voted through the department of industry and commerce budget.[66]

The intervention, however, was envisaged as a stop-gap measure – 'to meet emergency conditions'[67] – until a national film board, as recommended in the 1942 *Report of the inter-departmental committee on the film industry* and indeed promoted by Fr Devane,[68] was established. The conditions attached to the grant included that the members of the NFI 'be continued on the *same wide basis* [sic] as at present' (emphasis added); for the organization to maintain and increase voluntary support; that it cooperate with government departments in decisions as to which films would be purchased; that the government would have 'the right' to nominate a representative on the 'appropriate' committee of the institute, and that this person would concern himself with such work as was covered by the grant; and that government departments would have priority in the use of films purchased by the grant. The 'principal problem' as regards distribution and exhibition of educational films was the shortage of film projectors. Consequently, it was recommended that commercial cinemas be used for screening educational and propaganda films to schoolchildren at times other than the cinemas' ordinary (commercial) programme. If such cooperation was not forthcoming from the film trade, then 'legal provision' might be required to ensure such screenings.[69] Following the report, the minister for finance, Sean T. O'Kelly, in his 1945 budget allocated the NFI the full £2,000.[70] Shortly afterwards, Dr Quane and T. O'Conail of the department of education joined the NFI council as government representatives.[71] In this context, it is hardly surprising that in July 1945 Liam O'Leary reported to the IFS that the Irish Film Council was no longer in existence.[72]

Despite what Fathers Collier and Troy undoubtedly hoped for, Brigid Redmond did not resign from the NFI, and, ignoring McQuaid's caution, continued to be an awkward critic of the revised constitution. Vaughan, who wrote to McQuaid in October 1944 a week after Ms Redmond sought a meeting with the archbishop, described her as being 'in close collaboration' with Devane on whom he blamed her endless calls for 'reviews' of the draft constitution and accused her of failing to make 'one constructive suggestion' to the committee. Contradictorily, he added that she was suffering from a 'lack of interest' in the institute, which once again he blamed on Devane and the fact that she was missing him since his departure from Dublin. Despite the sidelining of Redmond and, more generally, of the vocationalist agenda, and the relative victory in relation to the NFI's eligibility for state-aid while still being allowed to adopt an exclusively Catholic executive, according to Vaughan the draft documents were not sufficiently explicit in articulating an exclusivist Catholic ideology, but contained, as he explained to McQuaid, the 'disturbing element' of a 'trend towards the State and the relegation of the Church to the background'. A memo, which he sent to McQuaid, detailed his and Troy's critique of the constitution. They not only rejected the possibility of affiliating or cooperating with other societies, but also the idea of taking over the censorship of films as it was beyond the NFI's scope and already was being dealt

with by the state, as well as the 'all-embracing aim' of 'encourag[ing] the use and development of the cinematograph in the national and cultural interests of the Irish People',
which they deemed 'as not being consistent with the tone of *Vigilanti Cura*' and 'being
subject to even anti-Catholic interpretation'.[73] While the latter aim was clearly a
Devane-type phrase, the ideas on cooperation with other bodies and stricter film censorship were ones repeatedly articulated by Devane.

On 9 November, Vaughan wrote to McQuaid once again, this time to say that a
group led by Gerald MacKeown (Gearoid MacEoin) BL, was planning to institute legal
proceedings to stop the use of the name 'National Film Institute'. He did not known
whether Brigid Redmond was involved, but reported she referred to the new group as
'The Catholic Social Service Group', a title which would have irked McQuaid as it was
similar to his Catholic Social Service Conference, and that she was 'playing into the
hands' of Muintir na Tíre.[74] Two days later, a draft of the constitution was passed by
the drafting committee, which voted four (Fagan, Piggott, Sheridan and Collier) to one
(Redmond) in favour. Redmond, who at this stage was completely marginalized, nevertheless, sought to assert her own position with McQuaid and on 14 November sent
him a twelve-page memo on the NFI's activities and problems.[75] She continued to complain about the narrow composition of the organization, and in a further communication on 9 February 1945 pointed out to McQuaid that the executive committee,
which consisted of her brother, Morgan Sheehy, Dermot O'Flynn, James Fagan and
Joseph Murphy, had 'no representatives of chief educational bodies, learned and scientific societies; the film trade; film associations, or government'.[76] Meanwhile, indicative of the importance of the Catholic ethos for the NFI and its regard for clerical recognition, Dermot O'Flynn, as chairman of the executive, had also written to McQuaid
and Bishops McNamee and Staunton seeking to put the NFI as an item on the hierarchy's agenda for their January 1945 meeting.[77]

On 10 February 1945, the NFI's organizing secretary/administrator, Sean
O'Sullivan,[78] the institute's first paid official who had taken over the executive activities formerly performed voluntarily by Brigid Redmond, sent McQuaid a copy of the
ballot paper for the election of the NFI's first nine-person executive.[79] While there is
no record within the McQuaid papers that he favoured any particular candidates on
the list of twenty-two, it is hard to imagine that he would have approached the election neutrally as only nine months earlier he had engineered the emasculation of the
original executive committee.

With a rigorous Catholic constitution in place, McQuaid may have felt he no longer
needed the same (clerical) personnel through whom the constitution had been moulded
to occupy positions within the executive committee, which, as is clear from his injunc-
tion to Fr Redmond, he believed should predominantly comprise of prominent lay
Catholics, namely, reliable, experienced professionals. It was, perhaps, as a result of
his influence, or even manipulation, that none of the five priests listed on the ballot
paper (Fathers Collier, Devane, Redmond, Troy and Vaughan), or, indeed, Brother F.X.
McCloskey, the editor of *Our Boys,* were elected. Though the NFI's Articles of Association allowed for nine members to be elected, only eight places were filled, with the

ninth place 'reserved' for GAA secretary Padraig O'Keefe who, as O'Sullivan told McQuaid the day after the election, was 'willing to serve' on the NFI's council, the new name for the executive.[80] Perhaps, given the direction which McQuaid, through Fathers Collier, Troy, Vaughan and others had succeed in imposing, the increasingly volatile Brigid Redmond was among those who failed to get elected.[81] The successful candidates, on the other hand, were four members of the previous executive: James C. Fagan, Joseph Murphy, Dermot J. O'Flynn, and Morgan Sheehy; principal teachers Dr Padraig T. Breathnach (of Naomh Peader [St Peter's] National School, Phibsborough, who, in a crossover of interests which further connected him to McQuaid, was appointed to the censorship of publications' board in 1950) and Patrick J. O'Hagan (of East Wall National School); John D. Sheridan (who had been a member of the constitution drafting committee); and Gabriel Fallon.

In April, Dermot O'Flynn was unanimously elected chairman of the organization, thus ending the debate surrounding its constitution, which was formally adopted two months later, and thus this executive was an interim one. The choice of O'Flynn was almost certainly encouraged by McQuaid. Not only was O'Flynn (as a prominent member of the Knights of St Columbanus,[82] the Catholic organization, which most often took the lead in calling for more restrictive film and book censorship and was a bastion of McQuaid's support) in regular correspondence with McQuaid on a wide range of issues, but also in May 1952 he was McQuaid's nominee to the censorship of publications' board[83] on which he served until 1957.[84] Finally, in June 1945, the NFI constitution was adopted and the list of subscribers (the equivalent to company shareholders, though, of course, the NFI was not a commercial or profit-making body) were led by experienced Catholic educationalists, including the influential academic and writer, Professor Alfred O'Rahilly, president of University College, Cork. Ironically, O'Rahilly had served as a member of the government's commission on vocational organizations and almost single-handedly refocused the outlook of the Catholic newspaper *The Standard*. He was also a member of the institute's council during 1945–7, though he appears not to have attended its meetings. Other subscribers to the company included the nine members of the interim executive – Padraig O'Keefe, Padraig Breathnach, Patrick O'Hagan, James Fagan, Gabriel Fallon, Joseph Murphy, Dermot O'Flynn, Morgan Sheehy, and John D. Sheridan – all of whom were appointed to the new board with O'Flynn elected as chairman and Fagan as vice-chairman; previous NFI chair Professor J.J. Piggott, St Patrick's, Drumcondra, who also served on the censorship of publications' board from 1946 to 1957, including as chair during 1956–57; and surgeon A.B. Clery, a confidante of McQuaid's, who was also elected to the council. Non-subscribers elected to the council included two religious – Fr Vaughan and Brother McCloskey – and T.J. Molloy.[85]

It took ten years from the time Fr Devane first publicly articulated the need for an Irish film institute until it was established. During that time, Devane held doggedly to a vocationalist agenda, seeking to involve all film interests, including non- and interdenominational groups, not least the IFS, as well as those in other areas of Irish cultural and social life such as the Gate and Abbey theatres, even Muintir, and the GAA.

Only the last one of these, the GAA, actually found a place in the new organization, and then perhaps only because its administrator, Padraig O'Keefe, a friend of de Valera's, was culturally and religiously conservative. Though Fr Devane's ideas resonated with Brigid Redmond, who fought a rearguard action, she was increasingly made irrelevant,[86] while by the 1940s Fr Devane was elderly and no longer operating at his full capacity. (He died in 1951.) Interestingly, there were no patrons of the incorporated body from 1945 to 1947, at which point Archbishop McQuaid was invited to become the institute's patron, a position he retained exclusively until his death in 1973.[87]

THE NATIONAL FILM INSTITUTE OF IRELAND, 1945–82

Adopting a careful methodical approach in its earlier years, the first task of the NFI council was to build up a library of educational films. While this was made possible largely through annual department of education grants,[88] which allowed it to purchase films, foreign embassies and national cultural institutions also donated material to the national body. In 1950, when it registered 3,722 film bookings,[89] its catalogue comprised of an impressive 941 films, almost five times the number listed in its first catalogue in 1946 when it included 148 sound and forty-eight silent films.[90] Within five years, in 1955, a full-time librarian, Seamus O'Connor, had been appointed to oversee the 1,500 strong-collection. This continued to develop such that in 1958 it had 1,628 films with 6,420 bookings, in 1960 it had 2,000 films, and in 1978 had double that number, 4,000 films.[91] Thereafter, the collection, which never expanded beyond its 1978 catalogue, increasingly fell into disuse as a consequence of television, which was making its presence felt from the mid-1960s, and the advent of video in the 1980s.

Designed to fill the void left by commercial cinema distributors, the film library consisted largely of documentaries and covered most subjects on the school curriculum. Consequently, it comes as no surprise that the educational sector was the institute's main market, though many other organizations relied on its services, the most important of which were farming-based groups, youth clubs and, following the development in the 1960s and 1970s of an Irish industrial base, industry and state bodies. Though the films were mostly of American or British origin as very few were produced in Ireland (a recurring complaint by NFI personnel during the 1940s and 1950s), when in the late 1940s the Irish government decided to finance occasional documentaries on such subjects as the modernization of agriculture, road safety and public health, the NFI was charged with producing them, a role it continued to fulfil until at least 1957.[92] Besides these public information films, the institute also produced and distributed two government-funded cultural documentaries. The first of these was *A Nation Once Again* (1946), a centenary film on the life and work of Thomas Davis and his relevance to contemporary Ireland, while the second was *W.B. Yeats – A Tribute* (1950), the first film to be funded by the department of foreign affairs' cultural relations' committee.[93]

Further indication of the institute's close engagement with government departments during the first two decades of the organization's existence (after which it became less relevant), can be seen in the distribution of the government-sponsored films and the NFI's role as an intermediary between the government and the film trade with which it also had firm links despite its promotion of moral classification of films.[94] In addition, the department of education also gave funding to the NFI to put Irish language soundtracks on imported films,[95] while the departments of health and local government contracted it to screen health and safety films in schools and other institutions, though by this time the NFI was already involved in exhibition having established mobile film units with portable generators. Through these units they screened agricultural and other informational films to rural audiences who otherwise would not have had the chance to see such films.[96]

From the outset, in order to neutralize the importance of the IFS and to consolidate its own role and enhance the importance and use-value of their film library, the NFI provided courses for teachers, through whom they hoped that they would be able to use the schools to develop a 16mm 'cinema' circuit. In 1946 they held their first summer school, which, mixing instruction in film projection with film appreciation for teachers, later became institutionalized as an annual event and often drew on the expertise of British Film Institute educationalists.[97] Initially, given that in the mid- to late 1940s, most Irish schools did not possess 16mm projectors, one of the institute's first tasks was to train teachers in the use of such equipment so that school principals would then have an incentive to purchase projectors, after which they could rent films from the NFI library. However, by the 1950s the NFI was complaining that schools were using their recently acquired projectors for entertainment only purposes. Aligned to the use of 16mm projectors in schools was the notion of 16mm 'cinemas', often run in parish halls under clerical control.

As early as 1946, the NFI sought to establish local 16mm film units, based on diocesan areas (that is, parishes), under the direction of the local bishop, but, in a manner similar to Muintir na Tíre, incorporating vocational categories. To this end, NFI secretary Sean O'Sullivan sent a circular to the bishops in July 1946 reporting that 'certain groups', a reference perhaps to the developing 16mm entertainment market at village level, or even the IFS, which were 'not subject to clerical guidance, intend to send travelling film units throughout the country for purely commercial purposes.' O'Sullivan wanted the bishops to restrict access to such units in parish halls and to support 'opposition that the institute can provide' by making diocesan priests aware of the aims and objects of the NFI, including its four mobile film units.[98] These units and their attendant 16mm activities, described by *Irish Cinema Quarterly* editor T.J.M. Sheehy, as 'for all who are interested in brightening rural life without urbanising it',[99] were ultimately envisaged as a form of Catholic Action and, indeed, portrayed as such by one commentator who saw them as an attempt 'to infuse the Christian spirit' and 'to offset … the frequently paganising influences of the large-scale commercial film industry.'[1] Though by 1948 six units had been set up in Galway, Cork, Waterford, Killarney, Monaghan and Dundalk, with plans for a further five in Wexford, New Ross, Dublin, Limerick and Clare, it appears that except for the two units in Dublin and Navan,[2] they were largely inactive. This is confirmed in the NFI's 1950 annual report. The document records its 'regret' that local units, which, by local activities, 'would have spread the influence of the institute … and would have brought a host of new members to our fold', had not brought the 'advantages' that the council had expected.[3]

Consequently, the areas with which the NFI's pursuit of Catholic Action became most clearly identified were in its moral classification of films (which had its roots in *Vigilanti cura*)[4] and in its approach to film 'appreciation'. These were expressed through its summer schools; its quarterly publication; its film reviewing panels and their published film reviews;[5] in its early years, its series of prestigious public lectures;[6] and its engagement with the French-based International Catholic Cinema Office (OCIC), which, originally formed in 1927, acted as a focal point for international Catholic thinking on the cinema. After contacting Bishop Staunton of Ferns, secretary to the Catholic hierarchy and one of the institute's original patrons, authorization was given for NFI secretary Sean O'Sullivan to attend the 1949 conference of the recently reinvigorated OCIC,[7] while the following year, the Catholic hierarchy in Ireland gave permission for the institute to become a full member of OCIC, with successive NFI chairmen thereafter usually attending the OCIC annual gatherings and serving on the organization's governing board.[8] NFI chairman James Fagan, for example, not only attended the 1951 Lucerne congress, the theme of which was 'The Christian film critic and his public';[9] the 1952 Madrid meeting when 'Film education' was the topic;[10] and the 1953 Malta convention;[11] but also the 1954 Cologne symposium when they discussed 'The moral classification of films'.[12] In response to an OCIC questionnaire for this conference, the NFI stated that the compilation and distribution of its weekly classification guide to schools, convents and colleges had proved too expensive to continue such that they were forced to introduce an annual subscription of 10s. whereupon they found that 'the response … was not as great as [they] had hoped'.[13] In any case, while at Cologne Fagan secured OCIC backing to hold the 1955 assembly under NFI auspices in Dublin.

Attended by representatives of twenty-four countries, the 1955 Irish event, which set out to explore 'the extent and influence of the moral classification of films', was opened by Archbishop McQuaid. In his address, he praised the NFI and, in keeping with his theological outlook, affirmed a doctrinal notion of moral classification,

> by moral, I mean, doctrinal classification, for morality is based on the doctrine that is the deposit of Faith, entrusted by her Divine Founder to the Church.[14]

Such a rigorous approach, as evidenced by the attention that McQuaid received as a regular guest at NFI annual general meetings until shortly before his death in 1973, was shared by many key NFI members, not least of whom was Fagan who stated that the NFI wanted to see the cinema in Ireland make 'its proper contribution to the advancement of our people, and [help] them to achieve that end, in the Divine Order of Things, for which we are all created.'[15]

Unsurprisingly, the NFI's *Quarterly*, which regularly published the OCIC congress reports and papers, also echoed this view with one late 1951 editorial stating that moral and aesthetic standards are not easy to come by, even on the moral side, and there will always be room for differences of opinion. But in this country the ten commandments will be a guide, and we can get help not just from our own consciences but from that national conscience that is the result of a long, unbroken Catholic tradition.[16]

Another NFI article argued that Ireland was

being swamped by the culture and philosophy of other English-speaking peoples and [consequently, Irish] minds [were] being shaped by England and America. This constant pressure from without cannot do much harm to people old enough to remember the struggle for national independence, but our children have little protection against it. And apart from the question of morals it is tragic that so far we have made no serious effort to secure some measure of control of a medium that is forming and shaping the minds of our children.[17]

Despite the NFI's calls for further controls on film, which relied moreover on fusing notions of nationality and Catholic morality within a broader socio-cultural context rather than on doctrinal certainties, their film reviews as published in the NFI's own *National Film Quarterly* were judged by McQuaid as not displaying a sufficiently robust Catholic moral perspective.[18] As a result, in 1956 he arranged, as Fagan reported in the journal, 'a special Course of instruction' for the members of the film reviewing panel.[19] Characteristically direct in his criticism, McQuaid deemed the NFI 'defective in its attitude to films from the Catholic point of view', and appointed Fr Dempsey and Dr O'Hare as chaplins to lecture NFI members, especially members of the film reviewing panel, on moral theology, Catholic philosophy of life as a whole, and on Catholic philosophy of art.[20] In fact, McQuaid went even further and 'especially appointed' teachers, businessmen, professional men and priests to the panel.[21]

In any case, as substantiated by the relatively large numbers continuing to attend cinemas, neither the NFI's position with regard to cinema (articulated in its reviewing classifications and its call for further restrictions), nor that of McQuaid fully dominated Irish thinking on the matter. While one newspaper described the NFI's film-reviewing panellists in 1955 as 'ever active busybodies',[22] on the whole, the press appears largely to have ignored the more extreme Catholicism of the institute's moral ratings, either out of fear of losing valuable advertising revenue from the cinema trade or, more likely, because none of the newspapers had full-time film reviewers who might have challenged the NFI with informed debate. One exception was writer Patrick Kavanagh, who complained in 1948 in his capacity as film critic of the Catholic newspaper *The Standard* that the NFI 'does not approve of criticism', and went to question the attitudes underpinning the organization. Noting that 'there seems to be ... too much of the priggish and jingoistic outlook about this body', he went on to suggest that they 'mean well' but 'lack, as a body, the free outlook which produces work of imagination'. Kavanagh concluded that its work was 'futile'.[23] The NFI's John D. Sheridan's[24] defensive response only elicited Kavanagh's acceptance that 'they are a benevolent soci-

ety with no interest in making money, but they are also unfortunately rather uninspiring.'[25]

Although the NFI, which attempted to pursue a thoroughly anti-commercial cinema
agenda while simultaneously seeking to present a positive Catholic film policy, undoubtedly served a negative and retarding function in terms of the development of an internationally informed film culture, not least through its refusal to accommodate Fr
Devane's vocationalist agenda but also in its determination to marginalize the more
broad-based progressive IFS, such that for thirty-five years the notion of an Irish film
institute was bound up with a narrow Catholic attitude to film and sexuality, nevertheless, it should also be acknowledged that, as J.H. Whyte[26] has commented,

> If a full survey were undertaken, it might appear that the Irish Catholic preoc-
> cupation with sexual morality in the [nineteen-] twenties, thirties and forties
> was only an extreme example of a trend ... found among the traditionally-
> minded people all over the world.

Furthermore, it should be noted also that neither the NFI nor the church necessarily
always reflected the most extreme Catholic viewpoint.

Elia Kazan's gritty *On the Waterfront* (1954), for example, was not only positively
reviewed by the NFI's *National Film Quarterly*,[27] with even the leather-jacketed boxer-
docker-enforcer played by Marlon Brando (rather than Fr Barry played by Karl
Malden), appearing on its front cover, but it received the OCIC's 1955 award for best
Catholic film during its Dublin congress. The OCIC citation highlighted 'the profound
action of the Church in the person of a priest [Fr Barry], who in the midst of shame-
fully exploited dockers, courageously undertakes to secure the triumph of social justice.'[28] The *Sunday Independent*, by contrast, refused to review the film. In a special
statement on the film-reviewing page, the editor, who objected to the film's 'horrible
and brutal' violence despite its having been toned down by the censor, recommended
that parents should not let their offspring see the film, claiming that 'the insidious penetration of this type of film can do untold harm, especially to young people.'[29]

Nevertheless, and not withstanding the institute's belief, articulated by their librarian as late as 1959, that their 16mm 'movement' with its eighty to one hundred parish
cinemas was 'a potential weapon in sufficient quantity to change the face of Ireland',[30]
the institute proved unable to impose the narrow preoccupations, alluded to by Whyte,
on yet another generation. Indeed, by the mid-1960s Ireland had changed to the point
where the NFI were little able to influence the culture. Not only had television and
new leisure activities brought new opportunities for consumers that negatively impacted
on cinema admission figures (diminishing since 1954), but also, more importantly, the
base from which the NFI had received its most loyal support – conservative, rural communities – was being eroded through emigration and internal migration. Despite the
institute's attempt to adapt to the new socio-economic imperatives by developing a
service of providing different types of films to industry and government training bodies,
its importance as a national organization continued to wane.

Meanwhile, the church itself was changing due to the liberalization set in train by the second Vatican council (1962–5), which, convened by Pope John XXIII and continued by Pope Paul VI, had attempted to restore the unity of the church, engage with other Christians and accept the challenges of a secular modern world. Even Dr McQuaid adapted to the changing circumstances by establishing a church film unit. He sent two of his diocesan priests, Fathers Joseph Dunn[31] and Des Forristal, for training in film techniques to New York for three months in 1959, and so began the Radharc (Look/ Sight) film unit. The first film made under the Radharc banner, *Lá 'le Bríde* (*St Brigid's Day*, 1960) won the NFI's award for outstanding Irish language film in 1960. The umbrella body, the Catholic Communications' Centre, Dublin, which offered training and other activities, developed as an extension of Radharc, though the film unit maintained a degree of independence.[32]

Finally, following NFI council election tussles in the early 1980s between a declining, even moribund, old guard and a new generation of secular and film-informed activists whose number included this book's principal author,[33] the NFI's direction was changed radically. Renamed the Irish Film Institute in 1983 (see chapter 6), its summer schools, which had been renewed in 1980 (with topics such as 'Film study and the Irish context'; 'Genre and film noir'; 'Film: entertainment, politics, form'; '21 years of RTÉ'; and 'Television drama'), introduced a more inclusive and internationally informed level of cinema and television debate to Ireland, thus contrasting with the innoculatory or prescriptive approach adopted by some lecturers at early NFI events. This institutional break eventually led in 1992 to the opening of the Irish Film Institute's premises at 6 Eustace Street, Dublin, with its two cinemas, a film archive, educational facilities, specialist film bookshop, and a bar and restaurant. Incorporating a number of key organizations such as Filmbase (until its move in the mid-2000s to larger nearby premises), access>CINEMA, and Media Desk, the centre has succeeding in becoming the focal point for film culture in Ireland.

THE PERENNIAL CONTROVERSY: CHILDREN AND THE CINEMA

The possible baneful effects of cinema on children have preoccupied moral reformers worldwide since the beginnings of cinema. Nevertheless, prior to the Second World War, little reputable independent scientific research had been carried out on the subject, and, thereafter, the reports that emerged were often contradictory and provoked disagreement over the methodologies employed, the findings and the interpretations drawn, such that in 1961 a UNESCO survey of the research literature produced by 400 writers from nearly thirty countries concluded that 'the one thing known with certainty' about children and the cinema 'is that we don't know anything *with certainty*', except 'the obvious fact that they have a persistent liking for it'.[34]

Despite the lack of corroborated international evidence and the fact that such research had never even been undertaken in Ireland, the assertion as to cinema's negative impact on young people was often given official voice in Ireland, and ranged from members of the Catholic clergy, who argued that cinema's 'corrupting influence [was] a frequent cause of juvenile crime',[35] to the churches more generally and the oireachtas, but also to the judiciary. Indeed, as already noted, in January 1935, during a hearing of the industrial schools' commission, Mr G.P. Cussen, a senior district court justice at the children's court, and chairman of the government enquiry, stated that there was an increase in crime by boys 'largely due to the pictures',[36] while Mrs M. Lynch, honorary secretary of the Child's Welfare Society, Cork, declared it was 'dangerous to allow children to go to gangster pictures'. However, during the 1930s, it was the educational sector and, in particular, the Irish National Teachers' Organization, that was most frequently to the fore when it came to criticism of children at cinemas. In 1933, the INTO passed a resolution at its annual conference calling for restrictions to be placed on the attendance of children at cinemas, while during their April 1935 assembly it approved a motion from P.J. O'Hagan, who criticized the availability of gangster and 'sex-appeal' films, urging the convening of a forum of educational and ecclesiastical authorities with a view to 'hastening legislation to regulate the admission of children in cinemas'.[37] Ten years later during another INTO annual conference, O'Hagan, who had by this time become a key figure in the NFI, declared in a clear admission of the campaign's failure that over the twelve years since the union had broached the subject of curtailing children's access to the cinema, the characters of a quarter-of-a-million children had been irreparable damaged.[38] It is probable that the INTO's renewed interest in the topic had been fuelled by campaigns at local level during the previous eighteen months.

In December 1943, both Tuam parish council and Nenagh council pressed for stronger control of films, with the latter voting in favour of the need of a regulation excluding under-14s from cinema entertainments at night, while Justice Kenny, speaking at a sitting of Longford's juvenile court, said that if parents did not do so, he would take steps to have children kept out of cinemas.[39] Throughout the following year, numerous local authority councils followed suit with resolutions calling for action to be taken on the issue. In Bray, Co. Wicklow, for example, a local priest drew up restrictions, adopted by the local authority, limiting children's attendance at cinemas.[40] (Smoking was also banned in cinemas, at this time, on the grounds that it hampered proper vision.)[41] On 11 September Wicklow county council passed a motion seeking controls on films that 'might endanger children's morals', while on the same day Waterford county council adopted a resolution demanding the grading of films as a means of 'protecting children'.[42] Despite the fact that the *Irish Press*, which carried an editorial on 'Children and the cinema' on 18 September, came out against any such restrictions on children, and cited Mr Justice H.A. McCarthy of Dublin's children's court, who opposed any bans on children's cinema-going,[43] local councils kept up the pressure with, for example, the general council of county councils provocatively calling on the minister for justice in September to indicate which films released in Ireland were unsuitable for children.[44] Subsequently, Limerick county council at its meeting on 30 October called for the prohibition of children attending gangster films,[45] while on 16 December Mayo county council pressed for restrictions on schoolchildren at late performances. Similarly, the Catholic boy scouts also sought legislation to control 'juveniles at cinemas and other amusements of a character which may tend to prejudice their physical, mental and moral welfare'.[46]

The following May, after the general council of county councils had passed a resolution pertaining to juvenile cinema attendance that supported the granting of limited certificates for certain films, the justice minister wrote to the council. In classic bureaucratic formulation, he admitted that 'the influence of the cinemas on children is sometimes injurious', but pointed out 'that the injury is caused more by too frequent attendance ... a matter for parents ... than by the quality of the films exhibited.'[47] While an editorial in the *Irish Times* seemed to concur, suggesting that 'unfortunately, many parents have not the time, the energy, or the desire to fulfil that responsibility', it went on to note that in many homes, the removal of children to the cinema for a couple of hours 'is the only hope of a rest for the mother, or – on Sundays – for the parents', and, importantly, added that

> one must wonder whether the children themselves suffer more harm from the
> example of Hollywood gangsters than from running wild in the streets. At least,
> the picture-house is warm.

It was a question, like tuberculosis and malnutrition, bound up with the standard of living. The *Times* concluded that the grading of films was perhaps the 'only solution' that the state could offer, but, nevertheless, the writer also seemed to be encouraging local councils to impose restrictions on the hours when children might attend.[48] By contrast, P.S. O'Hegarty, writing in the *Sunday Independent*, voiced his opposition to any 'special censorship for children', including the 'vexatious regulations' of cinema hours. Indeed, the prolific historical writer and secretary of the department of posts and telegraphs from 1922 to 1944, went so far as to say that the 'very strict' film censorship 'could do with some relaxation'.[49] As might have been expected, the government took no action,[50] but regardless, if the *Irish Times* is to be believed, by January 1946, juvenile delinquency was 'declining rapidly', with fewer children committing crimes 'being prompted to do so by the desire to get money for amusement'.[51] That same month a suggestion from, perhaps, an unexpected quarter aroused the government on the matter, but then it was in the context of Catholic-nationalist paranoia about England and Protestantism, rather than cinema or children per se.

In January 1946 J. Arthur Rank announced his acquisition of a majority stake in the Elliman-owned cinema chain. Given that it was Ireland's largest film exhibition company, the purchase generated considerable controversy from both small Irish exhibitors and Catholic writers on the cinema, such as T.J.M. Sheehy in the *Irish Catholic* (see chapter 3). In part, possibly motivated by a desire to soften this negative reaction, but also, no doubt, because of his experience in Britain where he had established highly-successful children's film clubs, which, usually held on Saturday mornings, included children's films, other entertainments and uplifting embellishments including talks on good citizenship and road safety, Rank proposed to establish similar children's cinema clubs in his newly acquired Irish cinemas. In anticipation of these developments, the Irish Film Society reported in December 1945 that its own children's film committee, discussed below, had been 'laying the groundwork' for a new organization, the Children's and Educational Film Association of Ireland (CEFA), to deal exclusively with films in education and entertainment. At its formative meeting on 18 January 1946, the very day Rank announced its takeover of the Elliman circuit of Irish cinemas, the CEFA council was to be chosen from panels representing primary, secondary and technical education, 'cultural' and 'sociological' workers, and members of the film trade.[52]

In early February, the NFI's John D. Sheridan met Rank to discuss the distribution in his cinemas of the NFI-produced/government-funded films, including the soon-to-be-released *A Nation Once Again*, but he also spoke to Rank about the possibility of running Saturday morning children's matinees in Ireland. As reported by Sheridan in the NFI council's minutes' book, Rank responded with the promise that he would take up the matter with the people concerned in London. Subsequently, on 28 March, NFI vice-chairman P.J. O'Hagan, council member John D. Sheridan and the organization's secretary, Sean O'Sullivan, met with Rank's closest associate, Odeon-Theatres' managing director John Davis, and Mr E. St John. Following the meeting, the NFI delegation prepared a two-page memo detailing twelve points of information revealed during the encounter. This was sent to Archbishop McQuaid by NFI chairman Dermot J. O'Flynn on 13 April.

It was stated that Rank was 'anxious' to extend to Ireland his children's film clubs, which, as emphasized by both Davis and St John, would have an Irish character, and include ten minutes of community singing, a cartoon, educational films on citizenship or safety, a talk by the club manager, a cowboy or wild-west feature, a serial, and slides on such topics as kindness to animals or brushing teeth. Rank would retain control of the matinees, but an advisory committee of adults, which he hoped would include representatives from the NFI and other organizations, would be formed, while all films would be previewed by the institute or the advisory committee by arrangement with the film censor.

Despite these apparently strict guarantees, the NFI report declared that it was 'not enamoured of the proposed scheme' and listed four objections. Firstly, it feared that despite the slight alterations in programming, the propaganda contained in the programmes would be alien in tendency; secondly, Saturday morning was usually set aside for children's confessions; thirdly, the proposed progamme would clash with when hurling and football leagues were usually played; and finally, it was noted that there was a very sharp difference of opinion among members of the teaching profession in England as to the merits or otherwise of such screenings. Worried that some other 'and far less desirable organisation' (a reference, no doubt, to the IFS and its children's committee, but equally applicable to the more broad-based CEFA) would step in and cooperate with Rank, which seemed determined to proceed with the scheme, it called for a quick decision on whether 'our attitude is to be one of opposition or co-operation'.[53]

Copies of the report were sent to Taoiseach Éamon de Valera, with whom the NFI also sought a meeting, and to Archbishop McQuaid. In the accompanying letter to

McQuaid, NFI chairman O'Flynn reported that the institute's 'general reaction' was disdainful of this 'importation from abroad – this maturing of to-morrow's audience for Mr Rank' and complained that the departments of education and justice 'will not lift a finger to "interfere with commercial interests".' He then asked how the NFI could prevent the proposal, and, if it went ahead, should the institute act on the advisory committee 'and strive to neutralize the influence as far as possible' or 'withdraw completely', thereby ensuring that the advisory committee would be the 'mixed grill' of the IFS's Comhairle na nÓg (he seemed to be unaware of the recently-formed CEFA).[54]

On 1 May, the NFI council's subcommittee on children's films sat (the last day on which there is any reference to Rank's children's clubs in the NFI minutes), and de Valera, who 'attached the greatest importance to this matter and desired that it should be examined as a matter of immediate urgency' with regard to its possible national and social implications, met an unofficial NFI delegation consisting of O'Flynn, O'Hagan and Padraig O'Keefe. Following the session, de Valera ordered his civil servants to examine the matter in relation to the provision of Article 40.6 of the constitution and 'such statutory powers, if any, as might enable the State to prevent the operation of Mr Rank's scheme or to regulate or control the scheme if put into operation'.[55] On 3 May, memos, to be replied to within the week, were sent to the departments of industry and commerce, justice, and education to ascertain their views on Rank's children's film scheme.

Industry and commerce sent an immediate and positive reply.[56] They could find no objection to the scheme provided there were no problems from an educational and social viewpoint, and envisaged no effect on the development of an Irish film industry. Consequently, they offered to engage in discussions with Rank, with whom they already had contacts. Justice's reply, five days later on 9 May, was similarly positive. Not only did it doubt whether the alien influence would be any greater than the alien influence of the films ordinarily attended by children, but also suggested that Rank's programmes might be beneficial in encouraging other exhibitors to programme films for children. Though it thought that films certified for children would need to be introduced, and that this would be problematic, it was also of the opinion that there were insufficient grounds for legislation on the matter. Accordingly, it was inclined to the view that Rank should be allowed to proceed with the scheme, but recommended that the NFI accept the invitation to join the advisory committee so as to ensure that 'no objectionable features are introduced into the programmes'.[57] The same day, the department of education also replied, but, identifying the question of control (and influence) as of primary importance, was not welcoming of the proposal.

It argued that as such programmes 'cannot fail to exercise an appreciable influence on ... those who regularly attend', allowing the 'Rank Combine' to control the matinees

> involves placing an important aspect of the education of our young people under the guidance of an outside authority over which neither the Church nor the Parents nor the State would have effective control.

Only with *complete* Irish control of the scheme would it be acceptable to education. Furthermore, and reflecting the impulse towards compulsion, which had been a feature of Irish language policy since independence, they demanded 'definite assurance that the national language will be accorded its rightful place on all the programmes'. It reported, erroneously perhaps, that cinema attendance among young people was 'casual and infrequent', but that such a scheme was bound to increase cinema-going, the desirability of which, from a social viewpoint, was questioned. It therefore concluded with a declaration of opposition to the Rank scheme unless it was

> under such effective native control as will ensure that our young people shall be brought under no influences other than those calculated to develop and strengthen in their growing consciousness a proper attitude towards religion, morality and patriotism.[58]

In order to resolve the issue and to emphasize his own concern about Rank's proposal, on 17 May de Valera circulated a memo to the members of the government. Entitled 'Films for children' the document outlined the scheme and the positions of the three government departments consulted. On 21 May the cabinet decided that de Valera and the minister for education, Thomas Derrig, should speak with Rank. To this end, on 7 June, the department of external affairs wrote to Ireland's high commissioner in London, J.W. Dulanty, who, it appears, then had a lengthy meeting with Rank and John Davis on 12 June during which he expressed de Valera's concerns, especially with regard to the Irish government's policy of restoration of the Irish language. While Dulanty formed the impression that Davis would be willing to proceed regardless of opinion in Ireland, Rank, by contrast, indicated his reluctance to go ahead with any scheme with which the taoiseach had misgivings. To allay any fears, Rank invited representatives from the Irish government or the Dáil, or, anyone whom de Valera suggested, to visit his British children cinema clubs, and even offered to meet with de Valera,[59] an invitation realized on 11 July when de Valera 'stressed the importance of the State and Church points of view in regard to the cinema as an educative influence'.

Having pointed out the denominational nature of Irish education and how conditions in Ireland differed from those elsewhere, de Valera asked Rank to consult with both the minister for education and religious authorities before submitting a plan tailored to the special educational conditions and needs of the Irish market. He also threatened that in such a serious matter state action might have to be taken if undesirable developments appeared likely to take place. Though it seems that Rank agreed to liaise with the department of education and the clergy with a view to proposing a revised scheme, two months later the taoiseach's department wrote to education enquiring as to whether Rank had been in touch with them. Education replied the following day stating that no communication had been made by Rank.[60] It appears, therefore, that de Valera's cautioning remarks led to Rank abandoning his interest in such a project. In contrast with the near-hysterical responses of the NFI, McQuaid and de Valera to the idea of Rank establishing children's film clubs in Ireland, the Protestant archbishop of Dublin praised Rank at the Irish Secondary Teachers' Association conference in Dublin at the end of April.[61]

Despite the scuppering of Rank's children's programmes, from a purist Catholic or NFI perspective, the IFS's children's committee and its associated organization, the CEFA, remained no less a threat to the minds of the nation's children. The IFS had been active in this area from the beginning of the 1940s and on 17 and 24 February 1940 had held a conference on 'The child and the cinema' at the Classic Cinema, Terenure, with papers delivered by, among others, Liam O'Leary ('The social respon-sibility of the film'), Louise Gavin Duffy ('Visual impressions') and Ernest Blythe ('Gaelic: the child and the film'). Designed to initiate 'constructive action' in the use of 'this great medium of entertainment and culture into proper channels which will render it a great service to the community',[62] it was, as one of the participants, school-teacher Áine Ní Chanainn, subsequently wrote, the 'first attempt' in Ireland 'to focus the attention of educationalists on the importance of the film in education'.[63] Shortly afterwards, an IFS children's film committee was formed. The committee, which iden-tified its activities as promoting the use of film in education and in juvenile entertain-ment, included Edward Toner (chairman), headmaster Cyril B. Parker (secretary); James J. Carey (treasurer); Pádraig Ó Nualláin; exhibitor and distributor Hubert McNally; B. Irene Grove; Máirtín Bean Uí Riain; Áine Ní Chanainn; and Abbey Theatre direc-tor Ernest Blythe. On 16 September 1942, during a children's film committee-spon-sored Dublin Mansion House lecture given by the director of the British Film Institute, Dr Oliver Bell, at which numerous educationalists attended, it was decided to form a teachers' group[64] (of the film society), which would study the implications of teaching with the aid of educational film, and a teachers' film production unit, which, under the direction of Pádraig Ó Nualláin, followed in the wake of the work of Frederick Phillips who had already produced 'the first' Gaelic cartoon and was then making a geography film, *Zones* (1942).[65]

In 1943 Comhairle na nÓg replaced the children's cinema committee, and incor-porated both the teachers' group and the teachers' production unit (also known as Cumann Déanta Scannáin Oideachais). The association, presided over by Justice Henry McCarthy, with vice-presidents Frank Hugh O'Donnell and E.A. Maguire, and with Liam O'Leary as its planning director, liaised with the Irish Theatre and Cinema Association with the aim of holding special matinees for children under 16 years-of-age at various suburban Dublin cinemas, and at which they would offer additional supervision. The first such event, targeted at the 7 to 16 year-old group, was held at Dublin's Olympia Theatre on 18 December 1943. Its success led Comhairle na nÓg and the Theatre and Cinema Association to form a joint committee – the Children's Film Council – which was charged with the promotion of children's matinee pro-grammes.[66] While these were envisaged as primarily entertaining, they would nonethe-less include at least one short film of special interest from a cultural or educational point of view.[67]

In May 1944, in an effort to influence national policy Comhairle na nÓg, which had expanded from organizing lectures and demonstrations on the value of educational

film and the use of visual aids, to making several teaching films and forming the educational film programme group, submitted a memorandum on 'The film in education'
to the minister for education. The document, drafted by Liam O'Leary, Morgan Sheehy
(listed under his Irish name, Tomás MacSithigh), Breandán Ó Sé and Áine Ní
Chanainn[68] starts by quoting (strategically perhaps) from *Vigilanti cura* vis-à-vis the
'power' of motion pictures. The cinema

> speaks by means of vivid concrete imagery which the mind takes in with enjoy-
> ment and without fatigue. Even the crudest and most primitive minds which
> have neither the capacity nor the desire to make the efforts necessary for abstract
> or deductive reasoning are captured by the cinema.[69]

In contrast to the majority Catholic approach, Comhairle na nÓg's memo goes on to
ignore the encyclical's 'moral' dictums and instead highlights *Vigilanti cura*'s positive
view of the medium. It states, therefore, in addition to providing recreation, films

> are able to arouse noble ideals of life, to communicate valuable conceptions,
> to impart better knowledge of the history and beauties of the Fatherland and
> of other countries, to present truth and virtue under attractive forms, to create
> or at least to favour understandings among nations, social classes and races and
> to champion the cause of justice, to give life to the claims of virtue and to con-
> tribute positively to the genesis of a just social order.[70]

Throughout, emphasis is placed on the value of visual education with film presented as 'a truly magic blackboard which holds interest and arouses imagination'.[71]
In discussing Irish language sound films, the memo commented that such films would
help connect Irish with the outside world, and, thus, lose the 'unfortunate tendency'
to regard it as something peculiar to the classroom.[72] Indeed, only five months later,
Conradh na Gaeilge, committed as it was to the restoration of the Irish language, held
a symposium on the importance of film in its sphere of interest. 'One of the first public
seminars of its type', it was addressed by a number of film society activists including
Ernest Blythe ('The film and national culture'), Liam O'Leary ('An Irish film industry'), and Áine Ní Chanainn ('The film in education') as well as Fr Collier ('Youth and
the cinema').[73] While Comhairle na nÓg's policy included the objective of encouraging 'a Cinema which will serve the best interests of the Child', it also declared a modernizing impulse as it 'stood for new methods in Irish education'.[74]

In 1945, the IFS's initiatives were compressed into the first Irish summer school of
visual education, which was addressed by the director of the Scottish Film Council, A.
Russell Borland, and Eilish McGinley, who had produced educational films in Glasgow.
Held at Dublin's Peacock Theatre between 30 July and 4 August, the school attracted
fifty teachers from all over the country and several of the Gaelic organizers from
Comhdháil Náisiúnta na Gaeilge, after which a pubic symposium was held at the
Mansion House. This event, presided over by Justice Henry McCarthy, represents one

of the rare occasions when IFS and NFI personnel shared a public platform. Speakers included Felix Hackett, Liam O'Leary, and Áine Ní Chanainn of the IFS; P.J. O'Hagan and Morgan Sheehy of the NFI (the latter having more fully aligned himself with the NFI); and independent film exhibitors Maurice Baum and Gerry Kirkham.[75]

The summer school demonstrated how in the area of education, children and cinema, the ever-practical film society had eclipsed the NFI, which had spent the previous two years worrying about and ensuring a sectarian constitution. But then, as suggested above, the IFS's activities had served to propel Catholic film activists into establishing the NFI in the first instance. Seeking to gain exclusive control over what it regarded as its legitimate sphere of authority – the education of and influence over children (and adults) – the NFI belatedly established an interim children's committee on 5 June 1946. It was, perhaps, in this context of asserting dominance in the field that the NFI through Morgan Sheehy met with McQuaid at Archbishop's House on 14 November 1946, five months after Rank had met de Valera, with the purpose of seeking guidance in relation to Rank's children's cinema clubs.[76] (There is, however, no record of what transpired at the McQuaid/Sheehy meeting.)

Despite the participation of a number of NFI members at the 1945 Mansion House event, which followed on from the IFS summer school, as Liam O'Leary pointed out in an article on Comhairle na nÓg in *Scannán* in September 1946, the NFI's 'co-operation has not always been forthcoming'. Not only did the NFI ignore an invitation to contribute a speaker to the 1945 summer school, in 1946 it also failed to inform Comhairle na nÓg/CEFA of its own plans with regard to children and the cinema even though it had to have been 'aware of our interest in any such project'.[77] Of course, the promoters of the NFI had decided well before then that given the IFS and/or its activists were unlikely to be brought under Catholic control, they would continue on a separatist Catholic agenda. Indeed, O'Leary's other comments in *Scannán*[78] further help to explain why the film society was so distrusted by the NFI, and why 'without giving any reason' it had declined to supply *Scannán*, as reported in its December 1946 issue, 'with news of its activities, despite repeated invitations'.[79] Even if other members of the IFS, which included such influential people as Ernest Blythe, Prof. Felix Hackett, respected statistician and senior civil servant Thekla Beere, Justice Kenneth Reddin (whose novel *Another Shore* was filmed in 1948), and Owen Sheehy-Skeffington, would not agree with O'Leary's characterization in *Scannán* of the Irish education system along Patrick Pearse's lines as being under oppressive state-control, many of those would have had no trouble if O'Leary had substituted in place of the state the Catholic Church, possibly the real object of O'Leary's ire. O'Leary also complained in an anti-censorship comment about the 'unhealthy state' in Ireland 'when even the reading of the adult is arbitrarily decided for him by a state institution which assumes that all vital writing is identical with pornography.' There was, O'Leary concluded, 'a great need for the introduction of social consciousness into Irish education'.[80]

The NFI, of course, was determined that any modification of Irish education or culture would follow from their Catholic social consciousness and within six months of this article being published, the NFI and McQuaid had achieved their objective. By

March 1947 it had been agreed that Comhairle na nÓg/CEFA would be dissolved and re-established as an NFI body with the then chairwoman of the committee – Áine Ní Chanainn – changing her allegiance to the NFI and subsequently becoming a NFI council member.[81] Though the reasons for this transformation are not clear, with even Ní Chanainn's booklet, *The pioneers of audio visual education in Ireland, 1940–1962* (1992), skirting over the institutional relationships between the IFS, CEFA, and NFI, it might have been motivated by the society's and CEFA's pragmatism. It was surely understood that in the prevailing politico-religious climate that a body under the NFI, an organization well positioned to penetrate the Catholic-dominated school system, rather than one associated with the IFS, was more likely to achieve its aims and receive state support. Interestingly, previous to this, the technical instructors of the NFI's 1946 summer school for primary, secondary and vocational teachers at the Catholic teacher training college, had included those associated with Comhairle na nÓg: Breandán Ó Sé, Desmond Toomey, Pádraig Ó Nualláin and H.J. Healy.[82] By 1950, the NFI's annual summer school, which had maintained an IFS crossover with regard to technical lectures and workshops, though not the moral or appreciative elements,[83] had been approved by the department of education, with any teachers in attendance allowed extra school leave. It is also plausible that the NFI's 'takeover' of the functions of Comhairle na nÓg came about due to undoubted pressure teachers within the organization must have been subjected to from the Catholic church. That said, it may have been orchestrated, for other undisclosed reasons, by Ní Chanainn, a teacher and later school principal, who came to play an active role especially in the dubbing of Irish language soundtracks on NFI-purchased foreign films. (It was probably because of her role as a Gaelic teacher and scholar that she was appointed a member of the first governing board of Irish radio and television, the RTÉ Authority, from 1960 to 1965.)

The NFI, keen to maintain its dominance in the area of children and education now that the IFS, despite having established a Junior Film Society by its 1951–2 season,[84] had largely returned to its primary objective of screening films otherwise unobtainable in the country, invited Mary Field, executive-officer of the newly established British organization, the Children's Film Foundation, to give a public lecture in 1953. The foundation had come about following the publication of the British government's interdepartmental report on *Children and the cinema*, which, two years in the making, concluded with the 'meagre result' that cinema's influence on children's minds was 'sometimes harmful'.[85] Though the NFI regarded the report (and the group it gave rise to) as opening up 'a new and important missionary field', some members felt that it only covered part of the Irish problem.

> We here in Ireland have a similar, if not more serious problem regarding children and the Cinema, a problem which we have not analysed from religious, moral or national aspects, let alone the five approaches [entertainment; physical effects; nervous reactions; psychological and moral effects; and the cinema and juvenile delinquency] to the question made by the British government.[86]

In the absence of any 'authoritative enquiry' in Ireland, Brigid Redmond, in an article published in *Studies* in 1956, notable for its rare sense of balance and refusal of the more emotional Catholicism of her former NFI colleagues,[87] looked to the various initiatives aimed at children in Europe and North America, including Rank's children's clubs with their one million weekly attendance. Following the example of countries such as Switzerland, Portugal and Canada, she suggested excluding under-16s from cinemas, with the justification that 'it is difficult ... to judge the harm done to young audiences by bringing them into contact with not only the brutal heroes of gangster films, but also the dubious fathers and mothers of "triangle" affairs'. However, she tempered this by proposing special shows for young audiences given that children need 'a long apprenticeship' to assimilate all the 'artifices' of the movies.[88]

For its part, the National Film Institute adopted a practical, if negative way to influence children's access to cinema. From 1951 it reviewed all current films in order to advise adults on the suitability or otherwise of films for children. It should be remembered, however, that in all cases, these films had been passed already by the Irish film censor, and given that limited certificates were something of an exception, were intended for general audiences. In 1954, in an attempt to further develop 'a conscientious and responsible public', one which 'might bring about better standards of cinema entertainment' by staying away from 'unworthy' films,[89] this reviewing system was formalized into moral classification. While initially only schools, colleges and convents were issued with the reviews, from the end of 1954, the monthly film ratings were released to all newspapers in the Republic. Though the institute supported the introduction of grading of films on the British model, this was resisted by the minister for justice on the grounds that it 'would arouse unhealthy curiosity'[90] in the films receiving restrictive ratings. Though not spelled out in detail, the NFI's support for grading was, presumably, limited to those films already passed by the Irish censor (for a general audience) and not to increase the number of films in circulation for a teenage or more mature audience, or admit to the screen a relaxation of Catholic and moral standards.

Of the 809 films viewed by panellists in the three sample years in the accompanying table, only just under half of the films, 402, were deemed suitable for general audiences; 360 were regarded as adult fare; a further 31 were deemed appropriate only for adults and adolescents; while 16 were categorized as objectionable in whole or in part, thus

National Film Institute of Ireland classification of films approved for public exhibition by the Irish film censor

Year	General	Adult	Adult & Adolescent	Objectionable	Objectionable in Part	Total Viewed
1955[91]	186	129		5	2	322
1958[92]	142	161		2	5	310
1963[93]	74	70	31	2		177

suggesting these films should have been banned. It is clear then that the NFI's reviewers, suitably theologically empowered by Dr McQuaid's lecturers on Catholic theology, art and morality, judged the national film censorship regime inadequate, even though it included on the censorship of film appeal board a nominee of Dr McQuaid's! Alice would indeed have felt she was looking through a most peculiar looking glass in Ireland.

Furthermore, the NFI also sought an extension of the censor's authority to encapsulate the general content of films, given that even though he screens out 'all that is openly dangerous', there remains, as an 1955 *National Film Quarterly* editorial argues,

> things which the censor's scissors cannot touch – attitudes, and tendencies and conventions, and the easy moral codes of the two big countries from which we buy the bulk of our films.[94]

This issue was somewhat addressed fifty years later, when, in 2004, the film censor (known from 2008 as the director of film classification), John Kelleher, established a website offering consumer information on all film releases.[95]

The effect of the institute's moral classification of films on audience attendance is difficult to measure. Though T.J.M. Sheehy organized occasional campaigns through the *Irish Catholic*, and even titled his paper to the Dublin OCIC congress 'Boycotting the films' in which he related the relative success of such campaigns,[96] there is frequent reference made to the statistic that one million Irish people continued to go to the cinema each week. In any case, it seems that notwithstanding that the film reviewing panel was twenty-to-thirty reviewers-strong at least in its early period, and reviewed all the current releases, which were then sent to all Irish newspapers from the end of 1954,[97] there was a resigned acceptance that it had little or limited impact. Nevertheless, the practice of issuing reviews continued until December 1974 by which time a modification in the NFI's more restrictive Catholicism had been affected by socio-economic, cultural and filmic changes in Ireland. However, an indication that the NFI's earlier approach had not completely vanished was given in a 1972 review of *The Last Picture Show* (Peter Bogdanovich, 1971), which received an Objectionable rating (the severest) by the reviewer, NFI Secretary George McCanny, who wrote

> That such a film should be shown in this country is further proof, if proof be needed of the ever increasing downward moral trend in the film world.[98]

By then, such views were seen as part of the past. The liberalization of film censorship, which had flowed from the policy of issuing limited certificates on a wide scale from 1965 onwards, had effectively answered most Catholic critics of the cinema, at least as regards the attendance of children at cinemas. Any controversies that surfaced in relation to the cinema tended in the main to come from a liberal or left wing perspective and were focused on seeking further liberalization of censorship.[99] In any case, by the 1990s the debate over cinema had largely shifted to other technologies, not least, the internet.[1]

ARCHBISHOP MCQUAID AND THE SCREENING OF RELIGIOUS THEMED FILMS

Archbishop John Charles McQuaid, in stark contrast to the experience of his predecessor – 'the silent Archbishop' Edward Byrne whose last years in office were beset by his struggle with Parkinson's disease – engaged on numerous occasions with the official film censor – Dr Richard Hayes (1940–54), Dr Martin Brennan (1954–6) and Liam O'Hora (1956–64) – or his deputy[2] on the matter of religious-themed films. This was despite the fact that McQuaid could already potentially indirectly influence the content of commercially available films released in Ireland as he, in the role of archbishop of Dublin, had a representative on the censorship of films appeal board (as had his Protestant counterpart). Additionally, though less often, renters, distributors and independent exhibitors, including priests and religious organizations, also approached McQuaid when it came to religious material, particularly with regard to documentary films.

While such a practice of consultation on the part of the censors arose primarily in response to McQuaid's controlling hand and interventionist approach, this is not to suggest that the censor prior to McQuaid's tenure as archbishop, Ireland's first official film censor, James Montgomery (1923–40), was any less sensitive to the issue of religion than his successors. Not only did Montgomery take 'the Ten Commandments as his Code',[3] but also when it came to religious films or films with a religious element, he would seek the advice of Monsignor Michael Cronin – a formidable Thomist scholar, who was professor of ethics and politics at University College Dublin, and, importantly, Byrne's nominated representative on the film censorship appeal board – and also the opinions of other clerics, a practice to which he refers in his reports. For example, in his report on *Cloistered* (Robert Alexander, 1936, France), a documentary on a convent of the Good Shepherd Order in France, he makes reference to having shown the film to 'some Catholics and high ecclesiastics', after which he points out that if it is passed, it will be with a limited certificate to be shown in 'such places as the Father Mathew Hall under the auspices of the "Fathers"' and that 'all scenes showing the Canon of the Mass, and the Holy Communion must be deleted'. To incentivize the renter to withdraw the film, he also promised to 'return the censorship fee'. The film was finally passed with Cronin's approval, and its certificate issued a few weeks later.[4]

Though it seems that many of Montgomery's decisions were taken on the basis of his own strict Catholicism, or with recourse to ecclesiastical advice, nevertheless, his report on John McCormick's farce, *Lost at the Front* (Del Lord, 1927), passed with cuts after appeal, indicates that he might have also felt pressure from the church: 'Cutting is a thankless task for *the priest-ridden censor*' (emphasis added).[5] Regardless, he was clear that all sacraments were to be treated with reverence and respect and followed to the letter the archbishop's diktat of not allowing in Dublin cinemas 'the Canon of the Mass, or the Monstrance in procession or Benediction'.[6] As a result, Montgomery cut a number of films, including, among others, *The Wedding March* (Erich von Stroheim, 1928),[7] *Call of the Flesh* (Charles Barbin, 1930),[8] the Shirley Temple vehicle, *The Little Colonel* (David Butler, 1935, USA),[9] documentaries such as Pathé's 1930s

Holy Ghost Fathers,[10] and even news items that featured any such sensitive material, including images of the pope, but more generally of the monstrance.[11] As might be expected, this censorious practice with regard to both fiction and non-fiction continued during McQuaid's time as archbishop,[12] even when the news items originated in or pertained to Ireland,[13] or the material was 'treated with due reverence in every way' such as in Hugh Calkins' 1941 documentary *The Eternal Gift*, which features the Catholic mass.[14] Nevertheless, it seems that the blood of Jesus was not always accorded the same treatment as His body, perhaps because it was already protected from sight by being within a container.[15] Furthermore, special privilege was retained for the Catholic Church and its emissaries. In 1953, for instance, the censor demanded cut from *Nactwache* (USA title, *Keepers of the Night,* Harald Braun, 1948, Germany) the 'R.C. [Roman Catholic] service and scene between the two clergymen', but wrote 'leave Protestant service'.[16] Given that neutral scenes of priests or Catholic rituals were so routinely cut, it is hardly surprising that if the Catholic clergy were deemed to be represented in a poor or negative light then the film would be cut.

No doubt as a consequence of Montgomery's acceptance of Catholic authority and his unambiguous censorship policy, there is very little material regarding film in Archbishop Byrne's papers. One rare example relates to an early sound film by Julien Duvivier, *Golgotha* (aka *Ecce Homo* and *Behold the Man,* 1935, France), starring Robert de Vignan as Jesus and Jean Gabin as Pontius Pilate. Described by *Variety* as 'an accomplishment that should bring world-wide prestige to the French film industry',[17] the film, which details the events of Holy Week, was denied a certificate for public exhibition in Ireland by Montgomery who opposed any representation of the materialization of Christ. In his reject report on the film, he noted that he 'never passed for general exhibition' films featuring the canon of the mass and views of the monstrance in benediction and procession. He judged that the Last Supper was 'too sacred' for screening while the 'awful realism of His Passion and Death, for commercial profit in an ordinary' cinema 'amount[ed] to blasphemy'.[18] Given that the film had been positively received by those within the broader international Catholic community, J.V. Hallessy of the Catholic Film Society of Ireland (CFSI) appealed the decision; however, when the appeal board upheld Montgomery's ruling, Hallessy sent a three-page letter to Archbishop Byrne in which he enquired as to why the film had been refused certification and also included testimonies from no less a figure than Cardinal Maglione, the Vatican's secretary of state. The letter pointed out that although the Holy See had not expressed an opinion on the film, positive reference to reviews of the film had been made in the church's newspaper, *L'Observatore Romano*. Furthermore, the 'competent' French, Italian and Belgian Catholic offices had been 'unanimous in their approbation' of the film,[19] while the International Catholic Cinema Office (OCIC), which had classified the film as an 'A', thereby allowing it to be shown in parochial churches, oratories, colleges and schools, deemed it to be 'excellent from every point of view'.[20] The reply from the archbishop's secretary, Fr H.G. McKernan, was discouraging in that it redirected the query about restrictions on films 'of Catholic composition' to the film censor.[21] Undaunted, Hallessy got Cardinal MacRory, archbishop of Armagh, who had approved the CFSI's constitution when the organization was formed in 1936, to write to the film censor on their behalf. But, Hallessy told McQuaid six years later, the censor wrote 'a most misleading letter containing numerous inaccuracies',[22] a reference perhaps to Richard Hayes' reaffirmation in 1942 of the decision to uphold the banning of *Golgotha*.[23] Less controversial requests to Archbishop Byrne were ones seeking permission to show the film *The Shepherd of the Seven Hills* (aka *No Greater Faith*, 1933)[24] during Lent 1935 as a fund-raiser for the Society of St Patrick for foreign missions, and the following year, the same group sought permission to show *The Blessings of the Holy Father* at Dublin's Mansion House for the same cause.[25]

In November 1943, following a telephone conversation some weeks earlier, the official film censor Richard Hayes, wrote to Archbishop McQuaid inviting him to his office to see 'a typical' Hollywood production.[26] On 4 November McQuaid took him up on the offer and joined Hayes for the screening of *Heaven Can Wait* (Ernest Lubitsch, 1943) in which an elderly playboy on arrival in Hades tells his transgressions to Satan who sends him to Heaven. Though on the day, Hayes passed it with seven cuts for general release,[27] it seems that under pressure from McQuaid, he subsequently explored with a senior department of justice official the possibility of withdrawing the film's certificate. While this was permitted under the Emergency Powers' Order if the film was deemed to infringe Irish neutrality, there was no such power under the 1923 Censorship of Films' Act to have an 'ordinary' certificate withdrawn. Hayes noted that the withdrawal of the American short, *Army Chaplin*, part of the RKO 'This is America' series, which he had passed the previous May, was 'different', as the renter, Walter McNally, 'a Catholic, consented to withdraw it after representations were made to him', and, thus, was more amendable to diocesan pressure. Hayes told McQuaid that he cut out 'a considerable number' of 'objectionable features' from *Heaven Can Wait*, including 'the man ogling the nurse towards the end of the picture'.[28]

Perhaps regretting his invitation to McQuaid to view a film with so many objectionable features from a strict Catholic perspective (there is even a reference to divorce in the film!), it was a little over five years before Hayes wrote to McQuaid again with another such invitation, this time to view the Oscar winning *Monsieur Vincent* (Maurice Cloche, 1947, France), about the seventeenth-century eponymous figure, St Vincent de Paul, the patron of the poor.[29] Once again, McQuaid accepted, and, following the viewing on 25 January 1949 of the film (which at times is historically inaccurate), Hayes passed it with five cuts.[30] Relations between the film censor's office and Archbishop's House seem to have continued on good terms, such that in December 1953, when the NFI secretary, Francis B. Ryan, wrote to McQuaid to seek support for the film classification scheme being established by the institute, Ryan characterized the relations as 'excellent'. Ryan's primary concerns were how the censor might perceive such a rating system given that the censor's office felt 'offended' having made, they believed, 'every effort to suit the censorship to the requirements of religion', and how it might jeopardize the 'close cooperation' between the Catholic authorities and the censor. Despite the possible consequences, McQuaid, who summoned Ryan to Drumcondra, permitted the NFI to establish the reviewing panels.[31]

The following year, 1954, McQuaid contacted the recently appointed censor Martin Brennan requesting that he 'do [him] the favour of calling' so that he might discuss with him his concerns regarding the Italian film about Maria Goretti, *Cielo Sulla Palude* (*Heaven Over the Marshes, The Life of Maria Goretti* [dubbed version]; Augusto Genina, 1949) and another title, not yet even submitted to the censor, 'a propagandist film', *Martin Luther* (Irving Pichel, 1953, USA/West Germany), which had 'already caused serious trouble in other countries'.[32] McQuaid's interest in the Goretti film was ignited when Elliman Films Ltd invited him to view it. Though he stated his objection 'in principle' to the film, which had been described in an accompanying leaflet,[33] following a further letter from B. Elliman, who was 'surprised' at McQuaid's position and hoped that if he saw it he would give it 'the same blessing … as it [had been given] in other countries where it [had] been received with great acclaim',[34] McQuaid sent a representative, Monsignor Michael O'Halloran of St Joseph's, Glasthule, to see the film.

O'Halloran grimly, if succinctly, reported back to McQuaid that he 'would ban it completely'. He noted that the censor, Martin Brennan, accompanied by his department of justice 'minder', Mr E.C. Powell, was 'very worried' by the film, which he decided he would cut in five or six places if he passed it at all, while two others in attendance, Mrs Carton and Mrs Keenan, there, it seemed, at O'Halloran's request, felt that the film should be passed with three or four cuts. Elliman, who was astonished at O'Halloran's response, told him that his company would not wish to handle any film that would offend religious feeling and hoped for some communication from the archbishop.[35] On 10 November, when McQuaid, following his return from a trip to Rome, saw O'Halloran's 'gravely disquieting' report, he wrote to Brennan asking him to visit. It is not known what happened between McQuaid and Brennan, but as is clear from film censor records, Brennan had actually banned the film ten days earlier, though he did not include any comment about the film in his report.[36] Given Elliman's desire not to offend the clergy, it is unsurprising that there was no appeal. It later transpired, however, that Fr Simone of the St Vincent de Paul Society, ignoring McQuaid's stricture on the screening of religious films, actually showed the 'awful film' about Maria Goretti, who had been canonized in 1948. This was revealed when Fr Simone was sponsoring the certificate for another Italian film, *Shadow on the Hill* (*Il Figlio Dell'Uomo; The Son of Man*, 1955), directed by Virgilio Sabel. Concerned at Sabel's 'reverent' seventy-minute life of Christ, which 'depicted in person' Our Lord, even though He 'does not speak', deputy film censor E.C. Powell contacted McQuaid and offered him or his representative a private viewing of the film. The archbishop replied that 'in principle, I have never sanctioned a film depicting' Our Lord or the Blessed Virgin.[37] Powell took the direction, and the film was banned; there was no appeal.[38]

A greater number of religious-themed films were being submitted by the late 1950s. Interestingly, it was not American films (such as the Hollywood 'epic' *The Ten Commandments* [Cecil B. De Mille, 1956] about which Monsignor O'Halloran and Dr O'Hare had been instructed 'to give *personal* opinion, [and] not to represent' the archbishop)[39] that caused most concern, but European productions. In April 1959

O'Halloran and O'Hare were dispatched by McQuaid to see the Italian film about cloistered life, *Suor Letizia* (*Sister Letizia*; *The Awakening*; *When Angels Don't Fly*; Mario Camerini, 1957). Though they found it 'excellent', it seems that one scene featuring a nun (played by Anna Magnani) 'showed perhaps too much affection' for an orphan boy.[40] In any case, Liam O'Hora had already decided to cut that scene (reel 9) and having agonized over the decision, passed the film with 'one of [his] rare "limited certificates"', noting in his report that 'this picture is not to be shown to persons under the age of 18.'[41] Indeed, another film that appears to have given O'Hora some concern was the French anti-capital punishment drama *We are all Murderers* (*Nous sommes tous des assassins*, André Cayatte, 1952), about which he may well have sought religious advice. One of the cuts he demanded was a scene involving 'a doctrinal argument between the priests, [which he believed] might, if shown here, cause trouble. The official R.C. teaching is that capital punishment is, in certain circumstances, justifiable.'[42]

A film that McQuaid would have been particularly interested in at this time was a documentary with drama inserts about the Holy Ghost Fathers, which had been submitted to the film censor in April 1959.[43] Liam O'Hora had told Archbishop's House that the religious order did not like the film, but when O'Halloran, Dr O'Hare and several Holy Ghost priests saw it, all except one agreed that it was 'an excellent film'. It was 'devotional in tone' and 'may serve to foster vocations, as it is adventurous in spirit'. It included an ordination scene, the burning down of a mission institution for boys, and the abduction of a catechist's wife by a pagan chieftain.[44] The following month O'Hora contacted McQuaid with regard to a German film with the English language title *One More Tomorrow* about a seminary priest, and Fred Zinnemann's highly praised *The Nun's Story* (1959).[45] Once again, O'Halloran was assigned to investigate, though both films seem to have been passed uncut. O'Halloran was also asked to adjudicate on *Say One for Me* (Frank Tashlin, 1959) in which a priest (played by Bing Crosby) in New York's theatre district prevents a young Catholic girl from entering the night club world and converts an alcoholic producer. O'Halloran, who noted that the film had been passed by the Legion of Decency, concluded that even though such a mixture of vaudeville and religion 'could be an objectionable grouping, in this case it seems to be well handled'.[46]

O'Halloran's presence was similarly requested during the censor's screening of *Song Without End* (Charles Vidor, George Cukor, 1960), about the life and loves of composer Franz Listz. However, O'Halloran was unable to attend and arranged for Dr J. O'Hare to deputize for him. The film was passed with just one cut; the line 'You and I find it easy to live in adultery' was deleted.[47] Even after a film was passed by the censor, O'Halloran's influence was such that he could effectively stop its screening. One such instance relates to a request by the committee for the reconstruction of Kylemore Abbey to be allowed to use the premiere of *Gigi* (Vincente Minnelli, 1958) to help in their fundraising. Though the film had been passed by the censor with three cuts,[48] O'Halloran, nevertheless, regarded its theme of Parisian life with 'its high-grade prostitutes' as 'not suitable as a premiere' with the result that the committee were forced to 'relinquish the scheme'.[49]

In December 1960, censor Liam O'Hora asked Archbishop McQuaid for the assistance of a priest with regard to deciding the fate of the adaptation of Sinclair Lewis' *Elmer Gantry* by Richard Brooks (1960). Monsignori O'Halloran and Glennon were assigned the task,[50] and, in a decision upheld by the appeal board, the film was banned.[51] Subsequently, O'Halloran was sent to see *The Singer not the Song* (Roy Baker, 1960, GB),[52] about a priest working in Mexico, on which occasion he was accompanied by recent recruit to filmmaking Fr Joseph Dunn of the church's Radharc film unit; and *King of Kings* (Nicholas Ray, 1961), once again with Glennon. This latter film, which had the additional frisson of Irish actress Siobhan McKenna playing the Virgin Mary, was described by O'Halloran as 'on the whole', offering 'a reverential record of Our Lady's Life'. It would, he suggested, create an overall good impression on 'the average man or woman (Catholic or atheist)'. He deemed McKenna's 'treatment of Our Lady [to be] full of reverence and dignity', but recommended that O'Hora cut part of Salome's dance before Herod, as he regarded this as 'not necessary'.[53] Monsignor R.J. Glennon, who also objected to the dance, took a more hostile approach to the film. He described it as 'unhistorical', found its 'many inaccuracies … exasperating', and judged the acting to be 'of a poor order'. Notwithstanding that McKenna was 'dignified throughout', she was, nonetheless, 'inadequate to requirements'. He accepted that Christ was presented as 'a man of peace, apostle of brotherly love', but noted that of 'Christ's claim to be God, there was not a single utterance' in the film. The 'cures shown are presented in a spooky fashion with Christ not even present and the audience wondering what is going on.' There was no attempt to relate the miracles to Christ's spiritual mission, Glennon commented, while 'any reference to the enmity of the Jewish leaders or people is scrupulously excluded'. He added that although it had been shot in Spain, 'a few shots of Palestine would have helped to compensate for so much stupidity'. While he conceded that the production could not be accused of blasphemy or irreverence, he concluded that it was a matter of speculation whether there was any 'sinister design' in presenting as the 'King of Kings a character who is immature and inept, measured by merely human standards'.[54] McQuaid in reply accepted Glennon's negative judgment that the film was 'terrible', and added that he had refused permission for the premiere of the film to be held in the Pro-Cathedral.[55]

In the letter in which Monsignor O'Halloran reviewed *King of Kings*, he also referred to *Le Defroqué* (*The Renegade Priest*, Léo Joannon, 1953, France), which, though banned in 1956, a decision upheld by the appeal board in 1957,[56] was about to be resubmitted to the censor. O'Halloran, who obviously had been involved in the original decision, described the film as 'a wonderful show', but feared that '*it did not suit the mentality of the Irish*' (emphasis added), and, as such, would 'cause scandal' even though it had received good reviews in the English and American Catholic press, as well as from French and Italian religious authorities. The distributor was offering to cut one scene in which the defrocked priest of the title '"consecrates" a glass of wine in a cheap dance hall', which 'gave rise to a controversy'. O'Halloran asked McQuaid: 'Was this a valid consecration?'[57] When resubmitted in 1962, O'Hora passed the film with an over-18s certificate, but, uniquely, confined its exhibition to the cities of Dublin, Cork and Limerick.[58]

A further correspondence between Liam O'Hora and the archbishop concerned *The Power and the Glory* (Henry Koster, 1956) in which Laurence Olivier plays, in O'Hora's words, 'a drunken dissolute priest who nevertheless faces martyrdom with dignity'.[59] The censor, whose intention it was to ban the film, phoned McQuaid to enquire as to whether he wished to see the film, but he had 'no [such] desire', and was 'very glad to see it thrown out'.[60] Worried that the appeal board might overturn his decision, he called Archbishop's House again and reported that there were two non-Catholics on the board, 'who only objected to violence on the films but not to sexual immorality'.[61] Yet, at times, even sex was less important to O'Hora than religion, and specifically the portrayal of Catholicism as is evident in his report on *The Criminal* (aka *The Concrete Jungle*, Joseph Losey, 1960, GB).[62] While no further action on the part of O'Hora or McQuaid seems to have been taken, the board upheld the censor's decision to reject *The Power and the Glory*.[63]

The fate of Alberto Gout's 'nudist' film adapted from *Genesis* entitled *Adam and Eve* (*Adán y Eva*, 1956, Mexico)[64] is interesting not just because it signalled a developing chasm between the official film censor and the appeal board, but also as it gives a further illustration of McQuaid's involvement with cinema. Though rejected by O'Hora,[65] the appeal board, much to O'Hora's chagrin, passed the film uncut. While this indicated for the official film censor, a 'most definite and indeed deliberate lowering of the standards than hitherto prevailed',[66] given that there was a sixteen-month gap between when O'Hora saw the film and when the appeal board did,[67] it was probable that the version viewed by the board had a number of the explicit or frontal nude scenes cut. Nevertheless, as Morgan Sheehy put it in an article in the *Irish Catholic* shortly after the film's release in December 1962, 'When I write "nude" I mean nude in the literal sense.'

Under the title of 'This film calls for a quiet boycott', Sheehy 'strongly condemn[ed]' the appeal board's action, suggesting that 'if this is taken as a[n] example of their considered judgement it is high time the Board was replaced'. He recommended that cinema managers refuse the film 'quietly' so as to avoid drawing attention to it, while local Catholic organizations should make it clear that

> if it is booked, they will QUIETLY organise a boycott and do everything in their power to see that the principle established that nude adult screen characters in any setting or story should not be classed as suitable entertainment for youngsters and adolescents.

Indeed, Sheehy reported that when he saw the film in a Dublin cinema, there were groups of 'adolescent morons' in attendance.[68] The following week, he returned to the topic with a strong attack on the 'inconsistency' of the appeal board, and on the civil servants and the ministers for justice who reacted 'like frightened horses at any suggestion of classification'. While in 'the old days' the refusal to grade films was 'unsatisfactory, but not over-stupid', in 1962 given that the era of 'family entertainment' had come to an end and cinema had become an 'essentially ... adult medium' catering to teenage and adult audiences, with 'moronic ideas of morality and "free love"', the idea of classification could no longer be dismissed. Though he did not go so far as to fully support a new dispensation, he, nevertheless, called on the minister for justice to engage with exhibitors to 'draw up a new schedule of operation' for film censorship.[69]

A month later, the editor of the *Irish Catholic* wrote to McQuaid on Sheehy's behalf drawing attention to his articles, as the film was still running in a Dublin cinema, though exhibitors outside Dublin were refusing to book it. The letter pointed out that the screening of such a film 'raises a big problem for all reviewers' and 'once it becomes known that nudity is permitted on Dublin screens' the floodgates would open for other such films 'of an even more blatant type'.[70] Replying the next day, McQuaid stated that 'the film got through in [his] absence', but in any case he had already 'taken effective action against it'. This entailed him seeing Dermot O'Flynn, chief knight of the Knights of St Columbanus, who was instructed to 'have laymen all over Ireland alerted to' the film and to reject it 'quietly'.[71] McQuaid also contacted Revd Thomas O'Donnell, his representative on the appeal board since October 1941 following McQuaid's reappointing Monsignor Cronin to the role of vice-general of the Dublin archdiocese. Admitting that he could not 'explain ... how the Appeal Board came to pass it', O'Donnell stated that he had tried 'very hard to reverse' the 'amazing' decision.[72] It is possible, however, that long before this, McQuaid had lost confidence in O'Donnell's effectiveness, as otherwise he would hardly have relied so heavily on Monsignor O'Halloran to engage with the film censor and others on censorship issues, at least as regards religious and theological topics, and to provide him with independent reports on individual films. Indeed, around this time, McQuaid asked O'Halloran to view *The Reluctant Saint* (Edward Dmytryk 1962), about St Joseph of Cupertino, to which he raised 'no objection';[73] *The Carmelites* (*Dialogue des Carmélites*, Philippe Agostini and Raymond Leopold Bruckberger, 1959, France/Italy);[74] and *The Cardinal* (Otto Preminger, 1963), a blockbuster religious film of the period, which traces the life of a young priest who confronts the Klu Klux Klan and, eventually, is appointed cardinal. In the case of the latter film, O'Halloran was accompanied by Monsignori O'Regan and Glennon.

Though Glennon was typically dismissive of the film's 'usual American blend of stupidity, sentiment and of course, sex', like the other two monsignori, he thought that to approve the film for release was 'the better of two evils', not least because there was nothing indecent, obscene or offensive in it, but, moreover, 'to ban the film would start off another campaign of the accusations that seem to be in season just now'. McQuaid commented simply, 'Just as I had expected'.[75] O'Halloran, for his part, assured McQuaid that 'the dignity of the priesthood [was] ... preserved throughout', while, when it came to issues involving a moral or theological dimension, such as when the cardinal's sister wants to marry a Jew who will not give 'the promises' (that is, the children to be brought up as Catholics), 'the correct' answers were given by the film. Nevertheless, he also pointed out that it was not suitable for under-18s and concluded that 'if films were graded in some way some small control of these problematical films could be obtained'.[76] Exactly a year later, in January 1965, grading of films was introduced when the minister for justice, Brian Lenihan, replaced all the members of the film censorship appeal committee. Uniquely, the new board had two Catholic priests – Revd John Desmond Murray, one of McQuaid's film 'spies' since the 1950s, and Jesuit Fr J.C. Kelly – however, when Fr Kelly went to Rome the following September he was replaced by architect Sam Stephenson, who had served briefly on the previous board. McQuaid's papers, which as regards film effectively end in 1964, do not record his attitude to these changes, but perhaps by this stage he had accepted that Irish society had changed irrevocably, not least through the cultural vector of television, which in terms of the production and exhibition of religious films had superseded the film industry. The archbishop could at least take comfort from the fact that one such television production company, perhaps the most important, was Radharc, the archdiocese's own film unit.

In keeping with his micro management of the archdiocese, Dr McQuaid monitored the distribution/exhibition of religious films in Dublin, including films held by the NFI, which, as the largest library of such films, had its own built-in monitoring system, and often assigned experienced clerics to provide private opinions on the theological content of such films. In addition, he was also approached directly by independent renters seeking advice and/or approval with regard to films, particularly documentaries, which had a religious aspect. One of the few independent Irish film distributors was Egan Film Service Ltd, based at 70 Middle Abbey Street, Dublin. Unable to secure big budget American or British films, Egan, along with companies such as Irish International Film Agency (which in 1950 had invited McQuaid to a private screening of a film about Pope Pius XI it was distributing),[77] and Abbey Films Ltd, were left to distribute 'B' films, continental European productions, or, when profitable, documentaries with a religious theme. When these latter films became available, companies such as Egan's sought episcopal sanction both to cover themselves against possible inadvertent theological transgressions, and to gain, for promotional purposes, an official imprimatur. As the 16mm film market developed from the 1940s onwards, commercial film companies were alert to the lucrative distribution network, especially in light of the National Film Institute's development, which was supported by the government. Thus, in 1942, Edward S. Hardiman, managing director of Egan's, wrote to Archbishop McQuaid to say that his company had secured the rights to 'two most unusual films', *The Immortal Song* (*Das Unsterbliche Lied*; *Silent Night*; *Stille Nacht, heilige Nacht*; Hans Marr, 1934, Switzerland/ Germany), based on the hymn 'Silent Night' and 'the only official version' of *A Visit to Lourdes*. The latter film, made under the auspices of Cardinal Gerlier, the former bishop of Lourdes, included scenes featuring a detachment of the Irish army, and Cardinal MacRory celebrating mass. Hardiman invited McQuaid to a private showing of the Lourdes film at the Astor Cinema, but the archbishop was unable to attend.[78]

Eleven years later, Hardiman wrote again to McQuaid. He highlighted his own 'pioneering' screenings of 'outstanding films bearing a religious background', including *Sanctuary of the Heart*,[79] *The Life of the Cure d'Ars*, and the OCIC 1950 award-winning *Isle of Sinners* (*Dieu a besoin des homes*; *God Needs Men*; Jean Delannoy, 1950, France),[80] but complained how these were not receiving the support of either the press or clergy. That week he was showing *Which Will Ye Have?* (USA title, *Barabbas the Robber*, Donald Taylor, 1949, GB) – a thirty-six-minute biblical story about the thief who was pardoned prior to Jesus being crucified to death – and *Angel on my Shoulder* (Archie Mayo, 1946), a feature drama in which the devil arranges for a deceased gangster to return to Earth for revenge, but who in his 'new body' seems compelled to do the right thing. Citing the archbishop of Canterbury's appreciation for such films as a means of popularizing religious topics within the ordinary cinema programme, Hardiman made an 'urgent appeal' to McQuaid to grant these films episcopal support, 'irrespective of any commercial value', so as to ensure that such screenings would not have to be discontinued. The archbishop's support would help other 'outstanding films', including *Miracle in Milan* (Vittorio de Sica, 1951, Italy) – which had been praised by the pope – to be released because 'under the present circumstances' with 'mediocre attendances' they could not be released. McQuaid, as ever, was succinct. He regretted that he could not 'regard it as advisable to interfere in a commercial project'.[81]

The archbishop's papers also includes correspondence with another independent company, Elba Films, 32–3 Lower Abbey Street, Dublin, which was the distributor of the successful Irish War of Independence feature film *The Dawn* (1936). In May 1945, having secured the distribution rights of *Monastery* (Robert Alexander, 1938), a documentary that explores two monastic orders – the monks of St Bernard, Switzerland, and Trappist monks at a French Canadian monastery – Elba wrote to McQuaid enquiring as to whether he would like to recommend any particular charitable association that might cooperate in the film's distribution. McQuaid 'regretted' that he could 'not see his way' to name such an organization. Given it was at this time that the NFI was being formally launched as a company, his refusal to identify the institute as even one among a list of possible candidates either suggested that he wished to distance himself from the NFI (which is in keeping with his wish that its board be made up predominantly of lay people), or more likely because he did not wish to encourage religious films, even though *Monastery* was written and narrated by Fr Michael Ahern SJ, a radio broadcaster and seismologist, and was dedicated to Cardinal William O'Connell, archbishop of Boston, and dean of the American hierarchy (with his authorization).[82] Supporting this view is the fact that in 1953 he refused the NFI his permission for it to purchase Walter Rilla's *Behold the Man* (aka *The Westminster Passion Play—Behold the Man*, 1951, GB), which was based on Walter Meyles and Charles P. Carr's play *Ecce Homo*, and featured Carr as Jesus. In line with his general opposition to religious subjects, especially ones that included the materialization of Christ, McQuaid simply responded to the NFI, which was wary about acquiring any religious-themed films without his approval,[83] that he did not want the film to be shown.[84] Even when faced by a body with impeccable Catholic credentials, McQuaid did not bow to pressure to allow (certain) religious films to be screened.

In 1949, the Catholic societies' vocational organization conference (CSVOC), an umbrella organization of thirteen member bodies including An Ríoghacht, CYMS, the

Knights of Columbanus and Maria Duce, wrote to McQuaid to inform him of their intention to screen at the Father Mathew Hall in November 1949 *The Sacrifice we Offer* (a documentary about the mass in relation to everyday life) and *Peace Work* (about a French Catholic factory).[85] In his reply, McQuaid was unequivocal, stating that 'no religious film, especially on the Mass, may be shown in public without previous viewing' by a vicar general of Dublin, 'and even then' the archbishop 'may consider it advisable not to permit [the] film to be shown'. 'If you choose' to continue with the screening, he told the CSVOC that they should arrange for Monsignor Boylan to view the material.[86] On 28 October, Boylan, whom McQuaid had assigned two years earlier along with Monsignor Dunne to view *My Sacrifice and Yours* for the NFI and which led to the NFI's purchase of the film,[87] viewed the *The Sacrifice we Offer*. In Boylan's report he described *The Sacrifice we Offer* as 'a good film' which presents a 'very detailed' showing of 'every action of the Mass. Nothing is hidden'. Boylan added that although he considered that the film could be shown to sodalities and similar religious groups, as well as being helpful for those engaged in advanced theological study, he did not think that it was suitable for a public theatre.[88]

Even before McQuaid had received Boylan's report, the CSVOC secretary, T.C. O'Gorman, had written to McQuaid pressing him for an early decision, as the film was due to be presented on 13 November.[89] Four days later, on 2 November, by which time the archbishop was in possession of the report, McQuaid's secretary replied saying that the archbishop would respond 'when he has satisfied himself' concerning the film, adding, in a cautionary tone, that 'it may be useful to remind you' that McQuaid 'has not encouraged or invited the entrance of this Film into our country', a clear signal that the film should be withdrawn.[90] It seems, however, by this time, on the evidence of a comment written on Boylan's letter of 31 October, that McQuaid had already made up his mind as the annotation reads, 'refused leave to view film as suitable'. Perhaps this remark was influenced by another, undated, commentary on the film attributed to H. Cathal McCarty, in which was noted that at least nine 'things' in the film's script could be improved. The critique also questioned whether it was 'desirable for Irish people' to see such a 'detailed visual instruction on the Mass' given that so often they are forced to see Mass said 'so hurriedly and imperfectly'.[91] Perhaps it was this implied criticism of Irish priests, which it should be noted, is made even more explicit in the contrast made to English priests, who, 'as a rule, say Mass much more slowly', that most influenced McQuaid's decision to deny the screening, though, in any case, he already had an adamant attitude towards film representations of Catholic religious ceremonies.

One further correspondence in relation to film in McQuaid's papers concerns an Italian film, *First Communion* (*Prima Comunione*, aka *His Majesty Mr Jones* and *Father's Dilemma*; Alessandro Blasetti, 1950), which was passed with four cuts by Richard Hayes in November 1952.[92] In 1953 Oona MacWhirter, public relations' officer of Irish Cinemas Ltd – one of J. Arthur Rank's companies – wrote to Archbishop McQuaid's secretary, Fr C. Mangan, to say that they were worried about the film, which was to be shown at Dublin's Regal Rooms, because its title might suggest that it was a religious film, although, in fact, it was a comedy written by Cesare Zavattini

– best known for his writings on and within neorealism – about a father's attempts to get a First Holy Communion dress for his daughter.[93] MacWhirter asked McQuaid to appoint someone to view the film, which had been retitled when screened in London as *His Majesty Mr Jones*, a title also demanded by the Irish film censor more than eight months after approving the film.[94]

Despite McQuaid's strictures on film, he was invited regularly to see new releases and premeires, mainly, though not always, religious ones, but it seems that usually he refused such offers. For example, in October 1944 he declined an invitation from Capitol and Allied Theatres' Patrick Farrell to attend a private screening of *Going My Way* (Leo McCarey, 1944), even though the invitation had been sent on the recommendation of the bishop of Ossory who felt that McQuaid might wish to see it and Farrell had assured McQuaid that Bing Crosby, who plays a priest in the film, was 'a Catholic of Irish descent'.[95] Similarly, he did not attend MGM's *The Last Chance* (Leopold Lindtberg, 1945, Switzerland), an anti-fascist film featuring an Englishman and an American who escape in 1943 from Italy to Switzerland;[96] an Odeon benefit screening for the Catholic Stage Guild (Ireland) of John Ford's *The Fugitive* (1947); an adaptation of Graham Greene's *The Power and the Glory*, which focuses on a priest;[97] or the premiere to which he was also invited of Ford's most famous Irish film, *The Quiet Man*, in June 1952.

Nevertheless, McQuaid saw privately at least one film, the follow-on to *Going My Way*, *The Bells of St Mary* (Leo McCarey, 1945), which he viewed on 4 February 1946, and about which he expressed his enjoyment. RKO's Robert McNally wrote to McQuaid after the screening stating that he was 'very pleased [he] enjoyed [the film] so much ... and as I mentioned to you, it would be a great honour and privilege to us to have you' at another private showing on 14 February.[98] It is not known whether McQuaid saw the film a second time, then or later, but it is an interesting feature of McQuaid's childhood biography that there is no mention of him attending the cinema in his home town of Cootehill, Co. Cavan, or, indeed, anywhere else. As a result, it is worthwhile imagining what McQuaid might have taken from *The Bells of St Mary's*, a film which could be deemed transgressive from a rigorous Catholic viewpoint.

Central to the *The Bells of St Mary's* is the relationship between Fr O'Malley (Bing Crosby) and head nun Sr Benedict (Ingrid Bergman) as the nuns try to save a run-down primary school. Two secular themes are clearly evident in the film. Fr O'Malley and Sr Benedict flirt throughout the film, down to the scene after she pleads to God for strength not to be bitter about being sent away from the school she loves. It is only as she is leaving with a heavy heart shortly afterwards that Fr O'Malley finally tells her that she is being sent away to clear up the tuberculosis detected on her lung, not because of her running of the school or any transgression (on her part). She smiles at him and expresses warmth for Fr O'Malley – she can always find him by dialling 'O', she tells him – and his looks at her reinforce the sense that in another genre they would have kissed, an expression of love that is anything but divine! The other theme in the film concerns 13-year-old Patricia, whose father deserted the family when she was born. When Patricia's mother comes to see Fr O'Malley he enquires how she has kept herself since her husband's disappearance – she dresses well and drives a car – and hints that a series of men have supported her. Through Fr O'Malley, who is streetwise and has a knowledge of the secular world of music in which area Patricia's father works, the couple are reconciled. However, when Patricia, who has deliberately failed her exams in order to remain within the safe clean cocoon of the convent-school, first sees the new couple she is unsure, and presumes the man to be just another 'friend' of her mother. Her fears are quickly allayed when, supported by the smiling presence of both Sr Benedict and Fr O'Malley, her mother assures her that this is her 'real Daddy', a clear implication that many other men had sought to play this part.

It is the absence of condemnation of Patricia's mother's behaviour and Fr O'Malley's encouragement of her to look after herself and to take personal responsibility for her life that is most striking when contrasted with McQuaid's rigorous patriarchal ideology. Indeed, it is perhaps the contradiction between the archbishop's private fantasies in relation to cinema and his public theological persona, which helps explain why he was very touchy about any publicity surrounding him and film. Even in 1943, when he accepted from Paramount Film Service a copy of the newsreel of the requiem service for the late Cardinal Hinsley at Westminster, it was 'on the strict explicit understanding that *no publicity* would be attached to the presentation' (emphasis added). When this condition was breached, seemingly inadvertently during a phone conversation to Archbishop's House, the film was returned. Eventually, McQuaid accepted an apology – but not a copy of the film – from Paramount's Dublin manager, Norman Barfield.[99]

CHAPTER 9

Irish Cinemas

'Being brought into town to the Metropole [Dublin] was a special event ... There was an exciting smell to the dark. There were velvet seats and shining curtains and someone showed you to your seat with a beam of light. It was nothing like being sent out to the pictures on a Saturday afternoon, out of your mother's way, to a cinema where the toilets stank and kids ran screaming up and down the aisles.' (Pat Murphy).[1]

THE CINEMA BUILDING

As Nuala O'Faolain writes, 'my memories are not of the art form of film, but of cinemas themselves ... Our aim was to see and sense and parade past members of the opposite sex. And then to end up beside each other, in the warm, anonymous dark ... Cinemas were the one place where young people had an excuse to be together in privacy.'[2] Though such a position in relation to the cinema is not universal, and, it should be said, largely limited to teenagers and young adults, it points to an essential truth that films are only part of what a cinema offers. It also makes clear what all cinemagoers instinctively know, that cinemas are, in the first instance, public rather than private spaces, even if, the darkness (and at times sumptuousness), and the images that flicker on the screen, moreover transport the viewer to a secret place, a place of fantasy and of desire. A place often suggested in the exotic names of the buildings themselves – Excel, Palace, Majestic, Arcadia, Regal, Coliseum, and Alhambra. Indeed, for writer Shane Connaughton, the cinema in Clones' Fermanagh Street 'was the best-named cinema in Ireland – or anywhere: the Luxor. It sounded luxurious. Perfumed. Sexy. It was.' However, in a comment that highlights that cinema has been always more of an imported culture in Ireland than a native one, he recalls how, a teacher of his, Father Gallagher, 'was furious with the name ... "It should have been an Irish name".'[3]

Consequently, any history of film or analysis of a specific film is necessarily incomplete without a consideration of the actual buildings used for film screenings, given that an integral part of the context shaping a film's reception is the venue itself. Such influencing factors include the cultural geography of the building's location, for example, its placement in or proximity to a socially unfashionable area would impact on

366

the type of clientele; the frequency of the screenings; the ideology of its management; the typical selection or genre of films screened; the level of supervision and regulation; the formal layout of its interior, which in a pre-multiplex era, particularly in major urban areas, was generally subject to clear social demarcations, with the rougher patrons occupying the 'wooders' at the front; the overall aesthetic choices and type of architecture, presuming it is a permanent venue and not a mobile or touring, fit-up theatre-cinema; its self-promotion and point of contact with the potential audience through advertising and ticket sales; and, of course, the pricing structure, and whether the somewhat apocryphal jam-jars were accepted as a form of currency.

While one of the characteristics of the contemporary multiplex is its privileging of uniformity (whether at the level of product, screening room, or audience), older single-screen venues, which ranged from the less than adequate hall with sparse furnishings, and often poor equipment and even poorer (scratched and worn) film product to the great opulent palaces of sin and sensuality, ironically, subject to closer regulation and higher levels of decorum,[4] allowed for a greater sense of difference both within the cinemas themselves and in relation to each other. According to Gerry Stembridge, writer-director of *About Adam* (2000), 'there were six cinemas in Limerick, all with distinguishing features. There was the Lyric[;] even as a kid, you knew the Lyric was a low-rent cinema, because it had wooden benches ...; the Royal ... [which] you entered behind the screen; the City Theatre .... a part-time cinema [which gave] away sweets with the cinema tickets ... ; [and] the three classier cinemas ... [which were] the Carlton[;] the Grand Central[;] ... [and surpassing all] the Savoy ... a beautifully ornate 1930s picture palace ... [where] everyone in the stalls could turn around and look at the rich people in the balcony who had paid extra.'[5]

It is this diversity, evident at times in a venue's screen size and seating capacity, that informs the list below.

(a) Remit of list

The list presented includes all known full-time and part-time cinemas, as well as many, if not all, of the 'rather drab' parish halls, which were 'a far cry from the picture palaces of the cities'[6] and other venues such as theatres and art centres where films were occasionally or are shown in Ireland. Cinemas due to open, even if under construction with completion dates estimated for 2011, such as for example the new six-screen Odeon and UCI cinema at the Point, Dublin, have not been included.[7] Similarly excluded have been venues offering viewing or conference facilities, such as found in numerous hotels, or institutions that regularly screen films (privately) to students including the many cinema or screening spaces in educational establishments.

In creating the list a number of sources have been used. Principal among these have been the British *Kinematograph Year Books*, abbreviated to *KYB*; the annual British Film Institute film and television handbooks, which, following the demise in 1971 of *KYB*, published a list of Northern Ireland cinemas; the *Cinema and theatre annual review and directory of Ireland, 1947* (Dublin: Parkside, n.d.), abbreviated to *1947 directory*;[8] a list compiled by *Showcase* 1968 ('List of all cinemas in Republic of Ireland & Northern Ireland', *Showcase*, March 1968:32–4);[9] and Neil Connolly and Maretta Dillon's report on cultural cinema, 2001. However, in all instances the information given in these publications has only been partial and at times, such as with regard to the *KYB* entries, inaccurate. Though *KYB* needs to be approached with caution as it often contain errors or omissions, such as cinemas not appearing for a number of years after their opening date and remaining listed after their closure, a sloppiness which may also apply to the personnel listed, it has been possible to supplement and modify a number of *KYB* entries by other sources, especially provincial newspapers, many of which are now online. With regard to the internet, the most useful website proved to be *Cinema treasures*. Seeking to gather information on cinema buildings internationally, it was helpful especially in relation to some of the Northern Ireland entries.

Notwithstanding the extent of the list produced below, and the substantial research carried out on a number of Irish cities including Dublin (by Keenan, 2005, Kearns and Maguire, 2006, and Zimmermann, 2007), Belfast (by Open, 1985 and Doherty, 1997), and Cork (McSweeney, 2007), all drawn upon and cited within the entries, there is a need for further investigation at village, town and city level to mine local authority and newspaper archives, and undertake oral history projects, in order to fill in the gaps and refine (and perhaps correct) the history of cinema buildings in Ireland. Nevertheless, what is presented is the first attempt at a comprehensive list of cinemas on the whole island of Ireland, and collates the information available at an international and national, if not always a local, level. It is therefore a work in progress.

(b) Further notes on the cinemas' list

(1) It should be noted that *KYB*'s data relates to information collected in the year *previous* to the date of the volume. Other dates in an entry indicate the first known change of name or the ownership of the venue.

(2) It has not always been possible to establish if cinemas with different names but on the same street or with similar addresses are in fact the one cinema.

(3) Where a number appears alone, such as 430, this refers to the number of seats in the cinema. Seat numbers have at times been rounded up or down (but by no more than 15 seats either way).

(4) All venues are single screen unless stated otherwise.

(5) • indicates venues operating as full-time cinemas in December 2010.

(6) + the latest known date on which we know that the cinema was still open; it is probable that it remained open for a period after that date.

(c) (Other) abbreviations used

1934 cinemas = an undated 1-page document of eighteen circuits, 'Cinema circuits (of two or more theatres) in Irish Free State', with a further 7-page list, 'Name of cinemas, address, seating capacity and remarks', which was compiled, it would seem in the mid-

1930s, given the inclusions and exclusions of known cinemas (for example, the *Strand Cinema*, George's Square, Balbriggan, which opened in February 1934 is included, while the *Drumcondra Grand Cinema*, which opened in October 1934, is not), and the fact that almost all venues listed were equipped for sound. It is most probable that Thekla Beere compiled this document while researching her statistical profile of Irish exhibition during 1934–5, the results of which were published in 1936. A copy of the document is held in IFI library.

arch = architect(s)
BFI = British Film Institute handbook
bm = booking manager
br = business representative/representing business management or control, often lessee
CRO = Company registration office, Dublin (www.cro.ie)
d = director(s)
DIA = Dictionary of Irish architects, 1720–1940 (www.dia.ie)
fb = film booker
gm = general manager
KYB = Kinematograph year book
l = lessee or licensee
m = manager
md = managing director
sec = secretary
mus d = musical director
narr = narrator
p = proprietor(s)
RPC = Restrictive practices commission's *Investigation into the supply and distribution of films* (1977).

LIST OF CINEMAS AND PUBLIC VENUES SCREENING FILMS IN IRELAND (BY COUNTY)

ANTRIM

Antrim
Antrim Cinema, Castle Street (1936–July 1958, aka *The Cinema* [*1947 directory*]), p: Antrim Cinema Ltd (*KYB*, 1945–71); br: Mr McGrogan (*1947 directory*); 14½ft proscenium (*1947 directory*); seats: 430 (*KYB*, 1936–44); 500 (*KYB*, 1945–52; *1947 directory*); 400 (*KYB*, 1953–9); programme: three times weekly (*1947 directory*); closed by Joseph Barr and James McGrogan to make way for *New Cinema*.[10]
• *Antrim Cineplex*, 1 Fountain Hill (28 October 1994–), 4 screens/788 (312, 232, 132, and 112) seats, independent cinema (*BFI*, 1996; Connolly and Dillon, 2001:73); 4 screens (2010).
Camden Cinema, Crumlin, br: Mr McElwaine (*1947 directory*).
Clotworthy House Arts Centre, Louth Road (*BFI*, 1991).
New Cinema, Castle Street (July 1958–1991), p: Antrim Cinema Ltd; opened by Joseph Barr and James McGrogan to replace *Antrim Cinema* (opposite); cost: £27,000; 400 (*KYB*, 1958–9); 300 (*KYB*, 1968–71).[11]
Picture House (1922–34; intermittent), p: Revd T. McCotter (*KYB*, 1922–4, 1934); twice weekly (*KYB*,

1922–4); Revd T. McGorian (*KYB*, 1925); reappears in *KYB* 1930–3, without details; sound installed in 1933.

Ballycastle
Masonic Hall (1899; McCole, 2005:appendix D).
New Cinema (*c*.1935–71, aka *Cinema* [*KYB*, 1953–64, *Showcase*, 1968]), p: AC Cinemas Ltd (*KYB*, 1937–8); Mr E.F. McCambridge, 3 Foyle Street, Derry, from 1945, 9 Castle Street (*KYB*, 1939–71, as br in *1947 directory*); seats: 400 (*KYB*, 1936–8), 450 (*KYB*, 1937–8), 500 (*KYB*, 1939–44, *1947 directory*), 397 (*KYB*, 1945–71).
The Picture House (*c*.1924–*c*.1932, listed as *McAllister Hall* in *KYB*, 1932–3), p: McAllister Picture Hall Co.; sec/m: E.J. Fogarty (*KYB*, 1925–33).

Ballyclare
Cinema (*c*.1921–71+; aka *Picture House*; *Reo Cinema* [*KYB*, 1952]; *New Reo Cinema* [*KYB* 1957–71, *Showcase* 1968]), p: H. McCrone (*KYB*, 1922–4); Ballyclare Cinema Co.; F. Blair (*KYB*, 1925–7, previously manager); no p/m listed *KYB*, 1929–32; James Menary, 133 Harppark Ave, Belfast (*KYB*, 1933–35); Maurice Logan, 35 Royal Avenue, Belfast (1934,[12] *KYB*, 1936–52); Reo Cinemas Ltd, 133 Royal Avenue, Belfast (*KYB*, 1958–71); fb: Mr McClintock, Supreme Cinemas, Ltd, 133 Royal Avenue, Belfast (*1947 directory*); 350 (*KYB*, 1936–41); 400 (*KYB*, 1942–52, *1947 directory*); 600 (*KYB*, 1958–71).

Ballymena
• *IMC Ballymena*, Larne Link Road (31 August 1998–), p: Ward Anderson, 7 screens/1,253 (342, 261, 160, 160, 109, 112, 109) seats (Connolly and Dillon, 2001:74; 2010).
Lyric Cinema (*c*.1932–*c*.1937), p: H.P. Cinemas, Northern Ireland, m/d: Harry Terry; films and occasional variety (*KYB*, 1933); m: Harry Percy (*KYB*, 1934); part of Supreme Cinemas circuit; p: Maurice Logan, Bertie Walsh, 35 Royal Avenue, Belfast; 700 (*KYB*, 1936–8).
Pictorium, 21 Calorm Street (*c*.1918–*c*.1920), p/m: John Gordon; 210 (*KYB*, 1919–21).
Picture House (*c*.1915–February 1937), p: Ballymena Picture Palace Co. Ltd (*KYB*, 1918–36); m: Sam Eagleson (*KYB*, 1919–38); 400 (*KYB*, 1918); 450 (*KYB*, 1919–20); 420 (*KYB*, 1921).[13]
Picture Palace (*KYB*, 1916–17). See *Picture House*.
Protestant Hall, opened September 1934 as cinema following redecoration, reseating and new equipment installed, by l: Maurice Logan, Bertie Walsh.[14]
Ritz (*c*.1936–), p: Union Cinemas Ltd, Regent Street, London (*KYB*, 1937–9); ABC after purchase of Union Cinema circuit in October 1937.
State Cinema, The Pentagon, Ballymoney Road (December 1935–mid-1970s; reopened *c*.1990–30 August 1998), p: State Enterprises Ltd, 133 Royal Ave, Belfast (*KYB*, 1941–71; *Showcase* 1968; though Supreme Cinemas Ltd listed in *1947 directory*); fb: Mr McClintock, Supreme Cinemas, Ltd, 133 Royal Avenue, Belfast (*1947 directory*); 1,100 (*KYB*, 1941–7); 1,000 (*KYB*, 1948–71); from *c*.1990 2 screens/381 (215 and 166) seats (*BFI*, 1991), p: Ward Anderson; closed day before opening of Ward Anderson *IMC Ballymena*;[15] demolished in 2006.
Town Hall (1915–18), (*KYB*, 1916–19), town clerk: Henry O'Harn (*KYB*, 1919).
Towers (December 1937–71+), p: Maurice Logan, Bertie Walsh and T.J. Furey of Supreme Cinemas circuit, 133 Royal Avenue, Belfast (*KYB*, 1939–71, *1947 directory*); fb: Mr McClintock, Supreme Cinemas, Ltd (*1947 directory*); 1,150 seats (*KYB*, 1942–71).[16]

Ballymoney
Ballymoney Picture House, Main Street (*c*.1918–*c*.1932), p/m: P.J. O'Kane (*KYB*, 1919–33), licensed also for music and dancing (*KYB*, 1919–20); 500 (*KYB*, 1919–20); 400 (*KYB*, 1921).
Cinema (*c*.1935–*c*.1967), 300 (*KYB*, 1936–68).
Palladium Cinema (*c*.1938–*c*.1971), p: J.N. Crawford (*KYB*, 1939–48, *1947 directory*); J.M. Crawford Cinemas Ltd, Castlereagh Road, Belfast (*KYB*, 1950–71; *Showcase* 1968); fb: Mr E. Crawford, *Castle Cinema*, Belfast (*1947 directory*); 400 (*KYB*, 1939–48); 500 (*KYB*, 1950–64).[17]
Presbyterian Hall (1899; McCole, 2005:appendix D).
Town Hall (1897–1902; McCole, 2005:appendix D)
YMCA Hall (*c*.1933), p: James Menary (*KYB*, 1934). Menary is also listed in *KYB*, 1938 only, as the operator of *New Kinema*. This may be the same venue listed as *Cinema*.

Belfast
ABC, Fisherwick Place. See *Ritz*.
ABC Film Centre, Fisherwick Place. See *Ritz*.
Albert Hall, Shankill Road (*c*.1915–16); 1,900; l: Revd H. Montgomery (*KYB*, 1916; 1917).

The Alexandra, Grosvenor Road/Durham Street. See *Coliseum*.

The Alhambra, 39–43 North Street (opened as a music hall, 1873; films as part of variety programme from *c*.23 November 1903, later full-time cinema to 10 September 1959; aka *New Alhambra, Royal Alhambra,* and *Alabama*), p: J. Hollingworth Elliott; Will White (1914–15);[18] Alhambra Theatres, Ltd (*KYB*, 1924–52; *1947 directory*); Odeon (Northern Ireland) Ltd (February 1955–9); m: W.G. Bradley (*KYB*, 1922); J. McDermott (*KYB*, 1926–8); fb: Ferris ('Paddy') Pounds, Whitehall Buildings, Ann Street, Belfast, 25ft proscenium (*1947 directory*); 980 (*KYB*, 1916–17); 800 (*KYB*, 1936–52). Damaged by fire on 10 September 1959; did not reopen as a cinema. 'In the post-war years the Alhambra acquired a reputation as a rather downmarket cinema that attracted an increasing number of rough or sleazy patrons.' (Doherty, 1997:26.)

Ambassador, 31-3 Cregagh Road (16 December 1936–4 March 1972); arch: John MacGeagh (*DIA*); p: D.D. Young (*KYB*, 1939–41); Mrs E. McGhie (*KYB*, 1943–6); W.J.E. & E. McGhie (*KYB*, 1948–61); Ambassador Cinema Co. Ltd (*KYB*, 1962–71; *Showcase* 1968); br: D.D. Young (*1947 directory*); long and spacious hall; 1,200 (*KYB*, 1939–41); 1,030 (*KYB*, 1943–61); 883 (*KYB*, 1970–1). In the 1960s it became the first Belfast cinema to specialize in sex films.[19]

Apollo, Ormeau Road/Agincourt Avenue (30 October 1933–1 December 1962),[20] arch: John McBride Neill in art deco style with additions in 1939 by Thomas McLean (*DIA*); p: J.H. McVea (1933–41); M. Curran & Sons (1941–56; *1947 directory*); Odeon (Northern Ireland) Ltd, Capitol Cinema, 405 Antrim Road, Belfast (1956–62);[21] fb: James Curran, Capitol Cinema, Antrim Road (*1947 directory*); 1,000 (*KYB*, 1935; *1947 directory*); 870 (*KYB*, 1945–55); 890 (*KYB*, 1957). First 'all talkie' cinema in Belfast.[22]

The Arcadian, 74½ Albert Street (1924–60, aka the 'Arc'), p: Arcadia Picture Theatre Co. with d: H. O'Kane, James Boyle, John O'Neill (*KYB*, 1925–37); Arcadia Picture Theatre, Ltd (*1947 directory*); m: John O'Neill (*KYB*, 1926–8); fb: Messrs Wilton & Barry, 20 Church Street, Belfast, 25ft proscenium and 24ft stage (*1947 directory*); 600 (*KYB*, 1936–55); 750 (*KYB*, 1956–60). See also *Arcadian Amusement Hall.*

Arcadian Amusement Hall, 80 Albert Street (cinema was in an alleyway behind Albert Street), (18 December 1912–*c*.1920); p: coal merchant John Donnelly (1912–*c*.1914); Joseph McCavana(gh) (*KYB*, 1916–17; previously manager from 1912); 650 (*KYB*, 1916–17); 1,000 (*KYB*, 1920). Along with the *Clonard* and the *Diamond*, it was bombed during the Troubles of the early 1920s, but reopened nearby in 1924 as the *Arcadian*.[23]

Assembly Hall, Fisherwick Place and Howard Street (*c*.1915–16); l: Henry Scott; 2,000 (*KYB*, 1916–17).

Astoria, Upper Newtownards Road (22 December 1934–17 August 1974); arch: Thomas McLean (*DIA*); p: M. Curran & Sons (*KYB*, 1935–57; *1947 directory*); Odeon (Northern Ireland) Ltd from 1955 (*KYB*, 1960–71; *Showcase* 1968); fb: James Curran, Capitol Cinema, Antrim Road (*1947 directory*); 1,070 (*KYB*, 1935–6); 1,240 (*KYB*, 1937–56); 1,300 (*1947 directory*); 1,260 (*KYB*, 1957). By the mid-1960s the once sumptuous cinema had become run-down.[24]

Avenue Cinema, Royal Avenue. See *Belfast Picture House.*

Belfast Cineplex, Kennedy Centre, Falls Road East. See *Cineworld; Belfast Omniplex.*

Belfast Empire Theatre of Varieties, 12–14 Victoria Square (*c*.1915–16), p: Alfred Edwards, seats: 1,450 (*KYB*, 1916–17).

Belfast Hippodrome, Glengall Place (*c*.1915–16), l: Martin E. Lynas, 3,000 (*KYB*, 1916–17).

Belfast News and Cartoon Cinema, Fisherwick Place, College Square East (17 December 1958–69).[25] See *Kelvin Picture Palace.*

• *Belfast Omniplex*, Kennedy Centre, Falls Road East (*c*. August 2010–; aka *Kennedy Centre Omniplex*; redevelopment of *Belfast Cineplex*), Omniplex Holdings/Ward Anderson; m: Diarmuid Kelly; 8 digital screens, third full digital cinema complex in Ireland. See *Cineworld.*

Belfast Picture House, 34 Royal Avenue, next to General Post Office (19 June 1911–23 October 1982; aka *The Picture House; The Regent* [1947–74]; *Avenue* [1974–82, but also earlier occasional nickname as in *Showcase* 1968]), p: Provincial Cinematograph Theatres Ltd, m: Mr Firth (1914–15);[26] J. Boughton (*KYB*, 1919–28); reopened 29 April 1929 with sound film *The Singing Fool*;[27] reopened November 1934 after refurbishment;[28] p: Northern Theatres (*1947 directory*); M. Curran & Sons (from September 1947), who renamed it the *Regent*;[29] Odeon (Northern Ireland) Ltd (from December 1956; *Showcase* 1968); after being damaged by IRA bomb in 1974, Odeon/Rank left the running of the cinema to an independent who renamed it *Avenue Cinema*; 29ft proscenium (*1947 directory*); 680 (1912);[30] 620 (*KYB*, 1917); 877 (*KYB*, 1919); 700 (*KYB*, 1920); 850 (*1947 directory*); 750 (*KYB*, 1948–53); 706 (*KYB*, 1954–7). In 1987 the building was demolished to make way for the Castle Court shopping centre. Though it was not in fact the first Belfast cinema it was one of the earliest central Belfast cinemas to have had no connection with the music hall and in 1914 was the first to present the kinetophone, 'an early attempt at rough synchronisation of sound and vision'.[31]

Belfast Picturedrome (aka *The Picturedrome*), 112 Mountpottinger Road (25 February³² 1911–30 May 1970); arch: Campbell & Fairhurst (1911), Robert Hill Sharpe (alterations 1928, 1930, 1931) and John McBride Neill (reconstruction in art deco style, 1934) (*DIA*); p: Mount Pottinger Cinemas Ltd (from *c.*1912; listed in *1947 directory*); Belfast Picturedrome Ltd (*KYB*, 1919); Irish Theatres; Odeon (Northern Ireland) Ltd (February 1955–; *Showcase* 1968); m: Ferris Pounds (1911–12); A. Graham Porter (from *c.*1919, *KYB*, 1920–3); James A. Fletcher (*KYB*, 1924); H. Crowley (*KYB*, 1925); M. Croly ([sic] *KYB*, 1926–8); br & fb: Ferris Pounds (*1947 directory*); 900 (*KYB*, 1916–17); 850 (*KYB*, 1918–21); rebuilt with 1,000 seats, opened November 1934 (*1947 directory*). The *Belfast Picturedrome* was the first major Belfast cinema to be built on one level, or in stadium-style.

Broadway Cinema, 278 Falls Road, Willowbank (12 December 1936–31 January 1972), arch: Thomas McLean, p: M. Curran & Sons (from opening until Rank take over, *1947 directory*); Odeon (Northern Ireland) Ltd (December 1956–; *Showcase* 1968); fb: James Curran, Capitol Cinema, Antrim Road (*1947 directory*); 1,500 (1936)³³; 1,380 (*KYB*, 1943–71); 1,200 (*1947 directory*); did not reopen as a cinema after being fire-bombed on 31 January 1972.

Cannon, Fisherwick Place. See *Ritz*.

Capitol, 407 Antrim Road (9 November 1935–11 January 1975), arch: Thomas McLean (*DIA*) p: Michael Curran & Sons; Odeon (Northern Ireland) Ltd (December 1956–; *Showcase* 1968); fb: James Curran (*1947 directory*); 1,300 (1935; *1947 directory*);³⁴ 1,000 (*KYB*, 1936–49); 1,094 (*KYB*, 1950–7).

Castle, 84 Castlereagh Road (1 October 1934–26 March 1966), arch: Thomas H. Guthrie (*DIA*) built on the site of a mission hall; alterations: John McBride Neill (1937); p: James M. Crawford (*KYB*, 1936–48); James M. Crawford Cinemas Ltd, 84 Castlereagh Road, Belfast (*KYB*, 1949–64), Crawford owned and managed the cinema until its closure;³⁵ 1,000;³⁶ 900 (*KYB*, 1936–64; *1947 directory*).

Castlereagh Cinema, p: D.D. Young (*KYB*, 1936–7).

Central Picture Theatre, 18–20 Smithfield (22 December 1913–58; aka *Smithfield Ritz*), converted from a jeweller's shop and in the early period had the most basic facilities; p: Central Belfast Picture Theatre Co., Ltd (*KYB*, 1916–23; *1947 directory*); m: H.P. Doherty, licensed for music and singing (*KYB*, 1919); Joseph McCavana (*c.*1920–4);³⁷ J.A. Howarth (*KYB*, 1925–8); 550 (*KYB*, 1916–17; 1920–1); 660 (*KYB*, 1919); 600 (*KYB*, 1935); 420 (*KYB*, 1945–7); 440 (*KYB*, 1948–58).

Cineworld, Kennedy Centre, Falls Road East (18 May 1991–9; as *Belfast Cineplex*, 1999—2010; aka *Cineworld Cineplex*), p: West Belfast Cineplex Ltd; developed by Curley family, 5 screens/1,007 (296, 190, 178, 178, 165) seats³⁸, site redeveloped as *Belfast Omniplex*, 2010.

Classic, 13–25 Castle Lane (24 December 1923–30 September 1961; *Gaumont* from 3 July 1950), arch: Samuel Stevenson (*DIA*); p: Classic Cinemas Ltd, 16 Chichester Street, Belfast;³⁹ Provincial Cinematograph Theatres Ltd (August 1928– February 1929); Gaumont British Theatres (February 1929–); Circuits Management Association, Albion House, 59 New Oxford Street, London WC1, a company controlled by the Rank Organization (1949–); m: Noel Hobart (*KYB*, 1924); Henry Houston (*KYB*, 1925); F. Sparkes (*KYB*, 1927–8); T.H. McDermott (*1947 directory*); fb: A.J. Jarrett, New Gallery House, London (*KYB*, 1927–44); 23ft screen (*1947 directory*); 1,600 (1,000 stalls; 600 balcony) seats; *KYB*, 1923); 1,730 (*KYB*, 1935); 1,810 (*KYB*, 1941–4); 1,807 (*KYB*, 1945–8); 1,775 (*KYB*, 1961). It was an extremely luxurious 'colonnaded four-storey building with semicircular entrance', whose manager and thirty-piece orchestra changed into evening dress after 5 o'clock' (*DIA*). It had a lot of extra features, including from 1927 a Wurlitzer organ, and from 1935, Ardente deaf aids.⁴⁰ Building demolished and replaced with BHS department store.

Classic, Fisherwick Place, College Square East. See *Kelvin Picture Palace*.

Clonard Picture House, 140 Falls Road (22 December 1913–30 March 1966; aka *Slieve Donard*), p: Clonard Hall Co. Ltd (*KYB*, 1916–23; *1947 directory*); m: J.J. Irvine (*KYB*, 1916–23); W.J. Hogan (*KYB*, 1922–8; *1947 directory*, which also lists him as fb); 32ft proscenium (*1947 directory*); 1,200 (*KYB*, 1916); 1,500 seats (*KYB*, 1921); 1,000 (*KYB*, 1936–44; *1947 directory*); 1,100 (*KYB*, 1945–61). One of Belfast's 'finest suburban cinemas' built before the First World War; its pit could accommodate twelve orchestral players.⁴¹ Westrex sound system introduced in 1931.

Coliseum Cinema, Grosvenor Road/Durham Street (30 November 1911–20 June 1959; formerly, *Alexandra Theatre*; and *Palladium* to 7 February 1915; *Coliseum* from 8 February 1915–20 June 1959. It was as the Coliseum [1915] that film became the dominant entertainment), p: John Lawson (*Palladium*); J.L. Jackson (*KYB*, 1916–17); Belfast Coliseum Ltd (addresses: 35 High Street, Belfast [*KYB*, 1924]/79 Donegall Street, Belfast [*1947 directory*]/Whitehall Buildings, Ann Street, Belfast [*KYB*, 1953–6]); Odeon (Northern Ireland) Ltd (from 1956, *KYB*, 1957); m: James Burt, licensed for music and dancing (*KYB*, 1919); C. Bourke (*KYB*, 1920–1); W.G. Harrington (*KYB*, 1922); Henry Houston (*KYB*, 1924); Samuel Boyd (*KYB*, 1925); Harold Buckley (*KYB*, 1926–31); Billy Branagh;⁴² fb: Ferris Pounds (*1947 directory*); 30ft stage (*1947 directory*); 1,600 (*KYB*, 1916); 1,200 (*KYB*, 1919); 1,400 (*KYB*, 1921); 1,000 (*KYB*, 1936–44); 900 (*KYB*, 1945–8).⁴³ It was the second Belfast cinema to instal sound (1930).

Comber Cinema (10 December 1957–77+; aka *Comber Picture Palace*), p: Dr A.O. Hyman and sister Mrs Rada Smith of Solar Group; built on site adjacent to *Comber Picture House*, owned by the same company and built to augment the facilities of the older cinema;[44] 400 seats; damaged by IRA fire bombs, 10 October 1977.[45]

Co-Operative Hall, Frederick Street (*c.*1915–16), p: Belfast Co-operative Society, Ltd, 600 seats (*KYB*, 1916–17).

The Cosy, 250–6 York Road. See *Queen's*.

Crumlin Empire (*KYB*, 1932–3).

Crumlin Picture House, Crumlin Road (23 March 1914–27 May 1972; aka *The Ranch*), arch: William J. Moore (*DIA*); p: Crumlin Picture House Ltd (*KYB*, 1916–71; *1947 directory*); m: A. George (*KYB*, 1920–8); screen 20ft x 15ft (*1947 directory*); 850 (*KYB*, 1916); 950 (*KYB*, 1917); 1,000 (*KYB*, 1918–21); 973 (*KYB*, 1936–66); 826 (*KYB*, 1967–8); 860 (*KYB*, 1970–1). Like other cinemas, it differentiated between plush seats and Wilton carpet for the more expensive parts of the house and hard benches and cork flooring in the cheap front stalls area. One of its innovations was the showing of children's matinees. The cinema closed after being bombed by the IRA.[46]

Curzon, 300 Ormeau Road, near Sunnyside Street (12 December 1936–23 September 1977; December 1977–9 April 1999), the third cinema designed by John McBride Neill (*DIA*); p: John Gaston (1936–73) and following his death in 1973, his sons John and Leslie became joint managing directors; Curzon Cinema (Belfast) Ltd (*KYB*, 1953–71; *Showcase* 1968); br: H. Sheppherd (*1947 directory*); screen: 26ft x 19½ft (*1947 directory*); 1,424 (*DIA*); 1,500 (*KYB*, 1940–60); 1,478 (*KYB*, 1961–71); 3 screens/1,013 (453, 360, and 200) seats (*BFI*, 1991); though fire-bombed by the IRA on 23 September 1977, the cinema reopened in December 1977; in 1982 it was converted to a three-screen complex, dividing the stalls in two, and keeping the balcony intact as a third screen; later in the 1990s, it was divided into five screens. It operated a Curzon children's cinema club from early 1950s, while in 1983 it was the first cinema in Northern Ireland to offer Dolby stereo sound. Projectionist William Wilson worked at the cinema from its opening for over fifty years, becoming chief projectionist in 1951. The building was demolished in 2003 to make way for Curzon apartment block.

Diamond Picture House, 35 Falls Road (7 February 1920–*c.*1959), p: Joe McKibben estate; J. McCann (*KYB*, 1922–8), 600 (*KYB*, 1953–61). The third cinema to be built by Joe McKibben, the *Diamond* was a long and narrow 'bottom-of-the-market' cinema with a small screen. Its 'ultra–local' status led it only to advertise its film shows outside the cinema.[47]

Duncairn Picture Theatre, 12 Duncairn Gardens (3 July 1916–22 November 1969; aka *Duncairn Super-Cinema*), arch: Frederick Turner Waddington; p: Duncairn Picture Theatre Co. (*KYB*, 1936–71; *1947 directory*: address at 157–61 North Street; *Showcase* 1968); m: W.J. Hogan;[48] Will White (*KYB*, 1922–36); fb: Messrs Wilton & Barry, 20 Church Street, Belfast (*1947 directory*); originally 1,200 (*DIA*); 950 (*KYB*, 1936–45); 1,000 (*1947 directory*]); 24ft proscenium (*1947 directory*); 830 (*KYB*, 1946–56); 826 (*KYB*, 1957–71). It was an 'extremely attractive and very large cinema' with the 'exceptional quality of the building and the originality of the design' commented on when opened. It had a tea lounge at the top of the staircase from where it was possible to view the films. It also incorporated into its design retail outlets on the ground floor.[49]

Duncairn Super-Cinema, 12 Duncairn Gardens. See *Duncairn Picture Theatre*.

East Belfast YMCA, 183 Albertbridge Road (*c.*1915–*c.*1916); p: Andrew MacMillan; 600 seats (*KYB*, 1916–17).

Electric Picture Palace, 19–21 York Street (22 August 1910–16 March 1915; aka *Silver Cinema* from 1912; *York Street Picture Palace*; *Picture Palace*; *Electric Picture Gallery*), p: Fred Stewart; m: L. Cooke; 500; 250 (*KYB*, 1916–17). When Stewart planned to open the larger *New York Cinema* the *Electric* was closed down, but it reopened in 1915 as *Silver Cinema* (*KYB*, 1916–17). The whole block was destroyed during a German bombing raid on 5 May 1941, and the site is now occupied by the College of Art.

Forum, 491–5 Crumlin Road (20 November 1937–28 January 1967), arch: John McBride Neill (*DIA*); p: Irish Theatres; Odeon (Northern Ireland) Ltd, 405 Antrim Road, Belfast (February 1955–; *Showcase* 1968); br & fb: Ferris Pounds, Ann Street (*1947 directory*); 1,250; single level cinema. Last cinema to be built in Belfast before the Second World War.[50]

Gaiety Theatre, 157–163 North Street (14 November 1916–56), p: Belfast Gaiety Picture Theatre Co. (*KYB*, *1947 directory*); m: J. Quinn (*KYB*, 1924–36; as br in *1947 directory*]); fb: W. Barry, Donegall Street, Belfast (*KYB*, 1941); George Lodge (*1947 directory*); 24ft proscenium (*1947 directory*); 968;[51] 800 (*KYB*, 1936–8); 1,000 (*KYB*, 1939–44); 900 (*KYB*, 1945–52). Servicing the lower end of the market, it also operated as a cine-variety house. Catering for the opposing religious and political constituencies of the Shankill and Falls Roads, Open (1985:43) reports that the week was divided, three days each, between the two groups. Sold to Woolworth's, April 1959, though during its last years it had deteriorated considerably.[52]

Gaumont, 13–25 Castle Lane. See *Classic*.

Gaumont, Lisburn Road, Finaghy (17 June 1955–7 June 1975; originally known as *Tivoli*, 1955–61, reverted to original name when Rank left in 1974), arch: John McBride Neill (*DIA*); p: Odeon (Northern Ireland) Ltd, the only cinema built by the Rank organization in Northern Ireland (listed in *Showcase* 1968); 900; 1,000.

Grand Opera House, Great Victoria Street (23 December 1895; opened in current design and as cinema, 3 October 1949; closed [due to bombing] on 7 April 1972, ceased to be used as a cinema; reopened, 15 September 1980), arch: Frank Matcham, p: Imperial Cinema and Cinematograph Theatres (1949–); Warden Ltd (1950s); Odeon (Northern Ireland) Ltd/Rank Organisation (1960–); 1,800 (*KYB*, 1961–71); 1,001 (1980–); restored as Grade A listed building during 1975–80; damaged again by bombs in 1991 and 1993; continues as live venue as it was never an ideal cinema space.

Great Northern Kinema. See *Kinema House*.

Grosvenor Hall, Grosvenor Road (*c*.1915–16, and again from September 1934), hall owned by Methodist church, 2,200 (*KYB*, 1916–17); 'talkie pictures at cheap prices',[53] 500 (*KYB*, 1935–6).

Grove, 194 Shore Road. See *Troxy*.

Hippodrome, Great Victoria Street, Grosvenor Road (2 November 1907 as a music hall; cinema from 1929–87; aka *Royal Hippodrome* [1935–8]; *Royal Hippodrome Cinema* [December 1938–61]; following modernization: *Odeon* [October 1961–74]; *New Vic* [1974–87]); arch: Bertie Crewe (London theatre architect); John McBride Neill (remodelling in 1961); p: ABC (from 1931, *KYB*, 1932–9); Hippodrome Belfast Ltd (*KYB*, 1939–41); G.L. Birch, Woodside, Holywood, Co. Down (*KYB*, 1941–52; as br in *1947 directory*); Royal Hippodrome (Belfast) Ltd (*KYB*, 1953–7); Odeon (Northern Ireland) Ltd/Rank Organisation (from 28 November 1960; *Showcase* 1968); l: Martin E. Lyons (1916); m: G.L. Birch; George Lodge (prior to takeover by Rank); 36ft proscenium and 26ft stage (*1947 directory*); 1,800 (*KYB*, 1935–57); 1,200 (*KYB*, 1961). It was one of the first music halls to include a projection box in its design (March 1929),[54] though its life as a cinema proper really began with ABC; damaged by IRA fire bombs on 23 September 1977, but reopened the following day; bingo hall from 1987–96. Demolished in 1996 and office block built on site.

Holy Cross Hall (16mm), Ardoyne, p: Holy Cross Committee (*KYB*, 1951–60).

IMAX, Odyssey Arena (29 November 2001–2007); screen: 82ft high x 62ft wide; 380 seats.

Imperial Picture House, Cornmarket (7 December 1914–28 November 1959), arch: Robert Lynn; p: Cllr Turner and James Barron; subsequently Mr Waterson (1915)[55] Ulster Kinematograph Theatres Ltd (*KYB*, 1922–60); George Lodge; m: B.N. McDowell (*KYB*, 1922–37); br & fb: George Lodge (*1947 directory*); reopened, October 1932 with 400 extra seats;[56] 1,800 (*KYB*, 1936); 1,000 (*KYB*, 1949–60). The *Imperial* 'was the most important cinema' in Belfast until the *Classic* was built in 1923.[57] The day after it opened the *Belfast Newsletter* recorded that not only did the cinema occupy a central site, but it left 'nothing to be desired'.[58]

Kelvin Picture Palace, Fisherwick Place, 17–18 College Square East (20 December 1910–1 January 1972; aka *Kelvin Picture House* [1934–43]; *New Kelvin Picture House* [1944–6]; *Mayfair* or *New Mayfair* [1946–57];[59] *Mayfair News and Cartoon Cinema*, or *Belfast News and Cartoon Cinema* [17 December 1958–69]; *Classic* [1970–2] at which time it was a popular art house cinema;[60] and 'Soldier's Home'[61]). The building was formerly the residence of scientist Lord Kelvin; p: Kelvin Picture Palace Co. (*KYB*, 1916); Raymond Stross Theatres[62] (from 1942, *KYB*, 1944–6; listed as fb with address Astoria House, 62 Shaftsbury Avenue, London, W.1 [*1947 directory*]); Mayfair Theatres Ltd (from 1946; *Showcase* 1968); Capitol & Provincial News Theatres (from 1959); Classic Cinemas Ltd, 100 Baker Street, London (from *c*.1963; *Showcase* 1968); m: J. Chapman, full licence (*KYB*, 1919–25); Captain A.V. Crothers (*KYB*, 1926–7). 632;[63] 500 (*KYB*, 1916); 700 (*KYB*, 1919), 650 (*KYB*, 1920); 500 (*KYB*, 1921, 1936); 550 (*KYB*, 1946); 500 (*1947 directory*); 467 (*KYB*, 1948); 369 (*KYB*, 1964–6). Destroyed by an IRA bomb on New Year's Eve, 1971.

• *Kennedy Centre Omniplex*, Falls Road East. See *Belfast Omniplex*.

Kinema House, Great Victoria Street (7 April 1914–*c*.16 March 1919; aka *Great Northern Kinema*),[64] arch: W.J. Roome; p: Great Northern Kinema Company; m: Alfred George; 550 (*KYB*, 1916); 600 (*KYB*, 1918–21).

Lido, 812 Shore Road, Greencastle (28 March 1955–70),[65] p: Troxy Cinemas (Belfast) Ltd (*KYB*, 1955–71; *Showcase* 1968); arch: John McBride Neill, it was Belfast's first post-Second World War cinema (*DIA*) and the first with CinemaScope (*KYB*, 1955–71); 1,025.[66] It was converted into a Catholic church.

Ligoniel Picture House (*c*.1918–24),[67] m: J. Baird, twice nightly (*KYB*, 1922–5); 300 seats; cinema and variety hall.

Lyceum, Antrim Road/New Lodge Road (11 December 1916–29 April 1966; aka: '*Likie*'), p: Irish Electric Palaces Ltd (*KYB*, 1918–23); Michael Curran,[68] and M. Curran & Sons (*KYB*, 1924–59); Odeon (Northern Ireland) Ltd (*KYB*, 1960–1); m: L.G. Harris (*KYB*, 1922–3), m: J. Curran (*KYB*, 1925–6); fb: James Curran, Capitol Cinema, Antrim Road (*1947 directory*); 950 (*KYB*, 1918, 1936–48); 850 (*1947 directory*); 707 (*KYB*, 1949–57); 850. The *Lyceum* was Michael Curran's share of the splitting of the original Irish Theatres circuit. It was the first Belfast cinema to show fully synchronous sound films on 20 November 1926.[69] After its closure, it was used as a film storage depot by Rank; it was destroyed by an IRA bomb in 1970.

The Lyric, 44–6 High Street. See *Panopticon*.

MacQuiston Institute, Cregagh Road (*c*.1915–16), p: J.W.A. Hamilton, 850 (*KYB*, 1916–17).

McQuiston Institute,[70] 35 High Street, m: J.A. Kirkpatrick, 1,000 (*KYB*, 1918–19).

Majestic, 204–22 Lisburn Road, at corner of Derryvolgie Avenue (25 May 1936–4 October 1975), arch: John McBride Neill (*DIA*); developed by independent operator John Gaston; bought by Union Cinemas chain; Union taken over in October 1937 by Associated British Cinemas (*1947 directory*); m: Hugh Finlay (1970s); 1,369 (1,000 in stalls; 369 in circle) (*KYB*, 1945–71). Premises later used as a furniture store.

Mayfair News & Cartoon Cinema, Fisherwick Place, College Square East. See *Kelvin Picture Palace*.

Midland Picture House, 7–9 Canning Street (6 March 1916–15 April 1941), arch: William J. Moore (*DIA*); p: McKibben Estate Ltd (1922–41); m: J.H. Craig (*KYB*, 1922–8); 1,200 (*KYB*, 1915); 1,500 (*KYB*, 1918–19); 2,000 (*KYB*, 1920–1); 600 (*KYB*, 1936–41). Occupying a prominent site close to York Street station, this last cinema built (and managed) by Joe Kibben was destroyed during a German bombing raid.

MGM, 14 Dublin Road (18 July 1993–; from 1995, *Virgin*; from October 1999, *UGC*; from January 2004, *Movie House*), p: Metro Goldwyn Meyer ((1993); Michael McAdam (2004) who was reported to have paid £5.5 million; 10 screens/2,501 (436; 354; 262; 264; 252; 272; 187; 187; 169; and 118) seats; original cost: £5 million, developed by the Sheridan Group; complex included Burger King and Chicago Pizza Pie factory when opened.[71]

• *Movie House*, 14 Dublin Road; chain includes City Side; Coleraine; Glengormley; and Maghera (2010). See *MGM*.

• *Movie House*, City Side retail park (formerly Yorkgate shopping centre), 100–150 York Street (30 September 1992–); originally operated independently by Film Network; p: Michael McAdam; 8 screens/1,340 (340; 230; 220; 160; 120; 90; 90; and 90) seats (*BFI*, 1996); *Cinema Treasures* gives original seating capacity as 1,450; 6 screens were added *c*.2000; 14 screens/2,574 seats (Connolly and Dillon, 2001:74).

New Alhambra Theatre, 39–43 North Street (*KYB*, 1916–17).

New Kelvin Picture House, Fisherwick Place, College Square East. See *Kelvin Picture Palace*.

New Mayfair, Fisherwick Place, College Square East. See *Kelvin Picture Palace*.

New Princess Picture Palace, 307 Newtownards Road (29 July 1912–2 April 1960; aka *New Princess Palace*; *New'n*), arch: Thomas Houston (*DIA*); p: Ferris Pounds (his first venture); Irish Electric Palaces Ltd; City & Suburban Cinemas Ltd (*KYB*, 1930–56); Odeon (Northern Ireland) Ltd, 13 Ann Street, Belfast (from February 1955); m: William Adorey (*KYB*, 1919–21); Ferris Pounds (*KYB*, 1922–8); A. Cowan, fb: Ferris Pounds, Whitehall Buildings, Ann Street (*1947 directory*); screen: 12ft x 15ft (*1947 directory*); 1,200 (*KYB*, 1915); 1,000 (*KYB*, 1916); 1,200 (*KYB*, 1919–21); 808 (*KYB*, 1945–55). The entrance featured coloured lights and a distinctive windmill–like tower.[72]

New Reo, Ballyclare (September 1956–), replaced *Reo*, p: Maurice Logan; 800; fifth new post-war cinema to be opened;[73] 1,000.[74]

New Royal Cinema, Arthur Square (Cornmarket). See *Royal Cinema*.

New Vic, Great Victoria Street (1974–87). See *Hippodrome*.

New York Cinema, 68 York Street (31 July 1916–*c*.31 December 1922), p: Fred Stewart/New York Cinema Ltd; m: George Stewart (1919–21); 700 (*KYB*, 1918; 1921); 750 (*KYB*, 1919); 800 (*KYB*, 1920); bombed by the IRA to stop its use as an emergency police station.[75] It has been suggested that there were two cinemas on York Street, both of which were owned by Fred Stewart, with the first perhaps open as early as 1915.[76]

Odeon, Great Victoria Street (1961–74). See *Hippodrome*.

• *Odeon*, Unit 13SF, Victoria Square shopping centre, Victoria Square (18 July 2008–), p: Odeon Theatres chain, 8 screens/1822 (465; 283; 254; 209; 204; 177; 128; 102) seats.[77]

Old Princess Palace, Newtownards Road. See *Princess Picture Palace*.

• *Omniplex*, Falls Road East. See *Belfast Omniplex*.

The Palladium, Grosvenor Road. See *Coliseum*.

Panopticon, (42–)44–6 High Street (22 February 1912–5 May 1941; aka the *Lyric*, [1924–41]); p: Fred

Stewart (*KYB*, 1919–24); reopened as the Lyric from 13 October 1924 after refurbishment and increased to 750 seats; further alterations by John MacGeagh (*DIA*) in 1930, 1932; p: D.D. Young (*KYB*, 1939–42); m: Thomas G Harris (*KYB*, 1926–7); 335 (1912);[78] 511 (*KYB*, 1916); 510 (*KYB*, 1918); 500 (*KYB*, 1920–1); 750 (1940).[79] Destroyed during German air raid on 5 May 1941.[80]

Park Cinema, Oldpark Road/Torrens Avenue (11 December 1936–71; reopened 1 May 1972–27 May 1972), arch: Thomas Robert Eagar (*DIA*); p: Supreme Cinemas (*KYB*, 1936–67); listed as C.E. Carter (*Showcase* 1968); Park Cinema (Belfast) Ltd (*KYB*, 1968–71); fb: Mr McClintock, Supreme Cinemas, Ltd, 133 Royal Avenue, Belfast (*1947 directory*); 1,200 (*KYB*, 1936–41); 1,000 (KYB, 1942–6) 960 (*KYB*, 1948–66); 642 (*KYB*, 1968; 1970).[81] An IRA bomb destroyed the cinema in May 1972.

People's Hall, York Street (*c*.1915–16), l: Revd W. McGuire, 1,200 (*KYB*, 1916–17).

Pictoria, Shaftesbury Square. See *Shaftesbury Pictoria*.

The Picturedrome, 112 Mountpottinger Road See *Belfast Picturedrome*.

The Picture House, Royal Avenue. See *Belfast Picture House*.

Popular Picture Theatre, 49–55 Lower Newtownards Road, bridge end (30 October 1917–Easter 1941 (destroyed by a German bomb); rebuilt 1947–January/February 1962; aka *Popular Picture House, Popular Picture Palace, 'the Pop'*), p: Popular Picture Palace Co. Ltd, 84 Castlereagh Road, Belfast; p/m: W.J. Hogan; licensed for music and dancing; 1,100 (*KYB*, 1920–1); 700 (*KYB*, 1948–66). Hogan was also owner of the *Clonard* and the *Savoy*. In spite of the lack of comfort, it was 'much loved' by the population of Ballymacarret.[82]

Princess Picture Palace, 308 Newtownards Road (16 September 1910–*c*.31 December 1926; aka *Old Princess Palace*, 1923–6), formerly a skating rink, p/m: W.T. Anderson (*KYB*, 1919–29), full licence (*KYB*, 1919); 1,250 (*KYB*, 1919); 1,200 (*KYB*, 1920–1). It catered for the lower end of the market and had extremely poor facilities.[83]

Queen's, 250–6 York Road (*c*.8 December 1915–15 April 1941; aka *The Cosy*; *Queen's Picture Theatre*; *Queen's Picture & Variety Theatre*), p: Belfast Gaiety Theatre Co. Ltd; m: J. Lowden (*KYB*, 1922–6); G.M. Loughrey (*KYB*, 1927–31); bm: Harry Wilton (*KYB*, 1928–33); 800 (*KYB*, 1935); 500 (*KYB*, 1940). It was destroyed during a German air raid on 15 April 1941.

• *Queen's Film Theatre*, 20–2 University Square Mews (14 October 1968–, brief closure in 1972); p: Queen's University, Belfast, brainchild of Michael Emmerson and Michael Barnes; m: Michael Open (from 1969 to 2004, except from 1974 to 1977 when Robert Caldicott held the position);[84] originally, 220 seat 'art' cinema; 252 (1985)[85]; though a lecture theatre was in use as a second screen since mid-1980s, a proper 88-seat second screen added in mid-1990s (Connolly and Dillon, 2001:74: 2 screens, 402 seats); refurbished in 2004. In April 2007 it became the first cinema in Northern Ireland to install a digital projector.

Raleigh Cinema, Dundrum (*KYB*, 1931–3).

Queen's Picture Theatre, 250–6 York Road. See *Queen's*.

Queen's Picture & Variety Theatre, 250–6 York Road. See *Queen's*.

Regal Cinema, 366–72 Lisburn Road, between Bawnmore Road and Lancefield Road (23 October 1935–7 January 1967), arch: Thomas McLean; p: M. Curran & Sons, 403 Antrim Road (*KYB*, 1936–58); Odeon (Northern Ireland) Ltd (from December 1956; *Showcase* 1968); fb: James Curran, Capitol Cinema, Antrim Road (*1947 directory*); 1,000 (*KYB*, 1936–58); 1,270 (*KYB*, 1939–41); 1,300 (*1947 directory*); 1,380 (*KYB*, 1942–9); 1,270 (*KYB*, 1950–8). Its huge neon sign was said to be the largest cinema sign in Ireland.[86] One of its innovations was that it offered books of cinema tickets (at reduced prices) that could be bought in advance.[87] Demolished 1982.

The Regent, Royal Avenue. See *Belfast Picture House*.

Reo (dates undetermined). See *New Reo*.

Rex Cinema. 205 Woodstock Road. See *Willowfield Picture House*.

Ritz, Fisherwick Place/Grosvenor Road (9 November 1936–1 July 1993; aka *Ritz Theatre*; *ABC* from August 1963; *ABC Film Centre* from 1981; *Cannon* from 1986),[88] arch: Leslie H. Kemp, Ernest F. Tulley, with steel work by Harland and Wolff; p: Ritz Belfast Ltd (Union Cinemas Group, Regent Street, London); Associated British Cinemas Ltd, Golden Square, London W1 (from October 1937–; *1947 directory*); Cannon (from 1986); 27ft stage and 49½ft proscenium (*1947 directory*); 2,219 seats (originally, the largest cinema in Ireland, complete with Compton organ);[89] 2,144 (1970); in 1985, 4 screens, 1,490 (550; 444; 281; 215) seats; destroyed by IRA incendiary bombs on 23 September 1977;[90] reopened in June 1981 as 4-screen *ABC Film Centre*; closed in 1993 and demolished in 1994 to make way for hotel.

Royal Alhambra, 39–43 North Street. See *The Alhambra*.

Royal Cinema, Arthur Square, Cornmarket (16 December 1916–late 1960s; aka *New Royal Cinema*), arch: conversion of the historic Theatre Royal into cinema, Bertie Crewe (*DIA*); p: Warden Ltd (Fred Warden), (*KYB*, 1916; 1922–57); m: Edward Clarkson (*KYB*, 1922–3); P.W. Whittle (*KYB*, 1924); Cecil King

(*KYB*, 1925, 1927–8); md: Fred W. Warden (*KYB*, 1926–9); br: Cecil M. King (*1947 directory*); screen: 22ft x 18ft (*1947 directory*); 1,200 (*KYB*, 1916; 1920–1); 1,100 (*KYB*, 1918); licensed for dancing and music (*KYB*, 1920); 953 (*KYB*, 1936); 968 (*KYB*, 1941–51); 956 (*KYB*, 1952–61); 920.

Royal Hippodrome, Great Victoria Street. See *Hippodrome*.

St George's Hall, 39 High Street (17 August 1908–16); p: Entertainment Halls Ltd, 1,500 (*KYB*, 1916–17). Originally a regular film venue, it stopped showing films in 1916 as it faced competition from more comfortable and attractive cinemas, such as the *Panopticon*, which opened just across the street in 1912.

St John's Parochial Hall Cinema, Falls Road (*c.*1951–*c.*1963), p: Revd D. Rhodes, PP (*KYB*, 1952–8); Revd L. Higgins, PP (*KYB*, 1959–71); 250 (*KYB*, 1952–64).

St Mary's Hall, Bank Street (*c.*1915–*c.*1916), 1,500 (*KYB*, 1916–17).

Sandro, 71–3 Sandy Row/address in *1947 directory*: 67a (January 1919[91]–2 September 1961), p: Sandro Theatres Ltd (*KYB*, *1947 directory*); m: Charles Rogers (*KYB*, 1922–7); fb: Mr McClintock, Supreme Cinemas, Ltd, 133 Royal Avenue, Belfast, 22ft proscenium (*1947 directory*); 670 (Doherty, 1997:103); 700 (*KYB*, 1936; *1947 directory*); 600 (*KYB*, 1949–51); 500 (*KYB*, 1952–61). A down market local cinema which in the early years did not have a proper cinema screen with films projected on the whitewashed front wall of the cinema, though the walls of the auditorium included ornate plaster mouldings decorated with sixteenth century scenes.[92] Used as a bingo hall from 1961 and subsequently rebuilt as a community centre.

Savoy, 294–6 Crumlin Road (5 November 1934–67); arch: Thomas McLean (*DIA*); p: Savoy P.H. Ltd with William J. Hogan as br & fb (*KYB*, *1947 directory*; company name listed in *Showcase* 1968); 36ft proscenium (*1947 directory*); 1,088 (*KYB*, 1935); 1,250;[93] 1,400 (*KYB*, 1941–4); 1,150 (*KYB*, 1945); 1,050 (*KYB*, 1946–61). Building used as car salesroom during 1967–97, and was demolished in July 2009.

Shaftesbury Pictoria, Shaftesbury Square (21 December 1910–17; aka *Pictoria*); p: Ulster Electric Theatres Ltd; 200 (*KYB*, 1916–17). The extremely small *Shaftesbury Pictoria* was the first Belfast cinema to introduce non-stop screenings from 3p.m. to 11p.m. It closed in 1917, probably as a result of competition from larger and more profitable cinemas. 'The films, like many of its patrons, were select, and the audiences often included ladies and families from the upper class areas nearby.'[94]

Shankill Picturedrome, 148 Shankill Road (19 December 1910–58; aka '*Wee Shankill*', '*Little Joe McKibben*') p: Shankill Picturedrome (Belfast) Ltd; Joseph McKibben (*KYB*, 1922–5); m: Miss Montgomery (*KYB*, 1925–6); Mrs Montgomery (*KYB*, 1927–8); fb: Mrs Newel, *West End Picture House* (*1947 directory*); 500 (*KYB*, 1916); 1,000 (*KYB*, 1918–19); 700 (*KYB*, 1920); 2,000 (*KYB*, 1921); 400 (*KYB*, 1936); 500 (*KYB*, 1941–61). No price increase from the coming of sound to its closure; it also supplied teas, the first Belfast cinema to provide this service.[95]

Silver Cinema, 19–21 York Street. See *Electric Picture Palace*.

Slieve Donard; 140 Falls Road. See *Clonard Picture House*.

Smithfield Ritz, 18–20 Smithfield. See *Central Picture Theatre*.

Stadium, 351–3 Shankill Road (16 October 1937–13 March 1976), arch: Robert Sharpe Hill (*DIA*); p: Irish Theatres Ltd; Odeon (Northern Ireland) Ltd (from February 1955, *KYB*, 1959–71; *Showcase* 1968); Belfast Cinemas; br & fb: Ferris Pounds (*1947 directory*); 1,400. With its 180ft long auditorium it was the longest cinema in Belfast.[96]

Star Palace of Variety, Church Street. See *Star Picture Palace*.

Star Picture Palace Church Street, between North Street and Donegall Street (14 September 1908–9; aka *Star Palace of Variety*) p: James W. Gyle, owner of adjoining public house and billiards' saloon known as 'The Office', which was converted to the *Star* one month after nearby St George's Hall started showing films; closed 1909, reverting to its earlier usage.[97] Capacity: 1,500. Open (1985:78–9) suggests that the closure of what was effectively Belfast's first full-time cinema may have been due to its inability to satisfy the safety requirements laid down in the Cinematograph Act 1909.

• *Storm Cinemas*, The Odyssey Pavilion, 2 Queen's Quay, (June 2006–). See *Warner Village Cinema*.

• *Strand Cinema*, 152–4 Holywood Road, Gelston's Corner (7 December 1935–19 November 1983; reopened with 4 screens in 1984); arch: John McBride Neill (*DIA*); p: Strand Cinema Co. Ltd/Union Cinemas Co., Regent Street, London (December 1935–October 1937, cited in *KYB*, 1937–9); Associated British Cinemas Ltd, Golden Square, London W1 (from October 1937–late 1970s cited in *KYB*, 1937–57; Open 1985:79–81; *1947 directory*); Sean Henry; 1,300 (*KYB*, 1937–9); 1,140 (*KYB*, 1945–50); 1,166 (*KYB*, 1951–7); (*KYB*, 1959–70); 1,168 (*KYB*, 1970); 4 screens/642 (276; 196; 90; and 80) seats (1984); 4 screens/625 seats (Connolly and Dillon, 2001:74); 4 screens, 2010. Damaged by IRA firebombs, 10 October 1977;[98] refurbished in 1999.

Tivoli, 2 Christian Place (off Albert Street/Irwin Street, Smithfield), opposite the *West Belfast Picture Theatre* (1 July 1918–*c.*1927, though not licensed after 1923) p: publican P.J. Kelly (*KYB*, 1922).[99]

Tivoli, Lisburn Road, Finaghy (17 June 1955–7 June 1975; aka *Gaumont* from 1961–74). See *Gaumont*.

Troxy, 194 Shore Road (24 October 1936–15 July 1977; *Grove* [1965–77]), arch: John McBride Neill (*DIA*); p: Troxy Cinemas (*KYB*, 1939–71)/Wilton & Barry (*1947 directory*); fb: Messrs Wilton & Barry, 20 Church Street, Belfast, 36ft proscenium (*1947 directory*); 1,300 (*KYB*, 1939–44; *1947 directory*); 1,154 (*KYB*, 1945–61); 1,164 (*KYB*, 1962–71). Its design allowed patrons to queue inside.
UGC, Dublin Road. See *MGM*.
Vue, Belfast, The Odyssey Pavilion. See *Warner Village Cinema*.
Virgin, Dublin Road. See *MGM*.
Warner Village Cinema, The Odyssey Pavilion, 2 Queen's Quay (May 2001–; as *Storm*, June 2006–), 12 screens/ 3,055 (476 to 155) seats, and a director's lounge with panoramic views of Belfast skyline and riverfront; operated from May 2003 by Vue Cinemas, but it was never rebranded under the *Vue* name; bought by Storm for an estimated €7 million in May 2006.[1]
Wellington Hall, Wellington Place (*c.*1915–16), p: D.A. Black; 1,500 (*KYB*, 1916–17).
West Belfast Picture Theatre, Christian Place (in alleyway behind 80 Albert Street), Smithfield (18 December 1912–22), p: John Donnelly (1912–14); J.M. Cavanagh (from 1914, *KYB*, 1920); West Belfast Picture Theatre Ltd (*KYB*, 1922–3); m: J.M. Cavanagh (1912–); Thomas Diamond; J. Quin (*KYB*, 1922–3); 1,000, licensed for dancing and music (*KYB*, 1919–20); 500 (*KYB*, 1921).
West End Picture House, 108 Shankill Road/Carlow Street (9 October 1913–60, aka: '*Big Joe McKibben*'), p: Joe McKibben, A. Craig & A. Newel (*KYB*, 1916–33); Mrs Craig, Mrs Newel & H.A. Newel (*KYB*, 1936–57; *1947 directory*); m: Miss E. McKibben (*KYB*, 1919–28); fb: Mrs Newel (*1947 directory*); 1,150 (*KYB*, 1916); 1,000 (*KYB*, 1918; 1920); 850 (*KYB*, 1919); 800 (*KYB*, 1921; 1940–59). The cinema remained in the McKibben family until it closed in 1960; like the *Shankill Picturedrome* it had stable prices from 1934 until its closure.
Willowfield Picture House, 205 Woodstock Road (20 December 1915–60; reopened, *c.*1970–3 as *Rex Cinema*); p: Willowfield Unionist Club (*KYB*, 1922–68; *Showcase* 1968); Rex Cinema (Belfast) Ltd, 185 Donegall Street, Belfast (*KYB*, 1970–1); m: R. Carothers (*KYB*, 1919–28; *1947 directory* [as R. Caruthers]); 1,000 (*KYB*, 1919–20; 1953–61); just over 800 (Open, 1985:83). In the 1970s it allowed local Pakistanis to occasionally screen Asian films.[2]
Windsor, Donegall Road (23 March 1935–70), arch: Thomas McLean (*DIA*); p: Underwood Entertainments Ltd (Open 1985:152; *KYB*; *Showcase* 1968); Irish Theatres, fb: Ferris Pounds, Whitehall Buildings, Ann Street (*1947 directory*); 1,250 (*KYB*, 1940); 1,270 (*KYB*, 1941); 1,000 (*KYB*, 1942–8); 1,250 (*KYB*, 1949–55); 1,240 (*KYB*, 1956–71).
Woodvale Hall, Cambrai Street (*c.*1915–16), 630 (*KYB*, 1916–17).
York Street Picture Palace, 19–21 York Street (22 August 1910–6 March 1915). See *Electric Picture Palace*.

Bushmills
Bush Cinema (*KYB*, 1944), br: Mr Smith, 300 (*1947 directory*).
Hamill Memorial Hall (1898–9, 1904; McCole, 2005:appendix D).
Orange Hall (*c.*1938–*c.*1943), p: H. Black; 300 (*KYB*, 1939–44).

Carnlough
Marine, p: John Kelly, *c.*300.

Carrickfergus
• *Carrickfergus Omniplex*, Unit 4, Rodgers Quay (22 April 2000–), p: Ward Anderson's Empire Cinemas chain, 6 screens, 1,200 seats/1,032 seats (Connolly and Dillon, 2001:74); 6 screens (2010).
The Castle Cinema[3] (*c.*1925–*c.*1928+; listed as closed in *KYB*, 1930–1; reopened by December 1936 with McGookin Brothers in charge, known as *Cinema*; aka *Ideal Cinema* [under which name it is listed in *1947 directory* and *Showcase* 1968] reappears in *KYB*, 1957 as *Castle*), p: William Nabney; three changes weekly (*KYB*, 1926–9); Thomas Nabney (as *The Cinema, KYB*, 1925–9); Ideal Cinemas (Northern Ireland) Ltd, 133 Royal Avenue, Belfast (*KYB*, 1939–71); br: Mr L. McGookin (*1947 directory*); 350 (*KYB*, 1939–71).
Cinema (December 1936–?), p: McGookin Brothers. See *Castle Cinema*.
Ideal Cinema (*c.*1946–7), p: Supreme Cinemas, 133 Royal Avenue, Belfast (*Showcase* 1968); br: Mr L. McGookin, 20ft proscenium, 545 (*1947 directory*). See *Castle Cinema*.
Rossleigh Cinema (*c.*1925–*c.*1932), m: R. Lee (*KYB*, 1926–8); no personnel listed *KYB*, 1929–33.

Cogry, Doagh
Picture House (*c.*1924–*c.*1933), p/m: Ivan McMeekin (*KYB*, 1925–33).[4]

Crumlin
Camlin (*c.*1947–*c.*1956), p: R.S. McIlwayne, The Bungalow ('Erindale', *KYB*, 1954–7). Crumlin; 400 (*KYB*, 1948–57).

Cushendal
Moyle, p: Daniel McAllister; 300.
Cushendall Cinema, br: Mrs Wann (*1947 directory*).

Dundonald
• *Dundonald Omniplex*, Eastpoint Entertainment Centre, Old Dundonald Road (19 December 2008–), 8 screens, at cost of GB£9 million.[5]
Metro, Woodstock Road/East Link (3 September 1956–61), designed by Oliver N. Wheeler; cost: £50,000; p: T.J. Furey; Supreme Cinema Group's thirteenth cinema; Sandro Theatres, 133 Royal Avenue, Belfast; 860;[6] 850 (*KYB*, 1957–61).

Dunloy
Cinema.

Glengormley
• *Movie House*, 13 Glenwell Road (September 1990–), p: Michael McAdam, 6 screens/906 (309; 243; 117; 110; 76; and 51) seats (*BFI*, 1992; Connolly and Dillon, 2001:74).

Larne
Electric Palace, Main Street (*c.*1916–*c.*1928; aka *Picture House*, 1925–September 1936), (though its first listing in *KYB* is in 1917, suggesting that it was operational from 1916, the *DIA* give 1911 as the date when architect Robert Sharpe Hill undertook the project, which was claimed as the first cinema in Northern Ireland),[7] arch: John McBride Neill; p: Irish Electric Palaces Ltd; Irish Theatres Ltd (*KYB*, 1930–7); m: C.S. Graves (*KYB*, 1919–21); Harry Aicken (1920–36); 600, licensed for music and dancing (*KYB*, 1919); 650 (*KYB*, 1920–1); 500.[8] 650 (*KYB*, 1936); replaced by *Regal* in 1937.
• *Larne Omniplex*, Port of Larne business park, Redlands Road (December 2010–), p: Ward Anderson, 8 screen/1,100 seats, cost: £5 million.[9]
McGarel Town Hall (*KYB*, 1916–17).
Naval Base Cinema, p: British Navy; m: Lieut. Locksley Clark; 450 (*KYB*, 1919).
Regal Cinema, 7 Curran Road (13 March 1937–May 2001), arch: John McBride Neill (*DIA*);[10] p: Ferris Pounds and J.Y. Moore of Irish Electric Palaces Ltd; John Hunter (*KYB*, 1938); Irish Electric Palaces, 79 Donegall Street, Belfast (*KYB*, 1939–57, address of Irish Electric Palaces in *KYB*, 1945–57: Whitehall Buildings, Ann Street, Belfast [p in *1947 directory* is given as Irish Theatres, with Ferris Pounds as fb]); Odeon (Northern Ireland) Ltd (*KYB*, 1958–71; *Showcase* 1968); m: H. Aicken (from 1937 to ?), who had managed *Electric Palace* since 1920; 900 (*KYB*, 1939–57); damaged by IRA firebombs, 8–9 October 1977;[11] 4 screens/760 (300; 220; 120; and 120) seats (*BFI*, 1996; Connolly and Dillon, 2001:74). Damaged by fire on 13 December 2008.

Lisburn
Lisburn Electric Picture Palace, Market Street (1914–*c.*1963; aka *Picture House*), originally built as a late eighteenth-century Wesleyan prayer house, p: Lisburn Electric Palace Ltd, m: V. Dornan (*KYB*, 1922–8; 1945–57 [p in *1947 directory* is given as Irish Theatres]); no personnel listed *KYB*, 1929–57; booked at Whitehall Buildings, Ann Street, Belfast (by Ferris Pounds, listed in *1947 directory*), (*KYB*, 1953–4); p (February 1955–): Odeon (Northern Ireland) Ltd (*KYB*, 1958–64; *Showcase* 1968); 23ft proscenium (*1947 directory*); 650 (*KYB*, 1936–:); 500 (*KYB*, 1953–4); 691 (*KYB*, 1955–7). Plans were drawn up for a cinema at Market Street by Thomas Houston in 1912, while in 1931 Lisburn Electric Palace engaged architect Robert Sharpe Hill with a budget of £6,000 (exclusive of heating and ventilation and using direct labour) to (re)build the Lisburn cinema (*DIA*); building now occupied by the Christian Workers' Union.
• *Lisburn Omniplex*, 5 Lisburn Leisure Park, Governors Road (10 October 1997—), p: Ward Anderson's Empire Cinemas chain, 12 screens/1,814 (487, 180, 132, 164, 259, 220, 66, 66, 66, 66, 42, 66) seats; increased to 14 screens/2,253 seats (Connolly and Dillon, 2001:74).
Picture House, Market Street. See *Lisburn Electric Picture Palace*.

Portglenone
Cinema, p: William Shields, Maghera, 300.
Town Hall (1898; McCole, 2005:appendix D).

Portrush
Majestic, 47–51 Main Street (7 April 1939–70; reopened 1977–80 as *Playhouse Cinema*; reopened 1993–2006; 2007–8; redeveloped as *The Playhouse*), p: Portrush Majestic Cinemas Ltd; Portrush Majestic Cinema Co. (*KYB*, 1941–7); Curran Theatres, Capitol, Antrim Road (*KYB*, 1948–57);

Odeon (Northern Ireland) Ltd (*KYB*, 1961–71; *Showcase* 1968); Michael McAdam (1988–95); McAdam temporarily reopened cinema in 2007–8;[12] d: William (Billy) James; Mrs James; and J. Curran; m: Norman M'Leod (1939);[13] br: William James, fb: James Curran, Capitol Cinema, Antrim Road (*1947 directory*); 780 (380 balcony; 400 stalls) seats (1939);[14] 700 (*KYB*, 1945–57); 360 (1977, in circle only; balcony in use as amusement arcade); 299 (*BFI*, 1991; 1996); in 1997, 50-seat screen was added, with former circle reduced to 315; 2 screens/364 seats (Connolly and Dillon, 2001:74). See *Playhouse Cinema*.

Picture House, Main Street (*c*.1918–*c*.1963), p: Portrush Estate Co. Ltd (*KYB*, 1919–64); m: R.A. Cooper, (*KYB*, 1919–28); licensed for music and dancing (*KYB*, 1919); no personnel listed *KYB*, 1929–48; 24ft proscenium (*1947 directory*); 650 (*KYB*, 1919); 700 (*KYB*, 1920–1); 620 (*KYB*, 1940); 654 (*KYB*, 1943); 700 (*KYB*, 1944); 650 (*1947 directory*); 600 (*KYB*, 1945–56); 587 (*KYB*, 1957); 545 (*KYB*, 1961–4).

- *Playhouse Cinema*, 47–51 Main Street (1970s–; formerly, *Majestic*; as *The Playhouse* from 2010); later 2 screens; temporarily reopened by Michael McAdam during April–August 2007; it was the cinema where he began his career; reconstructed in 2010 as bar, nightclub and 250-seat cinema/theatre/concert venue. See *Majestic*.

Ritz, p: William James (*KYB*, 1939–40); may be same as *Majestic*.

Randalstown

Picture House (*c*.1938–*c*.1958; aka *The Cinema* [*KYB*, 1941–52]), p: Supreme Cinemas, 35 (later, 133) Royal Avenue, Belfast, 300 (*KYB*, 1939–57); p: William Shields, Maghera; br: Maurice Logan, fb: Mr McClintock, Supreme Cinemas, Ltd, 133 Royal Avenue, Belfast, 500 (*1947 directory*).

Rathcoole

Alpha Cinema, Rathcoole Estate (Newtownabbey), (1 April 1957–November 1973); arch: John McBride Neill (*DIA*); p: A. Niblock, bookmaker Sammy Allen and Mrs Allen of Rathcoole (Entertainments) Ltd; 1,000 seats.[15] The cinema, opened by earl of Antrim, closed following its bombing by the IRA; became East Way social club, a loyalist men-only club.

Whitehead

Picture House (*c*.1938–October 1961; aka *Whitehead Cinema*), p: Supreme Cinemas, 35 [later, 133] Royal Avenue, Belfast (*KYB*, 1939–61); Maurice Logan (*KYB*, 1939–61); fb: Mr McClintock, Supreme Cinemas, Ltd, 133 Royal Avenue, Belfast (*1947 directory*); 500 (*KYB*, 1939–61), 350.

Travelling cinemas

BHMC Cinemas, Carnlough & Glenarm (*KYB*, 1941).

ARMAGH

Armagh

Armagh Omniplex. See *City Film House*.

Armagh Picture House, Russell Street (*c*.1914–*c*.1957; aka *Electric Picture Theatre*), arch: Thomas Houston (tender for rebuilding for Irish Empire Palaces, 1913), improvements in 1915 by Frederick William Higginbottom (*DIA*); p: Irish Empire Palaces Ltd (*KYB*, 1921–57); m: W.J.C. Neill (*KYB*, 1921–5); L.M. Ewing (*KYB*, 1926–8); fb: Mr H. Campbell, Irish Empire Palaces, 3 Grafton Street, Dublin (*1947 directory*); 20ft proscenium (*1947 directory*); 450 (*KYB*, 1921); 400 (*KYB*, 1936); 363 (*KYB*, 1945–57).

City Cinema, 8 Market Street (*c*.1916–63; aka *Armagh City Cinema*), p: J. Allen (*KYB*, 1925–6), m: J. Cauldwell (*KYB*, 1925–7); Irish National Forresters (*KYB*, 1927–31); George McKee (*KYB*, 1933); City Cinema (Armagh) Ltd (*KYB*, 1936; *1947 directory*); J. Kelly (*KYB*, 1944–66; listed as br in *1947 directory*); 400 (*KYB*, 1943); 317 (*KYB*, 1944–61).[16]

- *City Film House*, 25–37 Market Street (10 November 1995–29 June 2007; 2009–; aka *Armagh Omniplex*; *Armagh Cineplex*), joint venture between Diamond Cinemas Ltd and local council, 4 screens/650 seats; 790 (Connolly and Dillon, 2001:74). In 2008, it was taken over by Ward Anderson, who invested *c*. £1million in refurbishment, and it reopened in 2009 as *Armagh Omniplex*, part of the company's Empire Cinemas chain.

Cosy (*KYB*, 1932–3).

Marketplace Theatre and Arts Centre, Market Street; 397 (main auditorium), 120 (studio theatre), films screened by (access>CINEMA supported) Armagh City Film Club (2010).

New Cinema, p: Antrim Cinema, Ltd (*Showcase* 1968). Possibly, this is *New Cinema*, Antrim.

People's Palace (*KYB*, 1917).

Ritz Cinema, Market Street (1938–?, listed in *Showcase* 1968), p: Ritz Belfast Ltd (Union Cinemas Group), 15 Regent Street, London; Associated British Cinemas following its takeover of Union Cinemas in October 1937, 782; m: James McSorley (1937–);[17] after being destroyed by IRA bomb, *The Market Place, Armagh Theatre and Arts Centre* built on site.

Crossmaglen

Cinema (*c.*April 1944–71+), p: Parochial Hall Committee (*Showcase* 1968); opened by Richard Hayward;[18] p: HBE Cinemas Ltd, 133 Royal Avenue, Belfast (*KYB*, 1948–60); fb: Richard Hayward, 7 Bedford Street, Belfast (*1947 directory*); 280 (*KYB*, 1948–71).

Gilford

Dunbarton Cinema (*c.*1947–*c.*1962), p: Dunbar McMaster & Co. Ltd (*KYB*, 1948–55); Eltico Mills Ltd (*KYB*, 1961–3); 280 (*KYB*, 1948–55); 243 (*KYB*, 1956–61).

Keady

Scala Cinema, Granemore Road (*c.*1957–91+), p: Charles J. Mallon (*KYB*, 1958–71; *Showcase* 1968); 400 (*KYB*, 1958–61); 200 (*BFI*, 1991).
Keady Cinema, Town Hall, 7 Lake Road (*c.*1947–*c.*1956; aka *Town Hall Cinema*), p: Charles J. Mallon (*KYB*, 1948–57); 230 (*KYB*, 1948); 200 (*KYB*, 1949–51).
St Patrick's Hall (*c.*1962–71+), p: C.L. McKeone; 600 (*KYB*, 1963–71; *Showcase* 1968).

Lurgan

• *Centrepoint Cinemas* (aka *ESI Cinemas*), Multi-leisure complex, 24 Portadown Road (*c.* 1995–); 4 screens/828 (304; 254; 160; and 110) seats (*BFI*, 1996); 4 screens/695 (281, 182, 142, 90) seats or 769 (386, 135, 158, 90) seats (*Cinema Treasures* online; Connolly and Dillon, 2001:74).
Cinema and Hippodrome, Church Place, Main Street (?–*c.*20 August 1921), p: S. Hewitt; twice nightly (*KYB*, 1922); destroyed by fire in August 1922.[19]
Lyric Cinema (*c.*1933–71+), p: J.M. Murray (*KYB*, 1934–71; listed as J.A. McMurray [br/fb] in *1947 directory* and Mr J. M'Murray in *Showcase* 1968); 800 (*KYB*, 1948–60); 1,060 (*KYB*, 1961–2).
Picture House (*c.*1921–71+; aka *Foster's Picture House* [*KYB*, 1936–48]), p: J. Foster (*KYB*, 1922–37); Mr A. Foster (*KYB*, 1939–47; *1947 directory*); Ernest Foster, 41 Market Street (*KYB*, 1948–71; *Showcase* 1968); 500 (*KYB*, 1939–46); 600 (*KYB*, 1947–8); 700 (*KYB*, 1949–61).

Markethill

Cinema (*c.*1962), 5 nights per week, 1963.[20]
Olympic, Main Street (*c.*1949–*c.*1951), p: John Clarke, 360 (*KYB*, 1950–2).

Portadown

Catch My Pal Hall, Edward Street (*c.*1933–*c.*1935), first listed in *KYB*, 1934, 'run by a committee'; l: Robert Spence, Tandragee, Co. Armagh; cinema, 1936;[21] 290 (*KYB*, 1936). This seems to have been in the Town Hall, an 1890 building which currently has an in-house theatre with tiered seating. The *Town Hall* is also listed in *KYB*, 1916–17, as a cinema venue.
Picture House (*c.*1918–71+), p: Irish Empire Palaces Ltd, 52 Stafford Street, Dublin; Irish Empire Palaces, 3 Grafton Street, Dublin (*KYB*, 1934–71; *Showcase* 1968); m: William C. Summerson (*KYB*, 1919–33); fb: Mr H. Campbell, Irish Empire Palaces, 3 Grafton Street, Dublin (*1947 directory*); 18ft proscenium (*1947 directory*); 400 (*KYB*, 1919); 450 (*KYB*, 1920–1); 750 (*KYB*, 1936–41; *1947 directory*); 343 (*KYB*, 1942–61).
Regal Cinema, Bridge Street (*c.*1933–*c.*1985), p: Regal Cinema Ltd (*KYB*, 1934); Regal Theatres Ltd, 9 Garfield Chambers, Royal Avenue, Belfast (*KYB*, 1936–71 in *1947 directory* address: 277 Gardiels [sic?] Chambers; in *Showcase* 1968 address: 27 Garfield Chambers); Charles (Charlie) F. O'Dowda, Picture House, Royal Avenue, Belfast (*KYB*, 1934); James McCafferty; 900 (*KYB*, 1936–61); 1,200.
Savoy (*c.*1936–*c.*1965), p: Robert Spence; listed *KYB*, 1937–66.

Tandragee

New Cinema (*c.*1935–*c.*1936), p: Robert Spence (*KYB*, 1937), 320 (*KYB*, 1936–7).

CARLOW

Bagenalstown

Astor Cinema, Borris Road (26 April 1940–71+), p: Harry Godfrey Brown, E.D. Brown (*KYB*, 1949–71, just H. Godfrey listed in *Showcase* 1968); br: H. Godfrey Brown, 300 (*1947 directory*); screen: 12ft x 10ft (*1947 directory*); 350 (*KYB*, 1955); 300.

Palace Cinema (*c.*1929–*c.*1945; as *Cinema*, *KYB*, 1930–4, no personnel listed), p: Harry Godfrey Brown & O'Reilly (*KYB*, 1935); H. Godfrey Brown (*KYB*, 1936–46).

Borris
Borris Cinema (*c.*1948–*c.*1970; listed as temporarily closed in *KYB*, 1971), br/p: Revd J. O'Meara (*1947 directory*); Revd Joseph McDonnell, MA (*KYB*, 1949–50); Revd E. Kennedy (*KYB*, 1951–6); Revd D. Deady (*KYB*, 1957–61); Revd J. Meaney (*KYB*, 1962–4); Revd A. Murphy (*KYB*, 1965–7; *Showcase* 1968); Francis P. Kiernan, Borris (*KYB*, 1968–71); 12ft x 9ft proscenium (*1947 directory*); 250 (*KYB*, 1949–57); 140 (*KYB*, 1968–71).

Carlow
Assembly Rooms, Dublin Street (1912–17), later vocational school, and now county library, where Chris and Ralph Sylvester, professional vaudevillians, seeing that cinema might spell decline of their business, started live shows with film screenings from 1912 when they rented venue for £55 per annum.
Carlow Cineplex (*c.*2000–9; aka *Savoy Cineplex*)[22] Hanover (now Carlow) shopping centre, Kennedy Avenue, p: Ward Anderson, 3 screens/520 (248, 154, 118) seats.
• *Carlow Omniplex*, Fairgreen shopping centre, Barrack Street (12 November 2009–; aka *Carlow Cineplex*), p: Ward Anderson, 8 screens.
Cinema Palace, Burrin Street, where post office now stands (February 1915–26 December 1937; aka *Cinema Theatre*; *Palace Cinema*), p: Carlow Cinema Palace Ltd (*KYB*, 1917); Fred Thompson; James Murphy (*KYB*, 1919–21); Mr Hanna (*KYB*, 1922–9); Frank Slater (*KYB*, 1930–7); executors of late F. Slater (*KYB*, 1938); m: Michael J. Deasy, who moved to the Stephen's Green Cinema, Dublin, as manager in December 1935; 700 (*KYB*, 1938); 750, licensed for music and dancing (*KYB*, 1919); 600 (*KYB*, 1920–1);[23] destroyed by fire.
Coliseum, Upper Tullow Street (19 September 1941–76+), built on Ryan's coal yard; arch: Thomas Burke, Portlaoise; p/d: Fred Pollard, Kilkenny Road, Carlow; Fred McElwee, Station Road, Carlow; Mr J.L. Kelly; and Joe Egan, Portlaoise (*KYB*, 1946–55); p: F. Pollard & F. McElwee (*KYB*, 1955); Coliseum Cinema (Carlow) Ltd (CRO no. 16107; *KYB*, 1960–71; *Showcase* 1968); br: Mr F. Pollard (*1947 directory*); fb: John Egan, 24 Main Street, Maryborough [Portlaoise] (*1947 directory*); Leo Ward (1975–6);[24] 750; 800 (*KYB*, 1944–5); 700 (*1947 directory*); 850 (*KYB*, 1946–61).
Palace Cinema, Burrin Street. See *Cinema Palace*.
Ritz Cinema, 130–1 Tullow Street/side entrance on Charlotte Street (18 June 1938–?); replaced *Palace Cinema* which was destroyed by fire on 26 December 1937; arch: Bill O'Dwyer, Michael Scott & Associates (archiseek.com); p: Carlow Cinemas, Ltd (1938–46; *1947 directory*); Amalgamated Cinemas (Ireland) Ltd, 9 Eden Quay, Dublin (*KYB*, 1946–71; *Showcase* 1968); Tommy Heavey; Ward Anderson; m: P.J. Tyanan, fb: Michael J. Deasy (9 Eden Quay, Dublin) (*1947 directory*); 1,054 (*KYB*, 1939–61); 'Perhaps no other type of enterprise so faithfully indicates the prosperity of a town as the erection of a luxury premises can do. The Ritz represents the last word in cinema glamour.'[25]
Town Hall (1898–1905, McCole, 2005:appendix D; also later: *KYB*, 1916–17).
Visual, Centre for Contemporary Art & the George Bernard Shaw Theatre, Old Dublin Road (grounds of Carlow College), (autumn 2009–), arch: Terry Pawson Architects, London (cost £18 million), occasional venue for film, used by access>CINEMA affiliated club; 294 seat theatre, and 4 main gallery spaces.

Hacketstown
Cinema, occasional film shows, p: E. Bradley, Baltinglass.

Muine Bheag/Muinebeag see **Bagenalstown**

Rathvilly
Cinema, occasional film shows, p: E. Bradley, Baltinglass.

Tullow
Grand Central Cinema, Main Street (2 May 1940–76+), Grand Central Cinema (Tullow) Ltd (CRO no. 16127), p: Thomas Flynn, builder and garage owner, Church Street, Tullow, (*KYB*, 1941–71; *Showcase* 1968); m: Mr M. Mulhall (*Showcase* 1968); opening prices: 4*d.*, 1*s.*; 1*s.* 4*d.*; shows 6.30p.m. and 9p.m.; fb: M. Mulhall (1975–6);[26] screen: 17ft x 13ft (*1947 directory*); 500 (*KYB*, 1941–71); 400 (*1947 directory*).
Town Hall (*KYB*, 1930–3; no personnel); p: K. Gould (*KYB*, 1934 as *The New Hall*).
Tullow Cinema (*c.*1924–*c.*1939), p/m: R.J. Lawson (*KYB*, 1925–40), 350.[27]

CAVAN

Arva
Cinema (? to 1947), p: Edward McKiernan, 300. This 'established' cinema, which was subject to an annual rent of £16, was put up for sale in June 1947.[28]
Moonlight Pavilion is listed *KYB*, 1949–71 and *Showcase* 1968, as a cinema, though it seems to have been used primarily as a dance venue in the 1940s and 1950s; p: Mr E. McKiernan (*Showcase* 1968).
Temperance Hall (1904–5; McCole, 2005:appendix D and later including 1930s), in May 1936 the iron and timber building partly destroyed following ignition of nitrate film in exterior projection box while 180 were attending film show.[29]

Bailieborough/Bailieboro'
Excel Cinema, Henry Street (25 October 1943–71+), p: Excel Cinema Co. Ltd (CRO no. 10569; *KYB*, 1949–71; *Showcase* 1968); br: Paul Fegan (*1947 directory*); 550 (*KYB*, 1949); 450 (*1947 directory*, *KYB*, 1950–3); 400 (*KYB*, 1954–71).
Market House, Main Street, upper room, which runs length of building, was used for concerts, travelling cinema, theatrical performances and meetings; now a pubic library.
Town Hall (1934), 400.[30]

Ballyconnell
Star Cinema (17 November 1949–*c*.1971), p: Star Cinema, Ballyconnell, Ltd (CRO no. 12792), J.J. Clancy; 300; used as live venue after closing as cinema.
Paragon Cinema, br: Miss Kaye (*1947 directory*).

Ballyjamesduff
AOH Hall, 16mm venue for travelling cinemas.
Cinema (*KYB*, 1930; 1947),[31] 16mm venue for travelling cinemas, perhaps same as above.
Market Hall (1905; McCole, 2005:appendix D).

Belturbet
Erne Cinema, Holborn Hill (December 1947–71+), p: Erne Cinema, Belturbet, Ltd (CRO no. 11553; *KYB*, 1957–71; *Showcase* 1968), 477 (*KYB*, 1957–61). Construction of the cinema was begun in 1944 by William Stewart, who subsequently sold the premises to Erne Cinema, Belturbet Ltd for £2,000; the use of timber in the cinema's construction was not authorized by the dept. of industry and commerce and as such was subject of a court case shortly before the cinema opened.[32]
Town Hall (1901; McCole, 2005:appendix D; *c*.1930s/1940s), 300; venue for travelling cinema companies, not equipped for sound by 1940.[33]

Cavan
Cinema, Town Hall, Drumellis (1913–71+; aka *Town Hall Cinema*), p: Messrs Foster and Thompson;[34] Cavan Cinema Co. (*KYB*, 1919); Claude Nixon (*KYB*, 1920–1); Mr Stanley (*KYB*, 1930); Mr Verdon (*KYB*, 1936–8); Edward McKiernan, Drumelis (*KYB*, 1939–71; *Showcase* 1968); licensed for music and dancing (*KYB*, 1919); m: Claude Nixon (*KYB*, 1919–21); br: Edward McKiernan (*1947 directory*); 20ft stage and 16ft proscenium (*1947 directory*); 400 (*KYB*, 1919); 350 (*KYB*, 1921); 450 (1934);[35] 600 (*KYB*, 1939–71). In 1921 plans for a new cinema were drawn up by Patrick Brady (*DIA*).
Forester's Hall (1905; McCole, 2005:appendix D).
The Hall, Farnham Street, (1898–1904; McCole, 2005:appendix D; aka *The Old College*).
Magnet Cinema, Farnham Street (*c*.March 1936–*c*.1993; first listed in *KYB* 1936), p: Cavan Cinema Ltd (CRO no.8983; *KYB*, 1937–71; *Showcase* 1968); br: Mr C. McGriskin, md: A.W.Gordon (*1947 directory*); fb: Leo Ward (1975–7);[36] screen: 13ft x 18ft (*1947 directory*); 630/650 (*KYB*, 1937–71).
The Picture Lounge at the Gonzo Theatre, The Imperial, Main Street (7 July 2010–),weekly arthouse screnings, 4 m x 4 m HD screen.[37]
Protestant Hall (1905; McCole, 2005:appendix D).
• *Storm Cinemas*, Townpark Centre, Main Street (2000–; aka *Odeon/Storm*), p: Premier Productions/ Patrick O'Sullivan; Irish Leisureplex Entertainment Co./Entertainment Enterprises/Ciáran and Colum Butler (2008); l: Odeon Cinemas; 4 screens/775 seats[38]/815 (225; 228; 182; 180) seats.

Cootehill
St Michael's Cinema (*c*.1947–71+; as *Cinema* in *1947 directory*), p: J. Stanley, Boyne Cinemas Ltd, 450 (*KYB*, 1949–71; *Showcase* 1968); fb: Mr J.M. Stanley, 6 Peter Street, Drogheda (*1947 directory*).
Town Hall (1898–9; McCole, 2005:appendix D).

Kingscourt
Majestic (c.January 1944–71+), p: P. Macken (*KYB*, 1951–71; *Showcase* 1968); br: G. Macken, R. McGee (*1947 directory*); screen: 16ft x 12ft, 450 (*1947 directory*, *KYB*).

Virginia
Ramor Theatre (September 1999–), home to Film@ramor, which as of September 2010 was entering its sixth year (supported by access>CINEMA, 2010).
Town Hall Cinema (1947),³⁹ venue for travelling cinema companies.

Travelling Cinemas
Abbey Cinema Co. (1947).⁴⁰
Culate Cinemas (February 1947–), Hall cinemas in Carrigallen; Newtowngore; Swanlinbar; Bawnboy.⁴¹
Edward McKiernan: Town Hall, Bailiesborough; Belturbet; and Cavan (*KYB*, 1941–4).
Provincial Cinemas: Swanlinbar, Belturbet, Ballyjamesduff, Bailliesborough, and Drumshanbo and Carrigallen, Co. Leitrim (*KYB*, 1937; 1948).⁴²

CLARE

Ennis
• *Burren Cinema*, Station Road (9 May 1971–), Burren Cinema Co. Ltd (CRO no. 36707), p: Modern Irish Theatres; Michael Breen, fb: Paddy Melia (1975–7);⁴³ 2 screens.
Burren Twin Cinema. See *Burren Cinema*.
• *Empire Movieplex*, Parnell Street, 6 screens, 975 seats.⁴⁴
Gaiety Cinema (c.1947–71+; listed in *1947 directory* [no details, though elsewhere lists fb: Harry W. Culleton, 75 Middle Abbey Street, Dublin]), p: Ennis Cinemas Ltd, 9 Eden Quay, Dublin (*KYB*, 1950–71; *Showcase* 1968); 800 (*KYB*, 1952–61).
Glór (Arts and Entertainment Centre), Causeway Link (November 2001–), d: Katie Verling; 485 (main auditorium) and 60 (studio space); regular if limited film screenings, mostly via IFI and Glór cinema club, access>CINEMA supported (2010).
The Kinema, p: T. McGregor, Mayler Street, Cork; m: Miss E. Boland (*KYB*, 1923).
Picture House (c.1922–c.1926), p: Helena Gough (1926–7); (cited 'Helena Gouch', three changes weekly, *KYB*, 1923–5).
Rink Palace (c.1933), p: Mrs McGregor (*KYB*, 1934).
Town Hall Cinema (c.1913–c.1940s; listed in *1947 directory* [no details, though elsewhere lists fb: Harry W. Culleton, 75 Middle Abbey Street, Dublin]), p: Mrs McGregor (*KYB*, 1923–33) m: Miss K. Boland (*KYB*, 1924–8); 400 (1934), equipped for sound.⁴⁵ This may be the same venue as *The Kinema* above, while *Rink Palace* has also a single entry with Mrs McGregor as proprietor.⁴⁶

Ennistymon
Town Hall (1940s+–) p: Ennistymon Cinema Co. Ltd (CRO no. 11298), 1,000 seats, not equipped for sound; used by travelling companies (1934);⁴⁷ listed in *1947 directory* with br: Mr Browne, screen: 10ft x 12ft, 200, sound (population at that time 1,202).

Kildysart
Victory (?–c.1965) p: Thomas Kenny, 300.

Kilkee
Arcadia, O'Curry Street (September 1946–c.1968; aka *New Arcadia* [*1947 directory*]), p: Dr J.A. Kelly, Henry Street, Kilrush (*KYB*, 1950–64; *Showcase* 1968); br: Mr Williams (*1947 directory*); 600 (*1947 directory*); 495 (*KYB*, 1950–5); 460 (*KYB*, 1960–1).
Kilkee Cineplex (July 1999–?) 3 screens, 225 seats.⁴⁸
Olympia (c.1929–c.1960;1963–6 (summer only); aka *Olympic Hall*; listed *KYB*, 1930–4 (no personnel) and *KYB*, 1950–5); p: Charles Fitzgerald (*KYB*, 1950–5; *Showcase* 1968; as br in *1947 directory*); 800;⁴⁹ 450 (*KYB*, 1961–71); after being closed for a number of years, reopened as a cinema by John Lynch during summers 1963–6; became full-time ballroom in 1960s.
Town Hall Cinema (c.1924–50s), p: Carron Cinema Co. (*KYB*, 1927–38); Gennand (sic) Walkin (*KYB*, 1939); Dan Ryan, Ballinard, Clanmorris Avenue, Limerick (*KYB*, 1940–8); m: J.G. Carron (*KYB*, 1927–38); 500;⁵⁰ 300 (*KYB*, 1939–48).
The Picture House (c.1924–c.1931), p: Patrick Tubridy (*KYB*, 1925–6); W. Fagherty (*KYB*, 1930); M. Fagherty (*KYB*, 1931–2).

Killaloe
McKeogh's Hall (c.1934), 300 seats, used by travelling companies, not equipped for sound.[51]
Cinema (?–late 1950s), br: Mr Williams, Carlton Limerick (*1947 directory*, perhaps same Williams of Kilkee *Arcadia*); past p: Pat Ryan, perhaps same as *McKeogh's Hall*.

Kilrush
Mars Cinema, Francis Street (16 December 1950–January 1991), p: Patrick Turbidy (*KYB*, 1951–71; *Showcase* 1968); 850 (600 in stalls; 250 in balcony) seats; 650 (*KYB*, 1961–4); 500 (*KYB*, 1965–71).
Palace Theatre (c.1920–c.1950; aka *Palace Cinema*), p: P. & M. Turbidy (*KYB*, 1926–31); O. & M. Turbidy (*KYB*, 1932–4); Patrick Tubridy (*KYB*, 1935–50); 350 (1935–41; *1947 directory*); 500.[52]

Lahinch
Lahinch Community Centre, c.1964–9, small 35mm venue.

Milltown-Malbay
Central, p: Tom Malone; 250.
New Cinema, m: Dan Ryan, Marine Parade, Kilkee, screen: 10ft x 12ft, 190 (*1947 directory*).

Newmarket-on-Fergus
Central Cinema (c.1947–c.1962); listed in *1947 directory*), p: Richard Murray (*KYB*, 1949–71; *Showcase* 1968); screen: 12⅓ft x 9ft (*1947 directory*); 350 (*KYB*, 1949); 300 (*KYB*, 1950–71).

Scariff
Astor Cinema, p: Jimmy Tracey, owner of limeworks, 200; twice weekly, Wednesdays and Sundays; converted to Astor Ballroom in 1950s.

Sixmilebridge
Arch, p: M. Barron, 300.

Tulla
Tulla Cinema (1920s–98) p: John Byrne (*1934 cinemas*; *1947 directory*); 200/300; opened as a silent cinema; equipped for sound from c.1936; used occasionally by travelling companies, by 1947 it had programme changes twice weekly and a screen 12ft x 11ft. Closed with death of John Byrne in 1998, the last village cinema in Ireland.[53]

CORK

Ballincollig
• *Reel Picture House*, Time Square (1997–), 6 screens/1,277 seats, balcony seats in larger screens (associated with *Reel Picture House*, Blackpool, Cork).

Bandon
• *Bandon Cinema*, Market Street (c.1918–77+), p: Thomas J. Powell (*KYB*, 1919–33); T.J. Powell & Sons, Hill Terrace, Bandon (*KYB*, 1934); C.A. Powell, Knockbrogan (*KYB*, 1935–7); Bandon Cinema Co., Castle Park Road, Bandon (CRO no. 98276; *KYB*, 1938); T. Lowney (*KYB*, 1939–41); T. Lowney & J. O'Brien (*KYB*, 1942–59; br & fb: Thomas Lowney [*1947 directory*]); J. O'Brien (*KYB*, 1960–71; *Showcase* 1968; m: John O'Brien (*1947 directory*); fb: Sean Lowney (1976–7);[54] screen: 12ft x 12ft (*1947 directory*); 600 (*KYB*, 1919); 500 (*KYB*, 1920); 450 (*KYB*, 1935–7); 350 (*KYB*, 1938); 450 (*KYB*, 1942–59); c.600 (*1947 directory*); 500 (*KYB*, 1960–71).

Bantry
• *Bantry Cinemax*, The Quay (17 December 2005–), p: Stephen Keoghan, 3 screens/313 seats.
Rock Cinema (*KYB*, 1930–1).
Stella Cinema (27 April 1927–77+), p: Michael, Jack and Denis Murphy (brothers), (1927); W. McSweeney, Central Hotel, Bantry (*KYB*, 1935–45; address from 1939: The Square, Bantry); A. McSweeney, The Square (*KYB*, 1946–67; *1947 directory* which also lists him as fb); V. McSweeney (*KYB*, 1968–71; *Showcase* 1968); m: Walter Prendergast (1927); fb: S. Lowney (1977);[55] 500 (1927);[56] 398 (*KYB*, 1935–8);[57] 400 (*KYB*, 1939); 600 (*KYB*, 1942; 1946–61); 700 (*1947 directory*).

Bere Island
Cinema (1920s), Michael, Jack and Denis Murphy.[58]
Garrison Cinema, Bere Island (c.1929–c.1946; listed as closed in *KYB*, 1948), p: Garrison Welfare Board; Fort Berehaven, Bere Island (*KYB*, 1942–7).[59]

Blackpool
Blackpool Cinema, 70–4 Watercourse Road, Blackpool (2 November 1920–*c*.1927; later ropened as
    Lido, 25 October 1931–14 April 1962), Blackpool Cinema Co. (CRO 4992), p/m: Mrs Hussey, Cobh
    (*KYB*, 1921–3); p: William S. Spencer (*KYB*, 1924–8); films, live shows, Irish dancing, political ral-
    lies; refused a licence in 1926 because it did not meet basic standards required of an entertainment
    venue (lack of lighting, exit notices defective and seating not fixed or spaced), remained vacant for
    a number of years.[60] See also *Lido*.
Lido, 70–4 Watercourse Road (25 October 1931–14 April 1962; formerly, *Blackpool Cinema*, 1920–
    c.1927; later, *Palladium*, 1962–77+), p/m: Edward (Eddie) L. Coghlan, Dublin; 456 (1934);[61] 420
    (*KYB*, 1940–61; *1947 directory*); decorated in Venetian style, fitted out with latest equipment; pop-
    ular suburban cinema akin to, if better than, St Mary's Hall; accepted jam jars and bottles for admis-
    sion; by 1960s it had a bad reputation for rowdiness; Eddie Coghlan closed the cinema on 14 April
    1962, five days after a stabbing occurred in the cinema. See also *Blackpool Cinema* and *Palladium*.
Palladium, 70–4 Watercourse Road (June 1962–77+; formerly, *Blackpool Cinema*, 2 November 1920–
    c.1927; *Lido*, 25 October 1931–14 April 1962), p: Paddy Coughlan, hotelier; a new upmarket cinema
    with 450 seats, it became the first cinema in Cork to run Sunday matinees;[62] Edward (Eddie) L.
    Coghlan (*Showcase* 1968). 437 (*KYB*, 1963). See also *Blackpool Cinema* and *Lido*.
• *The Reel Picture*, Blackpool retail park (*c*.2008–; aka *Blackpool Cinema*), 7 screens/1,201 seats; 600
    car spaces; associated with *Reel Picture House*, Ballincollig.

Buttevant
Legion Hall, p: Kyrle Cahill, 250.

Capswell
New Picture Theatre (*KYB*, 1917).

Carrigaline
Oakwood Cinema (*c*.1969–77+), p: Oakwood Cinema Ltd (CRO no. 53870), Mr R. Cogan (*KYB*,
    1970); 400; fb: R. Cogan (1976).[63]

Carrigtwohill
Movie Junction, Fota retail park (opened on 19 November 2010); Ireland's first drive-in cinema; accom-
    modation for 100 cars; screen: 17 m x 20 m (approx. 2,500 sq. ft).[64]

Castlemartyr
Cinema (*c*.1948–71+), p: Reuben Hurst (*KYB*, 1949–71; *Showcase* 1968).

Castletown Bearhaven/Castletownbere
Beerhaven Cinema (*c*.1964–71+, listed *Showcase* 1968), 250 (*KYB*, 1965–9); 200 (*KYB*, 1970–1).
Cinema, p: O. Harrington (*KYB*, 1949–57), 250 (*KYB*, 1949–64). May be same venue as *Beerhaven
    Cinema*.

Charleville
The Pavilion, Main Street (*c*.1924–77+; aka *The Coliseum*),[65] p: J. Hurley (*KYB*, 1925–33); T.J. Hurley
    (*KYB*, 1936–41; 1945–71; *Showcase* 1968); fb: T. Hurley (1975–7);[66] 30ft deep stage and 30ft prosce-
    nium (*1947 directory*); 500 (1934);[67] 450 (*KYB*, 1938; *1947 directory*); 700 (*KYB*, 1943–6); 750
    (*KYB*, 1948); 500 (*KYB*, 1949–71).

Clonakilty
Clonakilty Cinema, Wolfe Tone Street (*c*.1925–*c*.2000), located in nineteenth century warehouse, p:
    Timothy Lowney & D.C. McCarthy (*KYB*, 1927–33); Timothy Lowney & Co. (*KYB*, 1934–71, just
    as T. Lowney in *Showcase* 1968); m: Timothy Lowney (*KYB*, 1927–33); br & fb: T. Lowney (*1947
    directory*); fb: S. Lowney (1977);[68] screen: 14ft x 12ft and stage: 25ft x 14ft (*1947 directory*); 370
    (1934);[69] 350 (*KYB*, 1937); 400 (*KYB*, 1939–63; 600 in *1947 directory*); 500 (*KYB*, 1964–71).
    Building demolished; site used for new hotel.
• *The Park Cinema*, Link Road (*c*.2001–), built as part of Quality Hotel development, 510 seats
    (Connolly and Dillon, 2001:72); 3 screens/355 (199, 96, 60) seats (2010).

Cloyne
The Cinema (*c*.1948–*c*.1968), p: Reuben Hurst, 300 (*KYB*, 1949–66; *Showcase* 1968).
Picture House (*c*.1929–*c*.1932), listed in *KYB*, 1930–3 (no personnel).[70]

Cobh (formerly Queenstown)
Arch Cinema (*c*.1934–*c*.1947; first listed in *KYB*, 1935, also listed in *1947 directory*), p: J.J. Frenett
    (*KYB*, 1936–48), 450–470 (*KYB*, 1935–46);[71] 400 (*KYB*, 1948).

Assembly Rooms, Queen's Hotel (*KYB*, 1916–17).

Baths Hall (aka *Baths Picture Palace*, *KYB*, 1917), p: J. Piper (*KYB*, 1916).[72]

Coliseum (*c.*1932–*c.*1947), p: Queenstown Picture House Ltd (*KYB*, 1933); 450 (*KYB*, 1935–7; 1934);[73] 480 (*KYB*, 1938–43); 417 (*KYB*, 1944–8).

Imperial Cinema (*c.*1916–? reappears in *KYB*, 1930), p: Queenstown Picture Co., 220 (*KYB*, 1916–17).

Ormonde Cinema (*c.*1952–*c.*1992; formerly *Tower Cinema*, *c.*1947–52), p: James Kavanagh, Ormonde Cinemas, Arklow; Ormonde Cinema Co. (Cobh) Ltd (CRO no. 13052; *KYB*, 1952–65; *Showcase* 1968); fb: Leo Ward (1975–6);[74] 480 (*KYB*, 1952–65).

Picture Theatre (*KYB*, 1916–17).

Tower Cinema (*c.*1947–52; renamed *Ormonde Cinema*, *c.*1952; listed as *Cobh Tower* in 1947 directory with F. McDonnell as br), p: James Kavanagh (*KYB*, 1949–51). See also *Ormonde Cinema*.

Queenstown Cinema, West Beach (*KYB*, 1916–17).

Cork

Alhambra, Cork Street, p: N. Long,[75] 500 (*KYB*, 1920).

Assembly Rooms, 22 South Mall (April 1896–1909 [irregular shows];[76] 27 December 1909–19 December 1964; aka *Assembly Rooms Cinema*; *Assembly Rooms Picturedrome*, *KYB*, 1929–38); p/m: Alex McEwan[77] (*KYB*, 1916–19; McEwan died, April 1919); licensed for dancing and music (*KYB*, 1919); p: Reid & Goodwin (*KYB*, 1935–7); Goodwin family (*KYB*, 1940); Assembly Rooms Cinema Ltd (*KYB*, 1945–71; *1947 directory*; *Showcase* 1968); m: Miss M.E. Spencer[78] (*KYB*, 1920–8; listed as br in *1947 directory*); 600 (*KYB*, 1917), *c.*1,000 (*KYB*, 1918–19); 800 (*KYB*, 1920–1); 730 (*KYB*, 1935–7); 670[79] (*KYB*, 1940; 1945–63); 607 (*KYB*, 1964–71). The building was demolished in 1970.

Bellevue Cinema, Military Road, opposite Collins Barracks (23 September, 1920–*c.*1925; later, *Gaiety Ballroom*, *c.*1925–64; *Cameo Cinema*, 1964–7; *Cameo Panorama Cinema*, September 1967–October 1985); arch: Chillingworth & Levie, builders, J. Kearns & Sons and decoration by J. O'Connell; Cork's first suburban cinema; p/m: Michael Pendergast (*KYB*, 1922); 450 (*KYB*, 1921); converted to *Gaiety Ballroom* in mid-1920.[80] See also *Cameo Cinema*.

Cameo Cinema, Military Road, opposite Collins Barracks (18 April 1965–7; *Cameo Panorama Cinema*, September 1967–October 1985; formerly, *Bellevue Cinema*, 23 September 1920–*c.*1925; *Gaiety Ballroom*, *c.*1925–64), p: Seamus Quinn, who converted *Gaiety Ballroom* back to cinema, which could double as a dancing venue; further renovations followed with the introduction of a curved 41ft x18ft panorama screen, and it reopened as the *Cameo Panorama Cinema* in September 1967; in 1972 children's cinema club on Saturdays; due to declining cinema audiences, in October 1983 Quinn converted premises to a discotheque, but showed occasional films. Closed fully as a cinema by 1985; knocked down *c.*2000 and an apartment block was built on the site.[81] See also *Bellevue Cinema*.

Capitol, Grand Parade (5 April 1947–21 January 1989; *Capitol Cineplex*, 11 August 1989–2 December 2005), arch: James Finbarre McMullen (*DIA*); p: The Capitol (Cork) Ltd, subsidiary of Capitol & Allied Cinemas, 4–8 North Princes Street, Dublin (*Showcase* 1968); Ward Anderson (from 1971);[82] m: Eddie McGrath, Clonmel (from 1947–81); Fred Hill (1981–92); Donal Kelly (1989–95); Patrick O'Brien (2005); fb: Peter Farrell (*1947 directory*); *c.*1,300 (*KYB*, 1948–61); 1,329 (*KYB*, 1968–71). Built on site of Grant's clothing and furniture store, which was destroyed by fire on 11 March 1942; lavish painting of Madonna and Child on ceiling of auditorium. In December 1974, the space that had been initially designed as a restaurant was transformed into a 105-seat cinema called the *Mini Capitol* (this became screen 6 of the new *Cineplex*); from 11 August 1989 reopened as 6-screen *Capitol Cineplex*; 1,083 (399, 177, 152, 151, 102, 102) seats; at cost of £1.75 million.[83]

Capitol Cineplex, Grand Parade. See *Capitol*.

City Hall (occasional film shows, aka *Municipal Buildings*, showed films during Easter Fete Speranza, 1897;[84] and *c.*1915–16) (*KYB*, 1916–17); 800 (*KYB*, 1917).

Classic, 11–12 Washington Street (28 December 1975–10 August 1989; formerly, *Ritz*, 13 August 1939–February 1974; *Washington Cinema*, January 1920–8 January 1928); p: Seamus Quinn; Abbey Films/Ward Anderson (from 1979).[85] See *Ritz*; *Washington Cinema*.

Clonmel Hall, p/m: A. McEwan (*KYB*, 1918–20).

Coliseum Cinema, King Street (now MacCurtain Street), (10 July 1913–4 April 1964), p: Southern Coliseum Ltd, 52 Stafford Street, Dublin (chairman, David Frame; address in *KYB*, 1935–55 as 3 Grafton Street, Dublin, while in *KYB*, 1960–71, 9 Herbert Place, Dublin; also listed in *Showcase* 1968), Cork's first custom built cinema; interiors based on the tomb of Egyptian King Tutankhamun; same proprietors as Phoenix Picture Palace and Electric, Talbot Street, Dublin;[86] m: M.J. Tighe (*KYB*, 1918–24); M.F. Reynolds (*KYB*, 1925); Harry J. Brett (*KYB*, 1926); A.E. Norwood (*KYB*, 1927–33); Stanley Cant (1947–); fb: Will Summerson, Picture House, Portadown (*KYB*, 1924); fb: Mr H.K.

Campbell (also fb for *Picture Houses* in Dundalk, Armagh and Portadown as well as *Coliseum* in Waterford, *1947 directory*); screen: 16ft x 13ft (*1947 directory*); 800 (*KYB*, 1918); licensed for dancing and music, *c.*690–700 (*KYB*, 1919–21; 1940–2; 1943–61);[87] in three areas with the sections progressively dearer to the back. Occasionally used for live music, including opera seasons in 1920s. From 1990, the building was used as a bowling alley and amusements' arcade.[88]

Cork Electric Theatre, 32 Maylor Street (27 December 1909–*c.*January 1910; March 1910–April 1911); p/m: Allan S. Davenport, lessee of Irish Electric Theatres Ltd; Mr C.F. Fielding, owner of an engineering and electrical company, Grand Parade, a supplier of magic lanterns and cinematographic material (March 1910–April 1911).[89]

• *Cork Omniplex*, Mahon Point shopping centre (2005–), p: Ward Anderson, 13 screens, stadium seating, 2,677 seats.

Father Mathew Picturedrome (27 December 1909–10; October 1912–?; aka *Father Mathew Hall*).[90]

• *Gate Multiplex*, North Main Street (1998–), p: Cado Ltd; 6 screens (2 digital), 1,084 seats, stadium seating, loop system for hard of hearing; temporarily closed in March 2007 because of an arson attack, which caused extensive damage;[91] associated cinemas are the *Gate* cinemas at Mallow and Midleton.

Half Moon Theatre, Emmet Place, located to the rear of Cork Opera House, it is a small flexible studio space (*c.*150) that occasionally offers film screenings; host to Cork Cine Club, access>CINEMA supported (2010).[92]

Imperial Cinema, 43–4 Old George's Street (later Oliver Plunkett Street), (7 February, 1913–3 July 1954; aka *Miah's*, after cinema's long–time commissionaire, Miah), p: John Hannon; Miss E. Hannon (*KYB*, 1922–3); Gertrude Hannon (*KYB*, 1924–9); l: Stephen Whelan, Grosvenor Place, Willington Road, Cork (*KYB*, 1930–55; see also *Washington*); m: J. Aughney (*1947 directory*); screen: 10ft x 8ft (*1947 directory*); 300 (*KYB*, 1919–21); 350 (*KYB*, 1935–55; though only listed as 279 in *1934 cinemas*); lost its 'premier' status by the 1920s and had become run down; appealed to child market, screening B movies/second–run; downstairs seating wooden benches; building became premises of Hannover Cycle Co.[93]

Kino Cinema, Washington Street (November 1996–November 2009), p: Michael Hannigan; art cinema; one screen, 188 seats. In 2003, the Cultural Cinemas Consortium (Arts Council and Irish Film Board) awarded *Kino* a €750,000 grant for its redevelopment, but the matching funding could not be raised, so the redevelopment did not take place; Hannigan announced its closure in October 2009, but despite widespread public support for its continuance, the cinema closed on its thirteenth anniversary.[94]

Lee Cinema, Winthrop Street (?–11 December 1920; 22 September 1921–8 April 1972; 19 November 1972– August 1989; aka *Lee Picture House* in *KYB*, 1921), p: Lee Cinema Ltd (CRO no. 5022; *KYB*, 1924–71; *Showcase* 1968); m: J. McGarry, (*KYB*, 1921); Mrs Dowling (*KYB*, 1924–5); E.P. Dowling (*KYB*, 1926–32); destroyed by fire 11 December 1920 (*KYB*, 1921); interiors gutted, reopened 22 September 1921; p: Madge O'Regan and Julia Scraggs, sold end of 1950s to Abbey Films/ Ward Andreson [*1947 directory* lists Stephen Whelan as prop. and Miss M. O'Regan as br]); m: J. Aughney (*1947 directory*); screen: 10ft x 8ft (*1947 directory*); *c.*450 (*KYB*, 1921; 1940–70);[95] 350 (*1947 directory*); cinema closed 8 April 1972 to downsize; reopened with single entrance on 19 November 1972, 2 screens/ 250 seats, and downstairs converted to a shop; until its closure in August 1989 it remained one of the most important second–run venues in the city.

Lee Picture House. See *Lee Cinema*.

Limerick Hall, p: Alex McEwan (*KYB*, 1918–20).

Opera House, Emmett Place (9 September 1896 presented Vitagraph films;[96] 25 January 1897–6 February 1897, Robert Paul and his animatographe; *c.*1915–26, occasional film seasons, or as part of cine-variety; listed in *KYB*, 1916–17); p: Cork Opera House Co. Ltd; m: Frank J. Pitt (*KYB*, 1920–7); 1,600 (*KYB*, 1918–19; 1921); 1,800 (*KYB*, 1920); destroyed by fire, 12 December 1955. The new *Opera House* (opened 31 October 1965) is the major venue used by the Cork Film Festival.

The Palace Cinema. See *The Palace Theatre of Varieties*.

The Palace Theatre of Varieties, King Street (now MacCurtain Street), (19 April 1897–), Professor Jolly's Cinematographe part of opening programme; films as part of variety programmes;[97] full-time cinema from June 1930 to June 1988; aka *The Palace Theatre*; *Palace Cinema*, 1930–88); p: Dan Lowry's Star of Erin Theatre of Varieties, Dame Street, Dublin (*KYB*, 1921–5); The Palace Theatre (Cork) Ltd (*KYB*, 1940–71; *Showcase* 1968); m: J. McGrother (*KYB*, 1921–5); J. McGrath (*KYB*, 1926–8); Richard McGrath (under whose management it became a dedicated cinema from June 1930); Bill Aherne (from mid-1930s, listed in *1947 directory* as William A. Aherne [br]); Dermot Breen (from 1956; Breen was first director of Cork Film Festival and Official Film Censor, 1972–8); fb: Leo Ward (1976);[98] screen: 19½ft x 15½ft (*1947 directory*); 1,500 (*KYB*, 1922; 1924), 995 (1934);[99] 1,000 (*KYB*, 1949–52; *1947 directory*); 600 (following replacement in December 1959 of wooden seats in balcony with soft seats); 952 (*KYB*, 1965–8); 930 (*KYB*, 1969–71). Sold to the Everyman Theatre Company and in 1990 reopened as a live show venue.[1]

Pavilion Cinema and Cafe, 80–1 Patrick Street (10 March 1921–August 1989); p: Tallon family, Rochestown Road; James Tallow (*KYB*, 1926–41); m: Fred Harford[2] (first manager, *KYB*, 1923–4); W. Wates (*KYB*, 1925); Ernest R. Wates (*KYB*, 1926–8; 1930s); first Cork cinema to convert to sound, 5 August 1929; first talkie, Al Jolson's *The Singing Fool*, drew in 12,000 patrons in five days; also live shows and orchestra; fire on 16 February 1930, stage, screen, loud speakers and much of interior destroyed; reopened in June 1930, but without a stage; p: James Tallon, Clontarf, Dublin; p: Pavilion Cinemas Ltd (*KYB*, 1939–48); Pavilion Cinema & Cafe Ltd (*KYB*, 1949–64); Mrs Murphy (*KYB*, 1954); Mrs Murphy, Mrs Donegan, Leo Ward and Kevin Anderson of Abbey Films (*Showcase* 1968); Abbey Films Ltd, 71 Middle Abbey Street, Dublin 1 (*KYB*, 1969–71; with Leo Ward, part-time manager); m: Kevin O'Donovan (*c.*1946–54; 1947 *directory*); Miss J. Kelleher (*Showcase* 1968); Donal Kelly (1980s); fb: Leo Ward (1974–6);[3] screen: 16ft x 12ft (1947 *directory*); 900 seats;[4] 1,000 (*KYB*, 1921–); *c.*777 (*KYB*, 1937–46);[5] *c.*770 (*KYB*, 1948, 1949–61, 1969–71).

Picture House, Patrick Street (*KYB*, 1916).

Ritz Cinema, 11–12 Washington Street (13 August 1939–February 1974; formerly, *Washington Cinema*, January 1920–8 January 1938; later, *Classic*, 28 December 1975–10 August 1989); arch: Anthony Fitzgibbon, replacement of building following fire in 1938 (*DIA*); p: Ritz (Cork) Ltd (*Showcase* 1968); d: Stephen Whelan, 3 Grosvenor Place, Wellington Road, Cork, cinema p; T.F. Meagher, 2 Ashton Lawn, Cork, company d;[6] br: Mr S. Whelan (1947 *directory*); 23ft proscenium (1947 *directory*); 568 seats (*KYB*, 1940–71; 1947 *directory*); badly designed, the screen was too high and not wide enough, but it had an exclusive contract for all first-run Warner Bros films, which lasted until 1950s; p from August 1966: Dublin-based Amalgamated Cinemas (Ireland) Ltd/Ellimans; despite modernization closed February 1974; reopened as the *Classic* on 28 December 1975.[7] See *Washington Cinema*; *Classic Cinema*.

St Mary's Hall, St Mary's Road (21 October 1912–*c.*1948); p: North Chapel (opposite hall); Revd Canon M. O'Sullivan, m: John F. Corkery (1912–*c.*1942;[8] *KYB*, 1920–8); Capitol and Allied Cinemas Ltd (from late 1940s); the last film screening when the cinema was under direct Catholic church control was *The Song of Bernadette* (1943), which was released in Ireland in 1944; plans to extend the venue in the 1940s were frustrated by an ESB substation behind the hall; sold to Cork corporation and knocked; 400 (*KYB*, 1918, first listing); 300 (*KYB*, 1920–2); 450 (1934).[9]

Savoy Cinema, 108 Patrick Street (12 May 1932–*c.*January 1975), p: Associated Irish Cinemas Ltd, 32 Shaftesbury Avenue, London WI (CRO no. 8027); md: J.E. Pearce (*KYB*, 1933–38); arch: Albert Walter Moore & Crabtree, Bradford, England; cost £148,000; built in seven months by the firm which constructed Savoy Dublin; over 1,000 employed in construction; included Compton organ; art deco exterior with lighted canopy; interior modelled on Venetian street; 2,249 seats; staff of 70; first m: John McGrath; subsequent p(s): Irish Cinemas Ltd, 19 Upper O'Connell Street, Dublin (from 1934, registered 17 November 1934; CRO no. 8828; *KYB*, 1937–45); Irish Cinemas Ltd/Metropole & Allied Theatres Ltd (January 1939); J. Arthur Rank-controlled Irish Cinemas Ltd (from 1946; 1947 *directory*; *Showcase* 1968 which gives address as 1/2 Poolbeg Street, Dublin); fb: Louis Elliman, Savoy Cinema, Dublin (1947 *directory*); 2,285 (1947 *directory*); host to Cork Film Festival from 1956; up to 1962, one million visited Savoy each year; by 1972, only 200,000; in 1971, with loss of 250/300 seats, cinema subdivided; last m: Renee Ahern; cinema turned into Savoy shopping centre and Cork dance studio in 1977.[10]

Southern Cinema Co., 32 Mayler Street, m: Donald McGregor (*KYB*, 1918–20).

Tivoli Picture Theatre, 21 Merchants Quay (November 1912–15); arch: Magahy (*DIA*); p: Tivoli Picture Theatre Ltd. (d: T. Fletcher, E. Buskley, J.J. McSwiney, F. O'Hanlon, J. Ballintemple);[11] Southern Coliseum Ltd (from 1914); reopened as an off-shoot of the Coliseum after being closed for some time;[12] 500 (*KYB*, 1916–17).

Triskel Arts Centre, Tobin Street (since 1986) (1978– expanded in 2010; part-time cinema space known as *Triskel Cinematek*), *c.*77 (Connolly and Dillon, 2001:66, 74); artistic director: Tony Sheehan (2010).

Washington Cinema, Washington Street (formerly Great George's Street), (January 1920–8 January 1938), uniquely, it was heated by a coal fuel fire gate under the screen; p: Washington Cinema Ltd (CRO no. 7784); J.T. Carpenter, H. and S. Whelan, J. French; md: J.T. Carpenter (*KYB*, 1924–8); m: W.B. Symes (*KYB*, 1921–3); 'just over' 300;[13] 350 (*KYB*, 1921–3); 298;[14] destroyed by fire, 28 January 1938, damage estimated at £4,000; p/m: Stephen F. Whelan, who acquired the adjoining premises, formed a new company with solicitor Thomas F. Meaghar, and opened new cinema, the *Ritz*, on 13 August 1939.[15] See *Ritz*; *Classic*.

Washington Picture House. See *Washington Cinema*.

Crookstown
Kilmurry Catholic Social Hall (1947 *directory*).

Doneraile
Casino Cinema (c.1947–71+; aka *The Cinema*), p: Tom Cooper, Killarney (*KYB*, 1949–55; listed as fb in 1947 *directory*); T.J. Sheehan (*KYB*, 1960–71; *Showcase* 1968), 400 (*KYB*, 1949–55); 500 (*KYB*, 1960–6), 395 (*KYB*, 1967–71).

Douglas
• *Cinema World*, Link Road (summer 1994–), p: Cinema World (Douglas) Ltd (CRO no. 206231); Cado Ltd; Tom O'Connor; Gate Cinemas, Cork (by 2008); 5 screens/1,152 seats, stadium seating; loop system for hard of hearing.

Dunmanway
Broadway Cinema (1936–May 2005; first listed, *KYB*, 1936), p: Barnabas Deane, Dunmanway (*KYB*, 1950–71; *Showcase* 1968); br: Mr B. Deane (1947 *directory*); fb: Barry Deane (1977);[16] screen: 14ft x 12ft (1947 *directory*); 400 (*KYB*, 1936–41); 450 (1934);[17] 400 (1947 *directory*); 250 (*KYB*, 1945); 350 (*KYB*, 1946–61); 280 (Connolly and Dillon, 2001:72).
Dunmanway Cinema (c.1925–c.1945), p: Mr Housett (*KYB*, 1934–46), 300.[18]

Fermoy
Cinema Theatre, Rathealy Road (c.1915–16; aka *Kinema*), p: Noble & O'Mahoney (or O'Mahony), 600 (*KYB*, 1916–17); contact: J.L. Pfounds,[19] 600 (*KYB*, 1918).
Cinema Palace Theatre, p: Messrs J.J. Bowen & Co. (*KYB*, 1922–33); may be same as *Cinema Theatre*.
Fermoy Community Youth Centre, Ashe Quay, occasional part-time cinema, 1 screen/77 seats (Connolly and Dillon, 2001:74).
Kinema, Patrick Street, m: J.L. Pfounds, 600 (*KYB*, 1919–20).
Kinema Assembly Rooms, Francis Street (c. 1920–October 1929;[20] aka *Kinema*, *KYB*, 1921–3; *Kinema Assembly Rooms*, *KYB*, 1924), p: J.S. Noble & R. O'Mahony (*KYB*, 1921–30), m: J. Holden, 400 (*KYB*, 1921); 300. See also *Cinema Theatre*.
Ormonde (c.1959–76+), p: Ormonde Cinemas (Fermoy), Ltd (CRO no. 13454; *KYB*, 1960–7; *Showcase* 1968); fb: Leo Ward (1975–6);[21] 400 (*KYB*, 1960–1).
• *Palace Cinema* (c.1938–; aka *Palace Hall*; *Palace Theatre and Hall*), p: M.A. O'Brien, The Manor, Fermoy; Dr O'Brien, Fermoy (*KYB*, 1939–71; 1947 *directory*; *Showcase* 1968); fb: Leo Ward (1976); 40ft proscenium (1947 *directory*); 600 (*KYB*, 1934–9); 400 (1934);[22] 500 (*KYB*, 1939–71).[23]
Royal Cinema (c.1944–71+), p: Patrick McGrath, 26A Pearse Street, Dublin (*KYB*, 1945–71, *Showcase* 1968, also listed as fb in 1947 *directory*, but at 27); 500 (*KYB*, 1945–64); 600 (1947 *directory*).

Glanmire
Cameo, Sarsfield Court, near Glanmire (1950s–c.1964; initially 16mm, later 2 x 35mm projectors installed), p: Seamus Quinn, 130 seats, converted from car garage.[24]

Kanturk
Cinema, Mill Street, listed *KYB*, 1930–4 (no personnel).
• *Cosey*, Watergate Street (c.1929–; aka *Cosy* in *KYB*, 1937–44; *Cosey Midiplex*; listed *KYB*, 1930–2 (no personnel)), p: Jeremiah O'Sullivan;[25] J. O'Sullivan & M.J. Bowman (*KYB*, 1933–39); J. O'Sullivan, Strand Street, Kanturk (*KYB*, 1940–8); Michael O'Riordan (1977–96+); br: Mrs O'Sullivan, fb: James J. Kavanagh, Ormonde Cinema, Arklow, 24ft proscenium (1947 *directory*); 300 (*KYB*, 1936; 1940–8);[26] 2 screens (1996);[27] 3 screens /248 seats (by 2001).[28] Possibly same venue as *Ormonde*.
Ormonde (c.1949–c.1968), p: James J. Kavanagh, Ormonde House, Arklow (*KYB*, 1950–5); Ormonde (Kanturk) Ltd (*KYB*, 1960–4; *Showcase* 1968); 400 (*KYB*, 1950–5; 1960–1).
Strand Cinema (c. 1929–; listed *KYB*, 1930–4 (no personnel)), p: Mr M.J. Bowman (1929);[29] perhaps same as *Cinema*.

Kinsale
Coliseum, King Street (c.1916–c.1933, listed also in 1947 *directory*), p: Southern Coliseums Ltd (*KYB*, 1917, 1922–3); br: J. Fitzgerald (1947 *directory*); m: D.P. Foley (*KYB*, 1919–27, 1931–4); licensed for music (*KYB*, 1919–20); 250.[30] See *Pier Cinema*, possibly a continuation of the *Coliseum* given J. Fitzgerald's involvement in both.
Pier Cinema (c.1949–77+), p: J. Fitzgerald, 6 Pearse Street; 340 (*KYB*, 1950–71; *Showcase* 1968); fb: S. Lowney (1977).[31] See *Coliseum*.

Macroom

Briery Gap Arts Centre, Main Street, 1 screen/*c.*200 (Connolly and Dillon, 2001:74; 2010); venue for Sulan Film Society; m: Ann Dunne (2010).
Castle Cinema (*c.*1934–*c.*1956; aka *Castle Ballroom*), br: J.J. O'Sullivan (*1947 directory*); 350 (1934,[32] *KYB*, 1950–7).
Cinema, school building, Lucey's Lane (by 20 September 1914–*c.*1935; originally opened on Sundays, Tuesdays, and Fridays; closed during summer 1914;[33] listed in *KYB*, 1930–3: no personnel), p: Maurice Logan & Bertie Walsh, 35 Royal Avenue, Belfast; 300 (*KYB*, 1936).
Palace Cinema (25 April 1953–74; 1975–29 March 1987; aka *Macroom Palace*), built on site of derelict house owned by Balwin family, p: Lucey and Pope; Denis Murphy (from 1975); fb: J. Lucey (*RPC*, 1975–7);[34] 400.

Mallow

Capitol Cinema, Fair Street (*c.*1933–77+), Capitol Cinema (Mallow) Ltd (CRO no. 31995); p: [W.] Robinson & [L.] Ward (*KYB*, 1934–70; *Showcase* 1968); fb: C. Napier (1976–7);[35] 350 (1934);[36] 300 (*KYB*, 1936–70; *1947 directory*).
The Central Hall, Main Street (*c.*1924–77+; aka *Central Cinema*; first listing, *KYB*, 1925); p/m: C.M. Donovan (*KYB*, 1925–36); Edward (Eddie) J. Donovan (*KYB*, 1939–71; *Showcase* 1968; br: Mr W. Donovan [*1947 directory*]); fb: Eddie Donovan (1975);[37] 515 (1934);[38] 400 (*KYB*, 1934–5); 300 (1936–40); 650 (*1947 directory*; *KYB*, 1950–2).
• *Gate Multiplex*, Market Square (April 2006–), 5 screens, 881.
Reel Cinema, Park West (aka *Reel Picture House*), 4 screens/446 seats (*c.*2001).[39]

Midleton

• *Gate Multiplex*, Market Green shopping centre (2006–), 5 screens, 710 seats.
Star Cinema, Broderick Street (*c.*1930–*c.*1944; as *Southern Star Cinema*, *c.*1944–7 [*1947 directory*]; as *Ormonde Cinema*, 1947–April 2006;[40] listed sometimes as *Cinema* and as *Star Cinema*), p: The Southern Star Cinema Co., Ltd (CRO no. 4724; *KYB*, 1931–55, *Showcase* 1968); Greenes (from 2000); br: Miss A. Hyde (*1947 directory*); m: Pat and Kathleen Greene (from 1980); fb: James Kavanagh, Ormonde Cinema, Arklow (*1947 directory*); Leo Ward (1975–6);[41] 15ft proscenium (*1947 directory*); 420 (1934);[42] 500 (*KYB*, 1935–44; *1947 directory*); 700 (*KYB*, 1951–5); 2 screens/328 seats (1980–2006).[43]

Millstreet

The Cinema (*c.*1947–71+; aka *West End Cinema* in *1947 directory*, first listed *KYB*, 1950), p: D. McSweeney (*KYB*, 1950–71; *Showcase* 1968; br in *1947 directory*); 420 (*KYB*, 1950–71).
The Cinema Hall, *c.*1934: 350; not equipped for sound.[44]
Central Cinema, br: Mr Cleere (*1947 directory*). Possibly *Cinema Hall*.

Mitchelstown

Central (*c.*1949–71+), p: Henry Delany, 400 (*KYB*, 1950–5); Thomas Roche, 400 (*KYB*, 1965–71; *Showcase* 1968).
Picture House,[45] listed, *KYB*, 1930–4 (no personnel).
Savoy Cinema (*c.*1932–*c.*1947), p: A.E. Russell, 400 (*KYB*, 1934–48); 750 (1934);[46] listed as closed, *KYB*, 1948.
Star Cinema, Church Road (*c.*1933–71+, listed in *1947 directory*), p: A.H. Sharp (*KYB*, 1934); G.H. Sharp (*KYB*, 1935–66); R.G. Sharp, Church Road (*KYB*, 1967–71; *Showcase* 1968); 400 (*KYB*, 1935–66; 450 in *1934 cinemas*); 300 (*KYB*, 1967–71).

Newmarket

Casino (*c.*1948–71+), p: Thomas G. Cooper, Killarney, 500 (*KYB*, 1949–71; *Showcase* 1968).

Passage West

Catholic Young Men's Society Hall (*c.*1938–71+; aka *The Cinema*; listed *Showcase* 1968), p: Revd T. McCarthy (*KYB*, 1939–48); Fr O'Flynn (*KYB*, 1949–55); 350 (1934);[47] 300 (*KYB*, 1949–55); 320 (*KYB*, 1960–71).

Queenstown, See Cobh.

Skibbereen

Cinema, 14 North Street (1912–77+), p: Brothers Michael, Jack and Denis Murphy (1927);[48] The Skibbereen Cinema Co. Ltd, Townsend Street, Skibbereen (CRO no. 10226; *KYB*, 1942–71; *Showcase* 1968); br & fb: Thomas Lowney (*1947 directory*); fb: C. McCarthy (1976–7);[49] 200 (1929);[50] 450 (*KYB*, 1942–57).

Coliseum, Mardyke Street (*c.*1923–*c.*1943), listed, *KYB*, 1930 (no personnel); p: M.S. O'Driscoll, 53
  Bridge Street (*KYB*, 1931–48, listed as br in 1947 *directory*); 200 (*KYB*, 1940; 1947 *directory*, though
  300 in 1934 *cinemas*); listed as closed in *KYB*, 1945–8.
Kinema (*c.*1915–16; aka *Picturedrome*), p: Dr Macura; Alex McEwan, Assembly Rooms, Cork.[51]
West Cork Arts Centre, Sutherland Building, North Street (1985–), new building planned for site of
  Wolfe's Bakery, off Townshend Street, film screenings every other Thursday, during winter and spring,
  programmed supported by access>CINEMA (2010).

Youghal
Abbey Cinema (later *Abbey Twin Cinema*), fb: Leo Ward (1975–6).[52]
Horgan's Picture Theatre, Friar Street (23 December 1917–71+; aka *Horgan's Picture Palace*), p: Horgan
  Brothers [James, Thomas and Philip Horgan] (*KYB*, 1925); Thomas Horgan[53] (*KYB*, 1926–38);
  Horgan Brothers (*KYB*, 1939–57); Marietta & Margaret Horgan (*KYB*, 1965–71; *Showcase* 1968);
  br: J. Horgan (1947 *directory*); fb: Leo Ward (from 1966); damaged in fire, *c.*10 August 1935; next
  door to *Hurst's Picture Palace* which was completely destroyed;[54] 16ft proscenium (1947 *directory*);
  600 (*KYB*, 1935–7, 1934);[55] 390 (*KYB*, 1940; 1945; 1947 *directory*); 650 (*KYB*, 1949–57).
• *Hurst's Picture Palace*, Friar Street (*c.* October 1914[56]–*c.*10August 1935; August 1936–; aka *Youghal
  Picture Palace*; *Regal*; from June 1997, *Regal Cineplex*), p: R. Hurst (from 1914, *KYB*, 1926; 1930–
  55); Shanly's Animated Pictures, King Henry's Road, Hampstead, London (*KYB*, 1921–5); executors
  of Mrs Z.B. Hurst (deceased) (*KYB*, 1955–7); p: Hurst Brothers Ltd (*KYB*, 1965–71; *Showcase* 1968);
  Harry Hurst (*c.*1990); m: Mr R.W.B. Nevill (1914); burnt down *c.*10 August 1935;[57] rebuilt; 16ft
  proscenium (1947 *directory*); 800;[58] 425 (*KYB*, 1935–55);[59] 630 (*KYB*, 1957–60; 1970); (from June
  1997), 3 screens/512 seats (Connolly and Dillon, 2001:72).
Regal Cinema. See *Hurst's Picture Palace*.
Strand Palace, 500 (1934).[60]

DERRY

Coleraine
Coleraine Picture Palace, Railway Road (*c.*1916–*c.*1980 [first entry, *KYB*, 1917]; original building
  demolished; new cinema, 1934–70s; aka *The Picture House* [*KYB*, 1937–52], *The Picture Palace*
  [1947 *directory*; *KYB*, 1958–60], *The Palace* [*KYB*, 1960–71]), p: Coleraine Picture Palace Co., Ltd
  (*KYB*, 1918–71; 1947 *directory*; *Showcase* 1968); Norman Christie; br: Mr D. Christie (1947 *directory*); m: Alex Douglas Sutherland (*KYB*, 1919–28); fb: Ferris Pounds, Whitehall Buildings, Ann
  Street, Belfast (1947 *directory*); screen: 16ft x 13ft (1947 *directory*); 600 (*KYB*, 1918); *c.*550 (*KYB*,
  1919–21); 850 (1934);[61] 500 (*KYB*, 1936–44; 1947 *directory*); 475/470 (*KYB*, 1956–71); licensed
  for music and dancing (*KYB*, 1919–20); converted to retail use. It is possible that it is for this cinema
  that James Kennedy submitted plans in 1914 (*DIA*).
• *Movie House*, Jet Centre leisure complex, Riverside Park South, Dunhill Road (as *Jet Centre Cinema*,
  August 1990–14 April 2005; as *Movie House* from 21 July 2006), p: Ward Anderson (from *c.*1997);
  Michael McAdam (purchased the 7 acre centre, July 2006); 4 screens/755 (286; 193; 152; and 124)
  seats (*BFI*, 1996, 722 seats in Connolly and Dillon, 2001:74); 6 screens/1,200 (from September 2006);
  2 more screens planned (2010).
Palladium, Society Street (October 1934–September 1936; October 1936–90) p: James Menary, 37
  North Parade, Belfast (*KYB*, 1935–43, listed as br in 1947 *directory*); Coleraine Palladium Cinema
  Co.; Raymond Stross Cinemas, College Street, Belfast (*KYB*, 1944–7); Irish Theatres Ltd (*KYB*, 1947–
  57, with fb: Ferris Pounds, Ann Street, Belfast (1947 *directory*); Odeon (Northern Ireland) Ltd (*KYB*,
  1958–71; *Showcase* 1968); destroyed by fire, September 1936;[62] 800 (1934);[63] 836 (1936);[64] 620
  (*KYB*, 1935–9); 950 (*KYB*, 1940–3; 1947 *directory*); 760/761 (*KYB*, 1944–57); 538 (*BFI*, 1991).
  Used as a bingo hall before being demolished in 2008 to make way for apartment building.
Picture House/Picture Palace. See *Coleraine Picture Palace*.
Terrace Row Lecture Hall (1898; McCole, 2005:appendix D).
Town Hall (1903; McCole, 2005:appendix D); *KYB*, 1916–17).

Derry
ABC Cinema, Market Street. See *Rialto Cinema*.
City Cinema, William Street (*c.*1932–71+; formerly, *City Picture House*; first listed *KYB*, 1933, as *City
  Picture House*), p: City Pictures Ltd (*KYB*, 1936–71; 1947 *directory*; *Showcase* 1968); br: William
  (Willie) Doherty (1947 *directory*); 25ft proscenium (1947 *directory*); 1,000 (*KYB*, 1936–71; 1947
  directory); 800.

- *Derry Omniplex*, Quayside Centre, Strand Road (29 November 1993–); built on the site of the *Strand Cinema*, p: Ward Anderson's Empire Cinemas chain, which operates as Omniplex Cinemas in Northern Ireland, 7 screens/1,395 (315, 270, 215, 215, 170, 120, 90) seats. See also *Strand*.

Empire Theatre (*c*.1919–20), p: Barney Armstrong, m: J. Mathers, 1,600, licensed for music and dancing (*KYB*, 1920–1). See also *Opera House*, same proprietor.

Midland Cinema, Waterside (*c*.1929–*c*.1961), pictures and variety; stage 18ft (*KYB*, 1929); l: W.L. James (*KYB*, 1930–2); M. Curran & Sons (*KYB*, 1937–57); p: Odeon (Northern Ireland) Ltd (*KYB*, 1958–62); fb: James Curran, Capitol Cinema, Antrim Road, Belfast (*1947 directory*); 850 (*KYB*, 1936–57; *1947 directory*).

- *The Nerve Centre*, 7–8 Magazine Street (1990–), multimedia arts centre, 1 screen/60 seats.

Odeon, Strand Road (*c*.1959–71+), p: Odeon (Northern Ireland) Ltd (*KYB*, 1960–71; *Showcase* 1968).

Opera House, Carlisle Road (opened, 1876–; in use as cinema from *c*.1915–40; aka *Opera House and Hippodrome*, listed in *1947 directory* as a current venue), p: W. Payne Seddon (*KYB*, 1916–17); Barney Armstrong with Edward Hart as manager (*KYB*, 1919, licensed for dancing and music); Rialto Theatres; City Pictures Ltd (*KYB*, 1936–9; *1947 directory*); fb: W.A. Fielder (Wardour Films, London) (*KYB*, 1931–4); 20ft stage and 26ft proscenium (*1947 directory*); 1,500 (*KYB*, 1916–17); 1,200 (*KYB*, 1919; 1936–9); 1,250 (*1947 directory*); destroyed by fire, 1940.[65]

- *Orchard Hall Cinema*, Orchard Street. See *Saint Columb's Hall*.

People's Hall, Barracks Street (*KYB*, 1916–17), p: Revd Herbert H. Cornish (*KYB*, 1918).

Palace Cinema. See *Picture Palace*.

Picture House. See *Picture Palace*.

Picture Palace, Shipquay Street (*c*.1915–71+; October 1927–; aka *Picture House*; *Palace Cinema*, *c*.1936–71+), p: Irish Living Pictures Co. Ltd (*KYB*, 1916–31); Ritz Belfast Ltd (Union Cinemas Group); Associated British Pictures Ltd, Golden Square, London W1 (from October 1937; *KYB*, 1942–5); Palace (Derry) Ltd (*Showcase* 1968); m: H.G. Harrington (*KYB*, 1921–, 1924–6); br: Mr W. Doherty (*1947 directory*); fb: J Boughton, London; (*KYB*, 1937–45); Palace (Derry) Ltd (*KYB*, 1948–71); 25ft proscenium, stage: 7ft deep (*1947 directory*); 450 (*KYB*, 1916–17); 800 (*KYB*, 1942–5; *1947 directory*); 900 (*KYB*, 1948–71); reopened October 1927 after £20,000 refurbishment and seating increased to 760.[66]

Rialto Cinema, Market Street (1918–2001; aka *Rialto Theatre*; *ABC Cinema* from 4 June 1960–76; as *Rialto Cinema*, 1976–83; listed in *Showcase* 1968), p: London Motion Pictures Co.; Rialto Theatres Ltd; Ritz Belfast Ltd (Union Cinemas Group), (from September 1936); Associated British Pictures Ltd, Golden Square, London W1 (October 1937–76; *KYB*, 1942–60); m: Charles Warrel; G.C. Cropper (*KYB*, 1923); William Arthur (*KYB*, 1924–8); fb: W.A. Fielder (Wardour Films, London) (*KYB*, 1931–2); screen: 17½ft (*1947 directory*); 650 (*KYB*, 1919–20); 500 (*KYB*, 1921); 800 (*KYB*, 1937–52); partly demolished in 1959 to build new *ABC Cinema* on site which opened on 4 June 1960; arch: C. J. Foster, Alan Morgan, Berry & Miller, 1,166 (*KYB*, 1961–6); bought by independent operator in 1976 who renamed cinema the *Rialto*; taken over by Derry city council in 1984 and renamed *Rialto Entertainment Centre*, with programming including films and stage shows, but closed in August 2001; building demolished in 2006 with site used for new shopping centre. *Millenium Forum Theatre* built on adjoining street.

- *Saint Columb's Hall*, Orchard Street (*c*.1914–; aka *The Hall*; *Orchard Hall Cinema*), p: London Motion Picture Co. (*KYB*, 1915); St Columb's Hall committee (*KYB*, 1930–1); P. Downey (*KYB*, 1963); m: George Watterson (*KYB*, 1919–20, licensed for music and dancing); W.L. James (*KYB*, 1921–3); J.P. McKenna (1924–5); sec: J. Bonner (*KYB*, 1926–30, 1932–4, 1937–8, 1941–61); screen: 18ft x 14ft (*1947 directory*); 800 (*KYB*, 1915); 1,500 (*KYB*, 1919); 1,400 (*KYB*, 1920); 1,000 (*KYB*, 1921); 1,100 (*KYB*, 1941; *1947 directory*); 980 (*KYB*, 1950–63).

- *Strand*, Strand Road (1934[67]–11 January 1975; *Odeon* from 1958; *Strand* from 1 December 1975–17 December 1992), p: M.E. Curran & Sons, Antrim Road, Belfast (*KYB*, 1937–57; listed as Strand Pictures (Derry) Ltd in *1947 directory*); Odeon (Northern Ireland) Ltd (from December 1956); fb: James Curran, Capitol Cinema, Antrim Road, Belfast (*1947 directory*); 1,350 (*KYB*, 1937); 1,050 (*1947 directory*); 1,077 (*KYB*, 1950–60); redeveloped in 1975 by independent operator as 2 screens/471 (293 and 178) seats (*BFI*, 1991). Building demolished in 1992 and 7 screen *Derry Omniplex* built on site, opened 29 November 1993, p: Ward Anderson; 1,362 (316; 252; 220; 220; 220; 132; 126; and 96) seats (*BFI*, 1996); 7 screens/1,375 seats (Connolly and Dillon, 2001:74).

- *Waterside Theatre*, Ebrington Centre, Glendermott Road, Waterside (21 December 2001–; site of old military/naval headquarters), 393 seats, used as both a cinema and a theatre.

West End Cinema (?–November 1927).[68]

Draperstown

Cinema, p: William Shields, Maghera; 300; fb: Mr E. Stuart, Park View house, Strabane (*1947 directory*).

Dungiven

• *Saint Canice's Hall*, 90 Main Street (*BFI*, 1991); closed in summer.
Cinema (1937–*c*.1971+; listed in *KYB*, 1939–44 as *Picture House*), p: Mr J. Hunter, Limavady;[69] William O'Hanlon, Marie House, Dungiven (*KYB*, 1945); William O'Hanlon, Market Street, Limavady (*KYB*, 1946–60); Charles O'Neill (*KYB*, 1961–71; *Showcase* 1968); fb: W. O'Hanlon, Regal Cinema, Limavady (*1947 directory*); 200/300 (*KYB*, 1939–44); 500 (*KYB*, 1945); 450 (*KYB*, 1946–60); 317 (*KYB*, 1961–3).
The Cinema, p: R. O'Neill (*KYB*, 1926); possibly the same as above.

Garvagh

Avon Cinema (*c*.1947–71+), p: Ralph Robertson, Ardonara, Garvagh (*KYB*, 1948–71; *Showcase* 1968); 275 (*KYB*, 1948–61).

Kilrea

Cinema (*KYB*, 1946), p: William Shields, Maghera; fb: Mr E. Stuart, Park View house, Strabane (*1947 directory*).

Limavady

Electric Kinema (*c*.1919–*c*.1927), p: Electric Kinema Co., m: D. Boyd (*KYB*, 1920–6); 400 (*KYB*, 1920); 350 (*KYB*, 1921). Listed until *KYB* 1928. Either this venue was at the Town Hall, or Electric Kinema Co. ran *The Picture House*, Town Hall, after the *Electric* closed, and before Frank Coghlan became proprietor of *The Picture House*, Town Hall.
The Picture House, Town Hall (*c*.1927°–*c*.1936), p: Electric Kinema Co. (*KYB*, 1929–30); Frank J. Coghlan, (*KYB*, 1931–7); 500 (*KYB*, 1934–7).
Regal (*c*.1938–96+), p: J. Hunter (*KYB*, 1939–66); p: Limavady Cinemas Ltd (*KYB*, 1968–71; *Showcase* 1968); William O'Hanlon; Colm Henry and Sean Henry; 600 (*KYB*, 1941–61); fb: W. O'Hanlon (*1947 directory*); 400 (*KYB*, 1965–7); 450 (*KYB*, 68–71); 368 (*BFI*, 1996); 650.
Roe, Roe Mill Road (*c*.1938–*c*.1943), arch: Mary Gilmer (*DIA*, 1937); p: J. Hunter (*KYB*, 1939–44); fb: W. O'Hanlon of *Regal* (*1947 directory*); listed as closed, *KYB*, 1944–57. See *Regal* (separate venue) and *Savoy*.
Saint Patrick's Hall Picture House (*c*.1921–*c*.1931; listed, *KYB*, 1930–2, no personnel), p: The Hall Picture Co with Frank J. Cog(h)lan as cinema manager (*KYB*, 1922–8); Bob Devlin, occasional variety; stage 11ft (*KYB*, 1929). Coghlan seems to have become proprietor of *The Picture House*, Town Hall, *c*.1929–30.
Savoy, br: Mr J. Hunter, 750 (*1947 directory*). See also *Regal/Roe* above and *Regal* in Larne and *Cinema* in Dungiven.
Town Hall. See *Picture House*, Town Hall.

Maghera

The Cinema, Main Street (*c*.1936–71+), p: Supreme Cinemas Ltd, 35 (and later, 133) Royal Avenue, Belfast, 300 (*KYB*, 1937–71; *1947 directory*; *Showcase* 1968); br: Maurice Logan, fb: Mr McClintock, Supreme Cinemas, Ltd, 133 Royal Avenue, Belfast, 18ft proscenium, 300 (*1947 directory*).
• *Movie House*, 51 St Lurach's Road, (1999–), p: Michael McAdam, 3 screens/433 seats (Connolly and Dillon, 2001:74).
Picture House (*c*.1930–*c*.1933), p: Frank J. Coghlan (*KYB*, 1931–4).

Magherafelt

• *Picture House*, Queen Street (*c*.1938–; aka *Cinema* from 1944; *Classic* from *c*.1990–*c*.2000 as 2-screen), p: Russell Lamont, p: Supreme Cinemas, 35 (and later, 133) Royal Avenue, Belfast (*KYB*, 1939–; *1947 directory*; *Showcase* 1968); br: Maurice Logan, fb: Mr McClintock, Supreme Cinemas, Ltd, 133 Royal Avenue, Belfast (*1947 directory*); 400 (*KYB*, 1939); 412 (*KYB*, 1940–8, *1947 directory*); 312 (*KYB*, 1949–71); 2 screens /330 (220, 100) seats.

Portstewart

Palladium Cinema, Society Street (*c*.1933–*c*.1956; aka *The Cinema*; address in *1947 directory*: Promenade), p: James Menary, 133 Haypark Avenue, Belfast (*KYB*, 1934–5); James Menary, 37 North Parade, Belfast (*KYB*, 1936–43); Raymond Stross Cinemas, College Square, Belfast (*KYB*, 1944–5; *1947 directory*); Irish Theatres Ltd, Whitehall Building, Ann Street, Belfast (*KYB*, 1946–57); br: Mr W. Dunlop, fb: Ferris Pounds, Whitehall Buildings (*1947 directory*); screen: 12ft x 14ft (*1947 directory*); 700 (*KYB*, 1936–43); *c*.410 (*KYB*, 1944–57); it was noted for its double seats at the back, which were carefully monitored by ushers to prevent any untoward behaviour!
Picture House (*c*.1918–*c*.1932), p/m: Peter Doherty, 300 (*KYB*, 1919–21); p/m: J. McCrory (*KYB*, 1922–33; listed McCory in *KYB*, 1925).

DONEGAL

Ardara
Ardara Cinema, p: Frank Quinn, Dunkineely, 200.

Ballybofey
Ritz (*c.*winter 1945/6–November 1980; reopened after refurbishment, 24 March 1981; subdivided with
  Balor Theatre/Arts Centre from December 1982 to June 2008), arch: John McBride Neill (*DIA*,
  1945); p: William Barry (*DIA*); Ballybofey Cinemas Ltd (*KYB*, 1957–70; *Showcase* 1968); Butt Hall
  Committee, Ballybofey (*KYB*, 1971); Leo Keeney (1981); fb: Mr W. Barry, Duinboy House, Lifford,
  Co. Donegal (*1947 directory*); L. Keeney (1975–7);[71] 550 (*KYB*, 1949–55); 534 (*KYB*, 1957–61). In
  1982 it was agreed by the Butt Hall Committee to reduce the size of the cinema by giving the rear
  portion of the *Ritz* to the Butt Drama Circle for the Balor Theatre.[72]

Ballyshannon
• *Abbey Arts and Cultural Centre*, Tirconnaill Street (14 October 2009–), 3 auditoria, 2 with 35mm
  projection and Dolby stereo sound, 394 (*c.*300 and *c.*100) seats (2010); film club screenings supplied
  by access>CINEMA.
Abbey Cinema (*c.*1928–95+), p: Ballyshannon Cinema Co. (CRO no. 11200; *KYB*, 1949–70; *Showcase*
  1968); Mr T.P. O'Connell, Astoria Ballrooms, Bundoran (*KYB*, 1971); Barney McLoughllin (1995);
  fb: T. O'Connell (1975–6);[73] 500 (*KYB*, 1949–70); 400 (*KYB*, 1971).
Cinema (*KYB*, 1930–3).
Erne Cinema (*c.*1946–71+), br: Frances Stewart (*1947 directory*); p: AC Cinemas (Ireland) Ltd, 800 (*KYB*,
  1949–71, *Showcase* 1968);[74] fb: Mr E.F. McCambridge, 9 Castle Street, Derry (*1947 directory*).
New Cinema (*c.*1935–?), 400 (*KYB*, 1936).
Picture House, p: J. Corry. This may be same as above as Corry had a cinema at Ballinahinch, Co.
  Down, in late 1920s/early1930s.
Rock Cinema (*c.*1932–*c.*1947), p: W. McMenanim, Stranolar, Co. Donegal (*KYB*, 1937–8); Revd C.B.
  Finnegan (*KYB*, 1939–48); 400 (*KYB*, 1937–8); 300 (*KYB*, 1939–48); part of the cinema was
  destroyed by fire in 1932.[75]

Bridgetown
King's Picture Palace, 59 James Street (*KYB*, 1917).

Buncrana
• *St Mary's Hall*, St Mary's Road (*c.* 1934–; aka: *Parochial Cinema, Parochial Hall, The Cinema*) p:
  Revd Peter Tracy, Railway Road (*KYB*, 1935–44, 1949–50); Revd J. McShane (*KYB*, 1945–8); Revd
  Monsignor McShane PP VF, St Oran's, Buncrana (*KYB*, 1951–61); Revd P. O'Brien (*KYB*, 1962–71;
  Showcase 1968); br: Mr J. Flanagan (of the committee, *1947 directory*); fb: O. Gallagher (1977);[76]
  22ft proscenium (*1947 directory*); 400 (*KYB*, 1935–44, 1949–50; *1947 directory*); 500 (*KYB*, 1943–
  8); 470 (*KYB*, 1951–61), 450 (*KYB*, 1962–71); 281; 320 (Connolly and Dillon, 2001:74; 2010).

Bundoran
• *Bundoran Cineplex*, Station Road (?–; *Eclipse Cinema* from July 2008), p: Eclipse Cinema Group
  (2008), 6 screens/976 seats.
Central Cinema Committee, 500 (*1947 directory*).
Eclipse Cinema. See *Bundoran Cineplex*.
Grand Central (*c.*1948–71+), p: St Joseph's Orphanage (*KYB*, 1949–56); Keeney Bros (*KYB*, 1957–71;
  Showcase 1968); fb: L. Keeney (1977);[77] 600 (*KYB*, 1949–56); 500 (*KYB*, 1957–71); may be same
  as above.
Hamilton Hall, m: T.J. Watts (1 July to October 1917).
St Patrick's Hall (*c.*1934–*c.*1947), p: R. McKiernan (*KYB*, 1935; 1939–48).

Carndonagh
Colgan Hall (*c.*1935–71+; first listed *KYB*, 1936), p: Trustees of Colgan Hall, Carndonagh, (*KYB*, 1938–);
  Revd James Boner PP (*KYB*, 1949–71; *1947 directory*; *Showcase* 1968); 404 (*KYB*, 1938– 500 *1947*
  directory).

Clonmany
St Mary's Parochial Hall, p: Fr Morris, 250.

Convoy
St Mary's Hall (*c.*1946–*c.*1968, listed in *1947 directory*), p: Fr T. Doherty, 300 (*KYB*, 1949–64; T.
  Doherty as Revd and CE in *Showcase* 1968).

Derrybeg
Astor (August 1958–84+; aka *Cinema*),[78] p: Tom & Mary McBride; fb: T. McBride (1975).[79]

Donegal
Four Masters Cinema (c.1946–77+; listed as *The Cinema*, KYB, 1949–54), p: Revd P.B. McMullen PP (KYB, 1949–54); Revd T. Doherty (KYB, 1955–67), m: Frank Muldoon, Diamond, Donegal (KYB, 1968–71; *Showcase* 1968); screen: 16ft x 12ft (1947 *directory*); 500 (1947 *directory*); 400 (KYB, 1949–54); 450 (KYB, 1955); 550 (KYB, 1960–1); 500 (KYB, 1962–71); fb: F. Quinn (1975–7).[80]

Dungloe
Cinema, p: Walsh & McGinley (KYB, 1934).
Parochial Hall, br: Daniel Sweeney (1947 *directory*).
Ritz, Main Street Lower (c.1962–71+), p: Wilton & Barry (KYB, 1960–3); Ritz (Dungloe) Ltd, Drumboy House, Lifford; 400 (KYB, 1963–71; *Showcase* 1968); site later used as car park.

Falcarragh
Strand Cinema (August 1958–);[81] p: Josephine Murray.

Glencolmcille
Parochial Hall, p: Fr James McDyer; 300.

Glenties
St Dominick's Hall, p: Barry & Shortt, Lifford; 200.

Killybegs
Ritz (c.1949–77+; aka *The Cinema*), p: Messrs Barry & Shortt, Drumloy House, Lifford, 300 (KYB, 1950–71; *Showcase* 1968); fb: W. Barry (1947 *directory*; 1975–7).[82]

Letterkenny
• *Century Cinemas*, Leckview Lane, Pearse Road (2001–), p: A.C. Cinemas (Ireland), Ltd; 8 screens/ 994 seats.
The Cinema (c.1925–c.1928), p/m: Joseph P. Gregg (KYB, 1926–9).
The Cinema, Market Hall (c.1934–c.1947; aka *Market Hall Cinema*), p: S. Molloy (KYB, 1934); Letterkenny Cinema Co. (KYB, 1935–48); 250 (KYB);[83] may be same as above.
Regional Cultural Centre (July 2007–), multi-purpose venue with full cinema facilities, offers film and digital media community and adult initiatives; host to access>CINEMA supported film club; cost: €5 million; 150 seats
La Scala, 16–18 Ramelton Road (c.1934–77+), p: AC Cinemas & City Pictures Ltd (KYB, 1935 as *New Cinema*; thereafter, *La Scala*); AC Cinemas (Ireland) Ltd (KYB, 1948–71; *Showcase* 1968); br: Mr J. McCombridge, 9 Castle Street, Derry (1947 *directory*); fb: Mr E.F. McCambridge, 9 Castle Street, Derry (1947 *directory*); W. Doherty (1975–7);[84] 240–250 (KYB, 1936–46; 1947 *directory*); 550 KYB, 1948–51); 850 (KYB, 1952–62); 600 (KYB, 1969–71); permission granted in 2004 to demolish building and erect retail units and offices on site.
Letterkenny Recreation and Cinema Hall (1925–7 May 1928), destroyed by fire.[85]
Letterkenny Cinema, Port Road, p: Mark Doherty (c.1990); 4 screens/637 seats.[86]
Picture House (c.1919–c.1924), p: Coon's Pictures, m: A.D. Coon (KYB, 1920); p/m: A.D. Coon (KYB, 1921–5).
Twin Cinemas (July 1980–), p: William Doherty, 2 screens.[87]

Lifford
• *Lifford-Strabane Cineplex*, Three Rivers Centre (?–July 2008; *Eclipse Cinema* from July 2008), p (2008): Eclipse Cinema Group; originally, 4 screens/714 (296, 211, 104 and 103) seats; 4 screens/684; 4 screens/680 seats;[88] 7 screens by 2008.
Ritz Cinema (c.1952–71+), p: Barry & Shortt Ltd, Main Street, Lifford, 350 (KYB, 1953–71; *Showcase* 1968).

Milford
La Scala (c.1946–90+ listed as *The Cinema* in 1947 *directory*), p: William O'Hanlon (KYB, 1950–5); William McElwee (KYB, 1955–71; *Showcase* 1968); fb: W. O'Hanlon, Regal Cinema, Limavady (1947 *directory*); A. McElwee (KYB, 1975–6);[89] F. McElwee (1990); 285 (KYB, 1950–5).

Moville
Beach Cinema (c.1967–75+), p: McAuley Brothers, Moville, 350 (KYB, 1968–71; *Showcase* 1968); fb: D. McAuley (1975).[90]
Coliseum, The Square (c.1946–71+), br: John Davis, fb: John Egan, 24 Main Street, Maryborough

[Portlaoise], screen: 12ft x 9ft, 500 (*1947 directory*); p: John Egan, 375 (*KYB*, 1949–71).
Ritz Cinema, Glebe Street (*c*.1942–*c*.1943), p: F.J. Farrell, Cloncoose, Longford (*KYB*, 1944); 300 (*KYB*, 1943), 400 (*KYB*, 1944).

Raphoe
Raphoe Cinema, p: Messrs Wilton & Barry, 350 (*KYB*, 1949–55; *Showcase* 1968); fb: Mr W. Barry, Duinboy House, Lifford, Co. Donegal (*1947 directory*); 274 (*KYB*, 1960).
Ritz Cinema, p: Messrs Wilton & Barry (*KYB*, 1957–70); 274 (*KYB*, 1957); may be same as *Raphoe*.

Rathmelton
Star Cinema, p: James McFadden, 350.

Travelling cinemas
Cannon's Cinema. Operating in Ballyshannon every Wednesday; Ballyboley every Tuesday; Donegal town every Sunday & Monday (*KYB*, 1937).

DOWN

Ballykinlar
Camp Cinema (*KYB*, 1934). As there is an army camp at Ballykinlar, this may have been a temporary or travelling cinema visiting the camp; however, it is also possible that it was the *Soldiers' Home*, which one might presume was another name or incarnation of *Sandes' Cinema* given that was the address of Miss Sandes of the *Sandes' Cinema*.
Sandes' Cinema (*c*.1925–*c*.1968), p: Miss Sandes (*KYB*, 1926–33); Miss Sandes, Soldiers Home (*KYB*, 1941–64, *Showcase* 1968); m: Miss Eva Maguire (*KYB*, 1926–9); three shows weekly (*KYB*, 1926–31); 250 (*KYB*, 1937); 600 (*KYB*, 1942); 630 (*KYB*, 1945–61); 600 (*KYB*, 1962–4).
Soldiers' Home, br: Miss McGuire, 450 (*1947 directory*). See *Sandes' Cinema*.

Ballynahinch
The Picture House (*c*.1925–*c*.1971+; listed in *1947 directory*), p: J. Corry, open Friday & Saturday, winter only (*KYB*, 1926–32); Mr B.H. Bloomfield, Scotch Street, Downpatrick (*KYB*, 1933–64, listed as fb in *1947 directory*); Frank & I. Hargreaves, 17 Larkfield Avenue, Belfast (*KYB*, 1965–71; F.&J. in *Showcase* 1968); 375 (*KYB*, 1936–9); 300 (*KYB*, 1940–61).

Ballywalter
Midlands Cinema (*c*.1936–*c*.1948; aka *Mid Ards Cinema* [*KYB*, 1942–9; *1947 directory*]), p: John Bell, The Cottage, Ballyhalbert (*KYB*, 1948); Mrs E.M. Bell, The Cottage, Ballyhalbert (*KYB*, 1949); 407 (*KYB*, 1948); 375 (*KYB*, 1949).
Tatler (*c*.1949–*c*.1963), p: H.C. Orr, Opera House Buildings, Hale Street, Coventry (*KYB*, 1950–64); H.C. Orr, Enterprise House, 141 Albany Road, Coventry (*KYB*, 1962–4); 379 (*KYB*, 1958–64).

Banbridge
Dromore Cinema, 70 Dromore Street (*c*.1924–71+), p: Thomas Larmour with Thursday, Friday, Saturday opening (*KYB*, 1924); James & R.W. Dale (*KYB*, 1925–48); R.W. Dale (*KYB*, 1949–71); 280 (*KYB*, 1936–57). See *Dromore Cinema*, Dromore.[91]
Iveagh Cinema, Hanratty Road (1955–March 2001; originally to be called the Ritz [*DIA*]; listed in *KYB*, 1957–71), arch: John McBride Neill; p: The Picture House (Banbridge) Ltd (*KYB*, 1957–71); Ward Anderson; 928 (*KYB*, 1957–61); 930 (*KYB*, 1962–71; *BFI*, 1991); 863 (1999);[92] 860 (Connolly and Dillon, 2001:74).
• *Iveagh Movie Studios*, 26 Downshire Place (May 2004–; aka *New Iveagh Cinema*), p: Dominic Quinn, 4 screens/700 seats (300, 200, 110, 100) seats (*Cinema Treasures*); 4 screens (2010); part of leisure complex, and used as live event venue.
Picture House (*c*.1915–*c*.1959), p: J.W. Finney (*KYB*, 1916); James U. Finney (*KYB*, 1918; 1922–39, Finney's address: Belmont, Banbridge [*KYB*, 1938]); Picture House (Banbridge) Ltd (*KYB*, 1941–60); Irish Theatres (*1947 directory*, with fb: Ferris Pounds, Ann Street, Belfast (*1947 directory*); m: Herbert Burton with one show nightly (*KYB*, 1926); 900 (*KYB*, 1916); 825 (*KYB*, 1936); 703 (*KYB*, 1937); 756 (*KYB*, 1941–8); 724 (1949–57); 695 (*KYB*, 1960).
Temperance Hall, Dromore Street (*KYB*, 1916–17).
Gilford Cinema, Dunbarton Street, relocated to Ulster Folk Museum, 2007.

Bangor[93]
Adelphi Cinema, 37 Main Street (1929–*c*.1959), p: James Menary & Bertie Walsh (*KYB*, 1931–3); Bertie

Walsh (*KYB*, 1934–7, listed as br in *1947 directory*); Adelphi Cinemas Ltd (*KYB*, 1931–44; 1942–4; 1951–60; *1947 directory*); Rialto Cinema Co., 37 Main Street, Bangor (*KYB*, 1945–50); fb: Mr McClintock, Supreme Cinemas, Ltd, 133 Royal Avenue, Belfast (*1947 directory*); while the *KYB* (1936, 1945–50, 1957–60)[94] variously lists the number of seats at 450/480/500, the *1947 directory* gives the venue's capacity as 1,300 with a 30ft proscenium.

Astor, Seacliffe Road.

• *Bangor Cineplex*, 1 Valentine Road, Castlepark (*c.*1992–; aka: *Bangor Multiplex*; *Bangor Omniplex*), p: Ward Anderson; initially, 4 screens/758 (287; 196; 163; and 112) seats; 7 screens, 1,172 seats (Connolly and Dillon, 2001:74); 7 screens (2010).

Maypole Cinema, Shore Street/ Marine Parade (1917–).

The Picture Palace, Quay Street (1915–October 1940; aka *The Palace*) p: Irish Electric Palaces Ltd, 79 Donegall Street, Belfast (*KYB*, 1919–38), m: Herbert Rogers (*KYB*, 1919–28); 700; 650 (*KYB*, 1919, 1921); 700 (*KYB*, 1920); 600 (*KYB*, 1936–40).[95]

Queen's Cinema, Queen's Parade (*c.*1952–9 October 1977), p: Queen's Cinema (Bangor) Ltd (*KYB*, 1953–71; *Showcase* 1968); Norman Ellison; 500 seats (*KYB*, 1953–70); 400 (*KYB*, 1971); damaged by IRA firebombs, 8–9 October 1977.[96]

Rialto (*KYB*, 1930).

The Tonic, 102 Hamilton Road (6 July 1936–83; aka *Odeon*), arch: John McBride Neill; p: John H. O'Neill, Hamilton Road, Bangor (*KYB*, 1937); Bangor Cinemas Ltd/M.E. Curran circuit, Antrim Road, Belfast (*KYB*, 1938–57; *1947 directory*); Odeon (Northern Ireland) Ltd (*c.*1957–74, listed *KYB*, 1958–70; *Showcase* 1968); Belfast Cinemas Ltd (1974–83); br: Francis Murray, fb: James Curran, Capitol Cinema, Antrim Road (*1947 directory*); screen: 27½ft (*1947 directory*); 2,250 (*KYB*, 1937); 2,001 (*1947 directory*). It was the second-largest cinema in Ireland at the time of its opening; cost £76,000; a Compton organ was installed in July 1936. Building demolished in 1992 following fire.

Tudor, Main Street (*c.*1960–71+), p: Adelphi Cinema Co., Ltd (*KYB*, 1962–71; *Showcase* 1968).

Castlewellan

The Cinema (*c.*1924–*c.*1928), p/m: B. Cusack (*KYB*, 1925–9); listed as closed in *KYB*, 1930–1.

Cinema (*1947 directory*, no details).

The Cosy (*c.*1924–33), p/m: F. Bosco (*KYB*, 1925–34).

Comber

Grand Cinema (*c.*1918–*c.*1931; listed as closed in *KYB*, 1932), p/m: A.J. White[97] (*KYB*, 1919–31); 700 (*KYB*, 1919–21); licensed for music and dancing (*KYB*, 1920).

Picture House, Castle Street (*c.*1935–71+), p: Comber Picture House Ltd (*KYB*, 1936–71; *1947 directory*; *Showcase* 1968); br & fb: Mr B.H. Bloomfield, Scotch Street, Downpatrick, 18ft proscenium (*1947 directory*); 300 (*KYB*, 1941; *1947 directory*); 358 (*KYB*, 1946–57); 399 (*KYB*, 1958–71).

Tudor, 22A Drumhirk Road (*c.*2000–), p: Noel and Roy Spence, 66–seat private cinema converted from an outhouse as tribute to original *Tudor*, Bangor.[98]

Crossgar

Crossgar Picture House, p: Paddy Morgan, Warrenpoint, 350 (*KYB*, 1930–3).

Donaghadee[99]

Picture House, 1 Manor Street (*c.*1918–*c.*1928; *c.*1932–5; aka *Arcadian Picture House*, 1928–*c.*1935; *Regal Cinema* from *c.*1936 to 1970s), p: R.J. Evans (*KYB*, 1919); p/m: E.J. Evans (*KYB*, 1921–5); l: Dan Fraser (*KYB*, 1926–9 gives spelling as Frazer); p: William Carlisle, 13 Shore Street, Donaghadee (from 1928, *KYB*, 1930–2);[1] p: T. McChesney, 15 View Street (from *c.*1932, *KYB*, 1933); occasional variety; p: T. Duffy (from *c.*1933; *KYB*, 1934–6); Solar Cinemas Ltd (*KYB*, 1937–66; *KYB*, 1946–52, cites the address for Solar Cinemas as 6[–14] Howard Street, Belfast, while in *KYB*, 1953–66 and *Showcase* 1968 it is given as 44(–46) Corporation Street, Belfast); B.R. Briggs (*KYB*, 1967–71); br: R.G. Carr, fb: Mr L. Hyman, Howard Street (*1947 directory*); screen: 14ft x 10ft (*1947 directory*); 400 (*KYB*, 1919; 1921); 500 (*KYB*, 1920); 300 (*KYB*, 1934; 1937–66); 270 (*KYB*, 1967–71). After closing as cinema, used as community centre; when new community centre was built beside *Regal*, cinema was demolished and site became a car park.

Downpatrick

Assembly Hall (*c.*1915–16) (*KYB*, 1916–17).

• *Eclipse Cinema*, 5 Owenbeg Avenue (June 2009–; aka *Downpatrick Cineplex*), p: Downpatrick Cineplex Ltd, 39C Church Street, Warrenpoint; Eclipse Cinema Group, md: Martin Barratt, Omagh; m: Maureen Daly; 6 screens/1,000 seats; cost: £4 million.

Grand Cinema, Market Street (December 1935–91+); p/m: Thomas (Tommy) Breen, The Corner House, Downpatrick (1935–51; *KYB*, 1937–52, *1947 directory*), p: Mrs A.M. Breen, The Corner House, Downpatrick (*KYB*, 1956–68; *Showcase* 1968); J.H. Breen, Saul Road, Lisheen (*KYB*, 1969–71); 570;[2] 560/550 (*KYB*, 1937–71; *1947 directory*); 450 (*BFI*, 1991).

Pavilion Cinema, Market Street (*c.*1925–35), p/m: Thomas Breen (*KYB*, 1926–36), 350 seats (*KYB*, 1936). Closed by Breen after opening of *Grand*.

Picture House (*c.*1921–4), m: W. Tweedie; once nightly (*KYB*, 1922–4); m: Thomas Breen (*KYB*, 1925). It is possible that this is the same cinema as the *Pavilion*.

Regal (*c.*1935–6); listed without details in *KYB*, 1936–7.

Dromore

Cinema (aka *Montague*), p: John E. Hurst; one show nightly (*KYB*, 1919–23), p: Eddie Montague; 300 (*KYB*, 1919); 200 (*KYB*, 1920); 250.

Dromore Cinema.[3] See *Town Hall*.

Town Hall (?–1976; aka *Dromore Cinema*), p: Mr Rodgers, electrician and employee of Dromore Electric Light and Power Co, pioneered film shows in *Town Hall*, p: James Dale, owner of chemist shop, Church Street/Bridge Street corner, succeeded by his son, Robert Dale, who continued to 1969; p (1969–76): David and Rosemary Harrison; br: R.W. Dale (*1947 directory*; as p in *Showcase* 1968); cinema was located on top floor of Town Hall, where public library is now situated.[4]

Orange Hall, p: Mr Hurst, 'Elsinore', Hillsborough Road, manager of Banbridge linen firm William Walker & Co., held films shows on Tuesdays, Fridays and Saturdays in Orange Hall, and later by Mr Lamour.

Holywood

Holywood Cinema, High Street (*c.*1921–71+; aka *Picture House*), p: J. McDonald (*KYB*, 1922–3); William MacDonald (*KYB*, 1924–32; 1934); reappears in *KYB*, 1940, p: J. Turner, The Lodge, Sydenham Avenue, Belfast (*KYB*, 1940–69; *Showcase* 1968); Holywood Cinema Ltd (*KYB*, 1970–1); 20ft proscenium (*1947 directory*); 500 (*KYB*, 1940–61); 450 (*KYB*, 1962–9); 400 (*KYB*, 1970–1).

Maypole Cinema, Short Street, (*c.*1932–*c.*1946), p: W.P. Noble, Coolbeg, Cultra, Co. Down (*KYB*, 1933–34); M.W. Kennedy & Co., 22–8 Academy Street, Belfast (*KYB*, 1936); Raymond Stross, Orchard Hill, Holywood (*KYB*, 1941–4); br: Henry McCormick (*1947 directory*); screen: 14ft (*1947 directory*); 450 (*KYB*, 1936); 350 (*KYB*, 1939–40; *1947 directory*); 425 (*KYB*, 1941–4).[5]

New Cinema (*c.*1933–*c.*1938), p: Mrs R.B. Noble, Knock (*KYB*, 1934–9); 500 (*KYB*, 1936–9); may be same as *Maypole Cinema*.

Town Hall (*KYB*, 1916–17).

Kilkeel

The Cinema, p: M. Fagherty (*KYB*, 1926–9); may be same venue as *Royal Cinema*.

The Cinema, br: Mr McGonigale, 250 (*1947 directory*); may be same venue as above, and hence possibly same as *Royal Cinema*, but given the name of the business contact is similar to that of the *Vogue*, it is possible that it refers to same building.

Protestant Council Hall (*c.*1927).[6]

Royal Cinema (?–February 1929; *c.*1932–*c.*1946;[7] reappears in *KYB*, 1933–47) p: John Rooney; 250 (*KYB*, 1933–47).

Mourne Cinema, appears in *KYB*, 1948–64, in name only; p: Mr W. McGonigle (*Showcase* 1968), may be same venue as *Royal Cinema*.

Vogue, 52 Newry Street (*c.*1941–*c.*1942; *c.*1947–7 September 2007; listed, *KYB*, 1942–3; reappears, *KYB*, 1948 in name only), p: William F. McGonagle & J. McCulla (*KYB*, 1949–64); John Quinn (*KYB*, 1949–60); 490 (*KYB*, 1949–60); 400 (*KYB*, 1961–2); 413 (*BFI*, 1991); 295 (Connolly and Dillon, 2001:74). The last single-screen cinema to operate in Northern Ireland; building later owned by Newry and Mourne county council.

Killyleagh

Cinema (*c.*1935–71+), p: Harold S. McMurray, Gweedore, Saul Road, Downpatrick (*KYB*, 1936–57; *1947 directory*), Harold S. McMurray, Quoile Road, Downpatrick (*KYB*, 1958–64; name only in *Showcase* 1968); W.F. McGonigle [see entries under Kilkeel], 47 Mill Road, Kilkeel (*KYB*, 1969–71); 300 (*KYB*, 1936–64); 280 (*KYB*, 1959–71).

Kircubbin

Amethyst Cinema.

Millisle

Millisle Cinema, p: Solar Cinemas Ltd, Belfast; 400.

Newcastle

Belle-Vue Cinema (*c*.1924–*c*.1929), p: F. Bosco (*KYB*, 1925–8); Jack Delius; dance hall (*KYB*, 1929); listed as closed, *KYB*, 1930.

Palace Picture House (*c*.1941–*c*.1960; aka *The Picture House*), p: B. Cusack (*KYB*, 1924–48); Robert Cusack (*KYB*, 1949–71; *Showcase* 1968 spelled as Cussack); Jack Corkin; m: J. Stevens (*KYB*, 1922–3); 300 (*KYB*, 1936–42; *1947 directory*); 350 (*KYB*, 1943–8); 400 (*KYB*, 1949–61).

Ritz (*c*.1939–71+), p: Mr F. McMurray, Lurgan, 500 (*KYB*, 1939–71; *1947 directory*); fb: Mr J.A. McMurray, Lyric Cinema Co., Lurgan (*1947 directory*);

Newry

Frontier Picture Palace, John Mitchell Place (*c*.1915–71+; aka *Frontier Cinema*), p: Irish National Foresters (*c*.1915–36); sec: J. Campbell (*KYB*, 1922–3); m: W. Campbell (*KYB*, 1926–8), l: M. Curran & Sons (1936–57; listed as p in *1947 directory* with James Curran, Capitol Cinema, Antrim Road as fb);[8] lease expiry in 1957 coincided with sale of Curran group to Odeon (Northern Ireland) Ltd; reopened December 1957 by James Cunningham, formerly house manager, Belfast Ritz, and his brother C.P. Cunningham;[9] p: Irish National Foresters (*KYB*, 1963–71; *Showcase* 1968); 1,200 (*KYB*, 1916–17); 800 (*KYB*, 1936–61; *1947 directory*); 650 (*KYB*, 62–4); 500 (*KYB*, 1968); 550 (*KYB*, 1969–71).

Imperial Picture Palace (*c*.1915–*c*.1960; aka *Imperial Palace*; first listed, *KYB*, 1916); p: T.C. Mistagh (sic) (*KYB*, 1919); p/m: Frank Murtagh (*KYB*, 1922–66, *1947 directory*); 400 (*KYB*, 1916–17); 350 (*KYB*, 1919–21); 320 (*KYB*, 1940–61); 750 (*1947 directory*).

• *Newry Omniplex*, Quays shopping centre, Albert Basin (11 June 1999–), p: Ward Anderson's Empire Cinemas chain, 9 screens/2,100 seats (Connolly and Dillon, 2001:74).

Newry Picture Palace, Canal Street (*KYB*, 1916–17); may be same as below.

Premier Picture Palace, Canal Street, 300 (*KYB*, 1916–17); may be same as above.

Ritz, p: Ward Anderson, 2 screens.

Savoy, Monaghan Street (October 1933–71+), p: James Finney;[10] Derek & J.U. Finney (*KYB*, 1934–40); Savoy (Newry) Ltd, Newry Street, Banbridge (*KYB*, 1942–71; *Showcase* 1968; listed as Irish Theatres in *1947 directory* with fb: Ferris Pounds, Whitehall Buildings, Ann Street, Belfast); 750–780 (until *c*.1952, *KYB*, 1936–41; 1944–53); 805 (*KYB*, 1954–68); 750 (*KYB*, 1969–71).

Savoy 2, Merchant's Quay, 2 screens/255 (197 and 58) seats (*BFI*, 1991).

Sean Hollywood Arts Centre, 1a Bank Parade, used by Newry FC, access>CINEMA member and registered with the British Federation of Film Societies (established in 2006).

Town Hall (*KYB*, 1916–17), may be same as *Newry Picture Palace* and/or *Premier Picture Palace*.

Newtownards

• *Movieland*, Circular Road/Blair Mayne Road South, beside Ards shopping centre (1992–), p: Ernie Watson, 2 screen/408 (236, 171) seats; later extended to 6 screens; 6 screens/989 seats (Connolly and Dillon, 2001:74). Compton organ from Ambassador (later Odeon) Cinema, Hounslow, Middlesex, England, installed over cinema foyer.

Palace, Francis Street (*c*.1917–37; aka *Palace Unity-De-Lux*, *KYB*, 1922–4; *Ritz* from 1937), p: Campbell Morrison & Bros (*KYB*, 1918–21); p/m: Campbell Morrison (*KYB*, 1922–9, 1931–4); p: Robert Morrison & Son (*KYB*, 1924–5); E.J. Morrison (*KYB*, 1927); m: Campbell Morrison (*KYB*, 1919–27); 350 (*KYB*, 1936–7); 500.[11]

Palace Unity-De-Lux. See *Palace*.

Picture House, Regent Street (*c*.1916–December 1921), p: Irish Electric Palaces Ltd, 500 (*KYB*, 1917); m: William McAdorey (*KYB*, 1919); H. Aitken, 450 (*KYB*, 1920–1); destroyed by fire, December 1919.[12]

Regent (*c*.1938–9 October 1977; aka *New Hall*, *KYB*, 1939–40), p: Louis Hyman, 44–6 Corporation Street, Belfast (*KYB*, 1939–41), Solar Cinemas Ltd, 6–14 Howard Street South, Belfast (*KYB*, 1942–71; *Showcase* 1968 with address 44 Corporation Street, Belfast); fb: Louis Hyman, Howard Street (*1947 directory*); 850 (*KYB*, 1941–69); 780 (*KYB*, 1970–1); destroyed by IRA firebombs, 8–9 October 1977.[13]

Ritz, Francis Street (1 March 1937–64; formerly *Palace*, *c*.1917–37; listed in *Showcase* 1968), p: Ritz Belfast Ltd (Union Cinemas Group); Associated British Pictures Ltd, Golden Square, London W1 (October 1937–64; *KYB*, 1944–64; *1947 directory*); 755 (*KYB*, 1947–8); 713/12 (*KYB*, 1949–64).[14]

Portaferry

The Cinema, High Street (*c*.1923–71+), p: John K. Hinds (*KYB*, 1925–44; *1947 directory*); café and dance hall (*KYB*, 1933); Agnes Hinds (*KYB*, 1949–54); Charles, John & W. Hines (*KYB*, 1955–7); John Wm. & Hugh Hinds (*KYB*, 1961–71; *Showcase* 1968); stage: 25ft x 15ft (*1947 directory*); 350 (*KYB*, 1925–32); 370/80 (*KYB*, 1941–71).

Rathfriland

Rathfriland Cinema, School Road (*c.*1947–71+), p: HBE Cinemas, 133 Royal Avenue, Belfast (*KYB*, 1948–71); p: Paddy Morgan, Warrenpoint; 300 (*KYB*, 1948–62); 250.

Warrenpoint

Foy, Slieve Foy Place (*c.*1947–*c.*1963; listed as *cinema* in *1947 directory* with fb as Richard Hayward, 7 Bedford Street, Belfast), p: HBE Cinemas Ltd, 133 Royal Avenue, Belfast (*KYB*, 1948–64; *Showcase* 1968); 385 (*KYB*, 1948); 400 (*KYB*, 1950); 450 (*KYB*, 1951–2); 350 (*KYB*, 1953–62).

The Town Hall (*c.*1923–*c.*1927), p: National Band and Picture Co.; M. Doran; m: J. Carr (*KYB*, 1925–8).

Palais De Danse and Cinema (*c.*1924–*c.*1944; aka *Garden Cinema*, *KYB*, 1926–31 and 1936–45), p/m: L. Jackson (*KYB*, 1925); p: J. Leicester Jackson, Seaview, Warrenpoint & T.H. Richardson, Athelbie Terrace (with Jackson as manager, *KYB*, 1926–31); J. Leicester Jackson (*KYB*, 1932–4); Cinema & General Finance Corporation Ltd, 29 Donegall Street, Belfast; 300 (*KYB*, 1936–45).

Travelling cinemas

Menet's Talkies. Dundrum, Co. Down (*KYB*, 1941–4).

DUBLIN

Balbriggan

Savoy Cinema, Dublin Street (19 December 1944–June 1974; reopened as *Europa*, 9 August 1974–7), p: Tailteann Theatres (Balbriggan) Ltd, also owners of the *Savoy*, Kells, and *Savoy*, Rush (*1947 directory*; *Showcase* 1968); Kevin and Adrian Cunningham (1974–7); br & fb: Mr E.G. Scanlan[15] (*1947 directory*), screen: 19ft x 12 ²/₃ft, 700 (*1947 directory*); 700 (*KYB*, 1949–53); 686 (*KYB*, 1954); 656 (*KYB*, 1955–69); 646 (*KYB*, 1970); 576 (*KYB*, 1971); 800.[16]

• *New Savoy Cinema*, 10 Mill Street, Harbour Mill development (October 2006–; aka *Savoy Cinema*), 5 screens/ 637 (63–125) seats, all digital, m: Martin Strong; put up for sale, 2007.[17]

Strand Cinema, George's Square, rear of Town Hall (25 February 1934–*c.*1970s), in periodic use by travelling cinema shows until *Strand* was established as full-time cinema by local priests Fr Doherty and Fr Joseph Hickey, the lessees who managed the business; fire in premises during film show, 28 January 1929; l: William Walsh (from 1941, listed in *1947 directory* as Walshe);[18] p: Thomas O Brien and William Walsh (*KYB*, 1954–6); 650 (*1947 directory*); 600 (*KYB*, 1949–53); 530 (*KYB*, 1954–6); listed as closed in *KYB*, 1956–61.

Town Hall (*c.*1912–34+), p: Skerries Electric Theatre Co.; d: I.I. Bradlaw, Thomas Flanagan.[19]

Ballsbridge/Sandymount

Assembly Picture Hall, 59 Serpentine Avenue (October 1912–*c.*December 1926; aka *Assembly Cinema Theatre* and *Assembly Picture Hall*; *Picture Hall*), p: Izidore Isaac Bradlaw, lessee of premises from October 1912.[20] This 'cinema' may have been an extension or outside building at the side of nos 59 and 59a Serpentine Avenue, houses owned by the O'Neill family. Thomas O'Neill and James F. O'Neill are identified as managers during 1915–26, at which time Pembroke urban council complained to James O'Neill that the cinema was in a state of disrepair and 'should be closed forthwith' until the repairs were carried out, but the premises seem to have ceased being used as a cinema from this time.[21] See also *Elmerville* and *Astoria*.

Astoria, 78 Serpentine Avenue (9 February 1935–*c.*22 December 1940; aka *Ritz Cinema*, 1940–2 September 1973 [listed in *1947 directory* & *Showcase* 1968]; *Oscar Film Theatre*, 18 October 1973–28 November 1976), purpose-built, p: James F. O'Neill, 66 St Helen's Road, Booterstown; Ritz Cinema Co. (1940–73); md: Percy Winder Whittle, 2 Oaklands Drive, Ballsbridge and director of *Regal Cinema*, Ringsend; John Francis Stokes, St Patrick's, Dundalk; David McKay, 5 South Frederick, Dublin. Whittle became the cinema's outright owner in 1946 (and acted as fb [*1947 directory*]); as part of the agreement with O'Neill, who also owned *Astoria*, Glasthule (August 1940–), the name of the cinema had to be changed to *Ritz*; m (1940–): Owen Dunne, former am, *Regal*, Ringsend;[22] p: G.J. Jay (*Showcase* 1968); Paddy Melia (1973–6, as *Oscar Film Theatre*);[23] converted to *Oscar Theatre*[24] (10 January 1977–*c.*16 April 1983); building later became Dublin's first Sikh temple; screen: 24ft x 18ft (*1947 directory*).

Elmerville, 'Elmville', 84 Serpentine Avenue (*c.*1919–23; *c.* 24 July 1924–34; aka *The Shed*; *O'Neill's Cinema*; *Cinema House*; *Picture House*), originally unlicensed cinema, 'a simple shed where pictures were shown at weekends';[25] p: Mr Callow, from whom, in 1923–4, James F. O'Neill of nearby 59a Serpentine Avenue leased the property, including a 'cinema' building measuring 210ft by 41ft sometimes referred to as *The Shed* due to its structure. O'Neill may have run daily programmes at this location as the *Picture House* until *c.*1934 when he built the *Astoria* at 78 Serpentine Avenue, where his *Assembly Picture Hall* was located, opening *c.*9 February 1935.[26]

Ballyfermot
Gala, 361–3 Upper Ballyfermot Road (23 November 1955–*c.*April 1973, occasionally listed for charity events or screenings until 1978, finally closed in 1980), arch: J.F. McCormack; p: Republic Pictures; first m: Mr J. Kelly, formerly of the *Lyric*, James's Street; 1,850/1,900 (including 350 in balcony); majority p (1968): Green Group/Ward Anderson; converted to a roller rink in 1981; two years later changed to a leisure centre. Planning permission was approved in 2005 for the building to be partly demolished to make way for apartments, retail outlets and a bingo hall.

Ballymun
Axis: Ballymun Arts & Community Resource Centre, Main Street (29 June 2001–), 240, regular film screenings mostly organized by Pictures Film Club in conjunction with access>CINEMA and IFI.

Blackrock
Blackrock Cinema Theatre, 13 Main Street (26 February 1914–*c.*1929–31; aka *The Grand Theatre*; *Blackrock Grand Picture Palace*), p: Maurice Elliman with m: Jacob Elliman; The Blackrock Picture Co. (*c.*1924–9) with md: John Hanna (*KYB*, 1925–31; 700; listed as closed in *KYB*, 1932); converted to McEvoy's bicycle shop and billiards hall. (McEvoy had previously owned the *Masterpiece*, Talbot Street.) See also *Regent*.

New Cinema, 7–9 Main Street (1 February 1973–11 October 1973; as *Globe Cinema* from 3 May 1974–29 March 1975), p: Dublin Film Institute, 46 Upper Baggot Street, Dublin 2; *c.* 200; now occupied by Roccia Nera restaurant (no. 9) and a Mexican bar/café (no. 7).[27]

Regent Cinema, 13 Main Street (24 February 1938–25 March 1961); arch: James V. McCrane; p: Associated Picture Houses (1944) Ltd (listed, 1947 *directory*), with d: Mr P.J. Whelan [md]; Mr J.J. Hickey; Mrs M. Hickey; Mr J.J. Fagan); Odeon (Ireland) Ltd (from 1948) br: George H. Kerins, 550, screen: 18ft x 14ft (1947 *directory*); 520–536 stadium seats; 556;[28] site now occupied by Café Java and beside Xtra-Vision (no. 11) in a new building, and beside O'Rourke's public house (no. 15).[29]

Blanchardstown
• *UCI Blanchardstown* (December 1996–), arch: Burke Kennedy Doyle; p: United Cinema International (1996–2004), thereafter lessee; Terra Firma Capital Partners (from October 2004); Irish Leisureplex Entertainment Co./Entertainment Enterprises/Ciáran and Colum Butler (from September 2006); 9 screens/2,455 (451, 437, 332, 263, 206, 206, 194, 183, 183) seats; 9 screens/2,463 seats.[30]

Cabra
Cabra Grand, 60–2 Quarry Road (16 April 1949–31 January 1970), arch: Henry J. and Samuel Lyons (*DIA*); p: Leonard Ging in association with Hubert McNally and his brother Dr Patrick McNally. Just before it opened, Ging sold the 1,634-seat cinema, along with most of his other exhibition interests, to Irish Cinemas Ltd (listed in *Showcase* 1968, address: 1/2 Poolbeg Street, Dublin). It had a 13m wide proscenium arch, one of the largest on the island. In May 1975 Gael Linn bought the cinema for use as a bingo hall, for which purpose it is still used.

Chapelizod
Ritz Cinema, Cinema Lane (8 August 1942–19 May 1945; as *Majestic*, 20 May 1945–57 [also listed under this name in *Showcase* 1968]; as *Oriel*, 21 April 1957–66), p: Mr G.W. Mordant (20 May 1945–57); Thomas O'Neill, chief projectionist of *Majestic*, and Mr A. Pope (21 April 1957–1966); 500 (1947 *directory*); entrance was via side of Mullingar public house; site now occupied by ML Manufacturers Ltd.[31]

Churchtown
Landscape Cinema, Landscape Road (9 April 1955–1 May 1957; November 1958–25 June 1965), p: James Brophy; 900, stadium-style; the cinema's closure in 1957–8 was connected in part with a dispute with trade union ITGWU over the employment of the proprietor's unqualified son as an operator.

Clondalkin
Tower Cinema, Monastery Road (9 April 1939–14 May 1977), Portlaoise exhibitors Mr J.L. Kelly and Joe Egan in association with Peter Ging converted the former premises of the Irish Omnibus Company into a 350 seat cinema; Ging bought out his partners in January 1941, and when he died the following year, his sons Larry and Tommy ran the cinema, which they extended in 1942 to 480/500 seats; br: Laurence (Larry) Ging, screen: 12ft, 480 (1947 *directory*); CinemaScope was installed in

1957. When Larry Ging died in 1964, his wife Lily ran the cinema with her sons until it closed in 1977 (nevertheless, Laurence Ging, Monastery Road, listed as p in *Showcase* 1968); building converted to shops.[32]

Ster Century, Liffey Valley shopping centre, Fonthill Road/New Lucan Road (16 July 1999; from 2005, *Vue*); p: Ster-Kinekor; Aurora Entertainment; SBC International Cinemas, owners from May 2003 of Warner Village cinemas in UK (from April 2005); management buy-out of company; 14 screens/3,814 (459, 425, 388, 336, 334, 283, 262, 259, 221, 198, 178, 176, 158, 137) seats; 14 screens/3,568 seats;[33] 4 screens were bigger than any other screen in Ireland, while screen 1 with a 195 square metre screen was the biggest multiplex screen in Ireland or Britain; 70 staff.[34] 2010: 14 screens/3,804 seats, gm: Nigel Drake.

• *Vue*, Liffey Valley shopping centre, Fonthill Road/New Lucan Road. See *Ster Century*.

Clontarf
Clontarf Electric Theatre, Town Hall, 61 Clontarf Road (18 July 1913–5 November 1921; as *Clontarf Cinema* from 19 September 1917 to 1918; 10 October 1921–5 November 1921; aka *Town Hall Cinema*), in 1900 the separate Clontarf district council was incorporated into Dublin city, thus making its town hall obsolete for official purposes, as a result of which it was used for concerts, dances, meetings, etc.; l (1917): David Morrison, 3 Whitehall Terrace, Clontarf; projection box destroyed when film caught fire in October 1917;[35] l (1921): Mr Forde. In addition to its periodic openings and closings, it was used on other occasions for short film runs. In 1926–7 the building was converted to St John the Baptist Catholic church, which opened on 28 August 1927. When a new church was built at the rear of the building in 1975 (now known as St Anthony's), the building reverted to being a community centre.[36]

Coolock
• *UCI Coolock*, 84 Malahide Road, Greencastle Road extension, Dublin 17 (30 July 1991–; aka *Odeon Coolock*), p: United Cinema International (1991–2004), thereafter lessee; Terra Firma Capital Partners owners of Odeon Cinema chain (October 2004–September 2006); Irish Leisureplex Entertainment Co./Entertainment Enterprises/Ciárán and Colum Butler (acquired in September 2006 with the other Dublin UCI cinemas in Blanchardstown and Tallaght, from Terra Firma/Odeon for €90 million); arch: Burke Kennedy Doyle; 10 screens/2,194 seats (297 x 2; 200 x 8); 10 screens/2,284 seats.[37]

Crumlin
Star, Kildare Road/ St Mary's Road (15 January 1953–11 December 1971, reopened, destroyed by [malicious] fire 5 September 1978),[38] p: Crumlin Cinema Co. (*Showcase* 1968); arch: Jones and Kelly; cost: £60/65,000; 1,750/1,800 (c.1,350/1,400 in stalls; 350/450 in balcony) seats; m: Kevin Cunningham (1978);[39] occasionally cine variety; after it closed, it was used as a 'Roller Rink'; was then bought by Gael Linn, which continues to use it as a bingo hall.

Dalkey
Dalkey Cinema, 37A Convent Road (c.1919–c.1931; aka *Kavanagh's Picture House*), p: John Kavanagh, a builder, 'an oblong-shaped wooden building with an A-shaped corrugated iron roof' was built on waste ground beside 37A; c.100 seats; now car-park at rear of Club bar, Coliemore Road.[40]

Dolphin's Barn
Leinster Cinema, 37B Dolphin's Barn Street (3 November 1936–18 May 1968; aka *The Leinster*),[41] arch: Robinson & Keefe; p: Daniel McAllister (and fb), 1,250 (1947 directory) stadium-style; p given as Leinster Cinema Ltd in *Showcase* 1968); later used as Dublin Ice Rink; building demolished in 2004 to make way for apartment block.
Rialto Cinema. See Rialto.

Drumcondra
Drumcondra Grand Cinema, 20–4 Upper Drumcondra Road (19 October 1934–24 March 1968; aka *Grand Cinema*), arch: Harry J. Lyons; decorated in silver and green with amber lighting; p: Leonard Ging (listed as br and fb in 1947 directory, with company name given – Drumcondra Grand Cinema Ltd); Irish Cinemas Ltd (from 1949); 1,038; 31ft proscenium, 1,200 (1947 directory); auditorium now houses a Tesco supermarket.

Dublin
Abbey Theatre, Abbey Street. While the 540-seat *Abbey Theatre* is listed in *KYB*, 1918–20, no other evidence has been uncovered that it was used as a venue for film screenings.
Abercorn Hall, 3 Harcourt Road. See *Picturedrome*.
Academy Cinema, 42 Pearse Street (13 March 1965–January 1977 and August 1977–19 November 1981; formerly *Antient Concert Rooms*, 1844–1920; *Palace*, 13 May 1920–3 December 1950; *Forum*,

4 December 1950–7 April 1956; *Embassy*, 9 April 1956–May 1964), p: Bertie McNally, John Farrelly and Thomas F. St John (who converted venue into *Academy* cinema); p: Dublin Cinema Group Ltd (*Showcase* 1968); Capitol and Allied Theatres group (at time of 1977 closure); Ward Anderson, who reopened cinema in August 1977; 640 (1965); from its reopening in 1977, concentrated on adult material, became a 'half-way house' between commercial films and the 'art' fare offered by the *Irish Film Theatre*; screened second-run features and films which the management felt had been under-exploited in city-centre first-run cinema; largely destroyed by fire in March 1994, planning permission for an office block on the site was approved in 2001 to the Ward Anderson group; the main building was restored and an office block built to the rear.[42] See also *Antient Concert Rooms*; *Palace Cinema*; *Forum*; *Embassy*.

Adelphi Cinema, 98–101 Middle Abbey Street (12 January 1939–69; 8 October 1970–3, 3 screens; 23 November 1973–30 November 1995, 4 screens); p: Associated British Cinemas on the site of the Plaza ballroom at a cost of £75,000 with 2,304 seats (parterre, 1,553; balcony (front circle) 276; balcony (back circle, 496) and standing room for 500; 2,326 (2,028 in stalls; 298 in balcony);[43] designed by ABC house architect William Riddell Glen working with Irish architect Robert Donnelly;[44] first m: Mr J.H. Hamilton, formerly of *Theatre Royal*; asst. m/later m: Harry Lush, 1943–81 (listed in 1947 *directory* as br).[45] The *Adelphi* also included a large stage, and it was there that such live performers as the Beatles (7 November 1963), the Rolling Stones and Gene Pitney performed. Following its closure in 1969 after takeover by EMI of ABC, it reopened in 1970 as Dublin's first triple cinema (Cinema 1, 614 seats, formerly the balcony, maroon; Cinema 2, 1,052 seats, formerly the stalls, bronze; Cinema 3, 360 seats, formerly the café, blue; cost £300,000). Adelphi 2 was subdivided into two screens and opened in November 1973, making a total of four screens; fb: D. O'Keefe (1974–6).[46] On 30 August 1976 incendiary devices damaged Adelphi 1, and it reopened on 10 September 1976. While at one point 18 girls sold ice-cream from the Fridge Room, as a result of a rationalization plan in May 1991 of the *Adelphi* and its sister cinema, the *Carlton*, 75 employees lost their jobs. When the *Adelphi* and *Carlton* closed permanently in November 1995, the 45 remaining employees were made redundant, and the site was incorporated into the expansion of the adjoining Arnotts' department store.[47]

Ambassador Cinema, Parnell Street (1954–99; formerly *Round Room*, *Rotunda*). See *Round Room*, *Rotunda*.

Ancient Order of Hibernians Cinema, 31 Parnell Square. See *AOH Cinema*.

Antient Concert Rooms, 42E Great Brunswick Street (now Pearse Street), (occasional film seasons from December 1898; aka *Palace*, 13 May 1920–3 December 1950; *Forum*, 4 December 1950–7 April 1956; *Embassy*, 9 April 1956–May 1964; *Academy Cinema*, 13 March 1965–13 January 1977, and from 3 August 1977–19 November 1981). In 1842 the site was acquired by the Society of Antient Concerts which adapted the interior to an 800-seat hall with a Telford organ, and gave the first performance on 20 April 1843 featuring extracts from Handel's *Messiah*. On the fashionable southside of river, it supplanted the previously popular Rotunda Rooms. Irish Academy of Music based here until own premises built on nearby Westland Row; in 1860s served as home for Philharmonic Society of Dublin; and in late nineteenth century, the Amateur Musical Society was based there. Periodically used for film screenings in early years of cinema, but following a visit by Dublin corporation's public health committee in 1913 restrictions were placed on its use as a cinema, including a ban on use of the gallery. Reopened by Dr Isaac Epell as the 600-seat *Palace* on 13 May 1920; mus. dir (from 1920): cellist John Mundy; renamed *Embassy* (1956–64) and then *Academy* (1965–81) when used as a full-time cinema; 640 seats. In 1980s it was used as a part-time theatre and infrequently as a cinema. Now part of an office complex.[48]

AOH Cinema, 31 Parnell Square (4 October 1920–mid-1920s), p: Irish National Foresters Co., 432 seats; later converted to a dance hall.[49]

Astor, 51 Lower O'Connell Street (27 March 1937–21/23 December 1946; formerly, *The Picture House*, 1910–17; *Sackville Picture House*, 1917–37); p: Capitol & Allied Theatres Ltd; m: Mr B. Murray; m: Bertie McNally (early 1940–6). See *The Picture House*.

Astor, 7–8 Eden Quay (12 March 1953–15 June 1984); converted from an auctioneering business by architect William O'Dwyer, it had 313 seats on the ground floor; p: Bertie McNally, son of singer Walter McNally, and who operated the *Astor*, O'Connell Street, until it closed in 1946; m: John R. Bools;[50] Tommy Gogan (195?–1961); specialized in early years in foreign-language films; opening film, Vittorio de Sica's *Bicycle Thieves*: 'Its aim is to supply a long-felt need amongst discriminating picturegoers – the presentation of top-class and specialised films, particularly Continental, which do not find their way into the commercial cinemas as a whole';[51] p: Astor Cinemas Ltd (*Showcase* 1968); Mrs Vogue McNally, widow of Bertie McNally, (from *c.*1976) and Ward Anderson, as partner with Mrs McNally; after Ward Anderson bought in, the programme went more mainstream; later a video store opened on the premises, but was converted along with the Ward Anderson-owned adjacent *Corinthian Cinema* into a nightclub, and the two cinemas were demolished in November 2002.

Broadway Cinema, Manor Street. See *Manor Street Picture House*.

Brunswick Cinema Theatre, 30 South Great Brunswick Street (now Pearse Street), (30 November 1911–c.1919), p: Irish Amusement Co., d: A. Sim, Maurice Elliman, 28 Lower Camden Street; I.I. Bradlaw, 57 Grafton Street; O.S. Baker; m: Captain John R. Smallman; p: Brunswick Kinema Theatre, Ltd (incorporated, 3 December 1914, with d: I.I. Bradlaw; William Petrie, merchant, Glasnevin; Joseph Harris, merchant, South Anne Street; Maurice Elliman, cinema manager, Dufferin Avenue, South Circular Road);[52] converted from former billiard saloon; 350, stadium seating;[53] 367;[54] from 1919, the premises were in use as the Brunswick Motor Exchange; an office block is now on the site.

Camden Picture House, 55 Lower Camden Street (25 October 1912–28 August 1948), arch: Rudolf Maximilian Butler; p: Alfred H. Poulter (also proprietor of the *Cinematograph Theatre*, Lower Sackville Street, and the *Empire Theatre*, Dame Street); Patrick Whelan and John Breslen (from 1928), following Whelan's death in 1944, Associated Picture Houses (1944) Ltd (*1947 directory*); Odeon (Ireland) Ltd closed it down shortly after purchasing it in 1948 as it was near their *Theatre de Luxe*, which the company had bought from the Ellimans in 1946;[55] fb: Louis Elliman, Savoy Cinema, Dublin (*1947 directory*); access to the cinema was via a long passageway under the screen; a solid-fuel stove provided heating to the poorly-equipped cinema, with wooden forms for the cheap seats; 354; 400 (*KYB*, 1916–19); 350 (*KYB*, 1920); 360 (*1947 directory*). Demolished, an office building, Matrix House, now stands on the site.

Cameo Cinema, 52 Middle Abbey Street (30 July 1976–15 March 1990), p: Michael Butler (1977); arch: Henry J. Lyons & Partners; conversion of former warehouse, cost: £37,000.[56]

Cameo Cinema Cafe, 43 Grafton Street (20 October 1949–52; 11 July 1952–December 1953; formerly the Bolero Café; from 1952, *Cameo Cinema*; *Cameo Continental Café*); opened using 16mm in 1949 showing 60 minutes of shorts as the Kinematograph Renters Society banned film renters from supplying the venue; hired educational films from National Film Institute, and Italian and French films; p: Mai Garvey (from 1949, 200,[57] art cinema policy from 11 July 1952);[58] Mr E. Hardiman, 6 Lower Fitzwilliam Street (1952–3, md, Egan Film Service Ltd, who died in early December 1953);[59] screenings continued until Christmas, but the venture seems to have closed by the end of 1953; a court case in July 1954 in which Bolero Cafés and Dorothy Begley sued Cameo Cinema Ltd seems to have concluded the venture.[60]

Capitol, Princes's Street (1 August 1927–9/11 March 1972; formerly, *La Scala Theatre & Opera House*). See *La Scala*.

Carlton Cinema Theatre, 52 Upper O'Connell Street (*c*. 27 December 1915–11 July 1936; aka *Irish National Picture Palace*; *Carlton Picture Palace*); originally known as *Irish National Picture Palace*, this was changed to (*New*) *Carlton Cinema Theatre* shortly afterwards; p: Carlton Cinema Ltd/ Frank W. Chambers, George P. Fleming;[61] m: F.W. Chambers; arch: Thomas E. MacNamara, included a tea lounge at the front decorated with mahogany panelling (*DIA*); damaged during 1916 Rising; m: T.P. Robinson (*KYB*, 1920); 600 seats; 480 seats (*KYB*, 1919); 460 seats (*KYB*, 1920); pulled down in 1936 to make way for a new *Carlton Cinema* (see next entry).

Carlton Picture House, 52–4 Upper O'Connell Street (16 April 1938–28 March 1976; as 3 screen complex, 27 August 1976; 4 screens from 27 June 1980 to 20 October 1994; aka *New Carlton Picture House*), the new *Carlton Cinema* incorporated two adjoining premises, nos 53 and 54, including the Dorset Institution and Repository for Plain and Fancy Needlework; 2,000 seats (1,500 in stalls; 500 in balcony); arch: John Robinson (of Robinson and O'Keefe), John Higginbottom supervised construction as Dublin corporation's surveyor of places of public resort, while steel framing was by Smith & Pearson (*DIA*), it had a classical façade incorporating two art-deco light beacons into sky, but following complaints from air traffic controllers at Dublin Airport, their use was discontinued, while musical instruments and Celtic motifs decorated the cinema and foyer; p: Ellis family (from beginning); Associated British Pictures, which established the Adelphi-Carlton group of cinemas, including the *Adelphis*, Middle Abbey Street and Dún Laoghaire (from 1959); EMI (from late 1960s); MGM; m: Thomas J. (Tommy) Gogan, former manager of *Pavilion Gardens*, Dún Laoghaire, and publicity manager of *Coliseum*, Henry Street (listed as br in *1947 directory*, which also notes screen size – 24ft x 18ft – seats –2,000 – and fb as Jack Ellis); Michael Neary (1950s–1970s).[62] In 1976, the auditorium was converted to a triple screen and four years later, the Charcoal Grill restaurant was changed to a 126-seat fourth screen, opening on 27 June 1980; subsequently, many uses were proposed for its redevelopment (relocation of the Abbey Theatre; a concert hall; multiplex), until in 2010 a huge shopping mall received planning permission which would include keeping the cinema's façade, but moving it further up O'Connell Street, but without a multiplex due to proximity of 17-screen *Cineworld*, Parnell Street.

Cinema Palace, 6 Townsend Street (*c.*1908, weekly screenings; 30 March 1909–*c.*1914, cine-variety; aka *Coffee Palace; Palace Theatre; The Palace; Picture Palace; Cinema Royal* from 23 December 1913), also a concert venue, opened as an irregular cinema in the premises of the Dublin Total Abstinence Society (from 1875) and the Dublin Temperance Institute in 1911 as an alternative to the public house. Coffee palaces, of which there were three in 1897, were establishments where temperance campaigners sought to wean drinkers off spirits with food and non-alcoholic drink and spiritual guidance. The *Cinema Royal*, in a hall at rear of premises, reopened, 30 March 1909 as *Cinema Palace*, m: Mr Erskine,[63] p: W. Butler of G. Butler & Sons, musical instrument makers, Monument House, O'Connell Bridge, owners of the *Thomas Street Picture House*; 500 seats; frequent inspections and demands for safety improvements by Dublin corporation's inspector of buildings led to its demise.[64] When Dublin Total Abstinence Society was wound up in November 1915, the building became offices for *Freeman's Journal*; demolished; site now occupied by office building beside *Screen Cinema*.

Cinerama, 42–6 Talbot Street. See *Dublin Cinerama Theatre*.

• *Cineworld*, Parnell Centre, Parnell Street. See *Virgin Cinemas Multiplex*.

The Coliseum, entrances 24 Henry Street and 29 Prince's Street North (5 April 1915–24 April 1916; aka *The Coliseum Theatre; The Picture Palace Theatre*), arch: Bertie Crowe, Francis R. Bergin; cost: £40,000; custom-built; 1,060 seats on the ground floor and 400 seats in the gallery and was granted a cinema licence in 1915 when its name was changed to *The Coliseum*; 3,000;[65] the main entrance was formerly Strahan's with two entrances: from Prince's Street for the pit (6*d.*) and gallery (3*d.*), with approach to the four boxes (15*s.* and 12*s.* 6*d.*), circle (1*s.*) and stalls (2*s.*) via Henry Street;[66] as a result of the cinema's proximity to the General Post Office, it was destroyed during the 1916 Rising. Derelict until 1925, it was rebuilt and occupied by the Dublin district postal controllers' office.

The Coliseum Picture House, 16–17 Redmond's Hill, between Aungier and Wexford streets (*c.*March 1910–28 August 1911; aka *The Coliseum Theatre of Living Pictures*), located between D. Ross, fish merchant, and William J. McEvoy, hat and cap manufacturer; p: Maurice Elliman; p/m: Richard ('Dickie') Graham; *c.*250 seats; following a fire in the exterior projection box on 28 August 1911, which did not cause casualties as no screenings were taking place, and from which the caretaker and his family escaped, the premises, made of pitch-pine and varnished wood, was completely destroyed and did not reopen as a cinema; the site was later occupied by Fannin's medical supplies.[67]

Coliseum Theatre, 24 Henry Street. See *The Coliseum*.

Corinthian Cinema, 4–6 Eden Quay (8 August 1921–18 January 1930; 17 May 1930–3 March 1993; aka *Corinthian Picture Theatre* [1947 directory], *New Corinthian*, 4 January 1956–3 July 1975; *Odeon* 1 & 2, 16 October 1975–12 November 1987; *Screen at O'Connell Bridge*, 13 November 1987–3 March 1993), arch: Thomas MacNamara[68] for James Coney Nolan and his family; structural alterations/additions: Jones & Kelly (1930) (*DIA*). A native of Mayo, Nolan returned from the West Indies in 1917 and established the Corinthian Picture Theatre Co., but died two months after the cinema opened; an attempt was made to blow up the cinema on 13 April 1923 during the civil war. In the late 1920s, the Corinthian Picture Co. was wound up when trading at a loss, and it was bought for £20,300 at auction in February 1930 by Maurice Elliman, George Nesbitt and P.A. Corrigan, all of whom were linked to the *Metropole* and *Theater De Luxe*;[69] it was redecorated and sound was installed; 794; 700;[70] renovated again in 1939, when a balcony was installed; in *1947 directory* the proprietor is listed as Dublin Kinematograph Theatre Ltd, 35–9 Lower O'Connell Street, while the fb is Louis Elliman (Savoy Cinema, Dublin); 841; it became part of Rank's interests in Ireland, Odeon (Ireland) Ltd, in 1946 after the Ellimans sold their cinema chain to Rank. It was relaunched on 4 January 1956 as the *New Corinthian*, and began to specialise in showing European films. Closed in June 1975 to be twinned as *Odeon* 1 and *Odeon* 2 with 323 and 200 seats;[71] m (1965–75): William D. King, whose father owned *Phibsboro Cinema* where William started work in 1928; closed temporarily in August 1985 when 'management regarded it as being overstaffed';[72] cinema known as 'The Corral' and 'The Ranch' due to specialisation in westerns; p (from 1983): Ward Anderson; name changed to *Screen at O'Connell Bridge* in 1987; closed permanently on 4 March 1993; along with adjoining *Astor*, also owned by Ward Anderson, it was demolished in November 2002 to make way for an entertainment, office and apartment complex.

The Corona Cinema, 71B Parnell Street. See *Cosy Cinema Theatre*.

Cosy Cinema Theatre, 71B Parnell Street, former premises of Irish American Tobacco Co., 'practically-adjoining' Mooney's public house (later Conway's), (March 1914–16; from 26 March 1919 known as *The Corona Cinema; The Corona Picture House*), arch: Orpen & Dickinson (*DIA*); p: Cosy Cinema (Ireland) Ltd (registered, 9 March 1914; d: R.L. Boyd, G.E. Lee and T. Mason), m: Mr Manley; 180;[73] 250 (*KYB*, 1916–17); 420; closed *c.* 1922; later converted for use by Academy of Irish Dancing; now a convenience store.

Curzon Cinema, Middle Abbey Street (8 August 1968–*c*.April 1988; as *Light House Cinema*, 11 November 1988–28 September 1996), arch: Henry J. Lyons & Partners; p: Michael Collins, 400; 2 screens from June 1982; in 1982, first Dublin cinema to introduce non-smoking areas. In 1970s and 1980s the *Curzon* and *Cameo* across the road became involved in a dispute with the Society of Film Distributors about access to first-run product;[74] building demolished in 1999 along with adjoining *Adelphi* to make way for extension to Arnotts department store. See also *Light House Cinema*.

Dame Street Picture House, 17 Dame Street (24 December 1912–20), former premises of wallpaper manufacturer; arch: Francis Bergin; p: Dame Street Picture House Ltd; m: J. Aherne; M. Lean; 360 (*KYB*, 1916–17); 300 (*KYB*, 1918–19); 420 (*KYB*, 1920); 275;[75] in 1927 it became the Official Film Censor's office and screening room; auditorium was later occupied by Chinese restaurant in building known as Noble House.[76]

DBC Picture House, 6–7 O'Connell Street. See *Grand Central*.

Denzille Private Cinema, 13 Denzille Lane (1997–), arch: Grafton Architects; 30 seats; now owned by Tyrone Productions.

Dorset Picture House, 22–3 Upper Dorset Street, at corner with Granby Row (13 May 1911–1981; aka *Shanly's Picture Hall*; *Dorset Picture Hall*; *Picture Palace Theatre*; renamed *Plaza Picture Hall* aka *Plaza Cinema* and *Plaza Picture Palace* after renovations [26 September 1927–October 1966]; renamed *Plaza Cinerama* [28 September 1967–15 January 1976]; continued as standard cinema until 2 July 1981), previously occupied by the Bethesda chapel (built, 1780s; deconsecrated 1908), and 'there was no attempt to disguise the fact';[77] arch: Bachelor and Hicks (*DIA*); p: William H. Shanly (with m: F.W. Sullivan); J.J. Farrell (*c*.1928 when known as *Picture Palace Theatre*, listed as br in *1947 directory* at which time 1,200 seats); in 1958, reconstructed as a modern cinema, arch: H.R. Lynch; 1,200;[78] in 1967, *Plaza Cinerama* conversion by Cinerama International Releasing Organization (*Showcase* 1968), plus incorporation of neighbouring building, with 754 seats at a renovation cost of £75,000; m: Mr T. Rooney, house m: Mr T. O'Leary (*Showcase* 1968) fb: Peter Farrell (*1947 directory*); T. Rooney (1975). It housed the *National Wax Museum* from 1983 to 2005, before its conversion to a hotel in 2008.[79]

Dublin Cinematograph Theatre, 51 Lower O'Connell Street. See *The Picture House*.

Dublin Cinerama Theatre, 42–6 Talbot Street (15 April 1963–10 March 1972; formerly, that is prior to its conversion to take the Cinerama 70mm format, it was known as *Electric*; *Dublin Electric Theatre*; *New Electric*; later *New Capitol*). The name had to be changed to *Superama* following the decision by the Cinerama Corporation to open in 1967 its own Dublin cinema, the *Plaza Cinerama*; p: Theatrerame Ltd; gm: Mr B. O'Reilly, hse m: Mr K. Nolan (*Showcase* 1968).

Dublin Electric Theatre, 42–6 Talbot Street. See *Electric Theatre*.

Dublin Picture Palace, 50 Thomas Street. See *People's Picture House*.

Electric Theatre, 42–6 Talbot Street (19 May 1911–1938; as *New Electric*, 14 April 1938–1963; *Dublin Cinerama/Superama Theatre*, 15 April 1963–10 March 1972; *New Capitol*, 11 March 1972–29 August 1974), p: Dublin Electric Theatres Ltd (incorporated, 26 January 1911; main shareholder/d: J.J. Farrell); 379; 450;[80] conversion from Farrell's tobacconist/stationary business, and boot and shoe warehouse, near Amiens Street railway station;[81] arch: George Moore; m: Frederick J. Orr (1911–16); P.K. Murtagh; balcony, 107 seats, installed, 1912:[82]450;[83]400 (*KYB*, 1919); 700 (*KYB*, 1920); demolished in 1938 after fire to make way for *New Electric*, p: Irish Kinematograph Co. (1920), Ltd (listed in *1947 directory*) /J.J. Farrell, fb: Peter Farrell (*1947 directory*); 1,700; in 1963, the *New Electric* was converted to Dublin's first *Cinerama* venue; p: Capitol & Allied Theatres Ltd. After being reopened temporarily as the *New Capitol*, it closed down permanently in 1974, after which it became a music venue and later a carpet showroom.[84]

Embassy Cinema, 42 Pearse Street. (9 April 1956–May 1965; formerly *Antient Concert Rooms*, 1844–1920; *Palace Cinema*, 13 May 1920–3 December 1950; *Forum*, 4 December 1950–7 April 1956; later, *Academy*, 13 March 1965–January 1977, and from August 1977– 19 November 1981), opened after undergoing extensive rebuilding and interior decoration, including installation of CinemaScope screen and sound; p: Capitol & Allied Theatres Ltd. The front of the building was rebuilt, a row of modern shops flanked by plate glass doors gave ingress to a spacious entrance foyer decorated and illuminated with diffused fluorescent lighting. A broad tiled passageway gave direct entrance to the stalls where the seating was planned to give every patron an uninterrupted view of the screen. The seats were of the armchair type, upholstered in crimson and pink fabric. A frame enclosed the wide screen, over which were crimson curtain drapes. From the foyer a wide stairway was constructed with a metal balustrade leading to a wide balcony, the front of which carried the original ornamentation. The general colour scheme was carried out in shades of pink, peach, Tuscan red, with cream introduced into the ceilings and floors. Lighting was of the gradual dim type, and the heating could be so adjusted as to give an even temperature in all weathers.[85] See also *Antient Concert Rooms*; *Palace Cinema*; *Academy Cinema*.

Empire Palace Theatre, Dame Street. See *Star of Erin Music Hall Theatre of Varieties*.

Father Mathew Hall, Church Street, occasional film shows, at least from October 1909, by Irish Animated Picture Co.[86]

Film Centre, O'Connell Bridge House, Burgh Quay/D'Olier Street (14 October 1966–23 November 1973; after refurbishment, 22 December 1973–2 February 1984), p: Michael Butler, who took over *Cameo Cinema Café* in 1952, and opened *Cameo*, Middle Abbey Street, in 1976; cinema space now occupied by bar.

Fine Arts Film Club, Eblana Theatre, Busarus (*c.* December 1962–21 April 1969), 150/230; originally opened as a theatre on 22 September 1959, in 1962, when the theatre was not in use, a Sunday night 'art' cinema was opened by Michael Collins who went on to open a full-time cinema with a similar policy, *International Film Theatre*.

Foresters' Hall, 41 Rutland (now Parnell) Square West. See *Irish National Foresters Hall Cinema*.

Forum, 42 Pearse Street. See *Palace Cinema*.

Fountain Picture Palace, 36–7 James's Street, opposite ornamental fountain monument, (26 February 1923– March 1941; as *Lyric Cinema*, 28 September 1941–23 June 1962; aka *Fountain Cinema*; *Fountain Picture House*), built on the derelict site of the former Phoenix brewery; cinema measured 80ft long x 37ft wide x 38ft high; 1,200; p: Irish National Picture Palaces Ltd, a subsidiary of Midland and Northern Industries Ltd, involving, among others, chairman William H. Flanagan who owned the *Electric Theatre*, Skerries, and other businesses; arch: Patrick J. Munden, who designed the *Sandford*, and was the company's managing director; m: Clifford Marston, who had transferred from the *Brunswick Cinema*; during the civil war, on 19 March 1923, a bomb exploded at the entrance, though no serious damage was done to the building; in April 1939 the company was wound up and the cinema sold for £14,500 to Associated Picture Houses, who renamed it the *Lyric Cinema* after being closed for renovations for 7 months in 1941. In the 1940s, it was bought by Mr D.M. McAllister, Shankill, Co Dublin, who ran it until it closed on 23 June 1962; m: Kevin Cunningham; fb: Dan McAllister, 550 (*1947 directory*). The building, in use for many years as a warehouse, was demolished in 2002 and 92 apartments were built on the site by Oaklee Housing Trust.[87]

Gaiety Theatre, South King Street (27 November 1871–), a prestigious patent theatre for drama and opera. From 21–4 October 1914 it screened the film of the South Pole expedition of Captain Scott for which it received a licence from Dublin corporation; in September 1916 it was the venue for the Irish premiere of D.W. Griffith's *The Birth of the Nation*; and from 11–30 March 1918, Griffith's *Intolerance*, with the usual theatre prices.

George's Hall, 63 South Great George's Street (*c.*1914–*c.*1920), p: Dublin Central Mission; in 1914 it was granted a licence to screen film on Saturdays; 70. Unique among Dublin venues, though common in Belfast, *George's Hall*, a Protestant venue, screened films (*Tom Brown's Schooldays; Miss Cinderella*; and *Romantic Betty*) on Christmas night, 1920.[88]

Grafton News and Cartoon Cinema, 72 Grafton Street. See *Grafton Picture House*.

The Grafton Picture House, 72 Grafton Street (17 April 1911–June 1913; after renovations, 5 February 1914–25 September 1932; following renovations, 14 October 1932–1959; aka *Grafton Street Picture House*; as *Grafton News and Cartoon Cinema* from 18 September 1959–1968; following refurbishment reverted to feature films, 3 May 1968–1 December 1973), arch: Richard Francis Caulfield Orpen (older brother of painter William); alterations and additions: Robinson & O'Keefe (1929, 1932) (*DIA*); p (1911–): Provincial Cinematograph Theatres Ltd; m (1911): H. Huish; 'the pretty tea room has become one of the gathering places of Dublin's fashionable *coterie*. It is difficult to get in of the evening.'[89] Closed 1913–14 for extensive renovations; m: Mr R.G. Bell (1914); M.N. Richardson (1919, *KYB*, 1920); Charlie M. Jones (1875–1961, for thirty years, listed in *1947 directory*); James McCarthy (from 1968); Jim Thorpe (1973). From 1930s owned by Ellis family (br: Jack Ellis, *1947 directory*); Maurice Baum ran cinema in late 1950s before it was acquired by the specialist cinema newsreel company, Capitol and Provincial Theatres, which renovated the cinema and reopened it as the *Grafton News and Cartoon Cinema* (name of company in *Showcase* 1968: the Classic Cinemas Ltd, 100 Baker Street, London W.1) In May 1968 the *Grafton* reverted to showing feature films, and in November 1972 it was sold to Irish Amalgamated Cinemas, a company owned by Geoffrey Elliman and Bertie McNally, but it closed on 1 December 1973;[90] became site of Principles' clothing store.

Grand Central Cinema, 6–7 Lower O'Connell Street (10 October 1921–13 September 1946; aka *Grand Picture House*; *DBC Picture House*), built on the site of the former Dublin Bread Company which was destroyed during the 1916 Rising. The neo-classical fronted building with an imposing glass canopy was designed by three teams of architects: O'Callaghan and Webb; Higginbottom and Stafford; and Vincent Kelly. Its steep raked balcony led some patrons to complain of vertigo;[91] p: Irish Kinematograph Co./J.J. Farrell; damaged by fire in 1930;[92] 620;[93] 550 (*KYB*, 1918–20); expanded to 708 seats during reconstruction;[94] destroyed by fire on 13 September 1946 (there had been an earlier fire in December 1933); in 1949 the site was sold to Hibernian Bank, and the building continues to be used as a bank. See also *Grand Cinema*, 8 Lower O'Connell Street.

Grand Cinema, 8 Lower O'Connell Street (26 October 1913–17 April 1916), part of Grand Hotel and restaurant building, arch: W. Higginsbottom; p: William Kay; 250; destroyed during the 1916 Rising; rebuilt on adjoining site of the Dublin Bread Company, 6–7 O'Connell Street, which was also destroyed during the Rising. See also *Grand Central Cinema*.

Grand Picture House, 5–7 Lower O'Connell Street. See *Grand Central Cinema*.

Green Cinema, 127 St Stephen's Green West. See *Stephen's Green Cinema*.

Hale's Tours, South Anne Street (1905–*c.*1908), p: Will C. Pepper; projectionist: Arthur Bursey; narr: Mike Nono; railway carriage type venue for showing *Hale's tours of the world* travelogues. Bursey later became a projectionist in the *Sackville Picture House*.[95]

Hibernian Electric Theatre, 113 Capel Street. See *Irish Cinema Theatre*.

IMAX Theatre, Parnell Centre, Parnell Street (5 June 1998–15 October 2000); 18m high screen; 370; developed by Sheridan Group, after closing was redeveloped and incorporated into adjoining *Virgin Cinemas Multiplex*.

International Film Theatre, Earlsfort Terrace (17 June 1966–October 1976; later, location of *Irish Film Theatre*), l (1966–77): Michael Butler; *c.*160.

Irish Cinema, 113 Capel Street. See *Irish Cinema Theatre*.

Irish Cinema Theatre, 113 Capel Street, next door to trades' hall (1911–19; aka *Irish Cinema* [*KYB*, 1916]; *Hibernian Electric Theatre* [*KYB*, 1917]), approved a licence in 1911, renewal was refused in 1912 until structural alterations were carried out (by arch: Orpen & Dickinson, *DIA*); p: Richard (Dickie) H. Graham; T. Mahoney, 350 (*KYB*, 1917); 'This little hall is very cosy and comfortable, and commands a goodly share of patronage.'[96] In 1913, cinema was fined £5 for showing films without a licence and was later fined £20 for disobedience of a court order. It was the only Dublin cinema premises in 1914 from where a licence was withheld due to the poor standard of the electrical fittings. It was granted a licence in 1915 subject to alterations being carried out. Also known as *Hibernian Electric Theatre* and it seems to have operated under both names until it closed in 1919, after which the premises became Milroy Brothers, confectioners; next door to *Torch Theatre*, which operated intermittently as a cine-variety venue during 1935–41.

• *Irish Film Institute*, 6 Eustace Street, Temple Bar (September 1992–), arch: O'Donnell & Twomey; p: Irish Film Institute; originally 2 screens/364 (258 and 106) seats; from January 2010, third screen with 58 seats added; building also houses Irish film archive; library; bookshop, bar and restaurant.

Irish Film Theatre, Earlsfort Terrace (8 March 1977–31 May 1984; former premises of *International Film Theatre*, l: Arts Council through subsidiary Irish Film Theatre Ltd; m Ronnie Saunders (1977–83); Irish Film Institute (1983–4); after many years being derelict, became popular music venue and nightclub with film screenings called *Sugar Club*, taking its name from original owners, Irish Sugar Co.; reducing original *c.*160 seats to 128.

Irish Kinematograph, 12–13 Mary Street. See *Mary Street Picture House*.

Irish National Foresters[97] *Hall Cinema*, 41 Rutland (now Parnell) Square West (1912–*c.*1919; aka *Irish National Foresters' Branch Hall Cinema*), 432 seats. Controversy surrounded its application for change of use to a cinema due to its proximity to St Kevin's House, a residence for Catholic girls, at no. 42, and St Mary's parish rectory at no. 39. There was also a Catholic nurses home at no. 34.

Irish National Picture Palace, 52 Upper O'Connell Street. See *Carlton Cinema*.

La Scala Theatre and Opera House, 4–8 Princes Street North (10 August 1920–31 July 1927; as *Capitol* from 1 August 1927–*c.*9 March 1972); p: Frank W. Chambers, who also had an interest in the *Carlton*; George Peter Fleming; built on site of the *Freeman's Journal* which was destroyed during 1916 Rising; arch: Thomas F. McNamara; included a ballroom, café, function rooms, lounges; circular marble foyer decorated in red and gold; 3,200;[98] 1,900 in stalls, double-cantilevered balconies, and 32 private boxes; 1,400;[99] m: T. Arthur Shields (Snr); mus. d: W.T. Mortimer; p (from 1926): J.J. Farrell/Capitol & Allied Cinemas Ltd.; l: Famous Lasky Film Services Ltd/Paramount Film Services Ltd (1 August 1927–1934); gm: Thomas ('Tony') C. Reddin; mus. d: Alex B. Fryer; br: B. Markey, fb: Peter Farrell, 2,000 (*1947 directory*); m: Mr K. Lehane (*Showcase* 1968); while it seems Paramount may have surrendered the lease on the *Capitol* in 1934, the cinema retained into the 1940s the slogan, 'The Home of Paramount Pictures'; the first sound feature to be shown in Ireland, *The Singing Fool*, opened there on 22 April 1929; in 1934, cine-variety policy changed to cinema only, changing again in 1943 to cine-variety, with variety ending on 29 October 1953; mus. d. (1943–): Frank Doherty; sold in 1972 for £300,000; demolished to make way for British Home Stores, BHS, later Penneys.[1] From 10 March 1972, the name *Capitol* continued as *New Capitol* in former *New Electric/Cinerama*, Talbot Street.

Light House Cinema, Middle Abbey Street (11 November 1988–27 September 1996; formerly, *Curzon*), p: Irish Film Institute and Neil Connolly; after opening of *Irish Film Institute* cinemas, 6 Eustace

Street, Connolly and Maretta Dillon ran cinema until it closed; 280 and 80 seats. Along with the adjoining *Adelphi*, it was incorporated into the redevelopment and expansion of Arnotts department store.

Light House Cinema, Smithfield (9 May 2008– 15 April 2011; aka *Lighthouse*), p: Light House Cinema Exhibition & Cinema Distribution Co. Ltd (CRO no. 103210); d: Neil Connolly, Maretta Dillon, David Collins, David Kavanagh, arch: Derek Tynan, DTA Architects; m: Neil Connolly, Maretta Dillon, 4 screens/614 (277, 153, 116, 68) seats (excluding 2 permanent wheelchair spaces in each room). The cinema was closed down when the High Court wound up the operating company because it had rent arrears of €156,856 and declared its inability to pay rent on the premises in 2011 of €200,000, twice the amount due during its first years in operation.[2]

Irish National Picture Palace. See *Carlton Cinema.*

Lyceum Picture Theatre, 45 Mary Street, Dublin 1. See *Volta Electric Theatre.*

Lyric Cinema, 36–7 James's Street. See *Fountain Picture Palace.*

Lyric Picture House, 36–7 James's Street. See *Fountain Picture Palace.*

Manor Street Picture House, 60–1 Manor Street, Stoneybatter (1914–19; as *Manor Cinema* from 10 May 1920– March 1929; as *Palladium Cinema* from 1 September 1929–1934; as *Broadway*, 1934– 11 August 1956); p: Associated Picture Houses (1944) Ltd (*1947 directory*); custom-built on derelict site, it was granted a licence in 1915, though it operated as a cinema from 1914; it was rebuilt in 1920 with 630 seats; 650 (*1947 directory*); and refurbished in 1929, occasional variety shows; fb: Louis Elliman, Savoy Cinema, Dublin (*1947 directory*); premises became a cooperage and is now home to Stoneybatter community training workshop/Fás.[3]

Mary Street Picture House, 12–13 Mary Street, intersection of Mary and Stafford (now Wolfe Tone) streets (19 December 1912–9/11 January 1959; aka *Irish Kinematograph*; *Mary Street Cinema*; *Picture Theatre*),[4] former premises of Beakey's cabinet-making factory, arch: George Luke O'Connor; p: Irish Kinematograph Co. (1920) Ltd, 6/7 Lr O'Connell Street/J.J. Farrell; m: Isaac Eppel;[5] m: Patrick Farrell (br in *1947 directory*); fb: Peter Farrell (*1947 directory*); 600; 800; a gallery with 122 seats was added in 1916, making total of 922; expanded again in 1931, 1,119 (still at this figure in *1947 directory*); it had panelled recessed walls, decorative arches and a curved ceiling, with cinema proper 105ft x 30ft;[6] site now an office block occupied by AXA insurance company.

Masterpiece Picture Theatre, 99 Talbot Street (27 July 1914–April 1916; rebuilt, 1916–54; aka *Masterpiece Cinema*; *Masterpiece Picture Palace*; *Masterpiece Theatre*), arch: George Luke O'Connor; p: Charles A. McEvoy (*KYB*, 1916–17);[7] Edward (Ed) Kay (1942, listed as br in *1947 directory*); 420; damaged during 1916 Rising; entrance damaged by bomb on 20 November 1925 when *Ypres* was being shown;[8] auction of fittings on 27 January 1954; building bought by Mr J.G. Costello, p. of drapery firm, O'Reilly & Co., North Earl Street; foyer turned into a drapery store and the main part of the building into a wholesale warehouse;[9] later used as a rehearsal space by Abbey Theatre and Team Theatre Company; now Carroll's gift shop.

Metropole Cinema, 35–9 Lower O'Connell Street (11 February 1922[10]–11 March 1972), built on the derelict site of the former Metropole Hotel (at no. 37 since 1834 when it was called Spadaccini's and later the Prince of Wales) which was destroyed during the 1916 Rising; arch: Audrey Vincent O'Rourke; p: Maurice Elliman/Irish Cinemas Ltd/Metropole and Allied Cinemas, Ltd; Odeon (Ireland) Ltd (1946–72); m: Abe Elliman; Mr M. Meehan (1967; *Showcase* 1968, which also lists ass m as Mr R. Smullen); br: F. Dowling, fb: Louis Elliman, screen: 17ft x 12ft (*1947 directory*); 883 (some reports suggest over 1,000 [1,000 in *1947 directory*]) seats on the ground floor; a restaurant on the first floor; and a dance hall on the upper floor; the domed ceiling of the cinema was decorated with scenes from William Shakespeare's plays;[11] sold to British Home Stores, which demolished the building, along with the adjoining *Capitol Cinema*, to make way for a store which is now occupied by Penneys; the name was continued at the *New Metropole*, which opened on 16 March 1972 at Townsend Street on part of the former *Theatre Royal* site.

The Mountjoy Variety and Picture Palace, Rutland [now Parnell] Place, Summerhill (17 May 1912–July 1912; aka *The Mountjoy Animated Picture and Variety Palace*), p: Dublin Sporting and Picture Club Ltd; m: Mr Fisher; having announced that the venue would reopen on 5 August 1912 after renovations and extensions, the *Mountjoy* may not have reopened, though it is listed in *KYB*, 1916.[12]

New Capitol, 46 Talbot Street. See *Electric Theatre.*

New Carlton Cinema Theatre, 52 Upper O'Connell Street. See *Carlton Cinema Theatre.*

New Carlton Picture House, 52–4 Upper O'Connell Street. See *Carlton Picture House.*

New Electric, 42–6 Talbot Street. See *Electric Theatre.*

New Metropole, 2 Townsend Street/16–19 Hawkins Street (16 March 1972–; 3 screens from December 1980; aka *Screen at College Street*; *Screen*), built by Rank Organisation on part of the site of the demolished *Theatre Royal*; arch: Thomas Bennett; H.J. Lyons & Partners; p: Odeon (Ireland) Ltd,[13] with Trevor Berry as manager; Ward Anderson (from 1983), who changed name to *Screen at College Street*; 783; 876; 878 seats; 3-screen/721 (256, 222 and 243) seats. In 2009 in time for celebrating its twenty-five years as the *Screen*, it was upgraded to digital.

New Regal Cinema, Hawkins Street. See *Regal Rooms Cinema*.

Odeon Cinema, Eden Quay. See *Corinthian Cinema*.

Olympia Theatre, Dame Street. See *Star of Erin Music Hall Theatre of Varieties*.

The Palace, 6 Townsend Street, Dublin 2. See *Cinema Palace*.

Palace Cinema, 42 Pearse Street, Dublin 2 (13 May 1920–3 December 1950; aka *Antient Concert Rooms*, 1844–1920; *Forum*, 4 December 1950–7 April 1956; *Embassy*, 9 April 1956–May 1964); *Academy*, 13 March 1965–19 November 1981), opened as a full-time cinema by Dr Isaac Eppel (1891–1942), a chemist who produced the first feature film about the Irish War of Independence, *Irish Destiny* (1926), emigrating to England shortly afterwards. His brother, Simon Eppel, ran the cinema thereafter; 600 (1920). See also *Antient Concert Rooms, Forum, Embassy, Academy*.

Palace Theatre, 6 Townsend Street. See *Cinema Palace*.

People's Picture House, 50 Thomas Street (11 May 1912–1920s; aka *People's Picture Palace*; *The Picture Palace*; *Dublin Picture Palace*), arch: T.J. Cullen; p: Dublin Picture Palace Co. Ltd/Butler family, musical instrument makers and retailers, and who leased the *Cinema Royal*, Townsend Street; 500 (1913); m: W. Butler; it operated initially as a six-day cinema with closure also during church services; due to absence of a telephone on the premises, a condition of Dublin corporation's licence, it was refused licences in 1916 and 1918 but is listed in *KYB*, 1917. Its location opposite a fire station was presented in mitigation; cinema premises now occupied by Centra retail store.[14]

People's Popular Picture Palace, Brunswick Street. See *Queen's Theatre*.

Phoenix Picture Palace, 7–9 Ellis Quay (3 December 1912–early 1913; after renovations, 3 March 1913–26 January 1957); p: Phoenix Picture Palace Co. (with d: H. Grundy; David Frame, 8 Granby Row, Dublin; A.T. Wright, Belfast; K. Mackay, Dundalk); Rudolph Aherne (early 1920s until his death in 1945); Capitol and Allied Theatres Ltd (1945–57); m: Cathal MacGarvey (1912–); J. Aherne (*KYB*, 1919–20); George H. Clitheroe; M.J. Tighe (*1947 directory*); fb: Peter Farrell (*1947 directory*); 730/750/850(*1947 directory*)/950 seats; after renovations, reopened with 1,200 seats on 3 March 1913, with *Quo Vadis?* showing from 7 April 1913.[15] In 2002 the building was saved from demolition. Although not a listed building, an inspector from An Bord Pleanála found that the building was 'worthy of retention and restoration having regard to the historical significance of its survival.' In 2000, the council had requested the developers to deposit at the Irish Architectural Archive a detailed record of the cinema, including a full-scale survey of its structural elements and interior and a full photographic record;[16] premises now occupied by Kings and Queens furniture store.

The Picture House, 51 Lower O'Connell Street (9 April 1910–1917; aka *Dublin Cinematograph Theatre*; *Provincial Cinematograph House*; *Sackville Picture House*, 1917–37; *Astor*, 27 March 1937–c.21 December 1946); p: Provincial Cinematograph Theatres Ltd; m: W.H. Huish; 233; 270; opened by Dublin city's Medical Officer of Health Sir Charles Cameron. It had a decorative ceiling, panelled red and white walls, carpeted floor, and green velvet seats. Afternoon tea was included in the admission price of 6*d*. to 1*s*. In 1917, the cinema was acquired by Robert Morrison who renamed it the *Sackville Picture House*; p: The Sackville Picture House Co. (1917–37, listed *KYB*, 1918–20); Capitol and Allied Theatres (1937–46, name changed to the *Astor*); m: Bertie McNally (early 1940s to 23 December 1946); now houses a McDonald's fast food restaurant. In 1953, McNally opened the *Astor*, Eden Quay.

The Picture House, 72 Grafton Street. See *Grafton Picture House*.

The Picture Palace, 50 Thomas Street. See *People's Picture House*.

Picture Palace, 6 Townsend Street. See *Cinema Palace*.

Picture Palace Theatre, 24 Henry Street. See *The Coliseum*.

Picturedrome, 3½ Harcourt Road, between Charlotte Street and Harcourt Road (October 1912–1922; aka *Abercorn Hall*), p: Entertainment Halls Co. Ltd. In same premises as the gospel hall, the *Abercorn Hall* (1884), had been built in the back yard of a shop, and was used occasionally for film screenings in early years of cinema. In 1911, it was fined for using cinematograph machines without spool boxes. The entrance was via a long passage beside O'Hara's shop, which had the *Picturedrome* sign above shop front. Sparsely furnished with bare floorboards and backless wooden forms for seats, it had a cheap admissions policy aimed at the working classes and poorer children. In 1917, the licence was transferred from A.T. White to Percy Daviez (Percy F. Davis listed in *KYB*, 1918); first m: James J. (Jimmie) Worth, who moved to *Princess*, Rathmines, in 1913; pianist: Nan Kerin. After closing in 1922, it became the premises of the Harcourt Social Club, and later was a billiard and bingo hall. In 1980s, the building was demolished to make way for Harcourt Centre offices.[17]

Pillar Picture House, 62 Upper O'Connell Street (2 December 1914–3 April 1938; reopened after renovations, 16 April 1938–25 March 1945), arch: Aubrey Vincent O'Rourke; p: The Irish Kinematograph Co./ John J. Farrell; opened as *Pillar Picture Theatre* with 372 (288 in stalls; 84 in gallery) seats;[18] by 1915, 400;[19] survived the 1916 Rising, but damaged on 17 March 1923 during civil war; for many years after closing was occupied by the Pillar Ice Cream Parlour; now houses a McDonald's fast food restaurant.

Plaza Cinema, 22–3 Upper Dorset Street. See *Dorset Picture House.*

Plaza Cinerama, 22–3 Upper Dorset Street. See *Dorset Picture House.*

Plaza Picture Hall, 22–3 Upper Dorset Street. See *Dorset Picture House.*

Plaza Picture Palace, 22–3 Upper Dorset Street. See *Dorset Picture House.*

Pravda Cinema, 35 Lower Liffey Street (closed summer 2010), part of a super-bar, entertainment venue, decorated with communist (Russian) murals on the walls, film club screenings; Pravda pub and Winding Stair restaurant bought from receiver for *c.*€1.3 million by Brian Montague who planned to relaunch it as a music venue;[20] in October 2010, the new more live entertainment based venue opened as The Grand Social, Bar and Venue, though a film club remains.

Premier Picture Palace, 50 Thomas Street. See *People's Picture House.*

Project Cinema Club, East Essex Street (1976–8), p: Project Arts Centre; fb: Kevin Rockett; Dublin's first cinema club operated as alternative 16mm venue with contextualized film seasons, including 'Brecht and the cinema', 'Feminism and cinema', and 'Film and Ireland'; 80 seats.

Provincial Cinematograph House, 51 Lower O'Connell Street. See *The Picture House.*

Pullman Studio, 29–35 Tirconnell Road. See *Inchicore Cinema.*

Queen's Theatre, Great Brunswick Street (now Pearse Street), (as 'cinema', 2 March 1908–1909; formerly, *Adelphi Theatre*, 1829–44; aka *People's Popular Picture Palace*), as a cine-variety theatre, its proprietor, H.C. Pearce, was granted a cinema licence in 1914; in 1930s and 1940s, films confined to Sunday nights; 22ft proscenium, 1,200 (*1947 directory*, at which time p listed as Dublin Kinematograph Theatres Ltd, with Louis Elliman as fb); following fire at Abbey Theatre in 1951, Abbey relocated to *Queen's* until 1966, during which time the Sunday film shows were discontinued; *Queen's* later demolished, office block now on site.

Regal Rooms Cinema, Hawkins Street (16 April 1938–1955; as *New Regal Cinema*, 18 August 1955– June 1962), part of the *Theatre Royal* complex, the Regal Rooms restaurant (23 September 1935) was built on the site of the former Winter Gardens; arch: Leslie Norton, London, with Scott & Good, Dublin. When the restaurant did not prove to be a financial success, converted to the *Regal Rooms Cinema* which opened on 16 April 1938; architects who oversaw conversion of restaurant to 750-seat cinema: Guy, Moloney and associates; dissatisfied with the earlier conversion, Rank employed architects O'Connor & Aylward to oversee the total reconstruction of the interior as the 929-seat *New Regal Cinema*, which opened on 18 August 1955, with both side balconies removed, resulting in better eye lines to screen. Cinema lengthened and broadened to provide extra accommodation and CinemaScope and VistaVision installed;[21] fb: Louis Elliman (*1947 directory*).

Regent Cinema, Findlater Place/Cathal Brugha Street (19 May 1967–3 March 1985), p: Cameo Cinema Ltd/ Michael Butler; Ward Anderson; cost: £60,000; 457; after being derelict for number of years, converted to nightclub, Back Lane, in 1996; later demolished and site redeveloped as Academy hotel.[22]

Round Room, Rotunda,[23] Cavendish Row/165 Parnell Street (1897–, increasingly regular film seasons, until full-time cinema *c.*1910; reopened 3 May 1920 after redecoration, improved seating; closed 31 October 1953; name changed to *Ambassador*, 23 September 1954–13 January 1977; reopened 29 April 1977–16 October 1988; reopened, 22 July 1994–29 September 1999; aka *Rotunda Picture House*), opened in 1767 primarily as a music venue to raise funds for the Lying-in Hospital (Rotunda); designed by John Ensor; one of the first locations used for film screenings; operated as an occasional and then full-time cinema by James T. Jameson's Irish Animated Picture Co. from early 1900s to 1916; p: William Kay (and his executors after his death), (October 1916–1940s, former proprietor of the *Grand Cinema*, 8 Lower O'Connell Street);[24] Capitol and Allied Theatres Ltd (by *c.*1946/47– 13 January 1977 with br as Peter Farrell [company's md, *1947 directory*] and with m as Mr W. Bergin, PC [*Showcase* 1968]); Green Group/Ward Anderson (April 1977–13 October 1988);[25] 736, including wooden benches (during Kay's time);[26] though Keenan (2005:16) states it was redesigned in early 1950s by architect William O'Dwyer, when a 500-seat balcony and private boxes were added, increasing the total seats to 1,222, the *1947 directory* gives the seating capacity as 1,200; uses after closing as cinema have included as music and exhibition (*Bodies*; *CSI interactive*, 2008–9) venue; plans to relocate ILAC shopping centre public library to building were announced in 2007.[27]

Sackville Picture House, 51 Lower O'Connell Street. See *The Picture House.*

• *Savoy Cinema*, 19 Upper O'Connell Street (29 November 1929–April 1969; as 2 screens, 19 November 1969–1975; 3 screens, 1975–9; 5 screens from 5 July 1979–1996; 6 screens/1,984 seats from 19 July 1996–), Ireland's premier first-run cinema was built on the site of the former Crown and Granville hotels, which were destroyed during the civil war; arch: Frederick Charles Mitchell (London) and

William Glen, with marble work by Harrison & Sons (*DIA*); cost: £200,000; Venetian decoration which was designed and executed by Mr W.E. Greenwood; p: Associated British Pictures (London);[28] Irish Cinemas Ltd (from 1933) with J.E. Pearce as md; Ellimans' Metropole & Allied Theatres Ltd (1939–46, this company had a controlling interest in Irish Cinemas Ltd); J. Arthur Rank when the company took a majority share in the Ellimans' exhibition interests (1946–83); m: Dan Tracy (1946–67);[29] Denis Byrne (from 1967); fb: Louis Elliman (*1947 directory*); the first Dublin cinema with CinemaScope when *The Robe* opened on 23 April 1954; *c.*2,800 (*1947 directory*); 150 employed in cinema and restaurant from 1929 to 1950s; damaged in fire, 1938; in 1969 it was first Dublin cinema to be converted to a twin screen with 1,072 and 780 seats at a cost of £400,000; in 1975 the restaurant was converted to a third screen with 200 seats; in 1979 it was adapted to take five screens; in 1983 the *Savoy* was bought by the Ward Anderson family exhibition interests, and a sixth screen was added in 1996. In 2005, especially its main screen, Savoy 1 with 780 seats, was restored to its 'classical' status at a cost of €2 million.

• *Screen at College Street*, 2 Townsend Street. See *New Metropole*.

Screen at O'Connell Bridge, Burgh Quay. See *Corinthian*.

Shanly's Picture Hall, 22–3 Upper Dorset Street. See *Dorset Picture House*.

Star of Erin Music Hall Theatre of Varieties, Dame Street (22 December 1879–27 February 1897; aka *Star of Erin Theatre of Varieties*; *Dan Lowrey's Music Hall*; *Star Theatre of Varieties*; *Empire Palace Theatre* from 15 November 1897; *Olympia* from 5 February 1923), 1,600 (1892); 1,750 (*1947 directory*); venue for first films to be screened in Ireland, 20 April 1896; thereafter, periodically screened films as part of cine-variety entertainments, while a regular Sunday evening film show became an established part of its programme, a practice that continued until 1969 (listed in *Showcase* 1968).

Stephen's Green Cinema, 127 St Stephen's Green West (18 December 1935–; 2 screens/517 [340 and 177] seats, 14 July 1972–9 November 1987; aka *Green Cinema*; listed in *Showcase* 1968), p: Stephen's Green Cinema Ltd; d: Frank J. McDonnell, BL, PC, md: Sir Thomas Robinson, (chairman); Robert G.H. Russell; William J. Barnett; m: Michael J. Deasy, who moved from *The Cinema*, Carlow; former site of the only Turkish baths in Dublin; front block: 27ft x 113ft deep; restaurant; arch: Jones & Kelly (*DIA*); plain frontage and art deco interior;[30] 1,496 (*c.* 1,000 on ground floor and *c.* 500 in balcony, *1947 directory*) seats; p (mid-1960s–): Green Group/Ward Anderson; building demolished in April 1989; site now occupied by Fitzwilliam hotel.

Strand Cinema, North Strand Road (16 April 1938–16 September 1944; after rebuilding, 16 March 1945–31 January 1970), arch: Henry J. Lyons; p: Strand Cinema Ltd; md (and fb): Leonard Ging (*1947 directory*); gm: Cyril Ging; company also owned *Fairview*, *Drumcondra* and *Sutton* cinemas; 500 (1938); in 1945, having acquired adjoining land, Ging extended the original cinema and the new *Strand* opened 16 March 1945 with 1,100 seats and 35ft proscenium (*1947 directory*). In 1949 Ging sold the *Strand* along with most of his other cinemas to Rank's Irish Cinemas Ltd (*Showcase* 1968); after closing as cinema, bought by Gael Linn, which used it as a bingo hall before it was converted to the Metro Bowling Alley;[31] demolished, except for façade, to make way for apartment block.

Superama Theatre, 42–6 Talbot Street. See *Dublin Cinerama Theatre*.

Theatre De Luxe, 84–6 Lower Camden Street (16 December 1912–March 1920; 4 September 1920–3 June 1934; 19 October 1934–29 June 1974; aka *New Super Theatre De Luxe*), arch: Frederick Hayes; p: Irish Amusements Ltd, registered, 16 October 1911, 30 Great Brunswick Street; d: Maurice Elliman, 28 Lower Camden Street; A. Sim; I.I. Bradlaw, 57 Grafton Street; O.S. Baker;[32] 400 (*KYB*, 1916); 500 (*KYB*, 1918); 1,000 (*KYB*, 1920); financial support was received from Camden Street business neighbours, the O'Rourkes and the Corrigans.[33] A narrow, compact building with an oriel window on the first floor. In 1920, the building was demolished and with the adjoining building, no. 85, an enlarged cinema with 1,200 seats was built at a cost of £30,000. On 19 October 1934, Dublin Kinematograph Theatres Ltd opened the *New Super Theatre De Luxe* with an art deco façade from a design by Alfred E. Jones of Jones & Kelly, 1,241/1,395 (with 16ft x 25ft screen, listed *1947 directory*)/1,500; md: Maurice Elliman; d: George J. Nesbitt (chairman), Peter A. Corrigan, Patrick I. Wall, Frances B. O'Rourke; John Crowley (secretary); in *1947 directory* Joseph Gilligan is named as br while Louis Elliman is listed as fb; p: Odeon (Ireland) Ltd (*Showcase* 1968); in 1975 bought by Gael Linn, along with the *Grand*, Cabra, *Grand*, Whitehall, and the *Strand*, Fairview, as bingo halls.[34] *Theatre De Luxe* became Ricardo's snooker hall, and in late 1990s was converted to De Luxe Hotel.

Theatre Royal, Hawkins Street (23 September 1935–30 June 1962), the original *Theatre Royal* opened on 18 January 1821, but it was destroyed by fire on 9 February 1880; the second *Theatre Royal* (1897–1934) received a cinematograph licence in 1910, p: Paragon Bioscope Co. Ltd. On 23 September 1935, J.E. Pearce's Dublin Theatre Group opened new *Theatre Royal* with 3,850 seats, stage 40ft deep (*1947 directory*), the largest theatre in the country, at a cost of £250,000; arch: Leslie C. Norton, London, in association with Dublin company Scott and Good. It combined an art-deco exterior with a Moorish-style 'atmospheric' interior. In 1939 Maurice Elliman took over the building, and it was sold to J. Arthur Rank as part of their acquisition of the Elliman cinemas and theatres in 1946. The theatre's programming policy consisted of 40 per cent cinema and 60 per cent theatre. Following the closure of the *Theatre Royal* on 30 June 1962 and the subsequent demolition of the building, the *New Metropole* was built on part of the site, the rest occupied by office blocks, Hawkins House and College House.[35]

Tivoli Cinema, 135–8 Francis Street (21 December 1934–c.September 1964; listed in *Showcase* 1968), arch: Vincent Kelly; p: Patrick J. Whelan; Tivoli Cinema Co., 1,700; cost: £8,000;[36] closed following Whelan's death in 1944, but reopened on 21 December 1944; br and fb: Dan McAllister (also of *Leinster Cinema*, Dolphin's Barn) (*1947 directory*); after being derelict for twenty years, redeveloped as a theatre and music venue which opened on a full-time basis in 1988; in 2005 planning permission was granted to demolish the building and allow redevelopment of the site for apartments and retail units, and as a live venue.

Tivoli Theatre, 12–13 Burgh Quay (28 October 1901–28 May 1928; aka *Grand Lyric Hall*, 27 November 1897–1901); 1,500; cine variety; m: Charles Jones; building acquired in 1930 by the Fianna Fáil party to produce their newspaper, the *Irish Press*; offices now occupy the site.[37]

UGC Cinemas, Parnell Centre, Parnell Street. See *Virgin Cinemas Multiplex*.

Virgin Cinemas Multiplex, Parnell Centre, Parnell Street (November 1995–2003; aka *UGC Cinemas*, November 2003–5; *Cineworld*, 2005–), p: MGM, which was bought by Virgin Cinemas; UGC, which bought Virgin; Cine UK, which bought UGC (January 2005); 9 screens/ 2,337 seats;[38] extended to 17 screens/ 3,348 (92 to 404) seats by November 2003 with UGC investing €13 million and incorporating adjoining IMAX theatre, which closed in 2000; café bar and children's party room.[39]

Volta Electric Theatre, 45 Mary Street (20 December 1909–1920; as *Lyceum Picture Theatre*, 10 May 1920–5 October 1947; aka *Volta Picture Theatre*, *Volta Picture House*), formerly a hardware store; p: International Cinematograph Society Volta (1909–July 1910); Provincial Cinematograph Theatres Ltd (from July 1910, with l: Irish Animated Picture Co. [1913]); J.J. Farrell and Bob O'Russ, who bought cinema for £875 (from September 1915, following period closed); Rudolph Ahearne (1945); Capitol and Allied Theatres Ltd (1945–7); br: Mr G.H. Porter, 202 Clontarf Road (*1947 directory*); m: James Joyce (20–30 December 1909); Lorenzo Novak (January–July 1910); W.H. Huish (from July 1910); Richard Bell (1912); fb: Peter Farrell, 320;[40] 420 (*1947 directory*); 600; at present part of the site occupied by Penneys retail store.[41] Long-regarded as Dublin's first full-time cinema because it continued largely uninterrupted as a cinema for forty-eight years; others lay claim to venues such as the *Rotunda*, with its long film seasons from 1902; the *Palace*, 6 Townsend Street (2 April 1909); the *Queen's Theatre* (1908–9), and even *Hale's Tours*, South Anne Street, as the 'first' cinema. Nevertheless the *Volta* was unique as a dedicated full-time commercial cinema: the *Queen's* offered cine-variety; *Hale's* did not offer fiction films; the *Palace* was a charitable/religious venue; and despite its huge importance in developing film exhibition in Dublin, the *Rotunda* was not a full-time cinema until after the *Volta* opened.

World's Fair Waxworks and Varieties, 30 Henry Street (as occasional film venue, May 1896–April 1916; aka *World's Fair*), site of waxworks exhibition (opened, 29 December 1892) and 6½d. store on ground floor and waxworks exhibition and cine variety venue on first floor (there was another waxworks at 6 Henry Street, Samuel's Bazaar, another 6½d. shop, which had an exhibition hall in 1911 with 47 seats); original p: Charles James, an American who was an alderman and high sheriff of Dublin; film screenings, May 1896; the waxworks was destroyed in a fire in April 1902, reopened 20 August 1902; thereafter cine variety venue only with shop continuing on ground floor; redeveloped in 1912 as a cine variety hall;[42] 194 seats; destroyed during 1916 Rising as it stretched back to Princes Street, rear of General Post Office; when the GPO was rebuilt, it incorporated not just the World's Fair, but also the derelict site of the Coliseum theatre (24 Henry Street);[43] premises facing on to Henry Street rebuilt as Sprengel brothers china stores; p: Robert W. Sprengel.

XD Theatre, Dr Quirkey's Good Time Emporium, Upper O'Connell Street, 18 seats (March 2009–) 4D 'ride' cinema.

Dún Laoghaire [formerly Kingstown]

Adelphi Cinema, 40–2 George's Street, (29 November 1947–16 May 1971); p: Adelphi (Dún Laoghaire) Ltd, subsidiary of Associated British Cinemas Ltd; The Plaza Ltd, 13 D'Olier Street, Dublin (*Showcase* 1968); EMI (*c.*1970–1); D. O'Keefe, 101 Middle Abbey Street, Dublin; m: T.J. Lawler (from 1947); V. Ball (*Showcase* 1968); 1,620 seats (*KYB*, 1953–66); 1,446 seats (*KYB*, 1967–71); included café; site developed as offices known as Adelphi Centre.

• *IMC Dún Laoghaire*, Bloomfields shopping centre, Lower Georges Street (November 1999–), p: Ward Anderson; m: Andrew Nelson; 12 screens/ 'over 1,700' (340 to 85) seats;[44] 12 screens/1,833 seats;[45] new small screen added in July 2010: 13 screens/1,947 seats.

Kingston Pavilion Gardens, Marine Road. See *Pavilion Cinema*.

Kingstown Picture House, 9–10 Upper George's Street/Mulgrave Street corner (17 April 1911–1 January 1950; aka *Dún Laoghaire Picture House*; *Picture House*), p: Sackville Picture House Co., Ltd with R. Morrison as manager (*KYB*, 1922–8); Associated Picture Houses (1944) Ltd (*c*.1945–50, *1947 directory*); br: C.D.G. McCrodden, fb: Louis Elliman, (*1947 directory*); originally, 268;[46] 315 (*KYB*, 1920); gallery added in 1920, 400/473; 453 (*c*.1936); 500 (*KYB*, 1937–44, *1947 directory*); 280;[47] screen: 14½ft x 10½ft (*1947 directory*). See also *Tatler*.

Pavilion Cinema, Marine Road (21 June 1903–13 November 1915; 7 July 1917–15 April 1939; 29 June 1940–10 November 1940; 12 April 1941–29 June 1974; aka *Pavilion and Gardens*), municipal theatre designed in style of Mississippi paddle steamer by C.A. Owen, used for cinema, variety, concerts; p: Pavilion (Kingstown) Ltd; Pavilion Gardens (Kingstown) Ltd with Sir Thomas Robertson, JP as chairman and director; Associated Picture Houses Ltd (1940–4); Associated Picture Houses (1944) Ltd (1944–8); Odeon (Ireland) Ltd (1948–74); m: Thomas Mannion (1903–); T.J. Gogan (*KYB*, 1923–8); Mr H. Kinsella (*Showcase* 1968); fb: Louis Elliman (*1947 directory*); 800 (1917); 820 (*KYB*, 1937); 840 (*KYB*, 1918–21); *c*.1,315 (*1947 directory* with screen: 20ft x 25ft; *KYB*, 1948–64); 1,033 (*KYB*, 1965–71); no personnel listed *KYB*, 1929–52; licensed for music and dancing (*KYB*, 1920); initially, small room used for film screenings; destroyed by fire in November 1915 and in 1940; after its closure in 1974, Dún Laoghaire Rathdown county council bought the building and ran it as a theatre until 1984; after fifteen years in disuse, the building was demolished in late 1990s to make way for apartment complex and new *Pavilion Theatre*, which opened on 7 December 2000.[48]

Tatler, George's Street/Mulgrave Street corner (26 January 1950–26 May 1950), Ireland's first news cinema in former premises of *Kingstown Picture House*, which closed on 1 January 1950; 280.[49]

Town Hall (1901–2; McCole, 2005:appendix D).

Dundrum

Apollo, Rosemount, Dundrum Road (21 April 1961–*c*. 26 February 1967; site formerly occupied by *Odeon*, 1 August 1944–1 June 1959), p: Kilmainham Cinema Co. See also *Sundrive Cinema*.

• *Movies @ Dundrum*, Dundrum shopping centre (30 September 2005–), p: Spurling and O'Gorman families; arch (structure): Burke Kennedy Doyle; (interior): McNally group; 12 screens/2,200 (96 to 440) seats; digital, 3D and 35mm projection.

Odeon, Rosemount, Dundrum Road (1 August 1944–1 June 1959); arch: Henry J. Lyons (*DIA*); p: Robert Graves Kirkham; br: H. Riley, fb: Gerry Kirkham (35 Upper Abbey Street, Dublin) & Joe Riley (Belmont Avenue, Donnybrook), screen: 18ft, 750 seats (*1947 directory*); *Apollo* built on site.

Fairview

Fairview Grand Cinema, 18 Fairview Avenue/Strand Road (18 November 1929–29 June 1974; aka *Grand Cinema*) p: Leonard Ging and partners Patrick Whelan and Joseph Lyons, it was the first of five suburban cinemas built by Ging (arch: Henry Lyons); 1,469. In 1933, the original single storey building was rebuilt, including the addition of a balcony, and a reorientation of the cinema with new entrance from Strand Road; further rebuilding in 1940s; 36ft proscenium, 1,400 seats, fb: Leonard E. Ging (*1947 directory*); p: Rank-owned Irish Cinemas Ltd, Hawkins House (from 1949, listed in *Showcase* 1968); m: George H. Kerns (or Kerins), ass m: Mr N. Fagan (*Showcase* 1968); auditorium split into two screens; since 1999 one of the screens has been used by Walt Disney's film distribution company Buena Vista International (Ireland) as a preview theatre; the other part of the building was knocked down in April 2005 to make way for an apartment block on Lower Fairview Avenue.

Finglas

Casino, Glasnevin Avenue, North Road (25 November 1955–28 September 1970), p: Finglas Cinema Ltd (subsidiary, St Stephen's Green Cinema Co., owners of the *Green Cinema*); Ward Anderson; arch: John E. Collins; opening ceremony performed by Revd R.J. Glennon, PP; 1,910 seats (1,418 in stalls; 492 in balcony); bought in September 1970 by Fergal Quinn of Superquinn who incorporated the cinema into existing supermarket by October 1971.[50]

Plaza, Janelle Shopping Centre (*c*.July 1993–*c*.February 1994).

Glasthule

Astoria, 29–31 Glasthule Road (5 August 1940–17 September 1957; 14 October 1957–14 June 1964; as *Forum* from 7 December 1971 to 26 August 1981; as twin-screen *Forum* from 16 November 1981 to 2 September 1999), p: Astoria Cinema Co. (incorporated, 18 April 1942; d: James O'Neill, former proprietor of *Astoria*, Serpentine Avenue; Robert Gerard Kirkham; and Vernon Alfred Walker. Walker's shares were later bought by Kirkham, and when Kirkham retired, O'Neill became sole owner of company); m: Des O'Keefe; 701 seats (*KYB*, 1944–61; *1947 directory*). After O'Neill's death on 17 February 1957, the cinema was closed on 17 September, after which it was renovated and reopened on 14 October 1957 by Kirkham's son, Robert Gerald; the new owners of the *Astoria* had a long association with Cinema and General Publicity, which handled screen advertising and NSS trailers.[51] Kirkham programmed many European films, but these were not sufficiently popular to maintain the cinema and it closed in 1964; *KYB*, 1963–6, identifies Kirkham's company as Associated Cinemas Ltd, 3 Suffolk Street, Dublin 2. Disused for four years, it was converted to the Caroline Club, but in 1968 it became a bingo hall. In 1971, exhibitor Barney O'Reilly bought the premises and re-established a cinema, naming it the *Forum* after a venue in which he had worked in Fulham, London. He installed the first automated projection facilities in Ireland, allowing the projection room to be run by one operator. A dispute with trade union ITGWU resulted, with O'Reilly going on hunger strike to assert his right to the new employment practice. In 1976, O'Reilly leased the *Forum* to the O'Gorman family who twinned the cinema in 1981; fb: A. O'Gorman (1976).[52] It was demolished in August 2002 and an office building (which retains the name of the Forum) and a convenience store occupy the site. *Forum*, 29–31 Glasthule Road. See *Astoria Cinema*.

Harold's Cross

Kenilworth Cinema, 314–18 Harold's Cross Road (30 July 1953–21 June 1976; as *Classic*, 4 October 1976–28 August 2003), arch: Peter D. Kavanagh (stadium style with *c.*1,100); p: Sundrive Cinemas Ltd (*Showcase* 1968); m: Thomas P. Gallagher; former m/fb: Albert Kelly leased the cinema from Sundrive and adopted the name the *Classic* when it was reopened on 4 October 1976; Kelly bought the cinema in 1978 and two years later twinned the cinema with 300 and 180 seats; 2 screens/497 seats.[53] From 1980 to its closure 23 years later, the *Classic* was famous for its screening every Friday night of *The Rocky Horror Picture Show*;[54] bought by German supermarket chain LIDL in September 2005, with plans to develop a discount store on the site, and with 18 apartments above the shop.[55] See also *Classic*, Terenure.

Inchicore

Inchicore Cinema, 29–35 Tyrconnell Road (25 November 1921–7 March 1980; as *Europa*, 7 June 1973–*c.*December 1976; as *Pullman Studio*, 19 December 1976–27 March 1980; aka *Inchicore Pullman Cinema*), p: Robert Graves Kirkham, a building contractor who also built and operated cinemas in Dundrum, Newbridge and Tuam; 450; when Kirkham died in 1950, his son, Robert Gerald Kirkham, ran the cinema; following various extensions, it had 776 seats by 1960 (723 in 1947 *directory*); p: Inchicore Cinema Ltd with directors, R.G. Kirkham and Ethel Riley (*Showcase* 1968); Ward Anderson leased the cinema in 1973 to Kevin and Adrian Cunningham, who changed the name to *Europa*; name changed to *Pullman Studio* in 1976 when it had armchair-style seating in the balcony; fb: Gerry Kirkham (35 Upper Abbey Street, Dublin) & Joe Riley (Belmont Avenue, Donnybrook), (1947 *directory*); demolished on 2 March 2005 following a planning application for apartments and a shop. See also *Astoria*, Glasthule.

Killester

Killester Cinema, 61 Collins Avenue East (3 August 1950–19 September 1970), arch: Munden & Purcell; p: Metropolitan Cinemas Ltd, 127 St Stephen's Green, a subsidiary of Stephen's Green Cinema Co. (*Showcase* 1968); m: Brian G. Flanagan, 1,300 seats.[56]

Kimmage

Sundrive Cinema, 24 Sundrive Road (*c.*19 September 1935–*c.*1958; reopened after renovations, 7 February 1959–*c.*12 May 1964 as *Apollo Cinema*; though still listed in *Showcase* 1968), p: Sundrive Cinemas Ltd (incorporated 12 March 1935 with d: Frederick Croskerry; Matthew Heron; William Callow (chairman; M. Heron listed as br and fb in 1947 *directory*); 750/700, 30ft proscenium (1947 *directory*); in 1954 cinema was sold to Leo Henry and George Frederick Kearns, cinema managers, and builder John J. Smith, who formed the Kilmainham Cinema Co.; renamed *Apollo* in 1959, and two other *Apollos*, in Walkinstown (1953), and Dundrum (1961), also owned by the company; public house and apartment block now on site.

Lucan

Premier Cinema (7 February 1945–1976+; *Grove* from 1975; aka *Panorama Cinema*); p: Lucan Cinema Ltd; d: Ronald Rice (1,243 shares; also cinema's fb, listed in 1947 *directory*), Danny O'Leary (350 shares), Vincent McMahon, civil servant, 10 Kenilworth Square, Dublin (1,285 shares); and Mrs Lily McMahon, 1 Grosvenor Place (1,285 shares); p (from 7 September 1953): Leo Ward and Kevin Anderson, 71 Middle Abbey Street, Dublin, the first cinema owned by the Ward Anderson group of companies (listed as Lucan Cinemas Ltd in *Showcase* 1968).
Prior to the erection of the cinema there was a travelling cinema based there run by the Rices. Since the early 1920s Englishman Rice, whose real name was Turner, and his wife Catherine (Kay) had a trav-

elling cinema and variety show; by the 1930s with employee Danny O'Leary they were concentrating on film shows and toured with three tractor-drawn caravans and a long dray that carried the cinema itself, a large collapsible tent; in Lucan, it was erected at the rear of Mary O'Malley's shop on Main Street and adjacent to the side wall of St Andrew's Church, with admission prices of 4*d*. and 8*d*.; when a son, Ronnie, was born in 1937, the family decided to settle in Lucan. When it was claimed that a large black dog was roaming the area as a result of one of Rice's conjuring tricks, angry locals burned down his cinema tent, though a new tent was acquired and the shows continued; later, Rice and others invested in Lucan Cinemas Ltd and bought a plot of land at the east end of the village where a proper cinema was built, even though it remained a cine-variety venue; by the time the company was incorporated, the Rices were managing a family café in Nottingham, England, but nevertheless continued to direct the *Premier* until it was sold in 1953; the Rices also developed the Lucan Printing Works; renovated by Ward Anderson in 1975; an Ulster Bank building and a block of apartments now stand on the site of the *Premier*.[57]

Malahide

Gem, Malahide Coal & Gasworks Yard (1940s, listed in *1947 directory* as *Cinema*, br: Mr J. O'Brien.), 'Pop' O'Brien had a caravan and trailer with a 'fit-up' cinema which he set up as a temporary structure, accommodating 30/40 people, in the coal and gasworks yard; in August 1940, O'Brien was given the first of a series of six-month cinema licences to operate from a large shed on the premises; this continued until 1944–5, but when O'Brien submitted a plan *c*.1946 for a new cinema on the site, the application was turned down by the local authority.[58]

Grand Cinema, Townyard Lane (12 March 1945–*c*.1962; aka *Ma Walshe's Cinema*; *Malahide Cinema*), p: Walshe family, also owners of 'Claddagh' public house and dance hall; m: Mrs ('Ma') Walshe; br: Mrs Neilon Walshe (*1947 directory*); K. Neilon Walsh, White House, Grove Road, listed as owner in *Showcase* 1968; *c*.1962 Albert Reynolds took control of the premises and converted it to the Showboat hotel and dance hall complex, which was destroyed by fire on 13 October 1969; later Mitchell's television sales and video rentals on site.

Mount Merrion

Stella Cinema, 64 Deerpark Road (28 July 1954–31 October 1976), opposition to the building of the cinema was intense from the residents of this middle class area; p: Deerpark Cinema Co. Ltd/James O'Grady, owner of the *Stella*, Rathmines; arch: Robert H. Dowling; 1,000; now occupied by Flanagans furniture store.

Naul, Fingal

The Seamus Ennis Cultural Centre (23 October 2001–), mixed-use venue, occasional film screenings, with access>CINEMA film club.

Phibsborough

Bohemian Picture Theatre, 154–5 Phibsborough Road (8 June 1914–30 March 1974; aka *Bohemiam Picture Palace*), purpose-built cinema on cleared site; arch: George Luke O'Connor; p/m: F.A. Sparling (to *c*. September 1914); Bohemian Picture Theatre Ltd (from 1931; *1947 directory*; *Showcase* 1968);[59] d: W.H. Freeman, J.J. Flood, Mrs M.P. McEntagart (*c*.1915); m: Ernest Matterson (formerly, *Panopticon*, Belfast; from September 1914); W.O. Ashton; P.O'Toole (from 1931, listed as br in *1947 directory*); fire in 1925 damaged the building, which reopened on 19 April 1925;[60] on 24 October 1927 fire destroyed the church organ, which had been installed in the cinema in December 1914;[61] 29ft proscenium, stage: 10ft x 22ft (*1947 directory*); 862 seats (682 seats on ground floor; 180 in gallery); 796 seats (616 in stalls; 180 in balcony, 1931, *1947 directory*); demolished in 1990s.

Phibsborough Picture House, 36 Madras Place (now 376 North Circular Road), adjoining Blacquiere Bridge/Madras Place (May 1914–25 January 1953; aka *Phibsboro' Picture Theatre*; *The Blacquire*); p: William King, Belcamp House, Raheny, a farmer, and John J. Farrell, Henry Hibbert and Thomas Wood, formed the Phibsboro Picture House Company in 1913 to build and operate the cinema from a design by Aubrey Vincent O'Rourke; m: Robert O'Russ (1914); John (Jack) A. King, brother of William King (*KYB*, 1920); fb: Louis Elliman, (*1947 directory*); 387 (1914–15); following reconstruction in 1915, it had 600 seats; 550 (*KYB*, 1918); 540 (*KYB*, 1919); 530 (*KYB*, 1920); 626 (*1947 directory*); 750;[62] in 1916 it was refused a licence due to the lack of a telephone at the cinema; in 1938 William King sold the cinema to Metropole and Allied Cinemas Co.;[63] p (from 1946): Odeon (Ireland) Ltd; demolished by Odeon (Ireland) Ltd in 1954 to make way for the *State Cinema*.

State Cinema, 374–6 North Circular Road (24 April 1954–29 June 1974), built on the site of *Phibsborough Picture House* and an adjoining building at a cost of £75,000–£100,000 by Odeon (Ireland) Ltd from a design by O'Connor and Aylward (*DIA*); 1,330; m: Michael Murray (from 1954); William D. King (from 1962);[64] p: John James McManus (from 1975); second Dublin cinema with

CinemaScope; pan-shaped auditorium, 80ft wide; 'finished in contemporary style relying mainly on proportion and treatment for effect as distinct from provision of excessive ornamentation. The main distinctive feature of the auditorium is the curved wall and ceiling treatment to the screen which eliminated entirely the previous highly ornamented treatment common to proscenium walls and around the screen. The general effect of the interior of the new cinema will result in the screen and auditorium forming the one unit and giving the impression to the patron that he is viewing an actual scene as distinct from looking at a heavily framed photograph';[65] in the 1950s it was used as weekly venue by Irish Film Society; owner from 1975 J.J. McManus, who already had four cinemas (in Enniskillen, Armagh, Monaghan and Sligo), paid over £100,000 and hoped to present live shows and theatre;[66] closed *c.* 1980; subsequently used as a carpet showrooms and for a time as an ice-rink which closed in 2000.

Portmarnock
Riverside (*c.*1951–*c.*1957), occasional screenings, mainly at weekends, in large wooden club house belonging to Riverside Golf Club; p: Charlie Dillon.[67]

Portrane
Dockery's Cinema, p: Mr Dockery, a local businessman with a butcher's shop, grocery, barber shop and fuel business; the cinema was located above and at rear of Dockery's shop, with salvaged tram seats affixed to floor; Grogan's supermarket now on site, though some original features of cinema remain.[68]

Ranelagh
Sandford Cinema, 35–6 Elm Grove/5 Lower Sandford Road (9 November 1914–1917; 26 December 1917–1924; reopened, 1 August 1924–1925 as the *Coliseum Cinema*; reopened, 5 October 1925– autumn 1926; reopened, 12 November 1926–5 April 1968 as *Sandford Cinema*, aka *Sandford Green*, reopened, 6 April 1968–18 February 1978 as *New Sandford*); arch: Patrick Munden (*DIA*); p: Sandford Cinema Co. (1914); John J. Healy (1917–24); Dublin Cinemas Ltd (from 1924); Suburbia Cinemas Ltd, br: Mr O'Connor, 634 (*1947 directory*, company listed in *Showcase* 1968); custom-built; first cinematograph licence was issued to H. Coleman; m: Whittle brothers; later converted to a bar and restaurant.[69]

Rathcoole
Rathcoole Cinema, Tay Lane (1930s–40s/early 1950s), p: Alfie Hudson, whose fit-up cinema with canvas tent had formerly been a travelling cinema show. Hudson moved from tent to hall at side of Glebe House, which belonged to Church of Ireland.[70]

Rathmines
Princess Cinema, 145 Lower Rathmines Road (orig. 3 Tourville), (24 March 1913–1914 as *Rathmines Picture Palace*;[71] *Princess Cinema*, 1914–2 July 1960; aka *New Princess Cinema*), arch: George Luke O'Connor (estimated cost £3,000 [*DIA*], purpose-built cinema); p: Rathmines Amusement Co. (1913– 30 April 1937, when company was wound up; cinemtograph licence first issued on 5 March 1913) with directors Izidore Isaac Bradlaw, a dentist with a practice in Grafton Street and Joseph Karmel; partnership of Albert E. Reglar, manager, *Princess Cinema*, and James Fearson (1937–8); from 1938: Princess Cinema Co. Ltd (incorporated on 15 December 1938), in which Anthony O'Grady, md of nearby *Stella Cinema*, bought Fearson's interest in the *Princess*; Reglar (25 per cent) and Stella Picture Theatre Co., owner of the *Stella Cinema*; by 1942, O'Grady was sole owner, with Reglar continuing as manager until late 1950s; last m: Michael Keegan; 952 (150 in balcony);[72] fb: Val Kinsella of the Stella (*1947 directory*); 700 (*1947 directory*);[73] sold to Jones Group, August 1960, used as a metal workshop; sold again, July 1981, and demolished on 22 January 1982 to make way for office block.[74]
Stella Cinema, 207–209 Lower Rathmines Road (29 January 1923–June 1978; after refurbishing, December 1978–27 September 1981; as twin, 22 February 1982–*c.*28 August 2004), arch: Higginbotham and Stafford; included dancehall on first floor, (*DIA*); p: Stella Picture Co. Ltd (incorporated, 1921); d: Anthony O'Grady, licensed vintner and grocer, 140 Leinster Road, Rathmines, and William Kay, cinema proprietor, Rothesay Cottage, Sutton, Co. Dublin; 1,350; second largest cinema in Dublin; m: Val Kinsella (by 1949, listed as fb in *1947 directory*); refurbished for £20,000 in 1978 by Anthony O'Grady, grandson of founder of cinema, with 330 seats on ground floor; sub-divided into a twin in 1981, with 280 and 180 seats; 2 screens/413 seats;[75] the O'Grady family continued to run the cinema until 2003 when it was bought by Ward Anderson who closed it in August 2004, ahead of developing the nearby *Swan Cinemas*.[76]
• *Swan Cinemas*, Swan Centre (December 2009–; *Swan Omniplex*), p: Dublin Cinema Group/Ward Anderson, 3 screens (first cinema in Dublin custom designed for digital), 571 seats.
Town Hall (31 December 1904–*c.*1923), *c.* 2,000 seats; l: James T. Jameson's Irish Animated Picture Co; occasional film seasons from *c.* 1902; in 1910s Jameson leased the premises as a full-time cinema,

though dispute with local council centred on refusal to allow Sunday opening, unlike in Dublin city;[77] projection box damaged when film caught fire during screening in September 1918.[78]

Rialto

Rialto Cinema, 27–31 South Circular Road (5 November 1936–29 August 1970), arch: F.J. Macaulay; p: Maurice Baum (also fb, *1947 directory*); Green Group/Ward Anderson (1967; as Abbey Films Ltd in *Showcase* 1968); 1,500 (*1947 directory*)/1,600 (1,000 in stalls, 500 in balcony) seats; in 1971 the property was bought for about £50,000 by Windsor Motors which used it as a car-salesroom.

Ringsend

The Rinn Cinema, 28 Fitzwilliam Street (14 November 1925–1934, during which the cinema closed for short periods, went into receivership, 2 October 1934; as *Regal Cinema*, 1936–10 January 1965), p: Cities Cinemas Ltd (incorporated, 7 August 1924); d: William Murphy (stevedore), Cambridge House, Cambridge Road, Ringsend; Michael Carrick (stevedore); William Byrne (builder); Padraig Tarrant (printer); John Doran (gm, insurance co.); Peter Sherry (spirit merchant); John Boyle (gm); cost: £10,000; arch: Thomas Francis McNamara, Pearse Street; Dr Andrew Charles, Merrion Square, investor in company, initiated court case seeking to recover £200 subscribed in company as he had not been given shares; co-opted to board but resigned when not issued with shares;[79] p: Percy Winder Whittle bought cinema from receiver (2 October 1934); Regal Cinema Co. (incorporated, 16 November 1936, with Percy Winder Whittle as majority shareholder [and acting as cinema's fb], listed in *1947 directory*); George Jay (1949); m: Owen Dunne; 22ft proscenium, 900 (*1947 directory*); in 1986 under CYTP programme, *Regal* was divided between a sound recording studios (downstairs) and upstairs a Fás training scheme, Ringsend community workshop; according to workshop newsletter, 'A Regal re-opening', 'the Rinn was built by the locals providing both money and endeavour for the cinema project'; later, Seamus Bourke (de Bourca), chief operator, and brothers Lorcan and Rick, changed name to *Regal*.[80]

Rush

Savoy Cinema, Sandy Road (4 April 1937–26 December 1953; reopened as *Tideway*, 17 July 1955–1973; as *Europa*, 22 April 1973–1977; listed *Showcase* 1968), former Foley-Keane dance hall; p: Tailteann Theatres Ltd (incorporated, 28 November 1935); original d(s): Margaret and Eugene Scanlon, merchants, Balbriggan; Anthony Conlon, Kells; Joseph Rooney, builder, Balbriggan; br & fb: Mr E.(G.) Scanlon (*1947 directory*); 500; destroyed by fire, 26 December 1953; p (from 1955): Abbey actress Marie Kean and her brother Michael Kean, who named new cinema after 'The Tideway', the last ship commanded by their father, Captain John Kean; subsequent owner: John Mulvey, a solicitor; l: Kevin and Adrian Cunningham (1973–7); the Cunninghams also leased the *Savoy*, Balbriggan (1973) and *Inchicore* (1974), renaming them *Europa*; destroyed by fire on 25 March 1979.

Santry

• *Santry Omniplex*, Omni Park shopping centre, Old Airport Road/Swords Road (March 1992–), p: Ward Anderson; expanded in summer 2003 to incorporate adjoining vacant Adventure World, increased from 10 screens (with 2,262 seats[81]) to 11 screens with 2,152 seats (screens from 53 to 610 seats).

Skerries

Electric Theatre, South Strand (1914–32; aka *Picture Palace*; *Star Electric Theatre*; *Skerries Electric Theatre*), p/m: William H. Flanagan; Skerries Electric Theatre Co. (*KYB*, 1919–33), d: I.I. Bradlaw; originally Sunday nights only; 500 seats (*KYB*, 1919).

Pavilion Cinema, South Strand (c.1933–1971+; aka *Pavilion & Cinema*), built on site of *Electric Theatre* (*KYB*, 1934–8); p: William H. Flanagan, New Street, Skerries (*KYB*, 1936); P.L. Flanagan, Imperial, Skerries (*KYB*, 1939–71; *1947 directory*; *Showcase* 1968); 16ft proscenium and 20ft stage (*1947 directory*); 400 (*KYB*, 1936); 550 (*KYB*, 1939–48; *1947 directory*); 700 (*KYB*, 1949–57); 550 (*KYB*, 1968–71); later converted to swimming pool.

Stillorgan

• *Ormonde*, Stillorgan Plaza, Lower Kilmacud Road (24 August 1954–30 July 1978, 1,000 seats; as 3 screen complex in new development, 5 February 1983–1977; 7 screens from April 1997–April 2011; July 2011–), p: J.J. Kavanagh, Ormonde cinema circuit; arch: Mr W.A. Maguire; 924; cost: £45,000; m & fb Andrew O'Gorman (*Showcase* 1968, *RPC* 1977);[82] sold to developers building Stillorgan Plaza shopping centre; AIB bank now on cinema site. A 3-screen complex with 230, 95 and 95 seats was included as part of new development; p (1983–): Andrew, Liam and Donal O'Gorman, who invested £1.5/2 million to increase complex to 7 screens, 1,018 (screens with 80 to 280) seats; m: Brian O'Gorman;[83] rented to and refurbished by UCI, July 2011.

Sutton
Sutton Grand, Howth Road/ Station Road, Sutton Cross (4 January 1937–16 September 1967), p:
Leonard Ging (and fb); 729/700 (*1947 directory*); in 1949 Ging sold his cinema circuit to Rank's
Irish Cinemas Ltd except the *Sutton Grand*; when Ging died in April 1952, his daughter Shirley ran
the cinema; the building was bought by the Quinn family in 1967 who converted it to a supermar-
ket; following a fire in 1980, the building was demolished, and an office block and a supermarket,
Superquinn, now occupy the site.

Swords
• *Movies @ Swords* (November 2006–), p: Spurling and O'Gorman families, 11 screens/1,780 seats.
Swords Cinema (1950s), p: Tom Bray; opened weekends only; cine variety; demolished, supermarket
built on site.[84]

Tallaght
UCI Tallaght, The Square shopping centre, Belgard Square South, Old Blessington Road (November
1990–March 2010), arch: Burke Kennedy Doyle; p: United Cinema International (1990–2004, there-
after lessee); Terra Firma Capital Partners (October 2004–September 2006); Irish Leisureplex
Entertainment Co./Entertainment Enterprises/Ciáran and Colum Butler (September 2006–2009);
Noel Smyth; 12 screens/ 2,697 (336 x2; 257 x2; 212; 197 x5; 157 x2) seats; 12 screens/2,980 seats.[85]

Terenure
Classic, 17 Rathfarnham Road (1 July 1938–19 June 1976), p: Sundrive Cinema Co. Ltd; d: William
Callow (chairman), F.H. Croskerry, M.D. Heron; 728; built on site of disused Blessington and Steam
Tramway Co. premises; renovated during July/August 1959, m: Matthew Albert Heron (1940s [br
and fb in *1947 directory*] to 30 April 1964); Albert Kelly (from 1964), who also managed the
Kenilworth, Harold's Cross, which was owned by Sundrive Cinemas Ltd, 30 Lower Ormond Quay,
as was the *Sundrive*, Kimmage; m: Mr M. Keegan (*Showcase* 1968); changed façade, reconstructed
by Everclear TV, which went bankrupt in 1984.[86] 760, screen: 17ft x 13ft (*1947 directory*).

Walkinstown
Apollo, 5 Harry Avenue (16 October 1953–*c*.25 May 1974) p: Leo Henry Kearns and George Frederick
Kearns, cinema managers, through Walkinstown Enterprises Ltd; 1,000 seats, stadium style.[87] See
also *Sundrive Cinema*, Kimmage.

Whitehall
Whitehall Grand Cinema, 396–402 Collins Avenue (31 July 1954–June 1974), arch: Henry J. Lyons;
p: Irish Cinemas Ltd (*Showcase* 1968); m: Rick Bourke (from 1954), formerly of the *Queen's Theatre*;
1,088; after closure as cinema, bought by Gael Linn which continues to use the premises as a bingo
hall.

Travelling cinemas
Bracey Daniel's Talkies, Howth, Rush, Kilcock and Leixslip (*KYB*, 1941).

FERMANAGH

Enniskillen
• *Enniskillen Omniplex*, Raceview, Factory Road (14 April 2000–; aka *Castle Centre*; *Enniskillen
Cineworld*), p: Ward Anderson's Empire Cinemas chain; originally built as Lakeland Forum
Entertainment Centre, after two IRA bombings during 1982–4, the centre was renamed Castle Park
Recreation Centre, it had 3 screens/625 (302; 193; and 130) seats (*BFI*, 1996); following another
bomb attack in January 1998, it was reopened in 2000 with 7 screens/1,200 seats, including a
'Premier' screen; 7 screens/1,062 seats (Connolly and Dillon, 2001:74).
Regal Cinema, Townhall Street (*c*.1936–1967; first listed in *KYB*, 1937); p: Enniskillen Cinemas, Ltd,
79 Donegall Street, Belfast (*KYB*, 1939–57, address in *1947 directory*: Whitehall Chambers, Ann
Street, Belfast); from February 1955, Odeon (Northern Ireland) Ltd (*KYB*, 1958–66; *Showcase* 1968);
br & fb: Ferris Pounds (*1947 directory*); m (November 1966–7): Kelvin Kerr; 32ft proscenium; *c*.790–
798 (*KYB*, 1942–57; *1947 directory*).
Ritz Cinema, 32 Forthill Street, beside Railway Hotel (*c*.1970–92); p: J.J. McManus; 450 (*BFI*, 1991).
Technical Hall (*KYB*, 1916–17).
Town Hall Cinema, Town Hall Street (*c*.1915–*c*.1956; first listed, *KYB*, 1916–17), Assembly Hall in
building converted to cinema, p: Dundealgan Electric Theatres, Ltd, Town Hall buildings, Dundalk
(d: Paddy Deary [Dundalk], Walter Slevin [Enniskillen], company also leased *Whitworth Hall*,

Drogheda and *Town Hall*, Dundalk; *KYB*, 1921–4, 1926–36; *1947 directory*); Con O'Mahony, St Helena, Dundalk (*KYB*, 1942–3); Eker Ltd,[88] St Helena, Dundalk (*KYB*, 1944–57); m: P.J. Slevin (*KYB*, 1922–4, 1926–8); no personnel listed *KYB*, 1929–41; br: Mr C. O'Mahony (*1947 directory*); 500 (*KYB*, 1936); *c.*400 (*KYB*, 1940–57).

Irvinestown
Adelphi, p: Scallan Brothers, 400.
Cinema, br/fb: Mr E. Stuart, Park View house, Strabane (*1947 directory*).

Lisnaskea
Astral (1958–71+), p: Clarke & Co.; 399 (*KYB*, 1958–61), 500; listed, *KYB*, 1958–71 & *Showcase* 1968.
Cinema, Main Street (*c.*1938–*c.*1956; listed as closed in *KYB*, 1942), p: D. Stewart (*KYB*, 1939–41); Raymond Stross, College Square East, Belfast (*KYB*, 1943); Messrs J. McCaffrey, H.H. Jordon, Matt O'Reilly, & T.A. Maguire (*KYB*, 1944); J. McCaffrey (*KYB*, 1948–57); br: John Caffrey (*1947 directory*); screen: 9½ft x 7½ft (*1947 directory*); 300 (*KYB*, 1939–41); 235 (*KYB*, 1943–4); 254 (*KYB*, 1945–52); 170 (*KYB*, 1953–7).

GALWAY

Aran Islands
Áras Éanna, Inis Oírr, an arts and heritage centre with 70-seat theatre, occasional film screenings.
Man of Aran Cinema, Kilronan, Inís Mór, 24 seats, access>CINEMA supported club based there.

Athenry
New Cinema, 350 (*KYB*, 1936).
Payne's Hall, Cross Street (*c.*1929–*c.*1934; first listed, *KYB*, 1930, as *Picture Theatre*), p: J. Payne (*KYB*, 1932–4); not equipped for sound and used only occasionally by travelling companies; 250 (1934).[89]
Ryan's Cinema Hall (1927).

Ballinasloe
Aisling, fb: Paddy Melia (1975–7).[90]
Central Cinema, Society Street (31 May 1942–1977+); p: Central Cinemas Ltd (CRO no. 9944; *Showcase* 1968); br: Mr Swanwyck (*1947 directory*); fb: Noel W. Swanwick (1976);[91] 600 (*1947 directory*); 500 (*KYB*, 1949–71).
Cinema (*KYB*, 1930).
Farming Society Hall (*KYB*, 1916–17).
Plaza Cinema, Society Street (*c.*1932–71+; formerly *Town Hall*), p: Revd T. Moloney (*KYB*, 1931–2); M.P. McGing, (*KYB*, 1933–39); The Clonfert diocesan trustees under the auspices of Ballinasloe Town Hall committee, St Michael's, Ballinasloe (*KYB*, 1941–71; *Showcase* 1968 in which is named Fr Dunne as admin.); screen: 16ft x 12ft (*1947 directory*); 500 (*KYB*, 1935–9), 450;[92] 550; 650 (*KYB*, 1949–71; *1947 directory*).

Clifden
Town Hall (dates undetermined).
Cinema (*1947 directory*).

Dunmore
Dunmore Cinema, p: J.J. Finnegan; 250.

Galway
Claddagh Palace, Lower Salthill (12 October 1975–28 September 1995, formerly *Estoria*), p: Ward Anderson, fb: Leo Ward (1975–7);[93] at opening, 2 screens/431 (300 and 131) seats;[94] later 111 seater 'mini' added; at closure, 3 screens/664 (385, 168 and 111) seats;[95] home to annual Galway Film Fleadh during 1989–94; demolished to make way for apartment block. See *Estoria*.
Cluain Mhuire, Monivea Road (part of GMIT [Galway-Mayo Institute of Technology]), Galway Film Centre, established in 1989, based there, community and education screenings. 200 (Connolly and Dillon, 2001:66).
Corrib Cinema Theatre, William Street. See *Empire Theatre*.
Court Theatre, Middle Street (*c.*March 1912–*c.*March 1923; aka *Court Picture House*), p: O'Shaughnessy & Sons/ E. O'Shaughnessy/ Mrs E. O'Shaughnessy (*KYB*, 1916–25); licensed for music and dancing (*KYB*, 1919–20); 600 (*KYB*, 1916–17); 500 (*KYB*, 1918–21).

Empire Theatre, William Street (*c*.August 1919–*c*.1934; formerly, *Gaiety Theatre*; *Corrib Cinema Theatre*, November 1934–23 March 1935; 28 July 1935–*c*. May 1936), p: Galway Cinemas, Ltd (md: Walter A. McNally, d: B. Armstrong, Mr D. Meldon; *KYB*, 1923); p: Walter A. McNally (*KYB*, 1924–35); Mrs. J.J. Leonard (from reopening in 28 July 1935);[96] m: J.J. Glynn (*KYB*, 1923–4), Miss O'Grady (*KYB*, 1927); bm: Harry O'Donovan (*KYB*, 1925), J.G. Pfounds (*KYB*, 1926); 900 (*KYB*, 1935; 1934).[97] Proprietors also owners of new *Savoy Cinema*, who put *Corrib* up for sale in April 1935, itself perhaps prompted by refusal of licence, later rescinded in January 1933 as on-going dispute with local council concerned rewiring and other safety matters;[98] even before the closing of the cinema, it was being used for boxing and other live entertainments and sports.

Estoria, Lower Salthill (22 November 1939–May 1975; following renovations and twinning, from 12 October 1975–28 September 1995, *Claddagh Palace*), arch: Hubert O'Connor (cost: £10,000); p: Estoria Cinema Co. Ltd; W.E. Egan & P.J. Mulligan (*KYB*, 1950–61); M.D. Burns & P.J. Mulligan, Estoria Cinema Co. Ltd, Ballina (*KYB*, 1963–71; *Showcase* 1968); Ward Anderson (from 1975); br & fb: P.J. Mulligan (*1947 directory*, also fb of *Estoria*, Ballina); *c*.775;[99] 753 (*KYB*, 1963–71); 620 (1975). See *Claddagh Palace*.

• *Eye Cinema*, Wellpark Retail Park, Dublin Road (March 2005–), arch: Douglas Wallace; p: Gerry Barrett;[1] 9 screens/1,989 (385; 166; 239; 273; 273; 239; 166; 124; 124) seats; digital projection.

Gaiety Cinema Theatre, William Street (31 October 1917–19; formerly *Galway Cinema Theatre*; later *Empire Theatre*), m: Mr J.P.S. McGurk.

Galway Cinema Theatre, William Street (April 1912–March 1915; aka *Cinema Theatre*; formerly, *The Rink* premises), p: Galway Cinema Ltd; d: Isidore J. Bradlaw; contact: Robert W. Simmons, a photographer; Robert Simmons, a shareholder in the company, rented the premises at £3 per week for up to ten years to Bradlaw; Albert H. Simmons, motor agent, was in dispute with Bradlaw in 1913 over continuing use of a covered archway and passage which led to the cinema but which they used for access to their own businesses; when rent arrears reached 18 weeks, Simmons took a case which led to the company's liquidation; accommodation *c*.1,000 (including standing);[2] 500–600 (*KYB*, 1918). See also *Tierney's Cinema Theatre*.

• *Galway Omniplex*, Galway Retail Park, Headford Road (10 November 1993–), p: Ward Anderson, originally 7 screens, later expanded to 11 screens/1,974 (372, 350, 212, 190, 175, 176, 133, 82, 68, 108, 108) seats; 11 screens/2,020 seats;[3] reduced to 10 screens.

Jade Winters Sex Cinema, Liosban Industrial Estate, Tuam Road (*c*.2007–), 24-seat room with booths for private screenings of pornographic films as part of sex shop; apparently Ireland's only such venue to which patrons paid €12 admission; local councillor Padraig Connelly campaigned for its closure, describing Galway as 'a city of culture, not of sleaze'; an attempt to gain a court order against venue thwarted by bringing successful prosecution with 30 days jail against Director of Film Classification John Kelleher in mistaken belief he was owner of the shop rather than simply the signature on the DVD/Video shop's official licence.[4]

Mall Cinema, Newtownsmith, p: Mall Cinema Ltd (CRO no. 10429).

Savoy Cinema, Eglinton Street (26 December 1934–1971+), rebuilding of Empire Theatre as cinema by Walter McNally's Provincial Cinemas, arch: Robinson & Keefe, estimated cost: £18,000 (*DIA*); p: Galway Cinemas Ltd, 75 Middle Abbey Street, Dublin (*KYB*, 1940–8); Galway Cinemas Ltd, 9 Eden Quay, Dublin (*KYB*, 1950–60); the cinema was opened by John McCormack, who sang at the event, and who was a friend of md Walter McNally, and was himself a well-known singer;[5] p: Amalgamated Cinemas (Ireland) Ltd, 9 Eden Quay, Dublin (*KYB*, 1961–71; *Showcase* 1968); m: Harry McMahon, who worked at *Savoy* from opening of cinema (*c*.1943–60, listed in *1947 directory* which also notes owner as Mr A. Culleton, Dublin, and fb as Harry W. Culleton [75 Middle Abbey Street, Dublin]);[6] m: Miss W. Mannion (*Showcase* 1968); screen: 21ft x 16¼ft (*1947 directory* 1,300 (*KYB*, 1935–8); 1,254 (*KYB*, 1939–45); 1,260 (*1947 directory*); 1,200 (*KYB*, 1946–61).

Tierney's Cinema Theatre, William Street (October 1916–?), p: Frederick Tierney. This venture seems to have been a temporary reopening of *Galway Cinema Theatre*.

• *Town Hall Cinema* (*c*.April 1910–), films screened there from at least 1910 by Jameson's Pictures/Irish Animated; contact: F. Hardiman (*KYB*, 1918); l: Mr Hardiman, Francis Street (*KYB*, 1934–64; *1947 directory*), p: Town Hall Cinemas/Ward Anderson; fb: Leo Ward (1975–6);[7] redeveloped with help of Galway Corporation in 1995–6 with 35mm projection installed and used as venue by Galway Film Society (4 February 1996–) and Galway Film Fleadh (the theatre reopened in October 1995); 28ft proscenium (*1947 directory*); 800 (*KYB*, 1918); 450 (*KYB*, 1934–41); 570;[8] 600 (*KYB*, 1942–64); 340 (Connolly and Dillon, 2001:66); 393 (2010).

Victoria Cinema Theatre, Victoria Place (*c*.1 August 1915–22 July 1926), p: Robert W. Mackie (*KYB*, 1919–24); Mr M.J.H. McGrath (*KYB*, 1924–8); m: Walter Clifton (*KYB*, 1919); licensed for music and dancing (*KYB*, 1919–20); 600 (*KYB*, 1919); 700 (*KYB*, 1920–1); cinema burned down on 20

July 1924; the fire was blamed on an electrical fault, with loss estimated at £8,000–£10,000;[9] premises put up for sale in September 1928;[10] listed *KYB*, 1929, as closed.

Gort

Central Cinema (*c*.1941–1971+), p: Daniel Ryan,[11] Marine Parade, Kilkee, Co. Clare (*KYB*, 1942–5); R.G. Kirkham, 35 Upper Abbey Street, Dublin (*KYB*, 1950–61); Christopher Fennessy (*KYB*, 1961–71; *Showcase* 1968); br: G. Kirkham, Dublin (*1947 directory*); screen: 12ft x 14ft (*1947 directory*); 500 (*KYB*, 1942–5); 250 (*1947 directory*); 450 (*KYB*, 1950–61); 260 (*KYB*, 1961–71).

Inverin/Indreabhán

Seanscoil Sailearna, host to film club Scannán Sailearna (2010).

Loughrea

Cinema (*c*.1926–; listed in *KYB*, 1930–3 [no personnel]); p: Mr Sweeney (*KYB*, 1934).
Town Hall Cinema, Barrack Street (*c*.1932–71+), arch: 1931–9, Ralph Byrne, conversion of town hall into cinema and ballroom (*DIA*); p: Loughrea Town Hall Ltd (*KYB*, 1936–43; *1947 directory*; *KYB*, 1952–71; *Showcase* 1968); Michael Timlin (*KYB*, 1944–51; listed as br in *1947 directory*); 10ft proscenium (*1947 directory*); 400 (1934);[12] 380 (*KYB*, 1936–43); 350–380 (*KYB*, 1944–71; *1947 directory*).

Moycullen

Basilica (13 December 1930–).

Oranmore

• *Oranmore Omniplex*, City Limits Entertainment Centre, behind the Maldron Hotel (March 2005–), p: Ward Anderson, 6 screens, 1,400 seats.[13]

Portumna

Coliseum, Clonfert Avenue, (*c*.1947–*c*.1956), p: John Egan, 24 Main Street, Maryborough (Portlaoise), 500 (*KYB*, 1948–57; *Showcase* 1968); Egan listed as fb in *1947 directory*.
Town Hall (*c*.1929–*c*.1947+), listed, *KYB*, 1930–8 (no personnel); hon. sec: M.C. Stronge, 800 (*KYB*, 1939–46, *1947 directory*); stage: 20ft (*1947 directory*).

Tuam

The Mall Cinema, The Mall (*c*.1919–?; reopened as sound cinema, 5 April 1931–1990+), Mall Theatre and Cinema Ltd (CRO no. 203606), p: Tuam Cinema Co. (*KYB*, 1919; 1922); Joseph O'Connor (*KYB*, 1919–27); Mrs M. O'Connor (*KYB*, 1938); Joseph McHugh, Tuam Cinema Co. (*KYB*, 1935–48); Mrs J. O'Connor (*KYB*, 1939–43); The Mall Cinema Ltd (*KYB*, 1944–71; *Showcase* 1968 with Mr P. O'Connor md); m/bm: Joseph O'Connor (*KYB*, 1919–37); Joseph McHugh (*KYB*, 1928–37); bm: Mrs J. O'Connor (*KYB*, 1938); fb: P.M. O'Connor, Jarlath's Terrace, Bishop Street, Tuam (*KYB*, 1944); P.M. O'Connor (*1947 directory*); P.M. O'Connor, 'Iona', The Mall, Tuam (*KYB*, 1970); P. O'Connor (1976–7);[14] 300 (*KYB*, 1919; 1922); 500 (*KYB*, 1920); 400 (*KYB*, 1921); 450 (*KYB*, 1935–70); 400 (*KYB*, 1971).
Odeon Cinema, Shop Street (*c*.1947–75+), p: Midland Amusement Ltd (*KYB*, 1949–71; *Showcase* 1968); br: Mrs Myra Walsh (*1947 directory*); fb: Gerry Kirkham (35 Upper Abbey Street, Dublin) & Joe Riley (Belmont Avenue, Donnybrook), (*1947 directory*); J. Doris (1975);[15] screen: 22ft x 16ft (*1947 directory*); 800 (*1947 directory*); 836 (*KYB*).
Town Hall (1898–1902; McCole, 2005:appendix D; listed, *KYB*, 1930–1 [no personnel]).

Travelling Cinema

Cinemobile (April 2001–), p: Fis na Milaoise Teoranta, subsidiary of Irish Film Institute, 100-seat mobile cinema funded by National Millenium Committee with grant of £531,000;[16] p: subsidiary of Irish Film Institute to cover whole island, with partners/funders Arts Council of Ireland, Irish Film Board, Northern Ireland Film Screen, Arts Council of Northern Ireland, RTE; administered from Cluan Mhuire, Galway; in first decade over 100,000 viewed films in cinema. See also *Cinema-North-West*.

KERRY

Ballybunnion

Savoy (*c*.1948–54), p: Ballybunnion Amusement Co., 250 (*KYB*, 1949); A. Blood–Smyth, 47 O'Connell Street, Limerick, 371 (*KYB*, 1950–5); Ballybunnion Cinema Ltd (CRO no. 17265); Michael Hanrahan; Brian Canney.
Cinema, br: Mr Carron (*1947 directory*).

Ballylongford
Cinema (1955–65): John Walsh, a national school teacher, 16mm, 1955–8; 35mm, 1958–65, *c*.200.
Walsh's Egg Store (*c*.late 1940s/50s), a long building at the edge of the village, screenings every Monday night.[17] See above.

Cahirciveen
• *Cahirciveen Community Cinema*, Community Centre (August 2003–), supported by Cahirciveen Community Resource Centre; co-ordinator: Karolien Verheyen.[18]
Cinema Theatre (*c*.1918–*c*.1925), p: The Cahirciveen Cinema Co., m: P.J. O'Riordan (*KYB*, 1923–6); 400 (*KYB*, 1919–22); licensed for dancing and music (*KYB*, 1919).
The Kingdom Cinema, Main Street (*c*.1926–71+), p: Patrick J. Gilsenan & Charles Troy (*KYB*, 1927–30); Charles Troy (*KYB*, 1931–52; *1947 directory*); J. & S. Breen (*KYB*, 1955–71; *Showcase* 1968); bm: P.J. Gilsenan (*KYB*, 1927–8); 18ft deep stage and 24ft proscenium (*1947 directory*); 340 (1934);[19] 400 (*KYB*, 1935; 1942; *1947 directory*); 350 (*KYB*, 1943); 420 (*KYB*, 1944–52; 1955–71).

Castleisland
Astor Cinema (*c*.9 October 1950–1976+; listed *Showcase* 1968), fb: S. O'Connor (1976);[20] 300 (*KYB*, 1953–71).
Carnegie Hall (*c*.1934–*c*.1947), 400 (*KYB*, 1935–48).
The Cinema (*c*.1934–*c*.1951; first listed in *KYB*, 1935), p: P. Coffey (*KYB*, 1939–52, Coffey, Picturedrome, Tralee as br & fb in *1947 directory*); Castleisland Cinema Co. (*KYB*, 1949–52); 300 (*KYB*, 1939–52);[21] 230 (*KYB*, 1949–52).

Dingle
• *Phoenix Cinema*, Dykegate Lane (*c*.1925–; listed as *Cinema* in *KYB*, 1936; 1939; 1940–8), p: J. Houlihan, Dingle (*KYB*, 1925–6); J. & J.C. Houlihan (*KYB*, 1926–34); Dingle Electric Light & Power Co. (*KYB*, 1949–55); John A. Moore, Dingle (*KYB*, 1960–71; *Showcase* 1968); Michael 'Francie' O'Sullivan (from 1980); br: J. Houlihan (*1947 directory*); 400 (1934);[22] 500/600 (*KYB*, 1925–71; *1947 directory*);[23] 200 (1980); 152 seats (Connolly and Dillon, 2001:72; 2010).

Farranfore
Gazette Picture Pavilion (aka *Picturedrome*; *Picture Pavilion*), p: Henry Gazett, 300 (*KYB*, 1916–18).

Kenmare
Arcadia Cinema (*c*.1947–71+), p: J. Quinlan & P.J. Arthur (*KYB*, 1950–5); J. Finnegan & B. McSwiney (*KYB*, 1961–71; *Showcase* 1968); br: P. Arthur (*1947 directory*); 323 (*KYB*, 1950–5); 300 (*KYB*, 1961).
Commercial Club (*c*.1915–17; aka *C&W Club Hall*), p: Commercial and Working Men's Club, 250–300 (*KYB*, 1918).
Carnegie Arts Centre, Shelbourne Street (November 2008–) multi-purpose arts venue, 140-seat theatre with full-size cinema screen, regular film screenings, affiliated to access>CINEMA (2010).

Killarney
Casino, East Avenue Road (*c*.1932–*c*.1996; formerly *East Avenue Hall*, as 3 screen *Three Lakes Cinema* from *c*. 1974–96), p: Thomas G. Cooper; on 20 September 1931, the third night of *East Avenue Hall* being used as a full-time cinema, it was destroyed by fire; nine months later Cooper opened a new cinema on the site, the *Casino*,[24] br & fb: T. Cooper (*1947 directory*, Cooper also booked the *Casino*s at Rathmore, Tramore and Doneraile; listed in *Showcase* 1968); fb: Leo Ward (1976–7);[25] 650 (1934);[26] 600 (*KYB*, 1935–71); 700 (*1947 directory*); demolished to make way for *Killarney Cineplex*. See *Killarney Picturedrome*.
• *Killarney Cineplex*, East Avenue Road (20 December 1996–; aka *Killarney Cineplex Cinema*), p: Ward Anderson, 4 screens/813 (316, 178, 172, 147) seats; 4 screens/848 seats.[27] In 2004 the cinema's manager was Tommy Cooper, grandson of Thomas G. Cooper, who directed *The Dawn* (1936) and who owned the *Casino*, on which site it was built; later 12 screens/1,947 seats.
Killarney Picturedrome, East Avenue Hall, East Avenue Road (*c*.1920–*c*.1927), m: Daniel MacMonagh (*KYB*, 1921–5), C. O'Keeffe (*KYB*, 1926–8); 900 (*KYB*, 1921).[28] See *Casino*; *Three Lakes Cinema*.
Town Hall Cinema (*c*.1910–*c*.1948, intermittently), l: James T. Jameson (1910s); James C. Houlihan, Dingle, Co. Kerry, 700 (*KYB*, 1941–8).

Killorglin
Carnegie Picture Hall (*c*.1919–*c*.1947), p: Picture Committee, sec: W. MacSweeney (*KYB*, 1920); p: Carnegie Trust Committee (*KYB*, 1921–34; *1947 directory*); m: W. MacSweeney (*KYB*, 1926–7); no personnel listed *KYB*, 1929–48; 280 (*KYB*, 1920); 500 (*KYB*, 1921); 200 (1934).[29]

Oisín, The Square (*c*.1947–98+), p: Patrick O'Shea, Lower Bridge Street, Killorglin (*KYB*, 1948–71; *Showcase* 1968; Mr O'Shea in *1947 directory*); O'Shea family (aka Duffy O'Sheas); Diarmuid O'Shea (1998); fb: D. O'Shea (1975);[30] 700 (*1947 directory*); 800 (*KYB*, 1948–71); O'Sheas also owned *Cinema*, Milltown, Co. Kerry, and *Oisín*, Glin, Co. Limerick.

Listowel

Astor Cinema (*c*.1929–77+; redeveloped as *Listowel Classic*), p: P. Coffey (*KYB*, 1934–41; 1950–71; *Showcase* 1968; *1947 directory* [as br & fb]); fb: Leo Ward (1975–7); 300 (1934);[31] 500 (*KYB*, 1934–71 [when listed]; *1947 directory*).
Gymnasium Hall (*KYB*, 1916–17).
• *Classic Movieplex*, Upper William Street (October 1987–), p: brothers Kieran and Pat Gleeson, third generation of family to own a cinema (father and grandfather ran *Regal Cinema*, Cappamore, Limerick); 2 screens/249 (*c*.160 and 80) seats;[32] runs art-house/alternative cinema club on Thursdays, similar programme to *Kino*, Cork, and Irish Film Institute, Dublin.[33]
Plaza Cinema (*c*.1941–*c*.1972), p: A. McSweeney (*KYB*, 1942–8, listed as fb in *1947 directory*); J. O'Sullivan (*KYB*, 1950–71; *Showcase* 1968); 600 (*KYB*, 1942–71); 700 (*1947 directory*).
St John's Arts & Heritage Centre, The Square, houses theatre, arts centre and tourist office; occasional film screenings, access>CINEMA club based there (2010).

Milltown

Cinema, p: O'Shea family (aka Duffy O'Sheas), also owned *Oisin* cinemas in Killorglin and Glin, Co. Limerick.

Rathmore

Casino (*c*.1947–*c*.1957), p: Thomas G. Cooper, Killarney, 450 (*KYB*, 1949–57, listed in *1947 directory* with Cooper as fb, no other details).

Tarbert

Shannon Cinema (*c*.1966–71+), p: Patrick J. Lynch, Tarbert, 200 (*KYB*, 1967–71).

Tralee

Concert Hall (1900–3; McCole, 2005:appendix D).
Picturedrome, Castle Street (*c*.1916–76+), p: Murphy & Coffey; aka Munster Cinemas; (*KYB*, 1917–31); P. Coffey (*KYB*, 1932–57, as br & fb in *1947 directory*); Mrs M. Gillooly (*KYB*, 1965–71; *Showcase* 1968); fb: Leo Ward (1975–6);[34] 300 (*KYB*, 1919–21); 558 (1934);[35] 900 (*KYB*, 1945–57); now a bookshop.
Theatre Royal, p: James & Sons (*KYB*, 1916–17); p/m: Patrick J. Cahill, licensed for music and dancing (*KYB*, 1919); p: P. Coffey (*KYB*, 1949–57); Mrs M. Gillooly, daughter of P. Coffey (*Showcase* 1968; *KYB*, 1970); m: W.J. Mullins, (*KYB*, 1920–1); 1,200 (*KYB*, 1919); 900 (*KYB*, 1920–1); 700 (*KYB*, 1949–71); now a bowling alley.
Thomas Ashe Memorial Hall (aka *Ashe Cinema*), (*c*.1929–70s), p: B. McSweeney (*KYB*, 1930–2); Mr A. McSweeney (*KYB*, 1933–66, listed also as fb *1947 directory*); 840 (1934);[36] 900 (*KYB*, 1936–66); 1,000 (*1947 directory*); 630–80 (early 1970s); used by the Tralee Film Society in the 1970s (as Michael Dwyer later related, the society 'couldn't afford a new screen, so we painted the back wall white – the clarity was so good that nobody noticed').[37] Now home to Kerry County Museum.
Tralee Omniplex, Ivy Terrace, Town Park, between Siamsa Tire and The Square (26 December 1994–2007), p: Ward Anderson; m: Roger Webb; 4 screens/897 (337, 204,192, 164) seats;[38] demolished autumn 2007. See below, new cinema in nearby site.
• *Tralee Omniplex*, Fels Point, Dan Spring Road (July 2007–), p: Ward Anderson; 8 screens/1,512 seats.

Valentia Island

Cinema, listed, *KYB*, 1930–1 (no personnel); listed as closed, *KYB*, 1932.

Waterville

New Cinema, listed, *KYB*, 1930–3 (no personnel).

Travelling cinemas

National Mobile Cinemas, which visited Ardbert, Kildorrery, Milltown, Boherbue, Castletownroche, and Coachford in 1950.[39]

KILDARE

Athy

Athy Picture Palace (*c*.1926–*c*.1947), p: Athy Picture Palace Ltd, d: Captain A.J. Hosie (*KYB*, 1927–48); 440;[40] 600 (*KYB*, 1930–48).

Grove Cinema (1957–94); *c.*1,000; built by local contractor George Nash; fb: Leo Ward (1975–7); closed after trespassers broke in and set fire to premises. Local man Ned Martin reopened it for a while, but it closed again; Graham Spurling reopened it, but in 1994 the *Grove* finally closed as a cinema; demolished in January 2004 to make way for LIDL supermarket.[41]

Savoy Cinema (*c.*1947–58), p: McNally Cinemas, Ltd (*1947 directory*); Roscrea & Athy Cinema Co. (*KYB*, 1949–57); br: Miss Kirwan, fb: Harry W. Culleton, 75 Middle Abbey Street, Dublin (*1947 directory*); screen: 19ft x 14½ft (*1947 directory*); 500 (*1947 directory*, *KYB*, 1949–57); 405.[42]

Town Hall (1902; McCole, 2005:appendix D).

Ballymore-Eustace

Cinema (*c.*1947–51), p: C. Clinton (*KYB*, 1949–52); br: Neil Clinton (*1947 directory*); 200 (*1947 directory*; *KYB*, 1949–52).

Carbury

Central, p: Charles Adams, 300.

Castledermot

Castle Cinema (*c.*1947–71+), p: Peter E. Murphy, 290 (*KYB*, 1949–71; *Showcase* 1968; also listed 1947 *directory*).

Celbridge

Cinema, fb: Roland Rice, Premier Cinema, Lucan (*1947 directory*).

Curragh

Camp Cinema (military only), 800 (*1947 directory*).

Curragh Picture Hall (*c.*1918–*c.*1971+), (*KYB*, 1919–22; aka *Picture House*, *KYB*, 1930–3; *Curragh Picture House*, *KYB*, 1934–8; *Picture Palace*, *KYB*, 1939–69; *Curragh Cinema*, *KYB*, 1970–1; listed in *Showcase* 1968), licensed for music and dancing (*KYB*, 1919–20); p: Southern Coliseum Ltd (*KYB*, 1919; 1921–); Curragh Picture House Ltd (*KYB*, 1920); Mrs K. Sylvester (*KYB*, 1946–8); Curragh Picture House Ltd, South Hill Avenue, Blackrock, Co. Dublin (*KYB*, 1949–71); Curragh Picture Co. Ltd (*Showcase* 1968); m: Chris G. Silvester (*KYB*, 1919–45); br: Chris Silvester (*1947 directory*); 750 (*KYB*, 1919–20); 650 (*KYB*, 1921); 600 (*KYB*, 1934–48); 544;[43] 450 (*KYB*, 1970–1).

Sandes Cinema, Curragh Camp (*c.*1929–*c.*1965; first listed in *KYB*, 1930–3), p: Sandes Soldiers Home (*KYB*, 1948); Maguire & Keenan (*KYB*, 1949–61); Sandes Soldiers' Home (*KYB*, 1963–6); m: Miss Magill (*KYB*, 1934–46; *1947 directory*); 450 (*c.*1934);[44] 400 (*KYB*, 1933; *1947 directory*); 500 (*KYB*, 1942–8); 600 (*KYB*, 1949–63); 500 (*KYB*, 1964–6). May be same as *Camp Cinema*.

Kildare

Electric Theatre, listed, *KYB*, 1930–3 (no personnel); l: Foy & McGovern, 480 (*KYB*, 1935); 350 (1934).[45]

The Picture House, p: James T. Jameson (*KYB*, 1925).

Star Cinema, Dublin Road, (*c.*1915–May 1918; ?–28 December 1925), destroyed by fire in 1918;[46] and in December 1925.[47]

Tower Cinema, The Square (*c.*1933–*c.*1967; listed *Showcase* 1968), p: Breslin & Whelan, 204 Pearse Street, Dublin, (*KYB*, 1934–44); Tower Cinema, Kildare (*KYB*, 1945–52); Walter Kehoe, Emo, Portarlington (*KYB*, 1955); Walter Kehoe, Milford, Co. Carlow (*KYB*, 1960–4); Joe Flanagan, the Diamond, Kildare town (last owner); m: John Kennedy (*1947 directory*); fb: Walter Kehoe, Jnr, Killone, Emo (*1947 directory*); 500 (*KYB*, 1937–42); 650 (*KYB*, 1943–52); *c.*700 (*1947 directory*; *KYB*, 1955; 1960–8); building incorporated into the Silken Thomas premises.

Kilcullen

Tower Cinema, br: James J. Byrne, Jnr, 350, screen: 15ft x 12ft, stage area: 18ft x 15ft (*1947 directory*); programme changed four times weekly, fb: Mr Walter Kehoe, Jnr, Killone, Emo, Portarlington (*1947 directory*).

Town Hall, fb: Paddy Melia, 200.

Monasterevan

Picturedrome (*KYB*, 1916–17), p: Harry McCormack, 300.

Naas

Cinema, listed in *KYB*, 1930 (no personnel); p: C.S. Silvester, Curragh Picture House, 300 (*KYB*, 1932–48); may be same as *Town Hall Cinema*.

Coliseum, North Main Street (15 February 1940–8 August 1972; aka *Dara Cinema*, which closed on 1 September 2007; first listed in *KYB*, 1942), built on site belonging to St David's House school; p:

Coliseum Cinema (Naas) Ltd (CRO no. 19523); Mr J.L. Kelly; T.A. Kelly and Joe Egan, Portlaoise (as Egan, Kelly and Kelty in *Showcase* 1968); Modern Irish Theatres (1972); Fran McCormack (2004); br & fb: John Egan, 24 Main Street, Maryborough [/Portlaoise] (*1947 directory*); fb: Paddy Melia (1975–6; also booking advertising manager in 2003);[48] 700 (*KYB*, 1949–71); 2 screens/450 seats (Connolly and Dillon, 2001:72); 2 screens (2003).[49]

Moat Theatre (1963, reopened following €3.2 million investment on 11 April 2003), 200 (2003), Naas film club (affiliated to access>CINEMA) is based there.

• *Storm Cinemas*, Maudlins on the Dublin Road (2005–), 5 screens, p: Premier Productions/ Patrick O'Sullivan; Irish Leisureplex Entertainment Co./Entertainment Enterprises/Ciáran and Colum Butler (2008); l (from 2008): Odeon Cinemas; from 2008 equipped with 5 digital projectors; 850 (348; 188; 134; 101 and 79) seats.

Town Hall (Cinema) (1902; McCole, 2005:appendix D; 1929–42; listed also in *1947 directory* with fb: John Egan, Maryborough [Portlaoise]), p: Chris Sylvester, Curragh, listed, *KYB*, 1931–5, 1937–48, 269 seats.[50]

Newbridge

Newbridge Picture House, Henry Street (*c.*1929–January 2006; aka *Picture House*, *KYB*, 1930–4; aka *Picture Palace*, *KYB*, 1937; aka *Palace Cinema*, *c.*1934–73; *Oscar Cinema*, 1973–2006), p: Curragh Picture Co. Ltd, Picture House Curragh Camp (*KYB*, 1953–71; *Showcase* 1968); l: Foy & McGovern Ltd; Michael Roycroft and unknown partner (from 1990 who converted cinema from 1 to 3 screens); br: J. McGovern (*1947 directory*); m: Michael Roycroft (1973); fb: Paddy Melia (1975–7);[51] 300;[52] 500 (*KYB*, 1934–50; *1947 directory*); 338 (Connolly and Dillon, 2001:72).[53] The decision to close the cinema in mid-January 2006 was influenced by a recent lack of good films.[54]

Odeon, Main Street (*c.*1941–*c.*mid-1970s; first listed in *KYB*, 1942); p: Newbridge Cinemas Ltd, booked at Veritas House, Lower Abbey Street, Dublin (*KYB*, 1943–4); Odeon Cinemas (*1947 directory*); Messrs Kirkham & Cecil Silvester (*KYB*, 1949–52),[55] Newbridge Cinemas Ltd (*KYB*, 1953–71; *Showcase* 1968); br: J.J. Watson (*1947 directory*); screen: 20ft x 18ft (*1947 directory*); *c.*620 (*KYB*, 1943–6; 1948–53, 650 in *1947 directory*); 720 (*KYB*, 1954–5).

Riverbank Arts Centre, Main Street (2001–), purpose-built venue includes a cinema, 180 seats (2010), access>CINEMA film club based there (2010).

• *UCI Newbridge*, Whitewater shopping centre, Main Street (January 2010–), 6 screens/ 1,001 (312, 250, 123, 112, 105, 99) seats.

Prosperous
Cinema, p: Ernie Price, 300.

Rathangan
Cinema, occasional cinema, p: Harry McCormack, Monasterevan.
The Cinema, br: Mr T. McGovern, Artillery Place, Newbridge (*1947 directory*).

KILKENNY

Ballyraggett
New Hall Cinema, not equipped for sound, 200 (1934;[56] *1947 directory*).

Callan
Gaiety Cinema, Green Street (*c.*July 1923–1971+; aka *Green View Cinema*; *Cinema*, *KYB*, 1925–31; *Gaiety*, *KYB*, 1942–3) p: William F. Egan, owner of garage and other businesses in town, and B. Aylward[57] (*KYB*, 1925–71; only W.F. Egan listed as br in *1947 directory*, and as p in *Showcase* 1968); screen: 15ft x 20ft (*1947 directory*); 400 (1934);[58] 450 (*KYB*, 1944–55); 500 (*1947 directory*); 400 (*KYB*, 1960–71).

Castlecomer
Deen (*c.*1960–71+), p: Castlecomer Cinema Co Ltd (CRO no. 15383; *KYB*, 1961–71; *Showcase* 1968); 500 (*KYB*, 1961–4); 400 (*KYB*, 65–7); 495 (*KYB*, 1968); 456 (*KYB*, 1969–71).
Hall Cinema (*c.*1935–*c.*1956), p: Quinn & McKenna (*KYB*, 1936–52); White, Quinn & McKenna (*KYB*, 1943–54); Quinn, McKenna & Fogarty (*KYB*, 1955–7); br: Mrs White (*1947 directory*); 16ft proscenium (*1947 directory*); 350 (*KYB*, 1936–52);[59] 400 (*KYB*, 1955–7).

Freshford
Odeon (*c.*1949–71+), p: O'Carroll & Dooley (*KYB*, 1950–5); Mr P. O'Carroll, Kilkenny (*KYB*, 1955–71; *Showcase* 1968); 400 (*KYB*, 1950–61).

Goresbridge
Rural Cinema, p: Mrs Ryan; 300.

Graiguenamanagh
Brandon Cinema, br: John A. Joyce, screen 14ft x 11ft (*1947 directory*).
Cinema (*KYB*, 1930–2; no personnel), in 1932 when the proprietor of the cinema applied for a dance licence, the police superintendent asked the judge to order that an appropriate number of Irish dances be included as there was 'too much "jazz" and "foreign" dancing in the town'. The judge hoped Irish dances would be included, but 'coercion never succeeded in Ireland, and he could not ask people to dance a dance if they did not want to.' The proprietor undertook to include Irish dances and the application was granted.[60]

Johnstown
The Cinema, not equipped for sound, 400 (1934).[61]

Kilkenny
Cinema (*c.*1916–*c.*1937), p: Kilkenny Cinema Co. Ltd (CRO no. 4174; *KYB*, 1917–38); m: T. Stallard (*KYB*, 1923, 1926–7); licensed for music and dancing (*KYB*, 1920); 400 (*KYB*, 1919–21); 728 (*KYB*, 1935); 700 (*KYB*, 1937).
• *Kilkenny Cineplex*, Jail Street, Fair Green (*c.*June 1998–; aka *Kilkenny Omniplex*), p: Ward Anderson, 4 screens/850 (316, 216, 172, 146) seats; 4 screens/808 seats.[62]
Kilkenny Theatre, Patrick Street (*c.*1915–71+; first listed, *KYB*, 1916); p: The Kilkenny Cinema Co. Ltd, Kilkenny, 700 (*KYB*, 1939–71; *1947 directory*; *Showcase* 1968).
Regent Cinema, William Street (*c.*1947–76+; first listed as *New Cinema* in *KYB*, 1950), p: Amalgamated Entertainments (Kilkenny) Ltd (*KYB*, 1950–5); Regina Cinema, Waterford (*KYB*, 1960–8; *Showcase* 1968); Abbey Films, 71 Middle Abbey Street, Dublin 1 (*KYB*, 1969–71); br & fb: Martin S. Breen (*1947 directory*); fb: Leo Ward (1974–6);[63] 1,020 (*KYB*, 1950–5); 1,100 (*KYB*, 1956–71).
Savoy (*c.*1941–March 1985; first listed, *KYB*, 1942), p: T. & R. Walsh, 20 North Main Street, Wexford (*KYB*, 1943–5); Savoy Cinema (Kilkenny) Ltd, 1 Lower Rowe Street, Wexford (CRO no. 9287; *KYB*, 1946–71); Amalgamated Cinemas Co. Ltd, Eden Quay (*Showcase* 1968); br: Mr J. Sherin (*1947 directory*); m: Miss K. Gilmartin (*Showcase* 1968); fb: R. Walsh (20 North Main Street) (*1947 directory*); Leo Ward (1977);[64] *c.*1,000 (*KYB*, 1943–61; 900 in *1947 directory*).
The Set Theatre, Langton House Hotel, John Street (2009–) 270/350, multi-purpose venue designed by David Collins Studio, London; Kilkenny FC is based there.

Mullinavat
The Electric Pictures, p: T.T. Bower, 350 (*KYB*, 1918).

Thomastown
The Concert Hall, not equipped for sound, 400 (1934).[65]
Tower Cinema (subsequently *Glenane Community Hall*), br: Mr Kelly, fb: Walter Kehoe, Jnr (Killone, Emo, Portarlington), 400, screen: 16ft x 14ft (*1947 directory*).

Urlingford
Cinema, listed, *KYB*, 1930–4 (no personnel).

Travelling cinemas
Billy Walsh's Picture Company, Kilmacow (July 1928), new regulations only allowed for travelling shows to remain six nights in any one location.[66]
Bracey Daniel's Picture and Variety Company, Piltown (July 1931).[67]
Bradley's and Shaw's Picture and Variety Company, Kilnaspic (March 1926).[68]
O'Brien's Picture and Dramatic Company, Fiddown, (October 1927).[69]
Sullivan's Cinema and Conjuring Show (September 1916).[70]

LAOIS (also Leix)

Abbeyleix
Coliseum (*c.*1947–68, listed *Showcase* 1968), p: John Egan, 500 (*KYB*, 1949–68); fb: John Egan, 24 Main Street, Maryborough [Portlaoise], (*1947 directory*).
Milo (*c.*1968–71+), p: Bernard Murray, 450 (*KYB*, 1969–71); m: Mr W. Gorman (*Showcase* 1968).

Maryborough, see **Portlaoise**

Mountmellick

Catholic Young Men's Society Cinema (*c.*1931–76+), p: CYMS (*KYB*, 1932–45; 1950–2; *1947 directory*); l: E.J. Breen (*KYB*, 1950–4); P.A. Fennelly, 28 Emmet Street, Mountmellick (*KYB*, 1955); Sean Keenan, 17 Patrick Street (*KYB*, 1965–; listed as m in *Showcase* 1968); br: Mr Breen (*1947 directory*); m: Michael Scott, Sarsfield Street, Mountmellick (*KYB*, 1970–1); fb: Michael Scott (1976);[71] 14ft proscenium (*1947 directory*); 350 (*KYB*, 1936–41; *1947 directory*);[72] 400 (*KYB*, 1942–5); 500 (*KYB*, 1946–8); 802 (*KYB*, 1949–55); 564 (*KYB*, 1965–71).

Electric Cinema (*c.*1918–*c.*1930; aka *Owenass Hall*), p: Mountmellick Electric Cinema Co. Ltd; licensed for music and dancing; m: William Lynch (*KYB*, 1919); N. Scully (*KYB*, 1920, 1922–8); 400 (*KYB*, 1919–21); no personnel listed *KYB*, 1929–31.

Mountrath

Coliseum Theatre (*c.*1947–*c.*1968), p (& fb): John Egan (*1947 directory*; *KYB*, 1949–66; *Showcase* 1968).

Elite Cinema, Main Street (*c.*1967–71+), p: Christopher McLoughton & Mrs E. McLoughton, 475 (*KYB*, 1968–71).

Park View Cinema, not equipped for sound, 250 (1934).[73]

Portarlington

Coliseum (*KYB*, 1945).

CYMS Cinema, not equipped for sound, 300 (1934).[74]

Electric Cinema (*c.*1929–47+: first listed, *KYB*, 1930, listed in *1947 directory*), p: W. Higgins, Patrick St, Portarlington, 500 (*KYB*, 1934–45); br: Mrs. W. Higgins (*1947 directory*). See also *Father Paul Murphy Hall*, Edenderry, Co. Offaly.

Savoy Cinema (*c.*1946–76+), p: McNally Cinemas, Ltd (*1947 directory*); Roscrea & Athy Cinema Co. (*KYB*, 1949–66; 1971; *Showcase* 1968); Mrs T. Kevin, Main Street, Templemore (*KYB*, 1967–70); br: W. Higgins (*1947 directory*); fb: Harry W. Culleton, 75 Middle Abbey Street, Dublin (*1947 directory*); Paddy Melia (1976–7);[75] screen: 20ft x 15ft (*1947 directory*); 700 (*1947 directory*); 600 (*KYB*, 1949–71).

Town Hall (first listing, *KYB*, 1916–17), 400; contact: CYMS (*KYB*, 1918); may be same as *CYMS Cinema*.

Portlaoise (formerly Maryborough)

Coliseum, Bull Lane (mid-1930s–12 December 1985;?–December 2000), p: Coliseum (Portleix) Ltd (*KYB*, 1939–71; *1947 directory*; *Showcase* 1968); br & fb: John Egan, 24 Main Street, Maryborough [Portlaoise] (*1947 directory*); fb: Paddy Melia (1975–6),[76] 600 (*1947 directory*); 350 (*KYB*, 1950–71); destroyed by fire, 12 December 1985;[77] reopened until December 2000, a week before opening of *Storm Cinemas* multiplex.

Dunamaise Theatre & Centre for the Arts, Church Street (May 1999–), purpose-built arts and theatre venue, d: Louise Donlon (2010); 240; occasional film screenings.

Electric Cinema, New Road (November 1914–2000+), p: Delaney family, Kellyville Park; P. Delany (*KYB*, 1933–44, 1950–5); Mrs N. Delany (*Showcase* 1968); PEP Cinemas Ltd (*KYB*, 1969–71; 2000);[78] m: P.J. Delany (*KYB*, 1927–33); br: J. Delany (*1947 directory*); 300 (*KYB*, 1935; 1934);[79] 400 (*KYB*, 1939–44, 1950–5); 450 (*1947 directory*); 255 (*KYB*, 1969–71). Narrow building with a single aisle down the centre; projector powered by gas; extended in mid-1920s to include adjoining building; balcony added by 1930s; sold in 1968;[80] renovated and reopened in April 2000.

Heath Cinema, Bull Lane, p: Michael Breen, Heath Cinema Co. Ltd (*c.*1990; CRO no. 106008). Possibly same as *Coliseum*.

• *Storm Cinemas*, Church Street (2001–; aka *Odeon/Storm*), p: Premier Productions/Patrick O'Sullivan; Irish Leisureplex Entertainment Co./Entertainment Enterprises/Ciáran and Colum Butler (2008); l (2008–): Odeon Cinemas; 5 screens/709 seats;[81] the largest room: 250 seats by late 2000s, all with digital projection.

Rathdowney

Cinema (possibly from *c.*1945)[82] fb: W. Smeaton (1976).[83]

LEITRIM

Ballinamore

Lyric Cinema (1946–*c.*1974; aka *Nicholas's*), p: Nicholas Keegan, 500 (*KYB*, 1949–71; *Showcase* 1968).[84]

Drumshanbo

Breffni Cinema (*c.*1948–71+), p: Ed McGowan, 200 (*KYB*, 1949–71; *Showcase* 1968).
Roxy Cinema, Carrick Road (Easter Sunday 1953–30 April 1967), p: Michael John Giblin;[85] demolished in May 2004.[86]

Manorhamilton

Park Cinema (aka *Cinema*, listed as name only in *1947 directory*), p: Kyle Armstrong; 400.

Mohill

Ritz Cinema, Glebe Street (*c.*1944–*c.*1970), p: Ballymahon Associated Cinemas circuit (*1947 directory*); Frank J. Farrell, Cloncoose, Longford (*KYB*, 1945, 1950–71; as Mr R.F. Farrell in *Showcase* 1968); m & fb: Frank J. Farrell (*1947 directory*, address: Ballymahon, Mullingar); screen: 10ft x 11ft (*1947 directory*); 400 (*KYB*, 1945, 1950–71; *1947 directory*); F.J. Farrell incorporated with 'Staffords' cinema, Longford (*KYB*, 1970).

Travelling cinemas

Barry's Hippodrome. Carrick-on-Shannon's first talking pictures were displayed by this company which visited Hugh Dolan's field on 24–5 September 1929.[87]
• *Cinema-North-West* (2007–; formerly, *c.*2005–2007, *Leitrim Cinemobile*; *Aisling Gheal Leitrim*), dedicated to provision of Irish and world cinema, weekly screenings in Manorhamilton; Carrick-on-Shannon; and also the south Sligo town of Tubbercurry at Humbert Street. Developed by Leitrim county council's directorate of community enterprise and Sligo county council's art department – Sligo Arts Service and supported by the Sligo county council library services;[88] based at Powellsboro, Tubbercurry, Co. Sligo.
George Coates, Manorhamilton, Co. Leitrim; Ballybofin; Donegal (*KYB*, 1941–4).
Leitrim Cinemobile. See *Cinema-North-West*.

LIMERICK[89]

Abbeyfeale

Abbey Cinema, Convent Street (*c.*1948–*c.*1993, listed *Showcase* 1968), p: Tobin Brothers, 520 (*KYB*, 1949–71); fb: D. Tobin (1976);[90] protected structure.[91]
Desmond Cinema (*c.*1947) br: [Patrick] O'Carroll-Nash, screen: 16ft x 12ft 350 (*1947 directory*). See *Desmond Cinema*, Newcastle West (also listed in *1947 directory*).

Ballylanders

Arcade, 300.

Bruff

Picture House (*c.*1915–*c.*1947), p/m: William B. Donovan (*KYB*, 1916–21); William O'Donovan (*KYB*, 1922–48; *1947 directory*); 500 (*KYB*, 1919); 200 (*KYB*, 1920).

Cappamore

Cappamore Cinema (*c.*1934–?), 400, not equipped for sound.[92]
Regal Cinema (1943–90), p: W. Gleeson (*Showcase* 1968); Edward (Eddie) Gleeson (1975–7);[93] 350 (*KYB*, 1949–71).

Doon

Capital Cinema (*c.*1955–?) Toher Street, p: Richard Keane, 300.

Drumcollogher

Church Street, an occasional venue in upstairs of wooden shed, 60ft x 20ft, cinema fire, 5 September 1926, 48 dead (see chapter 1).

Glin

Holley's Hall, not equipped for sound, 200 (1934).[94]
Oisín Cinema (1938–98+), p: O'Shea family (1938–); Patrick J. O'Shea, Oisín Cinema, Killorglin (*KYB*, 1952–65); Patrick J. Lynch, Tarbert, Co. Kerry (*KYB*, 1967–71; *Showcase* 1968); Diarmuid O'Shea (1998); 500 (*KYB*, 1952–61); in 2006, planning permission was sought by Jim and Carol Costello, Kilfergus, Glin, for the conversion of the cinema into eight apartments.

Granagh

One of the many locations for travelling picture shows into the 1950s. In this case, Brian Lyons' Super Talkies and Ben Bono's, Dublin, which included variety, came to Walshe's sandpit field near Chawke's

Cross. Other travelling visitors were the Hayes Brothers, whose tent and equipment were lost in a fire in the village, though they later returned; the McCormacks; Gazettes; and Courtneys.[95]

Hospital
Community Hall (aka *Muintír na Tíre Cinema*), p: local clergy, 300.

Kilfinane
Astor Cinema (formerly *Brennan's Hall*, used for dances, live shows and occasional [16mm] film shows), p: Sean Hyde, Tallow; 200.

Kilmallock
Friars Gate Theatre and Arts Centre (opened on site of *Curzon Cinema* in 1997), Sarsfield Street, 130 seats; film club based there, supported by access>CINEMA (2010).
Hall Cinema (*c*.1927–*c*.1947; aka *People's Hall*; listed, *KYB*, 1928–33, no personnel); p: Joe O'Connor; 14ft stage; dancehall (*KYB*, 1933); p: Kilmallock Co–Operative Friendly Society, 600 (*KYB*, 1934–48; *1947 directory*); 20ft stage (*1947 directory*).
Sarsfield Cinema (*c*.1947–77+; latterly known as *Curzon*; listed *Showcase* 1968, site redeveloped as arts centre in 1997, see above), p: Willie & Eddie Gleeson, Cappamore; br: Mr T. Howard (*1947 directory*); fb: Eddie Gleeson (1975–7);[96] 200 (*KYB*, 1950–71).
Super Grand Cinema (*c*.1938–*c*.1947), p: Howard (*KYB*, 1939–48). May be same venue as *Sarsfield Cinema*.

Limerick
Abbey Cinema, George's Quay, near Barrington's hospital (*c*.1922–12 April 1930), p: James J. Trehy, 23 Glenthworth Street (*KYB*, 1923–31); destroyed by fire on 12 April 1930.[97]
Astor Cinema, North Sexton Street, Thomondgate, p: O'Donoghue family.
Athenaeum Hall, Upper Cecil Street (intermittently from 24 December 1900; permanently from 1912 to 1937; reopened after renovations, 23 October 1937–November 1946; aka *Athenaeum Hall Picturedrome*; *Athenaeum Permanent Picturedrome*; *Athenaeum Picture Playhouse*; after extensive reconstruction, reopened as *Royal Cinema*, 17 November 1947–*c*.March 1985; first listing, *KYB*, 1916); contact: Alex McEwan (*KYB*, 1918); l/m: P.G. Cronin and family (1919–5 April 1941; *KYB*, 1920–41); 'pictures & variety' (*KYB*, 1929); p Thomond Cinema at £5 per week (April 1941–July 1941); Messrs O'Donoghue & Costello received short lease from owners vocational educational committee (VEC, March 1944); Royal Cinema (Limerick) Ltd/Martin Breen circuit, Waterford (from 1947; *Showcase* 1968); Mary Collins; Green Group/Ward Anderson; fb: Leo Ward (1975–6);[98] 600 (*KYB*, 1918); 400 (*KYB*, 1920–1); 450 (*KYB*, 1937); 500 (*KYB*, 1940; *1947 directory*);[99] 900 (*KYB*, 1950–71); one of the first films to be shown in the *Athenaeum* was in 1913 of a Garryowen versus University College Cork rugby match; under lease's '12 days' rule', venue had to be given over to citizens for twelve days per year for live entertainments; on 10 November 1930, two reels of Alfred's Hitchcock's film version of Sean O'Casey's play *Juno and the Paycock* were seized from the *Athenaeum* and burned in the street outside;[1] restored building opened as *Theatre Royal* in 1989; despite severe damage as a result of a fire on 6 March 1990, reopened on 3 February 1991 as a live venue, though closed again in 1997.[2]
Belltable Arts Centre, 69 O'Connell Street
Limerick Film Club, Belltable Arts Centre, 69 O'Connell Street (1975–; aka *Belltable Film Club*; *Limerick Filmhouse Centre*), based at the *Savoy* and *Grand Central* cinemas (to 2005), associated with *Irish Film Theatre-Limerick*, Roxboro, 1980–2, as *Belltable Film Club* associated with *Belltable Arts Centre* (established 1981, the first regional arts centre in Ireland), from 1982, using *Savoy* and *Grand Central* cinemas (to 2005), based at *Belltable Arts Centre* from 2005, fb: Declan McLoughlin, Pat Carroll, via access>CINEMA;[3] *Belltable* cinema known initially as *Limerick Filmhouse Centre*. Once weekly film screenings and other occasional film events. In 2003 the Cultural Cinema Consortium (Arts Council and Irish Film Board) awarded a €750,000 grant for art house cinema development at the centre, but this had not been utilized by 2010.[4] The *Belltable* is also host to the Fresh Film Festival which began in 1997; 100 (Connolly & Dillon, 2001:66). Declan McLoughlin and John O'Leary established the Limerick Film Archive at Kilmallock in 1992.
Carlton Cinema, corner of Henry Street and Shannon Street, (Easter Saturday 1940 [private opening]/Easter Monday 1940 [open to public]–1990, demolished in 2001), arch: Clifford, Smith & Newenham, Limerick; built on site of corn store; parterre and balcony;[5] p: Carlton Cinema (Limerick) Ltd (*KYB*, 1944–71; *Showcase* 1968); br: R. Williams (*1947 directory*); fb: Leo Ward (1974–6);[6] screen: 22ft x 18ft (*1947 directory*); 800 (*KYB*, 1944–55); *c*.675 (*KYB*, 1960–71). In 2003 Bank of Scotland signed a lease for a new six-storey office block on the old cinema site.[7]
City Theatre (1952–*c*.1970s). See *Ritz Cinema*.

Coliseum Cinema, O'Connell Street (November 1917–8 June 1953), p: Helena & Thomas Gough, m: Thomas Gough (*1947 directory*), screen: 18ft x 12ft (*1947 directory*); 550 seats (*KYB*, 1919–54);[8] *Belltable Arts Centre*, which opened in 1981, built on site.

Gaiety Kinema-De-Luxe, 45 O'Connell Street (*c.*1916–*c.*1929), p: P. McCarty & Sons (*KYB*, 1917–22); Messrs Sexton & Kerney (*KYB*, 1923); A.J. Sexton (*KYB*, 1924); m: Joseph J. McCarty (*KYB*, 1919); P.A. Smyth (*KYB*, 1920–1); N. Fogarty (*KYB*, 1926); l: P. Foy & R.W. O'Russ (*KYB*, 1927–9);[9] 400 (*KYB*, 1917); 470 (*KYB*, 1919); closed *KYB*, 1930.

Garryowen Cinema, Broad Street (1919–*c.*1930), m: S.A. McInerney (*KYB*, 1922–8), 'accommodation' for 450;[10] 350 (*KYB*, 1921–); no personnel listed *KYB*, 1929–31; listed as closed in *KYB*, 1932; became a furniture store.

Grand Central Cinema, Bedford Row (*c.*1922–2005; aka *Central Cinema*; from 1972, *Central Studio Cinema*), built on site of Primitive Wesleyan Methodist preaching house (1821); p: Paul & May Bernard (*KYB*, 1923–36); A.E Goodwin (*KYB*, 1937–55); National Cinemas Ltd, Limerick (*KYB*, 1960–70; *Showcase* 1968); Metropolitan Cinema Ltd (*KYB*, 1971); m: Paul Bernard (*KYB*, 1923–36); br: Mr B. Brien (*1947 directory*); fb: Leo Ward (1976);[11] 25ft proscenium (*1947 directory*); 600 (*KYB*, 1935; 1934);[12] 650 (*KYB*, 1937–61); after closing as commercial cinema, one of the locations for Belltable Film Club; redeveloped as offices and retail premises.

• *Limerick Omniplex*, Crescent shopping centre, Dooradoyle (December 1996–), p: Ward Anderson, 9 screens (December 1996); 12 screens (from September 1998); 1,814 (487, 180, 132, 164, 259, 220, 66, 66, 66, 66, 42, 66) seats; 12 screens/1,832 seats;[13] extensively refurbished in November 2005 to compete with *Storm* which had opened six months previously.

Lyric Cinema, Glenworth Street (1924–8 August 1976; formerly *Havergal Hall*; *Lyric Theatre*; aka *Limerick Hippodrome*, October–November 1924; first listed, *KYB*, 1931–3; demolished in 1982, used as a car park before becoming an apartment complex with casino on ground floor), art deco building, complete with a stage, which was used for occasional live shows (operas, plays, etc); p: Mr Ashleigh (*KYB*, 1934–41); J. Cronin (*KYB*, 1942–51; *1947 directory*); Amalgamated Cinemas (Ireland) Ltd, 9 Eden Quay, Dublin (*KYB*, 1952–71; *Showcase* 1968); Ward Anderson; m: Mr A. O'Sullivan (*Showcase* 1968); 900 (*KYB*, 1937); 600 (*KYB*, 1940); 800 (1934);[14] 900 (*KYB*, 1942–71; *1947 directory*).

Movieland. See *Roxboro Twin Theatres*.

Rink Palace, Wellesley Place, arch: William Smith, conversion of skating rink built in 1909 into a cinema (*c.*1911 [*DIA*]), listed in *KYB*, 1916–17.

Ritz Cinema/Theatre, Sexton Street (aka *City Theatre*, late 1940s to 1970s), Lorcan Bourke purchased the *Ritz* and in 1952 renamed it as the *City Theatre*; occasional film shows, manly continental films during 1960s and 1970s.

Roxboro Twin Theatres, Thomond shopping centre, aka Roxboro shopping centre, Roxboro Road (*c.*1976–83; aka *Movieland* [better-known local designation], *Movieland Twins*), p: Ward Anderson, who sublet one screen to Irish Film Theatre, Dublin, July 1980—December 1981, in failed regional art cinema policy; fb: Leo Ward (1976);[15] 2 screens (the city's first 2-screen complex); later snooker hall/amusement arcade.

Royal Cinema, Cecil Street. See *Athenaeum*.

Savoy Cinema, Bedford Row (19 December 1935–74; aka *Savoy Theatre*; became music/concert venue, *c.*1975–89); arch: Leslie C. Norton, who also designed Theatre Royal, Dublin; p: Irish Cinemas Ltd, 19 Upper O'Connell Street, Dublin (registered 17 November 1934; CRO no. 8828; *1947 directory*; *Showcase* 1968); d: J.E. Pearce, Ayeesha Castle, Killiney, Co. Dubin; Joseph X. Murphy, Ashurst, Mount Merion Avenue, Blackrock, Co. Dublin; James McCann, Simmonscourt, Dublin; Horace Moore; Fred W. Moore; m: James Sheil (1935, *1947 directory*);[16] p: Capitol & Allied Theatres Ltd (January 1939–January 1946); J. Arthur Rank's Odeon (Ireland) Ltd (January 1946–74); fb: Louis Elliman (*1947 directory*); screen: 24ft x 18³/₄ft (*1947 directory*); 1,650 (*KYB*, 1946); 1,483 (*KYB*, 1961–4); 1,465 seats (*KYB*, 1965–71); building demolished in 1989 and site redeveloped by Ward Anderson as *Savoy Centre*.

Savoy Centre, Bedford Row (July 1990–*c.*2002, aka *Savoy* [+ *Central Studio*]), built on site of demolished *Savoy Cinema*, p: Ward Anderson, 5 screens/1,002 (292, 226, 196, 156, 132) seats with a further screen across the road at the *Central Studio*; 6 screens/1,200 seats (Connolly and Dillon, 2001:73); 6 screens/1,650 seats (*Cinema Treasures*, 2010); demolished to make way for 94-bedroom Marriott Hotel, renamed Savoy hotel in 2009.

Shannon Cinema, George's Quay (1916–*c.*1921; first listed, *KYB*, 1917), p: The Shannon Cinema Co. Ltd (CRO no. 11219); Messrs Murphy and Coffey (*KYB*, 1919–22); m: J.P. McCaughey (*KYB*, 1919–22); 700 (*KYB*, 1919); 500 (*KYB*, 1920–1).

• *Storm Cinemas*, Castletroy shopping centre (19 May 2005–; *Odeon/Storm*), p: Premier Productions/

Patrick O'Sullivan; p (2008): Irish Leisureplex Entertainment Co./Entertainment Enterprises/Ciáran and Colum Butler; l (2008–): Odeon Cinemas; 8 screens/1,587 (434; 310; 199; 199; 159; 122; 86; 78) seats, wine bar.[17]

Theatre Royal, Henry Street (1841–23 January 1922), built by Joseph Fogerty (also owner), remained in family until it burnt down on 23 January 1922;[18] occasional film shows, which, as indicated from *KYB*, 1919, became a regular feature; p: M.W. Shanly, m: Joseph P. McKenna, (*KYB*, 1919–22); 800 (*KYB*, 1921).

Thomond Cinema, Nicholas Street (*c*.1936–71+; first listed, *KYB*, 1937–8), p: Thomond Cinemas, Ltd (CRO no. 9312; *KYB*, 1939–71; *1947 directory*; *Showcase* 1968); br: Mr Dillon (*1947 directory*); 600 (*1947 directory*); 500 (*KYB*, 1950–71); snooker hall now occupies site.

Tivoli Cinema, Assembly Mall, near Baal's Bridge, Charlotte's Quay (1916–24 July 1920; ?–1956; aka *Tivoli Picture Palace*, *KYB*, 1922), p/m: Paul Bernard (*KYB*, 1922–31); Paul & May Bernard (*KYB*, 1933–55); br & fb: Mr P. Coffey (of *Picturedrome*, Tralee, listed in *1947 directory*); 500 (1934);[19] 350 (*KYB*, 1935–55); damaged by fire on 24 July 1920.

Newcastle West

Desmond Cinema (*c*.1941–71+) p: J. [O']Carroll Nash (*KYB*, 1942); Patrick O'Carroll Nash, Demesne House, Newcastle West, 500 (*KYB*, 1943–71; *1947 directory*; *Showcase* 1968); screen: 14ft x 12ft (*1947 directory*).

Latchford's Cinema (*c*.1929–90+; aka *Latchford's Theatre*, *KYB*, 1930–3; later, *Lee's Cinema*), p: Mr [J.] Latchford (*KYB*, 1933–55; *1947 directory*); Mrs K. Latchford (*KYB*, 1965–71; *Showcase* 1968); Toss Lee (*c*.1990); 300 (1934);[20] 250 (*KYB*, 1936–71).

Lee's Cinema, Maiden Street (closed 2003; formerly, *Latchford's Cinema*), p: Toss Lee; 1 screen;[21] 190 seats.[22]

Picture House (*c*.1918–*c*.1930), p: The Enterprises; occasional variety; 15ft stage; 2 dressing rooms (*KYB*, 1930–1; no personnel); may be same as *Picture Palace*.

Picture Palace, p: William Phelan (1919–28); J.P. Roche (*KYB*, 1929); m: J.J. Phelan (*KYB*, 1919–25); M.J. Phelan (*KYB*, 1926–8); 500 seats, licensed for dancing and music (*KYB*, 1919); 450 (*KYB*, 1920); 350 (*KYB*, 1921).

St Ita's Hall, p: W. Phelan, 400 (*KYB*, 1917); may be same as *Picture House*.

Rathkeale

Central Cinema, Lower Main Street (*c*.1948–71+), p: Messrs Gazetts (*KYB*, 1949–71; *Showcase* 1968); 450 (*KYB*, 1949–57); façade has preservation order; it was proposed in 2006 that the derelict cinema be purchased by the local authority as a performing arts centre.

Travelling cinemas

Super Sound Cinema (Nelius Fraser): Abbeyfeale and Kilfinnane, Co. Limerick; Doneraile, Co Cork; Ennistymon and Milltown Malbay, Co. Clare; Newport, Co. Tipperary (*KYB*, 1941).

LONGFORD

Ballymahon

Cinema (December 1920–), p: Mr Connolly.[23]

Ritz Cinema, Main Street (1943–71+), p: F.J. Farrell, Cloncoose, Longford (*KYB*, 1944–8); Misses K. & B. Connelly (*KYB*, 1949–71; *Showcase* 1968); br: Miss K. Connnelly (*1947 directory*); screen: 11ft x 11ft (*1947 directory*); 450 (*KYB*, 1944–8); 400 (*1947 directory*; *KYB*, 1949–71).

Edgeworthstown

Auburn, p: Ward Anderson, 200.

Granard

Alpha Cinema (*c*.1949–*c*.1963), Granard Cinema Ltd (CRO no. 11645), p: Alan McDonald, 350 (*KYB*, 1950–64; *Showcase* 1968).

Lanesboro'

Plaza, p: Eddie Kelly; 300.

Longford

Adelphi (*c*.1948–71+), arch: Mr Devaney, Dublin (*DIA*); p: Cinemas Ltd (*KYB*, 1948–51); Midland Amusements Ltd, Bridge Street, Longford (*KYB*, 1952–71; *Showcase* 1968); 770 (*KYB*, 1948–61).

Hall, Church Street (1897–1904; McCole, 2005:appendix D).

Hibernian Cinema, p: Ward Anderson (*c*.1981).

• *Longford Omniplex*, Bridge Street (1998–; aka *Longford Cineplex*), p: Ward Anderson, 4 screens/622 (266, 140, 127, 89) seats; 681 seats.²⁴

Odeon, Bridge Street (9 October 1941–*c*.1996; redeveloped as *Longford Cineplex*), p: John Doris and Matthew J. Lyons, Midland Amusements Ltd, 35 Upper Abbey Street, Dublin, (*KYB*, 1942–51); Midland Amusement Ltd, Bridge Street, Longford (*KYB*, 1952–71; *1947 directory*; *Showcase* 1968); Ward Anderson (from 1981);²⁵ br: M.J. Lyons, screen: 25ft x 18ft (*1947 directory*); fb: Gerry Kirkham (35 Upper Abbey Street, Dublin) & Joe Riley (Belmont Avenue, Donnybrook), (*1947 directory*); J. Doris (1975–7);²⁶ 652 (*KYB*, 1942–51); 689 (*KYB*, 1952–61).

Palace Cinema (*c*.1933–*c*.1947), p: J Molloy (*KYB*, 1934); M.J. Lyons (*KYB*, 1935); br: M.J. Lyons (*1947 directory*); 250 (1934);²⁷ 600 (*KYB*, 1935–41; *1947 directory*).

Picturedrome, Kilashee Street, p: Joseph J. Stafford, (*KYB*, 1916–17).

Protestant Hall (1903; McCole, 2005:appendix D).

*Stafford's Cinema*²⁸ Main Street [Kilashee Street in *1947 directory*] (*c*.1915²⁹–*c*.1947), p/m: Joseph J. Stafford (*KYB*, 1919–33); K. Stafford, 1 Main Street, Longford (*KYB*, 1937–42); F.J. Farrell, Cloncoose, Longford (*KYB*, 1943–6, also listed as fb in *1947 directory*, but name as Frank J. Farrell and with address as Ballymahon, Mullingar); br: Miss P. Malone (*1947 directory*); screen: 12ft x 12ft (*1947 directory*); 300 (*KYB*, 1919–20); 320 (*KYB*, 1921); 300 (1934);³⁰ 450 (*KYB*, 1935); 325 (*KYB*, 1937–42); 430 (*KYB*, 1943–6); 400 (*1947 directory*); last listed in *KYB*, 1946.

LOUTH

Ardee

Bohemian Cinema, Tisdale Street (*c*.1933–40; new cinema building, 30 August 1940–1979; aka *Ardee Cinema*; listed in *Showcase* 1968), p: Ardee Cinema Ltd (CRO no. 9978); a small picture house originally run by the De La Salle Brothers, later taken over by Thorne family, who had set up a furniture factory in village in 1923, and where the furniture for the cinema was made and upholstered; in 1940, the Thornes built a new cinema beside their factory and retained name *Bohemian*; arch: J.F. McGahon & Sons, Dundalk; p: S. Markey (*KYB*, 1934–5); H.C. Thorne, S. Markey (*KYB*, 1937–9); H.C. Thorne (*KYB*, 1936, 1940), Ardee Cinema Ltd (*KYB*, 1941–6; CRO no. 9978); J.J. Thorne (*KYB*, 1949–54; *1947 directory*); Ardee Cinema Ltd (*KYB*, 1955–71), screen: 20ft x 16ft (*1947 directory*); 300 (*KYB*, 1936); *c*.225 (*c*.1938);³¹ *c*.450³² (*KYB*, 1948, 1965–8; 430 [*KYB*, 1969–71]); 480 (*1947 directory*); premises now used by Ardee concert band and for bingo sessions.

Young Men's Society Hall (1904–5; McCole, 2005:appendix D).

Carlingford

Abbey Cinema (20 June 1947–1971+) p: Carlingford Pictures Ltd, Newry Street, Carlingford, 500 (*KYB*, 1948–71; *Showcase* 1968, address as New Street).

Parochial Hall (*KYB*, 1930–4).

Drogheda

Abbey Cinema, Abbey shopping centre, West Street, beside old abbey (8 September 1937³³–26 February 1969; *c*.1970–1993; as *Abbey Cineplex*, 1993–2000), p: John G. Murphy, local garage owner, and Mary A. Murphy (*KYB*, 1939–55; *1947 directory*); Abbey Cinema Ltd (*KYB*, 1960–71; *Showcase* 1968); Ward Anderson; fb: Leo Ward (1975–7);³⁴ 1,000 seats including balcony; cinema burned down on 26 February 1969; rebuilt as 2 screens.

Abbey Cineplex. See *Abbey Cinema*.

Boyne Cinema, Fair Street (27 January 1919–February 1960; renamed *Savoy*, 1954), p: Joseph M. Stanley, newspaper proprietor (1919–32, *KYB*, 1923–32); Boyne Cinemas Ltd. (*KYB*, 1935–46); Joseph M. Stanley, 6 Peter Street, Drogheda (*KYB*, 1951, also fb listed in *1947 directory*); J.C. Stanley, 6 Peter Street, Drogheda (*KYB*, 1952); m: E.D. Kenny (*KYB*, 1924–28); br: J.C. Stanley (*1947 directory*); screen: 14ft (*1947 directory*); 450 (*KYB*, 1933); 400 (1934);³⁵ 330 (*KYB*, 1936–46; *1947 directory*); 450 (*KYB*, 1948–52). The *Boyne* got power initially from a steam-driven engine; in 1931, a diesel engine was installed, and it was not until 1952 that electricity was used.

Cinema House, Lawrence Street, (aka *Whitworth Hall*; *Town Hall*), p: Dundalgan Electric Theatres Ltd, 1,000 (*KYB*, 1916–17; reappears in *KYB* 1936 and 1938 without details.

• *Drogheda Omniplex*, Boyne Centre, Bolton Street (1997–), p: Ward Anderson; 6 screens/578; 579 (199, 161, 30, 81, 61, 47) seats; 6 sceens/785 seats (Connolly and Dillon, 2001:73.)

Droichead Arts Centre, Stockwell Street (1994–; originally opened in Scholes Lanes in 1989), mixed-use venue; home to access>CINEMA affiliated Droichead film club/society.

Electric Theatre, Fair Street (*c*.1911–?), p: Irish Provincial Electric Theatres Ltd registered in Dublin on 29 April 1911 with £3,000 capital in £1 shares to acquire and carry on the business of electric theatre proprietors, (1) by John F. Pinchin, L.E. Foster and J. Mackay under the style of 'Electric Theatre, Dundalk' Co. Louth; and (2), by J.F. Pinchin and Louisa Pinchin at Newry, Co. Down, under the style of 'Picture Palace, Newry'; private company; first d: John Mackay, Dundalk, John F. Pinchcin, Lansdowne Lodge, Holyhead, England; Louis E. Foster, Dundalk; qualification £100; registered; Market Street, Dundalk;[36] m: Mr Butler (1914);[37] may be same as *Boyne Cinema*.

Gate Cinema, Westgate (2 November 1944–December 1973), p: Drogheda Cinemas Ltd, d: Robert (Bob) McCabe, local businessman, and Donal O'Hagan, local solicitor (*KYB*, 1949–71, company also listed in *Showcase* 1968); 900 (*1947 directory*); 970 (*KYB*, 1949); 1,000 (*KYB*, 1952–69); 800 (*KYB*, 1970–1).

Oscars 1 & 2, p: Mr O. Cassidy (1975–6).[38]

Savoy Cinema, Fair Street (*c*.1954–71+; formerly, *Boyne Cinema*, 1919–54), p: John McGrane and T. Boylan, 420 (*KYB*, 1955–71; *Showcase* 1968).

Town Hall, Lawrence Street (aka *Whitworth Hall*; *Cinema House*), 380 (1934).[39]

Whitworth Hall, near St Lawrence Gate (1898–1905 [McCole, 2005:appendix D]; 1914–10 June 1939; aka *Cinema House*), l: Dundealgan Electric Theatres Ltd, Town Hall buildings, Dundalk, d: Paddy Deary; Walter Slevin (Enniskillen); m (1914–): Jack O'Mahoney, tobacconist, Shop Street, where cinema seats could be booked;[40] l: Dundealgan Electric Theatre Ltd, St Helena, Dundalk (*KYB*, 1935–8); 450 (*KYB*, 1935–8); 380 (*KYB*, 1939–41).[41]

Dundalk

Adelphi, Market Street (12 May 1947–*c*. June 1995; later, *IMC Dundalk*), arch: Robinson, Keefe & Devane, Dublin (*DIA*); p: Eastern Cinemas Ltd (*KYB*; *Showcase* 1968), d: Brian McGuinness, Donal O'Hagan, Jimmy Quinn, Eileen O'Hagan, Brian McGuinness (second person with same name); m: Brian Barry (from 1947, *KYB*, 1949–71); cine-variety; d. of Eastern Cinemas Ltd (1975): Mr R.F. Martin; p: Ward Anderson; 1,122;[42] 1,100 (*KYB*, 1949–52); 1,025 (*KYB*, 1955–71); 3 screens/479 (225, 148, 106) seats. See also *IMC Dundalk*.

Casino, fb (1976–7): Leo Ward.[43]

Dominican Hall (early 1950s), screened films for about three years but had to stop following objections from commercial cinema interests.[44]

Magnet (12 April 1938–1977+), converted from Pioneer Total Abstinence Hall/St Patrick's Hall; p: Revd J. Stokes Horn, administrator, St Patrick's, Dundalk (*KYB*, 1939–51); Revd J. McEvoy, administrator, St Patrick's (*KYB*, 1952); Revd T.F. MacDonald (*KYB*, 1953–5); Revd D. Campbell (*KYB*, 1961–71; *Showcase* 1968); fb: Revd Shiels (1975–7);[45] 600 (*KYB*, 1943; *1947 directory*); 750 (*KYB*, 1944–55; 1961–71).

• *IMC Dundalk*, Carroll Village, Longwalk (1999–; formerly *Adelphi*), p: Ward Anderson, 7 screens, 1,211 seats;[46] 7 screens/1173 (2010).

Oriel Cinema, Market Street, formerly Foresters Hall (*c*.1922–*c*.1951), p: Joseph M. Stanley (*KYB*, 1923–36); J.M. Stanley's Boyne Cinemas Ltd (*KYB*, 1937–52); m: J. McKeown (*KYB*, 1926–7); bm: E.D. Kenny (*Boyne Cinema*, Drogheda, also owned by J.M. Stanley) in *KYB*, 1926–8, 1930–6; br: Miss E.C Kenny (*1947 directory*); fb: Mr J.M. Stanley, 6 Peter Street, Drogheda, screen: 9ft x 12ft (*1947 directory*); 386 (1934);[47] 300 (*KYB*, 1936; 1943–52); 350 (*1947 directory*).

Park Street Cinema, Park Street (17 October 1912–21 February 1961; aka *Picture Palace*; *Picture House*), p: Irish Provincial Electric Theatres Ltd which leased from Messrs Hardy, seed merchants, a bread shop and bakery and converted it to a cinema (1912); m: William Perkins; m: L.E. Foster (December 1912), who had formerly taken pictures on tour with his Forester's Pictures to Carlingford, Omeath and Kilcurry in the interests of the 1912 Oriel bazaar held in Dundalk;[48] p: Irish Empire Palaces Ltd, 52 Stafford Street, Dublin (*KYB*, 1923–30, later address: 3 Grafton Street; *1947 directory*, this Grafton Street address is same as that for cinema's fb: Mr H.K. Campbell [*1947 directory*]) ; m: A.T. Wright (*KYB*, 1923–7); br: Stanley R. Cant, screen: 15½t x 11½ft (*1947 directory*); 600 (*KYB*, 1916–17); 427 (1934);[49] 450 (*KYB*, 1934–48); *c*.485 (*KYB*, 1942–55; *1947 directory*); destroyed by fire in 1961.

St Nicholas Hall, Philip Street (*c*.1927–71+), p: Fr T.F. McManus, St Patrick's, Dundalk (*KYB*, 1955); Fr T.F. McDonald (*KYB*, 1955–71; *Showcase* 1968); 600 (*KYB*, 1955).

Town Hall Cinema, Crowe Street (17 August 1912–1 June 1929; 1931–17 February 1947), p: Dundealgan Electric Theatres Co., Ltd, Town Hall Buildings, Dundalk (1912–31), d: Paddy Deary; Walter Slevin (Enniskillen); W.C. Robinson, 43 Castle Road, Dundalk (from 1931, *KYB*, 1933–41); Leo MacCarron, Clanbrassil Street, Dundalk (*KYB*, 1942–8); m: Eric Hornber (1912);[50] m: John Gormley (1919–30); br: D. McCarron; continuous programming from beginning; licensed for music and dancing (*KYB*, 1919); screen: 16ft x 13ft (*1947 directory*); 900 (*KYB*, 1919); 800 (*KYB*, 1920–

1); 840 (1934);[51] 900 (*KYB*, 1935–7); 800 (*KYB*, 1942–8); 700 (*1947 directory*); the cinema burned down on 17 February 1947.

Louth

Ceili Cinema (?–1956+), p: Gerry McArdle, garage owner; following government measures in 1932 to encourage tobacco growing, McArdle built a drying shed for tobacco; when the venture was abandoned, he converted the building into a cinema.

Tallanstown

Glyde Cinema.[52]

MAYO

Achill

Achill Head Cinema, p: John J. McMonagle, 300.

Balla

Cinema.

Ballina

Arcadia Picture Palace, Arran Street[53] (*c*.1924–*c*.1938), p: Tom Ryan (*KYB*, 1925–33), 500 (*KYB*, 1935–8).[54]

Astoria Cinema, Arthur Street (*c*.1931–) arch: Thomas McNamara, cost *c*.£8,000 (*DIA*).

• *Ballina Cineplex*,[55] corner of Mercy Road and Convent Hill (12 February 2004–), p: Ward Anderson, 6 screens; 1,300 seats; cost: €7 million.[56]

Estoria, Teeling Street (*c*.1934–*c*.September 2001; aka *Astoria*), arch: Hubert O'Connor; p: Estoria Cinema Co. (*KYB*, 1935–71; *1947 directory*; *Showcase* 1968); br & fb: P.J. Mulligan (*1947 directory*); fb: Miss R. Molloy (1975–7);[57] 20ft proscenium (*1947 directory*); 731 (1934);[58] 715 (*KYB*, 1935–61; *1947 directory*); 688 (*KYB*, 1962–71).

Opera Hall (*KYB*, 1916–17).

Savoy, Garden Street (1947–September 2001), arch: Robinson & Keefe, cost £35,000 (*DIA*); p: Ballina Cinema Co. (CRO no. 11403, *KYB*, 1949–52); Amalgamated Cinemas (Ireland) Ltd, 9 Eden Quay, Dublin (*KYB*, 1953–71; *Showcase* 1968), local (Mayo) directors, Mixie Murphy and J.P. Roughneen, Kiltimagh; 886 (*KYB*, 1949–52); 882 (*KYB*, 1955); 718 (*KYB*, 1953–62); sold in 1979 to local consortium which entered a distribution partnership with Ward Anderson, renovated the single screen cinema to become a twin cinema with shopping complex; 2 screens/257 (143 and 114) seats; put into voluntary liquidation and closed September 2001. Leo Ward commented that 'two screens cannot compete with seven screens [in nearby Castlebar]'.[59]

Town Hall Picture House, Arthur Street (*c*.1918–40s; aka *Picture House*; *Town Hall Cinema* in *1947 directory*), p: James Ahern, 400 (*KYB*, 1920); m: James McHale (*KYB*, 1923–33); 400 (*KYB*, 1919–22).

Ballinrobe

The Cinema (*c*.1924–31), p: D.J. O'Connor, Ballinrobe Cinema Co. (*KYB*, 1925–32).

Popular Cinema (*c*.1935–*c*.1955), p: J. Gammon; 380 (*KYB*, 1936; *1947 directory*); 360 (*KYB*, 1941–56). Possibly the Ballinrobe cinema designed by Joseph Gannon (*DIA*).

Rex Cinema (*c*.1956–*c*.1960), p: J. Collins, 300 (*KYB*, 1957–61).

Ritz Cinema (*c*.1962–71+), p: Mrs Drops (*KYB*, 1963–6); Ritz Cinema (Ballinrobe) Ltd (CRO no. 28509, *KYB*, 1970–1); messrs P. Ryder, H. Murphy, J. Staunton (*Showcase* 1968).

Robe Cinema, Main Street (1932–*c*.1947), p: Michael Walsh;[60] Miss Elizabeth Cooney; Miss Cooney & J. Walsh (*KYB*, 1939–48); 300 (*KYB*, 1935–48);[61] 4 shows weekly (*KYB*, 1933–34).

Town Hall, Abbey Street (*c*.1917–*c*.1923), p: Ballinrobe Town Hall Co. Ltd (*KYB*, 1918–24); m: Peter Morris (*KYB*, 1918–24); 300 (*KYB*, 1920–1).[62]

Ballyhaunis

New Cinema (*c*.1929–*c*.1933), p: John Conway, (*KYB*, 1930–4).

St Patrick's Hall (*c*.1947–*c*.1968), p: Revd J.J. Prendergast PP (*KYB*, 1949); Revd G.J. Chancellor Prendergast PP (*KYB*, 1950–60);[63] Revd T. Rushe (*KYB*, 1961–4; *Showcase* 1968); 470 (*1947 directory*); 350 (*KYB*, 1949–56); 400 (*KYB*, 1957–60); 323 (*KYB*, 1961–4).

Star, Clare Street (1948–2002), p: P.J. McGarry, 600 (1949–71; *Showcase* 1968); fb: Gerard McGarry (1975–6);[64] by 1997, (part?) owned by Ward Anderson; 2 screens; closed in 2002; the building was sold by Gerard McGarry in November 2006. While the sale price was not disclosed, the asking price was €380,000. A local businessman purchased the premises and there were plans to knock it down and build an office block.[65] A charity auction of its contents took place in December 2007.

Belmullet

Erris Cinema (?–1989) p: Peader Cafferty (alt. name/spelling: Seamus Cafferkey),[66] 200.

Áras Inis Gluaire, Belmullet civic centre (officially opened on 21 April 2007, digital cinema operational from 10 October 2008–); cost of centre: *c.*€6 million; home to Pictiúrlann Iorrais, the local film club, supported by access>CINEMA (2010), aka *Erris* cinema; 170 seats.[67]

Castlebar

Concert Hall (*c.*1915–*c.*1947; aka *Town Hall*), p: Dr Higgins DD (*KYB,* 1916–18); Revd Archdeacon, later Canon, Fallon (*KYB,* 1918–48); m: J. Corcoran (*KYB,* 1919–48); occasional shows, *c.*600 (*KYB,* 1918–25).

County Cinema, Spencer Street (5 March 1939–*c.*1993),[68] p: Augustus (Gussie) Bourke, The Bungalow, Marylands, Castlebar (*KYB,* 1940–8; listed as 'Bourne' in some issues of *KYB* and in *1947 directory*), arch: 'Tot' McGowan; fb: W. Bourke (1975–7);[69] 23ft proscenium (*1947 directory*); 680 (*KYB,* 1940–8).

Ellison Cinema (*c.*1921–*c.*1938), p: Bourke Bros (*KYB,* 1922, 1924–39); Bourke & Sons (*KYB,* 1923); m: Thomas Bourke (*KYB,* 1924–34); 270 (1934);[70] 400 (*KYB,* 1936–8).

Linenhall Arts Centre (moved into current building in 1986, supported by Arts Council from 1990), mixed-use venue, Linenhall film club, a member of access>CINEMA screens films on a fortnightly basis during autumn and spring seasons, digital, new screen (2010).

• *Mayo Movie World,* Moneen Street (1999–; refurbishing and upgrading to digital in 2009; aka *SGC Castlebar*), 7 screens, 970 seats;[71] largest cinema in Mayo.

Star Cinema (*c.*1921–), p: M. Brady (*KYB,* 1922–3).

Charlestown

Eurkea Cinema (*c.*1939–71+), p: The Eureka Cinema Company (Charlestown) Ltd (CRO no. 13457), P.A. Mulligan family; Louise, Marian, Joe, Luke Mulligan (*KYB,* 1949–71; only Mrs M. Mulligan listed in *Showcase* 1968); associated with *Estoria,* Ballina (*KYB,* 1970); br: Miss Mulligan (*1947 directory*); 244 (*KYB,* 1949–57); 450 (*KYB,* 1960–71); Luke Mulligan's coffin-making business was in an upper room adjoining the balcony entrance (http:towns.mayo-irleand.ie).

• *Town Hall Arts Centre,* film club affiliated to access>CINEMA, 2005.[72]

Claremorris

Central Cinema, James Street (*c.*1952–5 October 1997), p: Messrs Kileen & Gallagher (*KYB,* 1953–64; listed in *Showcase* 1968); br: Mr J. Gallagher, screen: 16ft x 14ft, 500 (*1947 directory*); 450 (*KYB,* 1953–66); 385 (*KYB,* 1968–71).[73]

Town Hall Cinema (*c.*1933–*c.*1951), listed in *KYB,* 1934, 1937–44 no personnel); p: Messrs Kileen & Gallagher (*KYB,* 1949–52); 250 (1934);[74] 300 (*KYB,* 1937–45); 500 (*KYB,* 1949–52).

Cong

Shandhill Cinema (*c.*1949–71+), p: Noel Huggard, 240 (*KYB,* 1950–71; *Showcase* 1968).

Kilmaine

Kilmaine Cinema, p: J.J. Gilmore, Brickens, Claremorris; 200.

Kiltimagh

Savoy Cinema (*c.*1946–71+), p: McNally Cinema Ltd (*1947 directory*); Kiltimagh Cinema Co. (CRO no. 11650; *Showcase* 1968); br: Miss R. Moore, fb: Harry W. Culleton (75 Middle Abbey Street, Dublin), screen: 20ft x 16ft, 620 (*1947 directory*); 600 (*KYB,* 1964–71).

Newport

New Cinema Theatre. (*c.*1929–*c.*1954; listed as *Cinema* in *KYB,* 1930–1, as *New Cinema Theatre* in *KYB,* 1932–4, and as *New Cinema* in *KYB,* 1935–55), pictures & variety; café; proscenium 17 feet; p: local clergy, 250 (*KYB,* 1945–55); *KYB,* 1955 lists venue as closed.

Newport Star Cinema, p: Star Cinemas Co. Ltd; p: John Duffy, 300.

Swinford

Lyric Cinema (*c.*1947–71+), p: D. Kelly & A.M. Bourke (*KYB,* 1957); D. Kelly (*KYB,* 1965–71; *Showcase* 1968); br: P.J. Feeney, screen: 14ft x 18ft, 500 (*1947 directory*); 400 (*KYB,* 1949–71).

Westport

Octagon Cinema, The Octagon (*c.*1923–71+; aka *New Cinema Theatre*), p: Stanton, Ruddy, Kenny &

Joyce (1924–48); Mrs P. Malone & James Ruddy (*KYB*, 1949–71; *Showcase* 1968); Sean Hoban; br: Miss Carney, screen: 10ft x 8ft (*1947 directory*); 430 (*KYB*, 1936–48); 500 (1934; *1947 directory*);[75] 430 (*KYB*, 1949–52); 550 (*KYB*, 1953–7); reopened for winter season on 4 September 1927 under a committee of members of Westport St Vincent de Paul Society showing *Pathé Gazette*; open on Sunday nights only in September, but Wednesday night from October; *The Road to Mandalay* opening film.[76]

Regal Cinema (1930s–49), p: Michael Hoban, burned down in 1949 and was replaced by Hoban's *The Ideal*.

The Ideal (1949–76+), p: Michael and Nonie Hoban; fb: Leo Ward (1975–6).[77]

• *Westport Cineplex*, James Street (15 April 2004–), p: Hoban family (Seán [formerly of the *Octagon*], Haulie, Joe and sister Claire (children of Michael and Nonie Hoban) and family friend, Leo Ward/Ward Anderson; cost: €2.5 million; 3 screens; 450 seats; situated beside the Westport leisure park in town centre; there had been a controversy when planning permission was approved in December 2001 because Hoban and Ward won out over *Mayo Movie World* which had a lower tender; Hoban and Ward's application, however, was deemed to be of a higher architectural rating and was successful on that basis.[78] It was the first time Westport had a cinema in two decades; film booking arranged by Ward Anderson cinema group.

MEATH

Asbourne

• *Showtime Cinema*, Ashbourne retail park (2009–), 6 screens/1,000+seats.

Athboy

Civic Cinema (*c*.1930–1), also dance venue (*KYB*, 1930–4).

St James's Hall (*c*.1936–*c*.1968), p (& fb): James Garry, 280 (*KYB*, 1937–64; *1947 directory*, *Showcase* 1968).

Clonard

Clonard Cinema (*c*.1945–*c*.1963), p: Thomas Gibney, 350 (*1947 directory*, *KYB*, 1949–64), also live venue.

Kells

Kells Cinema Theatre, Market Yard, entrances from Newmarket and Farrell streets, (*c*.6 June 1914–*c*.1936), p: James Carroll, who adapted an existing building owned by him at a cost of £200–£300, and which had been in occasional use as an entertainment venue, to a full time cinema.[79]

New Hall (December 1916–), p: Thomas Mason.

Cinema, listed *KYB*, 1930–1 (no personnel); perhaps same as *St Vincent's Hall*.

Phoenix Video Theatre (4 June 1983–),[80] advertised as Ireland's first full-time video cinema, this was a seven days per week operation that may have infringed the law.

St Vincent's Hall (*c*.1930–), listed *KYB*, 1930–41 (no personnel); p: St Vincent de Paul Society (*KYB*, 1932–5); Trustees, parochial committee (*KYB*, 1936–41, *1947 directory*); 15ft proscenium (*1947 directory*); 500 (*KYB*, 1936–41, *1947 directory*), also live venue.

Savoy Cinema, Suffolk Street (15 December 1936–6 June 1982; as *Oscar Cinema*, 1974–82), arch: Frank Gibney; p: Tailteann Theatres Ltd, Dublin Street, Balbriggan, Co. Dublin (*KYB*, 1950–71; *Showcase* 1968); Kells Cinema Co. Ltd; br & fb: Mr E. Scanlan, Dublin Street, Balbriggan (*1947 directory*); m: Michael Rycroft (1973); James Allen (to 1975); Raymond Lynch (1981); fb/gm: Patrick (Paddy) Melia (1974–82);[81] 550; 524 (*KYB*, 1971).

Navan

Catholic Young Men's Society Hall, granted a cinema licence in January 1915 (*KYB*, 1916–17).

Cinema Theatre, Academy Street (1914–28).

• *Diamond Screen Cineplex*, Navan shopping centre, Metges Lane, Kennedy Road (17 February 1998–; aka *Diamond Cinema 6*), 6 screens/930 seats; 935 seats.[82] See also *Diamond*, Monaghan.

Lyric Cinema, Brews Hill (7 December 1941–7 August 1951; after renovations to April 1997), arch: Thomas and John (father) McGahon, Dundalk (*DIA*); p: Navan Picture Palace Co. Ltd, Brews Hill, Ludlow Street, Navan (*Showcase* 1968); br & fb: Mr Kennedy (*1947 directory*); 857 (*KYB*, 1946–71); sold for *c*. £200,000, February 1997;[83] Morton Hall apartment block now on site. See *Navan Picture Palace* (seems to have same personnel, but separate venue).

Navan Picture Palace, Ludlow Street, (1914–July 1936; after renovations, 18 October 1936–9 February 1949; 10 August 1951–1998; aka *Palace Cinema*; *Picture Palace*),[84] p: Navan Picture Palace Co. Ltd

(*KYB*, 1919–41; 1949–71; *Showcase* 1968 address: Brews Hill, Navan); m: Robert Kennedy (1914–39);[85] William J. Kennedy (1939–49);[86] fb: W.R. Kennedy (*1947 directory*); William Kennedy (1975–7);[87] newly constructed building following fire on 9 February 1949 (arch: J.F. McGahon & Sons, Dundalk[88]); licensed for music and dancing (*KYB*, 1919); 18ft proscenium (*1947 directory*); 400 (*KYB*, 1919); *c*.350 (*KYB*, 1920–1; 1935–6; 1934);[89] 582 (*KYB*, 1940–4; 1949–55; *1947 directory*); 2 screens; before closing as a cinema, part of premises became video rental and retail store from 20 June 1988; later converted to a nightclub.
• **Solstice Arts Centre**, Railway Street (April 2006–), arch: Grafton Architects; 320 seat theatre; occasional films, access>CINEMA film club based there.

Oldcastle
Castle Cinema, Oliver Plunkett Street (9 April 1944–5 July 1981), p: Owen Clarke and Andrew Carolan (1944–); Castle Cinemas, Ltd (*1947 directory*); Owen Clarke, Paddy Kearney and family (end period of cinema); Jim Haghney and family (prior to closing);[90] m: Mr W. Clarke (*Showcase* 1968); fb: Harry W. Culleton, 75 Middle Abbey Street, Dublin (*1947 directory*); Owen Clarke (1975);[91] screen: 16ft, 650 (*1947 directory*); 558 (*KYB*, 1953–5); 600 (*KYB*, 1960); 458 (*KYB*, 1965–71).
Electric Cinema Theatre (22 January 1914–*c*.1933; aka *Oldcastle Cinema; The Cinema*), p: Charles (Charly) Fox (1914–28); Owen Clarke (from 1928); m: Patrick Kelly (1915); after 1916 it seems that the venue was called *The Cinema*; in April 1923, military guard in occupation of the cinema were fired on by a party of iregulars;[92] closed during summer; listed, *KYB*, 1930–4 (no personnel).[93]

Trim
Cinema, seems to have been in Town Hall or in other building owned by council;[94] listed, *KYB*, 1930–48 (no personnel); br & fb: James G. Garry, Athboy (*1947 directory*).
Royal Cinema, Emmet Street (15 September 1948–7 July 1974; temporarily reopened November 1974 after failing to sell), p James Garry, Athboy (*KYB*, 1949–67); Messrs Mangan & Fay (*KYB*, 1968–71); Margaret Fay, Market Street, and others (1974);[95] put up for sale in 1974; 400 (*KYB*, 1949); 500 (*KYB*, 1950–7); converted to supermarket which opened in November 1975.

MONAGHAN

Ballybay
Ballybay Cinema, p: Joseph K. Keelaghan, Ballybay, who had leased *Foresters' Hall* until *c.* 1944; upon his return from the USA where he had studied engineering he built, without a licence, a cinema near the church, and performances began by October 1947, at which point he was fined £500 for building without the local authority's consent;[96] as it was offered for sale in 1958, it must have overcome these planning difficulties; 500 (balcony, 140; centre, 200; front, 160) seats.[97]
Irish National Foresters' Hall/St Patrick's Hall, p: Keelaghan Bros (*1947 directory*); l: Joseph K. Keelaghan, Ballybay (*c*.1941–4);[98] Kevin J. Keelaghan (*KYB*, 1949–71; *Showcase* 1968); br: Mr O'Dowd (*1947 directory*); 240.
Luxor Cinema, p: Luxor Cinemas Ltd, 600 (*1947 directory*).

Carrickmacross
Gem Cinema (?–5 May 1938), p: Mrs J. Rogers, destroyed by fire on 5 May 1938.[99]
Oscar Cinema (*c*.1931–91).
Stella Cinema (*c*.1942–76+), p: Norman Lewis (*KYB*, 1945–55); P.J. Higgins (*KYB*, 1960–71; *Showcase* 1968); fb: H. Tunney;[1] screen: 18ft x 16ft (*1947 directory*); 500 (*1947 directory*; *KYB*, 1949–66); 480 (*KYB*, 1967–71).

Castleblaney
Castleblaney Cinema (*c*.1948–71+), p: Blaney Cinemas Ltd, 27 South Frederick Street, Dublin (*KYB*, 1949–71; *Showcase* 1968); br: Mr McGinn (*1947 directory*); *c*.500 (*KYB*, 1949–71).
Lyric Theatre, p: Mr A. McElroy, m: Mr A. Muldoon (*Showcase* 1968); fb: H. McElroy (1977).[2]
Picture House (*KYB*, 1917).

Clones
Electric Theatre, Church Street (*c*.1915–16), p: St Joseph's Hall committee, 500 (*KYB*, 1917); first listed, *KYB*, 1916.
Luxor Cinema, Fermanagh Street (*c*.November 1946–*c*.March 1974; listed in *Showcase* 1968; listed as *Cinema*, *KYB*, 1949–55),[3] p: Luxor Cinemas Ltd (*KYB*, 1949–64); fb: H. Tunney (1976);[4] 400 (*KYB*, 1949–52); 550 (*KYB*, 1954–5; 1960–7); 500 (*KYB*, 1968–70); 460 (*KYB*, 1971); in 1966, fire sparked

by an electrical fault caused minor damage to cinema just after children's Saturday matinee ended;[5] advertised for sale, March 1974;[6] used as live venue after closing as cinema.

Star Cinema (?–*c*.September 1985);[7] after closing as cinema used as live venue.

St Joseph's Temperance Hall, Church Hill (*c*.1930–*c*.1947; aka *Clones Parochial Cinema*; *Clones Cinema*), p: Clones Catholic Club (*KYB*, 1934–46, *1947 directory*); Revd J. Canon Marran PP, Claukeen House, Clones (*KYB*, 1948); 22ft proscenium (*1947 directory*); *c*.350 (*KYB*, 1938–48); first listed, *KYB*, 1931. In 1944–5, the cinema was segregated with males and females required to sit on either side of the aisle.[8]

Monaghan

Diamond Cinema, Diamond shopping centre (*c*.1939–2000+), p: Monaghan Cinema Ltd (*KYB*, 1945–8); Ken Dursey (*c*.1990); l: Martin Rennie, 384;[9] 350 (*KYB*, 1940–8). See also *Diamond Screen Cineplex*.

• *Diamond Screen Cineplex*, Diamond centre (2008–), 4 screens/770 seats.[10] See also *Diamond*, Navan.

Magnet Cinema (1939–71+), p: Monaghan Cinema Ltd (CRO no. 9641; *KYB*, 1942–3; 1950–71; as Amalgamated Cinemas (Ireland) Ltd in *Showcase* 1968); br: M. Rennie (*1947 directory*); cost: £7,000;[11] m: Miss M. Roberts (*Showcase* 1968); 500 (*KYB*, 1942–3); 600 (*KYB*, 1944–6); 700 (*1947 directory*, *KYB*, 1948–71); damaged by fire on 20 April 1964.[12]

Town Hall Cinema, Main Street (*c*.1924–*c*.1938), l: John Gormley; m: Martin Rennie (*KYB*, 1925–6); l/m: Martin Rennie (*KYB*, 1927–39); 450 (*KYB*, 1936).

OFFALY (aka King's County)

Banagher

Harp Cinema, not equipped for sound, 150 (1934).[13]

Shannon Cinema, Harbour Street (*c*.1947–71+), p: Shannon Cinema Co. Ltd (*KYB*, 1955–71, *Showcase* 1968); br: W.J. D'Alton, screen: 16ft x 12ft (*1947 directory*); 480 (*KYB*, 1955–71).

Birr

Aisling, fb: Paddy Melia (1975–7).[14]

Birr Kinema, Cumberland Street, p/m: Archibald Wright, 150 (*KYB*, 1919); 200 (*KYB*, 1920).

Birr Electric Picturedrome, Main Street (*c*.1919–*c*.1931), p: Birr Electric Picture Co.; Gilbert Powell, Newbridge Street (*KYB*, 1930–1); m: J.J. O'Meara (*KYB*, 1920–8); 350 (*KYB*, 1920); 300 (*KYB*, 1921); listed as closed in *KYB*, 1932.

Birr Theatre and Arts Centre, Oxmantown Hall (opened in July 2000–), mixed-use venue; an access>CINEMA film club with over 100 members based there (2010).

Cinema, Chronicle Hall, Cumberland Square (*KYB*, 1917).

Oxmanton Hall (*KYB*, 1916–17).

New Cinema, Brendan Street (*c*.1947–71+), p: Roscrea & Athy Cinema Co. (*1947 directory*; *KYB*, 1949–66; *Showcase* 1968); br & fb: Mr J. Barry, St Cronin's Terrace, Roscrea (*1947 directory*); m: Mr V. Conboy (*Showcase* 1968); 500 (*KYB*, 1949–50); 564 (*KYB*, 1951–2); 550 (*KYB*, 1965–6); 400 (*KYB*, 1967–8); 490 (*KYB*, 1969–71).

Rialto Cinema (*c*.1929–71+), first listed, *KYB*, 1930, p: Mr Murphy (*KYB*, 1934–41); W. Murphy (1935; 1942–8); J.J. Murphy (*1947 directory*; *KYB*, 1949–71; *Showcase* 1968); 570 (1934);[15] 500 (*KYB*, 1936–71).

Clara

Cinema (*c*.December 1925[16]–*c*.1947; first listed *KYB*, 1930–8 [no personnel]); p: Martin Fleming, Ballycumber, Co. Offaly (*KYB*, 1939–48, also listed in *1947 directory* as fb with address as Cinema, Moate); 550 (*KYB*, 1942–8); closed for summer in 1920s.

Edenderry

Father Paul Murphy Hall (*c*.1933–*c*.1944; aka *Star Cinema*, *KYB*, 1939–41), l: William Higgins, Barrow View, Portarlington (*KYB*, 1934–9); Sean O'Kelly, The Mart, Edenderry (*KYB*, 1939–41); 500 (*KYB*, 1939–40); 400 (*KYB*, 1941–5); last listed *KYB*, 1945.

Savoy, O'Connell Square (*c*.1945–90+), p: McNally Cinemas Ltd (*1947 directory*); Roscrea & Athy Picture Co. (*KYB*, 1948–50); Edenderry Picture Co. (*KYB*, 1951–71; *Showcase* 1968); fb: Harry W. Culleton, 75 Middle Abbey Street, Dublin (*1947 directory*); Eugene O'Brien (1975–7),[17] screen: 20ft x 15ft (*1947 directory*); 2 screens; *c*.700 (*1947 directory*; *KYB*, 1948–61).

Portarlington see **Laois** (lies on the border of County Laois and County Offaly).

Tullamore
Catholic Young Men's Society, Henry Street (*c.*1922–*c.*1940), p: CYMS – Cinematograph Association (1923–36); m: F. Slattery (*KYB*, 1923–34); 400 (*KYB*, 1936–41).
Foresters' Picture House (1924–), arch: George L. O'Connor and Thomas McNamara both credited (*DIA*); cost at time of tender in 1923, £6,052; listed in *KYB*, 1930–1 (no personnel).
Frontier Picture Palace, m: Andrew Gallagher, once nightly, three shows weekly (*KYB*, 1925).
Grand Central Cinema, Market Square (*c.*1931–71+), Grand Central Cinema (Tullamore) Ltd (CRO no. 69017), p: Messrs Mahon & Cloonan (*1947 directory*; *KYB*, 1932–49); Offaly Cinema Co. Ltd, High Street, Tullamore (CRO no. 12066; *KYB*, 1950–71; *Showcase* 1968); fb: A. Mahon (1975–7);[18] 12ft proscenium (*1947 directory*); 660 (1934);[19] 400 (*KYB*, 1935); 724 (*KYB*, 1940–66); 526 (*KYB*, 1967–71).
Palais De Luxe Cinema (1912), p: Denis Sweeney, local publican; m: John O'Connor; while the first night of opening had a full house, on the second day, a rival show arrived in the town, with the result that the *Palais* was a failure and it was decided not to continue; O'Connor subsequently took a successful court case to recover wages promised to him by Sweeney and his (unnamed) business partner.[20]
Ritz, High Street (*c.*1947–71+; aka *New Cinema* [*1947 directory*]), p: Mahon & Cloonan (of *New Cinema* [*1947 directory*]); Midland Cinema Co. (*KYB*, 1949); Offaly Cinema Co. Ltd, High Street (*KYB*, 1950–71; *Showcase* 1968); 1,000 (*New Cinema* [*1947 directory*]); 1,050 (*KYB*, 1950–67); 900 (*KYB*, 1968–71).
• *Tullamore Omniplex*, Bridge shopping centre (July 1995–), p: Ward Anderson, 6 screens/970 (289, 222, 166, 124, 120, 49) seats.[21]

ROSCOMMON

Ballaghadreen
Ariel Cinema (*c.*1947–*c.*1969; possibly same cinema as *St Mary's Hall* which is given as its address in *1947 directory*, and the cinema's proprietor is listed as Roxy Cinemas Ltd, also in *1947 directory*), p: Roxy Cinemas, Ltd (*1947 directory*); Revd J. Hunt (*KYB*, 1949–52); Revd T.A. McVann, administrator (*KYB*, 1953–70; *Showcase* 1968); br: Revd Dr Stenson (*1947 directory*); m: J. Macken, screen: 14ft x 11ft (*1947 directory*); 400 (*1947 directory*, *KYB*, 1949–70).
Estoria, Arthur Street.
Presbytery Cinema (*c.*1929–33, listed in *KYB*, 1930–4); became furniture store, 1986.
Roxy Cinema (*c.*1942–?), p: Roxy Cinemas Ltd & Picture House, Bray; 400 (*KYB*, 1943–5). See *Ariel Cinema*.
St Mary's Hall, Cathedral Street (1901; McCole, 2005:appendix D; and occasional venue); not equipped for sound; used occasionally by travelling companies, 500 (1934).[22] See *Ariel Cinema*.

Boyle
Abbey Cinema, Bridge Street (*c.*1939–90; from *c.*1990, *Crescent Cinema*), p: Abbey Cinema (Boyle) Ltd (CRO no.25854); John Lowe/John Lowe & Co. Ltd, Carrick-on-Shannon (1931–59; *Showcase* 1968);[23] Donal Farrell, The Crescent (*KYB*, 1968–71, *RPC*, 1977:108, 116); Brian Kelly, *Gaiety*, Carrick-on-Shannon (*c.*1990); m: John Callaghan (*1947 directory*); 600 (*KYB*, 1940–50); *c.*650 (*1947 directory*; *KYB*, 1951–6); 550 (*KYB*, 1957–67); 320 (*KYB*, 1968–71).
Boyle Picture Theatre, Bridge Street (*c.*1922–*c.*1938; aka *The Picture House*; from *c.*1939–*c.*1990, *Abbey Cinema*), p/m: Edward J. Tighe (*KYB*, 1926–31); p: John Lowe (*KYB*, 1932–9, from October 1931[24]); bm: Patrick J. Kilcullen (*KYB*, 1924–7); one show nightly (*KYB*, 1923–5); 320 (*KYB*, 1936). See *Abbey Cinema*.

Carrick-on-Shannon
Arcadia Cinema, Town Hall (*c.*1927–*c.*1937), closed in summer, first listed *KYB*, 1930–3 (no personnel); p: Mr B.A. McManus, 200 (*KYB*, 1934–8);[25] fire in operator's box on 11 February 1927 led to destruction of film.[26]
• *Carrick Cineplex*, Carrick retail and business park, Boyle Road (2006–); 4 screens/ 414 (49–171) seats, café-wine bar.
Cinema (*c.*1944–5), formerly armed forces hall; p: Raymond Stross, 1,000 (*KYB*, 1945).[27]
Gaiety Cinema, Bridge Street (*c.*1933–2004), p: John J. Flood, 61 Main Street (*KYB*, 1934–50, *1947 directory*); Dr J.F. O'Hanrahan, county hospital, Roscommon (*KYB*, 1950–71; *Showcase* 1968); 500 (*KYB*, 1935–9);[28] 350 (*KYB*, 1940–50); 427 (*KYB*, 1950–61); 450 (*KYB*, 1962–71), 135 (Connolly and Dillon, 2001:72).

The Picture House, Bridge Street (undetermined dates), p: Edward J. Tighe, High Street, Sligo.

Castlerea
Castle, fb: A. Robinson (1977).[29]
Cinema Hall, Main Street (*c*.1929–*c*.1934), listed *KYB*, 1930–4 (no personnel); not equipped for sound; used occasionally by travelling companies, 400 seats (1934).[30]
Regal Cinema (*c*.1947–71+), p: J. Bourke, 250 (*1947 directory*; *KYB*, 1949–71; *Showcase* 1968).

Roscommon
Blue Moon (*c*.1947–*c*.1968), p: H. Noel McCourt (*1947 directory*); Noel A. McCourt (*KYB*, 1949); H.I. & R. McCourt (*KYB*, 1950–2); Rose McCourt (*KYB*, 1955–69; *Showcase* 1968); Kelly family, *Gaiety*, Carrick-on-Shannon; 270 (*KYB*, 1949); 340 (*KYB*, 1951); 300 (*KYB*, 1952–7). (It is possible that this is Robinson & Keefe's 1947 designed cinema in Castle Street, *DIA*.)
Cinema, listed, *KYB*, 1930–4 (no personnel).
Harrison Memorial Hall (*c*.1915–*c*.1934), p: Harrison Memorial Trustees (*KYB*, 1916–17); 500 seats (*KYB*, 1918); not equipped for sound; used occasionally by travelling companies, 300 seats (1934).[31]
Music Hall (*KYB*, 1916–17).
Roscommon Arts Centre, Circular Road (2000–), purpose-built venue with 35mm projection facilities; 194; offers film screenings often in conjunction with IFI's education programme, and access>CINEMA supported film club which is based there (2010).
Roxy Cinema, The Square (*c*.1942–*c*.1947), p: Roxy Cinemas Ltd, 70 Middle Abbey Street, Dublin (*KYB*, 1943–8); 450.
Royal (*c*.1948–77+), p: Patrick C. Sweeney (*KYB*, 1949–57); Messrs O'Hanrahan, Rafferty & Sweeney, m: A. Robinson (*KYB*, 1965–71; *Showcase* 1968); fb: A. Robinson (1977); 700 (*KYB*, 1949); 661 (*KYB* 1950–7).[32]
Saint Coman's Hall (*KYB*, 1916–17).

Roxboro
Blue Moon Cinema, p: Bill Keane (*c*.1990).

Strokestown
The Club Cinema, Church Street, br: W.E. Chapman, screen: 12ft x 9ft, 250 (*1947 directory*).

Travelling cinemas
J. Carron: *Cinema*, Ballaghadereen; Glenamaddy; Castlerea; Roscommon (*KYB*, 1941).
Caslin's Company: *St Mary's Hall*, Ballaghadereen; *Goldsmith's Hall*, Elphin; *New Hall*, Strokestown; and *Town Hall*, Ballyhaunis, Co. Mayo (*KYB*, 1941).

SLIGO

Ballymote
Abbey Cinema, Teeling Street (1947–75; aka *Hibernian Cinema* [*1947 directory*]), p: John Conroy (*KYB*, 1949–62); Lynda Begley, Bartholomew Cryan (*KYB*, 1963–9; *Showcase* 1968); Ballymote Cinema Co. Ltd, Teeling Street, Ballymote (CRO no. 11460; *KYB*, 1970–1); screen: 12ft x 10ft, 350 (*1947 directory*; 520 (*KYB*, 1949–69), 500 (*KYB*, 1970–1); in 2010 plans were announced to restore the Art-Deco style cinema as a cultural centre with a 220-seat combined theatre and cinema auditorium.[33]
Picture House (*KYB*, 1930–3).

Enniscrone
Town Hall, p: J.J. Llewellyn, 400.

Sligo
• *Gaiety Cinema*, Wine Street (3 November 1935–1981; August 1981–1991 [3 screens]; 1991–June 1996 [4 screens]; demolished, rebuilt: August 1998–June 2002 [7 screens/887 seats[34]]; reopened, 6 December 2002 [12 screens][35]; aka *Gaiety Cinema Complex/GCG*), arch: John J. Robinson, R.C. Keefe, 8 Merrion Square, Dublin (original building); p: The Gaiety (Sligo) Ltd (from 1935, *1947 directory*; *Showcase* 1968); d: (all from Sligo): T.P. Toher, P.J. Henry, J.P. Moran, T. Mulligan, P.J. Burke, W.J. Maloney, M.A. Henry, M.J. Raftery; Martin A. Henry (died, 21 July 1991); brothers Dermot and Tom Mulligan who with John Henry designed the 2002 development; GCG (Gaiety Cinema Group, by 2008); m: M.J. Brady (1930s–late 1960s);[36] Miss N. McGoldrick (*Showcase* 1968); Paul Keegan (from 1998); br: Mr Paton (*1947 directory*); fb: N. McGoldrick (1974–6);[37] 1,000 (*KYB*, 1937–71; 750 in stalls; 250 in balcony); 12 screens/1,500 seats (rooms from 220 to 66 seats), 2002–. The *Gaiety Cinema* won an

award for best Irish cinema at the RAAM conference for the cinema industry in Glasgow, February 2005.[38] By November 2009 it was equipped with digital technology for showing 3D; Sligo Film Society (access>CINEMA member) based there (2010).
Gillooly Hall, l/m: Michael J. Tighe, 800.[39]
• *Model Arts and Niland Gallery*, The Mall, occasionally used for film screenings; closed from 2008 to April 2010 for a €6 million refurbishment. Film programme presented in partnership with the IFI, and others, including the Sligo Film Society and Cinema North-West.
Pavilion, Thomas Street (*c.*1920–*c.*1943), p: Kilgannon & Sons (*KYB*, 1921–37); G.P. Gaynor (*KYB*, 1938–44); m: J.P. Kilgannon (*KYB*, 1921); 450 (*KYB*, 1921); 416 (1934);[40] 500 (*KYB*, 1935–44); may be same as *Sligo Picture Palace*.
Picture Theatre, Thomas Street. See *Sligo Picture Palace*.
Savoy Cinema, Market Street (31 July 1932–1987+), p: Savoy Cinema Co (Sligo) Ltd (CRO no. 8239 and 15063, registered 16 March 1932); md: Thomas Walsh, Ballyshannon; Gerard Sweeney, Ballyshannon (*KYB*, 1933–42); Western Counties Theatres Ltd (*KYB*, 1943–6); Curran Theatres (*1947 directory*); Troxy Cinemas (Sligo) Ltd (*KYB*, 1948–71; as Amalgamated Cinemas (Ireland) Ltd in *Showcase* 1968); Seamus and Harry Monaghan (from November 1986);[41] br: Bernard O'Reilly (*1947 directory*); m: Miss M. Casey (*Showcase* 1968); fb: James Curran, Capitol Cinema, Belfast (*KYB*, 1943–6, *1947 directory*); J. McManus (1976);[42] screen: 20ft x 16ft (*1947 directory*); 1,000 (*KYB*, 1935); 850 (*KYB*, 1943–6); 800 (*1947 directory*, *KYB*, 1948–57); there was a strike over wages in March 1938.[43]
Sligo Picture Palace, Thomas Street (1913–*c.*1937; aka *Picture Theatre*; *Sligo Picture Theatre*), p: Kilgannon[44] & Sons Ltd (*KYB*, 1919–20; 1923–38); m: J.P. Kilgannon (*KYB*, 1919–20; 1923–8); 450 (*KYB*, 1919–20; 1922); 550 (*KYB*, 1921); 406 (1934)[45]; 500 (*KYB*, 1935–8); may be same as *Pavilion*.
Town Hall (1897–1905; McCole, 2005:appendix D).

Tubbercurry
Palace Cinema (*c.*1929–*c.*1933), listed, *KYB*, 1930 (no personnel); p: W. Durkin (*KYB*, 1931–4); pictures & variety; dance hall (*KYB*, 1931).
St Brigid's Hall (*c.*1947–71+), p: The Trustees (*KYB*, 1949–71; *Showcase* 1968); 500 (*1947 directory*; *KYB*, 1965–71).

TIPPERARY

Borrisokane
Borrisokane Cinema (*c.* October 1922–April 1923),[46] a former fever hospital close to Borrisokane workhouse renovated and converted into a cinema and dance hall; destroyed by fire *c.*17 April 1922.[47]
Cinema, br: Mr S. Shanahan (*1947 directory*).
Stella Cinema (16mm), David Clarke Memorial Hall, Mill Street (7 April 1957–May 1967), fb: schoolteacher Denis Gardiner, 234; 2/3 nights per week.[48]

Cahir
Capitol Cinema, Old Church Street (*c.*1951–71+), p: Capitol Provincial Cinemas Ltd, 4 North Princes Street, Dublin (*KYB*, 1952–68; *Showcase* 1968); Capitol Provincial Cinemas Ltd, 41 Nutley Lane, Ballsbridge, Dublin (*KYB*, 1969–71); 450 (*KYB*, 1952); 485 (*KYB*, 1955–68); 440 (*KYB*, 1969–71).
Savoy Cinema (*c.*1935–50; first listed, *KYB*, 1936, as *Cinema*), p: P. McGrath, 26A Pearse Street, Dublin, 400 (*KYB*, 1939–51, listed as fb in *1947 directory*); br: J.F. Walsh, 370 (*1947 directory*). Full-size screen, programme changed daily, and Sunday opening (*1947 directory*).
Town Hall (1901; McCole, 2005:appendix D), (*c.*1915–*c.*1920, first listed, *KYB*, 1916), p/m: Joseph Walsh & Sons (*KYB*, 1918); m: Joseph Walsh (*KYB*, 1919–21); licensed for dancing and music (*KYB*, 1920); occasional shows (*KYB*, 1921); 450 (*KYB*, 1918); 500 (*KYB*, 1919); 400 (*KYB*, 1920–1).

Carrick-on-Suir
Castle Cinema, Castle Street (*c.*15 February 1946–1975; from *c.*1975, *Strand*), p: Castle Cinemas Ltd (*1947 directory*; *KYB*, 1949–71), 74 Dame Street, Dublin (address from *KYB*, 1961 & *Showcase* 1968: 14 Marine Drive, Sandymount), fb: Patrick McGrath, Pearse Street, Dublin (*1947 directory*); C. Butler (1975; 1975–7, as *Strand*);[49] Liam Butler (1990); screen: 18ft x 14ft, 850 (*1947 directory*); 800 (*KYB*, 1949–55); *c.*915 (*KYB*, 1960–8); 898 (*KYB*, 1969–71); used as a venue for international boxing tournaments in the 1960s and 1970s.
The Cinema, Greenside, 400 (1934).[50]

Park View Cinema (1917–August 1947[51]), p: Patrick J. McGrath[52] (from 1917, *KYB*, 1925–33); Mr Daly (*KYB*, 1934–5); P. McGrath, 26A Pearse Street, Dublin (*KYB*, 1939–48, listed as fb in 1947 *directory*); Castle Cinemas Ltd, 14 Marine Drive, Sandymount, Dublin 4 (*KYB*, 1970); 300 (*KYB*, 1936–45, 1947 *directory*); 400 (*KYB*, 1948–55).[53]

Cashel

Cinema, Main Street (*c.*1924–*c.*2 January 1930), p: M.H. Hannigan. (*KYB*, 1925–33); destroyed by fire in January 1930 with damage estimated at £4,000.[54]
Rock (*c.*1934–77+), p: Mr Delahunty (*KYB*, 1934); P. Delahunty (*KYB*, 1939–52; 1947 *directory*); John Delahunty, Mitchel Street, Thurles (*KYB*, 1955–71; *Showcase* 1968), fb: Leo Ward (1975–7);[55] 600 (1934);[56] 500 (*KYB*, 1935–52); 550 (*KYB*, 1955–71).
Town Hall (1901; McCole, 2005:appendix D).

Clogheen

Ormonde Cinema, br: Mr. T. Duggan (*1947 directory*).

Clonmel[57]

Clonmel Cinema Theatre, rear, 35 Upper Gladstone Street (January 1913–*c.*1920; aka *Clonmel Electric Picture Palace*; *Picturedrome*), p: Whitney & Long, 600 (*KYB*, 1916–17). p: Roberto Lena, m: Gertie Lena, 750, licensed for drama, music and dancing (*KYB*, 1920); p/m: J.J. Trehy, 400 (*KYB*, 1921).
• *Clonmel Omniplex*, Kickham Street (*c.*2000–), p: Ward Anderson, 5 screens/709 (235, 138, 134, 99, 103) seats; 5 screens/782 seats.[58]
John Magner's Theatre, David Road, The Mall (*c.*1913, burned down in 1919; rebuilt in 1921, closed 2001; aka *Magner's Theatre*; *Clonmel Theatre*, *Regal Theatre*), arch: Alleyn Lovell (*DIA*), p: John Magner, (*KYB*, 1919–24); Clonmel (Associated) Theatre Co.[59] (*KYB*, 1931–41); William O'Keefe (*KYB*, 1932–41); m: R. Walsh, (*KYB*, 1919–24); gm: W.R. Symes (*KYB*, 1925–41); 700 (*KYB*, 1919–24); 900 (*KYB*, 1938–40);[60] fb: Leo Ward (1976),[61] 1,000; 3 screens/850 seats.
Oisín, O'Connell Street (1921–*c.*1970; aka *Oisín Theatre*), p: Messrs Morris & O'Keeffe (*KYB*, 1922–4); Clonmel (Associated) Theatre Co. (*KYB*, 1931); William O'Keefe (*KYB*, (1943–9); Ritz (Clonmel) Ltd, 9 Eden Quay, Dublin (*KYB*, 1950–71; *Showcase* 1968); m: W.B. Symes (*KYB*, 1924; 1931); 750 (1934);[62] 550 (*KYB*, 1943–62); 650 (*1947 directory*); 500 (*KYB*, 1963–70).
Picturedrome. See *Clonmel Cinema Theatre*.
Regal Theatre. See *John Magner's Theatre*.
Rink Theatre (*KYB*, 1916–17).
Ritz (1 March 1940–1971+),[63] arch: William (Bill) O'Dwyer, Michael Scott & Associates (International Modern style, *DIA*; archiseek.com); p: Louis Elliman's Ritz (Clonmel) Ltd, 9 Eden Quay, Dublin, m: P.J. Condron, fb: Michael J. Deasy (9 Eden Quay, Dublin) (*1947 directory*); 980 (*KYB*, 1942–9); 821 (*KYB*, 1950–71); credit union offices now located at site.
Tivoli, p: W.J. Hefferson (*KYB*, 1922–3).
Town Hall (1897–1902; McCole, 2005:appendix D).

Cloughjordan

Electric Picturedrome (*c.*1923).[64]

Fethard

Capitol Cinema (*c.*1947–*c.*1960), p: Fethard Cinemas Ltd, 4 North Princes Street, Dublin (*KYB*, 1952–66; *Showcase* 1968 gives company name as Capitol Provincial Cinemas Ltd, but with same address); fb: Patrick McGrath, Pearse Street, Dublin (*1947 directory*); 589 (*KYB*, 1952–61).

Nenagh

• *Ormond Cinema*, Saint Flannan Street, Summerhill (7 January 1923–; aka *Ormond Picture Palace*; *Ormond Cinema Hall*; *Ormond Cineplex*); p: William (Willie) F. Moloney, Summerhill; Ormond Cinema Co. (*KYB*, 1939–55); Noel Moloney; Eddie Gleeson, Cappamore (from December 2007); m: Edward Cahill (from 1922); William F. Moloney (*KYB*, 1926–8); fb: Michael J. Deasy, 9 Eden Quay, Dublin (*1947 directory*); 330 (1934);[65] 250 (*KYB*, 1933–55); 2 screens; 270 seats (Connolly and Dillon, 2001:73); 4 screens/431 seats (2010).
Rialto Cinema, Banba Square (1 September 1946–1 May 1976), arch: William F. O'Dwyer; p: Amalagamated Entertainments (Nenagh) Ltd, (*KYB*, 1949–59); Breen circuit, Waterford (*KYB*, 1960–71; *Showcase* 1968); Green Group/Ward Anderson; fb: Martin S. Breen (*1947 directory*); Leo Ward (1975);[66] 900 (*KYB*, 1949–71); in May 1977, Kilroy's department store opened in the former cinema.
Town Hall Cinema, Banba Square (built 1895; 26 September 1915–*c.*1947; 1984–6; aka *Electric Picture Palace*; *The Picture House*), p: Ormond Cinema Co./Messrs William F. Maloney, Nenagh, and W.J. Tooher, Cloughjordan (1915–*c.*1925);[67] p/m: Edward O'Kennedy (*KYB*, 1925–38);[68] Nenagh Cinema

Co. (*KYB*, 1939–41); E.D. Kennedy, Emmet Place, Nenagh (*KYB*, 1943–8; *1947 directory*); screen: 16ft x 12ft (*1947 directory*); 370 (1934; *1947 directory*);[69] 550 (*KYB*, 1935–6); 420 (*KYB*, 1939–41); 340 (*KYB*, 1943–8). On 22 March 1984, the *Town Hall Cinema* was reopened by Ted Boland, and seems to have continued until about December 1986; now location of *Nenagh Arts Centre* with 214 seat theatre, and thus remains a regular (though limited) film venue with screening supported by access>CINEMA via a film club.

Portroe
The New Hall, Mr R.D. Shouldice (*1947 directory*).

Roscrea
Powell's Cinema Hall, Main Street (?–28 November 1924; aka *Cinema*), p: Valentine Powell, destroyed by fire on 28 November 1924.[70] Another cinema was operating in Roscrea by April 1928. *Cinema*, listed, *KYB*, 1930–3 (no personnel).
Roscrea Cinema (September 1934–burned down, June 1959; rebuilt; reopened 24 February 1960–18 July 1982; aka *New Hall* [*KYB* 1935–44]; *New Cinema* [*1947 directory*; *Showcase* 1968]), p: Mr Moynihan (*KYB*, 1934; 1935–44); Roscrea & Athy Picture Co. Ltd, Glebe View, Roscrea; d: Billy Carroll, Bill Barry, Tom Kevin (*KYB*, 1945–55); Roscrea & Athy Picture Co. Ltd, Main Street, Templemore, Co. Tipperary (*KYB*, 1956–71; *Showcase* 1968); F. Williams (*KYB*, 1934); Alfie Clarke; Killarney Picture Co. (from 1977);[71] br & fb: Mr J. Barry, St Cronin's Terrace, Roscrea (*1947 directory*); fb: Paddy Melia (1975–7);[72] 550 (1934);[73] 200 (*KYB*, 1935–44); 500/600 (*KYB*, 1945–54); 600 (*KYB*, 1955–7).
Temperance Hall, refused a cinema licence in July 1933; first listed, *KYB*, 1934; sec: Joseph Brady (*KYB*, 1935); Joseph Bailey (*KYB*, 1936–8).

Templemore
Abbey Cinema (*c.*1928–75; aka *Abbey Theatre*), p: James Guilders (J. Guider in *KYB*, 1929–33; James Guidera, *KYB*, 1934–7, as *Picture House*); two shows weekly; pictures & variety; stage 21ft by 50ft; dressing rooms; p: Roscrea Athy Cinema Co., Roscrea (*KYB*, 1938–71; *Showcase* 1968); br: Mr J. Barry, m: Thomas J. Kevin (*1947 directory*); fb: Mr J. Barry (*1947 directory*); Paddy Melia (1975);[74] screen: 19ft x 17ft (*1947 directory*); 450 (*KYB*, 1938–47);[75] 500 (*1947 directory*); 550 (*KYB*, 1948–71); put up for sale in 1975.
Templemore Picture House (*c.*1919–*c.*1932; aka *Cosy Cinema*), p: George Moynan[76] (*KYB*, 1920–8); 450 (*KYB*, 1920); not listed *KYB*, 1929; *Picture House* listed, *KYB*, 1930–3 (no personnel).
Town Hall (1901; McCole, 2005:appendix D).

Thurles
Capitol Cinema, Castle Avenue (7 February 1949–1971; reopened 9 October 1971–*c.*2008), p: Capitol Provincial Cinemas Ltd, 4 Princes Street North, Dublin (*KYB*, 1952–7); Capitol Provincial Cinemas Ltd, 41 Nutley Lane, Dublin 4 (*KYB*, 1965–70; *Showcase* 1968, though address as 4 Princes Street, Dublin); Modern Irish Theatres Ltd (from October 1971); fb: Paddy Melia (from 1971); Leo Ward (by 1976);[77] 950 (*KYB*, 1952); 926 (*KYB*, 1955); 922 (*KYB*, 1957–68); 846 (*KYB*, 1969–71); 400;[78] 401 (Connolly and Dillon, 2001:73); 3 screens (by 2001).
• *IMC Thurles*, Thurles shopping centre, Slievenamon Road (9 April 2009–), p: Ward Anderson; 5 screens/751 seats; the forty-third screen in the *IMC* network.[79]
National Cinema (*c.*1924–*c.*1950; aka *National Theatre*), l/m: J.J. McGrath (*KYB*, 1925–8, died on 24 December 1925); l: Mrs J. McGrath (*KYB*, 1929–33); Thomas B. Daly (*KYB*, 1934–5); Patrick McGrath (*KYB*, 1937–51; *1947 directory*); 400 (*KYB*, 1934–5; 1934);[80] 500 (*KYB*, 1937–51).
New Cinema, Mitchel Street/ Slievenamon Road (*c.*1929–77; aka *New Theatre*), listed, *KYB*, 1930–3 (no personnel); p: Patrick Delahunty (*KYB*, 1934–55; *1947 directory*); J. Delahunty, New Cinema Thurles Ltd (*KYB*, 1957–71); M.J. Delahunty listed in *Showcase* 1968); Irish Film Theatre Co. (1977); fb: Leo Ward (1975–7);[81] 600 (*KYB*, 1935–57);[82] 800 (*KYB*, 1957–64); 850 (*KYB*, 1965–70);[83] building sold to Thurles Motors, which levelled cinema to make way for car salesroom.[84]
Source Arts Centre (2 October 2006–) 250, mixed-use flexible auditorium.

Tipperary
Aherlow, fb: Paddy Melia (1975–7).[85]
• *Excel Arts and Cultural Centre*, Mitchel Street (2001–), formerly, *Excel Cinema*; 2010: 3 screens/584 (362 [doubles as main theatre]; 144; 78) seats.
Excel Cinema,[86] Mitchel Street (1940–1980s, after fire; *Tipperary Excel Cinema*), listed, *KYB*, 1942–4, name only; p: W.G. Evans & Sons Ltd, 52 Main Street; 700 (*KYB*, 1945–71, *1947 directory*; *Showcase* 1968); redeveloped as *Excel Arts and Cultural Centre*.

Gaiety Theatre and Cinema (*c*.1964–71+), p: W.G. Evans & Sons Ltd, 600 (*KYB*, 1965–71; *Showcase* 1968).
Picturedrome, James Street (*c*.1920–3 January 1921;[87]?–*c*.1959), p/m: W.G. Evans (*KYB*, 1921–34), p: W.G. Evans & Son (*KYB*, 1936–44; 1960); licensed for dancing and music (*KYB*, 1919); m: Sadie Evans (*KYB*, 1921–8); 450 (*KYB*, 1920–1); 430 (*KYB*, 1935–6); 700 (*KYB*, 1960).
Tivoli, Henry Street (*c*.1921–*c*.1936), p: The Tivoli Picture Palace Co. Ltd; Bryan O'Donnell, Hill View, Tipperary (*KYB*, 1927–37); m: J. Heffernan (*KYB*, 1922–4; 1935); J. Harford (*KYB*, 1925–6); booked at hall by J. O'Donnell (*KYB*, 1927–32); 450 (1934);[88] 500.
Town Hall Cinema (*c*.1915–41; *KYB*, 1916–17; reappears, *KYB*, 1936–44 [no details]); 400 (1934),[89] interior destroyed by fire in 1941.

Travelling cinemas
Klondyke Picturedrome, Fair Green, Nenagh (1912–14), p: Harry Lyons.[90]

TYRONE

Aughnacloy
Picture House (*c*.1938–*c*.1963), p: J. Bell (*KYB*, 1939–41); Raymond Stross (1942);[91] Ernest G. Smith, Herbertville, Crilly, Aughnacloy (*KYB*, 1945–64); 300 (*KYB*, 1939–44); 267 (*KYB*, 1945–61).
The Valley Cinema (*c*. 1965–*c*.1968, listed in *Showcase* 1968), p: J. & G. Byers, The Diamond, Aughnacloy, 250 (*KYB*, 1966–8); p/m: George Byers (*Showcase* 1968).

Castlecaulfield
Castle Cinema (*c*.1951–71+), p: S.G. Wells (*KYB*, 1952–71; *Showcase* 1968), 200 (*KYB*, 1952–9); listed as *Cinema* in *KYB*, 1952.

Castlederg
Cinema (*c*.1940–71+), p: Wilton & Barry (*KYB*, 1941–2); Castlederg Cinemas Ltd, (*KYB*, 1943–71; *Showcase* 1968); Barry & Short Ltd, Lifford; br: W. McDevitt, fb: Messrs Wilton & Barry, 20 Church Street, Belfast; screen: 10½ft x 12½ft, 300 (1947 *directory*); 300 (*KYB*, 1941–71); 400.
Picture House, p: J. Stewart, 300 (*KYB*, 1939); most likely same venue as above.

Coalisland
Coalisland Picture House (*c*.1923–71+; aka *The Picture Palace*, *KYB*, 1934–7; *Coalisland Cinema*, *KYB*, 1939–71), p: Coalisland Picture House Ltd; Coalisland Cinema Co. (*KYB*, 1939–71; *Showcase* 1968); m: J.K. Stewart; one show nightly (*KYB*, 1924–6); bm: James J. Conway (*KYB*, 1926–33); br: Mr W.M. Barnard, 16ft proscenium (1947 *directory*); 300 (*KYB*, 1936); 270 (*KYB*, 1939–43; 1947 *directory*); 230 (*KYB*, 1944–57); 400 (*KYB*, 1959–64); 240 (*KYB*, 1965–71).

Cookstown
Cookstown Picture House (*c*.1918–*c*.1961; aka *Cookstown Electric Picture House*; *The Picture House*), p: Cookstown Electric Picture House Ltd (*KYB*, 1919); J.H. Donaghy (*KYB*, 1932); C.H. Donaghy, The Keep, Omagh (*KYB*, 1933–66); m: Patrick McLarnon (*KYB*, 1919); J.W. Fleming (*KYB*, 1921–3, 1926–31); br: Miss M. Marlowe, fb: Noel A. Donaghy, County Cinema, Omagh, screen: 16ft x 12ft (1947 *directory*); 200 (*KYB*, 1919), 230 (*KYB*, 1920); 400 (*KYB*, 1921); 460 (*KYB*, 1936); 400 (*KYB*, 1940–62).
Elect Picture Palace (*c*.1924–7), m: J. McElvogue (*KYB*, 1925–8).
Fair Hill Cinema, in 1920 A.M. Brennan provided designs for a cinema at this site (*DIA*).
Medway (*c*.1948–*c*.1956) p: T.A. Quinn[92] (*KYB*, 1952–7).
New Court House (*KYB*, 1916–17).
Phoenix Cinema (*c*.1967–71+), p: T.A. Quinn, 61 James Street, Cookstown; 384 (*KYB*, 1968–71).
• *Ritz Cinema*, 1–2 Burn Road (?; aka *Ritz Studio*; from 27 December 1999, *Ritz Multiplex*), p: Ward Anderson; 2 screens/320 (192 and 128) seats (*BFI*, 1991); 2 screens/334 (208, 126) seats. Original building demolished in May 1999; *Ritz Multiplex* built on site with 5 screens/830 (355, 200, 100, 95, 80) seats; building includes a restaurant, snooker hall and amusement arcade; 5 screens/800 seats (Connolly and Dillon, 2001:74).
Royal (*c*.March 1952–*c*.1968), p: T.A. Quinn[93] (*KYB*, 1952–66; *Showcase* 1968); 450 (*KYB*, 1952–7); 400 (*KYB*, 1958–60); 513 (*KYB*, 1969–66).

Dungannon
Astor Cinema, Market Square/George's Street (*c*.1946–90; aka *The Cinema*, *KYB*, 1936–46), p: L & W Cinemas Ltd, 35 and 133 Royal Avenue, Belfast (*KYB*, 1949–52); Astor & Castle Cinemas, Ltd, 133

Royal Avenue, Belfast (*KYB*, 1955–71; *Showcase* 1968); fb: Mr McClintock, Supreme Cinemas, Ltd, 133 Royal Avenue, Belfast (1947 *directory*); 500 (*KYB*, 1936–46); 600 (*KYB*, 1955–71); (*BFI*, 1991).

The Castle, Market Square (*c.*1933–*c.*1939; December 1946–71; first listed, *KYB*, 1934–7); reopened in 1946 after being requisitioned during war;[94] p: L & W Cinemas Ltd, 133 Royal Avenue, Belfast (*KYB*, 1950–3); Astor & Castle Cinemas Ltd, 133 Royal Avenue, Belfast (*Showcase* 1968).

Empire (*c.*1922–*c.*1925), p/m: R. Sully (*KYB*, 1923–5); m: W. Skeffington (*KYB*, 1926); 500, licensed for music and dancing (*KYB*, 1919–21).

Forresters' Hall (*c.*1915–*c.*1931 [*KYB*, 1916–17; 1930–2]).

• *Global Cinema*, Oaks Centre, Oaks Road (June 2000–), 6 screens/ 839 (255, 166, 129, 103, 95, 91) seats; 841 (Connolly and Dillon, 2001:74)

Picture House, p: J.C. Simpson (*KYB*, 1916).

Picture House (*c.*1932–*c.*1933; first listing, *KYB*, 1933); p: Maurice Logan & Wilton; fb: H. Wilton; p/m: Maurice Logan (*KYB* 1934); proscenium, 32ft wide.

Regal Cinema, Market Square, p: L & W Cinemas Ltd, 35 Royal Avenue, Belfast; br: M. Logn, 500 (1947 *directory*). Most likely same venue as *The Castle*, see above.

Saint George's Hall, George's Street (*c.*1915–*c.*1918; first listing, *KYB*, 1916); p: John C. Simpson, 200 (*KYB*, 1917; 1919).

Victory (16 December 1946–), former Orange Hall.[95]

Viceroy Cinema (*c.*1947–*c.*1960), p: Sydney Eikans, 411 (*KYB*, 1948–60); last listing *KYB*, 1961.

West End Picture Palace (*c.*1929–*c.*1936; listed, *KYB*, 1930–7), 500 (*KYB*, 1936).

Fintona

Pavilion (*c.*1947–*c.*1965), p: Henrys, Main Street, Fintona (*KYB*, 1948–52); J. & K. Henry, Main Street (*KYB*, 1953–66); 250 (*KYB*, 1948–57), 200 (*KYB*, 1958–60); 220 (*KYB*, 1961–6).

The Cinema, Main Street (*c.*1947–71+), p: Michael Kelly & P.P. McCaffrey; 250 (*KYB*, 1948–71); 300.

Fivemiletown

Classic Cinema, Bookborrow Road (*c.*1947–71+), p: Messrs McKeagney & MacMahon (*KYB*, 1948); Thomas McKeagney & Mrs M.E. McCaffrey (*KYB*, 1949–71; *Showcase* 1968); *c.*150 (*KYB*, 1948–62).

Moy

Olympic Cinema (*c.*1953–71+), p: Gilbert Clarke (*KYB*, 1954–71; *Showcase* 1968);[96] Frank Rafferty; 320.

Newtownstewart

Gorey Cinema (?–1970s) p: Philip R. Richardson, 300; p: T. Gouldson, St Couan's Road, Newtowntewart (*Showcase* 1968).

Omagh

County Cinema, Market Street (*c.*1938/39–71+), p: Charles H. Donaghy, Glenearne, Campsie, Omagh (*KYB*, 1941–53); County Cinema (Omagh) Ltd (*KYB*, 1954–71; *Showcase* 1968); br/fb: Noel A. Donaghy, County Cinema, Omagh, screen: 23ft x 16ft (1947 *directory*); *c.*820 (*KYB*, 1941–70); 775 (*KYB*, 1971); public information office now on site.

Omagh Picture House (*c.*1917–*c.*1924), p/m: Edith O. Millar (*KYB*, 1918 as Miller; 1922–5 as Millar); m: Mrs E.O. Smyth (*KYB*, 1926–31); 480 (*KYB*, 1918–19); 400 (*KYB*, 1920); 450 (*KYB*, 1921; 1925).

• *Omagh Studios*, 1–6 Drumquin Road (1976–; aka *Multiscreen Studios*), p: Philip R. Richardson; originally 2 screens, later extended to 4 screens/1,363 (800, 144, 300 and 119) seats (*BFI*, 1996); further 2 screens added in early 2000s by subdividing 800 seater, making largest of 6 screens, 305 seats, smallest 90; 6 screens/ 1,050 seats (Connolly and Dillon, 2001:74).

Picture House, 11–13 Market Street (*c.*1931–*c.*1960), p: James Menary & Bertie Walsh (*KYB*, 1932); Charles H. Donaghy (*KYB*, 1933–52, address as The Keep [*KYB*, 1933–34] and as Glenarne, Campsie [*KYB*, 1936–7; *KYB*, 1940–52]); N.A. Donaghy, County Cinema, Omagh (*KYB*, 1954–61); br/fb: N.A. Donaghy, ASSA, screen: 20ft x 16ft, 571 (1947 *directory*); 638 (*KYB*, 1941); 590 (*KYB*, 1942–50); 606 (*KYB*, 1951–61); last listed, *KYB*, 1961; now Supervalu supermarket.

Royal Assembly Hall (*KYB*, 1916–17).

Star Kinema, Sedan Avenue (*c.*1923–*c.*1946), p/m: J.E.C. Donnelly (*KYB*, 1924–32); Charles H. Donaghy (*KYB*, 1934–47, with addresses at The Keep [*KYB*, 1934] and Glenarne, Campsie, from 1936); 450 (*KYB*, 1937, 1940); 460 (*KYB*, 1941–7); not listed, *KYB*, 1948.

Strule Arts Centre, Town Hall Square (8 June 2007–; officially opened January 2008), cost: €10.5 million; 350–98 auditorium and 125-seat lecture/film theatre; home to Strule FC (access>CINEMA member, 2010).

Strabane

Pallidrome Picture Palace, Railway Road (*c*.1915–*c*.1935; first listed, *KYB*, 1916; aka *The Pallidrome*
[*KYB*, 1932]), p: H.F. Cooper (H. Cooper, *KYB*, 1922–31); Wilton & Barry (*KYB*, 1932–4); 600
(*KYB*, 1918; 1925); listed, *KYB*, 1936–9, closed when same company opened *Commodore.*
Commodore Cinema (*c*.1936–August 1981; March 1982–?), p: Wilton & Barry (*KYB*, 1940–7, 1947
    directory); Commodore Cinemas (Northern Ireland) Ltd (*KYB*, 1948–71); Mr D.H. Cooper (*Showcase*
    1968); destroyed by fire, August 1981; reopened, March 1982; 500 (*KYB*, 1937); 600 (*KYB*, 1940–
    6, 1947 *directory*); 700 (*KYB*, 1947–8); 750 (*KYB*, 1949–71).
• *Strabane Cineplex*. See *Lifford-Strabane Cineplex*, Lifford, Co. Donegal.
Town Hall (*KYB*, 1916–17).

Stewartstown

The Picture House (*c*.1924–*c*.1933), p/m: P. Corr (*KYB*, 1925–34).

Travelling cinemas

BHMC Cinemas, Draperstown (*KYB*, 1941).
Up-to-date Cinemas: Cookstown, Co. Tyrone; Kilree, Co. Derry (*KYB*, 1941–4).

WATERFORD

Cappoquin

Desmond Cinema (1945–2005+; aka *Ormonde Cinema*; *Cinema*), br: William McCarthy as *The Cinema*;
    James Kavanagh, Ormonde Cinema, Arklow (*1947 directory, Ormonde Cinema*); cine variety; listed
    in *KYB* as closed in 1963; served as parish church during renovation to St. Mary's in 1967; *Showcase*
    1968 lists it as *Desmond Cinema* with p: Mr. W. Gleeson; later a tyre centre and garage.

Dungarvan

Dungarvan Picture Palace, Bridge Street (*c*.1915–*c*.1947; aka *Crotty's Cinema*; *Bridge Cinema*), p:
    Daniel Crotty, garage and ironworks owner[97] (*KYB*, 1919–25); Daniel Crotty & Sons (*KYB*, 1927–
    9, 1939; as *Cinema*: *KYB*, 1930–7; 1941–8; 1947 *directory*);[98] m: David G. Hanly (*KYB*, 1919–20);
    David Healy (*KYB*, 1921–3); L.L. Crotty (*KYB*, 1924–5); m: Miss C. Crotty (*KYB*, 1926–8); fb: Miss
    M. Barry (*KYB*, 1924–5); Miss C. Crotty (*KYB*, 1926–8); br: Miss A. Crotty, 30ft proscenium, stage:
    23ft (*1947 directory*); 500 (*KYB*, 1919); 400 (*KYB*, 1920–1, 1935 (as *Cinema*); 1936–9); 950 (*KYB*,
    1942–8); 800 (*1947 directory*).
• *Old Market House Arts Centre*, Lower Main Street, venue for film club.
Ormonde Cinema, O'Connell Street (*c*.1944–September 2005), p: Ormonde Cinemas Ltd, Dungarvan
    (*KYB*, 1945); D.J. Crotty & James J. Kavanagh (*KYB*, 1948–55); in *1947 directory* the co-owner with
    Kavanagh is Miss Crotty); Mrs C. Falvey & J.J. Kavanagh (*KYB*, 1960–4; *Showcase* 1968); fb: James
    Kavanagh, Ormonde Cinema, Arklow (*1947 directory*); Leo Ward (1975–7);[99] 960 (*KYB*, 1948–55);
    2 screens/279 seats (2001).[1] By 1988, it was operating as Friday, Saturday, Sunday cinema;[2] refur-
    bished in 1989; permission was approved for the demolition of the cinema in 2006 to be replaced by
    a furniture store, 4 shop units and 10 apartments.[3]
• *SGC Dungarvan*, Dungarvan shopping centre, High Street (November 2005–), m: Graham Spurling;
    4 screens/467 seats; in 2006 cinema was upgraded to digital projection; by December 2007, was one
    of three Irish cinemas to have 3D projection (other two in Dublin) and silver screen; venue for
    access>CINEMA affiliated film club (2010).
Town Hall (*KYB*, 1916–17).

Kilmacthomas

Rainbow Cinema (*c*. January 1946–*c*.1971), p: Mr E. Hill (*1947 directory*; *KYB*, 1950–61); J. Barron
    (*KYB*, 1964–71; E. Barron in *Showcase* 1968); 500 (*1947 directory*); 300 (*KYB*, 1950–5); 329 (*KYB*,
    1960); 320 (*KYB*, 1961–71), also dances and other live events, especially by late 1960s.

Lismore

Palladium (*c*.1945–mid-1970s), p: Dr Daniel Healy MD, coroner for West Waterford (to at least 1964;
    Showcase 1968); screen: 17ft x 15ft, 250 (*1947 directory*); 350 (*KYB*, 1950–64).
Lismore Cinema (*c*.1926–36), listed in *KYB*, 1930–7 (no personnel).[4]

Tallow

Regal Cinema, Chapel Street (1924–75; aka *O'Brien's Picture Palace*, *KYB*, 1932–4), built as cinema-
    cum-dancehall by local Sheehan brothers for Daniel O'Brien in 1924; p Daniel & J. O. Brien (1924–
    c.1947, *KYB*, 1932–4); Sean Hyde (*c*.1947–74, *1947 directory*; *Showcase* 1968); 300 (*KYB*, 1949–
    71); bought mid-1940s by Sean Hyde, who continued to operate it as a cinema until O'Brien family

73 The 'co-operative cow-boy Horace' in Grace Gifford's cartoon is Horace Plunkett, founder of the Irish Agricultural Organisation Society, which promoted the modernization of Irish agriculture. While this undated cartoon (probably from the first half of the 1910s), is parodying the developing popularity of the western genre ('What the influence of the cinema may lead to!' is an imitation, perhaps, of popular cowboy star 'Broncho' Billy [Gilbert M. Anderson]), it could also be alluding to Plunkett's own role as a Wyoming rancher in the 1880s.

74 First programme of Dublin Cinematograph Theatre, Sackville (later O'Connell) Street, following a private screening on 8 April. A 'fashionable' venue with 270 seats, confirming the street as the premier location for cinemas, it was opened by major British exhibition company Provincial Cinematograph Theatres, which within months took over the struggling Volta and in 1911 opened the prestigious Grafton Street Cinema, Dublin and Belfast's Picture House. Among the eight films screened as part of the 75-minute programme were *The Cowboy and the Squaw* (1910), a western with G.M. Anderson ('Broncho' Billy) and Clara Williams; D.W. Griffith's *His Last Burglary* (1910).

75 Released in Rome on 1 October 1909, *Beatrice Cenci* was screened by James Joyce as part of the opening programme of the Volta, 45 Mary Street, Dublin, on 20 December 1909. This Italian advertisement declared it 'a true masterpiece of the Italian film industry, filmed in Castel Sant' Angelo in Rome where Beatrice Cenci was sentenced and executed. A premiere work of cinematic art from our company.'

76 The opening advertisement for the Kelvin Picture House, College Square East, Belfast.

DORSET
PICTURE HALL

Sole Proprietor - - M. W. SHANLY.

☞ This Theatre is fitted with THREE Distinct Sliding Apertures in the Roof and TEN side Ventilating Windows, which, together with the Electric Exhaust Fans, make it the Coolest Place of Entertainment in the town.

EXCLUSIVE NON-STOP PROGRAMME
From 2.30 to 10.30.
Sunday, 3 to 6.30.   8.30 to 10.30.

Mon., Tues. and Wed., Sept. 18th, 19th and 20th.

Great Irish Drama,
BRENNAN of the MOOR

A Powerful Drama. In Three Parts.

Brian O'Malley journeys to Dublin to ask for time in which to pay the mortgage on his father's estate. In spite of Brian's plea, the cruel creditor forecloses, and the shock of losing his home kills Brian's father. Later, Brian administers a well-deserved thrashing to Ward for insulting Ethel, and to be revenged, the Lieutenant disguises himself as a highwayman and tries to carry off the girl. He is frustrated by Brian, who tells Ethel that he is the notorious Brennan of the Moor, with the price of £1,000 on his head.

RED BIRD WINS
Sensational Racing Drama. In Two Acts.

Thurs., Fri. and Sat., Sept. 21st, 22nd and 23rd

The Fighting Chance
In Four Sensational Acts.

The Pit In Four Acts. Featuring Wilton LacKaye. Supported by Cail Kane and Milton Lills.

Cycles can be stored without charge, but no legal obligation is undertaken in the event of damage or loss,

USUAL PRICES.

W. H. WEST, Printer, 45a Capel Street, Dublin.

77 This typical early cinema playbill for M. William Shanly's Dorset Picture Hall advertises a multi-item film programme with top billing given to the 'Great Irish Drama', the 1913 film, *Brennan on the Moor* with Barney Gilmore playing the Irish nobleman-bandit. The poster also draws attention to the cinema's efficient ventilation systems, and the provision of free bicycle storage. (Many multiplexes later in the century similarly promoted their car-parking facilities.)

78 In 1915, having been shown in Dublin (from April 1914) and Belfast, the Kinetophone visited the Coliseum, King Street, Cork, with short lectures featuring Thomas Edison, including *Few Shamrocks from Ireland*. A short-lived phenomenon, the Edison-designed Kinetophone combined sound (recorded on an over-sized cylinder) and image with the projector driven by the phonograph, but due to poor operation frequently the sound and image did not synchronize exactly. The Coliseum's regular film programme included two First World War dramas made during the first few months of the war, *A Daughter of Belgium* and *The Coward*.

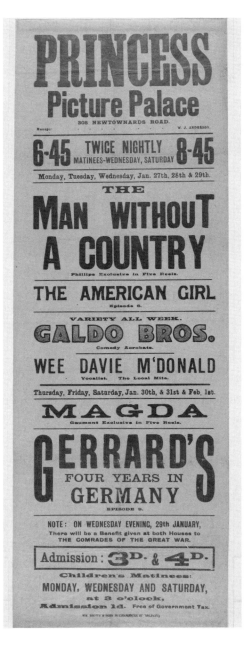

79 An anti-pacifist film, *The Man Without a Country* (Ernest C. Warde, 1917), based on an 1863 short story, was shown for three days along with a serial and some variety items for the low admission price of 3*d*. and 4*d*., with children's matinees only 1*d*. at Belfast's Princess Picture Palace, a down market cinema with poor facilities. The second half of the week continued the war film theme, while the venue also hosted a benefit for 'Comrades of the Great War'.

80 During September/October 1916 Irish audiences had a chance to see *The Birth of a Nation* (1915), the ground-breaking drama of the American civil war and its aftermath directed by D.W. Griffith, considered the father of classical film, when it was shown at the Gaiety Theatre, Dublin. As befitting the prestigious middle-class venue, the screenings were accompanied by a full symphony orchestra.

81 La Scala Theatre and Opera House, just off O'Connell Street, Dublin, was opened by John J. Farrell and partners on 10 August 1920 with 3,200 seats and thirty-two boxes. The luxurious building included tearooms, a lounge and a bar on each floor, a ballroom, smoke and dressing rooms, and a ground-floor restaurant.

82 The Metropole, Dublin, which adjoined La Scala, was opened on 11 February 1922 by Maurice Elliman and partners. With about 1,000 seats, the premises also contained a restaurant and a dance hall. The cinema's domed ceiling featured scenes from the plays of William Shakespeare. Both cinemas were built on sites derelict since the 1916 Rising.

83 Promotional leaflet for *The Thief of Bagdad* (Raoul Wlash, 1924) at the Shannon Cinema, Athlone. The image makes clear the exotic and erotic pleasures, real or imagined, afforded by cinema. The film opened in Ireland at Dublin's La Scala the previous April. Such leaflets were standard material produced by production and distribution companies and were easily customized.

CAPITOL THEATRE

(Late LA SCALA).

PRINCE'S STREET, - - - DUBLIN.

GRAND OPENING PROGRAMME.

WEEK COMMENCING MONDAY, AUGUST 1st, 1927.

HAROLD LLOYD in "The Kid Brother"

A PARAMOUNT RELEASE.

84 Cover of the opening programme of Dublin's Capitol Theatre / Cinema, formerly La Scala, but then being operated by Paramount, who remained the lessee until at least 1934. Inside the programme, general manager Thomas C. Reddin promised 'The entire world will be combed to obtain all that is best in Music, Screen Drama and Stage Presentations.'

CORINTHIAN THEATRE,

EDEN QUAY, DUBLIN. ... ... 'PHONE 3864
Manager : - - - - - - ERIC NOLAN

WEEK COMMENCING SUNDAY FEBRUARY 6th.

RONALD COLMAN
RALPH FORBES, NEIL HAMILTON
AND A CASTE OF OVER 2,000 IN—

BEAU GESTE

by Major P. C. WREN.

The Greatest Novel Ever Filmed.

RONALD COLMAN and RALPH FORBES
in " BEAU GESTE "

DIRECT FROM ITS RECORD-BREAKING SUCCESS OF 150
PERFORMANCES AT THE PLAZA THEATRE, LONDON.

85 Banned by film censor James Montgomery because of its negative representations of the French Foreign Legion, *Beau Geste* was passed with cuts by the censorship of films appeal board and opened at Dublin's Corinthian Cinema in February 1927. The cinema, which was designed by Thomas F. McNamara and opened in 1921, was twined in 1975, by which time it had lost its neo-classical façade, and renamed the Odeon. Later, new owners Ward Anderson renamed it as the Screen at O'Connell Bridge.

86 Juxtaposition of rural and urban in Galway in April 1936 at which time *A Notorious Gentleman* (Edward Laemmle, 1935), a legal drama, was being shown at the Town Hall Theatre and *The White Cockatoo* (Alan Crosland, 1935), a story of inheritance, impostors and mistaken identity set in France, was at the Corrib Cinema. Such billboards were used as a cheaper and more accessible means of advertising than newspapers.

87 May 1963 programme for the Erne Cinema, Ballyshannon, Co. Donegal, complete with prices. Most regional cinemas produced similar handbills, while in addition many such cinemas advertised their programmes in the windows of local businesses.

STELLA
CINEMA, RATHMINES

Proprietors   -   The Stella Picture Theatre, Ltd.

Telephone: 91281.   -   -   -   Manager: V. Kinsella

HOURS OF OPENING:

Monday, Tuesday, Thursday, Friday:
                6.30 to 10.30 (Continuous)

Wednesday and Saturday - 3 to 10.30 (Continuous)

Sunday   - -   Two performances at 3 and 8.30
                Doors open at 2.30 and 8

Programme

Week Commencing

Sunday, 16th Jan., 1949

Prices of Admission   -   2/6, 1/8, 1/3 and 1/-
(Including Tax)

The Management reserve the right to refuse admission to any person. No money returned. Tickets are sold subject to the right of the Management to alter the programme.

Western Electric
MIRROPHONIC
SOUND SYSTEM
THE STANDARD SOUND SYSTEM OF THE WORLD

The Sound Projection Apparatus used in this Theatre is Leased from Western Electric Co., Ltd., Bush House, London, W.C.2.

Rapid Printing Co., Ltd., Dublin.

88 Programme for the Stella Cinema, Rathmines, from 1949 advertising films for the weeks commencing 16 and 23 January, and forthcoming attractions. The four main films in the four programmes listed, which ran from Sunday to Wednesday, or Thursday to Saturday, were the 1942 film adaptation of W. Somerset Maugham's *The Moon and Sixpence*, the 1947 film noir *Kiss of Death*, the 1948 thriller *The Iron Curtain* starring Dana Andrews and Gene Tierney, and John Galsworthy's *Escape* (1948) in which Irish actor Cyril Cusack appeared in a supporting role. The cinema opened in 1923 and closed in 2004.

89 First programme for the Galway Film Fleadh 1989. Considered as one of the big film festivals in Ireland, it is an important platform, especially for young (Irish) filmmakers and animators, and, with its relaxed atmosphere and workshops it has become a lively talking shop for filmmakers and producers.

90 Foyle Film Festival's inaugural programme, 1987. Begun as a community-event it maintains a mixture of workshops and discussion strands involving academics, filmmakers and cultural activists with film screenings. It has grown significantly since its beginnings and has expanded the number and range of films screened.

91 Ireland's main film festival aimed at children and young people, Cinemagic, was first presented in Belfast in 1989 while from 2008 an annual sister event has been held in Dublin. As well as (preview) screenings, Cinemagic offers workshops for schools, special film events, the Cinemagic Young Filmmaker Competition, the young festival jury, and masterclasses in various aspects of television and filmmaking.

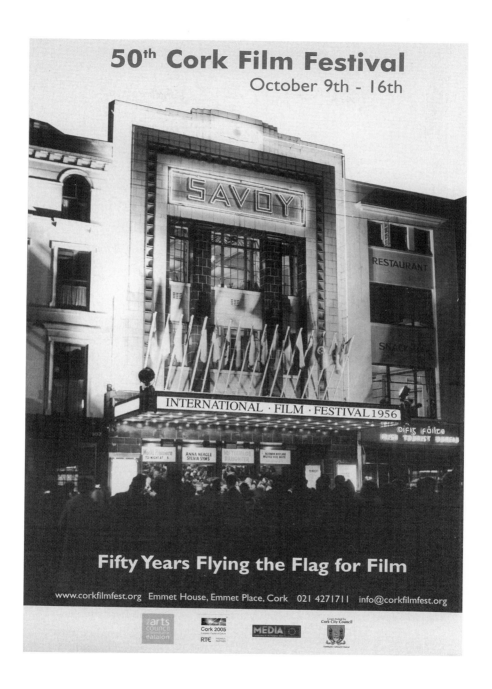

92 Cork Film Festival's fiftieth anniversary, 2006 advertisement. Though founded in 1956 by Dermot Breen, it was revitalized and given sharper focus and became a more significant festival in international film terms from 1986.

Metro Goldwyn Mayer

ARS GRATIA ARTIS

TRADE MARK

CINEMAS
THE BIGGEST NAME IN HOLLYWOOD
presents

DUBLIN'S ULTIMATE CINEMA EXPERIENCE

THE MGM
EIGHT SCREEN MULTIPLEX
PARNELL STREET

Building commences Spring 1993
Doors open Summer 1994

BEST WISHES TO THE
8th DUBLIN FILM FESTIVAL

93 While the 1993 Dublin Film Festival, programmed by Martin Mahon with just under 150 films, proved successful, by the end of the decade the festival, founded in 1985 by Michael Dwyer and Myles Dungan, had begun to lose its identity and in 2001 ended. The promised multiplex by MGM did not in fact materialize until 1995 and then under the name of Virgin. It was subsequently bought by UGC who redeveloped it in 2003 as Ireland's first and only megaplex. In 2005 it was acquired by Cine UK and rebranded as Cineworld.

94 Though cinema experimented with 3D as early as the 1920s when plastigrams were enjoyed by Irish audiences, and again, during the 1950s until the process was eclipsed by various widescreen formats that offered a different kind of immersion in the image, certainly more dramatic than television, it was only in the late 2000s that a more generalized shift of Hollywood to 3D became a real possibility particularly in the wake of the success of James Cameron's *Avatar* (2009) and given that 3D films are resistant to piracy.

95 While 4D theatre, which is 3D with the additional experience of movement introduced, akin to a roller coaster ride, appears a relatively recent phenomenon and is largely limited to theme parks, the process recalls the early Hale's tours in the 1900s when patrons sat in cinema halls designed as railway carriages and viewed images of phantom train-rides. One such theatre operated in Dublin from 1907 to 1909. This is an advert for the Irish Republic's first 4D venue, which opened in 2009.

96 The 1990s and 2000s saw an explosion of film and other festivals throughout all parts of Ireland. Dublin's cutting edge Darklight Festival is quite different to the other, more conventional festivals in that it incorporates new media and explores the boundaries between film and art, and as such digital film and animation take centre stage. Begun in 1999, it held its twelfth annual festival in October 2010.

bought it back again in 1974; closed in 1975 and knocked down to allow extension of O'Brien family garage and car sales business.[5]

Tramore

Carousel Cinema (April 1981–*c*.1991; aka *The Carousel*), p: John (Jack) Piper; 2 screens/284 (180 and 104) seats, summertime only. Jack Piper is great grandson of Bill and Emily Piper (see *Piper's Picture Palace* and *Strand Cinema*); used as a music venue and discotheque prior to being a cinema; by 1997 was being used as a bingo hall.[6]

Casino (12 February 1942–3 January 1948; formerly *Cosy Picture House*), p & fb: Thomas G. Cooper, Killarney (*1947 directory*).

Cosy Picture House, Strand Road (1926–*c*.1930; aka *Palace Cinema*; later *Casino*), p: John McGurk; 'almost directly opposite' *Strand*.[7] While in London at the 1924 Wembley exhibition, McGurk bought the Sierra Leone Palace, one of the event's most attractive buildings, and had it shipped to Ireland. It was erected for the August 1926 Tramore racing festival as a multi–purpose hall for dancing, skating, concerts and film shows.[8]

Grand Central Cinema, (1981–3), 2 screens.[9]

Pavilion Hall (*c*.August 1912–), p: Tramore amusement committee/Mr Sharples; cine-variety; films supplied by Irish Animated Picture Co., Rotunda, Dublin, which also supplied a projectionist/operator; in August 1915, hall hired for weekend film shows by Johnny McGurk (see also *Cosy*); *KYB*, 1917.

Piper's Picture Palace, Strand Road (*c*.1910–*c*.1918; Piper built new dance hall in 1922), p: Bill Piper; 300.

Rex Cinema, Main Street/Market Street corner (24 September 1945–14 March 1971; *c*.1975–19 December 1977), built on cleared site of Halley's butchers; arch: William O'Dwyer; p: Amalgamated Entertainments (Tramore) Ltd (*KYB*, 1949–55, md: Mr H.S. Breen [*1947 directory*]); Martin Breen circuit (*KYB*, 1957–71; *Showcase* 1968); Michael Kavanagh (1970s); p: Richard Fitzgerald, Mr E. Khedouri, Tramore; Mr E. O'Meara, Wexford;[10] m: Frank O'Beirne (1950s); fb: Martin S. Breen (*1947 directory*); CinemaScope (June 1955); put up for sale in 1971; 700 (*1947 directory*; 1970);[11] building remained derelict for many years,[12] later occupied by video rental shop; and Cahill's shop.[13]

Strand Cinema (1918–30s), p: Emily Piper (*KYB*, 1919–43);[14] m: Christopher J. Power (*KYB*, 1919–26), pianist: Dodie Harris, bm: J.J. O'Shaughnessy (*KYB*, 1926–43); 400 (*KYB*, 1920); McCormack's amusement arcade now stands on the site.

Waterford

Broad Street Cinema, Broad Street/26 Barronstrand Street (*c*. August 1915–26 November 1933; *Savoy Cinema* from 27 November 1933–1937),[15] first licence issued, 4 August 1915, no Sunday opening; p: Waterford Cinema Co. Ltd, 18 Merchant's Quay, Cork (CRO no.6096; *KYB*, 1917–37); Messrs Patton & McGregor, who paid 1,500 guineas at auction for building (from 14 November 1928);[16] m: George Hay (1914–23, *KYB*, 1919–20); R. Latimer (*KYB*, 1926–8); l: Messrs Hamilton & McGregor at annual rent of £208 (1928);[17] no personnel listed *KYB*, 1929–38; 800 (*KYB*, 1917); 750 (*KYB*, 1919), 700 (*KYB*, 1920); 850 (*KYB*, 1921); 800 (*KYB*, 1935); with the change of name in 1933, it seems as if the cinema was only redecorated in a Spanish style; demolished and rebuilt as *Savoy Cinema* (see below), which opened on 13 December 1937.

Coliseum, Adelphi Quay (1912–?; reopened, 9 April 1917–*c*.1966; aka *Rink Picture Palace*), formerly an ice rink which opened on 2 May 1910, but, in common with other such venues, the ice rink craze went into decline and the rink closed on 17 February 1912; as cinema; p: (Irish?) Animated Picture Co.; Isadore I. Bradlaw & J. Grandy; Waterford Cinema Palace Ltd (*KYB*, 1917–33; some errors in spellings of names in *KYB*); p: Amusements Ltd, 3 Grafton Street, Dublin (*KYB*, 1943–57; *1947 directory*); Amusements Ltd, 9 Herbert Place, Dublin (*KYB*, 1960–71; *Showcase* 1968); m: A.J. Harris Whitney (*KYB*, 1922–4, 1926–8); fb: Mr H.K. Campbell (*1947 directory*); licensed for dancing and music (*KYB*, 1919–20); no personnel listed, *KYB*, 1934–42; br: Miss E. Kerr, screen: 17½ft x 14½ft (*1947 directory*); 1,000 (*KYB*, 1919–20); 950 (1934);[18] 700 (*KYB*, 1935); 1,132 (*KYB*, 1943–57); 1,103 (*KYB*, 1955–7): 872 (*KYB*, 1960); after closing as a cinema, used as a live venue, including for boxing; Waterford Harbour Board subsequently used it as a storage facility; site later redeveloped.

• *Garter Lane Arts Centre*, 5 & 22A O'Connell Street, venue for film society/ access>CINEMA programmes, 2010: 164 seats.

The Picture Palace, John Street, new cinema designed by George Jephson for Mr Bowers at premises formerly owned by auctioneers, Walsh; contact: T.T. Bower, 900 (*KYB*, 1918).

Regal Cinema, The Glen (8 February 1937–*c*.March 1971), built on site of Matterson's Bacon Cellar; p: Martin S. Breen, Bridge Hotel, Waterford (*KYB*, 1938–); Amalgamated Entertainments (Waterford) Ltd (*KYB*, 1953–7); Breen circuit, Waterford (*KYB*, 1960–71; *Showcase* 1968); m: Mr Manahan (from 1937); fb: Martin S. Breen (*1947 directory*); 1,380;[19] 1,300 (*KYB*, 1938–60, *1947 directory*); 1,400;[20] put up for sale in 1971.[21]

Regina Cinema, Patrick Street (1 April 1957–28 February 1985; 3 screens from 1976; refurbished, 1985–6), built on site of O'Brien's Model Bakeries; arch: William M. O'Dwyer, Dublin; cost: £60,000;[22] p: Martin K. Breen (Jr) (*KYB*, 1957–71; listed as Breen circuit, Waterford in *Showcase* 1968); Ward Anderson (from 1985); fb: Leo Ward (1974–7);[23] 1,400 (*KYB*, 1957–); 1,500.[24] See *Waterford Cineplex*.

Rink Picture Palace, Adelphi Quay, cinema licence, 1913.[25] See *Coliseum*.

Savoy Cinema, Broad Street (13 December 1937–*c.*1978), built on site of *Broad Street Cinema/Savoy Cinema*, arch: Robinson & Keefe (*DIA*), p: Waterford Cinema Co Ltd, 33–34 Anglesea Street, Dublin (*KYB*, 1940–52); p: Waterford Cinema Co., 7 Eden Quay, Dublin (*KYB*, 1953–71; *Showcase* 1968); m: Frank Devlin (from 1937, *1947 directory*); fb: Harry W. Culleton, 75 Middle Abbey Street, Dublin (*1947 directory*); 866 (1934);[26] 1,200 (*KYB*, 1940–57);[27] after closing as cinema, was, temporarily, a live venue; Savoy Entertainment Centre from 1979; lobby area now houses a fast food restaurant.

• *Storm Cinemas*, Railway Square (8 June 2007–; *Odeon/Storm*), p: Premier Productions/Patrick O'Sullivan; Irish Leisureplex Entertainment Co./Entertainment Enterprises/Ciáran and Colum Butler (from 2008); l: Odeon Cinemas; 8 screens, 1,112 seats, stadium seating;[28] part of the Railway Square development – a significant residential, retail and office development on 1.29 acres. In 2003, the company had been given the approval for an 11-screen cinema.[29] The 0.75 acre cinema site running adjacent to St John's River was bought in 2002 from Tesco Ireland for €1.4m by a Cork based consortium led by businessman Roy O'Hanlon; access>CINEMA supported film club (Waterfordfilmforall) uses venue (2010).

Theatre Royal (*c.*1915; 1929–56), first listed, *KYB*, 1916; from 1 January 1929 for 30 years, Laurence Breen was granted a lease to venue at annual rent of £100;[30] l: Martin S. Breen, Bridge Hotel, Waterford, 900 (*KYB*, 1935–56; *1947 directory*, also listed as fb);[31] in 1952, Bridget Breen wrote to Waterford corporation seeking to surrender the lease three years early due to the uneconomic cost of renovations demanded by the fire officer;[32] stage: 26ft x 18ft (*1947 directory*).

Waterford Cineplex, Patrick Street (22 December 1993–*c.*2007; redevelopment of *Regina Cinema*; Ward Anderson/Amalgamated Entertainment Waterford Ltd; 5 screens/987 (306, 188, 174, 185, 134) seats/999 seats (Connolly and Dillon, 2001:73); further redevelopment announced in 2008, though venue remained closed in 2010.[33] See *Regina Cinema*.

Travelling cinemas

Toft's, Strand Road, Tramore (summer; 1901–), canvas-topped, portable wooden building.

Watson's Pictures, Theatre Royal, Waterford (January and May/June 1913).[34]

WESTMEATH

Athlone

Adelphi Cinema (*c.*1949–79; formerly *Adelphi Theatre & Cinema*, 1945–9), arch: Owen Doyle (1946, *DAI*); p: Athlone Cinemas Ltd, Ballymahon, Co. Longford (*KYB*, 1946–50; *Showcase* 1968); br: Miss Farrell, fb: Frank J. Farrell (*1947 directory*); Paddy Melia (1975–7);[35] 900 (*KYB*, 1946–50); 950 (*KYB*, 1951–7); later a furniture store.

Athlone Showcase (*c.*1990), p: Patrick O'Sullivan.

Dean Crow Theatre & Arts Centre, Chapel Street (refurbished and reopened in 2000), 460 seats, Athlone film club based there (2010).

Electric Cinema, Longworth Hall (*KYB*, 1917).

Garden Vale Cinema (*c.*1928–*c.*1944), l: Carron Bros (*KYB*, 1929–33); Mr Shercliffe (*KYB*, 1934–8), Eppel & Weiner (*KYB*, 1939–45), 400 (1934).[36]; 500 (*KYB*, 1934–45).

• *IMC Athlone*, Golden Island shopping centre (1998, newly refurbished), p: Ward Anderson, 6 screens/1,054 seats (300, 188, 165, 128, 136, 137); 1,078 (Connolly and Dillon, 2001:73).

Oscar Cinema, Longford Road (1970s), p: Oscar Cinema (Athlone) Ltd (CRO no. 44902).

Ritz (14 February 1940–84), arch: William (Bill) O'Dwyer, Michael Scott & Associates (International Modern style with superstructure built on piers; carved wooden figures on either side of proscenium by Lawrence Campbell, RHA [*DIA*]; archiseek.com), p: Western Cinemas Ltd/Amalgamated Cinema (Ireland) Ltd, 9 Eden Quay, Dublin (*1947 directory*; *Showcase* 1968), md: Louis Elliman; Ward Anderson; Loughlin family, Ritz Amusements; br: John Duffy (*1947 directory*); fb: Michael J. Deasy, 9 Eden Quay, Dublin (*1947 directory*); Geoffrey Elliman (1976); 977 (*KYB*, 1942–4), 987 (*c.*750 stalls; *c.*250 balcony; *KYB*, 1945–8); 1,000 (*KYB*, 1941–8), 1,050 (*1947 directory*; *KYB*, 1949–50), 975 (*KYB*, 1951–2); 935 (*KYB*, 1955), 882 (*KYB*, 1957–71);[37] demolished in December 1999; an apartment block and other facilities were built on the site.

Shannon Cinema (*c.*1924–*c.*1947; as *Savoy*, *c.*1939–*c.*1947; aka *Fr Mathew Hall*), p: Barnadonald Preston (1925–6); Gallagher Bros (*KYB*, 1925–34); m: J. Gallagher (*KYB*, 1925–32); p: Captain Elton Knight (*KYB*, 1940–8); 500.

Castlepollard
Mahon's Cinema (c.1917–).[38]
St Michael's Hall, p: Eugene Courtney, 300.

Kilbeggan
St James's Hall (c.1949–71+), p: Kilbeggan Parochial Committee (*KYB*, 1950–71; *Showcase* 1968); 500 (*KYB*, 1950–2); 450 (*1947 directory*; *KYB*, 1955–61).

Moate
Martin's Cinema (c.1947–71+), p: Martin Fleming (*1947 directory*, which also lists him as fb; *KYB*, 1950–66);[39] Brigid Fleming & Mrs Roche (*KYB*, 1968–71; *Showcase* 1968); 500 (*KYB*, 1950–66); 300 (*KYB*, 1968–71).
Tuar Ard Arts Centre, Church Street (2000–), mixed-use venue, hosts film seasons, affiliated to access>CINEMA.

Mullingar
Coliseum Cinema. See *National Picture Palace*.
County Cinema (c.November 1941–?; aka *Counties Cinemas*), p: *Counties Cinemas Ltd*, br: T. Whelahan, 700; screen: 17ft x 13ft (*1947 directory*); may be same venue as *Hibernian Cinema*.
Hibernian Cinema, Castle Street (c.January 1945–1988; reopened, March 1989–c.1997, as 2 screen *Ritz Cinema*, 1998–?), p: Counties Cinemas Ltd, 70 Middle Abbey Street (*KYB*, 1946–71); Ward Anderson; fb: Leo Ward (1975–6);[40] m: Marie Carroll (from 1978); 721 (*KYB*, 1946–8); 770 (*KYB*, 53–71); 920 (*KYB*, 1949–52); 2 screens/310 (198 and 110) seats[41]/ 308 seats (Connolly and Dillon, 2001:73).
• *IMC Mullingar*, Lakepoint Centre, Delvin Road (2002–), p: Ward Anderson, 6 screens/1,022 seats (2010).
Mullingar Cinema Theatre, County Hall (opened on 29 April 1913; first film show, 19–26 May 1913 with *From the Manger to the Cross* [1912]; aka *County Hall Cinema*); p: Excelsior Picture Co. (11 September 1913);[42] John Fitzmaurice (from c. November 1913); l: J.R. Downe (*KYB*, 1934–7), Patrick Shaw (*KYB*, 1938–45); 700 (*KYB*, 1934–7), 500 (*KYB*, 1938–45). Film shows seem to have ceased around the time of a successful prosecution in April 1944 against Westmeath county council and exhibitor Thomas Whelehan, Mullingar, of breaches of the Cinematograph Act 1909, relating to seating arrangements in the hall;[43] refurbished as *Mullingar Arts Centre*; opened 1 January 1999.
National Picture Palace, beside Healy's, Dominick Street (c.1914–31; following refurbishment, renamed *Coliseum* [22 February 1931–1958]; aka: *National Theatre*), p: Mr P.J. Brady (1917); management changed 1915; m: Michael Hope (1917);[44] p/m: John Fitzmaurice (*KYB*, 1920–32); p Edward M. Morton (1931–);[45] Healy Bros (*1947 directory*; *KYB*, 1933–52); Counties Cinemas Ltd (*KYB*, 1953–71; *Showcase* 1968); 350 (1934);[46] 450 (*KYB*, 1935), 680 (*KYB*, 1945); 450 (*1947 directory*); 314 (*KYB*, 1955).
National Theatre. See *National Picture Palace*.
Ritz Cinema, Castle Street. See *Hibernian Cinema*.

Tyrellspass
CYMS Parochial Hall, 400.

Travelling cinemas
Toft's Electric Picture Palace, Fair Green, Mullingar (March 1913).[47]

WEXFORD

Bunclody
Central Cinema.

Duncannon
Cinema, br: P.J. Walsh, 400, programme changed three times weekly (*1947 directory*).

Enniscorthy
The Abbey Theatre, m: T.T. Bower, 500 (*KYB*, 1918); may be same venue as below.
Abbey Picture House (1915–c.1920),[48] m: Mr T. McCarthy (*KYB*, 1921).
Athenaeum Picturedrome, Castle Street (c.1912[49]–) (*KYB*, 1916–17), 600, m: T.T. Bower[50] (*KYB*, 1918). The *Athenaeum* (1892), the new town hall, was later extended to include a theatre/concert hall (1896) and a skating rink, ball court and gymnasium (1908).
Astor Cinema (c.1938–77+) p: T. Doyle (*KYB*, 1939–69); Astor Enterprises Ltd (*KYB*, 1970–1); 700 (*KYB*, 1950–71); fb: A. Doyle (1975–7).[51]

Cinema, Water Street; listed *KYB*, 1930–2 (no personnel).
Grand Central Cinema (*c*.1932–*c*.1947), p: K.G. Gould (*KYB*, 1933–48); 279 (1934).[52]
Picture Hall (*KYB*, 1916–17).
• *SGC Enniscorthy*, Temple Shannon (formerly *Slaney Plaza*), 3 screens/530 seats (Connolly and Dillon, 2001:73), 3 screens (digital) (2010). Other *SGC*s are at Castlebar and Dungarvan.
Slaney Plaza. See *SGC Enniscorthy*.

Ferns
Castle Cinema (*c*.1959–*c*.1967), p: Ferns Cinema Ltd (CRO no. 12452; *KYB*, 1960–8; *Showcase* 1968), 500 (1960–8).

Gorey
• *Movies @ Gorey*, Raheenagurren East, on the Courtown Road (June 2010–), p: Phil Brennan, local businessman, in association with Spurling Cinema Group, owners of *SGC Enniscorty/Slaney Plaza*, 7 screens (all 3D capable) /1,200 seats.
Ormonde Cinema (*c*.1939–76+), p: James J. Kavanagh, Ormonde House, Arklow (*KYB*, 1940–64; *Showcase* 1968); fb: James Kavanagh, Ormonde Cinema, Arklow (*1947 directory*); A. O'Gorman;[53] 600 (*KYB*, 1940–61, *1947 directory*).
Picturedrome (*KYB*, 1917).
Town Hall (*c*.1918–*c*.1944), p: Gorey Cinema Co. (*KYB*, 1919–20; 1922); licensed for music and dancing (*KYB*, 1919–20); town commissioners (*KYB*, 1921–, 1925–33); Charles O'Brien, 40 Lower Newtown, Waterford (*KYB*, 1934–7); m: town clerk (*KYB*, 1921–, 1925–33); l: T.A. Carvon, Gorey Cinema (*KYB*, 1938–45); 200 (*KYB*, 1919–20; 1938–45); 600 (*KYB*, 1921).

New Ross
Cinema, South Street, p: Messrs C. Kavanagh & J. Sheehan; m: J. O'Kennedy, 900, licensed for dancing and music (*KYB*, 1919–20); may be same as *Town Hall*; may also be Alleyn Lovell's 1914 designed cinema (*DIA*).
Ritz Cinema (*c*.1947–76+), p: New Ross Co. (*1947 directory*); Amalgamated Entertainments (New Ross) Ltd, (*KYB*, 1949–55); Breen Circuit, Waterford (*KYB*, 1960–71; *Showcase* 1968); br: Martin Breen (*1947 directory*); fb: Martin S. Breen (*1947 directory*); Leo Ward (1974–6);[54] 850;[55] 600 (*KYB*, 1949–51); 750 (*KYB*, 1952–71).
St Michael's Theatre, Centre for the Arts. See *Town Hall*.
Savoy Cinema. See *Town Hall*.
Town Hall (*c*.1918–*c*.1940; as *Savoy Cinema*, *c*.1943–57), formerly a church (1806–1902), converted to town hall before it opened as a cinema; p: New Ross Cinema Co. (*KYB*, 1919–41; 1944–8); m: John O'Kennedy (*KYB*, 1919); J. Sheehan (*KYB*, 1926); J. Ward (*KYB*, 1927–37); licensed for dancing and music (*KYB*, 1919); 800 (*KYB*, 1919); 600 (*KYB*, 1920–1; 1940; 1944–8);[56] closed as a cinema in 1957; refurbished as *St Michael's Theatre* in 1999; in 2002 theatre expanded to create arts centre with art gallery, and in March 2003, a cinema was added; 329-seat theatre, 50-seat studio venue.

Newtownbarry
The Cinema, p: George Bradley, 300 (*KYB*, 1949–52).

Wexford
Abbey Cinema, Lower Georges Street (1946–90+), p: Amalgamated Entertainments (Wexford) Ltd (1949–71; *Showcase* 1968); initial cost: site: £1,000; to build: £21,511; 1,200;[57] Ward Anderson; m (1948): Captain Thomas Whelan; fb: Leo Ward (1974–6).[58]
Capitol Cinema, South Main Street/King Street (February 1931–?; 1980–*c*.21 March 1985; aka *New Capitol* [*KYB*, 1932–6]), p: Staffords; T. Doyle (*KYB*, 1936); Capitol Cinema (Wexford) Ltd (CRO no. 8527; *1947 directory*, *KYB*, 1937–57; *Showcase* 1968; d: Thomas Doyle, St John's Road, Wexford; Thomas Walsh, 63 North Main Street, Wexford; Richard Walsh, Laurence Kirwan, William Ffrench, James Galvin, John Galvin); Ward Anderson's Amalgamated Entertainments (Wexford) Ltd and Abbey Films Ltd (from 1980); br: T. & R. Walsh,[59] fb: R. Walsh (20 North Main Street), 24ft proscenium (*1947 directory*); 762 (1934);[60] 750 (*KYB*, 1936–57).
Cinema Palace, Harper's Lane/Hay's Lane/Cinema Lane (7 December 1914–1971+; aka *Royal*), formerly a warehouse for salvaged goods, d: M.J. O'Connor, local solicitor, and A.T. Wright, who controlled 29 cinemas and was head of distributors Films Ltd; arch: George L. O'Connor (*DIA*); p: Wexford Cinema Palace Ltd (CRO no. 6050; *KYB*, 1917–57; *Showcase* 1968); m: Charles E. Vize, a photographer (1914–; *KYB*, 1921–7),[61] Richard (Dick) W. Latimer (*1947 directory*; *KYB*, 1932–46; 1955–71); screen: 20ft (*1947 directory*); 600 (*KYB*, 1917; 1935; 1955–71); 650 (*KYB*, 1919–21; *1947 directory*); 750 (*DIA*).[62]

CYMS Concert Hall, Common Quay Street; the Gaelic League was reprimanded by the organizing committee for showing films on 19 December 1911; Mr Cosgrove of 'Ireland's Own Animated Picture Co.' was given permission to show a passion play film on 1 and 2 January 1913 at rent of 15s. per night; only other films shown in hall were in 1957 and 1962.[63]

Municipal Hall (*KYB*, 1916–17).

Picture Hall, Abbey Square (1915–).

Royal Cinema. See *Cinema Palace*.

Savoy Cinema, The Square, Redmond Road (?–July 2008; aka from early 1990s, *Savoy Cineplex*; *Wexford Cineplex*), p: Ward Anderson, 3 screens/622 (300, 196, 126) seats.[64]

Theatre Royal and Picturedrome, High Street (first screening possibly on 29 March 1902 by Irish Animated Picture Co, followed by others;[65] regular film shows from *c*.1915–*c*.1930; aka *Royal Theatre*), p: Theatre Royal Cinema (Wexford) Ltd (CRO no. 9669); Alex M. Ewan (*KYB*, 1916–17); representatives of the late E.P. Ronan (*KYB*, 1918); Wexford Cinema Palace Ltd (*KYB*, 1920–1); m: C.E. Vize, full licence (*KYB*, 1919–21, 1924–8); no personnel listed, *KYB*, 1929–31; 700 (*KYB*, 1916–); the venue for Wexford Festival Opera from its foundation in 1951; building demolished and replaced by 2 auditoria/947 (771 and 176), Wexford Opera House (16 October 2008–).

Wexford Arts Centre, Cornmarket, occasional film venue; opened as arts centre in 1974; access>CINEMA affiliated club, the Picture House, meets there.

Wexford Cineplex, The Square, Redmond Road. See *Savoy Cinema*.

• *Wexford Omniplex*, Rosslare Road, Drinagh (4 July 2008–), p: Ward Anderson, 8 screens/1,577 seats (largest room, 320); cost: €9 million;[66] promoted as Ireland's first fully digital cinema, it requires no projectionist as it is entirely run by computer, though it has one 'old-style' 35mm projector. The cinema is located adjacent to LeisureMax, a recreational centre that includes Wexford's first bowling alley, which opened in December 2007.

WICKLOW

Arklow

Electric Picture House (*c*.1929–39), p: A McGowan (*KYB*, 1934–8); P. Sweeney, 500 (*KYB*, 1940).

• *Gaiety Cinema*, Bridgewater shopping centre, North Quay (October 2007–), p: Gaiety Cinema Group, 9 screens/1,590 seats.

Gaiety Cinema (*c*.1918–*c*. September 1941), p: M. Gowar and Co. (*KYB*, 1919); P. Sweeney (*KYB*, 1935–42); 400 (*KYB*, 1919); 500[67] (*KYB*, 1935–42); put up for sale on 8 October 1941; 550.[68]

Kynoch Hall (1898; McCole, 2005:appendix D).

Marlborough Hall (1900; 1902–3; McCole, 2005:appendix D; *c*.1915–25, listed in *KYB*, 1916–26); p: Col. Proby; m: C.T. Evans (*KYB*, 1920–6); 500 (*KYB*, 1918–26).

Ormonde, Parade Ground, 53 Upper Main Street (*c*.1938–*c*.1982; 1988–2003), p: James Kavanagh (*KYB*, 1939–68; *Showcase* 1968, and fb); 25ft proscenium, 20ft deep stage (*1947 directory*); 600 (*KYB*, 1940–5, *1947 directory*); 550 (*KYB*, 1949–68); closed early 1980s, and reopened in 1988 by Ward Anderson, who twinned cinema, 260 (180 and 80) seats.[69]

Paramount Cinema (*c*.1942–77+), p: James Kavanagh's Ormonde cinema circuit[70] (*KYB*, 1957–68, *Showcase* 1968); fb: James Kavanagh (*1947 directory*); A. O'Gorman (1975–7),[71] 450 (*KYB*, 1943–64).

Baltinglass

Carlton (*c*.1944–72+), p: Edward Bradley, 300 (*KYB*, 1949–71; *Showcase* 1968). There was also a cinema in Baltinglass in 1924.[72]

Ritz Cinema, br: Mr Bradley (*1947 directory*); possibly same as *Carlton*.

Bray

Assembly Hall/Assembly Rooms (1901; McCole, 2005:appendix D).

Mermaid Arts Centre (31 August 2002–), occasional film shows; upgraded to digital in 2009; 242 seats, 35mm.

Gaiety Cinema Theatre, sold by Mr MacArthur to Mr J.M. M'Dowell, solicitor, in trust (1920).[73]

Panorama Cinema, Albert Avenue (1968–71+; aka *Panorama Theatre*; formerly *Roxy Cinema*), p: Michael Collins/Amalgamated Bray Cinema Ltd, 500 (*KYB*, 1970–1); put up for sale, 29 March 1988.

The Picture House, Quinsboro' Road (*c*.1916–*c*.1963), p/m: J.E. MacDermott (*KYB*, 1918–37); Maurice Baum, 70 Middle Abbey Street, Dublin (*KYB*, 1938–64, also listed as fb in *1947 directory*); br: A.S. Popham (*1947 directory*); licensed for dancing and music (*KYB*, 1920); screen: 16ft x 12ft (*1947 directory*); 450 (*KYB*, 1918–26); 400 (*KYB*, 1921); 550 (*KYB*, 1936); 600 (*KYB*, 1938–64); 450.[74]

Roxy Cinema, Albert Avenue (*c*.1927–*c*.1968; *Panorama* from 1968–71+), p: Maurice Baum, 70 Middle
   Abbey Street, Dublin (*1947 directory* [also lists him as fb]; *KYB*, 1948); East Coast Cinema Ltd, 34
   Lower Abbey Street, Dublin (*KYB*, 1951–66); A.P. Popham, Bray (*KYB*, 1960–9); A.A. Popham
   (*Showcase* 1968); m: A.S. Popham (*1947 directory*); 630 (*KYB*, 1948); 600 (*KYB*, 1951–69).
Royal Cinema, Quinsboro' Road (26 December 1935–28 June 2007; aka *Odeon; Bray Royal Cineplex*
   as 7 screens), arch: Vincent Kelly; p: Bray Royal Cinema Ltd (CRO no. 51990); Associated Picture
   Houses Ltd (*KYB*, 1939–46, *1947 directory*); Odeon (Ireland) Ltd (*KYB*, 1948–71; *Showcase* 1968);
   Michael Collins, Film House, Liffey Street, Dublin; m: Mr T.P. Gallagher (to 1946); A. Saunders (from
   1946); fb: Louis Elliman (*1947 directory*); Colman Conroy (1976);[75] 1,058 (*KYB*, 1948–56); 929
   (*KYB*, 1957–63); 721 (*KYB*, 1964–71); 900 (Connolly and Dillon, 2001:73).
Star Cinema, Albert Avenue (*c*.1934–*c*.1945), p: John Lowe (*KYB*, 1939–41); Thomas G. Cooper, Casino
   Cinema, Killarney (*KYB*, 1942–6); 450 (*KYB*, 1935–41); 500;[76] 650 (*KYB*, 1942–6); offered for sale,
   January 1940.[77]

Carnew
Cinema (*c*.1947–*c*.1964), p: Carnew Cinema Co.; James Kavanagh, Ormonde Cinema Arklow, 500
   (*1947 directory; KYB*, 1949–65).

Greystones
Ormonde Cinema, Victoria Road (3 May 1947–July 2007; aka *New Cinema* [*1947 directory*]; *Screen
   by the Sea Cinema*), arch: William O'Dwyer, Dublin; p: Ormonde Cinema (Greystones) Ltd (CRO
   no. 11828); James J. Kavanagh (*1947 directory*) and H.R. Henry[78] (*KYB*, 1950–4, 1960–4); James
   Kavanagh, Ormonde House, Arklow (*KYB*, 1955–9); Ormonde Cinema (Greystones) Ltd (*Showcase*
   1968); Ossie Spurling (*c*.1990); fb: A. O'Gorman (1975–6);[79] original *Ormonde Cinema* put up for
   sale, June 1953;[80] cinema put up for sale, July 1975; 675 (1947); 620 (*KYB*, 1950–5); 400 (*KYB*,
   1955–9); 615 (*KYB*, 1956–61); 120 (Connolly and Dillon, 2001:73); in later years, only balcony area
   operated as cinema, with part of lower floor used as funeral parlour; exterior used in 'film censorship' episode of tv series *Father Ted*.
Picture House, Harbour Road (*c*.1934–*c*.1947), first listing, *KYB*, 1935; p: J. Hipple, Coolagad,
   Greystones (*KYB*, 1938–48; *1947 directory*), 150 (*KYB*, 1935);[81] 210 (*KYB*, 1937–48).
St Kilian's Hall, Trafalgar Road, p: Mr Hipple (*KYB*, 1934).

Rathdrum
Ormonde (*c*.1945–71+), p: Rathdrum Cinema Co. Ltd, Ormonde Cinema, Arklow (CRO no. 11212;
   KYB, 1949–71; *Showcase* 1968); fb: James Kavanagh, Ormonde Cinema, Arklow (*1947 directory*);
   380 (*KYB*, 1946–8); 280 (*KYB*, 1960).

Rathnew
Picture Palace (*KYB*, 1917).

Tinahely
Courthouse Arts Centre (built in 1843, opened as a centre for arts, culture and heritage in January
   1996), occasional film screenings, access>CINEMA film club based there (2010).

Wicklow
Abbey Cinema, Wentworth Place (*c*.1946–*c*.1977; ?–1994), p: Wicklow Cinema Co. Ltd (CRO no.
   10316; *KYB*, 1949–70); Waldorf Associated Cinemas (Drogheda), (*KYB*, 1971); br: William Clarke
   (*1947 directory*); fb: J. Davis (1977);[82] screen: 20ft x 16ft, 660 (*1947 directory*); 714 (*KYB*, 1949–
   57); put up for sale in 1977;[83] 2 screens/259 seats (Connolly and Dillon, 2001:73).
Assembly Hall (1897–1905; McCole, 2005:appendix D).
Excelsior Cinema, Fitzwilliam Square (*c*.1922–*c*.1938), p: Mr. Dobell;[84] p: John J. Clarke; listed, *KYB*,
   1930–44 (no personnel); 500 (*KYB*, 1935); 350 (*KYB*, 1936–45); 300;[85] in 1938 announced that a
   new cinema with ballroom attached was to be built on site of *Excelsior*;[86] *Rialto* built on site.
Rialto Cinema, Fitzwilliam Square (*c*.1942–*c*.1979), p: Rialto Cinema (Wicklow) Ltd (CRO no. 10317;
   Showcase 1968); in 1942, John C. Oakes and W.J. McHugh, 36 Dawson Street, Dublin, acquired
   the business from John J. Clarke, Rossanagh, Rathnew;[87] put up for sale in 1947, 800 seats;[88] (*KYB*,
   1943–69); Waldorf Associated Cinemas (*KYB*, 1970–1); m: J.J. Clarke, br/contact/fb: Maurice Baum,
   screen: 16ft x 12ft (*1947 directory*); 750 (*KYB*, 1943–54); 730 (*1947 directory*); 694 (*KYB*, 1955–
   7); 702 (*KYB*, 1960).

Travelling cinemas
Star Company, operating generally in the midlands, but no regular schedule. Portable equipment. J.
   Duffy Jr, Aughrim, 1941, (*KYB*, 1937–41.)

APPENDIX

Irish Cinema and Other Statistics

INTRODUCTION

Although there is no one single, reliable, complete source of statistical data available on cinema in Ireland, nevertheless, there is still a considerable amount of information that has been published in official publications, trade journals and by individual researchers. These tables have drawn on all these sources, though greatest weight has been given to data compiled by official sources, as well as instances where private research appears thorough, as in the case of the comprehensive profile of Irish film exhibition prepared by statistician Thekla Beere in 1934–5. Statistics that appear unreliable or differ significantly from contemporary patterns have been relegated to footnotes. As with most areas of market research, since the late 1980s, corporate researchers have undertaken more regular and comprehensive data collection with regard to film exhibition in Ireland.

LIST OF TABLES

1. Cinemas (cinemas/cinema screens from 1968)
2. Irish Free State/Republic of Ireland cinema seats
3. (a) Irish Free State/Republic of Ireland admissions per head and European ranking
   (b) Northern Ireland admissions
4. Cinema admissions
5. (a) Irish gross box office revenue (in pounds/punts)
   (b) Republic of Ireland gross box office revenue (in euro)
6. Weekly household expenditure on cinema-going as a proportion of all entertainments and sports, 1951–2000
7. Irish Free State/Republic of Ireland cinema taxes (in pounds)
8. Northern Ireland cinema taxes (in pounds)
9. Irish Free State/Republic of Ireland repatriated profits (in pounds)
10. Numbers employed, 1936–81
11. Irish population statistics, 1901–2009
12. Average annual earnings, 1926–2004

13. (a) Top 10 films at Republic of Ireland box office to 2000
   (b) Films released in Republic of Ireland with gross box office over €5 million (2001–10)
   (c) Top 10 films at the Republic of Ireland box office (1997–2010)
   (d) Irish produced and Irish themed films at Irish box office (all island)

Table 1: Cinemas (cinemas/cinema screens from 1968)[1]

Year	Whole Island	Irish Free State/Éire Republic of Ireland	Dublin	Northern Ireland	Belfast
1909	1		1		
1913[2]			9		
1914			25[3]		
1916[4]	149	87	27–30	62	33
1917			18[5]		
1918			20[6]		
1919			19[7]		
1921			27[8]		
1922			28[9]		
1923[10]		150	31[11]		
1929[12]		180			
1930[13]	265		31		28
1934[14]					27
1935[15]		189	34		
1935[16]		190	36		
1936[17]				119	
1937[18]		200			
1938[19]		200			
1939[20]		220			
1940[21]		199	41		
1943[22]		240	48		
1944[23]	368	260		108	
1945[24]		280			
1945[25]		212	42		
1947[26]	368	256	44	112	
1950[27]		284	41		
1951[28]		278	49		
1952[29]		283			
1955[30]		289	45		
1958[31]		300			
1960[32]		284	43		
1962[33]		324			
1965[34]		271	38		
*1968[35]	349/	262/	87/		
1970[36]		242/	36/		
1975[37]		/196			
1976[38]		161/	24/		
1977[39]		177/			

Year	Whole Island	Irish Free State/Éire Republic of Ireland	Dublin	Northern Ireland	Belfast
1980[40]		/163			
1985[41]		/135			
1986		/140			
1987[42]		/140			
1988[43]		/145			
1989[44]		/160			
1990[45]		/172			
1991[46]		/192			
1992[47]		81/189	16/66		
1993[48]		79/184			
1994		76/201			
1995		65/197			
1996		63/215			
1997		62/228			
1998		64/261			
1999		64/299			
2000		69/313			
2001[49]		/322	/98		
2002		/326			
2003		/329		/144[50]	
2004		68/335		/158[51]	
2005[52]	80/	65/352	12/	23/150[53]	6/
2006		69/401[54]	/117	/154[55]	
2007		72/435[56]		23/151[57]	
2008		/415		24/166[58]	
2009				25/171[59]	

* From 1968 the number to left of forward slash refers to cinemas, and to the right, refers to cinemas screens.

1 The most complete lists of Irish cinemas are found in the annual *Kinematograph Year Book, Film Diary and Directory*, later abbreviated to *Kinematograph Year Book*, and renamed *Kinematograph and Television Year Book*, and in text as *KYB* (1914–71). Although a valuable aid in that the lists offer names and locations of cinemas as well as often including personnel and seating capacity, nevertheless *KYB* lists not only have omissions but they include theatres (such as the *Gaiety*, where films were rarely shown) and often fail to differentiate between full-time cinemas and town or parish halls where seasons of films were generally screened using the substandard 16mm gauge. In recent years, lists compiled by screen advertising companies and as were published in the 2000s in the *Irish Times* in its weekly entertainment guide *The Ticket*, give all cinema sites (though not the number of screens in each complex or capacity) on the island of Ireland in which commercially screened films were being shown. See part three of this book for details of cinema buildings. 2 *KYB*, 1914:322. 3 Number of Dublin corporation annual cinema licences (four of these for theatres). 4 *KYB*, 1916:410–12. 5 Number of Dublin corporation annual cinema licences. 6 Ibid. 7 Ibid. 8 Dublin city and immediate suburbs. 9 Dublin corporation licences. 10 Kevin O'Higgins, *Dáil debates*, vol. 3, col. 763, 10 May 1923. 11 This number is for the greater Dublin area. 12 Mary Manning, 'The talkies', *Irish Statesman*, 7 Dec 1929:268–9. 13 *KYB*, 1930:544–51. 14 *KW*, 13 Sept 1934:30. 15 *KYB*, 1935:613–19. In *Film Daily*, 14 March 1935, it is stated that there were 181 cinemas, of which 160 were wired for sound. There were 3 travelling shows touring in the midlands, Donegal and in the south. 16 Beere, 1935–6:85. 17 According to Sir Dawson Bates, minister of home affairs, speaking in the NI house of commons (following his department's collating of information supplied by local authorities), there were 101 permanent cinemas, 18 occasional licences, and 3 travelling exhibitions, the latter are not included in

the table. (*Belfast Telegraph*, 27 Nov 1936:11.)   18 Liam O'Leary, quoted, *TC*, 14 April 1937. *TC*, 7 April 1937, stated that there were 160 cinemas, while *The Cinema*, 10 Feb 1937, quoting the *Irish Catholic*, reported 200.   19 Nathan D. Golden, chief, motion picture division, *Review of foreign film markets during 1938*, bureau of foreign and domestic commerce, US dept of commerce, March 1939.   20 *Report of the inter-departmental committee on the film industry*, March 1942:7, NAI.   21 *KYB*, 1940:639–45.   22 *KW*, 13 Jan 1944:90.   23 Information from *Motion picture markets, Europe: Éire*, US dept of commerce inquiry reference service, 1944:1, and *Motion picture markets, Europe: Northern Ireland*, US dept of commerce inquiry reference service, 1944:77. (Figures given include theatres.)   24 'Approximately 280 motion-picture theatres … and all are wired for sound', digested from a report by C.M. Gerrity, US vice consul, Dublin, 'Postwar potentialities for motion-picture equipment in the United Kingdom and Éire', industrial reference service, US dept of commerce, vol. 3, part 3, 'Motion pictures and equipment', no. 19:3.   25 *KYB*, 1945:550–7.   26 *Cinema and Theatre Review*, 1947.   27 *KYB*, 1950:470–9. *KW*, 21 July 1949, reported that there were 300 16mm exhibitors, including in schools, institutions and commercial locations. *Screen Digest*, hereafter *SD* gives figure of 300 cinemas (Nov 1991:250) and 290 cinemas (Sept 1992:202).   28 Includes theatres. *Daily Film Renter*, 21 Jan 1955.   29 Cinema and General Publicity, *The Irish audience for screen advertising* (1952), summary of findings, *TC*, 9 June 1953.   30 *KYB*, 1955:418–29. *SD* (Nov 1991:250) gives figure of 327 cinemas.   31 There were 'over 300 conventional cinemas' and 220 16mm locations, especially mobile cinemas along western seaboard (*KW*, 30 Jan 1958).   32 *KYB*, 1960:406–17. *SD* gives figure of 290 cinemas (Nov 1991:250) and 220 cinemas (Sept 1992:202).   33 Restrictive practices' commission, *Report of enquiry into the supply and distribution of cinema films*, 1978:17 (hereafter *RPC*).   34 *KYB*, 1965:359–69. *SD* (Nov 1991:250) gives figure of 250 cinemas.   35 *Showcase*, March 1968:32–3. Ten ROI cinemas were described as 'halls', while a number NI venues were also parochial halls. The many local, or even village-level cinemas included in *Showcase* may not have been included in *KYB*.   36 *KYB*, 1970:297–300. *SD* gives figure of 240 cinemas (Nov 1991:250) and 237 screens (Sept 1992:202).   37 *SD*, Nov 1991:250.   38 *Report of investigation by the examiner of restrictive practices into the distribution of cinema films*, 1977:71–7. The Dublin figures were: city centre, 12; suburbs, 6; and county, 6. *SD*, Nov 1991:250, gives a figure of 196 screens for 1975; this is considerably more than the reliable figure in the examiner's report.   39 *RPC*, 1978:17. This report states that 87 cinemas had closed since 1971, of which 30 closed in 1976.   40 *SD*, Oct 1990:230; Sept 1992:202.   41 Ibid.   42 *SD*, Oct 1990:230; *SD*, Sept 1992:202, gives figure of 160 cinemas.   43 *SD*, Oct 1990:230.   44 MEDIA Salles [hereafter cited as MS], number of cinemas and of screens tables, *European Cinema Yearbook*, 2008 (http://medi-asalles.it) [hereafter cited as *ECY*] used as source for 1989 to 2007 inclusive, however, the number of cinemas are only given from 1992, and are absent for years 2001–3 inclusive. With regard to 1989 see also *SD*, Sept 1992:20. RSA Advertising as published in *Big Ticket*, film magazine's promotional issue, c.1994, and *SD*, Oct 1990:230, give figure of 146.   45 *SD* (Nov 1991:250 and Sept 1992:202) gives figure as 171; RSA Advertising as published in *Big Ticket*, c.1994, gives a figure of 170 screens.   46 *In Production* (hereafter *IP*), March/April 2004:13. *SD*, Sept 1992:202 gives figure of 173. RSA Advertising as published in *Big Ticket*, c.1994, gives a figure of 170 screens.   47 Cinema Media and RSA Advertising as published in *Big Ticket*, c.1994, which gives a figure of 186 screens.   48 RSA Advertising as published in *The Big Ticket*, c.1994.   49 *IP*, March/April 2004:13, gives the figure as 57 cinemas, this would suggest too dramatic a fall and so has not been included in table.   50 Table 6.6, admissions per screen and per person by region, *UK Film Council Statistical Yearbook*, 2003–4:35, hereafter *FCSY*.   51 Tables 7.4 and 7.5, *FCSY*, 2004–5:41.   52 List as published in the *IT*, 16 Dec 2005, the ticket:14–16; MS *ECY*, 2007.   53 Tables 7.4 and 7.5, *FCSY*, 2005–6:47. According to table 7.7 (ibid. 48) 114, or 76% (slightly more than the UK average of 73%), of these were in multiplexes.   54 MS tables (number of cinemas and of screens), *ECY*, 2008. Carlton Screen Advertising, Jan 2007, gives the figure as 375 screens. Carlton gives the screens of the other major Irish cities and counties including Cork: 61 screens; Limerick: 12; Galway:18; and Waterford: 9. The rest of the country had 158 screens.   55 Table 9.4, *FCSY*, 2006–7:82. There were 32,264 admissions per screen, the lowest in the UK (the highest were the North East with 54,776 and London with 53,659), and a total of 4,968,719 admissions.   56 MS tables (number of cinemas and of screens), *ECY*, 2008.   57 Table 9.4, *FCSY*, 2008:68. There were 34,864 admissions per screen, the lowest in the UK, and 3.1 admissions per person, the third highest of the UK's 13 regions, next to London (3.4) and central Scotland (3.3), while the lowest was 2.2 (recorded in 3 regions).   58 Table 10.4, *FCSY*, 2009:76. There were 32,765 admissions per screen, or a total of 5,439,000, representing 3.1 admissions per person where the average was 2.7 across all UK regions.   59 Table 9.4, *FCSY*, 2010:69. There were 33,360 admissions per screen, or a total of 5,705,000, representing 3.2 admissions per person where the average was 2.8 across all UK regions.

Table 2: Irish Free State/Republic of Ireland cinema seats

Year	Number of seats	Average seats per screen	Inhabitants per screen	Annual admissions per seat
1934[1]	111,438	586		
1939[2]	140,000			
1944[3]	120,000	461		
1989[4]	35,448	222	21,969	197
1990	40,176	234	20,389	184
1991			18,338	
1992	37,853	200	18,770	219
1993	38,129	207	19,399	247
1994	39,089	194	17,827	266
1995	39,402	200	18,262	250
1996	48,838	227	16,838	235
1997	44,025	193	16,031	261
1998	49,591	190	14,153	250
1999	*c.*53,000	*c.*180	12,482	*c.*230
2000	58,708	188	12,070	254
2001			11,904	
2002			11,963	
2003			12,048	
2004			12,023	
2005			11,674	
2006[5]	66,786	178	10,496	
2007	*c.*70,000	*c.*161	9,914	*c.*262
2008	*c.*73,033			250

1 Beere, 1935–6:85, 88. 2 *Report of the inter-departmental committee on the film industry*, March 1942:7, NAI. 3 *Motion picture markets, Europe: Éire*, US dept of commerce inquiry reference service, 1944:1; *Motion picture markets, Europe: Northern Ireland*, US dept of commerce inquiry reference service, 1944:77. 4 MEDIA Salles, number of inhabitants per screen; number of seats; number of admissions per seat; and number of seats per screen tables, *European Cinema Yearbook*, 2008 and 2009. This is the source for 1989 to 2008 inclusive, though see note 5 for 2006. 5 Carlton Screen Advertising, Jan 2007; MEDIA Salles, ECY, 2007.

Table 3a: Irish Free State/Republic of Ireland admissions per head
and European ranking

Year	Admissions per head	Euro ranking	Year	Admissions per head	Euro ranking
1923[1]	2.45		1994	2.90	1
1934[2]	6.14		1995	2.73	1
1939[3]	9.43		1996[14]	3.17	2
1944[4]	7.1		1997	3.14	2
1951[5]	16.1		1998	3.35	2
1956[6]	18.0		1999[15]	3.32	2
1960[7]	14.6		2000	3.94	2
1970[8]	6.9		2001[16]	4.16	2
1980[9]	2.79	11	2002[17]	4.44	2
1985[10]	1.27	14	2003[18]	4.40	2
1988[11]	1.69	8	2004	4.29	2
1989[12]	1.99	7	2005	3.99	2
1990[13]	2.11	4	2006	4.24	2
1991	2.29	2	2007	4.26	2
1992	2.34	1	2008[19]	4.14	2
1993	2.63	1			

1 Based on the admission figure of 7.3m. and the 1926 population of 2,971,992. As the Irish population remained fairly constant at almost 3m. during the years 1926 to 1971, choosing such figures in
close proximity to the admissions data will not alter significantly the admissions per head figure
(adm.p.h.). 2 Beere, 1935–6:96, gives the per capita figure as 6. A more refined view, based on her
admissions figures, and the 1936 population of 2,968,420, gives it as 6.14. 3 Based on the admission
figure of 28m. given in the *Report of the inter-departmental committee on the film industry*, March
1942:7, and the 1936 population of 2,968,420. 4 Based on the admission figure of 21m. and the 1946
population of 2,955,107. 5 Based on the admission figure of 47.8m. and the 1951 population of
2,960,593. 6 Based on the admission figure of 52.1m. and the 1956 population of 2,898,264. 7 Based
on the admission figure of 41.2m. and the 1961 population of 2,818,341. 8 *Screen Digest*, Nov
1991:251 (hereafter *SD*). 9 *SD*, Oct 1990:231. Spain was ranked no. 1 with 4.71adm.p.h. Ratings
refer to the 17 countries of western Europe. *SD*, Nov 1991:251, gives figure of 3.2. 10 Ibid. France
was ranked no. 1 with 3.17adm.p.h. *SD*, Nov 1991:251, gives figure of 1.7. 11 Ibid. Norway was
ranked no. 1 with 2.74adm.p.h. *SD*, Nov 1991:251, gives figure of 1.7. 12 MEDIA Salles, annual frequency per capita table, *European Cinema Yearbook*, 2008 (http://www.mediasalles.it.), used for years
1989 through to 2007 and hereafter cited as MS table, *ECY*. With regard to 1989 see also *SD*, Oct
1990:231, which reports figure of 1.97. Norway was ranked no. 1 with 2.98adm.p.h. *SD*, Nov 1991:251,
gives figure of 2. 13 MS table, *ECY*, 2008. *SD*, Nov 1991:251, gives figure of 2.10. Norway was
ranked no. 1 with 2.7adm.p.h. 14 MS table, *ECY*, 2008. *IT*, 15 May 1998:business 2, citing EU survey,
gives figure as 3.2. Note that it is only from 1996 that Iceland's per capita cinema-going was included,
so it can be deduced that Ireland only held the number one position on the basis of a statistical absence.
15 MS table, *ECY*, 2008. *SD, 1999*, quoted, *Film Ireland*, April/May 2000:10, gives figure as 3.30. The
USA had 5.6adm.p.h. in 1999. 16 MS table, *ECY*, 2008. *IT*, 3 April 2003: ticket 28, citing Eurostat,
the Statistical Office of the European Communities, Luxembourg, giving figure of 4.20. 17 MS table,
ECY, 2008. *IT*, 19 March 2004:4, citing Dodona Research, gives figure as 4.4. Iceland had the highest
cinema-going per head of population. 18 MS table, *ECY*, 2008. *In Production*, March/April 2004:13,
gives figure of 4.17. Iceland with 7.29adm.p.h. was Europe's highest. Table 6.6, *UK Film Council
Statistical Yearbook, 2003–4*:35, gives the NI admissions per head as 3.4 (the third highest of the 13
regions). However, with 9 screens per 100,000 inhabitants (the highest in the UK), unsurprisingly, NI
had the lowest admissions per screen at 37,276 compared to London's high of 61,492, where there were
6.5 screens per 100,000. 19 MS table, *ECY*, 2009.

Table 3b: Northern Ireland admissions[1]

Year	Per screen	Per person	Year	Per screen	Per person
2003	37,276	3.4[2]	2007	34,864	3.1
2004	34,104	3.2	2008	32,765	3.1
2005	32,804	2.9	2009	33,360	3.2
2006	32,264	2.9			

1 *UK Film Council Statistical Yearbook* (FCSY) 2003–10, inclusive. 2 While this figure is in table 6.6, FCSY, 2003, if you take the 2009 *European Cinema Yearbook* admissions' figure for 2003 of 5,367,800 and divide it by NI's population of 1,703,000, admissions per person is 3.15. This provides yet further evidence that all statistics need to be treated with caution. Nevertheless, the slightly inflated figure may be explained in part by the fact that *FCSYs* tend to include box office revenues for 6 to 8 weeks into the year in which the volume is published.

Table 4: Cinema admissions

Year	Whole Island	Irish Free State/Éire /Republic of Ireland	Dublin	Northern Ireland
1917[1]	20,000,000			
1923[2]		7,300,000		
1934[3]	36,400,000			
1934/35[4]		18,250,000	11,000,000	
1939[5]		28,000,000		
1943[6]		22,000,000		
1944[7]		21,000,000		
1950[8]		46,100,000		
1951		47,800,000		
1952[9]		49,100,000		
1953		50,700,000		
1954		54,100,000		
1955		50,900,000		
1956[10]		52,100,000		
1957		49,800,000		
1958		45,600,000		
1959		43,800,000		
1960[11]		41,200,000		
1965[12]		30,000,000		
1970[13]		20,000,000		
1975[14]		15,000,000		
1976[15]		5,400,000		
1980[16]		9,500,000		
1982[17]		11,400,000		
1984[18]		14,000,000		
1985[19]		4,500,000		
1986[20]		5,000,000		
1987[21]		5,200,000		

Year	Whole Island	Irish Free State/Éire /Republic of Ireland	Dublin	Northern Ireland
1988[22]		6,000,000		
1989[23]		7,000,000	2,500,000	
1990[24]		7,400,000		
1991[25]	10,397,100	8,084,100	4,219,300	2,313,000
1992[26]	10,710,700	8,258,700	4,612,100	2,452,000
1993[27]	12,800,100	9,310,100	5,319,700	3,490,000
1994[28]	14,251,500	10,422,500	5,657,500	3,829,000
1995[29]	13,272,700	9,836,700	5,163,900	3,436,000
1996[30]	15,282,000	11,480,200	5,709,400	3,801,800
1997[31]	15,339,100	11,491,300	5,173,600	3,847,800
1998[32]	16,437,300	12,386,800	5,902,600	4,050,500
1999[33]	16,442,931	12,452,400	5,917,889	3,990,531
2000[34]	19,389,365	14,885,700	7,188,080	4,503,665
2001[35]	20,773,500	15,941,500	7,817,600	4,832,000
2002[36]	22,824,800	17,319,400	8,517,400	5,505,400
2003[37]	22,799,600	17,431,800	8,600,000	5,367,800
2004[38]	22,649,700	17,261,900	8,489,554	5,387,800
2005[39]	21,315,000	16,395,000	7,990,440	4,920,000
2006[40]	22,822,279	17,854,100		4,968,719[41]
2007[42]	23,630,202	18,365,700		5,264,502[43]
2008[44]	23,668,000	18,229,000		5,439,000[45]
2009[46]	23,174,000	17,654,000		5,520,000

1 Commission of enquiry, National Society of Public Morals, cited, *Irish Limelight*, Nov 1917:12. 2 Kevin O'Higgins, minister for home affairs, *Dáil debates*, vol. 3, col. 763, 10 May 1923. 3 Simon Rowson, 'The value of remittances abroad for cinematograph films', *Journal of the Royal Statistical Society*, vol. XCVII, part V, 1934:638–9. Rowson estimated that total box office income in Britain was £40.2m. (less £6.7m. for entertainments tax), leaving a net of £33.5m. (p. 628). This figure was for Britain only, but as Rowson comments, 'in film matters – and despite the separate political existence of the Irish Free State and Northern Ireland – the United Kingdom is still united.' He goes on to say, 'As the number of cinemas in Ireland numbers about 3 per cent of the number in Great Britain, and as the average earning power for films in Ireland is generally assumed by the distributors as being worth about 3 per cent of the total, and the average price of admission is somewhat lower than in Great Britain, we may safely increase the Great Britain total for admissions by about 700,000 per week. This brings the total for Great Britain and Ireland to 19.25 million per week ... Including Ireland, therefore, the net value of the admissions would have to be increased from £33.5 [million] to nearly £35 million for Great Britain and Ireland' (p. 638). 4 Beere, 1935–6:96. Prior to Beere's analysis, wildly inaccurate admissions figures were attributed to cinemas. For example, Dublin's Savoy opening souvenir programme (1929) says that 'nearly' 2m. visited the cinema weekly in the Irish Free State. Beere also says that the often-quoted figure of 300,000 per week (15.6m. annually) attributed to Dublin was 'a gross exaggeration' (Beere, 1935–6:97). 5 *Report of the inter-departmental committee on the film industry*, March 1942:7, NAI. 6 B.G. Moriarty, 'The cinema as a social factor', *Studies*, vol. 33:45–6. 7 *Motion picture markets, Europe: Éire*, US dept of commerce inquiry reference service, 1944:1. 8 In notes attached to the figures for the 1950–60 period as compiled by the central statistics office and published in *Irish Trade Journal and Statistical Bulletin*, vol. XXXVI, no. 1, March 1961:19, a number of qualifications are made given that the figures were extrapolated from entertainments tax receipts during the period when various exemptions were introduced. As the journal comments, 'it is not known to what extent these changes affected the figures for admissions and receipts.' Most likely, the effect on the totals would have been to underestimate both sets of statistics. Nevertheless, there is a dramatic difference between the CSO figures for the 1950s and all those previously published. This March 1961 issue (p. 19) of the

Irish Trade Journal and Statistical Bulletin is used for 1950 to 1960 inclusive.   9 A survey, *The Irish audience for screen advertising*, published by the company that dominated Irish cinema screen advertising, Cinema and General Publicity, in 1953 reported that 50,180,000 attended the cinema annually; that the average Irish cinema sold 3,400 seats weekly, 41% of capacity; and that one-third of the total Irish population went to the cinema weekly. (See summary of findings, *TC*, 9 June 1953.) In a speech in 1952 on 'Catholics and the cinema', Revd J. Lynch stated that 45m. went to the cinema annually. (*Christus Rex*, vol. 18, no. 1:14–29.)   10 In 1956, Brigid Redmond stated that 50m. attended the cinema annually (*Studies*, vol. 45:222).   11 *Screen Digest* (hereafter *SD*), Nov 1991:252, gives a figure of 38m. for 1960, though the source is not noted. In contrast, *SD*, Sept 1992:205, gives the 1960 figure as 41m. As a result, this, and the figures published in *SD* for 1965, 1970, 1975 and 1980 should be treated with caution, and be regarded as an overestimate, especially as no source is given.   12 *SD*, Nov 1991:252; Sept 1992:205.   13 Ibid.   14 *SD*, Nov 1991:252.   15 *RPC report*, 1977:17, states that it was 'widely accepted' that total cinema attendance in 1976 was only 10% of its 1954 level. Given that the revenue commissioners estimated that cinema admissions in 1954 were 54.1m., their highest ever, admissions in 1976 were about 5.4m.   16 *SD*, Oct 1990:226; Nov 1991:252; Sept 1992:205. Previously, *SD*, Aug 1989, gave a figure of 11.5m.   17 *SD*, Aug 1989. In light of the revision later of other figures for the 1980s published in this issue of *SD*, this figure must also be treated with some scepticism.   18 See previous note.   19 Cinema Media and RSA Advertising as published in *Big Ticket*, *c.*1994; *SD*, Oct 1990:226; Nov 1991:252; Sept 1992:205. Previously, *SD*, Aug 1989, gave a figure of 11.6m.   20 Cinema Media; *SD* (Oct 1990:226, Sept 1992:205). *SD*, Aug 1989, gives a figure of 11m.   21 Cinema Media; *SD* (Oct 1990:226, Sept 1992:205). *SD*, Aug 1989, gives a figure of 10.5m.   22 Cinema Media; *SD* (Oct 1990:226, Nov 1991:252). *SD*, Aug 1989, gives a figure of 10m.   23 MEDIA Salles, admissions table, *European Cinema Yearbook*, 2008 (hereafter MS table, *ECY*); *SD*, Oct 1990:226, Nov 1991:252, Sept 1992:205.   24 MS table, *ECY*, 2008; *SD*, Nov 1991:252, Sept 1992:205.   25 Source for 1991 to 1996 figures in this table: Cinema Media/Taylor Nelson AGB (ROI) and Cinema Media/Gallup (NI) (1997). *SD* (Sept 1992:205) gives the 1991 ROI figure as 8.08m. (as in MS table, *ECY*, 2008); RSA Advertising/Adelaide cites 8m.   26 MEDIA Salles, *White Book of the European Exhibition Industry*, vol. 1, annex 2 – Ireland and a 'general overview' of Ireland compiled from various sources give the ROI 1992 figure as 7,850,000, a figure also given by Mike Casey, 'No Cinema Paradiso', *IT*, 17 April 1993. However, both RSA Advertising/Adelaide and MS table, *ECY*, 2008, give a somewhat higher similar figure of 8.25m. and 8.3m. respectively.   27 MS table, *ECY*, 2008, gives a figure of 9.4m.   28 MS table, *ECY*, 2008, gives a figure of 10.4m.   29 MS table, *ECY*, 2008, gives a figure of 9,837,000.   30 MS table, *ECY*, 2008 gives a figure of 11.48m.; Cinema Media/Taylor Nelson AGB (ROI) and Cinema Media/Gallup (NI) (1997); 'Key cinema statistics', sources: CAA/Nielsen EDI/Society of Film Distributors (*c.*2006), which give NI figure as 3,795,800. Brian Carey reported in 1997 that admissions per screen per annum increased from 36,000 in 1986 to 53,000 in 1996. (Carey, *Sunday Business Post*, 29 June 1997:10.)   31 *In Production*, April 1999:16, citing its source as Carlton Screen Advertising/Taylor Nelson MRBI/EDI; 'Key cinema statistics' (2006); MS table, *ECY*, 2008 (11,491m.). See also *Sunday Tribune*, 9 Nov 2003:B5.   32 *In Production*, April 1999:16, citing its source as Carlton Screen Advertising/Taylor Nelson MRBI/EDI; 'Key cinema statistics' (2006); *Sunday Tribune*, 9 Nov 2003:B5.   33 'Key cinema statistics' (2006) gives Dublin figure as 5,898,600. See also *Sunday Tribune*, 9 Nov 2003:B5. MS table, *ECY*, 2008, gives ROI figure as 12,390,000, while IBEC's *Audiovisual Federation Review*, 2003, gives all Ireland figure as 16,380,000.   34 'Key cinema statistics' (2006) gives Dublin figure as 7,238,500. See also *Sunday Tribune*, 9 Nov 2003:B5. MS table, *ECY*, 2008, gives ROI figure as 14,886,000, while IBEC's *Audiovisual Federation Review*, 2003, gives all Ireland figure as 19,500,000.   35 'Key cinema statistics' (2006); *Sunday Tribune*, 9 Nov 2003:B5. IFTN.ie gives the Dublin figure in 2001 as 8,619,500, and national figure as 17,854,100, citing Carlton Screen Advertising/Taylor Nelson MBRI/Nielsen EDI; MS table, *ECY*, 2008, gives ROI figure of 15,942,000.   36 MS table, *ECY*, 2008; 'Key cinema statistics' (2006). *IT*, 29 Jan 2004:28, citing Nielsen EDI and Carlton Screen Advertising. See also *Sunday Tribune*, 9 Nov 2003:B5; *Sunday Business Post*, 3 Aug 2003.   37 'Key cinema statistics' (2006) gives Dublin figure as 8,369,354. See also *In Production*, March/April 2004:13 and *IT*, 19 March 2004:4 (two articles by Ted Sheehy, which cite research consultants Dodona Research); Emmet Oliver, 'Record crowds boost cinema group earnings', *IT*, 8 June 2004:18; MS table, *ECY*, 2008, gives ROI figure as17,432,000; 'Exhibition', *UK Film Council Statistical Yearbook, 2003–4* (hereafter *FCSY*).   38 'Key cinema statistics' (2006); MS table, *ECY*, 2008, gives ROI figure of 17,262,000; Table 7.4, *FCSY*, 2004–5, gives NI admission figure as 5,387,965, with only 34,104 admissions per screen (the lowest UK regional rate, and almost half London's admission per screen of 60,837; this is explained by the fact that the region has a particularly high number of screens per head of population and not a result of low cinema-going rates; in fact, NI ranks among the top cinema-going regions).   39 'Key cinema statistics' (2006); UK Film Council website, 2006. NI accounted for 3% of the British and NI total; MS table, *ECY*, 2008, gives a ROI figure of 16,396,000. Table 7.4, *FCSY 2005–6*:47, gives the NI admission figure as 4,920,551, with 32,804 admissions per screen.   40 MS table, *ECY*, 2009.   41 Table 9.4, *FCSY, 2006–7*:82.   42 MS table, *ECY*, 2009.   43 Table 9.4, *FCSY, 2008*:68.   44 MS table, *ECY*, 2009.   45 Table 10.4, *FCSY, 2009*:76. NI with 3.1 admission per person in 2008 was the third highest of the UK's 13 regions, while its admissions per screen at 32,765 remained the lowest in the UK.   46 MS table, *ECY*, 2009. Table 9.4, *FCSY, 2010*, gives figure of 5,705,000 admissions for NI, though its box office totals include period to 21 February 2010.

Table 5a: Irish gross box office revenue (in pounds/punts)[1]

Year	Whole Island	Republic of Ireland	Year	Republic of Ireland
1934[2]	1,500,000		1983[10]	23,500,000
1934/5[3]		895,000	1985[11]	16,000,000
1939[4]		1,000,000+	1987[12]	13,000,000
1944[5]		2,630,000	1988[13]	15,000,000
1950[6]		3,235,000	1989[14]	16,000,000
1951		3,342,000	1990[15]	18,000,000
1952		3,420,000	1991[16]	20,000,000
1953[7]		3,622,000	1992[17]	20,000,000
1954		4,095,000	1993	24,000,000[18]
1955		3,999,000	1994	30,000,000[19]
1956		4,367,000	1995	27,600,000[20]
1957		4,355,000	1996	40,250,000[21]
1958		4,165,000	1997	40,250,000[22]
1959		4,070,000	1998	44,600,000[23]
1960		3,930,000	1999	47,020,000[24]
1980[8]		17,600,000	2000	47,600,000[25]
1981[9]		26,000,000	2001	65,400,000[26]

1 Irish box office statistics have been divided into two tables with 5a, denominated in pounds (sterling) and from 1979 punts, covering the period to 1989 and 5b, denominated in euro, the period 1990 to 2009. The euro was adopted by Ireland when the punt (decoupled from sterling in 1979 when Ireland joined the European exchange rate mechanism), was fixed at £1 to €1.27 from 1 January 1999, though the physical currency was not introduced until 1 January 2002. Caution needs to be adopted when applying this rate of exchange retrospectively, or, indeed, to the pound sterling.   2 Simon Rowson, 'The value of remittances abroad for cinematograph films', *Journal of the Royal Statistical Society*, vol. XCVII, part V, 1934:638. This figure is net of entertainments tax.   3 'These figures do not take into account free admissions, nor any admissions in respect of which there might have been an evasion of entertainments tax' (Beere, 1935–6:96).   4 'Box office receipts are calculated to have been well over £1 million.' (*Report of the inter-departmental committee on the film industry*, March 1942:7, NAI.)   5 *KW*, 13 Jan 1944:88.   6 *Irish Trade Journal and Statistical Bulletin*, vol. XXXVI, no. 1, March 1961:19. A note draws attention to the fact that changes in entertainments tax districts and rates during the 1950s do not allow for a consistent comparison of the figures. The journal's table is the source for table 5a for years 1950 to 1960 inclusive.   7 A survey, *The Irish audience for screen advertising*, published by the leading Irish cinema screen advertising company, Cinema and General Publicity, in 1952, reported that £3.5m. was paid at the Irish box office annually. (Summary of findings, *TC*, 9 June 1953.)   8 *Screen Digest* (hereafter *SD*), Oct 1990:228, also gives a figure of US$36.2m. While the same amount is given in *SD*, Nov 1991:254, *SD*, Sept 1992:208 lists US$42m. This difference may reflect changing exchange rates.   9 Muiris MacConghail, chairman, Irish Film Board, stated that the state company, Industrial Credit Company, had calculated Irish box office receipts at IR£26m. (*Proceedings of public hearing*, 4 April 1982, Dublin: Irish Film Board, 1982:39.)   10 *Report of the Irish Film Board, 1983*, estimated that between IR£20m. and IR£27m. was

the gross income of Irish cinemas. The figure in the table takes the mid-point of this range, IR£23.5m.
11 Leo Ward, quoted *Evening Press*, 4 Jan 1985. *SD*, Oct 1990:228 and Nov 1991:254, give figures of
IR£11.3m. and US$14.1m., but *SD*, Sept 1992:208, reports US$17.4m.   **12** *SD*, Oct 1990:228; *SD*, Nov
1991:254, and Sept 1992:208, also give a figure of US$21.8m.   **13** *SD*, Oct 1990:228. *SD*, Nov 1991:254,
and Sept 1992:208, also give a figure of US$22.9m.   **14** MEDIA Salles, *European Cinema Yearbook* [here-
after MS, *ECY*], *2003* and IBEC's *Audiovisual Federation Review* [hereafter *AVFR*] 2003. *SD*, Oct
1990:228, gives a figure of IR£17.5m. *SD*, Oct 1990:228, also gives a figure of US$24.8m., while *SD*
gives a figure of US$24.8m. (*SD*, Nov 1991:252; Sept 1992:208). MS *ECY*, *2007* gives the figure as
€20.912m.   **15** MS *ECY*, *2003* and IBEC's *AVFR*, 2003. John McGee, *Business and Finance*, 11 Oct
1990:42, says box office came to 'about £25m a year'. *SD*, Nov 1991:252 and Sept 1992:208, give figure
as US$31.8m.   **16** MS *ECY*, *2003* and IBEC's *AVFR*, 2003. *SD*, Sept 1992:208, gives a figure of
US$34.7m.   **17** MS *ECY*, *2003* and IBEC's *AVFR*, 2003, give a figure of £20m., the same as in 1991.   **18**
MS *ECY*, *2003* and IBEC's *AVFR*, 2003. *Film Ireland*, April/May 2000:10, gives the all island figure for
1993 as £20.9m., which is less than the ROI figure given in the column. The source of this figure is cited
as 'industry statistics', though no specific source is given. This table also has the following figures that
may be compared with those in this column: 1994: £28m.; 1995: £26m.; 1996: £34m.; 1997: £35.3m.;
1998: £50m.; and 1999: £63.7m. Only the last two figures are greater than those published for these years
in MS *ECY* and in IBEC's *AVFR*.   **19** MS *ECY*, *2003*, and IBEC's *AVFR*, 2003.   **20** Ibid.   **21** MS *ECY*,
2009. IBEC's *AVFR*, 2003.   **22** Ibid. IBEC gives a figure of £40,250,000, the same as for 1996.   **23** *IT*,
19 March 2004:4, citing source as IAPI Adspend, Dodona Research; MS*ECY*, *2003*, and IBEC's *AVFR*,
2003.   **24** MS *ECY*, *2003*, and IBEC's *AVFR*, 2003. See also *IT*, 19 March 2004:4. All the figures are net
of VAT and concession purchases.   **25** MS *ECY*, *2003*.   **26** Ibid.

Table 5b: Republic of Ireland gross box office revenue (in euro)[1]

Year	Republic of Ireland	Year	Whole Island	Republic of Ireland
1990	23,258,000	2000		76,184,000[4]
1991	26,157,000	2001		83,041,000[5]
1992	27,027,000	2002		93,500,000[6]
1993	30,303,000	2003		97,500,000[7]
1994	37,831,000	2004		100,900,000
1995	33,403,000	2005		94,400,000
1996	53,537,000	2006	135,352,887[8]	114,814,000
1997	53,221,000	2007	145,536,799[9]	112,767,000
1998	56,540,000[2]	2008		104,000,000
1999	59,703,000[3]	2009		124,600,000

1 While the Irish pound/punt was not formally linked to the euro until 1999 at the exchange rate of £1
to 1.27, MEDIA Salles in the *European Cinema Yearbook*s (hereafter MS *ECY*), from which this column
is taken, and others have retrospectively converted the Irish currency to euros to allow for a longer term
comparative profile of Irish exhibition. MS, gross box office revenue table, *ECY*, *2008*, was used for
years 1990 to 2007 (excluding 1998, see note below); MS, gross box office revenue table, *ECY*, *2010*,
for years 2008 and 2009.   **2** MS table, *ECY*, 2007. See also *IT*, 19 March 2004:4, citing source as IAPI
Adspend, Dodona Research.   **3** *ECY*, 2008. See also *IT*, 19 March 2004:4. The figures are net of VAT
and concession purchases.   **4** *ECY*, 2008. *IT*, 19 March 2004:4, and IBEC's *Audiovisual Federation
Review* [hereafter *AVFR*], 2003, give the figure as €76.2m.   **5** *ECY*, 2008. *IT*, 19 March 2004:4, and
IBEC's *AVFR*, 2003, give the figure as €83m.   **6** *ECY*, 2008; IBEC's *AVFR*, 2003. *IT*, 19 March 2004:4,
gives figure as €91m.   **7** *ECY*, 2008; IBEC's *AVFR*, 2003; *IT*, 29 Jan 2004:28, citing Nielsen EDI and
Carlton Screen Advertising. See also *IT*, 19 March 2004:4. Concession sales of soft drinks and confec-
tionery grew by 82% from €17.4m. in 1998 to €31.7m. in 2003. Gross cinema advertising revenue,
mostly booked through Carlton Screen Advertising, was €10m. in 2003.   **8** Ted Sheehy, *Film Ireland
online*, posted 30 Jan 2009.   **9** Ibid.

Table 6: Weekly household expenditure on cinema-going as a proportion of all entertainments and sports, 1951–2000

Year	All house-holds	Urban (u) house-holds	Rural (r) house-holds	Total expenditure on entertainments and sports	Cinema as % total	Television expenditure
1951–2[1]	3.14s.			5.61s.[2]	55.9	
1965–6[3]	3.15s.			8.6s.[4]	36.6	2.33s.[5]
1973[6]		£0.236	£0.069		30.4 (u) 11.7 (r)[7]	£0.14 (u) £0.134 (r)[8]
1980	£0.289[9]	£0.378[10]	£0.158[11]	£1.868[12]	18.1 (u) 10.1 (r)[13]	£0.30
1987		£0.333[14]	£0.148[15]		9.7 (u) 5.3 (r)[16]	
1994–5	£0.52[17]	£1.33[18]	£0.64[19]	£4.43[20]		£2.55 (u) £1.04 (r)[21]
1999 –2000	€2.25[22]					€3.50[23]

1 *Household budget inquiry, 1951–2:*9 (Dublin: Stationery Office).　2 The other expenditure was on the-atre, 0.49s. (8.7% of total); dancing, 0.95s. (16.9%); admission to games, 0.66s. (11.7%); and other enter-tainments, 0.37s. (6.5%). Pocket money to children was 0.72s. per week.　3 *Household budget inquiry, 1965–6,* Aug 1969:7.　4 The other expenditure was on theatre, 0.36s. (4.1% of total); dancing, 2.69s. (31.2%); sports and games, 0.85s. (9.8%); and other entertainments, 1.55s. (18%).　5 Television and radio rental expenditure was 2.33s. per week (73.9% of the cinema admissions' expenditure).　6 *Household budget survey* [hereafter *HBS*] 1973, vol. 3, p. 17 (urban), and vol. 4, p. 17 (rural).　7 The total expenditure on entertainments in urban areas was £0.775 per week, and in rural areas, £0.589 per week. The other expenditure in urban areas was on theatre, £0.057 (7.3% of total); dancing, £0.311 (40.1%); sports and games, £0.102 (13.1%); and other entertainments, £0.069 (8.9%); and in rural areas: theatre, £0.016 (2.71% of total); dancing, £0.409 (69.4%); sports and games, £0.064 (10.8%); and other entertainments, £0.031 (5.2%).　8 Television and aerial rental.　9 *HBS,* 1980:17.　10 Ibid., 38.　11 Ibid., 29.　12 Ibid., 19.　13 The total expenditure on entertainments in urban areas was £2.079 per week and in rural areas, £1.554 per week. The other expenditure in urban areas was on theatre, £0.191 (9.1% of total); dancing, £0.808 (38.8%); sports and games, £0.352 (16.9%); and other entertainments, £0.350 (16.8%); and in rural areas: theatre, £0.046 (2.9% of total); dancing, £0.886 (57%); sports and games, £0.250 (16%); and other entertainments, £0.214 (13.7%).　14 *HBS,* 1987:25.　15 Ibid., 125.　16 The total expenditure on entertainments in urban areas was £3.421 per week and in rural areas, £2.771 per week. The other expenditure in urban areas was on theatre, £0.426 (12.4% of total); dancing, £1.089 (31.8%); sports (participation), £0.749 (21.8%); sports (spectator), £0.227 (6.6%); and other entertain-ments, £0.597 (17.4%); and in rural areas: theatre, £0.181 (6.5% of total); dancing, £1.369 (49.4%); sports (participation), £0.276 (9.9%); sports (spectator), £0.284 (10.2%); and other entertainments, £0.513 (18.5%).　17 *HBS,* 1994–5, vol. 1, p. 45. The total expenditure for all households for all enter-tainments in the state was £4.43 per week. The other expenditure was on theatre, £0.55 (12.4% of total); dancing, £1.35 (30.4%); sports (participation), £0.76 (17.1%); sports (spectator), £0.47 (10.6%); and other entertainments, £0.78 (17.6%).　18 Cinema and theatre are combined. *HBS,* 1994–5, vol. 2, p. 77. Total cinema and theatre expenditure was £1.07 per household in the state, while dancing accounted for £1.30 per week (26.5% of total entertainment expenditure).　19 Cinema and theatre are combined. *HBS,* 1994–5, vol. 2, p. 159. Total cinema and theatre expenditure was £1.07 per household in the state, while dancing accounted for £1.47 per week (39.9% of total entertainment expenditure).　20 *HBS,* 1994–5, vol. 1, p. 45.　21 Rental for television and video. Other all households' expenditure per week included £0.15 for videos, £0.47 for audio tapes, and £0.32 for CDs.　22 Cinema and theatre are combined. *HBS,* 1999–2000:69 (final report). The weekly household expenditure on other activities included dancing, €1.73 per week; other entertainment, €4.32; (photographic) film development, €0.59; mobile phone, €3.07; and fixed-line phone, €10.18.　23 Television and video rental and aerial subscription.

Table 7: Irish Free State/Republic of Ireland cinema taxes[1] (in pounds)

Year	Total ET (entertainment tax)	Cinema ET	Cinema ET as % of total ET	Custom duty	Cinema ET and custom duty
1925	179,023			13,148	
1926	169,522			13,244	
1927	159,022			15,204	
1928	156,080			17,375	
1929	140,225			18,902	
1930	154,901			22,388	
1931	173,327			20,382	
1932	165,400			40,612	
1933	173,327			48,004	
1934	196,030			48,751	
1935	205,743			53,821	
1936	249,614			63,408	
1937	282,510			54,463	
1938	306,932			61,304	
1939	326,367			63,666	
1940	327,800	247,800	75.6	56,975	304,775
1941	336,800	257,500	76.5	55,801	313,301
1942	375,700	282,600	75.2	55,718	338,318
1943	453,500	334,300	73.7	52,173	386,473
1944	524,000	372,867	71.2	42,063	414,930
1945	584,489	406,532	69.6	47,921	454,453
1946	687,050	486,070	70.7	67,441	553,511
1947	641,349	524,100	81.7	67,039	591,139
1948	887,834	791,154	89.1	67,937	859,091
1949	1,129,543	997,154	88.3	69,019	1,066,173
1950	1,234,319	999,154	80.9	79,094	1,078,248
1951	1,277,445	1,026,309	80.3	72,473	1,098,782
1952	1,357,238	1,100,614	81.1	87,031	1,187,645
1953	1,279,000	1,200,000	93.8	69,481	1,269,481
1954	1,295,000	1,265,000	97.7	67,132	1,332,132
1955	1,341,345	1,245,987	92.9	64,941	1,310,928
1956	1,361,583	1,278,351	93.9	61,700	1,340,051
1957	1,608,257	1,397,086	86.9	62,711	1,459,797
1958	1,527,027	1,288,167	84.4	61,145	1,349,312
1959	1,524,947	1,298,002	85.1		
1960	1,244,386	1,148,265	92.3		
1961	879,000	780,878	88.8		
1962	828,162	730,385	88.2		
1963	467,167	416,567	89.2		

1 Information on ROI entertainments tax (abolished with effect from October 1962) and on excise duty (ended in 1958) was published in the annual reports of the revenue commissioners.

Table 8: Northern Ireland cinema taxes (in pounds)[1]

Year	Total ET	Year	Total ET
1922	34,058	1943	509,483
1923	81,326	1944	728,133
1924	90,513	1945	751,790
1925	102,513	1946	724,833
1926	105,278	1947	727,927
1927	97,926	1948	n/a
1928	68,241	1949	709,880
1929	57,875	1950	663,237
1930	65,659	1951	665,867
1931	70,960	1952	708,628
1932	66,794	1953	698,632
1933	61,590	1954	695,280
1934	61,094	1955	693,431
1935	65,521	1956	640,781
1936	62,057	1957	675,957
1937	69,650	1958	533,734
1938	75,295	1959	284,168
1939	74,698	1960	199,611
1940	77,286	1961	140,989
1941	150,180	1962	28,024
1942	245,964		

1 Information regarding NI entertainments tax can be found in annual official publications and covers the year to 31 March. Thus, the entry for 1922 is from the period 1 April 1921 to 31 March 1922.

Table 9: Irish Free State/Republic of Ireland repatriated profits[1] (in pounds)

Year	Repatriated Profits	Year	Repatriated Profits
1931[2]	130,000	1956	902,000
1932	n/a	1957	924,000
1933	160,000	1958	876,000
1934	165,000	1959	878,000
1935	135,000	1960	938,000
1936	165,000	1961	980,000
1937	200,000	1962	980,000
1938	216,000	1963	1,000,000
1939	219,000	1964	800,000
1940	219,000	1965	910,000
1941	243,000	1966	849,000
1942	287,000	1967	1,115,000
1943	330,000	1968	1,100,000
1944	374,000	1969	1,200,000
1945	376,000	1970	1,200,000
1946	423,000	1971	1,300,000
1947	453,000	1972	1,300,000
1948	650,000	1973	1,900,000
1949	650,000	1974	2,100,000
1950	650,000	1975	1,800,000
1951	650,000	1976	2,200,000
1952	650,000	1977	2,000,000
1953	712,000	1978	3,000,000
1954	832,000	1979	3,800,000
1955	845,000	1980	4,200,000

1 Figures for repatriated profits are described as 'Net outflow in respect of cinema films' in the publications of the central statistics office. Sources: *Irish Trade Journal and Statistical Bulletin* (ITG): June 1939:76, Sept 1942:106, Dec 1947:148, June 1951, March 1957:2, June 1959:74, June 1961:52; and *Irish Statistical Bulletin* (ISB): June 1965:96, Sept 1969:165, Dec 1973:221, Dec 1977:233, Dec 1979:328, June 1982:199. Since 1980 no separate figures have been published for film rentals. The composite figure now published under the heading of 'Other Services' covers a range of activities unrelated to film. Though not explicitly stated, it appears that the net outflow figures include television rentals of films. Since the 1960s this would have included RTÉ fees paid for screening imported films and programmes. 2 Estimates based on entertainments tax, most of which is in respect of cinemas. Allowances made for expenses of distributors and for imports of film already accounted for in trade statistics, and excludes import duty. While it is not stated explicitly in the accompanying notes, the figures in table 9 most likely include the earnings from exhibition by British companies, most especially ABC and Rank. The amounts repatriated do not, of course, reflect the total earnings of foreign distribution and exhibition companies in Ireland. Distributors were obliged to pay excise duty, film censorship fees, office running costs and taxes (depending on whether the company availed of the reciprocal taxation arrangements between Ireland and Britain whereby a British-registered company operating in Ireland could opt to pay tax in Britain). It is not known how much these represented of total income, though one estimate put renters office costs at 10% of income. Though the extent of the film censorship costs are similarly unknown, like excise duty, the film censor's fees may have been passed on indirectly to the exhibitors through higher percentage charges. Even if this practice did not exist, foreign distributors and exhibitors who, in the case of Rank at least, were often part of the same company, repatriated sums which in Irish terms were substantial.

Table 10: Numbers employed, 1936–81

Year	Entertainment & Sport[1]	Cinema & Film Production	Theatres & Broadcasting	Total All Industries
1936	6,722	2,444[2]		1,235,424
1946	9,665	3,586[3]		1,227,745
1951	10,912	2,718	1,369	1,217,106
1961	10,986	2,587	1,469	1,052,539
1966	11,153	2,102	2,290	1,065,987
1971	10,851[4]	1,660	2,884	1,054,839
1981	6,529[5]	739[6]	4,033	1,271,122

1 Entertainment and sport not only includes the two categories listed in the two adjoining columns but also horseracing (subcategory 3); sweepstakes, lotteries etc. (4); bookmaking (5); and 'other entertainment and sport (6). The source for this table is the *Census of population*, vol. 1: *Industries*. 2 1936 has only one category: Cinema, theatres, film production, etc. 3 1946 has only one category: Cinema, theatres, film production, etc. Figures for 1936 and 1946 are not comparable owing to the transfer of a subgroup of persons (1,577) in 1946 from 'other finance' to 'other entertainment and sport'. In 1945, the 1,500 members of the Irish Transport and General Workers' Union employed in film exhibition and distribution threatened all-out strike when a renter employed non-union labour. A closed shop was won by the union. With the decline in exhibition and distribution from the late 1950s onwards, the power of the ITGWU in film exhibition and distribution declined accordingly. This decline was compensated for by increased membership from the developing film production industry and RTÉ. By 1979 the union had only 34 members in film distribution, 36 projectionists and 276 cinema staff as members. However, film industry members numbered 232 while there were 615 members in RTÉ. In the 1980s the gap between the numbers employed in exhibition/distribution and in film production continued to widen, though with the advent of multiplexes from the late 1980s onwards, the ITGWU, by then known as SIPTU, increased its membership in both the exhibition and newly revitalized film production sectors. 4 Entertainment and sport is retitled 'recreational services'. The categories remain the same. 5 This figure is arrived at by combining the separate categories: horseracing (1,075), bookmaking (1,700), sweepstakes and lotteries (338), and other recreational activities (3,416). 6 Cinema and film production is retitled cinemas and film studios. It is not known whether independent film producers are also included in this category.

Table 11: Irish population statistics, 1901–2009[1]

Year	Ireland	Irish Free State/Éire/ Rep. of Ireland	Northern Ireland	Dublin city[2]	Belfast	Cork
1901	4,458,775			290,638	349,180	76,122
1911	4,390,219			304,802	386,947	76,673
1926	4,228,533	2,971,992	1,256,561	394,089	415,151	78,490
1936		2,968,420		472,935		93,322
1937			1,279,745		438,086	
1936–7	4,248,165					
1946		2,955,107		506,051		89,877
1951	4,331,514	2,960,593	1,370,921	575,988	443,671	112,009
1956		2,898,264		584,483		114,428
1961	4,243,383	2,818,002	1,425,042	595,288	415,856	115,689
1966	4,368,777	2,884,002	1,484,775	650,153	398,405	125,383
1971	4,514,313	2,978,248	1,536,085	679,748	416,679[3]	134,430
1981		3,443,405				
1991	5,103,555	3,525,719	1,577,836		236,116	
2001			1,685,267		232,319	
2002		3,917,203				
2006		4,239,848		506,211		119,418
2009	6,239,446(e)	4,450,446(e)	1,789,000(e)			

1 Main source: W.E. Vaughan and A.J. Fitzpatrick, *Irish historical statistics, population, 1821–1971*, Dublin: RIA, 1978. 2 By 1901 Dublin had increased according to the boundaries defined in the census from 3,733 acres in 1891 to 7,911 acres in 1901. The Dublin boundary increased further in the following years with the former independent urban districts of Rathmines and Rathgar, Pembroke and Howth, included in the Dublin table from 1926 onwards, while the legally defined boundaries of the city and suburbs are included from 1951. 3 Vaughan and Fitzpatrick, 1978:12. Raymond Gillespie and Stephen A. Royle (*Irish historic towns atlas, no. 12, Belfast, part 1, to 1840*, Dublin: RIA with Belfast city council, 2003:7), give a figure of 362,082 for Belfast in 1971, and state that the 1981 figure is unreliable due to the Troubles.

Table 12: Average annual earnings, 1926–2004[1]

Occupation	1926	1938	1947	1975	1984	1996	2004
All employees	£133.12	£128.21	£212				€37,819
All manufacturing	£136.24						
All services	£129.48	£131.18	£213.48				
Industry				€3,894	€15,730	€26,824	
Distribution				€2,636	€14,052	€21,902	
Financial				€4,235	€22,406	€37,432	
Brewing	£157.56						
Printing	£110.24						
Local authority	£92.04	£101.07	£155.80				

1 Irish Free State/Éire/Republic of Ireland/twenty-six counties only. Sources: Central statistics office, *Censuses of industrial production*, 1916 and 1929 (CSO, 1933); 1937 (CSO, 1939); 1938–44 (CSO, n.d.); 1945–7 (CSO, n.d.); and *Labour costs surveys*, 2000 (CSO, July 2002) and 2004 (Dec 2006).

Table 13a–13d: Top Grossing Films at Republic of Ireland Box Office

This section includes (a) top 10 films at Irish box office to 2000; (b) films released in Ireland with gross box office over €5 million (2001–10); (c) top 10 films at the Irish box office (1997–2010); and (d) Irish produced and Irish themed films at Irish box office.

Please note that no adjustment has been made to the figures for inflation, changes in the admission price, or the increased number of screens on which films could be shown during the period. Number of screens refers to first week's release.

*Indicates that film continued on release in following year. In these cases the total box office of the two years is combined in the year of release.

The exchange rate from the Irish pound/punt to the euro was at the rate of IR£1 to €1.27 when the Irish pound (punt) entered the euro currency area. However, conversion from sterling (the currency in use of Northern Ireland), is at a different and constantly fluctuating rate. This may produce some distortion of the figures when Northern Ireland's sterling region is included with the euro area of the Republic of Ireland. However, where possible, the figures are drawn from the euro conversions made by film trade statisticians, which will often take an annual average, such as the Oanda average exchange rate, for a particular year. These fluctuations of the euro-sterling exchange rates may also account for some differences between figures published in these tables and elsewhere.

Table 13a. Top 10 Films at Republic of Ireland Box Office to 2000[1]

The first film to pass £1 million (€1.27m.) at the Irish box office was *Porky's* (1982). '*Crocodile' Dundee* (1986) broke the Irish box office record with £1.81m. (€2.3m.). The first film to pass £2 million (€2.53m.) was *The Commitments* (1990). In 1994 *In the Name of the Father* took £2.3m. (to mid-March), making it at the time the second most successful film ever at the Irish box office after *Jurassic Park* (1993).[2]

1. *Titanic* (1998), £7,546,204 (€9,552,156).
2. *Michael Collins* (1996), £4.04m. (€5.11m.).
3. *Star Wars, Episode 1: the Phantom Menace* (1999), £3.53m. (€4.47m.).
4. *The Full Monty* (1997), £3.26m. (€4.13m.).
5. *Toy Story 2* (2000), £3.15m. (€3.99m.).
6. *Jurassic Park* (1993), £3.12m. (€3.95m.).
7. *Independence Day* (1996), £2.91m. (€3.68m.).
8. *The Sixth Sense* (1999), £2.64m. (€3.34m.).
9. *There's Something about Mary* (1998), £2.55m. (€3.23m.).
10. *Gladiator* (2000), £2.50m. (€3.16m.).

Table 13b. Films Released in Republic of Ireland with Gross Box Office
over €5 million, 2001–10

Avatar (2009–10; 2D & 3D & special edition), €8,702,770.
Shrek 2 (2004), €7,793,242.
The Lord of the Rings 3: the Return of the King (2003–4), €7,436,713.
The Lord of the Rings: Fellowship of the Ring (2001–2), €6,736,622.
Mamma Mia! (2008), €6,311,000.
Harry Potter and the Philosopher's Stone (2001–2), €6,076,749.
The Lord of the Rings: the Two Towers (2002–3), €5,756,363.
Toy Story 3 (2010; 2D & 3D), €5,720,478.
The Simpsons' Movie (2007), €5,400,000.
The Dark Knight (2008), €5,301,000.
Meet the Fockers (2005), €5,160,000.
Harry Potter and the Chamber of Secrets (2002–3), €5,151,011.
Charlie and the Chocolate Factory (2005), €5,110,000.
Bridget Jones' Diary (2001), €5,073,596.

Table 13c. Top 10 Films at the Republic of Ireland Box Office, 1997–2010

1997[1]
1. *The Fully Monty** (1997–8), £3.26m. (€4.13m.).
2. *The Lost World*
3. *My Best Friend's Wedding*
4. *Ransom*
5. *Sleepers*
6. *Bean*
7. *Men in Black*
8. *Jerry Maguire*
9. *Liar, Liar*
10. *Batman and Robin*

1998[2]
1. *Titanic* (91 screens; 39 weeks on release), £7,546,204 (€9,552,156).
2. *There's Something about Mary** (48 screens; 25 weeks on release, 1998–9), £2,559,090 (€3,239,354).
3. *Saving Private Ryan** (75 screens; 32 weeks on release, 1998–9), £2,007,522 (€2,541,167).
4. *Dr Dolittle** (58 screens; 35 weeks on release, 1998–9), £1,836,388 (€2,324,541).
5. *Armageddon* (87 screens; 12 weeks on release), £1,615,998 (€2,045,567).
6. *Godzilla* (80 screens; 11 weeks on release), £1,412,690 (€1,788,215).
7. *The General* (45 screens; 16 weeks on release), €1,738,373.
8. *As Good as it Gets*, £1.3m. (€1.65m.)
9. *The Wedding Singer* (9 screens; 12 weeks on release), £1,299,649 (€1,645,125).
10. *The Butcher Boy*, €1,433,669.

1999[3]
1. *Star Wars, Episode 1: the Phantom Menace* (89 screens; 23 weeks on release), £3,531,372 (€4,470,091).
2. *Notting Hill* (66 screens; 21 weeks on release), £2,487,724 (€3,149,017).
3. *Austin Powers: the Spy who Shagged Me* (77 screens; 10 weeks on release), £2,345,450 (€2,968,924).

4. *American Pie** (60 screens; 1999–2000), £2,261,542 (€2,862,711).
5. *The Sixth Sense** (78 screens; 1999–2000), £2,139,721 (€2,708,507).
6. *The World Is Not Enough** (67 screens; 1999–2000), £1,822,974 (€2,307,562)
7. *A Bug's Life* (74 screens; 29 weeks on release), £1,744,564 (€2,208,308).
8. *Waking Ned* (40 screens; 20 weeks on release), €2,193,419.
9. *The Rugrats Movie* (64 screens; 24 weeks on release), £1,617,907 (€2,047,983).
10. *Shakespeare in Love* (50 screens; 15 weeks on release), £1,479,325 (€1,872,632).

2000[4]
1. *Toy Story 2* (97 screens; 24 weeks on release), £3,158,643 (€3,998,282).
2. *Gladiator* (65 screens; 20 weeks on release), £2,985,945 (€3,779,677).
3. *Meet the Parents** (71 screens; 13 weeks on release, 2000–1), £2,598,445 (€3,289,170).
4. *American Beauty* (51 screens; 14 weeks on release), £2,403,469 (€3,042,365).
5. *Angela's Ashes* (80 screens; 11 weeks on release), £2,205,493 (€2,791,763).
6. *Mission Impossible II* (90 screens; 9 weeks on release), £1,830,312 (€2,316,850).
7. *What Lies Beneath** (55 screens; 9 weeks on release, 2000–1), £1,721,494 (€2,179,106).
8. *Scary Movie* (81 screens; 10 weeks on release), £1,638,245 (€2,073,727).
9. *Chicken Run* (78 screens; 24 weeks on release), £1,528,644 (€1,934,992).
10. *Stuart Little** (75 screens; 26 weeks on release, 2000–1), £1,480,199 (€1,873,669).

2001[5]
1. *The Lord of the Rings: Fellowship of the Ring** (124 screens; 14 weeks on release, 2001–2), €6,736,622.
2. *Harry Potter and the Philosopher's Stone** (140 screens; 24 weeks on release, 2001–2), €6,076,749.
3. *Bridget Jones' Diary** (72 screens; 24 weeks on release), £4,008,151 (€5,073,596).
4. *Shrek* (100 screens; 23 weeks on release), £3,546,591 (€4,489,355).
5. *Gladiator* (re-released) (12 screens; 2 weeks on release), £2,939,801 (€3,721,267).
6. *American Pie II* (85 screens; 11 weeks on release), £2,529,860 (€3,202,354).
7. *Hannibal* (83 screens; 8 weeks on release), £2,096,308 (€2,653,554).
8. *What Women Want* (74 screens; 9 weeks on release), £2,039,460 (€2,581,594).
9. *Cats and Dogs* (66 screens; 22 weeks on release), £2,000,335 (€2,532,069).
10. *Cast Away* (64 screens; 9 weeks on release), £1,770,796 (€2,241,513).

2002[6]
1. *The Lord of the Rings: the Two Towers** (119 screens; 21 weeks on release, 2002–3), €5,756,363.
2. *Harry Potter and the Chamber of Secrets** (144 screens; 19 weeks on release 2002–3), €5,151,011.
3. *Monsters Inc.** (122 screens; 19 weeks on release), €4,594,848.
4. *Spider-Man** (86 screens), €4,581,315.
5. *Ocean's Eleven** (82 screens; 14 weeks on release), €4,022,123.
6. *Die Another Day** (68 screens; 15 weeks on release 2002–3), €3,696,023.
7. *Star Wars, Episode II: Attack of the Clones* (73 screens; 17 weeks on release), €3,371,548.
8. *Austin Powers in Goldmember* (91 screens; 7 weeks on release), €3,290,761.
9. *Scooby-Doo* (80 screens; 20 weeks on release), €3,062,210.
10. *Minority Report* (68 screens; 13 weeks on release), €2,845,594.

2003[7]
1. *The Lord of the Rings 3: the Return of the King** (124 screens; 14 weeks on release, 2003–4), €7,436,713.
2. *Finding Nemo** (115 screens; 15 weeks on release), €4,454,877.
3. *Veronica Guerin** (61 screens; 15 weeks on release), €4,020,924.

4. *The Matrix Reloaded* (108 screens; 12 weeks on release), €3,971,790.
5. *Love Actually** (95 screens; 15 weeks on release), €3,826,138.
6. *Bruce Almighty* (90 screens; 13 weeks on release), €3,589,785.
7. *American Pie – The Wedding* (99 screens; 10 weeks on release), €3,540,995.
8. *Elf** (75 screens; 11 weeks on release, 2003–4), €3,205,865.
9. *Gangs of New York* (84 screens; 11 weeks on release), €3,140,623.
10. *Pirates of the Caribbean* (87 screens; 15 weeks on release), €2,789,355.

2004[8]
1. *Shrek 2** (145 screens; 14 weeks on release), €7,793,242.
2. *Harry Potter and the Prisoner of Azkaban** (138 screens; 17 weeks on release), €4,281,129.
3. *Bridget Jones: The Edge of Reason** (106 screens), €4,250,000.
4. *The Day after Tomorrow* (115 screens; 14 weeks on release), €3,698,908.
5. *Spider-Man 2* (83 screens; 7 weeks on release), €3,474,218.
6. *Shark Tale** (105 screens; 7 weeks on release), €3,260,000.
7. *The Incredibles** (130 screens), €3,180,000.
8. *The Passion of the Christ* (46 screens; 10 weeks on release), €2,966,217.
9. *Troy* (108 screens; 10 weeks on release), €2,835,661.
10. *Starsky & Hutch* (92 screens; 8 weeks on release), €2,483,750.

Shrek 2 broke the record with its first weekend's take of €2.7m. at 145 screens around the country. The previous record was *American Pie II* with €898,000 (2001).

2005[9]
1. *Charlie and the Chocolate Factory** (62 screens), €3,980,788.
2. *Meet the Fockers** (56 screens), €3,951,125.
3. *Harry Potter and the Goblet of Fire** (2005–6), €3,738,835.
4. *The Chronicles of Narnia: the Lion, the Witch and the Wardrobe** (2005–6), €3,469,152.
5. *Star Wars, Episode III: Revenge of the Sith** (60 screens), €2,894,447.
6. *Madagascar* (62 screens), €2,677,128.
7. *War of the Worlds* (61 screens), €2,614,904.
8. *The Wedding Crashers* (51 screens), €2,483,336.
9. *Mr and Mrs Smith* (53 screens), €2,238,268.
10. *Nanny McPhee** (2005–6), €2,140,383.

2006[10]
1. *Pirates of the Caribbean: Dead Man's Chest* (60 screens), €3,915,525.
2. *Casino Royale*, €3,793,239.
3. *The Wind that Shakes the Barley* (51 screens), €3,701,417.
4. *Walk the Line* (29 screens), €3,671,740.
5. *The Da Vinci Code* (61 screens), €3,603,752.
6. *Borat*, €3,560,142.
7. *Ice Age 2: the Meltdown* (59 screens), €2,636,818.
8. *The Departed*, €2,124,547.
9. *The Devil Wears Prada*, €2,074,235.
10. *Chicken Little* (59 screens), €1,883,573.

2007[11]
1. *The Simpsons Movie,** €5.4m.
2. *Shrek the Third,** €4.5m.
3. *Harry Potter and the Order of the Phoenix*, €3.5m.
4. *Spider-Man 3*, €3.5m.

5. *Pirates of the Caribbean: At World's End*, €3.4m.
6. *Ratatouille*, €2.9m.
7. *The Bourne Ultimatum*, €2.9m.
8. *Transformers*, €2.4m.
9. *Knocked Up*, €2.3m.
10. *Die Hard 4.0*, €2.3m.

2008[12]
1. *Mamma Mia!** €6,311,000.
2. *The Dark Knight*,* €5,301,000.
3. *Quantum of Solace*,* €4,147,000.
4. *Sex and the City*,* €4,142,000.
5. *Indiana Jones and the Kingdom of the Crystal Skull*, €3,644,000.
6. *Kung Fu Panda*, €3,099,000.
7. *In Bruges*, €3,036,000.
8. *Hancock*, €2,895,000.
9. *High School Musical 3: Senior Year*, €2,709,000.
10. *Wall-E*, €2,250,000.

2009[13]
1. *Avatar** (2D & 3D & Special Edition, 34 screens), €8,702,770 (€2,488,663 in 2009).
2. *The Hangover* (59 screens), €4,888,249.
3. *Up* (24 screens), €4,059,981.
4. *Slumdog Millionaire* (24 screens), €4,057,973.
5. *Harry Potter & the Half-Blood Prince* (65 screens), €3,806,535.
6. *Ice Age 3: Dawn of the Dinosaurs* (22 screens), €3,543,924.
7. *Twilight Saga: New Moon* (62 screens), €2,870,621.
8. *Transformers: Revenge of the Fallen* (61 screens), €2,666,516.
9. *Marley & Me* (61 screens), €2,420,040.
10. *Bruno* (60 screens), €2,332,227.

2010[14]
1. [*Avatar*, €6,214,107 (included in 2009 total)]
2. *Toy Story 3* (2D & 3D), €5,720,478.
3. *Shrek Forever After* (2D & 3D), €4,387,508.
4. *Inception*, €3,938,334.
5. *Alice in Wonderland* (2D & 3D), €3,542,625.
6. *Sex and the City 2*, €3,263,031.
7. *Harry Potter and the Deathly Hallows: part 1*, €3,088,593.
8. *The Twilight Saga: Eclipse*, €2,756,918.
9. *Iron Man 2*, €2,125,132.
10. *It's Complicated*, €2,020,003.

---

1 Carlton Screen Advertising. 2 Ibid.; *In Production* (cited as *IP*), Nov 1998 and Feb 2000:18–19; *IT*, 18 Dec 1998:14. 3 *IP*, Feb 2000:18; *IT*, 17 Dec 1999:15; *IT*, 20 Dec 2000:ticket 3; *Sunday Tribune*, 24–6 Dec 1999:10. 4 *IP*, Feb 2001:20. 5 *IP*, Feb 2002 and Feb 2003. Unpublished Carlton Screen Advertising, 'Top 25 ROI box office successes' of 2001, 2002, 2003 and 2004 (in possession of authors) give lower figures than in this table for ROI, with source credited to ACNielsen EDI. For example, gross box office for *Shrek* is given as £2.8m. for ROI in comparison with *IP*'s £3,546,591. The CSA figures have not been included here as they are 'estimated' and 'converted into euros from sterling', with the exchange rate not given. 6 *IP*, Feb 2003:14. 7 *IP*, Jan 2004. 8 *IP*, Nov/Dec 2004; *IT*, 7 Jan 2005: ticket 28. 9 Carlton Screen Advertising; Pearl and Dean; Nielsen EDI; *IT*, 6 Jan 2006, ticket 28. 10 Carlton Screen Advertising/Nielsen EDI. 11 Ibid. 12 Ibid. 13 http://www.carltonscreen.ie/Cinema-Data/BoxOffice. 14 Ibid.

Table 13d. Irish Produced and Irish Themed Films at Irish Box Office (all island)[1]

1. *Michael Collins* (no. 1 of all films released, 1996), €5,139,473.
2. *The Wind that Shakes the Barley* (51 screens; no. 3 of 2006), €4,134,909.
3. *Veronica Guerin* (61 screens; no. 3 of 2003), €4,020,924.
4. *Gangs of New York* (84 screens; no. 9 of 2003), €3,140,623.
5. *In the Name of the Father* (1993), €3,063,954.
6. *In Bruges* (no. 7 of 2008), €3,036,000.
7. *Angela's Ashes* (80 screens; 11 weeks on release, no. 5 of 2000), €2,800,525.
8. *The Commitments* (no. 1 of 1990), €2,764,953.
9. *Intermission* (41 screens; 24 weeks on release, 2003-4; no. 12 of 2003), €2,506,172.
10. *In America* (41 screens; 12 weeks on release, 2003-4), €2,221,580.
11. *Waking Ned* (40 screens; no. 8 of 1999), €2,193,419.
12. *The Departed* (no. 8 of 2006), €2,124,547.
13. *Man about Dog* (41 screens; 9 weeks on release, no. 11 of 2004), €2,102,499.
14. *The Field* (1990), €1,886,351.
15. *The General* (45 screens; no. 7 of 1998), €1,738,373.
16. *A Further Gesture* (1997), €1,737,210.
17. *Into the West* (1992), €1,501,076.
18. *The Butcher Boy* (1997), €1,433,669.
19. *The Van* (1996), €1,402,719.
20. *The Magdalene Sisters* (31 screens; 17 weeks on release, 2002-3), €1,391,909.
21. *Circle of Friends* (1995), €1,367,141.
22. *My Left Foot* (1989), €1,126,303.
23. *The Boxer* (1998), £800,000 (€1,016,207).
24. *Breakfast on Pluto* (38 screens; 2005), €981,256.
25. *The Crying Game* (1993), €965,958.
26. *Some Mother's Son* (1996), €950,000.
27. *When Brendan Met Trudy* (30 screens; 9 weeks on release, no. 42 of 2001), €945,292.
28. *Dancing at Lughnasa* (42 screens; no. 30 of 1999), €834,870.
29. *A Love Divided* (30 screens; 1999-2000, no. 36 of 2000), €780,800.
30. *Agnes Browne* (60 screens; 9 weeks on release, 1999-2000; no. 79 of 1999), €700,391.
31. *About Adam* (42 screens; 8 weeks on release, 2001), €678,265.
32. *Song for a Raggy Boy* (36 screens; 7 weeks on release, 2003), €659,878.
33. *I Went Down* (1997), €645,208.
34. *This is my Father* (17 screens; no. 49 of 1999), €643,270.
35. *Tara Road* (44 screens; 2005), €601,625.
36. *Inside I'm Dancing* (33 screens; 5 weeks on release, 2003-4), €587,492.
37. *Mickybo and Me* (28 screens; 2005), €565,547.
38. *Hunger* (30 screens; 2007), €561,508.
39. *Spin the Bottle* (4 screens; 10 weeks on release, 2003-4), €521,270 in 2003.
40. *Adam and Paul* (15 screens; 6 weeks on release, 2004), €489,693.
41. *Evelyn* (2003), €462,215.
42. *Mystic River* (16 screens; 2003), €455,828.
43. *When the Sky Falls* (52 screens; 6 weeks on release, 2000), €405,671.
44. *The Nephew* (38 screens; 1998), €363,420.
45. *Divorcing Jack* (31 screens; 1998), €333,949.
46. *His & Hers* (8 screens; 2010), €325,000.[2]
47. *Perrier's Bounty* (2010), €323,000.
48. *Garage* (2007), €305,952.

49. *Last of the High Kings* (1996), €303,800.
50. *Ned Kelly* (51 screens; 4 weeks on release, 2003), €299,706.
51. *Ordinary Decent Criminal* (41 screens; 5 weeks on release, no. 14 of 2000), €291,828.
52. *City of Ember* (45 screens; 2008), €290,543.
53. *Leap Year* (2010), €278,500.
54. *Once* (8 screens; 2007), €272,559.
55. *Strength and Honour* (4 screens; 2007), €258,468.
56. *The Actors* (40 screens; 6 weeks on release, 2003), €246,575.
57. *Shrooms* (5 screens; 2007), €245,141.
58. *The Most Fertile Man in Ireland* (15 screens; 2001), €239,829.
59. *Ondine* (2010), €226,930.
60. *Accelerator* (15 screens; 2001), €225,817.
61. *The Run of the Country* (1995), €215,190.
62. *Ugly Duckling and Me* (2007–8), €214,431.
63. *Nora* (2000), €201,571.
64. *The Closer You Get* (34 screens; 3 weeks on release, 1999–2000), €199,408.
65. *Studs* (2006), €199,264.
66. *Kisses* (12 screens; 2008), €180,000.
67. *Ella Enchanted* (48 screens; 2005), €164,916.
68. *Cowboys and Angels* (2003), €156,292.
69. *H3* (16 screens; 2001), €156,066.
70. *Borstal Boy* (32 screens; 4 weeks on release, 2000), €145,131.
71. *How about You* (2007), €135,000.
72. *The Tiger's Tail* (2006), €130,554.
73. *Disco Pigs* (26 screens; 2001), €129,200.
74. *Saltwater* (26 screens; 4 weeks on release, 2000), €125,886.
75. *Waveriders* (9 screens; no. 139 of 2009), €113,409.
76. *A Film With Me In It* (12 screens; 2008), €112,431.
77. *Boy Eats Girl* (35 screens; 2005), €107,014.
78. *Dead Bodies* (29 screens; 3 weeks on release, 2003), €103,413.
79. *Pavee Lackeen* (4 screens; 2005–6), €102,687.
80. *Broken Harvest* (1994), c.£80,000 (€101,270).
81. *Blind Flight* (20 screens; 1 week on release, 2004), €98,415.
82. *League of Gentlemen* (51 screens; 2005), €95,788.
83. *The Boys and Girl from County Clare* (2006), €93,700.
84. *An Everlasting Piece* (37 screens; 2 weeks on release, 2001), €91,313.
85. *Tristan and Isolde* (2006), €89,886.
86. *Nothing Personal* (1995), c.€88,610.
87. *Kings* (10 screens; 2007), €86,000.
88. *The Secret of Kells* (24 screens; no. 151 of 2009), €80,039.
89. *The Front Line* (2006), €78,537.
90. *A Man of No Importance* (1994), c.£60,000 (€75,960).
91. *Goldfish Memory* (7 screens; 5 weeks on release, 2003), €74,702.
92. *Sweety Barrett* (12 screens; no. 121 of 1999), £57,195 (€72,398).
93. *On the Nose* (36 screens; 2001), €66,360.
94. *On the Edge* (30 screens; 2001), €56,205.
95. *32A* (2008), €55,000.
96. *The Last September* (6 screens; 2000), €54,827.
97. *Felicia's Journey* (1999), €50,892.
98. *Korea* (1995), c.€50,630.
99. *Heartlands* (8 screens; 2003), €49,591.

100. *The Escapist* (7 screens; 2008), €47,190.
101. *Happy Ever Afters* (30 screens; no. 174 of 2009), €46,348.
102. *Trouble with Sex* (2 screens; 2005), €46,038.
103. *Speed Dating* (4 screens; 2007), €44,264.
104. *Rat* (4 screens; 5 weeks on release, 2000), €42,758.
105. *Headrush* (10 screens; 2005), €41,676.
106. *Southpaw* (7 screens; no. 139 of 1999), €39,744.
107. *Night Train* (1999), €39,381.
108. *Trojan Eddie* (1996), *c.*€37,970.
109. *The Mighty Celt* (2005), €36,171.
110. *Isolation* (2006), €35,191.
111. *Mapmaker* (5 screens; 9 weeks on release, no. 147 of 2002), €34,415.
112. *Honeymooners* (5 screens; 2004), €33,143.
113. *If I Should Fall from Grace?* (4 screens; 2001), €30,239.
114. *The Pipe* (2010), €29,224.
115. *Middletown* (2006), €28,735.
116. *Pyjama Girls* (2010), €25,000.
117. *Country* (7 screens; 5 weeks on release, 2000), €24,995.
118. *Titanic Town* (4 screens; 1998), €23,739.
119. *Savage* (2010), €22,000.
120. *Freeze Frame* (5 screens; 2004), €20,000.
121. *Situations Vacant* (19 screens; no. 200 of 2009), €18,197.
122. *The Heart of Me* (5 screens; 2003), €18,000.
123. *Saviours* (5 screens; 2008), €16,974.
124. *Cracks* (3 screens; no. 204 of 2009), €16,817.
125. *How Harry Became a Tree* (4 screens; 1 week on release, no. 169 of 2002), €16,776.
126. *The Mystics* (6 screens; 2003), €16,373.
127. *The Halo Effect* (8 screens; 2004), €16,243.
128. *Flick* (4 screens; 4 weeks on release, 2000), €16,094.
129. *The Yellow Bittern* (7 screens; no. 207 of 2009), €14,849.
130. *Small Engine Repair* (3 screens; 2007), €14,323.
131. *Wide Open Spaces* (9 screens; no. 210 of 2009), €14,277.
132. *Crushproof* (4 screens; no. 167 of 1999), €13,226.
133. *Gold in the Streets* (1997), €13,148.
134. *Swansong* (2010), €12,023.
135. *Bloom* (7 screens; 2004), €11,900.
136. *Snakes and Ladders* (1998), €11,460.
137. *Last Days in Dublin* (1 screen, 2 weeks on release, no. 188 of 2002), €10,296.
138. *Ulysses* (1 screen, banned 1967; released, 2001), €9,849.
139. *Five Minutes to Heaven* (4 screens; no. 225 of 2009), €9,649.
140. *Eamon* (2010), €9,500.
141. *Love and Rage* (1 screen, 2 weeks on release, no. 190 of 2002), €9,330.
142. *The Boy from Mercury* (1997), £6,457 (€8,173).
143. *The Fifth Province* (2 screens; 1999), £6,060 (€7,670).
144. *Best* (16 screens; 2000), €7,530.
145. *Trafficked* (2010), €7,300.
146. *I Could Read the Sky* (1 screen, 2 weeks on release, 2000), €6,588.
147. *Colony* (2010), €6,493.
148. *Rocky Road to Dublin* (1 screen; 1968; re-released 2005), €6,422.
149. *Crossmaheart* (1 screen, 1999), €6,075.
150. *Bogwoman* (1 screen, 1999), €5,954.

151. *Dead Meat* (1 screen, 2004), €5,545.
152. *Helen* (1 screen; no. 259 of 2009), €5,178.
153. *Summer of the Flying Saucer* (2008), €4,633.
154. *All Souls' Day* (1997), €4,212.
155. *The Sun, the Moon, and the Stars* (1996), €3,669.
156. *Words Upon the Window Pane* (1995), €2,658.
157. *Cherrybomb* (2010), €2,300.
158. *Anton* (2008), €2,000.
159. *The Fading Light* (2010), €1,771.
160. *Ailsa* (1995), €1,645.
161. *The Last Bus Home* (1 screen, 1999), €1,265.
162. *Double Carpet* (1 screen, 1998), €1,007.

1 Various sources, including *In Production* (cited as *IP*) and Nielsen EDI (now Rentrak), and with the assistance of the Irish Film Board. Some earlier *IP* issues and other sources sometimes are different to those quoted here, which may reflect currency movements, or may only include ROI figures. See *IT*, 14 Dec 1998:14; 'Box office figures for Irish and Irish interest films from 1999 to 2003', *IP*, Oct 2003:19; also *IP*, Jan 2004:23; Feb 2001:20; Oct 2001:21; and Nov/Dec 2004:14 (which includes 1999–2003 combined figures for ROI and NI). Some figures have been drawn also from Ted Sheehy, *Film Ireland online*, 30 Jan 2009. In comparing these films, it should be borne in mind that these are the earnings from a film's original cinema release; they do not attempt to compensate for the changes in the number of screens on which a film might have been released; and no allowance has been made for ticket price inflation. 2 *His & Hers* was the most successful opening weekend at the Light House, Smithfield, with €40,000 (*IT*, 3 Sept 2010:ticket 3).

CODA

'I look up to Sean [Fitzpatrick] and Bernard [McNamara], but I wouldn't look up to the sharks at all.'

Colum Butler, 2008[1]

That business is an endlessly fluid activity, which can be driven by the search for the ultimate deal or adrenalin fix as much as an interest in the actual business, service, or product being traded, is something that became clear to many observers during the Celtic Tiger years and to all in the context of the economic collapse in Ireland in the late 2000s, which, ultimately caused by reckless bank lending (not least by Sean Fitzpatrick's bank, Anglo Irish) and inadequate state regulation of the sector, led to the Irish republic losing economic sovereignty at the end of 2010. Indeed, it was doubly appropriate that a 2008 book celebrating success stories of private Irish business entitled the career piece on Colum Butler of Leisureplex Group/Entertainment Enterprises Group, 'The fun of the deal'.

1 Michael Gaffney and Colin O'Brien, *That'll never work... success stories from private Irish business*, Dublin: Mercier, 2008:131.

As discussed in the text, in autumn 2006, Colum and Ciáran Butler, at the time the owners of a number of entertainment centres in Ireland, as well as food franchises including Starbucks Ireland, entered into the Irish cinema exhibition market when they acquired UCI's three Irish cinemas, and, shortly afterwards, five of the six Storm cinemas, which gave them control of just over sixty screens. However, according to Colum Butler, one of the key factors driving the UCI deal with private equity group Terra Firma Capital Partners was the 'longer term property value'[2] of the assets, which was unfortunate for the Butlers given that within months the property bubble burst, though before that, in another bit of lucrative deal-making, they sold Tallaght UCI. In that context, it is perhaps unsurprising that 2011 saw them begin to disengage from owning cinema exhibition buildings.

In a somewhat ironic move, in June 2011, Terra Firma not only repurchased the UCI complexes at Blanchardstown and Coolock, which have combined annual admissions of two million, and the new UCI in Newbridge at the Whitewater Shopping Centre, which opened in 2009, but the five Storm/Odeon cinemas. Furthermore, it has been agreed that Terra Firma will also run, under the UCI/Odeon banner, the new nine- and six- screen cinemas at Charlestown shopping centre, Finglas, Co. Dublin, and at The Point, Dublin, for which EEG had signed leases. Additionally, in a separate, unrelated deal, Terra Ferma has signed a lease to rent the Ormonde complex, Stillorgan, Co. Dublin, which they refurbished and in July 2011 reopened. Thus, Europe's largest exhibition company with over 2,000 screens at 217 sites across Europe, 857 at 110 sites in Britain and Ireland, will have 77 screens (including the Charlestown and Point complexes) in Ireland.

When these enormous deals, worth tens of millions of euro, are put side by side with the struggle independent and cultural cinemas have to raise modest sums to provide a diversity of cinema experiences, the gulf between the transnational and the local can seem acute. The demise of the Kino, Cork, in 2009; the prohibitive rent on the four-screen Light House, Smithfield, which caused its closure in 2011; and the ongoing struggle facing Solas, Galway, to establish what would be the only art house cinema in the republic outside Dublin, demonstrates that alternative venues to the multiplex will remain rare into the future. Nevertheless, the proliferation of festivals, the outreach programmes of the IFI (often in conjunction with access>CINEMA), and that a number of multiplexes, not least Galway's Eye, regularly screen alternative or minority interest films, means that art-house or non-mainstream, films will continue to reach a wide audience.

2 Ibid., 138

Notes

PROLOGUE

1. May Nevin 'His masterpiece', *Virgo Potens*, September 1929:260 (258–62).
2. The coupling of food, particularly popcorn and ice cream, with film is a theme that is returned to throughout, especially in chapter 5. For now, it is enough to quote writer Maeve Binchy recalling her encounter with the pictures in the 1950s, 'And popcorn came in during those days. I hated it – I still do – but I ate buckets of it because everyone else thought it was great', while television and radio presenter Gay Byrne, notes how when he was assistant manager of the Strand Cinema, North Strand Road, Dublin, at the time of the release of *Roman Holiday* (William Wyler, 1953) not only did the cinema break all records for ticket sales but also for ice cream sales. (Binchy in McBride and Flynn [eds], 1996:19; Byrne in ibid., 51.) In addition to the cinema concession stand, or the uniformed sellers with their trays of Orange Maid ice pops (and other ice creams), sweets and chocolate, several of the bigger cinemas also had restaurants. According to Kathleen Quinn, who worked in a number of Dublin cinemas in the 1930s (the Adelphi, Abbey Street; the Capitol, Prince's Street; and the Savoy), the Savoy '*was* the place to eat' (in ibid. 51).
3. As Guy Debord writes in *Society of the Spectacle* (Detroit: Black & Red, 1983, orig. 1967), 'the spectacle presents itself ... as an instrument of unification ... [yet] the unification it achieves is nothing but an official language of generalized separation.' (p. 3) Elsewhere he argues that 'Separation is the alpha and the omega of the spectacle.' (p. 25) Related, but at a less abstract level, one can consider the effect that a film such as *Henry: Portrait of a Serial Killer* (John McNaughton, 1990), has on the collective audience. Given that the film's most 'normal' and socially-'stitched in' character, and the one with whom the audience identifies, is the murderer, the film contributes to an erasure of the communal grammar that binds societies, and yet the modes of distribution and exhibition demand that such grammar or 'trust' exists in order for the audience to gather in the cinema in the first place.
4. Dublin-born Mary (May) Josephine Nevin (1907–80) was a prolific writer of short stories, poems and articles for Catholic journals and newspapers in Ireland and the US from the late 1920s to the early 1950s. She wrote only two novels, *The girls of sunnyside* (Dublin: Talbot, 1933, republished NY, 1935) and *Over the hills* (Dublin: Talbot, 1935), both of which were well received. Though included in Brian Cleeve's *Dictionary of Irish writers* (fiction, first series), 1966; Cork: Mercier, 1967:98, and the revised version of this, Anne M. Brady & Brian Cleeve, *A biographical dictionary of Irish writers*, Mullingar: Lilliput, 1985:175; she has been omitted in more recent academic reference works, notably the *Field Day anthologies* (vols 4 and 5).
5. Dr John Charles McQuaid to Fr John Redmond, 20 February 1943, Dr McQuaid papers, DDA.
6. See McBride and Flynn (eds), 1996, where this point is remembered by a number of the contributors.

CHAPTER 1

1. *Irish Limelight*, vol. 1, no. 1, January 1917:1.
2. For a discussion of the Queen's and its programme, see Ryan, 1998:123–44; Morash, 2004; orig. 2002; and Cheryl Herr (ed.), *For the land they loved: Irish political melodrama, 1890–1925*, Syracuse: Syracuse UP, 1991.
3. *Dublin Evening Mail*, 29 February 1908:4; 3 March 1898:6; *Evening Telegraph*, 29 February

1908:8. There were ten entrance prices at the Queen's, ranging from 2*d.* to 2*s.* The theatre closed in March 1907 for refurbishment and reopened on 2 March 1908. It closed again in January 1909 and reopened the following October, once more as a theatre.

4. *Dublin Evening Mail*, 23 March 1908:2 (advert.).

5. See Rockett, 2004, for an account of Holloway's film censorship activities.

6. Denis Gifford, *The British film catalogue, 1895–1970*, no. 01757, Newton Abbott: David & Charles, 1973.

7. The film was released in Australia on 26 December 1906; it was *c.*4,000ft, or approx. forty minutes. See Rockett, 1996:86–7, or www.tcd.ie/irishfilm, for an outline of the film's content and a detailed note on its production.

8. *Joseph Holloway diaries*, 2 March 1908:220–1, MS 8523, NLI.

9. *Evening Telegraph*, 3 March 1908:2.

10. Early cinema, however, shares much with the panorama, not least in that it is a spectacle based entertainment. The influence of the panorama (which, it must be remembered, enjoyed a revival at the end of nineteenth century, but largely disappeared with the rise of film as the dominant entertainment of the twentieth century), is apparent in a number of other aspects, including in its reception by audiences, the choice of subjects, the interests in similar special effects, and the accompaniment by musicians. In addition, a series of circular panorama films were produced by the Edison Mfg Company using a special circular panorama camera. In 1901 and 1902 they produced over twenty such films including *Circular Panorama of Electric Tower* (*c.*August 1901; 100ft), which was filmed at the Pan-American Exposition; *Circular Panorama of Mauch Chunk, Pennsylvania* (catalogue listing: July 1901; 200ft); and *Circular Panorama of Niagara Falls* (catalogue listing: July 1901; 100ft), which is described in the Edison summary as 'taken from Goat Island. Shows a panoramic view of the Rapids above the Horseshoe Fall, the entire Horseshoe, with the Canadian shore in the background. The camera then turns, looking down the Whirlpool below the Horseshoe Falls, showing the Suspension Bridge in the background; passes the American Falls and ends by looking up the Rapids above the American Falls'. Indeed over 250 films with panorama in their title were in circulation in the first decade of cinema. A number of these are Irish subjects, including *Panorama of the Lakes of Killarney from Hotel* (Warwick Trading Company, 1903, 75ft, GB) and *Panorama of Queenstown* (Warwick Trading Company, 1903, 75ft, GB). While one film by Edison, recorded by Edwin S. Porter and A. White, entitled *Panoramic View of Electric Tower from a Balloon* [at the Pan-American Exposition, Buffalo, NY] (August 1901, 75ft) took the novel step of placing the camera in an ascending and then descending balloon, a similar but more elaborate film was imagined by Raoul Grimoin-Sanson's cineorama, exhibited at the Paris Exposition. Cited by Angela Miller (1996:68) and Raymond Fielding ('Hale's Tours: ultrarealism in the pre-1910 motion picture', *Smithsonian Journal of History*, 3, 1968–9:101–21), the cineorama, used ten film projectors to create a full circular film of a view from a balloon presented on a circular screen similar to Robert Barker's original panorama. See *The American Film Institute catalog: film beginnings, 1893–1910, film entries*, vol. A, compiled by Elias Savada, Lanham, MD/London: Scarecrow, 1995.

11. Musser, 1994:429–30; *IT*, 28 May 1907:6 (advert.).

12. 'Man who showed first movie in Dublin' [sic], *Dublin Evening Mail*, 17 September 1955.

13. See promotional image of Hale's Tours in Barnes, vol. 1, 1998:41.

14. Nevertheless, as Angela Miller (1996:58) notes, many of the people involved with Hale's 'pleasure railways' went on to become important players in the film industry. These include Sam Warner, later co-founder and owner of Warner Bros; Adolph Zukor, president of Paramount Pictures; and Carl Laemmle, founder and head of Universal Pictures Corporation.

15. *Dublin Evening Mail*, 17 September 1955; *IT*, 4 June 1907:4 (advert); 6. Bursey was later projectionist at the Sackville and Astor cinemas, and was projectionist for the opening of the Theatre de Luxe. He also operated the Curragh Camp cinema, but with the advent of sound became an electrical contractor. The experience offered by Hale's Tours has been incorporated in various rollercoaster rides. In Dublin the XD theatre, presented by Dr Quirkey's 'good time' Emporium, located on Upper O'Connell Street, has been offering similar rides since March 2009. It is Ireland's first eighteen-seat XD theatre and is promoted as '4D' or '4D motion ride experience'. Not only do the extra-large comfortable well spaced industrially or fun-ride seats, complete with side bars and safety belts, move in synch with the images on the screen, but also additional air machines, and complementary lighting are used to complete the experience of the coaster-ride. Furthermore, because the films do not try to go beyond the ride-aesthetic it delivers an experience that actually succeeds in tricking the body and not just the eyes into believing the experience is real. In 2010, it had five ride-films (*Cosmic Race, Haunted Mine, The Adventures of Jett and Jin, Cosmic Coaster*, and *Coaster Canyon*, with the latter two particularly effective) each of which lasts approximately five minutes,

with shows every eight to ten minutes, seven days per week from 10a.m. to 11p.m., with an admission charge of €5.

16. It closed down in 1916 under financial pressure from more comfortable and attractive cinemas.
17. Open, 1985:78–9.
18. This account is drawn usually from Richard Ellmann's 1959 biography, *James Joyce* (revised ed. with corrections, Oxford: Oxford UP, 1983; orig. 1959), though most of the Volta story appeared in Herbert Gorman's much earlier 1940 book *James Joyce* (New York: Octagon, 1974; orig. 1940). However, there is no contemporary verification of Eva's contribution; she is not mentioned in this regard by Gorman, who interviewed James on various matters; nor does she appear in Patricia Hutchins' slightly later (1951) account ('James Joyce and the cinema', *Sight and Sound*, vol. 21, no. 1, August–September 1951: 9–12). Similarly, there is no mention of Eva's role in the published *Letters of James Joyce* (vol. 2, ed. by Richard Ellmann, London: Faber and Faber, 1966), thirty-five of which cover the period while he was in Dublin organizing the cinema premises. Indeed, it was not until 1953, forty-four years after the Volta opened, when Eva was interviewed by Ellmann, that such a comment was recorded. McKernan in McCourt (ed.), 2010:21, gives the Volta's seating as 320.
19. Advertisement in *Cinefono e RFC*, no. 77, 18 September 1909, reproduced in Aldo Bernardini, *Cinema muto italiano* vol. 3, *Arte, divismo e mercato, 1910/1914*, Roma-Bari: Editori Laterza, 1982:49.
20. *FJ*, 21 December 1909:10.
21. An example of the extrapolation of the Volta films to Joycean texts without any evidence of Joyce's role in the programming policy of the cinema is to be found in Keith Williams, 'Cinematic Joyce', *James Joyce Broadsheet*, no. 57, October 2000. This approach also permeates aspects of John McCourt (ed.), *Roll away the reel world: James Joyce and cinema*, Cork: Cork UP, 2010, though in fairness to archivist Luke McKernan (ibid., 15–27), in particular, who has researched the Volta film programme for the December 1909–April 1910 period, he qualifies speculations about who selected the films for the Volta with an acknowledgment that 'we should be wary' of associating Joyce with any of the Volta's films after March 1910 (ibid., 24), though we would put Joyce's disengagement from the cinema's programming earlier than this. Also, unfortunately, though the conference which led to this publication took place in Trieste no effort seems to have been made to establish which of the films screened at the Volta, including *Beatrice Cenci*, were shown in that city prior to Joyce's departure for Dublin, or, indeed, after he returned in early January 1910. It is unlikely that he played a role in selecting films for the Volta *after* he returned to Trieste, since he was suffering from severe irisitis and remained in a semi-darkened room for two months after his return. Nevertheless, given Trieste's importance as a distribution gateway to the Austro-Hungarian empire, and the fact that it had 21 cinemas in 1909 (Schneider in ibid., 29), makes it likely that such a heavily promoted film as *Beatrice Cenci*, and, indeed, many of the other films shown in Dublin and released in 1909, would have been shown in that city even prior to Joyce's departure for Dublin. Notwithstanding what is implied by those writing about Joyce and the Volta, the only evidence that he played any further part in the cinema venture is that a February 1910 expenses sheet for the Volta exists, as is discussed below, though it remains to be confirmed if this is in Joyce's hand-writing, as McKernan suggests (ibid., 21.).
22. For a fuller discussion of Joyce and Shelley, see Kevin Rockett, 'Something rich and strange: James Joyce, *Beatrice Cenci* and the Volta', *Film and Film Culture*, vol. 3, 2004:21–34.
23. Ettore Schmitz to James Joyce, 15 June 1910, *Letters of James Joyce*, vol. 2, 1966:286.
24. *Bioscope*, 7 October 1909:92.
25. It was one reel (315m/1,033ft).
26. *Bioscope*, 9 October 1909:92. As no copy of the film seems to have survived, all discussion has to be based on English and Italian paper records. A number of other filmed versions of the Beatrice Cenci story have been filmed. One, a French film, *Beatrice [or Beatrix] Cenci* (Albert Capellani, 1908), predates the Cines' production, and conceivably could have been the film screened at the Volta. Later Italian productions include *Beatrice Cenci* (Gerolamo Lo Salvo, 1910); *Beatrice Cenci* (Baldassare Negroni, 1926); *Beatrice Cenci* (Riccardo Freda, 1956); and *Beatrice Cenci* (Lucio Fulci, 1969).
27. According to *Bioscope*.
28. Article 2, contract dated 16 October 1909 signed by Joyce, cited Schneider in McCourt (ed.), 2010:37. In addition to this stay of fifteen days, Joyce had also been contracted to get a cinema licence and to find a suitable premises by 5 November.
29. James Joyce to Theodore Spicer-Simon, 8 June 1910, *Letters*, vol. 2, 1966:285. The inflammation was perhaps brought on by the bad weather and stress. He left Ireland with his sister Eileen and returned to Trieste where he spent almost two months in bed in a half-dark room.

30. James Joyce to Nora Barnacle, 25 October 1909, *Letters*, vol. 2, 1966:254.
31. James Joyce to Nora Barnacle, 27 October 1909, *Letters*, vol. 2, 1966:255.
32. James Joyce to Stanislaus Joyce, 2 December 1910, *Letters*, vol. 2, 1966:270.
33. Butler's and O'Shaughnessy's role in the issuing of licences, and the attendant issues of film censorship during the 1910s, are discussed in Rockett, 2004. By 1914, twenty-five licences for showing films were being issued annually by Dublin corporation, most of which were for full-time cinemas, including the Rotunda and the Volta.
34. 'Dublin Cinematograph Volta', *Bioscope*, 30 December 1909:23.
35. *Dublin Evening Mail*, 20 December 1909:2.
36. 'Italian Bioscope company invades Dublin', *Bioscope*, 23 December 1909:37. This report claims that the cinema's backers had twenty-three 'film-producing factories, situated in different countries', though this may simply mean that they had *access* to the productions of twenty-three companies.
37. Ibid.
38. On unemployment in Dublin during this period, see O'Brien, 1982:209–13. The *Irish Times* estimated in 1909 that 7,000 heads of households in Dublin were unemployed, leaving 20,000 people in destitution. (*IT*, 6 April 1909, cited in O'Brien, 1982:211.)
39. James Joyce to Stanislaus Joyce, 23 December 1909, *Letters*, vol. 2, 1966:279–80.
40. McKernan in McCourt (ed.), 2010:20–1.
41. Scholes 1405, James Joyce collection, Cornell University Library, box 3, folder 14, with dates December 1909, January 1910, February 1910, cited by McKernan in McCourt (ed.), 2010:21, 207, who reports that the February 1910 sheet is in Joyce's handwriting, a somewhat surprising statement considering Joyce was in Trieste from early January.
42. *World's Fair*, 17 December 1910:12, cited, McKernan in McCourt (ed.), 2010:21.
43. Erik Schneider in McCourt (ed.), 2010:28–40, includes details of the business activities of the key figures in the venture: Vincenzo (Giuseppe) Caris, Giovanni Rebez, Antonio Machnich (who in 1907 filed for bankruptcy which meant that he could not do business in Trieste), and Lorenzo Novak. Schneider concludes that it was the competing agendas of these four plus Joyce that doomed the venture to failure as much as the choice of films. Indeed, not only was Novak planning to open a cinema in Portorose near Trieste, but also he was being encouraged to leave Dublin for Bucharest to help Machnich run the Volta there as well as to help Machnich establish his own cinema in the city, while Joyce measured his time in Dublin and was only committed by the 16 October 1909 contract to stay there for fifteen days after the cinema opened, though his eye problem caused him to leave a day earlier. This same contract also reserved for Joyce the management of the cinema during August to September. However, as the Volta was sold within seven months of opening, this clause, which would have allowed the Italian manager to return home and give Joyce a paid annual holiday in his home city, was never activated (ibid., 37.).
44. Knowing their market, Provincial screened predominantly American and British films, but the company then seems to have closed and then rented out the down-market Volta. By 1913, ironically, Irish Animated Picture Co. was the licensee, and the premises continued as a cinema until the late 1940s.
45. Luke McKernan, 'James Joyce's cinema', *Film and Film Culture*, vol. 3, 2004:7–20. A slightly revised version of this filmography is included in McCourt (ed.), 2010:187–203. McKernan records that the films were imported directly from Trieste. This necessitated the intertitles being translated from the Italian and given as a handout. However, such a 'clumsy presentation and risky cost-cutting' seems surprising given that many of the films would have been available in English-language versions in London, with, for example, as noted above, *Beatrice Cenci* being reviewed in the British trade paper *Bioscope* two-and-a-half months before it was shown at the Volta. (McKernan in McCourt (ed.), 2010:18.)
46. Hiley, 2002:116.
47. Ibid., 116.
48. Ibid., 114–15.
49. One of the main rinking companies was Crawford-Wilkins' rinks with a presence in twenty-six cities in Britain and Ireland, including in Dublin and Belfast (*IT*, 6 September 1909:7). The main Dublin rink was the Earlsfort Terrace Rink (aka American Roller Skating Rink), which had been opened by 1879 (as part of a revival of the first skating craze of the mid-1870s [*IT*, 27 January 1879:1]), while in Belfast it was the Belfast Roller Skating Rink, Cliftonville Road. A roller skating company was formed in Limerick to acquire and operate a rink at Wellesley Place, Limerick. It cost £4,000 and could accommodate 3,000 skaters and 1,000 spectators. It opened in November 1909 (*IT*, 14 August 1909:8; 22 November 1909:8). This rink was converted to the Rink Palace Cinema in 1911 (*Irish*

Architect & Contractor, 1, 15 April 1911:159). By then, Dublin already had a number of rinks including the City Pavilion, Bridge Street, which had opened in November 1908 (*IT*, 30 November 1908:6), while in autumn 1909 alone four new rinks had been opened there. These were the Olympia, in the great hall of the RDS, Ballsbrige (opened on 25 October, it was second in size only to London's Olympia and had a skating surface of 26,000 sq ft); the Skating Rink, Rotunda Gardens, on the site of the old Asphalte Rink which had opened in 1874 (the lessee was Frank W. Chambers, 18 Upper Sackville Street, who was already owner of several billiard rooms and later became involved in film exhibition); the Palace Rink, Rathmines, which, operational by November 1909, opened on an elevated site opposite the town hall (*IT*, 8 October 1909:4); and the Kingstown Pavilion Roller Skating Rink which opened in October (*IT*, 19 October 1909:5).

No new rinks seem to have opened after the end of 1909 and as a 1912 *IT* article noted 'the popularity of the skating rink proved ephemeral. For a time all Dublin "rinked" by day and by night, … But soon the rinks disappeared, and now roller skates are relegated to small boys on suburban footpaths.' (*IT*, 21 December 1912:6.) The 1909–10 craze followed on from a much earlier one in the mid 1870s. In 1875 there was a skating rink in Kingstown (*IT*, 14 July 1875:7), and, as already mentioned, one at the Rotunda Gardens (*IT*, 13 October 1877:4), while Rathmines' Ice and Roller Skating Rink was looking forward to a revival of skating and reopened on 26 December 1878 (*IT*, 24 December 1878:5).

50. *IT*, 21 December 1912:6.   51. Ibid.   52. Hiley, 2002:118.
53. See J.J. Farrell entry in Patrick Maume, *The long gestation: Irish nationalist life, 1891–1918*, New York: St Martin's, 1999:228.
54. Charles Duff, *Ireland and the Irish*, London: T.V. Boardman, 1952:120. Duff also recalls that to add to the casual ambience of the Volta, the man who played the upright piano 'refreshed himself with Guinness' stout from a cup which, to complete the deception, had a saucer to go with it.'
55. The chapel dating back to the 1780s and rebuilt in 1840 following the Big Wind of 1839 continued as a place of worship until 1908 when it was secularized. Part of the building had been used as an asylum for female orphans and also served as a tenement. (Kearns and Maguire, 2007:350.)
56. He installed 17,000 seats round the bandstand in Hyde Park, London. Among the Irish venues that he 'chaired' were the Phoenix Park and Kingstown.
57. Charles E. Kelly, 'Dublin cinema memories' in *Cinema Ireland, 1895–1976*, Dublin: Dublin Arts Festival, 1976:17. Though this booklet does not carry an editor credit, it was compiled by Liam O'Leary, the main organizer behind this pioneering exhibition held in Trinity College Dublin.
58. 'Dorset Picture Hall', *Irish Builder and Engineer*, vol. 53, no. 10, 13 May 1911:317.
59. In 1981 it ceased operating as a cinema and became the National Wax Museum, which closed in 2005.
60. These were the Avenue Picture Palace, Butt Street, Camden Town, London, a former Baptist chapel; St George's Hall, Ramsgate; Wellington Hall, Dover; Victoria Hall, Weston-Super-Mare; and the Picturedrome, Sutton. The circuit's general manager was Thomas Lenton. (See 'A flourishing circuit', *Bioscope*, 18 May 1911:321, which says that Shanly had a total of seven cinemas.)
61. A.J. Harris Whitney, managing director, Sandford Cinema, to Seacome Mason, town clerk, Rathmines and Rathgar urban district council, 4 August 1916, DCA.
62. *FJ*, 21 May 1915:2.
63. As described by Provincial's chairman, *Bioscope*, 14 March 1912:766.
64. 'Re-building in Grafton Street: the new picture house, No.72', *Irish Builder and Engineer*, vol. 53, no. 3, 4 February 1911:66; 'Another picture house at Dublin', *Bioscope*, 20 April 1911:101.
65. Low, 1997:18–19; orig. 1949. See also discussion of running costs of Volta in this chapter, p. 20.
66. 'The new aluminium screen', *Dublin Evening Mail*, 12 April 1910:4. The Picture House's first regular programme consisted of *The Eruption of Mount Etna*; *Pals*, an animal story; *His Last Burglary*, a drama; *Dancing Tabloids*, a comedy; *Winter Sports in the Vosges Mountains*; and *Cowboy and Squaw*. See plate 74 for inaugural presentations.
67. *Film Index*, 15 October 1910.   68. *Bioscope*, 14 March 1912:766.
69. *Bioscope*, 10 October 1912.
70. *Bioscope*, 23 September 1915. Closed during 1915 and in 1919, it reopened in 1920 as the Lyceum Picture Theatre, and continued as a cinema until 27 October 1947 at which time it was owned by Capitol and Allied Ltd, which had bought the property in 1945 following the death of its then owner Rudolph Ahearne. It has since been demolished and the site is now occupied by Penneys' retail store.
71. *Irish Builder and Engineer*, vol. 55, no. 4, 15 February 1913:115. In 1913, Provincial's ambitions extended to a second Belfast cinema to be erected on the site of the premises of Messrs B. Hyam in High Street and 'Linder's' in Corn Market, but these plans were abandoned, because, *Irish Builder* commented, 'the scheme was a rather ambitious one, and would hardly have given an adequate

return on the money it would have involved.' (*Irish Builder and Engineer*, vol. 54, no. 6, 15 March 1913:175.)

72. 'Provincial Cinematograph Theatres, Limited', *Bioscope*, 14 March 1912:766–9.
73. 'Employers and employees', *Bioscope*, 15 February 1912:421.
74. *Bioscope*, 4 April 1912:17. It is not known whether Huish realized his ambition to open cinemas in Ireland.
75. *Cinema Year Book*, London: 1915:94ff.
76. This was the number of cinema licences issued by Dublin corporation in 1914. Only four of these twenty-five venues – Theatre Royal, Tivoli Theatre, Empire Theatre and Queen's Theatre – were not exclusively or primarily devoted to film screenings.
77. This figure was given in the *Irish Builder and Engineer*, vol. 56, no. 7, 28 March 1914:191, as the number of buildings in Dublin [city] 'carrying on cinematograph displays'.
78. Ibid.
79. *Irish Builder and Engineer*, 8 November 1913:713.
80. Worldwide in 1913 it was estimated that there were 60,000 cinemas, 15,700 of which were in the USA, and 4,000–4,500 in Britain by 1914. (Low, 1997:21–3.)
81. Open, 1985:29. In 1919, Provincial had bought the Grand Central hotel with the intention of converting it into another cinema, including a restaurant and offices. (*Bioscope*, 7 August 1919:105.) The project does not appear to have been realized.
82. A number of cinemas, however, were destroyed during the rising including the Grand Cinema, 8 Lower O'Connell Street, which had opened on 23 October 1913 as part of the Grand Hotel and restaurant building; the custom-built cine-variety venue, Coliseum, 24 Henry Street/29 Princes Street North, which opened on 5 April 1915, also known as the Picture Palace Theatre; and the World's Fair Waxworks and Varieties, 30 Henry Street, where films had been shown from May 1896, and which Robert W. Sprengel opened as a 194-seat cinema in 1914.
83. Kearns, 2004:8–9.
84. *Evening Telegraph*, 25 March 1913:5. According to this report, Worth had been working in different areas of the cinema business for five years.
85. Kelly in O'Leary (ed.), 1976:16. Access to the Picturedrome was via a long passage beside a shop.
86. *Bioscope*, 10 October 1912.
87. Kearns, 2004:12.   88. *Evening Herald*, 20 July 1914:4.
89. I.I. Bradlaw was one of the directors of Irish Amusement Company which on 1 December 1911 opened the 300-seat Brunswick Cinema Theatre, 30 Great Brunswick Street (Pearse Street), discussed below. He also leased the Assembly Rooms, Sandymount, as a cinema in 1912, and planned a new venue in Kingstown.
90. *FJ*, 7 June 1910:9.   91. *Bioscope*, 10 October 1912:111.
92. 'Original Irish Animated Pictures', *Sunday Independent*, 6 April 1930:2.
93. *Kinematograph and Lantern Weekly*, 5 October 1916:53.
94. Unpublished Elliman family memoir, Liam O'Leary collection, NLI.
95. '"Father of Irish film trade"', *Evening Herald*, 3 March 1952:3. In 1940 the Irish Trade Benevolent Fund made a presentation to Elliman, 'the father of the industry', to mark his thirty years in the cinema business. It was reported that he had entered the business in 1910 when he opened the Coliseum, Redmond's Hill. (*IT*, 17 April 1940:4.)
96. 'The cameraman in the case', *IT*, 24 September 1984:10. This statement was made by RTÉ cameraman Godfrey Graham, a grandson of Dickie Graham.
97. The venue had received a Dublin corporation licence in March 1910. 'Serious fire in Dublin; picture theatre gutted', *FJ*, 29 August 1911:4; *IT*, 29 August 1911:6; *Evening Telegraph*, 28 August 1911. As no film was being screened at the time, and the caretaker and his family escaped, no one was injured. Nevertheless, the premises, made of pitch-pine and varnished wood, was completely destroyed. It did not reopen as a cinema and the site was later occupied by Fannin's medical supplies. According to a profile of the 'shy, unassuming' Elliman in 1931, he 'opened' the Redmond's Hill cinema, an enterprise which followed on from his activities in the 'fruit trade', and became known as a travelling exhibitor, visiting 'several towns throughout Ireland' with a show that also included 'well-known boxers'. (*Talkie Topics and Theatrical Review*, vol. 1, no. 2, 18 March 1931.)
98. For example, it was Elliman (with his solicitor, J.W. Davis), who appeared in the Southern Police District Court on 15 March 1910 on the occasion of the successful application for a cinema licence for the Coliseum, while Davis appeared before the recorder at Green Street Courthouse later in the month seeking a music licence, which was granted. It seems that the music licence was a temporary one until July only. (*IT*, 16 March 1910:3.) Nick Harris presents an alternative, but not referenced, time-line in which Maurice Elliman 'began his career in the motion picture business less than a year

after his arrival in Dublin' in 1900 when 'he rented a room in Camden Street and showed films with a hand-operated projector on a makeshift screen erected on one of the walls' for fifteen to twenty children at a time with a 1*d.* admission price. (Nick Harris, *Dublin's Little Jerusalem*, Dublin: A. & A. Farmer, 2002:79.)

99. Harris, *Dublin's Little Jerusalem*, 2002:79; Keenan, 2005:38.

1. Bought by Gael Linn in 1975 it became a bingo hall, then Ricardo's Snooker Hall, while in the late 1990s it was converted into the De Luxe Hotel.

2. Both Keenan, 2005:66 and Kearns and Maguire, 2007:251, suggest the Metropole had 1,000 seats.

3. *IT*, 3 January 1962:5.   4.   *Evening Press*, 1 February 1992:3.

5. It would seem that it was also known as Hibernian Electric Theatre, and was next door to the Trades' Hall. It was approved for a licence in 1911.

6. In 1912 it was refused a licence until structural alterations were carried out; in 1913 it was fined for operating without a licence and later for disobedience of a court order; and in 1914 it was the only Dublin city premises to be refused a licence due to the poor standard of the electrical fittings. Nevertheless, *Bioscope* found 'this little hall … very cosy and comfortable, and [it] commands a goodly share of patronage.' (*Bioscope*, 10 October 1912). In 1915 it was finally granted a licence subject to alterations being carried out. The cinema closed in 1919 when the premises became a confectioner's premises. See 'The cameraman in the case', *IT*, 24 September 1984:10. The date of 1906, however, when both cinemas with which he was associated are reported to have opened, is incorrect. Dickie Graham's main profession was dancing instruction.

7. 'Fire in a Dublin cinema hall: narrow escape of operator and assistant', *IT*, 23 October 1917:5.

8. In that year, Dublin corporation also became responsible for New Kilmainham, Drumcondra and Clonliffe, and Glasnevin. It was not until 1930 that boundaries were further expanded to include Rathmines and Pembroke, Cabra, Killester, Clonskeagh, and Terenure.

9. 'Fire at Rathmines Town Hall: cinematograph operator's escape', *IT*, 19 September 1918:3.

10. 'Fire in Dublin cinema', *IT*, 29 July 1920:6.

11. 'Reopening of Bohemian Picture House', *IT*, 18 April 1925:9. This reopening with improvements in accommodation followed a considerable closure.

12. 'Dublin cinema fire; Bohemian partly destroyed; Brigade captain injured', *IT*, 25 October 1927:7.

13. *Dáil debates*, vol. 32, cols 1440–1, 27 November 1929. Mr Cooney raised the issue. The cinema, however, received a certain amount of publicity a few months later when another minor fire broke out in the early hours of the morning with a considerable number of seats badly burned. ('Dublin cinema fire; discovery early this morning', *IT*, 11 January 1930:9.) It was expanded from 550/620 seats to 708 seats during reconstruction, but was finally destroyed by fire on 13 September 1946.

14. 'Fire fighting in the Free State; lack of equipment in country towns; unobserved cinema regulations', *IT*, 28 January 1930:11.   15.   Ibid.

16. '"Great laxity": fire appliances in cinemas', *IT*, 24 January 1929:5. He also took the opportunity to commend Sergeant Meagher and Guard Deegan for their action in having proceedings instituted against McCormack.

17. It transpired that she had received a licence from Belfast corporation, and no prosecution took place. Another travelling circus, that of Mrs Duffy, had been cautioned two months earlier for breaches of the act. However, one of the problems facing travelling circuses was in getting licences from the corporation due to administrative difficulties. 'Breaches of Cinematograph Act 1909', CSORP/1914/11239, NAI.

18. *Munster Express*, 26 November 1926:3.

19. 'Safety of picture houses', *IT*, 8 September 1926:8. The letter was written in the wake of the Drumcollogher fire, which is discussed below in the main text.

20. 'Fire fighting in the Free State', *IT*, 28 January 1930:11.

21. *Southern Star*, 2 May 1918:6.   22.   *IT*, 29 December 1925:6.

23. *Bioscope*, 3 January 1920:115.   24.   *IT*, 22 August 1922:3.

25. *Nenagh Guardian*, 1 November 1924:2; *IT*, 29 October 1924:9. Gaumont Film Co. later sought, unsuccessfully, to force Powell to pay for the rent of films contracted prior to the cinema being burned down. (*Nenagh Guardian*, 30 May 1925:5.)

26. *Connacht Tribune*, 24 July 1926:9, 10, 16; *IT*, 21 July 1926:7; 24 July 1926:9. The fire was blamed on an electrical fault (fused wires in the operation box), with the loss estimated at between £8,000 and £10,000. Within a few hours both the cinema and the adjoining building were destroyed.

27. *Irish Independent*, 8 May 1928:7.

28. *Southern Star*, 5 October 1929:7.

29. *Sligo Champion*, 4 January 1930:7. Damage was estimated at £4,000.

30. *Limerick Leader*, 12 April 1930; *IT*, 12 April 1930:10.   31.   *IT*, 14 May 1932:5.

32. *Daily Film Renter*, 10 August 1935.   33. *KW*, 1 October 1936:21.
34. Owned by Mrs J. Rogers, it was destroyed by fire on 5 May 1938. For accounts of the fire, see
    Meath Chronicle, 7 May 1938:10; *Anglo-Celt*, 23 April 1938:11; *Irish Independent*, 22 April
    1938:8.
35. Destroyed by fire on 28 January 1938 with damage estimated at £4,000.
36. Examples of such fires include at the Pavilion Cinema and Café, Patrick Street, Cork, in 1923 (*IT*,
    15 March 1923:9); at Limerick's Coliseum, O'Connell Street, in 1927 where some film was
    destroyed and there was limited damage to the projection box (*IT*, 5 March 1927:5); at Leitrim's
    Town Hall, Carrick-on-Shannon, where 10,000ft of film was destroyed, also in 1927 (*IT*, 19
    February 1927:8); at the City Cinema in Armagh in 1928 (*IT*, 6 Dec 1928:8); and at the Queen's
    Picture Theatre, York Road, Belfast, where a fire in the lantern room was put out even before the
    fire brigade arrived (*IT*, 8 July 1929:11). Another one in Belfast was at the Royal Cinema in
    December 1940 when the stage and screen were damaged, though the combination of the asbestos
    fire curtain and the fire brigade contained the fire to a limited area. (Belfasthistoryproject.com.)
37. 'Safety of picture houses', *IT*, 8 September 1926:8. The letter was written in the wake of the
    Drumcollogher fire, which is discussed below in the main text.
38. Another who had sustained injuries during the fire died ten days later. The same initial number of
    forty-eight also lost their lives fifty-five years later when on St Valentine's Night 1981 the Stardust
    dance hall in Dublin's northside Artane district caught fire. In an echo of this incident, the situa-
    tion was made much worse by barred windows and locked exit doors.
39. On 13 August 1927, at the Limerick city district sessions, the proprietors of the Coliseum, Grand
    Central, Athenaeum and Abbey cinemas were prosecuted by the corporation for contravening the
    1909 Cinematograph Act by having exit passages obstructed with chairs such that visitors congre-
    gated there. The defendants were fined £1 each by District Justice Flood. ('The cinematograph act:
    Limerick proprietors fined', *IT*, 27 August 1927:5.)
40. Despite regulations regarding safety, disastrous fires have been all too frequent in the international
    history of film exhibition. From May 1897 (when a fire during a film show at a charity bazaar in
    Paris killed a great many dignitaries) onwards there have been hundreds of cinema fires, with a
    great number of fatalities. Examples include a fire in January 1908 in Barnsley, England, in which
    16 lost their lives; another on New Year's Eve 1929, when 71 children died in Paisley, Scotland;
    and yet another at Le Select Cinema, Rueil-Malmaison, France, which killed 87 in 1947. More
    recent fires have tended to be in non-western countries: in 1977, the Xinyang cinema fire in Xinjiang,
    China, killed 694 people; in 1979, the Cinema Rex fire (suspected arson) killed 438 in Abadan,
    Khuzestan, Iran; in 1983, the Cinema Statuto fire in Turin, Italy, killed 64; in 1977, the Uphaar
    cinema fire, Green Park, New Delhi, in which 59 were killed; in 1999, a fire at a two-storey build-
    ing with a cinema complex in Yogyakarta, Central Java, Indonesia, resulted in 75 deaths; and in
    2000, the Tiantang cinema fire in Jiaozuo, Henan, China, killed 74.
41. It has been reported often that it was Cecil B. De Mille's *The Ten Commandments* (1923) that was
    being shown that night, but this was not the case. Perhaps, only an association with the Old
    Testament could subsequently explain the tragedy. The main film, *The White Outlaw*, was accom-
    panied by a two-reel comedy, *Baby be Good*.
42. Barney Keating, *Newcastlewest Observer*, July 1980, reprinted in Jim Kemmy (ed.), *The Limerick
    compendium*, Dublin: Gill and Macmillan, 1997:213–16; Denis O'Shaughnessy, *Limerick: 100 sto-
    ries of the century*, Limerick, 2000:124–8. See also letter from Denis O'Shaughnessy, *IT*, 26 February
    2003. Contemporary accounts may be found in *Irish Independent*, 8 September 1926:7, and 10
    September 1926:7; *Cork Examiner*, 8 September 1926; and *IT*, 8 September 1926, though all Irish
    and international newspapers carried reports of the fire in the week following the tragedy.
43. *Bioscope*, 10 April 1929:40.
44. *Southern Star*, 5 October 1929:7. The cinema room was capable of holding about 300 patrons.
    Despite the efforts of the Cork fire brigade the Francis Street building was destroyed, nevertheless,
    the adjoining (dwelling) houses were saved. The fire was first noted at around 6a.m., and the build-
    ing was unoccupied.
45. See Rockett, 2004, for the details of the struggle over censorship in Dublin during the 1910s.
46. *Bioscope*, 13 August 1925:80.
47. *Irish Builder and Engineer*, vol. 54, no. 25, 7 December 1912:699.
48. *Irish Builder and Engineer*, 8 November 1913, reported this figure a year before the cinema opened,
    with 288 in the stalls and 84 in the gallery. After it opened, the same publication (vol. 57, no. 5,
    27 February 1915:98) gave the seat number as 'about 400'.
49. *Dublin Evening Mail*, 4 December 1914:2 (advert.). The cinema seems to have opened two days
    before this first advertisement appeared in the *Mail*.

50. *Dublin Evening Mail*, 11 February 1915:6.
51. *Irish Builder and Engineer*, vol. 57, no. 5, 27 February 1915:98.
52. The Pillar Picture House closed on 3 April 1938 for renovations and reopened two weeks later, on 16 April 1938.
53. William King's son, William D. King, started work in the Phibsboro cinema, and at the time of his retirement in 1975, he had been manager of the Corinthian since 1965, by which time he had worked for Odeon (Ireland) Ltd for thirty-seven years. (See *Evening Press*, 3 July 1975; *Evening Herald*, 5 July 1975.)
54. *Bioscope*, 18 May 1916:845. 55. Kearns and Maguire, 2007:201.
56. Keenan, 2005:62.   57. Open, 1985:78–9.   58. Ibid., 3.
59. *Irish Builder and Engineer*, vol. 53, no. 5, 4 March 1911:145.
60. Open, 1985:32. See also *Irish Builder and Engineer*, 3 January 1914:17.
61. Open, 1985:50. It closed *c.*16 March 1919.   62. Ibid., 46.
63. *Belfast Newsletter*, 8 December 1914:3. Designed by Mr R.E. Forbes CE, the original owners of the Imperial were Councillor W.G. Turner and James Barron.
64. *Kinematograph and Lantern Weekly*, 25 March 1915:89. While many cinema staff stayed at the same venue for several years, uniquely, Portadown projectionist Billy Branagh came to the Coliseum in 1915 and remained with the cinema until it closed in 1959, at which time he was manager. (Open, 1985:34.)
65. The other directors of the Phoenix were J. Mackay, Dundalk; David Frame, 8 Granby Row, Dublin, who, as will become clear, became a leading figure in early exhibition and was a director of the New Electric, Talbot Street; H. Goodbody; and H. Grandy (Dublin). Notwithstanding the geographical distribution of the directors, Sherlock described the 'whole enterprise [as] purely a Dublin one'. He went on to say that 'anything that tended to the betterment of the working classes had his support, and that rational and intelligent amusement was to be provided in that neighbourhood at very cheap rates was a gratifying thing.' He added that he agreed with the recorder that cinemas should not be granted licences 'indiscriminately' because 'if the market was overrun it might develop into a class of enterprise that respectable citizens could not give their support to.' (*FJ*, 4 December 1912:10). The *Dublin Evening Mail* (3 December 1912:6) carried a slightly different version of the lord mayor's speech, and added that he said the 'needs of the district' would be taken into account when a licence was granted. Though Sherlock was mayor from 1912 to 1915, this apparently sympathetic policy towards cinema was not pursued by Dublin Corporation. Indeed, Sherlock, who presided at a major vigilance committee gathering on 1 July 1912, was not particularly supportive of cinema. (See Rockett, 2004:44, for an account of that event.) See also Kearns and Maguire, 2007:340–4.
66. *The Free Press*, 12 December 1914:6.   67. Open, 1985:43.
68. Ibid., 40–1.   69. *Southern Star*, 4 June 1910:4.
70. *Southern Star*, 12 November 1910:5.   71. *Southern Star*, 6 July 1912:5.
72. *Echo*, 14 December 1912:11. The theatre had opened on 31 May 1910.
73. *Echo*, 14 February 1914:10.
74. *Echo*, 10 January 1914:8. See also Condon, 2008:161–5.
75. Maurice Butler, '"Are you goin' to the pictures?" Dublin 1913–1989', unpublished, 1969, 2-page document at Irish Film Institute library.
76. See Albert B. Daniels, *'Five and nine': recollections of the touring shows of Ireland*, Donegal: Donegal Democrat, 1991. As with many undocumented and unreferenced family histories written by amateur historians, the reliability of the recollections, especially of the accuracy of the claim of 'Ireland's first film show' (Daniels, 1991:10), casts doubt on the text. 'Professor Jolley' (sic) is said to have visited Ireland with his film projector around 1889!
77. David O'Riordan, 'The travelling picture shows' in Pat O'Donovan (ed.), *Knockfeena and District Annual Journal*, vol. 3, 1991.
78. See Kevin Rockett, 'A bus journey' in McBride and Flynn (eds), 1996:90–2.
79. This seems to have been a particular issue for exhibitors in Northern Ireland who complained that 16mm exhibitors organized village and town hall circuits as rivals to their operations, and since such 16mm shows were not liable for entertainments tax, they were deemed to have an unfair commercial advantage. According to a *Kine Weekly* report in 1946, there were hundreds of 150- to 500-seat halls available at very low rentals which were being used by 16mm units to give double feature shows in villages and towns. It was claimed that some units had twenty-two halls in their circuits (*KW*, 7 February 1946:14). Pressure continued to be maintained throughout the late 1940s (*The Cinema*, 5 February 1947:14; *KW*, 6 February 1947:35; 14 October 1948:14) and in the 1950s when 16mm clubs were expanding to the point where they were 'dangerous to the trade' because not only could

they show films on Sundays, but they also were 'encroaching on the preserve of the cinemas in showing films on week-nights'. (*KW*, 19 June 1958:76.)

80. *Bioscope*, 28 May 1914:95.   81. Low, 1997:41.   82. Ibid., 41–2.
83. Ibid., 80–4.   84. Ibid., 47.
85. 'Pictures in Ireland', *Bioscope*, 29 February 1912:593.   86. Low, 1997:53–7.
87. *Irish Builder and Engineer*, vol. 55, no. 8, 12 April 1913:250. It was run by a Mr Young in 1915.
88. *Kinematograph and Lantern Weekly*, 18 February 1915:23.
89. *Bioscope*, 20 April 1916.   90. *Bioscope*, 18 October 1917:135.
91. *Irish Limelight*, January 1917:11.   92. *IT*, 21 December 1912:6.
93. Hiley, 2002:122.   94. Ibid., 123.   95. Ibid., 120.
96. The members also included exhibitor George J. Nesbitt, a director of Theatre de Luxe; G.H. Marsh; P.J. Kearns, men's representative; and Thomas Murphy, trades council representative.
97. Reports of the case against the three men were carried in the *IT*, 8 October 1913:9, and *Irish Independent*, 8 October 1913:2. Both papers report that the case was adjourned for a week, and since no further article was published, it is possible that the case was subsequently dismissed.
98. William Butler Yeats' poem 'September 1913' offers a poignant summation of the state of Ireland at this time, one that is equally relevant for contemporary Ireland. The first verse is as follows: 'What need you, being come to sense,/But fumble in a greasy till/And add the halfpence to the pence/And prayer to shivering prayer, until/You have dried the marrow from the bone?/For men were born to pray and save:/Romantic Ireland's dead and gone,/It's with O'Leary in the grave.' O'Leary refers to the Fenian leader John O'Leary (1830–1907).
99. The poster is in the department of prints and drawings, NLI. While the ITGWU was forced to admit defeat in the Lock-Out, the struggle established trade unions as a central part of Irish society and the ITGWU grew to become the country's largest union, and is now known as SIPTU. The effects of the Lock-Out on attendances at public entertainments in Dublin, especially cinema, are too obvious to need spelling out. Set during this period, James Plunkett's novel *Strumpet city* (1969) and RTÉ's seven-part television adaptation of the book (1980) were both hugely popular. For a discussion of the television series, see Martin McLoone, '*Strumpet city*: the urban working class on Irish television' in Martin McLoone and John MacMahon (eds), *Television and Irish society: 21 years of Irish television*, Dublin: RTÉ/IFI, 1984:53–88.
1. Daly, 1985:76.
2. Paddy Crosbie, *Your dinner's poured out! Boyhood in the twenties in a Dublin that has disappeared*, Dublin: O'Brien, 1985:145; orig. 1981.
3. Luke McKernan, 'Diverting time: London's cinemas and their audiences, 1906–1914', *London Journal*, vol. 32, no. 2, July 2007:137. See also Luke McKernan, 'A fury for seeing: cinema, audience and leisure in London in 1913', *Early Popular Visual Culture*, vol. 6, no. 3, November 2008:271–80; Luke McKernan, '"Only the screen was silent …" memories of children's cinemagoing in London before the First World War', *Film Studies*, no. 10, spring 2007:1–20. These articles were developed out of the AHRB Centre for British Film and Television Studies' London Project, of which McKernan was one of the research fellows, and which mapped out the film business in London during 1894–1914.
4. Doherty, 1997:63–4.
5. Éamonn MacThomáis, *Me jewel and darlin' Dublin*, Dublin: O'Brien, revised ed., 1994:16; orig. 1974.
6. McGuinness, 1999:130.   7. Doherty, 1997:64.
8. Commission of enquiry, National Society of Public Morals, cited in *Irish Limelight*, vol. 1, no. 11, November 1917:12.
. 9. *Irish Limelight*, vol. 1, no. 6, June 1917:2. Globally, there were about 60,000 cinemas at this time.
10. Beere, 1935–6:96.   11. *Census of population*, 1911 and 1926.
12. Beere, 1935–6:97, suggests that in 1934–5 there were 11 million admissions valued at £550,000 in Dublin, including the adjoining borough of Dún Laoghaire.
13. *IT*, 12 October 1915:3.   14. Doherty, 1997:102.
15. *Irish Limelight*, vol. 1, no. 11, November 1917:13. Thomas H. Ince's *Civilization* was also shown at the Gaiety from 19 November 1917. The writer reported that s/he had seen it four times.
16. *FJ*, 4 March 1913:10.   17. Crosbie, 1985:123.
18. Kearns and Maguire, 2007:340, give the figure as 750.
19. The Phoenix was taken over in the early 1920s by Rudolph Aherne, who ran it until his death in 1945, at which time, Capitol and Allied Theatres, a Farrell company, bought it. Kearns and Maguire (2007:344) suggest that it closed on 26 January 1957, but elsewhere (340) state that it closed in 1958. It is now occupied by Bargaintown/Kings and Queens furniture store.

20. Crosbie, 1985:121–2. Similar behaviour is recalled by actor John Kavanagh as occurring when he was a child in his local cinemas. In the Princess, Rathmines, for example, where it was practice that two children would share a single seat or three or four be squashed into the many double seats (popular with couples in the evenings), thus extending its capacity to almost twice the amount, the noise of the kids was 'absolutely deafening … The ushers were like ringmasters. You'd need cattle prods to keep some of the kids in check. They'd piss on the floor and the auditorium would be raked – they'd follow the trickle back up from the screen to the source. Dangerous times… And it there was a balcony, they' be throwing things down on top of you, cigarette butts and stuff.' (See John Kavanagh in McBride and Flynn [eds], 1996:115.) See also Thaddeus O'Sullivan in this collection (118–20) who notes that 'if we had to queue in the rain beforehand, the [Princess] would be like a steam bath from the wet clothes, and the stuffy damp smell would be nearly unbearable.' (119)
21. Ibid., 141–2. For another account of Dublin working-class life, though from a slightly later period, see Dominic Behan, *Teems of time and happy returns*, London: William Heinemann, 1961; reprinted (following its adaptation as an RTÉ television series), Dublin: Repsol, 1979.
22. As land tenure activist and MP William O'Brien put it in the house of commons in 1883, temperance advocates were a 'sect of puritans, who wished to impose their opinions forcibly on the Irish people, and who desired to treat the Irish people as though they were dipsomaniacs, and needed to be put under restraint.' He went on to argue that the proposed statutory restrictions would fall most heavily on the working classes, thus 'debarring them of one of the few enjoyments they had.' (Quoted, Malcolm, 1983:262.)
23. Malcolm, 1986:234.   24. Malcolm, 1983:48.   25. Ibid.
26. Malcolm, 1986:179–80. Subsequently, in addition to maintaining the coffee bar, the Dublin Total Abstinence Society developed a restaurant and hotel on the same site.
27. *Evening Herald*, 31 March 1909.   28. Kearns and Maguire, 2007:85–7.
29. Uniquely, and because Christmas Day 1920 happened to fall on a Saturday, St George's Hall opened on that day. Its advertised film programme consisted of *Tom Brown's Schooldays*; *Miss Cinderella* and *Romantic Betty*. (Kearns and Maguire, 2007:177–8.) While Dublin cinemas were closed on Christmas Day (a condition of Dublin corporation's cinema licence), those in Belfast seem to have been permitted to open on Christmas Day, but not on Sundays. The difference can be explained by the dominant religious ethos in the two cities, with (Protestant) George's Hall seemingly following Belfast's example.   30. See Rockett, 2004:49, 54.
31. See David R. Williams, 'Never on Sunday: the early operating of the Cinematograph Act of 1909 in regard to Sunday opening', *Film History*, vol. 14, no. 2, 2002:186–94.
32. The plasticizers, which made the safety film pliable, evaporated too rapidly.
33. Low, 1930:105–6.   34. See Rockett, 2004:49–51.
35. A.J. Harris Whitney to Seacome Mason, 9 February 1917.
36. *Dublin corporation reports*, vol. 1, 1912:287.
37. Of course, if no music accompanied the film, a venue with a six-day music licence and a seven-day cinema licence, theoretically, could show films on Sundays without breaching the music licence. However, the recorder seems to have interpreted his powers as requiring a venue to close on Sundays if it did not have a music licence.
38. Thomas O'Shaughnessy (1850–1933) was an experienced member of the Irish Bar, to which he was called in 1874, and to the English Bar by Middle Temple in 1894. Following the abolition of the recordership in 1924, O'Shaughnessy became a high court judge, but resigned the following year. He received a knighthood in 1927. The post of recorder, both its ancient/honorary version and a post-1971 statutory system, continues to be in use in England and Wales where 1,400 such posts are occupied. The position of recorder has been seen as a part-time though prestigious activity for fully qualified solicitors or barristers with ten years or more experience before the courts and is regarded as a stepping stone to a full judicial appointment as a circuit court judge. The post of recorder of Dublin was re-activated in the 2000s when the *Irish Times* legal affairs correspondent and barrister Carol Coulter was appointed temporarily to the post.
39. *Dublin corporation reports*, vol. 1, 1912:287–8.
40. See Rockett, 2004:37–42, for an account of how the recorder attempted to prohibit the release of *From the Manger to the Cross* (1912) in 1913. His failure to stop the film's release led to pressure being applied on Dublin corporation to include in its annual cinema licence conditions controlling the content of films being publicly exhibited in the city.
41. *IT*, 3 April 1913:10.
42. 'Dublin Sunday opening', *Kinematograph and Lantern Weekly*, 8 April 1915:37.
43. Memorial from Dame Street Picture House Ltd to lord lieutenant, 22 July 1913, CSORP/1915/2211; NAI.

44. Cornelius Kiernan, Dublin Metropolitan Police to chief secretary, 26 July 1913, CSORP/1915/2211; NAI.
45. *Kinematograph and Lantern Weekly*, 8 April 1915:37. When Elliman refused to accept the limited licence, the recorder threatened to withdraw completely the offer of a licence.
46. *Kinematograph and Lantern Weekly*, 8 April 1915:37. In its report, the *Irish Independent*, 30 March 1915, did not use the words 'humbler type' with its implication of working-class Protestants.
47. *Dublin Evening Mail*, 9 October 1918:3.
48. The *IT* (11 August 1920:5), *Dublin Evening Mail* (7 August 1920) and *Irish Builder and Engineer* (14 August 1920:530) give the number of seats as 3,200. The *FJ* (11 August 1920:3) does not mention the seat capacity, while *Dublin Evening Mail* (11 August 1920:2) describes the building as having a 'beautiful and wonderful artistic auditorium' and as being an 'epoch-making event in Theatreland so far as Dublin is concerned'. More recently, both Keenan, 2005:56, and Zimmermann, 2007:112, set the number of seats at 1,900, while Kearns and Maguire, 2007:62, state 1,400 seats, but none of these three books provide a source for the information given.
49. *Irish Limelight*, vol. 2, no. 4, April 1918:4; *Irish Builder and Engineer*, vol. 62, no. 18, 14 August 1920:530.
50. See *Dublin Evening Mail*, 9 October 1918:3. The identity of the applicant was not revealed in the press report, but when examined by his counsel, Mr Healy KC, he said that he founded the Rotunda Rink and had several other similar interests in the city, including the Carlton Picture House. His intention was to provide 'legitimate drama' (opera and drama), variety and cinema. The reference to the Carlton suggests that the applicant was either Frank W. Chambers or George P. Fleming, later manager of La Scala, as both of these were the principals behind the Carlton when it opened in 1915. Edward Shortt, secretary for Ireland, approved a twenty-one-year patent application on 4 March 1919, and forwarded it to London. The document with the king's approval was lodged in the Irish high court on 24 November 1919. (Copies of documents in Liam O'Leary collection, NLI.)
51. John Burke to Superintendent, 'C' Division, Dublin Metropolitan Police, Store Street, Dublin, 14 October 1920. CSORP/1920/23518, NAI.
52. Inspector Byrne, Dublin Metropolitan Police, Store Street, to chief crown solicitor, 27 October 1920; CSORP/1920/23518; NAI.
53. La Scala patent memo; CSORP/1920/19253, 19 November 1920, in ibid.
54. Chief commissioner, Dublin Metropolitan Police, to under-secretary, 6 January 1921, CSORP/1920/23518; NAI.
55. Chief commissioner, Dublin Metropolitan Police, to under-secretary, 2 February 1921, CSORP/1920/23518; NAI.
56. *FJ*, 21 May 1915.
57. Sam W. Dixon to Seacome Mason, 23 February 1915, DCA.
58. H. Coleman to F.P. Fawcett, 16 June 1914, DCA. Despite this assurance of good behaviour, the Sandford was fined £2 within two weeks of opening for not having a cinema licence. (*Evening Telegraph*, 21 November 1914:4.)
59. 'Sunday opening of cinemas', *Dublin Evening Mail*, 30 June 1915:2.
60. Seacome Mason to William J. Shannon, 1 July 1915, DCA.
61. William J. Shannon to Seacome Mason, 9 July 1915, DCA.
62. Seacome Mason to managers of the Sandford and Princess cinemas, 14 July 1915, DCA.
63. Nathan Karmel to Seacome Mason, 15 July and 22 July 1915, DCA.
64. Sandford Cinema to Seacome Mason, 27 July 1915, DCA.
65. James T. Jameson to Seacome Mason, clerk UDC, Town Hall, 6 January 1916; copy in Liam O'Leary collection, NLI.
66. Kearns, 2004:101.   67. Kearns and Maguire, 2007:198.
68. Kearns, 2004:102.
69. Revd E.H. Lewis-Crosby to Seacome Mason, 27 October 1915, DCA. Lewis-Crosby (1864–1961), though an establishment figure (during 1908 to 1921 he was chaplain to the lord lieutenant), during his tenure as rector of Drumcondra parish prior to moving to Rathmines, he took the 'unheard of' decision of appointing a female deaconess, and while in the 'pro-British' Rathmines parish 'took the unpopular step of interceding with the government on behalf of parishioners arrested during the 1916 rising', for which, later, he was praised by Éamon de Valera. (Jude McCarthy, 'Ernest Henry Cornwall Lewis-Crosby', *Dictionary of Irish biography*, 2009, accessed online.)
70. 'Cinema shows on Sundays', *FJ*, 4 November 1915:2.
71. Hugh Higginson to Seacome Mason, 4 January 1916, DCA. As part of its report on the UDC meeting, the *Irish Times* (6 January 1916:3) reprinted most of Higginson's statement which had been sent to Mason in advance of the meeting.

72. C.A. Alford, honorary secretary, to Seacome Mason, 8 January 1916, DCA.
73. Letter to Seacome Mason, 27 January 1916, DCA.
74. I.I. Bradlaw to chairman, Rathmines and Rathgar UDC, 2 February 1916, DCA.
75. Nathan Karmel to Seacome Mason, 14 February 1916, DCA.
76. Letter to Seacome Mason, 28 January 1916, DCA.
77. George Griffin, honorary secretary, Charleston Road Methodist church, to UDC, 27 January 1916.
78. Resolution of 7 February 1916, DCA.
79. Statement of 8 February 1916, DCA.
80. T. Kennedy to Seacome Mason, 21 February 1916, DCA.
81. Seacome Mason to William Shannon, 21 February 1916, DCA.
82. Rathmines and Rathgar Ratepayers' Association to UDC, 2 March 1916, DCA.
83. Text of UDC resolution, 1 March 1916, DCA.
84. Seacome Mason to Superintenant Kiernan, 'E' Divison, Dublin Metropolitan Police, Rathmines police station, 27 March 1916, DCA.
85. Nathan Karmel to Seacome Mason, 16 May 1916, DCA.
86. One of the shareholders was the premises' landlord. There were also debentures of £450, making the total investment, excluding any repayments to the builder (at £50 per quarter, no more than £150 since the cinema opened), of about £4,000. The profile of the Sandford's investors confirms that investment in independent cinemas in this period, as was the case in Britain, usually came from middle-class locals.
87. A.J. Harris Whitney to Seacome Mason, 4 July 1916.
88. Seacome Mason to A.J. Harris Whitney, 2 August 1916.
89. The concert proposal was made to Karmel by Desmond Fitzgerald. It was the recorder who had the authority to issue such music licences. (Nathan Karmel to Seacome Mason, 20 October 1916, DCA.)
90. A.J. Harris Whitney to Seacome Mason, 9 February 1917.
91. The liquidator accepted Healy's offer on 11 December 1917.
92. John Healy to Seacome Mason, 4 March 1919, DCA.
93. Seacome Mason to Nathan Karmel, 7 February 1919, DCA.
94. 'Sunday opening at Kingstown', *IT*, 16 January 1919:2. Canon Kennedy's comments, which mirror those of the religious delegation that met with the Rathmines and Rathgar UDC in November 1915, confirm that in those cases where detailed information is available during this period (the *From the Manger to the Cross* controversy and the Rathmines Sunday opening struggle) the institutionalized Protestant churches were much more forthright in their campaigns than their Catholic counterparts. This report, seemingly erroneously, refers to the proprietor of the Kingstown cinema as George, rather than Robert Morrison.
95. Nathan Karmel to Seacome Mason, 11 September 1920, DCA.
96. *IT*, 15 February 1923:11. It measured 110ft long by 51ft wide. According to Kearns and Maguire, 2007:483, in 2004, the year it closed, the Stella was said to be the oldest cinema in Dublin with two screens.
97. *The Leader*, 15 January 1927:566.   98. *KW*, 24 November 1932.
99. *Bioscope*, 15 October 1914, cited by Williams, 2002:193.
 1. Patrick Buckland, *The factory of grievances: devolved government in Northern Ireland, 1921–39*, Dublin: Gill & Macmillan, 1979:81, 86. See also *Ulster year books*, and R.J. Lawrence, *The government of Northern Ireland: public finance and public service, 1921–1964*, Oxford, 1965.
 2. Peter Murray, 'Citizenship, colonialism and self-determination: Dublin in the United Kingdom 1885–1918', PhD, Trinity College Dublin, 1987:266–7.
 3. Ibid., 267.
 4. Section 1, Finance (New Duties Act) 1916, 6 & 7 George V, chapter 11. The tax came into effect from 15 May 1916.
 5. Low, 1950:109–10.
 6. Beere, 1936:91, includes a table of changes of entertainment tax from 1917; section 3, Finance Act 1917, 7 & 8 George V, chapter 31.
 7. Beere, 1936:91. The original 1918 rates are listed in section 11, Finance Act 1918, 8 & 9 George V, chapter 15.
 8. Beere, 1936:91. Section 7, Finance Act 1919, 8 & 9 George V, chapter 32.
 9. Margaret Dickinson and Sarah Street, *Cinema and state: the film industry and the British government, 1927–84*, London: BFI, 1985:8.
10. *Irish Limelight*, vol. 1, no. 1, January 1917; vol. 1, no. 12, December 1917:6. See also 'Taxation' subsection, chapter 3, in this book.
11. 'More taxation', *Irish Limelight*, vol. 2, no. 1, January 1918:6.

12. *Irish Limelight*, vol. 2, no. 1, January 1918:6. Five months later the magazine informed readers that the act caused 'several' cinemas to close. (*Irish Limelight*, vol. 2, no. 5, May 1918:9.)
13. *Irish Limelight*, vol. 2, no. 6, June 1918:6.
14. *Bioscope*, 6 January 1916. Chambers home address was 'Tullyallen', Clontarf, Co. Dublin, while Fleming's was Drimnagh House, Inchicore, Co. Dublin.
15. The other members of the delegation were Fred Sparling (Bohemian Picture House); I.I. Bradlaw (Rathmines Amusements Co. Ltd); and T.P. Robinson (Carlton Cinema).
16. *Bioscope*, 23 November 1922:44.
17. 'How the Rebellion affects the industry; Will cinemas close down?', *Bioscope*, 2 December 1920:9.
18. The cinema was closed again in 1919 for a period because of another influenza scare.
19. The receipt books are held in the Horgan collection, IFI library.
20. 'Cinema notes; educating the public', *IT*, 31 December 1921:8.
21. *IT*, 8 October 1921:9.
22. Public health committee, Dublin corporation, 1923, no. 144, 24 April 1923. The building was destroyed again in September 1946 when it was hit by lightning.
23. *IT*, 8 October 1921:9.
24. 'Christmas films', *IT*, 27 December 1921:7.   25. See Rockett, 2004:318.
26. The cinema suffered unintentional damage when on St Patrick's night, 17 March 1923, an explosion designed to disable a power line supplying the La Scala Theatre occurred causing the back doors of the cinema to be blown off and considerable damage to the plasterwork. Members of the orchestra also suffered minor injuries. As the screen was not damaged, the film show continued even though a hole was visible beneath the screen to the back street beyond. What may have encouraged the Irregulars to choose that particular night was that there was a high-profile boxing match between Englishman Mike McTigue and Sengelese/Parisian Monsieur or 'Battling' Siki taking place at La Scala that attracted international media attention. Though McTigue was adjudicated the winner by the referee, the views expressed in the *Sunday Independent* (18 March 1923:2) suggest Siki was the better fighter. According to Kearns and Maguire (2007:70–1) the nearby Carlton also suffered an attack during the civil war.
27. *Dublin Evening Mail*, 13 April 1923:3. Two armed men placed a landmine in the empty auditorium, but the fuse burnt itself out before detonation.
28. 'Terrific explosion in Dublin; attempt to blow up Grand Central Cinema', *Dublin Evening Mail*, 27 April 1923:3.
29. Having been rebuilt following the rising, the attack on the Masterpiece seems to have been motivated by a republican protest at the cinema's screening of *Ypres* (Walter Summers, 1925). The bomb caused considerable damage, not least the destruction of the foyer; the gates were torn down; the vestibule walls damaged; the box-office destroyed; and the windows and doors, including of neighbouring premises, were blown out. The screen and auditorium were undamaged as a result of the long corridor leading into the cinema proper. The police subsequently charged a man who was part of the armed gang which four days earlier had entered the cinema and seized the film. (See Rockett, 2004:319; Kearns and Maguire, 2007:247–8). Some time later, the Bohemian was damaged by a bomb being thrown at the cinema on 12 May 1935 (*IT*, 14 May 1935:5), while in Belfast, persistent rioting during the summer of 1935 led to the imposition of a 10p.m. curfew order in July 1935 and four cinemas being closed for up to a week. (*KW*, 25 July 1935:19.)
30. Open, 1985:23.   31. *Bioscope*, 7 September 1922:42.
32. Open, 1985:73.   33. Ibid., 40.
34. 'The cranks campaign against the cinema', *Irish Limelight*, vol. 1, no. 7, July 1917:1; vol. 1, no. 9, September 1917:8.
35. *IT*, 8 October 1921:9.   36. *KW*, 8 January 1920.
37. *IT* 15 October 1921:9.   38. *Bioscope*, 18 March 1920:116.
39. The Belfast office was at 93 Donegall Street.
40. *Bioscope*, 8 May 1919:9; 7 August 1919:105.
41. *Bioscope*, 5 June 1929:54.   42. *Bioscope*, 18 July 1928:56–7.
43. *KW*, 28 June 1945:8.
44. *Bioscope*, 19 September 1930:43; 24 September 1930:54; 19 November 1930:42.
45. Low, 1971:72.   46. Ibid., 73.
47. The film production company was formed in 1916 by the merger of Adolph Zukor's Famous Players and Jesse L. Lasky's Feature Play Company to supply W.W. Hodkinson's Paramount Pictures, the distribution arm with which it merged. In 1919 the company entered exhibition and by the end of the 1920s controlled hundreds of cinemas in America. In 1927, the corporate name was changed to Paramount Famous Lasky Corporation and in 1930 to Paramount Publix Corporation. (See Ephraim

Katz, *The international film encyclopedia*, London: Papermac (Macmillan), 1982:400, 893–4; orig. 1979.)

48. Chaplin joined Keystone Film Co. in 1913, where in 1914 he was being paid $150 per week; he moved to Essanay, where he was paid $1,250 per week; and before the end of 1916, he moved to Mutual Film Corporation, where he was paid $10,000 per week. (Richard Koszarski, *An evening's entertainment: the age of the silent feature picture, 1915–28*, Berkeley/Los Angeles/London, 1994:263–5; orig. 1990.)

49. Thompson, 1985:83.   50. Ibid., 83–4.

51. Beere, 1935–36:99.   52. See note 47, p. 495.

53. Low, 1971:51. In 1926 it had two seven-year cinema leases in Birmingham.

54. George P. Fleming (*c.*1881–1950) was also engaged in the paper manufacturing business and became a long-time vice-chairman of Capitol and Allied Theatres Ltd. Beside his cinema interests, he was a 'fine' youth soccer player, and was known in Irish boxing circles as an amateur boxer and member of the committee of the Irish Amateur Boxing Association. He also founded its professional equivalent, the Éire Boxing Board of Control, and was vice-president of the Dublin Rifle Club. He died at his daughter's house, Mary Tower Fleming, 'The Shieling', Croner, Mount Nugent, Co. Cavan. See obituary in *Irish Press*, 3 February 1950:9.

55. *Sunday Independent*, 21 April 1929:2.

56. *KW*, 15 October 1931:53; 16 July 1931:34.

57. *KW*, 15 November 1934:22.

58. Low, 1971:84.   59. Eyles, 2005:11.   60. *KW*, 17 May 1945:25.

61. The cinema's first manager was Thomas ('Tony') C. Reddin, who had formed a film distribution agency in Dublin in 1919, and had been appointed La Scala's general manager and director of entertainment by J.J. Farrell the following year. He continued in that post when Paramount took over the venue in 1927, and in the early 1930s moved to England where, in 1934, he opened the new Paramount theatre, Liverpool. During his career with the company, he designed, produced and directed more than 350 stage shows for the Paramount theatre circuit. He was also director for fifteen years of the West End Plaza and Carlton theatres, as well as director of publicity and advertising for the company, handling all of Britain and Ireland. He retired in 1968, returned to live in Ireland in 1975, and died on 2 February 1979. In his early career, like exhibitor Leo Ward (discussed in chapter 4), he had played professional soccer (for Bohemians). In addition, he recorded about twenty songs on the Imperial and Decca labels, most famously, 'Mrs Mulligan, the Pride of the Combe', well before Jimmy O'Dea made this song his signature tune, a fact always acknowledged by O'Dea himself. His daughter was the London theatrical agent Joan Reddin. (Biographical note by Peter Tynan O'Mahony, 8 February 1979, Liam O'Leary collection, NLI.) See also interview with Tony Reddin, *Evening Herald*, 13 November 1962:7.

62. Beere, 1935–6:99.   63. *Bioscope*, 24 April 1924:44.

64. See Rockett, 2004:73–4   65. See official film censor's annual reports, NAI.

66. Low, 1971:92.   67. Ibid., 95.

68. Ibid., 91. See Thompson, 1985:211–12, for the various European quotas during the years 1921–34.

69. Low, 1971:106.   70. Ibid., 101.

71. *Dáil debates*, vol. 3, col. 763, 10 May 1923. The Savoy Cinema's opening souvenir programme in 1929 stated that the annual Dublin total of cinema admissions was 10.4 million, or 200,000 per week. As noted above, Thekla Beere reported that there were up to 11 million admissions annually in Dublin in the mid-1930s. (Beere, 1935–36:96–7.)

72. While talking of cinemas in Dublin, in the same sentence he said, 'and you have daily an average of 20,000' admissions, though later when referring to the whole country he used the same figure. (*Dáil debates*, vol. 3, col. 763, 10 May 1923.)

73. Open, 1985:52.   74. *Sunday Independent*, 5 May 1929:2.

75. 1,000 patrons attended 12p.m. screenings. *Sunday Independent*, 12 May 1929:2. *The Singing Fool* was followed by Paramount's first talkie, *The Doctor's Secret* (William C. De Mille, 1929), from J.M. Barrie's play *Half an hour*.

76. Open, 1985:62; *Bioscope*, 1 May 1929:41.

77. *Sunday Independent*, 28 June 1929:2.   78. Beere, 1935–6:96.

CHAPTER 2

1. *Report of the inter-departmental committee on the film industry*, 1942:14, NAI.

2. The proportion of American films in the British market declined during the following few years,

only to gain a dominant position again by the early sound era, such that they accounted for 75 per cent of the British market in 1930. (Thompson, 1985:213, 218.) If anything, the percentage of American films in Ireland was even greater than in Britain given the relative unpopularity of British films for nationalist and ideological reasons.

3. See Low, 1950:116–18, for a discussion of the formation and early activities of the Kinematograph Renters' Society of Great Britain and Ireland, which was established in 1915.

4. See Rockett in Rockett et al., 1987:32–8, for a discussion of General Film Supply.

5. Leah was described as the 'originator or mentor of animated cartoons … The work is quite the equal of anything hitherto offered by foreign producers.' (*Irish Limelight*, January 1918:16.)

6. Arthur Flynn, 'Early films in Ireland – 2', *IT*, 19 March 1975:10.

7. *Irish Limelight*, August 1917:18–19.

8. See Rockett in Rockett et al., 1987:7–12.

9. *Irish Limelight*, October 1917:19.

10. *Irish Limelight*, December 1917:1.

11. The film was praised for its 'transcendent beauty' (*Evening Herald*, 16 March 1920:3) and as a 'remarkable historical picture … [which was] the outcome of Irish minds, hands and hearts' (*IT*, 16 March 1920:9). See also Rockett in Rockett et al., 1987:37–8; and Rockett 1996:9–10.

12. *KW*, 8 March 1934:22.

13. A leading figure within film exhibition in Ireland, his Irish-born offspring also remained to the fore of the sector until the 1970s. See also **chapter** 1.

14. See **chapter** 1 for a more complete detailing of both companies' interests in Ireland, north and south. Provincial Cinematograph Co. also bought the Volta (1910), but never incorporated the venue into its overall programming structure. It sold the cinema to a consortium including John J. Farrell in September 1915 for £875 (*Bioscope*, 23 September 1915).

15. Rank, for its part, having renamed the Classic in 1950 as the Gaumont, embarked on an expansion of its Northern Irish interests throughout the 1950s.

16. Eyles, 1993:19.

17. Thekla Beere (1901–91), a graduate of Trinity College Dublin, joined the Irish civil service in 1924, and except for a study period in the US as a Rockefeller scholar during 1925–7, after which she resumed her career as a civil servant in the department of industry and commerce, she remained in state service until her retirement in 1966. In 1943, she was appointed a principal officer. She was only the second woman to reach this position since the foundation of the state, and the appointment represented her first major promotion in a regime designed to discriminate against women given that upon marriage a woman had to resign from the civil service. (This is perhaps why she never married.) Ten years later in 1953, she was made assistant secretary of industry and commerce, continuing her responsibilities for transport and marine issues. Finally, in 1959, she was appointed secretary of the department of transport and power, the first woman to hold such a job in the history of the Irish state. When she retired, she maintained a busy public life, serving, for example, as a member of the Devlin commission on the public service; a board member of the *Irish Times* Trust; and as the first chairwoman of the ground-breaking commission on the status of women (1970–2), whose report had a major influence on government policy. See Anna Bryson, *No coward soul: a biography of Thekla Beere*, Dublin: Institute of Public Administration, 2009.

18. 'President opens the Savoy', *Irish Independent*, 29 November 1929:11. This article lists the attendees at the opening event.

19. The building, as noted in the previous **chapter**, was on the site of the Crown and Granville hotels, both of which had been destroyed during the civil war.

20. *Savoy Cinema Souvenir Programme*, 29 November 1929:6, NLI.

21. The souvenir programme does not give a figure for the number of seats, though the *Irish Independent*, which carried a photo of John Maxwell, J.E. Pearce, William McGaw (general manager of Associated British Cinemas), and Fred Knott (general manager of Savoy cinema), reported it was 'capable of holding' 3,000 people. (*Irish Independent*, 'Lovely palace of pleasure', 29 November 1929:7; 3 [photo].) Keenan, 2005:76, puts its capacity at 2,900 seats. At the time of the Savoy's reopening after refurbishment in 2006, it was reported in an article about then owners Ward Anderson that the original Savoy had 2,792 seats. (Rose Doyle, 'Lights, cameras all action at city's premier cinema', *IT*, 25 January 2006:commercial property, 2)

22. Souvenir programme, 1929:22.

23. A silent government-sponsored tourist and industrial promotional film *Ireland* was also shown on the opening night. John Maxwell told the press that music would be added to the film and that it would be shown in ABC's 110 cinemas, though it is not known whether this happened. (*Irish Independent*, 29 November 1929:3.)

24. 'National asset; Dublin's palatial new cinema', *Saturday Herald*, 30 November 1929:4. See also *Sunday Independent*, 1 December 1929:2.

25. When formed on 17 July 1930, the directors of AIC were J.E. Pearce, Abraham Lincoln Rhodes, Horace Moore and Fred Moore. See Associated Irish Cinema Ltd file, dissolved companies list no. 8027, NAI. He is sometimes erroneously referred to as J.G. or J.R. Pearce in news reports. Little is known about Pearce until his appearance in relation to the Savoy and ABC, though a John Edward Pearce was an actor on the London and Dublin stages during 1909–10 as 'Crampton' in Bernard Shaw's *You Never Can Tell*. (*Times*, 11 May 1909:8; *IT*, 22 February 1910:2.)

26. Eyles, 1993:18. Reciprocal taxation arrangements between the Irish and British governments allowed foreign-registered companies to avoid paying Irish tax, as will be discussed in relation to distributors later in this chapter.

27. At this time, 19 August 1930, the 100,000 £1 preference shares and 133,000 1s. ordinary shares were distributed as follows: Dean Estate Ltd, of which Horace Moore was a director; Picture House (Doncaster) Ltd, 49,000 preference and 22,000 ordinary shares; Moontree Ltd, of which Horace Moore was a director, 4,000 preference and 4,000 ordinary; Picture House (Workshop) Ltd, 1,000 preference; Abraham Lincoln Rhodes, 25,000 ordinary; J.E. Pearce, a director of ABC and twenty-two other companies, 32,998 ordinary; Beatrice Rose Beresford, 10,000 ordinary; Fred Moore, Horace Moore and Frederick William Moore, 4,000 ordinary each. Two things are clear from this list: Almost all, if not all, shares were held by British-based investors, and some of these held other exhibition interests. See Associated Irish Cinema Ltd file, dissolved companies list no. 8027, NAI.

28. The loan was dated 20 February 1933. (Associated Irish Cinema Ltd file, dissolved companies list no. 8027, NAI.)

29. Pearce had 223,997 shares (almost 40 per cent of the 60,000 £1 ordinary shares) and Fred, Horace and John R. Moore, each had 12,000 shares. (Dublin Theatre Co. Ltd file, dissolved companies list no. 7311, NAI.)

30. *KW*, 8 March 1934:22. The new directors of Dublin Theatre Co. were J.E. Pearce, Horace Moore and Frederick William Moore, while Gerald A. Ellis was company secretary. A member of the film exhibition family, Ellis was also secretary and from August 1935 licensee, of the Savoy, Dublin, with the licence having been transferred from the cinema's manager Desmond Murphy (*KW*, 15 August 1935:19). Desmond Rushton was director of publicity (*KW*, 26 September 1935:3). Dublin Theatre Co. Ltd file, dissolved companies list no. 7311, NAI.

31. Pearce resigned from AIC on 6 July 1938 to be replaced by Frederick William Moore and Mrs Maxie Binns. The company ceased business by October 1944 and was dissolved on 27 July 1945. (Associated Irish Cinema Ltd file, dissolved companies list no. 8027, NAI.) Pearce also disengaged from the Dublin Theatre Co., selling 33,597 shares to Eustace J. Scott on 20 April 1938 and resigning from the company on 27 January 1939.

32. *KW*, 29 November 1934:23. See also *IT*, 19 January 1946:1. ABC's Associated Irish Cinemas and Irish Cinemas Ltd were both named in March 1935 as joint parties in a malicious damages' court case following damage by armed republicans to the Savoy cinema's screen during a screening of a royal wedding film. (*KW*, 21 March 1935: 23.)

33. The first Theatre Royal, Hawkins Street, opened in 1821, but was destroyed by fire in 1880. The second, built on the same site, opened in 1897 and was demolished in 1934. The third Theatre Royal opened on 23 September 1935. It was designed by London architect Leslie C. Norton in association with Dublin company Scott and Good, one of whose principals, Michael Scott, oversaw the project. It combined an art-deco exterior with a Moorish-style 'atmospheric' interior. The Regal Rooms restaurant was built as part of the complex, but when it did not prove to be a financial success it was converted into the 750-seat Regal Cinema, which opened on 16 April 1938.

34. *KW*, 9 December 1937:14.

35. *KW*, 2 February 1939:5. The directors of Dublin Theatre Co. from 27 January 1939 were all directors of Irish Cinemas Ltd. These were Maurice Elliman; George Joseph Nesbitt (also director of the Claremorris Bacon Co., New Ireland Assurance Co. and The Slane Brick Co.); Patrick Ignatius Wall (of the Central Hotel, Exchequer Street, Dublin, and Gaiety Theatre Ltd); and John Joseph Roche (also a director of Irish Cinemas Ltd as well as managing director of J.J. Roche & Co. Ltd and the Dublin Drug Co. Ltd). All but Roche were also directors of Metropole and Allied Cinemas Ltd. The last and only major block of Dublin Theatre company shares not to be owned by Irish Cinemas – the 23,597 shares owned by company secretary Edward J. Shott – were sold to Irish Cinemas on 16 May 1939, as a result of which it owned all but 1,400 of the 60,000 ordinary shares in Dublin Theatre Co. See Dublin Theatre Co. Ltd file, dissolved companies list no. 7311, NAI.

36. Dublin Theatre Co. continued until 1947 when it went into voluntary liquidation after J. Arthur

Rank took over Irish Cinemas Ltd. See Dublin Theatre Co. Ltd file, dissolved companies list no. 7311, NAI.

37. Elliman also had had interests in the Blackrock Cinema Theatre, 13 Main Street, Blackrock, which opened on 28 February 1914 with 700 seats, and was run by John Hanna in the 1920s before closing in 1929; Brunswick Cinema Theatre, 30 Great Brunswick Street (Pearse Street) which was opened by Irish Amusement Company on 1 December 1911, though closed by 1919; and perhaps from the 1930s, the Camden Picture House, 55 Lower Camden Street, Dublin.

38. The Corinthian, Eden Quay, Dublin, which opened in 1921 and wound up in the late 1920s as it was trading at a loss, was bought at auction in February 1930 for £20,300 by Maurice Elliman, George Nesbitt and P.A. Corrigan, all of whom were linked to the Metropole and Theatre de Luxe (*Saturday Herald*, 8 February 1930:7). Following redecoration and the installation of sound it reopened. It was further renovated in 1939 when a balcony was erected. The Ellimans sold the cinema in 1946 to Rank who controlled it through Odeon (Ireland) Ltd. From 1975 to 1983 it was known as the Odeon. From 1983 to 1993 Ward Anderson controlled the cinema (as well as the adjoining Astor cinema from 1985, with which it was merged) and renamed it the Screen at O'Connell Bridge. The combined cinemas were later redeveloped as a non-cinema entertainment venue.

39. Opened by Maurice Elliman's Dublin Kinematograph Theatres Ltd on Lower Camden Street on 16 December 1912 the cinema had only 400 seats. However, seating capacity tripled in 1920 when it was rebuilt and extended onto an adjoining site. Following further transformation by Dublin Kinematograph Theatres Ltd on 19 October 1934, the cinema, boasting an art deco façade from a design by Alfred E. Jones of Jones & Kelly and with 1,241 seats, was reopened as the New Super Theatre de Luxe. At the time the directors of Dublin Kinematograph Theatres Ltd were Maurice Elliman (managing director), George J. Nesbitt (chairman), Peter A. Corrigan, Patrick I. Wall, and Frances B. O'Rourke, with John Crowley as secretary. Two years later, Elliman bought the Gaiety Theatre and installed his son Louis as managing director.

40. In 1938 Metropole and Allied Cinemas Co. bought the Phibsboro, 36 Madras Place (now 376 North Circular Road), from William King and upgraded it to 'super' status with 1,500 seats. (It had originally opened in 1914 with only 387 seats, though by the end of the following year there were 600 seats.)

41. This is the figure published when Rank took over the Elliman cinemas in 1946; see next chapter. ('Rank's may buy more Irish cinemas', *KW*, 31 January 1946.) This figure is higher than the information recorded in the cinemas' list (part 3 of this book), where the eight cinemas had approximately the following number of seats in the late 1930s: Metropole (883–1,000); Corinthian (794); Theatre de Luxe (1,241); Phibsboro (750); Regal (750); Savoy, Dublin (2,792); Savoy, Cork (2,249); and Savoy, Limerick (1,650), making a total of between 11,109 and 11,226 cinema seats. Of course, the number of seats in these venues may have been increased between 1939 and 1946.

42. 'Booking merger in Éire; "A squeeze out" against A.B.C.; Ellimans buy into Irish cinemas', *KW*, 2 February 1939:5.

43. *Irish Press*, 17 February 1937:2. Adelphi Ltd was also interested in the purchase and renovation of the Pavilion, Dún Laoghaire, perhaps because both Freeman and Middleton as residents of Monkstown and Glenageary, respectively, lived within a mile of the cinema.

44. *Irish Press*, 13 January 1939:7, which also names William M.M. Curtis as a director of Adelphi Ltd; *IT*, 13 January 1939:3, photo of Adelphi manager J.H. Hamilton. The long-serving manager of the Adelphi from about 1950 to his retirement in 1981 was Harry Lush. During his time as manager, the Beatles played their only Irish concert at the cinema in November 1963. See obituary of Harry Lush, *IT*, 21 May 2005:12. The cinema cost £75,000 to build.

45. Despite the obvious safety issues involved, cinemas (and theatres, where the practice originated) were permitted to allow patrons stand at the sides or back of the venue during a show. In the case of the Adelphi, those standing could account for over 20 per cent of a full house. This may help to explain the discrepancies in the capacity of the Savoy mentioned in note 21 above, or, indeed, in other cinemas (see also note 41).

46. Perhaps Maxwell had been offered the circuit before talks began with Metropole and Allied Cinemas, but he declined the offer.

47. A list of Irish cinema circuits, that is, those with two or more cinemas, most likely compiled in 1934, lists the following 17 circuits: 1) Grand Central; Mary Street Picture House; and Pillar Picture House, Dublin; 2) Metropole, Corinthian, and Theatre de Luxe, Dublin; 3) Grafton Picture House and Carlton Cinema, Dublin; 4) Empire Theatre, Galway, and Golden Vale, Athlone; 5) Boyne Drogheda; Oriel, Dundalk, and Town Hall Cinema, Cavan; 6) Navan Picture House and Kells Picture House, Co. Meath; 7) Grand Central and Tivoli cinemas, Limerick; 8) Pavilion Picture

House, Sligo; the Theatre, Sligo; and Boyle Cinema, Co. Roscommon; 9) Savoy Cinema, Waterford, and Town Hall Cinema, Ennis; 10) Stella Cinema, Bantry, and Ashe Memorial Hall, Tralee; 11) Arch Cinema, Cobh, and Coliseum, Skibbereen; 12) Savoy cinemas, Dublin and Cork; 13) Theatre Royal, Waterford, and Town Hall Cinema, New Ross; 14) Picturedrome, Tralee, Castleisland Cinema, Castleisland, and Listowel cinema, Co. Kerry; 15) New Cinema, Thurles, and Rock Cinema, Cashel, Co. Tipperary; 16) Picture House, Dun Laoghaire; Picture House, Camden Street; and Broadway Cinema, Manor Street, Dublin; 17) Capitol Cinema, Wexford and Grand Cinema, Enniscorthy, Co Wexford. (Undated 1-page document, 'Cinema circuits (of two or more theatres) in Irish Free State', with a further 7-page list, 'no. of cinemas, address, seating capacity and remarks'. This document was probably compiled by Thekla Beere while researching her statistical profile of Irish exhibition during 1934–5, the results of which were published in 1936. A copy of the cinemas document is held in IFI library.

48. Three of the cinemas – the Majestic, Ritz and Strand – were in Belfast; two – the Palace and Rialto – were in Derry; while there were Ritzes in Armagh town and Newtownards, Co. Down.

49. *KW*, 13 January 1944:82. ABC's Northern Ireland manager Jack D. Russell had moved to Belfast from England in October 1935 to open Union's Strand Cinema. When the exhibitors' group, the White Cinema Club, was transformed in 1942 into the Belfast branch of the Cinema Exhibitors' Association, Russell became its first chairman.

50. Eyles, 1993:24.   51. *KW*, 3 July 1931:55.   52. *KW*, 22 November 1945.

53. 'Death of Louis Elliman', *Irish Press*, 16 November 1965:7. This article says that Maurice Elliman was Latvian.

54. *KW*, 8 February 1940.   55. See www.archiseek.com.

56. Rothery, 1991:192. See Rockett 2004, image 5, for an exterior view of the Ritz, Athlone.

57. Ritz, 130–1 Tullow Street, Carlow, opened by Carlow Cinema Ltd of the same address, on 18 June 1938. It is listed in 1940 as having 1,054 seats. By 1955 the holding company was Amalgamated Cinemas (Ireland) Ltd, 9 Eden Quay, Dublin, the same address as other Elliman linked companies. The holding company of the Athlone Ritz was Western Cinemas, also of 9 Eden Quay, but by 1960 the proprietor is cited as Amalgamated Cinemas (Ireland) Ltd, at the same Eden Quay address, suggesting at least some level of continuity. Louis Elliman's Ritz (Clonmel) Ltd, which owned the Clonmel Ritz, and later the 550-seat Oisin, Clonmel, opened by William O'Keefe in 1945, was also at 9 Eden Quay, as was Ennis Cinemas Ltd, which owned Clare's Gaiety Cinema (800 seats in 1955). In addition, Amalgamated Cinemas was owned, wholly or partly, by Geoffrey Elliman and Bertie McNally in the 1950s. However, Harry W. Culleton, general manager, McNally Cinemas Ltd, 75 Middle Abbey Street, in 1947 was booking films for nine cinemas, including the Savoys in Waterford, Galway, Portarlington (Co. Laois), Athy (Co. Kildare), Kiltimagh (Co. Mayo) and Edenderry (Co. Offaly); the Castle, Oldcastle, Co. Meath; Town Hall, Ennis, Co. Clare; and Gaiety, Ennis. (*Cinema and theatre annual review and directory of Ireland, 1947*, c.1947:57.) The confused state of the ownership of cinemas and bookers of films (not always the same), as well as the fluidity of ownership from decade to decade, makes it difficult to track such changes, especially as the private limited companies under which almost all operated are usually unhelpful in understanding these issues. Furthermore, there is generally an absence of any data on income and expenditure of venues in such company files.

58. *IT*, 18 June 1938:4.   59. *KW*, 7 February 1935:27.

60. Rothery, 1991:193.

61. A copy of the programme may be found in the Liam O'Leary collection, NLI.

62. As discussed in chapter 3, the 1970s saw the gradual erosion of the company, marked not least by the closure in 1972 of their flagship cinema, Dublin's Capitol.

63. The site was later developed as a branch of the Hibernian bank.

64. 'Four new Dublin picture houses; 7,000 additional seats in Éire capital', *KW* supplement, 12 May 1938:21.

65. The Phoenix continued as a cinema until 1960.

66. There were 1,500 seats in the stalls and 500 in the balcony.

67. These housed the Dorset Institution and Repository for Plain and Fancy Needlework.

68. The directors were identified by *KW* ('British control in Dublin?; Carlton protest', *KW*, 8 April 1937:15) as Jack Ellis, M. McCabe, T.P. Robinson (solicitor), and John J. Robinson. The publication of the names, all Dubliners, was the result of a resolution passed by the Gaelic Athletic Association claiming that those behind the venture were not Irish.

69. Keenan, 2005:82, puts the number of seats at 1,200.

70. Keenan, 2005:90, puts the number of seats at 720, he also gives the date as 1936. The cinema actually opened on 4 January 1937.

71. Keenan, 2005:90, puts the number of seats at 1,100.

72. *Talkie Topics and Theatrical Review,* no. 2, 11 March 1931:3. As the Grand Central is most closely associated with Maurice Elliman at this time, it may be that following a fire at the cinema in January 1930, McNally became involved or took it over. The other Dublin cinemas in which McNally had an interest have not been identified.

73. *KYB* variously puts the Savoy's seating capacity at 1,300 seats (1935–38); 1,254 seats (1939–45); and 1,200 seats (1946–61).

74. See Walter McNally's obituary in *IT,* 27 August 1945:3.   75. *IT,* 8 September 1945:4.

76. Though Maurice Baum may have been British born, his father John had been a distributor of films in Ireland as early as 1901, and he took over from his father in 1936. Maurice set up National Film Distributors in 1943, but following a period when his interests mainly focused on exhibition, he reinstated the company in 1962, by which time he had relinquished his interests in the Corinthian, Grafton, and Rialto cinemas. (*Showcase,* March 1969:13.)

77. There were 1,000 seats in the stalls and 500 seats in the balcony.

78. *KW,* 16 November 1944:38.   79. *KW,* 23 April 1936:25.

80. *KW,* 11 November 1943:33.   81. *KW,* 8 March 1945:16.

82. *Irish Independent,* 22 December 1934:10. See also Kearns and Maguire, 2007:515–20. As a cinema, the Tivoli closed in September 1964.

83. The approximately 700-seat Astoria, Glasthule, opened on 6 August 1940 and ran as a cinema until 1999, apart from closures in 1957 (when O'Neill died), from 1962 to 1971 (when it lay unused or was used as a bingo hall), and in 1981 (when it was being twined). Its name was changed by new owner Barney O'Reilly in 1971 to the Forum. See Keenan, 2005:104–5; Kearns and Maguire, 2007:42–4.

84. The proprietors had promised 'clean' films only. The proceedings from the opening programme of two religious films were donated to the African missions. (*TC,* 9 November 1936.) The Leinster closed in 1969.

85. The Regent opened on 24 February 1938. See Whelan's obituary, *KW,* 21 September 1944:7.

86. The Tower opened on 9 April 1939. In 1941 Ging bought out Egan and Kelly, and in 1942 the cinema passed on Ging's death to his sons Larry and Tommy, though later Larry took over. It was extended in 1942 to 500 seats and finally closed in 1977. See Keenan 2005:102–3; and Kearns and Maguire, 2007:528–46.

87. After Whelan's death, Daniel McAllister of Shankill, Co. Dublin, bought the cinema and ran it until it closed in June 1962. See Keenan, 2005:72–3; and Kearns and Maguire 2007:163–7.

88. *KW,* 23 November 1944:35.   89. *KW,* 8 March 1945:16.

90. *Cinema and Theatre Annual Review and Directory of Ireland, 1947, c.*1947:57–8.

91. This information is gleaned from Kavanagh's notepaper included in Archbishop McQuaid's papers, DDA. The reason Kavanagh wrote to McQuaid was to alert him to the imminent release of Elia Kazan's *A Streetcar Named Desire* (1951), which he had seen in Belfast some months earlier. While the film was unlikely to pass the Irish censor without cuts, 'no matter how much it was censored', Kavanagh told McQuaid, 'I would not book it for any of my Cinemas as I feel I have certain responsibilities to my own and other people[']s children.' Erroneously informed, Kavanagh told McQuaid that he understood that the film had been passed uncut by the Irish censor, and he asked the archbishop to investigate the matter. He added that even though the censor was, 'as a rule', 'very strict and it is rarely that a film of this type reaches the Irish public, ... it has happened occasionally.' He suggested that the appeal board should have at least one representative from among the 'Catholic Provincial Cinema owners, the great majority of whom feel as I do about this matter.' He concluded by asking McQuaid to treat his letter 'as strictly confidential' because 'it would be very hurtful to me in business with the Film Renters if it were known that I brought this matter before your Grace.' McQuaid investigated and wrote to Kavanagh three weeks later to say that the censor had cut the film 'very heavily', and he thanked him for his 'expression of ... carefulness, especially in regard to young [people] and trust[ed that] you will have God's blessing [for] all you do to present only worthy films.' (James J. Kavanagh to Dr McQuaid, 30 August 1952; margin note by Dr McQuaid dated 19 September 1952 on letter from James Kavanagh, 30 August 1952, Dr McQuaid papers, DDA.) Although *Streetcar* had been passed with twenty-seven cuts by the film censor in February 1952, six months before Kavanagh wrote to McQuaid, it was not released in the Irish Republic until the following December. For a discussion of this decision and the treatment of other adaptations of the plays of Tennessee Williams in the 1950s and 1960s, see Rockett, 2004:130–6.

92. *KW,* 13 September 1934:30.

93. The combined number of seats in the three venues was about 4,729.

94. *Irish Independent,* 3 April 1935:5.

95. *Irish Independent,* 16 July 1942:3. See *Irish Independent,* 15 July 1942:3.

96. According to *KYB* (1947–57), Coleraine's Palladium, Society Street, was also owned by Irish Theatres Ltd.
97. In the *IT* obituary for Finney, it notes that apart from opening cinemas in Banbridge, Newry and Belfast, and acting as director of Irish Theatres Ltd, he introduced electricity for public and private use in Co. Down; took a keen interest in sport, including boxing, association football and hockey; was a prominent member of the Masonic order; and was a past provincial grand organist of Down. (*IT*, 11 February 1942:2.)
98. *Irish Independent*, 15 November 1912:6.   99. *KW*, 13 January 1944:87.
 1. Obituary of Michael Curran in *Irish Independent*, 21 September 1940:8.
 2. *KW*, 15 August 1935:19. James, nevertheless, retained ownership of the city's Midland cinema.
 3. Open, 1985:22. He notes it was sold to the Curran circuit around 1941, but it must have been sometime earlier given that the *Irish Independent*, 21 September 1940:8, states that at the time of Michael Curran's death at age 70 in September 1940, the circuit had six Belfast cinemas.
 4. Open, 1985:140, 23–4; Doherty, 1997:41–3.
 5. The figure given for the seating varies from 1,270 (listed in a number of *KYB*s) to 1,380 (also in *KYB* and in Open, 1985:148).
 6. Some reports cite the Regal's address as 366–72 Lisburn Road.
 7. Open, 1985:66–7. Both the Astoria and the Regal were designed by Thomas McLean, as well as the Capitol.
 8. Open, 1985:26.   9.   Doherty, 1997:141.
10. Wright was mentioned in *Irish Limelight* in April 1917:12, in relation to Films Ltd (film distributors), as the 'first to do business in Ireland'.
11. Curran, the eldest of ten children, left school at 12 years old, and having earned £100 installing street lighting for Queen Victoria's 1900 state visit to Dublin, started an electrical contracting business. By 1910 with the help of four of his brothers, all electricians, he had established Curran Bros, electrical engineers, as a successful company. He diversified into electricity generation with power stations in Portadown, Ballyclare and Whitehead. When local councils/the Northern Electricity Supply Board, took over his power stations in the early 1930s, he concentrated on his cinema interests. He married in 1900, and had seven children, six boys and one girl.
12. Open, 1985:52.   13. Doherty, 1997:140–1.   14. *TC*, 5 March 1947:31.
15. *KW*, 13 January 1944:87.   16. Doherty, 1997:71.   17. *KW*, 13 January 1944:82.
18. Ibid., 87.   19. *KW*, 3 September 1936:7.
20. *KW*, 30 August 1956:9; 6 September 1956:7; 27 September 1956.
21. *KW*, 13 September 1934:30. As noted above, Maurice Curran bought the Strand in 1935.
22. *KW*, 12 December 1935:17.
23. Similar 'overseating fears' were raised in the south, such as in 1936 with the opening of the Dublin suburban Leinster and Rialto cinemas, and during the planning of the city centre Carlton 'super'. (*KW*, 24 September 1936.)
24. *KW*, 30 July 1936:17.   25. *KW*, 2 September 1937:17.
26. *KW*, 6 October 1938:22.   27. *KW*, 15 December 1938:17A.
28. *KW*, 4 April 1937:24A.   29. *KW*, 25 March 1939:24.
30. *KW*, 28 December 1944:19.   31. Low, 1985:5.   32. *KW*, 8 March 1945:16.
33. *KW*, 13 January 1944:82. The patrons of the Troxy were of 'a better middle-class residential type', no doubt a reflection of admission prices ranging from 9d. to 2s., which were somewhat above the charges of the Curran circuit in Belfast.
34. In fact William Cosgrave himself had been sentenced to death for his part in the rising, but this sentence was later commuted to penal servitude for life and he was released in December 1916 as part of the general amnesty of Sinn Féin prisoners.
35. Between 1932 and 1942, an average of 12,000 houses a year were built with state aid, compared to less than 2,000 per year in the previous nine years. As Lee notes, 'The building boom created employment, consolidated working-class support for the government and helped alleviate a social scandal.' It also began a long association of Fianna Fáil with the building and property development industry. (Joseph Lee, *Ireland, 1912–1985, politics and society*, Cambridge: Cambridge UP, 1989:193.)
36. Land annuities paid to the British government were in effect the repayments of loans by those who, with British state help, had bought their farms under the Land Acts from 1870 onwards. This process dismantled many of the landed estates from the English colonial plantation period when land had been confiscated without recompense for the native, especially Catholic, Irish. After the establishment of the Irish Free State, the Irish exchequer collected the sums and forwarded them to London. While the Cumann na nGaedheal government honoured these unpopular repayments, in the lead

up to the 1932 general election Fianna Fáil declared that if elected it would withhold the annuities from the British government. De Valera's refusal to pay the annuities was based on the argument that the agreements were invalid as they had never been ratified by the Dáil. Furthermore, he reasoned that Ireland's exemption from contributing to the UK's public debt had included the payment of land annuities. When the Irish government on 1 July 1932 withheld the payment from Britain, the British government reacted by imposing a 20 per cent tariff on the selling price of all Irish agricultural exports. Ireland retaliated with a duty of 5 per cent payable on certain British products. The effect on Irish agriculture, as well as the farming and farm-labouring community generally, was devastating and in turn led to an increase in emigration to Britain. The 'war' ended with the signing of the Anglo-Irish agreement in March 1938. While Ireland conceded a £10 million settlement to Britain, in a triumph for de Valera, the British agreed to withdraw from southern Irish naval bases, thus confirming his vision of Ireland as a free independent sovereign state that could adopt an independent foreign policy. The economic tariffs on both sides were largely removed, but, importantly, there was a provision for the protection of certain products.

37. Mark Tierney, *Modern Ireland*, Dublin: Gill and Macmillan, 1978:201. See Lee, *Ireland, 1912–1985*, 1989:184–201. Various measures were introduced to help the unemployed, including the Unemployment Assistance Act and the National Health Insurance Act, both 1933.

38. The wages' book records the payment of £7 to 'management' which is interpreted here as being the manager's weekly wages.

39. The pages from the Stella's wages' book can be found in the Liam O'Leary collection, NAI. More than a decade later in 1939, the chief projectionists in the top class 'AA' cinemas in Northern Ireland were being paid only £5 per week following a wages' agreement between the NATKE trade union and local exhibitors, while the chief projectionist in the lowest class 'D' category cinemas received only half that amount. Usherettes were being paid from £1 5s. in 'AA' houses, but only 16s. in 'D' cinemas. (*KW*, 5 May 1938:26; 5 January 1939:11; 9 January 1939:24.)

40. Lasky's *The Busybody* (from 1 January 1931) cost £20 or 25 per cent of the gross box office take (whichever was the greater); *Murder Will Out* (Clarence Badger, 1930; from 4 January 1931) cost £15; the seventy-six minute long *Showgirl in Hollywood* (Mervyn LeRoy, 1930; from 11 January 1931) cost £30; *New York Nights* (Lewis Milestone, 1929; from 1 February 1931) cost £20; *The Dawn Patrol* (Howard Hawks, 1930; from 22 February 1931) cost £30 or 33.3 per cent of the gross box office take (whichever was the greater); *Anna Christie* (Clarence Brown, 1930; from 25 June 1931) cost £20; *Morocco* (Josef von Sternberg, 1930; from 22 to 25 November 1931) cost £35; *Hell's Angels* (Howard Hughes, 1930; continued from 17 to 20 January 1932) cost £30; *The Yankee at King Arthur's Court* (USA title *A Connecticut Yankee*, David Butler, 1931; from 20 March 1932) cost £20; *The Front Page* (Lewis Milestone 1931; 3 April 1932) cost £25; *Frankenstein* (James Whale, 1931; from 12 June 1932) cost £20; *Bad Girl* (Frank Borzage, 1931; from 3 July 1932) cost £20; *The Public Enemy* (William Wellman, 1931; from 8 September 1932) cost only £10; and *A Night Like This* (Tom Walls, 1932; from 16 October 1932) cost £25. (Liam O'Leary collection, NAI.)

41. The pre-release of *City Lights* in London in 1931 had caused 'much bitterness' when it was booked for twenty weeks at 60 per cent with a minimum guarantee of £40,000, while ABC paid 50 per cent for it after others sought to hold out for 33.3 to 40 per cent (Low, 1985:4).

42. In the case of the *City Lights'* screening, the accompanying short gangster film *Teacher's Pet* at 1,891ft cost £2 17s. 6d., *Pathé News* cost £1, as did Wardour's 800ft *Musical Medley*, while additional hire costs of £1 10s. and £4 are also listed. The contrast with the economics of the small rural cinema can be deduced from the hire costs of double bills fifteen years later. In 1946, William McElwee's small, 285-seat La Scala Cinema in Milford, Co. Donegal, paid British Lion £2 6s. 10d. for the hiring of the double bill *Cassanova in Burlesque* (Leslie Goodwins, 1944) and *Deerslayer* (Lew Landers, 1943) from 11 January 1946; £3 11s. 4d. the following May for *Port of Forty Thieves* (Joseph Santley, 1944) and *Three Little Sisters* (Joseph English, 1944); and £4 6s. 6d. a month later for *Call of the South Seas* (John English, 1944) and what appears to be *Sing Your Way Home* (Anthony Mann, 1945). (Liam O'Leary collection, NAI.)

43. *Bioscope*, 9 October 1929:36.   44. Doherty, 1997:51, 83, 94.

45. Ibid., 94. In turn these organists were made redundant in the 1950s as the organs and their pipes were removed from cinemas to make way for the wider screens needed for CinemaScope.

46. *Bioscope*, 20 May 1931:38: It also pointed out that country cinemas were only beginning 'in real earnest' to make the change. *Bioscope* had reported in February 1931 that four or five Belfast cinemas had yet to convert to sound (*Bioscope*, 18 February 1931:44).

47. *Bioscope*, 7 October 1931:42.   48. *Bioscope*, 15 October 1930:38.

49. *KW*, 20 September 1934:18.

50. *KW*, 13 April 1934:42. The dinner took place in Belfast. Guest speaker Plunket Greene, president of the British-based Incorporated Society of Musicians, said that while they had looked to the cinema as the one stronghold of the professional musician, with sound cinema came 'canned music'.
51. *IT*, 31 December 1931:5.
52. May Nevin, *Over the hills*, Dublin: Talbot, 1935:183.
53. Beere, 1936:94.   54. *Dáil debates*, vol. 39, col. 1584, 8 July 1931.
55. More than a decade after its introduction *KW* reported that 'the real bone of contention, and it is one that makes both the circuits and the independents alike in the cities and villages "really burn up", is the ten per cent surcharge imposed by the KRS from the first week's takings to cover import duties. Exhibitors say that this is grossly unfair, and an arbitrary figure.' (*KW* 13 January 1944:90.)
56. During the Dáil debate, Patrick W. Shaw of the ruling party, Cumann na nGaedheal, reported that as the distributors had already notified the exhibitors that they would displace any such increased duty on them (*Dáil debates*, vol. 39, col. 1462, 2 July 1931), he called for an amendment allowing exhibitors to pass on to cinemagoers any surcharge that might be placed on them indirectly by the act. While the opposition spokesman on finance, Fianna Fáil's Seán MacEntee, opposed this concession as it would in effect mean a passing on of the tax 'from the foreign film producer to the native Irish public' (*Dáil debates*, vol. 39, col. 1584, 8 July 1931), the amendment, accepted by the minister for finance, Ernest Blythe, whom the exhibitors had lobbied on the issue, was later approved by the Dáil.
57. *Dáil debates*, vol. 39, col. 1584, 8 July 1931.   58. *KW*, 14 April 1932:55.
59. *KW*, 30 May 1935:18.
60. Seán MacEntee, minister for finance, quoted in Beere, 1936:92.
61. Crowds gathered outside the cinema on opening night, but only four entered. On the second night, the attendance was slightly better, but those who went in were booed and cat-called by the crowd outside. (*KW*, 15 August 1935:19.)
62. Beere, 1936:92.
63. Beere, 1936:94. See appendix, tables 7 and 8 for entertainment tax receipts.
64. Seán McEntee, quoted in Beere, 1936:92.   65. *KW*, 30 May 1935:18.
66. Beere, 1936:90.   67. Ibid., 83.   68. *KW*, 23 April 1936.
69. Beere, 1936:90.   70. Ibid., 97.
71. Ibid., 96. See appendix, table 4 on cinema admissions, see also tables 3a and 3b concerning admissions per head and European ranking.
72. Ibid., 97
73. Simon Rowson, address to the Royal Statistical Society on 17 December 1935, 'A statistical survey of the cinema industry in Great Britain in 1934', *Journal of the Royal Statistical Society*, vol. 99, 1936:67–129.
74. Beere, 1936:85.   75. Ibid., 89.
76. Ibid., 96.   77. Ibid.
78. Ibid., 93, 96–7; Rowson, 1936, quoted in Rachael Low, 1985:2. It is possible that Beere underestimated box office receipts as a government enquiry discussed below recorded that box office in 1939 was 'well over' £1 million, though she felt the need to argue that 18.25 million admissions was not a high figure.
79. This is the figure reported by the joint ITCA/NAIDA committee, which had been set up to counter 'alien penetration' in Irish film exhibition. See 'Drive against British cinema circuits', *TC*, 18 January 1937.
80. Peter de Loughrey (Cumann na Geadheal, Carlow-Kilkenny), *Dáil debates*, vol. 39, col. 1471, 2 July 1931.
81. 'Free State blaze', *Daily Film Renter*, 10 August 1935.
82. The Horgan cinema account books are at IFI.
83. Dr Kiernan responding to Thekla Beere's paper at the Statistical and Social Inquiry Society of Ireland, in Beere 1936:108.
84. J.A.P. [James A. Power], *The Standard*, 6 March 1939:16. The KRS had also faced down similar British co-operative or trade-induced combines, including the large and unwieldy body the Cinema Exhibitors' Association, which had attempted to resist the percentage system imposed with the coming of sound. As Rachael Low comments, the CEA with its 3,000–4,000 members, was 'an ineffective body which tried to represent at the same time the interests of the many independent showmen and [those] of the big circuits. The latter were themselves associated with renting companies and their interests were totally different to those of the small showmen. The CEA's disunity and lack of support for joint action was as marked as the unity of purpose and effectiveness of the KRS.' (Low, 1985:3.)

85. *The Standard*, 13 March 1936.
86. Despite having a similar name to the British exhibitors' body, the Theatre and Cinema Association, the Irish organization was wholly independent of the British society.
87. In March 1935, Erskine Childers (1905–74), eldest son of the author and patriot Robert Erskine Childers, was appointed as NAIDA secretary, a post that appears to have had duties similar to that of administrator. At the time of appointment he was advertising manager of the Fianna Fáil newspaper, the *Irish Press*. From 1938, for thirty-five years, he served continuously as a TD, occupying various ministries in the Dáil including, from 1969 to 1973, that of tánaiste (deputy prime minister). He was elected president of Ireland in succession to Éamon de Valera in 1973 and died in office in 1974.
88. The event received five pages of coverage in the *Irish Press*.
89. *Irish Press*, 5 March 1935:6.
90. *Irish Press*, 19 December 1936:13.
91. *TC*, 22 December 1936:l; *The Cinema*, 22 December 1936; *KW*, 22 December 1936.
92. *TC*, 22 December 1936:l.
93. *IT*, 14 January 1937:4; *The Cinema*, 18 January 1937; *TC*, 18 January 1937; 'Penetration in the Free State; nationalism as a state policy', *KW*, 21 January 1937:41; 'Free State's case against combines', *KW*, 28 January 1937:39.
94. *IT*, 25 April 1935.
95. *IT*, 14 January 1937:4; 'Anti-combine campaign in Dublin', *KW*, 2 September 1937:17.
96. 'Plaza site taken over', *Irish Press*, 17 February 1937:2. William M.M. Curtis, as well as W.M. Middleton, are named in this report as directors of Adelphi Ltd.
97. The McGrath family was the most prominent name associated with the Sweepstakes.
98. Margaret Dickinson and Sarah Street, *Cinema and state: the film industry and the British government, 1927–84*, London: BFI, 1985:101.
99. *IT*, 14 January 1937:4.
1. *KW*, 5 May 1938:26.
2. This was the comment made by T.J.M. Sheehy when J. Arthur Rank took over the Elliman circuit in 1946. See T.J.M. Sheehy, 'Consequences of Mr Rank's move', *Irish Catholic*, 24 January 1946.
3. *IT*, 12 January 1939:2, 3; *Irish Press*, 11 January 1939:5; 13 January 1939:6–7 (advertising feature); *IT*, 13 January 1939:5. J.H. Hamilton, formerly of the Theatre Royal and the Gaiety, was the cinema's first manager.
4. In a departmental memo from finance to the taoiseach's department in 1937, sent in response to Fr Devane's proposal for a film enquiry, finance opposed any restriction on the supply of cinema films: 'The inevitable result of failure to cater for [established audience] taste must be depleted attendances at cinemas, with consequential losses on entertainments tax' of which cinemas provided £230,000 of the £290,000 collected in 1936. The minister for finance at the time was Seán MacEntee. The memo, signed by J.J. McElligott, secretary of the department of finance, 14 July 1937, also pointed out that excise duty would be effected by any quota of foreign films. The document is in department of the taoiseach file S10136, NAI.
5. *TC*, 18 January 1937.
6. By the late 1930s, most of the running of the business was being done by J.J.'s sons Patrick and Peter.
7. *KW*, 13 January 1944:89.
8. Besides the Theatre Royal in Dublin, Elliman's cinemas included the Savoy, Metropole, Queen's, Corinthian, Theatre de Luxe and Phibsboro, while outside of Dublin, he controlled the Savoys in Cork and Limerick, and the Ritzes in Clonmel, Athlone and Carlow.
9. Martin Quigley Jr, 'Exhibition in Éire', *Motion Picture World*, 4 September 1943:56.
10. *KW*, 8 March 1934. Another priest exhibitor was Fr Flynn, who opened the Parochial Hall Cinema, Kilbeggan, Co. Westmeath, in 1945. The films to be shown there were being selected 'under the direction of the priests' and the programmes would be 'clean and healthy' and as such were intended as 'a counter-attraction to the demoralising influence' of a great many modern cinemas. ('Priests sponsor Éire kinema', *KW*, 26 April 1945:54B.)
11. 'Association to protect Éire exhibitors; independents will unite; delegates to meet government', *KW*, 23 March 1939:9.
12. *KW*, 17 December 1936:30.
13. Open, 1985:40–1.
14. *KW*, 7 November 1935:35.
15. *Bioscope*, 4 June 1925:55.
16. Unlike other industries it had a ready supply of attractive venues for social events and an endless stream of high-profile premiere films.
17. *Bioscope*, 21 November 1928:50. The ball attracted 1,000 people in its inaugural year, 1929. It started at 11.30p.m. and continued until dawn.
18. See chapter 3. Nevertheless, it should be noted that the rate of entertainment tax in Northern Ireland remained consistently below that set in the Irish Free State.

19. *KW,* 12 January 1933:17.   20.   *KW,* 30 May 1940:19.
21. The censorship controversy and such key films as *Frankenstein* (1931, which was among the first titles of the horror renaissance and expansion during the thirties), *The Green Pastures* (1936, which combined the powerful elements of race and religion), and the Irish political titles *Ourselves Alone* (1936) and *The Informer* (1935) – all banned by Belfast corporation's police committee – are comprehensively dealt with in John Hill's *Cinema and Northern Ireland: film, culture and politics,* 2006.
22. *Bioscope,* 9 April 1930:44; 3 December 1930:44. In such instances the police remained powerless, unless the local council had also banned the film.
23. *KW,* 1 December 1932:14.   24.   *KW,* 2 May 1935:27.
25. Ibid.   26.   *KW,* 11 July 1935:19.
27. Catholic attitudes to the cinema in the 1920s and 1930s are outlined in chapter 7.
28. *KW,* 12 September 1935:14.   29. *KW,* 26 September 1935:23.
30. *KW,* 3 October 1935:32.
31. *KW,* 17 October 1935:12. This report erroneously says the required distance was 300 *yards,* though this was corrected in its following issue (*KW,* 24 October 1935:31).
32. *Belfast Newsletter,* 2 November 1935:10; *Irish News,* 2 November 1935:3; *KW,* 2 November 1935:10.
33. *KW,* 7 November 1935:35.
34. *KW,* 9 April 1936:23. There was a sequel to these events six years later when a questioner in the Northern Ireland parliament enquired about Bates' possible conflict of interest in the Stadium Cinema decision. He admitted that in his capacity as a solicitor he had registered Irish Theatres Ltd on 28 March 1935, but he had never acted for Shankill Stadium Co. Ltd, which was registered a year later by 'an entirely different solicitor'. (*The Cinema,* 5 August 1942:12.)
35. *KW,* 23 July 1942:3, 39.
36. In his Lenten pastoral of 1937, Dr Kinanne, bishop of the diocese of Waterford and Lismore, gave an anti-cinema response to a recent court judgment by Judge Sealy KC of the Dungarvan circuit court in February 1937. Judge Sealy, recognizing the value of Sunday cinema opening, particularly as Sunday was the only day on which agricultural workers were free to attend entertainments, granted an appeal by exhibitor Daniel Crotty, who had been fined £1 for opening his cinema on a Sunday, something forbidden in his licence. As *KW* noted, the decision 'caused general satisfaction' among Free State exhibitors since Sunday shows were, 'in general, the greatest source of revenue' in cinemas. (*KW,* 11 February 1937:37.) Nevertheless, a minority, including Dr Kinnane, was enraged by the ruling.

    Dr Kinnane, who believed that Sunday closing of cinemas was 'in the public interest', contrasted 'innocent and health-giving' amusements, which were encouraged by the church 'provided they [were] indulged in with due moderation and [did] not interfere with normal recognised devotion', with those, including cinema, horse-racing and dog-racing, which were 'out of harmony with the holiness associated with the Lord's Day.' Castigating Judge Sealy's 'extraordinary decision', which broke the 'long-standing' practice in the diocese of Sunday closing, Dr Kinnane condemned the cinema as 'demoralising', observed that civil judges had 'frequently' drawn attention to its 'baneful influence on adolescents' and suggested that if Sunday opening were allowed he would act to ensure his congregation would not patronize the cinemas by giving Sunday opening 'the protection of absolute prohibition'. Betraying his hostility to the urban, he stated that the court's decision 'presumes to assert that in the public interest country people ... should be lured to towns to spend hours in the unhealthy atmosphere ... watching a travesty of life portrayed by Hollywood artistes!' ('Cinema shows on Sunday; Bishop's strong protest; General tendency demoralising', *IT,* 8 March 1937:7.)
37. Such as at Limerick in 1927 and Dundalk, where Sunday closing was replaced in the 1930s after sustained pressure from exhibitors aggrieved that church-run organizations could open on Sundays while they could not (*KW,* 3 December 1936:39), with a new form of restrictions. To the annoyance of exhibitors, Dundalk council stipulated in 1932 that the proceeds from Sunday shows had to be donated to charity (*KW,* 24 November 1932:30), a practice favouring the Magnet cinema, which was opened by a priest in 1936. According to *KW,* not only had the Magnet unrestricted opening, but also it received favourable rental terms (*KW,* 31 December 1936:37). In late 1938 renewed efforts were made to have the restriction – one of the few in the country – removed (*KW,* 6 October 1938:22), but this did not occur until the mid-1940s.
38. *KW,* 11 March 1937:37.
39. See 'Cinema on Sunday', *Sight and Sound,* vol. 3, no. 9, spring 1934:41.
40. From a survey carried out by the film trade publication *The Cinema,* 1 January 1947:8.

41. *Bioscope*, 20 March 1929:54.   42. *Bioscope*, 25 March 1931:56.
43. *KW*, 15 December 1932:21.
44. The curate had also proposed to show *From the Manger to the Cross* (Sidney Olcott, 1912), which had been reissued with a soundtrack in 1932. While the council rejected the *Angelus*, his own committee rejected *From the Manger to the Cross* on the basis that it would not draw an audience. Steeped in controversy, the film was seen as a 'Protestant' version of the story. (*KW*, 25 December 1938:17A.) For a discussion of the controversy surrounding the film's release in Dublin in 1913, see Rockett, 2004:37–42.
45. In 1935, Belfast's police committee turned down a free Sunday showing of *Modern Palestine*. (*KW*, 7 February 1935:27.)
46. *KW*, 12 January 1933:17.   47. *KW*, 15 February 1934:17.
48. *KW*, 17 May 1934:7.   49. *Northern Whig*, 9 January 1935:9.
50. *KW*, 24 January 1935:34; 14 February 1935:19.
51. *Armagh Guardian*, 15 February 1935:5; 3 March 1935:4. The White Cinema Club was annoyed that the Armagh exhibitors 'had cut the ground from beneath the feet of the club by seeing the commissioner and accepting a compromise in regard to Saturday matinees, Sunday opening and censorship.' (*KW*, 3 March 1935:25.)
52. *Northern Whig*, 15 March 1935:7; *KW*, 21 March 1935.
53. *KW*, 28 March 1935:27.
54. In the style of Irish Free State censors' secrecy about film titles, the attack on the film did not disclose the film's title! (*Armagh Guardian*, 5 April 1935:6.)
55. *KW*, 6 June 1935:20B.   56. *KW*, 1 October 1936:21.
57. *KW*, 13 February 1936:29.   58. *Irish News*, 10 December 1935:5; *KW*, 19 December 1935:15.
59. *KW*, 14 May 1936:33.   60. *KW*, 16 July 1936:50; 11 February 1937:37.
61. *KW*, 9 July 1936:31; 16 July 1936:50; 23 July 1936:2.
62. *KW*, 25 March 1937:16.   63. *KW*, 13 January 1938:33; 12 May 1938:29.
64. It seems that exhibitors were given a free hand with regard to opening hours. (*Bioscope*, 2 January 1929; *Bioscope*, 9 April 1930:44.)
65. *KW*, 11 April 1946:16. The Classic and Ritz, among other cinemas, already closed on Christmas Day. (*KW*, 28 November 1946:19.)
66. *KW*, 17 May 1934:7.   67. *KW*, 26 March 1936:24.
68. *Bioscope*, 9 April 1930:44.
69. In July 1929 *Bioscope* (24 July 1929) reported that one third of Ulster's cinemas were closed at that time for annual summer holidays or as a result of a heat wave. See also *Bioscope*, 28 May 1930:52.
70. *KW*, 5 May 1938:26.
71. As already noted, in Armagh, for instance, though commissioner Hanna maintained a ban on Sunday film shows, a solider was permitted to bring a companion to the Sunday concerts. (*Armagh Guardian*, 12 January 1940:5.)
72. *KW*, 2 May 1940.   73. *KW*, 16 May 1940.
74. *Newtownards Spectator*, 23 November 1940:5, 8.
75. *Newtownards Spectator*, 28 September 1940:5; *KW*, 10 October 1940:17.
76. *KW*, 16 May 1940:24.   77. *KW*, 19 September 1940:19.
78. *KW*, 30 May 1940:19. Coleraine, however, was inconsistent. It approved limited Sunday opening, but reversed that decision in May 1941, stating that a town petition had resulted in 2,397 votes against Sunday opening and only 492 in favour (*KW*, 29 May 1941:8). Accordingly, it refused a request by the military for the use of Coleraine Town Hall, but intimated that it would prefer if the military issued a legal order to requisition the cinema (*TC*, 15 April 1942:19). Resuming its flip-flop policy it granted permission to the Palladium in September 1942 to run Sunday cinema shows for troops (*KW*, 17 September 1942:14).
79. Ballymena 'once again' rejected the application for Sunday opening, despite a plea in person from a military officer. (*KW*, 19 September 1940:19.)
80. *KW*, 19 December 1940:10.   81. *KW*, 10 October 1940:17.
82. *KW*, 19 December 1940:10.   83. Ibid.
84. *KW*, 22 January 1942:42.   85. *KW*, 5 December 1940:22.
86. *KW*, 19 December 1940:10.   87. *KW*, 22 January 1942:42.
88. *KW*, 19 March 1942:12. Twenty members failed to vote, no doubt concerned at their prospect for re-election to the council.
89. *KW*, 19 March 1942:12.
90. *KW*, 26 March 1942:12. The vote was twenty-eight to thirteen against Sunday opening.
91. *TC*, 8 April 1942:25.   92. Ibid.

93. *KW*, 13 November 1941:5.   94. *KW*, 11 December 1941:26; 18 December 1941:23.
95. *KW*, 25 June 1942:12.
96. For a decade after the war, the Imperial was known for its Sunday screenings for troops. (Open, 1985:49.)
97. *TC*, 30 August 1942:27.   98. *KW*, 24 September 1942:1; 8 October 1942:5.
99. *KW*, 18 November 1943:37.
 1. *KW*, 10 August 1944:11; *TC*, 3 May 1944:27.
 2. *TC*, 14 April 1944:3; *KW*, 20 April 1944:17.
 3. *KW*, 3 February 1944:14A   4. *TC*, 30 August 1944:18.
 5. *TC*, 7 September 1944:13.
 6. *KW*, 9 September 1944:45. See also *KW*, 14 September 1944:1 for a report on the Ritz ban, which was resented and protested against by the Northern Ireland trade union movement but welcomed by the Presbyterian church.
 7. Quoted in *TC*, 20 September 1944:21.   8. *KW*, 9 November 1944:45.
 9. *KW*, 22 February 1945:32D; 15 February 1945:11.   10. *KW*, 12 April 1945:39.
11. *KW*, 5 April 1945:8.   12. *KW*, 16 August 1945:53.
13. *TC*, 5 September 1945:29.
14. Attempts to dilute the resistance to Sunday opening at times were made with recourse to high, uplifting or cerebral art. Michael Curran, a member of the province's most prominent exhibition family by the mid-1940s and managing director of Bangor Cinemas Ltd, successfully appealed, at Newtownards quarter sessions, a council decision not to grant a licence for Sunday night symphony concerts at his Tonic cinema. During the sitting, his counsel was careful to declare that 'nothing in the nature of popular melodies or stuff of that kind' nor 'jazz or light comics' would be played. It was clear during the hearing that while Curran would have regarded comedian Jimmy O'Dea as being more commercially viable, he was realistic enough to know that entertainment of that type had little chance of being accepted by the court. (*Newtownards Spectator*, 27 October 1945:3.) Undeterred by the council's refusal to grant a Sunday licence by twelve votes to five, Curran, like others in Belfast and elsewhere, sought to appeal to the county court under the provisions of the Northern Ireland Local Government Act 1934. (*KW*, 18 October 1945:36.)
15. *KW*, 9 May 1946:25.
16. Gordon Duffield, 'The cinema industry is fighting for its life', *Belfast Telegraph*, 14 February 1958:4. Many cinema clubs ran 16mm shows on Sundays.
17. *KW*, 29 October 1959:30.   18. *KW*, 16 June 1966:14.
19. Cinemas that were already in the planning stage or for which sites had been acquired invariably remained undeveloped.
20. *KW*, 29 March 1945:16.   21. *KW*, 16 November 1944:38.
22. *KW*, 17 September 1942:7.   23. *KW*, 28 September 1944:25.
24. *KW*, 22 November 1945.
25. Though *KW* reported in 1944 that there had been no strike or stoppage in the industry for twenty-five years (*KW*, 13 January 1944:90), in fact there had been a cinema strike in 1928. This strike, perhaps the country's first such major dispute, developed in part from personality differences between J.J. Farrell, proprietor of Dublin's Grand Central cinema, and its chief operator, Charles McEvoy, an experienced technician. What seems to have occurred is that McEvoy, who had been working for Farrell for twenty years, was disciplined for smoking a cigarette out of the window of the projection box facing into the auditorium. Rejecting Farrell's censure and eventual dismissal, McEvoy and other workers, who were members of the Workers' Union of Ireland, engaged in a bitter and protracted strike lasting two months. McEvoy and seven others were found guilty and fined under the Dublin Police Act 1842 of 'threatening, abusive and insulting behaviour' of fellow workers and cinema patrons during the strike, occasioning their dismissal. In all, 113 employees, including those at five other Farrell cinemas, were on strike, with the union later seeking reinstatement of the eight defendants. (*Evening Herald*, 11 July 1928; 'Dublin cinema strike', *IT*, 7 September 1928; 'Dublin cinema dispute', 8 September 1928; *KW*, 3 December 1928.) See chapter 1 for an account of the strike at the Theatre de Luxe, Dublin, in 1913.
26. *The Cinema*, 5 December 1945.   27. See Rockett, 2004:363.
28. Maurice Baum, 'Booking problems of Éire managers', *KW*, 11 January 1945:93. At the time, Baum was vice-chairman of the ICTA and booking manager of Dublin Cinemas Ltd.
29. *KW*, 27 December 1945:30.
30. *KW*, 21 September 1944:7. In September 1944 the electricity ration was increased from 40 to 90 per cent, thus allowing for the restoration of normal working hours. However, bus and tram services in Dublin were still ending at 9.30p.m.

31. *Report of the inter-departmental committee on the film industry*, March 1942:6 (unpublished), NAI.
32. *The Cinema*, 6 February 1939.   33. See note 17, p. 497 above.
34. No significant recommendations were made on altering the statutory or administrative functions of the office of official film censor. Indeed, the department of justice refused to join the committee on the basis that it was satisfied with the operation of the censorship regime.
35. The section featured thirteen national examples of how cinema operated under state control. Such state control was a central policy objective of Fr Devane and is discussed in more detail in **chapters** 7 and 8.
36. *Dáil debates*, vol. 91, col. 2081, 16 November 1943; vol. 92, cols 674–5, 14 December 1943; vol. 93, cols 2107–8, 3 May 1944.
37. While the KRS is mentioned in relation to the blacklisting of certain exhibitors who were deemed to be non-compliant with the conditions set by distributors, the information cannot be reasonably considered sensitive or libellous.
38. For a discussion of Lemass' film policy, see Rockett in Rockett et al., 1987:96–100, and Flynn, 2005:166–90.
39. *Report of the inter-departmental committee on the film industry*, 1942:7.
40. In 1938 Dublin corporation had refused a request from exhibitors who sought to stop the granting of a licence for the construction of a new cinema stating that its licensing powers only extended to matters of construction and design.
41. The committee stated that 'a reasonable amount of competition is regarded as desirable.' *Report of the inter-departmental committee on the film industry*, 1942:8.
42. *Report of the inter-departmental committee on the film industry*, 1942:8.
43. Ibid., 9.   44. Ibid., 9–10.   45. Ibid., 10
46. Ibid., 11   47. Ibid., 12.
48. As American producers wished to avoid paying British import duty, the dominant practice was the sending of a single negative to Britain from which copies would be made, only one or two of which would be for the Irish market.
49. American films represented about 80 per cent of the films distributed in Ireland.
50. *Report of the inter-departmental committee on the film industry*, 1942:12.
51. *KW*, 15 August 1935:19. Its offices were at 112 Marlborough Street, Dublin.
52. *KW*, 24 September 1936.   53. *KW*, 15 September 1938:19.
54. *Report of the inter-departmental committee on the film industry*, 1942:13.
55. Ibid.
56. Companies incorporated in the United Kingdom and carrying on business in Ireland paid tax in the UK, while those incorporated in Ireland and carrying on business in Britain paid tax in Ireland.
57. *Report of the inter-departmental committee on the film industry*, 1942:14.
58. Ibid., 16. By 1945, this surcharge had been reduced to 7.5 per cent for American films and 5 per cent for British films. (*KW*, 11 January 1945:93.)
59. While not referring back to the 1924 distributors' boycott over the administration of film censorship that had led to a six-months' withdrawal from the Irish market, it reported on the action taken by American companies in Mexico and Italy 'when State measures threatened their interests.'
60. *Report of the inter-departmental committee on the film industry*, 1942:17.
61. The idea of a film hire tax and a standard renting contract had been made in Beere's 1936 paper (Beere, 1936:100–1).
62. Such a view also accords with Beere's 1936 analysis when she praised the few outlets for continental European films in Ireland in the 1930s, instancing the Irish International Film Agency for 'some very fine German films' recently shown (Beere 1936:102). Beere was also involved in the Irish Film Society.
63. *Report of the inter-departmental committee on the film industry*, 1942:17. Though a production levy on box office receipts known as the Eady levy was introduced in Britain in 1951, in 1968 when Ireland's first statutory investigation of the Irish film industry was established, the exhibitors and distributors joined the committee only after a guarantee was given that there would be no discussion of a production levy on box office receipts. The issue resurfaced in 1996 when Lelia Doolan, chair of the statutory agency the Irish Film Board, called for a levy on cinema seats in order to provide secure funding for Irish films. (Michael Foley, 'Cinema levy call to help finance film production', *IT*, 30 November 1996:16.) Three years later, when Ossie Kilkenny, chair of the strategic review group of the Irish film industry and, from later in 1999, chair of the Irish Film Board, proposed that a 5 per cent levy be placed on cinema admissions and on videos as a means of financing Irish films, arts minister Síle de Valera vetoed the proposal. The minister's stance was taken 'fol-

lowing extensive lobbying from some film companies and distributors opposed to the levy's intro-duction.' (See Richard Oakley, 'De Valera vetoes cinema ticket levy', *Sunday Tribune*, 5 December 1999:5. See also Philip Molloy, 'Cinema ticket levy to fund expansion', *Irish Independent*, 5 August 1999:3. Most of the journalistic comment was hostile to the proposal: Ian Kilroy, 'Film goers face new cinema levy', *Sunday Tribune*, 25 July 1999:5; Eamon Timmins, *IT*, 4 August 1999:6; Eamon Timmins, *IT*, 5 August 1999:9; Mary Carr, 'Don't shoot the film fans', *Evening Herald*, 7 August 1999:4; Jonathan Philbin Bowman, *Sunday Independent*, 15 August 1999:13; Philip Howick, 'What a really good idea', *Evening Herald*, 6 August 1999:14; and from Fine Gael arts' spokesman Brian Hayes, *Irish Independent*, 7 August 1999:3.) The report's full title is *The strategic development of the Irish film and television industry, 2000–2010: final report of the film industry review group to the minister for arts, heritage, gaeltacht and the islands*, Dublin: Stationery Office, 1999.

64. *Report of the inter-departmental committee on the film industry*, 1942:14.
65. Beere reported that 'the average earning power for a film in Ireland is assumed by the distributors to be worth only about 3% of the total for Great Britain and Ireland.' (Beere 1936:101.)
66. *Report of the inter-departmental committee on the film industry*, 1942:13.
67. Ibid., 16.
68. Some renting was carried out on a fixed or 'flat rate' such as X pounds per screening.
69. Film contracts would state whether or not a particular film was exclusive, and for what length of time it was exclusive to a particular venue.
70. *Report of the inter-departmental committee on the film industry*, 1942:15.

CHAPTER 3

1. Colman Conroy, former manager of Savoys in Dublin, Cork and Limerick, and personal assistant to Louis Elliman, quoted, 'Colman Conroy memories', *Evening Herald*, 31 August 1972:11.
2. Opening programme, Strand, Liam O'Leary collection, NAI.
3. The film's distributor was Gaumont-British. Screened in a trade show in October, it went on gen-eral release in May 1936. Though it was well received, confirming Rank's opinion on the nature of distribution, it was given few screenings.
4. The company was registered with capital of just over a quarter of a million pounds, while the board included Lindenburg, Rank and L.A. Neel, who was film producer Max Schach's colleague from Capitol. Woolfe was able to consider setting up the new operation as he was guaranteed product from Schach, whose associates included Herbert Wilcox. (Wilcox, who had been born in Cork, had helped to found in the mid-1920s Elstree Studios where Rank's first feature film was made. He was also head of British and Dominion Film Corporation, an important production company during the interwar period with links in the 1930s to both Paramount and United Artists. The company was eventually incorporated into Rank's organization.)
5. According to Rachael Low (1985:210) the GCFC was registered in Britain in March 1936.
6. In November 1939, Odeon Theatres had already leased the Paramount cinemas at Leeds, Manchester and Newcastle, as well as the four London suburban Astorias.
7. In 1956, Rank agreed to pay Paramount £1,850,000 over twenty years for their freehold and leas-ing interests of the seven cinemas. (Eyles, 2005:52.)
8. Eyles, 2005:11. While Rank announced that he wanted a few more cinemas, in fact he never reached the permitted total.
9. Though it is beyond the immediate scope of this book, during 1947–8 when there was an effective eight-month boycott of the British market by American companies following the imposition of penal import duty of 75 per cent on foreign films, Rank massively increased film production, investing nearly £10 million in forty-seven films. However, by the time the films were ready for release, the duty, introduced to stem distributors repatriating profits ($70 million in 1947) at a time of eco-nomic crisis in Britain, was lifted. This resulted in an influx of American product, which once again outperformed British films at the box office. A compromise with Hollywood studios had been bro-kered which reduced to $17 million the annual sum allowed for repatriation annually, with the bal-ance to be invested in Britain. (See Roy Armes, *A critical history of British cinema*, New York: Oxford UP, 1978:171–2.)
10. See ibid., 171. Despite the sharp decline in the 1950s in the scale and quantity of its films compared to its 1940s productions, Rank produced a number of popular, if modest, films, including the *Doctor* series.
11. Eyles, 2005:39.
12. Raymond J. Raymond, 'Behind the special relationship: Anglo-American commercial rivalry in Ireland, 1939–45', *Administration*, vol. 34, no. 3, 1986:364–5.

13. *Daily Film Renter*, 13 November 1946. The figures were compiled by the department of industry and commerce.
14. *KW*, 16 August 1945:61.　15. *TC*, 7 August 1945.
16. As Diane Collins records in *Hollywood down under: Australians at the movies, 1896 to the present day* (New South Wales/London: Angus and Robertson, 1987:17), Rank's entry into the Australian market in 1946, when it bought the second-largest Australian film chain, confirmed foreign dominance within Australian film exhibition. In 1930, Fox Film Corporation of America had taken over Australia's largest exhibition circuit. In a comment that could equally apply to Ireland, Collins states that 'for more than 30 years the two major exhibition circuits were to be wholly or substantially foreign-owned.' In Ireland's case the two foreign exhibition players were Rank and ABC.
　　In passing, it is worth noting another aspect of the Australian film experience. While Ireland had an estimated 21 million admissions in 1944 (USA department of commerce inquiry reference service, *Motion picture markets: Europe; Éire*, 1944:1), Australia had 151 million admissions in 1945 (Collins, 1987:213), even though its population was less than two-and-a-half times that of Ireland. The per capita disparity between the two countries may in part be explained by the effects of a war-time boom and the presence of large numbers of American soldiers in Australia, while Ireland's supply of films was restricted by Emergency Powers Orders. Nevertheless, these factors can hardly account for an Australian per capita cinema attendance three times that for Ireland.
17. 'Mr Rank may build studio in Ireland', *IT*, 20 December 1945:1.
18. Opened in 1936 by film impresario Alexander Korda, the largest production facility in Britain complete with seven sound stages and a Technicolour laboratory, it was merged with Rank's nearby Pinewood Studios in 1939.
19. Both the Theatre Royal and Regal Rooms were controlled by the Dublin Theatre Company, a wholly owned subsidiary of the public company Irish Cinemas, which, as noted in **chapter 2**, had been established in 1934 to take over the assets of Associated Irish Cinemas.
20. 'J.A. Rank acquires big Irish cinema interest', *IT*, 19 January 1946:1. In 1946, the directors of Irish Cinemas Ltd were John McCann, chairman; George J. Nesbitt, vice-chairman; Maurice Elliman, managing director; J.J. Roche; P.J. Wall; and Horace Moore.
21. *Daily Film Renter*, 21 January 1946.　　22. *IT* 21 January 1946:5.
23. *IT*, 19 January 1946:6.　　24. *IT* 4 February 1946:5.
25. T.J.M. Sheehy, *Irish Catholic*, 10 January 1946:1; T.J.M. Sheehy, 'Mostly about Mr Rank', *Irish Catholic*, 17 January 1946:1. Sheehy had made comments about Rank's expansion into Ireland periodically in his column during the previous year.
26. T.J.M. Sheehy, 'Monopoly is dangerous', *Irish Catholic*, 11 April 1946:1.
27. *KW*, 2 May 1946:17.　　28. Quoted in *KW*, 2 May 1946:17.
29. T.J.M. Sheehy, *Irish Catholic*, 11 April 1946:1.
30. 'Mr Rank's exemplary character does not come into this question' as he put it. (T.J.M. Sheehy, *Irish Catholic*, 11 April 1946:1.)
31. T.J.M. Sheehy, 'Mostly about Mr Rank', *Irish Catholic*, 17 January 1946:1. Sheehy hoped that such films would also be released in Dublin.
32. T.J.M. Sheehy, 'My interview with Mr Rank', *Irish Catholic*, 7 February 1946:1, 5. The children's cinema clubs were the main subject of the interview. This issue is discussed in chapter 8.
33. Rank's Irish deal', *The Cinema*, 27 March 1946.
34. *Dáil debates*, vol. 100, col. 3, 20 March 1946.
35. Paul Bew and Henry Patterson, *Seán Lemass and the making of modern Ireland, 1945–66*, Dublin: Gill and Macmillan, 1982:20.
36. The company was a reconstitution of Patrick Whelan's Associated Picture Houses Ltd, following his death in 1944.
37. Department of industry and commerce memo for the government, August 1950:1, in department of the taoiseach file S14892A, NAI.
38. 'Camden closes down after 36 years', *Evening Herald*, 28 August 1948.
39. Department of industry and commerce memo for the government, August 1950:2, in department of the taoiseach file S14892A, NAI.
40. *Irish Catholic*, 24 March 1949:1; 31 March 1949:l.
41. *Dáil debates*, vol. 114, col. 2227, 5 April 1949.
42. Department of industry and commerce memo, August 1950:2, department of the taoiseach file S14892A, NAI.
43. Ibid., 3.
44. These individuals, including Louis Elliman, who handled the Rank-owned cinemas, are listed as trade bookers in the *Cinema & theatre annual review and directory of Ireland 1947*, 1947:55–9.

As is the case throughout the history of Irish cinemas, where buying and selling of cinemas was an ongoing activity, there are overlapping directorships and at times unclear ownership patterns.

45. The discussion by the Catholic hierarchy took place on 18 April 1950. Bishop Staunton to John A. Costello, 21 April 1950, department of the taoiseach file S14892A, NAI.

46. John A. Costello to Bishop Staunton, 25 April 1950, quoted, department of the taoiseach file S14892A, NAI.

47. Department of the taoiseach to department of industry and commerce, 23 May 1950, department of the taoiseach file S14892A, NAI.

48. Department of industry and commerce to department of the taoiseach, 16 June 1950:2, department of the taoiseach file S14892A, NAI.

49. Eyles, 2005:29. Given that the decline in admissions continued with a further 228 million gone by 1953, it is clear that the issue of product was not the only factor behind the decline. The increasing availability of television and other leisure activities, as well as the demographic shift to the suburbs where new cinemas were slow to be built, were the main catalysts behind the decline.

50. The company through which Rank owned this new 1,088-seat Dublin cinema was Irish Cinemas Ltd. This brought Rank's total seat number in the Republic to 24,319.

51. Eyles, 2005:61. It is unclear whether Rank's single cinema in Northern Ireland, Belfast's Classic, known from 1950 as the Gaumont, is being treated here as part of the British/UK figure, though Eyles (2005:61) treats Rank's Northern Ireland acquisitions in the mid-1950s as 'overseas'.

52. The Coliseum was put up for sale in 1957, but remained unsold in 1959 when a price of £11,000 was put on it. (*KW*, 29 January 1959:21.)

53. Eyles, 2005:61. According to *KW*, 12 July 1956:34, the deal with George Lodge's Irish Theatres Ltd was concluded in February 1956, and was for eleven cinemas at a cost of £500,000.

54. *KW*, 1 August 1946:22; *TC*, 30 July 1946:9. An undisclosed 'hitch' affected the deal (*KW*, 6 March 1947:26), and almost immediately the M.J. Curran circuit bought the cinema and took it over in August 1947. (*TC*, 5 March 1947:31.)

55. 'Curran-Rank handover bid', *KW*, 12 July 1956:34. A 1,000-seat cinema in the Rathcoole housing estate, Belfast, was being completed by Currans, while two other Belfast cinemas were planned: a 1,600-seater in Andersonstown and a 1,300-seater in the Cregagh housing estate. However, in September 1957, the Currans' decision not to renew the lease on the Frontier, Newry, was a signal that they had left the cinema business altogether. (*KW*, 26 September 1957:7. See also Eyles, 2005:61–2.)

56. Gaumont, formerly the Classic, 13–25 Castle Lane, Belfast.

57. *KW*, 28 February 1946:18.

58. Following renovations, the cinema reopened in October 1961 with 1,150 seats.

59. In addition, duties of 8*d*. per foot of negative and 0.5*d*. raw stock (the latter impacting on the costs of home production) were charged, though, following demands by the KMA (Kinematograph Manufactures' Association) these rates were reduced to 5*d*. and 0.33*d*. respectively. (*KYB*, 1916:21; *Bioscope*, 16 December 1915:1193.) To help protect Britain as a world film market, two years later, bonded film stores were opened where bulk film could be broken down and films screened, cut, titled or retitled without duty being paid. (See Low, 1950:111–13.) This meant, for example, that in the case of Ireland after 1922, importing an American film through London, the established route, only one duty would be charged to the film. In other words, the American film was subject to no import duty in Britain so long as it was kept in the bonded warehouse and the Irish distributor would only pay import duty to the Irish government if the Irish film censor passed the film for release. If the censor rejected the film, no import duty would be incurred, as the film would be returned to the British bonded store. If the film was cut, only the actual footage of film passed would be charged.

60. For example, in one month in spring 1917, the British film censors passed for exhibition 405,000 feet of foreign films and only 27,000 feet, or 6.25 per cent, of new British film. (Low, 1950:66.)

61. American films accounted for 92 per cent of film imports into Britain in 1915 and 98 per cent in 1916 (Low, 1950:40). The custom duty was charged on all imported film, even film shot by British production companies working overseas. In 1919, a preferential duty was introduced for such British-produced film. In *KYB*, 1923:23, it is stated that 'the British producer has obtained considerable relief ... as regulations have been framed by the Customs authorities permitting import into this country by payment of only one-third of a penny per foot, as against five pence per foot, on negative film exposed by a British producing unit.' In the 1923 Finance Act, this was extended to include films in which 75 per cent of the artists were British.

62. A film could not be admitted to this preferential rate unless a minimum of a quarter of the labour was done within the British empire. (Beere, 1936:99.) Later, the 10 per cent surcharge seems to have been imposed on all feature films.

63. With effect from 1 October 1918, ET rates were as follows. Seats under 2*d*.: 0.5*d*. tax; seats 2.5*d*. to 3*d*.: 0.5*d*. tax (a decrease of 0.5*d*.); seats 3*d*. to 4*d*.: 1*d*. tax (unchanged); seats 4.5*d*. to 7*d*.: 2*d*. tax (a reduction of 1*d*. on 6.5*d*. to 7*d*. seats); seats 8*d*. to 1*s*.: 3*d*. tax (unchanged); seats 1*s*. 1*d*. to 2*s*.: 4*d*. tax (unchanged); seats 2*s*. 1*d*. to 3*s*.: 6*d*. tax (unchanged); seats 10*s*. 6*d*. to 15*s*.: 2*s*. tax. In October 1919, the tax on the 4.5*d*. base ticket price was reduced from 2*d*. to 1.5*d*. These rates remained unchanged in the Irish Free State until 1931, with the exception of tickets costing 4*d*. or less being made exempt from tax in 1928, a situation which pertained until 1947. In all cases the seat price is the base price without duty added. See Beere, 1936:91.
64. Hugh Pollock, *Northern Ireland parliamentary debates*, vol. 4, col. 1048, 21 May 1924.
65. James Augustine Duff, ibid., cols 1058–9, 21 May 1924.
66. Sir Crawford McCullagh, ibid., col. 1118, 26 May 1924.
67. Samuel Kyle, ibid., vol. 6, cols 525–6, 12 May 1925.
68. Joseph Devlin, ibid., cols 527–8, 12 May 1925. 69. Ibid., col. 529.
70. Hugh Pollock, ibid., col. 530, 12 May 1925. 71. Ibid., cols 531–2.
72. Hugh Pollock, ibid., vol. 7, col. 1669, 14 October 1926.
73. Hugh Pollock, ibid., vol. 8, col. 1334, 11 May 1927. 74. Ibid., col. 1333.
75. Hugh Pollock, ibid., col. 1417, 12 May 1927.
76. Hugh Pollock, ibid., col. 1332–3, 11 May 1927.
77. Joseph Devlin, ibid., col. 1379, 12 May 1927.
78. Joseph Devlin, ibid., vol. 9, col. 2014, 23 May 1928.
79. Hugh Pollock, ibid., col. 2067, 22 May 1928.
80. *Bioscope*, 22 March 1929:32; 20 March 1929:54; 27 February 1929:54.
81. *Bioscope*, 26 February 1930:44; 12 March 1930:44; 26 March 1930:52.
82. *Bioscope*, 18 February 1931:4. 83. *Bioscope*, 13 May 1931:40.
84. *Bioscope*, 23 September 1931:46.
85. The rates for the more expensive seats in the period from August 1918 to the meeting in 1926 (and, with some small exceptions, to October 1932) were: 6.5*d*. to 7*d*. seats: 2*d*. tax; 8*d*. to 12*d*. seats: 3*d*. tax; 1*s*. 1*d*. to 2*s*. seats: 4*d*. tax; and 2*s*. 1*d*. to 3*s*. seats: 6*d*. tax. (In all cases the seat price listed is that before duty was added; see Beere, 1936:91.)
86. *Bioscope*, 25 March 1926:44. The report names one of the delegation as I.I. Bradlaugh, but this is almost certainly a misspelling of Bradlaw.
87. Effective from 1 October 1931, tax on seats priced 5*d*. to 5.5*d*. (excluding duty) was reduced from 2*d*. (the rate since October 1917) to 1.5*d*. (25 per cent reduction); tax on seats priced 8*d*. (excluding duty) was reduced from 3*d*. (the rate since October 1917) to 2*d*. (33 per cent reduction); tax on seats priced 1*s*. 1*d*. (excluding duty) was reduced from 4*d*. (the rate since October 1917) to 3*d*. (25 per cent reduction); and tax on seats priced 2*s*. 1*d*. to 2*s*. 2*d*. (excluding duty) was reduced from 6*d*. (the rate since October 1917) to 4*d*. (33 per cent reduction). (Beere, 1936:91.)
88. While the tax rate on seats priced 4.5*d*. to 7*d*. remained static in August 1935, with the exception of the 6.5*d*. seats which rose by only 0.5*d*. to 2*d*., all dearer seats rose considerably with tax rates increased from increases of 50 per cent to 125 per cent. Seats 8*d*. attracted an increase of 1.5*d*., from 2*d*. to 3.5*d*. which represented a 75 per cent increase (though from October 1917 to October 1931 the tax had been 3*d*.); 8.5*d*. seats also had a 3.5*d*. tax applied (an increase of 0.5*d*.); an increase of 50 per cent effected 9*d*. to 11.5*d*. seats which now had a tax of 4.5*d*. (since October 1917 these had attracted a duty of 3*d*.); 1*s*. seats moved from the rate of 3*d*. set in October 1917 to 6*d*. (100 per cent increase); 1*s*. 1*d*. to 1*s*. 6*d*. increased by 2*d*. to 6*d*. (50 per cent); 1*s*. 7*d*. to 1*s*. 8*d*. increased by 5*d*. to 9*d*. (125 per cent); 1*s*. 9*d*. to 1*s*. 10*d*. increased by 3*d*. to 9*d*. (50 per cent); 1*s*. 11*d*. to 2*s*. increased by 7.5*d*. to 1*s*. 1.5*d*. (125 per cent; though prior to October 1932 from October 1917 the tax had only been 4*d*., if benchmarked against this figure the increase was almost 240 per cent); and 2*s*. 1*d*. to 2*s*. 11*d*. increased by 4.5*d*. to 1*s*. (50 per cent); and finally, the tax on 3*s*. seats doubled from the rate set in October 1932 to 1*s*. 6*d*., however this was three times the rate of 6*d*. set in October 1917. (In all cases the seat price listed above is that before the addition of duty.) (Beere, 1936:91.)
89. In July 1936 the tax on seats priced 6.5*d*. was returned to its pre-August 1935 level of 1.5*d*.; the tax on 8*d*. and 8.5*d*. seats was reduced by 0.5*d*. to 3*d*.; and the tax on 9*d*. seats reduced by 1.5*d*. to 3*d*. (Beere, 1936:91.)
90. By 1939 ET revenue was £326,367. During the same decade, custom duty increased from £22,388 in 1930 to £63,666 in 1939. See appendix, table 7.
91. *KW*, 28 May 1936:28.
92. British house of commons, *Parliamentary debates*, fifth series, vol. 363, 23 July 1940:663. The other ET rates were: 6.25*d*. to 7*d*.: 1*d*. tax; 7*d*. to 7.75*d*.: 1.25*d*. tax; 7.75*d*. to 8.75*d*.: 2*d*. tax;

8.75*d*. to 11*d*.: 3*d*. tax; 11*d*. to 1*s*. 2*d*.: 4*d*. tax; 1*s*. 2*d*. to 1*s*. 5*d*.: 5*d*. tax; 5*d*. tax for the first 1*s*. 5*d*. and an additional 2*d*. for every 6*d*. or part of 6*d*. over 1*s*. 6*d*.

93. *Northern Ireland parliamentary debates*, vol. 23, 6 August 1940:1898–9; *KW*, 5 December 1940:22.

94. From 10 May 1942, British ET rates doubled, except where the amount of the payment including the duty already charged did not exceed 7*d*. (British house of commons, *Parliamentary debates*, fifth series, vol. 379, col. 145, 14 April 1942.)

95. British house of commons, *Parliamentary debates*, fifth series, vol. 388, cols 980–2, 12 April 1943.

96. *Northern Ireland parliamentary debates*, vol. 26, 18 May 1943:626–7.

97. *KW*, 6 June 1935:20B.

98. Frank Aiken, minister for finance, *Dáil debates*, vol. 105, cols 2241, 2243, 7 May 1947. The rates of entertainments tax from 15 August 1947 (amending subsection (2) of section 11 of the 1936 Finance Act, no. 31 of 1936): 4*d*. to 4.5*d*.: 1.5*d*. tax; 4.5*d*. to 6*d*.: 2*d*. tax; 6*d*. to 7*d*.: 3*d*. tax; 7*d*. to 9*d*.: 5*d*. tax; 9*d*. to 1*s*. 0.5*d*.: 7.5*d*. tax; 1*s*. 0.5*d*. to 1*s*. 4*d*.: 10*d*. tax; 1*s*. 4*d*. to 2*s*.:1*s*. 3*d*. tax; 2*s*. to 2*s*. 10.5*d*.: 2*s*. 1.5*d*. tax; 2*s*. 10.5*d*. to 4*s*.: 3*s*. tax; 3*s*. tax on first 4*s*. and 3*s*. for every additional 4*s*. or part of 4*s*. (Financial resolution no. 6 – excise, *Dáil debates*, vol. 105, 7 May 1947.)

99. Frank Aiken, *Dáil debates*, vol. 108, col. 1047, 29 October 1947.

1. The rates of entertainments tax from 16 January 1948 (amending subsection (2) of section 11 of the 1936 Finance Act (no. 31 of 1936), and replacing subsection (2), section 10 of the 1947 Finance Act (no. 15 of 1947), were: 4*d*. to 5*d*. (3*d*. tax); 5*d*. to 6*d*. (4*d*. tax); 6*d*. to 6.5*d*. (5.5*d*. tax); 6.5*d*. to 8*d*. (8*d*. tax); 8*d*. to 10*d*. (10*d*. tax); 10*d*. to 1*s*. 1*d*. (1*s*. 3*d*. tax); 1*s*. 1*d*. to 1*s*. 4*d*. (1*s*. 8*d*. tax); 1*s*. 4*d*. to 1*s*. 6*d*. (2*s*. tax); 1*s*. 6*d*. to 1*s*. 9*d*. (2*s*. 6*d*. tax); 1*s*. 9*d*. to 2*s*. (3*s*. tax); and 2*s*. to 3*s*. (4*s*. 6*d*. tax); 3*s*. to 4*s*. (6*s*. tax); and 6*s*. tax for every additional 4*s*. or part of 4*s*. (Financial resolution no. 8, excise, *Dáil debates*, vol. 108, col. 1045, 29 October 1947.)

2. James Everett, *Dáil debates*, vol. 105, col. 2286, 7 May 1947.

3. Daniel Morrissey, *Dáil debates*, vol. 108, col. 1046, 29 October 1947. Both Everett and Morrissey became ministers in the inter-party government formed on 18 February 1948.

4. Fianna Fáil leaders engaged in a virulent denunciation of the film, which featured three of the party's most prominent figures, including leader Seán MacBride. See Rockett, 1987:76–80.

5. 'Éire's fight against E.T. is real Irish', *Daily Film Renter*, 18 February 1948.

6. *Dáil debates*, vol. 111, cols 1049–51, 15 June 1948.

7. See appendix for the annual sums of ET collected, table 7 (Irish Free State/Republic of Ireland) and table 8 (Northern Ireland).

8. 'Éire tax rebate increases 16mm shows', *KW*, 21 July 1949. This figure includes those projectors in use in schools and other institutions apart from ordinary commercial users. In its 1945 report on the 'Postwar potentialities for motion-picture equipment in the United Kingdom and Éire', the industrial reference service of the USA department of commerce (vol. 3, part 3, no. 19, August 1945:3–4) reported that few primary or secondary schools, and only three technical schools, had motion-picture sound equipment. However, 'there is a definite trend towards the use of visual education in schools' and a good market for 16mm equipment was anticipated in the post-war period. Nevertheless, 'generally speaking, the public in Éire has only reached the experimental state with 16mm films.' In 1958, *KW* reported (30 January 1958), that there were 220 16mm locations, most of which operated as mobile cinemas, particularly along the western seaboard. In addition, there were 400 projectors in schools, colleges, hospitals and other institutions.

9. *KW*, 21 July 1949.

10. Commercial 16mm shows were liable to tax in the normal way, so this promotion is somewhat misleading. However, 16mm *educational* film shows were free of tax, and, as is discussed in chapter 8, the National Film Institute of Ireland was to the forefront in distributing such 16mm films. However, some 16mm operators seem to have tried to disguise commercial film shows as ET tax-free educational events.

11. See *KW*, 20 March 1958.

12. British house of commons *Parliamentary debates*, fifth series, vol. 449, col. 73, 6 April 1948.

13. Confining it to venues of under 200 people meant that it was designed to 'prevent any drawing off of patrons from places of entertainment in … cities and towns still subject to tax.' (Major J.M. Sinclair, *Northern Ireland parliamentary debates*, vol. 32, col. 1267, 5 May 1948.)

14. Ibid., col. 1268.   15. *Dáil debates*, vol. 113, cols 1527–8, 15 December 1948.

16. Minister for finance Patrick McGilligan argued that 'for all practical purposes the only entertainments held in these areas which are subject to duty are cinema shows and ciné-variety performances. They are operated either by resident exhibitors or by mobile film units, and it has been represented to me that the promoters find it extremely difficult to meet expenses, and that any profits are extremely meagre. There is no doubt that these entertainments do much to brighten life in rural

areas.' The concession cost about £21,000 in 1949 and £25,000 in a full year. In the same budget, the minister removed import duty on newsreels as a means of encouraging distributors to renew imports, which had ceased during the Second World War. Ireland was in 'the unique position that no news-reels are shown here'. (*Dáil debates*, vol. 115, col. 476, 4 May 1949.) Following the publication of the 1951 census of population, some areas found that the 500 population limit had been breached, thus depriving the area of the ET exemption. As a result, the 1953 Finance Act provided for a two-year extension in the use of the 1946 census data for the purposes of such population limits. (*Dáil debates*, vol. 140, cols 708–15, 8 July 1953.)

17. Major J.M. Sinclair, *Northern Ireland parliamentary debates*, vol. 33, cols 875–6, 17 May 1949.
18. Major J.M. Sinclair, ibid., vol. 35, col. 1033, 16 May 1951.
19. Major J.M. Sinclair, ibid., vol. 36, col. 994, 28 May 1952. The revised rates are listed in cols 1008–9.
20. Brian Maginnis, ibid., vol. 38, col. 1801, 1816–17, 4 May 1954.
21. Brian Maginnis, ibid., vol. 39, col. 1384, 17 May 1955.
22. George Boyle Hanna, ibid., vol. 40, col. 1350, 22 May 1956.
23. In the main, the cinemas were charging admission prices as low as 4*d.* tax free, with the tax rising from 1.5*d.* on a 6*d.* seat to 5*d.* on a 1*s.* 3*d.* seat. 'Ireland has its ET troubles', *TC*, 17 April 1953.
24. The 1951 order was lifted by minister for industry and commerce, Seán Lemass. See 'Seat prices "decontrolled" – in Ireland', *TC*, 26 January 1953.
25. *TC*, 17 April 1953.
26. *Dáil debates*, vol. 138, col. 1211, 6 May 1953; vol. 139, col. 262, 28 May 1953. The new ET rates effective from 1 September 1953 were: 4*d.* to 4.5*d.*: 0.5*d.* tax; 4.5*d.* to 5*d.*: 1*d.* tax; 5*d.* to 6.5*d.*: 1.5*d.* tax; 6.5*d.* to 8*d.*: 2*d.* tax; 8*d.* to 9*d.*: 3*d.* tax; 9*d.* to 10.5*d.*: 4.5*d.* tax; 10.5*d.* to 1*s.*: 6*d.* tax; 1*s.* to 1*s.* 1*d.*: 7*d.* tax; 1*s.* 1*d.* to 1*s.* 3*d.*: 9*d.* tax; 1*s.* 3*d.* to 1*s.* 5*d.*: 10*d.* tax; 1*s.* 5*d.* to 1*s.* 6*d.*: 1*s.* tax; over 1*s.* 6*d.*: 1*s.* tax on the first 1*s.* 6*d.* and 3*d.* tax for every additional 3*d.* or part of 3*d.* (Section 4, 1953 Finance Act, no. 21 of 1953.)
27. *TC*, 12 May 1953.
28. Section 6 of the 1953 Finance Act provided for the repayment of one-half of the entertainments duty paid in respect of entertainments which were wholly cinematographic performances and which, while not qualifying for existing exemption in respect of entertainments which were wholly of an educational character, could be said to be educational in the sense that they encouraged or facilitated the study of languages. It provided for relief where at least one-third of the entertainment consisted of Irish language films or where one-half consisted of films in, for example, a continental language.
29. *Dáil debates*, vol. 169, col. 183, 18 June 1958.
30. Section 16 of the 1956 Finance Act provided an exemption from entertainments duty for any entertainment consisting wholly of an Irish language film show.
31. *Dáil debates*, vol. 145, cols 563–4, 21 April 1954. See appendix, table 7.
32. *Dáil debates*, vol. 161, col. 951, 8 May 1957. The ET scale with effect from 1 August 1957 was: 5*d.* to 5.5*d.*: 0.5*d.* tax; 5.5*d.* to 6*d.*: 1*d.* tax; 6*d.* to 7.5*d.*: 1.5*d.* tax; 7.5*d.* to 8*d.*: 2*d.* tax; 8*d.* to 8.5*d.*: 2.5*d.* tax; 8.5*d.* to 10*d.*: 3*d.* tax; 10*d.* to 11.5*d.*: 4.5*d.* tax; 11.5*d.* to 1*s.* 1*d.*: 6*d.* tax; 1*s.* 1*d.* to 1*s.* 2*d.*: 7*d.* tax; 1*s.* 2*d.* to 1*s.* 4*d.*: 9*d.* tax; 1*s.* 4*d.* to 1*s.* 5.25*d.*: 10*d.* tax; 1*s.* 5.25*d.* to 1*s.* 7*d.*: 1*s.* tax; 1*s.* 7*d.* to 1*s.* 8*d.*: 1*s.* 1*d.* tax; 1*s.* 8*d.* to 1*s.* 9*d.*: 1*s.* 3*d.* tax; 1*s.* 3*d.* tax for the first 1*s.* 9*d.* and 0.5*d.* tax for every additional 0.5*d.* or part of 0.5*d.* (Section 12, Finance Act 1957, no. 20 of 1957.)
33. *KW*, 27 February 1958:28.
34. *Dáil debates*, vol. 167, col. 643, 23 April 1958.
35. *Variety*, 16 April 1958; 'Rank's Irish cinemas maintain profits', *KW*, 24 October 1957:7.
36. *Dáil debates*, vol. 167, col. 610, 23 April 1958.
37. *Dáil debates*, vol. 174, col. 360, 15 April 1959. Section 7 of the 1955 Finance Act had reduced from 35 per cent to 25 per cent the minimum proportion of a cine-variety programme in a patent theatre which had to consist of a personal performance so that the entertainment might qualify for the 30 per cent repayment of entertainment duty allowable under the Finance Act of 1948, subsection (10), section 4, paragraph C. At that time, the minister for finance told the senate that 'the qualifying conditions [were] intended mainly to help the management of Dublin's Theatre Royal to maintain the stage show as part of the theatre's entertainment and so preclude as far as possible the danger of unemployment amongst musicians, stage hands, etc.' (*Seanad debates*, vol. 45, col. 12, 30 June 1955.)
38. *Dáil debates*, vol. 174, col. 360, 15 April 1959. The ET rates from 1 August 1959 were 8*d.* to 8.5*d.*: 0.5*d.* tax; 8.5*d.* to 9*d.*: 1*d.* tax; 9*d.* to 9.5*d.*: 1.5*d.* tax; 9.5*d.* to 11*d.*: 2*d.* tax; 11*d.* to 1*s.* 0.5*d.*: 3.5*d.* tax; 1*s.* 0.5*d.* to 1*s.* 2*d.*: 5*d.* tax; 1*s.* 2*d.* to 1*s.* 3*d.*: 6*d.* tax; 1*s.* 3*d.* to 1*s.* 5.5*d.*: 7.5*d.* tax; 1*s.* 5.5*d.* to 1*s.* 7*d.*: 9*d.* tax; 1*s.* 7*d.* to 1*s.* 8.5*d.*: 10.5*d.* tax; 1*s.* 8.5*d.* to 1*s.* 10*d.*:11*d.* tax; 1*s.* 10*d.* to

1s. 11d.: 1s. 1d. tax; 1s. 11d. + : 1s. 1d. for the first 1s. 11d. and 0.5d. for every additional 0.5d. or part of 0.5d. (Section 17, Finance Act 1959, no. 18 of 1959.)

39. Labour Party deputy Denis Larkin pointed out that many urban cinemas were in as difficult a financial state as the provincial ones, adding that there had been 'a very substantial falling-off in attendances' to such an extent that there was 'quite a serious danger of a number of them actually closing.' (*Dáil debates*, vol. 176, col. 227, 30 May 1959.)

40. *Dáil debates*, vol. 176, col. 226, 30 May 1959.   41. *KW*, 11 September 1958:9.

42. Cinema entertainments tax revenue was £1,288,167 in 1958 and £1,298,002 in 1959, a difference of only 0.76 per cent. (See appendix, table 7.)

43. *Irish Trade Journal and Statistical Bulletin*, no. 1, vol. 36, March 1961:19. A note accompanying the table draws attention to the fact that the figures are not comparable over the whole period 1950–60 due to changes to entertainments tax introduced in the 1954 Finance Act. This is a slightly revised table, and with the addition of 1960, to that carried in ibid., vol. 35, no. 1, March 1960:41.

44. *KW*, 8 September 1960:1.   45. *Dáil debates*, vol. 180, cols 631–2, 640–3, 16 March 1960.

46. *KW*, 7 April 1960:9.

47. *KW*, 27 October 1960:9. See also 'Irish cinemas are gloomy about tv', *KW*, 9 November 1961:9. This had risen from an estimated 7,000 television sets in 1956. (Robert Savage, *Irish television: the political and social origins*, Cork: Cork UP, 1996:48.)

48. *KW*, 13 December 1962:144.

49. For a discussion of the first night of Irish television, see Lelia Doolan, Jack Dowling and Bob Quinn, *Sit down and be counted*, Dublin: Wellington, 1969. See also Martin McLoone and John MacMahon (eds), *Television and Irish society: 21 years of Irish television*, Dublin: RTÉ/IFI, 1984:149–50, in which Eamon de Valera's address on the opening of Telefís Éireann is included.

50. See tables in appendix 2 in McLoone and MacMahon (eds), *Television and Irish society*, 1984:150, for information on the number of television sets in the Republic of Ireland; the rural/urban divide; and the ratio of single channel to multi-channel for the years 1963, 1966, 1971, 1976, 1981 and 1983.

51. *KW*, 2 April 1964:7.

52. The company had already opened a number of news cinemas in London (at transport hubs such as the airport and Victoria and Waterloo railway stations), Liverpool, Manchester, Sheffield, Leeds and Glasgow.

53. *KW*, 25 December 1958:7.

54. Another news cinema had been planned as part of Dublin's Busáras complex, Store Street. Though planning for the central bus station project began in 1946, it was not completed until 1953 and the basement 'cinema' was not opened until 1959. However, the venue was operated exclusively as a theatre until 1962 at which time the Fine Arts Cinema Club was formed, which screened foreign films on Sundays, a practice that ran until the end of the decade.

55. *KW*, 1 October 1959:9. In May 1968 the Grafton reverted to showing feature films, and in November 1972 it was sold to Irish Amalgamated Cinema, a company owned by Geoffrey Elliman and Bertie McNally, but it closed for good on 1 December 1973 and a department store was built on the site.

56. *Dáil debates*, vol. 181, cols 162–3, 27 April 1960.   57. *KW*, 5 May 1960:1.

58. *KW*, 16 February 1961:9.   59. *KW*, 23 March 1961:9.

60. *KW*, 27 April 1961:6, gives the twelve-month ET figure to 31 March 1961 as £1,146,000, though the 1961 full year figure as recorded in appendix, table 7, gives the total ET figure as £879,000, with the cinema ET figure at £780,878, or 88.8 per cent of the total.

61. *KW*, 25 May 1961:1.

62. *KW*, 8 June 1961:9.

63. This may have been the first cinema strike since 1928, though on that occasion, as is outlined in chapter 2, the strike was over the dismissal of a worker for alleged transgressive behaviour (smoking in the projection room). On other occasions, such as when the trade union demanded a 'closed shop' agreement following the employment of non-union labour in renters' offices in 1945, the strike was averted when the employers conceded to the demand.

64. *KW*, 22 June 1961; 29 June 1961:9.

65. The top Dublin price was 4s. 3d. (*KW*, 17 August 1961:9; *IT*, 1 August 1961:1.)

66. *KW*, 14 June 1962:8.

67. *Dáil debates*, vol. 194, cols 1589–90, 10 April 1962; *KW*, 11 October 1962:9.

68. *KW*, 12 March 1964:7. See also *IT*, 1 August 1961:1.

69. *KW*, 22 February 1962:6. In 2007 it was decided to demolish the main office building (Hawkins House) on this site, though this had not happened by 2010.

70. It was subsequently converted into a three-screen cinema and later its name was changed to the Screen at College Street. It is still operating as a cinema.

71. *KW*, 2 April 1964:7.   72. See revenue commissioners' annual reports.

73. Philip Molloy, '23 pc VAT "causing cinema closures"', *Irish Press*, 15 February 1985:1; Philip Molloy, 'Can film monopoly be broken?'; 16 February 1985:3.

74. Captain Terence O'Neill, *Parliamentary debates*, vol. 41, cols 1247–8, 1251, 21 May 1957.

75. *KW*, 6 March 1958:14.   76. *KW*, 24 April 1958:7.

77. *KW*, 15 May 1958:26. ITV (whose licence was granted under an act of parliament) with the BBC (operating under royal charter) essentially operated as a broadcasting duopoly until 1982 when Channel 4 commenced. Though the latter carried commercials, it operated according to the principles of public service broadcasting.

78. Terence O'Neill, *Northern Ireland parliamentary debates*, vol. 42, cols 1046–7, 28 May 1958. While the minister announced in his budget speech that the ET rate was to be reduced to one-third of 1*s*. 1*d*. inclusive price, in the motion giving legal effect to the ET changes, it is stated that the ET chargeable from 9 June 1958 'shall be equal to one-half of the amount (if any), by which the amount of the payment, excluding the amount of the duty, exceeds' 1*s*. 1*d*. (Ibid., vol. 42, col. 1059, 28 May 1958.) See also *KW*, 12 June 1958:9.

79. Rex Cathcart, *The most contrary region: the BBC in Northern Ireland, 1924–1984*, Belfast: Blackstaff, 1984:174.

80. Ibid., 185. The first live television transmissions from Northern Ireland were from a mobile outside broadcasting unit in October 1955, but it was not until 1957 that a permanent live facility was available.

81. UTV, however, did not have a newsroom until October 1962. (Cathcart, *The most contrary region*, 1984:187.)

82. Cathcart, *The most contrary region*, 1984:200.

83. *KW*, 20 June 1963:8.   84. *KW*, 23 April 1959:9.   85. *KW*, 28 April 1960:36.

86. O'Neill had claimed that there were only four net closures, or 3 per cent of cinemas in the period, whereas there had been 1,029, or 23 per cent, net closures in Britain between January 1956 and December 1959. (Terence O'Neill, *Northern Ireland parliamentary debates*, vol. 46, col. 1703, 24 May 1960.)

87. The year previously, in 1959, the British government rejected the CEA's plea for tax relief.

88. Terence O'Neill, *Northern Ireland parliamentary debates*, vol. 46, col. 1703, 24 May 1960; *KW*, 26 May 1960:1.

89. 'N.I. industry bitter about Budget', *KW*, 2 June 1960:127.

90. *KW*, 9 June 1960:1, 38; 16 June 1960:11; 14 July 1960: supplement 35.

91. *KW*, 4 August 1960:6.   92. *KW*, 11 August 1960:9.

93. *KW*, 16 February 1961:1.

94. Terence O'Neill, *Parliamentary debates*, vol. 48, col. 2190, 23 May 1961.

95. *KW*, 12 October 1961:9. However, the cinema reopened in 1962 as the Strand with CinemaScope installed. (*KW*, 8 November 1962:7.)

96. *KW*, 22 March 1962:8.   97. *KW*, 6 December 1962:13.

98. *Irish Independent*, 17 December 1963:5.   99. *KW*, 13 January 1944:88.

1. *Motion picture markets: Europe – Éire*, inquiry reference service, USA department of commerce, 1944:1.

2. *World trade and commodities*, USA department of commerce, 1950.

3. The venues to which they sold advertising comprised 82 per cent of Ireland's cinema seats.

4. *TC*, 9 June 1953. This report mistakenly stated that Ireland had 2 million cinema seats.

5. *World trade and commodities*, USA department of commerce, 1950. The annual amount that could be spent on repairs was limited to £500.

6. The site had been acquired by Leonard Ging and brothers Hubert and Dr Patrick McNally in April 1946. Designed by architect Henry J. Lyons and, on his death, son Samuel, it was completed in March 1949. Just as it was finished it was bought by Irish Cinemas Ltd. A small number of other cinemas were opened or reopened even earlier. The Premier Cinema, Lucan, Co. Dublin, which was envisaged as both a cinema and a theatre complete with a large stage, opened in February 1945, while the Strand Cinema (and Theatre), North Strand, Dublin, as noted above, reopened after a complete reconstruction in March 1945. Sometime around 1948 the Pavilion, Skerries, north Co. Dublin, also opened, but a cinema had operated there as early as 1914. (See part 3 of this book.)

7. Nevertheless, it seems that the Medway, Cookstown, Co. Tyrone, opened *c*.1948 (*KW*, 6 March 1952:9). The cinema, owned by T.A. Quinn, was not of the scale or importance of the Lido and may have been an already existing premises. Indeed, other cinemas in Tyrone opened even earlier

but were not new buildings. The Castle, Dungannon, reopened in 1946 having being requisitioned during the war (*KW*, 12 December 1946:38), while the Victory, also in Dungannon, opened on 16 December 1946 in the former Orange Hall (*KW*, 12 December 1946:38).

8. *KW*, 7 April 1955:9.

9. The group already controlled twelve cinemas (*KW*, 27 September 1956). The owner of the Dundonald cinema was T.J. Furey, while his co-director, Maurice Logan, was named as the owner of the New Reo, Ballyclare. The precise relationships within the group are not known.

10. *KW*, 28 March 1957:7.

11. A documentary about McBride Neill, *The Uncle Jack* (1996), was made by his nephew, acclaimed documentarist John T. Davis, and Sé Merry Doyle.

12. The directors of the Solar group were Dr A.O. Hyman and his sister Mrs Rada Smith. ('Six new halls testify to N. Ireland's confidence', *KW*, 26 December 1957:12.)

13. *KW*, 10 July 1958:9.

14. In addition to the three new buildings, a fourth cinema also opened. The Ambassador Cinema opened on 23 September 1954 following extensive renovations, refurbishment and technical upgrading of the Round Room, Rotunda, Parnell Street.

15. Quoted in Keenan, 2005:114.   16. *KW*, 11 April 1957:8.

17. *KW*, 21 August 1958:10.

18. The decline in British box office began following the peak year of 1946 when 1,635 million tickets were sold. In 1950, 1,396 million were sold, a drop of 15 per cent on 1946. By 1955, this had declined to 1,182 million, a further drop of 15 per cent on 1950. In 1960, only 501 million tickets were sold. See Patricia Perilli, 'Statistical survey of the British film industry' in James Curran and Vincent Porter (eds), *British cinema history*, London: Weidenfeld and Nicolson, 1983:372.

19. The figures in the tables slightly underestimate receipts and admissions as they do not take account of the cinemas in rural areas and small provincial towns, which were exempt from entertainments tax in the 1950s. These omissions, though, would hardly constitute even as much as 5 per cent of the cinema's audience at this time.

20. The agreement between trade union ITGWU and the employers reached in March 1947 averted a large-scale strike of cinema workers. The agreement provided for the following wage rates: chief operators, £5 5s. (old rate) to £8 2s. 6d. (new rate) weekly; second operators, £4 5s. (old rate) to £6 6s. (new rate); third operators, £3 15s. (old rate) to £5 (new rate); fourth operators, £4 15s. (new rate); chief ushers, £4 (old rate) to £5 15s. (new rate); ushers, £3 17s. 6d. (old rate) to £5 (new rate); usherettes, £2 2s (old rate). to £2 15s. (new rate); cashiers (females), £2 7s. 6d. (old rate) to £3 12s. 6d. (new rate); chief male cleaners, £4 15s. (new rate); day cleaners, £4 5s. (new rate); female cleaners, £2 2s. (new rate);; stage hands, spot men and fly men, £5 (new rate); and barmaids, £2 (old rate) to £3 (new rate). ('Thousand film workers in big pay increases', *TC*, 18 March 1947.)

21. Gerry O'Hanlon, 'Population change in the 1950s: a statistical review' in Dermot Keogh, Finbarr O'Shea and Carmel Quinlan (eds), *The lost decade: Ireland in the 1950s*, Cork: Mercier, 2004:73,75; Pauric Travers, '"There was nothing for me there": Irish female emigration, 1922–71', in Patrick O'Sullivan (ed.), *Irish women and Irish migration*, the Irish world wide series, vol. 4, Leicester: Leicester UP, 1995:148; *Report of the commission on emigration and other problems, 1948–1954*, Dublin: Stationery Office, 1954:116.

22. Travers, '"There was nothing for me there"' in O'Sullivan (ed.), 1995:149.

23. O'Hanlon, 'Population change in the 1950s' in Keogh et al. (eds), *The lost decade*, 2004:76.

24. *Report of the commission on emigration*, 1954:19.

25. O'Hanlon, 'Population change in the 1950s' in Keogh et al. (eds), *The lost decade*, 2004:75.

26. Maxwell Sweeney, *KW*, 9 April 1959:9.

27. Based on 912 million admissions.

28. Based on 1,585 million admissions and, as there was no census of population between 1931 and 1951, the 1951 British census population of 48,854,000.

29. Based on 1,181 million admissions (three-quarters that of 1945) and the 1951 census of population.

30. Based on 500 million admissions and the 1961 census of population of 51,284,000.

31. Based on the 1961 population figure of 2,818,300, the per capita Irish admissions rate in 1960 had dropped to 14.6.

32. Curran and Porter (eds), *British cinema history*, 1983:372.

33. According to T.J.M. Sheehy in 1948 (T.J.M. Sheehy, 'Towards an Irish film industry', *Irish Monthly*, September 1948: 418), there were 320 places where films were shown but 'only about 150 count as a real market.' He added that £600,000 was 'the approximate maximum which could be collected in present conditions for films here in Ireland.' He also said that 'any good feature film which

earns £3–5,000 in Ireland is a good box office draw.' Though it is not clear from Sheehy's article, it is possible, especially in light of the figures estimated by the central statistics office for 1950–60, that Sheehy was referring to exhibitors' net income. If his figure is regarded as being in any way accurate it suggests that Irish exhibition made a dramatic improvement in the first half of the 1950s.

34. *Census of distribution, 1951–54*, Dublin: CSO, 1956:xlvii; 172–4. The general principle followed in the survey was to include establishments used or hired out for commercial entertainment, but to exclude any establishments such as parochial halls used exclusively for social and non-profit making activities. Most of these 'establishments' were cinemas. The figure for box office receipts excludes amounts in respect of theatres (except cine-variety) and of cinemas located outside areas in which entertainments tax was payable. In terms of box office receipts, the survey notes, the coverage attained was at least 90 per cent.

35. *Census of distribution, 1951–54*, 1956:xlviii; table 33, 174.

36. *Census of distribution, 1956–59*, Dublin: CSO, 1962:272.

37. Table 36, *Census of distribution, 1956–59*:275. £460,000 was taken by kiosks during performances, and £124,000 from other receipts.

38. Table 35, *Census of distribution, 1956–59*:274.

39. Table 37, *Census of distribution, 1956–59*:276.

40. Table 33, *Census of distribution, 1956–59*:272.

41. H.E. Browning and A.A. Sorrell, 'Cinemas and cinema-going in Great Britain', *Journal of the Royal Statistical Society*, vol. 117, 1954:136, table 3 cited by Philip Corrigan, 'Film entertainment as ideology and pleasure: a preliminary approach to a history of audiences', in Curran and Porter (eds), *British cinema history*, 1983:25.

42. In 1951 Ireland had only sixteen admissions per head, see appendix, table 3. It is possible that Dublin at this time had somewhere in the region of forty-five to fifty cinema visits per head. This estimate, though apparently high, is based on trends and figures from 1936 to 1951. While Beere estimated annualized cinema-going figures of twenty-three visits in Dublin against six visits nationally in 1936 given that in 1951 Dublin had 55 per cent of box office, or admissions of 26.29 million and a population (including its suburbs and Dún Laoghaire) of 634,500, or 21.4 per cent of the whole population of 2,960,600 (increased in relation to 1936 by 18.13 per cent so that it had now an additional 3.26 per cent of the national population), if worked out proportionally this results in Dublin having fifty-three visits per head. However, when adjusted to take account of the fact that Dublin had more first-run and quality cinemas, and, more generally, comprised a greater proportion of dearer tickets (increased at a higher rate through the various changes in ET), a fairer figure might be forty-eight visits, against sixteen visits nationally. See *Report of the commission on emigration*, 1954:13.

43. The data for *The Irish audience for screen advertising* (1953) was collected during 1952 and early 1953.

44. *TC*, 9 June 1953.

45. Despite this drop, in 1950 Britain's rate of cinema attendance remained far higher than Ireland's. Regional differences were also important in Britain, where Scotland, northern England and south Wales were the areas of highest cinema attendance. As late as 1960, Scotland had twenty-seven cinema visits per capita, while London had only twenty, a pattern also evident in the 1930s, as noted in chapter 2. In the same year, as noted above, the Irish per capita rate was just under fifteen admissions per year (14.6). (See Philip Corrigan, 'Film entertainment as ideology and pleasure' in Curran and Porter (eds), *British cinema history*, 1983:32.)

46. Des Hickey, 'The growth of the specialist cinema', *Showcase*, March 1968:29.

47. *Variety*, 16 April 1958.

48. *KW* advertisement, 27 March 1958; 10 April 1958:6.

49. See tables 33–40, *Census of distribution, 1955–59*, Dublin: CSO, 1962:272–9; and tables 60–57, *Census of distribution, 1955 and services, 1966; final report: wholesale trade and services*, Dublin: CSO, 1971:98–104.

50. Restrictive practices commission, *Report of enquiry into the supply and distribution of cinema films*, Dublin: Stationery Office, 1978:17.

51. Ibid., 18.

52. Odeon (Ireland)'s 1965 profit before taxation was £307,418, while in 1968 this had increased to £410,650. (See Odeon (Ireland) Ltd annual reports.)

53. See annual reports of Rank Organisation and its Irish subsidiaries.

54. This figure was given by Muiris MacConghaile, Irish Film Board chairman, when he spoke at the premiere of Cathal Black's Irish independent feature *Pigs* (1984) of the 'scandal' of this repatriated box office income. 'MacConghaile attack on film "scandal"', *IT*, 11 October 1984; '£20m a year

cinema profit is "exported"'. *Evening Press*, 11 October 1984:4; '£20m receipts at Irish cinema "sent abroad"', *Irish Press*, 11 October 1984:4; 'Make more films here', *Irish Independent*, 11 October 1984:2.

55. The Irish Film Board's annual report for 1983 estimated gross income of Irish cinemas between £20 million and £27 million. Given that usually approximately one-third goes to distributors, repatriated profit was certainly no more than £9 million. (*Report of the Irish Film Board, 1983*.) The actual amounts of repatriated profits during the period 1931–80 may be found in appendix, table 9.

56. *Nudist Paradise* (Charles Saunders, 1958, GB), though originally banned, it was passed for public exhibition in 1962. (*KW*, 18 October 1962:8.)

57. *KW*, 18 April 1963:8. Of course, it would be naïve to interpret this comment as endorsing cinema since it was probably motivated by the strong anti-gambling strain in Northern Ireland Protestantism.

58. See Ray Zone, *Steroscopic cinema and the origins of 3-D film, 1838–1952*, Lexington, KY: UP of Kentucky, 2007; a short overview is given by Ben Walters, 'The great leap forward', *Sight and Sound*, vol. 19, no. 3, March 2009:38–43 (also included are interviews by Nick Roddick with Jeffrey Katzenberg of DreamWorks Animation, 40–1, and Tom Charity with director Joe Dante, 42).

59. 'Varied fare at Bohemian' (advert.), *Irish Independent*, 27 October 1925:8.

60 Metropole cinema programme for *The White Shadow* (Graham Cutts, 1923), 1 September 1924.

61. 'What are plastigrams?', Metropole programme for *The White Shadow*, 1 September 1924:9, NLI.

62. *The Spectator* quoted in ibid.

63. 'What are plastigrams?', Metropole programme, 1 September 1924:9, NLI.

64. Indeed, even as late as 1951, the major studios refused to invest in the process when it was put on the market in the form of Milton and Julian Gunzburg's Natural Vision. (Belton, 1992:114–15.)

65. Following the return of 3D in the 2000s the possibility of creating a 3D experience without the need to wear special glasses is becoming more and more a possibility. Several companies, including 3ality and Dimension Technologies Inc., have produced systems in which no glasses are needed. See Niamh Creely, '3D Wars', *Film Ireland*, no. 122, May/June 2008:25.

   Indeed, while much media comment has tended to positively welcome 3D, one of the few less than enthusiastic voices has been Donald Clarke of the *IT*, who, surprise, surprise, is a spectacle wearer! ('Stage struck: what's so great about 3-D', *IT*, 5 June 2009:B32.) He is not alone; the principal author of this study, Kevin Rockett, also suffers visual impairment and as a result cannot enjoy the 3D experience. In fact, according to the Eyecare Trust (cited by Jonathan Brown and Kevin Rawlinson, '3D: cinematic revolution or just a trick of the light?' *Independent*, 23 March 2010) one in eight (or 12 per cent) of people have a visual impairment and thus cannot appreciate 3D or experience some level of visual discomfort or headaches as a result of watching 3D images. Of course, aside from the problems of wearing at times (ill-fitting) glasses (and it should be noted that the new twenty-first century ones are plastic with greyish polarized lens and not the 1950s style cardboard with red and blue thin plastic filters), the issue remains that 3D 'when it's done badly … can give you a headache.' (Sandy Climan, chief executive officer at 3ality, the digital film company behind U2 3D, quoted by Ian Campbell, 'The third dimension', *IT*, 2 April 2010.)

66. Oboler returned to this process at the end of his career when, under the pseudonym of Alf Silliman Jr, he wrote and directed the 3D, 'X'-rated, porn film *The Stewardesses* (1969). The process used to create the 3D effect was Stereovision, which could not go out of synch.

67. John Belton, 'Technology and innovation' in Geoffrey Nowell-Smith (ed.), *The Oxford history of world cinema*, Oxford: Oxford UP, 1996:266. This method creates a stereoscope image from two colour layers that are superimposed, but offset. It was popular in comics. Of all the methods (including anaglyphic, polarization and alternate-frame sequencing) of creating stereoscope film images with the use of glasses, it was polarization that almost completely dominated the market.

68. Ironically, the film's director had only one eye and so was unable to appreciate the film's stereoscopic quality.

69. 3D films include Columbia's *Man in the Dark* (Lew Landers, 1953), which, complete with a roller-coaster ride and numerous objects hurled at the audience such as scissors, knives and falling bodies, tells of a convict who has his brain operated on to rid him of his criminal tendencies; Jack Arnold's *It came from Outer Space* (1953), the first science fiction film to be shot using this process, and his *Creature from the Black Lagoon* (1954) as well as its sequel, *Revenge of the Creature* (1955), which, released just after the end of the golden period of 3D, did well at the box office; William Cameron Menzies' horror film *The Maze* (1953) about a man-frog; Warner Bros' follow-up to their *House of Wax*, *Phantom of the Rue Morgue* (Roy Del Ruth, 1954), which was based on Edgar Allen Poe's short story; the pro-peace western *Hondo* (John Farrow, 1953) starring John Wayne in which the 3D effects are used for psychological reasons as well as the more visceral ones whereby arrows shoot into the audience; MGM's musical *Kiss Me Kate* (1953); and *Dial M For Murder* (Alfred

Hitchcock, 1954, re-released in 3D format in 1982). Columbia was the only studio to use 3D for slapstick.

70. In the 1960s few 3D films were released and these were generally of the cheaper anaglyphic exploitation variety. For William Castle's *Thirteen Ghosts* (1960) audiences had to use a 'ghost viewer' which had two transparent squares, one of which was tinted red (the ghost viewer), and the other blue (the ghost remover). Julian Roffman's *The Mask* (aka *The Eyes of Hell*, 1961), though shot in 2D and in black and white, had a colour sequence in anaglyphic 3D. There was revived interest in 3D in the 1980s with many IMAX cinemas screening (70mm) documentaries in 3D. Once more patrons donned polarized glasses to see reissues of films such as *House of Wax* as well as a new batch of films such as *Friday the 13th Part 3* (Steve Miner, 1982), *Jaws 3-D* (aka *Jaws 3*, Joe Alves, 1983) and *Amityville 3D* (Richard Fleischer, 1984). More recently new systems have been used to create a 3D effect. While James Cameron, using the Reality Camera System (which is for HDTV cameras rather than film) has released a number of films including *Ghosts of the Abyss* (aka *Titanic 3-D: Ghosts of the Abyss*, 2003), *Spy Kids 3D: Game Over* (Robert Rodriguez, 2003) and *The Adventures of Sharkboy and Lavagirl in 3-D* (Robert Rodriguez 2003), another digital system, REAL D, based on circular (rather than the older technique of linear) polarization, is proving popular. Releases in that format include Disney's animations *Chicken Little* (Mark Dindal, 2005), *Meet the Robinsons* (Stephen J. Anderson, 2007), and *Beowulf* (aka in USA *Beowulf: An IMAX 3-D Experience*, Robert Zemeckis, 2007).

71. The fact that 3D involved the use of two projectors, which could only take roughly one hour of film, thus requiring films to have an intermission within that hour so as to refill the projectors, was clearly a negative factor. Furthermore, as it involved the use of two prints that had to be exactly synchronized, therefore greater care had to be taken with screening it (or indeed repairing it). If the prints were even slightly out of synch, the film would be unwatchable or cause headaches and eyestrain.

72. Belton, 1992:114.

73. Later films, including *Jaws 3-D* (1983), which were filmed using the Arrivision SD system whereby only a single camera was used but with a special twin-lens adapter, did not need two projectors. They could be screened in any theatre through a regular projector providing that the cinema obtained a relatively inexpensive lens adapter.

74. See Eyles, 2005:39–40, for 3D in Britain, particularly with regard to the Rank and ABC circuits.

75. 'Cinemascope for two Dublin houses' [Savoy and State, Phibsboro], *Dublin Evening Mail*, 16 March 1954:5.

76. By May 2010, Europe's first fully digital 3D multiplex cinema opened at St Catherine's Walk, Carmarthen, Wales with all screens 3D. Meanwhile in Ireland, one quarter of the screens using Carlton Screen Advertising, the biggest seller of cinema advertising space in Ireland, were digital (100 of 400 screens). Despite this, there has not yet been a single 3D Irish cinema commercial. See Catherine O'Mahony, 'Carlton focuses its sights on an improved year', *Sunday Business Post*, 9 May 2010.

77. This was the first live action concert in 3D. See Niamh Creely, 'Getting U in 2 3D', *Film Ireland*, no. 122, May/June 2008:22–5.

78. The idea of exploring the psychological and expressive possibilities of the medium is something which most of the new batch of 3D directors are interested in. As Joe Dante has said, he would like to invert the notion of the audience (joyfully, if fearfully) recoiling from oncoming objects to reaching in to the dimensional world, which is after all a more natural way of seeing. (Quoted by Tom Charity, 'Deep space', *Sight and Sound*, vol. 19, no. 3, March 2009:42.) Of course, 3D is particularly suited to the virtual reality world of gaming.

79. Ten of its twelve screens were compatible with 3D. (Denis Clifford, 'Encounters of the third kind', *IT*, 19 October 2007:ticket, 8–9.)

80. This can be contrasted against the number of 3D films screened between July and the end of December 2009 alone in Ward Anderson cinemas in Ireland: eight. These were *Ice Age: Dawn of the Dinosaurs* (3 July); *G-Force* (31 July); *Final Destination* (28 August); *Cloudy with a Chance of Meatballs* (18 September); *Toy Story* (2 October); *Up* (16 October); *A Christmas Carol* (6 November 2009); and *Avatar* (18 December).

81. Ian Campbell, 'The third dimension', *IT*, 2 April 2010. Of course 3D has been especially prevalent in computer-generated animation with films such as *Toy Story*, *Ice Age*, *Shrek*, *Bolt*, *Monsters vs Aliens*, *Up* and the pioneering 2004 *Polar Express*.

82. Cameron's first foray into 3D was with his short film *Terminator 2, 3D Battle Across Time* (1996) for Universal Studios theme park.

83. Michael Lynton, chairman and chief executive of Sony Pictures, quoted, Ian Campbell, *IT*, 2 April 2010.

84. See www.digital cinemareport.com. Information drawn from Media Salles and European Audiovisual Observatory.
85. Ben Walters, 'The great leap forward', *Sight and Sound*, vol. 19, no. 3, March 2009:43. Writing in April 2010, Ian Campbell stated that it is expected that there will be 7,000 3D cinemas by the end of 2010. (Campbell, *IT*, 2 April 2010.) Real D, a 3D production and exhibition company whose technology is used in 97 per cent of 3D cinemas, anticipates a total market of 15,000 screens. As of autumn 2008 they had equipped 1,500 screens across thirty countries, and in 2009 were estimating that by spring 2010 they would have equipped up to 6,000. (Ben Walters, *Sight and Sound*, vol. 19, no. 3, March 2009:39.)
86. 'IMC installs 3D screens', *IT*, 11 March 2009.
87. *IT*, 12 June 2009:ticket 3.
88. There were 67 3D screens in the Republic of Ireland, and this was expected to rise to 70 by year's end. Meanwhile in Northern Ireland 19 screens or 11 per cent were 3D, with a forecast digital integration by end of 2010 set at 24 screens or 14 per cent of all screens in Northern Ireland. The number, as of March 2010, of digital screens was Republic of Ireland: 109 screens (25 per cent; set to increase to 150 screens or 33 per cent); and Northern Ireland: 29 screens (17 per cent; set to increase to 40 screens or 23 per cent). Carlton Screen Advertising website (carltonscreen.ie).
89. Spanish communications group Telefonica and electronics manufacturer Philips demonstrated a prototype 3D television in 2008 that did not require the wearing of bi-coloured glasses to generate the 3D effect. ('Standby for 3-D television', *IT*, 14 July 2008:C53. See also Ian Campbell, *IT*, 2 April 2010, and 'In your face action', 30 July 2010:business 6, for an assessment of the competing 3D home entertainment technologies.)
90. Jonathan Brown and Kevin Rawlinson, '3D: cinematic revolution or just a trick of the light?', *Independent*, 23 March 2010.
91. While the England–Wales Six Nations rugby match, 6 February 2010, Europe's first live 3D sports broadcast, was screened in cinemas only in April 2010, Sky launched its 3D television channel with live coverage of the Premier League (Manchester United versus Chelsea). The March 2010 England–Ireland rugby match in 3D was shown in the Savoy, Dublin. According to Mark Anderson, 'the results were spectacular' and the combination of 3D, Dolby surround sound and the big screen 'really blew the audience away'. He added, by way of a more general comment about 3D, that 'the feedback from cinema-goers has been fantastic.' (*Sunday Independent*, 23 May 2010.)
92. Cited in Belton, 'Technology and innovation' in Nowell-Smith (ed.), *Oxford history of world cinema*, 1996:265. As Belton notes, Cinerama was not alone in exploiting the interactive or potentially participatory nature of the technology. While 3D promised 'a lion in your lap' and 'a lover in your arms' (*Bwana Devil*), CinemaScope boasted that it 'puts YOU in the picture' and Todd-AO declared 'you're in the show with Todd-AO' (Belton, 1992:165).
93. As Henry Hathaway, who directed the first part of the first narrative feature in Cinerama, complained: 'That goddamned Cinerama … do you know a waist shot is as close as you could get with that thing?' (Quoted in *Halliwell's film guide*, 7th ed., London: Paladin Grafton, 1990:487.)
94. See Belton, 1992:94–5.
95. *Commonweal* 57 (21 November 1952:165), cited, Belton, 1992:104. See also Belton, 1992:92ff.
96. Ibid., 99; see also 91ff.
97. *Evening Press*, 15 April 1963:8 (advert.). An earlier *Evening Press* (12–13 April 1963:8) full-page advertisement with an image of a roller-coaster entitled 'A new era in Irish entertainment' repeated the Cinerama tag-line, 'It actually puts YOU in the picture', and continued, 'you are suddenly part of an entertainment experience of a lifetime! You will find yourself swept right into the picture, surrounded by sight and sound. Not one, but three projectors perform their breathtaking magic – and through twelve speakers stereophonic sound surrounds you from all sides of the theatre … this is a whole new world opening up and *engulfing* you.' The visceral thrill of the roller-coaster ride was attested to by reviewers of the first show.
98. *KW*, 28 February 1963:8.
99. Prior to its incarnation as a cinema and waxworks, it had been a prayer meeting room. Despite attempts to close the venue from the late 1990s and 2000, and a change of ownership of the exhibition in 2001, it was only in summer 2005 that the waxworks were forced to move to make way for a hotel. Plans to reopen were hampered, not least by the robbery in July 2007 of a number of figures when damage to other sculptures was also sustained with an estimated loss of €1 million. A new waxwork museum opened in October 2009, not in Smithfield as had been anticipated (the developers of the cultural quarter there had deemed such an attraction 'kitsch'), but in the more centrally located historic landmark Armoury building, Foster Place, just off College Green/Dame Street. (They took possession of the building the previous April.) Under the name of the Wax

Museum Plus, and under the management of recording entrepreneur Paddy Dunning, owner of Grouse Lodge studios, the privately owned museum comprises new features including interactive (non-wax) sections on Irish scientists and inventors, and on (music) recording. The main body of the museum, however, is devoted to waxworks and considerable thought and effort has gone into creating an educative experience whereby Irish history is rendered in wax. There is also an Irish writers' room; Irish cultural, media and sporting personalities rooms; as well as chambers of horrors, and a space dedicated to popular stars and icons. While the collection includes many of the older wax figures, most of which have been given a facelift, it has been complemented by more assured sculptures with greater likeness and sense of life. The head sculptor is P.J. Heraty who has worked with the museum since its opening in 1983. See Pol O Conghaile, 'Wax works', *IT*, 20 April 1999:13; Fiona Dillon, 'Solo Ronan lays down some really hot wax', *Evening Herald*, 18 March 2000:3; Olivia Doyle, 'Get the last of your wax dummies', *Sunday Tribune*, 19 March 2000:5; Bríd Higgins Ní Chinnéide, 'Waxworks museum break-in a setback to anticipated reopening', *IT*, 31 July 2007:8; Rosita Boland, '"Frankenstein needs underpants": mixing politicians pop stars and popes with monsters, movies and music the newly revamped National Wax Museum has finally achieved the right combination of cool and kitsch', *IT*, 9 October 2009:17. The Waxwork Museum's own website includes a selection of radio and press reviews (waxmuseumplus.ie).

1. *Showcase*, July–September 1971:40. Sixteen of them were Pullman seats.
2. The directors of Capitol and Allied in 1971 were the company's managing director Thomas ('Tom') St John, John Farrell, John M. Farrell, and Richard Cox-Johnston.
3. Belton, 1992:113.
4. Nine days later, MGM's Empire, Leicester Square, which had been the first in Britain to announce their move to widescreen, also presented their films in widescreen; others soon followed. However, many of the films screened had not been photographed as widescreen and so 'suffered badly from being cut off at [the] top and bottom.' (Eyles, 2005:40.)
5. The film had record-breaking box office figures and proved to be a major success. By mid-April 1954, it grossed over $29.5 million. (Belton, 1992:137.)
6. Paramount developed Vista Vision, 'a large-negative-area camera process which, when reduced onto 35mm film, produced an image with a 1.66:1 aspect ratio.' (Belton, 1992:124.) It produced a sharp image, was compatible with traditional modes of production and exhibition, and offered greater flexibility to theatres, which could project in aspect ratios ranging from 1.33:1 to 2:1. (Belton, 1992:125.)
7. Belton, 1992:136, 140. See also Michael Allen, 'From *Bwana Devil* to *Batman Forever*: technology in contemporary Hollywood cinema' in Steve Neale and Murray Smith (eds), *Contemporary Hollywood cinema*, London: Routledge, 1998.
8. Belton, 1992:140; Belton, 'Technology and innovation' in Nowell-Smith (ed.) *Oxford history of world cinema*, 1996:266.
9. The directional quality of such a screen 'served to reduce scatter and to improve overall screen brightness' by as much as two times that of a usual screen for the same value of projector illumination. (Belton, 1992:148.)
10. See Eyles, 2005:41–2.
11. It had a four-week run. The film showed at the Odeon Newcastle for five weeks during which it attracted 190,615 paid admissions, while when screened at the Odeon Glasgow 50,000 attended during the first week alone. (Eyles, 2005:41–2.)
12. *Dublin Evening Mail*, 16 March 1954:5.
13. 'Theatre adapted to presentation of CinemaScope', *IT*, 24 April 1954:13.
14. The other problem with the process was the issue of not being able to comfortably or fully see the screen. Seats near the front of the screen and more generally those within the stalls, if they were not sufficiently raked, often presented problems for the patrons.
15. Keith Duggan, 'Plucky Irish set to skate on thin ice in Europe', *IT*, 24 February 1999:20. See profile of State owner John James McManus in *Irish Independent*, 8 June 1975.
16. Rank had argued that British cinemagoers did not want stereophonic sound and, indeed, it was their refusal to install stereo in more cinemas that ultimately led to the row between Rank and Fox. Other Hollywood studios proved more flexible than Fox and did not demand that their productions be accompanied by stereophonic sound. Even Fox relented (though not in relation to Rank) and issued mono as well as stereo versions of their films. (Eyles, 2005:42.)
17. Belton, 1992:162.
18. The film version of Richard Rogers and Oscar Hammerstein's 1943 Broadway musical *Oklahoma!* premiered in October 1955.
19. Quoted in Belton, 1992:168.

20. By September 1957 there were 46,544 CinemaScope cinemas.
21. Belton, 1992:279n15.   22. *KW*, 8 January 1959:9.
23. *KW*, 25 December 1958:22.   24. *KW*, 14 April 1960:26.
25. *KW*, 10 December 1959:7. Cinemeccanica 70/35mm multi-purpose projection equipment (with 18-inch diameter automatic Super Zenith arc lamps) was installed at the Regal, along with a Perlux screen. Cinemeccanica was designed to take all currently available motion picture systems, with easy and quick changeover from one system to the other. (*KW*, 24 December 1959:6.)
26. The far more rapid decline in British admissions during 1955–9 can be attributed to television in the main. (Eyles, 2005:52–3.)
27. Cited in Eyles, 2005:53.
28. As Eyles notes, ABC, unlike Rank, generally allowed independents to take over its discarded cinemas. (Eyles, 2005:55.) This 'barring' practice was not unique to Britain and was a feature of certain Irish cinema disposals in the 1970s and 1980s, in particular.
29. *KW*, 31 December 1959:9.   30. Eyles, 2005:66.   31. Ibid., 92.
32. Paul Tansey, 'Questions at a.g.m. of Irish Cinemas', *IT*, 22 March 1974:14. As part of its retrenchment in Ireland in the 1980s, Rank sold College House in 1981. See 'Rank sells city centre cinemas', *IT*, 10 September 1983:7.
33. The cinemas sold were the Fairview, Whitehall, State, Cabra and Strand cinemas in Dublin and the Savoys in Cork and Limerick. (Irish Cinemas Ltd annual report to 31 October 1975.)
34. *KW*, 14 June 1962.   35. *KW*, 20 March 1958.   36. *KW*, 17 April 1958:10.
37. www.screen daily.com, 4 January 2007. Following the dissolution of the partnership, also known as UIP, Universal Pictures International (UPI) appointed from January 2007 David Burke, formerly of independent distributors Eclipse Pictures and Clarence Pictures, as head of its new Dublin office.
38. There was a 50 per cent drop in audiences during the decade from the mid-1950s to the mid-1960s (*Showcase*, November 1967:8), and further decline during the following decade such that total cinema attendance in 1976 was about one-tenth that of 1954. (*Report of RPC enquiry*, 1978:17.)
39. *Report of RPC enquiry*, 1978:18.   40. Ibid.
41. One screen had 1,070 seats, the other 780 seats.
42. The political tension in the country at the time led the company to put only the letters BHS over the store, knowing how potentially provocative the word British would be in the context of the Northern troubles.
43. *Showcase*, June 1969:5.   44. *Showcase*, November 1967:8.
45. *Irish Statistical Bulletin*, vol. 48, no. 4, December 1973:221; vol. 52, no. 4, December 1977:233. See appendix, table 9.
46. These figures are based on the Irish Film Board's estimate of the gross income of Irish cinemas being between £20 million and £27 million, usually one-third of which goes to distributors. (*Report of the Irish Film Board, 1983*.)
47. Ted Sheehy, 'Distribution in Ireland', *Filmbase News*, no. 5, April/May 1988:12.

CHAPTER 4

1. Kevin Anderson, quoted, Rose Doyle, 'Cinema man a star of movie distribution company', *IT*, 29 September 2004: commercial property 2.
2. He was an employee of an independent film distributor in Dublin. See McSweeney, 2003:36–7. He moved to Manchester on 10 June 1939.
3. On returning home he first played with Drumcondra Juniors, then joined Shamrock Rovers at Milltown, Dublin, but after only three matches he moved to Drumcondra, where he received £4 per week. (This compares with the £6 per week he was paid at Manchester City at which time he played on the club's second team; the maximum wage in England was £8.) After the war, Manchester City demanded that he return to fulfill the terms of his contract, but he persuaded the club to give him a free transfer if he found another footballer to take his place. Though they finally agreed, when Ward's transfer came through it was to the Waterford club in which Ward's replacement had been based. Luck was on Ward's side and after three months the Waterford club went into liquidation, thus allowing Ward to once again return to Drumcondra with which he remained until 1949. He was part of the team that won the FAI Cup in 1943 and again in 1946. Despite this, the Manchester City museum, perhaps reflecting the terms of Ward's original contract with the club, note that he was there from 1939 through to 1948 when he was released during the 1948 close season. (See 'The medals many be gone but the memories will last forever: Leo Ward, Ireland's oldest FAI Cup winner, takes Alison O'Riordan on a trip down memory lane', *Sunday Independent*, 18 July 2010.)

4. Thomas Anderson, Kevin's father, died when his son was only 2 years old; Thomas' widow, Martha, subsequently married John Ward who had also been married. Leo was the first-born child of the second family. There were ten children in total.
5. Prior to that, Anderson worked in the civil service and with builders' providers T. and C. Martin. See interview with Anderson by Rose Doyle, *IT*, 29 September 2004:commercial property 2.
6. A number of accounts cite different dates: Rose Doyle and later Alison O'Riordan, Leo Ward's granddaughter, who interviewed Kevin Anderson in 2004 (*IT*, 29 September 2004), and in 2009, respectively (Alison O'Riordan, 'A good movie at the cinema is just the ticket to beat the doom', *Sunday Independent*, 7 June 2009), state that Abbey Films was set up as early as 1940 following Ward's return from England. In another article by O'Riordan (*Sunday Independent*, 27 January 2008), Leo Ward is quoted as saying that he was eleven years in distribution before they started up Abbey Films, while it is pointed out that he became immersed in the cinema business with his elder half-brother in 1949. Hugh Oram (*IT*, 13 January 2000: property 28) reports that the company was set up in 1947, while Ian Kehoe (*Sunday Business Post*, 12 June 2005:10) and others suggests the early 1950s. It seems that Ward and Anderson were certainly working together throughout the 1940s and that, at least from the late 1940s, the company was becoming well established. Abbey Films Ltd was not officially registered as a company until 15 July 1954.
7. The benefit match between Drumcondra and Belfast's Distillery was played in Dublin's Dalymount Park on 9 August 1946. Though Ward scored for Drumcondra in the first half, Distillery won by three goals to two. ('Benefit for popular soccer player', *IT*, 7 August 1946:2; 'Distillery beat Drumcondra in Ward benefit match', 10 August 1946:2.) The 'big "gate"' received by Ward is generally quoted as being £500. (*Sunday Business Post*, 29 June 1997:10; 11 July 1999:10; 12 June 2005:10; *Sunday Independent*, 18 July 2010.) To put this sum in context, in 1946 the average annual income (wages and salaries) of the 167,420 'persons engaged' in all industries and services was £185, though given that 2,276 proprietors, working in business, are included in this total, the 'average worker's' income would have been somewhat lower. (*Census of industrial production*, 1945–47, Dublin: Stationery Office, pr. 123. n.d. Almost fifty years later, in 2004, average wages and salaries across all sectors was €37,819 [€33,393 in the private sector, and €46,953 in the public sector] CSO, *Labour costs survey*, 2004, Dublin: Stationery Office, December 2005:vi. By then, the number engaged in industry and services had increased more than ten-fold to about two million.) Interestingly, Ward remembers the score as 2–1 to Drumcondra. (See Alison O'Riordan, *Sunday Independent*, 18 July 2010.)
8. Brian Carey, 'Rolling the celluloid credit lines', *Sunday Business Post*, 29 June 1997:10.
9. This film, the company's first, was co-produced with an independent UK film company. Though the film involved Peter Hunt, George Fleishmann and Liam O'Leary, according to Anderson it 'wasn't much good, but the words were wonderful!' (*IT*, 29 September 2004:commercial property 2.) In 1954, Abbey Films produced *Beatha Ui Raghallaigh/The Life of Riley*, a public information film made for the department of health, while in 1955, Anderson approached the department of foreign affairs seeking backing for a documentary on the Irish in London. Copies of *Who Fears ..?* and *Beatha* are held at the Irish Film Archive. In the 1980s, when Kevin Anderson was a member of the Irish Film Board, from his own resources, he gave financial support to one of the most interesting short films of the period, Siobhan Twomey's *Boom Babies* (1988), but he is not listed on the credits. This film concerns a cross-class relationship set in Dublin in which the female protagonist is seeking to break away from her family's traditional notions of employment as she works as a car mechanic.
   In 1983, Kevin Anderson's son Paul, having already negotiated a deal with Sandy Howard to film part of *KGB – The Secret War* (Dwight H. Little, 1986) in Ireland, announced the formation of a consortium of investors, Emerald Productions, to finance film production in Ireland with the hope to part-finance four pictures a year for international distribution. Since then, Paul Anderson has been executive producer of *After Midnight* (Shani S. Grewal, 1990), which was produced by Lazer Entertainments (Ireland) Ltd. Leo Ward's son, Paul Ward, has engaged in financing films, including *Peaches* (Nick Grosso, 2000), through his involvement with Stone Ridge, a production company set up by Ronan Glennane, a former employee of Ward Anderson. Abbey Films distributed the film.
10. As would define Ward Anderson's business approach, the films were paid for in cash. (Alison O'Riordan, *Sunday Independent*, 18 July 2010.) Butcher's Film Service, a renting and equipment company, which occasionally produced and financed films, dates back to 1897 and was still active as late as the 1960s. See Tom Ryall's entry in Brian McFarlane (ed.), *The encyclopedia of British film*, London: Methuen, 2003:98.
11. The Irish film censor also cut *The Hills of Donegal* in two places. 'Reel 9: Cut from words – "Your mother, was Daniel's mother ..." down to "How can you?" Reel 9: Cut words "I want to see her

– my sister."' (Reserve 7194, no. 22284, 15 December 1947, NAI.) These cuts were designed to suppress the adulterous relationship between Eileen's mother and Daniel's father.

12. Ian Kehoe, 'Screen team', *Sunday Business Post*, 12 June 2005:n10.

13. Cork-born Jack Doyle (1913–78), who enjoyed early success as a boxer, but was disqualified during a British heavyweight title bout, became famous as the playboy husband of two Hollywood actresses, Judith Allen, and Movita, a Mexican starlet who left Doyle in 1945 to marry Marlon Brando. Doyle appeared in *McGlusky the Sea Rover* (1934), which was partly filmed in Arklow, Co. Wicklow, and in which he plays a Scottish sea captain; and in *Navy Spy* (1937).

14. Alison O'Riordan, *Sunday Independent*, 7 June 2009.

15. The film, which was reissued in 1943, was a remake of the 1934 film *Danny Boy*. This film was co-produced and co-directed by Oswald Mitchell.

16. This is most probably Oswald Mitchell's 1937 film for which he also co-wrote the story. An edited version of this film, only fifty-five minutes long, was re-released in 1940, while a sequel/remake to the film, also called *Rose of Tralee*, but directed by Germain Burger, was released in 1942. It was seventy-seven minutes long, less than three minutes shorter than Mitchell's original version. The 1942 version was also re-released in 1944 (with 1,365ft/*c*.fifteen minutes, cut) and again in 1948.

17. Though an article in the *Evening Press*, 4 January 1985, refers to *Danny Boy and the Rose of Tralee* as being one film, there is no film of this title and, therefore, the poster to which the reporter refers as hanging in Leo Ward's office is most likely advertising the two films as a double bill. Depending on which version of *Rose of Tralee* was shown, the combined running time would have been at most 160 minutes (80 and 80 mins); 158 minutes (80 and 78 mins) or 135 minutes (80 and 55 mins). In 1943, the *Rose of Tralee* was cut by the Irish censor under the Emergency Powers Order. (See film censors' decisions, reserve 5522, no. 17910, 29 April 1943, NAI.)

18. This was the distribution arm of Anglo-Amalgamated, 'a small but resourceful production/distribution company', set up by Nat Cohen and Stuart Levy in 1945. For an overview of the company see Brian McFarlane (ed.), *Encyclopedia of British film*, 2003:19–20. Anglo-Amalgamated was bought by EMI in 1971.

19. Leo Ward quoted in Alison O'Riordan, *Sunday Independent*, 27 January 2008.

20. Kevin Anderson in *IT*, 29 September 2004:commercial property 2. One long-term acquaintance of Ward described him as being 'married to cinema'. (Quoted in Daire O'Brien, 'Ward Anderson: cinema's secret empire', *Business and Finance*, 11 June 1992:13.) Fittingly, it was he rather than his half-brother Kevin Anderson who was awarded the Volta by the Jameson Dublin International Film Festival in 2008 for his contribution to the Irish cinema-going landscape. As festival director Gráinne Humphreys said, 'having named the Festival Career Achievement Award after the first cinema in Ireland – The Volta Picture Theatre – it is only fitting that Leo Ward, co-owner of the oldest surviving city centre cinema, the Savoy Cinema on O'Connell Street, receives the accolade. With over 60 years in the film business, through both cinemas and his distribution company Abbey Films, Leo's passion for film has helped shape Irish cinema and we are delighted to mark his achievements with this award.' (Quoted, Alison O'Riordan, *Sunday Independent*, 27 January 2008.)

21. On the death of cinema manager Kevin O'Donovan in 1954, Mrs Murphy, unable to find a suitable replacement, asked Leo Ward to manage the cinema. He agreed to come once a month to oversee the cinema and book films. He was deemed to be extremely successful and as a consequence Mrs Murphy later sold Ward Anderson a 50 per cent share in the business and within ten years Ward Anderson bought the outstanding 50 per cent. The cinema, which opened in 1921 with D.W. Griffith's *The Greatest Question*, continued until 1989, but its famous restaurant closed in 1985. (McSweeney, 2003:36–8.)

22. As well as being a prolific investor, he has been one of the Irish stock market's most vocal and litigious shareholders. As one article reported, 'If there is a row at an agm of an Irish-quoted company, you could probably put money that Anderson is behind it.' (Quoted, Ian Kehoe, *Sunday Business Post*, 12 June 2005:n10.)

23. Kevin Anderson, quoted in *IT*, 29 September 2004:commercial property 2.

24. A representative of one of the big American distribution houses has said that 'Leo is a very tough negotiator, he's one of the old school. You just sit down and thrash it out with him.' According to Albert Kelly, chairman of the Independent Cinema Association, Leo would '"knock the corners off you" in defending his own company's interests.' (*Sunday Business Post*, 11 September 1999:10.)

25. As one reporter noted in 1999, although Paul Ward and Paul Anderson run the various related companies, often separately, 'as far as the industry is concerned, Leo Ward is still the boss ... [He] has retained responsibility for negotiating with distributors.' In the words of an industry colleague: 'Leo *is* Ward Anderson.' (Declan Walsh, 'The force is strong in the warrior behind Ireland's film screens',

Sunday Business Post, 11 July 1999:10.) While Leo might be Ward Anderson, according to commentators, 'Ward Anderson *is* the cinema business in Ireland.' (Quoted in Brian Carey, 'Stars of the silver screen', *Sunday Tribune*, 7 November 1999:5.) Leo Ward's continuing interest in cinema was reflected in his appearance at the Light House Cinema on 30 November 2009 (by then 90 years old), when the film classifier, John Kelleher, screened, to an invited audience, his final film before retirement. In contrast to Ward, Kevin Anderson retired from the day-to-day running of the business in 1995, although he remains a shareholder. (John Mulligan, 'Tribute to veteran shareholder (93)', *Irish Independent*, 2 July 2008.)

26. Ian Kehoe, *Sunday Business Post*, 12 June 2005:10.
27. By summer 2010 the Omniplex Cinema group controlled cinemas in Armagh, Bangor, Belfast, Carlow, Carrickfergus, Clonmel, Cork, Derry, Drogheda, Dublin (four), Dundonald, Enniskillen, Galway (two), Kilkenny, Limerick, Lisburn, Longford, Newry, Tralee, Tullamore and Wexford.
28. *Evening Press*, 4 January 1985.
29. Leo Ward, 'Enterprise in the provinces', *Showcase*, March 1968:30.
30. See Ronan McGreevy, 'Indie cinemas condemn royalty charges', *IT*, 25 February 2010. IMRO is seeking to replace a tiered system of royalty fees with a blanket 1 per cent levy on gross box-office takings, and also proposing that this be backdated five years. According to small cinema operators, such a change, perhaps amounting to a five- to seven-fold increase, 'will absolutely crucify' them, while larger multiplexes under the new scheme would actually end up paying considerably less than previously. Paul Anderson has said that it would mean that his company would have to pay an extra €260,000 which would wipe out the profit in seven of their smaller cinemas. He argued that 'Ireland has a great tradition of cinemas in small towns. These cinemas never wrote this into their equations or into their business plans. Now they are being hit by a 400 per cent to 500 per cent increase.' The current rates are: cinemas in towns of less than 15,000 pay €425 per screen per year, while in more populated areas, cinemas with four screens or less pay 0.6 per cent of gross-box office, with larger multiplexes paying 1.5 per cent.
31. In 1970 Mesdames M. and A. Horgan informed the cinema trade complaints' committee that had it not been for Mr Ward's assistance they would have had to close their cinema, Horgan's theatre, Youghal, Co. Cork. (*Report of investigation by the examiner of restrictive practices into the distribution of cinema films*, unpublished, Dublin: Restrictive Practices Commission, 1977:7, hereafter, *RPC investigation*).
32. This is not true of all such cinemas. Seamus Quinn's high spec Cameo in Cork, for example, from the late 1960s onwards showed mainly adult European films.
33. Leo Ward, 'Enterprise in the provinces', *Showcase*, March 1968:30.
34. Kevin Anderson in Rose Doyle, *IT*, 29 September 2004:commercial property:2.
35. *KW*, 27 July 1961.
36. Ian Kehoe, *Sunday Business Post*, 12 June 2005:10. According to an unpublished interview in 1995 with Harvey O'Brien (UCD), Paul Ward said the overdraft was £8,000 and the proprietor was willing to sell it for another £2,000–£3,000.
37. The whole family worked at the cinema at least on Sundays when 700/800 tickets were sold, and some of the employees had the day off. (Rose Doyle, 'Trade names: lights, cameras and all action at city's premier cinema', *IT*, 25 January 2006:44.)
38. In the *Kinematograph* annuals, 1955–69, inclusive, the Lucan cinema is listed as the Premier with 290 seats and the proprietor is Lucan Cinemas, Ltd, while in the year book of 1970, it is listed as the Grove with 750 seats and the proprietor is still Lucan Cinemas, Ltd. According to an *IT* article, Paul Anderson renovated the cinema in 1967. (Rose Doyle, *IT*, 25 January 2006:commercial property 2.)
39. Des Hickey, *Showcase*, January 1968:29.
40. Besides the ones mentioned in the main text, other Dublin cinemas owned by Ward Anderson included the Star, Crumlin (1,750 seats), which closed in 1971 but seems to have reopened, and was destroyed by a fire in 1978, and, from 1968, the Gala, Ballyfermot (1,850 seats), which finally closed in 1980.
41. Mrs Scraggs and Miss O'Regan offered Ward Anderson an option to buy the Lee Cinema, Winthrop Street, in the late 1950s. Ward and Anderson downsized the cinema in 1972, and thereafter it became the most important of all Cork's second-run houses. It closed in 1989. (McSweeney, 2003:37, 71–4).
42. Initially Mrs Murphy made a 50/50 arrangement with Ward and Anderson in the 1950s, but they bought it outright within the decade. (McSweeney, 2003:37.)
43. According to Anderson, the 400-seat Grand Central in Limerick took business from the 2,000-seat Savoy opposite as a result 'of a slow cashier' at the Grand Central. '[P]eople would see the long queue and think there was a better film … in the Central and cross over.' (Rose Doyle, *IT*, 29

September 2004:commercial property 2.) According to the *Kinematograph* annuals, 1937–61, the Grand had either 600 seats (1935; 1940), or 650 seats (1937–61), thereafter (*KYB* to 1971), no seating capacity is given. It is first listed by *KYB* in 1923, so it opened in 1922 or earlier. The only cinema in Limerick that had a similar number of seats was the Thomond, which had about 500.

44. *Showcase*, October 1967:19.
45. Ward bought the distribution rights to the first seven James Bond films for £500. (Ian Kehoe, *Sunday Business Post*, 12 June 2005:10.)
46. The interest of the directors and the immediate family in the share capital of the company as of 31 October 1976 is listed below. The figures in brackets are the shares as of 31 October 1975. Kevin T. Anderson: 542,984 ordinary shares, 12,763 preference (135,746 ord., 12,763 pref.); Leo Ward: 208,176 ordinary shares, 1,134 preference (51,284 ord., 1,134 pref.); Paul Anderson: 92,964 ordinary shares (21,250 ord.); and Maurice Le Gear: 18,160 ordinary shares (4,540 ord.). The only change to directorial holdings from October 1976 to July 1977 was the acquisition of an additional 2,200 ordinary shares by M. Le Gear. The directors were not aware of any other holdings of more than 5 per cent.
47. Pre-tax profits for years ending 31 October. 1975: £384,298; 1974: £186,709; 1973: £92,184; 1972: £75,027; 1971: £71,597; 1970: £72,856; 1969: £54,310; 1968: £37,973; 1967: £21,928; and 1966: £19,233.
48. 'Green Group buys equity holdings in three cinemas', *IT*, 8 July 1977:12.
49. 'Someone keeping little secrets in this "Mills & Boon" tale?', *IT*, 6 July 1978:13; 'SE adopts tough policy on relisting Green Group', *IT*, 1 August 1978:12.
50. Bill Murdoch, 'Board of Green Group bids for outstanding shares', *IT*, 6 September 1978:14.
51. *IT*, 1 August 1978:12.
52. Bill Murdoch, 'Vocal minority fails to carry day at Green AGM', *IT*, 30 July 1977:14.
53. *IT*, 1 August 1978:12.   54. Bill Murdoch, *IT*, 6 September 1978:12.
55. Nevertheless, he understood that this was something secondary to the strategy employed by the directors who wished to use the cash for a future acquisition.
56. Bill Murdoch, *IT*, 6 September 1978:12.
57. Eoin McVey, 'Shareholders in Green Group to appeal to court', *IT*, 26 February 1979:14.
58. Bill Murdoch, *IT*, 6 September 1978:12.
59. Section 204 of the Companies' Act, 1963.
60. Eoin McVey, *IT*, 26 February 1979:14.   61. *IT*, 1 and 2 January 1979:15.
62. According to Gene Kerrigan (a cinema projectionist for thirteen years who was about to be made redundant with the sale of the Ambassador), Capitol and Allied Ltd was controlled at this time by New Hibernia Investment Trust, which in turn was controlled by Leopold Joseph Ltd, a British merchant bank, which felt it was not receiving a sufficiently high rate of return on these investments and had decided to sell the properties two years earlier. (Gene Kerrigan, 'Dublin's silent screens', *IT*, 13 December 1976:14.)
63. The *RPC report*, 1978:19, describes Ward Anderson as having 'interests in' cinemas in Inchicore, Ballyfermot, Lucan and Rathmines, probably meaning the company/ies did not have outright ownership of the premises at this time. Nevertheless, it seems that following the acquisition of Capitol and Allied Theatres in 1977, they had acquired the outstanding 50 per cent interest in Crumlin Cinemas (which had net tangible assets of £71,518 and average annualized pre-tax profits over the period 1973–6 of £16,456) for £36,000. (As early as 1974, having increased their holdings in the Crumlin Cinema to 50 per cent in 1970, they expressed an interest in buying it outright. [See 'Green Group shows large expansion', *IT*, 13 February 1970:14; 'Green Group share asset value now at 220p', *IT*, 12 April 1974:17. The cinema was destroyed by fire in 1978, but following a malicious damages case against Dublin corporation, Crumlin Cinemas, Ltd was awarded £30,000 plus costs, see cinemas' list, part 3.]) Also at this time, in 1977, Ward Anderson, through the Green Group, acquired the outstanding 50 per cent in Republic Cinemas, which had net tangible assets of £75,894 and average annualized pre-tax profits over the period 1973–6 of £3,052, for only £20,000. (It is rare that such information concerning the price at which a cinema is acquired, the asset value of a cinema seat, or the multiple of revenue by which a cinema is bought, is revealed. Figures are reported in 'Green Group buys equity holdings in three cinemas', *IT*, 8 July 1977:12. The article is based on the Green Group's annual report for the year ending 31 October 1976. Summary figures of trading profits, dividends, taxation, capital expenditure, cash flow, etc. for the years ending 1974, 1975 and 1976 are given at the end of the article.) In 2003, as is discussed below, Ward Anderson took over the Stella, Rathmines, perhaps as part of a strategy to close it down as it sought planning permission for a multiplex in the nearby Swan shopping centre which it owned.
64. See McSweeney, 2003:125–6.

65. According to the annual report to 31 October 1976 it was acquired for a 'nominal' sum. See *IT*, 8 July 1977:12.
66. This list draws on appendix 1 of the *RPC investigation*, 1977:71–7, which focuses on the ownership of cinemas and booking of films in 1976.
67. *Report of enquiry into the supply and distribution of cinema films*, Dublin: Stationery Office, 1978:17 (hereafter, *RPC enquiry*).
68. Leo Ward, *Showcase*, March 1968:30.   69. *RPC investigation*, 1977:3–9.
70. Road show films were excluded from this. (*RPC investigation*, 1977:10–12.)
71. *RPC investigation*, 1977:15. Four months later, another such complaint was addressed to the examiner.
72. Quoted, *RPC investigation*, 1977:16; Godfrey Fitzsimons, 'Support your local cinema', *IT*, 12 January 1976.
73. *RPC investigation*, 1977:17–18; 'Small cinemas "being muscled out"', *Evening Herald*, 20 January 1976:3.
74. *RPC investigation*, 1977:18–19.
75. Exhibitors made no complaint about IFRA members 'because the films were considered to be relatively unimportant; their commercial value was peripheral.' (*RPC investigation*, 1977:35.)
76. *RPC investigation*, 1977:24.
77. The following companies are listed in the examiner's report as being 'associated in the sense that' Leo Ward and Kevin Anderson were 'directors of all of them and in most cases both are directors': Securities Trust Ltd; Lucan Cinemas Ltd; Wicklow Cinema Ltd; Counties Cinema Ltd; Auburn Hall Ltd; Palace Theatre (Cork) Ltd; Lee Cinema Ltd; Pavilion Cinema & Café Ltd; National Cinemas Ltd; Carlton Cinema (Limerick) Ltd; Cinema Television Ltd; Abbey Films Ltd; National Electric & Cinema Equipment Co. Ltd; General Film Distributors Ltd; Amusements Ltd; Irish Empire Palace Ltd; Fire Fighting Equipment Ltd; Paramount Fashions Ltd; Southern Coliseums Ltd; Coliseum Cinema (Carlow) Ltd; Green Group Ltd; Finglas Cinemas Ltd; and Metropolitan Cinemas Ltd. Additionally, the Green Group, of which both men were directors, held 50 per cent equity in the following companies: Cinema and General Publicity Ltd; Crumlin Cinemas Ltd; Republic Cinemas Ltd; and Amalgamated Entertainments (Waterford) Ltd. In turn, Amalgamated Entertainments (Waterford) Ltd held the entire ordinary share capital in a further series of 'Amalgamated Entertainments' companies located in Kilkenny, Regina (Waterford), New Ross, Wexford, Nenagh and Tramore, as well as Cinema Palace Wexford Ltd (non-trading) and 50 per cent in Royal Cinema (Limerick) Ltd. Furthermore, Ward also booked for a number of cinemas not operated by Ward Anderson companies. (*RPC investigation*, 1977:20–1.)
    In the period 1974–77 (*RPC investigation*, 1977:106–206, see also 71–7), Leo Ward booked (though not necessarily exclusively) for over fifty cinemas, which are listed below by county. *Carlow*: Coliseum; *Cavan*: Magnet; *Cork city*: Capitol, Palace, Pavilion, and Lee; *Co. Cork*: Ormonde (Midleton), Ormonde (Cobh), Abbey (Youghal), Palace and Ormonde (Fermoy); *Dublin*: Grove/Panaroma (Lucan), Pullman (Inchicore), Green Cinema and Regent (Dublin city centre); *Galway*: Claddagh Palace, Town Hall, Savoy, and Estoria; *Kerry*: Picturedrome (Tralee), Theatre Royal (Tralee), Lakes (Killarney), and Astor (Listowel); *Kildare*: Grove (Athy); *Kilkenny*: Regent, and Savoy; *Limerick*: Royal, Grand Central/Central Studio, Carlton, Roxoboro Twin Theatres, and Movieland; *Louth*: Casino (Dundalk), and Abbey (Drogheda); *Mayo*: Star (Ballyhaunis), and Ideal (Westport); *Offaly*: Aisling (Birr), Savoy (Edenderry), and Ritz (Tullamore); *Tipperary*: Rock (Cashel), Regal (Clonmel), Ritz (Clonmel), Capitol (Thurles), New Cinema/New Theatre (Thurles), Rialto (Nenagh), and Oscar (Roscrea); *Waterford*: Regina (Waterford city), and Ormonde, Panorama, Oscar (all Dungarvan); *Westmeath*: Hibernian (Mullingar); *Wexford*: Abbey (Wexford town) and Ritz (New Ross); *Wicklow*: Panorama (Bray).
78. *RPC investigation*, 1977:25.   79. *RPC enquiry*, 1978:20.
80. 'We prefer to be film renters instead of cinema proprietors – it's an easier business. We lost money in cinemas in the hope that the situation would improve.' (Kevin Anderson, quoted, Gary Culliton, 'Nothing green about the screen tycoon', *IT*, 13 November, 1984:15.)
81. *RPC investigation*, 1977:44; *IT*, 3 December 1977:8; *Irish Press*, 2 December 1977:6; *Irish Independent*, 3 December 1977; *Irish Press*, 6 December 1977:9; 8 December 1977; 'Film distributors seek High Court declaration', *IT*, 8 December 1977:8.
82. Quoted in an Irish Cinemas Association response, *RPC investigation*, 1977:27.
83. The £2 million investment by the three groups was spent on rebuilding/dividing cinemas, installing new equipment, and providing new seating and fittings. (*Report of enquiry*, 1978:22.)
84. *RPC investigation*, 1977:27–8.   85. Ibid., 28.
86. *RPC enquiry*, 1978:38.   87. Ibid., 38.

88. Ibid., 42–3.
89. The final version of the PAC's terms of reference is set out in *RPC enquiry*, 1978:66–75.
90. *RPC enquiry*, 1978:45. 91. Ibid., 42.
92. Ibid. 93. *RPC investigation, 1977*:50.
94. Colman Conroy began his cinema career as house manager at Dublin's Savoy in 1932, and later worked in the Savoys in Cork and Limerick. He became personal assistant to Louis Elliman, and in November 1960, a director of Odeon (Ireland) Ltd and Irish Cinemas Ltd. (See 'Colman Conroy memories', *Evening Herald*, 31 August 1972:11.)
95. These were Modern Irish Theatres Ltd; Killarney Cinema Co. Ltd; Burren Cinema Co. Ltd; Thurles Cinema Co. Ltd; Portlaoise Cinema Co. Ltd; Naas Cinema Co. Ltd; Ballinasloe Cinema Co. Ltd; Tipperary Cinema Co. Ltd; and Kells Cinema Co. Ltd. (*RPC investigation, 1977*:22.)
96. *RPC investigation, 1977*:22. A cinema owned by the circuit in Killarney never opened, while the Green Group operated one in Thurles by 1976.
97. These were Amalgamated Cinemas (Ireland) Ltd; Ballina Cinemas Ltd; Carlow Cinemas Ltd; Ennis Cinemas Ltd; Galway Cinemas Ltd; Monaghan Cinema Ltd; Ritz (Clonmel) Ltd; Savoy Cinema (Sligo) Ltd; Waterford Cinema Co. Ltd; Western Cinemas Ltd; Hibernian Films Ltd; Astor Cinema Ltd; Grafton Cinemas Ltd; Clonbur Investment Co.; and Amalgamated Services Ltd. (*RPC investigation, 1977*:22.)
98. Their other cinemas in Carlow, Clonmel, Cork, Ennis, Galway, Kilkenny, Limerick, Waterford and Wexford were either closed down or leased. (*RPC investigation, 1977*:23.
99. *RPC investigation, 1977*:34.
1. Ibid., 36. 2. Ibid. 3. Ibid., 41.
4. Ibid. 5. Ibid., 43. 6. Ibid., 46.
7. Ibid., 63.
8. Kevin Rockett, 'The case against the KRS', *In Dublin*, no. 32, 29 July–11 August 1977:27.
9. *RPC investigation, 1977*:67–8. 10. Ibid., 70.
11. The examiner sent out 190 questionnaires but received only 52 completed replies, an indication, once again, of the decades-old secrecy being maintained by exhibitors.
12. *RPC enquiry*, 1978:15. 13. Ibid. 14. Ibid., 36.
15. Ibid., 32. 16. Ibid., 12. 17. Ibid., 32.
18. Although Ward Anderson denied that they were themselves party to any agreement elsewhere in the country, they felt that 'there was an agreement in respect of Dublin city centre.' (*RPC enquiry*, 1978:32.)
19. *RPC enquiry*, 1978:61. 20. Ibid., 58. 21. Ibid., 62.
22. Ibid., 58. 23. Ibid., 62–3. 24. *RPC investigation, 1977*:67.
25. *RPC enquiry*, 1978:60–1. 26. Ibid., 62.
27. The production allocation committee (PAC) had to meet within six weeks of receiving an application. It was to consist of two distributors' representatives, two exhibitors' representatives, and a chairman appointed by the Irish advisory committee of the Society of Film Distributors Ltd (SFD, formerly the Kinematograph Renters Society), with a quorum comprising of one distributors' representative, one exhibitors' representative, and the chairman. Decisions were to be reached by a majority of members present and voting. A representative of the examiner could attend all meetings of the PAC and the appeals' tribunal as an observer. Representatives of the Irish Cinema Association (ICA) and the Society of Cinema Exhibitors (SCE), if one of the parties is a member, the IAC (of the SFD), and the Irish Film Renters Association (IFRA) could also attend as observers. The costs involved in the running of the PAC and the appeals' tribunal were to be met by the IAC and IFRA in a proportion to their market share. (Fair practice rules, 'Supply and distribution of cinema films', Restrictive Practices Commission, 1978. See terms of reference and procedures for PCA, appendix 3, *RPC enquiry*, 1978:66–75.)
28. 'Cinema men again accuse big circuits', *Evening Press*, 5 June 1979:1.
29. Philip Molloy, '"Fair play for cinemas" order', *Evening Press*, 17 November 1984.
30. Philip Molloy, 'Can film monopoly be broken?', *Irish Press*, 16 February 1985:3.
31. In 1984, Michael Butler sought planning permission for the conversion of both the Film Centre and the Cameo to amusement arcades, but this was turned down by the corporation. (Frank Kilfeather, 'Closing cinemas worry council', *IT*, 12 September 1984:13.) The Cameo eventually closed down in 1990, though, by then, the Curzon had reopened as the Light House.
32. Clare Cronin, 'Cork's Cameo up for sale', *Cork Examiner*, 5 January 1984. It fully closed as a cinema in 1985.
33. *Sunday Independent*, 3 December 1978:5.
34. The company also owned Sundrive Cinema, Sundrive Road, Kimmage.

35. See Albert Kelly's obituary, *IT*, 30 July 2005:12. See also Roisín Ingle, 'Camp farce ages with a swagger', *Sunday Tribune*, 14 April 1996:5.
36. 'Cinemas reopen as films make a comeback', *Irish Press*, 12 June 1980.
37. Michael Dwyer, 'Healthy outlook to Irish industry', *Screen International*, 26 February 1983:10.
38. 'Rank sells city centre cinema', *IT*, 10 September 1983:7; 'Proposed sale of Dublin city cinemas referred to examiner', 7 April 1984:18; 'Cinemas takeover approved', 12 June 1984:16. While the Savoy and Odeon were freehold, the Metropole was at a nominal rent of £100 per year, the latter status not something favoured by Ward Anderson as they planned possible commercial property ventures on cinema sites, as would later happen with the Corinthian complex.
39. Leo Ward, quoted, *Evening Press*, 4 January 1985.
40. Paul Anderson, quoted, Rose Doyle, *IT*, 25 January 2006:commercial property 2.
41. Following the acquisition of the Rank cinemas in 1983, the Dublin city centre cinemas (open and closed) owned by Ward Anderson were the Savoy (five screens; six from 1996); Corinthian/Screen at O'Connell Bridge (two screens; closed 1993); New Metropole/Screen at College Street (three screens); Ambassador (one screen; closed 1999); Regent (one screen; closed March 1985); Academy (one screen; closed 1981); Green (two screens; closed 1987); and Astor, Eden Quay (one screen; closed 1984). By 2010, it had retained as cinemas only the Savoy (six screens) and Screen at College Street (three screens), though the opening in December 2009 of the three-screen Swan cinemas in the near centre city middle-class suburb of Rathmines brought its central Dublin screens to twelve. This is due to double when the St Stephen's Green shopping centre cinema opens.
42. *Evening Press*, 4 January 1985.
43. Ibid. In the same interview, Leo Ward pointed out that although he was also a distributor, he never took, nor would he have been allowed to take, advantage of this in terms of his role as an exhibitor. 'Producers whom I represent here want their profits maximised by having their films placed in the most appropriate cinemas regardless of who owns them.'
44. Paul Anderson quoted in *Evening Press*, 4 January 1985.
45. *Evening Press*, 4 January 1985; '£1 cinema brings back crowds', *IT*, 18 July 1984:8.
46. Ian Kehoe, *Sunday Business Post*, 12 June 2005:10.
47. *IT*, 13 August 1999:13; Michael Dwyer, 'Five new custom built screens in D'Olier St.', 13 June 1999:11.
48. *IT*, 20 June 1997:11.   49. *Evening Press*, 4 January 1985.
50. Gary Culliton, 'Nothing green about the screen tycoon', *IT*, 13 November 1984:15.
51. 'Doyle buys cinema', *IT*, 30 October 1987:24.
52. The project was to be designed by Dublin based RKD architects. 'Green cinema site to be filled', *IT*, 9 May 2002:property 18. See also 'Scots haven't skimped on Stephen's Green HQ', 31 March 2005:16.
53. See Frank McDonald and Kathy Sheridan, *The builders: how a small group of property developers fuelled the building boom and transformed Ireland*, London: Penguin, updated ed., 2009; orig. 2008.
54. Neil Callanan, 'Andersons plan €9m cineplex on roof of Stephen's Green centre', *Sunday Tribune*, 17 January 2010; Jack Fagan, 'Food court for top of St Stephen's Green centre', *IT*, 2 June 2010.
55. Frank Kilfeather, 'Famous cinema may become financial centre', *IT*, 12 July 1988:12; 19 September 1988.
56. *IT*, 1 September 2007:4.
57. See Fintan O'Toole, *IT*, 31 January 2009:B2. *CSI: The experience,* an interactive exhibition, also featured at the venue from 15 August 2009.
58. It seems that Ward Anderson bought into and/or booked for the Astor from the late 1970s following the death of Bertie McNally, after which the programme went more mainstream. His widow, Vogue McNally, who had been carrying on the business since her husband's death eight years earlier, said in 1984 that she could no longer afford to keep the cinema open and closed it, saying, 'I can't keep things going in the present difficult times' (*Evening Herald*, 16 June 1984), at which point Ward Anderson seems to have bought the cinema outright.
59. The Astor Cinema was redeveloped by 2006 as Astor House, with a basement comedy theatre – Murphy's Laughter Lounge – a bar and restaurant, three floors of offices and two floors of apartments. From 1998, the Laughter Lounge comedy club had been housed in the adjoining old Screen at O'Connell Bridge, formerly the Corinthian. (Jack Fagan, 'Quayside bar to set new benchmark', *IT*, 15 February 2006:commercial propery 4.)
60. Ces Cassidy, 'Are we looking at the last picture show?', *Irish Independent*, 1 October 1982:8.
61. 'Taped movie explosion kills cinema plans', *Evening Press*, 11 August 1981:3.
62. *Irish Independent*, 1 October 1982:8; *IT*, 10 August 1982:8.

63. *Evening Press*, 4 January 1985.
64. Leo Ward, quoted, *Evening Press*, 4 January 1985. In another *Irish Press* article (16 February 1985:3), he is quoted as estimating that the exchequer took about £3 million from the cinema exhibitors in 1983 and £2.5 million in 1984.
65. Ray Comiskey, 'Cinemas with no queues', *IT*, 10 August 1982:8.
66. *Screen International*, 26 February 1983:10.
67. Philip Molloy, 'Can film monopoly be broken?', *Irish Press*, 16 February 1985:3.
68. It was in recognition of the difficulties facing smaller cinemas (vis-à-vis video and their delayed access to film product) that the minister of finance, Bertie Ahern, kept the VAT rate on cinema tickets in 1992 at 12 per cent. (Daire O'Brien, 'Ward Anderson: cinema's secret empire', *Business and Finance*, 11 June 1992:14.)
69. Ian Kehoe, 'Record year for Irish film', *Sunday Business Post*, 28 December 2004:3.
70. *IT*, 10 September 2004: ticket 32.
71. *IT*, 7 January 2005: ticket 28.
72. For details of box office revenue for Irish-theme films, see appendix, table 13d. Though there was a decline in the success of Irish films in terms of annual box office during the late 2000s, with ten Irish films released in 2007 earning a total of just under €2 million, twelve in 2008 earning a total of just under €1.4 million, and ten in 2009 earning only just under €0.6 million. However, the thirteen releases during January–November 2010 took €1,278,217, the top grossing film being the critically acclaimed documentary *His & Hers* (Ken Wardrop) which took €325,000. (See also 'Box office breakdown', *IT*, 3 June 2010.)
73. Quoted, Gretchen Friemann, 'Battle of the titans – the multiplex in Ireland 10 years on', *Film Ireland*, no. 80, April/May 2001:31.
74. Quoted by Daire O'Brien, *Business and Finance*, 11 June 1992:13–14.
75. 'Silver screen enjoying another golden age', *IT*, 15 May 1998:finance 2.
76. The cinema opened in 1947. Husband and wife team, Pat and Kathleen Greene, who bought it in 2000, had run it from 1980. When it closed it had the same cinema seats and carpet as it had in 1980 when it was converted into a two-screen cinema. To mark its closing, Ryan Tubridy broadcast his RTÉ radio one morning show live from the cinema. (Eoin English, 'End of an era as curtain closes on cinema', *Irish Examiner*, 6 April 2006.)
77. Emma Cullinan, 'Old-style interior in new Dundrum cinema', *IT*, 2 November 2005:commercial property 6.
78. Monika Unsworth, 'Cinema gets back its Art Deco glory', *IT*, 25 October 1999:4.
79. Brendan McGrath, 'Video firm classic of boom and bust', *IT*, 9 October 1996:16.
80. They invested £4 million in equity and an arrangement was made to restructure the company's bank borrowings over a five-year period. (Brendan McGrath, 'Video firm classic of boom and bust', *IT*, 9 October 1996:16.)
81. Brendan McGrath, 'Xtra-vision video rental group sold for £20m', *IT*, 9 October 1996:16.
82. Emmet Malone, 'Screen drama', *IT*, 1 July 1994: business this week, 12.
83. Given that the company's cash flow in 1995–6 was £5 million, and according to industry experts the selling price would normally be four times the cash flow, it is likely that Blockbuster paid £20 million. (Brendan McGrath, *IT*, 9 October 1996:16.)
84. At this time, Viacom also owned UCI, Paramount and MTV.
85. Brendan McGrath, *IT*, 9 October 1996:16.
86. For the year ending 31 December 1997, the company's pre-tax profit was £2.24 million, or a 9 per cent profit margin, though after tax and goodwill amortization, profit was £258,000. In 1996, there was a loss of £508,000. (Nick Webb, 'Will technology kill the video store?', *Sunday Tribune*, 5 March 2000:6.)
87. Jamie Smyth, 'Xtra-vision restructures after losing top management', *Sunday Tribune*, 10 October 1999.
88. Siobhán O'Connell, 'IBEC's portrait of a video renter', *Sunday Business Post*, 22 December 1996:9.
89. 2001 was the first year in America that DVD sales, which constituted 52 per cent of the $10.3 billion American consumers spent on buying films, outpaced VCR sales. (Klinger, 2006:59.)
90. *Sunday Times*, 14 February 2010. For a 2004 comparative survey of eight Irish video/DVD clubs and comparison with five foreign stores, see *IT*, 19 November 2004:21.
91. *Sunday Tribune*, 7 December 2003:B3.
92. Derek O'Connor, 'Digital killed the video store', *IT*, 15 July 2005:B5.
93. John Mulligan, *Irish Independent*, 24 November 2007.
94. The additional €12 million payable to Blockbuster was contingent on Xtra-vision's profits reaching a certain figure. However, although the company made an operating profit of €1.1 million on

turnover of €52.9 million in the period immediately following the sale (that is from 18 August 2009 to 3 January 2010), it was just under the figure that would have triggered the top price of €32 million. (Laura Slattery, 'Operating profit of more than €1m for Xtra-vision', *IT*, 23 October 2010.)

95. It was second time round for Pageant since it had become majority owner of Xtra-vision when it was taken private in 1994 by a consortium involving investment funds HSBC Private Equity and 3i, at which time O'Grady-Walshe, a former finance director of bookmakers Paddy Power, was Xtra-vision's managing director. In 1996, they sold the business to Blockbuster. (Arthur Beesley, 'Pageant and NCB take over Xtra-vision in €32m deal', *IT*, 29 August 2009.)

96. Furlong was a founder of DVD distribution business Pilton, of which sendit.com was a subsidiary, and, as noted in the text, was sold to DCC in 2005 for €42.5 million. Furlong's and business partner Norman Lyons' career stretches from cable television installer National Cable Vision in the 1970s to the early video distribution in the 1980s before involvement with Blackstar and sendit.com in the 1990s and 2000s. For a profile of Furlong's business activities since the 1970s, including property developments, see *Sunday Tribune*, 19 June 2005.

97. *IT*, 29 August 2009; *Sunday Business Post*, 30 August 2009.

98. Laura Slattery, 'Operating profit of more than €1m for Xtra-vision', *IT*, 23 October 2010; Barry O'Halloran, 'Xtra-vision near to clearing €7m debt', *IT*, 25 November 2010. The articles note that the purchase price of €20 million involved taking a bank loan of €7 million. This loan was paid back by the end of 2010, and, notwithstanding the depressed nature of the retail market, particularly after September 2010, the company was still expecting to make a profit.

99. Alison Healy, 'Cancer society gives warning on sunbeds', *IT*, 6 July 2002:3.

1. Shane Coleman, 'Mellowed but still motivated', *Sunday Tribune*, 15 September 1996:10. See also Shane Coleman, 'Chartbusters chief denies sell-off is imminent', *Irish Independent*, 18 April 1996: business and recruitment 6.

2. Ray Managh, *IT*, 8 January 2009.

3. For the story of the boom and bust Irish property bubble, see Frank McDonald and Kathy Sheridan, *The builders*, 2009. Kelly's public justifications for his playing of the property 'game' over four decades, and his display of wealth despite massive bank debts, made him a regular subject of negative media comment.

4. The mechanism for this is the National Asset Management Agency (NAMA), a state agency charged with realizing in the long term the value of the assets, at least equivalent to the state's purchase of them through its acquisition of the 'toxic' loans.

5. Though Moviemagic's website (www.moviemagic.ie, accessed in February 2010), claimed that it had over twenty stores, only nineteen locations were listed, of which eleven were in Dublin and three in the adjoining county Meath, with one store each in Kildare, Wicklow, Wexford, Limerick and Mallow. At that time, videos and DVDs were renting for €12.68 each, or three for €38.09.

6. Such threats included video-on-demand; online subscription rental online; and video/DVD sales, and those from supermarkets/large retail outlets (such as Smyths toy stores and electrical outlets including Power City), which drove prices down. Until the late 1990s, European video and DVD prices, on average, were one-third higher than American prices.

7. The importance of the computer games market can be gauged from the Irish profile of Texas-based GameStop Corp., the largest such retailer in the USA, which in 2008 had fifty-eight shops in Ireland and Britain, eleven of them in Dublin. With 288 employees in 2007 (up from 182 the previous year), it generated pre-tax profits in 2007 of €3.6 million on turnover of €75.7 (up from €35.4 million in 2006), as a result of the launch of Sony's PlayStation 3 games' console, the continuing popularity of Microsoft's X-Box 360, and 'unprecedented demand' for Nintendo's Wii and DS products. GameStop's entry to Ireland occurred in 2003 when it took a controlling interest in Gamesworld, a distribution business founded in 1994 that had eleven shops. (*IT*, 18 December 2008:19.)

8. Ciarán Hancock, 'Xtra-vision held talks with Tesco on disposing of stores', *IT*, 27 February 2008.

9. www. xtravision.ie/stores, accessed December 2010. It emerged from examinership in July 2011.

10. *IT*, 8 January 2009; 23 January 2009:business 2; *Evening Herald*, 8 January 2009.

11. Murphy had stopped a post-dated cheque for €42,973 to the company.

12. *IT*, 28 January 2009. See also, *IT*, 24 April 2009:4.

13. *IT*, 31 July 2010:16.

14. *IT*, 29 October 2010:business 1; 30 October 2010:16. Another article in the *Times*, also on 29 October 2010, gave the number of employees as 170 (this was the number in 2009 when it went into examinership). It pointed out while DVDs had declined further, the tanning part of the operation had been affected by the growing concerns over the dangers tanning booths could cause to health.

15. Managing director Carlos Marco hoped that Original Video might become the '"New" Blockbuster'. (Carlos Marco quoted in 'Manufacturing Irish innovation', *Irish Entrepreneur*, April 2007.)
16. *Irish Independent*, 3 April 2006; *Shelf Life*, 15 June 2006.
17. *Liffey Champion*, 27 April 2007.
18. *Irish Entrepreneur*, April 2007; *Clare Champion*, 17 August 2006.
19. *Nenagh Guardian*, 14 April 2007; *Tipperary Star*, 7 April 2007.
20. www.original-video.com.
21. This figure is reported in Gavin Daly, 'Exceptional expenses hit profits at Sendit.com', *Sunday Business Post*, 7 August 2005, and Dick O'Brien, 'Job cuts at Sendit.com have led to increase in profits', *Sunday Business Post*, 24 February 2008. While the number of employees is not given in Douglas Keatinge, 'Star trek', *Sunday Tribune*, 7 May 2000:7, the article gives 130 as the number of countries in which it has clients.
22. Douglas Keatinge, *Sunday Tribune*, 7 May 2000:7.
23. Brendan Munnelly, *Evening Herald*, 15 September 1998:18.
24. Simon Carswell, 'Amazon jumps the gun on movie releases', *Sunday Business Post*, 7 November 1999:12.
25. See Gavin Daly, *Sunday Business Post*, 7 August 2005.
26. As well as sendit.com, Pilton's subsidiaries at the time of the company's purchase by DCC included NCVD Distribution, a Dublin-based video and DVD distributor; CGS Distribution, which distributes games; and VHS Distribution, a Belfast video and DVD firm. Pilton was incorporated into DCC's IT distribution division, which made an operating profit of €27.5 million on sales of €878.2 million in the year to end of March 2005. Pilton was viewed by DCC as complementary to the firm's subsidiary Gem Distribution, which sells entertainment and consumer products in Britain. (Gavin Daly, *Sunday Business Post*, 7 August 2005.)
27. Turnover for the year ending January 2005 had been over GB£8 million. (*Sunday Business Post*, 7 August 2005.)
28. Dick O'Brien, *Sunday Business Post*, 24 February 2008.
29. Prices vary little between the various companies. In spring 2008, most Irish online rental companies were offering two films per month for €8; an unlimited number of films, sent one at a time, for €8–€13; two at a time for €14–€18; three at a time for €19–€25; and four at a time for €27–€32. Generally companies offer two-week free trials.
30. Orla O'Sullivan, 'Will online DVD kill our video stores?', *Irish Independent*, 23 February 2006.
31. 'Digital deliverance', *IT*, 27 June 2002:53. Its packages were one DVD at a time for €25 per month; two DVDs at a time for €33 per month; and three DVDs at a time for €40 per month.
32. *Irish Independent*, 23 February 2006.
33. Smaller players in the Irish market include Rentastic, launched in January 2005, and Online DVD rental owned by investors Mark Beggs and Martin Gavin in Dublin and Christopher Stuart in Wexford. Online DVD rental is the company behind the rental of movies and games on the Movies@ website which was launched in July 2010.
34. Brian O'Connell, 'And what will no longer be here by 2020?', *IT*, 2 January 2010.
35. Their activities in Britain led them to be accused of running misleading prize promotions, while the Irish regulator closed down another McCannon company, Parcel Plus, in April 2004 for sending 'misleading postcards telling recipients to phone a premium rate line for details of a package awaiting delivery.' (Kieron Wood, 'Dublin brothers reported for renting out retail DVDs', *Sunday Business Post*, 10 September 2006:14.)
36. Ibid.   37. *IT*, 10 January 2006:16.
38. 'About Moviestar', www.moviestar.ie, April 2008. This website is no longer functioning following the takeover by Screenclick.com of Moviestar.ie in January 2009.
39. The arrangement is that a film can be downloaded and kept for one month. (Charlie Taylor, 'Moviestar to launch download service', www.enn.ie, 10 April 2008.) Content was to be provided by the BBC, the Biography Channel and others. (John Collins, 'Apple to sell new release films on iTunes', *IT*, 3 May 2008:8.) Of course, downloading of illegally acquired recently released feature films is the primary concern for production companies in the 2010s, and has replaced illegal copying and selling of DVDs as the film industry's main piracy issue.
40. Charlie Taylor, www.enn.ie, 10 April 2008.
41. See 'Online DVD rental little guys disappear', www.choosedvdrental.co.uk.
42. www.screenclick.com; http://dvdclub.irishtimes.com, accessed February 2010. Other LoveFilm 'white label' services and partners provided by LoveFilm include the *Guardian* newspaper's Sofa Cinema; W.H. Smith Movies Direct; Tesco DVD Rental; and Odeon Direct-Service with the Odeon cinema chain. The issue of online DVD rental 'unlimited' plans has been the subject of some con-

troversy, as, in practice, some of those who seek rapid replacement of returned DVDs under an unlimited plan have been 'throttled' by companies such as Screenclick. Given fast postal delivery times, it is possible that a client could receive so many shipments in a month that the cost of delivery to the company would be greater than the subscription fee, thus making the customer unprofitable. As a result, companies favour low volume customers who request fewer DVDs per month. Companies such as Netflix and Screenclick have been accused of deliberately slowing down shipments to high demand users, and this is particularly relevant in the case of a film in high demand when a low volume customer will receive priority over a high volume one. As a result, high demand customers may not get replacement DVDs on the day a returned DVD arrives. Some online renters have inserted 'fair use' clauses in contracts. Indeed such terms led to LoveFilm being investigated by the UK's Advertising Standards Authority (ASA) over their use of the word 'unlimited' in advertising. To avoid being accused of 'throttling' – a complaint against LoveFilm concerning 'throttling' was upheld by the ASA in 2006 – some companies have instituted a 'cap' on rental numbers with additional shipping charges applying once the 'cap' is reached. While Blockbuster declared in 2006 that it did not practice 'throttling', its terms and conditions give the company power to restrict product allocation to customers. (See 'Online video rental', *Wikipedia.org*, with website reference links.)

43. *Irish Independent*, 23 February 2006.
44. In 2000 it was estimated that only 1,000, or about a quarter, of the films made in America each year are distributed. (Kate Stable, 'Indie exposure', *Sight and Sound*, April 2000:5.)
45. Jamie Allen, 'The golden age of the short: shorts move from film-class project to big time on the Web', www.CNN com, 15 May 2000, cited by Klinger, 2006:195.
46. Klinger, 2006:197.
47. John Collins, 'Apple to sell new release films on iTunes', *IT*, 3 May 2008:8.
48. Marie Boran, 'Moviestar.ie brings Ireland's first download service', www.silicon republic.com/news, 10 April 2006.
49. As Anderson recalls, 'When I was growing up we had an outing to the cinema around twice a week.' Quoted, Alison O'Riordan, 'A good movie at the cinema is just the ticket to beat the doom', *Sunday Independent*, 7 June 2009.
50. Quoted in John Mulligan, 'Cinema boss Spurling is relishing chance to keep reeling in the public', *Irish Independent*, 8 July 2010.

CHAPTER 5

1. Bruno Frydman, 'Exporting the multiplex model to Europe: the experience of AMC', *The impact of multiplexes on the cinema market and on their environment*, Amsterdam – Cinema Expo International, 15 June 1998 (wwwmediasalles.it/expo98), cited in Hanson, 2007:176.
2. Gomery, 1992:100. It should be noted, though, that well before the 1960s, shops formed an integral part of some cinema projects. Examples in Belfast include the Duncairn Cinema, which opened in 1916; the Troxy, with six shops, opened in 1936; and the Forum, Crumlin Road, which opened the following year. (See Open, 1985:40–4.)
3. Philip Molloy, 'Provincial cinemas moving to multiplex', *Irish Press*, 30 December 1987:3. By the 2000s, the Abbey, Wexford, had been sold and one of the town's first apartment developments was built on the site. In the early 1990s Ward Anderson had developed the three-screen Savoy Cineplex, Redmond Square. This closed in 2008 when their eight-screen, 1,550/1,600-seat, €9 million Omniplex opened at LeisureMax, a recreational centre which incorporated Wexford's first bowling alley, in the suburb of Drinagh. (Maria Pepper, 'Projected July opening for €9 million Omniplex', *Wexford People*, 9 January 2008.)
4. McSweeney, 2003:132. The state-of-the-art cinema, renamed the Capitol Cineplex, had six screens.
5. Some set the minimum at eight screens by which efficiencies of scale are achieved. (*Screen Digest*, May 1996:106.)
6. While Britain's first multiplex cinema, the 2,000-seat, ten-screen complex in Milton Keynes, north of London, which cost GB£7.7 million, had a radical pyramid design, few multiplexes thereafter risked such investment. Nevertheless, as Gomery points out in his 1992 study, the Cineplex Odeon chain and United Artists theatre chain, were both favouring a postmodern look, while some in the American industry were suggesting that film exhibition might return to the mini-movie palaces of the past. (Gomery, 1992:115.)
7. Michael Dwyer, 'Let there be light', *IT*, 25 April 2008:ticket 4–5. For a discussion of haptic space, see Juhani Pallasmaa, *The eyes of the skin: architecture and the senses*, Polemics series, London: Academy, 1996.

8. Hanson, 2007:159.
9. Ciarán Hancock, 'The multiplex effect', *Sunday Times*, 26 October 2003:business, 9.
10. Bruno Frydman cited in Hanson, 2007:176. See note 1, p. 535.
11. Such was the uncertainty within the market in the wake of the establishment of NAMA (referred to in chapter 4) that in 2010 bookmaker Paddy Power offered odds as to which of the big developers would open their cinema first. The Bailey brothers' Bovale Developments, which plans to open a nine-screen cinema at Charlestown shopping centre in Finglas came in first at 4/5; Bernard McNamara's Tallaght complex at 7/4; while Treasury Holdings' Spring Cross multiplex was at 4/1. (See 'Developers outline cinema complex plans for Dublin', *Irish Independent*, 21 July 2010.) The Bovale Charlestown project represents a €135 million investment, with an expected 500 jobs created in the construction, the cinema is due to be run by UCI. The first phase of the centre was completed in 2007 and cost €150 million. (See Ciarán Hancock, 'Bovale to spend €135m expanding Finglas centre', *IT*, 11 November 2009.) The Tallaght multiplex is due to be operated by UCI (Donal Buckley, 'McNamara to build €100m Tallaght cinema complex', *Independent*, 30 June 2010), while the nine-screen Ballymun cinema, which will be completed as part of the first phase of construction, will be run by Vue, which currently runs one of Ireland's largest cinemas at Liffey Valley ('Multiplex cinema to open in Ballymun', *IT*, 8 June 2010; Neil Callanan, 'Vue to open cinema in new Ballymun centre', *Tribune*, 6 June 2010; see also 'Permission secured for Ballymun Town Centre redevelopment', 21 September 2009, www.businessand leadership.com accessed 25 July 2010.) Of course, the ongoing recession may mean that some, if not all, of these developments may not be built.
    Another multiplex more likely to open is the twelve-screen Ward Anderson Stephen's Green cinema. Though Stephen's Green shopping centre is not of the scale of the complexes cited above, and is without such entertainment leisure facilities as are planned for in these other centres (a bowling alley, for example, will be included at Ballymun, while a Leisureplex complex will be in Finglas), Stephen's Green, nevertheless, is a busy shopping centre, whose current top floor will be converted to a food hall to complement the cinemas which will be above the centre.
12. Fintan Tierney of commercial agents Lambert Smith Hampton, quoted in Edel Morgan, 'Screens multiply, but moviegoers want more', *IT*, 21 June 2001:commercial property 4. In America during the late 1960s the importance of the cinema as a means of generating additional footfall made the presence of a cinema at a shopping centre a commercial necessity for all shopping complexes. (Paul Monaco, *The sixties, 1960–1969*, History of the American cinema, vol. 8, Berkeley: University of California, 2001:50. See also Friedberg, 1993; and Gomery, 1992.) A Singapore survey of over 1,000 shoppers in nine centres confirmed that 'both physical size and the presence of a Cineplex enhance the magnetism of suburban shopping centers.' (Joseph T.L. Ooi and Loo-Lee Sim, 'The magnetism of suburban shopping centers: do size and Cineplex matter?', *Journal of property investment and finance*, vol. 25, no. 2, 2007:111–35.)
13. Ooi and Sim, 'The magnetism of suburban shopping centers', 111–35.
14. Quoted in Emma Kennedy, 'Multiplexes dominate in €17.8m [sic] box office battle', *Sunday Business Post*, 5 August 2007.
15. Douglas Gomery, 'Thinking about motion picture exhibition', *Velvet Light Trap*, no. 25, spring 1990:6.
16. Friedberg, 1993:122.
17. *Jaws*, which radically reshaped future booking patterns, opened simultaneously on 464 screens in the summer of 1975. By 1990, it was not unusual for a film to be saturation-booked in 2,000 theatres, thereby necessitating about ten times the number of prints than for a 1940s 'A' film. (See Richard Maltby, '"Nobody knows everything": post-classical historiographies and consolidated entertainment', and Douglas Gomery, 'Hollywood corporate business practice and periodizing contemporary film history', both in Steve Neale and Murray Smith (eds), *Contemporary Hollywood cinema*, London: Routledge, 1998.)
18. As was pointed out in 'Silver screen enjoying another golden age', *IT*, 15 May 1998, 'with the demise of cinemas such as the Light House and Adelphi in Dublin there are fewer theatres willing to show non-commercial or artistic movies'.
19. Brendan McCaul, managing director of Buena Vista International (Ireland), quoted by Gretchen Friemann, 'Battle of the titans – the multiplex in Ireland 10 years on', *Film Ireland*, no. 80, April/May 2001:31.
20. Lir Mac Cárthaigh and Esther Terradas in conversation with Margaret Taylor, UGC's managing director, 'Beyond the block buster' *Film Ireland*, no. 96, January/February 2004:25.
21. Friemann, *Film Ireland*, no. 80, April/May 2001:31.
22. Cited by Michael Hannigan of the Kino, Cork, in *Film Ireland*, no. 80, April/May 2001:31.
23. Gomery, 1992:106. During Christmas and Easter school holidays they also offered a free baby-sit-

ting service whereby parents could buy a cinema ticket for the child to see a Disney reissue while the parents could go off for the duration of the movie. Apart from regular special children's screenings (kids' clubs) in many Irish cinemas on Saturday and Sunday mornings/early afternoons (and in some cinemas including the Ormonde, Stillorgan every day during school holidays), in the 2000s many Irish cinemas introduced special parent and toddler screenings. While these screenings offer mostly adult-oriented fare they are unlike regular film screenings as pre-schoolers are welcome, and it is 'OK for babies to sleep, feed & cry', and as the Ormonde cinema, Stillorgan, website also states, 'where it's OK for moms to feed & change baby without the glaring eyes of others.' Introduced first in Ireland in 2004 by Ruth Spurling (of the Ormonde and Movies@) it remains popular and as of summer 2010 was (generally) priced at €7.00 (inclusive of tea/coffee). 'Reel parents' operates at Movies@ Dundrum and Swords, and the Ormonde Stillorgan, while 'Baby boom' operates at a number of IMC cinemas, including Dún Laoghaire and Dundalk. See Deirdre Falvey, 'Will the monsters bawl?' *IT*, 28 August 2004: magazine 19, who describes it as 'a good, civilized idea, that works.' See Anna Carey, 'Box-office babies', *IT*, 7 August 2010: magazine 7, on baby-friendly screenings at the Light House, Dublin.

24. Leo Ward, quoted, 'Credits rolls for glorious cinemas', *IT*, 20 June 2001:A4.
25. Derek O'Connor, 'How the audience steals the show', *IT*, 12 November 2002:13.
26. The high level of noise output makes whispering impossible. On the other side, one *IT* reader in response to a letter complaining about the over-amplification of cinemas and asking why sound levels were so high, wrote that 'perhaps it's to combat the noise of latecomers looking for seats in the darkness, sweets being unwrapped and chewed, popcorn being devoured, cans of drink being popped open – and even the odd mobile phone or two going off for good measure.' (Linda Cusack, 'Noise levels in cinemas', *IT*, letters, 1 March 2001: 17.) See also Joe Patton, 'Noise levels in cinemas', *IT*, letters, 26 February 2001:17.
27. According to Douglas Gomery, by the 1980s 'talking and constant commotion had become the order of the movies in the [American] mall.' (Gomery, 1992:101.)
28. Donald Clarke, 'Screen sensation', *IT*, 19 April 2003:magazine 4.
29. Mark Anderson, operations manager of Ward Anderson, talking to Donald Clarke, 'Lowering the tone', *IT*, 24 April 2003:ticket 7. See also Paul Lambert, 'Does jamming mobiles break the law?', *Sunday Business Post*, 6 April 2003; Hugh Linehan, 'Law obliges cinema to stop using mobile phone jammer', *IT*, 26 April 2003:4.
30. Adrian Weckler, 'Celluloid fans take on the noise', *Sunday Business Post*, 20 August 2006.
31. Allocated seating only is available since beginning of 2010 at IMC Dún Laoghaire.
32. Acland, 2003:115, citing article in *Variety*, 11 April 1990:13. Other booking innovations have included Canalnumedia Ireland's FilmLine, Ireland's first interactive voice response (IVR) cinema listings and booking service, which, with the support of iTouch, was launched in early 2001 (see *Waterford News & Star*, 14 February 2001), while in August 2006 UCI Tallaght introduced a new service whereby customers who purchased tickets online were sent mobile phone text messages with a unique barcode.
33. Susan Cross, director of communications for the National Association of Concessionaires, quoted in Anne Gilbert, 'The cult of corn', *In Focus*, January 2006, www.insightcinema.org, 3 May 2008.
34. See Gomery, 1992:79–82.   35. Ibid., 113.
36. Acland, 2003:99, citing article by John W. Quinn, 'Exhibs bellied up to candy/popcorn bar at ShoWest's Trade Fair', *Variety*, 25 February, 1988:9.
37. 'Industry boss calls for alternative to junk food at movie theatres', *Irish Examiner*, 18 March 2010.
38. According to Professor Donal O'Shea, consultant endocrinologist at St Columcille's Hospital, Dublin, speaking in 2010, a quarter of the Irish population is obese. ('Industry boss calls for alternative to junk food at movie theatres', *Irish Examiner*, 18 March 2010.)
39. Fiona Looney, 'Why going to the movies can turn you into a tub', *Sunday Tribune*, 27 March 2005:3. Drink portions are similarly excessive with a typical large fizzy drink served in Irish cinemas containing the same amount of calories as two pints of alcohol, while according to a recent *Irish Examiner* report some US cinemas offer 64-ounce drinks that are thirteen times the size of the drinks offered in the 1940s. ('Industry boss calls for alternative to junk food at movie theatres', *Irish Examiner*, 18 March 2010.)
40. 'Industry boss calls for alternative to junk food at movie theatres', *Irish Examiner*, 18 March 2010.
41. *Statistical Abstract of Ireland*, 1972–3:231, 271.
42. Damien O'Donnell, 'Cinema film distribution and exhibition in Ireland', *Irish Communications Review*, vol. 2, Dublin: DIT, 1992:8.
43. Catherine Cleary, 'Exponential growth needed to fill seats at the multiplex', *IT*, 9 February 1996:business this week 3.

44. Brian Carey, 'Rolling the celluloid credit lines', *Sunday Business Post*, 29 June 1997:10.
45. Joe Humphreys, 'Silver screen enjoying another golden age', *IT*, 15 May 1998:business this week 2.
46. Edel Morgan, 'Screens multiply, but moviegoers want more', *IT*, 21 June 2001:commercial property 4.
47. Gretchen Friemann, *Film Ireland*, no. 80, April/May 2001:30.
48. Kathy Sherdian, 'Ireland goes to the movies', *IT*, 25 November 1995:weekend 3.
49. See table, 'Cinema revenues and costs 1998–2003',Ted Sheehy, 'Future looks bright for Irish cinemas – large and small', *IT*, 19 March 2004:4.
50. *MEDIA Salles*, gross box office table, *European Cinema Yearbook*, 2008. See also Barry O'Halloran, 'UCI Irish division reports 14% rise in pre-tax profits', *IT*, 5 January 2005:17.
51. *Sunday Times*, 3 April 2005:10.
52. See table, Ted Sheehy, *IT*, 19 March 2004.
53. Ciarán Hancock, 'The multiplex effect', *Sunday Times*, 26 October 2003:business 9.
54. The exhibitor-distributor split was usually about 60 to 65 per cent (exhibitor) to 35 to 40 per cent (distributor).
55. Though this figure, cited by *Independent on Sunday*, 4 December 1994, and quoted in Hanson, 2007:177, is in relation to the British market, there is no significant difference in the mark up in both jurisdictions.
56. 'Silver screen enjoying another golden age', *IT*, 15 May 1998:business 2.
57. *Sunday Tribune*, 13 June 1999:3.
58. Kathy Sherdian, *IT*, 25 November 1995:weekend 3.
59. *Sunday Tribune*, 13 April 2003:41.
60. In 2009, combined UK and Republic of Ireland gross box office revenue was £1,127 million from 173.5 million tickets, of which UK box office alone was £944 million, or 88.19 per cent, of the total for the two islands. However, the figure includes revenue generated to 21 February 2010 for 2009 releases, suggesting that the division between the two jurisdictions is approximately ten to one. (Table 1.4, *UK Film Council statistical yearbook, 2010*:11, http://rsu.ukfilmcouncil.org.uk.)
61. *UK Film Council statistical yearbook, 2009*, http://rsu.ukfilmcouncil.org.uk.
62. Table 1.4, *UK Film Council statistical yearbook, 2010*:11, http://rsu.ukfilmcouncil.org.uk.
63. See also David Clerkin, 'Cinemas reel in the punters', *Sunday Business Post*, 19 March 2006.
64. 'Postman thrown out of cinema for buying his own (much cheaper) sweets elsewhere', *Daily Mail*, 19 February 2008.
65. Luke Roberts of Cineworld quoted in *Daily Mail*, 19 February 2008. While cinema operators such as Pat Ryan, general manager of Carlow Cineplex, speaking in 2009, often draw attention to similar policies operating in public houses and restaurants by saying that bringing food into the cinema is the equivalent of 'bringing a sandwich into a restaurant', it is important to point out that the primary reason of visiting a cinema is not to eat or drink, and as such while one could argue that many restaurants demand a corkage fee on wine brought by the patrons, a more accurate comparison given that the link between cinema and food is not an intrinsic one, as is food and drink, but one created largely by the industry, might be whether such establishments allow their patrons bring in their own books/newspapers/DSs, or, perhaps more fairly as public phones are often provided in such establishments, mobile phones. (See Pat Ryan, quoted, 'Dad's fury as sweets binned in cinema', *Nationalist*, 4 February 2009.) Ultimately, of course, it is an issue of profit and whether cinemas for economic reasons should be rebranded as dining-cinemas.
66. John Mulligan, '3-D adds a new dimension to Cineworld box office income', *Irish Independent*, 8 January 2010. Their box office receipts for 2009 rose even more dramatically and were 16.8 per cent up on 2008. The rise in sales and box office more than compensated for the loss in advertising income.
67. 'Dad's fury as sweets binned in cinema', *Nationalist*, 4 February 2009.
68. 'Cue the profits for big screen ad agencies', *Sunday Times*, 3 April 2005:10. This figure was also given by David Clerkin, 'Cinemas reel in the punters', *Sunday Business Post*, 19 March 2006, and Ted Sheehy, *IT*, 19 March 2004. During 1998–2003, gross cinema advertising revenue rose from €4.7 m. in 1998 to €10 m. in 2003 (Table, 'Cinema revenues and costs 1998–2003', Ted Sheehy, *IT*, 19 March 2004.) As in other areas of the economy, the cinema advertising business 'endured a tough couple of years during 2008 to 2009, with advertising revenue falling 15 per cent in 2009 alone. In 2010, a 30-second advertisement shown for six weeks at every screening in all seventy-one cinemas across more than 400 screens serviced by Carlton Screen Advertising, the dominant company, cost €73,000, including the *c.*€4,000 cost of converting a television commercial to 35mm. It was anticipated that Carlton would take over advertising rights for the Vue at Liffey Valley and

the Eye at Galway, from Pearl and Dean, thus creating a monopoly advertising supplier for Irish cinemas. (Siobhan O'Connell, *IT*, 17 June 2010.)

69. Andrew McKimm, 'There's something for everyone on 17 screens', *Sunday Independent*, 23 November 2003:living, 17.
70. Lir Mac Cárthaigh and Esther Terradas, *Film Ireland*, no. 96, January/February 2004:24.
71. See Monaco, *The sixties, 1960–1969*, 2001:48–50. For a general history of the multiplex in America, see Gomery, 1992:93–114.
72. *Box Office*, 29 May 1961:6, cited in Monaco, *The sixties, 1960–1969*, 2001:48. By 1960, there were already twenty-five such cinemas. (*Variety*, 24 August 1960:3.)
73. Warner Bros International Theatres, for example, was integrated with Warner Bros; United Cinemas International (UCI) with Paramount and Universal; and MCA with its own Universal.
74. Hanson, 2007:152.
75. In addition to the 1,550 screens of Cineplex Odeon, MCA also had acquired Plitt (692 screens); Septum (48 screens); Essaness (41 screens); Sterling Recreation Organization (100 screens, but licenses pictures for an additional 30 screens); and Neighborhood (76 screens). Included in table of distributors' theatre acquisitions, 1986–87, in Wasko, 1995:178; orig. 1994.
76. Aljean Harmetz, 'Hollywood starts an invasion of Europe's booming market', *New York Times*, 11 January 1990:C19, cited, Wasko, 1995:234.
77. The best-known cinema chain brand with which the Massachusetts-based company is associated is Showcase. The first Showcase cinema in Britain was opened in 1988 in Nottingham.
78. In 1986 the domestic market was 65 per cent of the total, but, by 1991, it had been reduced to almost parity with the foreign market and was at 53.2 per cent. (Wasko, 1995:220.)
79. Quoted, Wasko, 1995:234.
80. *Screen Digest*, May 1996:107; MEDIA Salles, *European Cinema Journal*, international ed., no. 2, June 1999:1. The latter publication puts the 1991 figure for the eighteen countries of western Europe at 625 million admissions.
81. See Acland, 2003:134–6.
82. *The Hollywood Reporter*, May 1991:S–4, quoted in Hanson, 2007:145.
83. *Screen Digest*, May 1996:107. See also MEDIA Salles, *European Cinema Journal*, international ed., no. 2, June 1999.
84. See Hanson, 2007:146–8.
85. Damien Kiberd, 'Breaking onto the screen', *Sunday Tribune*, 5 July 1987:21.
86. Ray Comiskey, 'Multiplexes; cinemas of the future?', *IT*, 2 May 1988:14. See also Comiskey, 'Why is film-going in Ireland so depressing?', 10 August 1987:10.
87. This figure was given in a judgment on 25 July 1997 by the valuation tribunal following an appeal by UCI against the determination of the commissioner of valuation in fixing a rateable valuation of £3,000 on the Coolock cinemas. The tribunal reduced the RV to £1,825 following examination of rates paid by other Dublin cinema complexes. See appeal no. VA96/2/040 under Valuation Act 1988 at www.valuation-trib.ie.
88. Jill Kerby, 'Monarch to build £5m complex', *IT*, 5 May 1988:18. These figures later proved to be somewhat exaggerated.
89. See Michael Dwyer, 'Plans for giant Dublin cinemas', *IT*, 8 December 1988:16. Indeed when the Coolock cinema opened in July 1991, Dwyer quoted Ian Grey, marketing managing of UCI, who viewed the Coolcock and Tallaght multiplexes as fitting the company's 'pro forma' very nicely. 'The population exists there, the road links and the public transport are very good, and there was no existing cinema.' *IT*, 31 July 1991:6.
90. 87 per cent of the population were under 40 years of age. 'Welcome to the Square', *Square Times*, October 1990:2.
91. Taoiseach Charles Haughey officially opened the centre on 23 October 1990. See Jackie Gallagher, 'Tallaght in carnival mood as 45,000 attend The Square opening', *IT*, 24 October 1990:5.
92. Tony Parker, 'Shopping centre space increases by 35%', *IT*, 17 October 2001:34.
93. 'Robinson opens 12-screen cinema', *IT*, 28 November 1990:14. It opened to the public on 30 November.
94. 'Welcome to the Square', *Square Times*, October 1990:2–3.
95. 'Tallaght[:] A new lease of life', *Square Times*, October 1990:4. The article also notes that the developers spent £700,000 on a footbridge linking residents in isolated housing estates to the centre. A schematic map included in the *Square Times*, October 1990:15, illustrates The Square's accessibility via the N4, the N7, the N81 and the Belgard Road, from (in a clockwise direction) Castleknock/Blanchardstown; Inchicore/Ballyfermot/Bluebell; South Circular Road/Crumlin/city centre; Rathgar/Rathmines/city centre; Dundrum/Mount Merrion/Dún Laoghaire; Firhouse;

Springfield/Blessington; Baldonnell/Rathcoole/Naas/Newbridge; Clondalkin/Lucan/Leixlip; and Lucan-Leixlip.

96. See Hanson, 2007:146–8.
97. John McGee, 'Screening for Mercy!', *Business and Finance*, 11 October 1990:42.
98. Ibid.
99. By 2002 there were only forty-seven independent cinemas nationally. Rose Doyle, 'The *Rocky Horror* road to success', *Irish Independent*, 22 May 2002.
 1. Michael Dwyer, *IT*, 31 July 1991:6.
 2. *Moving Pictures International*, 17 January 1991:12, quoted, Hanson, 2007:160–1.
 3. Daire O'Brien, 'Ward Anderson: cinema's secret empire', *Business and Finance*, 11 June 1992:13.
 4. Sally Beckett, director of publicity at Warner Village, cited, *Observer*, 27 September 1998, and quoted in Hanson, 2007:161.
 5. Leo Ward quoted, Joe Humphreys, 'Silver screen enjoying another golden age', *IT*, 15 May 1998:business 2.
 6. 'UCI multiplex for Blanchardstown centre', *IT*, 26 April 1995:commercial property 24.
 7. Brian Carey, 'Happy year at UCI', *Sunday Business Post*, 12 February 1995:2. The figure of £12,715 is converted back from a CSO table which retrospectively gives the wage equivalents in euro: €16,096 converted at rate of £1= €1.27. With a similar conversion, the average industrial wage in 1992 was £17,500 (equivalent to €22,151), which is arrived at by extrapolating the wages and salaries element (82.8 per cent) from the total labour costs per employee in 1992 of £21,023 (€26,612). In distribution, the total labour costs per employee was £15,247 (€19,300), making the average wages and salaries £12,715 (€16,096), 83.4 per cent of the total. (Central Statistics Office, *Labour costs survey, 2000*, Dublin: Stationery Office, July 2002:viii.)
 8. *Film Ireland*, no. 57, February/March 1997:11. The rent for the cinemas was said to be £4 million per annum.
 9. *Screen Digest*, May 1996:111.
10. British Screen was founded by Simon Perry, who in 2006 became the Irish Film Board's chief executive; Alistair Gregory; and Marc Samuelson. The group's most notable achievement was the development of London's Greenwich cinema, the biggest-grossing three-screen cinema outside London's West End in 1991.
11. Ralf Ludemass, 'Alternative Ulster', *Screen International*, 4 October 1991:13.
12. 'Work to start on £30m leisure centre in central Dublin', *IT*, 20 January 1993:commercial property 20.
13. Frank Khan and Liz Allen, 'Final curtain falls at the Adelphi', *Irish Independent*, 1 December 1995:5. For a nostalgic piece on the visit of the Beatles to the Adelphi in 1963, see *Sunday Tribune*, 5 November 1995:magazine 6–7.
14. The move back into the city is a feature of later multiplexes. In Britain in the period from 2001 to 2004, there was a 20 per cent increase in city or near-city multiplexes. According to a 2003 report by the London Assembly cited in Hanson, 2007:157, only two cinemas were built in out-of-town locations around London since 1998, while twelve were built in the city centre, a reflection of British government policy as developed during 1993 to 1997. The scale of city centre Dublin does not allow for similar comparisons. Nevertheless, the development in the early 2000s of Railway Square in Waterford is another example of the move away from suburban or 'out-of-town' developments. (See 'Eight-screen multiplex cinema for Railway Square', *Waterford News & Star*, 1 May 2003.) The Waterford city cinema operated by Storm Cinemas opened on 8 June 2007. The proposed twelve-screen Ward Anderson complex on top of Dublin's Stephen's Green shopping centre, announced in 2010, discussed below, also fits this policy.
15. While the Sheridan Group paid £2.5 million plus costs for the site, they sold part of the site for £625,000 on which apartments were built; the carpark for £3.5 million; while it was expected that they would get £4.1 million for the nine-screen cinema. The project took four-and-a-half-years to be realized. (See Shane Coleman [interviewing Peter Curistan, managing director of Sheridan Group], 'Cinema plan an inner city success', *Irish Independent*, 8 February 1996:business 3. See also Jack Fagan, '£15m leisure complex for Dublin's inner city', *IT*, 6 February 1992:1.
16. 'Bank to sell Irish cinemas', *IT*, 2 February 1995:19; Siobhan O'Connell, 'Virgin boss expands his empire to north Dublin', *Sunday Business Post*, 19 November 1995:7, 8.
17. The letting was for a term of thirty-five years and the rent was subject to review on a five-yearly basis. Quoted in judgment of the valuation tribunal issued on 25 July 1997 with regard to appeal no. VA96/2/040, UCI. http://www.valuation-trib.ie/categories/theatre. cinema/VA962040.htm.
18. 'UGC buys film arms of Virgin', *IT*, 19 October 1999:17.
19. Ian Kehoe, 'Cineworld profits jump', *Sunday Business Post*, 12 November 2006.

20. Hanson, 2007:166.
21. 'Belfast launch for blind-deaf cinema', *BBC News*, 4 January 2002, web: news.bbc.co.uk. Designed by UK company DTS, subtitles relay dialogue and describe various accompanying sounds for the deaf or hard of hearing, while headphones with extra narration describing the visuals are provided to blind or poorly sighted people.
22. Quoted in ibid. The ticket prices for the special screenings were the same as for all other screenings. Movie House's efforts have been recognized, as is evident in one (anonymous) blogger's comments following the opening of Belfast's new Odeon cinema in Belfast's Victoria Square in 2008, 'Let us hope that the hideous new Odeon … is a financial disaster. [C]ontinue to support Ulster's indigenous cinema chain the Movie House. [T]hose chaps kept the silver screens flickering during the dark years …' posted 26 July 2008; lordbelmontinnorthernireland.blogspot.com.
23. As late as 2006, letter-writer Maria O'Gorman from Limerick answered the question posed in the *Irish Examiner*, 'is cinema dead?' 'Yes, it is – at least for those who are deaf and hard of hearing. … We need subtitles to follow films, so we have to wait for them to come out on DVD. In Dublin, subtitles are shown at one cinema, but this is a limited service. In Limerick, we have a new cinema complex, but it has no system in place for the use of subtitles.' (*Irish Examiner*, 4 Feburary 2006.)
24. Six of these were in Dublin: Cineworld, Movies@ Dundrum, Movies@ Swords, Ormonde Cinema, UCI, and the Vue. The remaining cinemas were Tom O'Connor's Reel Cinema, Cork; the Eye, Galway; Mayo Movie World, Ashbourne Showtime, Meath; SGC, Waterford; and UCI, Kildare. However, it should be pointed out that though UCI is listed as one cinema, it has branches at both Blanchardstown and Coolock, while Movies@ is also in Gorey, Wexford. Cinemas in Belfast in which subtitles are available, include Belfast Odeon, Movie House (Yorkgate), Queen's Film Theatre, and Village Cinemas (Storm) at the Odyssey centre. Elsewhere in Northern Ireland subtitles are available at the IMC, Ballymena, Co. Antrim; Iveagh Movie Studio, Banbridge, Co. Down; and the Omniplexes at Carrickfergus, Enniskillen, Lisburn and Newry. This list no doubt will grow particularly in the context of digitally equipped cinemas. See *Disability Federation of Ireland newsletter*, April 2010 online. (disability-federation.ie)
25. See Eoin English, 'Deaf community heralds new era with first subtitled film screening', *Irish Examiner*, 6 March 2010.
26. Gerald Morgan, 'Owner of new cinema deserves an Oscar' (letter), *Irish Examiner*, 11 March 2010.
27. *Sunday Tribune*, 13 June 1999:business 3. Ster also stated that it intended to open a second multiplex, a sixteen-screen, 3,400-seater near Santry, north Dublin, in 2000, but this did not materialize. See Charles Hogan, 'Heavy marketing planned for new cinemas', *Sunday Business Post*, 11 October 1998:16.
28. *Sunday Tribune*, 13 June 1999:3. In 2003 the Irish and British assets of Ster were sold to Aurora Entertainment in a management buyout, and in 2005 sold again to Vue Entertainment, the third-largest operator in Britain leading to further consolidation of the market.
29. David Clerkin, 'Cinemas reel in the punters', *Sunday Business Post*, 19 March 2006.
30. Gretchen Friemann, *Film Ireland*, no. 80, April/May 2001:30.
31. Anna Coogan, 'We're mad about the multiplexes!', *Evening Herald*, 1 April 1999:30. Besides the Ster Century complex, Ward Anderson's IMC Dún Laoghaire with 1,733 seats, discussed below, also opened in 1999. There were 19,066 cinema seats in Dublin in 1998.
32. O'Brien lists the group's major companies as Torgyle, Abbey Films, Fairfax (which could be interpreted as a cryptic reference to the elusive character in John Boorman's 1967 thriller *Point Blank*), Amalgamated Cinemas, Green Group, General Film Distributors, Dublin Cinema Group (which operates the Savoy), and Cinema and General Publicity. (Daire O'Brien, 'Ward Anderson: cinema's secret empire', *Business and Finance*, 11 June 1992:14.)
33. Brian Carey, 'Rolling the celluloid credit lines', *Sunday Business Post*, 29 June 1997:10.
34. While many of these companies are directly related to cinema, including cinema advertising companies, and those that deal in cinema equipment or fit-out cinemas, others such as Lucan Printing Works and Potter Demolition and Contractors have nothing to do with cinema at all. (Brian Carey, 'Stars of the silver screen', *Sunday Tribune*, 7 November 1999:5.) In 2005, Kevin Anderson increased his stake in the Carlow-based engineering company Oglesby & Butler to 24.8 per cent. (*IT*, 16 November 2005:finance 16. See also see also David Clerkin, 'Cinema boss ups Oglesby shares', *Irish Examiner*, 17 August 2004), a stake which was increased in 2010 to 49 per cent, making a takeover bid by Kevin and Thomas Anderson mandatory. (*IT*, 3 November 2010.)
35. In terms of directorships, Kevin Anderson was involved in forty-four in 2005; his son, Paul, thirty-three; and Leo Ward, twenty-eight (though this number varies). (Ian Kehoe, 'Screen team', *Sunday Business Post*, 12 June 2005.) Similarly, Declan Walsh reported six years earlier, 'It would be easier to negotiate a labyrinth with a blindfold on than to get to grips with the detail of the Ward Anderson

empire ... A small army of accountants would be needed to decipher the entire group of accounts for over 60 companies.' (Declan Walsh, 'The force is strong in the warrior behind Ireland's film screens', *Sunday Business Post*, 11 July 1999:10.)

36. Kevin Anderson in Rose Doyle, 'Cinema man a star of movie distribution company', *IT*, 29 September 2004:property 2.
37. Brian Carey, 'Stars of the silver screen', *Sunday Tribune*, 7 November 1999:5.
38. Declan Walsh, *Sunday Business Post*, 11 July 1999:10.
39. *Sunday Tribune*, 11 March 2001:7. The bulk of this article is a reprint of extracts from Brian Carey's 1999 article quoted above.
40. *Sunday Tribune*, 13 April 2003:41.
41. *Sunday Tribune*, 11 April 2004:34.
42. *Times*, 'rich list' 2006. These values gave them a ranking of joint 172nd place; however, if combined they would have come in joint 89th position.
43. *Times*, 'rich list' 2007.
44. Following five years of unbroken capital growth in Irish commercial property prices to the first quarter of 2007, these gains were wiped out in eighteen months. From the market peak to mid-2010, values dropped by 58 per cent, returning commercial property prices to mid-1999 levels. (*IT*, 28 July 2010:19.)
45. Tony Deane, *Box Office*, 1997.   46. Hanson, 2007:151.
47. Paul Ward, quoted, David Brophy, 'Future growth in cinemas will be in regional centres', *Sunday Tribune*, 27 March 2005:commercial property 15.
48. Hugh Oram, 'Dún Laoghaire's new theatres of dreams; The future looks good', *IT*, 13 January 2000:property 28.
49. Simon Carswell, 'Profits drop by half at cinema group', *Sunday Business Post*, 3 August 2003.
50. Mark Anderson, quoted, 'Projected July opening for €9 million omniplex.' *Wexford People*, 9 January 2008:3. The article discussed the opening of a multiplex in Drinagh, Co. Wexford.
51. The complex includes an eighteen-lane bowling alley, interactive laser games, an American-style diner and a four-level bar, Vertigo. See Fiona Tyrrell, 'Galway's multiplexes multiply on the east of the city', *IT*, 13 April 2005:commercial property 4; 'Ward Anderson releases new cinema in Galway', *Sunday Tribune*, 3 April 2005:property 11.
52. Ian Kehoe, 'Omniplex cinema firm's value doubles', *Sunday Business Post*, 16 September 2007. For details of earlier profits and assets, see Ian Kehoe, 'Cinema group has profit of €1.7m', *Sunday Business Post*, 28 August 2005.
53. To confuse matters, the word 'cineplex' has been used by other exhibitors, including independent Michael Collins' Bray Cineplex, which closed on 28 June 2007 (*Bray People*, 21 June 2007), and Eclipse Cinemas/Bundoran Cineplex.
54. An €8 million Omniplex cinema was built in Carlow as part of the second phase of the Fairgreen shopping centre. ('New nine-screen cinema for Carlow as part of Fairgreen phase two plans', *Carlow Nationalist*, 10 November 2004.) The limited number of screens in Carlow until the opening of the Omniplex meant that audiences were denied (or made to wait for) many of the top movies. Leo Ward was quoted in the *Carlow Nationalist* in 2003 as saying, 'the only reason we can't play all the movies on the release date is because there are only three screens in [the Cineplex] Carlow. ...There's nothing sinister in it. We try to do our very best and are anxious to play all the pictures at the time they are released.' ('Lack of film screen keeps Carlow audiences out of the cinema picture', *Carlow Nationalist*, 13 March 2003.)
55. *IT*, 23 March 2005:42; *Sunday Business Post*, 27 March 2005:property 16; David Brophy, 'Future growth in cinemas will be in regional centres', *Sunday Tribune*, 27 March 2005:commercial property 15. The Mahon Point centre had fifty retail outlets and three restaurants, but following its completion in 2009, was expanded to include a hotel, leisure centre, high-tech industrial park and offices. By 2010, it had more than 70 retail units and restaurants.
56. The cinema cost £1.3 million to build. (See Brian Carey, *Sunday Tribune*, 7 November 1999:5.)
57. 'In the first week we [Ward Anderson] had 12,000 admissions. It turned Tralee into one of the biggest cinema-going populations in the world at 17 visits a year.' (Mark Anderson, quoted, 'Projected July opening for €9 million omniplex.' *Wexford People*, 9 January 2008:3.)
58. While there is a four-screen cinema in Carrick-on-Shannon known as a Cineplex this is not a Ward Anderson cinema, while a three-screen Cineplex in Westport is co-owned with the Hoban family. This €2.5 million, three-screen, 450-seat cinema, beside the Westport leisure park, was officially opened on 3 June 2004. The project involved Haulie Hoban, his siblings Seán, Joe and Claire, as well as family friend Leo Ward. Film booking for the Cineplex is arranged by the Ward Anderson cinema group while Carlton Advertising, which at that point operated over 90 per cent of the coun-

try's cinema advertising, arranges the cinema's advertising. ('Westport's new cineplex prepares to open its doors', *Western People*, 14 April 2004; 'Night at flicks in Westport', *Western People*, 10 June 2004. By way of aside, by 2010 Carlton Advertising's business covered 97 per cent of Ireland's cinemas.)

59. Ward, cited by Catherine Cleary, 'Exponential growth needed to fill seats at the multiplex', *IT*, 9 February 1996:business this week 3.

60. Rose Doyle, 'Trade names: lights, cameras and all action at city's premier cinema', *IT*, 25 January 2006:44

61. Ian Kehoe, *Sunday Business Post*, 12 June 2005:10.

62. Paul Ward, quoted, Hugh Oram, 'Dún Laoghaire's new theatres of dreams; The future looks good', *IT*, 13 January 2000: property 28.

63. Jack Fagan, 'The Square in Tallaght to get €300 million extension', *IT*, 9 November 2005:58.

64. *Screen Digest*, May 1996:105.

65. MEDIA Salles, *European Cinema Journal*, international ed., no. 2, June 1999:1.

66. Emma Kennedy, 'Multiplexes dominate in €17.8m [sic] box office battle', *Sunday Business Post*, 5 August 2007. As the box office was not worth 17.8 million, but several multiples of this it is possible that admission amounted to 17.8 million.

67. Acland, 2003:113.

68. MEDIA Salles, *European Cinema Journal*, international ed., no. 2, June 1999:1, 3.

69. Acland, 2003:136. This was subsequently surpassed by others, including two twenty-screen complexes at Manchester and Sheffield in 1999 and by Warner Bros' thirty-screen, 6,500-seat cinema in Birmingham's Star City in July 2000, which was credited at the time as Europe's largest such complex. (Hanson, 2007:155–6.)

70. See Sean O'Riordan, 'Plans for first drive-in cinema get go ahead', *Irish Examiner*, 23 July 2010; 'Drive-in cinema gears up for launch', 11 November 2010; Brian O'Connell, *IT*, 23 November 2010. Previous promises of a drive-in cinema in Ireland failed to come to pass. In 2004, for example, announcements were made regarding the opening in March 2005 of such a venue at the Wellpark centre on the Dublin Road, Galway. In the end a nine-screen cinema, the Eye, opened instead. (See Gillian Nelis, 'Drive-in cinema for Galway', *Sunday Business Post*, 21 November 2004.)

71. It was the world's thirty-sixth such theatre.

72. Bill Tyson, 'Mega movie screen opens', *Evening Herald*, 26 February 1998:12; Sarah Binchy, *Sunday Business Post*, 10 May 1998:11.

73. Hugh Linehan, *IT*, 16 September 2000:weekend 4.

74. Quoted, Shane Coleman, 'Cinema plan an inner city success', *Irish Independent*, 8 February 1996:business 3.

75. Stephen McMahon, 'Imax failed to light up Parnell St', *Sunday Business Post*, 22 October 2000.

76. For background on the Sheridan group, see interview with its chief executive, Peter Curistan in Shane Coleman, *Irish Independent*, 8 February 1996:business 3.

77. Edel Morgan, 'UGC to take over IMAX in £10 million revamp', *IT*, 28 November 2001:commercial property 3.

78. James Bartlett, 'The health of cinema in Belfast', *Film Ireland*, no. 85, February/March 2002:10.

79. Lir Mac Cárthaigh and Esther Terradas, *Film Ireland*, no. 96, January/February 2004:25.

80. Quoted, Patrick Butler, 'Monster cinema aims for maximum visual impact', *IT*, 12 November 2003:property 4. See also Ciarán Hancock, 'The multiplex effect', *Sunday Times*, 26 October 2003:business 9.

81. See 'Developer makes major changes to Carlton site plan', *IT*, 5 November 2008:3; 'Carlton cinema site development "could undermine character of O'Connell St"', 4 April 2009; 'Approval for development of Carlton site', 27 March 2010.

82. Nevertheless, as is discussed in the next **chapter**, the decision in 2001 by the Dublin Film Festival to locate there was a last gasp error by a dying organization.

83. Margaret Taylor, quoted, Helen Boylan, 'UGC broadens our film horizons', *Sunday Business Post*, 23 November 2003:4. See also Andrew McKimm, 'There's something for everyone on 17 screens', *Sunday Independent*, 23 November 2003:living 17.

84. Helen Boylan, 'UGC broadens our film horizons', *Sunday Business Post*, 23 November 2003:4.

85. Their Cineworld Unlimited Card (excluding London's West End cinemas) has a twelve-month minimum subscription. It was initially priced at €15.99 per month, but by 2010 it had risen to €19.99, or €239.88 annually.

86. Michael Dwyer, 'Loyalty hits new releases', *IT*, 2 September 2000:weekend 7. A huge success in UGC's native France, the scheme was banned by the culture minister in May 2000, but a few months later the competition commission ruled that it did not constitute unfair competition.

87. Joe McNamee, 'Most cinemas to miss gay cowboy hit', *Irish Examiner*, 28 January 2006.
88. Michael Dwyer, 'Some *Sex and the City* fans face abstinence due to release dispute', *IT*, 29 May 2008:1. Other films that have been refused include *The Golden Compass* (Chris Weitz, 2007), *A History of Violence* (David Cronenberg, 2005), *Hairspray* (2007), and *The Departed* (Martin Scorsese, 2006), as well as Irish films *August Rush* (Kirsten Sheridan, 2007) and *Hotel Rwanda* (Terry George, 2004).
89. Examples with regard to 2004 are included in Michael Dwyer, 'Major UK releases bypass Ireland,' *IT*, 15 April 2004:28.
90. Ian Kehoe, 'Irish arm of British cinema chain loses €1.2m', *Sunday Business Post*, 31 October 2004.
91. Conor Brophy, 'Blockbusters boost UCI profits', *Sunday Tribune*, 9 November 2003:business 1, 5.
92. Ian Kehoe, *Sunday Business Post*, 31 October 2004.
93. Ian Kehoe, 'Cineworld profits jump', *Sunday Business Post*, 12 November 2006.
94. Simon Carswell, *IT*, 29 September 2007:18.
95. *Irish Independent*, 10 February 2010, which also says the Sheridan Group bought the 3.8 acre site for €3 million in 1993.
96. *Belfast News Letter*, 9 February 2010. Curistan's refocusing on Dublin may have been prompted by what can only be characterized as a sectarian attack on his company. Under privilege in the house of commons in February 2006, Peter Robinson, Democratic Unionist MP, and now the DUP party leader and first minister of the Northern Ireland government executive, claimed, without offering any proof, that the Sheridan Group was involved in money laundering for the IRA. This allegation 'severely damaged' the Sheridan Group and came after the company had been named as the pre-ferred developer in June 2005 of the £100 million Laganside development on the east side of the Lagan river. However, in December 2006, and without allowing Sheridans to respond, the preferred development status was withdrawn by the Laganside development authority. Rejecting the allega-tion, Curistan sought a judicial review of the decision, which proved unsuccessful, though the judge said that the IRA 'dirty money claim [was] "baseless"'. (David Gordon, *Belfast Telegraph*, 28 January 2008. See also *Sunday Business Post*, 24 December 2006.) Ironically, Robinson may have done Curistan a favour because the allegation and the judicial review rumbled on into 2008, by which time the full blast of the commercial property recession was clear.
    Curistan, born *c*.1956, at Hatfield Road, off the Ormeau Road, Belfast, later moved to Andersonstown, and studied economics and accountancy at Queen's University. He worked for accountants Price Waterhouse before leaving to become a businessman. He subsequently became a director of mineral exploration company Andaman Resources, and set up his own accountancy consultancy. One night in 1986, after failing to get to see that year's cinema hit, *Crocodile Dundee*, he decided that Belfast needed a multiplex, an idea that led to the founding of the Sheridan Group in 1989. He signed up cinema operators Cannon, and eventually the Dublin Road multiplex opened in 1993. Despite the scale of the Parnell Centre, Dublin, the biggest project in which the Sheridan Group was involved in as the largest private investor was the GB£100 million Belfast Odyssey Arena, which included a 10,000-seat ice-hockey venue as well as a multiplex with Sheridan IMAX operating there from 1999 to 2007. In 2007, the Sheridan Group sold its interest in the Odyssey to major Dublin property developer Noel Smyth for €150 million. The Sheridan Group also devel-oped a £12 million waterfront complex in Bournemouth, England, and other developments in Belfast. In 2002, Curistan was awarded an honorary doctorate by Queen's University and was later named the Institute of Directors' Northern Ireland's entrepreneur of the year. (*Belfast Telegraph*, 10 January 2007; *Sunday Independent*, 31 July 2005; Hugh Oram, 'What's the big deal?', *Shopping Centre*, 10 September 2007:6, accessed online at www.shopping-centre.co.uk.)
97. Paddy Barrett, 'Irish exhibition booms', *Screen International*, 17 January 1997:4.
98. *The national recovery plan, 2011–2014*, Dublin: Stationery Office, November 2010.
99. Douglas Keatinge, *IT*, 1 December 1999:commercial property 5.
 1. Ciaran Carty, *Sunday Tribune*, 7 September 2003:artlife 2. It is said by Carty that cinema-going in Ireland had increased by more than by 138 per cent during the previous decade. See also Andrew McKimm, 'There's something for everyone on 17 screens', *Sunday Independent*, 23 November 2003:living 17.
 2. MEDIA Salles, *European cinema yearbook 2003*; *2008*; Ciarán Hancock, 'The multiplex effect', *Sunday Times*, 26 October 2003:business 9, gives the 1991 admission figure as 7.1 million
 3. Rentrak EDI (formerly Nielsen EDI) on www.carltonscreen.ie; *IT*, 3 June 2010. See appendix, table 15c for national box office figures.
 4. *Sunday Tribune*, 4 February 1996:3.
 5. Conor Brophy, 'Blockbusters boost UCI profits', *Sunday Tribune*, 9 November 2003:business 5; Barry O'Halloran, 'UCI profits edge up as cost of sales rises sharply', *IT*, 9 January 2004:2. In

2001, UCI's Irish operation recorded a loss of €510,000, but this was after it paid a €5 million dividend to its parent company, UCI Multiplex, which is based in Holland.

6. Barry O'Halloran, 'UCI profits edge up as cost of sales rises sharply', *IT*, 9 January 2004:2.

7. Nick Webb, *Sunday Independent*, 14 November 2004:section 5, business 1; Barry O'Halloran, 'UCI Irish division reports 14% rise in pre-tax profits', *IT*, 5 January 2005:17.

8. John Mulligan, 'Dublin's Ster Century cinema complex could fetch 20m', *Sunday Tribune*, 2 February 2003:business 12.

9. Ciarán Hancock, 'The multiplex effect', *Sunday Times*, 26 October 2003:business 9.

10. 'Multiplexes falling victim to their own success', *IT*, 10 May 2000:4; Norma Cohen, 'No silver lining for silver screens in the US', *IT*, 20 June 2001:commercial property 4; both reproduced from *Financial Times*.

11. Joe Humphreys, 'Silver screen enjoying another golden age', *IT*, 15 May 1998: business this week 2.

12. Stannifer, a UK company, had already received planning permission for an eight-screen cinema in Santry.

13. Fintan Tierney of commercial agents Lambert Smith Hampton, quoted, Edel Morgan, 'Screens multiply, but moviegoers want more', *IT*, 21 June 2001:commercial property 4.

14. Quoted, *IT*, 21 June 2001:commercial property 4.

15. David Brophy, 'Future growth in cinemas will be in regional centres', *Sunday Tribune*, 27 March 2005:commercial property 15. The full list of Ward Anderson cinemas is listed in the main text.

16. Ciarán Hancock, 'Ward Anderson buys Dublin's Stella cinema', *Sunday Times*, 9 November 2003. At that time, filed accounts for Dublin Cinema Group showed a deficit of €151,850 in the nineteen months to the end of March 2003, but the net assets of the business were valued at just under €1.2m, which presumably takes into account the property's value. (See Ian Kehoe, *Sunday Business Post*, 12 June 2005:10.) A proposal by Highfield Estates Ltd to demolish the Stella Cinema and replace it with a four-storey building incorporating a fitness centre on the ground and first floors, and shops facing Lower Rathmines Road, with four apartments above was approved by Dublin city council, but in early 2009 local residents, who were concerned, among other things, that there was asbestos in the roof appealed to An Bord Pleanala. (See Edel Morgan, 'Locals appeal demolition of Stella cinema', *IT*, 29 February 2009.) The building remained intact, if derelict, at the end of 2010.

17. Ian Kehoe, 'Eight-screen cinema planned for Rathmines', *Sunday Business Post*, 22 August 2004:5.

18. Fiona Tyrrell, 'Plans for nine-screen cinema at Swan Centre in Rathmines to go to council', *IT*, 6 January 2005:8.

19. Neil Callanan, 'Ward Anderson lodges new cinema bid', *Sunday Business Post*, 8 July 2007.

20. Compiled by Mary Hetherington, 'A selective guide to developments in your area', *IT*, 17 April 2008, property/planning & development.

21. iftn.ie news release, 18 August 2009; interview with Omniplex operations manager Mark Anderson, iftn.ie, 7 January 2010.

22. Neil Callanan, 'Andersons plan €9m cineplex on roof of Stephen's Green centre', *Tribune*, 17 January 2010; and Jack Fagan, 'Food court for top of St Stephen's Green centre', *IT*, 2 June 2010.

23. Jack Fagan, 'Food court for top of St Stephen's Green centre', *IT*, 2 June 2010. In the article Fagan noted that the planning application for the Omniplex was due to be lodged shortly by joint owners of the centre, Irish Life and Pierse Molony. (See also Neil Callanan, 'Andersons plan €9m cineplex on roof of Stephen's Green centre', *Tribune*, 17 January 2010). It is intended that the construction will be relatively quick as most of the cinema's structure will be built off-site. The use of lightweight materials will mean that further supports to the shopping centre will not be needed. Though it is not envisaged as a particularly easy build given that the shopping centre will remain open, the problems posed will not be so different from those incurred during the building of the Swan cinema at the Rathmines shopping centre.

24. Based on the admission prices charged by IMC Dún Laoghaire. Hugh Oram, 'Dún Laoghaire's new theatres of dreams', commercial feature – IMC Cinemas, *IT*, 13 January 2000:28: adults: £3.75 (/€4.75, before 6p.m.); £5.30 (/€6.71, after 6p.m.); students/OAPs (before 7p.m.): £3.75 (€4.75); children: £3.30 (€4.18); Saturday and Sunday children's early show £1.75 (/€2.22, all tickets including for accompanying adults). January 2008: adults: €7 (before 6p.m.); €9 (after 6p.m.); students/OAPs: €5.50; children: €5.50; Saturday and Sunday children's early show €3 (all tickets including for accompanying adults). December 2010: adults: €7.30 (before 6p.m.); €9.30 (after 6p.m.); students/OAPs/children: €6; unemployed (over-18s): Monday to Friday before 5p.m., €4 (or €5 for 3D, 3D glasses €1).

25. Quoted, Ted Sheehy, 'Future looks bright for Irish cinemas – large and small', *IT*, 19 March 2004.

26. Such tickets are bought with a minimum commitment of a year.

27. Such transactions often preclude the customer from availing of special discounts.
28. Emma Kennedy, 'Multiplexes dominate in €17.8m [sic] box office battle', *Sunday Business Post*, 5 August 2007.
29. Emmet Oliver, 'Record crowds boost cinema group earnings', *IT*, 8 June 2004:18.
30. Matthew Goodman, 'Cinema sector is shaken by Ster sale', *Sunday Times*, 11 July 2004.
31. 'Irish jewel in cinema group sold cheap', *Sunday Tribune*, 3 August 2003:business 2. Inflexion may have also taken on debt as part of the transaction.
32. Matthew Goodman, *Sunday Times*, 11 July 2004.
33. Tom Bawden, 'Hands launches bid for £400m cinema chain', *Times*, 17 February 2004.
34. See Neil Callanan, 'Tchenguiz may bid for UCI', *Sunday Business Post*, 15 February 2004:6; 'Sale of UCI expected to bring in €740m', *Sunday Tribune*, 15 February 2004:3.
35. *Sunday Independent*, 14 November 2004: business 5. Terra Firma Capital Partners was owned by Legal and General Ventures and the deal was brokered by financier Guy Hands, who bought troubled music company EMI in August 2007 just before the 'credit crunch' took hold. According to Tom Bawden ('Hands launches bid for £400m cinema chain', *Times*, 17 February 2004), in February 2004 Vue was owned by Legal & General Ventures, Boston Ventures, and Clarity Partners.
36. Matthew Goodman, *Sunday Times*, 11 July 2004.
37. Cine-UK, which managed the Cineworld chain, had been owned by JP Morgan Partners, N.M. Rothschild and Botts & Co.
38. 'Carlton wins UGC contract', *Sunday Business Post*, 20 February 2005:23.
39. Michael Dwyer, 'Dublin multiplexes change hands', *IT*, 6 May 2005:ticket 32. In 2004, Dodona Research deemed UGC Parnell Street as the company's most profitable cinema in the UK and Ireland. Turnover in 2002 was GB£4.4 million (*c.*€6.5 m.), an increased of 14 per cent on the previous year. (Ted Sheehy, *IT*, 19 March 2004.)
40. Matthew Goodman, 'Big screen changes hands', *Sunday Times*, 1 May 2005.
41. Michael Dwyer, *IT*, 8 April 2005:ticket 7.   42. See www.ukfilmcouncil.org.uk.
43. Though separate box office figures are not issued for Northern Ireland, the admissions figures for 2004 was 5,387,000, or 31 per cent of the Republic of Ireland's 17,261,900. If it is presumed for this exercise that admission prices are roughly comparable for the two parts of Ireland, the Northern Ireland admissions can be said to be worth approximately €31 million, thus producing an all-island box office figure for 2004 of about €132 million; however, prices generally are higher in the south than in Northern Ireland. One researcher has put the 2007 all-island figure at over €145 million, when the Republic of Ireland figure was €112,767,000, suggesting Northern Ireland accounted for about 23 per cent of the total. (Ted Sheehy, *Film Ireland online*, 30 January 2009). Taking Northern Ireland's lower percentage of the total, the 2004 all-island figure, therefore, would be approx. €123 million. However, the *Film distributors yearbook, 2010* gives the Northern Ireland gross box office for 2009 as GB£25.9 million and that for the Republic of Ireland as GB£110.7 million, giving an all-island figure of GB£136.6 million, suggesting Northern Ireland was worth only 18.9 per cent of the total. (www.launchingfilms.com.)
44. Michael Dwyer, *IT*, 7 January 2005:ticket 28.
45. The value of the seven-screen cinema was estimated at £1.5 million.
46. *Irish Independent*, 13 April 2000:e-Thursday 9. The cinema re-opened under the UCI brand in July 2011.
47. John Mulligan, 'Cinema boss Spurling is relishing chance to keep reeling in the public', *Irish Independent*, 8 July 2010. In 1976 builder Ozzie Spurling bought the local cinema in Greystones, Co. Wicklow, which he used as a hardware store. Ward Anderson approached him with the idea of reopening the cinema, and so began a relationship whereby the Spurlings redeveloped sites that Ward Anderson selected for cinemas. In the mid-1990s they parted amicably. Ozzie's son, Graham Spurling, is currently the principal figure in the group, which also includes Ozzie and two of Graham's sisters.
48. Jack Fagan, 'Cinema letting agreed for Dundrum centre', *IT*, 7 May 2003:commercial property 2.
49. The first phase of the complex opened in 2001. ('Movies @ to lease 11-screen cinema at the Pavilions', *IT*, 24 May 2006:commercial property 4.)
50. According to one survey reported in the *Irish Examiner*, as a result of the recession, two out of three people are going less to the cinema (Niamh Hennessy, 'Two in five people dating less since the recession hit', *Irish Examiner*, 28 April 2010). However, according to Carlton Screen Advertising admissions in 2010 were up on 2009 with March 2010, when there were 1.5 million admissions, registering a 15 per cent increase on March 2009. (John Mulligan, 'Cinema boss Spurling is relishing chance to keep reeling in the public', *Irish Independent*, 8 July 2010.) While according to Paul Anderson, speaking in early 2010, the cinema market in general is 'lousy' and no business has

remained unaffected by the economy, 'cinema has held up reasonably well' and has survived better than most businesses. (Quoted in Neil Callanan, 'Andersons plan €9m cineplex on roof of Stephen's Green centre', *Tribune*, 17 January 2010.) Nevertheless, UCI (Ireland), owned by the Butler brothers, recorded a loss of €641,000 for the financial year ending 31 July 2008, with shareholders funds falling from almost €2.2 million to just over €1.5 million. In 2007 losses were €200,000. Their average number of employees also fell from 110 to 98. (See 'Butlers' cinema company lost €641,000 in last financial year', *Sunday Tribune*, 28 March 2010.) Despite fears that 2010 would continue a downturn, Carlton reported in May 2010 that its current revenue was up 2 to 3 per cent, though, of course, this was up on 2009 figures which were down on the previous year's figures by 10 to 15 per cent. (Catherine O'Mahony, 'Carlton focuses its sights on an improved year', *Sunday Business Post*, 9 May 2010.)

51. *Argus*, 18 February 2009.
52. See John Mulligan, 'Cinema boss Spurling is relishing chance to keep reeling in the public', *Irish Independent*, 8 July 2010. This aspect of the business is operated through the Irish company Online DVD Rentals owned by Mark Beggs, Martin Gavin and Christopher Stuart.
53. Cado Ltd also owns Cinemaworld in Douglas, Co. Cork.
54. It was part of the Gaiety Cinema Group, which also owns the nine-screen Gaiety, Arklow.
55. Michael Dwyer, 'Irish cinemas join the digital age', *IT*, 12 May 2006:ticket 32. See also digitalcinema.ie. For a discussion of the limits of digital projection by an experienced 35mm projectionist, see Brian Guckian, 'Can digital get the full picture?', *IT*, 16 February 2006:14. See also Donald Clarke, *IT*, 13 April 2005:16, which recalls the announcement by a subsidiary of American digital exhibition company, Avica Technologies, Thurles-based Digital Cinema Ltd, that it was going to make Ireland the 'world's first digital cinema nation' by installing 515 projectors in 105 sites throughout the country during the following twelve months. This did not happen. See also another article on Avica and digital cinema, 'Cinema technology firm uses Ireland as its springboard into Europe', *Sunday Business Post*, 11 July 2004.
56. According to Justin Comiskey ('Strong run of commercial sales in Kildare area', *IT*, 6 September 2006) the complex, beside the new Maudlins House Hotel at Naas Business Park on the Dublin Road, was original envisaged as a six-screen facility of 17,562 square feet (1,626 square metres).
57. The Whitewater saga led to an unprecedented local campaign demanding a cinema complex and generated dozens of newspaper articles far too numerous to cite; see, for example, Vicki Weller, 'Residents gear up for court fight over Whitewater cinema', *Kildare Nationalist*, 18 October 2007 for a summary article, though the newspaper published many articles on the issue.
58. *Leinster Leader*, 11 November 2009. Developers Ballymore Properties continued to insist that they were seeking to have a large multiplex built at another location, and that such a complex might be built at a later date. In the meantime, Riverbank Arts Centre installed in 2009 a high-definition cinema system, though its screenings would be confined to digital and video formats. (www.kildare.ie, 21 August 2009.)
59. www.artscouncil.ie
60. *Digital cinema in Ireland*, 2008:25–7, 39. In the UK, the Film Council announced in 2004 the funding of a 'digital screen network' (DSN) in which it funded the installation of digital projection equipment for 238 screens (in 209 cinemas), at a cost of £11.7 million, or about £49,000 per unit. It estimated that when fully realized, DSN would increase by 4 million the audience for specialized film, compared to 10 million before DSN. By contrast to the use of the DSN-funded equipment without restrictions, DCL charges additional fees for the showing of alternative content. (*Digital cinema in Ireland*, 28.)
61. Kevin Cummins, Avica operations director in Europe, estimated in 2004 that digital cinema technology had the potential to cut distribution costs by between 50 and 90 per cent. At that time in Ireland, the annual cost of making and distributing master copies to local cinemas was more than €8 million. (Ailbhe Jordan, 'Cinema technology firm uses Ireland as its springboard into Europe', *Sunday Business Post*, 11 July 2004.)
62. Michael Dwyer, *IT*, 8 April 2005:ticket 7; Fiona Tyrrell, 'Galway's multiplexes multiply on the east of the city', *IT*, 13 April 2005:commercial property 4.
63. Elaine O'Regan, '€10m Limerick cinema', *Sunday Business Post*, 19 September 2004, reported the possibility of the multiplex having six more screens added, though this did not happen.
64. David Clerkin, 'Storm cinemas group buys Belfast cineplex', *Sunday Business Post*, 28 May 2006.
65. The scheme was developed by Railway Square Ltd owned by Cork property developers Roy and Dave O'Hanlon and Bill Keighry. ('Railway Sq. to feature eight-screen cinema', *Waterford News & Star*, 16 February 2007; Ella Shanahan, '€80 million mixed-used Waterford scheme nears completion', *IT*, 25 April 2007.)

66. 'Cineplex to battle back with major facelift', *Waterford News & Star*, 19 October 2007.
67. *Waterford News & Star*, 5 October 2007, which registers nearby residents' objections to how the development would change their area. Planning permission was secured in June 2008. (See *Waterford News & Star*, 20 June 2008.) The developer is Parker Green International.
68. See chapter 7 of *That'll never work: success stories from private Irish business* by Mike Gaffney and Colin O'Brien, Dublin: Mercier, 2008, for an overview of Colum Butler and the Leisureplex group.
69. 'Odeon-UCI acquires more Irish multiplexes', *IT*, 25 April 2008:ticket 3.
70. As well as the Leisureplex complexes, the brothers also own the Irish franchises for the TGI Friday's and Hard Rock Cafe restaurant chains, while a third brother, Tom, was behind the expansion of the Quasar electronic war game, which has become a feature of the family's Leisureplex outlets. An indication of the value of these sites is illustrated by the €65 million the brothers received from major property company Treasury Holdings for the Stillorgan Leisureplex site after they failed to get planning permission for a fifteen-storey mixed-use development there. Treasury already owned substantial properties in the area. Early investors along with the Butler brothers in LeisureCorp., which owned the worldwide manufacturing and distribution rights for the Quasar game, were accountant Ossie Kilkenny and U2 manager Paul McGuinness. (Mark Paul and Brian Carey, 'Ireland: Butlers pay €90m in UCI cinema deal', *Sunday Times*, 17 September 2006:section 3, business 1.)
71. Arthur Beesley, 'Storm cinema group sells five of its outlets', *IT*, 10 April 2008:21.
72. Neil Callanan and Ian Kehoe, 'Developer in multimillion euro High Court battle', *Sunday Business Post*, 10 December 2006. The complexity of the transactions and apparent double-dealing by some of those involved around the Tallaght shopping redevelopment reached the high court in July 2009 when Noel Smyth sued two developers (Larry O'Mahony and Thomas McFeely, a former IRA hunger striker in the Maze prison), who, despite having agreed to sell Smyth a strip of land, joined forces with Liam Carroll which in turned stopped Smyth from proceeding with the expansion and redevelopment of the Square and adjoining lands. Tallaght was the least of Carroll's woes by this time, as his property empire came crashing down from August 2009 onwards with up to €2.8 billion in debts, of which personal liabilities amounted to €260 million. (*Sunday Tribune*, 14 June 2009; *Sunday Business Post*, 12 July 2009; *IT*, 15 July 2009:4; 16 July 2009; *Evening Herald*, 12 August 2009; *Irish Independent*, 23 October 2009; 5 November 2009. For a career profile of Smyth, see Hugh Oram, 'What's the big deal?', *Shopping Centre*, 10 September 2007:6, available at www.shopping-centre.co.uk.) On 29 June 2010 Smyth lost his €140 million damages case against O'Mahony, McFeely and Carroll. (See Mary Carolan, Noel Smyth loses €140 million damages case over centre', *IT*, 30 June 2010:finance.)
73. 'UCI Tallaght cinema to close', movies.ie/news.
74. United Cinemas International (Ireland) is actually owned by UCI cinema operators Colum and Ciarán Butler, though the cinemas are leased to Odeon.
75. Despite the recession and the fact that cinemas, particularly in Dublin and on the east coast more generally, have reached or are near reaching saturation point, a former major property player, Bernard McNamara, lodged a planning application in November 2009 for a major leisure and retail complex at Belgard Road, Tallaght, which would serve as a challenge to Noel Smyth's plans to redevelop The Square. The leisure component would include a fourteen-screen multiplex and a bowling facility on the former Woodies' site at Belgard Square East. (*Irish Independent*, 4 November 2009.) Even though two months later, a group of investors in one of McNamara's projects secured a record Irish personal judgment against him of €62.5 million, causing his personal and business affairs to unwind somewhat (*Sunday Independent*, 28 February 2010), by the end of June 2010 plans to start building the new complex were announced. (Donal Buckley, ' McNamara to build €100m Tallaght cinema complex', *Irish Independent*, 30 June 2010.)
76. Ibid.
77. Simon Carswell, 'Profits drop by half at cinema group', *Sunday Business Post*, 3 August 2003.
78. Colm Keena, 'Movies profitable for Ward Anderson group', *IT*, 5 November 2005:17.
79. Ian Kehoe, 'Eight-screen cinema planned for Rathmines', *Sunday Business Post*, 22 August 2004:5; similar article by Emmet Oliver, 'Record crowds boost cinema group earnings', *IT*, 8 June 2004:18.
80. 'Dublin Cinema in €1m profit slump', *Sunday Times*, 19 June 2005.
81. Mark Paul, 'Cinema chain goes back into the black', *Sunday Times*, 4 June 2006.
82. 'Cinema giants rolls out profits', *Sunday Times*, 13 August 2006.
83. Ciarán Hancock, 'Reel success for cinema owners', *IT*, 30 May 2008. The owners paid themselves the same dividend as in 2006 – €100,000 – but directors' emoluments decreased from €350,000 to €300,000. At this time, both Paul Anderson and Paul Ward owned 250 ordinary shares.
84. Colm Keena, *IT*, 5 November 2005:17. The ownership structure of Torgyle in 2004 was that Kevin

Anderson, by then 90 years old, had 315 shares; Paul Anderson (37 years old), 65 shares; and 86-year-old Leo Ward, 120 shares.

85. 'Cinema giants rolls out profits', *Sunday Times*, 13 August 2006.

86. Ian Kehoe, *Sunday Business Post*, 22 August 2004:n5i.

87. Ciarán Hancock, 'Little things', *IT*, 23 April 2010.   88. Ibid.

89. Harry Leech, 'Industry hotting up for a blockbuster season of sequels', *Sunday Independent*, 23 May 2010.

90. Acland, 2003:135.

91. *Sunday Tribune*, 13 April 2003:41.

92. *Sunday Tribune*, 11 April 2004:34.

93. Colm Keena, *IT*, 5 November 2005:17.

94. David Clerkin, 'Irish group to buy 11 British cinemas', *Sunday Business Post*, 13 October 2005, a similar article also by Clerkin, 'Ward Anderson given go-ahead for €80m takeover of cinema chain', is featured in *Irish Examiner*, 1 November 2005.

95. David Clerkin, 'Ward Anderson buys six British cinemas for €40m', *Sunday Business Post*, 22 January 2006; David Clerkin, 'Ward Anderson rebrands British cinemas', *Sunday Business Post*, 2 April 2006.

96. Table 9.11, *UK Film Council Statistical Yearbook, 2010*:74, www. ukfilmcouncil.org.uk. The four largest UK cinema chains in 2009 were Odeon with 840 screens at 106 sites; Cineworld, 773 screens at 76 sites; Vue with 641 screens at 67 sites; and National Amusements with 274 screens at 21 sites.

97. David Clerkin, *Sunday Business Post*, 2 April 2006. Also in 2006, another group of Irish investors, Pat Chesser, Pat Whelan, and Paul Hanby, with no background in cinema, bought for GB£28 million another prestigious Leicester Square cinema, the Odeon. Their intention was to redevelop the cinema as a multiplex along with restaurants, bars, offices and apartments. (Jack Fagan, 'Irish buy London cinema for over €40m', *IT*, 22 February 2006:commercial property 4.) Following the acquisition of further property adjoining the Odeon, the partnership lodged an application to demolish the cinema and other buildings to make way for two new cinemas with 660 seats, restaurants, apartments, and a hotel. This project dovetails with Westminster council's plan, ahead of the 2012 Olympics, to make Leicester Square the centre of cinema in Britain, something which will not only aid this project, but also Ward Anderson's presence in the area. (Jack Fagan, 'Irish investors plan €250 million London scheme', 11 June 2008:property 4.) Other activities by Irish investors involving entertainment in Britain include the purchase in 2005 of the high profile Savoy Theatre, London, and its resale in 2006. (Jon Myles, http:/www.irishabroad.com/news/irishpost, accessed 6 February 2008.)

98. A more recent move into England has been made by Northern Ireland developer, the Benmore Group, which in summer 2010 announced plans to develop a £200 million leisure complex including a multi-screen cinema, on a 50-acre brownfield site in Speke, near Liverpool airport. See 'NI firm unveils £200m plan for Liverpool', *BBC News, Liverpool*, 2 July 2010, bbc.co.uk/news.

CHAPTER 6

1. Mary Leland, 'The man who makes the festival tick', *IT*, 31 August 1970:6.
   Published just prior to the fifteenth Cork International Film Festival, Leland expands on the statement quoted above by noting how one 'festival night when the crowds outside the Savoy, [having grown] tired of waiting for a recognizable "star", cheered instead, with immense gusto and goodwill, all the local dignitaries, the councillors, the committee [and] the blushing PR man who were trapped in unaccustomed evening dress in the arc lights on the steps.'

2. It has not proved possible to find any information on this film; however, an American comedy drama with an Egyptian narrative, *An Arabian Knight*, made in 1920 by Charles Swickard, features Soada as a leading character.

3. Mary Manning, 'A Dublin film society', *Irish Statesman*, 4 January 1930:352.

4. *Irish Statesman*, 4 January 1930:350.

5. While countless books and articles explore this, particularly in relation to the dominant ideology of classical Hollywood cinema in terms of its content, form and exhibition, a good introduction to the subject is Jean-Luc Comolli and Jean Narboni's 1969 *Cahiers du cinéma* article, 'Cinema/ideology/criticism', reprinted in Gerald Mast, Marshall Cohen and Leo Braudy (eds), *Film theory and criticism: introductory readings*, fourth ed., New York and Oxford: Oxford UP, 1992:682–9.

6. In 1932 he became Fianna Fáil's first minister for finance.

7. *Dáil debates*, vol. 39, cols 1464–6, 2 July 1931. *Storm over Asia* ran at the Sackville Cinema, Lower O'Connell Street, for three weeks during October/November 1930.

8. Ms E.M. Coulson to Diarmuid O'Hegarty, 11 February 1930, dept of the taoiseach file S6002, NAI.
9. Diarmuid O'Hegarty to H. O'Friel, 11 February 1930, dept of the taoiseach file S6002, NAI.
10. Detective branch, metro division, to Diarmuid O'Hegarty, 27 February 1930, dept of the taoiseach file S6002, NAI.
11. Diarmuid O'Hegarty to Ms E.M. Coulson, 19 February 1930, dept of the taoiseach file, S6002, NAI. According to the police report, the group had met twice at 66 Waterloo Road, Mary Manning's home, and once, on 20 February, at 75 Leinster Road, where Lilian Dalton lived, suggesting a very well placed police informant.
12. Detective branch, metro division, to Diarmuid O'Hegarty, 27 February 1930, dept of the taoiseach file S6002, NAI.
13. Import duty on *Potemkin* at 1,740m would have amounted to approximately £24.
14. John Hill, 2006:65.
15. Bert Hogenkamp, *Deadly parallels: film and the left in Britain, 1929–30*, London: Lawrence and Wishart, 1986:36–7.
16. Nevertheless, the London county council banned it again in January 1930 after rescinding an earlier decision to allow the November screening.
17. *Belfast Newsletter*, 14 October 1930:6.   18. Hill, 2006:64–71.
19. Bert Hogenkamp, *Deadly parallels*, 1986:5, citing the newspaper of the Communist Party of Great Britain, *Daily Worker*, 26 May 1930:49.
20. Liam O'Laoghaire, *Irish Catholic*, 20 June 1936:6.
21. Though mostly known as Liam O'Leary, during this period he used the Irish version of his name, Liam O'Laoghaire. The anglicized version is used throughout this text.
22. Report of IFS honorary secretary to 1956 annual general meeting looking back over the society's first twenty years. (IFS minutes, Liam O'Leary collection, NAI.)
23. Its European premiere in Berlin was postponed due to censorship intervention, but it eventually took place on 29 April 1926. The reaction to the film was overwhelmingly enthusiastic. It was released in twenty-five cinemas in Berlin alone, and ran for a year. It was shown in ten other major German cities and fifty copies of the film were in distribution. Its American premiere a month later also followed censorship delays, but *Potemkin* was hailed as the year's best film. See Yon Barna, *Eisenstein*, London: Secker & Warburg, 1973:110–11; orig. 1966.
24. Hogenkamp, *Deadly parallels*, 1986, contains a detailed account of the British workers' film societies and their struggle to show Soviet films, while Don MacPherson (ed.), *Traditions of independence: the British cinema in the thirties*, London: BFI, 1980, includes contemporary documents on the treatment of Soviet films in Britain. See also Jen Samson, 'The Film Society, 1925–39' in Charles Barr (ed.), *All our yesterdays: 90 years of British cinema*, London: BFI, 1986:306–13.
25. MacPherson, *Traditions of independence*, 1980:111.
26. The copy of *Potemkin* had come from London where 9.5mm, 16mm, and 35mm copies of the film were available from film distribution company Kino since December 1933, and from the Progressive Film Institute by March 1936. (MacPherson, *Traditions of independence*, 1980:213.)
27. Liam O'Leary, 1976:40.
28. Though not identified by O'Leary, this sailor is thought to be Ivan Beshoff (1882–1987), a Russian immigrant to Ireland in 1913 whose name remains associated with a number of fish and chips shops in Dublin, the first of which he opened in North Strand in the 1940s. (See *Dictionary of Irish biography*, dib.ie.)
29. 'Ban on Dublin film display', *Irish Independent*, 24 February 1936:6.
30. *Irish Catholic*, 20 June 1936:6. O'Leary wrote in 1976 that 'there was a Government ban on further showings' of the film (O'Leary, 1976:40). In programme notes on the film when screened in November 1986 at the Academy Cinema, Dublin, to mark the fiftieth anniversary of the foundation of the Irish Film Society, O'Leary wrote that 'on a technically further showings of the film were banned by the Dept. of Justice and hysteria broke loose amongst the more conservative journals of the city.' As a result, *Potemkin* does not appear to have been included in any subsequent film society programme, at least until the 1960s, though Eisenstein's *The General Line* (1929), *October*, *Strike* (1925), and *Alexander Nevsky* (1938), as well as Pudovkin's *Mother* and *Storm over Asia*, were all shown as part of the IFS's 16mm 'B' programme between the 1949/50 and 1958/59 seasons, while Eisenstein's *Ivan the Terrible*, part 1, was screened on the main, or 'A', programme during the 1950/1 season, with part 2 of the film shown during the 1959/60 'A' season. In addition, a number of other Soviet films were shown on both the 'A' and 'B' programmes in the late 1940s and during the 1950s.
31. *IT*, 25 February 1936:4.

32. *Irish Independent*, 22 February 1936:6.
33. J.V.H. [J.V. Hallessy], 'Spreading deadly poison; first Soviet propaganda film in Ireland', *Irish Catholic*, 13 June 1936:5.
34. See Rockett, 2004:66–7.
35. In Ireland the Catholic Film Society of Ireland (CFSI), established in the late 1930s, faded out by 1945 before they had even embarked on any screening programme, while a separate body, the Irish Catholic Film Society, and incorporating Dublin Theatre Players, sent a circular in May 1951 seeking subscriptions for the making of an anti-communist film from a script by American film director Myron C. Fagan. The other promoters of the society were William Cowley (president), James Thornton (vice-president), and Fr Denis Fahey CSSp (spiritual director). (A copy of the circular was sent to Archbishop McQuaid, Dr McQuaid papers, DDA.) Meanwhile, a dedicated Catholic body, the National Film Institute of Ireland was established in 1943 with the purpose of educating and guiding Catholics in relation to film, as is outlined in **chapter 8**.
36. Ferdinand Valentine, OP, *Irish Catholic*, 27 June 1936:5.
37. J.V.H. [J.V. Hallessy], *Irish Catholic*, 4 July 1936:7.
38. Liam O'Laoghaire, 'Russian films in Ireland', *Irish Catholic*, 20 June 1936:6. This letter was a response to J.V.H.'s 13 June article,
39. Liam O'Laoghaire, 'Reactionary red herrings', *Irish Catholic*, 4 July 1936:2.
40. Liam O'Laoghaire, 'In defence of *Potemkin*', *Irish Catholic*, 11 July 1936:2.
41. J.V.H. [J.V. Hallessy], 'Soviet film propaganda', *Irish Catholic*, 18 July 1936:2.
42. An attempt was made during 1938–45 to gain official church recognition for the Catholic Film Society of Ireland (CFSI). The catalyst for this organization was the acquisition of the distribution rights of *Golgotha* (aka *Ecce Homo*; *Behold the Man*, Julien Duvivier, 1935, France) by J.V. Hallessy, based in Youghal, Co. Cork, which is discussed in **chapter 8**. (The director of the organization in Northern Ireland was J.P. McConville, a solicitor based in Lurgan, Co. Armagh.) While the CFSI had been approved in 1938 by the head of the Irish church, Cardinal MacRory of Armagh, and its objects and plans had been submitted to the general meeting of the Irish bishops in June 1938, Hallessy regarded the distribution of *Golgotha* as 'the corner-stone' of their work as it would provide the resources to build up the organization. (J.V. Hallessy to Archbishop Byrne, 18 September 1939, Dr Byrne's papers, DDA.) Nevertheless, with the banning of the film for public exhibition in Ireland, and the advent of war delaying any alternative plan, the CFSI waited until 1945 before seeking recognition for the organization from Archbishop McQuaid, but, as is outlined in **chapter 8**, he was unlikely to facilitate them, given that he had just helped to establish a dedicated Catholic body, the National Film Institute of Ireland. (J.V. Hallessy to Archbishop McQuaid, 9 February 1945, including four-page memo on the organization, Dr McQuaid papers, DDA.) Fr H.G. McKernan told Hallessy that McQuaid was 'not prepared to grant ... formal approval' of the organization. (Fr H.G. McKernan to J.V. Hallessy, 19 February 1945, Dr McQuaid papers, DDA.) Though Hallessy wrote again to McQuaid taking the opportunity to complain that the film censor's decision in relation to *Golgotha* 'was greatly tinged with Jansenism' (J.V. Hallessy to Archbishop McQuaid, 22 March 1945, Dr Quaid papers, DDA), there is no recorded reply in the McQuaid papers, and the CFSI effectively disappeared. Film censor Richard Hayes viewed *Golgotha* on 20 August 1942. In rejecting the film, he commented that 'on account of the nature of the Subject (materialisation of the figure of Christ etc) a certificate cannot be granted for this picture.' (Reject 1556, film censors' records, NAI.)
43. Liam O'Laoghaire, 'The film society movement in Ireland', *The Bell*, vol. 15, no. 3, December 1947:57.
44. *The Bell*, vol. 15, no. 3, December 1947:58.
45. Obituary of Patrick Carey, who died in 1994, by Tom Hayes, *Film West*, no. 23, winter 1995:34.
46. See Rockett, 2004:355–61.
47. Liam O'Leary collection, NLI.
48. In 1930, one showing of a feature film cost about £10 in rent and a further £10 in transport, insurance and other expenses.
49. In 1947, Liam O'Leary suggested that the optimum number of members for 16mm screenings in the average Irish town was 200.
50. Liam O'Laoghaire, *The Bell*, vol. 15, no. 3, December 1947:62.
51. John Gerrard, 'Film societies in Ireland', *Sight and Sound*, vol. 17, no. 67, autumn 1948:133.
52. Liam O'Laoghaire, *The Bell*, vol. 15, no. 3, December 1947:61.
53. The project won the Irish Film Society School of Film Technique's script award, but it seems that the film was either never completed or has been lost. Rushes of the film are held at the Irish Film Archive.

54. Irish Film Society records, Liam O'Leary collection, NLI.
55. Liam O'Laoghaire, *The Bell*, vol. 15, no. 3, December 1947:59.
56. See Rockett, 2004:73ff.
57. Liam O'Laoghaire, *The Bell*, vol. 15, no. 3, December 1947:59.
58. The film was banned after the renter refused to accept the Irish film censor's extensive cuts (29 February 1956), and the decision was upheld by the appeal board on 10 April 1956. (Record 30844, film censors' records, NAI.)
59. Rejected by film censor Martin Brennan, the ban was upheld after appeal (13 March 1956). Resubmitted in 1961, it was passed with four cuts dealing with Zampano's relationships with women, by film censor Liam O'Hora. (Record 35345, reserve 10359, 8 June 1961, film censors' records, NAI.)
60. Rejected by the film censor (reject 2778, 8 December 1970), the ban was upheld after appeal (18 January 1971). (Film censors' records, NAI.)
61. *Brief Encounter* had been rejected by film censor Richard Hayes in 1946 (reject 1828, record 20392), and the ban was upheld after appeal (9 April 1946). It was resubmitted to the film censor in 1962 and a certificate for public exhibition was issued on 4 January 1962 (film censors' records, NAI).
62. Richard Hayes, 13 March 1946, reject 1828, record 20392, film censors' records, NAI.
63. Report by Mullingar branch of IFS to IFS 1954 annual general meeting. (Liam O'Leary collection, NLI.)
64. Conor Sweeney, 'The Irish Film Society in the '70's', *Hibernia*, 8 October 1971:23.
65. Dublin branches 1972/3 season: Dublin University Trinity College (440); College of Technology, Bolton Street/Kevin Street (114); University College Dublin (296); University Halls (72); Milltown Park (25); and Guinness' (*c.*200). (Irish Film Society honorary secretary's report, 38th season, 1973–4:9–10.)
66. Several reasons were put forward for this decline ranging from 'five day week, T.V., censorship (lack of), not sufficient publicity'. (Irish Film Society honorary secretary's report, 38th season, 1973–4:2.)
67. It was suggested that the Junior Film Society be reactivated; this happened during 1974–5 when it had six shows. Indeed, during the 1973–4 season a number of pilot schemes were tested, including a one-day seminar on film appreciation. (Irish Film Society honorary secretary's report, 38th season, 1973–4:3.)
68. Irish Film Society honorary secretary's report, 38th season, 1973–4:9–10.
69. Irish Film Society honorary secretary's report, 39th season, 1974–5.
70. Irish Film Society honorary secretary's report, 40th season, 1975–6:1, 9.
71. See Fergus Linehan, 'Why a National Film Centre?' *IT*, 6 February 1975:10, which discusses the proposal and features an architect's drawing of the proposed Irish Film Centre.
72. *Hibernia*, 19 August–1 September 1977.
73. R.F. (Ronnie) Saunders, honorary secretary's report, Irish Film Society, 40th season, 1975/6.
74. According to the Irish Film Society honorary secretary's report, 40th season, 1975–6:9, the Tralee branch 'exceeded all expectation' and was close to 300 members. In 1973–4 it was 100, double its previous season.
75. For an overview of his career, see Hugh Linehan, 'Film festival founder and critic Michael Dwyer dies', *IT*, 2 January 2010:9; and Hugh Linehan 'A true star of Irish film', *IT*, 4 January 2010:14. For a report on his funeral, see *IT*, 6 January 2010:3.
76. Ray Comiskey (*IT*, 13 August 1977:12) listed among the potential new member societies as those at Killarney; Dundalk; Naas; Furbo; Wexford Arts Centre; Carrickmacross; Tralee; Limerick; University College Cork; St Patrick's, Drumcondra, Dublin; and National College of Art and Design, Dublin.
77. Ray Comiskey, 'Booming film societies', *IT*, 16 November 1978.
78. These were located at Athlone; Baileborough; Bandon; Bolton Street College of Technology, Dublin; Bray; Carrick; Carrickmacross; Carrick-on-Shannon; Clonmel; College of Marketing & Design, Dublin; Connemara; Cork; Donegal; Drogheda; Dublin University [Trinity College]; Dundalk; Dungloe, Co. Donegal; Dún Laoghaire; Galway; Kevin Street College of Technology, Dublin; Kilkenny; Killarney; Limerick; Longford; Mayo; Mullingar; National College of Art and Design, Dublin; National Institute of Higher Education, Limerick; Nenagh; North Clare; Roscrea/Birr; Sligo; Tipperary; Tralee; Tullamore; University College, Cork; University College, Dublin; Waterford; and Wexford. Source: Federation of Irish Film Societies, 13 May 1980, information sheet, authors' private papers. At that point the president was Eddie Toner; Paudie Commane of the Tralee Film Society was chair; honorary secretary was Paddy Lyons (Dún Laoghaire Film Society); and honorary treasurer was Pat Carroll (NIHE). Assistant to FIFS administrator, Michael Dwyer, was Ted Sheehy. These thirty-nine branches had a combined membership in excess of 7,000. Ten months

later, the *NVS* [National viewing sessions] '81, Great Southern Hotel Galway, 13–15 March 1981, put the number of affiliated societies at forty-six, rising to forty-nine for the following season. However, the number of societies fluctuated throughout the 1980s, something which can be explained by the fact that some of them were formed without a sustainable or sufficient number of members and were unable to survive, or had periodic phases of dormancy, particularly in the recessionary 1980s.

79. These were located at Athlone; Baileborough; Bandon; Bantry; Bolton Street College of Technology, Dublin; Bray; Cahir; Carrickmacross; Carrick-on-Shannon; Cavan; Clonmel; College of Commerce, Rathmines, Dublin; College of Marketing & Design, Dublin; Connemara; Cork; County Kildare; Crawford School of Art, Cork; Drogheda; Dundalk; East Cork; Fermoy; Galway; Gorey; Hirschfield Centre, Dublin; Kells; Kenmare; Kilkenny; Killarney; Longford; Maynooth; Mullingar; National College of Art and Design, Dublin; National Institute of Higher Education, Dublin (now Dublin City University); National Institute of Higher Education, Limerick (now University of Limerick); Nenagh; Newcastle West; New Ross; North Clare; Portlaoise; Roscrea/Birr; Sligo; Tralee; Tuam; Trinity College Dublin; Tullamore; University College, Cork; University College, Dublin; Waterford; Wexford. Source: *NVS* [National viewing sessions, Limerick Inn, 12–14 February 1982] '82, FIFS, 1982.
80. Philip Molloy, *Irish Press*, 11 September 1978:9.
81. Incidentally, this film did not get a general release in Dublin.
82. Michael Dwyer, *IT*, 8 September 1989:12.
83. The first of these was held in Carrickmacross and essentially acted as a social bonding weekend, which was attended by 150 or more of the societies' key personnel.
84. *IT*, 9 January 1982:12. Still a feature of access>Cinema in the 2000s, these later became known as the National Viewing Sessions.
85. Michael Dwyer, *IT*, 8 September 1989:12.
86. It varied from 45,403 admissions in 1992/3 to 32,669 admissions the following season, but rose to 42,069 in 1996/7. (Federation of Irish Film Societies, *Film societies in Ireland: upgrading to 35mm projection systems*, final report, December 1997:4–5. This report was prepared by Neil Connolly and Maretta Dillon of the Light House cinema.)
87. Connolly and Dillon, *Film societies in Ireland*, 1997:5.   88. Ibid., 7.
89. Ibid., 16. Indeed, a permanent, two-machine 35mm system was costed at £42,133. (Connolly and Dillon, *Film societies in Ireland*, 1997:14.)
90. Michael Finlan, 'Restored town hall reopens as theatre', *IT*, 2 February 1996:5.
91. Following the refurbishment of Kiltimagh's Town Hall Theatre, Co. Mayo, after an absence of a cinema screen for almost forty years, cinema returned to the district in November 2002 when the Kiltimagh Film Club was launched there.
92. *A development plan for the Federation of Film Societies Limited*, 1998:21 (unpublished), access>CINEMA archive.
93. Press release, launch of access>CINEMA at Cork Film Festival, 13 October 2001. These were at Arts & Community Resource Centre (AXIS), Ballymun, Dublin; Rockabill FS, Skerries, Co. Dublin; Midnight Court FS, Scariff, Co. Clare; Cinematek, Triskel Arts Centre, Cork; Kinsale FS, Co. Cork; Sulán FS, Briary Gap Theatre, Macroom, Co. Cork; West Cork Arts Centre, Skibbereen, Co. Cork; Letterkenny Arts Centre, Co. Donegal; Galway FS, Town Hall Theatre, Galway; Letterfrack FS, Co. Galway; Riverbank Arts Centre, Newbridge, Co. Kildare; Kenmare FS, Co. Kerry; Dunamaise Film Club, Laois; Belltable Film Club, Limerick; Linenhall Arts Centre, Castlebar, Co. Mayo; Sligo FS, Model Arts Centre and Niland Gallery, Sligo; South Tipperary Arts Centre, Clonmel; Waterford FS, Garter Lane Arts Centre; Wexford FS, Wexford Arts Centre; and Tinahely Courthouse, Tinahely, Co. Wicklow.
94. The report, published in 2002, was jointly commissioned by the Arts Council, the Irish Film Board, and Enterprise Ireland in association with the Northern Ireland Film Council.
95. Press release at Cork Film Festival, 13 October 2001.
96. Michael Dwyer, *IT*, 9 October 2003:ticket, 8.
97. For an up-to-date list see www.accesscinema.ie. In September 2010, the list was as follows:
    Leinster: Eleven were in Dublin: Ranelagh FC; Rathmines First Friday FC; Rockabill FS, Skerries; The Seamus Ennis Cultural Centre, Naul; The Science Gallery FC, Trinity College; Tallaght FC; Clondalkin InterCulture FC; Axis Ballymun; Friends of the Eldery, Bolton Street; Dalkey FC; and Dolphin's Barn FC. Four in Wicklow: Mermaid Arts Centre, Bray; Wicklow FC, Grand Hotel; Conary FC; and Courthouse Arts Centre, Tinahely. Three in Wexford: The Picture House, Wexford Arts Centre, Cornmarket; Slaney Plaza, Enniscorthy; and St Michael's Theatre, New Ross. One in Kilkenny: Kilkenny Film Club, The Set Theatre. Two in Carlow: Blackstairs Film Society, Rahanna, Borris; and Carlow Visual Centre, Old Dublin Road. Four in Kildare: Maynooth FC, NUI;

Riverbank Arts Centre, Newbridge; Naas FC, The Moat Theatre; and Athy FC. One in Meath: Solstice Arts Centre, Navan. One in Louth: Droichead Arts Centre, Stockwell Street. One in Laois: Dunamaise Arts Centre, Portlaoise. One in Offaly: Birr Theatre and Arts Centre. Two in Westmeath: Tuar Ard Arts Centre, Moate; and Athlone FC, Dean Crow Theatre. (None in Longford.)

Munster: Five in Kerry: Cinemobile–Caherciveen FC; Samhlaíocht, Tralee; St John's Arts & Heritage Centre, Listowel; Club Zoom, Carnegie Arts Centre, Kenmare; and Kenmare FS, Carnegie Arts Centre. Twelve in Cork: West Cork Arts Centre, Skibbereen; Sulán FS, Briery Gap Cultural Centre, Macroom; The Caha Centre, Beara; Kinsale FC; Blackrock Castle Observatory FC, Blackrock; Cinemax, Bantry; Clonakilty FC; Bandon FC; East Cork Cinema Club, Cobh; Comharchumann Forbartha Mhuscraí; Cork Cine Club, Half Moon Theatre; and Crosshaven FC. Four in Limerick: Belltable Film Club, Belltable Arts Centre; Friars Gate Theatre, Kilmallock; Drum Row Village Centre, University of Limerick; and Newcastle West FC. Three in Waterford: Garter Lane Arts Centre; SGC Dungarvan; and Waterfordfilmforall, Storm Cinemas. Four in Tipperary: The Source Arts Centre, Thurles; Cloughjordan Cine Club; Excel Arts and Cultural Centre, Tipperary Town; and Nenagh Arts Centre. Two in Clare: Glór Irish Music Centre, Ennis; and Midnight Court FS, Scariff.

Connacht: Six in Galway: Letterfrack FS; Man of Aran Cinema, Inís Mór; Cinemobile–Portumna FC; Club Scannáin Sailearna, An Cheathrú Rua; Galway FS, Town Hall Theatre; and Gort Vibes Cinema Club, Gort. Five in Mayo: Linenhall Arts Centre, Castlebar; Westport FC; Achill FC; Arás Inis Gluaire, Belmullet; and Ballina FC, Barrett Street. One in Roscommon: Roscommon Arts Centre. One in Sligo: Sligo FS (at Gaiety Cinema). One in Leitrim: Glens Centre FC, Manorhamilton.

Ulster: One in Armagh: Armagh FC, Marketplace Theatre. One in Cavan: Ramor Theatre, Virginia. Two in Donegal: The Abbey Centre, Ballyshannon; and Regional Cultural Centre, Letterkenny. One in Down: Newry FC, Sean Hollywood Arts Centre. One in Fermanagh: Fermanagh FC, Enniskillen. One in Monaghan: Clones FS. One in Tyrone: Strule FC, Strule Arts Centre, Omagh. (None in Antrim or Derry.)

This gives a total membership of eighty-three, which compares to seventy-two in June 2008, Leinster increased by ten, with a substantial rise in Dublin; Munster increased by only three, though the number of societies in Cork rose from six to twelve, perhaps a reflection of the loss of the Kino; Ulster increased from six to eight; while only Connacht saw a decrease from eighteen to fourteen.

98. Maretta Dillon, quoted, Gemma Tipton, 'What goes around', _IT_, 20 April 2007:ticket 8.
99. In addition, the organization seeks to undertake a lobbying/advocacy role within the larger arts and film sector and to support the work of Irish filmmakers.
1. Maretta Dillon, quoted, Gemma Tipton, _IT_, 20 April 2007:ticket 8.
2. For an outline of access>CINEMA's activities, see interview with Maretta Dillon, the [then] organization's director, 'Beyond the arthouse', _Film Ireland_, no. 108, January/February 2006:25.
3. Access>CINEMA has been a member since 2004 of Europa Cinemas, which was set up in 1992 to provide financial support to 35mm cinemas committed to programming European films, as well as promoting European films for young people. See www.europa-cinemas.org and access>CINEMA website. In November 2008, at the time of the award, access>CINEMA was working with over sixty groups.
4. Access>CINEMA, _Viewing Sessions 2010_ brochure, 19–21 March 2010; Sinéad Gleeson, 'Welcome to film club', _IT_, 6 July 2010; and members as listed on website, September 2010.
5. _Northern Whig_, 7 January 1929:5; _Bioscope_, 9 January 1929:71.
6. _Bioscope_, 16 January 1929:53.
7. _Bioscope_, 17 April 1929:45. See also _Bioscope_, 27 February 1929:54.
8. _Bioscope_, 9 October 1929:36.
9. _IT_, 13 June 1930:4.
10. _British Film Institute Northern Ireland Branch Bulletin_, no. 1, December 1934:1; _KW_, 5 December 1935:18.
11. The basis for this estimate is not given, so it must be treated with caution. Indeed, if the figure is taken as weekly attendance, thus giving 5.2 million per annum in Belfast, half Dublin's 11 million admissions in 1934–5 (Beere, 1936:97), which seems quite low for a city of comparable size and with a relatively well-paid skilled industrial workforce: Belfast city had a population of 438,086 in 1937, while Dublin had slightly more with 472,912 in 1936. If taken as a daily figure, then Belfast at 36.5 million annual admissions would have had twice the cinema attendance of the whole of the Irish Free State (18.25 million in 1934–35), which is also an unlikely scenario.
12. _British Film Institute Northern Ireland Branch Bulletin_, special issue, June 1936.
13. _KW_, 29 October 1936:45.

14. *KW*, 17 December 1936:30.   15. *KW*, 21 January 1937:41.
16. *KW*, 25 March 1937:16. Like other such societies, the problem of a suitable venue remained.
17. *KW*, 4 March 1937:24A.
18. *Belfast Newsletter*, 25 March 1937:5.
19. *KW*, 1 December 1938:28; *British Film Institute Northern Ireland Branch Bulletin*, vol. 3, no. 4, April 1937:2.
20. Hill, 2006:164   21. Rockett, 2004:114–15.
22. *Sight and Sound*, winter 1942:83.
23. *Sight and Sound*, spring 1943:109.
24. John Gerrard, 'Film societies in Ireland', *Sight and Sound*, vol. 17, no. 67, autumn 1948:133. According to Liam O'Laoghaire, the principals in the BFS were 'the late' Ian McClelland and Hazel Hackett. (O'Laoghaire, *The Bell*, vol. 15, no. 3, December 1947:56.)
25. O'Laoghaire, *The Bell*, vol. 15, no. 3, December 1947:58; *Sight and Sound*, spring 1949:39.
26. www.northernirelandscreen.co.uk, general news, 11 April 2007, accessed 6 February 2008.
27. *KW*, 26 February 1959:9.
28. Described by the film censor as 'sordid and immoral', it was refused certification (reject 2161, 16 August 1957), though the appeal board allowed it through 'provided the embrace of the woman by the bandit [was] substantially shortened and that all references to "seduction" [were] eliminated.' (Appeal board decision, 20 September 1957, film censors' records, NAI.)
29. Although the film, which embodied many of the elements of neo-realism, used non-professional actors and location shooting, was not a cheap production. Though it cost a considerable 100 million lire and elaborately creates 'an illusion of technical poverty', as Millicent Marcus writes, it, nevertheless, 'reflects a conscious ideological *prise de position* against the spectacular conventions of the commercial cinema.' (Millicent Marcus, *Italian film in the light of neorealism*, Princeton: Princeton UP, 1986:57.) The story also is seemingly very simple, but nonetheless allows for a complex, often pathos-ridden examination of reality, and in a sense the journey to find the stolen bike is a great odyssey. See 'De Sica's *Bicycle thief*: casting shadows on the visionary city' in Marcus, ibid., 54–75.
30. *KW*, 26 February 1959:9.
31. Maxwell Sweeney, *KW*, 13 April 1961:9. Gogan had entered the film business in 1916 in Dublin and 'for many years' had managed the Pavilion, Dún Laoghaire, before moving back to the city to manage the Carlton. Later, he was sales supervisor for Odeon (Ireland) Ltd, and subsequently appointed by Bertie McNally to manage the Astor. A few months before his death, he was made president of the Irish Film Society. (*KW*, 13 April 1961:9.) The Astor continued as a cinema until 1984.
32. *IT*, 17 September 1962:8.   33. *IT*, 25 March 1963:8.
34. Fergus Linehan, 'Falling standards', *IT*, 10 August 1964:8.
35. *IT*, 4 January 1965:8.   36. See Rockett, 2004:175–87.
37. Its opening film was the acclaimed Greek tragedy *Electra* (Michael Cacoyannis, 1961, Greece).
38. The film censor passed the film with one cut. (Record 37863, reserve 10967, 2 April 1965, film censors' records, NAI.)
39. Banned by the film censor (reject 2593, 14 February 1967), it was later passed with cuts and an over-18s certificate after appeal. The initial appeal board meeting was deferred pending viewing by the entire board (3 April 1967) and it was passed on 1 May 1967 with four cuts mainly dealing with sexual activity. (Reserve 11263, film censors' records, NAI.)
40. The film censor imposed cuts and an over-18s certificate, but this was appealed (record 39152, reserve 11296, 15 August 1967; reviewed on 27 September 1967). The film was passed after appeal with one cut (Anne and Jean Louis in bed in nude in reels 10–11 was to be 'trim[ed]') and an over-18s certificate was issued. (Appeal board decision, reserve 11304, 4 December 1967, film censors' records, NAI.)
41. 'Feminism and cinema', Project Cinema Club programme bulletin, January–March 1978.
42. Ray Comiskey, 'Mammoth event at Project', *IT*, 14 July 1978.
43. The short-lived 16mm Ha'penny Film Club, based at Temple Bar Studios in the 1980s, and run by Trish McAdam and Jane Gogan, had a similar programming approach to PCC, though without the critical cultural contexualizing of PCC. Another short-lived 1980s' initiative was the Metropolis Film Club, named after the successful art house video retail outlet Metropolis run by John Dick and showing films on video.
44. See Fergus Linehan, 'The Irish Film Theatre', *IT*, 12 January 1977:8, which features an interview with Saunders.
45. The other members of the first board were Tom Owens (chairman), Kathleen Barrington, Tiernan MacBride (filmmaker and activist), Colm O'Briain (director, Arts Council), Brian Quinn, and

Richard Stokes (dept of the taoiseach). Like the others listed, Toner had also been a member of the DFS council until the 1975/6 season (Irish Film Society honorary secretary's report 40th season 1975/6:9), its last, as the Irish Film Theatre opened in what would have been during its 41st season. Though some other members of the DFS, including Michael Cassidy, struggled to maintain the IFS/DFS identity for a few years, it had been bypassed by both the FIFS and IFT developments.

46. *A report to members of the Arts Council on the activities of the Irish Film Theatre Ltd during the term of office of the first board of directors, 1977–9*:5, IFI.

47. G.O. Tigheagh, dept of justice, to Colm O'Briain, director, Arts Council, 3 March 1977, included as appendix 1, p. 13, in ibid., IFI.

48. Ibid.

49. This issue came to the fore in 1995 when the Irish Film Institute planned to give an extended run to the banned film *Natural Born Killers* (Quentin Tarantino, 1994). When made aware of the screenings by film censor Sheamus Smith, the dept of justice threatened legal sanction against the organization if the film was shown because the audience base of the 'private club' would be considerably extended by the screenings. (See Rockett, 2004:256–9.)

50. Film censor's record 43976, reject 3142, 23 January 1979, film censors' records, NAI.

51. Film censor's reject 3005 (7,844ft), 20 March 1973. Resubmitted in 1979 (7,740ft), when it was issued with an over-18s certificate with two cuts: from 'You see, Doctor, up there in the mountains' to 'It was the greatest lay I ever had', and the 'Intercourse with large rye bread' scene. (Record 44237, reserve 12959, 22 February 1980, film censors' records, NAI.)

52. Film censor's record 42343, reserve 12252, with two cuts and a general certificate. (1 August 1974, film censors' records, NAI.)

53. Initially passed with an over-18s certificate and eight cuts (including copulation; girls' discourse on St Augustine and the Virgin Mary; and action with mechanical doll). (Film censor's record 43588, reserve 12795–6, 12 October 1977.) Dermot Breen subsequently banned the film. (Reject 3119, 6 December 1977). However, in July 1982 the appeal board passed the film with two cuts for over-18s. (Film censors' records, NAI.)

54. Film censor's reject 2891, 4 September 1972. There was no appeal. (Film censors' records, NAI.)

55. Banned by the film censor (reject 2833, 21 July 1971), it was passed with eleven cuts and an over-16s certificate on appeal. (Appeal board decision, reserve 11698, 4 October 1971, though the limited certification was deferred pending a response from the distributor who was allowed to propose variations of the cuts proposed and the certificate proposed.) Eventually, the film was passed uncut for over-18s under the 'seven year rule' for resubmissions. (10 October 1978, film censors' records, NAI.)

56. Film censor's reject 2888 (27 July 1972); the ban was upheld after appeal (28 September 1972).'On a rough estimate [the] cuts total [was] about 2,500–3,000ft. Consequently, any attempt to consider this film for, even limited viewing, would be impossible as the total footage is in the region of about 9,000ft.' (Censor's report to appeal board, 28 September 1972, film censors' records, NAI.)

57. Film censor's reject 3083, 5 March 1976, film censors' records, NAI.

58. Film censor's reject 3082, 4 March 1976, film censors' records, NAI.

59. Peter Cowie (ed.), *50 Major film-makers*, London: Tantivy; South Brunswick/New York: A.S. Barnes and Company, 1975:38. Film censor's reject 3171, 17 November 1981; ban upheld after appeal, 11 December 1981; rehearing of appeal, 22 January 1982. Eventually, in 2009, John Kelleher, the new title for the film censor, invited members of the Jameson Dublin International Film Festival to attend one of his last screenings in the censor's film theatre in Harcourt Terrace (before moving the IFCO's screening room to Light House 4, Smithfield) to reassess *Last Tango* … The ban on the film was lifted and it was given an over-18s certificate. (*IT*, 25 February 2009.)

60. Film censor's reject 2765 (9 September 1969); passed with cuts and over-18s certificate after deferred appeal board meeting (5 October 1970): appeal board reserve 11609 (22 December 1970); and appeal board reserve 11613 (4 January 1971, film censors' records, NAI).

61. Film censor's reject 2603 (11,880 feet), 26 October 1967; ban upheld after appeal (11 December 1967); resubmitted in 1977: reject 3121 (9,900 feet), 8 December 1977. *Ulysses* was shown on RTÉ in 1984 and eventually was given a certificate in 2000 when it was rated 15PG. (Film censors' records, NAI.)

62. John McSweeney, 2003:123.

63. *A report to members of the Arts Council on the activities of the Irish Film Theatre during the term of office of the first board of directors, 1977–9*:8. An undated revised and expanded income/expenditure table for 1977–81 inclusive, probably from 1982, is included in IFT files at IFI library. It is these latter figures that are used here.

64. Connolly and Dillon, 2001:14.

65. *IFT News*, vol. 4, no. 1, January 1981. By the time of its first anniversary its membership had reached 1,400.

66. *IFT News*, vol. 4, no. 3, March 1981:14.

67. *IFT News*, vol. 5, no. 1, January 1982:1.

68. Declan Hassett, 'Arts Council funds cinema in Cork and Limerick', *Irish Examiner*, 25 July 2003.

69. 'New format for festival', *Irish Press*, 6 October 1982; 'Film festival to lack glitter', *IT*, 6 October 1982; 'Film festival goes ahead', *Cork Examiner*, 6 October 1982; Ray Comiskey, 'Film festival reprieve', *IT*, 4 November 1982.

70. Ray Comiskey, 'Last chance at Cork?', *IT*, 20 September 1984.

71. The other members of the second IFT board included chairman Tiernan MacBride, Christina Albertini, Maura Clarke, David Collins, John Hill, Fergus Linehan, Evelyn Mahon, Tommy McArdle, Richard Tobin and Edward Toner.

72. Director's report, IFT board meeting, and IFT board minutes, thirty-third meeting of the board, 1 November 1982; IFT files at IFI library.

73. Philip Molloy, 'Irish Film Theatre in danger of closing', *Evening Press*, 6 January 1983.

74. Minutes of IFT board meeting (34th), 10 January 1983, IFI library.

75. Minutes of IFT board meeting (35th), 14 February 1983, IFI library.

76. Minutes of IFT board meeting (36th), 11 April 1983, IFI library.

77. Minutes of IFT board meeting (36th), 11 April 1983, reconvened 25 April 1983, IFI library.

78. Minutes of IFT board meeting (37th), 9 May 1983, IFI Library. See also Ray Comiskey, 'What went wrong with the IFT?', *IT*, 12 May 1983, which includes interviews with MacBride, Saunders and O'Briain.

79. Letter from Ronnie Saunders to James Whyte, 17 August 1983; copy in Tiernan MacBride papers, IFI library.

80. Minutes of IFI extraordinary meeting, 27 April 1983.

81. Minutes of IFI board meeting, 11 May 1983.

82. Minutes of IFI board meeting, 17 April 1984.

83. Document prepared by Neil Connolly, IFI board meeting, 17 January 1984.

84. Quoted in Johnny Gogan, 'The Light House', *Film Base News*, no. 10, December 1988/January 1989: 4.

85. Document presented to IFI board, 12 April 1989.

86. Minutes, IFI board meeting, 27 July 1988.

87. IFI board minutes, 15 February 1989.

88. Chairman's report, 42nd annual general meeting, IFI, 28 April 1990.

89. *Irish Film Institute Plans for 1991 and application to the Arts Council for grant-in-aid*, December 1990:12.

90. Michael Dwyer, *IT*, 24 December 1993:13.

91. While the buildings acquired from the Society of Friends/Quakers cost only £205,000, of which IFI contributed £55,000 from the net proceeds of the sale of its building at 65 Harcourt Street, with the balance paid by the Arts Council and Irish Film Board, the more substantial sums were raised by a building development board. Construction began in autumn 1991,and the building opened to the public in September 1992. In spring 1993, after the opening of the Irish Film Centre on 25 September 1992, the IFI (responsible for the operation of the cinemas and the archive) and the Irish Film Centre Building Ltd (or IFCB, responsible for the physical facilities, bar/restaurant, rents and maintenance including security) were merged under the film institute banner, and Shelia Pratschke was appointed director of the newly named Film Institute of Ireland, a cumbersome name later changed back to Irish Film Institute. For background and an overview of the project, see 'Irish Film Centre', *Film Ireland*, issue 31, September/October 1992:10–13. Developments at IFI in the 1980s and 1990s are outlined more fully in note 33, p. 582.

92. 'Cinema appeals store's plan', *IT*, 19 January 1996:11. See also Ciaran Carty, 'Don't let the light out on world cinema', *Sunday Tribune*, 20 August 1995:*Tribune magazine* 16; Michael Dwyer, 'Light House goes dark', *IT*, 6 September 1996:11.

93. www.lighthousecinema.ie. See also Neil Connolly and Maretta Dillon talk with Michael Open, 'From the Light House … to the Light House', *Film Ireland*, no. 122, May/June 2008:18–20.

94. 'Consistently thoughtful' (Ted Sheehy) and Michael Dwyer ('commendably thoughtful'), quoted, *Film Ireland*, no. 122, May/June 2008:20.

95. www.lighthousecinema.ie. See *Film Ireland*, no. 122, May/June 2008:19–20, for a discussion of the type of films preferred.

96. When first opened, the smaller cinema had 117 seats. A third screen with fifty-eight seats was added upstairs in January 2010.

97. 'The Irish Film Centre', a supplement to the *IT*, 22 September 1993:4.
98. For an interview with Mick Hannigan, see Eileen Battersby, 'The flag carrier', *IT*, 8 October 1998:15.
99. For an interview with Pete Walsh, see 'Behind the screen', *Film Ireland*, no. 108, January/February 2006:24.
1. *IT*, 4 August 1994:2.
2. Director's report, IFI 46th annual general meeting, 9 November 1995:4. Put in the context of the Republic of Ireland box office revenue of €34,940,000 in 1995, the IFI cinemas represented about 1.2 per cent of total national box office. (MEDIA Salles *European Yearbook 2003* and IBEC's *Audio Visual Federation Review*, 2003, give a figure of £27.6 million. MEDIA Salles *European Yearbook 2007* gives the figure as €33,403,000.)
3. Niamh O'Sullivan, chairperson's report, IFI's 46th annual general meeting, 9 November 1995:1.
4. Irish Film Institute financial statements for year ended 31 December 2007.
5. Director's report, IFI's 59th annual general meeting, 8 December 2008.
6. IFI *five year plan*, first draft, November 1995:25–6.
7. For a report on the eighth Carte Noire French Film Festival (13–22 November 2007), see *Film Ireland*, no. 119, November/December 2007:10, while Sarah Griffin reports on the 2009 festival, 'Par excellence: The IFI French Film Festival, 2009', *Film Ireland*, online, December 2009, accessed September 2010.
8. For a report on the fifteenth Gaze Dublin International Lesbian and Gay Film Festival (2–6 August 2007), which was programmed by Michele Devlin, previously of the Belfast Film Festival, see *Film Ireland*, no. 118, September/October 2007:10. The seventeenth event was previewed in *IT*, 24 July 2009:ticket 13. The festival was also known as Outlook and Look Out! The eighteenth festival took place at the Light House cinema from 29 July to 2 August. See *Film Ireland* online.
9. See Horrorthon website, which includes festival programmes from 2001. In October 2009, shortly before Cork's Kino shut, Mick Hannigan hosted Cork's first horror film festival, Shockers.
10. For a report on the sixth festival (13–16 September 2007), see *Film Ireland*, no. 118, September/October 2007:9, while the expanded 15–18 April 2010 festival featuring twenty-two documentaries, nineteen of which were premieres, is previewed in *Film Ireland* online. The magazine's online entry detailing the award winners, reported a 'massive 23% rise in box office income compared to 2009's festival' with many of the screenings completely sold out. See also ifi.ie for the festival's own website.
11. 'A decade at the IFC', *Tenth anniversary programme*, August/September 2002:30–1.
12. IFI financial statements for the year ended 31 December 2008:25, IFI.
13. IFI director's report, annual general meeting, 15 July 2009, IFI.
14. Philip Molloy, 'Subsidy urged for art house cinemas', *Irish Independent*, 27 April 1998:6.
15. See access>CINEMA website for a complete list, the branches in Northern Ireland are located in Fermanagh (1), Tyrone (1), Down (1) and Armagh (1); neither Antrim nor Derry have film societies affiliated to the organization. The shift way from 16mm to DVD and 35mm was complete by the early 2000s.
16. For example, they jointly organized the Bealtaine 2010 film tour, which comprised of screenings at over fifty venues.
17. Film studies was introduced into the secondary school curriculum as part of the English course in the 1990s. The engagement of young people with the cinema is evident not just in terms of their attendance at cinemas, clubs or festivals, but also in their commitment to filmmaking (seen in their participation in such initiatives as access>CINEMA's Zoom and Limerick based Fresh Film Festival dedicated to showcasing the work of young filmmakers), and even film exhibition as highlighted in a transition year project by students at Coláiste na Sceilige, which set up a cinema in Caherciveen, Co. Kerry. The community cinema was officially launched in summer 2003 by local government minister John O'Donoghue. (See *The Kingdom*, 20 August 2003.) Another group of transition students (from Scoil Chriost Rí, Laois) under the banner Zoom Anonymous, a subsidiary of Zoom, have also created a small company, which in January 2010 screened films in the Dunamaise Arts Centre targeted at teenagers (see Mary Kavanagh, 'Zoom Anonymous presents film for teenagers', *Leinster Express*, 19 Januray 2010), while in October 2010 as part of Ireland's first Kurdish Film Festival, a programme of short Kurdish films was presented by transition year students from Carrick-on-Shannon Community School.

    Though film studies had been available as a subject within third-level institutions from the 1980s, notably as part of the National Institute of Higher Education/Dublin City University's communications' degree, but also the various NCAD (National College of Art and Design) art and design degrees, and, of course, the more specialized practical film courses at the College of

Commerce, Rathmines and School of Art, Dún Laoghaire, the first dedicated film studies under-graduate degree only became a reality in 2003 with Trinity College's BA in film studies, eleven years after the first MA in film studies was established in University College Dublin (UCD) in 1992, and fourteen years after the first doctorate in the area of either film studies or media studies was awarded in Ireland, north or south, when in 1989 the co-author of this study Kevin Rockett received his D.Phil in film studies from the University of Ulster.

Other factors have also contributed to an increased cinema literacy and better appreciation of film, not least, television, video and DVD, as well as more adventurous programming in art and mainstream cinemas, and the increasing number of festivals.

18. Perhaps the most interesting or radical of the various alternative or cultural film clubs set up is the experimental or Avant-Garde Film Club founded in Dublin in 2008 by Aoife Desmond, Alan Lambert, Esperanza Collado, Donal Foreman and Katie Lincoln. It offers contextualized screen-ings of classic and rare alternative films on a monthly basis in informal settings, such as in the upstairs of the Ha'penny Bridge Inn or the Odessa Club. More recently the club has also worked in association with the Cork Film Centre and the IFI. See Experimental Film Club website/blogs.

19. Previously co-organizers access>CINEMA and Bollywood Ireland had worked together to bring titles such as *Monsoon Wedding* to venues in Galway, Waterford, Carlow, Limerick and Fermanagh.

Another festival with which access>CINEMA has been involved, the (annual) Japanese Film Festival, which started in November 2008 and toured a number of venues including the Town Hall Theatre in Galway (2009), University of Limerick (2009), and Cork's Kino (2008; 2009) also played at the commercial venues of Limerick's Storm cinemas (2008) and Cineworld, Dublin (2008; 2009).

20. 'Kieran delivers the reel deal with creative new film club', *The Kingdom*, 27 October 2005. The cinema has also been a venue for the Kerry Film Festival.

21. *Film Ireland*, no. 55, October/November 1996:9.

22. See Rosita Boland, 'Moving moving pictures', *IT*, 19 May 2001:5. Other supporters of the initia-tive include the Irish Film Board, ESAT Fusion, ESB, Irish Film Institute, RTÉ, the Arts Council of Ireland, and the National Lottery through the Arts Council of Northern Ireland. See Cinemobile website.

23. http://www.cinemobile.net.

24. *Sligo Weekender*, 2 October 2007. See also *Sligo Weekender*, 23 May 2006, and *Roscommon Herald*, 21 June 2006. See also website cinemanorthwest.com, accessed September 2010. Previous to this, since its launch by Sean Kielty in 2001, it had played a regular programme of mainstream films.

25. The first Adaptation Festival took place in 2005. Each year it focuses on a writer (or writers or theme) and screens various adaptations of their work. The list to date includes John McGahern, William Trevor, Enda O'Brien, Roddy Doyle, Bernard MacLaverty and Jennifer Johnston, and in 2010, the theme of the Border and the work of Eugene McCabe, Shane Connaughton and Thaddeus O'Sullivan.

26. This is operated with partners the Model in Sligo, Darklight Film Festival and the art/music/tech-nology collective Synth Eastwood. The inaugural event, which took place in June 2010, profiled the work of Cartoon Saloon (producers of the Irish, Oscar-nominated and multi-award winning *The Secret of Kells* directed by Tomm Moore and Nora Twomey, 2009) and veteran animator Jimmy Murakami (*When the Wind Blows*, 1986). It also featured other animations from around the world including *Ponyo* (Hayao Miyazaki, 2008, Japan) from the renowned Studio Ghibli, and *Lost and Found* (Philip Hunt, 2008, UK).

27. Recognized at the Galway Film Fleadh in the Best Irish Feature Film category in 2009, following a two-week run in the Light House (September 2010), the film was released at various venues in the north-west through the cinemobile (Cinema North-West).

Another 'cinemobile', Sol Cinema, though somewhat unique, visited Dublin in March 2010 during the St Patrick's Festival. It is a solar-powered cinema that is a converted small caravan and can seat eight adults. It is equipped with a LED projector. See sol cinema website, which includes a number of links and reviews. The 15 Second Film Festival also have a two-seater mobile picture palace, see text.

28. *IT*, 29 November 1996:13. For a discussion of the Kino in the context of other developments in Irish and European exhibition and production, see Rod Stoneman, 'The Kino in the age of the mul-tiplex', *The Cork Review*, 1997:28–30; also Connolly and Dillon, 2001, especially pages 16, 35–7, 42–3.

29. Connolly and Dillon, 2001:42.

30. See also Hugh Linehan, *IT*, 28 June 2002:16.

31. The city, next in size to the capital, had a population in 2002 of 123,062, which compares to Galway city's 65,832, Limerick city's 54,023, and Waterford city's 44,594. See CSO 2002 census figures.

32. *IT*, 25 July 2003:3; Declan Hassett, 'Arts Council funds cinema in Cork and Limerick', *Irish Examiner*, 25 July 2003.

33. Quoted, Declan Hassett, *Irish Examiner*, 25 July 2003.

34. Conversation with co-author Kevin Rockett, June 2008.

35. See various articles in the *Irish Examiner*, notably Dan Buckley's 'Cork's arthouse Kino cinema facing its final reel' (29 October 2009) and his 'Curtain goes down on Kino cinema' (27 November 2009).

36. Michael Dwyer, 'Let there be light', *IT*, 25 April 2008:ticket 4–5.

37. 'We don't have [digital] because we can't afford it.' Neil Connolly quoted, *IT*, 25 April 2008:ticket 4–5; Connolly and Dillon, *Film Ireland*, no. 122, May/June 2008:19.

38. See www.artscouncil.ie.

39. Neil Connolly and Maretta Dillon talk with Michael Open, *Film Ireland*, no. 122, May/June 2008:18.

40. The group behind the project is Solas Galway Picture Palace Teoranta. Its members include Lelia Doolan (chair); actress Fionnuala Flanagan; Joe McMahon and Bridie McMahon of the film society; Miriam Allen, director of the film fleadh; Norma Flaherty of the arts centre; Henry Comerford; Michael Mooney; and Tracy Geraghty, formerly of the film centre and now Solas project manager.

41. See Lorna Siggins, 'Galway welcomes Claddagh cluster', *IT*, 5 January 2008:weekend 8.

42. London Economic and Dodona Research, *Study of the specialised cinema sector*, London, March 1997, see Connolly and Dillon, 2001, especially 33–4.

43. CSO census of population 2006. It is thought that by 2011, Galway city's population might reach 85,000. The 2006 figure is already a ten per cent increase on the 2002 figure of 65,832.

44. Connolly and Dillon, 2001:34.

45. *IT*, 24 March 2009:3; *Galway Independent*, 25 March 2009; *Galway Advertiser*, 9 July 2009; Irishconstruction.com, 14 September 2009; Margaret O'Brien, 'Galway city races ahead', *Sunday Business Post*, 28 June 2009:Galway supplement, 1, 2.

46. Quoted in Deirdre O'Shaughnessy, 'Cinema decision slammed', *Galway Independent*, 25 March 2009; and Kernan Andrews, 'Divided views emerge over new art house cinema for Galway', *Galway Advertiser*, 26 March 2009.

47. 'Summer sees some screen time for kids', *IT*, 2 July 2010:ticket.

48. Filmclub was founded in Britain in 2006 by BAFTA winning filmmaker Beeban Kidron and writer Lindsay Mackie 'to explore cinema's ability to revolutionise the hearts, minds and visions of young people.' Its partners include Lovefilm, the online DVD rental company; the *Guardian*; Film Education and UK Film Council, and in Northern Ireland, where, as of 2010, it was still in a pilot stage, it was supported by the department of culture, arts and leisure, Northern Ireland Screen, and Cinemagic. See www.filmclub.org.

49. *Ponyo* had been already screened as part of the 2009 Japanese Film Festival, which opened at the Town Hall Theatre, Galway, on 31 October before moving on to University of Limerick, Cork's Kino and Dublin's Cineworld. It was organized by the Japanese embassy, access>CINEMA and the Ireland Japan Association.

50. Anna Carey, 'Tough critics', *IT*, 7 August 2010:magazine 7. The screenings take place one day every other week.

51. Deirdre O'Shaughnessy, 'Cinema decision slammed', *Galway Independent*, 25 March 2009.

52. The Irish Tourist Board quoted in Furlong, 2009:169. See chapter 7, 'Taking tourism seriously, 1951–1960', an earlier version of this appeared in D. Keogh, F. O'Shea and C. Quinlan (eds), *The lost decade, Ireland in the 1950s*, Cork: Mercier, 2004:162–86.

53. Morash, 2004:209–11.

54. The group was taken subsequently, by Rolls Royce, on a trip to the nearby town of Midleton.

55. Cork Film Festival website; *Irish Times Pictorial*, 29 June 1957:12; Jack McQuillan to Seán Lemass, *Dáil debates*, vol. 162, cols 1122–3, 25 June 1957. A follow-up article in the *IT* featured an interview with Adams' husband, Prince Vittorio Massimo, who claimed to be a descendant of Roman general Maximus, driver of Hannibal from Italy. He supported his wife's desire for a milk bath: 'The Irish had more milk than they could use since they couldn't make cheese from it. Irish milk was too fat for cheese', he contended. The princess told the journalist that she had drawn her inspiration for the milk bath from Poppaea, Nero's mistress, who bathed in asses' milk, after being told there was a glut of milk and asked that it be thrown into the bath. ('More about the milk bath', *Irish Times Pictorial*, 21 September 1957:6.)

56. Members of the first committee included Senator Mrs J. Dowdall; Richard Breathnach, a lecturer at University College Cork; R.B. Beamish, managing director of brewing company Beamish; Commandant J.J. Casley; Major F. O'Donoghue, a 1916 Rising veteran; Harbour commissioner R.B. Sinnott; and S. Fitzgerald, LLD.

57. *IT*, 28 May 1956:1.   58. Ibid.
59. *IT*, 26 September 1959:1; 3 October 1959:12; 'Danish film banned', *Irish Independent*, 26 September 1959:1.
60. *IT*, 8 December 1959:1.
61. *IT*, 25 September 1967:1; *Sunday Press*, 24 September 1967; *Sunday Independent*, 24 September 1967:1; 'Film row; Breen explains', *Irish Press*, 25 September 1967:5; *IT*, 25 September 1967; *Sunday Times*, 15 October 1967. Later, the film's director described the committee behind the decision as 'puritanical, narrow-minded [and] jelly-livered' and suggested that they 'confine themselves to films on coalmines.'
62. *Irish Independent*, 28 August 1968; *IT*, 6 September 1968:14.
63. *IT*, 4 September 1968:9.
64. *Evening Herald*, 30 September 1979; *Evening Press*, 30 September 1979; *Irish Independent*, 30 September 1979. A decade later, Davis was honoured by CFF: *Irish News*, 18 September 1989; *Cork Examiner*, 5 October 1989; *IT*, 6 October 1989:12.
65. *Cork Examiner*, 15 September 1969, 1, 16; *IT*, 15 September 1969:11; 16 September 1969:1; 17 September 1969:21; 'Bishop urged festival body to withdraw film', *Cork Examiner*, 16 September 1969:11.
66. When eventually passed for public exhibition in Ireland in 1972, two cuts were made to the film, both of which concerned nude or bed scenes, though the distributor had made a further cut to the film's first reel prior to its submission to the censor. (Film censor's record 41356, reserve 11810, over-18s, 12 June 1972, NAI.)
67. While two of the cuts were for 'language' ('fuck' and 'damn'), the scene with 'Bobby' climbing out of the pool nude was also cut. (Reserve 11797, 22 May 1972, film censors' records, NAI.)
68. 'Audience walks out in protest at abortion film', *Evening Press*, 10 June 1975:3; *IT*, 12 June 1975:10.
69. See Rockett, 2004:251.
70. *Cork Examiner*, 29 September 1988; *Evening Press*, 29 September 1988; *Evening Echo*, 29 September 1988; *IT*, 30 September 1988:7; *Irish Independent*, 30 September 1988:5; *Evening Echo*, 3 October 1988; *Cork Examiner*, 4 October 1988 (Des O'Sullivan's article is reprinted in Breakwell and Hammond [eds], 1990:40–2); *Evening Echo*, 4 October 1988; *Irish Independent*, 4 October 1988:1; *Cork Examiner*, 5 October 1988; *In Dublin*, no. 310, 13–26 October 1988. The Cork 'vigil' followed in the wake of a similar one in London's West End three weeks earlier. (*IT*, 10 September 1988:7.)
71. See documentary by Pat Butler on Cork Film Festival, RTÉ, 2005 (series producer: Sarah Ryder, programme producer: Edel O'Brien).
72. Ibid. The festival's late night drinking club was strictly members and black-tie only, a rule which remained largely intact until the 1980s. Among those who objected to the club's social formality were British documentarist Paul Rotha and filmmaker Louis Marcus, who is originally from Cork.
73. Godfrey Fitzsimons, 'Cork Film Festival to remain in hands of amateurs, says Breen', *IT*, 19 June 1978:9. Ironically, this article was printed just below a piece accompanied by a photograph describing a garda raid on the festival's club, which, to the embarrassment of the *hoi polie*, including the lord mayor and a minister for state, pointed out that drinking was not allowed anywhere in the state after midnight on Saturday night.
74. See *IT*, 12 October 1994:4; *IT*, letters, 18 October 1994:13; *IT*, letters, 25 October 1994:13; *IT*, letters, 21 October 1994:13; *IT*, letters, 28 October 1994:13. During the week-long event, 162 films had been screened, 33 were feature films, 30 were documentaries and short features, while 99 were shorts.
75. Michael Dwyer, *IT*, 23 October 1998:13.
76. For a report on the fifty-second Corona Cork Film Festival, see *Film Ireland*, no. 119, November/December 2007:9.
77. For a report on the fifty-fourth Corona Cork Film Festival (1–8 November 2009), see *Film Ireland*, no. 131, winter 2009/10:11.
78. See Corona Cork Film Festival website, which includes an archive. The fifty-fifth event is previewed in *Film Ireland*, no. 134, autumn 2010:40. *Film Ireland* online also includes festival reports.
79. See Donald Clarke, 'Southern spotlight on home movies', *IT*, 12 November 2010:18.
80. *Dublin Film Festival programme*, 12–19 September 1985.
81. One of the three seasons offered by the festival was designed to tie in with the Dublin Theatre Festival. (*Dublin Film Festival programme*, 12–19 September 1985.)
82. Myles Dungan, *3rd Dublin Film Festival programme*, 28 October–5 November 1987:4.
83. The sponsors included RTÉ, Aer Lingus, Jury's Hotel, Wang, Telecom Éireann, Animotion (IRL), Harp Lager, Windmill Lane, Strongbow Productions/Green Apple Productions.

84. Dublin Film Festival press release, 5 November 1987; Charles Hunter, *IT*, 9 November 1987:14.
85. While arguably this was the first opening with an Irish made film, previously Thaddeus O'Sullivan's short drama *The Woman who Married Clark Gable* (1985, Ireland), was shown in the first film festival as the complement film to the gala opening presentation of *Desperately Seeking Susan* (Susan Seidelman, 1985), while John Huston's *The Dead* (1987, USA, UK), the well regarded adaptation of James Joyce's germinal story and starring largely an Irish cast, opened the third film festival.
86. Michael Dwyer, *4th Dublin Film Festival, 26 Oct–4 Nov 1988*, programme p. 3. For a critical overview of Neil Jordan and his relationship to Irish cinema, see Rockett and Rockett, *Neil Jordan: exploring boundaries*, Dublin: Liffey, 2003.
87. Films screened were *Blue Collar* (1978), *The Hardcore Life* (1988), *American Gigolo* (1980), *Cat People* (1982), *Mishima* (1985), *Light of Day* (1987), *Patty Hearst* (1988) and *Taxi Driver* (Martin Scorsese, 1976).
88. Previous retrospectives under Mahon's programming included those on Oliver Stone and Theo Angelopoulos, 1992; American Independent John Sayles and Finnish director Aki Kaurismäki, 1993; actor Jeremy Irons and Russian auteur Alexander Rogozhkin, 1994; horror director Abel Ferrara, 1995; French director Bertrand Tavernier, 1995; and British director Terry Gilliam, 1996.
89. *IT*, 12 December 1997:15.
90. Mary Carr, *Evening Herald*, 24 February 1998:18; Michael Dwyer, 'Facing festival facts', *IT*, 13 March 1998:13. In 1997 the Ambassador had been used for a single screening, while the IFC was used for a number of screenings, as was the Savoy. In 1996, additional venues included the Light House and for retrospective screenings, UCI Tallaght and Coolock. In 1995, supplementary screening venues (to the Screen) included the Savoy, the Adelphi, the IFI, UCI and the Ambassador (for the opening film only).
91. *IT*, 30 October 1998:13; *IT*, 5 April 2000:10.
92. *IT*, 30 April 1999:13.
93. Hugh Linehan, *IT*, 3 April 1999, Dublin Film Festival supplement:3; Ciaran Carty, *Sunday Tribune*, 4 April 1999:review 6.
94. Mary Carr, *Evening Herald*, 28 June 1999:22.
95. Michael Dwyer, 'Film festival director resigns', *IT*, 2 September 1999:4; Hugh Linehan, 'Testing times ahead for film festival', *IT*, 3 September 1999:13; Joanne Hayden, 'Irish films are out of the picture', *Sunday Business Post*, 2 April 2000:35.
96. See interview with Taylor: Hugh Linehan, *IT*, 5 November 1999:13. Taylor had been interviewed for the job in 1997, but withdrew his application for personal reasons.
97. At this stage the board consisted of Clohessy, Boorman, Cox, filmmaker Paddy Breathnach, FIFS administrator Brenda Gannon, John Given, RTÉ's William F. Harpur, Buena Vista marketing manager Trish Long, and film censor Sheamus Smith, with Paddy Pouch joining the board the following year.
98. Joanne Hayden, 'Irish films are out of the picture', *Sunday Business Post*, 2 April 2000:35.
99. Philip Molloy, 'Putting the film festival back in the picture', *Irish Independent*, 6 April 2000:15. See also Ian O'Doherty, 'Film fans reeling by flimsy festival fare', *Evening Herald*, 3 April 2000:24.
1. Michael Dwyer, 'Festival misses the mark', *IT*, 21 April 2000:15.
2. Michael Dwyer, 'The show must go on,' *IT*, 28 November 2002:ticket 6. See also Grainne Cunningham and Philip Molloy, 'Shutters come down on festival', *Irish Independent*, 9 February 2002:3.
3. Retrospectively, Dwyer wrote a somewhat ironic report on a seminar on the role of a film festival in Dublin held at the 2001 event. He concluded that there had been too much talking about the DFF and the time was 'overdue for action, to find the remedy to cure this wounded animal.' (Michael Dwyer, 'What price film festival?', *IT*, 2 May 2001:ticket 5). He could hardly have imagined that eighteen months later he would step forward and effectively start it all again for a second time.
4. Local brewery Murphy's, owned by Heineken, was Cork's title sponsor during 1996–2001, while Corona, another beer took over this role in 2006. As noted, Miller beer became the title sponsors of the DFF for the final two years (2000–1) of the event, and, indeed, it was reported that one of the reasons the festival failed in 2002 was Miller's withdrawal of sponsorship. (Cunningham and Molloy, 'Shutters come down on festival', *Irish Independent*, 9 February 2002:3.) ACC Bank, repositioning itself from being an agricultural bank and seeking new markets among young urbanites, became a DFF sponsor from 1991, and as principal sponsor, lent the festival its name from 1995 until 1997 inclusive in a deal worth £90,000 per annum. (Mary Carr, *Evening Herald*, 24 February 1998:18.)
5. The other board members were Dwyer; film producer Arthur Lappin; film production manager Mary Alleguen; Sue Bruce-Smith, formerly of BBC Films and Film Four International, and then

head of production at Little Bird films; independent distributor Niamh McCaul of Eclipse Pictures; Martine Moreau of the cultural service of the French embassy; Rory Concannon, formerly of the Cork Film Festival and then head of marketing at the Abbey Theatre; Gordon Judge, an entertainment lawyer; and Gaby Smith, an accountant for Dublin arts' organizations.

6. Donald Clarke, 'Remaking a film festival', *IT*, 11 March 2003:14; 18 March 2003:16. See also Hugh Linehan, *IT*, 27 February 2003:ticket 2.

7. *IT*, 24 January 2004:weekend review, 8.

8. In 2003 there was a retrospective of the films of Claire Denis. (Michael Dwyer, *IT*, 28 January 2005:ticket, 4.)

9. Hugh Linehan, *IT*, 25 February 2004:14.

10. In 2007 the festival entered a new three-year deal with sponsors Jameson valued at over €1.5 million. (*Film Ireland*, no. 114, January/February 2007:8.)

11. See report, *Film Ireland*, no. 120, January/February 2008:8.

12. Donald Clarke, 'Late founder Dwyer to have reel presence at Dublin film festival', *IT*, 29 January 2010:3. A report of the 2010 festival is featured in *Film Ireland*, no. 132, spring 2010:40.

13. Initially it was a complementary strand of the arts' festival, but its move to the Town Hall theatre following the closure of the Claddagh Palace in the 1990s meant that it had to shift to the week immediately preceding the arts' festival. However, by that time the sheer scale of the film component suggested it was more appropriate as an independent festival.

14. By June 1989 Irish submissions totalled fifty-nine, or 10 per cent of Europe's total. The help was particularly important as the Irish Film Board had closed down. (Michael Dwyer, *IT*, 28 July 1989:12.)

15. Michael Dwyer, *IT*, 24 July 1992:9.

16. Brendan Gleeson replaced Annette Bening who cancelled just prior to the fleadh for person reasons.

17. Galway Film Fleadh programme, 2004:5.

18. For a review of the programme see Donald Clarke, 'The west wing', *IT*, 2 July 2010:ticket 12; 'Galway fleadh ends in tears', *IT*, 16 July 2010:ticket 10. See also Galway Film Fleadh website.

19. The other members of the first committee were Margo Harkin, Julie Barber, Denis Bradley, Gillian Coward, Anne Crilly, Joe Nicholas, Declan McGonagle, Martin McLoone, Gerry McLaughlin, Brendan McMenamin and Charles Sweeney.

20. Brendan MacMenamin, Foyle Film Projects chairperson, *Festival '89 Derry programme*, 1989:2. The other members of the organization's committee were filmmakers Anne Crilly, Margaret Gallagher, Siobhan Twomey, Elaine Farthing and Jim Curran; Derry City council visual arts' officer Declan McGonagle; visual artist Moira McIver; and art education and community liaison worker Pauline Ross.

21. The Nerve Centre later displaced Film Projects as the festival's organizer. (Hugh Linehan, 'Agreeable ambiguities', *IT*, 1 May 1998:13.)

22. Helen Meany, 'Does the image have the last word?', *IT*, 28 November 1996:16. This report on the tenth festival includes an account of the event's exploration of the relationship between literature and film.

23. Hugh Linehan, 'Agreeable ambiguities', *IT*, 1 May 1998:13. For a report on the 2005 festival, the eighteenth, see *Film Ireland*, no. 108, January/February 2006:9.

24. Thomas Arnold Fanning, *Film Ireland*, no. 96, January/February 2004:10.

25. For a report on the eighteenth festival in 2005, see *Film Ireland*, no. 108, January/February 2006:9.

26. Michael Open, report on nineteenth festival in 2006, *Film Ireland*, no. 114, January/February 2007:10.

27. See report, *Film Ireland*, no. 120, January/February 2008:8; also preview, *Film Ireland*, no. 119, November/December 2007:8.

28. In 2010, the main venues were the Nerve Centre, Orchard Cinema, and Derry Omniplex. Associated facilities were Café Nervosa, City Hotel, Tower Hotel, Void Gallery, Strule Arts Centre and Letterkenny Arts Centre.

29. For an overview of the festival (including programmes), see festival's own website.

30. For a discussion of the films shown, see Gerry McCarthy, 'Snapshots of a nation at war', *Sunday Times*, 2 September 2001:culture, 6–7.

31. See *Film Ireland*, no. 97, 2004:10.

32. Donald Clarke, "Everything is politics', *IT*, 1 April 2005:ticket 5.

33. Michael Open, *Film Ireland*, no. 109, March/April 2006:9.

34. In 2007, the popularity of purveyors of alcoholic drinks as film festival sponsors continued with Jameson Irish Whiskey adding Belfast to its stable following its title sponsorship of Dublin in 2003. Orange had been Belfast's previous sponsor.

35. Michael Open, *Film Ireland*, no. 116, May/June 2007:10.
36. www.belfastfilmfestival.org., accessed June 2008.
37. *Film Ireland*, no. 128, May/June 2009:10.
38. See *Film Ireland*, no. 132, summer 2010:6; report by Michael Open in *Film Ireland* online; and www.belfastfilmfestival.org., accessed September 2010. As an aside, a special event, 'A-Z of Belfast Cinemas', was presented at the April 2010 festival by Brian Henry Martin in memory of James Doherty (1920–2008).
39. See Michael Open, *Film Ireland*, no. 118, September/October 2007:8 (forty-fifth event) and, more generally, (Ulster Bank) Belfast Festival at Queen's website.
40. Report in *Film Ireland*, no. 107, November/December 2005: 10 (preview in no. 106:8). In 2008 the festival was held in Waterford.
41. See lughfilm.com. It was dedicated to screening maritime films.
42. For a report on the October 2005 festival, see *Film Ireland*, no. 108, January/February 2006:10; for a report on the seventeenth festival in November/December 2007, see *Film Ireland*, no. 120, January/February 2008:9 (preview in no. 119, November/December 2007:8).
43. Quoted on Cinemagic's website which was promoting its seventeen-day event in November/December 2005 (accessed June 2006). The twentieth anniversary (Coca-Cola) Cinemagic Festival in November 2010 boasted more than 100 film screenings from all over the world, and over fifty workshops, competitions, master-classes and other events. See cinemagic.org.uk.
44. See *Film Ireland*, no. 122, May/June 2008:9. Cinemagic (Dublin and Belfast) attracts over 20,000 people annually.
45. *Film Ireland*, no. 123, July/August 2008:52; See www.lightsout.ie.
46. For reports on the various years, see *Film Ireland,* no. 125, November/December 2008:8 (fourteenth); *Film Ireland*, no. 119, November/December 2007:8 (thirteenth); *Film Ireland*, no. 114, January/February 2007:8 (twelfth); *Film Ireland*, no. 108, January/February 2006:8 (eleventh). See *Film Ireland* online, and Junior Film Fleadh website (galwayfilmfleadh.com/junior).
47. The board of directors of the Limerick Irish Film Festival were Siobhan O'Donoghue, Tom Garavan, Trish Long, Michael Murphy, Gerry Stembridge and Aidan Corr. See *IT*, 12 April 1996:2 for a report on the second year's festival.
48. For festival reports see *Film Ireland*, no. 116, May/June 2007:10 (tenth); *Film Ireland*, no. 121, March/April 2008:9 (eleventh); *Film Ireland*, no. 128, May/June 2009:10 (twelfth) and *Film Ireland* online (filmireland.net), 24 March 2010 entry. Founded by Jayne Foley in 1997, it has become a resident company at the Belltable Arts Centre. Grant aided by the Arts Council of Ireland, its board of directors (as of 2010) comprised of Jayne Foley, Brendan Maher, Donal Foreman (previous Fresh winner, 2003), Alicia McGivern, Pat Shortt and Tony Tracy. According to its website (www.freshfilmfestival.net), Fresh hosts International Film Shares, creates opportunities for filmmakers to travel and network on an international level, provides workshops, produces various showcases, and hosts Ireland's Young Filmmaker awards. (www.freshfilmfestival.net, accessed June 2008.) *Film Ireland*, no. 128, May/June 2009:10. The 2009 Young Filmmaker of the Year, Nicholas Sheridan, won the award for *The Grim Trials of Vida Novak*. That year there were 180 competitive film entries in all categories.
49. http://www.fis.ie, the film project for primary schools. For a report on the third festival, see 'Outstanding pupils are animated by success of film', *Laois Nationalist*, 15 November 2007.
50. For festival reports see *Film Ireland*, no. 108, January/February 2006:10 (fourth festival); *Film Ireland*, no. 120, January/February 2008:9 and no. 119, November/December 2007:9 (sixth festival); *Film Ireland*, no. 124, September/October 2008:7 (seventh festival); *Film Ireland*, no. 130, September/October 2009:10 (seventh festival). See www.clonesfilmfestival.com.
51. Geraldine Zechner, quoted, *Film Ireland*, no. 134, autumn 2010:40, preview of ninth festival, 'Ireland's biggest little film festival'.
52. 'Festival to take Laois by storm', *Laois Nationalist*, 24 September 2002; 'Wonderfully mixed bag makes arts festival a huge success', *Laois Nationalist*, 11 November 2002.
53. See report, *Film Ireland*, no. 120, January/February 2008:10; preview, no. 119, November/December 2007:8. For reports on the second Waterford Film Festival, see *Film Ireland*, no. 125, November/December 2008:8 and no. 126, January/February 2009:10. The fourth event is previewed in *Film Ireland*, no. 134, autumn 2010:40. See waterfordfilmfestival.com.
54. Imagine in conjunction with Storm Cinemas and Waterford Film for All presented the French Film Festival, 2007.
55. Sponsored by the University of Limerick and Ulster Bank enablement fund, the event, which had as its theme identities in twenty-first century Ireland, was initiated by Dr Tina O'Toole, assistant dean of humanities. Planned to celebrate a cross-institutional humanities' college day on 7 March 2007, the four-day festival was organized by Dr O'Toole and Dr Kate Boulay (dept of languages

& cultural studies) in collaboration with the university's students' union and a festival committee that included staff and students in the college of humanities.

56. Rebecca Kemp, *Film Ireland*, no. 96, January/February 2004:22–3.
57. *IT*, 30 September 2005:ticket 32. See also Rebecca Kemp, *Film Ireland*, no. 108, January/February 2006:38.
58. For a report on the eighth festival, see *Film Ireland*, no. 120, January/February 2008:9 (previewed in *Film Ireland*, no. 118, September/October 2007:9). By 2010, O'Mahony was expecting close on 10,000 people to attend. (*Film Ireland*, no. 134, autumn 2010:40.)
59. See *Film Ireland*, no. 124, September/October 2008:9; no. 126, January/February 2009:10; no. 134, autumn 2010:40; and *Film Ireland* online (filmireland.net). See also Kerryfilmfestival.com.
60. *Film Ireland*, no. 131, winter 2009/2010:10.
61. Quoted in *Film Ireland*, no. 134, autumn 2010:40. As was reported in *Film Ireland* online, the Kerry Film Festival has joined with a number of film festivals in Spain, Italy, Sweden, Canada, the UK and America in an attempt to promote Irish short films. See 'Irish Films at [the] Rushes Soho Shorts Festival [London]', 29 July 2010, filmireland.net.
62. *Film Ireland*, no. 119, November/December 2007:10 (previewed in *Film Ireland*, no. 118, September/October 2007:9; and under the title 'Kerry International FF', *Film Ireland*, no. 116, May/June 2007:8). Regarding the second Dingle Film Festival, see *Film Ireland*, no. 123, July/August 2008:10 (preview) and no. 125, November/December 2008:11 (report); for the third (10–13 September 2009) see *Film Ireland*, no. 131, winter 2009/10:9 (preview).
63. See news.dinglefilmfestival.com, accessed September 2010. For a report on the 2010 March festival, see Rebecca Kemp, *Film Ireland* online, filmireland.net.
64. www.dinglefilmfestival.com. In 2010, the board of directors were Ned Dowd, producer; Mandy Kean, Soho House, London; Tom Hogan; David Chipperfield, producer; Maurice Galway; and John Naughton, secretary. For coverage of the 2009 event, see *Film Ireland*, no. 129, July/August 2009:12 (preview).
65. For a preview of the sixth festival, which bridges the gap between studio and independent filmmaking, held in May 2009 at a new larger venue, the Ulster History Park, see *Film Ireland*, May/June 2009:9. See www.midulsterfilmfestival.com.
66. *IT*, 30 June 2006:ticket 32; and 'Sound+Vision 2009: Dylan on Screen', 15 June 2009, wordpress.hotpress.com. While 2010 was a year of transition in the context of the venue and funding, as of September 2010 the organizers were looking forward to a full festival in 2011.
67. The first event included thirty films from fifteen countries, while the second complemented the main programme with recent Irish-language films. The third festival featured, alongside its main film programme of over twenty films, including a special Polish season, various master-classes, seminars on such topics as filmmaking for social change, and the future of distribution. For festival reports, see *Film Ireland*, no. 116, May/June 2007:8 (preview of second festival); *Film Ireland*, no. 122, May/June 2008:8 (preview of third festival); for a preview of the fourth event in June 2009, see *Film Ireland*, May/June 2009:8; the fifth (which represented twenty-nine countries) is reported in *Film Ireland*, no. 133, summer 2010:38 (see also 34–5).
68. Report in *Film Ireland*, no. 106, September/October 2005:10; the second festival in 2006 is reported on in *Film Ireland*, no. 112, September/October 2006:8.
69. *Film Ireland*, no. 115, March/April 2007:7.
70. Second event held in June 2007 previewed in *Film Ireland*, no. 116, May/June 2007:9.
71. 'It's lights, camera and action for Sligo's short film festival', *Sligo Weekender*, 6 September 2005. Films from Ireland and around the world, between one and thirty-five minutes in length, were screened in five categories (fiction, documentary, animation, experimental digital video art, and amateur), while (aspiring) filmmakers had the opportunity of attending a questions and answers session with director Brendan Muldowney and producer Conor Barry. See also report in *Film Ireland*, no. 106, September/October 2005:10.
72. First Minicinefest (30 September 2006) used the cinemobile and is previewed in *Film Ireland*, no. 112, September/October 2006:9. The third Minicinefest was held in September 2008 as part of the fourth Ranelagh Arts Festival. See also Ranelagh Arts Festival website; 'Cine-Café "all shorts" film show', mylocalnews.ie, accessed September 2010.
73. The project is also supported by Northern Ireland Screen, and Queen's University, Belfast. Northernirelandscreen.com; 'Funding boost for 15 second film festival', *IFTN News*, 5 October 2009, iftn.ie; and 15SecondFilmFestival.com.
74. The area is without a cinema and so relies on the cinemobile and the Harbour View. See festival's own website, while a review of the 2010 event, when a programme of Mexico's best shorts as well as local interest films were included, can be found in *Film Ireland*, no. 133, summer 2010:38.

75. Previewed in *Film Ireland*, no. 118, September/October 2007:9.
76. See *Film Ireland*, no. 116, May/June 2007:7.
77. Guests have included Mbye Cham, professor of African film, Howard University, Washington (2007); filmmaker Jeta Amata (2007); and actors Presley Chweneyagae (2006), who starred in the Oscar winning *Tsotsi*, which premiered there; Bonnie Henna (2007) of *Catch a Fire*; and *Eastenders'* star Rudolf Walker (2009). See festival website, carlowafricanfilmfestival.com.
78. *Film Ireland*, no. 122, May/June 2008:8.
79. See *Film Ireland* online and festival website (kffcarrickonshahannon.wordpress.com). The programme included a selection of Kurdish shorts chosen by transition year students from Carrick Community School, as well as a panel discussion featuring some Kurdish directors (including Doug Aubrey, Binevsa Berivan, Miraz Bezar, Peri Ibrahim and Chiman Rahimi). All events were free.
80. A related festival, in that it surveyed the best of cutting-edge technology, was Resfest. Focusing on the new 'sights and sounds and moving image innovations [...] from the biggest to the smallest screen, [...] live music to music videos to machinima' (*Film Ireland*, no. 101, November/December 2004:8), it was an international (North-American based) touring festival rather than an Irish-based event and first came to Dublin (and the IFI) in its eight year in November 2004. In 2006, ten years after it had been established, it disappeared.
81. The tenth festival (26–29 June 2008) featured actor, writer and filmmaker Crispin Hellion Glover as its guest of honour; a number of workshops in conjunction with Screen Training Ireland; symposia; and various screenings and special events, including the 15-second Film Festival Picture Palace (referred to above) and outdoor late night screenings, with work by internationally acclaimed Irish artist and filmmaker Paddy Jolley; and the making of its closing presentation during the actual festival – an experimental documentary portrait of Dublin by director Lenny Abrahamson and others.
82. See darklight-filmfestival.com. See also Hugh Linehan, 'Let there be Darklight', *IT*, 27 May 1999:14; *Film Ireland*, no. 101, November/December 2004:8 (preview of Darklight 5, 17–21 November 2004); *Film Ireland*, no. 116, May/June 2007:34; *Film Ireland*, no. 122, May/June 2008:8 (Darklight 10, 26–29 June 2008 previewed).
83. Frank McDonald, *IT*, 4 July 1996:property 9. Other buildings in the square include the Gallery of Photography, which 'evoke[s] a Box Brownie camera', and the National Photographic Archive, both of which were designed by the Irish Film Centre architects O'Donnell and Twomey.
84. See www.darklight.ie/festival.
85. See entry in Yoram Allon, Del Cullen and Hannah Patterson (eds), *Contemporary North American film directors: a Wallflower critical guide*, London: Wallflower, second ed., 2002:559–60; orig. 2000.
86. See http://www.celticfilm.co.uk. For reports on the Celtic Media Festival, see *Film Ireland*, no. 122, May/June, 2008:7, 9 (twenty-ninth on 16–18 April 2008 in Galway); and *Film Ireland*, no. 132, spring 2010 (preview of the thirty-first festival on 21–3 April).
87. See belfastfestival.com, accessed 21 September 2010.
88. Michael Dwyer, 'Too much of a good thing?', *IT*, 23 April 1999:13.
89. Donald Clarke, 'Ireland feasts on festivals', *IT*, 26 October 2007.

CHAPTER 7

1. Fr Richard S. Devane SJ, 'Proposals for a censorship code in Éire', c.1940, Archbishop McQuaid papers, DDA.
2. Ultramontanism triumphed with the first Vatican Council (1870) and its definition of papal infallibility. See John Bowden (ed.), *Christianity: the complete guide*, London: Continuum, 2005:1043.
3. Inglis, 1987:138. See also Bowden (ed.), *Christianity*, 2005:259–61.
4. Bowden (ed.), 2005:1016.
5. John Healy, *Maynooth College: its centenary history*, Dublin: Brown and Nolan, 1895:283, quoted in Inglis, 1987:137.
6. See Bowden (ed.), *Christianity*, 2005:1190–4, 1312.
7. James M. Byrne, 'Thomism' in Bowden (ed.), *Christianity*, 2005:1194.
8. Ibid.
9. Michael Cronin was an international authority on Thomist theology: his PhD was published as *The science of ethics* (1909), the same year as he became the first professor of ethics and politics at University College Dublin. In 1930, Archbishop Edward Byrne appointed him vicar-general of the Dublin archdiocese, a position reconfirmed by Archbishop McQuaid in 1941. His book, *Primer of*

the principles of social science (1927), an anti-modernist tract, was widely distributed among the Catholic laity, the fourth revised edition of which was published in 1956 (Dublin: M.H. Gill).

10. Fr Louis Billot SJ was professor of dogmatic theology at the Gregorian University, Rome, and from 1911, a cardinal.

11. Fr Fahey, as a student of Billot, subscribed to the integralist belief that the Revelation as a body of truths delivered by God to the Apostles and their bishop-successors had been placed before the faithful to be accepted without question. His other books include *The mystical body of Christ in the modern world* (1935); *The rulers of Russia* (1938); *Money, manipulation and the social order* (1944); *The mystical body of Christ and the reorganisation of society* (1945); *The kingship of Christ and the conversion of the Jewish nation* (1953); and *The church and farming* (1953). Fahey established the extreme Catholic group *Maria Duce* in 1945. See Finín O Driscoll, 'In search of a Christian social order: the impact of social Catholicism in Ireland' in T.M. Devine and J.F. McMillan (eds), *Celebrating Columba: Colm Cille á Cheiliúradh, Irish-Scottish connections, 597–1997,* Edinburgh: John Donald, 1999:115.

12. Cooney, 1999:44–5. See also Fr Denis Fahey, 'The mission of St Thomas Aquinas', *Catholic Bulletin,* May 1925:491–506.

13. John Feeney, *John Charles McQuaid: the man and the mask,* Dublin/Cork: Mercier, 1974:7–8.

14. Fr R.S. Devane SJ, *The failure of individualism: a documented essay,* Dublin: Richview/Browne and Nolan, 1948:229. Europe's crisis, according to Devane, was a consequence of its religious, political and economic 'nihilistic individualism or atavism that had its origin mainly in the Protestant Reformation of the sixteenth century, and for which the Renaissance, to some extent, paved the way'. According to this argument there had been four centuries during which society had been 'steadily disintegrating under the growing force of this triple composite evil', until it was now 'in danger of complete collapse'. (Ibid., xvi.)

Richard Stanislaus Devane (1876–1951), born in Limerick at 29 William Street, was the eldest son of Cornelius Devane, a well-known merchant and Joanna (née McCormack) Devane. He had two brothers and two sisters. He was educated at the Sacred Heart College; Crescent College, Limerick (1891–3); St Mungret College (1893–94); St Munchin's seminary; and St Patrick's, Maynooth, where he was ordained a priest in 1901. During 1901–4, he worked on the 'English mission' at St Patrick's church, Middlesborough, Yorkshire. On his return to Ireland in 1904, he became, for fourteen years, curate of St Michael's, Limerick, which was a large, working-class district. While there, he was involved in parochial work with the St Vincent de Paul Society and temperance sodalities for men and women; kept in close touch with labour circles, on whose behalf he initiated a series of lecturers; wrote for *The Leader*; was responsible for the licence regulating cinema shows in Limerick under the Cinematograph Act 1909, which was adopted by Limerick borough council; and was a member of the Limerick technical committee. During 1904–14 he was also chaplain to the local British army garrison, and helped to launch a campaign against 'evil literature'.

In 1918, he entered the Society of Jesuits at St Stanislaus College, Tullamore, and in 1920 'he made his religious profession'. His first appointment was to the newly founded Retreat House for working men, Rathfarnham Castle, of which he became its first director in 1922, a post he held for a decade, and he returned as director from 1945, staying there until his death in 1951. During 1933–44, he was attached to the Retreat House, Milltown Park. Besides his activities in film and book censorship campaigns, discussed in the main text, he was also involved in legislative changes for the 'legal redress for mother and offspring of irregular unions' (1930); public dance halls (1935); criminal law amendments relating to young people (1935); and the children's bill, in particular 'the education of nomads' (1942). His funeral was attended by Liam Cosgrave, parliamentary secretary to the taoiseach; Margaret Pearse, mother of Patrick Pearse; Major Vivion de Valera, son of Éamon de Valera; Sean Brady; and writer and broadcaster Annraoi Ó Liatháin, president of the Gaelic League and of An Coiste Náisiúnta Agóide. (*Irish Press,* 23 May 1951:7; 26 May 1951:4; 'Death of a noted Jesuit', *Irish Independent,* 24 May 1951:7; *IT,* 24 May 1951:5.)

15. Whyte, 1980:35, orig. 1971.

16. Joseph G. Ambrose, *The Dan Breen story,* Dublin/Cork: Mercier, 1981:47–8.

17. See Kevin Rockett, 'Representations of Irish history in fiction films made prior to the 1916 Rising' in Laurence M. Geary (ed.), *Rebellion and remembrance in modern Ireland,* Dublin: Four Courts, 2001:224–8. Both of these films, made by the Kalem film production company, can be viewed online at www.tcd.ie/Irishfilm.

18. See Bowden (ed.), *Christianity,* 2005:700, 891.

19. J. Waldron (past president and founder member), 'An Ríoghacht; a retrospect', *Irish Monthly,* vol. 87, no. 924, June 1950:274–80.

20. An Ríoghacht's programme, quoted, Cooney, 1999:64.

21. Éamon de Valera later consulted both Fathers Cahill and McQuaid when drafting the 1937 Constitution of Ireland. Nevertheless, as Finín O Driscoll comments, de Valera 'was much more preoccupied with attempting to break the link with Britain than with reconstructing Irish society according to the thinking of Fr Edward Cahill and those who thought like him.' (O Driscoll, 'In search of a Christian social order' in T.M. Devine and J.F. McMillan (eds), *Celebrating Columba*, 1999:117. See also *Irish Monthly*, 87, no. 924, June 1950:278.)

22. Dr McQuaid became president of the school in 1931, a post he retained until 1940 at which time he was appointed archbishop of Dublin, a position he held until 1971.

23. Cooney, 1999:64. Both Cahill and Fahey had been influenced by the most reactionary elements of continental Catholicism, the latter becoming a supporter of the *Action Française* movement while studying in France at the time of the anti-Jewish Dreyfus affair. See O Driscoll, 'In search of a Christian social order', in T.M. Devine and J.F. McMillan (eds), *Celebrating Columba*, 1999:133.

24. This notion is expressed most completely in his 1929 book *Freemasonry and the anti-Christian movement.*

25. Fr Cahill, *Ireland's peril*, Dublin: M.H. Gill, 1930:21.

26. Pastoral issued, 2 March 1924, *Irish Catholic directory*, 1925:559.

27. Ibid. On 4 January 1928, a modest dress and deportment crusade was launched in Limerick. (*Irish Catholic directory* 1929:560.)

28. Pastoral issued 2 March 1924, *Irish Catholic directory*, 1925:563.

29. Pastoral issued 29 September 1927, *Irish Catholic directory*, 1928:605.

30. Pastoral issued 6 October 1925, *Irish Catholic directory*, 1926:597.

31. Pastoral address, 15 August 1927, *Acta et decreta concilii plenarii episcoporum Hiberniae, 15 Augusti 1927*, Dublin: Browne and Nolan, 1929:142.

32. Ibid.141.

33. Pastoral issued 1 August 1927, *Irish Catholic directory*, 1928:596.

34. *Irish Catholic*, 21 February 1931:2.

35. Ibid., 7. Though Dr Mageean lived in Belfast there is little evidence to suggest that Northern Ireland, even though it operated under different laws to the Free State, had a culture any more 'immoral' than the Free State's.

36. The delegation that met O'Higgins on 28 February 1923 included representatives of the Irish Vigilance Association, the Priests' Social Guild, the Church of Ireland and the Presbyterian Church, as well as Devane's fellow Jesuit, Fr Tomkin, Milltown Park. See Rockett, 2004:64.

37. Fr R.S. Devane, 'Indecent literature: some legal remedies', *Irish Ecclesiastical Record*, vol. 25, 5th series, 1925:182–204; *Irish Ecclesiastical Record*, vol. 28, 1926:357–77; Fr R.S. Devane, 'Suggested tariff on imported newspaper and magazines', *Studies*, vol. 16, 1927:546, 552, 554, in which he reported that there were 53 juvenile weeklies and 24 juvenile fortnightlies and monthlies, and 250 other weeklies imported from England. In one shop alone in a Dublin slum, 145 English juvenile papers were sold weekly. Devane retained an interest in this issue all his life: one of his last publications was a booklet, *The imported press: a national menace – some remedies*, Dublin: James Duffy & Co., 1950.

38. In 1925 in the *Irish Ecclesiastical Record*, vol. 25, 5th series, 1925:185, Fr Devane justified such vigilante action with recourse to the justification offered by, of all people, Ulster Unionist leader Sir Edward Carson with regard to the 1912 Ulster gun-running that 'there are illegalities which are not crimes.' For a discussion of the events in Limerick in 1911, and of the vigilance committee publications' agitation more generally, see Louis Cullen, *Eason & son: a history*, Dublin: Eason & Son, 1989, and for the related film censorship campaigns during the 1910s, see Rockett, 2004.

39. Fr Devane proposed a 33.3 per cent or 50 per cent tariff on magazines of the popular class and of 100 per cent on foreign dailies. (See Michael Adams, *Censorship: the Irish experience*, Alabama: University of Alabama, 1968:37.)

40. Kieran Woodman, *Media control in Ireland, 1923–1983*, Galway: Officina Typographica, Galway UP, 1985:42.

41. Fr R.S. Devane, 'The menace of British combines', *Studies*, vol. 19, 1930:53–69.

42. Interestingly, Fr Devane never served as a member of either the publications or film censorship appeal boards, despite the fact that both boards always included a Catholic clergyman.

43. *Irish Catholic*, 7 January 1922:5.

44. 'Juvenile crime increase', *Irish Press*, 15 January 1935:3. Another contributor to the hearing said that it was 'dangerous to allow children to go to gangster pictures'. Writing the following week in the *Irish School Weekly*, the journal of the Irish National Teachers' Organization (INTO), its editor, John D. Sheridan, dismissed the concern with gangster films and sought to focus attention on the 'sex film'. He argued that 'Gangster pictures may harm one child in a hundred, but sex pictures

have a definitely bad effect on every child who sees them. Bracketing these two classes of pictures in a general condemnation is like bracketing pimples and tuberculosis as dangers to the health of the nation.' (*Irish School Weekly*, vol. 37, no. 4, 26 January 1935:84.)

45. 'The cinema', *Irish Press*, 23 January 1935:10.
46. The evidence about gangster films required an investigation into 'how far separate performances for children could be arranged' in the Irish Free State. (*Irish Press*, 23 January 1935:10.)
47. Clearly unfamiliar with the details of the Censorship of Films Act 1923, neither the *Irish Press* nor any other publication drew attention to the fact, until the 1950s, that films were released for a general or universal only audience. The issue was not resolved until 1965 when the policy on grading of films was changed by the minister for justice, Brian Lenihan. (See Rockett, 2004.) The first official film censor, James Montgomery (1923–40), never once issued a limited certificate, such as the British 'A' for adults, or 'H' for horror, but banned or cut films according to his imagined experience of the effect it might have on the youngest child. He believed that limited certificates 'would excite morbid and unhealthy curiosity' in those films thus restricted. (James Montgomery, 'Film censorship in the Irish Free State', 9 December 1936:2, unpublished paper, office of film classification, Dublin.)
48. *Irish Press*, 6 February 1935:1. The *Press* also reprinted on page one its 23 January editorial which precipitated the exhibitors' action.
49. 'An evil', ibid., 6.
50. 'The cinemas action' (editorial) and 'Cinema proprietors' action' (letter), *Irish Press*, 7 February 1935:10.
51. 'Comhairle and Dublin cinemas', *Irish Press*, 11 February 1935:7.
52. 'Public bodies pledge support', *Irish Press*, 18 February 1935:1–2.
53. 'Council and films', *Irish Press*, 26 February 1935:2.
54. 'The cinema evil; *Irish Press* hypocrisy', *An Phoblacht*, vol. 10, no. 8, 23 March 1935:1. The article argued that the *Press* 'did not go to the roots of the cinema evil' in Ireland. Not only was cinema 'the greatest Anglicising force in the country' and offered representations of 'shady alien modes of life', but also 'its continued depictions of British imperialist functions and British War Office propaganda displays' were designed 'to make Irish youth "sensible" of the British connection.' As a result, it accused the *Press* of having failed to protest 'at the attempt to link [Ireland] with a recent British Royal wedding by showing on the screen the crazed adulation of foolish English people.' Furthermore, it complained, when Irish republicans 'showed in no uncertain manner their determination to prevent these Imperialist film displays' (attacking the cinemas or threatening the managers where the film was being shown), 'there was no note of approval sounded by the *Irish Press*.' For more on the republican anti-British campaign, which climaxed during 1935–7, see Kevin Rockett, 'From radicalism to conservatism: contradictions within Fianna Fáil film policies in the 1930s', *Irish Studies Review*, vol. 9, no. 2, August 2001, 160, and Rockett, 2004:317–25.
55. *Dáil debates*, vol. 56, cols 394–8, May 1935. See also 'Mr Dillon and cinema', *Irish Press*, 4 May 1935:9.
56. 'Films for children', *Irish Press*, 25 February 1935:1.
57. 'County councils and cinemas', *Irish Press*, 22 February 1935:7, 8.
58. 'Jesuit's plea for reform of cinema'; *Irish Press*, 16 February 1935:9.
59. See Fr Richard S. Devane SJ, *Challenge from youth*, Dublin: Browne and Nolan, 1942.
60. 'A "clean film" campaign', *Irish Press*, 14 February 1935:1.
61. Three other clergymen shared the platform with Revd Dudley. These were Fr Sweeney OMI, Revd G. Sullivan, and Revd Dr Doyle, while Mr S. Walsh and Terence de Vere White were also there. Dudley's lecture was entitled 'The cinema – curse or blessing?'
62. Quoted, *Irish Press*, 18 February 1935:1.
63. 'Threat of pagan films to world; Catholic Action called for', *Irish Press*, 18 February 1935:7.
64. In moving the vote of thanks to Fr Dudley, Joseph A. Power, film reviewer with the *Irish Independent*, suggested that the Gaeltacht was 'a very good antidote to the evil influence of the films.' Such Irish-Irelander sentiments were hardly shared by cinemagoers but help to put in context Power's own support for Irish films. See Rockett et al, 1987:62. It is perhaps significant that Fr Devane did not feature in these events.
65. The resolution went on to state that though 'a film may be freed from what is indecent, or obscene, … owing to its essential character [it might] remain a menace to the religious, national and cultural interests of the Irish people.' ('An Ríoghacht plan to control cinemas', *Irish Press*, 23 March 1935:7.)
66. An indication of the conservative nature of the leadership of the INTO is suggested by their secretary, Mr M.P. Linehan, a lecturer on Catholic social teaching, who led the transformation of the Labour Party constitution by 1940 to make it acceptable to the Catholic hierarchy through deleting its references to a 'workers' republic. (Whyte, 1980:83–4.)

67. *Irish School Weekly*, vol. 37, no. 19, 11 May 1935:457.
68. *Irish School Weekly*, vol. 37, no. 18, 4 May 1935:423.
69. *IT*, 11 and 12 June 1935:6, 8.
70. Editorial, 'Cinema and the people', *Irish Press*, 12 June 1935:6. See also 'Central cinema control', *Irish Press*, 11 June 1935:7.
71. *Irish Independent*, 11 June 1935:6. See also 11 June 1935:7.
72. *Standard*, 14 June 1935:8.   73. *Dublin Evening Mail*, 11 June 1935:4.
74. Quoted, *The Cinema*, 26 June 1935:24.
75. *TC*, vol. 44, no. 3033, 18 June 1935.
76. *The Cinema*, 26 June 1935:24.
77. Lord abbot of Mount Mellary, Calcius O'Connell, proposed a call for stricter censorship. (*The Cinema*, 24 June 1935.)
78. The Catholic body An Ríoghacht (The League of the Kingship of Christ) demanded legislative restrictions on Sunday opening of cinemas. (*The Cinema*, 21 November 1935.)
79. This resolution, proposed by the Finglas cumann, was included on the agenda of the Fianna Fáil ard fheis in November 1935, though it seems not to have been debated. (*Irish Press*, 27 November 1935:1.)
80. *The film in national life: being the report of an enquiry conducted by the commission on educational and cultural films into the service which the cinematograph may render to education and social progress*, London: George Allen and Unwin, 1932. Membership of the commission, which held conferences in 1929 and 1930, included representatives of government departments, and of educational, scientific and social organizations, as well as independent commentators. Among the commission's thirty-six members who were not representatives of government departments was the Irish writer St John Irvine.
81. Dr Cornelius Lucey, 'The message of the social encyclical', *Irish Ecclesiastical Record*, 5th series, vol. 52, August 1938:113. He explained that while the pope 'is qualified by his office to speak authoritatively only on matters of faith and morals, it follows that the subject-matter of an encyclical will be one in which religious or moral issues of one kind or another are involved.' However, since 'encyclicals are not usually made vehicles for infallible pronouncements, still their teaching has to be accepted as the official teaching of the Church.' In other words, through free will Catholics could come to recognize the 'truth' of the encyclical.
82. Unlike in other European countries, the Catholic social movement did not begin to develop fully in Ireland until after independence and the encyclical gave both a focus and an impetus to the movement in Ireland.
83. This was the preferred term in Ireland, as it enabled a distancing from 'fascist' corporatism in Spain, Portugal and Italy. As John Whyte argues, though, corporatism was not confined to Catholicism, having a long tradition in Europe, especially in France and Austria. (See Whyte, 1980:67–8.)
84. This 'special position', which was subsequently decreed by the courts as conferring no legal privilege, fell short of what the clergy both in Ireland and Rome would have ideally liked. Furthermore, the same article also recognized by name other religions existing in Ireland at this time. In 1972 the clause was removed following a constitutional referendum.
85. In November 1995, a second closely fought referendum on divorce resulted in a 'no fault' divorce, following five years of separation, being introduced under the Family Law Act 1996. This came into effect from February 1997.
86. O Driscoll, 'In search of a Christian social order' in T.M. Devine and J.F. McMillan (eds), *Celebrating Columba*, 1999:115–16.
87. *The use and misuse of films* [trans. encyclical letter, *Vigilanti cura*, issued, 29 June 1936], London, Catholic Truth Society, July 1936:6–7.
88. Ibid., 9.   89. Ibid., 10–11.
90. Ibid., 11.   91. Ibid., 15–22.
92. For the history of the Catholic church's role in American film censorship, see Gregory D. Black, *Hollywood censored: morality codes, Catholicism and the movies*, Cambridge: Cambridge UP, 1994, and Gregory D. Black, *The Catholic crusade against the movies, 1940–1978*, Cambridge UP, 1997. For the views of Irish censors on the American 'clean screen' campaigns, see Rockett, 2004:97–104.
93. 'Nation and cinema', *IT*, 8 April 1937:8.   94. *IT*, 10 April 1937:8.
95. Fr Richard Devane SJ, 'The cinema and the nation', *Irish Press*, 10 April 1937:8. In the same issue, the *Irish Press* published a report of a Peacock theatre meeting at which Liam O'Leary spoke on the limited range of films available to Irish cinemagoers, while Fr Devane and Professor Felix Hackett also contributed. Judge Kenneth Reddin chaired the meeting. ('Good films not seen', *Irish Press*, 12 April 1937:6.)

96. *TC*, 14 April 1937.
97. Eoin P. Ó Caoimh to Fr Devane, 22 April 1937; Fr Devane to Éamon de Valera, 22 April 1937. The de Valera/Devane correspondence and related memos may be found in department of the taoiseach file S10136, NAI.
98. The members of the proposed delegation were named by Devane as: Professor Felix Hackett, National University of Ireland, and honorary secretary, Royal Dublin Society; Professor Drew, principal, Agricultural College, Glasnevin; Mrs Cosgrave, member of Dublin Corporation; Helena Moloney, president, Trades Union Congress; Cu Uladh, president, Gaelic League; S.P. O'Grady, president, Irish National Teachers' Organization; Dermod O'Brien, president, Royal Hibernian Academy; Padraig O'Keefe, secretary, Gaelic Athletic Association, 1929–64; P. O'Maille, secretary, An Fianna; E.J. Little, a senior magistrate; George Cussen, retired, senior magistrate; Dr M. Russell, medical officer of health; and Right Revd Herbert Kennedy, dean of Christ Church cathedral. Fr Devane hoped that Dr Thrift, vice-provost of Trinity College, could also be present. He indicated that the delegation would be introduced by members of the three political parties. (Fr Devane to Éamon de Valera, 22 April 1937, dept of the taoiseach file S10136, NAI.)
99. P.S. O Muireadhaigh to Fr Devane, 22 May 1937, 'Correspondence on film censorship, 1939–1941', Fr Devane papers, Irish Jesuit Archive, Dublin.
1. Fr Devane to Éamon de Valera, 29 May 1937, dept of the taoiseach file S10136, NAI.
2. Britain's absence from this list of countries is not due to any nationalist antagonism towards the British Film Institute but to the BFI's semi-private status. Indeed, Fr Devane was regularly in contact with the very conservative director of the BFI, Oliver Bell, and he spent a month at the BFI in 1939.
3. John Leydon, secretary of the dept of industry and commerce, to dept of finance, 12 June 1937, dept of the taoiseach file S10136, NAI.
4. Industry and commerce to president's dept, 24 June 1937, dept of the taoiseach file S10136, NAI. Neither of these letters made reference to Devane's request for an enquiry, and thus they avoided a direct refutation of his proposal.
5. Dept of justice to president's dept, 2 July 1937, dept of the taoiseach file S10136, NAI.
6. Dept of finance to dept of industry and commerce, 14 July 1937, dept of the taoiseach file S10136, NAI.
7. Dept of agriculture to president's dept, 11 August 1937, dept of the taoiseach file S10136, NAI.
8. Dept of local government and public health to president's dept, 28 July 1937, dept of the taoiseach file S10136, NAI.
9. Dept of finance to president's dept, 16 November 1937, dept of the taoiseach file S10136, NAI.
10. Departmental note, 19 November 1937, dept of the taoiseach file S10136, NAI.
11. Minute, president's dept, 21 December 1937, dept of the taoiseach file S10136, NAI.
12. Éamon de Valera and Fr Devane met in the taoiseach's department on 16 January 1938 and again on 10 February 1938, dept of the taoiseach file S10136, NAI. (From 1 January 1938, the president and the executive council were renamed taoiseach and cabinet, respectively. Henceforth, president is the title of a largely ceremonial post the holder of which is elected by universal suffrage for a seven-year term.)
13. Terms of reference of the interdepartmental committee on the film industry, undated (margin note of 16 February 1938, version shown to Fr Devane), dept of the taoiseach file S10136, NAI.
14. Fr R.S. Devane SJ, 'National film control (Ireland: section 1): the problem in Éire!', *Standard*, 25 October 1940:7. This was the fifth article in a series which began on 27 September 1940:3. These articles followed on from another series of articles by Devane which appeared in the *Irish Times* in summer 1940 and were mainly concerned with Scandinavian cinema: 15 June 1940:11; 20 June 1940:11; 22 June 1940:13; and 6 July 1940:11. Two other series of articles by Devane had appeared in the *Irish Independent* on 18 April 1939:14, 19 April 1939:9, and 20 April 1939:13 (on film censorship); and on 18 May 1939:8, 19 May 1939:8, and 20 May 1939:8 (on children and the cinema).
15. Dept of the taoiseach file 10136, NAI.
16. *Report of inter-departmental committee on the film industry* (unpublished), March 1942:54.
17. Fr R.S. Devane SJ, 'Official steps taken to control films in the national interest, 'Correspondence on film censorship, 1939–1941' file, Fr Devane papers, Irish Jesuit Archive, Dublin.
18. A covering letter enclosing the memo is dated 16 May 1939, 'Correspondence on film censorship, 1939–1941' file, Fr Devane papers, Irish Jesuit Archive, Dublin.
19. *Irish Independent*, 18 April 1939:11.
20. Fr R.S. Devane, 'Official steps taken to control films in the national interest', 16 May 1939, 'Correspondence on film censorship, 1939–1941' file, Fr Devane papers, Irish Jesuit Archive, Dublin.
21. Two Irish government reports have given accounts of certain (restrictive) trade practices (such as block booking; blind booking; operation of contracts; and surcharges), which both independent

exhibitors and state authorities tried (unsuccessfully) to stamp out or ameliorate during cinemas' most successful periods. These practices are cited in *Report of the inter-department committee on the film industry,* 1942:15–16. In the restrictive practices commission's *Report into the supply and distribution of cinema films* (1978:26–31), the often-complex film distribution arrangements of a later era are described. These depended on the location and size of a cinema, and whether films were first-run or second-run, issues that could effect rental charges; flat-rate rentals (fixed fee per screening or per week); 'nut' rentals (how takings on major box office films are distributed between exhibitor and distributor); 'break figures' (rental charges based on percentage of box office takings); and small town and parish hall variations. Within these arrangements further changes could be triggered depending on how a film performed at the box office.

22. Fr R.S. Devane SJ, 'Official steps taken to control films in the national interest', 16 May 1939, and undated related memo to interdepartmental committee on the film industry, 'Correspondence on film censorship, 1939–1941' file, Fr Devane papers, Irish Jesuit Archive, Dublin.

23. Fr R.S. Devane SJ, 'Proposals for a censorship code in Éire', Dr McQuaid papers, DDA. Two months after McQuaid's consecration as archbishop of Dublin on 27 December 1940, Devane sent him a related memo, 'Notes on censorship problems', including details of the American Production Code prepared for the interdepartmental committee, and other documents (not discovered at DDA), probably including the sixteen-point programme. (Fr Devane to Dr McQuaid, 24 February 1941, DDA.) Fr Devane made a handwritten amendment to the 'Notes on censorship problems' memo, changing that the interdepartmental committee had been sitting 'for many months', thus suggesting it was written in 1938, to 'since 1937'. In 'Proposals for a censorship code in Éire', Devane also made suggestions concerning the attendance of children at cinemas, which is discussed below, and the use of travelling film projects, which became part of the National Film Institute of Ireland's activities. For a discussion of Montgomery's proposals in the 1920s on 'stage Irish' representations, see Rockett, 2004:91–3. Montgomery was opposed (as would be all subsequent Irish censors), to a detailed code along the American or British models.

24. Fr R.S. Devane SJ, 'Notes on censorship problems', p. 6, Dr McQuaid papers, DDA.

25. In one of the articles in his *Irish Independent* series in April 1939, 'Quebec sets example for Ireland', he largely ignored the other two codes in favour of Catholic Quebec. (*Irish Independent,* 20 April 1939:13.)

26. Ibid., 8.

27. Fr R.S. Devane SJ, 'Official steps taken to control films in the national interest', 16 May 1939, and undated related memo to interdepartmental committee on the film industry, 'Correspondence on film censorship, 1939–1941' file, Fr Devane papers, Irish Jesuit Archive, Dublin.

28. Fr R.S. Devane SJ, 'Proposals for a censorship code in Éire', p.5, Dr McQuaid papers, DDA.

29. *Irish Independent,* 18 April 1939:14.

30. *Irish Independent,* 20 April 1939:13.

31. Quoted, *The Cinema,* 10 February 1937.

32. *Irish Catholic,* 11 February 1937:6; *The Cinema,* 10 February 1937.

33. Quoted, *The Cinema,* 10 February 1937.

34. Pastoral letters, 19 February 1939, *Irish Catholic directory,* 1940:632–3.

35. Besides Lyons these were Archbishop Thomas Gilmartin of Tuam to Fr Devane, 3 June 1939; Bishop Jeremiah Kinane of Waterford to Fr Devane, 2 June; Bishop Mageean to Devane 19 June; Bishop William MacNeely of Raphoe to Fr Devane, 16 June; Bishop McNamee of Ardagh, 16 June; Bishop James Roche of Cloyne to Fr Devane, 13 June; and Bishop Patrick Collier of Ossory to Fr Devane, 13 June. ('Correspondence on film censorship, 1939–1941' file, Fr Devane papers, Irish Jesuit Archive, Dublin.)

    Most of these bishops, as already noted, had recorded strong condemnations of cinemas and dance halls, among other public leisure pursuits, during their bishoprics. Both Bishops Morrisroe and Gilmartin, at least, had been very active in campaigning for restrictive legislation on public dance halls. The Public Dance Halls Act was passed in 1935 and it has been suggested that it was introduced following representations from 'some members of the hierarchy' (Whyte, 1980:50). Fr Devane, who wrote on the dance halls in 1931, was also a propagandist for restrictions on the dance halls and had a role in the introduction of the act, perhaps as an unofficial adviser to the hierarchy. See Fr Devane, 'The dance-hall; a moral and national menace', *Irish Ecclesiastical Record,* 5th series, vol. 37, February 1931:170–94.

36. Fr Devane to Bishop Patrick Lyons, 8 June 1939, 'Correspondence on film censorship, 1939–1941' file, Fr Devane papers, Irish Jesuit Archive, Dublin.

37. Bishop Patrick Morrisroe of Achonry to Fr Devane, 28 June 1939, 'Correspondence on film censorship, 1939–1941' file, Fr Devane papers, Irish Jesuit Archive, Dublin.

38. Fr Devane to Dr McQuaid, 24 February 1941, DDA.
39. Bishop Patrick Lyons to Fr Devane, 29 June 1939, 'Correspondence on film censorship, 1939–1941' file, Fr Devane papers, Irish Jesuit Archive, Dublin.
40. Fr Devane to Dr McQuaid, 5 May 1941, Archbishop McQuaid papers, DDA.
41. Bishop Patrick Lyons of Kilmore to Fr Devane, 14 September 1940, 'Correspondence on film censorship, 1939–1941' file, Fr Devane papers, Irish Jesuit Archive, Dublin.
42. Bishop Patrick Lyons of Kilmore to Fr Devane, 27 October 1940, 'Correspondence on film censorship, 1939–1941' file, Fr Devane papers, Irish Jesuit Archive, Dublin.
43. Unidentified correspondent to Devane, 27 September 1940; Bishop Lyons to Fr Devane, 16 December 1940, suggesting they see Richard Hayes early in 1941.
44. See Rockett, 2004:109ff.
45. Fr Devane to Dr McQuaid, 5 May 1941, Dr McQuaid papers, DDA.
46. SFX to Fr Devane, 7 July 1939, 'Correspondence on film censorship, 1939–1941', Fr Devane papers, Irish Jesuit Archive, Dublin. In a further letter of 21 September 1939 Devane revealed a revised strategy whereby, not knowing that the government had already acted to introduce further powers of censorship under an Emergency Power Order to last for the duration of the war (see Rockett, 2004:334ff.), he suggested that a bill introducing such regulations could be proposed 'under the guise of neutrality and propaganda'. He also recommended that coinciding with the Dublin meeting of bishops on 10 October a delegation of Catholic religious should meet with both the enquiry committee and the minister for justice.
47. S.A. Roche to Fr Devane, 10 March 1941. The letter had been prompted by Devane, who had sent Roche a copy of Martin Quigley's book *Decency in movies* (New York: Macmillan, 1937) on 7 March 1941, and, indeed, he offered to send Archbishop McQuaid a copy of it two months later, since Quigley was 'one of the greatest authorities on films in the world.' (Fr Devane to Dr McQuaid, 5 May 1941, Dr McQuaid papers, DDA). While Diarmaid Ferriter describes Roche as being 'fawning' in his correspondence with McQuaid, nevertheless, this must be seen in the context of Roche's successful resistance of the attempts by Devane and his episcopal allies to considerably expand the film censorship regime. His 'fawning' may have been strategic. (Diarmaid Ferriter, *Occasions of sin: sex & society in modern Ireland*, London: Profile, 2009:305.)
48. S.A. Roche, 14 October 1937, dept of the taoiseach file S10136, NAI.
49. Fr Devane to Dr McQuaid, 24 February 1941, DDA, Dr McQuaid papers, DDA.
50. Fr Devane to Dr McQuaid, 5 May 1941, Archbishop McQuaid papers, DDA.
51. Dr McQuaid to Fr Devane, 18 June 1941, 'Correspondence on film censorship, 1939–1941' file, Fr Devane papers, Irish Jesuit Archive, Dublin.

CHAPTER 8

1. Francis Ryan BL, secretary of the National Film Institute of Ireland, 'Film appreciation' lecture delivered at Macra na Tuaithe, Cahir, Co. Tipperary, August 1956, and reported in 'Film censorship no guarantee against transgression of Catholic moral principles', *The Nationalist (and Munster Advertiser)*, 1 September 1956.
2. Letter from Fr Devane to Éamon de Valera, 16 October 1939, which was mainly concerned with parish councils; note penned by P.S. Ó Muireadhaigh on extract of 16 October letter after de Valera and Devane met on 20 October. The taoiseach's office wrote to industry and commerce on 21 October. (Dept of the taoiseach file S10136, NAI.)
3. Dept of industry and commerce to taoiseach's dept, 15 November 1939. (Dept of the taoiseach file S10136, NAI.)
4. Though the report remained cautious about such a venture as 'the erection of a studio ... would be to a very large extent speculative', it suggested the possibility of assisting in the development of existing facilities, such as Tom Cooper's Killarney enterprise, which produced *The Dawn* (1936), and which was 'the only establishment in the country which [could] properly [be] regarded as a film studio.' (*Report of the inter-departmental committee on the film industry*, 1942:20.)
5. It was considered that any attempt to elaborate the general principles with a detailed code would be 'imprudent and impracticable'. (*Report of the inter-departmental committee on the film industry*, 1942:45–6.)
6. *Dáil debates*, vol. 91, col. 2081, 16 November 1943; vol. 92, cols 674–5, 14 December 1943; vol. 93, cols 2107–8, 3 May 1944.
7. For an account of the various private, mostly unrealized, studio proposals made to the dept of industry and commerce from the 1930s to the 1950s, see Kevin Rockett, 'Cinema in Ireland', vol. 1,

D.Phil. thesis, University of Ulster, Coleraine, 1989:182–235; and Kevin Rockett, 'An Irish film studio', in Rockett et al., 1987:95–8.

8. MacEoin is sometimes cited as Gerald MacKeown.

9. The other members in attendance were Val Clery, a technical school photography teacher; J. Boyne; Charles Cherry, Irish Elect. Medical Co.; T. Holmes; B.M. Mulvey of the College of Science; and Captain (later Commandant) Art Cullen, a solicitor, The Curragh. Mrs Boyne was another 'visitor'.

10. Brigid Redmond, *The golden age*, Browne and Nolan, 1928:5. Armagh, the national 'seat' of the Irish Catholic church, is described as 'the Christian capital of Ireland' and 'the metropolis of western civilisation' (1928:5).

11. The film's actual name may be *Thou Art a Priest Forever*, which was filmed by Fr Collier and features a group of seminarians being ordained as priests, and their visit to the Scholasticate of the Missionary Oblates of Mary Immaculate, Co. Kilkenny. However, if the production date of 1945 as recorded in the Irish Film Archive, where a 16mm copy of *Thou Art a Priest Forever* is held, is correct, then this is not the same film as *The Making of a Priest*, but another.

12. Minutes of meeting, 14 February 1943, 'Films general – censorship', Dr McQuaid papers, DDA.

13. Fr Redmond to Archbishop McQuaid, 17 February 1943, Dr McQuaid papers, DDA.

14. John Feeney, *John Charles McQuaid: the man and the mask*, Dublin/Cork: Mercier 1974:7. Feeney continues that 'certainly, like many of his contemporaries in the 1930s, Dr McQuaid was somewhat anti-Semitic and suspicious of contact with Protestantism.'

15. Cooney, 1999:135. The Catholic Social Service Conference was formally inaugurated under Dr McQuaid's patronage in April 1941 and had as its central aims, 'supplementing and supporting the State during the Emergency; providing means of employment and supplying the needs of those who were in distress; channelling public effort and goodwill into a single agency; and mobilising all available resources for the common good.' (Cooney, 1999:136.) While McQuaid's contributions to social welfare were numerous, the CSSC was arguably the most striking. See also Whyte, 1980:77ff; orig. 1971.

16. Note by Dr McQuaid after seeing Fr Redmond on 19 February 1943, Dr McQuaid papers, DDA.

17. Dr McQuaid to Fr Redmond, 20 February 1943, Dr McQuaid papers, DDA.

18. National Film Institute of Ireland aims and objects, 28 February 1943, Dr McQuaid papers, DDA. Enclosed was a list of film books and reports held by the organization. Of the thirty titles listed more than half were concerned with film in the classroom, with an additional number focusing on the sociology of cinema, including Martin Quigley's *Decency in motion pictures* (1937), and a further seven devoted to 'amateur' film technique, of which Pudovkin's *Film technique* (1933) was the best known. The three periodicals held were *Sight and Sound*, *Catholic Film News* and *Movie Makers*, the magazine of the New York-based Amateur Cinema League.

19. Fr Redmond to Dr McQuaid, 26 May 1943, Dr McQuaid papers, DDA.

20. McQuaid to Fr Redmond, 27 May and 28 May 1943, Dr McQuaid papers, DDA.

21. Fr Redmond to Dr McQuaid, 28 May and 13 June 1943, Dr McQuaid papers, DDA.

22. Fr Redmond to Dr McQuaid, 24 June 1943, Dr McQuaid papers, DDA.

23. Brigid Redmond to Dr McQuaid, 18 August 1943, with margin note by Dr Quaid instructing one of his staff, Fr C. Mangan, to reply that he agreed to the invitation, Dr McQuaid papers, DDA. By then, additional NFI patrons were reported to Dr McQuaid as Dr Patrick Lyons, bishop of Kilmore; Dublin's lord mayor, Mr M. O'Sullivan; Mr T. O'Connell, director of agriculture; Professor Drew, Albert College; and Professor Alfred O'Rahilly, University College Cork. In response, Brigid Redmond, honorary secretary, NFI, wrote to Dr McQuaid on 23 August 1943.

24. Feeney, *John Charles McQuaid*, 1974:8.

25. Fr R.S. Devane SJ, 'The problem in Éire!', *The Standard*, 25 October 1940:7.

26. *Irish cinema handbook*, Dublin: Parkside, 1943. Devane is not credited as advisory editor, but in late November 1943 Devane sent a copy of the book to Éamon de Valera and in the accompanying letter stated that he had not only suggested the idea to printers/publisher Cahill & Co. but also had acted as advisory editor. (Fr Devane to Éamon de Valera, 29 November 1943, dept of the taoiseach file S10136, NAI.)

27. In Hayes' own parish, Bansha, Co. Tipperary, a vocationalist council consisting of twenty-five members was made up of five groups: farmers, farm labourers, trade unions, business and professional men, and unemployed. Hayes' 'vocationalist' model was influenced by the Flemish clergy's *Boerenbond* producers' cooperative movement, and later, as Muintir na Tíre took on a more educational/analytical role vis-à-vis the problems of rural Ireland, the French Catholic farmers' movement, the *semaines rurales* (rural weeks). By 1941, in response to wartime shortages, Muintir's guilds employed 1,000 men in food and turf production. (See Whyte, 1980:69.)

28. The complexity of Muintir's and, indeed, Fr Hayes' ideology, including his admiration for Italian fascist leader Benito Mussolini, is explored in Eoin Devereux, 'John Hayes (1887–1957) founder of Muintir na Tíre', *Old Limerick Journal*, summer 1998:34–6. Devereux points to the 'abundance' of correspondence between Hayes and de Valera in dept of the taoiseach file S10816, NAI.

29. In April 1943, before McQuaid was publicly associated with the NFI, Fr Hayes wrote to Fr Redmond to say that Muintir na Tíre 'would cooperate in every way' with the NFI, and praised their activities: 'You have a great work in hand, and something must be done, however small, to counteract the cinema.' A copy of the letter was forwarded to Dr McQuaid. (Fr John M. Hayes to Fr Redmond, 26 April 1943, Dr McQuaid papers, DDA.) A month later in his report to Dr McQuaid, he reported that Fr Hayes had 'signified his willingness to cooperate with [the NFI's] work.' (Fr Redmond to Dr McQuaid, 26 May 1943, DDA.) Indeed, even earlier, in April 1943, Muintir's organizing secretary, Barry Walsh, had contacted the NFI seeking advice about film equipment. (Brigid Redmond to Bishop Lyons, president, Muintir na Tíre, 12 December 1943, Dr McQuaid papers, DDA.)

30. See Benedict Kiely, 'Story of a film unit', *The Standard*, 31 August 1945:5. Writing in *Studies*, Fr Hayes explained that the idea of the cooperative film society was 'to show clean healthy and educational films – especially to rural people.' Alienated from contemporary cinema, he commented that he had seen 'children roar with laughter in a picture-house at scenes which, in my young days, I would have thought sinful', adding somewhat wistfully that 'perhaps, the rising generation are more theologically correct, but I prefer the extra clean outlook of former days.' He called for positive action by the state, church and parents to 'make the Cinema a power of real good.' (*Studies*, vol. 33, 60–1.)

31. A former government minister, Blythe, was, at the time, also W.B. Yeats' successor as director of the Abbey Theatre.

32. Brigid Redmond to Bishop Lyons, president, Muintir na Tíre, 12 December 1943:3, Dr McQuaid papers, DDA.

33. Reported by Redmond in a nine-page letter to Muintir's president, Bishop Lyons, in December 1943, a copy of which was sent to Dr McQuaid. Brigid Redmond to Bishop Lyons, president, Muintir na Tíre, 12 December 1943:2, Dr McQuaid papers, DDA.

34. Brigid Redmond to Bishop Lyons, president, Muintir na Tíre, 12 December 1943:4, Dr McQuaid papers, DDA. Redmond's representation of the IFS as being anti-Catholic, dominated as it was by Protestants, and being leftist or pro-communist with 'half' their 1942 programme comprising of 'Soviet Propaganda' films (though this was inaccurate), highlighted in her biased reporting of the meeting, ensured that episcopal prejudice against the IFS would be reinforced. For example, she reported that IFS members 'jeered at the invocation' *Virgo potens, ora pro nobis* used in the NFI masthead, and regarded it both as 'an empty formula' with no meaning for them, and as a form of objectionable 'flag-waving'.

35. Fr Redmond to Dr McQuaid, 10 September 1943, Dr McQuaid papers, DDA.

36. Dr McQuaid to Fr Redmond, 16 September 1943, Dr McQuaid papers, DDA. In response to another query from Redmond, McQuaid told him that the practice in the Dublin archdiocese was 'to refuse permission to show any film which portrays Our Divine Master or Our Blessed Lady.' (Ibid.)

37. Brigid Redmond to Bishop Lyons, president, Muintir na Tíre, 12 December 1943:5, Dr McQuaid papers, DDA. On the day after this letter was written, IFS member, civil servant Thekla Beere, was appointed principal officer in industry and commerce. It was only the second occasion since the foundation of the Irish state that such a (high-ranking) post (in any department) was given to a woman. (Anna Bryson, *No coward soul*, Dublin: Institute of Public Administration 2009:73–4.)

38. Irish Film Society records, Liam O'Leary collection, NLI.

39. Shortly before this, the speakers at a Muintir na Tíre 'Fireside chat and film show' in Dublin's Mansion House included Barry Walsh; J. Sheehy, manager of Muintir's film unit; and the IFS's Edward Toner and Liam O'Leary, who spoke of the support accorded to them by Muintir in provincial towns. 'No mention' was made of the NFI, as Redmond complained to Bishop Lyons. (Brigid Redmond to Bishop Lyons, 12 December 1943:6, Dr McQuaid papers, DDA, *IT*, 19 November 1943:3; *Irish Press*, 20 November 1943:3.)

40. The issue of the restoration of the Irish language had become more topical since Éamon de Valera's now infamous 1943 St Patrick's Day address in which he referred to rural Ireland, 'comely maidens', etc., and which has served in the modern period as a dismissive contrast of rural Ireland with modern, urban Ireland. Prompted by the speech, most of which was concerned with the Irish language, a group called Comhlucht Scannán Glórach na h-Éireann, with an address at 'Na Tri Luin', 55 Dame Street, Dublin, wrote to de Valera two months later, proposing, among other things, the

making and exhibition of Irish language films for schools and cinemas. The organization's Eoin O'Maolchalainn also wrote to Archbishop McQuaid seeking his support for 'the movement' from Catholic school managers because 'the eventual result of this work will be that only clean films will be shown to the Youth of the country.' McQuaid's request for further information on the project, including the names of the directors of the company, does not seem to have been replied to. The four film projects identified for production were the presenting of the principal 1916 events; the Dáil and Seanad in session; Irish national industries; and 'modern Ireland in colour'. (Eoin O'Maolchalainn to Éamon de Valera, 21 May 1943 [translation of Irish-language letter]; Eoin O'Maolchalainn to Archbishop McQuaid, 22 May 1943, Dr McQuaid papers, DDA.)

41. Brigid Redmond to Dr McQuaid, 16 May 1944:5, Dr McQuaid papers, DDA; Irish Film Society records, Liam O'Leary collection, NAI.
42. Brigid Redmond to Bishop Lyons, 12 December 1943:6, Dr McQuaid papers, DDA.
43. Ibid., 3.
44. Walsh had gone to see the UK representative in Dublin during the summer, 'and had protested against the British allocation of film to [the NFI] as a distributing body for Éire.' (Brigid Redmond to Bishop Lyons, 12 December 1943:8, Dr McQuaid papers, DDA.)
45. Quoted, Brigid Redmond to Bishop Lyons, 12 December 1943:8, Dr McQuaid papers, DDA.
46. Ibid.
47. Patrick Lyons to Brigid Redmond, 15 December 1943, Dr McQuaid papers, DDA.
48. Fr Devane to Éamon de Valera, 29 November 1943, dept of the taoiseach file S10136, NAI.
49. *Irish cinema handbook*, 1943:37.
50. *Report of the inter-departmental committee on educational films*, set up by the minister for education on 31 December, 1943, 15 June 1944:2, Dr Michael Quane papers, MS 17,984, NLI.
51. 'Conditions mentioned by Dr Quane ... to the Hon. Secretary [Brigid Redmond], National Film Institute, upon which a Government grant in aid might be given to the National Film Institute', undated, c.February–mid-March 1944 (that is, after 31 January meeting with the interdepartmental committee and before Brigid Redmond sent it to Dr McQuaid on 20 March), one-page document in 'NFI boxes', Dr McQuaid papers, DDA.
52. Dr McQuaid to Fr Redmond, 23 March 1944, Dr McQuaid papers, DDA.
53. Fr Collier to Dr McQuaid, 21 April 1944, 'NFI boxes', Dr McQuaid papers, DDA.
54. Brigid Redmond to Dr McQuaid, 16 May 1944:11, 'NFI boxes', Dr McQuaid papers, DDA.
55. A department of education inspector at the time and one of the most prolific writers on film matters in Ireland during the 1940s and 1950s with a regular column in the *Irish Catholic* and a contributor to *The Standard*, Sheehy's writings were often reprinted in other Catholic monthly or quarterly journals. He also edited the NFI's first regular publication, *Irish Cinema Quarterly* (1948–9), and contributed to its successors, *National Film Quarterly* (1950–56), *Irish Film Quarterly* (1957–9) and *Vision* (1965–8). (The last three have no editorial credits). Sheehy and John D. Sheridan were the only two active writers on film who were associated with the NFI during this period. Gabriel Fallon only contributed one article to the fifty-two issues of these publications seen by the authors.
56. Fr Collier to Dr McQuaid, 28 May 1944. Fr Collier's address to the 28 April meeting may be found in 'NFI boxes', Dr McQuaid papers, DDA.
57. Troy's dictatorial and crude instructions to Brigid Redmond were made worse when he and Vaughan went to the hospital on 6 May, shortly after Fr Redmond had an operation, to interrogate him about NFI activities.
58. Brigid Redmond to Dr McQuaid, 16 May 1944:11, 'NFI boxes', Dr McQuaid papers, DDA.
59. Brigid Redmond to Dr McQuaid, 31 May 1944:3, 'NFI boxes', Dr McQuaid papers, DDA.
60. Memo, 19 May 1944, 'NFI boxes', Dr McQuaid papers, DDA.
61. Fr Collier to Dr McQuaid, 25 May 1944, 'NFI boxes', Dr McQuaid papers, DDA.
62. In the fourteen-page letter Redmond wrote to McQuaid on 16 May 1944:5, which in part detailed the activities undertaken by her brother and herself in securing facilities for the NFI, she praised Fr Devane whose 'vast knowledge' and 'useful contacts' were of 'great value' to them, but, in a political distancing move, also criticized Devane for not being able 'to initiate and follow a deliberate programme or act in cooperation with a committee.' She charged that his visits to government departments and 'lack of discretion and judgement sometimes caused us great anxiety', such as, for example, when he urged the NFI to invite the two IFS members to a meeting. Nevertheless, while admitting that Devane, within three or four months of the institute's formation in early 1943, was urging the executive committee to retire and to be replaced (along vocationalist lines) by a number of representative people, she also pointed out that in light of the unexpected challenge for government recognition by the Irish Film Council, the NFI's executive committee itself recognized that it needed to bring in (unnamed) influential persons 'whose views would carry weight' and which

would demonstrate to the government that the institute was capable of fulfilling the functions of a national film institute. In both cases, however, it was envisaged that the constitution would 'completely safeguard our Catholic rights and ideals.' (Brigid Redmond to Dr McQuaid, 16 May 1944:3–5, Dr McQuaid papers, DDA.)

Fr Devane, in his letter to Éamon de Valera in November 1943 informing him of the establishment of the NFI, sought to assert his own role in its formation, noting his activity in promoting such an institute since 1937. He complained, in an unquestionable allusion to the IFS, Muintir na Tíre and the Irish Film Council, that 'other bodies are now adopting these ideas and setting up rival institutes, and it is well that something should be done to prevent this and to allow the body that originally put forward the idea of an Institute to function unhampered.' Part of Fr Devane's proposal was that a central government body be set up with a national director of films with an assistant. 'I am now wondering', he mused, 'has this suggestion been the cause or the occasion of much of the recent interest in setting up Film Institutes under various guises', notwithstanding the wholly voluntary nature of the Irish Film Society. (Fr Devane to Éamon de Valera, 29 November 1943, dept of the taoiseach file S10136, NAI.) Fr Devane's request for exclusive rights over a film institute received short shrift from industry and commerce to whom the taoiseach's department sent a copy of the letter. It reported that it had no statutory power to prevent the establishment of other bodies along the lines of the National Film Institute. (Dept of industry and commerce to dept of the taoiseach, 18 January 1944, dept of the taoiseach file S10136, NAI.) Fr Devane's (and, of course, Dr McQuaid's) complaint against the Irish Film Society was that it was a non-sectarian, secularist body, as Liam O'Leary described it. While Fr Devane could praise O'Leary in print in 1942 (*Scannán*, no. 6, 1942), his offer to him of the post of secretary of the NFI was dependent on two conditions being met: firstly, that he could prove his bona fides as a committed Catholic, and secondly, that he would sever his connection with the film society. O'Leary declined the offer. As noted, the NFI cut off all contact with the IFS, even to the point of not providing the society's main publication, *Scannán*, with any information about its activities, ignoring an invitation to provide the magazine with an article on its policy (*Scannán*, vol. 1, no. 5, August 1946:28; vol. 2, no. 3, December 1946:32). Regardless, in September 1946, *Scannán* carried a positive report of the NFI's summer school, but then, as noted in the text, many of those involved in teaching the technical courses were IFS members. (*Scannán*, vol. 1, no. 6, September 1946:1, 42.)

63. Fr Collier to Dr McQuaid, 28 April 1944, 'NFI boxes', Dr McQuaid papers, DDA. Collier commented that he did not know who 'prompted' Quane to come to him. It can be speculated that the 'prompter' was his minister, Thomas Derrig, the conservative and Irish-Irelander minister for education since 1931, and with whom McQuaid had had satisfactory dealings since at least 1933–4, while a tussle with Dublin's vocational education committee schools' ban on nuns teaching domestic economy was resolved in 1941 with Derrig's help in McQuaid's favour. (See Cooney, 1999:83–4, 137–40.)

64. Brigid Redmond to Dr McQuaid, 31 May 1944, 'NFI boxes', Dr McQuaid papers, DDA. The interdepartmental committee had met with the Irish Film Council's Ernest Blythe (IFS), Mr J. Sheehy (Muintir na Tíre and University College Cork extension committee), and film exhibitor Joseph Stanley during the previous week. (Ibid.)

65. Dr McQuaid to Brigid Redmond, 1 June 1944, 'NFI boxes', Dr McQuaid papers, DDA.

66. *Report of the inter-departmental committee on educational films*, 1944:2–4, Dr Michael Quane papers, MS 17,984, NLI.

67. Ibid., 1.

68. Fr Devane concurred with the view that the institute should only be seen as an interim measure prior to the establishment of a state film board. (Fr Devane to Éamon de Valera, 29 November 1943, dept of the taoiseach file S10136, NAI.) Such an Irish film board was not established for almost forty years, and then in very different circumstances when, as outlined below, the NFI itself was undergoing profound changes. We can only imagine what Irish cinema might have become at a much earlier stage had the Irish Film Society and/or the Irish Film Council been given the resources in the 1940s to develop a creative film culture rather than the state supporting the NFI, which pursued a Catholic defensive-protectionist and propagandist agenda.

69. *Report of the inter-departmental committee on educational films*, 1944:4–5, Dr Michael Quane papers, MS 17,984, NLI.

70. The fact that the grant came through the dept of education rather than industry and commerce suggests that the latter, hostile from the beginning to the clerical role in film policy, most probably rejected the report's recommendation despite having two civil servants on the committee.

71. *KW*, 6 June 1945.

72. Irish Film Society records, Liam O'Leary collection, NAI.

73. Fr Vaughan to Dr McQuaid, 20 October 1944, Dr McQuaid papers, DDA.

74. Fr Vaughan to Dr McQuaid, 9 November 1944, Dr McQuaid papers, DDA.
75. Brigid Redmond to Dr McQuaid, 14 November 1944, Dr McQuaid papers, DDA.
76. Brigid Redmond to Dr McQuaid, 9 February 1945, Dr McQuaid papers, DDA.
77. Dermot O'Flynn to Dr McQuaid, 12 December 1944, Dr McQuaid papers, DDA
78. Sean O'Sullivan held the post until 1953, and was succeeded by Francis B. Ryan, while Desmond Hand was secretary from 1964 to 1967. Later, George McCanny, a retired army captain, held the post until a professional arts' administrator, David Kavanagh, formerly an Arts Council officer, was appointed to the reformed institute as its first director in 1983.
79. Sean O'Sullivan to Dr McQuaid, 10 February 1945, Dr McQuaid papers, DDA.
80. Sean O'Sullivan to Dr McQuaid, 15 February 1945, Dr McQuaid papers, DDA.
81. The others who failed to get elected were Owen Cowey and John Riordan, national school teachers; Hugh Fitzpatrick, a solicitor; Patrick Linnane, a civil servant; Dr Conor Martin; Miss K. O'Sullivan, principal, Coláiste Mhuire le Tigheas; and Prof. John Piggott. Brigid Redmond, in her last act as an officer of the institute, sent a further lengthy memo to Dr McQuaid on 3 March 1945, Dr McQuaid papers, DDA.
82. In June 1960, he became the organization's supreme knight, a position he held until June 1966. (Evelyn Bolster, *Knights of Saint Columbanus*, Dublin: Gill and Macmillan, 1979:131, 137.)
83. There are further crossovers between NFI personnel and other activities in which McQuaid was involved. For example, Prof. Piggott, the chairman of the 'reformed' NFI constitution drafting committee, was appointed to the censorship of publications' board in 1946, and became its chairman in 1957, though he was forced to resign in controversial circumstances later that year (See Michael Adams, *Censorship: the Irish experience*, Alabama: University of Alabama, 1968:102ff.) P.T. Breathnach was appointed to the censorship of publications' board in 1950, though he died the following year; and accountant E.P. McCarron, a member of the first executive in 1943, was a member of the censorship of films appeal board during 1950–60.
84. At this time, O'Flynn, an economist, was managing director of a Dublin contracting firm. Among other activities in which O'Flynn and McQuaid worked 'closely' together was the provision of a boys' holiday home at Balbriggan, Co. Dublin, while O'Flynn was commended by McQuaid in 1954 for his work in using the knights to organize a national campaign against 'obscene' films, including his trying to get banned a film about a prostitute, *Behind Closed Shutters*. (Cooney, 1999:247, 283, 328; Adams, *Censorship*, 1968:222.)
85. It has not been determined if this is Tony Molloy, the author of children's adventure books, including *Caught in the callows* (1944) and *The quest of O–17* (1946).
86. Nevertheless, she retained an interest in film matters. See, for example, Brigid Redmond, 'Films and children', *Studies*, vol. 45, 1956:227–33.
87. Sean O'Sullivan to Dr McQuaid, 2 December 1947; Fr C. Mangan, secretary, Archbishop's House, to Sean O'Sullivan, 2 December 1947, Sean O'Sullivan to Fr C. Mangan, 8 December 1947, Dr McQuaid papers, DDA. McQuaid left office as archbishop on 2 January 1972 and died on 7 April 1973. The next patron of the (by then) Irish Film Institute was President Mary Robinson in the 1990s. Ironically, much of her work has been committed to dismantling the institutional surveillance and psychological terror most starkly represented by McQuaid's activities.
88. The annual grant to the NFI was £2,000 from 1946–7 to 1948–9; it was reduced to £1,000 during 1949–53 (a time of severe economic stress in Ireland); and raised in 1954–5 to £1,500. By 1966, the grant was £5,250, while its 1983 allocation was £13,000.
89. *National Film Quarterly*, vol. 1, no. 4, March 1951:24. Ní Chanainn, 1992:33, gives the 1950 figure as 859 films with almost 7,000 bookings. Though this booklet carries Ní Chanainn's name on its cover, inside Breandán MacGiollarnáth is credited as editor, and he explains in a foreword that he put the book together from her notes, press cuttings and reminiscences.
90. Ní Chanainn, 1992:33.
91. *Irish Film Quarterly*, vol. 3, no. 1, April 1959:17; Ní Chanainn, 1992:33–4.
92. Among the NFI-produced films were a series of ten short films on safety made for the department of local government during 1949–51, which included *Mr Careless Goes to Town* and *Safe Cycling*, both of which were scripted by Liam O'Leary and shot by George Fleischmann in 1949; *Science and the Farmer* (George Fleischmann, 1952) for the department of agriculture; a series of films for the department of health 1950–53, including *Voyage to Recovery* (Gerard Healy, 1952) on tuberculosis; and *Where Does the Money Go?* (aka *Cá n-Imíonn an t-Airgead?*, Gerard Healy, 1954) for the dept of posts and telegraphs. (A later film, *Our Money at Work/An t-Airgead ag Obair*, with a script by Healy and directed by Colm O'Laoghaire in 1957 was also produced by the NFI for posts and telegraphs.) In addition, the NFI produced short versions of All-Ireland hurling and football championship finals from 1949 to 1968. (See Ní Chanainn, 1992:35.) For the broader context of

documentary and drama-documentary during the 1940s and 1950s, see Harvey O'Brien, *The real Ireland: the evolution of Ireland in documentary film*, Manchester: Manchester UP, 2004.)

One of the few Irish film production companies of the period, Hibernia Pictures Ltd, complained to the minister for industry and commerce when it was told that it was government policy to give such work to the NFI. Hibernia had made a road safety film, *Next Please*, in 1948, and when an advertisement was published in August 1948 calling for tenders for two more films, the company's tender was rejected after the NFI was awarded the contract. Hibernia's M.W. O'Reilly wrote to the minister pointing out that if the NFI secured all the government work, 'then our hope of survival is slender, as owing to the limited [Irish] market ... we must necessarily rely on the real source of employment for sponsored work', namely, government departments. The company regarded it as unfair that a private enterprise should have to compete with the 'subsidised' NFI for such work. The alternative was that Hibernia should be treated 'no less favourably' than the NFI 'where subsidies are concerned'. McQuaid responded after being sent a copy of the letter that Hibernia had sent to the minister by saying that he could not consider it his duty to enquire into the matter unless it can be shown to him that the NFI or any other Catholic group 'was guilty of unfair methods', and if such was shown then he offered to use his 'good offices to secure justice'. He proposed that the matter be taken up with the government and the NFI. (M.W. O'Reilly to the minister for industry and commerce, 24 January 1949; M.W. O'Reilly to Archbishop McQuaid, 1 and 9 February 1949; Archbishop McQuaid to M.W. O'Reilly, 4 February 1949, NFI boxes, Dr McQuaid papers, DDA.) By the 1960s, a new generation of television and film-school trained Irish producers and directors emerged to compete for government film contracts, and in the process the close ties that previously existed between the government and the NFI were loosened.

93. For details on these and other films mentioned here, see www.tcd.ie/Irishfilm.
94. *National Film Quarterly*, vol. 2, no. 4, March 1952:12.
95. The NFI received sums varying from £500 when the grant was introduced in 1951 to £1,000 in 1971 when it was discontinued for this purpose and for the production of filmstrips for use in classrooms. Six short films with dubbed Irish commentaries were issued in 1948. Written by T. O Rabhartaigh, chief inspector of secondary schools, and spoken by Padraic Ó Connaire of the Dáil translation committee, they included *An Dochtúir Jenner* (Dr Jenner, the discoverer of vacination); *An tAthair Damien* (Fr Damien, the leper colony missionary); *Alfred Nobel*; *Sean-Mhurioca* (The Old South); and *Fear Eachtach* (Servant of mankind, Thomas Edison). It also made dual Irish and English versions of a number of government-sponsored films. Patrick Kavanagh commented in the *Standard* that 'the films, incidentally, were poor, while the Gaelic commentary never let up throughout the showing of the pictures. That may be enthusiasm for the old language, but it defeats the purpose. The Spirit of Literature and Art is not bigoted for any particular language, for it is the same spirit in any language dress. Would the National Film Institute, which has funds, give a young man the chance to make a film that wasn't safely dead?'
    Irish sound tracks were also put on films dealing with animal life, children of other lands, regional geography and nature study, thirty of which were dubbed into Irish during 1953 to 1959. The related development of making filmstrips of specifically Irish interest in the 1950s under the supervision of a joint committee of the NFI and the department of education led to nine such strips being produced. In the 1960s, Pádraig Ó Nualláin continued this activity and produced *1916* (1966); *Móin*, on the peat industry; one on art, and *Pattern and Texture* (1968). Other filmstrips focused on Aer Lingus (*Ireland Takes Wings*) and Dean Swift. (Ní Chanainn, 1992:39–40.)
96. By 1950, for example, three mobile projection units were engaged on a whole-time basis in the showing of health films in schools and parochial halls throughout the country for the department of health, while a fourth unit undertook a seven-month long campaign for the department of agriculture. In all that year, 1,135 such showings were organized: 962 for the department of health, and 173 for agriculture. (*National Film Quarterly*, vol. 1, no. 4, March 1952:25.)
97. While the 1951 and 1952 courses were run by the British Film Institute, the 1953 one was delivered by Irish lecturers, a change perhaps explained by an editorial in *National Film Quarterly*, which declared: 'it must be remembered' that in Ireland 'film appreciation does not mean what it does in Britain' for 'film appreciation must be coloured by moral standards as well as by cultural standards, and its purpose is spiritual as well as artistic.' (*National Film Quarterly*, vol. 4, no. 2, September 1953:4.) It would be thirty years, in the very different environment of critical film studies in the early 1980s, before BFI lecturers once more participated in NFI summer schools.
98. Sean O'Sullivan circular to bishops, 4 July 1946, Dr McQuaid papers, DDA. Of course, 16mm documentaries on worthy subjects and religious topics in parish halls had little chance of displacing popular commercial films, unless, of course, as O'Sullivan seemed to be suggesting, commercial 16mm circuits were denied access to such halls.

99. *Irish Cinema Quarterly*, vol. 1, autumn 1948:3.
1. The same writer, Revd Reginald Walker CSSp, also proposed a method of proliferation whereby groups of towns and villages 'could be localised in a "cell"' working 'in conjunction with the parish council' until individual units were 'ready to break off and "cell-out" on their own' just like 'the "Commies"' method. As he put it, 'the children of light must not be above taking a lesson in procedure from the Mammon of Iniquity.' (Revd Walker CSSp, 'Ways and means', *National Film Quarterly*, vol. 1, no. 1, June 1950:5.)
2. *Irish Cinema Quarterly*, vol. 1, autumn 1948:25; *National Film Quarterly*, vol. 4, no. 3, December 1953–January 1954; *Irish Cinema Quarterly*, no. 3, 1949:4–6; *National Film Quarterly*, March 1955:17.
3. NFI annual general meeting report, 9 February 1950, McQuaid papers, DDA.
4. As noted, this 1936 encyclical letter promoted the Legion of Decency and the work of the Catholic Reviewing Office in the United States, which issued a widely distributed list of current films classified according to a moral code.
5. While John J. Dunne had a regular 'Current films' column in *National Film Quarterly* from December 1951, this activity was superseded by the film-reviewing panel, which began in summer 1953 (*National Film Quarterly*, vol. 5, no. 1, December 1954:1). 'Selected critics' reviewed all current releases, and these reviews were sent to secondary schools, convents and colleges throughout the country with the intention of encouraging those connected with such institutions to stay away 'from films which [were] unworthy of support'. (*National Film Quarterly*, vol. 4, no. 4, April 1954:28.) The reviewing panel was praised by T.J.M. Sheehy at the 1954 NFI annual general meeting, an event attended by McQuaid when he blessed the NFI's new premises at 65 Harcourt Street, Dublin. (*National Film Quarterly*, vol. 4, no. 4, April 1954:4.)
6. On 27 May 1947, Robert Thom, head of the audio-visual department at Manchester University, spoke on 'The film in education'. On 11 May 1948, John Grierson spoke on 'The place of a small country in international film production', which was later published in *Studies* as 'A film policy for Ireland' (vol. 37, no. 147, September 1948:283–91). On 23 February 1950, André Ruszhowski, secretary-general of OCIC, the international Catholic cinema office, spoke on 'Religion and the film', which was later published as an NFI pamphlet. On 8 November 1951, W.J. Ogoe, film critic, *Catholic Herald* (London), spoke on 'A Christian approach to moving pictures' with panellists Gabriel Fallon and Roger McHugh. See reports of meeting, 'She genuflected in the Savoy' and 'Scot threw bricks at screen', *Standard,* 16 November 1951, and text of lecture in *National Film Quarterly*, vol. 2, no. 3, December 1951:20–8; vol. 2, no. 4, March 1952:16–21, 32–3; and vol. 3, no. 1, June 1952:14–18. In 1953, Mary Field of the Children's Film Foundation spoke on 'The responses of children to entertainment film'.
   The NFI also organized public symposia. In 1947, one was held on 'The film – its use and abuses'. In 1950, two public events concerned 'Youth and the cinema'. The participants included the foreign affairs' minister, Sean MacBride; *Irish Times* editor R.M. Smyllie; Irish Film Society chairman James Dooge; the director of the Pioneer Total Abstinence Association, Fr Sean McCarron SJ; lawyer Cearbhaill O Daillaig, later president of Ireland; and W.O'B. Fitzgerald SC. In 1951, a discussion on the same topic was addressed by Séan Lemass and chaired by Professor Michael Tierney. Ever alert to controversy, the NFI secretary even sought the archbishop's approval regarding the lecture titles. Thus, in 1952, Fr Burke, the director of the Catholic Film Institute, London, was due to give a lecture under NFI auspices entitled 'Catholic Action and cinema'. McQuaid responded positively to Sean O'Sullivan's request for approval of the lecture, provided the title was changed: 'In this diocese we do not use the term ... Catholic Action', he replied. Duly chastened, O'Sullivan wrote again to Archbishop House to propose the alternative title of 'Dare we ignore the cinema?' 'I agree', responded McQuaid. (Sean O'Sullivan to Dr McQuaid, 3 June 1952; Dr McQuaid to Sean O'Sullivan, 4 June 1952; Sean O'Sullivan to Revd L. Martin, Archbishop's House, 27 June 1952; Dr McQuaid to Sean O'Sullivan, 1 July 1952, Dr McQuaid papers, DDA.)
7. NFI council minutes, 6 July 1949. The OCIC already had held two conferences but the Second World War acted to put the organization into abeyance until 1947.
8. *National Film Quarterly*, vol. 1, no. 4, March 1951:27. On a visit to Dublin in February 1952, the secretary-general of the OCIC, André Ruszhowski, who was giving a lecture at University College Dublin on 'Lights and shadows of the religious film', had sought a meeting with McQuaid through the NFI's Sean O'Sullivan, but he was unable to arrange this. (André Ruszhowski to Sean O'Sullivan, 15 February 1950, Dr McQuaid papers, DDA.)
9. James C. Fagan, 'Report from the OCIC annual congress', *National Film Quarterly*, vol. 2, no. 2, September 1951:14–20. 'It was the first attempt at an international meeting of film critics to discuss the better definition of their role and of their responsibility from the Christian viewpoint.' (Ibid., 20.)

10. James C. Fagan, *National Film Quarterly*, vol. 3, no. 2, September 1952:13–16. J.P. Murphy, NFI vice-chairman, also attended the conference.
11. James C. Fagan, *National Film Quarterly*, vol. 4, no. 4, April 1954:10.
12. James C. Fagan, *National Film Quarterly*, vol. 4, no. 6, September 1954:13–15.
13. 'Replies to O.C.I.C. questionnaire as to the exten[t] and influence of moral classification of films', 1954:2, Dr McQuaid papers, DDA. Films on release, all of which would have been classified by the censor as 'general' or for universal audiences (only about ten 'adult' certificates were issued before 1965), were reclassified in four categories by the NFI reviewing panel: for general audiences; adult entertainment; objectionable in part; and completely objectionable.
14. 'Address of His Grace the Archbishop of Dublin to the International Catholic Cinema Congress', *National Film Quarterly*, vol. 5, no. 5, September 1955:11.
15. James C. Fagan, 'The institute's aims', *National Film Quarterly*, vol. 1, no. 2, September 1950:16.
16. *National Film Quarterly*, vol. 2, no. 3, December 1951:4.
17. 'Films for children', *National Film Quarterly*, vol. 4, no. 3, December 1953–January 1954:5.
18. For example, these would have included reviewers G. (*On the Waterfront* and *The Wages of Fear*); V. (*Night People* and *The Caine Mutiny*), H. (*Hell and High Water*); F. (*Romeo and Juliet*; *The Belles of St Trinian's* and *Kiss Me Kate*) in *National Film Quarterly*, vol. 1, December 1954:15–17, 21–4. While *On the Waterfront* and *The Caine Mutiny* were recommended for adults only, the overall tone of the reviews could be characterized as descriptive and impressionistic, such as would appear in a contemporary national newspaper, with the litmus test words 'Catholic' and 'moral' totally absent from the discussions.
19. James Fagan, *National Film Quarterly*, vol. 6, no. 1, March 1956:12.
20. Dr McQuaid, no date, *c.*May 1956, NFI boxes, Dr McQuaid papers, DDA. McQuaid's insistence on NFI control of any Catholic film activity is reflected in his response to the setting up of an independent body, the Apostolica Film Group, in 1955. Though the group seems to have had no clear policy, resources or direction, McQuaid instructed Fr Ernest Monks, St Theresa's Presbytery, Donore Avenue, South Circular Road, Dublin, to bring the group under NFI control, 'only let it be control', McQuaid added (handwritten note, 11 May 1955, DDA). After successfully carrying out the archbishop's instructions, Fr Monks told Fr Liam Martin at Archbishop's House that he had informed the group 'they had already infringed the laws of the Diocese by showing a film without permission.' He had also held a meeting with Desmond F. Brennan, president of the London group, which was part of the Catholic Film Institute and who seems to be have been the motivator behind the Dublin body. At a meeting with the NFI, Brennan agreed that the Dublin Apostolica organization 'would remain a separate entity under the control' of the NFI. However, Monks 'warned' Brennan that 'on no account were any of the original members of the Group to be on the Committee [of the NFI] eventually to be formed.' (Fr Martin to Fr Monks, 28 March 1955; Fr Monks to Fr Martin, 4 May 1955; Fr Martin to Fr Monks, 12 May 1955, Dr McQuaid papers, DDA.) Two years later, Brennan gave a lecture, 'Seeing is believing', to the congress of the Irish convent primary teachers, at which time the Apostolica Film Group remained affiliated to the NFI. (*Irish Film Quarterly*, vol. 1, no. 2, June 1957:18–21.)
21. *National Film Quarterly*, vol. 6, no. 4, December 1956:33.
22. Cited, *National Film Quarterly*, vol. 6, no. 1, March 1956:6–7.
23. Patrick Kavanagh, 'Film notes', *Standard*, 20 February 1948:5.
24. John D. Sheridan, 'National Film Institute and Mr Kavanagh's criticism', *Standard*, 5 March 1948:3.
25. Patrick Kavanagh, 'Film notes', *Standard*, 19 March 1948:5. By contrast, in his weekly column in the *Standard*, which ran from 22 February 1946 to June 1949, Kavanagh, whose novel *Tarry Flynn* (1948) was published during this time, consistently praised the Irish Film Society, even reporting conversations he had had with IFS members, including Liam O'Leary. (See, for example, *Standard*, 7 January 1949:3.) Straying beyond the traditional role of a newspaper reviewer (that is, largely descriptive summary only), he broadened the scope of the position to encompass social, cultural and institutional discourses, something which led to ongoing controversy with letter writers either attacking or supporting this extension of his role as critic. One of his targets was fellow columnist, theatre critic Gabriel Fallon, who shared the same page as Kavanagh. At the same time, he often failed to review current releases as he determined they were not worth watching! As he put it in October 1947, 'of the other films [being released that week] little can be said that would not be a waste of paper and ink.' (*Standard*, 17 October 1947:5.) What is perhaps somewhat surprising is that even in his first column he declared his preference for comedy, citing Popeye, Laurel and Hardy, Abbott and Costello, and the Marx Brothers, whose 'glorious lunacy' he later praised (*Standard*, 17 January 1947:7), as his favourites. Another theme of his articles was his regret at the lack of a native film industry, something that resurfaced when such British feature films as *Hungry Hill*,

Captain Boycott, *Saints and Sinners* and *Another Shore* were released, and which he reviewed in a highly critical manner. The film he commented on most favourably was Laurence Oliver's *Hamlet* (1948), which he saw four times. In July 1949, an anonymous writer, Scannán, replaced Kavanagh as the *Standard*'s film critic.

26. Whyte, 1980:34.
27. *National Film Quarterly*, vol. 5, no. 1, December 1954:15–16.
28. *National Film Quarterly*, vol. 5, no. 5, September 1955:13.
29. The editor, 'A brutal film: our attitude', *Sunday Independent*, 10 October 1954:11. The NFI warned that despite the film having been censored, it remained unsuitable for children. (*National Film Quarterly*, vol. 5, no. 1, December 1954:16.) The Irish film censor cut the film in four places. (See Rockett, 2004:137–8, 230.)
30. Seamus O'Connor, 'Quarterly jottings', *Irish Film Quarterly*, vol. 2, no. 4, January 1959:7–9.
31. Earlier that year McQuaid had sent Dunn on a television production course run by the BBC in Manchester. Clearly, McQuaid was planning ahead given that Ireland had not even published its broadcasting bill, and that Telefís Éireann had yet to be established. (See O'Brien, *The real Ireland*, 2004:159.)
32. Joseph Dunn, *No tigers in Africa! recollections and reflections on 25 years of Radharc*, Dublin: Columba, 1986. See also O'Brien, *The real Ireland*, 2004:158–61.
33. The impetus for change at the NFI came during 1978–80 from David Collins, at the time the Arts Council's first film officer, and who later became a film producer. The strategic objectives of the reformed institute, defined as cultural rather than moral, included its secularization and thus the specifically Catholic context of its constitution, especially *Vigilanti cura* as its reference point, was removed. Another objective was to professionalize the institute's moribund administration, something encouraged and financially supported by the Arts Council. This was realized through the appointments of Martin McLoone (now professor of media studies at the University of Ulster, Coleraine) as its first film education officer, and sometime later, in 1983, of former Arts Council officer David Kavanagh as its first director. (Later in the decade, McLoone was succeeded as education officer by Stephanie McBride, now a lecturer in communications at Dublin City University.) By then, Ciaran Benson, author of the well-regarded *The place of the arts in Irish education* report (Dublin: Arts Council, 1979), and now retired professor of psychology at University College Dublin, had been elected chairman, a position he held from 1982 to 1984, at which point this volume's principal author took over and remained chair until 1991.

   Among those who joined the council of the institute (renamed the Irish Film Institute in 1983) during this developmental phase, some of whom remained on the council until the mid to late 1990s were: Luke Gibbons, now a professor in the department of English, NUI, Maynooth; Michael Dwyer, later film correspondent, *Irish Times*; Kevin Barry, now professor of English, NUI, Galway; Tiernan MacBride, formerly chair of the Irish Film Theatre; Niamh O'Sullivan, later chair of the institute, and professor of visual culture, National College of Art and Design; Martha O'Neill, chair of Filmbase and later chair of the institute; filmmaker Donald Taylor Black, now artistic director of the National Film School, Dún Laoghaire Institute of Art, Design and Technology; RTÉ personnel Con Bushe and Peter Feeney; filmmaker Pat Murphy; and Michael Hannigan, then and now director of the Cork Film Festival, and owner of the Kino art cinema, Cork, 1996–2009.

   The task facing these and others on the IFI council was to create the conditions for the establishment of an Irish film centre, something which began properly when in 1987 the IFI acquired the 12,000 square foot premises at 6 Eustace Street in Dublin's Temple Bar, from the Society of Friends/Quakers for £205,000, having sold its own building at 65 Harcourt Street, with the balance being provided by the Irish Film Board and the Arts Council. To realize the project, in 1990 the Arts Council set-up a development board, Irish Film Centre Building Ltd., comprising of three of its own council members (academic Richard Kearney, chairman, Gate theatre director Michael Colgan and U2 manager Paul McGuinness), as well as film activist, producer and lecturer Lelia Doolan, and chairperson of the Irish Film Board in the 1990s, filmmaker Louis Marcus, and the IFI chairperson as an ex-officio member, and with Laura Magahy as project manager from 1989. After the building was opened in September 1992 by Taoiseach Albert Reynolds, the IFI and the development boards were merged under the IFI banner. In the early 1990s the name was changed to the Film Institute of Ireland, but within five years its name reverted to Irish Film Institute.
34. *The influence of the cinema on children and adolescents: an annotated bibliography*, reports and papers on mass communications, no. 31, Paris: UNESCO, 1961:5. Another survey of the literature on the effects of film and television is André Glucksmann, *Violence on the screen: a report on research into the effects on young people of scenes of violence in films and television*, trans. Susan Bennett, London: British Film Institute Education Department, February 1971; orig. 1966. See

also Annette Hill, *Shocking entertainment: viewer response to violent movies*, Luton: John Libbey, 1997.

35. Fr J. Gannon SJ, 1936 lecture, quoted, editor, 'The problem of juvenile crime; influence of unemployment, dances, and cinemas', *Irish Catholic*, 21 March 1936:5.

36. 'Cinema causing boys to form gangs', *Irish Press*, 15 January 1935:3. Later, Justice Cussen associated himself with Fr Devane's campaigns for restrictions on the cinema and he prepared a memorandum on the topic.

37. Editorial, 'Film and the people', *Irish Press*, 30 April 1935:6. Unsurprisingly, the *Irish Catholic* in its own inimitable fashion weighed in. See, for example, 'The cinema and the child: the need for drastic action', *Irish Catholic*, 18 May 1935:5.

38. *KW*, 12 April 1945. The issue had arisen also at the previous year's INTO conference when a delegate praised Cork's Youghal town council for imposing restrictions on juveniles attending local cinemas. ('Juvenile ban urged in Éire', *KW*, 27 April 1944.)

39. 'Child crime in Éire placed at cinemas' door', *TC*, 10 December 1943:3, 26.

40. *KW*, 1 June 1944. Provincial newspapers lent their support to these campaigns with, for example, the *Westmeath Independent* calling for the prohibition of youngsters from attending the cinema except for 'specially arranged matinees' at which comedies or educational films would be shown. (*KW*, 18 May 1944.)

41. The banning of smoking in all (enclosed) working places was introduced on health grounds in March 2004 by Fianna Fáil's minister of health, Micheál Martin, though smoking had already been banned in some public places, including cinemas, hospitals, schools, restaurant kitchens, planes and some trains by the late 1980s.

42. *Irish Independent*, 12 September 1944:3.

43. Editorial, 'Children and the cinema', *Irish Press*, 18 September 1944:2. MacCarthy said that the cinema was 'wrongly ... blamed ... for any of the evil results of delinquency.' He added that 'the good the cinema does, even in its present imperfect form, is far better than if it did not exist at all'. See also 'Éire judge defends the cinema', *KW*, 7 September 1944.

44. 'Films for children', *IT*, 28 September 1944:2.

45. *Irish Independent*, 30 October 1944.

46. 'Films for children' (dept of the taoiseach file S13555, NAI), contains details of some of these resolutions, as well as activity in relation to J. Arthur Rank's proposal for film clubs, discussed below.

47. 'Why films are not graded', *IT*, 4 May 1945:3.

48. 'Child and cinema', *IT*, 5 May 1945:3. See also 'Children and cinemas: Éire's minister's view', *TC*, 15 May 1945:19. The issue was also of concern in Northern Ireland where a magistrate at Belfast summons' court, Mr McCoy, in April 1940 suggested that under-15s should be barred from attending cinemas after a 12-year-old was charged with theft. The boy was placed under probation for two years during which time he was forbidden from entering a cinema. Six months later, a 13-year-old boy appeared in Belfast children's court on twelve charges of theft valued at £4, and offered the defence that he wanted the money to go to the cinema. He was also placed on probation and banned from cinema-going for a year. (Belfasthistoryproject.com.)

49. P.S. O'Hegarty, 'The child's view defended', *Sunday Independent*, 27 May 1945:4. See also 'Cinemagoing by children is defended', *The Cinema*, 6 June 1945.

50. Indeed, it did not permit grading of films for another twenty years. See Rockett, 2004.

51. 'Rapid decline in juvenile delinquency', *IT*, 14 January 1946:8.

52. Irish Film Society records, Liam O'Leary collection, NLI.

53. 'Report of interview with Mr John Davis', 28 March 1946, and covering letter from Dermot J. O'Flynn to Dr McQuaid, 13 April 1946, Dr McQuaid papers, DDA.

54. Dermot J. O'Flynn to Dr McQuaid 13 April 1946, Dr McQuaid papers, DDA.

55. Memo, 2 May 1946, dept of the taoiseach file S13555, NAI. No record has been discovered as to whether Archbishop McQuaid spoke with de Valera on the matter between receiving the NFI report and the taoiseach's meeting with the delegation just over two weeks later, though the memo concerning the 28 March meeting with Davis and St John sent to McQuaid was also given to de Valera.

56. Secretary, dept of industry and commerce to secretary of dept of the taoiseach, 4 May 1946. (Dept of the taoiseach file S13555, NAI.)

57. S.A. Roche, secretary, dept of justice to secretary, dept of the taoiseach, 9 May 1946. (Dept of the taoiseach file S13555, NAI.)

58. Micheál Beathnach, secretary, dept of education to secretary, dept of the taoiseach secretary. (Dept of the taoiseach file S13555, NAI.)

59. J.W. Dulanty to secretary, dept of external affairs, 13 June 1946. (Dept of the taoiseach file S13555, NAI.)

60. M. Ó Muimhneachain, secretary, dept of the taoiseach to secretary, dept of education, 12 September 1946; dept of education to taoiseach's dept, 13 September 1946. (Dept of the taoiseach file S13555, NAI). See also editorial, 'Films for children', *Irish Press*, 24 April 1946:4, which called for coop-eration between educationalists and film producers in arranging special screenings for children.
61. *The Cinema*, 1 May 1946.
62. Irish Film Society circular, 10 February 1942, quoted, Ní Chanainn, 1992:8.
63. Ibid.
64. Liam O'Leary credits Cyril Parker, who used teaching films in his school in Blackrock, Co. Dublin, as the inspiration behind this group. (Liam O'Laoghaire, *Invitation to the film*, Tralee: Kerryman, 1946:128.)
65. Ní Chanainn, 1992:9.
66. *Evening Herald*, 30 December 1943, cited Ní Chanainn, 1992:10. The members of the Children's Film Council were Mairín Cregan, Bean Uí Riain, Áine Ní Chanainn, B. Ó Seaghdha and Edward Toner of Comhairle na nÓg, Leonard Ging, Colman Conroy (Metropole & Allied Cinemas), Maurice Baum and Gerry Kirkham (Odeon Cinemas) of the ITCA. (Ní Chanainn, 1992:10.)
67. Reported in circular issued by Comhairle na nÓg, 5 North Earl Street, Dublin, cited in Ní Chanainn, 1992:10.
68. Reported by Ní Chanainn, 1992:13. The full text of the memo is included in Ní Chanainn, 1992:54–8.
69. Ní Chanainn, 1992:54.   70. Ibid.
71. Ibid., 55.   72. Ibid., 57.
73. Ní Chanainn, 1992:29. See also 'Films unsuitable for children', *IT*, 26 October 1944:2.
74. *Scannán*, vol. 1, no. 6, September 1946:37.
75. Ní Chanainn, 1992:14, 20–2.
76. T.J. Sheehy was at Archbishop's House on 14 November 1946, NFI boxes, Dr McQuaid papers, DDA.
77. Liam O'Laoghaire (ed.), 'Comhairle na n-Óg, Children's and Educational Film Association Review', *Scannán*, vol. 1, no. 6, September 1946:36. The names Comhairle na nÓg and CEFA were inter-changeable by this time, and the organization operated from 39 Harcourt Street, rather than the IFS's premises at 5 North Earl Street, Dublin. Despite O'Leary's attack on the NFI, its rival summer school at St Patrick's Training College, Drumcondra, was prominently reported in the same issue of *Scannán* ('Summer school for teachers', *Scannán*, 1, 42), perhaps a reason why editorial control of the magazine changed with the next issue. *Scannán* seems to have continued as an independent journal under the auspices of the Portlaoghaise [Portlaoise] Film Society and was edited by the soci-ety's secretary, Richard Delaney, who had written for *Documentary Newsletter*, and with four trustees (Liam O'Leary, Peter G. Sherry, an industrial chemist who worked for Clondalkin Paper Mills, and Edward Toner) was editor of the IFS's publications, as well as contributing to a wide range of journals, including *Sight and Sound*. *Scannán*'s editorial advisers included Gordon Clarke, Sighle Ní h-Iarnain, Pearse Hutchinson, Kevin O'Kelly, Colm O'Laoghaire, Liam O'Leary, T.J.M. Sheehy, Peter G. Sherry and Charles Whelan. Significantly, under the new dispensation it carried the subtitle, 'a critical review of the cinema'. Giving additional focus to this group's interest in Irish and international cinema was the publication in late 1946 of O'Leary's *Invitation to the film*, the first single authored book-length study of the cinema published in Ireland. In that book, O'Leary gave a somewhat caustic view of the NFI and its beginnings during the previous three years, about which O'Leary would have been well informed: 'Its early growing pains threatened to nullify any work such an organization could have accomplished, but I understand drastic re-adjustment has taken place and it is hoped that the new Institute will help to foster co-operation between all Irish Film workers and avoid those displays of egotistical self-assertion which have hitherto hindered the path of national progress in many spheres.' (O'Leary, 1946:8.) Of course, we now know that such a democratic wish was not forthcoming from a body whose reference point was a papal encyclical and its chief policymaker a *rigorous* and powerful Catholic prelate.
78. *Scannán*, vol. 1, no. 6, September 1946:36, 42.
79. *Scannán*, vol. 2, no. 3, December 1946:32.
80. *Scannán*, vol. 1, no. 6, September 1946:42.
81. NFI minutes, 19 March 1947. The NFI minutes merely record the fact of the change. No doubt pleased at this turn of events, by the end of the year, McQuaid had agreed to become the NFI's patron.
82. Ní Chanainn, 1992:23.
83. In 1947, Liam O'Leary lectured on documentary film, while practical demonstrations, backing up the film technique course delivered by Denis Forman of the Central Office of Information (and later the director of the British Film Institute), were given by Ó Sé, Toomey, Ó Nualláin and Donal

O'Carroll. In 1949 from 11 to 16 July, H.J. Healy directed a (technical) course for technical and vocational teachers. (See Ní Chanainn, 1992:23.) Though Eilish McGinley, from Glasgow, who had spoken at the inaugural 1945 IFS summer school, gave a lecture on 'Youth and the Cinema', generally speaking, when lectures strayed beyond the technical they were given by NFI stalwarts such as, in 1950, Morgan Sheehy ('The film in adult education') and Áine Ní Chanainn ('Training the child in film appreciation'). (See teachers' training course [24–9 July, 1950] programme in Ní Chanainn, 1992:24.) Indeed a special 'film appreciation' course was run in 1953 which was addressed by J.C. Fagan ('The film among the arts'), Seamus Rossiter, Ballyfermot Vocational School ('The influence of the film'), D.J. O'Flynn ('Film appreciation') and Áine Ní Chanainn ('Film appreciation for schools'). (Ní Chanainn, 1992:26.)

84. At a meeting of its executive committee on 25 October 1951 to discuss 'The child and the cinema' it was decided to establish a junior film society operating on 16mm for secondary school boys and girls, and, as a result, the society continued some of the policies of the earlier children's committee. (IFS minutes, Liam O'Leary collection, NLI.)

85. *National Film Quarterly*, vol. 4, no. 5, July 1954:14.

86. *National Film Quarterly*, vol. 4, no. 3, December 1953–January 1954:5.

87. The word Catholic does not appear in the article as she chose to emphasize 'social sense and moral responsibility'.

88. Brigid Redmond, 'Films and children', *Studies*, vol. 45, 1956:229.

89. *National Film Quarterly*, vol. 4, no. 4, April 1954:28.

90. Minister for justice, Gerald Boland, *Dáil debates*, vol. 98, col. 306, 17 October 1945; vol. 143, col. 2020, 10 December 1953.

91. *National Film Quarterly*, vol. 6, no. 1, March 1956:21.

92. *Irish Film Quarterly*, vol. 3, no. 1, April 1959:17–21.   93. Ní Chanainn, 1992:46.

94. *National Film Quarterly*, vol. 5, no. 1, March 1955:5.   95. See www.ifco.ie.

96. T.J.M. Sheehy, 'Boycotting the films', *National Film Quarterly*, vol. 6, no. 1, March 1956:16–26. In this article, Sheehy relates how he drew on the word 'boycott' (born nearly a century before in Ireland 'when a group of harassed peasantry found themselves victims of the oppressive behaviour of a powerful, greedy and tyrannical alien landlord') to restrict certain films being distributed in Ireland, that is, after they had been approved by Ireland's censorship regime (which was regarded as being too relaxed by many NFI and other Catholic commentators including Sheehy, but which, in reality, as has since been clearly shown, was extremely strict, and far more oppressive than elsewhere, including in Britain). Boycotts had been used only occasionally by OCIC members due to a concern that such a tactic might arouse undue publicity for a film. Though the majority of film reviewers were Catholic, 'only in exceptional cases do they concern themselves with comment on moral aspects of the film.' As a result, Sheehy used his articles in the *Irish Catholic* and in the monthly the *Pioneer*, neither of which took film trade advertisements 'on principle', to criticize films from a Catholic moral perspective.

Sheehy details how he mounted a 'full blast campaign' against *Duel in the Sun* (King Vidor, 1946), which led to one circuit refusing to book it, while provincial exhibitors told him they, too, would not book it, resulting in the release of the film being postponed and later abandoned. (During the film's long censorship process in Ireland during 1947–8, the censor clocked up thirty-three cuts, probably the main reason why the film was not released at the time. [Censor's reserve 7056–7, 14 May 1947, and reserve 7214–16, 23 January 1948, NAI.] It was resubmitted to the censor in 1961 when its was passed with three cuts, including of the film's rape scene, which was 'drastically curtail[ed]'. [Censor's record 35257, reserve 10350, censor's decision, 2 May 1961, NAI.]) According to Sheehy, *Forever Amber* (Otto Preminger, 1947), the book of which had been banned by the censorship of publications' board, was not even offered for release in Ireland due to his actions. As regards *Bitter Rice* (Giuseppe de Santis, 1948, Italy), he regretted that he 'failed to move early enough', but his 'late campaign prevented numerous country cinemas from booking it.' When released on 16mm, 'my immediate condemnation gained practically 100 per cent cancellation of bookings in the small 16mm country theatres.' *Bitter Rice* was released as *The Harvesters*, a title change insisted on by film censor Richard Hayes, who made ten cuts to the film, including of Silvana's suggestive dance at the film's beginning. (Censor's record 25389, reserve 7822–3, censor's decision, 27 September 1950. The certificate was issued on 3 October 1950 and the distributor was Egan Film Service.) As for *Salome* (William Dieterle, 1953), Sheehy used his contacts with distributors to stymie its release, while he succeeded in having the words 'Corpus Christi' deleted by distributor 20th Century-Fox from *Three Coins in the Fountain* (Jean Negulesco, 1954) following its approval by the censor, who cut kisses from the film. (Censor's record 29408, reserve 8726, censor's decision, 17 August 1954; certificate issued, 27 October 1954.)

Despite Sheehy's obvious commitment to a strict Catholic film censorship regime, Archbishop McQuaid commented when the NFI's secretary, Francis B. Ryan, reported in 1956 that while the institute's reviewing panel found the French film *Lovers at Midnight*, then running at the Astor cinema, Dublin, 'objectionable', the *Irish Catholic* had regarded it as containing 'nothing objectionable'. This observation prompted McQuaid to comment that it was 'not the first worry from that direction.' (Francis B. Ryan to Dr McQuaid, 2 March 1956; Dr McQuaid to Francis B. Ryan, 25 March 1956.) It was shortly after this that McQuaid appointed Fr Dempsey and Dr O'Hare to lecture NFI personnel on Catholic theology and art, as discussed above.

A more subtle form of Catholic film reviewing was to be found in the *Furrow*, for which Fr Peter Connolly, a lecturer in English language and literature at Maynooth College, had been reviewer since December 1955. See, for example, his 'Censorship and moral classification of film', reprinted in *Irish Film Quarterly*. In light of the increased availability of continental European films, he argued for the introduction of adult film certificates, something Catholic activists did not always agree on, though he warned that liberalism 'tends to presuppose a wholly adult society'. (*Irish Film Quarterly*, vol. 1, no. 1, March 1957:27.) For the broader context, see Rockett, 2004.

97. *National Film Quarterly*, vol. 5, no. 1, March 1955:6–7.
98. G. McC (George McCanny), *Film Review*, July 1972:46. The film censor passed the film with three cuts. (Besides deleting the words 'fuck' and 'damn', 'Bobby' climbing out of a swimming pool nude was also cut). (Reserve 11797, 22 May 1972, film censors' records, NAI.)
99. The last major instance of the Irish clergy battling against cinema was with regard to *The Last Temptation of Christ* (Martin Scorsese, 1988), which the then recently appointed archbishop of Dublin, Dr Desmond Connell, sought to have banned. However, it was passed uncut with an over-18s certificate. (See Rockett, 2004:251.)
  1. See Rockett, 2004:271–316.
  2. One figure was Mr E.C. Powell, a civil servant in justice, who deputized from time to time as official film censor from at least 1951 to the late 1950s and initiated O'Hora into the role in 1956 following Martin Brennan's death. See Rockett, 2004.
  3. Thomas P. Gallagher, 'Our first film censor', in *Irish cinema handbook*, 1943:93. See Rockett, 2004, for an account of Montgomery's work as film censor.
  4. Distributor British Lion accepted the cuts and the film was released. James Montgomery viewed the film on 17–18 June 1937; it was reviewed on 19 June 1937 with Monsignor Michael Cronin in attendance; and the certificate was issued on 16 July 1937. (Record 11869, reserve no. 3858; 21 June 1937, film censors' records, NAI.)
  5. James Montgomery, 29 September 1927, film censors' records, NAI.
  6. Cited in James Montgomery's report on *Holy Ghost Fathers*, which was passed following the deletion of the benediction. (6 November 1937, film censors' records, NAI.)
  7. James Montgomery, record 1896 and 34668; reserve 680, 30 October 1929; review and certificate issued, 14 November 1929.'In the church scenes there are incidents that are anything but reverent. … [T]he sacred ceremonies … display the cynical disregard of Hollywood for the sincere feelings of Catholics. The Elevation, and the bells for it, [and] … the full view of the Monstrance must come out.' (James Montgomery, 30 October 1929, film censors' records, NAI.)
  8. As well as demanding the title to be changed to *Singer of Seville*, views of the altar showing the monstrance during the singing of 'Tantum Ergo' had to be deleted. (Record 3494 and 8088; reserve 1215; censor's decision, 8 January 1931; review, 12 February 1931, film censors' records, NAI.)
  9. 'A joke about a sacrament will not be tolerated in this country … there must be no allusion to baptism.' (James Montgomery, record 9194 and 19684; reserve 3374, 24 June 1935; reviewed, 26–27 June 1935; certificate issued on 2 July 1935, film censors' records, NAI.)
 10. James Montgomery, records 12344 and 16375; reserve 3933, 6 November 1937; reviewed, 23 November 1937; appeal board viewing and certificate issued, 25 February 1938.
 11. Movietone 220a: In Lourdes item, 'the entire shot showing the Monstrance being exposed, and blessing the pilgrims must be deleted.' (James Montgomery, reserve 2489, 24 August 1933.) Super Sound 35/02: Film of 1935 Eucharistic congress in which benediction was cut. 'By order of the Archbishop this must NEVER be shown in a picture house.' (James Montgomery, reserve 3186, 7 January 1935.) Movietone News 447, from which the pope and the monstrance were cut. (James Montgomery, reserve 3966, 30 December 1937, film censors' records, NAI.)
 12. While a complete list would be beyond the scope of the book, fiction films cut include *La Femme du Boulanger* (Marcel Pagnol, 1938, France) from which an entire chapel scene with a priest's sermon was cut (Richard Hayes, record 17783, reserve 5467–8, 11 March 1943); the spoof documentary *Yellow Caesar* (Alberto Cavalcanti, 1941) from which a shot of a priest celebrating mass was cut (Richard Hayes, record 20484, reserve 6746, 5 April 1946); *Joan of Paris* (Robert Stevenson,

1942), from which a priest reciting a psalm was cut (Richard Hayes, record 20506, reserve 6751, 10 April 1946); *Monsieur Verdoux* (Charles Chaplin, 1947), which had among its cuts, 'flippant and irreverent words – "Why not? After all, it belongs to Him"' – and Priest saying '*Agitorium in nomine dominae quae facil kalum et tenam* ...' (Richard Hayes, record 22223, reserve 7181, 24 November 1947, film censors' records, NAI.)

In a documentary on the Lourdes' shrine viewed by the censor in October 1941, cuts were demanded to the administration of Holy Communion, and views of the monstrance and the elevation of the Host. Nevertheless, understanding the greater emotional impact of the close-up, he noted that 'the *long* shot of this need *not* be cut'. (In this way the blood of Christ was often allowed as it was shielded from the audience, contained as it was in the chalice. Censor's decision, reserve 4903, 7 October 1941.) Thus, close-ups of the monstrance or the elevation of the Host were cut from a number of documentaries in the 1940s and 1950s: *Story of the Pope* (in which a close-up of the monstrance was cut) (Richard Hayes, record 25165, reserve 7778, 18 July 1950); *Faith in Wales*, a drama, (close-up of monstrance cut) (Richard Hayes, record 26043, reserve 7973, 2 May 1951); *Weekend with God* (close-ups of monstrance and Host, as well as administering Communion) (Richard Hayes, record 26073, reserve 7984, 15 May 1951 and 4 March 1952); and *Pilgrimage to Fatima* (monstrance and Host) (Richard Hayes, record 26519, reserve 8105, 18 October 1951).

13. *Irish News*: Corpus Christi at Bandon. 'Cut out Monstrance shot (3 times) including the Benediction scene (this is the third shot)', (Richard Hayes, 30 June 1941); *Irish News*: 'Cut shot of Priest drinking from Chalice at Mass', though in conformity with Second World War censorship restrictions, this film also had cut from it references to 'fallen comrades ... who fell on French coastline near Dieppe.' (Richard Hayes, reserve 5290, 19 October 1942.) *Universal Irish News no. 177*: 'Cut shots of Monstrance in item "Mr De Valera in Portugal".' (Richard Hayes, reserve 8553, 5 October 1953.)

14. According to Richard Hayes, 'This picture shows the entire ritual of Holy Mass. There is nothing objectionable in the film from a Catholic viewpoint – the subject is treated with due reverence in every way. But I consider the selection of the Holy Sacrifice unsuitable as a subject for a cinema, either public or private. (I may add that high Church authorities agree with my view as regards this.)' (Record 16913, reject 1531, 21 March 1942, 1,582ft, 16mm, film censors' records, NAI.)

15. In *Fatima Gown*, shots of administering of Communion with a priest raising the Host, which were followed by the raising of the chalice, were to be cut, though the latter was *not* to be cut. (Richard Hayes, record 27106, reserve 8222, 4 April 1952.) Indeed, as can be seen from the censor's remarks with regard to *El Capitán de Loyola* (*Loyola, the Soldier Saint*, José Díaz Morales, 1949, Spain), the issue of visibility was key: 'In [the] last reel curtail [the] shot where [the] Host is shown – a distant shot of [it] may be allowed to appear.' (Richard Hayes, record 27298, reserve 8276, 20 June 1952.) A similar comment is made on *Sanctuary of the Heart*, from which close-ups of the Host were cut. (Richard Hayes, record 27572, reserve 8336, 15 October 1952.)

16. Other cuts to *Nactwache* included the scene where Revd Heger says, 'We want to build a house for God', while all shots of the Catholic priests were to be cut. (Richard Hayes, record 28675, reserve 8595, 2 December 1953.)

17. Quoted, Roy Kinnard and Tim Davis, *Divine images: a history of Jesus on the screen*, New York: Citadel, 1992:57.

18. James Montgomery, reserve 1358, 23 November 1938. See also Rockett, 2004:82–4 on the censoring of religious films.

19. Cardinal Maglione to J.V. Hallessy, 8 May 1939, Archbishop Byrne papers, DDA.

20. General secretary, OCIC, to Minerva Films, Rome, 14 April 1939, Archbishop Byrne papers, DDA.

21. Fr H.G. McKernan, secretary, Archbishop's House, to J.V. Hallessy, 21 September 1939, Archbishop Byrne papers, DDA. A margin note titled 'reply' on Hallessy's 18 September letter recorded that 'His Grace has absolute confidence in the Irish Film Censor.'

22. J.V. Hallessy to Dr McQuaid, 22 March 1945, Dr McQuaid papers, DDA.

23. Richard Hayes wrote that 'the materialisation of the figure of Christ' ensured that a certificate could not be granted to the film. (Reject 1556, 20 August 1942, film censors' records, NAI.)

24. Before being issued with a censor's certificate, shots of the monstrance and of Communion were cut from the film. (James Montgomery, record 28426, reserve 2515, 12 September 1933, certificate issued on 22 November 1933, film censors' records, NAI.)

25. P.J. Whitney, St Patrick's, Kiltegan, Co. Wicklow, to Archbishop Byrne, 23 February 1935, and P.J. Whitney to Fr Dunne, Archbishop's House, 5 March 1936, Archbishop Byrne papers, DDA. No information on the content of the film has been discovered.

26. Richard Hayes to Archbishop McQuaid, 1 November 1943, Dr McQuaid papers, DDA.

27. Richard Hayes, record 18378, reserve 5798, 4 November 1943, reviewed, 7 December 1943, film censors' records, NAI.

28. Richard Hayes to Archbishop McQuaid, 18 February 1944, Dr McQuaid papers, DDA. See also Rockett, 2004:342, 456, on *Army Chaplin*.
29. Richard Hayes to Fr Mangan, Archbishop's House, 15 January 1949, Dr McQuaid papers, DDA.
30. Richard Hayes, record 23283, reserve 7426, 26 January 1949, film censors' records, NAI.
31. Francis B. Ryan to Dr McQuaid, with McQuaid note, 11 December 1953, Dr McQuaid papers, DDA.
32. Dr McQuaid to Martin Brennan, 10 November 1954. McQuaid was alert to the fact that while one of the film's producers was the high-profile American Louis De Rochement, who is best known as producer of *March of Time*, Germany's Lutheran Church Productions was co-producer through Lothar Wolff. It does not seem that the film was submitted to the Irish censors.
33. Dr McQuaid to B. Elliman, 22 October 1954, Dr McQuaid papers, DDA.
34. B. Elliman to Dr McQuaid, 25 October 1954, Dr McQuaid papers, DDA.
35. Michael O'Halloran to Dr McQuaid, 1 November 1954, Dr McQuaid papers, DDA.
36. Martin Brennan, reject 2036, 1 November 1954. Another film about the young saint, *St Maria Goretti*, was passed with two cuts (both involving shots of the Host) nine months earlier. (Richard Hayes, record 28864, reserve 8622, 3 February 1954, film censors' records, NAI.)
37. James MacMahon, film censor's office, to McQuaid, with McQuaid's commentary, 20 April 1956, Dr McQuaid papers, DDA.
38. E.C. Powell, undated, *c.*April/May 1954, film censors' records, NAI.
39. Dr McQuaid note following phone call from Liam O'Hora asking that Dr McQuaid send two representatives to view the film, 24 February 1958; reply given to Miss Gleeson, secretary, film censor's office, 25 February 1958, Dr McQuaid papers, DDA.
40. Unsigned internal note to Dr McQuaid, 28 April 1959, Dr McQuaid papers, DDA.
41. Liam O'Hora, record 33617, reserve 9940, 15 April 1959, film censors' records, NAI.
42. Liam O'Hora, record 32964, reserve 9743, 24 July 1958, film censors' records, NAI.
43. It is possible, but very unlikely, that this was the Pathé 1937 film, *Holy Ghost Fathers,* cited above, which James Montgomery had passed with cuts (6 November 1937).
44. Dr Desmond Williams, Archbishop's House, to Dr McQuaid, 2 April 1959; Monsignor O'Halloran to McQuaid, 8 April 1959, Dr McQuaid papers, DDA.
45. Dr Desmond Williams to Dr McQuaid, 22 May 1959, Dr McQuaid papers, DDA.
46. Desmond Williams to McQuaid conveying Monsignor O'Halloran's phone report, 1 July 1959, Dr McQuaid papers, DDA.
47. Liam O'Hora, record 34821, reserve 10210, 21 September 1960, film censors' records, NAI; memo, Archbishop's House, 19 September 1960, Dr McQuaid papers, DDA.
48. Liam O'Hora, record 33502, reserve 9902, 4 March 1959, film censors' records, NAI.
49. Unsigned, conveying telephone message from Monsignor O'Halloran to Dr McQuaid, Archbishop's House, 1 September 1959, Dr McQuaid papers, DDA.
50. Leo Quinlan, Archbishop's House, to Dr McQuaid, 15 December 1960, Dr McQuaid papers, DDA.
51. Reject 2342, 15 December 1960; appeal board decision, 18 April 1961, film censors' records, NAI. O'Hora commented that it had 'caused offence in every country where there are even vestigial traces of Christianity.' The reject decision was confirmed by O'Hora's successor Christopher Macken in 1964, but eventually the (new) appeal board in 1965 passed it with six cuts. (Christopher Macken, reject 2460, 20 July 1964; appeal board reserve 11028, 23 July 1965, when the decision was deferred; 1 September 1965; appeal allowed, 12 October 1965, with over-18s certificate.)
52. *The Singer not the Song*, which is set in 1950s' Mexico, features an Irish priest, Fr Michael Keogh (John Mills), who is caught between the attentions of the secret love of Locha (Mylène Demongeot) and the church-hating controller of the town, Ancelto (Dirk Bogarde). In his report detailing the ten cuts he demanded, censor Liam O'Hora commented that 'the Renter will appreciate that I am taking a chance in passing this picture at all. The theme is a controversial one; in fact in this country one that is rather beyond the pale.' (Reserve 10290, 16 February 1961.)
53. Monsignor Michael O'Halloran to Dr McQuaid, 30 October 1961, Dr McQuaid papers, DDA.
54. Monsignor R.J. Glennon to Dr McQuaid, 31 October 1961, Dr McQuaid papers, DDA.
55. Dr McQuaid to Monsignor Glennon, 2 November 1961. John O'Regan of Curia Archiepiscopalis Dublinensis wrote a three-page report on the film, and while feeling that an opportunity was missed to convey the divinity of Christ, nevertheless, because of 'the lively Faith of our people ... it can be safely asserted that its public showing in Ireland will do no injury to that' (30 October 1961). McQuaid wrote on the cover of this report that 'under the Act, we must tolerate its unreality, inaccuracy and poverty' (31 October 1961), Dr McQuaid papers, DDA.
56. Liam O'Hora, reject 2132, 12 November 1956; appeal board decision, 8 January 1957, film censors' records, NAI.

57. Monsignor Michael O'Halloran to Dr McQuaid, 30 October 1961, Dr McQuaid papers, DDA.
58. Liam O'Hora, record 35827, reserve 10460, 4 January 1962, certificate issued on 7 February 1962, film censors' records, NAI.
59. Liam O'Hora, reject 2398, 15 May 1962, film censors' records, NAI.
60. Leo Quinlan, Archbishop's House, to Dr McQuaid, 21 May 1962, Dr McQuaid papers, DDA.
61. Leo Quinlan note, 23 May 1962, on letter of 21 May, Dr McQuaid papers, DDA.
62. 'Firstly, I should remark that this picture has been shown nowhere in the world to children. It has in fact been condemned in all countries by prison authorities and youth supervisors. Secondly, I have not rejected this picture because of its sex or violence alone. In point of fact I believe I might have cut it successfully if only sex and violence were involved. However, my greatest problem has been the fact that every nasty character in the film – including the sadistic prison officer – is a Catholic and certain facets of Catholic worship and behaviour are presented in a most controversial light. I refer particularly to the blatantly disrespectful conduct of Mass, the nude pin-ups in the prison cell *vis-à-vis* the statues of the Blessed Virgin, etc. I could not see my way to pass this picture, with or without cuts.' (Liam O'Hora to appeal board, 15 November 1960; reject 2335, 8 November 1960, appeal board decision, 15 November 1960.) Earlier, deputy censor E.C. Powell had, in a decision also upheld by the appeal board, banned *The Prisoner* (Peter Glenville, 1955, GB) because of its treatment of the cardinal and religion in general. (Deputy film censor E.C. Powell, reject 2055, record 30152, 26 May 1955; appeal decision, 18 October 1955, film censors' records, NAI).
63. Appeal board decision, 29 May 1962, film censors' records, NAI.
64. See Rockett, 2004:157.
65. Liam O'Hora, record 35165, reject 2350, 13 February 1961, film censors' records, NAI.
66. Film censor Liam O'Hora's report to minister for justice, 31 January 1963, Office of Film Classification, Dublin.
67. Censorship of films appeal board decision and film censor Liam O'Hora's report, 26 June 1962. See Rockett, 2004:411n29.
68. T.J.M.S. 'Films and TV', *Irish Catholic*, 6 December 1962.
69. T.J.M.S. 'Films and TV', *Irish Catholic*, 13 December 1962.
70. The editor, *Irish Catholic* to Dr McQuaid, 11 January 1963, Dr Quaid papers, DDA.
71. Dr McQuaid note on letter of 11 January 1963 from *Irish Catholic* editor, 14 January 1963, Dr McQuaid papers, DDA.
72. Revd Thomas O'Donnell to Dr McQuaid, 15 January 1963, Dr Quaid papers, DDA.
73. Monsignor O'Halloran to Dr McQuaid, 21 July 1962, Dr Quaid papers, DDA.
74. Monsignor O'Halloran to Dr McQuaid, 10 May 1963, Dr Quaid papers, DDA.
75. Monsignor R.J. Glennon to Dr McQuaid, 11 January 1964, and note by McQuaid on Glennon's 11 January correspondence, 13 January 1963, Dr Quaid papers, DDA.
76. Monsignor O'Halloran to Dr McQuaid, 11 January 1964, Dr Quaid papers, DDA.
77. John Hanlon to Dr McQuaid, 19 July 1950, Dr Quaid papers, DDA.
78. E. Hardiman to Dr McQuaid, 6 May 1942, note on same, Dr Quaid papers, DDA. This is probably the film *Lourdes*, which was passed with cuts by film censor James Montgomery in October 1941, thus making it the Irish 'official version' of the film. Montgomery's cuts to the film were in accordance with his policy of not permitting sacraments to be shown publicly; thus, shots with Holy Communion being administered; the elevation of the Host (a long shot was allowed); pilgrims kissing a wall; and all front views of the monstrance in a procession of the blessed sacrament, were all cut. (Reserve 4903; 17 October 1941.) Five months earlier, the short *Miracle at Lourdes* had been banned by Montgomery, a decision upheld after appeal (film censor's reject 1471, 13 May 1941; appeal board decision, 10 June 1941), on the basis that the film 'seems to have the definite object of disproving the miracle at Lourdes as being the result of direct or indirect divine intervention. The sceptical, if not rationalistic, tones of the narrator would offend the religious susceptibilities of the majority of the ordinary Irish cinema audience.' McQuaid had told film censor Richard Hayes in November 1943 that he was 'very worried' about the forthcoming *Song of Bernadette* (Henry King, 1943). (Dr McQuaid note on letter from Richard Hayes to Archbishop McQuaid, 1 November 1943, Dr McQuaid papers, DDA.) Clerical scepticism of the apparition, as expressed by the dean of Lourdes, was among the six cuts made to the film by the censor in March 1944 (Richard Hayes, reserve 5938, 14 March 1944, reviewed, 21 March 1944, 3 April 1944, 25 April 1944, 2 May 1944), which is discussed in Rockett, 2004:121–2.
79. *Sanctuary of the Heart*, a feature drama, had been released by Egan Film Service, though shots of the Host had to be cut. (Richard Hayes, reserve 8336, 15 October 1942, film censors' records, NAI.)

80. *Isle of Sinners*, a feature drama, was passed with nine cuts. (Richard Hayes, reserve 8516, 27 July 1953, film censors' records, NAI.)
81. E. Hardiman to McQuaid, with added comment by McQuaid, 26 October 1953, Dr McQuaid papers, DDA. Hardiman incorrectly called the film *Miracle of Milan*.
82. Elba Films to Dr McQuaid, 20 May 1945; Dr McQuaid to Elba Films, 4 June 1945, Dr McQuaid papers, DDA.
83. In 1946 the NFI sought advice on *My Sacrifice and Yours*. The archbishop dispatched Monsignori Boylan and Dunne to view the film after which it got their approval and that of the archbishop. (Monsignor P. Dunne to Dr McQuaid, 16 September 1946 and Sean O'Sullivan, NFI secretary, to Dr McQuaid, 16 September 1946, with Dr McQuaid's note approving purchase, 17 September, Dr McQuaid papers, DDA.)
84. Sean O'Sullivan, NFI secretary, to Fr C. Mangan, Archbishop's House, 28 July 1953, Dr McQuaid papers, DDA.
85. T.C. O'Gorman, honorary secretary, CSVOC, to Dr McQuaid, 3 October 1949, Dr McQuaid papers, DDA.
86. McQuaid note on T.C. O'Gorman letter of 3 October 1949, Dr McQuaid papers, DDA.
87. See note 83, above.
88. Monsignor Boylan to Dr McQuaid, 31 October 1949, Dr McQuaid papers, DDA.
89. T.C. O'Gorman to Dr McQuaid, 29 October 1949, Dr McQuaid papers, DDA.
90. S.M. to T.C. O'Gorman, 2 November 1949, draft note on letter of 29 October 1949, Dr McQuaid papers, DDA.
91. H. Cathal MacCarthy, 'The Sacrifice We Offer', undated, Dr McQuaid papers, DDA.
92. Richard Hayes, report 27685, reserve 8356, 28 November 1952, film censors' reports, NAI,
93. Oona MacWhirter to Fr Mangan, 6 July 1953, Dr McQuaid papers, DDA.
94. Richard Hayes, report 27685, reserve 8504, 11 July 1953, film censors' reports, NAI.
95. Patrick Farrell to Dr McQuaid, 14 October 1944, Dr McQuaid papers, DDA. Ironically, Irish actor Barry Fitzgerald, who also plays a priest in the film, was from a Protestant background.
96. MGM to Dr McQuaid, 13 March 1946, Dr McQuaid papers, DDA.
97. Odeon (Ireland) Ltd to Dr McQuaid, 30 September 1948; Dr McQuaid to Odeon (Ireland) Ltd, 4 October 1948, Dr McQuaid papers, DDA. *The Fugitive* had been passed with ten cuts. (Richard Hayes, reserve 8169, 22 January 1952.)
98. Robert McNally to Dr MacQuaid, 28 January 1946; Robert McNally to Dr McQuaid, 5 February 1946. Dr McQuaid papers, DDA.
99. David E. Ross to Dr McQuaid, 30 March 1943; Dr McQuaid to Paramount Film Service, 17 April 1943; Fr R.A. Glennon, secretary, Archbishop's House, to Norman Barfield, 17 April 1943; Dr McQuaid to Barfield, 20 April 1943, Dr McQuaid papers, DDA.

CHAPTER 9

1. Dublin-born film director and scriptwriter whose work includes *Maeve* (1982), *Anne Devlin* (1984) and *Nora* (2000), in Stephanie McBride and Roddy Flynn (eds), 1996:132–3.
2. Nuala O'Faolain in ibid., 94.   3. Shane Connaughton in ibid., 108–9.
4. Three contrasting views are represented by John Quinn: 'And there, careless of grease-pocked wooden seats/Oil-soaked sawdust and icy draughts/We surrendered to the celluloid world' (in ibid., 73); Fr Brian D'Arcy, who in his recollection of the Regal Cinema, Enniskillen, remarks it was a good cinema and the projector *rarely* broke down (emphasis added, in ibid., 103); and politician Mary O'Rourke who writes: 'I can vividly recall the Aladdin's Cave that was the glittery glory of the Ritz cinema in Athlone' (in ibid., 72).
5. Gerry Stembridge in ibid., 86–7.
6. John MacMahon, commissioning editor for educational films, RTÉ, in Stephanie McBride and Roddy Flynn (eds), 1996:23, reminiscing on visits to such a hall in Ballyheigue, Co. Kerry, which he recalled was 'a long narrow building, with benches towards the front and somewhat more comfortable seats at the back.' Despite its less than salubrious design, 'every week, however, it was transformed by the power of the projector.' Indeed, very often the buildings were less than ideal, but then as another contributor to McBride and Flynn's 1996 book states, despite visiting many regular cinemas in later life it was his childhood visits to the 'fit-up cinema with a leaky roof in a field of foot-high grass' for which he retains a special affection (John Quinn of RTÉ, in ibid., 26).
7. Such a list includes, in Dublin, Ward Anderson's 12-screen Omniplex, St Stephen's Green centre (it is suggested that initial rent will be around €1 million); UCI, Charlestown complex, Finglas (a 9-

screen facility as part of the second phase of the Charlestown project developed by Tom and Michael Bailey of Bovale Developments); UCI/Leisureplex, Tallaght (UCI/Leisureplex has committed to occupy 145,000 sq ft, or 56 per cent of a new shopping and leisure complex being developed by Bernard McNamara for a lease period of 25 years); and Vue, Spring Cross complex, Ballymun (by June 2010 Vue Entertainment agreed with developers Treasury Holdings to operate new multiplex; the cinema is intended to be built as part of phase one of the construction). Outside the capital, the most progressed cinema is Galway's *Solas, the Picture Palace,* 15 Lower Merchant's Road, Spanish Arch. Referred to in chapter 6, the cinema will be run by the Solas Picture Palace Teoranta and brings together representatives from Galway Film Society, Galway Film Fleadh, Galway Film Centre and Galway Arts Centre. It is envisaged to have 3 screens/*c.*340 seats. Other cinemas include ones in Naas, Co. Kildare (in December 2009 it was reported that Superquinn was intending to build a new mixed-use development in Naas incorporating a supermarket, offices, shops, an 8-screen cinema and an underground car-park. According to Superquinn's chairman, 'There are a lot of people interested in coming on board with the project, particularly for the cinema and leisure development.' [Ian Kehoe and Gavin Daly, 'Superquinn planning large new multi-use development in Naas', *Sunday Business Post,* 27 December 2009]); Fermoy, Co. Cork (on Courthouse Road, Ballyjamesduff Properties plan to build a major retail development complete with a 5-screen cinema); Old Cork Marts site, also in Cork (where developers the Shipton Group plan to build another mixed use development including a 7-screen cinema [*Evening Echo,* copy in *breakingnews.ie* 8 May 2008]); Lugatemple, Claremorris, Co. Mayo (a 5-screen cinema with seating for 687 people, planned since 2009 [*Western People,* 24 June 2009]); and in Roscommon at Roxboro (John Farrell is seeking planning permission for a change of use of part of an existing retail/wholesale development [*Roscommon Herald,* 31 March 2010]), and at the Centre Point retail park, Circular Road (where Flix Leisure are seeking to open a 6-screen, all digital, cinema as part of leisure centre).

8. The actual directory of films is found on pp 63–79, while a list of trade bookers is included on pp 55–61.

9. The *Showcase, 1968* list does not include seat numbers, so if a reference to *Showcase* appears after seat numbers, it is only to avoid splitting a reference.

10. *KW,* 10 July 1958:9; 14 August 1958:28; *KYB,* 1958–64.

11. *KW,* 10 July 1958:9; *KYB,* 1958–64; *BFI,* 1991.

12. *KW,* 9 September 1934:30.

13. Closed February 1937 by Supreme Cinemas Ltd (*KW,* 11 February 1937:37; 9 December 1937:14). Possibly the same venue as the *Picture Palace.* This cinema name is listed in *KYB,* 1939–42; then in *KYB,* 1950 as Mill Street with p: Theatre Supplies Ltd, 133 Royal Avenue, Belfast; 500 seats; then listed as closed in *KYB,* 1951–7.

14. *KW,* 13 September 1934:30.   15. *KW,* 5 December 1935:8.

16. *KW,* 9 December 1937:14.   17. *KYB,* 1939, spells Crawford's name as Crowford.

18. *Kinematograph and Lantern Weekly,* 7 January 1915:51.

19. Open, 1985:21.

20. 'A striking building, the main elevation of which has been designed upon modernistic lines.' (*KW,* 16 November 1933:31.)

21. *KW,* 27 December 1962:9.   22. Open, 1985:22.

23. Ibid., 23; see photo in Doherty, 1977:48. Open says that this cinema was also known as the *West Belfast Picture Theatre,* though both the *Arcadian* and the *West Belfast Picture Theatre* are listed separately in *KYB,* 1920.

24. Open, 1985:24.   25. *Daily Cinema,* 3 December 1958:5.

26. *Kinematograph and Lantern Weekly,* 7 January 1915:51.

27. *Bioscope,* 1 May 1929:41.   28. *KW,* 15 November 1934:22.

29. *TC,* 5 March 1947:31.   30. *Bioscope,* 14 March 1912:766.

31. Open, 1985:59; see 58–63.   32. 25 March 1911 given as date in *DIA.*

33. Open, 1985:24.   34. *KW,* 7 November 1935:25.

35. Open, 1985:28; fb in *1947 directory* is given as Mr E. Crawford.

36. *KW,* 11 October 1934:18. Reference to a Winters as a partner with Crawford was made, but this name does not appear in *KYB.*

37. According to *KYB,* 1920, the proprietor was J. McCanana, while in *KYB,* 1921–4, it is listed as J. McCanava. It is likely that these were the same person, and is most probably Joseph McCavana (sometimes spelled as McCavanagh) who managed the *Arcadian* from its opening in the 1910s and later ran a number of cinemas. See Open, 1985:23.

38. Connolly and Dillon, 2001:74.

39. The directors of Classic Cinemas Ltd in 1923 were W.K. Gibson (chair); Mr H. Smylie, J.P. (vice

chair); Sir Crawford McCullough, MP; Mr S. Donald Cheyne, JP (*KYB*, 1924); *Bioscope*, 3 January 1924:52. *KYB*, 1936–48 cites 'Fitted with ARDENTE Deaf Aids & Wurlitzer Organ.' The site is now occupied by British Home Stores.

40. Open, 1985:29–31.   41. Open, 1985:32; photo in Doherty, 1997:51.

42. Open, 1985:35.

43. Open says that projectionist Billy Branagh, who came to the cinema in 1915, became the cinema's manager and remained in that position until it closed in 1959, though he is not listed as manager in any issue of *KYB*. (Open, 1985:34)

44. *KW*, 26 December 1957:12.   45. *IT*, 11 October 1977:5.

46. Open, 1985:36.   47. Ibid., 40.   48. Ibid., 41.

49. Ibid., 40–1.   50. Open, 1985:42.   51. Ibid., 143.

52. *KW*, 23 April 1959:9.   53. *KW*, 13 September 1934:30.

54. *Bioscope*, 22 March 1929:32.

55. *Kinematograph and Lantern Weekly*, 7 January 1915:51.

56. *KW*, 26 October 1932:37.   57. Open, 1985:46.

58. *Belfast Newsletter*, 8 December 1914, quoted Open, 1985:49.

59. *KW*, 7 November 1946:20.   60. Open, 1985:50.

61. Ibid., 144.   62. *KW*, 26 February 1942:30.

63. Open, 1985:144.   64. Ibid., 50.   65. Ibid., 50–1.

66. *KW*, 7 April 1955:9.   67. Open, 1985:51.

68. *KYB*, 1924–8, lists the proprietor as W. Curran, but this is probably a mistake as the owner seems to have been Michael Curran.

69. Open, 1985:52. In March 1930 it went 'all talkie'.

70. It is not known whether these were two separate screening venues, or whether there is an error in the *KYB* listings.

71. *IT*, 19 July 1993:4.   72. Doherty, 1997:39; Open, 1985:54.

73. *KW*, 30 August 1956:9.   74. *KW*, 27 September 1956:10.

75. Doherty, 1997:69.   76. Open, 1985:54; 41.

77. John Heaney, *IT*, 7 March 2008:11.

78. Open, 1985:146.   79. Ibid., 146.

80. William J. Moore is recorded as the architect of a cinema on High Street in 1911, which was a conversion by Alex Murduch (Culligree Road) of the extensive premises of house furnishers C. Millar & Co. (*DIA*). It is possible that this is the *Panopticon*.

81. Ibid., 147.   82. Ibid., 63.   83. Ibid., 64.

84. In 2004 Michael Open retired. See Ted Sheehy, 'Open to retire from Belfast's Queen's Film Theatre', *Screen Daily*, 21 September 2004; also Open, 1985:64–6.

85. Open, 1985:148.   86. Ibid., 67.   87. Ibid.,

88. *Irish News*, 10 November 1936:6; *KYB*, 1936–71.   89. Open, 1985:69.

90. Fionnuala O'Connor, 'What's not on', *IT*, 28 September 1977:8.

91. *Bioscope*, 6 February 1919:117.

92. Open, 1985:73; Doherty, 1997:103.

93. *KW*, 15 November 1934:22; according to Open, 1985:74, there were 1,000 seats in the stalls and 250 in the balcony.

94. Doherty, 1997:126–7.   95. Open, 1985:75.   96. Ibid., 150.

97. Doherty, 1997:122–3.   98. *IT*, 11 October 1977:5.

99. Open, 1985:85, 151.

1. David Clerkin, 'Storm Cinemas Group buys Belfast cineplex', *Sunday Business Post*, 28 May 2006.

2. Open, 1985:85.

3. This entry combines the *KYB* entries for *Castle Cinema*, *Cinema* and *Ideal Cinema*, as the separate *KYB* entries appear to be complementary.

4. *Bioscope*, 1 May 1929:41.   5. *IT*, 20 December 2008:10.

6. *KW*, 30 August 1956:9; 6 September 1956:7.

7. In that year, 1911, at least two plans for electric cinemas were drawn up by Peter William Cahill, for Lurgan, and for Portadown (Irish Provincial Theatres); it seems that neither were built. (*DIA*.)

8. *KW*, 12 April 1934:31.   9. *Larne Times*, 20 May 2010.

10. *KW*, 25 March 1937:16,   11. *IT*, 11 October 1977:5.

12. www.breakingnews.ie, 18 April 2007.

13. *KW*, 20 April 1939:19.   14. *KW*, 20 April 1939:19.

15. *KW*, 4 April 1957:9.   16. *KYB*, 1925–66; *KW*, 18 April 1963:8.

17. *KW*, 9 December 1937:14; *KYB*, 1937–71.

18. *KW*, 20 April 1944:17.   19. *IT*, 22 August 1922:3.   20. *KW*, 18 April 1963:8.

21. *KW*, 14 May 1936:33.   22. Connolly and Dillon, 2001:72.

23. Photo of cinema reproduced in *The Nationalist Centenary, 1883–1983*, p. 37; manager seems to have been Valentine Kavanagh, though not listed in *KYB*, 1921.

24. *RPC*, 1977:106, 109, 114, 115.   25. *IT*, 18 June 1938.

26. *RPC*, 1977:107, 115.   27. *1934 cinemas*, IFI.   28. *Anglo-Celt*, 7 June 1947:5.

29. *Meath Chronicle*, 16 May 1936:1.   30. *1934 cinemas*, IFI.

31. *Anglo-Celt*, 12 April 1947:4.   32. *Anglo-Celt*, 11 October 1947:2, 8.

33. *1934 cinemas*, IFI.   34. *Bioscope*, 27 February 1913:631.

35. *1934 cinemas*, IFI.   36. *RPC*, 1977:106, 109, 111, 114.

37. *The Anglo-Celt*, 7 July 2010.

38. Connolly and Dillon, 2001:72.

39. *Anglo-Celt*, 12 April 1947:4.   40. *Anglo-Celt*, 25 January 1947:4.

41. Ibid.   42. *Anglo-Celt*, 25 September 1948:4.

43. *RPC*, 1977:107, 110, 112, 115.   44. Connolly and Dillon, 2001:72.

45. *1934 cinemas*, IFI.

46. *Town Hall Cinema* reappears in *KYB*, 1950–1,with proprietor Ennis Cinemas, 500 seats. This may be a mistake in relation to the Ennis Cinemas Ltd owned *Gaiety Cinema*, which opened around this time. Entries for Ennis, Kilkee and Kilrush have drawn from Harvey O'Brien, 'Of palaces and planets', MA dissertation, UCD, unpublished, 1994.

47. *1934 cinemas*, IFI.   48. Connolly and Dillon, 2001:72.

49. *1934 cinemas*, IFI.   50. Ibid.   51. Ibid.

52. Ibid.

53. Information supplied by John Lynch (Clieveragh, Listowel), who was a projectionist and exhibitor in Kilkee in the 1960s.

54. *RPC*, 1977:108, 117. Listed in *KYB* as *Cinema Hall* (in 1920 and periodically from 1934 to 1971); listed also as *Cinema Bandon* from 1969–71.

55. *RPC*, 1977:108.   56. *Southern Star*, 30 April 1927:4.

57. *1934 cinemas*, IFI   58. *Southern Star*, 30 April 1927:4.

59. Cited as *Cinema* in *KYB*, 1930–9.   60. *RPC*, 1977:110–17.

61. *1934 cinemas*, IFI.

62. *RPC*, 1977:116–17; *KYB*, 1963–71, continued to list E.L. Goghlan as the cinema's proprietor.

63. *RPC*, 1977:108

64. See Sean O'Riordan, 'Plans for first drive-in cinema get go ahead', *Irish Examiner*, 23 July 2010; 'Drive-in cinema gears up for launch', 11 November 2010; Brian O'Connell, *IT*, 23 November 2010.

65. *KYB*, 1925, lists *The Coliseum* with proprietor J. Hurley, but this is most likely to have been a mistake as J. Hurley is listed from *KYB*, 1926, as proprietor of the *Pavilion*, with no further *KYB* entries for *The Coliseum*. Of course, another possibility is that Hurley changed the name of the venue between 1924 and 1925.

66. *RPC*, 1977:108, 116.   67. *1934 cinemas*, IFI.   68. *RPC*, 1977:108.

69. *1934 cinemas*, IFI.

70. Listed under Midleton, Co. Cork. This entry and *Cinema* may be the same venue.

71. *1934 cinemas*, IFI.   72. *Kinematograph and Lantern Weekly*, 7 January 1915:51.

73. *1934 cinemas*, IFI.   74. *RPC*, 1977:108, 109, 111, 116.

75. It is possible that N. Long is the same person as the Mr Long for which a cinema was to be erected in 1921 at 27 Cook Street, Cork. (*DIA*.)

76. Films were shown during fair in aid of the Munster Convalescent Home (McSweeney, 2003:86).

77. According to *Bioscope*, 18 December 1913:1207; 13 November 1913, McEwan also had cinemas in Limerick and Waterford.

78. Her surname is spelled Spender in *KYB*, 1922–5.   79. *1934 cinemas*, IFI.

80. McSweeney, 2003:7; 118–19.   81. Ibid., 118–26.

82. *Showcase*, April–June 1971:31

83. McSweeney, 2003:49–57; *IT*, 2 December 2005:2; Connolly and Dillon, 2001:72, give seats as 1,021.

84. McSweeney, 2003:4.   85. Ibid., 82–3.

86. *Bioscope*, 2 October 1913; 13 November 1913.   87. *1934 cinemas*, IFI.

88. McSweeney, 2003:58–66   89. Ibid., 5–6.

90. *Cork Examiner*, 27 December 1909; 4 January 1910; McSweeney, 2003:6.

91. *Irish Examiner*, March 27, 2007.

92. *Irish Independent*, 1 October 2010.

93. McSweeney, 2003:96–102.

94. Declan Hassett, 'Arts council funds cinema in Cork and Limerick', *Irish Examiner*, 25 July 2003; Michael Dwyer, *IT*, 25 July 2003:3. See also Rod Stoneman, 'The Kino in the age of the multiplex', *Cork Review*, 1997:28–30.
95. *1934 cinemas*, IFI.   96. McSweeney, 2003:4.
97. Professor Jolly's cinematographe was one of the acts. *Cork Examiner*, 28 April 1897; *IT*, 20 April 1897; *Cork Examiner*, 23 January 1897; Watters and Murtagh, 1975:170.
98. *RPC*, 1977:107.   99. *1934 cinemas*, IFI.   1. McSweeney, 2003:39–48.
2. Harford was a former Abbey Theatre actor. (McSweeney, 2003:29.)
3. *RPC*, 1977:111, 114.   4. McSweeney, 2003:29. 5. *1934 cinemas*, IFI; *1947 directory*.
6. *IT*, 16 August 1939:2.   7. McSweeney, 2003:77–82.
8. Ibid., 108. *KYB* gives a number of other versions of Corkery's name, all of which are wrong: J.F. Cirkeny (*KYB*, 1919); J.F. Corkary (*KYB*, 1922–5), and J.O. Corkerry (*KYB*, 1926–8).
9. *1934 cinemas*, IFI.
10. McSweeney, 2003: 11–28; *IT*, 13 May 1932:5; *Bioscope*, 26 May 1932; Mary Leland, 'Goodbye to the Golden Land…', *IT*, 19 September 1973:9; Elgy Gillespie, 'The Savoy Cinema, Cork', *IT*, 23 July 1976.
11. *Bioscope*, 6 February 1913:423.
12. *Bioscope*, 10 December 1914:1111; McSweeney, 2003:6–7.
13. McSweeney, 2003:75.   14. *1934 cinemas*, IFI.
15. *Cinema and Theatre Construction*, February 1939; McSweeney, 2003:75–8; *KYB*, 1930–8, lists J.T. Carpenter as the cinema's managing director, while McSweeney 2003:77, cites Whelan as owner and managing director of the *Washington*.
16. *RPC*, 1977:108.   17. *1934 cinemas*, IFI.
18. *Southern Star*, 22 August 1925:8, when cinema was put up for sale.
19. As Founds (sic) is listed for *Kinema*, Rathenly (sic) Road (*KYB*, 1918), this could be either *Kinema*, Rathealy Road, or *Kinema*, Patrick Street. Of course, it is possible that Pfounds took over *Cinema Theatre*, Rathealy Road, and then established a new venue at Patrick Street.
20. At 6a.m. on 2 October 1929, when the *Cinema*, Francis Street, was empty, a fire completely gutted the building in which the cinema was on the upper floor, with a garage and stores underneath. While the origin of this fire is unknown, the location of the cinema on the upper floor of a building is reminiscent of the Drumcollogher cinema fire five years earlier in which forty-eight people died. (*Southern Star*, 5 October 1929:7.)
21. *RPC*, 1977:109, 111, 114.   22. *1934 cinemas*, IFI.   23. *RPC*, 1977:106.
24. McSweeney, 2003: 82, 120. Seamus Quinn also ran a travelling cinema at Ballincollig, Berrings, Coachford, Killeagh and Lady's Bridge. After moving to Cork city, Quinn opened the *Cameo*, Military Road, in December 1964, initially as a ballroom, but installing the projectors from the old *Cameo*, Glanmire, to allow the venue to be used also a cinema from April 1965. (McSweeney 2003:120–1.)
25. *Southern Star*, 11 January 1930:7.   26. *1934 cinemas*, IFI.
27. *IT*, 17 April 1996:10.   28. Connolly and Dillon, 2001:72.
29. *Southern Star*, 2 November 1929:7.   30. *1934 cinemas*, IFI.
31. *RPC*, 1977:108.   32. *1934 cinemas*, IFI.
33. *Southern Star*, 16 May 1914; 19 September 1914:6.
34. *RPC*, 1977:108, 116.   35. Ibid., 107, 112.   36. *1934 cinemas*, IFI.
37. *RPC*, 1977:116.   38. *1934 cinemas*, IFI.
39. Connolly and Dillon, 2001:72.
40. It is possible that the Ormonde was a new cinema entirely, as B. O'Flynn & Sons designed a new cinema on Broderick Street in 1947 (*DIA*).
41. *RPC*, 1977:107, 109, 111, 116.   42. *1934 cinemas*, IFI.
43. Connolly and Dillon, 2001:72; 'End of an era as curtain closes on cinema', *Irish Examiner*, 6 April 2006; Carlton Screen Advertising, January 2006.
44. *1934 cinemas*, IFI.
45. This is most likely either to be the *Savoy* or *Star* cinemas, both of which have *KYB* entries from 1934.
46. *1934 cinemas*, IFI.   47. Ibid.   48. *Southern Star*, 30 April 1927:4.
49. *RPC*, 1977:112,116.
50. *Southern Star*, 24 August 1929:12, when cinema was put up for sale.
51. *Southern Star*, 31 July 1915:1; 22 January 1916:5.
52. *RPC*, 1977:106, 109, 111, 114, 115.
53. Thomas Horgan died in 1948. See 'Death of Irish film pioneer', *Youghal Tribune*, 2 October 1948.
54. *Daily Film Renter*, 10 August 1935.

55. *1934 cinemas*, IFI.   56. *Bioscope*, 29 October 1914; 11 February 1915:526.
57. 'Free State blaze', *Daily Film Renter*, 10 August 1935.
58. *Bioscope*, 29 October 1914.
59. See *Bioscope*, 29 October 1914; 10 December 1914:1111; *Daily Film Renter*, 10 August 1935. 400 seats in *1934 cinemas*, IFI.
60. *1934 cinemas*, IFI.   61. *KW*, 13 September 1934:30.
62. *KW*, 1 October 1936:21.   63. *KW*, 13 September 1934:30.
64. *KW*, 15 October 1936:37.   65. *KW*, 24 October 1940:15.
66. *Bioscope*, 20 October 1927:58.   66. *KW*, 15 August 1935:19.
68. *Bioscope*, 24 November 1927:67–8.   69. *KW*, 9 December 1937:14.
70. *Bioscope*, 17 November 1927:66–7.   71. *RPC*, 1977:108, 113, 116.
72. *Donegal Democrat*, 4 December 1982:17. 73. *RPC*, 107,116.
74. *KYB*, 1960, lists the proprietor as City Cinemas, Derry. All other *KYB* entries give owner as cited.
75. *IT*, 14 May 1932:5.   76. *RPC*, 1977:110, 116.   77. Ibid., 112.
78. *KW*, 21 August 1958:10. This cinema is referred to as Derrybeg-Falcarragh, though these are two distinct villages about ten miles apart.
79. *RPC*, 1977:116.   80. Ibid., 108; 112, 116.
81. *KW*, 21 August 1958:10. This cinema is referred to as Derrybeg-Falcarragh, though these are two distinct villages about ten miles apart.
82. *RPC*, 1977:108, 110, 112, 115. The address of Barry in *1947 directory* is mistakenly written as Duinboy House.
83. *1934 cinemas*, IFI.   84. *RPC*, 1977:107, 110, 112, 115.
85. *Irish Independent*, 8 May 1928:7.   86. Connolly and Dillon, 2001:72.
87. *Donegal News*, 19 July 1980:20.   88. Connolly and Dillon, 2001:72.
89. *RPC*, 1977:108, 116.   90. *RPC*, 1977:116; *KYB*, 1968–71, spells surname as McCauley.
91. The *1947 directory* lists the *Dromore Cinema* owned by James & R.W. Dale and with 280 seats as being in Dromore.
92. *Belfast Newsletter*, 29 March 2001.
93. In 2008, North Down museum launched a permanent exhibition, 'The great days of cinema', which focused on cinemas in Bangor.
94. *Bioscope*, 21 August 1929:60; also listed in *KYB* as *Adelphi Kinema*.
95. The cinema was destroyed by fire in October 1940. (*KW*, 10 October 1940:17.)
96. *IT*, 11 October 1977:5.   97. *KYB*, 1919, lists proprietor as R.J. White.
98. See Roisín Ingle, 'Silver screen dreamer', *IT* magazine, 9 December 2000.
99. As there is no entry for *Picture House* in *KYB*, 1930–2, and there is for *Arcadian Picture House*, it is probable that it is the same venue for both cinemas, especially as William Carlisle is associated with both names. In addition, the third listed cinema for Manor Street, the *Regal*, begins its listing in *KYB*, 1937, the year after *Picture House* ceases to be listed.
 1. *Bioscope*, 12 September 1928:3, records a change of ownership in 1928 from Dan Fraser to William Carlisle.
 2. *KW*, 7 November 1935:35; 5 December 1935:8.
 3. There also seems to have been a *Dromore Cinema*, 70 Dromore Street, Banbridge, Co. Down.
 4. Harold Gibson, 'Days of the silver screen in Dromore', *Dromore and District Local Historical Group Journal*, vol. 2, 1992.
 5. *KW*, 26 February 1942:30.   6. *Bioscope*, 17 November 1927:66–7.
 7. *Bioscope*, 27 February 1929:54.   8. *KW*, 20 August 1936:21.
 9. *KW*, 26 December 1957:12.   10. *KW*, 12 October 1933:13.
12. *KW*, 11 March 1937:37.   13. *Bioscope*, 3 January 1920:115.
14. *IT*, 11 October 1977:5. The *1947 directory* list *Regal Cinema* with br: Louis Hyman, which is possibly a misprint of *Regent Cinema*, as no Newtownards cinema with this name appears elsewhere.
15. *KW*, 4 April 1937:214A.
16. While the directory lists the br as R.G. this appears to be a mistake and elsewhere in the book is recorded E.G. or Eugene.
17. See Kearns and Maguire, 2006:454–7.
18. *Fingal Independent*, 14 May 2007.   18. Ibid., 487–90.
19. The company was prosecuted in 1912 under the Cinematograph Act 1909, for breaches of public safety (Maguire and Kearns, 2006:334). See also *KW*, 8 March 1934.
20. *Bioscope*, October 1912.
21. Clerk, Pembroke urban council, to James F. O'Neill, 13 December 1926, following council decision on 8 November 1926, DCA, quoted Kearns and Maguire, 2006:27; 20–30.

22. *Evening Herald*, 9 February 1935; see also Kearns and Maguire 2006:418–29.
23. *RPC*, 1977:115.
24. Maev Kennedy, 'Cinema into theatre', *IT*, 5 January 1977:8.
25. Kearns and Maguire 2006:22, also 20–36.
26. See Kearns and Maguire, 2006:22–7, 420, 423; *Dublin Evening Mail*, 28 July 1924 (advert.).
27. See advert., *Evening Press,*11 October 1973. This is not the same premises as *Regent* and *Grand* cinemas, which were at 13 Main Street.
28. *KW*, 13 April 1961:9; *KYB*, 1957–61.
29. *Evening Herald*, 25 February 1938; Kearns and Maguire, 2006:409–12.
30. Connolly and Dillon, 2001:72.
31. See Kearns and Maguire, 2006:304–6. From 1922, temporary or makeshift premises were used to screen films, including in school play-shed; a wooden hut at rear of Keenan's public house; and a portable building used by the local priest where the Texaco garage now stands; in 1940s, Fr McMahon ran film shows in the parochial hall. By then, a custom-built cinema had been erected.
32. See Maguire and Kearns, 2006:528–46.
33. Connolly and Dillon, 2001:72.
34. *IT*, 9 July 1999:13; *Sunday Business Post*, 6 June 1999:33; *IT* health supplement, 30 April 2004; 'Carlton wins UGC contract', *Sunday Business Post*, 20 February 2005; www.myvue.ie/cinmas/facilities, accessed, April 2010.
35. *IT*, 23 October 1917:5.   36. See Kearns and Maguire, 2006:98–105.
37. Connolly and Dillon, 2001:72.
38. *IT*, 12 May 1981:16; report on malicious damages case, award to Crumlin Cinema £30,000 plus costs.
39. 'Firemen stoned at blaze', *IT*, 7 April 1981:13.
40. See Kearns and Maguire, 2006:129–33.
41. *TC*, 9 November 1936.
42. *IT*. 4 August 1977; Robert O'Byrne, 'Films, fish oil feature in "ancient" history of the Academy Concert Rooms and cinema', *IT*, 22 February 2001:property 18. See also Kearns and Maguire, 2006:312–24, and Keenan, 2005:54.
43. Zimmermann, 2007:45–6.
44. *Irish Press*, 11 January 1939; 21 January 1939; *DIA*.
45. Harry Lush was associated with the Adelphi from 1943 when appointed assistant-manager; in 1944, he was appointed manager and held the position until 1981. He was born in Co. Sligo; received a BA Mod. in Celtic Languages, TCD; taught Irish at St Columbus College, Rathfarnham; and was a member of the Irish language commission.
46. *RPC*, 1977: 109, 111, 114.
47. Colman Cassidy, 'Jobs blow to city cinemas; Success of suburban multiplexes blamed', *Evening Press*, 16 September 1992:3; Katherine Donnelly, 'Suburban jobs for redundant cinema staff', *Evening Herald*, 2 July 1992: 18; Kathryn Rodgers, 'It's adieu to the Adelphi', *Irish Independent*: 28 November 1995: Dubliners, 10–11.
48. Elgy Gillespie, 'The Academy and the Ambassador cinemas', *IT*, 30 November 1976:10; Robert O'Byrne, *IT*, 22 February 2001:property 18.
49. See Kearns and Maguire, 2006:6–7.   50. Ibid., 40.
51. *Sunday Independent*, 1 March 1953:8.   52. Kearns and Maguire, 2006:51.
53. *Evening Herald*, 29 November 1911; *Evening Mail*, 1 December 1911, cited Kearns and Maguire, 2006:50.
54. *Bioscope*, 1 November 1911; 10 October 1912. *Bioscope*, 7 December 1911, seemingly erroneously, gives the seating as 685.
55. 'The Camden closes down after 36 years', *Evening Herald*, 28 August 1948. Some accounts suggest the Ellimans were partners in the cinema from the 1930s, though this may be a confusion with the Ellimans' nearby Theatre de Luxe.
56. *RPC*, 1977:112.   57. *IT*, 22 September 1949:5.
58. *IT*, 9 July 1952:5.   59. *IT*, 5 December 1953:7.
60. *IT*, 2 July 1954:7.   61. *Bioscope*, 6 January 1916.
62. See obituary for manager Michael E. Neary, C.O.K., *IT*, 4 October 1989. Renamed the *New Carlton* on 16 April 1938 with 2,000 seats. Converted to triple screen in 1976 with loss of 700 seats; in 1980 Carlton 4 was added with 126 seats. See Pat Liddy, 'Dublin today', *IT*, 15 August 1984.
63. *Evening Herald*, 31 March 1909.   64. Kearns and Maguire, 2006:86.
65. Zimmerman, 2007:69.
66. *Irish Builder and Engineer*, 'Premier Palace Theatre (Dublin)', 16 August 1913:536, reports on a

more ambitious building than seems to have been built. The theatre was to be used more for varieties than cinematographic exhibitions. At a cost of £40,000, it was to cover 3,200 sq ft, the stage was be as large as any of the exiting theatres in Dublin with a proscenium of 43ft wide and 28ft high; and with twelve dressing rooms and twelve private boxes. The cinematograph enclosure was to be placed at the back of the upper circle, with the winding room adjoining, while there were to be 2,210 seats: 920 on ground floor, same as Theatre Royal; gallery, nearly 700; circle 500. See *FJ*, 10 April 1915; *IT*, 5 April 1915:7; 6 April 1915:3.

67. 'Serious fire in Dublin; picture theatre gutted', *FJ*, 29 August 1911; *Evening Telegraph*, 28 August 1911.

68. Thomas MacNamara also designed plans for a cinema in South Great George's Street in 1919 for (Nolan's) Corinthian Picture Co. (*DIA*).

69. *Saturday Herald*, 8 February 1930; *Irish Independent*, 10 May 1930.

70. Zimmermann, 2007:71.

71. 'It's the last picture show – and the end of a cinematic era', *Evening Herald*, 5 July 1975; Zimmermann, 2007:72.

72. 'City's Odeon cinema to shutdown', *Evening Herald*, 12 July 1985:17.

73. *Irish Builder and Engineer*, 16 August 1913:536. See also Kearns and Maguire, 2006:117–19.

74. 'Curzon is refused new films', *Evening Press*, 1 and 2 January 1985.

75. Zimmermann, 2007:75.

76. See *Dublin Evening Mail*, 21 December 1912.

77. Charles E. Kelly, 'Dublin cinema memories' in O'Leary, 1976:17. See also 'An unwanted church', *FJ*, 28 August 1913.

78. Zimmermann, 2007:78. 79. See Kearns and Maguire, 2006:350–6.

80. Zimmermann, 2007:81.

81. *Bioscope*, 25 May 1911. *KYB*, 1919–20, gives the address as 45 Talbot Street.

82. *Bioscope*, 25 April 1912. 83. Kearns and Maguire, 2006:263.

84. See 'Capitol cinema to close down', *Evening Press*, 1 August 1974.

85. *Evening Press*, 9 April 1956; *Irish Press*, 14 January 1964; 'Embassy will be retained as cinema', *Evening Herald*, 9 June 1964.

86. Kearns and Maguire, 2006:150–1. See also chapter 7 for attempt to screen films there in the 1950s.

87. While Kearns and Maguire, 2006:163, give the company structure as noted in text, Keenan, 2006:72, identifies the cinema company as Fountain Picture House Co., with the principals as listed in text. 'Like many of the cheaper cinemas at the time, it attracted boisterous patrons and was poorly appointed' (Keenan, 2005: 72); Kearns and Maguire, 2006;163–7; E.M. Stafford, *Between the fountain and the gate*, Dublin.

88. Kearns and Maguire, 2006:178.

89. *Bioscope*, 10 October 1912; *Bioscope*, 28 May 1914:95. Kinetophone films – singing, talking, and reciting, 'were very popular with patrons, and it was a difficult matter to get a seat any time after 6 o'clock without waiting for some time.'

90. 'Grafton cinema is sold', *Irish Press*, 7 November 1973; *Irish Independent*, 6 November 1973. The cinema was bought by merchant bank Equity Securities Ltd for *c*.£200,000.

91. Keenan 2005:62.

92. *IT*, 11 January 1930:9. According to *Talkie Topics and Theatrical Review*, vol. 1, no. 2, 11 March 1931, Walter McNally was managing director of the Grand Central, as well as three unidentified other Dublin cinemas, and ones in Galway, Athlone and Westport.

93. Zimmermann, 2007:91. 94. Ibid., 76.

95. M. Kinsella, letter to the editor, *Evening Herald*, 2 July 1963.

96. *Bioscope*, 10 October 1912.

97. The Ancient Order of Foresters 'were mainly professional and business men, often in the greybeard stage, finding a relaxation from the humdrum of life in the myth of the native pine, the ash and the oak, and dressing up in a half-military half-woodland style. Their quaint and romantic kind of racialism gives colour to the Cyclops Episode in *Ulysses*, and it is caricatured by [Sean] O'Casey in the character of Uncle Peter in *The Plough and the Stars*'. (Watters & Murtagh, 1975:24.) The Irish National Foresters, founded in 1877, was an off-shoot of the Ancient Order of Foresters.

98. *Dublin Evening Mail*. 7 August 1920. 99. Kearns and Maguire, 2006:62.

1. 'The death of the Capitol', *IT*, 17 March 1972:10; *Evening Herald*, 2 March 1972.

2. *Irish Times*, 16 April 2011:3.

3. Kearns and Maguire, 2006:239–42.

4. *Dublin Evening Mail*, 21 December 1912. Obituary of George P Fleming, vice-chairman Capitol and Allied Theatres Ltd, (daughter, Mary Tower Fleming), *Irish Press*, 3 February 1950.

5. The manager may also have been J.J. Eppel or Simon Eppel, brother of Isaac. See also *Palace Cinema*, 42 Pearse Street.
6. *Irish Builder and Engineer*, vol. 54, 7 December 1912:699.
7. See *Irish Limelight*, vol. 2, no. 7, July 1918:1; drawing included of Charles McEvoy, proprietor and manager of Masterpiece.
8. *Irish Independent*, 10 November 1925:6; 17 November 1925:6, which covers raid on cinema on tenth, followed by arrest and charging of two men. On 20 November, three men planted a mine at the cinema's entrance, and half an hour later two plain-clothes policemen were shot and wounded, leading to six arrests. (ibid., 21 November 1925:7.)
9. *Irish Press*, 28 January 1954. See also Kearns and Maguire, 2006:247–50.
10. *IT*, 13 February 1922.
11. See *Bioscope*, 8 May 1919; 11 September 1919, on *Metropole*, *Corinthian* and *La Scala* being built. *FJ*, 4 February 1922:9; *IT*, 6 February 1922 (over 1,000 seats), 13 February 1922.
12. See *Bioscope*, 11 July 1912.
13. See interview with Odeon Ireland's Theatre controller Colman Conroy, *Sunday Independent*, 12 March 1972; and *Evening Press*, 14 March 1972.
14. See Maguire and Kearns, 2006:337–9.
15. *FJ*, 4 December 1912; 7 May 1913; *Dublin Evening Mail*, 30 November 1912:3; 3 December 1912:6.
16. Neil Callanan, 'Picture Palace site is saved', *Sunday Business Post*, 9 June 2002.
17. *Bioscope*, 10 October 1912:111; Charles E. Kelly, 'Dublin cinema memories' in O'Leary, 1976:16; Keenan, 2005:32; Kearns and Maguire, 2006:345–6.
18. *Irish Builder and Engineer*, 8 November 1913, reported that the *Pillar* would have 372 seats, 82 of which were to be in the gallery.
19. *Irish Builder and Engineer*, 27 February 1915:98.
20. *Irish Independent*, 26 May 2010: commercial property.
21. *Dublin Evening Mail*, 19 August 1955.
22. See *Evening Press*, 27 March 1967; *Evening Herald*, 27 February 1985.
23. The Pillar Room, Rotunda, is a smaller venue within the same complex, with distinctive marbled pillars. Together, the two rooms were often referred to as the Concert Rooms, Rotunda, or simply the Rotunda. Another part of the complex is occupied by the Gate Theatre.
24. *Kinematograph and Lantern Weekly*, 5 October 1916:53.
25. *IT*. 4 August 1977; Kieran Phillips, 'Sad last picture show', *Evening Press*, 29 October 1988:6.
26. Keenan 2005:16.
27. 'Landmark venue to host new €8m Dublin library', *IT*, 1 September 2007:4. See also 'Dublin cinema to be financial centre', *IT*, 19 September 1988; Frank Kilfeather, 'Famous cinema may become financial centre', 12 July 1988:12.
28. *Irish Independent*, 29 November 1929; *Saturday Herald*, 30 November 1929.
29. 'Tribute to cinema manager', *Evening Herald*, 8 February 1967; 'An Irishman's Diary', *IT*, 21 November 1969, on conversion to twin screen; Hugh Lambert, 'Night of the first picture show', *Sunday Press*, 27 July 1975:8, on being tripled; Donald Clarke, 'Lowering the tone', *IT*: the ticket 7, on Savoy 1. The Savoy 2 reopened after 'extensive renovations' on 1 July 1994 (*IT*, 1 July 1994:12); Kearns and Maguire, 2006:458–67.
30. *IT*, 19 December 1935.
31. Gay Byrne, *Sunday Independent*, 23 November 2003:living 18: Byrne was assistant manager at the *Strand* when *Roman Holiday* was shown.
32. *Bioscope*, 2 November 1911:367.   33. Keenan, 2005:38.
34. *In Dublin*, no. 83, 16 August 1979; 'Deluxe cinema gets £20,000 programme change', *Sunday Independent*, 12 August 1979.
35. See also, Kearns and Maguire, 2006:439–46.
36. 'New Tivoli Cinema', *Irish Independent*, 22 December 1934.
37. See also Kearns and Maguire, 2006:515–27.   38. Connolly and Dillon, 2001:72.
39. 'Nine-screen cinema for city', *Evening Press*, 26 January 1994; 'Monster cinema aims for maximum visual impact', *IT*, 12 November 2003:B4.
40. Luke McKernan in McCourt (ed.), 2010:21.
41. *Bioscope*, 23 December 1909; 30 December 1909; 10 October 1912; 23 September 1915; Liam O'Leary, *IT*, 8 January 1980.
42. *Evening Telegraph*, 21 December 1912.
43. See Kearns and Maguire, 2006:1; 566–70.   44. *IT*, 13 January 2000:28.
45. Connolly and Dillon, 2001:72.   46. Zimmermann, 2007:109.

47. Kearns and Maguire, 2006:502–3.   48. Ibid., 326–31.
49. Ibid., 502–3.
50. *IT*, 23 September 1970:14; 19 October 1971:14; *Showcase*, October/December 1970:24; Kearns and Maguire, 2006:82–3, say the cinema did not fully close until 28 September 1979, so perhaps the 400-seat balcony area was a cinema during the 1970s.
51. *KW*, 24 October 1957.
52. *RPC*, 1977: 112. See also Kearns and Maguire, 2006:42–4.
53. Connolly and Dillon, 2001:72.
54. Rose Doyle, 'The Rocky Horror road to success', *Irish Independent*, 22 May 2002.
55. Neil Callanan, *Sunday Business Post*, 18 September 2005.
56. *Evening Herald*, 29 July 1950; 29 February 1950.
57. See Kevin Murray, *Some Lucan memories*, cited by Kearns and Maguire, 2006:360–74.
58. Kearns and Maguire, 2006:174–6.
59. Thre is a drawing of F.A. Sparling in *Irish Limelight*, vol. 1, no. 8, August 1917:1. See also *Irish Builder and Engineer*, 16 August 1913:536.860. Sparling became manager of the *Sandford* from 18 April 1915.
60. *IT*, 18 April 1925:9.
61. 'Dublin cinema fire', *IT*, 25 October 1927; reprinted, 25 October 1997.
62. Kearns and Maguire, 2006:476.
63. Letter from son, William Dermot King, *Evening Press*, 12 January 1971; John J. Dunne, '"The End" for another cinema', *Evening Press*. 21 January 1981.
64. *Evening Herald*, 30 June 1962, which reported that the *State* was being given first-run status.
65. *IT,* 24 April 1954. Such a description of course not only propels us forward to the immersive experience forgrounded in the world of virtual reality and indeed 3D cinema, but also backwards to Robert Barker and the panorama.
66. 'Northerner breaks into Dublin cinema circuit', *Sunday Independent*, 8 June 1975.
67. Kearns and Maguire, 2006:430.   68. Ibid., 357–8.
69. See ibid., 447–53.
70. Ibid., 386–8. *Irish Builder*, vol. 54, November 1912:664; vol. 55, 1 February 1913:83.
71. It has not been possible to discover why the *Rathmines Picture Palace* closed for a number of months so soon after opening, and then reopened as the *Princess*. See also Kearns, *The Prinner*, 2005.
72. *Bioscope*, 14 November 1912; 7 December 1912; 3 April 1913; 27 November 1913. See *Bioscope*, 13 August 1925:80, on redecoration of cinema after ink-throwing incident as protest against screening of film of Prince of Wales. *Irish Builder*, vol. 54, November 1912:664; vol. 55, 1 February 1913:83.
73. Kearns, 2005:45; Adrian McLoughlin, 'The picture palaces', *Evening Press*, 19 September 1977.
74. See Kearns, 2005; Kearns and Maguire, 2006:375–82. Kearns worked in the *Princess*, 1952–6.
75. Connolly and Dillon, 2001:72.
76. See *Sunday Independent*, 3 December 1978:5; Kearns and Maguire, 2006:483–6.
77. *Bioscope*, 10 October 1912:111.   78. *IT*, 19 September 1918:3.
79. *Irish Independent*, 26 November 1927.
80. See Kearns and Maguire, 2006:395–401; *Evening Press*, 4 January 1965.
81. Connolly and Dillon, 2001:72.   82. *RPC*, 1977: 107, 111, 117.
83. *Screen International*, 26 February 1983:10; *Sunday Business Post*, 11 May 1997:12.
84. Kearns and Maguire, 2006:500–1.   85. Connolly and Dillon, 2001:72.
86. *Irish Press*, 1 July 1938; 'Cinema for sale', *IT*, 30 January 1984.
87. See Kearns and Maguire, 2006:15–19.
88. *KYB*, 1949–57, gives the company's name as Ekn Ltd; however, the address is the same for the company as well as for proprietor Con O'Mahony.
89. *1934 cinemas*, IFI.   90. *RPC*, 1977:107, 110, 115.
91. Ibid., 107, 112.   92. *1934 cinemas*, IFI.
93. *RPC*, 1977:106, 109, 111, 113.
94. *Connacht Sentinel*, 10 October 1975:16; 17 October 1975:23.
95. *Connacht Sentinel*, 26 September 1995:1.   96. *Connacht Sentinel*, 9 July 1935:3.
97. *1934 cinemas*, IFI. McNally gave an undertaking to Galway corporation in 1933 to make alterations and improvements costing £2,000 to the cinema, including a new asbestos roof and a fire exit. (*KW*, 12 January 1933:17.)
98. *Connacht Tribune*, 7 January 1933:9; 14 January 1933:28.
99. 776 seats in *Connacht Tribune*, 25 November 1939; *KYB*, 1950–61; 764 in *1947 directory*.
 1. *IT*, 13 April 2005:commercial property 4.

2. *IT*, 29 March 1913:11; *Connacht Tribune*, 30 January 1915:7; 6 March 1915:8.
3. Connolly and Dillon, 2001:72.
4. *Irish Independent*, 19 May 2008; *Galway Independent*, 16 July 2008; *Connacht Sentinel,* 18 May 2010:11; 8 June 2010:5; *City Tribune*, 1 October 2010:6.
5. *Galway Observer*, 15 December 1934.
6. *City Tribune*, 15 March 1985:9.
7. *RPC*, 1977:108, 109, 111, 114, 115.   8.   *1934 cinemas*, IFI.
9. *Connacht Tribune*, 24 July 1926:9, 10, 16; *IT*, 21 July 1926:7; 24 July 1926:9.
10. *Connacht Tribune*, 15 September 1928:1.
11. When Ryan was found guilty in 1947 of not complying with entertainments tax requirements, he was fined £2,950. It was reported that he also owned cinemas in Athenry, and Ahascragh, Co. Galway; Milltown-Malbay, Co. Clare; and Athleague, Co. Roscommon. (*Connacht Tribune*, 10 May 1947:6.) This followed a similar offence at the cinema in 1944. (*Connacht Tribune*, 11 November 1944:6.)
12. *1934 cinemas*, IFI.   13.   *IT*, 13 April 2005: commercial property 4.
14. *RPC*, 1977: 107; 112.   15.   Ibid., 115.
16. *Sunday Independent*, 21 November 1999:6.
17. Brendan Kennelly in McBride and Flynn (eds), 1996:49.
18. *The Kingdom*, 5 August 2004; 20 August 2003.   19.   *1934 cinemas*, IFI.
20. *RPC*, 1977:116.   21.   *1934 cinemas*, IFI.   22.   Ibid.
23. See also *IT*, 21 June 2001.   24.   *Kerryman*, 10 April 1987:28.
25. *RPC*, 1977:106, 109, 111, 113, 114, 115.   26.   *1934 cinemas*, IFI.
27. Connolly and Dillon, 2001:72.
28. Though *KYB*, 1935–48, listed Picturedrome with 750 seats during this period, this is perhaps a confusion with *Casino* at same location.
29. *1934 cinemas*, IFI.   30.   *RPC*, 1977:116.   31.   *1934 cinemas*, IFI.
32. Connolly and Dillon, 2001:72.   33.   *The Kingdom*, 27 October 2005.
34. *RPC*, 1977:106, 109, 111, 114, 116.   35.   *1934 cinemas*, IFI.
36. Ibid.   37.   Michael Dwyer in McBride and Flynn (eds), 1996:123.
38. Connolly and Dillon, 2001:72: 4 screens/919 seats.
39. *Kerryman*, 12 August 1950:14.   40.   *1934 cinemas*, IFI.
41. *RPC*, 1977:106, 109, 111, 114. *Kildare Nationalist*, 8 January 2004, states that the opening of the *Grove* led to the closure of *Bob's* cinema. John Berry who worked at Grove for twenty-one years recounts some of his memories in *Kildare Nationalist*, 15 January 2004.
42. *KW*, 28 August 1958:9.   43.   *1934 cinemas*, IFI.   44.   Ibid.
45. Ibid.   46.   *Southern Star*, 2 May 1918:6.
47. *IT*, 29 December 1925:6.   48.   *RPC*, 1977:107, 109, 111, 114, 115.
49. Paddy Melia, booking/advertising manager of *Dara* cinema, quoted, *Kildare Nationalist*, 9 November 2003. See also *Kildare Nationalist*, 16 September 2004, for a report on a fire which broke out in the cinema's foyer.
50. *1934 cinemas*, IFI.   51.   *RPC investigation*, 1977:107, 110, 112, 114.
52. *1934 cinemas*, IFI, which calls it the *Palace Cinema*.
53. See *Kildare Nationalist*, 3 October 2003; 18 May 2005.
54. *Kildare Nationalist*, 19 January 2006.
55. See also *Kildare Nationalist*, 4 December 2003.   56.   *1934 cinemas*, IFI.
57. *Munster Express*, 16 June 1923:5.   58.   *1934 cinemas*, IFI.
59. Ibid.   60.   *IT*, 9 May 1932:5.   61.   *1934 cinemas*, IFI.
62. Connolly and Dillon, 2001:72.
63. *RPC*, 1977:106, 109, 111, 114, 115.   64.   Ibid., 108, 112.
65. *1934 cinemas*, IFI.   66.   *Munster Express*, 6 July 1928:5.
67. *Munster Express*, 31 July 1931:8; 7 August 1931:8.
68. 'The cinema is, no doubt, a rare treat to the inhabitants of rural districts far from towns. Many of the dwellers in country districts live miles from town, and the cinema show is a great novelty to them.' The company was next visiting Harristown, Waterford. (*Munster Express*, 26 March 1926:5.)
69. *Munster Express*, 28 October 1927:5. The company was moving on to Templeorum after a two-week stay at Fiddown.
70. *Munster Express*, 9 September 1916:5.   71.   *RPC*, 1977:170.
72. *1934 cinemas*, IFI.   73.   Ibid.   74.   Ibid.
75. *RPC*, 1977:107, 110, 112.   76.   Ibid., 107, 109, 112, 114.
77. *Evening Press*, 13 December 1985; *Laois Nationalist*, 14 April 2000.

78. *Laois Nationalist*, 14 April 2000.
80. *The Nationalist*, 7 June 1968.
82. In 1945 Patrick Munden drew up plans for a cinema in Rathdowney (*DIA*).
83. *RPC*, 1977:170
84. See Tommy Moran, 'Nicholas's: a view from the gods', *Leitrim Journal*, 1976:24–5.
85. *Leitrim Observer*, 11 October 2006. Ned McKiernan, Cavan, and Ned McGowan, Drumshanbo, provided mobile cinemas in the village before a permanent cinema opened. Dermot Grey, Drumshanbo, 'brought his Marian portable picture shows to almost every hall in the county.' (Ibid.)
86. *Anglo-Celt*, 6 May 2004:15.
87. *Leitrim Observer*, 21 September 1929.
88. 'Leitrim's mobile flicks extend to Tubbercurry', *Sligo Weekender*, 2 October 2007.
89. The Limerick entries were read by and in a number of instances further refined by Declan McLoughlin, December 2010.
90. *RPC*, 1977:170.   91. See www.lcc.ie.   92. *1934 cinemas*, IFI.
93. *RPC*, 1977:108, 112, 116   93. *1934 cinemas*, IFI.
95. David O'Riordan, 'The travelling picture shows', in Pat O'Donovan (ed.), *Knockfeena and district annual journal*, vol. 3, 1991:35.
96. *RPC*, 1977:108, 112, 116.
97. *Limerick Leader*, 12 April 1930; *IT*, 12 April 1930:10.
98. *RPC*, 1977:106, 115.   99. *1934 cinemas*, IFI.
 1. *Limerick Chronicle*, 11 November 1930; 25 November 1930.
 2. This account of the *Athenaeum* draws on James McMahon, "If walls could talk", The Limerick Athenaeum – the story of an Irish theatre since 1852', online, 2010.
 3. Rachael Finucane, *Limerick Independent*, 12 March 2008.
 4. Declan Hassett, 'Arts council funds cinema in Cork and Limerick', *Irish Examiner*, 25 July 2003.
 5. See *Limerick Leader*, 23 March 1940, on opening of cinema.
 6. *RPC*, 1977:109, 111, 114.
 7. *Sunday Business Post*, 24 August 2003:18, includes a photo of the derelict cinema.
 8. *1934 cinemas*, IFI.
 9. These may have been the lessees following an advert. seeking to let the 400 seat cinema in 1924. (*IT*, 16 May 1924:12.)
10. *IT*, 6 November 1920:10. This figure was included in an advertisement in which the owner was seeking to sell the cinema as a 'going concern'.
11. *RPC*, 1977:107.   12. *1934 cinemas*, IFI.
13. Connolly and Dillon, 2001:73.   14. *1934 cinemas*, IFI.
15. *RPC*, 1977:112.   16. *Limerick Leader*, 14 December 1935.
17. See '€10m Limerick cinema', *Sunday Business Post*, 19 September 2004. Original plans were for 14 screens to be in place by Christmas 2005, but this was not realized.
18. *Limerick Leader*, 25 January 1922.   19. *1934 cinemas*, IFI.
20. Ibid.   21. See *IT*, 21 June 2001.   22. Connolly and Dillon, 2001:73.
23. *Westmeath Examiner*, 18 December 1920:6.   24. Connolly and Dillon, 2001:73.
25. *Longford Leader*, 13 February 1981.   26. *RPC*, 1977:112, 115.
27. *1934 cinemas*, IFI.
28. It is possible that *Cinema* and *Staffords Cinema* are the same venue, while J.J. Stafford's *Picturedrome* may have been his first cinema.
29. An advertisement in the *IT*, 25 October 1915:1, seeking a violist for the cinema, suggests the cinema opened around this time. *Picturedrome*, Kilashee Street, seems to have been an earlier Stafford cinema.
30. *1934 cinemas*, IFI.   31. Ibid.
32. *Dundalk Democrat*, 31 August 1940:4. See Canice O'Mahony, *Democrat & People's Journal*, 3 May 1997:24. O'Mahony is a former Dundalk county engineer whose father and uncle worked in Dundalk cinemas. Ardee resident Benny Matthews, a former patron of the *Bohemian*, created a miniature cinema in his back garden shed using one of the two original 35mm Kalee II projectors from the *Bohemian* and 15 flip-up seats from the *Magnet*, Dundalk, to screen films. (*Argus*, 13 June 1997:43.)
33. See *Drogheda Independent*, 11 September 1937:6. At opening of cinema, Dr Lyons, bishop-elect of Kilmore, commented that Sunday closing of cinemas had been respected in the town for forty years due to the wishes of a 'venerable' local clergyman, but the previous year Sunday evening opening had been permitted after religious services, and this had worked satisfactorily.
34. *RPC*, 1977:106, 109, 113, 114, 115. See also *Drogheda Independent*, 18 September 1937.

35. *1934 cinemas*, IFI; *Democrat & People's Journal*, 3 May 1997:24.

36. *Bioscope*, 11 May 1911:271.   37. *Bioscope*, 28 May 1914:95.

38. RPC, 1977:99, 100.   39. *1934 cinemas*, IFI.   40. *Bioscope*, 28 May 1914:95.

41. Canice O'Mahony, *Democrat & People's Journal*, 3 May 1997:24.

42. *Dundalk Democrat*, 17 May 1947:2, on opening.   43. *RPC*, 1977:106, 109, 111, 113.

44. *Democrat & People's Journal*, 3 May 1997:24.   45. *RPC*, 1977:106, 110, 114.

46. Connolly and Dillon, 2001:73.   47. *1934 cinemas*, IFI.

48. See *Democrat and People's Journal*, 12 October 1912:4. See also reference to him with regard to *Electric Theatre*, Drogheda.

49. *1934 cinemas*, IFI. See *Drogheda Democrat*, 19 October 1912:4, on opening of cinema. Another travelling film show from this period and area is Farney's Cinema Co. which visited Carrickmacross in October 1912 with the Carpentier versus Klaus fight film. See *Drogheda Democrat*, 19 October 1912:3.

50. *Dundalk Democrat*, 12 October 1912. See also Jim Garry, *The streets and lanes of Drogheda*, Drogheda: Old Drogheda Society, c.1999.

51. *1934 cinemas*, IFI.

52. Canice O'Mahony, *Democrat & People's Journal*, 3 May 1997:24.

53. *Western People*, 18 February 2004, gives the cinema's location as Tone Street.

54. *KYB*, 1934, cites this cinema as *Astoria*; p: T. Ryan. This may have been an error in relation to the *Estoria*, Teeling Street.

55. 'A magnificent stone-fronted glass and concrete structure girdled with a necklace of quad poster niches.' (*Western People*, 18 February 2004.)

56. Discussions for a cinema multiplex date back at least to August 2001. (See *Western People*, 16 August 2001 and 29 August 2001.)

57. *RPC*, 1977:110, 112, 115.   58. *1934 cinemas*, IFI.

59. Quoted, 'Ballina site sought for major cinema complex', *Western People*, 16 August 2001.

60. In December 1933, Walsh was fined £50 at Ballinrobe district court for failing to issue cinema tickets with entertainments tax stamps, a not uncommon prosecution in rural Ireland. (*Connacht Tribune*, 23 December 1933:6.)

61. *1934 cinemas*, IFI.

62. *KYB*, 1919, gives the number of seats as 1,000 seats, which is almost certainly an error.

63. It is probable that *KYB*, 1949, is in error as regards the name of Fr Prendergast, and this was corrected the following year.

64. *RPC*, 1977:107, 116.   65. *Western People*, 22 November 2006.

66. 'Sliver screen lights up in Erris', *Western People*, 15 October 2008.

67. Ibid.

68. The cinema was closed by 1993 when it was the subject of criticism as it was a derelict site lowering the tone of the street. In April 2005, Castlebar town council, having bought the site in 1999 from County Enterprises Ltd for €300,000, sold it to property developers Alan Park Properties for over €1.3 million. (*Western People*, 27 April 2005.) The undeveloped cinema was sold for the third time in 2006. (*Western People*, 26 April 2006; 21 June 2006; *Mayo News*, 19 September 2006.)

69. *RPC*, 1977: 110; 112; 116.   70. *1934 cinemas*, IFI.   71. Connolly and Dillon, 2001:73.

72. *Western People*, 14 September 2005.   73. *Western People*, 1 Octoebr 1997.

74. *1934 cinemas*, IFI.   75. Ibid.   76. *Mayo News*, 2 September 1992.

77. *RPC*, 1977: 106; 109; 111; 115; *Western People*, 14 April 2004.

78. *Western People*, 12 December 2001; 14 April 2004. Official opening: 3 June 2004 (*Western People*, 10 June 2004).

79. *Meath Chronicle*, 25 April 1914:5; 16 May 1914:5. The council's building inspector objected to a licence being issued because of inadequate exits, despite assurances that the buiding was satisfactory. The council issued a one-month provisional licence. (*Meath Chronicle*, 6 June 1914:2.)

80. *Meath Chronicle*, 28 May 1983:23.   81. *RPC*, 1977:106, 110, 112, 115.

82. Connolly and Dillon, 2001:73.

83. *Meath Chronicle*, 5 April 1997:11.

84. Listed in *KYB*, 1946–8, as Tringate Street   85. *Meath Chronicle*, 1 April 1939:6.

86. William Kennedy (aged 45), also owned the *Lyric*, Navan, and was principal of Meath vocational education school; his mother and his sister were killed in the fire that destroyed the cinema on 9 February 1949. Mr Kennedy died after he re-entered the burning building having seen his wife and two children to safety. (*Anglo-Celt*, 12 February 1949:12.)

87. *RPC*, 1977:107, 110, 112, 116.

88. *Meath Chronicle*, 4 August 1951:5.

89. *1934 cinemas*, IFI.   90. *Meath Chronicle*, 31 October 1981:20.
91. *RPC*, 1977:116.   92. *Meath Chronicle*, 28 April 1923:1.
93. *Meath Chronicle*, 24 January 1914:5.
94. *Meath Chronicle*, 11 October 1930:7.
95. *Meath Chronicle*, 16 November 1974:11.   96. *Anglo-Celt*, 1 November 1947:1.
97. *Anglo-Celt*, 22 February 1958:6.   98. *Anglo-Celt*, 1 November 1947:1.
99. *Meath Chronicle*, 7 May 1938:10; *Anglo-Celt*, 23 April 1938:11; *Irish Independent*, 22 April
    1938:8.
 1. *RPC*, 1977:108, 116.   2. Ibid., 108.
 3. There is a single entry, *KYB*, 1930, for *Cinema*, a word that does not reappear until *KYB*, 1949. It
    is not known if this is the same premises.
 4. *RPC*, 1977:108.   5. *Anglo-Celt*, 4 November 1966:1.
 6. *Anglo-Celt*, 15 March 1974:10.   7. *Irish Press*, 24 August 1985.
 8. *Anglo-Celt*, 26 August 1944:2; 17 March 1945:23.   9. *1934 cinemas*, IFI.
10. Connolly and Dillon, 2001:73.
11. *Anglo-Celt*, 2 December 1939:4.   12. *Anglo-Celt*, 25 April 1964:1.
13. *1934 cinemas*, IFI.   14. *RPC*, 1977:107, 110, 112, 115.
15. *1934 cinemas*, IFI.   16. *Westmeath Examiner*, 28 November 1925:4.
17. *RPC*, 1977:106, 110, 111, 115.   18. Ibid., 108, 109, 111, 115.
19. *1934 cinemas*, IFI.   20. *IT*, 26 November 1912:8.
21. Connolly and Dillon, 2001:73.   22. *1934 cinemas*, IFI.
23. *Leitrim Observer*, 19 September 1931:4.   24. Ibid.
25. *Leitrim Observer*, 29 June 1929:1.   26. *IT*, 19 February 1927.
27. *KW*, 22 February 1945:32D.   28. *1934 cinemas*, IFI.
29. *RPC*, 1977:108, 113.   30. *1934 cinemas*, IFI.   31. Ibid.
32. *RPC*, 1977:108, 113.
33. *Sligo Champion*, 27 May 2009; 12 May 2010: 20 October 2010.
34. Connolly and Dillon, 2001:73.
35. 'Gaiety opens twelve screen complex', *Sligo Weekender*, 4 March 2003. Officially opened on 5
    March 2003.
36. *Sligo Champion*, 26 October 1935:5; listed in *KYB*, 1937–71.
37. *RPC*, 1977:106, 109, 112, 114, 117.
38. *Sligo Weekender*, 13 November 2002; 11 December 2002; 3 April 2003; 22 February 2005.
39. *Bioscope*, 27 February 1913:631. Venue named after Dr Gilhooly, Catholic bishop of Sligo.
40. *1934 cinemas*, IFI.
41. *IT*, 17 February 1987:16.   42. *RPC*, 1977:118.
43. *Irish Independent*, 15 March 1938.
44. *Bioscope*, 27 February 1913:631, spells this name as Gilbannon, presumed here as a mistake.
45. *1934 cinemas*, IFI.   46. *Nenagh Guardian*, 14 October 1922:2.
47. *IT*, 19 April 1923:8.
48. Prior to the *Stella*'s opening, in 1936 Vincent Byrne rented the *Clarke Hall* for a three-month film
    season, while in the late 1940s, *Brereton's Hall* was used for occasional film shows. Eventually, the
    parish priest, Canon (later Dean) Cahill spearheaded a local committee which established the *Stella*,
    with money earned earmarked for improving the existing parish church or for erecting a new one.
    (See Doorley, n.d. [*c*.2002] 43ff.), 'At no stage did the Canon exercise any form of censorship.'
    (Ibid., 50.) *Stella Days*, a film directed by Thaddeus O'Sullivan based on these events, began film-
    ing in late 2010, with Martin Sheen as the priest. (*IT*, 2 November 2010).
49. *RPC*, 1977:116, as Castle; *RPC*, 1977:107, 110, 112, as *Strand*.
50. *1934 cinemas*, IFI.
51. 'Closing for alterations', according to *Munster Express*, 22 August 1947:4. It is unclear whether it
    reopened, and subsequent *KYB* listings, especially of prioprietor Patrick McGrath and Castle
    Cinemas Ltd, are identical for the *Park View* and *Castle* cinemas, suggesting that this may be a mis-
    take in *KYB* as the *Park View* may not have reopened considering McGrath had opened the *Castle*
    sixteen months earlier. To complicate matters, the *Park View* as well as the *Castle* are referred to
    as the *Strand* in the 1970s.
52. *Irish Limelight*, September 1917:7. In 1923, McGrath was prosecuted in 1923 for non-compliance
    with the collection of entertainments tax. (*Munster Express*, 21 April 1923:4.) During the court
    hearing, it was revealed that the box office receipts for the cinema during the week of 19 May 1923
    were £34, while expenses were £30 12s. 2d., with tax of a further £5 12s., making a loss of £1 2s.
    2d. on the week if the full tax was paid. (*Munster Express*, 2 June 1923:6.) The impulse in such

financially marginal cinemas not just in the 1920s, but through the following decades, was to try to evade paying the tax whenever possible. This is attested to by the frequency with such cases appeared in provincial courts.

53. *KYB*, 1970, gives the cinema's seat number as 898, the same as it does for the *Castle*, suggesting on-going confusion between the two names, perhaps even in *RPC*, 1977.
54. *Sligo Champion*, 4 January 1930:7; 11 January 1930:7.
55. *RPC*, 1977:106, 109, 112, 115.   56. *1934 cinemas*, IFI.
57. *KYB*, 1949–52, lists a *Cinema* in Clonmel, Co. Monaghan, even though no such place exists in that county. This is a further reminder that the *KYB* listings are far from being infallible.
58. Connolly and Dillon, 2001:73. Plans by Ward Anderson to develop a nine-screen complex as part of the second phase development of the Showgrounds shopping centre were turned down by Bord Pleanala in 2010. (*The Nationalist*, 2 November 2010.)
59. *Clonmel Theatre*, aka *John Magner's Theatre* and the *Oisín Cinema* were amalgamated under the name Clonmel (Associated) Theatre Co. *c.*1924 (*KYB*, 1924–9), with general manager W.B. Symes, by new proprietor William O'Keefe.
60. *1934 cinemas*, IFI.   61. *RPC*, 1977:106, 109, 111, 114, 116.
62. Ibid.   63. *KW*, 8 February 1940; *KYB*, 1942–71.
64. *Nenagh Guardian*, 3 February 1923:5.   65. *1934 cinemas*, IFI.
66. *RPC*, 1977:114.   67. *Nenagh Guardian*, 2 October 1915:2,6.
68. In October/November 1922, Edward O'Kennedy wrote to Nenagh urban council suggesting use of the hall be divided between his cinema company and Ormond, a proposal to which the council agreed. (*Nenagh Guardian*, 11 November 1922:5.) It seems Ormond may not have used the Town Hall after this time, and the council reported difficulty in collecting rent arrears of £25. (*Nenagh Guardian*, 9 June 1923:5.) However, it seems that when *Ormond Cinema* opened, O'Kennedy took over *Town Hall Cinema*. Both O'Kennedy and Ormond proprietor William Maloney were found guilty in December 1927 of failing to issue an admission ticket stamped with the entertainment tax charge. (*Nenagh Guardian*, 24 December 1927:2.)
69. *1934 cinemas*, IFI.
70. *Nenagh Gaurdian*, 1 November 1924:2; *IT*, 29 October 1924:9. Gaumont Film Co. later sought unsuccessfully to force Powell to pay for the rent of films contracted before the cinema was burned down. (*Nenagh Guardian*, 30 May 1925:5.)
71. *Nenagh Guardian*, 24 July 1982:7.   72. *RPC*, 1977:107, 110, 112, 116.
73. Listed as *The Cinema*, *1934 cinemas*, IFI.   74. *RPC*, 1977:116.
75. *1934 cinemas*, IFI.
76. Moynan was fined for failing to comply with entertainment tax regulations. (*Nenagh Guardian*, 6 June 1925:5.)
77. *RPC*, 1977:106, 109, 111.
78. J. Kennedy, *A chronology of Thurles, 580–1978*, revised and updated, n.d (1978), p. 71; orig. Thurles: Tipperary Star, 1945.
79. *IT*, 11 March 2009.   80. *1934 cinemas*, IFI.
81. *RPC*, 1977:108; 112; 114.   82. *1934 cinemas*, IFI.
83. See three photo sequence of the demolition of the cinema in 1978 in J. Kennedy, *A chronology of Thurles, 580–1978*, 1978:76.
84. *Nenagh Guardian*, 15 October 1977:5.   85. *RPC*, 1977:107, 110, 112, 115.
86. It was opened by bicycle shop owner Mr Evans, following a fire in Tipperary town in 1940 that destroyed the town's cinema. It had 'baskets of flowers suspended from the hugely jutting ledge that formed a roof above pale marble steps, and a motif of butterflies on curtains that marvellously changed colour several times before each programme began.' (William Trevor in McBride and Flynn (eds), 1996:127.) This cinema provided the inspiration behind Trevor's novella, *Nights at the Alexandra*, New York: Harper & Row, 1987.
87. The cinema burned down after two boys fell asleep in it, and in order to find their way out in the darkness they lit a match, which set fire to nitrate film. The boys were rescued, but the cinema was destroyed. (*Nenagh Guardian*, 8 January 1921:4; 15 January 1921:4; 29 January 1921:3.)
88. *1934 cinemas*, IFI.   89. Ibid.
90. *Nenagh Guardian*, 28 September 1912:2; 27 June 1914:2,3.
91. *KW*, 8 October 1942:11.   92. *KW*, 6 March 1952:9.   93. Ibid.
94. *KW*, 12 December 1946:38.   95. Ibid.
96. *KW*, 18 April 1963:8, carried an advertisement for a cinema for sale, which is most likely the *Olympic* as it seems to have been the only cinema in Moy.
97. Patrick C. Power, *A history of Dungarvan*, Dungarvan, Co. Waterford: de Paor, 2000:241. While

this book places Crotty's investment in a cinema in the early 1920s, newspaper advertising suggest Crotty ran this or another venue in 1915 or earlier. In 1923, Crotty was fined for non-compliance with entertainment tax collection. (*Munster Express*, 2 June 1923:4.)

98. *KYB*, 1930–7 and 1941–8, list *Cinema*, p: Daniel Crotty & Sons, so it is presumed that *Cinema* and *Dungarvan Picture Palace* are the same venue with 400 seats for both places, since, with the exception of 1937, *KYB* does not list both names in the same year.

99. *RPC*, 1977:106, 109, 111, 114.

1. Connolly and Dillon, 2001:73. 2. *Cork Examiner*, 5 April 1988.

3. *Waterford News & Star*, 7 April 2006.

4. The only entry in the *Munster Express* for *Lismore Cinema* was when in 1926 it reported that local gardaí visited the cinema when the society melodrama *The Golden Bed* (Cecil B. De Mille, 1925, USA) was being shown and 'after an interview with the management, an abrupt termination took place, and the hall was emptied in a short space of time.' (*Munster Express*, 17 September 1926:2.) As the film does not seem to have been submitted to the Official Film Censor (see censor's record, www.tcd.ie/Irishfilm), this cryptic comment may relate to the proprietor showing the film without a censorship certificate, something which has to be displayed on the screen before a film can be shown in public.

5. *Waterford News & Star*, 7 April 2006. In reporting on a non-fatal projection box fire, *Munster Express*, 31 May 1946:4, referred to the cinema as the *Royal*, perhaps another name by which it was known..

6. *Munster Express*, 10 April 1981:15.

7. Pat Kiely, 'Silver screens in Tramore', unpublished, states *Cosy* and *Strand* cinemas both closed with advent of sound cinema, though *KYB* continues to list *Strand* until 1948. McGurk brought a libel case against Thomas Collins, manager of Mrs Piper's entertainment, where McGurk had worked until 1921 when he set up his *Marque de Danse*. McGurk alleged that Collins told a former republican activist that he had harboured Black and Tans and had informed to Dublin Castle during the War of Independence. As a result of the allegations, McGurk's place was boycotted in 1922, though evidence in the case suggested that a new Piper's dance hall built in 1922 might have contributed to the decline in business. The case was dismissed before the evidence for the defence was heard. (*Munster Express*, 9 June 1923:5.)

8. Andy Taylor, 'Echoes from an eggshell', 1990:81.

9. *Screen International*, 26 February 1983:10.

10. *Munster Express*, 8 February 1980:1, reports plans by Richard Fitzgerald to reopen the cinema for the summer season.

11. *Munster Express*, 12 March 1948:7; 25 June 1971:2.

12. *Munster Express*, 2 May 1980:12; 9 December 1983:49.

13. See Andy Taylor, 'Echoes from an eggshell', 1990:79–86. Taylor was a projectionist in the *Rex*.

14. Emily Piper built the *Strand* when her husband Bill died. Though locals Pat Kiely and Andy Taylor (ibid.) say the *Strand* and *Cosy* closed at the beginning of the sound era, and Tom Cooper opened the *Casino* in 1942 at a different location, *KYB* lists *Strand* as open until 1947, by which time it lists Cooper as proprietor, even though he reopened the *Cosy*, not the *Strand*, as the *Casino*, the name he used for all of his cinemas.

15. *Waterford News*, 24 November 1933.

16. *Munster Express*, 16 November 1928:5.

17. *Munster Express*, 2 November 1928:5, when cinema was being sold due to death of owner of building, James A. Power.

18. *1934 cinemas*, IFI. 19. *Munster Express*, 12 March 1948:7.

20. Combined area residents' association with assistance from Andy Taylor, *Ballybricken and thereabouts*, Waterford, July 1991:89.

21. *Munster Express*, 25 June 1971:2. 22. *Waterford News*, 5 April 1957:2.

23. *RPC*, 1977:108, 109, 111, 113, 114, 115.

24. *Ballybricken and thereabouts*, July 1991:90–1. See *KW*, 11 April 1957, on opening of cinema; and *Irish Press*, 15 February 1985:1, on closing of cinema.

25. *Munster Express*, 31 May 1913:8. 26. *1934 cinemas*, IFI.

27. *Ballybricken and thereabouts*, July 1991:90.

28. *Waterford News & Star*, 8 June 2007; 16 February 2007.

29. *Waterford News & Star*, 1 May 2003; 11 July 2003.

30. *Munster Express*, 9 November 1928:7. Writing in 1956, Richard (Dick) W. Latimer, by then manager of the *Cinema Palace*, Wexford, for twenty-five years, recalled that while working for Laurence Breen, leesee of the Theatre Royal, the first film shown there was *The Singing Fool*, 'which set up

a record figure for the week's receipts that has never been beaten by any film in Waterford City to this day'. Latimer also recalled that in spring 1929 while he was also manager of the *Broad Street Cinema*, he screened the first sound film shown in Waterford when Walter McNally, accompanied by an American projectionist and with portable amplification equipment, showed *Syncopation*, *Mother's Boy* and *The Leathernecks* there. (*Munster Express*, 8 June 1956:6.). Latimer died less than three motnhs after writing this letter to the paper (ibid., 24 August 1956:6).

31. *1934 cinemas*, IFI.
32. 'Surrender of Theatre Royal lease', *Waterford News*, 13 January 1956. Martin Breen died in November 1952.
33. *Waterford News & Star*, 5 October 2007; 19 October 2007. Ward Anderson's focus seems to have shifted to the possibility of building a new mulpliex as part of a new shopping centre on the former Waterford Crystal sports grounds at Ballinaneeshagh, the opposite side of the city to where Storm's Railway Square multiplex is located. In an interview in October 2007, Paul Anderson indicated that Waterford Cineplex for which they were planning a major multi-million facelift with work due to begin in 2008, might be rebranded as Waterford Ominiplex. ('Cineplex to battle back with major facelift', *Waterford News & Star*, 19 October 2007.)
34. *Munster Express*, 11 January 1913:5; 28 June 1913:5.
35. *KYB*, 1946–71; *RPC*, 1977:107, 110, 114.   36. *1934 cinemas*, IFI.
37. *RPC*, 1977:112; *IT*, 18 November 1999:2, includes a photo of the partly-demolished cinema; *KYB*, 1941–71. The strategy at this and the Ritz, Clonmel, was to screen first-class films recently shown in Dublin in luxury conditions for low admission prices: 4*d*., 1*s*., 1*s*. 4*d*.; 1*s*. 8*d*. Thee was no Sunday opening in Clonmel, which, with Waterford, were the only areas with no Sunday opening in Eire at this time. (*KW*, 8 February 1940.)
38. *Westmeath Examiner*, 31 March 1917:7.
39. Listed as *Cinema*, *KYB*, 1950–66.
40. *RPC*, 1977:106, 109, 111, 114. See Tom Widger, 'Miracle at Mullingar', *Sunday Tribune*, 31 March 1985, and *What's On Sunday, Mr Fitz?* Radio Éireann documentary on the cinema.
41. *Westmeath Examiner*, 11 March 1989:12.
42. *Westmeath Examiner*, 6 September 1913:4.
43. *Westmeath Examiner*, 22 April 1944:5.
44. *Westmeath Examiner*, 3 February 1917:7. It seems that the cinema licence was in the name of John Fitzmaurice and in 1917 was transferred to Michael Hope. (*Westmeath Examiner*, 6 January 1917:8.)
45. *Westmeath Examiner*, 21 February 1931:5.   46. *1934 cinemas*, IFI.
47. *Westmeath Examiner*, 22 March 1913:4.
48. *Kine & Magic Lantern Weekly*, 6 May 1915.
49. Anne Marsh, *The Atheneum, Enniscorthy: a stroll down memory lane, 1892–2004*, c.2005, reports that a film show with a concert and lecture was held on 4 February 1912.
50. As Bower is listed as manager both of the *Abbey* and the *Athenaeum*, the former may be the same venue as latter.
51. *RPC*, 1977:107, 110, 112, 115.   52. *1934 cinemas*, IFI.
53. *RPC*, 1977:107, 115.   54. Ibid., 106, 109, 111, 114.
55. *Munster Express*, 12 March 1948:7.   56. *1934 cinemas*, IFI.
57. In the hearing concerning an appeal against the valuation of the cinema in which these figures were reported, revenue commissioner Mr. J.J. Hogan reported that the average valuation in provincial towns was three shilling per cinema seat; in cities such as Limerick it was three to four shillings per seat; while Dublin's valuation was 30*s*. per seat. The judge reduced the cinema's annual valuation from £190 to £180. (*Munster Express*, 12 March 1948:7.)
58. *RPC*, 1977:106, 109, 111, 114, 115.
59. Actually written as Welsh in directory list, but Walsh in booker section of directory. In this part of the country the name Walsh is pronounced Welsh.
60. *1934 cinemas*, IFI.
61. Vize, 52-years-old, was killed in a road accident on 17 July 1927. (*IT*, 18 July 1928:8.)
62. *1934 cinemas*, IFI. See *The Free Press*, 12 December 1914:6, on opening. See Liam O'Leary, 'Reminiscences of a Wexford filmgoer, 1923–1928', *Journal of the Wexford Historical Society*, no. 11, 1986–7.
63. Michael A. O'Rourke, *History of the Wexford Catholic Young Men's Society, 1855–2008*, vol. 1, Enniscorthy: Breffni, 2008:218.
64. Connolly and Dillon, 2001:73.
65. *Bioscope*, 21 March 1912, reports on Mr E.P. Ronan, proprietor of the *Theatre Royal*, showing a selection of drama films.

66. 'Eight-screen cinema opens', *Wexford Echo*, 3 July 2008; *Sunday Business Post*, 6 July 2008; *Wexford People*, 9 January 2008:3.
67. *1934 cinemas*, IFI.
68. *Irish Independent*, 27 September 1941:6; 6 October 1941:6.
69. Connolly and Dillon, 2001:73.
70. *1947 directory*: lists V. Kavanagh as br.   71. *RPC*, 1977: 107, 110, 115.
72. *Irish Independent*, 25 February 1924.
73. *Irish Independent*, 15 May 1920:6.   74. *1934 cinemas*, IFI.
75. *RPC*, 1977:107, 109, 111, 117.
76. *1934 cinemas*, IFI.   77. *Irish Independent*, 15 January 1940:11.
78. *Irish Independent*, 5 May 1947:5.   79. *RPC*, 1977:107; 116.
80. *Irish Independent*, 1 July 1953:14.   81. *1934 cinemas*, IFI.
82. *RPC*, 1977:108.   83. *Irish Independent*, 19 July 1977:17.
84. *Irish Independent*, 1 July 1922:4.
85. *1934 cinemas*, IFI. It was announced in 1938 that a new cinema was to be built on the site of the *Excelsior*. (*Irish Independent*, 8 October 1938:12.) This did not happen until 1942 when Rialto Cinema (Wicklow) Ltd was established by John J. Clarke to take over from his own *Excelsior Cinema*, and which was sold the same year. (*Irish Independent*, 22 April 1942:4.)
86. *Irish Independent*,8 October 1938:12.
87. *Irish Independent*, 22 April 1942:4. J.J. Clarke died in April 1951.
88. *Irish Independent*, 5 July 1947:11.

Select Bibliography

Acland, Charles R., *Screen traffic: movies, multiplexes, and global culture*, Durham/London: Duke UP, 2003.

Belton, John, *Widescreen cinema*, Cambridge, MA/London: Harvard UP, 1992.

Beere, Thekla J., 'Cinema statistics in Saorstát Éireann', *Journal of the Statistical and Social Enquiry Society of Ireland*, 89th session, 1935–6:83–110.

Breakwell, Ian and Paul Hammond (eds), *Seeing in the dark: a compendium of cinemagoing*, London: Serpent's Tail, 1990.

Cinema and theatre annual review and directory of Ireland, 1947, Dublin: Parkside, n.d. [c.1947].

Condon, Denis, *Early Irish cinema, 1895–1921*, Dublin: Irish Academic, 2008.

Cooney, John, *John Charles McQuaid: ruler of Catholic Ireland,* Dublin: O'Brien, 1999.

Corbett, Kevin J., 'Empty seats: the missing history of movie watching', *Journal of Film and Video*, vol. 50, no. 4, winter 1998–9:34–48.

Daly, Mary E., *Dublin – the deposed capital: a social and economic history, 1860–1914*, Cork: Cork UP, 1984.

[Devane SJ, Richard S. (ed.),] *Irish cinema handbook*, Dublin: Parkside, 1943.

Docherty, David, David Morrison and Michael Tracey, *The last picture show? Britain's changing film audiences*, London: BFI, 1987.

Doherty, James (additional material: Tom Thompson), *Standing room only: memories of Belfast cinemas*, Belfast: Lagan Historical Society, 1997.

Doorley, Michael, *Stella days, 1957–1967: the life and times of a rural Irish cinema*, Tipperary: Dubhairle, n.d. [c.2002].

Eyles, Allen, *ABC: the first name in entertainment*, London, Cinema Theatre Association, 1993.

Eyles, Allen, *Gaumont British cinemas*, London, Cinema Theatre Association, 1996.

Eyles, Allen, *Odeon cinemas 1: Oscar Deutsch entertains our nation*, London, Cinema Theatre Association, 2002.

Eyles, Allen, *Odeon cinemas 2: from J. Arthur Rank to the multiplex*, London: Cinema Theatre Association, 2005.

Field, Mary, *Good company: the story of the children's entertainment film movement in Great Britain, 1943–1950*, London: Longmans, 1952.

Flynn, Roddy, 'A semi-state in all but name? Seán Lemass's film policy' in Brian Girvin and Gary Murphy (eds), *The Lemass era: politics and society in the Ireland of Seán Lemass*, Dublin: UCD, 2005.

Friedberg, Anne, *Window shopping: cinema and the postmodern*, Berkeley/Los Angeles/Oxford: University of California, 1993.

Fuller, Kathryn H., *At the picture show: small-town audiences and the creation of movie fan culture*, Washington DC/London: Smithsonian, 1996.

Fullerton, John (ed.), *Celebrating 1895: the centenary of cinema*, London: John Libbey, 1998.

Furlong, Irene, *Irish tourism, 1880–1980*, Dublin: Irish Academic, 2009.

Gerrard, John, 'Film societies in Ireland', *Sight and Sound*, vol. 17, no. 67, autumn 1948.

Gomery, Douglas, *Shared pleasures: a history of movie presentation in the United States*, London: BFI, 1992.

Gomery, Douglas, 'US film exhibition: the formation of a big business' in Tino Balio (ed.), *The American film industry*, revised ed., Madison: University of Wisconsin, 1985:218–228.

Grau, Oliver, *Virtual art: from illusion to immersion*, Cambridge, MA/London: MIT, 2003; orig, Berlin 2001.

Grieveson, Lee, 'Fighting films: race, morality and the governing of cinema, 1912–1915', *Cinema Journal*, vol. 30, no. 1, autumn 1998:40–72.

Grieveson, Lee, '"A kind of recreation school for the whole family": making cinema respectable', *Screen*, vol. 42, no. 1, spring 2001:64–76.

Hanson, Stuart, *From silent screen to multi-screen: a history of cinema exhibition in Britain since 1896*, Manchester: Manchester UP 2007.

Hanson, Stuart, 'Spoilt for choice? multiplexes in the 90s' in Robert Murphy (ed.), *British cinema of the 90s*, London: BFI, 2000:48–59.

Hark, Ina Rae (ed.), *Exhibition: the film reader*, London: Routledge, 2002.

Hiley, Nicholas, 'Nothing more than a "craze"': cinema building in Britain from 1909–1914' in Andrew Higson (ed.), *Young and innocent: the cinema in Britain, 1896–1930*, Exeter: Exeter UP, 2002.

Hill, John, *Cinema and Northern Ireland: film, culture and politics*, London: BFI, 2006.

Kearns, George P., *The Prinner: the story of the Princess cinema, Rathmines and other Dublin picture palaces and cinemas*, Dublin, n.d. [2005].

Kearns, George P., and Patrick Maguire, *A to Z of all old Dublin cinemas*, Dublin, n.d. [c.2006].

Keenan, Jim, *Dublin cinemas: a pictorial selection*, Dublin: Picture House, 2005.

Kessler, Frank and Nanna Verhoeff, *Networks of entertainment: early film distribution, 1895–1915*, Eastleigh: John Libbey, 2007.

Klinger, Barbara, *Beyond the multiplex: cinema, new technologies, and the home*, Berkeley/Los Angeles/London: University of California, 2006.

Kuhn, Annette, 'Memories of cinemagoing in the 1930s', *Journal of Popular British Cinema*, no. 2, 1996:100–20.

Lalor, Brian (gen. ed.), *The encyclopaedia of Ireland*, Dublin: Gill and Macmillan, 2003.

Low, Rachael, *The history of the British film*, 7 vols, London: George Allen & Unwin 1948–85, reissued in 1997 by Routledge (London). Vol. 1, *1896–1906* (with Roger Manvell, 1948); vol. 2. *1906–1914* (1949); vol. 3, *1914–1918* (1950); vol. 4, *1918–1929* (1950); vol. 5, *Documentary & educational films of the 1930s* (1979); vol. 6, *Films of comment and persuasion of the 1930s* (1979); vol. 7, *Film making in 1930s Britain* (1985).

McBride, Stephanie and Roddy Flynn (eds), *Here's looking at you, kid! Ireland goes to the pictures*, Dublin: Wolfhound, 1996.

McCourt, John (ed.), *Roll away the reel world: James Joyce and cinema*, Cork: Cork UP, 2010.

McGuinness, Des, 'Media consumption and Dublin working-class cultural identity', PhD, Dublin City University, 1999.

McSweeney, John, *The golden age of Cork cinemas*, Cork: Rose Arch, 2003.

Morash, Christopher, *A history of the media in Ireland*, Cambridge: Cambridge UP, 2010.

Ní Chanainn, Áine [edited by Breandán MacGiollarnáth], *The pioneers of audio visual education in Ireland, 1940–1962*, Ballina: Western People, 1992.

O'Brien, Joseph V., *Dear dirty Dublin: a city in distress, 1899–1916*, Berkeley/Los Angeles/London: University of California, 1982.

O'Connor, Barbara and Michael Cronin (eds), *Tourism in Ireland: a critical analysis*, Cork: Cork UP, 1993.

[O'Leary, Liam (ed.)], *Cinema Ireland, 1895–1976*, Dublin: Dublin Arts Festival, 1976.

O'Leary, Liam, *Cinema Ireland, 1896–1950*, Dublin: NLI, 1990.

Open, Michael, *Fading lights, silver screens: a history of Belfast cinemas*, Antrim, Northern Ireland: Greystone/W.G. Baird, 1985.

Powell, Hudson John, *Poole's myriorama! a story of travelling panorama showmen*, Bradford on Avon, Wiltshire: ELSP 2002.

Rockett, Kevin, Luke Gibbons and John Hill, *Cinema and Ireland*, London: Croom Helm, 1987; Routledge, 1988.

Rockett, Kevin with Emer Rockett, *Irish film censorship: a cultural journey from silent cinema to internet pornography*, Dublin: Four Courts Press, 2004.

Rockett, Kevin (compiler and ed.), *The Irish filmography: fiction films, 1896–1996*, Dublin: Red Mountain Media, 1996. Updated and expanded to include non-fiction films, published online at www.tcd.ie/irishfilm.

Rothery, Sean, *Ireland and the new architecture, 1900–1940*, Dublin: Lilliput, 1991.

Stokes, Melvyn and Richard Maltby (eds), *American movie audiences: from the turn of the century to the early sound era*, London: BFI, 1999.

Stokes, Melvyn and Richard Maltby (eds), *Hollywood abroad: audiences and cultural exchange*, London: BFI, 2004.

Thompson, Kirstin, *Exporting entertainment: America in the world film market, 1907–1934*, London: BFI, 1985.

Thornton, Niamh and Richard Hayes (eds), *James Joyce and cinema*, special issue, *Film and film culture*, vol. 3, 2004.

Waller, Gregory A. (ed.), *Moviegoing in America: a sourcebook in the history of film exhibition*, Oxford: Blackwell, 2002.

Wasko, Janet, *Hollywood in the information age: beyond the silver screen*, Austin: University of Texas, 1995; orig. 1994.

Whyte, J.H., *Church and state in modern Ireland, 1923–1979*, 2nd ed., Dublin: Gill and Macmillan, 1980; orig. 1971.

Williams, Christopher (ed.), *Cinema: the beginnings and the future: essays marking the centenary of the first film show projected to a paying audience in Britain*, London: University of Westminster, 1996.

Williams, David R., 'Never on Sunday: the early operating of the Cinematograph Act of 1909 in regard to Sunday opening', *Film History*, vol. 14, no. 2, 2002:186–194.

Zimmermann, Marc, *The history of Dublin cinemas*, Dublin: Nonsuch, 2007.

REPORTS

Arts Council of Ireland, *The cultural and economic trends of cinema in Ireland and Wales*, Dublin: Arts Council, 2004.

Connolly, Neil and Maretta Dillon, *Developing cultural cinema in Ireland: a report commissioned by the Arts Council/an Chomhairle Ealaíon, the Irish Film Board/Bord Scannán na hÉireann, and Enterprise Ireland in association with the Northern Ireland Film Commission*, Development Resource Documents series, no. 5, Dublin: Arts Council of Ireland, 2001.

Digital cinema in Ireland, Dublin: Arts Council of Ireland, 2008.

Federation of Irish Film Societies, *Film societies in Ireland: upgrading to 35mm projection systems*, final report, December 1997. This report was prepared by Neil Connolly and Maretta Dillon.

Report of the inter-departmental committee on the film industry, March 1942 (unpublished), NAI.

Report of investigation by the examiner of restrictive practices into the distribution of cinema films, RPC (unpublished), Dublin, 1977.

Report of enquiry into the supply and distribution of cinema films, RPC, Dublin: Stationery Office, 1978.

The strategic development of the Irish film and television industry, 2000–2010: final report of the film industry review group to the minister for arts, heritage, gaeltacht and the islands, Dublin: Stationery Office, 1999.

Ireland

DONEGAL

Derry

DERRY

ANTRIM

Belfast

TYRONE

FERMANAGH

ARMAGH

DOWN

SLIGO

MONAGHAN

LEITRIM

CAVAN

MAYO

ROSCOMMON

LONGFORD

LOUTH

MEATH

GALWAY

WESTMEATH

Galway

OFFALY

DUBLIN

Dublin

KILDARE

CLARE

LAOIS

WICKLOW

CARLOW

Limerick

KILKENNY

LIMERICK

TIPPERARY

WEXFORD

KERRY

WATERFORD

Waterford

CORK

Cork

Land over 300m OD

N

0   50 miles

0   80 km

Index of Cinema Locations

Abbeyfeale, Co. Limerick 430
Abbeyleix, Co. Laois 429
Achill, Co. Mayo 436
Antrim, Co. Antrim 369–70
Aran Islands, Co. Galway 421
Ardara, Co. Donegal 395
Ardee, Co. Louth 434
Arklow, Co. Wicklow 453
Armagh, Co Armagh, 380
Arva, Co. Cavan 383
Asbourne, Co. Meath 438
Athboy, Co. Meath 438
Athenry, Co. Galway 421
Athlone, Co. Westmeath 450
Athy, Co. Kildare 425–6
Aughnacloy, Co. Tyrone 446

Bagenalstown, Co. Carlow 381
Bailieborough/Bailieboro', Co. Cavan 383
Balbriggan, Co. Dublin 401
Balla, Co. Mayo 436
Ballaghadreen, Co. Roscommon 441
Ballina, Co. Mayo 436
Ballinamore, Co. Leitrim 429
Ballinasloe, Co. Galway 421
Ballincollig, Co. Cork 385
Ballinrobe, Co. Mayo 436
Ballsbridge/Sandymount, Co. Dublin 401–2
Ballybay, Co. Monaghan 439
Ballybofey, Co. Donegal 395
Ballybunnion, Co. Kerry 423
Ballycastle, Co. Antrim 370
Ballyclare, Co. Antrim 370
Ballyconnell, Co. Cavan 383
Ballyfermot, Co. Dublin 402
Ballyhaunis, Co. Mayo 436–7
Ballyjamesduff, Co. Cavan 383
Ballykinlar, Co. Down 397
Ballylanders, Co. Limerick 430
Ballylongford, Co. Kerry 424
Ballymahon, Co, Longford 433
Ballymena, Co. Antrim 370
Ballymoney, Co. Antrim 370

Ballymore-Eustace, Co. Kildare 426
Ballymote, Co. Sligo 442
Ballymun, Co. Dublin 402
Ballynahinch, Co. Down 397
Ballyraggett, Co. Kilkenny 427
Ballyshannon, Co. Donegal 395
Ballywalter, Co. Down 397
Baltinglass, Co. Wicklow 453
Banagher, Co. Offaly 440
Banbridge, Co. Down 397
Bandon, Co. Cork 385
Bangor, Co. Down 397–8
Bantry, Co. Cork 385
Belfast, Co. Antrim 370–8
Belmullet, Co. Mayo 437
Belturbet, Co. Cavan 383
Bere Island, Co. Cork 385
Birr, Co. Offaly 440
Blackpool, Co. Cork 386
Blackrock, Co. Dublin 402
Blanchardstown, Co. Dublin 402
Borris, Co. Carlow 382
Borrisokane, Co. Tipperary 443
Boyle, Co. Roscommon 441
Bray, Co. Wicklow 453–4
Bridgetown, Co. Donegal 395
Bruff, Co. Limerick 430
Bunclody, Co. Wexford 451
Buncrana, Co. Donegal 395
Bundoran, Co. Donegal 395
Bushmills, Co. Antrim 378
Buttevant, Co. Cork 386

Cabra, Co.Dubin 402
Cahir, Co. Tipperary 443
Cahirciveen, Co. Kerry 424
Callan, Co. Kilkenny 427
Cappamore, Co. Limerick 430
Cappoquin, Co. Waterford 448
Capswell, Co. Cork 386
Carbury, Co. Kildare 426
Carlingford, Co. Louth 434
Carlow, Co. Carlow 382

Carndonagh, Co. Donegal 395
Carnew, Co. Wicklow 454
Carnlough, Co. Antrim 378
Carrickfergus, Co. Antrim 378
Carrickmacross, Co. Monaghan 439
Carrick-on-Shannon, Co. Roscommon 441–2
Carrick-on-Suir, Co. Tipperary 443–4
Carrigaline, Co. Cork 386
Carrigtwohill, Co. Cork 386
Cashel, Co. Tipperary 444
Castlebar, Co. Mayo 437
Castleblaney, Co. Monaghan 439
Castlecaulfield, Co. Tyrone 446
Castlecomer, Co. Kilkenny 427
Castlederg, Co. Tyrone 446
Castledermot, Co. Kildare 426
Castleisland, Co. Kerry 424
Castlemartyr, Co. Cork 386
Castlepollard, Co. Westmeath 451
Castlerea, Co. Roscommon 442
Castletown Bearhaven/Castletownbere, Co. Cork 386
Castlewellan, Co. Down 398
Cavan, Co. Cavan 383
Celbridge, Co. Kildare 426
Chapelizod, Co. Dubin 402
Charlestown, Co. Mayo 437
Charleville, Co. Cork 386
Churchtown, Co. Dublin 402
Clara, Co. Offaly 440
Claremorris, Co. Mayo 437
Clifden, Co. Galway 421
Clogheen, Co. Tiperary 444
Clonakilty, Co. Cork 386
Clonard, Co. Meath 438
Clondalkin, Co. Dublin 402–3
Clones, Co. Monaghan 439–40
Clonmany, Co. Donegal 395
Clonmel, Co. Tipperary 444
Clontarf, Co. Dublin 403
Cloughjordan, Co. Tipperary 444
Cloyne, Co. Cork 386
Coalisland, Co. Tyrone 446
Cobh (formerly Queenstown), Co. Cork 386–7
Cogry, Doagh, Co. Antrim 378
Coleraine, Co. Derry 392
Comber, Co. Down 398
Cong, Co. Mayo 437
Convoy, Co. Donegal 395
Cookstown, Co. Tyrone 446
Coolock, Co. Dublin 403
Cootehill, Co. Cavan 383
Cork, Co. Cork 387–9
Crookstown, Co. Cork 390
Crossgar, Co. Down 398
Crossmaglen, Co. Armagh 381
Crumlin, Co. Antrim 378

Crumlin, Co. Dublin 403
Curragh, Co. Kildare 426
Cushendal, Co. Antrim 379

Dalkey, Co. Dublin 403
Derry, Co. Derry 392–3
Derrybeg, Co. Donegal 396
Dingle, Co. Kerry 424
Doagh, Co. Antrim *see* Cogry, Doagh, Co. Antrim
Dolphin's Barn, Co. Dublin 403
Donaghadee, Co. Down 398
Donegal, Co. Donegal 396
Doneraile, Co. Cork 390
Doon, Co. Limerick 430
Douglas, Co. Cork 390
Downpatrick, Co. Down 398–9
Draperstown, Co. Derry 393
Drogheda, Co. Louth 434–5
Dromore, Co. Down 399
Drumcondra, Co. Dublin 403
Drumcollogher, Co. Limerick 430
Drumshanbo, Co. Leitrim 430
Dublin, Co. Dublin 403–14
Dún Laoghaire (formerly Kingstown), Co. Dublin 414–15
Duncannon, Co. Wexford 451–2
Dundalk, Co. Louth 435–6
Dundonald, Co. Antrim 379
Dundrum, Co. Dublin 415
Dungannon, Co. Tyrone 446–7
Dungarvan, Co. Waterford 448
Dungiven, Co. Derry 394
Dungloe, Co. Donegal 396
Dunloy, Co. Antrim 379
Dunmanway, Co. Cork 390
Dunmore, Co. Galway 421

Edenderry, Co. Offaly 440
Edgeworthstown, Co. Longford 433
Ennis, Co. Clare 384
Enniscorthy, Co. Wexford 451
Enniscrone, Co. Sligo 442
Enniskillen, Co. Fermanagh 420–1
Ennistymon, Co. Clare 384

Fairview, Co. Dublin 415
Falcarragh, Co. Donegal 396
Farranfore, Co. Kerry 424
Fermoy, Co. Cork 390
Ferns, Co. Wexford 452
Fethard, Co. Tipperary 444
Finglas, Co. Dublin 415
Fintona, Co. Tyrone 447
Fivemiletown, Co. Tyrone 447
Freshford, Co. Kilkenny 427

Galway, Co. Galway 421–3
Garvagh, Co. Derry 394
Gilford, Co. Armagh, 381
Glanmire, Co. Cork 390
Glasthule, Co. Dublin 415–16
Glencolmcille, Co. Donegal 396
Glengormley, Co. Antrim 379
Glenties, Co. Donegal 396
Glin, Co. Limerick 430
Goresbridge, Co. Kilkenny 428
Gorey, Co. Wexford 452
Gort, Co. Galway 423
Graiguenamanagh, Co. Kilkenny 428
Granagh, Co. Limerick 430–1
Granard, Co. Longford 433
Greystones, Co. Wicklow 454

Hacketstown, Co. Carlow 382
Harold's Cross, Co. Dublin 416
Holywood, Co. Down 399
Hospital, Co. Limerick 431

Inchicore, Co. Dublin 416
Inverin/Indreabhán, Co. Galway 423
Irvinestown, Co. Fermanagh 421

Johnstown, Co. Kilkenny 428

Kanturk, Co. Cork 390
Keady, Co. Armagh, 381
Kells, Co. Meath 438
Kenmare, Co. Kerry 424
Kilbeggan, Co. Westmeath 451
Kilcullen, Co. Kildare 426
Kildare, Co. Kildare 426
Kildysart, Co. Clare 384
Kilfinane, Co. Limerick 431
Kilkee, Co. Clare 384
Kilkeel, Co. Down 399
Kilkenny, Co. Kilkenny 428
Killaloe, Co. Clare 385
Killarney, Co. Kerry 424
Killester, Co. Dublin 416
Killorglin, Co. Kerry 424–5
Killybegs, Co. Donegal 396
Killyleagh, Co. Down 399
Kilmacthomas, Co. Waterford 448
Kilmaine, Co. Mayo 437
Kilmallock, Co. Limerick 431
Kilrea, Co. Derry 394
Kilrush, Co. Clare 385
Kiltimagh, Co. Mayo 437
Kimmage, Co. Dublin 416
Kingscourt, Co. Cavan 384
Kinsale, Co. Cork 390
Kircubbin, Co. Down 399

Lahinch, Co. Clare 385
Lanesboro', Co. Longford 433
Larne, Co. Antrim 379
Letterkenny, Co. Donegal 396
Lifford, Co. Donegal 396
Limavady, Co. Derry 394
Limerick, Co. Limerick 431–3
Lisburn, Co. Antrim 379
Lismore, Co. Waterford 448
Lisnaskea, Co. Fermanagh 421
Listowel, Co. Kerry 425
Longford, Co. Longford 433–4
Loughrea, Co. Galway 423
Louth, Co. Louth 436
Lucan, Co. Dublin 416–17
Lurgan, Co. Armagh 381

Macroom, Co. Cork 391
Maghera, Co. Derry 394
Magherafelt, Co. Derry 394
Malahide, Co. Dublin 417
Mallow, Co. Cork 391
Manorhamilton, Co. Leitrim 430
Markethill, Co. Armagh 381
Midleton, Co. Cork 391
Milford, Co. Donegal 396
Millisle, Co. Down 399
Millstreet, Co. Cork 391
Milltown, Co. Kerry 425
Milltown-Malbay, Co. Clare 385
Mitchelstown, Co. Cork 391
Moate, Co. Westmeath 451
Mohill, Co. Leitrim 430
Monaghan, Co. Monaghan 440
Monasterevan, Co. Kildare 426
Mount Merrion, Co. Dublin 417
Mountmellick, Co. Laois 429
Mountrath, Co. Laois 429
Moville, Co. Donegal 396–7
Moy, Co. Tyrone 447
Moycullen, Co. Galway 423
Muine Bheag/Muinebeag *see* Bagenalstown
Mullinavat, Co. Kilkenny 428
Mullingar, Co. Westmeath 451

Naas, Co. Kildare 426–7
Naul, Fingal, Co. Dublin 417
Navan, Co. Meath 438–9
Nenagh, Co. Tipperary 444–5
New Ross, Co. Wexford 452
Newbridge, Co. Kildare 427
Newcastle, Co. Down 400
Newcastle West, Co. Limerick 433
Newmarket, Co. Cork 391
Newmarket-on-Fergus, Co. Clare 385
Newport, Co. Mayo 437
Newry, Co. Down 400

Newtownards, Co. Down 400
Newtownbarry, Co. Wexford 452
Newtownstewart, Co. Tyrone 447
Oldcastle, Co. Meath 439
Omagh, Co. Tyrone 447
Oranmore, Co. Galway 423

Passage West, Co. Cork 391
Phibsborough, Co. Dublin 417–18
Portadown, Co. Armagh 381
Portaferry, Co. Down 400
Portarlington, Co. Laois 429
Portglenone, Co. Antrim 379
Portlaoise (formerly Maryborough), Co. Laois 429
Portmarnock, Co. Dublin 418
Portrane, Co. Dublin 419
Portroe, Co. Tipperary 445
Portrush, Co. Antrim 379–80
Portstewart, Co. Derry 394
Portumna, Co. Galway 423
Prosperous, Co. Kildare 427

Queenstown, see Cobh

Randalstown, Co. Antrim 380
Ranelagh, Co. Dublin 418
Raphoe, Co. Donegal 397
Rathangan, Co. Kildare 427
Rathcoole, Co. Antrim 380
Rathcoole, Co. Dublin 418
Rathdowney, Co. Laois 429
Rathdrum, Co. Wicklow 454
Rathfriland, Co. Down 401
Rathkeale, Co. Limerick 433
Rathmelton, Co. Donegal 397
Rathmines, Co. Dublin 418–19
Rathmore, Co. Kerry 425
Rathnew, Co. Wicklow 454
Rathvilly, Co. Carlow 382
Rialto, Co. Dublin 419
Ringsend, Co. Dublin 419
Roscommon, Co. Roscommon 442
Roscrea, Co. Tipperary 445
Roxboro, Co. Roscommon 442
Rush, Co. Dublin 419

Santry, Co. Dublin 419
Scariff, Co. Clare 385
Sixmilebridge, Co. Clare 385

Skerries, Co. Dublin 419
Skibbereen, Co. Cork 391–2
Sligo, Co. Sligo 442–3
Stewartstown, Co. Tyrone 448
Stillorgan, Co. Dublin 419
Strabane, Co. Tyrone 448
Strokestown, Co. Roscommon 442
Sutton, Co. Dublin 420
Swinford, Co. Mayo 437
Swords, Co. Dublin 420

Tallaght, Co. Dublin 420
Tallanstown, Co. Louth 436
Tallow, Co. Waterford 448–9
Tandragee, Co. Armagh 381
Tarbert, Co. Kerry 425
Templemore, Co. Tiperary 445
Terenure, Co. Dublin 420
Thomastown, Co. Kilkenny 428
Thurles, Co. Tipperary 445
Tinahely, Co. Wicklow 454
Tipperary, Co. Tipperary 445–6
Tralee, Co. Kerry 425
Tramore, Co. Waterford 449
Trim, Co. Meath 439
Tuam, Co. Galway 423
Tubbercurry, Co. Sligo 443
Tulla, Co. Clare 385
Tullamore, Co. Offaly 441
Tullow, Co. Carlow 382
Tyrellspass, Co. Westmeath 451

Urlingford, Co. Kilkenny 428

Valentia Island, Co. Kerry 425
Virginia, Co. Cavan 384

Walkinstown, Co. Dublin 420
Warrenpoint, Co. Down 401
Waterford, Co. Waterford 449–50
Waterville, Co. Kerry 425
Westport, Co. Mayo 437–8
Wexford, Co. Wexford 452–3
Whitehall, Co. Dublin 420
Whitehead, Co. Antrim 380
Wicklow, Co. Wicklow 454

Youghal, Co. Cork 392

TRAVELLING CINEMAS

Co. Antrim 380
Co. Cavan 384
Co. Donegal 397
Co. Down 401
Co. Dublin 420
Co. Galway 423
Co. Kerry 425
Co. Kilkenny 428

Co. Leitrim 430
Co. Limerick 433
Co. Roscommon 442
Co. Tipperary 446
Co. Tyrone 448
Co. Waterford 450
Co. Westmeath 451
Co. Wicklow 454

General Index

The general index is confined to parts one and two of the book.
Numbers in bold refer to plates.

Abbey Cinema, Drogheda 96, 165
Abbey Cinema, Limerick 31, 489n
Abbey Cinema, Wexford 165, 194
Abbey Cinema, Wicklow 165
Abbey Cinema, Youghal 165
Abbey Films Ltd 159–60, 163, 165, 168, 169,
    172, 180, 211, 264, 361, 525–26n, 529n,
    541n
Abbey Theatre, Dublin 15, 120, 323, 335, 347,
    575n
ABC Cinema, Derry (formerly Rialto) 125, 140
ABC Film Centre, Belfast (formerly Ritz) 206
Abercorn Hall, Dublin 27, 29
Aberdeen, Lady 27
Aberdeen, Lord 27
About Adam (2000) 367
Abrahamson, Lenny 566n
Academy Cinema, Pearse Street, Dublin 165,
    179, 241, 251 (*see also* Palace Cinema,
    Brunswick [Pearse] Street, Dublin, aka Antient
    Concert Rooms and Embassy)
ACC Bank (sponsor) 277, 562n
access>CINEMA 244–6, 265, 269, 286, 290,
    341, 481, 553–54n, 558n, 559n, 560n *see also*
    Federation of Irish Film Societies (FIFS)
ACCESS scheme 268
Accident (1967) 251, 555n
Adam and Eve (*Adán y Eva*, 1956) 359
Adams, Dawn 271, 560n
Adaptation Festival 266, 559n
Adelphi Cinema, Dundalk 165
Adelphi Cinema, Dún Laoghaire 95, 121, 141,
    157
Adelphi Cinema, Middle Abbey Street, Dublin
    76, 94, 111, 121, 154–5, 157, 172, 207, 241,
    262, 312, 540n
Adelphi-Carlton group 125, 157, 169, 171–2,
    175, 176, 203, 205, 207
Adelphi Ltd 76, 94, 499n, 505n
Advance Vision 186, 189
Adventures of Sharkboy and Lavagirl in 3D, The
    (2003) 521n
African Film Festival, Galway 289 *see also*

Dublin African Film Festival, and Carlow
    African Film Festival
After Midnight (1990) 525n
Agostini, Philippe 360
Ahearne, Rudolph 78, 486n, 491n
Ahern, Bertie, 532n
Ahern, Fr Michael 362
Ai No Borei see Empire of Passion
Ai No Corrida see Empire of the Senses
Aiken, Frank 121, 131–2.
Aiseirghe (1941) 239
Aitken, Mr R.G. 67
Akerman, Chantal 280
Albert Hall, Belfast 37
Albertini, Christina 253, 557n
Alburn Real Estate Capital 226
Alexander, Robert 353, 362
Alexander Nevsky (1938) 550n
Alexandra Theatre, Belfast 36, 81
Alfred Nobel 779n
Algar, Michael 181
Alhambra, Belfast 81, 124, 139
Ali, Muhammad 264
Alice in Wonderland (2010) 151, 208
Alleguen, Mary 562n
Allen, Miriam 280, 282, 560n
Allen, Woody 254
Alliance Française Cork 286
Allsecure Ltd 204
Almodóvar, Pedro 261
Alpha, Rathcoole, Co. Antrim 141
Amalgamated Cinemas (Ireland) Ltd 79, 122,
    156, 500n, 541n
Amata, Jeta 566n
Amateur Cine World Competition 239
Amazon.com 188–9
Ambassador Cinema (Rotunda) 78, 152–3, 165,
    179, 278, 518n
Ambrosio, Arturo 21–2
AMC (American Multi-Cinema Corporation)
    193, 195, 198, 201–3, 205, 211
Amelio, Gianni 279
American Moving Picture Company 48

American Multi-Cinema Corporation *see* AMC
American Optical 154
American Roller Skating Rink, Dublin 485n
Amityville 3D (1984) 521n
An Dochtúir Jenner (Doctor Jenner) 579n
An t-Airgead ag Obair (1957) 578n
An tAthair Damien (Father Damien) 579n
An Ríoghacht, 296, 304, 362, 569n, 570n
Anderson, Caroline 291
Anderson, Kevin 158, 159–75, 178–9, 191, 211, 226, 249, 548–49n, 33
Anderson, Mark 198, 212, 522n, 542n
Anderson, Martha 525n
Anderson, Paul 160, 162, 178, 212, 220, 227–8, 525–26n, 528n, 541n, 546n, 548–49n, 36
Anderson, Thomas 525n
Anderson, Thomas 227, 541n
Anderson, W.T. 34
Andrews, J.M. 83, 130
Angel on my Shoulder (1946) 362
Angelopoulos, Theo 562n
Angelus, The (c.1938) 100
Anglo-Amalgamated Film Distributors 160, 526n
Anglo-Irish Treaty 1921 60, 295–6
Anna Christie (1930) 503n
Another Country (1984) 178
Another Shore (1948) 280, 349, 582n
Another Way (1982) 259
Antal, Nimród 245
Anthony and Cleopatra (1913) 40
Antient Concert Rooms *see* Palace Cinema, Brunswick [Pearse] Street, Dublin
Antrim Cinema, Castle Street 142
Apollo, Belfast 81, 82, 124, 247
Apostolica Film Group 581n
Apple Corp. 191
Arabian Nights (1974) 255
Arcadian Cinema, Belfast 97
Ardavín, César Fernández 273
Ardmore Studios 273
Argyle, John 160
Aristotle 294
Armagh Omniplex 151
Army Chaplin 355
Arts Council/An Chomhairle Ealaíon (Republic of Ireland) 224, 242, 244, 253, 256, 258–60, 263–5, 267–9, 274, 276–7, 279, 290, 553n, 557n, 564n
Arts Council of Northern Ireland (ACNI) 248, 265, 285, 289
Arts plan, 1995–97 265
Assembly Hall, Belfast 37
Assembly Rooms Picturedrome, Cork 32
Assembly Rooms, Sandymount, Dublin 487n
Associated British Cinemas (ABC) 73–6, 80–1,

85, 92, 94–5, 104, 111, 116–17, 121, 125, 140, 154–5, 157–8, 161, 202–3, 302, 312, 510n
Associated British Pictures Corporation (ABP) 26, 73–4, 84–5, 94
Associated Cinema Properties Ltd 121
Associated Cinemas Ltd 309, 511n *see* Associated Picture Houses Ltd
Associated Irish Cinemas Ltd (AIC) 75–6, 302, 498n
Associated Picture Houses Ltd 80, 120, 511n
Associated Provincial Picture Houses Ltd 26
Association of Provincial Exhibitors (APE) 95–6 *see* Irish Provincial Cinema Owners' Association (renamed)
Association of Secondary Teachers of Ireland (ASTI) 329, 332, 347
Astor Cinema, Eden Quay, Dublin 79, 142, 176, 179, 241, 250–1, 499n, 531n
Astor Cinema, Enniscorthy, Wexford 96
Astor Cinema, Listowel, Kerry 165
Astor Cinema, O'Connell Street, Dublin 78, 79, 361
Astoria Cinema, Ballsbridge, Dublin 80
Astoria Cinema, Belfast 82, 124, 502n
Astoria Cinema, Glasthule, Dublin 80, 162, 501n
Astra (film distributors) 67
Asylum 239
Athenaeum, Limerick 489n
Athy urban district council 302
Atlas Cine Supply Co. 133
Atlas Film Company 232
Atlas Venture 188
Atomfilms 191
Attenborough, Richard 172
Au Revoir, les Enfants (1987) 243
Aubrey, Doug 566n
Aughnacloy Picture House 102
Augustine of Hippo 293
Augustus (1640) 293
Aurora Cinemas / Aurora Entertainment 221, 541n
Australia 510n
Avalos, Stefan 291
Avant-Garde/Experimental Film Club, Dublin 559n
Avatar (2009) 151, 521n
Avica Technologies 547n
Awakening, The see *Suor Letizia*

Bachelor and Hicks (architects) 23
Bacon, Lloyd 69
Bad Girl (1931) 503n
Bagnalstown cinema, Co. Carlow 88, 504n
Bailey, Michael 591n
Bailey, Tom 591n

Baker, O.S. 28
Baker, Roy Ward 271, 358
Baker's Wife, The see *La Femme du Boulanger*
Ballina Cineplex 212
Ballymena council 103
Ballymoney council 103
Ballymore Properties 547n
Band, Harry 180
Bangor Cinemas Ltd 82, 508n
Barabbas the Robber see *Which Will Ye Have?*
Barber, Julie 563n
Barbin, Charles 353
Barfield, Norman 365
Barker, Robert 228, 483n
Barnacle, Nora 19
Barnes, Michael 249
Barr, Joseph 142
Barrett, Gerry 224
Barron, James 490n
Barrow Trust Ltd 124
Barry, Conor 565n
Barry, Kevin 582n
Barry, W.J. 96
Barry Lyndon (1975) 171
Basco, Miss 30
Bass, Murray 98
Bass, William 25
Bastow, Charleton and Co. 164
Bates, Kathy 282
Bates, Dawson 81, 97, 99, 506n
Battersea Power Station complex, London 214
Battle of Waterloo, The (1913) 40
Battleship Potemkin, The (1925) 229, 231, 232, 233, 235, 236, 550n
Baum, John 501n
Baum, Maurice 79, 80, 107, 121, 349, 501n, 508n, 584n
BBC see British Broadcasting Coporation
Beamish, R.B. 560n
Beatha Ui Raghallaigh (1954) 525n
Beatles, The 540n
Beatrice Cenci (1909) 17–8, 21–2, 484n, 75
Beattie, Mr 246
Beere, Thekla 45, 65, 74, 89–90, 92–3, 108–9, 145–6, 327, 349, 369, 497n, 500n, 509n, 519n, 554n, 575n, 25
Beggs, Mark 534n, 547n
Behold the Man (1951) 362
Beineix, Jean-Jacques 258
Belfast (Arts) Festival 249, 285
Belfast Coliseum Ltd, 36
Belfast Co-Op Wholesale Society, Yorkgate leisure and retail complex see City Side, Belfast
Belfast Corporation 59, 97–9, 103–5, 140, 149, 232, 248

Belfast (Dublin Road) multiplex 207–8, 215
Belfast Film Festival 249, 284–5, 558n, 564n
Belfast Film Institute Society (BFIS) 247–8
Belfast Film Society (founded 1928; joined with Provincial Film Society of Ireland in 1929) 246
Belfast Film Society (BFS; founded 1937) 247, 555n
Belfast Gaiety Picture Theatre Co. 36
Belfast Independent Video see Northern Visions
Belfast Odyssey Arena 544n
Belfast Omniplex see Kennedy Centre multiplex
Belfast Picture House, 25, 26, 35, 67, 69, 71, 73, 82, 87, 104, 124, 206, 486n
Belfast Picturedrome Ltd 35
Belfast Picturedrome 124
Belfast Roller Skating Rink 485n
Bell, Desmond 283
Bell, Oliver 319, 347, 571n
Belles of St Trinian's, The (1954) 581n
Bells of St Mary, The (1945) 364–5
Belltable Arts Centre 257, 267, 289
Belton, John 153, 154, 520n, 522–23n
Belton, Patrick 302
Benigni, Roberto 178
Benmore Group 549n
Bennett, Ronan 283
Benson, Ciaran 582n
Beowulf (2007) 150, 521n
Beresford, Beatrice Rose 498n
Berger, Ludwig 86
Bergman, Ingmar 262
Bergman, Ingrid 364
Berivan, Binevsa 566n
Berlin Film Festival 271
Berlin: Symphony of a Great City (1927) 229
Bernard, F. 322
Bertolucci, Bernardo 254, 255
Beshoff, Ivan 550n
Bethesda chapel, Dublin, 23
Bew, Paul 119–20
Bezar, Miraz 566n
Bibal, Robert 248
Bicycle Thieves (1948) 250, 555n
Bierce, Ambrose 239
Billot, Fr Louis 294, 567n
Binchy, Maeve 482n
Binns, Mrs Maxie 498n
Binoche, Juilette 287
Bioscope's 'Paddy' 40, 41
Birch, G.L. 105
Birchhall Investments 185
Birmingham Film Festival 263
Birth of a Nation, The (1915) 45, 80
Bitter Rice (1948) 585n
Black and Tans 32

Black, Cathal 245
Black, Donald Taylor 582n
Black, D.A. 37
Blackrock Cinema Theatre, Dublin 28, 52, 80, 499n
Blackrock College, Dublin 296
Blackstar Films 187–8, 533n
Blackstone (private equity group) 208, 216, 221
Blanchardstown multiplex 203, 204 *see also* UCI Blanchardstown
Blanchardstown shopping centre 203–4, 206
Blasetti, Alessandro 363
Blessings of the Holy Father, The 355
Blier, Bertrand 255, 257
Blithe Spirit (1944) 118
Blockbuster 183–5, 187–8, 532–33n
Blockbuster Entertainment (Ireland) Ltd *see* Blockbuster
Blu-Ray 184
Blue Light, The (1932) 236
Blythe, Ernest 129, 324, 327, 347–9, 504n, 575n, 577n
Bodies exhibition 179
Bogdanovich, Peter 272, 352
Bohemian Picture House, Dublin 26, 29, 54, 55, 149, 495n
Boland, Gerald 316, 318
Bollywood Ireland 559n
Bolt (2008) 521n
Bond, Jack 272
Bondermann, David 188
Bong, Joon–ho 245
Bono, Ben 38
Boom Babies (1988)
Boorman, John 245, 277, 562n
Boot, Sir Charles 116
Bord Fáilte/Irish Tourist Board 273–4
Borzage, Frank 67
Boston Ventures 222, 546n
Botts & Co. 546n
Bovale Developments 590–1n
Bowden, Tony 187–8
Bowen, Mr 30
Boy from Mercury, The (1996) 277
Boylan, Msgr 363, 590n
Boyle, Jimmy 97
Boyne Cinema, Drogheda 96
Boyne Cinemas Ltd 96
Boyne, J. 574n
Boyne, Mrs. 574n
Box, Muriel 245
Bradbury Films Ltd 67
Bradlaw, Izidore Isaac 27, 28, 56, 129, 487n, 495n, 6
Bradley, Denis 563n
Brady, Erina 239

Brady, John 102
Brady, Sean 567n
Branagh, William (Billy) 490n
Brando, Marlon 340
Brase, Col. Fritz 74
Braun, Harald 354
Bray Cineplex 542n
Breathnach, Paddy 181, 562n
Breathnach, Padraig T. 335-6, 578n
Breathnach, Richard 560n
Breen cinema circuit /family 80, 122, 142, 162
Breen, Dan 295, 567n
Breen, Dermot 270–4, 26
Breen, Laurence 605n
Breen, Martin 80, 122,
Brennan, Desmond F. 581n
Brennan, Martin 353, 356, 552n
Brennan, Miss 86
Brennan, Patrick 32
Brent Walker 163
Bridge Too Far, A (1977) 172
Brief Encounter (1945) 241, 552n
Britannia's Message (1914) 72
British and Dominion Film Corporation 510n
British Board of Film Censors (BBFC) 49, 70, 97, 106, 232–3
British Broadcasting Corporation (BBC) 136, 139, 191, 582n
British Entertainments Tax Abolition League 126
British Federation of Workers' Film Societies 232
British Film Institute (BFI) 238–9, 243–4, 246–9, 257, 278, 306–7, 312, 319, 326, 337, 347, 579n, 584n
British Film Institute (BFI), Northern Ireland branch 246–7 *see also* Belfast Film Institute Society (BFIS)
British International Pictures (BIP) 73–4
British Land 219–20.
British Lion Film Corporation 84, 140, 156
British National Films 116, 160
British Paramount News 117
British Screen 540n
Broadway Cinema, Belfast 82, 124
Broadway Cinema, Manor Street, Dublin 26, 120
Brokeback Mountain (2005) 216
Brophy, James 142
Brooke, Basil 105
Brooke, Lady 247
Brooks, Richard 358
Brosnan, Pierce 282
Brown, Simon 287
Bruce Lee films 163
Bruce, Lenny 254
Bruce-Smith, Sue 562n
Bruckberger, Raymond Leopold 360

Brunswick Cinema Theatre 28, 52, 487n, 499n
Brunswick Motor Exchange 28
Bruton, John 176
Buena Vista International Ireland 181
Buena Vista Social Club, The (1999) 264
Buñuel, Luis 236, 254, 255
Burger, Germain 526n
Burke, David 524n
Burke, Fr (Catholic Film Institute, London) 580n
Burke, John 53
Burke Kennedy Doyle (architects) 204
Burn After Reading (2008) 275
Bursey, Arthur 16, 483n
Burton, Tim 151, 208
Bushe, Con 582n
Busy Bee DVD 190
Busybody, The (c.1930) 503n
Butchers/ Butcher's Film Service, London, 67, 160, 525n
Butler, Ciáran 225–6, 481, 548n
Butler, Colum 225–6, 480–1, 548n
Butler, David 353
Butler, G., and Sons 48
Butler, Maurice 38
Butler, Michael 175–6, 251, 530n
Butler, Tom 217
Butler, Walter 19, 29, 30
Bwana Devil (1952) 150, 522n
Byrne, Alfie 80, 97, 304
Byrne, Edward, archbishop of Dublin 353–5, 566n
Byrne, Gabriel 282, 287–8,
Byrne, Gay 482n
Byrne, Joan 253

Ca n-Imíonn an t-Airgead? (1954) 578n
Cabinet of Dr Caligari, The (1919) 232
Cabiria (1914) 21, 45
Cabra Grand Cinema, Dublin 79, 120, 141
Cado Ltd 223, 546n
Caduta Degli Dei, La see *Damned, The*
Caffrey, David 275
Cahill, A.J. 269
Cahill, Fr Edward 296, 304, 568n
Caine Mutiny, The (1954) 581n
Caldicott, Robert 249
Caldwell, J.C. 177
Calkins, Hugh 354
Call of the Flesh (1930) 353, 586n
Call of the South Seas (1944) 503n
Cambridge (financial services group)183
Camden Picture House, Dublin 499n
Cameo Cinema, Cork 165, 176, 256, 527n, 58
Cameo Cinema, Dublin 175–6, 251, 530n
Camerini, Mario 357
Cameron, James 151, 521n

Campa (1942) 239
Campbell, Caroline 290
Campbell, H.K. 84, 122
Campo Viejo Spanish Film Festival 266
Cannes Film Festival 270, 278
Cannon Cinema, Fisherwick Place, Belfast 206
Cannon Group 157, 203, 205–7, 544n
Canterbury Tales, The (1972) 255, 556n
Capital Irish Film Festival, Washington DC 291
Capitol and Allied Theatres 78, 79, 152, 158, 165, 179, 364, 486n, 491n, 496n, 523n, 528n
Capitol and Provincial Cinemas, Ltd 78
Capitol and Provincial News Theatres 136
Capitol Cinema, Belfast 82, 124, 502n
Capitol Cinema/Theatre, Dublin 53, 69, 71, 73, 95, 122, 152, 157, 61, 84 see also La Scala
Capitol Cinema, Thurles, Tipperary 165, 223
Capitol Cineplex, Cork 535n
Capitol (Cork), Ltd 78
Capitol, Cork 165, 194, 205
Captain Boycott (1947) 582n
Cardinal, The (1963) 360
Carey, Brian 210–1
Carey, James J. 347
Carey, May 237, 23
Carey, Patrick 237
Carey, William D. 237
Caris, Vincenzo (Giuseppe) 485n
Carley, John 52, 56
Carlow African Film Festival 289–90, 566n
Carlow Cinema Ltd 77, 500n
Carlow Cineplex 200, 538n, 542n
Carlow Omniplex 542n
Carlton Cinema, Dublin 62, 78, 95, 122, 125, 157, 207, 215–6, 555n see also Adelphi-Carlton
Carlton Cinema, Limerick 165, 367
Carlton Cinema, London 68
Carlton Screen Advertising 220, 538n, 542n, 546n
Carmelites, The (1959) 360
Carné, Marcel 238, 248
Carney, John 287
Carnival in Flanders see *La Kermesse Héroïque*
Carr, Charles P. 362
Carrick-on-Shannon Cineplex 542n
Carrick-on-Shannon Community School 558n
Carrick-on-Shannon Town Hall 489n
Carroll, Liam 225–6, 548n
Carroll, Pat 552n
Carry On films 160, 163
Carson, Edward 568n
Carstairs, John Paddy 140
Carter, Clifford 246
Carton, Mrs 356
Cartoon Saloon 559n
Casanova (1974) 254–5, 556n

Casanova in Burlesque (1944) 503n
Caserini, Mario 17
Cashel Cinema 31
Cashman, J. 320
Casino Cinema, Doneraile, Co. Cork 122
Casino Cinema, Dundalk 165
Casino Cinema, Finglas, Dublin 142
Casino Cinema, Killarney, Co. Kerry 122, 165
Casino Cinema, Rathmore, Co. Kerry 122
Casino Cinema, Tramore, Co. Waterford 122
Casley, Commandant J.J. 560n
Cassavetes, John 255
Cassidy, Michael 556n
Castle Cinema, Dungannon 518n
Castle Cinema, Ferns 80
Castle Cinema, Oldcastle, Co. Meath 122
Catholic Boy Scouts 239, 343
Catholic Communications' Centre 341
Catholic Educational Cinema Company 301
Catholic Film Institute (London) 580n
Catholic Film Society (London) 235
Catholic Film Society of Ireland (CFSI) 235,
    354–5, 551n
Catholic Reviewing Office (USA) 580n
Catholic Social Service Conference 321, 324,
    334, 574n
Catholic Social Service Group 334
Catholic Social Welfare Bureau 321
Catholic Societies' Vocational Organization
    Conference (CSVOC) 362–3
Catholic Stage Guild (Ireland) 364
Catholic Truth Society 300
Catholic Young Men's Society (CYMS) 320–1,
    362.
Cavan Town Hall Cinema 96
Cavanagh, Joseph 35
CAVIAR *see* Cinema and Video Industries
    Audience Research
Cayatte, André 357
Celtic Film & Television Festival *see* Celtic
    Media Festival
Celtic Media Festival 290–1, 566n
Censorship of Films Act 1923, 59, 69, 97, 233–
    4, 253, 271, 300, 313–17, 355
Censorship of Films Appeal Board 272, 294,
    316, 352–4, 358–61.
Censorship of Publications Act 1930, 300
Censorship of Publications' Board 301, 335,
Central Belfast Picture Theatre Ltd 35
Central Hall, Colne, Lancashire 23, 34
Central Office of Information 584n
Central Picture Theatre, Belfast 35, 138
Central Studio, Limerick 165
Cet Obscur Objet du Désir see *That Obscure
    Object of Desire*
Cham, Mbye 566n

Chambers, C.W. 1
Chambers, Frank W. 62, 493n, 2
Chambers, Richard, Dr 324–6
Channel Four (Ch4) 256, 283
Chapayev (1934) 248
Chaplin, Charlie 41, 63, 68, 87, 236, 496n
Charlemont, Lord 247
Chartbusters 185–7
Chess Player, The (1938) 237
Chesser, Patrick (Pat) 549n
Chicken Little (2005) 521n
Child's Welfare Society 342
Childers, Erskine 93–4, 505n
Children and the cinema (report) 350
Children's and Educational Film Association
    (CEFA) 344–5, 347, 349–50, 584n *see also*
    Comhairle na nÓg (IFS children's commitee)
Children's Cinema Clubs (Rank) 119, 343–6,
    349, 351
Children's cinema committee *see* Comhairle na
    nÓg
Children's Film Council 347, 584n
Children's Film Foundation (GB) 350, 580n
Chipperfield, David 565n
Christmas Carol, A (2009) 521n
Christopher, James 287
Church of Ireland 568n
Churchill, Winston 105
Chweneyagae, Presley 566n
CIC *see* Cinema International Corporation
Cielo Sulla Palude (1949) 356
Cine-UK chain 208, 221, 546n.
Cinema and General Publicity Ltd 141 147, 163,
    541n
Cinema and Hippodrome, Lurgan 30
Cinema and Video Industries Audience Research
    (CAVIAR) 257
Cinema Holdings Ltd 227
Cinema International Corporation (CIC) 156,
    171–2, 202–3, 205
Cinema North-West *see* Cinemobile
Cinema Palace, Carlow 31, 77
Cinema Palace, Dublin 48
Cinema Palace, Wexford 36
Cinema Royal, Dublin 48
Cinema trade complaints' committee (CTCC)
    166–8, 172
Cinemagic, Belfast 269, 286, 560n, 564n, 91
Cinemagic, Dublin event 286
CinemaScope 141, 142, 150, 153–5, 161, 503n
Cinematograph Act 1909, 15, 19, 23, 29, 30, 32,
    33, 49–50, 57, 59, 84, 97
Cinematograph Exhibitors' Association (CEA)
    39, 56, 66, 102, 104, 106–7, 138–40, 500n,
    504n
Cinematograph Films Act 1927, 70

Cinemobiles (including Cinemobile 2000, and Leitrim Cinemobile/Aisling Gheal Liatroma/Cinema North-West) 224, 266–7, 269, 287, 72

Cineplex circuit *see* Omniplex and Ward Anderson

Cineplex Odeon Corporation 194, 197, 199, 201–3, 535n, 539n

Cineplex Odeon Multiplex, Toronto 194, 197

Cinerama 150–4, 522n

Cinerama Group 23, 152

Cinerama Theatre, Talbot Street, Dublin *see* Dublin Cinerama Theatre

Cinergy Film Festival 288

Cines 18, 21, 40, 41

Cineworld 200, 216–7, 220–1, 227, 266, 538n, 549n *see also* Blackstone

Cineworld, Belfast *see* Kennedy Centre multiplex

Cineworld, Dublin 208, 216–7, 220–1, 266, 289, 543n, **69** *see also* Parnell Street multiplex

Cineworld, Glasgow 194

Cineworld, Stockport, England 200

Circuits Managements' Association Ltd (CMA) 121, 124 (*see* Odeon and Gaumont)

Circular Panorama of Electric Tower (1910) 483n

Circular Panorama of Munch Creek, Pennsylvania (1901) 483n

Circular Panorama of Niagara Falls (1901) 483n

City Cinema, Armagh 101, 489n

City Lights (1931) 86–7, 503n

City Lights Leisureplex, Oranmore, Galway 212

City Pavilion (roller skating rink), Dublin 486n

City Side Retail Park (and multiplex), York Street, Belfast 207–8

City Theatre, Limerick 367

Claddagh Palace, Galway 165, 280–1, 563n

Clair, René 233

Clann na Poblachta 121, 132

Clare Board of Health 302

Clarence Pictures, Dublin (distributors) 524n

Clarity Partners 222, 546n

Clark-Brown, T.S. 87

Clarke, Donald 292, 520n

Clarke, Gordon 584n

Clarke, Maura 557n

Clarkson, Patricia 282

Classic Cinema, Belfast 26, 36, 66, 73, 87, 97, 104, 121, 507n, 512n

Classic Cinema, Cork 165

Classic Cinema, Harold's Cross, Dublin *see* Kenilworth Cinema

Classic Cinema, Terenure, Dublin 80, 168, 176, 238, 347

Classic cinemas 66

Classic Movieplex, Listowel, Co. Kerry 266

Clerkin, David 209

Clery, A.B. 335

Clery, Val 574n

Climan, Sandy 520n

Cloche, Maurice 271, 355

Clockwork Orange, A (1971) 255

Clohessy, Lewis 276–8, 562n

Cloistered (1936) 353, 586n

Clonard Hall Company 35

Clonard Picture House, Belfast 35, 36, 65, 87

Clones Film Festival 286–7

Clonmel Omniplex 213, 223

Clontarf Town Hall 29, 31

Cloran, J. 1

Cloudy with a Chance of Meatballs (2009) 521n

Clouse, Robert 171

Cluster.net 291

Coburn, James 303

Cobweb, The (1917) 41

Coen Brothers 275

Cogan, Patrick 133

Cogan, R. 165

Cogan, T.J. 1

Cohen, Nat 526n

Coleman, H. 54

Coleman, Rob 291

Coleraine council 103, 104, 507n

Colgan, Michael 582n

Coliseum Cinema, Carlow 165

Coliseum Cinema, Cork 66, 78

Coliseum Cinema, Grosvenor Road, Belfast 36, 81, 124, 207, 490n, 512n

Coliseum Cinema, Limerick 489n

Coliseum Cinema/Theatre, Henry Street, Dublin 26, 62, 487n

Coliseum Theatre of Living Pictures, Redmond's Hill, Dublin 28, 29, 487n

Collado, Esperanza 559n

College of Commerce, Rathmines/Dublin Institute of Technology 558–59n

Collier, Fr Daniel 320–2, 326, 330–5, 348, 574n, 577n

Collier, Patrick, bishop of Ossory 315, 321 323, 326, 572n

Collins, Darryl 187

Collins, David 253, 276–8, 557n, 582n

Collins, Diane 511n

Collins, Michael, 175–6, 251, 542n

Collins, Pat 281

Colonial Picture Combine 15

Columbia 156, 167

Columbia-Warner Distributors Ltd 167, 171–2

Comber Cinema/Picture Palace, Belfast 142

Comerford, Henry 560n

Comerford, Joe 280

Comfort, Lance 140

Comhairle le Leas Óige 332

Comhairle na nÓg/Irish Film Society Children's Cinema/Film Commitee 239, 241, 344–5, 347–50, 584n *see also* Children's and Educational Film Association of Ireland (CEFA)
Comhdháil Náisiúnta na Gaeilge 332, 348
Comhlucht Scannán Glórach na h-Éireann 575n
Comin' through the Rye (1916) 41
Comiskey, Ray 180, 203, 252
Commane, Paudie 552n
Commercial and Industrial Property 156
Commitments, The (1991) 181
Comradeship see *Kameradschaft*
Concannon, Rory 279, 563n
Concrete Jungle, The see *Criminal, The*
Connaughton, Shane 366
Connell, Dr Desmond, archbiship of Dublin, 586n
Connerty, Michael 290
Connolly, Matt 197
Connolly, Neil 244, 246, 259–62, 267, 269, 278, 368
Connolly, Fr Peter 586n
Conradh na Gaeilge 348
Conroy, Colman 115, 170, 510n, 530n, 584n
Constitution of Ireland 1937 111, 307, 309, 313–4, 318, 325, 345, 568n, 570n
Control of Manufacturers Acts 85, 94, 111, 119
Conway, Dr A.W. 323
Cooder, Ry 264
Coogan, Steve 289
Cooke, Maeve 246
Cookstown council 103
Coon, A.D. 14, 71
Cooney, Eamon 29
Cooper, Thomas G. (Tom) 92, 112, 122, 573n
Co-Operative Film Society 324
Coppola, Francis 260
Corcoran, Vincent 280
Cork choral festival 270
Cork corporation / city council 32, 267–8
Cork Enterprise Board 267
Cork Film Centre 559n
Cork Film Festival (CFF) 229, 256–8, 263, 267, 269, 270–5, 276, 279, 281, 288, 560–1n, 563n, 28, 92
Cork French Film Festival 286
Cork Omniplex 151
Corinthian Cinema, Dublin 64, 65, 75, 118, 129, 138, 157, 158, 177, 499n, 531n, 18, 85
Corish, Brendan 135
Cornfield, John 116
Corona (sponsor) 275, 289, 562n
Corona Fastnet Short Festival, Schull, Cork 289
Corr, Mr (Dublin councillor) 302
Corr, Aidan (Board of directors, Limerick Film Festival) 564n
Corrigan, Patrick A. 499n
Corrigans' undertaker 28
Cosgrave, Liam 567n
Cosgrave, Mrs (Dublin corporation) 571n
Cosgrave, William T. 74–5, 85, 230, 324, 502n
Costello, John A. 122–3,
Coulson, Ms E.M. 230–1
Court Laundry (1917) 73
Courtney family 38
Coward, Gillian 563n
Cowell, George E. 230
Cowey, Owen 578n
Cowley, William 551n
Cox, Tom 277, 562n
Cox-Johnston, Richard 523n
Coyne, R.C. 329
Craigavon, Viscount 129
Craobh na L'Aiseirghe 239
Crawford, Mr 97
Crawford-Wilkins' rinks 485n
Creagán Centre, An, Co. Tyrone 288
Creature from the Black Lagoon (1954) 520n
Credit Lyonnais 207–8
Cregan, Mairín 584n
Crichton, Charles 280
Crilly, Anne 563n
Criminal, The (1960) 359, 589n
Crocodile Dundee (1986) 544n
Crofton, Harry 165
Cronin, Msgr Michael 294, 353, 360, 566–67n, 586n
Crosbie, Paddy 46–7, 491n
Crosby, Bing 137, 357, 364
Crosland, Alan 74
Crossley Clitheroe, J. 247
Crotty, Daniel 506n
Crouching Tiger, Hidden Dragon (2000) 264
Crowley, John (director) 181
Crowley, John (exhibitor) 499n
Crumlin Picture House, Belfast 34, 35, 65
Crumlin Picture House Ltd 35
Cu Uladh 571n
Cukor, George 357
Cullen, Art 574n
Cullen, Cardinal Paul 293
Culleton, Harry W. 122, 500n
Culliton, Gary 178
Cultural Cinema Consortium 224, 267–8
Cumann Déanta Scannáin Oideachais 239, 347
Cumann na nGaedheal 85, 87, 303, 502n, 504n
Curia Archiepiscopalis Dublinensis 588n
Curistan, Peter 215, 217, 540n, 544n
Curley's Cinemas 207
Curragh Picture House 66
Curran, Fred 82

Curran, James 83
Curran, Jim 563n
Curran, Michael 71, 81–3, 502n, 3, 13
Curran, Michael (junior) 508n
Curran circuit 34, 81–4, 512n
Curran Theatres Ltd 82, 124
Curtis, William M.M. 499n, 505n
Curtiz, Michael 82
Curzon Cinema, Belfast 206
Curzon Cinema, Dublin 175, 176, 241, 251, 258, 260
Cusack, Cyril 159
Cussen, George P. 301, 304, 342, 571n, 383n

D'Arcy, Fr Brian 590n
Dáil Éireann 29, 71, 88, 91, 119, 120, 133, 230, 231, 271, 303, 320, 346,
Daldry, Stephen 282
Dalton, Geoffrey 239, 23
Dalton, Lilian 230, 550n
Dalton, Thomas 42–3
Daly, Aidan 180
Daly, Gerry 253
Daly, Mary 43
Dame Street Picture House, Dublin 51–2, 54, 66
Damned, The (1969) 255, 556n
Dan Lowrey's Music Hall *see* Star of Erin
Dance School (1946) 239
Daniel, Martin 282
Daniels' family 38, 490n
Dann, C. 96
Danny Boy (1941) 160, 526n
Dante, Joe 521n
Darklight Film Festival 270, 290–1, 559n, 566n, 96
Das Unsterbliche Lied see *The Immortal Song*
Davies, Terence 261
Davis, John (Rank/Odeon) 117–18, 147, 156, 344, 346, 583n
Davis, John T. (filmmaker) 272, 283, 518n
Davis, J.W. (solicitor) 487n
Davis, Thomas 336
Davis, Tim 587n.
Davy, John H. 149
Dawn, The (1936) 92, 112, 122, 311, 362, 573n
Dawn Patrol, The (1930) 503n
Daylight Saving Time Act 61
DCC [Development Capital Company] Group plc 188, 534n
De Mille, Cecil B. 356, 32
de Paul, St Vincent 355 *see also* St Vincent de Paul Society
de Rochemont, Louis 588n
de Sica, Vittorio 250, 362
de Toth, André 150
de Valera, Éamon 108, 230, 296, 303, 309–11,

318–19, 324, 328–9, 336, 344–6, 349, 503n, 568n, 571n, 573n, 574–77n, 583n
de Valera, Síle 509n
de Valera, Vivion 567n
de Vere White, Terence 569n
de Vignan, Robert 354
Dean, James 245
Dean Estate Ltd 498n
Deane, Seamus 283
Deasy, Michael J. 77, 122
Deasy, Seamus 282
Debord, Guy 482n
Decameron, The (1971) 255, 556n
December Bride (1990) 262
Decoin, Henri 250
Deerslayer (1943) 503n
Defroqué, Le (1953) 358
del Toro, Guillermo 245
Delahunty, P. 96
Delaney, Richard 238, 584n
Delannoy, Jean 262
Democratic Unionist Party 49
Dempsey, Fr 339, 586n
Denham Film Studios 118
Dennehy and Dennehy Designs Ltd 267
Denzille Private Cinema 197–8
Derrig, Thomas 332, 346, 577n
Derry city council 103, 105
Desmond, Aoife 559n
Desmond Cinema, Cappoquin, Co. Waterford 80
Deutsch, Oscar 116
Desperately Seeking Susan (1985) 562n
Devane, Fr Richard Stanislaus 93, 95, 108, 294, 296, 299–307, 309–26, 328–31, 333–6, 340, 567–78n, 21
Developing cultural cinema in Ireland (report) 244, 265, 267, 269
Devereux, Eoin 575n
Devils, The (1971) 255, 556n
Devlin, H. 246
Devlin, Joseph 127–9
Devlin, Michele 285, 558n
Dewhurst, George 64
Dial M for Murder (1954) 520–21n
Diamond Picture House, Belfast 65, 66, 207
Dick, John 555n
Dieu a besoin des homes see *Isle of Sinners*
Digital Cinema Ltd (DCL) 223–4, 547n
Digital Hub, Dublin 290
Digital Theatre Systems (DTS) 223–4, 541n
Digital versatile disc (DVD) 182–92
Dignan, John, bishop of Clonfert 318, 323
Dillon, James 303
Dillon, Maretta 244–6, 262, 267, 269–70, 278, 368

Dillon, Matt 282
Dingle Film Festival 288, 565n
Disney Corporation 150, 155, 189, 191
Distant Voices, Still Lives (1988) 261
Diva (1981) 258, 260
Divide and Conquer 105
Divorce American Style (1967) 251
Divorcing Jack (1998) 275
Dixon, Sam W. 54
Dmytryk, Edward 360
Dobbyn, Seamus 304
Dobler, George 76
Doctor's Secret, The (1929) 496n
Dodona Research 200, 220, 269
Doherty, James 82
Donaghy, Noel 138
Donlon, Phelim 259
Donnelly, John 35
Donnelly, Robert 76
Donnybrook Fair 47
Dooge, James 580n
Doolan, Lelia 268, 280–1, 509n, 516n, 560n, 582n
Doras Luimní 289
Dore, Philip 87
Dorgan, Theo 258, 274, 276
Dornhelm, Robert 277
Dorset Picture Hall *see* Dorset Picture House
Dorset Picture House, Dublin 23, 52, 54, 17, 77
Dougan, Albert 138
Dougherty, Revd J.O. George 51
Douglas, Senator James G. 230
Douglas, John Harold 230
Dowd, Ned 565n
Dowdall, Mrs J 560n
Dowling, Revd J.P., OP 51
Dowling, Jack 516n
Downing, Patrick 32
Doyle, Jack 160, 526n
Doyle, P.V. 179
Doyle, Revd. Dr 569n
Doyle, Roddy 181, 283
Doyle, Sé Merry 518n
Doyle, T. 96
Drake, Nigel 195
DreamWorks 151
Dreville, Jean 237
Drew, Professor (Albert College) 571n, 574n
Dreyer, Carl 229
Dromcolliher *see* Drumcollogher
Drowning by Numbers (1988) 261
Druid Theatre, Galway 268
Drum, Con 320
Drumcollogher 'cinema' 31–2, 59
Drumcondra FC 159
Drumshanbo traditional music festival 270

DTA Architects 194
Dublin African Film Festival (DAFF) 289
Dublin and South of Ireland Cinematograph Exhibitors' Association (DSICEA) 53–4, 62, 66, *see also* Theatre and Cinema Association of Ireland
Dublin Central Mission 48
Dublin Cinema Group (DCG) 210–11, 219, 226, 545n
Dublin Cinemas Ltd 508n
Dublin Cinematograph Theatre *see* Picture House, O'Connell Street, Dublin
Dublin Cinerama Theatre, Talbot Street, Dublin 152
Dublin corporation / city council 19, 28, 29, 50–1, 57, 59, 61, 66, 97, 109, 204, 268, 276–7, 279, 302
Dublin Film Festival (1986–2001) 178, 260, 275–9, 561–52n, 93
Dublin Film Festival (2003–) *see* Dublin International Film Festival
Dublin Film Society (1930) 229–33, 246
Dublin Film Society (DFS) 241–2, 250, 253, 556n *see also* Irish Film Society (IFS)
Dublin International Film Festival (DIFF; 2003–) 270, 275, 279–80, 288, 526n, 28
Dublin Kinematograph Theatres Ltd 28, 75, 499n
Dublin Little Theatre Guild 232–6, 249
Dublin Metropolitan Police (DMP) 50, 52, 53
Dublin Police Act 1842, 508n
Dublin Road, Belfast multiplex 544n
Dublin Theatre Company 75, 498–9n
Dublin Theatre Festival 270, 276, 561n
Dublin Theatre Players 551n
Dublin Total Abstinence Society 48, 492n
Dudley, Revd Owen 304, 569n
Duel in the Sun (1946) 585n
Duff, Charles 486n
Duff, James Augustine 126
Dufferin and Ava, Marquis of 246–7
Duffield, Gordon 106
Duffy, Martin 277
Duffy, Mrs (travelling circus) 488n
Duffy & Co., James (solicitors) 309
Dukes, Alan 180
Dulanty, J.W. 346
Dunamaise Arts Centre 558n
Duncairn Picture Theatre, Belfast 36, 96, 141, 535n
Duncairn Picture Theatre Co 36
Dundalk Film Festival *see* Cinergy Film Festival
Dundalk town council 506n
Dundalk Town Hall Buildings 38
Dundealgan [Dundalk] Electric Theatres Ltd 38
Dundonald Omniplex 151

Dundrum cinema *see* Movies@Dundrum
Dungan, Myles 276–7
Dunn, Fr Joseph 341, 358,
Dunne, Msgr 363, 590n
Dunning, Patrick (Paddy) 523n
Dunseith, T.R. 97
Durwood, Stanley H. 201
Duvivier, Julien 247, 354
DVD 182–92
dvdrentals.ie 188 *see* Screenclick.com
Dwyer, Michael 242–3, 275–81, 552–53n, 562n, 582n, 27
Dylan, Bob 288
Dzigan, Efim 248

Eagle-Lion Distributors Ltd 84, 123
Ealing Studios 117
Earlsfort Terrace Rink 485n
Early Bird, The (1936) 112
Earthquake (1974) 171
East Lynne (1913) 40
Easter Amusements in Ulster (1929) 246
Easy Street (1917) 236
Eblana Theatre, Dublin 250
Ecce Homo (film) see *Golgotha*
Ecce Homo (play) 362
Echo Park LA (2006) 245
Eclipse Pictures, Dublin (distributors) 524n, 563n
Edison Company 40, 41
Educational Film Programme Group 239
Edukators, The (2004) 245
Edward Holdings 224
Egan, Joseph 80, 501n
Egan, John 122
Egan Film Service Ltd 361, 589n
Egymásra Nézve see *Another Way*
Eisenstein, Sergei 229, 232
Ekk, Nikolai 247
El Capitán de Loyola (1949) 587n
Elba Films 362, 590n
Electra (1961) 555n
Electric Palace, Larne 81, 82, **44**
Electric Picture Palace, Belfast 34
Electric Theatre, Dublin 23, 33, 50, 52, 54, 66, 78, 122 *see* New Capitol
Elizabeth II 139
Elliman family / cinema chain 42, 75–6, 80, 84, 92–3, 95, 110–11, 118–20, 125, 129, 158, 168, 302, 343–4, 356 505n *see also* individual members
Elliman, Abe 28, 52, 118, 158, 1
Elliman, B. 356
Elliman, Edward 170, 530n
Elliman, Geoffrey 118, 170, 500n, 516n, 530n
Elliman, Jacob 43, 52

Elliman, Jack 118
Elliman, Louis 28, 76–7, 79, 84, 118, 158, 499n, 511n, 530n, 32
Elliman, Maurice 27–8, 33, 42–3, 52, 64, 73, 75–6, 88, 95, 118, 302, 487–9n, 501n, 511n, 1
Elliman, Max 1
Ellis family, 26, 73, 78, 80, 302 *see also* Jack Ellis
Ellis, Gerald 118
Ellis, Jack 78, 122, 500n
Ellmann, Richard 21
Elmer Gantry (1960) 358, 588n
Elstree Studios 73, 116, 510n
Embassy *see* Academy, Pearse Street, Dublin.
Emerald Productions 525n
Emergency Powers Order 107, 143, 355, 511n, 573n
EMI 157, 163, 169, 171
Emmerson, Michael 249
Employers' Federation, Ireland 42
Empire, Leicester Square, London 228, 523n
Empire of Passion (1978) 255
Empire of the Senses (1976) 255
Empire Theatre, Dublin 53, 228 *see also* Star of Erin
Empire Theatre/Cinema, Galway 79
Ennis Cinemas Ltd 500n
Ennis Town Hall 122
Ennis urban district council 302
Enniskillen local council 100
ENSA 104
Enter the Dragon (1973), 171
Enterprise Ireland 553n
Enterprise Zone projects (UK) 204
Entertainment Enterprises Group (Ire) 225, 480–1
Entertainment Film Distributors (EFD) 216
Entertainment Halls Ltd 16
Entertainments tax (ET) 58, 60–1, 85, 87–92, 96, 109, 114, 126–43, 155, 161, 311
Epell, Dr Isaac 64
Erne Cinema, Ballyshannon 87
Essanay Manufacturing Film Company 41 68
Eternal Gift, The (1941) 354, 587n
Eternal Mask, The see *Ewige Maske, Die* 238
Eucharistic Congress, 1932 301
Europa Cinema 554n
European Audiovisual Observatory 184
European Motion Picture Company 67
Eurostat 218
Everett, James (Jim) 131, 271.
Everything You Always Wanted to Know about Sex ... (1972) 254, 556n
Ewige Maske, Die (1935) 238
Express Film Agency 67
Eye Cinema, Galway 197, 201, 223, 225, 265–6, 481, 543n, **66**

Face of the Cat, The (1958) 250
Faces of the Children see *Visages d'Enfants*
Fagan, James C. 322, 334–5, 338–9, 585n, 22
Fagan, Myron C. 551n
Fahey, Fr. Denis 294, 296, 552n, 566–69n
Fahy, Justice 30
Failure of individualism, The (1948) 294
Fair trade commission 166 *see also* restrictive
  practices commission
Fairfax (Ward Anderson company) 541n
Faith in Wales (c.1951) 587n
Fallon, Gabriel 331–2, 335, 576n, 581n
Famous Lasky Film Services Ltd 68 *see also*
  Paramount Film Service Ltd
Famous Players-Lasky Corporation 67, 68 *see
  also* Paramount
Fanfare (1958) 272
Farrell, Colin 29
Farrell family 28, 78, 80, 92, 95, 110, 122, 158,
  161 *see also* individual members
Farrell, F. 1
Farrell, John 523n
Farrell, John J. 23, 25, 27 28–9, 33–4, 53, 56,
  64, 66, 69, 78, 80, 88, 95, 129, 496–7n, 508n,
  1
Farrell, John M. 523n
Farrell, Patrick (Paddy) 78, 95, 364, 505n, 1
Farrell, Peter 78, 505n
Farrow, Graeme 249, 291
Farthing, Elaine 563n
Fassbender, Michael 282, 287
Father Mathew Hall, Dublin 353, 363
Fatima Gown (c.1951) 587n
Fawcett, F.P. 54
Fear Éachtach (*Servant of mankind*, Thomas
  Edison) 579n
Federation of Irish Film Societies (FIFS, including
  access>CINEMA, the name under which it
  was reorganized in 2001) 242–46, 253, 265,
  269, 286, 290, 341 552–54n, 556n
Federation of Irish Manufacturers 108
Feeney, John 294, 574n
Feeney, Peter 582n
Féile Beochan 286
Fellini, Federico 240, 254
Fermanagh council 104
Fermoy 'cinema' 31, 32, 489n
Ferrara, Abel 562n
Feyder, Jacques 236–7, 238
Ffrench, N.J. 93
Fianna Fáil 85, 87, 93, 119, 124, 132, 231, 271,
  301–3, 306, 570n
Field, Mary 350, 580n
Fields, Bill 183
15-Second Film Festival 289, 566n
Film Booking Offices Ltd 67, 68

Film Centre, O'Connell Bridge House, Dublin
  175–6, 251, 530n
Film Council (UK) 249, 266
Film in Ireland: the role of the Arts Council 265
Film in national life, The (1932) 307
Film Institute of Ireland 582n *see* Irish Film
  Institute
Film Network 207
Film Services Ltd 41
Film Society, London 230, 232
Film Society of Northern Ireland 246
Filmbank 243
Filmbase 290, 341, 582n
Filmclub (UK) 269, 560n
Films Ltd (distributor) 36, 502n
Final Destination (2009) 521n
Finance (New Duties) Act 1915 (GB & I) 125
Finance (New Duties) Act 1916 (GB & I) 60–1,
  126
Finance Act 1917 (GB & I) 61
Finance Act 1918 (GB & I) 61, 513n
Finance Act 1919 (GB & I) 61
Finance Act 1923 (GB) 512n
Finance Act 1931 (IFS) 87–8, 125, 130, 513n
Finance Act 1932 (IFS) 125, 300
Finance Act 1935 (IFS) 130, 513n
Finance Act 1936 (IFS) 130–1, 513n
Finance Act 1939 (IFS) 126, 237–8 513n
Finance Act 1940 (GB) 130, 513–14n
Finance Act 1940 (NI) 130, 514n
Finance Act 1942 (GB) 130, 514n
Finance Act 1943 (GB) 130, 514n
Finance Act 1943 (NI) 131, 514n
Finance Act 1943 (Éire) 131, 514n
Finance Act 1947 (Éire) 131, 514n
Finance Act 1947 (Éire; supplementary budget)
  131, 514n
Finance Act 1948 (Éire) 132, 514n
Finance Act 1948 (NI) 133, 514n
Finance Act 1949 (ROI) 133, 514n
Finance Act 1949 (NI) 133, 515n
Finance Act 1953 (ROI) 134, 515n
Finance Act 1955 (ROI) 515n
Finance Act 1956 (ROI) 135, 515n
Finance Act 1957 (ROI) 135, 515n
Finance Act 1957 (NI) 138–9, 517n
Finance Act 1958 (ROI) 126, 135
Finance Act 1958 (NI) 517n
Finance Act 1959 (ROI) 135, 515–16n
Finance Act 1960 (ROI) 136
Finance Act 1960 (GB) 140, 517n
Finance Act 1960 (NI) 140
Finance Act 1961 (NI) 140
Finance Act 1962 (ROI) 137, 516n
Fine Arts Cinema Club, Dublin 250–1, 516n
Fine Gael 271, 303

Finney, James U. 81, 502n
Fior Uisce (*Water Wisdom*, 1962), 273
First Communion see *His Majesty Mr Jones*
First National 76
First National Exhibitors' Circuit (FNEC) 68, 69
First National Pathé 73
Fís Film Festival (FFF) 286
Fishing Village (1940) 239
Fitzgerald, Barry 590n
Fitzgerald, Desmond 494n
Fitzgerald, S. (CFF committee), 560n
Fitzgerald, Sandy (arts administrator) 276
Fitzgerald SC, W. O'B. 580n
Fitzgerald-Kenney, James 29
Fitzpatrick, Hugh 331, 578n
Fitzpatrick, Sean 480–1
Fitzsimons, P. (doorman) 86
Fitzsimons, Patrick J. (Dublin Theatre Guild
    director) 236, 23
Flaherty, Nora 560n
Flanagan, Fionnuala 560n
Flanagan, Fr John 300
Flavin, Colin 284
Fleishmann, George 525n
Fleming, George P. 62, 69, 493n, 496n
Flix Leisure 591n
Flood, Justice 31
Flynn, Emmett J. 63
Flynn, Fr, Kilbeggan, Co. Westmeath 505n
Foley, Jayne 564n
Foolsmate (1940) 237
For Ireland's Sake (1912) 295
Forbes, Bryan 255
Forbes, R.E. (architect), 490n
Forbidden Relations (1983) 260
Ford, John 152, 364
Forde, Sean 312
Forde, William 32
Foreman, Donal 559n, 564n
Forever Amber (1947) 585n
Forman, Denis 584n
Forman, George 264
Forsythe, John 43
Forum Cinema, Crumlin Road, Belfast 81, 124,
    535n
Forum Cinema, Glasthule, Co. Dublin 167, 177,
    222, 501n *see also* Astoria
Fosse, Bob 254
Foster, Dr 246
Fountain Cinema, Dublin 80, 129
4 *Adventures of Reinette & Mirabelle* (1987) 261
Fox Film Corporation 68, 69, 511n, 523n (*see*
    20th Century-Fox)
Fox Movietone News 71
Foyle Film Festival 283–4, 291, 90
Foyle Film Projects 283, 563n

Frame, David 56, 62, 66, 490n
Franco, General 234, 299
Frankenheimer, John 152
Frankenstein (1931) 503n, 506n
Frears, Stephen 282, 288
Freeman, William H. 76, 94, 499n
Freemasonry and the anti-Christian movement
    296
French Film Festival (IFI) 264, 558n
French National Cinema Control Board 312
Frenchman's Creek (1944) 69
Fresh Film Festival 257, 269, 286–7, 558n, 564n
Friç, Martin 238
Fricker, Archdeacon 55
Fricker, Brenda 287
Friday the 13th Part 3 (1982) 521n
From the Manger to the Cross (1912) 45, 492n,
    507n
Front Page, The (1930) 503n
Frontier Cinema, Newry 82, 124, 512n
Fugitive, The (1947) 364, 590n
Fugitive Places (2007) 282
Funeral of Edward VII 27
Furey, T.J. 83, 518n
Furlong, Nicholas (Nicky) 185, 188, 533n
Further Gesture, A (1997) 277
Fusano Properties 268

G-Force (2009) 521n
Gabin, Jean 238, 354
Gaelic Athletic Association (GAA) 93, 275, 299,
    304, 323, 332, 335–6, 500n
Gaelic League 309, 323
Gaiety Cinema, Arklow 547n
Gaiety Cinema, Belfast 36
Gaiety Cinema, Ennis, Co. Clare 122, 500n
Gaiety Cinema Group 547n
Gaiety Cinema, Sligo 223
Gaiety Theatre, Dublin 45, 53, 76–7, 304, 499n,
    80
Gala Cinema, Ballyfermot, Dublin 142, 165,
    527n
Gallagher, Margaret 563n
Gallagher, Patrick 178
Gallagher, Fr 366
Gallagher, Mr (solicitor, NFI treasurer) 323
Gallery of Photography 566n
Galway, Maurice 287–8, 565n
Galway Arts Centre 268, 591n
Galway Arts Festival 269, 280–1
Galway Cinemas Ltd 79
Galway city council 268
Galway City Museum 268
Galway Film Centre 268, 591n
Galway Film Fleadh 244–5, 268–9, 279, 280–2,
    283, 288, 591n, 30, 89

Galway Film Society 241, 243, 244, 268, 280, 289, 591n
Galway Multiplex Ltd 227
Galway (city) Omniplex (Headford Road) 151, 212–3, 227, 281
Galway One World Centre 289
Galway Town Hall, 165, 224, 244, 281, 289, 30
Game Group Corporation 185, 533n
Gamestation stores 185
GameStop stores 533n
Gamesworld stores 533n
Gannon, Brenda 562n
Garavan, Tom 564n
Garden Cinema, Warrenpoint 106
Garland, Judy 137
Garnett, Tay 152
Garter Lane Arts Centre, Waterford 244
Gast, Leon 264
Gaston, James 97, 98
Gate Multiplex, Cork 223, 275
Gate Theatre, Dublin 323, 335
Gaumont 26, 40, 41, 67, 73–4, 76, 78, 80, 116, 121, 153, 155, 488n
Gaumont Cinema, formerly Classic, Belfast 26, 121, 512n
Gaumont Cinema, formerly Tivoli, Belfast 124
Gavin, Martin 534n, 547n
Gavin Duffy, Louise 347
Gay and Lesbian Film Festival, 264, 275, 558n
Gaze *see* Gay and Lesbian Film Festival
Gazettes travelling cinema 38
Gem Cinema, Carrickmacross 31
Gem Distribution 534n
General, The (1998) 245
General Cinema Finance Corporation (GCFC) 116
General Council of County Councils 342–3
General Film Distributors (GFD) 84, 116, 163, 541n
General Film Supply (GFS) 41, 67, 72–3
General Line, The (1929) 550n
General Theatres Corporation 116
Generation, A (1954) 250
Genina, Augusto 356
George's Hall, Dublin 48, 52
George V 53
Geraghty, Tracy 560n
Gerasimov, Sergei 248
Gerlier, Cardinal 361
Geronomi, Clyde 155
Get Out Your Handkerchiefs (1978) 257
Getting It Up see *Les Valseuses*
Gibbons, Cedric 101
Gibbons, Luke 582n
Gibney, Alex 282
Gifford, Grace 73

Gigi (1958) 357
Gilliam, Terry 562n
Gilmartin, Thomas, archbishop of Tuam, 298, 572n
Ging, Larry 501n
Ging, Leonard 78–80, 115, 120, 501n, 517n, 584n, 1
Ging, Peter 80
Ging, Thomas (Tommy) 501n
Given, John 562n
Glatzer, Richard 245
Gleeson, Brendan 282
Gleeson, John 32
Gleeson, Kieran 266
Glen, William Riddell 76
Glenaan, Kenneth 245
Glengormley multiplex *see* Movie House cinema chain
Glennane, Ronan 525n
Glennie, Sarah 264
Glennon, Msgr R.J. 358, 360
Glover, Crispin Hellion 566n
Glover, Jeremy 188
Godard, Jean-Luc 273
Goethe Institute 276
Gogan, Jane 555n
Gogan, Nicky 290
Gogan, Thomas J. (Tommy) 79, 94, 250, 555n
Goggin, W.R. 37
Going My Way (1944) 364
Going Places see *Les Valseuses*
Gold, J. 87
Golden age, The 320
Golden Bed, The (1925) 606n
Golden crest, The 320
Goldwyn, Samuel 68
Golgotha (1935) 354–5, 551n, 587n
Gomery, Douglas 193, 535–37n
Good Shepherd Order 353
Goodbody, H. 490n
Goretta, Claude 255
Goretti, Maria 356
Gorey multiplex (Movies@Gorey) 223
Gorky, Maxim 231
Gorman, Herbert 484n
Gout, Alberto 359
Grafton News and Cartoon Cinema, Dublin 136
Grafton Station, Dublin 16
Grafton Street Picture House / Grafton Cinema, Dublin 21, 24, 25, 26, 45, 73, 78, 122, 136, 231, 302, 516n, 46
Graham, Mr 246
Graham, Richard (Dickie) H. 28, 29, 487n
Granada Television 155
Grand Central Cinema, 6/7 O'Connell Street, Dublin 26–7, 29, 33–4, 64, 65, 78, 79

Grand Central Cinema, Limerick 367, 489n, 527–28n
Grand Central Cinema, Tramore, Co. Waterford 180
Grand Cinema, 8 Lower O'Connell Street, 27, 34, 59, 62, 487n
Grand Cinema, Drumcondra, Dublin 78, 120, 162, 369
Grand Cinema, Enniscorthy, Co Wexford 500
Grand Cinema, Fairview, Dublin 78, 120, 138.
Grand Cinema, Whitehall, Dublin 124, 142
Grand Opera House, Belfast 45
Grand Prix (1966) 152
Grandy, H. 490n
Grangers 67
Grapevine Arts Centre, Dublin 276
Gray, Miss 86
Gray, George JP 97, 103
GRE Properties 204
Great Brunswick Street Picture House, Dublin *see* Brunswick Cinema Theatre
Great Northern Kinema Company 35
Greatest Question The (1919) 526n
Green Cinema, Dublin *see* Stephen's Green Cinema
Green Group Ltd 156, 160, 162–5, 169, 171, 178–9, 203, 210–11, 220, 541n
Green Isle Film Agency 41
Green Pastures, The (1936) 506n
Green Property Co. 203
Greenaway, Peter 261, 275
Greene, Graham 364
Greene, Kathleen 182, 532n
Greene, Patrick 182, 532n
Greene, Plunket 504n
Greene, Roger 327
Greenwich Cinema, London 540n
Greenwood, Mr W.E. 74
Gregory, Alistair 540n
Gregson, John 271
Grey, Ian, 539n
Grierson, John 247, 580n
Griffith, D.W. 45
Griffith, Kenneth 280
Grim Trials of Vida Novak, The (2009) 564n
Grimoin-Sanson, Raoul 483n
Grokenda Holdings 212
Grosvenor Hall, Belfast 98, 248
Grove, B. Irene 347
Grove Cinema, Athy, Co. Kildare 165
Grove Cinema (formerly Premier), Lucan, Co. Dublin 162, 165, 527n
Guardian's Sofa Cinema 534–35n
Guazzoni, Enrico 21, 40
Guckian, Brian 547n
Guitry, Sacha 238, 248

Gundogdu, Mustafa 290
Guth Gafa Documentary Film Festival 288, 565n

Haanstra, Bert 272
Hackett, Felix 349, 570n, 571n
Hackett, Hazel 555n
Haggard, Piers 272
Haig, Charles 246
Haldane, Bert 40
Hale's Tours 16, 483n
Half Moon Theatre, Cork 268
Hallessy, J.V. 234–5, 354–5, 551n, 587n
Hamilton, J.H. 499n, 505n
Hamilton, J.W.A. 37
Hamlet (1948) 582n
Hampton, Christopher 282
Hanby, Paul 549n
Hand, Desmond 578n
Hands, Guy 221, 546n
Hanlon, John 159–60, 327
Hanlon, Tommy 112
Hanna, George Boyle 100–1, 134, 507n
Hanna, John 499n
Hannigan, Michael (Mick) 258, 263, 267–8, 274–6, 582n, 24
Ha'penny Film Club 555n
Happy Hooker, The (1975) 171
Happy Warrior, The (1917) 41
Hardiman, Edward S. 361, 590n
Harkin, Margo 283, 563n
Harland and Wolff 82
Harma & Co. 41
Harper, William (Bill) F. 562n
Harrelson, Woody 282
Harrison, Mr L. 309, 312
Harvesters, The (1948) see *Bitter Rice*
Harwood, Ronald 282
Hathaway, Henry 152, 522n
Hayes Brothers 38
Hayes, Frederick 28
Hayes, Fr John M. 324–5, 328, 574–75n
Hayes, Richard (film censor) 240–1, 316–7, 353, 355, 363, 551–52n, 585–7n, 589–90n
Hayward, Richard 327
Healy, H.J. 350, 585n, 22
Healy, John 58
Heaven Can Wait (1943) 355
Heaven Over the Marshes see *Cielo Sulla Palude*
Heimat series (1979–84) 276
Helix Theatre, Dublin 286
Hell and High Water (1954) 581n
Henna, Bonnie 566n
Henrick, Seán 272
Henry V (1944) 118
Henry VIII 294
Henry: Portrait of a Serial Killer (1990) 482n

Hepworth, Cecil M. 39, 41, 72
Hepworth Company 40–1
Heraty, P.J. 523n
Hernon, P.J. 323
Hess, Hermann 254
HgCapital 221
Hibbert, Henry 33
Hibernia Pictures Ltd 579n
Hibernian Cinema, Mullingar 165
Hibernian Electric Theatre, Dublin 488n
Hibernian Films Ltd 41
Hichie, Ethel Mary 271
Hickey, James 276–8
Higginbottom and Stafford (architects) 34, 59
Higgins, Michael D. 268, 281
Higginson, Hugh 56
High Spirits (1988) 277
High Wycombe multiplex, England 203
Highfield Estates Ltd 545n
Hiley, Nicholas 22, 42
Hill, George Roy 171–2
Hill, John 232, 247, 283, 506n, 557n
Hills of Donegal, The (1947) 160, 525n
Hinds, Seán 275
Hinsley, Cardinal 365
Hippodrome, Belfast *see* Royal Hippodrome,
   Belfast
His & Hers (2009) 245, 532n
His Majesty Mr Jones (1950) 363–4
His Rival's Necklace (1907) 15–6
Hisamatsu, Seiji 271
Hitchcock, Alfred 73
HMV 185
Hoban family, Westport, 542n
Hockbaum, Werner 238
Hogan, Tom 288, 565n
Hogan, W.J. 36
Hogenkamp, Bert 550n
Holland, Agnieszka 282
Holloway, Joseph (architect, diarist) 15–6
Holloway, J.J. (NAIDA president) 93
Holly, Katie 290
Holmes, T. 574n
Holy Ghost Fathers (c.1937) 354, 586n, 588n
Holy Ghost Fathers 322, 354, 357
Home Guard 103
HomeVision 191
Hondo (1953) 520n
Hope, Bob 137
Horgan, Conor 245
Horgan, James 62, 15
Horgan, Joseph 15
Horgan, Philip 62
Horgan's Picture Theatre, Youghal 31, 62–3, 91–
   2, 167, **16**, **47**, **48**
Horgan, Thomas 62

Horrorthon, Dublin 264, 558n
Horseman in the Sky, A 239
Host, The (2006) 245
House of Fortescue, The (1916) 41
House of Wax (1953) 150, 520–21n
How the West Was Won (1962) 152
How to Marry a Millionaire (1953) 153–4
HSBC Private Equity 183, 533n
Huish, W.H. 25–6
Humphreys, Gráinne 279, 526n
Hungry Hill (1947) 581n
Hunt, Peter 525n
Hunter, John 103
Hurleys of Charleville 31
Hurst, Mr H. 167
Hurst's Picture Palace, Youghal 31, 62, 91, 167
Huston, Angelica 282
Huston School of Film and Digital Media 289
Hutchins, Patricia 484n
Hutchinson, Pearse 584n
Hutton, Clayton 118
Hutton Collins 221
Hyman, Dr A.O. 518n

I am on Trial (1956) 271
I Can't, I Can't (1969) 272, 561n
Ibrahim, Peri 566n
Icahn, Carl 185
Ice Age: Dawn of the Dinosaurs (2009) 521n
Ideal Cinema, Westport 165
Ideal Film Renting Co 41
Ideal Films 67
iFilm.net 191
IFI *see* Irish Film Institute
Il Figlio Dell'Uomo see *Shadow on the Hill*
ILAC shopping centre, Dublin 179, 204, 207
IMAX cinemas 214–15, 521n, 544n
IMC (Irish Multiplex Cinemas) 151, 160, 198,
   212–3, 220–1
IMC Dún Laoghaire 180, 194–5, 198, 201, 209,
   212–3, 266, 545n
IMDb 188
IMF see International Monetary Fund
Imitation of Life (1959) 163
Immortal Song, The (1934) 361
Impact Films Ltd 163, 168
Imperial Picture House, Cornmarket, Belfast 36,
   104, 508n
IMRO *see* Irish Music Rights Organization
In America (2002) 181
In Bruges (2008) 181
In the Days of St Patrick (1920) 73
In the Woods see *Rashomon*
Inchicore Cinema, Dublin 64, 122
Incorporated Association of Film Renters 39
Incorporated Society of Musicians 504n

Incubus (1965) 272
Independent Cinemas' Association of Ireland (ICAI) 177, 180, 205, 526n
Independent Film Distributors Ltd 168
Independent Film Renters' Association (IFRA) 168, 170, 172, 173
Independent Newspapers 42
Independent Television (ITV) 139, 155
Industrial Light & Magic 284
Industrial schools' commission 301, 342
Inflexion 221
Informer, The (1935) 506n
Ingram, Rex 281
Inside I'm Dancing (2004) 275
Inter-departmental committee on the film industry 108–14, 121–2, 300, 306, 310–16, 318–20, 329–30, 332–3
Intermission (2003) 181
International Catholic Cinema Office *see* OCIC
International Cinematograph Society Volta 17
International Federation of Film Producers 274
International Festival of Celtic Film *see* Celtic Media Festival
International Film Theatre, Dublin 241, 251, 253
International Monetary Fund (IMF) 218
International Youth Year Committee [1985] 276
Invitation to the Film (1946) 584n
Ireland (1929) 497n
Ireland Takes Wings (1968) 579n
Ireland's peril 296
Irish advisory committee (IAC) of the KRS *see* KRS
Irish Aid 289
Irish Amalgamated Cinema 516n
Irish Amusement Company 28, 487n, 499n
Irish Animated Picture Co. 27, 37–8, 39, 485n
Irish audience for screen advertising, The (1953) 141
Irish Catholic directory 296
Irish Cine Club 320–1
Irish Cine Institute 320
Irish Cinema Association (ICA) 66, 132, 135, 137–8, 166, 168–70, 172, 177, 530n *see also* Irish Theatre and Cinema Association (ITCA); Theatre and Cinema Association of Ireland; Independent Cinemas' Association of Ireland (ICAI); Association of Provincial Exhibitors (APE); Irish Provincial Cinema Owners' Association.
Irish Cinema Handbook (1943) 323, 328, 574n
Irish Cinema Quarterly (1948–9) 337–8, 576n (*see also National Film Quarterly* [1950–6] and *Irish Film Quarterly* [1957–9])
Irish Cinema Theatre, Capel Street, Dublin 29, 52
Irish Cinemas Ltd 75–6, 78–9, 93–4, 117–21, 137, 142, 147–8, 155–6, 302, 363, 498–9n, 511–12n, 517n, 524n

Irish Competition Authority 196, 214, 220
Irish Deaf Society 208
Irish Destiny (1926) 64, 70
Irish Electric Palaces Ltd 81–2
Irish Events newsreel (1917–20) 41, 72–3
Irish Film Archive *see* Irish Film Institute (IFI)
Irish Film Board (1981–), 181, 224, 258, 265–6, 269, 276–7, 280–1, 509n, 519–20n, 524n, 553n, 557n, 563n
Irish Film Board (original name of Irish Film Council, 1943–4) 327
Irish Film Centre (IFC) *see* Irish Film Institute (IFI)
Irish Film Centre Building Ltd 557n
Irish Film Council 326–7, 332–3, 576–7n
Irish Film Institute (IFI) 52, 201, 215, 224, 259–67, 269, 275, 278–9, 286, 290, 341, 481, 556n, 557–59n, 578n, 582n, 40, 65
Irish Film Institute (IFI) Family Festival 269
Irish Film Quarterly (1957–9) 338, 576n
Irish Film Renters Association (IFRA) 530n
Irish Film School (part of IFS) 239
Irish Film Service 67
Irish Film Society (IFS) 92–3, 126, 236–42, 247, 249–50, 253, 309, 321, 323–33, 335, 337, 340, 344, 347–50, 551–2n, 555–56n, 575n, 577n, 580n, 581n
Irish Film Theatre (IFT) 242–3, 251–61, 265, 276, 555–56n
Irish Film Theatre, Limerick (IFT Limerick) 257–9
Irish Film Theatre Ltd, 253
Irish Hospitals' Trust Films 327
Irish International Film Agency 112, 159–60, 249, 327, 361, 509n
Irish Kinematograph Cinema, Mary Street, Dublin 33
Irish Kinematograph Co. 78
Irish Music Rights Organization (IMRO) 161, 527n
Irish National Foresters 124
Irish National Foresters' Hall, Dublin 51
Irish National Teachers' Organization (INTO) 300, 304–5, 326, 329, 332, 342, 568–69n, 583n
Irish Pilgrimage to Lourdes (1917) 73
Irish Provincial Cinema Owners' Association 123, 162 *see also* Association of Provincial Exhibitors
Irish Red Cross 324, 332
Irish School of Film Technique *see* Irish Film School 239
Irish School Weekly 305, 322, 568–69n
Irish Technical Officers' Association 329
Irish Theatre and Cinema Association (ITCA) 88, 93–6, 107, 108, 129, 136–7, 166, 168,

239, 302, 319, 347, 504n, 505n, 584n *see also* Irish Cinema Association (ICA)
Irish Theatres cinema circuit (Northern Ireland) 34, 35, 67, 81, 82
Irish Theatres Ltd *see* Irish Theatres cinema circuit 67, 81, 98–9, 124, 506n, 512n
Irish Transport and General Workers' Union (ITGWU), 42, 107, 137, 518n
Irish Vigilance Association 300, 568n
Irons, Jeremy 282, 287, 562n
Isle of Sinners (1950) 362, 590n
It Came from Outer Space (1953) 520n
It's a Mad, Mad, Mad, Mad World (1963) 152
Italian Straw Hat, The (1927) 233
Ivan the Terrible, part 1 (1944) 550n
Ivanovsky, Alexander V. 248

Jacobson, Johan 272
Jacqueline (1956) 271
James, Billy 82, 83
James Bond films 163
Jameson (sponsor) *see* Dublin International Film Festival
Jameson, James T. 25, 27, 37–8, 41, 55, 67, 78, 84, 12
Jancsó, Miklós 254, 255
Jánošík (1936) 238
Jansen, Cornelius 293
Japanese Film Festival 559n, 560n
JARFID 156
Jarman, Derek 255
Jaws (1975) 172, 196, 536n
Jaws 3–D (1983) 521n
Je Vous Salue Marie (1983) 273
Jeffers, Oliver 269
Jeffs, Fred A. 301
Jennings, J.J. 22
Jet Centre Cinema, Coleraine 208 *see* Movie House chain
J.H. Vavasseur 163
Joan of Paris (1942) 586–7n
Joannon, Léo 358
Joffé, Alex 271
John XXIII, Pope 341
Johnston, Denis 23
Jolley, Paddy 566n
Jolson, Al 71
Jones, Alfred E. 28, 499n
Jones [Alfred Edwin] & [Stephen Stanislaus] Kelly (architectural partnership, 1919–51) 28, 77, 142, 499n.
Jordan, Neil 92, 181, 277, 562n
Joseph of Cupertino, St 360
Joseph Rank Ltd 115
Jouvet, Louis 238
Joyce, Eva 17

Joyce, James 15, 17–22, 484n
Joyce, Stanislaus 19, 20
J.P. Morgan Partners 546n
Judge, Gordon 563n
Junior Dublin Film Festival 264, 269, 286,
Junior film festivals (including Cinemagic, Dublin, Galway, IFI, Fresh, Fís) 264, 269, 286–7
Junior Film Society (part of Irish Film Society) 241, 350, 552n, 585n
Junior Galway Film Fleadh 286
J.V.H. *see* J.V. Hallessy
J.Y. Moore Ltd 67 *see also* John Yeats Moore

Kalem Company 73
Kameradschaft (1931) 236
Kamisaka Shirô no Hanzai see *I am on Trial*
Kanievska, Marek 178
Karlovy Vary International Film Festival 290
Karmel, Joseph Michael 27
Karmel, Nathan 27, 55, 56, 57, 58, 59, 88
Kaurismaki, Aki 562n
Kavanagh, David 259–60, 578n, 582n, 24
Kavanagh, James J. 80, 122, 501n,
Kavanagh, John 492n
Kavanagh, Patrick 339–40, 579n, 581–2n
Kavanagh, Peter D. 142
Kavanagh, Valentine 593n
Kay, George 129
Kay, William 27, 34, 55, 59
Kazan, Elia 340
Kealy, T.S. 312, 329
Kean, Mandy 565n
Kearney, Niall 188–9
Kearney, Richard 582n
Kearns, P.J. 491n
Keating, Tony 185
Keenan, Austin (examiner of restrictive practices) 167–74, 210
Keenan, Mrs 356
Keepers of the Night see *Nactwache*
Kehoe, Ian 211
Keighry, William (Bill) 547n
Kelleher, John 352, 527n
Kelly, Albert 167, 176–7, 205, 526n, 531n, 34
Kelly, Fr J.C. 361
Kelly, J.L. 80, 501n
Kelly, Ned 15
Kelly, P.J. 36
Kelly, Paddy 186
Kelly, Vincent 34
Kelvin Picture Palace, Belfast 34–5, 87, 104, 42, 76
Kemp, Rebecca 287
Kenilworth Cinema, Harold's Cross, Dublin 142, 167–8, 176–7, 205, 34
Kennedy, Councillor T. 57

Kennedy, Herbert (canon of Mariners' church, Kingstown, and later dean of Christ Church Cathedral) 58, 304, 494n, 571n
Kennedy, Mr (secretary, ITCA) 129
Kennedy, Michael J., TD 303
Kennedy Centre shopping centre, Belfast 207
Kennedy Centre multiplex, Belfast 207, 213
Kenny, Justice 342
Kensit, Patsy 206
Kerr, C. 246
Kerrigan, Gene 528n
Kerry county council 287
Kerry Film Festival *see* Samhlaíocht Kerry Film Festival, *see also* Dingle Film Festival
Keystone Film Co. 41
Kézdi-Kovács, Zsolt 260
KGB – The Secret War (1986) 525n
Kiarostami, Abbas 282
Kiberd, Damien 203
Kid, The (1921) 63
Kid Brother, The (1927) 69
Kiernan, Cornelius 52, 57
Kieslowski, Krzysztof 262
Kildare urban district council 302
Kilkeel council 103
Kilkenny corporation 302
Kilkenny, Ossie 509n
Killarney Cineplex 206, 213
Killester Cinema, Dublin 142
Killing of a Chinese Bookie, The (1976) 255
Kilrea Cinema, Co. Derry 106
Kilroy, Godfrey 41
Kiltimagh Film Club, Co. Mayo 553n
Kiltimagh Town Hall Theatre, Co. Mayo 553n
Kinane, Dr Jeremiah, bishop of Waterford and Lismore 506n, 572n
Kinema Assembly Rooms, Fermoy 31
Kinema House, Belfast 35–6
Kinematograph Exhibitors' Society 93
Kinematograph Manufacturers' Association 39, 512n
Kinematograph Renters Society (KRS) 62, 66–7, 72, 88, 93, 108, 114, 140, 166–76, 319, 504n, 509n, 530n
Kinepolis group 214
King, E. 81
King, Henry 154
King, J.J. 7
King, Michael Patrick 216
King, William 33, 490n, 499n
King, William D., 490n
King and Country (1964) 251, 555n
King of Kings (1961) 358
King of the Khyber Rifles (1954) 154
Kingship of Christ, according to the principles of Saint Thomas Aquinas, The (1931) 294

Kingstown Ltd 77
Kingstown Pavilion Roller Skating Rink, Dublin 486n
Kino Cinema, Cork 258, 267–9, 275, 481, 559n
Kino (distribution company) 550n
Kinofest 290
Kirkham, Robert Gerald (Gerry) 122, 349, 584n
Kirkham, Robert Graves 64
Kiss Me Kate (1953) 520n, 581n
Kitty from Coleraine 246
Knights of St Columbanus 335, 360, 363, 578n
Knott, Fred 497n
Kontroll (2003) 245
Korda, Alexander 511n
Koster, Henry 153, 359
Kramer, Stanley 152
Kreplin, Dr Dietrich 276
Krupp family 255
Kubrick, Stanley 171
Kurdish Film Festival (London, New York, Dublin) 290, 558n, 566n
Kurosawa, Akira 250
Kyle, Samuel 127, 513n

L&G Ventures 222
L'Atalante, (1934) 262
La Bandera (1935) 247
La Chatte (1958) see *The Face of the Cat*
La Dentellière see *The Lacemaker*
La Femme du Boulanger (1938) 248, 586n
La Grande Illusion (1937) 238
La Kermesse Héroïque (1935) 238
Lá 'le Bríde (*St Brigid's Day*, 1960) 341
La Notte di San Lorenzo see *Night of San Lorenzo*
La Scala and Opera House, Dublin 26–7, 32, 52–3, 55, 59, 64, 65, 68–9, 73, 493n, 81
La Scala Cinema, Milford, Co. Donegal 503n
La Strada (1954) 240, 250, 552n
La Tragédie de la Mine see *Kameradschaft*
Lacemaker, The (1977) 255
Lakes Cinema, Killarney, Co. Kerry (*see also* Casino, Killarney) 165
Lambert, Alan 559n
Land Without Bread (1932) 236
Landscape Cinema, Churchtown, Dublin 142
Lang, Fritz 233, 248, 277
Lange, Jessica 282
Laois Arts Festival 287
Lappin, Arthur 562n
Larkin, Denis 516n
Larkin, Jim 231, 232
Larne council 103
Las Hurdes see *Land Without Bread*
Last Broadcast, The (1998) 290–1
Last Chance, The (1945) 364

Last Picture Show, The (1971) 272, 352, 561n
Last Tango in Paris (1972) 255, 257, 556n
Last Temptation of Christ, The (1988) 273, 586n
Laverty, Paul 282
Law of Desire (1987) 261
Le Gear, Maurice 528n
Le Joueur d'Echecs see *The Chess Player*
Le Quai des Brumes (1938) 238, 248
Le Roman d'un Tricheur see *The Story of a Cheat*
League of the Kingship of Christ, The *see* An Ríoghacht
Leah, Jack 72, 497n
Lean, David 117, 118, 241
Lee, Ang 216, 264
Lee, Joseph Jack 271
Lee Cinema, Cork 30, 162, 165, 167, 527n
Leech, W.H. 246
Legal and General Ventures 546n
Legion of Decency 308, 357, 580n
Legion of Mary 233, 321
Leicester Square Theatre, London 116
Leigh, Mike 287
Leinster, The, Dolphin's Barn 80, 122
Leisen, Mitchell 69, 153
Leitrim county council 266
Lelouch, Claude 251
Lemass, Seán 94, 109, 119–21, 306, 311–12, 320, 580n
Lenardon, Guido 20, 21
Lenihan, Brian 361, 569n
Lennon, Peter 251
Lenny (1974) 254, 556n
Leo XIII, Pope 294
Leopold Joseph Ltd 528n
Les Assassins du Dimanche (1956) 271
Lesbian and Gay Film Festival, 264, 275, 558n (*see also* Galway Film Fleadh queer seasons, 282)
Letterkenny Recreation and Cinema Hall, 31
Levi & Sons 67
Levin, Henry 152
Levy, Stuart 526n, 547n
Lewis-Crosby, Revd Ernest Henry 55, 493n
Lewis, Gordon J. 71–3
Lewis, Sinclair 358
Ley del Deseo, La see *Law of Desire*
Leyden, John 326
Lido Cinema, Greencastle, Belfast 141
Life and Death of Colonel Blimp, The (1942) 118
Life is Beautiful (1997) 178
Life of Riley, The (1954) 525n
Life of the Cure d'Ars, The (c.1950) 361
Liffey Valley Multiplex, Clondalkin, Co. Dublin 195, 204, 209, 219, 221–2 *see* Ster and Vue

Lightbox Animation Festival 266, 269, 288–9
Light House Cinema, Abbey Street, Dublin 197, 244, 260–2, 264, 278, 530n
Light House Cinema, Smithfield, Dublin 194, 197, 224, 246, 261–4, 268, 270, 290, 481, 558n
Light House Cinema Exhibition and Distribution Co. Ltd. 262
'Lights Out!' (IFI junior festival) 286
Limerick county council 302, 342,
Limerick Film Forum 257
Limerick Filmhouse Centre 257, 267
Limerick Irish Film Festival 564n
Limerick Omniplex 151
Lincoln, Katie 559n
Lindenburg, Paul 116, 510n
Lindtberg, Leopold 364
Linehan, Fergus 250–1, 557n
Linehan, Hugh 283–4
Linehan, M.P. 569n
Linnane, Patrick 578n
Lisburn Omniplex 151
Lisburn Picture House 124
Listz, Franz 357
Little, F.J. 571n
Little Colonel (1935) 353, 586n
Little Jules Verne, A (1907) 21
Little Theatre, St Stephen's Green, Dublin 233, 236 *see* Dublin Little Theatre Guild
Loach, Ken 181
Locke, John 295
Lodge, George 124, 138–40, 512n
Logan, Joshua 155
Logan, Maurice 83, 518n
Logue, Michael, Cardinal archbishop of Armagh 297
Lombard Ireland Bank 187
London county council 49, 50, 51, 69, 232
London Film Festival 256
Long, Sergeant 32
Long, Trish 562n, 564n
Lord, Del 353
Lorentz, Pare 238, 247
Losey, Joseph 251, 359
Lost and Found (2008) 269, 559n
Lost at the Front (1927) 353
Lough Neagh Hotel, Lurgan 101
Louis XV 248
Lourdes (c.1941) 589n
Louth, Newry and Mourne Film Commission 288
Love and Rage (1999) 245
LoveFilm International Ltd 189–91, 534–33n
Lovers at Midnight (*Les Amants de Minuit*, 1953) 586n
Low, Rachael 23, 67, 69, 84
Lowell Rich, David 163

Loyalty League 100
Lubitsch, Ernest 86, 355
Lucan, Arthur 160
Lucan Cinemas Ltd 527n
Lucan Printing Works 541n
Lucey, Cornelius, bishop of Cork 272, 307, 570n
Luck of the Irish, The (1935) 112
Lumber Camp (c.1907) 16
Lurgan council 101
Lush, Harry 499n
Luther, Martin 294
Lutheran Church Productions 588n
Lux (production/distribution company) 40
Luxor Cinema, Clones 366
Lyceum Cinema, Belfast 36, 71, 82, 124
Lyceum Picture Theatre, Dublin 486n
Lynam, Joan 325–6
Lynch, Claire 275
Lynch, Jack 274
Lynch, John (exhibitor/projectionist) 10, 593n
Lynch, John (actor) 282
Lynch, Mrs M. 342
Lynton, Michael 199
Lyons, Brian 38
Lyons, Harry J. (architect) 78–9, 517n
Lyons, Joseph 78
Lyons, Norman 533n
Lyons, Patrick, bishop of Kilmore 315–16, 318,
  326–8, 574–5n
Lyons, Patrick (academic) 174
Lyons, Patrick (Dún Laoghaire Film Society)
  552n
Lyons, Samuel (architect) 517n
Lyric Cinema, High Street, Belfast 34, 35, 98,
  106
Lyric Cinema, Dublin 80, 122
Lyric Cinema, Limerick 367

McAdam, Michael 207–8, 38
McAdam, Trish 555n
McAllister, Daniel (Dan) M. 122, 162–3, 501n
McAnally, Ray 280
McArdle, Tommy 557n
MacAvin, Josie 282
MacBride, Sean 580n
McBride, Stephanie 582n
MacBride, Tiernan 258, 555–57n, 582n
McBride Neill, John 141, 518n
McCabe, John 186–7
McCabe, M. 500n
McCabe Builders 187
McCafferty, Nell 275, 283
McCann, John 75–6, 511n
McCanny, George 352, 586n
McCarey, Leo 364
McCarron, E.P. 322–23, 578n

McCarron, Fr Sean 580n
McCartan, Pat 276–7
McCarthy, Justice Henry A. 342, 347–8, 583n
McCarty, Charles 174
McCarty, H. Cathal 363
McCaul, Brendan 181
McCaul, Niamh 563n
McClelland, Ian 555n
McCloskey, Brother F.X. 334–5
MacConghaile, Muiris 519n
McConnon, Gavin 189, 534n
McConnon, Iain 189, 534n
McConville, J.P. 551n
McCormack, Augustus 30
McCormack, John 67, 353
McCormack, J.F. 142
McCormack family 38
McCourt, Kevin C. 1
McCoy, Mr 583n
McCrane, James V. 80
McCullagh, Crawford, MP 36, 97, 126
McDermott, Felim 281–2
MacDermott, J.E. 11
McDermottroe, Conor 266
MacDonagh, Martin 181
McDonald, Frank 533n
McDonnell, F.J. BL, PC 77, 1
McElligott, J.J. 310, 505n
McElwee, William 503n
MacEntee, Seán 88–9, 134, 230, 237, 310–11,
  316, 504n
MacEoin, Gearoid 320, 323–4, 574n
McEvoy, Alan 217
McEvoy, Charles 508n
McEvoy, Emer 215
McEvoy, E.J.C. 312, 316, 329
McEwan, Alex 10
McFeely, Thomas 548n
MacGabhainn, Liam 306
McGarvey, Cathal 9
McGaw, William 497n
McGee, John 205
McGilligan, Patrick (Paddy) 132, 271, 514–15n
McGinley, Eilish 348, 585n
MacGiollarnáth, Breandán 578n
McGivern, Alicia 564n
McGlusky the Sea Rover (1934) 526n
McGonagle, Declan 563n
McGrath, Brendan 183
McGrath, J. 1
McGrogan, James 142
McGuinness, Des 44
McGuinness, Paul 582n
McGuire, Revd W. 37
McHugh, Roger 580n
McIver, Moira 563n

McKenna, Siobhan 358
MacKeown, Gerald *see* Gearoid MacEoin
McKernan, Luke 21, 44, 484–5n, 491n
McKernan, Fr H.G. 354
McKibben, Joe 35, 36, 66
MacKinnon, Gillies 275
McLaughlin, Bernie 284
McLaughlin, Gerry 563n
McLean, Thomas (architect) 502n
McLeod, Norman Z. 248
MacLochlainn, Alf 253
McLoone, Martin 283, 516n, 563n, 582n
McLoughlin, David 277, 279
McMahon, Bridie 560n
MacMahon, Revd C. 322
McMahon, Joe 280, 560n
MacMahon, John 516n, 590n
McMahon, Fr 596n
McMenamin, Brendan 563n
MacMillan, Andrew 37
McNally, Hubert (Bertie) 79, 152, 179, 250,
    347, 516–17n, 531n, 555n
McNally, Dr Patrick 79, 517n
McNally, Robert 364
McNally, Walter (d. 1945) 67, 79–80, 84, 355,
    500–01n, 1
McNally, Walter (1970s) 170
McNally, Vogue 179, 531n
McNally Cinemas Ltd 500n
McNamara, Bernard 226, 548n, 480–1, 591n
McNamara, Thomas F. 64
McNamee, James, bishop of Ardagh and
    Clonmacnoise 297, 314–6, 318, 334, 572n
MacNeely, William, bishop of Raphoe 572n
MacNeill, James (governor general) 230–1
MacNiocaill, Seoirse 312
McQuaid, John Charles (dean of studies/presi-
    dent, Blackrock College; archbishop of
    Dublin) 294, 296, 315–16, 318, 321–36,
    338–9, 341, 344–6, 349, 352, 353–65, 501n,
    566–68n, 572n, 573–85n, 587–90n, 20
MacRory, Joseph, bishop of Down & Connor;
    cardinal archbishop of Armagh 298, 354, 361,
    551n
McShane, Kitty 160
MacSithigh, Tomás *see* T.J.M. (Morgan) Sheehy
McSweeney, John 256, 368
MacSwiney, Mary 65
McWalter, Dr BL 43
McWeeney, Dr E.J.T. 329
MacWhirter, Oona 363–4
McVea, J.H. 82
McVey, Eoin 164
Machnich, Antonio 20, 485n
Machuca (2004) 245
Mackay, Colin 194

Mackay, J. 490n
Macken, Christopher 251, 588n
Macnas 269
Macquiston Institute, Belfast 37
Macra na Tuithe 573n
Madame X (1965) 163
Magahy, Laura 582n
Magdalene Sisters, The (2003) 275
Mageean, Daniel, bishop of Down and Connor
    299, 315, 568n, 572n
Maggi, Luigi 21–2
Maginnis, Brian 134, 515n
Maglione, Cardinal 354
Magnani, Anna 357
Magnet Cinema, Cavan 165
Magnet Cinema, Dundalk 79, 506n
Maguire, Conor 323
Maguire, E.A. 347
Maguire, Patrick 368
Maher, Brendan 564n
Mahon, Evelyn 557n
Mahon, Martin 277–8, 562n
Mahon Point Omniplex, Cork, 212–13, 219,
    542n
Mahony, J. 329
Majestic Cinema, Belfast 81, 98, 125, 140
Majestic Cinema, Portrush 82, 124
Making of a Priest, The (c.1942) 320, 574n
Makk, Károly 259
Malcolm, Elizabeth 48
Malden, Karl 340
Malle, Louis 243
Man About Dog (2004) 181
Man and a Woman, A see Un Homme et une
    Femme
Man in the Dark (1953) 520n
Manchester City football club 159
Mandoki, Luis 282
Mangan, Fr C. 363, 574n
Mann, Daniel 240
Manning, Mary 229, 230, 550n
Mannon's Acre (1944) 237, 239
Manor Street Picture House, Dublin 26
Mansion House, Dublin 236, 304–5, 327, 347–
    9, 355, 575n.
Mantz, Paul 152
Marco, Carlos 534n
Marcus, Louis 280, 561n, 582n
Margey, H. 93–4, 118
Maria Duce 363
Marriage of William Ashe, The (1916) 41
Marseillaise, La (1937) 248
Marsh, G. H. 491n
Marshall, George 152
Marshall, Mr (Provincial Cinematograph
    employee) 25

Marshall, P. (Irish Cine Club member) 320
Martin, Dr Conor 578n
Martin, Fr Liam 581n
Martin, Micheál 583n
Martin-Jones, C.M. 53–4
Martin Luther (1953) 356, 588n
Marton, Andrew 152
Marx Brothers 248, 581n
Mary Street Picture House, Dublin 33, 52, 54, 78
Mask, The (1961) 521n
Mason, Seacome 54–8, 59
Massard, Yves 271
Massimo, Vittorio Prince 560n *see also* Dawn Adams
Master of Men, A (1917) 41
Masterpiece Picture Theatre, Dublin 62, 65, 495n
Mathew, Fr Theobold 48, 51
Maxwell, John 74–6, 94, 312, 497n, 499n
Mayfair Cinema, Belfast 136
Mayfair Entertainment 210
Maynooth College 586n
Mayo, Archie 362
Mayo Board of Health 302
Mayo county council 342
Mayo Movie World, Castlebar 223
Maypole Cinema, Holywood, Co. Down 106
Maysles, Albert 285
Maze, The (1953) 520n
MCA (Music Corporation of America), 202, 539n
Meaney, Colm 282
Medem, Julio 279
MEDIA '92 programme 280
Media Desk 341
Medway, Cookstown, Co. Tyrone 517n
Meet the Robinsons (2007) 521n
Meeting House Square, Dublin 290, 63
Mekas, Jonas 280
Melia, Patrick ('Paddy') 170, 530n
Menehan, Richard 43
Mermaid Arts Centre, Bray 224, 245
Merrill Lynch 221
Messiah, The (Handel) 321
Metro Cinema, Dundonald 83, 141
Metro-Goldwyn-Mayer (MGM) 69, 152, 157, 205, 207–8, 364, 523n
Metropole and Allied Cinemas Company Ltd 28, 33, 75–6, 93, 118, 302, 498–9n, 584n
Metropole Cinema, O'Connell Street, Dublin 26–7, 28, 64, 75, 89, 118, 149–50, 157, 366, 499n, 19, 50, 82
Metropole Cinema, Townsend / Hawkins Street, Dublin *see* New Metropole
Metropolis Film Club 555n

Metropolitan Cinemas Ltd 142
Meyles, Walter 362
MGM *see* Metro-Goldwyn-Mayer
Michael Collins (1996) 92, 181, 473, 477
Michael Curran & Sons 81–2
Michael Scott & Associates 77
Mid-Ulster Film Festival 288
Middlesex county council 50
Middleton, William M. 76, 94, 499n, 505n
Midland Cinema, Derry 82, 83, 124
Midland Picture House, Belfast 36, 106
Miles, Sarah 288
Miller (beer; film festival sponsor) 278, 562n
Miller, Angela 483n
Miller, Liam 277
Miller, Rebecca 287
Mills & Allen 163
Milne, Karl 199, 219
Milne Barbour, J., MP 247
Minerva Films (Rome) 587n
Minicinefest short film competion 289, 565n
Minnelli, Vincente 357
Miracle in Milan (1951) 362
Miramax 189
Mise Éire (1959) 135, 273
Mr Careless Goes to Town (1949)
Mitchell, F.C. 74
Mitchell, Maurice 84
Mitchell, Oswald 160, 526n
Mix, Tom 137
Miyazaki, Hayao 269
Modern Palestine (*c.*1934) 507n
Móin (*Turf*) 579n
Molloy, Philip 176, 278
Molloy, T.J. 335, 578n
Moloney, Helena 571n
Monarch Properties Ltd 203–4
Monastery (1938) 362
Monkey Business (1931) 248
Monks, Fr Ernest 581n
Monsieur Verdoux (1947) 587n
Monsieur Vincent (1947) 355
Monsters vs. Aliens (2009), 151, 521n
Montagu, Ivor 230
Monte Carlo (1931) 86
Montgomery, Revd H. 37
Montgomery, James (official film censor, 1923–40) 15, 70, 96, 230, 233–4, 240, 303, 310, 313, 316–7, 353–4, 569n, 572n, 586–87n, 589n
Montrose, Professor 247
Moody, Mr (musical director) 86
Moody Jnr, Mr (musician) 86
Mooney, Michael 560n
Moontree Ltd 498n
Moore, Frederick (Fred) William 75, 498n

Moore, Horace 75–6, 498n, 511n
Moore, I. 82
Moore, John R. 498n
Moore, John Yeats 81, 98, 3
Moore, Lady 247
Moore, Tomm 270
Moore, William J. 592n
Moreau, Martine 563n
Morocco (1930) 503n
Morris, James 31
Morrison, Boyd 246
Morrison, George 135, 273
Morrison, Louis 246
Morrison, Robert 26, 58, 64
Morrisroe, Patrick, bishop of Achonry, 315, 572n
Morrissey, Daniel 120–2, 131–2
Moss and Stoll circuit 24 (H.E. Moss of Moss and Thornton, and Oswald Stoll owner of the Provincial Hall circuit)
Moss and Thornton 188, 228
Moss Empires 67
Mother (1926) 231, 232, 550n
Mount Pottinger Cinemas Ltd 35
Mount Pottinger Picturedrome *see* Belfast Picturedrome
Movie House cinema chain 207–8, 541n
Movie House, City Side, Belfast 207, 70
Movie Magic 186, 533n
Movie Junction (drive-in cinema) Cork 214, **64**
Movieland, Limerick 165, 257
Movieoke 285
Movies@Cinemas chain, 191, 223, 266 *see* Movies@Dundrum
Movies@Dundrum, Co. Dublin 150, 182–3, 194, 209, 219, 222–4, 534n, 537n, 546n, **68**
Movies@Gorey 223
Movies@Swords, Co. Dublin 223, 537n
Moviestar.ie 189, 534n
Moyne committee 70
Muintir na Tire 324–30, 332, 334–5, 337, 574–75n, 577n
Muldowney, Brendan 565n
Mullen, Peter 275
Mulligan, P.J. 96
Mulvey, B.M. 574n
Muncer, Ernest 152
Munden, P.J. (exhibitor) 88, 129
Munden, Patrick J. (architect) 601n
Murakami, Jimmy T. 559n
Murder Will Out (1930) 503n
Murdoch, Bill 164
Murphy, Canon 58
Murphy, Mrs (Cork exhibitor)160, 526n
Murphy, Cillian 288
Murphy, Deirdre 217
Murphy, Desmond 498n

Murphy, Ian 217
Murphy, J.G. (exhibitor) 96
Murphy, John (Parnell Partnership, 2000s) 217
Murphy, John Xavier (director, Bank of Ireland, d.1937) 75
Murphy, Joseph 322, 334–5, 22
Murphy, Michael 564n
Murphy, Pat 366, 582n
Murphy, Richard 183, 186–7
Murphy, Thomas 491n
Murphy, Vinny 207
Murphy, William Martin 42
Murphy's (beer, film festival sponsor) 275, 562n
Murray, Revd John Desmond 361
Musical Story (1940) 248
My Left Foot (1989) 181
My Sacrifice and Yours (c.1946) 363, 590n

Nactwache (1948) 354, 587n
Nair, Mira 282
Napoleon III 248
Nation Once Again, A (1946) 336, 344
National Agricultural and Industrial Development Association (NAIDA) 93–5, 108
National Amusements (USA exhibition company) 202
National Asset Management Agency (NAMA) 533n
National Association of Theatrical and Kine Employees (NATKE) 102, 138
National Association of Theatrical Employees (NATE) 43
National Centre for Technology in Education 286
National College of Art and Design (NCAD) 558n
National Electric and Cinema Equipment Co 163
National Film Distributors Ltd 121, 168, 501n
National Film Institute of Ireland (NFI) 237, 321–41, 342, 344–6, 349–52, 355, 361–3, 551n, 572n, 573–8n, 584n *see also* Irish Film Institute
National Film Quarterly (1950–6) 338–40, 352, 576n, 579n, 580n
National Film School, Dún Laoghaire Institute of Art, Design and Technology (NFS, DLIADT) 286, 582n
National Films Ltd 67
National Institute of Higher Education/Dublin City University 558n
National Library of Ireland 253
National Lottery 277
National Organization of Cinematograph Operators 49
National Photographic Archive, Dublin 566n
National Wax Museum, Dublin 152, 486n, 522–23n

Nationalist Party of Northern Ireland 127
Natural Born Killers (1994) 556n
Naughton, John 565n
Navan Film Festival 288
Navy Spy (1937)
Naylor, Miss 86
NCB Stockbrokers 183, 185, 533n
NCVD Distribution 534n
Neel, L.A. 510n
Neeson, Liam 287
Negulesco, Jean 153
Nelson's Pillar, Dublin 33
Nenagh town council 342
Nero (1909) 21–2
Nerve Centre, Derry 283–4, 563n
Nesbitt, George Joseph 43, 88, 93–4, 491n, 498–9n, 511n
Netflix 188, 190, 535n
Nevin, May 13, 87, 482n
New Antrim Cinema, Castle Street 142
New Capitol Cinema, Dublin 152
New Cinema, Thurles, Tipperary 96, 165
New Egyptian Hall, Piccadilly 34
New Electric Cinema, Dublin 78, 152 *see* Dublin Cinerama Theatre
New Hibernian Investment Trust 528n
New Metropole Cinema, Dublin 138, 156, 157, 158, 177, 531n *see also* Screen at College Street, Dublin
New Princess Palace, Belfast 34, 81, 124, 139
New Reo Cinema, Ballyclare, Co. Antrim 83, 141, 518n
New Super Theatre de Luxe, Dublin 28
New Teacher, The (1939) 248
New York Cinema, Belfast 34
New York Nights (1929) 503n
Newcastle town council 103
Newry Omniplex 151
Newtownards town council 103
Newtownbreda shopping centre, Belfast 204
Next Please (1948) 579n
Ní Bhriain, Doireann 277
Ní Chanainn, Áine 327, 347–50, 578n, 584n, 585n, 22
Ní h-Iarnain, Sighle 584n
Nicholas, Joe 563n
Night Like This, A (1932) 503n
Night Mail (1936) 247
Night of San Lorenzo (*The Night of the Shooting Stars*, 1982) 259
Night People (1954) 581n
1916 (1966) 579n
N.M. Rothschild (bank) 546n
No Greater Faith see The Shepherd of the Seven Hills
Noah's Ark (1929) 82

Nolan, Eric 129
Nono, Mike 16
Nordisk 41
Northern Ireland Business Innovation Centre 291
Northern Ireland Film and Television Commission 249
Northern Ireland Film Council 266, 553n
Northern Ireland Labour Party 127
Northern Ireland Local Government Act 1934 508n
Northern Ireland parliament 106, 126–7, 138–9
Northern Ireland Screen 560n
Northern Theatres 26
Northern Visions 283
Norton, Leslie C. 498n
Norton, William 142
Nosferatu (1922) 299
Nous sommes tous des assassins see We are all Murderers
Novak, Lorenzo 20, 21, 485n
Noy, Wilfred 41
Nudist Paradise (1958) 520n
Nun's Story, The (1959) 357
Nutgrove shopping centre 204

O'Briain, Colm 259, 555–57n
O'Brien, D. (exhibitor) 88
O'Brien, Daire (reporter) 210
O'Brien, Dermod 571n
O'Brien, Harvey 579n, 582n
O'Callaghan and Webb (architects) 34
Ó Caoimh, Eóin P. 309, 312
O'Carroll, Donal 584–5n
O'Ceallaigh, Caoimhín 239
O'Ciarbhain, Fergus 239
O'Conail, T. 333
Ó Connaire, Padraic 579n
O'Connell, Brian 189
O'Connell, T. 574n
O'Connell, William (cardinal, Boston) 362
O'Connor, Derek 290
O'Connor, George (exhibitor) 88
O'Connor, George Luke (architect) 27, 33
O'Connor, Mr (cinema manager) 58
O'Connor, J.S. TD 119
O'Connor, Pat 277
O'Connor, Seamus 336, 340
O'Connor, Tom 208, 224
O Daillaig, Cearbhaill 580n
O'Doherty, Revd J. 95–6
O'Doherty, Thomas, bishop of Galway 297
O'Donnell & Twomey (architects) 566n
O'Donnell, Damien 275
O'Donnell, Frank Hugh 347
O'Donnell, Revd Thomas 360
O'Donoghue, Major F. 560n

O'Donoghue, Siobhan 564n
O'Donovan, Kevin 526n
O Driscoll, Finín 307, 568n
O'Dwyer, Bill 77
O'Faolain, Nuala 366
O'Farrell, Paul 230–1
O'Flynn, Dermot J. 322, 331, 334–5, 344–5, 360, 578n, 585, 22
O'Friel, H. 230
O'Gorman family 167, 176, 222–3
O'Gorman, Andrew 167, 177, 37
O'Gorman, T.C. (CSVOC secretary) 363
O'Grady, Anthony 55, 59, 176
O'Grady, Anthony (Tony; grandson of above) 167, 176
O'Grady, Frank 188–9
O'Grady, S.P. 571n
O'Grady Walshe, Peter 183, 185, 533n
O'Hagan, Patrick J. 304–5, 335, 342, 344–5, 349, 22
O'Halloran, Áine 278
O'Halloran, Msgr Michael 356–8, 360
O'Hanlon, Dave 547n
O'Hanlon, Gerry 518n
O'Hanlon, Roy 547n
O'Hanlon, W. 84
O'Hara, Maureen 282, 287
O'Hare, Dr 339, 356–7, 586n
O'Hegarty, Diarmuid 230–2
O'Hegarty, P.S. 343
O'Higgins, Kevin 71, 300, 568n
O'Hora, Liam 353, 357–9, 552n, 586n, 588n, 589n
O'Keefe, Padraig 93, 304, 335–6, 345, 571n
O'Keefe, William 500n 604n
O'Kelly, Kevin 584n
O'Kelly, Seán T. 270–1, 333.
Ó Laoghaire, Colm 241, 273, 584n
O'Leary, Liam 92–3, 232–6, 238–40, 253, 281, 323, 327, 333, 347–9, 525n, 550n, 570n, 575n, 577n, 581n, 584n, 23, 24
Ó Liatháin, Annraoi 567n
O'Mahoney, Mr (cinema manager) 38
O'Mahony, Jason 287–8
O'Mahony, Larry 548n
O'Mahony, Peter 190
O'Maille, P. 571n
O'Maolchalainn, Eoin 576n
O Meadhra, Seán 236, 23
Ó Muireadhaigh, P.S. 309, 573n
O'Neill, Miss 86
O'Neill, Captain Terence 138–40, 517n
O'Neill, James 80
O'Neill, Martha 582n
Ó Nualláin, Pádraig 347, 350, 579n, 584n, 22
O Rabhartaigh, T. 579n

O'Rahilly, Alfred 335, 574n
O'Regan, Miss 527n
O'Regan, Msgr John 588n, 360
O'Reilly, Barney 167, 501n
O'Reilly, David 290
O'Reilly, Frank 304
O'Reilly, M.W. 579n
O'Reilly, Sally-Anne 281
O'Riordan, David 38
O'Rourke, Aubrey V. 33
O'Rourke, Francis B. 499n
O'Rourke, Mary 590n
O'Russ, Robert (Bob) 25, 33
Ó Sé, Breandán 348, 350, 584n
Ó Seaghdha, B. 584n
O'Shaughnessy, Thomas Lopdell KC (recorder, Dublin) 19, 50–2, 54, 58, 59, 492–3n
O'Shea, Diarmuid 182
O'Sullivan, Fionnuala 170, 530n
O'Sullivan, Miss K. 578n
O'Sullivan, Louis 170, 530n
O'Sullivan, M. (lord mayor of Dublin, 1943)
O'Sullivan, Michael (investor, 2000s) 217
O'Sullivan, Niamh 582n
O'Sullivan, Patrick 225
O'Sullivan, Robin 257–8, 272, 274,
O'Sullivan, Sean 334–5, 337–8, 344, 578n, 579–80n, 590n
O'Sullivan, Thaddeus 262, 281, 492n
O'Toole, P.J. 88, 1
O'Toole, Peter 282
Oakwood Cinema, Carrigaline, Cork 167
Oboler, Arch 150, 520n
OCIC (International Catholic Cinema Offfice) 338, 340, 352, 354, 361, 580n, 585n, 587n
October (1928) 232, 550n
Odeon Cinemas / Circuit / Odeon Theatres Ltd 26, 69, 116, 118, 121, 153, 155, 157, 225–7, 344, 364, 510n (*see* Odeon-UCI)
Odeon Direct Service 534–35n
Odeon Cinema, Eden Quay, Dublin (formerly Corinthian) 157–8, 176, 177, 531n
Odeon Cinema, Derry (formerly Strand) 124
Odeon Cinema, Dundrum, Co. Dublin 122
Odeon Cinema (formerly Royal Hippodrome), Great Victoria Street, Belfast 125
Odeon Cinema, Leicester Square, London 153, 549n
Odeon Cinema, Longford 122
Odeon Cinema, Tottenham Court Road, London 153
Odeon Cinema, Tuam, Co. Galway 122
Odeon Cinema, Victoria Square shopping centre, Belfast 541n
Odeon (Ireland) Ltd 117, 120–1, 142, 148, 155–7, 169, 171, 175–7, 490n, 499n, 519n, 590n

Odeon (Northern Ireland) Ltd 124, 139
Odeon-UCI 225–7, 481
Offaly Board of Health 302
Office of Fair Trade ([British] OFT) 227
Oglesby & Butler 541n
Ogoe, W.J. 580n
Oisín Cinema, Killorglin, Co. Kerry 182
Oke, Ade 290
Oklahoma! (1955) 154–5, 523n
Olcott, Sidney 45
Old Mother Riley series (1937–52) 160
Oldpark Ratepayers' Association 99
Olivier, Laurence 118, 359, 582n
Olympia (roller skating rink), Dublin 486n
Olympia Theatre, Dublin 129, 347
Omagh Picture House 106
Omagh rural council 102
Omniplex chain (/Omniplex Holdings) 151, 160,
    211–3, 220, 223, 227–8, 527n *see* Ward
    Anderson, also individual cinemas
On the Waterfront (1954) 340, 581n
On With the Show (1929) 74
One Hundred Mornings (2009) 245
One More Tomorrow 357
Online DVD Rental (onlineDVDrental.ie)183,
    190, 534n
Online Rentals Ltd 189
Open, Michael 36, 249, 285
Opera House, Cork 268, 274–5
Opera House, Derry 106
Orange Order 100, 102, 106
Orchard Hall Cinema, Derry 283
Organization for Economic Co-operation and
    Development (OECD) 218
Oriel Cinema, Dundalk 96
Original Video 187, 534n
Orlando (1992) 261
Ormond Cinema, Nenagh, Co. Tipperary 122
Ormonde Cinema, Arklow, Co. Wicklow 80
Ormonde Cinema, Carnew, Co. Wicklow 80
Ormonde Cinema, Cobh, Co. Cork 80, 165,
Ormonde Cinema, Dungarvan, Co. Waterford
    80, 165,
Ormonde Cinema, Fermoy, Co. Cork 80, 165,
Ormonde Cinema, Gorey, Co. Wexford, 80
Ormonde Cinema, Greystones, Co. Wicklow, 80
Ormonde Cinema, Kanturk, Co. Cork 80
Ormonde Cinema, Midleton, Co. Cork 80, 165,
    182,
Ormonde Cinema, Rathdrum, Co. Wicklow 80
Ormonde Cinema, Stillorgan, Dublin 80, 142,
    167, 177, 222, 481, 537n
Ormonde family 37
Ormsby Scott, S. 62
Oscar Cinema, Carrickmacross, Co. Monaghan
    180

Oshima, Nagisa 255
Oska Bright (festival) 285
Our Boys (publication) 334
Our Country (1948) 132
Our Lady's Choral Society 321
Our Land in Story 320
Our Money at Work (1957) 578n
Ourselves Alone (1936) 506n
Over the hills (novel) 87
Owens, Tom 555n

Pabst, G.W. 236, 280
Padre Padrone (1977) 255
Pageant Holdings 185, 533n
Pagnol, Marcel 248
Paisley, Rev. Ian 49
Pal, George 152
Palace Cinema, Bangor 106
Palace Cinema, Brunswick [Pearse] Street,
    Dublin 54, 64 *see* Academy
Palace Cinema, Cork 165
Palace Cinema, Derry 125
Palace Cinema, Edinburgh 23
Palace Rink, Rathmines, Dublin 486n
Palace Theatre/Cinema, Townsend Street, Dublin
    48
Palladium Cinema (formerly Coliseum), Belfast
    36
Palladium Cinema, Coleraine 31, 124, 507n
Palladium Cinema, Portstewart, Co. Derry 124
Pallidrome Cinema, Strabane 100
Pan Loaf, The (1994) 275
Panavision (Super / Ultra Panavision) 152, 154
Pandora's Box (1929) 280
Panopticon Cinema, Belfast 34, 35
Panorama of Queenstown (1903) 483n
Panorama of the Lakes of Killarney from Hotel
    (1903) 483n
Panoramic View of Electric Tower from a
    Balloon (1901) 483n
Pan's Labyrinth (2006) 245
Paramount 68, 69, 73, 116–17, 153, 156, 191,
    205, 365, 495–6n, 510n, 523n, 532n, 539n
    see also Cinema International Corporation
    (CIC)
Paramount Cinema, Arklow 80
Paramount Famous Lasky Corporation 86, 495n
Paramount Film Service Ltd 68, *see also* Famous
    Lasky Film Service Ltd
Paramount on Parade (1930) 86
Paris, Texas (1984) 178
Park Cinema, Old Park Road, Belfast 83
Park Street Cinema, Dundalk 60
Parker, Alan 181, 288
Parker, Cyril B. 347, 584n
Parnell Street Multiplex, Dublin 194, 196–7,

201, 204–5, 207–9, 214–7, 278, 289, 544n, 69 (aka Virgin; UGC; Cineworld)
Parochial Hall Cinema, Kilbeggan Co. Westmeath 505n
Pasolini, Pier Paola 240, 255
Passion of Joan of Arc, The (1928) 229
Pastrone, Giovanni 21, 45
Pathé 39, 40, 41, 67, 73, 353
Pathé Gazette 71
Pather Panchali (1955) 250
Pattern and Texture (1968) 579n
Patterson, Henry 119–20
Paul VI, Pope 341
Pavilion Cinema, Kingstown [later Dún Laoghaire] 29, 58, 77, 93–4, 120, 499n, 555n
Pavilion Cinema, Skerries, Co. Dublin 517n
Pavilion Cinema and Café, Cork 31, 160, 162, 165, 489n, 57
Peace III (EU fund) 290
Peace Work (c.1949) 363
Peaches (2000) 525n
Peacock Theatre (part of Abbey Theatre) 348
Pearce, J.E. (John Edward) 75–6, 497–8n
Pearse, J.R. [J.E. Pearce?] 1
Pearse, Margaret 567n
Pearse, Patrick, 349, 567n
Peck, Cecilia 288
Peck, Gregory 288
Pedelty, Donovan 112
People's Hall, Belfast 37
Pepper, Will C. 16
Perisano, Sal 183
Perry, Simon 540n
Peters, Harry 37
Petrie, William 43
Phantom of the Rue Morgue (1954) 520n
Phibsborough Picture House 33, 54, 75, 118, 142, 153, 490n, 499n
Phibsboro Picture House Company 33
Phillips (distributors) 67
Phillips, Frederick 67
Phoenix Cinema, Dublin 36, 45–7, 52, 54, 66, 78, 122, 490n
Phoenix Film Ltd 67
Pichel, Irving 356
Picturedrome, Belfast 35, 81
Picturedrome, Dublin 27, 52, 487n
Picturedrome, Kerry 165
Picture House, Bray 79, 121
Picture House, Camden Street, Dublin 23–4, 52, 54, 56, 120
Picture House (Doncaster) Ltd 498n
Picture House, Kingstown (later Dún Laoghaire) 58, 120, 136
Picture House, Larne 81
Picture House, Magherafelt 83

Picture House, Newtownards 30
Picture House, O'Connell Street, Dublin 21, 24, 25, 26, 45, 58, 64, 73, 78, **43, 74**
Picture House, Royal Avenue *see* Belfast Picture House
Picture House (Workshop) Ltd 498n
Picture Palace Theatre *see* Dorset Picture House
Picture Palace Theatre, Henry Street, Dublin 26
Piggott, Professor John J. 331, 334–5, 578n
Pilgrimage to Fatima (c.1951) 587n
Pilis, J. 1
Pillar Picture House, Dublin 33, 53, 65, 78, 490n, 495n, 45
Pilton (video distributor) 188, 533–34n
Pinewood Studios 116, 511n
Pinter, Harold 251
PintSize Film Festival 289
Pioneers of audio visual education in Ireland, 1940–1962, The 350
Pius X, Pope 294
Pius XI, Pope 295, 321, 324, 361
PlayStation, 186
Plaza Cinema, London 68
Plaza Cinema, Dublin 23, 122, 152
Plaza Cinerama, Dublin 23, 152
Plaza Picture Hall, Dublin 23
Plow that Broke the Plains, The (1936) 247
Plunkett, Horace 73
Plunkett, James 491n
Podeswa, Jeremy 282
Point multiplex, Milton Keynes, England 195, 202–3, 535n
Polar Express (2004) 521n
Pollock, George 147, 273
Pollock, Hugh 126–9
Ponyo (2008) 269, 559n, 560n
Popular Picture Palace Ltd 36
Popular Picture Theatre, Belfast 36
Port of Forty Thieves (1943) 503n
Port of Shadows see *Le Quai des Brumes*
Portal, Lord 116
Portlaoghaise [Portlaoise] Film Society 584n
Portrush Picture House 97
Portrush Playhouse (formerly Majestic) 208 *see* Movie House chain
Portrush town council 104
Portstewart town council 103
Potter, Sally 261
Potter Demolition and Contractors 541n
Pouch, Paddy 562n
Poulter, Alfred H. 23–4, 54
Pounds, Ferris ('Paddy') 34, 35, 81–2, 98
Powell's Cinema Hall, Roscrea 30–1
Powell, E.C. 356, 586n, 589n
Powell, Michael 117, 118
Powell, Valentine, 488n

Powell, Victor 138
Power, Joseph A. 93, 569n
Power and the Glory, The (1956) 359, 364
Power City 533n
Pratschke, Sheila 263, 557n
Premier Cinema, Lucan, Co. Dublin 162, 517n
Preminger, Otto 360
Préparez vos Mouchoirs see Get out your
  Handkerchiefs
Presbyterian church 568n
Pressburger, Emeric 117, 118
Priests' Social Guild 300, 568n
Prima Comunione see His Majesty Mr Jones
Prime (2005) 223
Primedia 221
Princess Cinema, Rathmines 26, 27, 28, 43, 52,
  54–8, 59, 492n
Princess Picture Palace, Belfast 34, 79
Prisoner, The (1955) 589n
Private Vices & Public Virtues (1976) 255
Product allocation committee (PAC) of IAC *see*
  KRS
Production Code Administration 308, 313
Progressive Film Institute 550n
Project Arts Centre 252
Project Cinema Club (PCC) 252–3, 254, 555n
Provincial Cinematograph Theatres Ltd 21, 22–
  3, 24–6, 35, 52, 64, 73–4, 78, 116, 485–7n
Provincial Film Society of Ireland 246
Provincial Picture House *see* Picture House,
  O'Connell Street, Dublin
Public Dance Halls Act 1935, 301, 572n
Public Enemy, The (1931) 503n
Public Health Act 1890, 50–1
Pudovkin, Vsevolod 230, 231, 232, 235, 574n
Pullman Cinema, Inichore 165
Purcell, Noel 271
Purcell family 38
Putapish, J.M. 1

Quadragesimo anno (1931 papal encyclical) 296,
  307, 324, 326
Quaker Meeting Room, Dublin 51, 52, 53, 262,
  65
Quane, Dr Michael 329, 332–3, 576n, 577n
Quas primas (1925 papal encyclical) 295–6
Queen's Cinema, York Road, Belfast 36, 106,
  489n
Queen's Film Theatre (QFT), University Square,
  Belfast 206, 248–9, 267, 285
Queen's Theatre, Dublin 15–16, 53, 75–6, 118,
  120, 482–3n
Quiet Man, The 364
Quigley, Martin 573n, 574n
Quinceañera see Echo Park LA
Quinlan, Dr 331, 332

Quinn, Aidan 282
Quinn, Bob 280, 516n
Quinn, Brian 555n
Quinn, John 590n
Quinn, Kathleen 482n
Quinn, Seamus 165, 256, 527n, 594n
Quinn, T.A. 517n
Quo Vadis? (1913) 21, 37, 40

Radharc Film Unit 341, 358, 361
Radio Pictures 67
Radio Telefís Éireann (RTÉ) 136, 241, 276, 277,
  296, 305, 341, 350, 582n
Rag Doll (1960) 140
Rahimi, Chiman 566n
Raimu 248
Ramor Film Festival 289
Ranelagh Arts Festival 289
Rank group 73, 79, 115–25, 135, 137–9, 141,
  147–8, 153–8, 161, 169, 171–2, 177, 202,
  343–7, 349, 351, 363, 510–12n, 519n, 523n,
  531n *see also* Odeon group, Odeon (Ireland)
  and Irish Cinemas Ltd
Rank, J. Arthur 84, 94, 115–25, 343–7, 349,
  363, 498n, 510n (*see* Rank Group)
Rank, Joseph 115
Rank Screen Services, Ltd 139
Rank Xerox 155
Rashomon (1950) 250, 555n
Rathmines Amusement Company 27
Rathmines and Rathgar urban district council
  50, 54–6, 57, 59
Rathmines Ice and Roller Skating Rink, Dublin
  486n
Rathmines Picture Palace, Dublin 26, 27
Rathmines Ratepayers' Protection Association
  55–6, 57
Rathmines Town Hall 27, 29, 31, 54–5, 59
Ravey, Pastor 98
Ray, Nicholas 245, 358
Ray, Satyajit 250
Rea, Stephen 277
RealD 151, 521–22n
Rebel Without a Cause (1955) 245
Rebez, Giovanni 485n
Reddin, Joan 496n
Reddin, Thomas (Tony) C. 496n
Reddin, (Justice) Kenneth 349, 570n
Redmond, Brigid 320, 322, 324–36, 351, 574–
  78n
Redmond, Fr John 320–3, 325–6, 328–331, 334,
  574–77n
Reefer and the Model (1988) 280
Reel Cinema group 224
Reel Pictures, Blackpool, Co. Cork 223–4
Regal Cinema, Belfast 82, 104, 124, 502n

Regal Cinema, Clonmel, Tipperary 165, 172, 194

Regal Cinema, Enniskillen 81, 100, 124

Regal Cinema, Larne 124

Regal Cinema, Portadown 51, 52

Regal Cinema, Waterford 80

Regal Cinema, Youghal 167 *see* Hurst's Picture Palace

Regal (Rooms) Cinema, Dublin 76, 118, 137, 156, 363, 498n, 524n

Regan, Charles 152

Regent Cinema, Royal Avenue, Belfast (formerly Belfast Picture House) 82, 124

Regent Cinema, Blackrock, Dublin 80, 120, 162,

Regent Cinema, Kilkenny 165

Regent Cinema, Newtownards 103

Regent Cinema, Findlater Place, Dublin, 165, 179, 251–2.

Regina Cinema, Waterford 142, 165, 225

Reiniger, Lotte 238

Reitz, Edgar 276

Religious Film Society 115

Reluctant Saint, The (1962) 360

Remontons les Champs-Élysées (1938) 248

Renoir, Jean 238, 248

Rentastic 534n

RenTel Ltd 155–6

Report of enquiry into the supply and distribution of cinema films 169, 173–4

Report of the inter-departmental committee on the film industry 72, 109–14, 319–20, 329, 333

Report of the investigation into the distribution of cinema films 171, 173–4

Republic Cinemas 528n

Republic Pictures 142

Rerum novarum (1891 papal encyclical) 307

Rescued by Rover (1905) 39

Research Services Ltd 141

Resfest 566n

Restrictive practices commission 148, 165–77, 210, 530n

Reynolds, Albert 262, 582n

Reynolds, McCarron & Co. 323

Revenge of the Creature (1955) 520n

Rex Cinema, Tramore, Waterford 80

Rhodes, Abraham Lincoln 498n

Rialto Cinema, Derry 125 *see* ABC Cinema, Derry

Rialto Cinema, Dublin 79, 121

Rialto Cinema, Nenagh, Tipperary 165

Rialto Cinema, Wicklow 79, 121

Rice, Ignatius J. 50–1

Richies, Ian 205

Riefenstahl, Leni 236

Riley, Joe 122

Rilla, Walter 362

Rink Palace Cinema, Limerick 485–6n

Ríoghacht, An 296, 304, 362, 569n, 570n

Riordan, John 578n

Rithie [Richie?], G. 1

Ritz Cinema, Armagh 125

Ritz Cinema, Athlone 77, 122, 590n, 62

Ritz Cinema, Ballsbridge, Dublin 80

Ritz Cinema, Belfast 76, 81, 87, 104–5, 125, 154–5, 206, 507–8n, 53, 54

Ritz Cinema, Carlow 77, 122, 500n

Ritz Cinema, Clonmel, Tipperary 77, 122, 165, 500n

Ritz Cinema, New Ross 80, 165

Ritz Cinema, Newtownards, Co. Down 125

River, The (1937) 238

Riverbank Arts Centre, Newbridge, Co. Kildare 547n

RKO Radio Pictures 79, 156, 355, 364

Road to Life, The (1931) 247

Robb, Mr C.A. 67

Robe, The (1953) 153, 154

Robeson, Paul 92

Robinson, Alan 278

Robinson, John J. (Carlton, Dublin) 500n

Robinson, Mary 204, 578n

Robinson, Peter 544n

Robinson, T.P. (Carlton, Dublin) 495n, 500n

Robinson, Sir Thomas W. 77

Robinson and O'Keefe (architects) 78

Robson, Mark 171

Roche, James, bishop of Cloyne, 572n

Roche, John Joseph 498n, 511n

Roche, Stephen A. 316–18, 573n

Rock Cinema, Ballyshannon 31

Rock Cinema, Cashel 96, 165

Rockett, Kevin 252, 260, 484n, 490n, 520n, 559n, 567n, 569n, 573n, 582n, 25

Rocky Horror Picture Show, The (1975) 177

Rocky Road to Dublin, The (1968) 251

Roeg, Nicholas 282

Rogers [Richard] and [Oscar] Hammerstein 155

Rogers, Will 32

Rogozhkin, Alexander 562n

Rohmer, Eric 261

Roman Holiday (1953) 482n

Romeo and Juliet (1954) 581n

Rooks, Conrad 254

Rooney (1958) 147

Roosevelt, Franklin D. 238

Rory O'More (1911) 295

Roscrea Temperance Hall 96

Rose, David 1

Rose of Tralee 160, 526n

Rose of Tralee Festival 287

Rose Tattoo, The (1955) 240, 552n

Rosi, Francesco 276
Ross, Mike 200
Ross, Pauline 563n
Rossiter, Seamus 585n
Rotha, Paul 561n
Rothery, Sean 77
Rotunda, Dublin 15 17 19 20 21, 27, 29, 37, 55, 59, 78, 86, 122, 129, 152, 518n *see also* Ambassador
Roughneen, Peter 170, 530n
Rourkes' Bakery 28
Rousseau, Jean-Jacques 295
Rowson, Simon 90
Roxboro Twin Theatres, Limerick 165, 257
Roxy Cinema, Ballaghadereen, Co. Roscommon 79
Roxy Cinema, Bray 79, 121
Royal Air Force 104
Royal Cinema, Bray 120
Royal Cinema, Cornmarket, Belfast 36, 489n
Royal Cinema, Limerick 165, 367
Royal Cinema, Tralee, 165
Royal Hippodrome, Belfast 15, 34, 76, 104–5, 125
RTÉ *see* Radio Telefís Éireann
Rumble Fish (1983) 260
Run Lola Run (1998) 264
Rushton, Desmond 498n
Russell, Dr M. 571n
Russell, Jack D. 500n
Russell, Ken 254, 255, 276
Russell Borland, A. 348
Ruszhowski, André 580n
Ruttledge, Patrick 310, 315–16, 318
Ruttmann, Walter 229
Ryan, Francis B. 355, 573n, 577n, 586n, 22
Ryan, Frank 244
Ryan, James 134–6
Ryan, Pat 538n

Sabel, Virgilio 356
Sackville Picture House *see* Picture House, O'Connell Street, Dublin
Sacrifice we Offer, The 363
Safe Cycling (1949) 578n
St Bartholomew's church, Drumcollogher 32
St George's Hall, Belfast 16, 34
St John, Mr E. 344, 583n
St John, Thomas (Tom) 523n
St Joseph's Temperance Hall, Monaghan 79
St Maria Goretti (c.1953) 588n
St Mary's Hall, Belfast 37, 105, 247
St Michael's Cinema, Cootehill 96
St Patrick's Training College, Dublin 584n
St Stephen's Green shopping centre 178–9, 531n, 536n, 590n

St Vincent de Paul Society 321, 356
Saints and Sinners (1949) 582n
Sally's Irish Rogue (1958) 273
Salome (1953) 585n
Samhlaíocht, An 287
Samhlaíocht Kerry Film Festival 287–8, 565n
Samuelson, Marc 540n
San Francisco Film Festival 287
Sanctuary of the Heart (c.1952) 361, 587n, 589n
Sandford Cinema, Ranelagh, Dublin 23, 50, 54–7
Sandford Cinema Co. Ltd, 54
Sandro Cinema, Belfast 66, 83
Sandro Theatres Ltd 66
Sandys, Revd D. 55
Santry Omniplex, Dublin 151, 209
Saoirse? (Freedom? 1961) 274
Saunders, R.F. (Ronnie) 253, 257–9, 274, 552n
Savage, Robert 516n
Savoy Cinema, Athy 122
Savoy Cinema, Cork 75, 118, 121, 157, 274, 28, 49
Savoy Cinema, Dublin 26–7, 66, 71, 74–5, 77, 78, 84–5, 87, 94, 118, 147–8, 153–5, 157–8, 176–8, 181, 198, 213, 215, 226, 279, 482n, 496n, 526n, 531n, 33
Savoy Cinema, Edenderry, Offaly 122
Savoy Cinema, Galway 79, 122, 165
Savoy Cinema, Kiltimagh, Mayo 122
Savoy Cinema, Limerick, 118, 121, 157, 205, 367
Savoy Cinema, New Ross, Wexford 80
Savoy Cinema, Newry, Down 81
Savoy Cinema, Portarlington, Laois 122
Savoy Cinema, Sligo 83
Savoy Cinema, Waterford 122
Savoy Cineplex, Wexford 535n
Savoy Station, Dublin 16
Savoy Theatre, London
Savoy Theatre of Varieties, Dublin 16
Sawbridge Ltd 220
Say One for Me (1959) 357
Sayles, John 562n
SBC International 222
Scaggs, Mrs 527n
Scannán 238, 241, 349, 577n, 584n
Schlesinger, John 255
Schmitz, Ettore 18
Schneider, Erik 485n
Schofish, Mr 86
School of Art/Dún Laoghaire Institute of Art, Design & Technology 559n
Schrader, Paul 277, 282, 562n
Schumacher, Joel 181
Science and the Farmer (1952) 578n
Scola, Ettore 277
Scorsese, Martin 273

Scotia-Barber Distributors 171, 172
Scott, Campbell 282
Scott, Eustace J. 498n
Scott, Henry 37
Scott, Michael 77, 498n
Scott [Michael] and [Norman Douglas] Good (architectural partnership, 1931–6) 498n
Scottish Film Council 348
Screen at College Street, Dublin 177–8, 213, 215, 224, 260, 264, 276, 278–9, 517n
Screen at O'Connell Bridge, Dublin 177, 179, 499n
Screen by the Sea, Greystones, Co. Wicklow 223, 546n
Screenclick.com 188–91, 535n
Screen on the Hill, London 178
ScreenSelect 189
Screen Training Ireland 566n
Seagate (sponsor) 284
Sealy, KC, Judge 506n
Sean-Mhurioca (*The Old South*) 579n
Sebastian, Fr 320, 322
Sebastiane (1976) 255
Secret of Kells, The (2009) 270, 560
Sellar, Ian 280
Sellers, Antony 281
sendit.com 188
Separation (1968) 272
Seven Wonders of the World (1956) 152
Sex in the City (2008) 216
Sgarro, Nicholas 171
SGC Castlebar *see* Mayo Movie World
SGC Dungarvan 223
SGC Enniscorthy 223
Shadow on the Hill (1955) 356
Shaftesbury Pictoria 34–5
Shankill Baptist Tabernacle 98
Shankill Picturedrome 34–5
Shankill Picturedrome (Belfast) Ltd 34–5
Shankill Stadium Co. Ltd. 99, 506n, 56
Shanley, Dr J.P. 323
Shanly, M. William 23, 486n
Shanly's Picture Hall, Dublin 23
Shannon, William 54, 57
Shannon Cinema, Athlone 83
Sharman, Jim 177
Shaw, Patrick W 504n
Sheehan, Donal 275
Sheehan, Jack 327
Sheehy, J. (Muintir na Tire film unit) 575n, 577n
Sheehy, T.J.M. (Morgan; journalist) 119, 331, 334–5, 337, 343, 348–9, 352, 359–60, 518–17n, 576–7n, 580n, 584n, 585–6n
Sheehy, Ted (journalist) 552n
Sheehy-Skeffington, Owen 327, 349
Shell Ireland (sponsor) 276

Shelley, Percy Bysshe 17–8
Shellshock Rock (1979) 272
Shepherd of the Seven Hills, The (1933) 355, 587n
Sheridan, Jim 181, 287–9
Sheridan, John D. 305, 322, 334–5, 339, 344, 568n, 576n
Sheridan, Kathy 533n
Sheridan, Kirstin 287
Sheridan, Nicholas 564n
Sheridan Group 207–8, 215, 217, 540n, 544n
Sherlock, Lorcan G. 36, 490n
Sherry, Peter G. 239, 584n
Shipton Group 591n
Shockers film festival, Cork 558n
Shortt, Edward 493n
Shortt, Pat 564n
Shott, Edward J. 498n
ShoWest 199
Showgirl in Hollywood (1930) 503n
Shrek (521n
Siddharta (1972) 254, 556n
Sight and Sound Ltd 156
Silent Light *see* Super 8 film festival
Silent Night *see* The Immortal Song
Silliman, Alf (pseud. Arch Oboler) 520n
Sim, A. 28
Simone, Fr 356
Sinclair, Major M.T. 133–4
Sing Your Way Home (1945) 503n
Singer not the Song, The (1960) 358, 588n
Singer of Seville *see* Call of the Flesh
Singing Fool, The (1928) 69, 71, 39
Sinkins, Melchior A.A. 83
Sinn Féin 272, 272, 303, 502n
Sinnott, R.B. 560n
Sirk, Douglas 163
Skating Rink, Rotunda Gardens, Dublin 486n
Skibbereen Town Hall 37
Skinny Wolves 290
Sky Movies 184
Slaney Plaza, Wexford *see* SGC Enniscorthy
Sleeping Beauty (1959) 155
Slieve Donard Cinema, Belfast 35
Sligo Short Film Festival 288, 565n
Smiles of a Summer Night (1955) 262
Smith, Clifford 32
Smith, Gaby 563n
Smith, Mrs Rada 518n
Smith, Sheamus 556n, 562n
Smyllie, R.M. 580n
Smyllie, Sydney 124
Smyth, J.G. 246
Smyth, Noel 226, 544n, 548n
Smyths toy stores 533n
Soada (n.d.; 1920s) 229

Society of Cinema Exhibitors (SCE) 168, 170 (*see* ITCA)
Society of Film Distributors (SFD) 170, 530n
Society of Friends/Quakers 51–3, 262, 557n, 582n
Society of Professional Musicians, Northern Ireland 87
Society of St Patrick for foreign missions 355
Solar Group 142
Solas Galway Picture Palace Teoranta 268–70, 481, 560n, 591n
Somers, Brendan 183
Sommarnattens Leende see *Smiles of a Summer Night*
Song for a Raggy Boy (2003) 275
Song O' My Heart (1930) 67
Song of Bernadette (1943) 589n
Song of Freedom (1936) 92
Song of the Little Road see *Pather Panchali*
Song Without End (1960) 357
Sons of John Bull (1914) 72
Sony Corp. 186, 191, 199
Sound + Vision festival, Ballina 288
Sound of Music, The (1965) 152
South Pacific (1958) 155
Southern Television 155
Spanish Film Festival *see* Campo Viejo Spanish Film Festival
Sparling, Frederick A. 55, 495n, 8
Special Powers Act (Northern Ireland) 232
Spicer–Simon, Theodore 484n
Spider-man (2002, 2004, 2007) 199
Spielberg, Steven 172
Spione (*Spies*, 1928) 233
Sprengel, Robert W. 487n
Spurling family 222–3
Spurling, Graham 191, 546n
Spurling, Ossie 546n, 37
Spurling, Ruth 537n
Spurlock, Morgan 199
Spy Kids 3D: Game Over (2003) 521n
Stabovoi, Georgi 232
Stadium Cinema, Belfast 81–2, 124, 56
Stafford, Brendan 237
Stanley, Joseph M. 96, 327, 577n
Stanley, Major Rupert 247
Star Cinema, Crumlin, Dublin 142, 165, 527–28n
Star Cinema, Kildare 30
Star Picture Palace, Belfast 16, 34
Star of Erin Music Hall, Dublin 24, 188, 228 see also Empire, Olympia
Star of Ulster (1938) 112
Star Wars films 291
Starvation in Dublin 60
State Cinema, Phibsboro, Dublin 142, 153–5, 240

Staunton, James, bishop of Ferns 122–3, 323, 326, 334, 338
Stella Artois (sponsor) 249, 284
Stella Cinema, Mount Merrion, Dublin 142, 167, 176
Stella Cinema, Rathmines, Dublin 55, 59, 86–7, 165, 176, 219, 226, 494n, 528n, 545n, 88
Stella Picture Co. Ltd, Dublin 59
Stembridge, Gerry 289, 367, 564n
Stepford Wives (1974) 255
Stephen's Green Cinema, Dublin 77, 122, 142, 162, 163, 165, 168, 170, 176, 178–9, 220, 55
Stephen's Green Cinema Company Ltd 77, 142
Stephen's Green Multiplex 179, 213, 220.
Stephenson, Sam 361
Stephenson Gibney and Associates 152
Ster Century 195, 200, 209, 219, 221–2, 541n
Ster Century, Liffey Valley, Dublin 209, 219, 221–2, *see* Liffey Valley Multiplex
Ster Kinekor 209
Stevens, Leslie 272
Stewart, Fred 34
Stewardesses, The (1969) 520n
Strick, Joseph 255
Strike (1925) 550n
Stillorgan shopping centre, Dublin 204
Sting, The (1973) 171–2
Stokes, Richard 556n
Stokes Horn, Fr J. 79
Stoll, Oswald 67
Stone, Oliver 562n
Stone Ridge (production company) 525n
Stoneman, Rod 281
Story of a Cheat, The (1936) 238
Story of Dublin, The (c.1921) 320
Story of the Kelly Gang, The (1906) 15
Story of the Pope (c.1950) 587n
Strabane town council 100
Strand Cinema, Balbriggan, Co. Dublin 369
Strand Cinema, Belfast 81, 125, 140, 182, 194, 206, 500n
Strand Cinema, Derry 82, 83, 103, 124, 213, 283
Strand Cinema, Dublin 79, 115, 120, 482n, 517n
Stranger Knocks, A (1959) 272
Stranger than Fiction Documentary Film Festival 264, 266
Streetcar Named Desire, A (1951)
Stringfellow, Peter 217
Storm cinema chain 223, 225
Storm multiplex, Waterford 540n, 547n
Storm Over Asia (1928) 230, 231, 549n, 550n
Stross, Raymond 104
Strumpet City (novel, 1969; television series, 1980) 491n
Stuart, Christopher 534n
Studio Ghibli 269

Sullivan, Fr G. 569n
Summa theologica 294
Summerfield, F.M. 93
Sundance Film Festival 287
Sunday Bloody Sunday (1971) 255, 556n
Sunday Entertainment Act 1932, 100
Sunday Observance Acts (1625–1780) 49
Sunday Performance (Temporary Regulations)
    Act 1931, 100
Sundrive Cinema, Kimmage, Dublin 530n
Sundrive Cinema Ltd 80, 176
Suor Letizia (1957) 357
Super 8 film festival, Cork 275
Super Size Me (2004) 199
Superama, Talbot Street, Dublin 152
Superquinn 591n
Supreme Cinemas Ltd 81, 83, 140, 141, 591n
Sutherland KT, duke of 246
Sutton Grand Cinema, Dublin 78, 162
Swan Centre Cinema, Rathmines, Dublin 213,
    219–20, 266
Swansong: The Story of Occi Byrne (2009) 266,
    559n
Sweeney, Charles 563n
Sweeney, Fr 569n
Sweeney, Jarleth 186
Sweeney, Maxwell 135, 145
Sylvester, Chris 96, 1
Synth Eastwood 290, 559n

Tait, Charles 15
Take 1 241
Tallaght multiplex (later UCI Tallaght) 193, 195,
    203–6 209, 213, 217, 225–6, 278
Tallaght shopping centre (the Square) 186, 203–
    4, 209, 226, 539–40n, 548n
'Tan.ie' 186
Tarrant Venture Capital 188
Tarry Flynn (1948) 581n
Tarzan and his Mate (1934) 101
Tashlin, Frank 357
Tatler Cinema, Dún Laoghaire, 136
Tavernier, Bernard 562n
Taviani, Paolo 255, 259
Taviani, Vittorio 255, 259
Taylor, Donald 362
Taylor, Harry E. 27
Taylor, Margaret 201, 215
Taylor, Paul 278, 562n
Tchenguiz, Robert 221
Telefís Éireann 136, 582n *see also* Radio Telefís
    Éireann (RTÉ)
Temperance Hall and Coffee Palace, Dublin
    Total Abstinence Society 48
Ten Commandments, The (1956) 356
Ten Days Leave (1917) 72

Ten Days that Shook the World (1928) 232
Teorema see *Theorem*
Temple Bar Cultural Trust 269
Temple Bar Film Festival 288
Temple Bar Renewal and Development Act 1991,
    262
Temple, Shirley 353
Templemore urban district council 302
Terminator 2, 3D Battle Across Time (1996)
    521n
Terra Firma Capital Partners 221, 225, 227, 481,
    546n
Tesco 185, 186
Tesco DVD Rental 534–35n
Testament of Dr Mabuse, The (1933) 248
Tetzlaff, Ted 152
That Obscure Object of Desire (1977) 255
Theatre and Cinema Association of Ireland *see*
    Irish Theatre and Cinema Association
Theatre & Cinema Association, The (Ireland) *see*
    Irish Theatre and Cinema Association
Theatre de Luxe, Dublin, 28, 42–3, 52, 54, 56,
    75, 118, 120, 240, 499n
Theatre Royal, Belfast 36
Theatre Royal, Dublin 45, 48, 75–7, 118, 135,
    137, 150, 155–6, 498n, 515n
Theatre Royal, Tralee 37–8
Theatre Royal, Waterford 80, 142
Theatres' Act 1843 49
Theorem (1968) 240, 552n
These are the Times (1949) 239
They Live by the Sea (1942) 239
Thirteen Ghosts (1960) 521n
This is America series (1943) 355
This is Cinerama (1952) 151–2
This Other Eden (1959) 245
Thom, Robert 580n
Thomas Aquinas, St 294
Thompson, Walter 152
Thorn-EMI group 157, 203
Thornton, F. Martin 41
Thornton, James 551n
Thou Art A Priest Forever (1945) 574n
Thou Shalt Not Kill (1975) 273
3D 149–51, 180, 191, 208, 214, 222, 224, 520–
    22n, 545n, **94**
3-D: Ghosts of the Abyss (2003) 521n
3i 183
Three Coins in the Fountain (1954) 585n
Three Colours trilogy (*Blue* [1993], *Red* [1994]
    and *White* [1994]) 262
Three Little Sisters (1944) 503n
Thrift, W.E.E. 55, 571n
Tibradden (1943) 239
Tierney, Michael 323, 580n
Tiger's Eye Film Festival, Limerick 287

Tighe, Michael 5
Titanic (1998) 151, 182
Tivoli Cinema, Dublin 80, 122, 501n
Tivoli Cinema, Finaghy, Belfast 124, 141
Tivoli Cinema, Limerick 30, 499n
Tivoli Cinema, Smithfield, Belfast 36,
Tivoli Theatre, Burgh Quay, Dublin, 231
Tobin, Richard 557n
Todd-AO 152, 154–5, 522n
Todd, Mike 154
Tom Brown's Schooldays (1916) 492n
Tomkin, Fr 568n
Toner, Edward (Eddie) 236, 253, 323, 347,
    552n, 557n, 575n, 584n
Tonic Cinema, Bangor 82, 103, 124, 508n
Tonight We Sing (1953) 153
Toomey, Desmond 350, 584n
Torgyle Holdings 164, 210–11, 226–7, 541n,
    548n–49
Toronto Film Festival 279, 288
Tory Island Maritime Film Festival 286
Tóstal, An 270
Tower Cinema, Clondalkin, Co. Dublin 80, 501n
Town like Alice, A (1956) 271
Town Planning Act 1931, 99
Towne, Robert 282
TPG (venture capital company) 188
Tracy, Tony 564n
Tragic Story of Beatrice Cenci, The 17–18, 21
Tralee Omniplex 542n
Tralee Theatre Royal 37–8
Travers, Pauric 518n
Treasury Holdings 225, 591n
Treaty of Limerick 1691, 43
Trinity College Dublin 10, 11, 51, 55, 154, 230,
    238, 239, 241, 486n, 497n, 552n, 553n,
    559n, 571n
Trip through the Canadian Rockies, A (c.1907)
    16
Triskel Arts Centre, Cork (including Cinematek)
    269, 275, 286,
Triumph of the Will (1936) 236
Trojan Eddie (1996) 275
Troxy Cinema, Shore Road, Belfast 84, 149,
    535n
Troxy Cinemas (Belfast) Ltd 141
Troy, Fr M.C. 330–5, 576n
Tsotsi (2005) 566n
Tuam parish council 342
Tucci, Stanley 282
Turin, Viktor 236
Turksib (1928) 236
Turn of the Tide (1935) 116
Turner, Lana 163
Turner, W.G. 490n
Turnover tax 138 *see also* VAT

20th Century-Fox 107, 123, 153–4, 156, 171–2,
    191, 585n
Two Days (1927) 232
2RN 296, 305, 309 *see* RTÉ
Twomey, Nora 270
Twomey, Siobhan 525n, 563n
Tykwer, Tom 264

U2 150
U2 3D (2007) 150
Uchitel see *The New Teacher*
UCI (United Cinemas International), 199, 202,
    205–7, 209–10, 212–15, 217–9, 221, 223,
    225–8, 278, 481, 532n, 539n, 548n
UCI Blanchardstown 203–4, 206, 209, 217, 219,
    223, 225, 278, 481
UCI Coolock 195, 203–6, 209, 212, 217, 219,
    225, 278, 481, 539n
UCI Tallaght 193, 195, 203–6, 209, 213–14,
    217, 219, 225–6, 278, 481, 591n
Údarás na Gaeltachta 281
UGC (Union Générale Cinématographique)194,
    196–7, 201, 207–8, 214–7, 221, 227–8, 543n,
    546n *see also* Parnell Street multiplex and
    Belfast (Dublin Road) multiplex
Uí Riain, Bean 347, 584n
UIP (United International Pictures) 180, 216,
    524n
Uisce Beatha (*Water of Life*, 1972) 273
Ulster Bank (festival sponsor) 291, 564n
Ulster Television (UTV) 136, 138, 139, 208,
    517n
Ulster Unionist Party 126
Ulysses (1967) 255, 556n
Un Chapeau de Paille D'Italie (1927) see *The
    Italian Straw Hat*
Un Homme et une Femme (1966) 251, 555n
Un Missionnaire (1955) 271
UNESCO 341
Union Cinemas chain 76, 81
Union Générale Cinématographique *see* UGC
United Artists 117, 167, 171–2, 205, 510n, 535n
Universal 69, 116, 123, 150, 156, 191, 202, 205,
    539n *see also* Cinema International
    Corporation (CIC)
Universal Pictures International 524n
University College Dublin 559n
Use and misuse of films, The 307–8

VAT (value added tax) 138, 180–1, 188, 200,
    261, 517n, 532n
Vagabond King, The (1930) 86
Valentine, Fr Ferdinand, OP 235
Valseuses, Les (1974) 255
Vasilyev, Georgi 248
Vasilyev, Sergei 248

Vaughan, Fr D. 331, 333–5, 576n.
Vavasseur *see* J.H. Vavasseur
Velvet Underground 288
Venice Film Festival 271
Venus Peter (1989) 280
Veronica Guerin (2003) 181
VHS Distribution 534n
Viacom, 221, 532n
Victoria Cinema Theatre, Galway 30–1
Victory Cinema, Dungannon 518n
Video Island 189
Vidor, Charles 357
Vigilanti cura (1936 papal encyclical) 236, 307–8, 321–3, 325–6, 334, 338, 348, 582n
Vigo, Jean 248, 262
Virgin company interests 194, 207–8, 213, 278
   see Parnell Street multiplex and Belfast
   (Dublin Road) multiplex
Virgin multiplex, Parnell Street, Dublin *see*
   Parnell Street multiplex
Virgin multiplex, Dublin Road, Belfast, *see*
   Belfast (Dublin Road) multiplex
Visages d'Enfants (1925) 236–7
Visconti, Luchino 255
Vision (1965–8) 576n
Visit to Lourdes, A (1930s) 361
Visszaesök see *Forbidden Relations*
Vista Vision 154, 523n
Vitagraph 40, 41, 67, 68
Vivendi Universal Studios 221 183
Vizi Privati, Pubbliche Virtù see *Private Vices &
   Public Virtues*
Volta Cinema 15–22, 23, 24–5, 25, 33, 34, 35,
   50, 52, 73, 78, 484–5n, 497n, 526n, 41
von Stroheim, Erich 353
von Trotta, Margarethe 276
Voyage to Recovery (1952) 578n
Vue Entertainment 215, 221–2, 225, 541n, 591n
   see also Vue, Liffey Valley and Warner Village,
   Odyssey Pavilion
Vue, Liffey Valley, Dublin 195, 209, 222, 67 *see
   also* Liffey Valley Multiplex, Vue
   Entertainment

Wages of Fear, The (1952) 581n
Wagner, Richard 74
Wajda, Andrzej 250
Walker, Norman 116
Walker, Revd Reginald 580n
Walker, Rudolf 566n
Wall, Patrick Ignatius 498n, 511n
Waller, Fred 151
Walls, James 137
Walsh, Aisling 275
Walsh, Barry 325, 327–8, 575n, 576n
Walsh, John (RPC enquiry chairman) 174

Walsh, John (property developer)186
Walsh, Peter (Pete) 263
Walsh, Roisin 23
Walsh, Mr S. 569n
Walsh, V. (Bertie) 83
Walton, James 235
War Comforts Fund 103
Ward Anderson group 110, 151, 159–75, 175–
   180, 182, 194, 198, 203, 205–7, 209–13,
   216–7, 220, 222, 225–8, 257, 260, 264, 276,
   280–1, 497n, 499n, 524–33n, 535–36n, 545–
   49n, 590n *see also* Ward (Leo and Paul) and
   Anderson (Kevin and Paul) and
Ward, John 525n
Ward, Leo 138, 158–79, 180, 197, 203, 205–6,
   211, 219, 226, 249, 525–26n, 541–22n, 549n,
   31 *see also* Ward Anderson
Ward, Paul 160, 163, 178, 199, 211–13, 219–20,
   525–26n, 548n, 35 *see also* Ward Anderson
Warden, Fred 36
Wardour Films Ltd 73
Wardrop, Ken 245
Warner Bros 76, 150, 185, 191, 202, 207, 214–
   5, 539n
Warner Village cinema, Odyssey Pavilion, Belfast
   221–2, 225,
Warnock, J.E. (Edmond) 105
Warren, Jack 72
Washington Cinema, Cork 31
Water of Life (Uisce Beatha, 1972) 273
Water Wisdom (Fior Uisce, 1962), 273
Waterford Arts Festival 287
Waterford county council 342
Waterford Film Festival 287
Waterford Film for All 564n
Waterford Light Opera Festival 270
Watt, Harry 154, 247
Wax Museum Plus, Dublin 522–23n
W.B. Yeats – A Tribute (1950) 336
We are all Murderers (1952) 357
We from Kronstadt (1936) 248
Wedding March (1928) 353, 586n
Wedding Night (1969) 272, 561n
Weekend with God (*c.*1951) 587n
Weekend with Lulu (1961) 140
Weiler, Lance 290–1
Weingartner, Hans 245
Weir, H. 246
Weisker Brothers 41, 67
Welles, Orson 254
Wellington Hall, Belfast 37
Wenders, Wim 178, 264
West Belfast Community Arts Festival 284
West Belfast Film Festival 278, 284
West Belfast Picture Theatre 35, 65
West End Picture House, Belfast 35

West of Zanzibar (1954) 154
Western Cinemas Ltd 77, 500n
Western Import Co. Ltd 67, 68
Westfront 1918 (1930) 236
Westmoreland, Wash 245
Weston, Charles 40
Westport Cineplex, Co. Mayo 542n
Wexford Omniplex 151, 535n
Wexford Opera Festival 279
Whelan, Charles 584n
Whelan, Patrick J. (exhibitor, d.1944) 78, 80,
    309, 511n, 1
Whelan, Pat (investor, 2000s) 549n
When We Were Kings (1996) 264
Where Does the Money Go? (1954) 578n
Where No Vultures Fly (1952) 154
Which Will Ye Have? (1949) 362
White Outlaw, The (1925) 32, 489n
White, Will 36, 96
White Cinema Club 83, 96–7, 101–4, 128–9,
    500n, 507n
Whitehead Cinema (later Strand), Co. Antrim 83
    140, 517n
Whitewater shopping centre / cinema,
    Newbridge, Co. Kildare 223, 262, 547n
Whitney, A.J. Harris 57–8
Whitten, Norman 41, 72–3, 4
Whitworth Hall, Drogheda, Co. Louth 38
Who Fears to Speak of '98? (1948) 159
W.H. Smith Movies Direct 534–35n
Why We Fight 105
Whyte, James 259
Whyte, J.H. 340, 570n, 572n
Wicklow county council 342
Wiene, Robert 232
Wilcox, Herbert 510n
Wilde, Ted 69
William of Orange 294
Williams, Keith 484n
Williams, Tennessee 501n
Willowfield Unionist Club 36
Willowfield Picture House, Belfast 36
Wills, J. Elder 92
Wilson, Frank 41
Wilton, Harry 84
Winchurch Investments Ltd 187
Wind that Shakes the Barley, The (2006) 181
Windsor Cinema, Belfast 81
Winter Festival, Irish Film Theatre, Dublin 256
Winter Gardens, New York 117

Winterbottom, Michael 282
Winters, Mr 97
Wired 291
Wise, Robert 152
Wolff, Lothar 588n
Woman Who Married Clark Gable, The (1985)
    562n
Wonderful World of the Brothers Grimm, The
    (1962) 152
Wood, Andrés 245
Wood, Thomas 33
Woodvale Hall, Belfast 37
Woolf, C.M. 116
Workers' Film Guild (WFG) 232
Workers' Film Society, London 232
Workers' Union of Ireland 231, 508n
World Witness Film Festival 289
World's Fair Picturedrome, Henry Street, Dublin
    52, 62, 152
World's Fair Waxworks and Varieties, Henry
    Street, Dublin 487n
Worth, James J. 27
Wright, Andy T. 36, 82, 502n
Wright, Basil 247

Xantus, János 259
XD Theatre, Dublin 483n, 95
Xtra-vision 183–6, 189, 532–33n

Yankee at King Arthur's Court, The (1931) 503n
Yankee in King Arthur's Court, A (1920) 63
Yasmin (2004) 245
Yellow Caesar (1941) 586n
YMCA, East Belfast 37
Yorkin, Bud 251
YouTube 191
Young, D.D. 98
Younger, Ben 223
Your dinner's poured out! 46–7
Ypres (1925) 495n
Yule, Lady 116
YWCA, Rathmines 56–7

Zavattini, Cesare 363
Zéro de Conduite: Jeunes Diables au College
    (1933) 248
Zinnemann, Fred 154
Zones (1942) 347
Zoom 245, 558n *see also* access>CINEMA
Zukor, Adolph 68, 69, 1